Frommer's®

W9-BSB-391

POSTCARDS

FROM

NEW ENGLAND

In fall, pumpkins cover the ground at hundreds of farm stands like this one in Maine. For more information on New England's seasons, see chapter 2. © Richard V. Procopio/ New England Stock.

Faneuil Hall Marketplace lights up the nighttime skyline in Boston (top). Beacon Hill is home to many of the city's stateliest homes (bottom). See chapter 4. Top photo: © William Johnson Photography; bottom photo: © Chuck Pefley/Tony Stone Images.

The Appalachian Trail crosses through sections of Maine, New Hampshire, Vermont, western Massachusetts (above), and Connecticut on its way to Georgia. But you don't have to hike the whole thing to enjoy the bucolic splendor; there are plenty of great day hikes. See chapters 8, 9, 11, 12, and 13. © Kindra Clineff Photography.

Fall foliage season brings every imaginable color to the region, whether it's the orange and yellow of the trees near Concord (above), or the crimson red of newly harvested cranberry bogs in Nantucket (opposite, top). See chapters 5 and 7. Both photos © Kindra Clineff Photography.

The Hancock Shaker Village serves lunches based on traditional recipes in summer and fall. See chapter 8. © Kindra Clineff Photography.

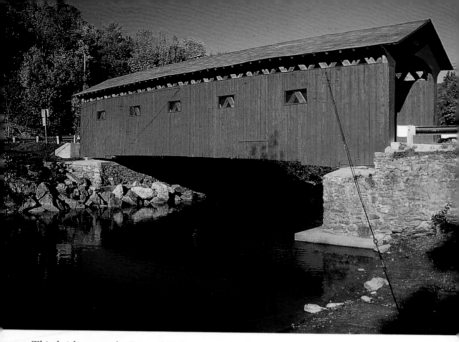

This bridge over the Battenkill River is one of more than 100 covered bridges in Vermont. See chapter 11. © Jim Schwabel/New England Stock.

The Kancamagus Highway in New Hampshire is one of New England's most stunning drives. Sabbaday Falls (above) is one of dozens of stops along the way where you can pause to hike, swim, or simply enjoy the surroundings. See chapter 12. © Brooks Dodge/New England Stock.

It's no accident that the Stockbridge General Store looks straight out of a Norman Rockwell painting: The artist lived here for 25 years, and a museum of his work is just down the block. See chapter 8. © Kindra Clineff Photography.

In winter, thoughts turn to skiing (opposite), antiquing (left), and tapping maple trees for their oh-so-sweet syrup (bottom). Vermonters will tell you their state is the best for all three activities, but you can find serious competition in New Hampshire, Maine, and western Massachusetts. See chapters 8, 11, 12, and 13. Photo opposite: © Brooks Dodge/New England Stock; both photos on this page: © Kindra Clineff Photography.

Spring in New Hampshire is fleeting, but beautiful, especially in the White Mountains. See chapter 12. © William Johnson/New England Stock.

Volunteers in period costumes reenact the "shot heard 'round the world" and other events from the Battle of Lexington every April 19 (a local holiday known as Patriots Day in and around Boston). See chapter 5. © James Lemass Photography.

Maine has countless lighthouses that prevent ships from crashing into its more than 3,000 miles of coastline. See chapter 13.   © Kindra Clineff Photography.

Summer is a time for relaxing outdoors on a blanket. Enjoy the sounds of the Boston Symphony Orchestra at Tanglewood (above), or the roar of the surf on Cape Cod (opposite). See chapters 6 (for Cape Cod beaches) and 8 (for Tanglewood). Photo above: © Jeff Greenberg/ New England Stock; photo opposite: © Kindra Clineff Photography.

No visit to New England is complete without a shore dinner: a cup of clam chowder, a steamed lobster, corn on the cob, and a slice of blueberry pie, usually for under $20. You can find some variation on this menu in parts of New Hampshire, Cape Cod, and Boston's North Shore (above), but the tastiest lobsters, freshest blueberries (opposite), and cheapest prices are without a doubt in Maine. See chapter 13. Photo above: © Kindra Clineff Photography; photo opposite: © Jeff Greenberg/New England Stock.

Parts of Maine are so uncrowded you can have a lake all to yourself. See chapter 13. © *Peter Cole/New England Stock.*

Frommer's® 2000

New England

by Wayne Curtis, Herbert Bailey Livesey, Marie Morris & Laura M. Reckford

with Online Directory by Michael Shapiro

MACMILLAN • USA

ABOUT THE AUTHORS

Wayne Curtis (chapters 2, 3, 11 through 13, and the Appendix) is the author of *Maine: Off the Beaten Path* (Globe Pequot) and numerous travel articles in newspapers and magazines, including the *New York Times, National Geographic Traveler,* and *Outside.* He lives in Portland, Maine, where he endeavors to support local microbreweries and minor-league baseball.

Herbert Bailey Livesey (chapters 8 through 10) is a native New Yorker and a former NYU administrator. After leaving his career in higher education, he worked briefly as an artist before devoting himself to writing full time. He is the author of several travel guides, nine books on education and sociology, and a novel.

Marie Morris (chapters 4 and 5) is a native New Yorker and a graduate of Harvard College, where she studied history. She has worked for the *New York Times, Boston* magazine, and the *Boston Herald,* and is also the author of *Frommer's Boston.* She lives in Boston, not far from Paul Revere.

Laura M. Reckford (chapters 6 and 7) is a writer and editor who lives on Cape Cod. Formerly the managing editor of *Cape Cod Life Magazine,* she has also been on the editorial staffs of *Good Housekeeping Magazine* and *Entertainment Weekly.*

MACMILLAN TRAVEL

Macmillan General Reference USA, Inc.
1633 Broadway
New York, NY 10019

Find us online at **www.frommers.com**

Copyright © 1999 by Macmillan General Reference USA, Inc.
Maps copyright © by Macmillan General Reference USA, Inc.

ISBN 0-02862982-5
ISSN 1044-2286

Editor: Alice Fellows
Production Editor: Suzanne Snyder
Design by Michele Laseau
Staff cartographers: John Decamillis, Roberta Stockwell
Additional cartography: Ortelius Design, Carolyn Casey
Page Creation by Melissa Auciello-Brogan, Sean Monkhouse, and Angel Perez
Photo Editor: Richard Fox

SPECIAL SAL.ES

Manufactured in the United States of America

5 4 3 2 1

Contents

iii

5   Side Trips from Boston: Lexington & Concord, the North Shore & Plymouth   130

by Marie Morris

6   Cape Cod   182

by Laura M. Reckford

7   Martha's Vineyard & Nantucket   251

by Laura M. Reckford

8   Central & Western Massachusetts   291

by Herbert Bailey Livesey

List of Maps

AN INVITATION TO THE READER

In researching this book, we discovered many wonderful places—hotels, restaurants, shops, and more. We're sure you'll find others. Please tell us about them, so we can share the information with your fellow travelers in upcoming editions. If you were disappointed with a recommendation, we'd love to know that, too. Please write to:

Frommer's New England
Macmillan Travel
1633 Broadway
New York, NY 10019

AN ADDITIONAL NOTE

Please be advised that travel information is subject to change at any time—and this is especially true of prices. We therefore suggest that you write or call ahead for confirmation when making your travel plans. The authors, editors, and publisher cannot be held responsible for the experiences of readers while traveling. Your safety is important to us, however, so we encourage you to stay alert and be aware of your surroundings. Keep a close eye on cameras, purses, and wallets, all favorite targets of thieves and pickpockets.

WHAT THE SYMBOLS MEAN

✪ Frommer's Favorites

Our favorite places and experiences—outstanding for quality, value, or both.

The following abbreviations are used for credit cards:

AE	American Express	ER	EnRoute
CB	Carte Blanche	MC	MasterCard
DC	Diners Club	V	Visa
DISC	Discover		

The following abbreviation is used in hotel listings:
MAP (Modified American Plan): Sometimes called half board or half pension, this room rate includes breakfast and dinner (or lunch, if you prefer).

FIND FROMMER'S ONLINE

Arthur Frommer's Budget Travel Online (www.frommers.com) offers more than 6,000 pages of up-to-the-minute travel information—including the latest bargains and candid, personal articles updated daily by Arthur Frommer himself. No other Web site offers such comprehensive and timely coverage of the world of travel.

The Best of New England

One of the greatest challenges of traveling in New England is choosing from an abundance of superb restaurants, accommodations, and attractions. Where to start? Here's an entirely biased list of our favorite destinations and experiences. Over years of traveling through the region, we've discovered that these are places worth more than just a quick stop when we're in the area. They're all worth a major detour.

1 The Best of Small-Town New England

- **Marblehead** (Mass.): The "Yachting Capital of America" has major picture-postcard potential, especially in the summer, when the harbor fills with boats of all sizes. From downtown, a short distance inland, make your way toward the water down the narrow, flower-dotted streets. The first glimpse of blue sea and sky is breathtaking. See chapter 5.
- **Chatham** (Mass.): Located on the "elbow" of the Cape, right on Nantucket Sound, Chatham is proof that Main Street USA is alive and well on the Cape. Families throng here in the summer to enjoy the beach and to browse through shops brimming with upscale arts, crafts, and other unique gifts. In summer, visitors and locals come together every Friday night for great outdoor concerts, while the looming Chatham Lighthouse, built in 1828, keeps a close eye on the Atlantic. See chapter 6.
- **Edgartown, Martha's Vineyard** (Mass.): For many visitors, Edgartown *is* Martha's Vineyard, its regal captain's houses and manicured lawns a symbol of a more refined way of life. Roses climb white picket fences, and the tolling of the Whaling Church bell signals dinnertime. By July, gleaming pleasure boats fill the harbor passing Edgartown Lighthouse, and shops overflow with luxury goods. Edgartown's old-fashioned Fourth of July parade harkens back to small-town America, as hundreds line Main Street cheering the loudest for the floats with the most heart. It's a picture-perfect little town, a slice of homemade apple pie to go with nearby Oak Bluff's hot fudge sundae. See chapter 7.
- **Stockbridge** (Mass.): Norman Rockwell made a famous painting of the main street of this, his adopted hometown. Facing south, it uses the southern Berkshires as backdrop for the sprawl of the Red Lion Inn and the other late-19th-century buildings that make up the commercial district. Then as now, they service a beguiling mix of unassuming saltboxes and Gilded Age mansions

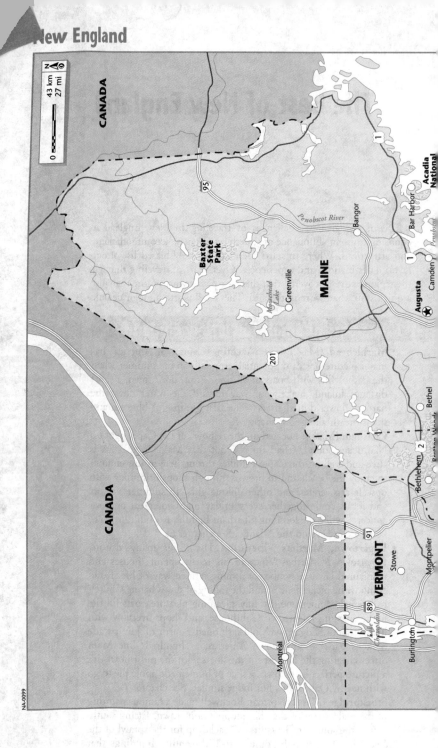

NA-0099

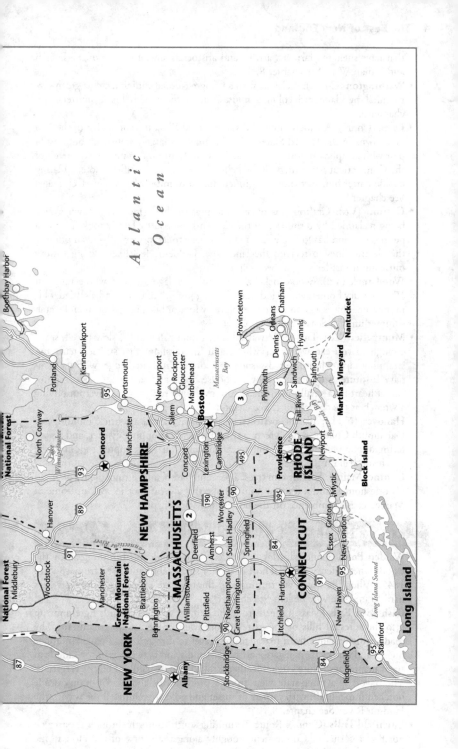

that have sheltered farmers, artists, and aristocrats since the days of the French and Indian Wars. See chapter 8.

- **Washington** (Conn.): A classic, with a Congregational church facing a green surrounded by clapboard colonial houses, all of them with black shutters. See chapter 9.
- **Essex** (Conn.): A widely circulated survey voted Essex tops on its list of the 100 best towns in the United States. That judgment is largely statistical, but a walk past white clapboard houses to the active waterfront on this unspoiled stretch of the Connecticut River rings all the bells. There is not an artificial note, a blaring cookie-cutter franchise, nor a costumed docent to muddy its near-perfect image. See chapter 9.
- **Grafton** (Vt.): Grafton was once a down-at-the-heels mountain town slowly being reclaimed by termites and the elements. A wealthy family took it on as a pet project, and has lovingly restored the village to its former self—even burying the electric lines to reclaim the landscape. It doesn't feel like a living history museum; it just feels right. See chapter 11.
- **Woodstock** (Vt.): Woodstock has a stunning village green, a whole range of 19th-century homes, woodland walks leading just out of town, and a settled, old-money air. This is a good place to explore by foot or bike, or to just sit and watch summer unfold. See chapter 11.
- **Montpelier** (Vt.): This is the way all state capitals should be: slow-paced, small enough so you can walk everywhere, and full of shops that still sell nails and strapping tape. Montpelier also shows a more sophisticated edge, with its Culinary Institute, a theater showing art-house films, and several fine book shops. But at heart it's a small town, where you just might run into the governor buying a wrench at the corner store. See chapter 11.
- **Hanover** (N.H.): It's the perfect college town: handsome brick buildings of Dartmouth College, a tidy green, a small but select shopping district, and a scattering of good restaurants. Come in the fall and you'll be tempted to join in the touch football on the green.
- **Castine** (Maine): Soaring elm trees, a peaceful harborside setting, plenty of grand historic homes, and a few good inns make this a great spot to soak up some of Maine's coastal ambience off the beaten path. See chapter 13.

2 The Best Places to See Fall Foliage

- **Walden Pond** (Concord, Mass.): Walden Pond is hidden from the road by the woods where Henry David Thoreau built a small cabin and lived from 1845 to 1847. When the leaves are turning and the trees are reflected in the water, it's hard to imagine why he left. See chapter 5.
- **Bash Bish Falls** (Mass.): Head from the comely village of South Egremont up into the forested hills of the extreme southwest corner of Massachusetts. The roads, which change from macadam to gravel to dirt and back, pass handmade houses and quirky Congregational chapels, and wind between crimson clouds of sugar maples and white birches feather-stroked against banks of black evergreens. The payoff is a three-state view from a promontory above a 50-foot cascade notched into a bluff, with carpets of russet and gold stretching all the way to the Hudson River. See chapter 8.
- **Litchfield Hills** (Conn.): Route 7, running south to north through the rugged northwest corner of Connecticut, roughly along the course of the Housatonic River, explodes with color in the week fore and aft Columbus Day. It's something to see the fallen leaves whirling down the foaming river. See chapter 9.

- **I-91** (Vt.): An interstate? Don't scoff (the traffic can be terrible on narrow state roads). If you like your foliage viewing wholesale, cruise I-91 from Brattleboro to Newport. You'll be overwhelmed with gorgeous terrain, from the gentle Connecticut River valley to the sloping hills of the Northeast Kingdom. See chapter 11.
- **Route 100** (Vt.): Route 100 winds the length of Vermont from Readsboro to Newport. It's the major north-south route through the center of the Green Mountains, and it's surprisingly undeveloped along most of its length. You won't have it to yourself along the southern stretches on autumn weekends, but as you head further north you'll leave the crowds behind. See chapter 11.
- **Aboard the M/V *Mount Washington*** (N.H.): One of the more majestic views of the White Mountains is from Lake Winnipesaukee to the south. The vista is especially appealing as seen from the deck of the *Mount Washington,* an uncommonly handsome 230-foot-long vessel that offers a variety of tours through mid-October, when the lake is trimmed with a fringe of fall color along the shoreline. See chapter 12.
- **Crawford Notch** (N.H.): Route 302 passes through this scenic valley, where you can see the brilliant red maples and yellow birches high on the hillsides. Mount Washington stands guard in the background, and in fall is likely to be dusted with an early snow. See chapter 12.
- **Camden** (Maine): The dazzling autumn colors that cover the rolling hills are reflected in Penobscot Bay on the east side, and in the lakes on the west. Ascend the coastal peaks for views out to the color-splashed islands in the bay. Autumn is usually a week or two later on the coast, so you can stretch out your viewing pleasure. See chapter 13.

3 The Best Ways to View Coastal Scenery

- **Strolling Around Rockport** (Mass.): The town surrounds the small harbor and spreads out along the rugged, rocky coastline of Cape Ann. From the end of Bearskin Neck, the view is spectacular—fishing and pleasure boats in one direction, roaring surf in the other. See chapter 5.
- **Getting Back to Nature on Plum Island** (Mass.): The Parker River National Wildlife Refuge in Newburyport offers two varieties of coastal scenery: picturesque salt marshes packed with birds and other animals, and gorgeous ocean beaches where the power of the Atlantic is evident. See chapter 5.
- **Biking or Driving the Outer Cape** (Mass.): From Eastham through Wellfleet and Truro, all the way to Provincetown, Cape Cod's outermost towns offer dazzling ocean vistas and a number of exceptional bike paths, including the Province Lands, just outside Provincetown, that are bordered by spectacular swooping dunes. See chapter 6.
- **Heading "Up-Island"** (Martha's Vineyard, Mass.): Many visitors to Martha's Vineyard never venture beyond the port towns of Vineyard Haven, Oak Bluffs, and Edgartown. Though each has its charms, the scenery actually gets a lot more spectacular "up-island," in towns like Chilmark, where you'll pass moorlike meadows and family farms surrounded by stone walls. Whether biking or driving, follow State Road and the scenic Moshup Trail to the westernmost tip of the island, where you'll experience the dazzling colored cliffs of Gay Head, and the quaint fishing port of Menemsha. See chapter 7.
- **Cruising Newport's Ocean Drive** (R.I.): After a tour of the fabulously overwrought "cottages" of the hyper-rich that are strung along Bellevue Avenue, emerging onto the shoreline road that dodges the spray of the boiling Atlantic is a

cleansing reminder of the power of nature over fragile monuments to the conceits of men. To extend the experience, take a 3.5-mile hike along the Cliff Walk that skirts the edge of the bluff commanded by the largest mansions. See chapter 10.

- **Biking Route 1A from Hampton Beach to Portsmouth** (N.H.): You'll get a taste of all sorts of coastal scenery pedaling along New Hampshire's minuscule coastline. Begin with sandy beaches, then pass rocky headlands and handsome mansions before coasting into the region's most scenic seaside city. See chapter 12.
- **Kayaking Merchant's Row** (Maine). The islands between Stonington and Isle au Haut, rimmed with pink granite and capped with the stark spires of spruce trees, are simply spectacular. Exploring by sea kayak will get you to islands inaccessible by motor boat. Outfitters offer overnight camping trips on the islands. See "Enjoying the Great Outdoors" in chapter 13.
- **Hiking Monhegan Island** (Maine). The village of Monhegan is clustered around the harbor, but the rest of this 700-acre island is all picturesque wildlands, with miles of trails crossing open meadows and winding along rocky bluffs. See chapter 13.
- **Driving the Park Loop Road at Acadia National Park** (Maine). This is the region's premier ocean drive. You'll start high along a ridge with views of Frenchman Bay and the Porcupine Islands, then dip down along the rocky shores to watch the surf crash against the dark rocks. Plan to do this 20-mile loop at least twice to get the most out of it. See chapter 13.
- **Cruising on a Windjammer** (Maine): See Maine as it was first seen for centuries—from the ocean looking inland. A handsome fleet of sailing ships departs from various harbors along the coast, particularly Rockland and Camden. Spend from a night to a week exploring the dramatic shoreline. See chapter 13.

4 The Best Places to Rediscover America's Past

- **Paul Revere House** (Boston, Mass.): The history of the American Revolution is often told through stories of governments and institutions. At this little home in the North End, you'll learn about a real person. The tour is self-guided, allowing you to linger on the artifacts that hold your interest, and is particularly thought-provoking. Revere had 16 children with two wives, supported them with his thriving silversmith's trade—and put the whole operation in jeopardy with his role in the events that led to the Revolutionary War. See chapter 4.
- **The Old State House** (Boston, Mass.): Built in 1713, the once-towering Old State House is dwarfed by modern-day skyscrapers. It stands as a reminder of British rule (the exterior features a lion and a unicorn) and its overthrow—the Declaration of Independence was read from the balcony, which overlooks a traffic island where a circle of bricks represents the site of the Boston Massacre. See chapter 4.
- **Faneuil Hall** (Boston, Mass.): Although Faneuil Hall is best known nowadays as a shopping destination, if you head upstairs instead of out into the marketplace, you'll be transported back in time. The second-floor auditorium is in tip-top shape, and park rangers are on hand to talk about the building's role in the Revolution. Tune out the sound of sneakers squeaking across the floor, and you can almost hear Samuel Adams (his statue is out front) exhorting the Sons of Liberty. See chapter 4.
- **"Old Ironsides"** (Boston, Mass.): Formally named the USS *Constitution,* the frigate was launched in 1797 and made a name for itself battling Barbary pirates

and seeing action in the War of 1812. Last used in battle in 1815, it was periodically threatened with destruction until a complete renovation in the late 1920s started its career as a floating monument. The staff consists of sailors on active duty who wear 1812 dress uniforms, conduct tours, and can answer just about any question you throw at them. See chapter 4.

- **The Old North Bridge** (Concord, Mass.): British troops headed to Concord after putting down the uprising in Lexington, and the bridge (well, it's a replica) stands as a testament to the Minutemen who fought there. The Concord River and its peaceful green banks give no hint of the bloodshed that took place here. On the path in from Monument Street, placards and audio stations provide a fascinating narrative. See chapter 5.
- **Plymouth Rock** (Mass.): Okay, it's a fraction of its original size and looks like something you might find in your garden (especially if your garden is in rocky New England soil). Nevertheless, Plymouth Rock makes a perfect starting point for exploration. Close by is the *Mayflower II,* a replica of the alarmingly small original vessel. The juxtaposition reminds you of what a dangerous undertaking the Pilgrims' voyage was, something to keep in mind as you explore the town. See chapter 5.
- **Sandwich** (Mass.): The oldest town on Cape Cod, Sandwich was founded in 1637. Glassmaking brought notoriety and prosperity to this picturesque town in the 19th century. Visit the Sandwich Glass Museum on Main Street for the whole story, or one of the town's glassblowing studios. Don't leave without visiting the 76-acre Heritage Plantation, which has a working carousel, a sparkling antique-car collection, and a wonderful collection of Americana. See chapter 6.
- **Nantucket** (Mass): It looks like the whalers just left, leaving behind their grand houses, cobbled streets, and a gamut of enticing shops offering luxury goods from around the world. The Nantucket Historical Association owns over a dozen interesting properties open for touring, and the well-stocked Whaling Museum is one of the most fascinating sites in the region. Tourism may be rampant, but not its tackier side effects, thanks to stringent preservation measures. Time has not so much stood still here as vanished: You can relax into island time, dictated purely by what you feel like doing next. See chapter 7.
- **Deerfield** (Mass.): Arguably the best-preserved colonial village in New England, Deerfield has scores of houses dating back to the 17th and 18th centuries. None of the clutter of modernity has intruded here. Fourteen houses on the main avenue ("The Street") can be visited through tours conducted by the organization known as Historic Deerfield. See chapter 8.
- **Newport** (R.I.): A key port of the clipper trade long before the British surrendered their colony of "Rhode Island and Providence Plantation," Newport retains abundant recollections of its maritime past. In addition to its great harbor, clogged with cigarette boats, tugs, ferries, and majestic sloops, the City by the Sea has kept three distinctive enclaves preserved: the waterside homes of colonial seamen, the hillside Federalist houses of port-bound merchants, and the ostentatious mansions of America's post–Civil War industrial and financial grandees. See chapter 10.
- **Plymouth** (Vt.): President Calvin Coolidge was born in this high upland valley, and the state has done a superb job preserving his hometown village. You'll get a good sense of the president's roots, but also gain a greater understanding of how a New England village works. Don't miss the cheese shop still owned by the president's son. See chapter 11.

- **Shelburne Museum** (Shelburne, Vt.): Think of this sprawling museum as New England's attic. Located on 45 acres on the shores of Lake Champlain, the Shelburne Museum not only features the usual exhibits of quilts and early glass, but whole buildings preserved like specimens in formaldehyde. Look for the lighthouse, the railroad station, and the stagecoach inn. This is one of northern New England's "don't miss" destinations. See chapter 11.
- **Saint-Gaudens National Historic Site** (Cornish, N.H.). Sculptor Augustus Saint-Gaudens has been overshadowed by his contemporary, Daniel Chester French, but his works were extraordinary and prolific. You'll learn all about the man and the artistic culture of the late 19th and early 20th century during tours of his studio and house, located in the peaceful Connecticut River Valley of southwest New Hampshire. See chapter 12.
- **Portsmouth** (N.H.): Portsmouth is a salty coastal city that just happens to boast some of the most impressive historic homes in New England. Start at Strawbery Banke, a historic 10-acre compound of 42 historic buildings. Then visit the many other grand homes in nearby neighborhoods, like the house John Paul Jones occupied while building his warship during the Revolution. See chapter 12.
- **Sabbathday Lake Shaker Community** (New Gloucester, Maine): This is the last of the active Shaker communities in the nation. The 1,900-acre farm, about 45 minutes outside of Portland, has a number of exceptional buildings, including a handful dating back to the colony's founding in 1793. Visitors come to view examples of historic Shaker craftsmanship and buy locally grown Shaker herbs to bring home. See chapter 13.

5 The Best Literary Landmarks

- **Concord** (Mass.): Concord is home to a legion of literary ghosts. Homes of Ralph Waldo Emerson, Nathaniel Hawthorne, Henry David Thoreau, and Louisa May Alcott are popular destinations, and look much as they did during the "flowering of New England" in the mid–19th century. See chapter 5.
- **Salem** (Mass.): Native son Nathaniel Hawthorne might still feel at home here. A hotel and a boulevard bear his name, the Custom House where he found an embroidered scarlet "A" still stands, and his birthplace is open for tours. It has been moved into the same complex as the House of the Seven Gables, a cousin's home that inspired the classic novel. See chapter 5.
- **The Outer Cape** (Mass.): In the last century, the communities at the far end of the Cape—Wellfleet, Truro, and particularly Provincetown—were a veritable headquarters of bohemia. Henry David Thoreau walked the 28 miles from Eastham to Provincetown and wrote about it in his classic *Cape Cod*. In the 1920s, Henry Beston spent a year living in a beach cottage and recorded his experience in *The Outermost House,* a great primer for your Cape vacation. Distinguished literati such as Edna St. Vincent Millay, Mary McCarthy, Edmund Wilson, Tennessee Williams, Norman Mailer, and many others have also taken refuge among the dunes here. See chapter 6.
- **Robert Frost Farm** (Franconia Notch, N.H.). Two of the most famous New England poems—"The Road Not Taken" and "Stopping by Woods on a Snowy Evening"—were composed by Robert Frost at this farm just outside of Franconia. Explore the woods and read the verses posted along the pathways, then tour the farmhouse where Frost lived with his family earlier this century. See chapter 12.

6 The Best Activities for Families

- **Visiting the Museum of Science** (Boston, Mass.): Built around demonstrations, experiments, and interactive displays that never feel like homework, this museum is wildly popular with kids—and adults. Explore the exhibits (this can fill a couple of hours or a whole day), then take in a show at the planetarium or the Omni Theater. Before you know it, everyone will have learned something, painlessly. See chapter 4.
- **Free Friday Flicks at the Hatch Shell** (Boston, Mass.): Better known for the Boston Pops' Fourth of July concert, the Esplanade is also famous for family films (*The Wizard of Oz* or *Pocahontas,* for example) shown for free on Friday nights in summer. The lawn in front of the Hatch Shell, an amphitheater usually used for concerts, turns into a giant, carless drive-in movie as hundreds of people picnic and wait for the sky to grow dark. See chapter 4.
- **Exploring the Museum of Fine Arts** (Boston, Mass.): Parents hear "magnificent Egyptian collections" but kids think: "Mummies!" Even the most hyper youngster usually manages to take it down a notch in quiet, refined surroundings (you may have seen this phenomenon in fancy restaurants), and the collections at the MFA simultaneously tickle visitors' brains. Admission is free to those under 18. See chapter 4.
- **A Trip to Woods Hole** (Mass.): For junior oceanologists, this is the place to be. You can try the hands-on exhibits at the Woods Hole Oceanographic Institute, observe experiments at the Marine Biological Laboratory, explore the touch tanks at the country's oldest aquarium, and even collect crucial data with the "Ocean Quest" crew. See chapter 6.
- **Whale Watching off Provincetown** (Mass.): Boats leave Provincetown's MacMillan Wharf throughout the day for the 8-mile journey to Stellwagen Bank National Marine Sanctuary, a rich feeding ground for several types of whales. Kids will be entertained by on-board naturalists who set the stage for the show-stoppers. But nothing can prepare you or the little ones for the thrill of spotting these magnificent creatures feeding, breaching, and even flipper slapping. Hands down, the best outfit in town is the **Dolphin Fleet** (☎ **800/826-9300**), which is affiliated with the Center for Coastal Studies. See chapter 6.
- **An Afternoon of Deep-Sea Fishing:** Charter fishing boats these days usually have high-tech fish-finding gear—imagine how your kids will react to reeling in one big bluefish after another. The top spots to mount such an expedition are Barnstable Harbor or Rock Harbor in Orleans, on Cape Cod; Point Judith, at the southern tip of Rhode Island; and the Maine coast. See chapters 6, 10, and 13, respectively.
- **Riding the Flying Horses Carousel in Oak Bluffs** (Martha's Vineyard, Mass.; ☎ **508/693-9481**): Some say this is the oldest carousel in the country, but your kids might not notice the genuine horsehair, sculptural details, or glass eyes. They'll be too busy trying to grab the brass ring to win a free ride. After your ride, stroll around the town of Oak Bluffs. Children will be enchanted with the clustered "gingerbread" houses, a carryover from the 19th-century revivalist movement. Community sings and concerts—some big-name—still take place at the open-air **Trinity Park Tabernacle** (☎ **508/693-0525**). See chapter 7.
- **Biking Nantucket** (Mass.): Short flat trails crisscross the island, and every one leads to a beach. The shortest rides lead to Children's Beach with its own playground and Jetties Beach; older kids will be able to make the few miles to Surfside and Madaket. The rest of the vacation will be a big hit too. Looking like a

toy town in all its preserved 19th-century primness, Nantucket also has a striped lighthouse, and a turn-of-the-century movie house, and two old-fashioned soda fountains complete the idyll. See chapter 7.

- **A Learn-to-Ski Vacation at Jiminy Peak** (Mass.): More than 70% of Jiminy Peak's trails are catered toward beginners and intermediates, making it one of the premier places to learn to ski in the East. The mountain is located in the heart of the Berkshires, near Mount Greylock. See chapter 8.
- **Visiting Mystic Seaport and Mystic Marinelife Aquarium** (Conn.): The double-down winner in the family-fun sweeps has to be this combination: performing dolphins and whales, full-rigged tall ships, penguins and sharks, and river rides on a perky little 1906 motor launch are the kinds of G-rated attractions that have no age barriers. See chapter 9.
- **Visiting the Montshire Museum** (Norwich, Vt.): This handsome and modern children's museum, in a soaring, barnlike space on the Vermont–New Hampshire border, has a long afternoon's worth of interactive exhibits that put the wonder back into science. Afterward, stroll the nature trails along the Connecticut River. See chapter 12.
- **A Stay in Weirs Beach** (N.H.): This is the destination your kids would pick if you weren't so bossy. Weirs Beach on Lake Winnipesaukee offers passive amusements like train and boat rides that appeal to younger kids, and plenty of active adventures for young teens—like go-cart racing, waterslides, and video arcades. Their parents can recuperate while lounging on the lakeside beach. See chapter 12.
- **A Ride on Mount Washington Cog Railroad** (Crawford Notch, N.H.): It's fun! It's terrifying! It's a great glimpse into history. Kids love this ratchety climb to the top of New England's highest peak aboard trains that were specially designed to scale the mountain in 1869. As a technological marvel, the railroad attracted tourists by the thousands a century ago. They still come to marvel at the sheer audacity. See chapter 12.
- **A Trip to Monhegan Island** (Maine): Kids from 8 to 12 years old especially enjoy overnight excursions to Monhegan Island. The mail boat from Port Clyde is rustic and intriguing, and the hotels are an adventure. Leave at least one afternoon to sit atop the high, rocky bluffs scouting the glimmering ocean for whales.

7 The Best Country Inns

- **Hawthorne Inn** (Concord, Mass.; ☎ **978/369-5610**): This inn rings all the bells. Everything—the 1870 building, the garden setting a stone's throw from the historic attractions, the antique furnishings, the eclectic decorations, the accommodating innkeepers—is top of the line. See chapter 5.
- **The Old Farm Inn** (Rockport, Mass.; ☎ **800/233-6828**): Here's the perfect resolution of the eternal country-or-beach debate. It's surrounded by trees but just a short walk from the ocean, on the outskirts of a picturesque coastal town. See chapter 5.
- **Captain's House Inn** (Chatham, Mass.; ☎ **800/315-0728** or 508/945-0127): An elegant country inn that positively drips with good taste, this is among the best small inns in the region. Most rooms have fireplaces and elegant paneling and antiques throughout; they're sumptuous yet cozy. This may be the ultimate spot to enjoy Chatham's Christmas Stroll festivities, but you may need to book your room a couple of years in advance. See chapter 6.
- **Charlotte Inn** (Edgartown, Martha's Vineyard, Mass.; ☎ **508/627-4751**): Edgartown tends to be the most formal enclave on Martha's Vineyard, and this

anglicized compound of exquisite buildings is by far the fanciest address in town. The rooms are distinctively decorated: one boasts a baby grand, another its own thematic dressing room. The conservatory restaurant, **l'étoile** (☎ **508/ 627-5187**), is among the finest you'll find this side of France. See chapter 7.

- **The Wauwinet** (Nantucket, Mass.; ☎ **800/426-8718** or 508/228-0145): Far from the bustle of Nantucket Town and nestled between a bay beach and an ocean beach, this opulently restored landmark offers the ultimate retreat. The inn's atmosphere is both intimate and lavish, with attentive service and exquisite furnishings. Everything a summering sybarite could want is close at hand, including tennis courts, a launch to drop you off on your own secluded beach (part of a 1,100-acre wildlife refuge), and an outstanding New American restaurant called Topper's. See chapter 7.
- **Mayflower Inn** (Washington, Conn.; ☎ **860/868-9466**): Not a tough call at all for this part of the region: Immaculate in taste and execution, the Mayflower is as close to perfection as any such enterprise is likely to be. A genuine Joshua Reynolds hangs in the hall. See chapter 9.
- **Griswold Inn** (Essex, Conn.; ☎ **860/767-1776**): "The Gris" has been accommodating sailors and travelers as long as any inn in the country, give or take a decade. For all that time, it has been the focus of life and commerce in the lower Connecticut River valley, always ready with a mug of suds, a haunch of beef, and a roaring fire. The walls are layered with nautical paintings and memorabilia, and there is music every night in the schoolhouse-turned-tavern. See chapter 9.
- **Blueberry Hill Inn** (Goshen, Vt.; ☎ **800/448-0707** or 802/247-6735): In search of the perfect Vermont getaway? This remote, casual inn on a quiet byway surrounded by national forest is a great retreat for those who love the natural world. There's hiking and swimming in summer, skiing in the winter. See chapter 11.
- **Pitcher Inn** (Warren, Vt.; ☎ **888/867-8424** or 802/496-6350): One of the newest New England inns (built in 1997) is also one of the best. It combines traditional New England form and scale with modern and luxe touches, plus a good dollop of whimsy. See chapter 11.
- **Twin Farms** (Barnard, Vt.; ☎ **800/894-6327** or 802/234-9999): Just north of Woodstock may be the most elegant inn in New England. Their rates may cause facial tics, but you'll certainly be pampered here. Novelist Sinclair Lewis once lived on this 300-acre farm, and today it's an aesthetic retreat that offers serenity and exceptional food. See chapter 11.
- **Windham Hill Inn** (West Townshend, Vt.; ☎ **800/944-4080** or 802/ 874-4080): New innkeepers have added welcome amenities like air-conditioning in the rooms and a conference room in the barn while still preserving the antique charm of this 1823 farmstead. It's at the end of a remote dirt road in a high upland valley, and guests are welcome to explore 160 private acres on a network of walking trails. See chapter 11.
- **Balsams Grand Resort Hotel** (Dixville Notch, N.H.; ☎ **800/255-0600** or 603/255-3400): The designation "country inn" is only half-correct. You've got plenty of country—it's set on 15,000 acres in far northern New Hampshire. But this historic resort is more castle than inn. The Balsams has been offering superb hospitality and gracious comfort since 1866. It has two golf courses, miles of hiking trails, and, in winter, its own downhill and cross-country ski areas. See chapter 12.
- **Claremont** (Southwest Harbor, Maine; ☎ **800/244-5036** or 207/244-5036). The 1884 Claremont is a Maine classic. This waterside lodge has everything a

Victorian resort should, including sparely decorated rooms, creaky floorboards in the halls, great views of water and mountains, and perfect a croquet pitch. The dining room's only so-so, but Southwest Harbor has other dining options. See chapter 13.

- **Goose Cove Lodge** (Sunset, Maine; ☎ 207/348-2508): Guest at this remote cluster of cottages along a pristine Maine cove are pampered with a rustic elegance. Spend your day exploring the coast in the lodge's boats, or wandering the adjacent nature preserve. Come evening, you'll be fed well in the lovely dining room overlooking the cove. See chapter 13.
- **The White Barn Inn** (Kennebunkport, Maine; ☎ 207/967-2321): Much of the White Barn staff hails from Europe, and guests are treated with a continental graciousness. The rooms are a delight, and the meals (served in the barn) are among the best in Maine. See chapter 13.

8 The Best Moderately Priced Accommodations

- **Newbury Guest House** (Boston, Mass.; ☎ 617/437-7666) and the **Harborside Inn** (Boston, Mass.; ☎ 617/723-7500): These sister properties would be good deals even if they weren't ideally located—the former in the Back Bay, the latter downtown. Rates even include breakfast. See chapter 4.
- **Harvard Square Hotel** (Cambridge, Mass.; ☎ 800/458-5886 or 617/864-5200): Smack in the middle of Cambridge's most popular destination, this hotel is a comfortable place to stay in a great location. See chapter 4.
- **John Carver Inn** (Plymouth, Mass.; ☎ 800/274-1620 or 508/746-7100): This hotel is centrally located, whether you're immersing yourself in Pilgrim lore or passing through on the way from Boston to Cape Cod. Ask about the "Passport to History" packages for a good deal. See chapter 5.
- **Isaiah Hall B&B Inn** (Dennis, Mass.; ☎ 800/736-0160 or 508/385-9928): Nestled amid oak trees in Dennis Village, not far from Cape Cod's historic Old King's Highway, this B&B has been welcoming visitors to this part of Cape Cod for more than 50 years. The inn and its gregarious owner are popular with actors starring in summer stock at the nearby Cape Cod Playhouse. Guests enjoy country-cozy rooms and a communal breakfast served on a 12-foot cherry table in the dining room. See chapter 6.
- **Nauset House Inn** (East Orleans, Mass.; ☎ 508/255-2195): This small, romantic 1810 farmhouse is like a sepia-toned vision of old Cape Cod. Recline in a wicker divan surrounded by fragrant flowers while the wind whistles outside. Better yet, stroll 10 minutes to Nauset Beach and take a quiet walk as the sun sets. Your genial hosts also prepare one of the finest breakfasts in town. See chapter 6.
- **Lighthouse Inn** (West Dennis, Mass.; ☎ 508/398-2244): A classic 1930s beachside resort, now run by the third generation, this homey little complex has everything a family could require, at affordable prices: comfy cottages, a calm strip of beach, plus a pool, tennis and volleyball courts, miniature golf and other lawn games, and a game room. Kids can enroll in a structured play program (for a slight surcharge); dinner is a communal feast, all the better to befriend other families. See chapter 6.
- **Tollgate Hill Inn** (Litchfield, Conn.; ☎ 800/445-3903 or 860/567-4545): No sacrifices in comfort will be made when you stay here, and you'll enjoy the marvelously atmospheric 1745 tavern that serves thoroughly up-to-date eclectic fusion cuisine. On weekends, they have live jazz, and Sunday brunch beside the fireplace in winter couldn't be more New England. See chapter 9.

- **Beech Tree** (Newport, R.I.; ☎ **800/748-6565** or 401/847-9794): Arrive on Friday afternoon at the Beech Tree in Newport and they sit you down to a complimentary bowl of chowder, fresh bread, and a glass of wine. Breakfast the next morning, huge and cooked to order, makes lunch irrelevant. All rooms have air-conditioning, TVs, and phones, unlike most B&Bs. See chapter 10.
- **Inn at Mad River Barn** (Waitsfield, Vt.; ☎ **800/631-0466** or 802/496-3310): It takes a few minutes to adapt to the spartan rooms and no-frills accommodations here. But you'll soon discover that the real action takes place in the living room and dining room, where skiers relax and chat after a day on the slopes, and share heaping helpings at mealtime. Rooms with breakfast are $65 for two in summer, and $95 in winter. See chapter 11.
- **Thayers Inn** (Littleton, N.H.; ☎ **800/634-8179** or 603/444-6469): This historic inn stands proudly along busy Main St. of the unpresupposing White Mountain town of Littleton. It's not overly elegant, but with all rooms under $80 it's one of the best deals for those seeking an in-town base in the mountains. See chapter 12.
- **Philbrook Farm Inn** (Shelburne, N.H.; ☎ **603/466-3831**): Go here if you're looking for a complete getaway. The inn has been taking in travelers since the 1850s, and they know how to do it right. The farmhouse sits on 1,000 acres between the Mahoosuc Mountains and the Androscoggin River, and guests can hike with vigor or relax in leisure with equal aplomb. Rooms for two are $145 or under, and that includes both breakfast and dinner. Ask about discounts for longer stays. See chapter 12.
- **Driftwood Inn** (Bailey Island, Maine; ☎ **207/833-5461**): Where else can you find rooms at the edge of the rocky Maine coast for about $75? This classic shingled compound dates from 1910 and offers mostly rooms with shared bath. But it's worth that small inconvenience for the views alone. See chapter 13.
- **Maine Idyll Motor Court** (Freeport, Maine; ☎ **207/865-4201**). The 20 vintage motor court cottages have all the classic appeal of an old-time vacation, and have been kept up spotlessly. No phones, no credit cards, and no frills, but solid value with rates ranging from $44 to $70. The downside? Traffic sounds from the nearby interstate. See chapter 13.

9 The Best Restaurants

- **Aujourd'hui** (Boston, Mass.; ☎ **617/451-1392**): The exquisite setting, spectacular view, telepathic service, and, of course, marvelous food combine to transport you to a plane where you might not even notice (or care) how much it's costing. See chapter 4.
- **Rialto** (Cambridge, Mass.; ☎ **617/661-5050**): This is a don't-miss destination if your plans include fine dining. The contemporary setting is a great match for chef Jody Adams's inventive cuisine, and the service is efficient without being too familiar—surely a draw for the visiting celebrities who flock here. See chapter 4.
- **The Regatta at Falmouth-by-the-Sea** (Falmouth, Mass.; ☎ **508/548-5400**): Perched over Falmouth Harbor, this soft-hued, candlelit dining room features exquisite nouvelle and fusion cuisine in an atmosphere that's more relaxed than reverential. What also distinguishes the Regatta is old-fashioned sensational service, in which your genial host table-hops, and wait staff are expertly trained. Signature dishes include a memorable crab-and-corn chowder, plus succulent lamb *en chemise*. See chapter 6.
- **Òran Mór** (Nantucket, Mass.; ☎508/228-8655): Climb up the stairs of this historic building and prepare yourself for a somewhat extravagant dining experience.

Chef/owner Peter Wallace has created an intimate setting for his creative international cuisine, served with utmost professionalism. The best sommelier on the island will assist you in choosing a wine to go with your elegant meal. See chapter 7.

- **Truc Orient Express** (West Stockbridge, Mass.; ☎ 413/232-4204): The artists and craftspeople who live in this funky Berkshires hamlet deserve something out of the prevailing red-sauce and red-meat mode. They get it in this converted warehouse, with eye-opening Thai, Vietnamese, and Southeast Asian dishes that rarely emerge from kitchens this far west of Ho Chi Minh City. Tastes range from delicate to sinus-clearing, and the service is sweetly diffident. See chapter 8.
- **Amberjacks Coastal Grill** (Norwalk, Conn.; ☎ 203/853-4332): Think Duval Street in Key West—that's where the chef/owner honed his craft before moving to this cooler shore. Such transplantations rarely work, but his uncommonly flavorful assemblages rouse weary palates. The menu leans to tropical fruits and aquatic denizens of the Caribbean, fired or freshened with Asian spices. See chapter 9.
- **Union League Café** (New Haven, Conn.; ☎ 203/562-4299): This august setting of arched windows and high ceilings is more than a century old and was long the sanctuary of an exclusive club. It still looks good, but the tone has been lightened into an approximation of a Lyonnais brasserie. The moderately priced menu observes the southern French tastes for curry, olive oil, pastas, lamb, and shellfish. See chapter 9.
- **Scales & Shells** (Newport, R.I.; ☎ 401/846-3474): Ye who turn aside all pretension get yourselves hence. There isn't a frill or affectation anywhere near this place, and since the left end of the wide-open kitchen is right at the entrance, there are no secrets, either. What we have here are marine critters mere hours from the depths, prepared and presented free of any but the slightest artifice. This might well be the purest seafood joint on the southern New England coast. See chapter 10.
- **Chantecleer** (Manchester Center, Vt.; ☎ 802/362-1616): Swiss chef Michel Baumann has been turning out dazzling dinners here since 1981, and the kitchen hasn't gotten stale in the least. The dining room in an old barn is magical; the waitstaff helpful and friendly. It's a great spot for those who demand topnotch continental fare, but don't like the fuss of a fancy restaurant. See chapter 11.
- **Hemingway's** (Killington, Vt.; ☎ 802/422-3886): Killington seems an unlikely place for serious culinary adventure, yet Hemingway's will meet the loftiest expectations. The menu changes frequently to ensure only the freshest of ingredients. If it's available, be sure to order the wild mushroom and truffle soup. See chapter 11.
- **T. J. Buckley's** (Brattleboro, Vt.; ☎ 802/257-4922): This tiny diner on a dark Brattleboro sidestreet serves up outsize tastes prepared by talented chef Michael Fuller. Forget about stewed-too-long diner fare; get in mind of big tastes blossoming from the freshest of ingredients prepared just right. See chapter 11.
- **Firepond** (Blue Hill, Maine; ☎ 207/374-9970): The lovely setting along a brook in the middle of one of Maine's loveliest villages is just the prelude. The food is also exceptionally well-prepared, a mix of New American fare with earthy seasonings. See chapter 13.
- **Robinhood Free Meetinghouse** (Robinhood, Maine; ☎ 207/371-2188): Don't be alarmed by the vast fusion menu that seems to draw from every continent save Antarctica. Chef Michael Gagne pulls it off, and with tremendous flair. The setting is superb—a spare, 1855 Greek Revival meetinghouse set miles from anywhere. See chapter 13.

- **White Barn Inn** (Kennebunkport, Maine; ☎ 207/967-2321): The setting, in an ancient, rustic barn, is magical. The tables are floor-length tablecloths, and the chairs feature imported Italian upholstery. The food? To die for. Enjoy entrees such as grilled duckling breast with ginger and sun-dried cherry sauce, or a roast rack of lamb with pecans and homemade barbecue sauce. See chapter 13.

10 The Best Local Dining Experiences

- **Durgin-Park** (Boston, Mass.; ☎ 617/227-2038): A meal at this landmark restaurant might start with oysters, and it might start with a waitress slinging a handful of napkins over your shoulder, dropping a handful of cutlery in front of you, and saying, "Here, give these out." The surly service usually seems to be an act, but it's so much a part of the experience that some people are disappointed when the waitresses are nice (as they often are). In any case, it's worked since 1827. See chapter 4.
- **Woodman's of Essex** (Essex, Mass.; ☎ 800/649-1773): This North Shore institution, one of the busiest restaurants anywhere, is not for the faint of heart—or the hard of artery, unless you like eating corn and steamers while everyone around you is gobbling fried clams and onion rings. The food at this glorified clam shack is fresh and delicious, and a look at the organized pandemonium behind the counter is worth the (reasonable) price. See chapter 5.
- **The Menemsha Bite** (Martha's Vineyard, Mass.; ☎ 508/645-9239): It's usually places like "The Bite" that we crave when we think of New England. This is your quintessential "chowdah" and clam shack, flanked by picnic tables. Run by two sisters employing their grandmother's recipes, this place makes superlative chowder, potato salad, fried fish, and so forth. The food comes in graduated containers, with a jumbo portion of shrimp topping out at around $25. Those in the know bring their picnic dinner over to nearby Menemsha Beach, where the sunsets are awesome. See chapter 7.
- **Abbott's Lobster in the Rough** (Noank, Conn.; ☎ 860/572-9128). Places like Abbott's abound along more northerly reaches of the New England coast, but here's a little bit o' Maine a Sunday drive from Manhattan (it's a short but baffling drive from Mystic Seaport). This frill-free Sound-side institution is an expanded shack with wooden picnic tables inside and out, featuring seafood by the bucket. Shore dinners rule, so roll up sleeves, tie on napkins and feedbags, dive into bowls of clam chowder and platters of boiled shrimp and steamed mussels, and dunk hot lobster chunks in pots of drawn butter. See chapter 9.
- **The Very First (Well, Probably) Burgers** (New Haven, Conn.): Not a lot of serious history has happened in New Haven, but boosters claim a lock on a couple of bedrock fast food essentials—it was here, they insist, that hamburgers as we know them were invented in 1900. The venue was **Louis' Lunch** at 261-263 Crown St. (☎ 203/562-5507), a boxy little brick luncheonette that lives on, moved from its original site in order to save it. The patties are freshly ground daily, thrust into vertical grills, and served on white toast. Garnishes are tomato, onion, and cheese. No catsup and no fries, so don't even ask. See chapter 9.
- **Wooster Street Pizza** (New Haven, Conn.): New Haven's claim to America's first pizza is a whole lot shakier, but it has few equals as purveyor of the ultrathin charred and bubble-crusted variety of what they still call "apizza" in these parts, pronounced "ah-peetz." Old-timer **Frank Pepe's** at 157 Wooster St. (☎ 203/ 865-5762) is usually ceded top rank among the local parlors, but it is crowded at

the summit by such contenders as **Sally's** at 237 Wooster St. (☎ **203/624-5271**) and the upstart **Brü Rm** at 254 Crown St. (☎ **203/495-1111**). See chapter 9.

- **Johnnycakes and Stuffies** (R.I.): Sooner or later, most worthy regional food faves become known to the wider world (witness Buffalo wings and Cajun popcorn). The Ocean State still clutches a couple of taste treats within its borders. "Johnnycakes" are flapjacks made with cornmeal, which come small and plump or wide and lacy, depending upon family tradition. "Stuffies" are the baby-fist–size quahog (*kwa*-hog or *koh*-hog), clams barely known elsewhere in New England. The meat is chopped up, combined with minced bell peppers and bread crumbs, and packed back into both halves of the shell.
- **Blue Benn Diner** (Bennington, Vt.; ☎ **802/442-5140**): This Bennington favorite, housed in a classic 1945 Silk City diner, has a barrel ceiling, acres of stainless steel, and a vast menu. Make sure you don't overlook specials scrawled on paper and taped all over the walls. And leave room for a slice of delicious pie, like blackberry, pumpkin, or chocolate cream. See chapter 11.
- **Al's** (Burlington, Vt.; ☎ **802/862-9203**): This is where Ben and Jerry go to eat french fries—as does every other potato addict in the state. See chapter 11.
- **Common Ground** (Brattleboro, Vt.; ☎ **802/257-0855**): There's no finer memorial to Brattleboro's hippie heritage than this vegetarian and whole food cooperative, where you can get everything from a simple meal of beans and tortillas to the rather more creative marinated sea vegetable salad. See chapter 11.
- **Chauncey Creek Lobster Pier** (Kittery Point, Maine; ☎ **207/439-1030** or 439-9024): Chauncey's is one of the most popular lobster pounds in the state, not the least because the Spinney family, which has been selling lobsters here since the 1950s, takes such obvious pride in their place. Lobster, served hot and fresh, is the specialty, of course, but they also serve up steamed mussels and clams. See chapter 13.
- **Portland Public Market** (Portland, Maine; ☎ **207/228-2000**): Newly opened in 1998, this wonderful, airy market features some of the best of what Maine raises, grows, and harvests. Get some food for chewing while on the hoof, or settle in at the seafood cafe or the upstairs dining area. See chapter 13.

11 The Best of the Performing Arts

- **Symphony Hall** (Boston, Mass.; ☎ **617/266-1492**): Home to the Boston Symphony Orchestra, the Boston Pops, and other local and visiting groups and performers, this is a perfect (acoustically and otherwise) destination for classical music. See chapter 4.
- **Hatch Shell** (Boston, Mass.; ☎ **617/727-9547**, ext. 555): This amphitheater on the Charles River Esplanade plays host to free music and dance performances and films almost every night in the summer. Around the Fourth of July, the Boston Pops provide the entertainment. Bring a blanket to sit on, and maybe a sweater. See chapter 4.
- **Boston's Theater District:** The area's performance spaces are in the midst of a nearly unprecedented boom, and this is the epicenter. Previews and touring companies of Broadway hits, local music and dance troupes, and other productions of every description make this part of town hop every night. See chapter 4.
- ***The Nutcracker*** (Boston, Mass.): New England's premier family-oriented holiday event is Boston Ballet's extravaganza (☎ **617/695-6955** for tickets). When the Christmas tree grows through the floor, even fidgety preadolescents forget that they think they're too cool to be here. See chapter 4.

- **Comedy Connection at Faneuil Hall** (Boston, Mass.; ☎ 617/248-9700): Even in the Athens of America, it's not all high culture. The biggest national names and the funniest local comedians take the stage at this Quincy Market hot spot. See chapter 4.
- **The Berkshire Theatre Festival** (Stockbridge, Mass.; ☎ 413/298-5576): An 1887 "casino" and nearby converted barn mount both new and classic plays from June to late August in one of the prettiest towns in the Berkshires. Name artists on the order of Joanne Woodward and Dianne Wiest are often listed as actors and directors in the annual playbill. See chapter 8.
- **Jacob's Pillow Dance Festival** (Becket, Mass.; ☎ 413/243-0745): Celebrated dancer/choreographer Martha Graham made this her summertime performance space for decades. Her partner in the endeavor was Ted Shawn, for whom the main stage is named. Guest troupes are among the world's best, often including Dance Theatre of Harlem, the Merce Cunningham Dance Company, and the Paul Taylor Company, supplemented by repertory companies working with jazz, flamenco, or world music. See chapter 8.
- **Tanglewood** (Lenox, Mass.; ☎ 617/266-1492 in Boston, 413/637-5165 in Lenox): By far the most dominating presence on New England's summer cultural front, the music festival that takes place on this magnificent Berkshires estate is itself in thrall to the Boston Symphony Orchestra and its director, Seiji Ozawa. While the BSO reigns, room is made for such guest soloists as Jessye Norman and Itzak Perlman as well as practitioners of other forms, from jazz (Dave Brubeck) to folk music (James Taylor) and the Boston Pops. See chapter 8.
- **Shakespeare & Company** (Lenox, Mass.; ☎ 413/637-3353): Edith Wharton's turn-of-the-century mansion and estate are host to multiple performances of works by her, contemporary playwrights, and especially, the Bard. From late May to Labor Day, the plays are presented at two outdoor amphitheaters and two indoor stages. Performers are highly professional in technique and range, but since big-name stars are rarely in evidence, ticket prices aren't too steep or hard to get. See chapter 8.
- **The Williamstown Theatre Festival** (Williamstown, Mass.; ☎ 413/597-3400): Classic, new, and avant-garde plays are all presented during the late-June–through– August season at this venerable festival. There are two stages, one for works by established playwrights, the smaller second venue for less mainstream or experimental plays. There is usually a Broadway headliner on hand; Frank Langella has been a frequent presence. See chapter 8.
- **The Norfolk Chamber Music Festival** (Norfolk, Conn.; ☎ 860/542-3000): A century-old "Music Shed" on the Ellen Battell Stoeckel Estate in this Litchfield Hills town shelters such important chamber performance groups as the Tokyo String Quartet and the Vermeer Quartet. Young professional musicians perform morning recitals. See chapter 9.
- **Summer in Newport** (R.I.): From Memorial Day to Labor Day, only a scheduling misfortune will deny visitors the experience of an outdoor musical event. In calendar order, the highlights (well short of all-inclusive) are: the July Newport Music Festival, the Rhythm and Blues Festival on the last July weekend, the August 2-day Ben & Jerry's Folk Festival and 3-day JVC Jazz Festival, and the 2-day Irish Music Festival toward the end of September. See chapter 10.
- **The Marlboro Music Festival** (Marlboro, Vt.; ☎ 215/569-4690 off-season, 802/254-2394 summers): Pablo Casals participated in this highly regarded festival between 1960 and 1973. He's gone, but today, you can hear accomplished masters and talented younger musicians in a 700-seat auditorium amid the

rolling hills of southern Vermont. Performances are held weekends mid-July to mid-August. See chapter 11.

- **The Maine Festival** (Brunswick, Maine; ☎ **207/772-9012**): What started as a counterculture celebration of Maine people and crafts has evolved into a popular mainstream event. Performers ranging from leggy and lithe dancers to rumpled blues artists. They're joined by poets, artists, and craftspeople, who gather from throughout Maine at this pretty coveside park the first weekend in August. See chapter 13.

12 The Best Destinations for Antique Hounds

- **Charles Street** (Boston, Mass.): Beacon Hill is one of the city's oldest neighborhoods, and at the foot of the hill is a thoroughfare that's equally steeped in history. Hundreds of years' worth of furniture, collectibles, and accessories jam the shops along its 5 blocks. See chapter 4.
- **Main Street, Essex** (Mass.): The treasures on display in this North Shore town run the gamut, from one step above yard sale to one step below nationally televised auction. Follow Route 133 west of Route 128 through downtown and north almost all the way to the Ipswich border. See chapter 5.
- **Route 6A: The Old King's Highway** (Cape Cod, Mass.): Antique buffs, as well as architecture buffs and country-road connoisseurs, will have a field day along scenic Route 6A. Designated a Regional Historic District, this former stagecoach route winds through a half-dozen charming Cape Cod villages and is lined with scores of antique shops. The largest concentration is in Brewster, but you'll find good pickings all along this meandering road, from Sandwich to Orleans. In addition, rigid preservation regulations have saved several centuries' worth of historic houses ranging from colonial to Victorian. See chapter 6.
- **Sheffield** (Mass.): This southernmost town in the Berkshires is home to at least three dozen dealers in collectibles, Americana, military memorabilia, 18th-century clocks, English furniture of the Georgian period, silverware, weather vanes . . . even antique birdhouses. Most of them are strung along Route 7, with a worthwhile detour west along Route 23 in South Egremont. See chapter 8.
- **Brimfield Antique and Collectible Shows** (Brimfield, Mass.): This otherwise tranquil and undistinguished town west of Sturbridge erupts with three monster shows every summer, in mid-May, mid-July, and early September. Upward of 3,000 dealers set up tented and tabletop shops in fields around town. Call ☎ **413/283-2418** for details, and make room reservations far in advance. See chapter 8.
- **Woodbury** (Conn.): More than 30 dealers strung along Main Street offer a diversity of precious treasures, near-antiques, and simply funky old stuff. American and European furniture and other pieces are most evident, but there are forays into crafts and assorted whimsies as well. Pick up the directory of the Woodbury Antiques Dealers Association, available in most of the shops. See chapter 9.
- **Newfane & Townshend** (Vt.): A handful of delightful antiques shops are hidden in and around these picture-perfect towns. But the real draw is the Sunday flea market, held just off Route 30 north of Newfane, where you never know what you'll turn up. See chapter 11.
- **Portsmouth** (N.H.). Picturesque downtown Portsmouth is home to a half-dozen or so antique stores and some fine used book shops. For more meaty browsing,

head about 25 miles northwest on Route 4 to Northwood, where a dozen good-size shops flank the highway. See chapter 12.

- **Route 1, Kittery to Scarborough** (Maine). Antiques scavengers delight in this 37-mile stretch of less-than-scenic Route 1. Antiques minimalls and high-class junk shops alike are scattered all along the route, though there's no central antique zone. See chapter 13.

2

Planning a Trip to New England

by Wayne Curtis

This chapter covers the nuts-and-bolts travel information you'll need before setting off on your New England journey. Browse through this section before you hit the road, and you stand a good chance of avoiding some of the common travel headaches that befall less-prepared travelers.

1 The Regions in Brief

BOSTON Oliver Wendell Holmes dubbed Boston the "Hub of the Universe," and the label stuck. Today, "The Hub" is the region's largest and most historic city. This metropolis of brick, leafy trees, and sea-gulls still exerts it allure, and is an important stop for travelers on any trip to New England.

CAPE COD & THE ISLANDS The ocean is writ large on Cape Cod, a low peninsula with miles of sandy beaches and grassy dunes that whisper in the wind. The carnival-like atmosphere of Province-town is a draw, as are the genteel charms of Nantucket and Martha's Vineyard, two islands just offshore.

THE BERKSHIRES Massachusetts' rolling hills at the state's western edge are home to historic old estates, graceful villages, and an abundance of festivals and cultural events, including the Tanglewood Music Festival and Jacob's Pillow Dance Festival.

THE PIONEER VALLEY Extending from the Vermont border in the north to the Connecticut border in the south, the area takes its name from the early settlers who arrived here in the 17th century. Among the many picturesque towns is unspoiled Historic Deerfield.

THE LITCHFIELD HILLS The historic northwest corner of Con-necticut has sleepy villages, hidden hiking trails, and a surfeit of New England charm just a couple of hours from New York City.

CONNECTICUT COAST The eastern coast is home to the his-toric towns of Mystic and New London, where you can get a glimpse of the shipbuilding trade at the Mystic Seaport Museum and the navy submarine base in nearby Groton.

NEWPORT, RHODE ISLAND AREA The lifestyles of those once truly rich and famous are on parade in Newport, once home to the likes of the Astors, Vanderbilts, and Auchinclosses. A tour of the oceanfront mansions will open your eyes.

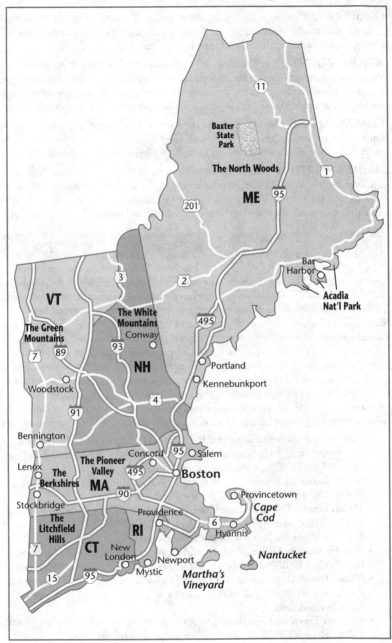

GREEN MOUNTAINS Extending the length of Vermont from Massachusetts to Canada, this mostly gentle chain of forested hills and low mountains offers good hiking, scenic backroad drives, and superb bicycling.

WHITE MOUNTAINS Starting in the mid–19th century, New Hampshire's White Mountains attracted travelers seeking to experience the grandeur of the rugged, windswept peaks and explore the forests dotted with glacial erratics and clear, rushing streams. New England's best backcountry hiking and camping is found here.

COASTAL MAINE Maine's rocky coast is the stuff of legend, art, and poetry. The southern coast features most of the state's beaches. Further "down east," you'll find rocky headlands and Acadia National Park, New England's only national park.

MAINE'S NORTH WOODS Consisting of millions of acres of uninhabited terrain, the North Woods is almost entirely owned by timber companies who harvest trees to feed their mills. Within this vast tree plantation are pockets of undisturbed wildlands that recall the era when Thoreau paddled and portaged his way north.

2 Visitor Information

New England's leading cash crop is the brochure. Shops, hotels, inns, museums and even restaurants invariably feature racks of colorful pamphlets touting local sights and accommodations. These mini-centers can be helpful in generating ideas for spur-of-the-moment excursions, but for a more comprehensive overview you should head for the state information centers or local chambers of commerce. Addresses and phone numbers are provided for each region in the chapters that follow. If you're a highly organized traveler, you'll call in advance and ask for information to be mailed to you several weeks before you set out on your trip. If you're like the rest of us, you'll swing by when you reach town and rifle through the racks as the staff is trying to close up for the day.

All six states are pleased to send out general visitor information packets and maps to travelers who call or write ahead. Here's the contact information, including web addresses. (All Web sites have links allowing you to request visitor packets on-line.)

- **Connecticut Office of Tourism,** Department of Economic and Community Development, 505 Hudson St., Hartford, CT 06106 (☎ **800/282-6863** or 860/270-8081). Web: **www.state.ct.us/tourism**.
- **Maine Office of Tourism,** 33 Stone St., 59 State House Station, Augusta, ME 04333. (☎ **888/624-6345**). Web: **www.visitmaine.com**.
- **Massachusetts Office of Travel and Tourism,** State Transportation Building, 10 Park Plaza, Suite 4510, Boston, MA 02116. (☎ **800/447-6277** or 617/973-5500). Web: **www.mass-vacation.com**.
- **New Hampshire Office of Travel and Tourism,** P.O. Box 1856, Concord, NH 03302 (☎ **800/258-3608** or 603/271-2343). Web: **www.visitnh.gov**.
- **Rhode Island Department of Economic Development,** 1 W. Exchange St., Providence, RI 02903 (☎ **800/556-2484** or 401/277-2601). Web: **www.visitrhodeisland.com**.
- **Vermont Travel and Tourism,** 134 State St., Montpelier, VT 05602 (☎ **800/837-6668** or 802/828-3237). Web: **www.travel-vermont.com**.

3 When to Go

THE SEASONS

The well-worn joke about New England's weather is that it has just two seasons: winter and August. There's a kernel of truth to that, especially in the north, but it's mostly a canard to keep outsiders from moving here. In fact, the seasons are one of those elements that make New England so distinctive.

SUMMER   Peak summer season runs from July 4 to Labor Day. Crowds surge into New England's tourist areas in the mountains and along the coast for the two months between these two holidays, and activity remains frenetic through Labor Day evening, when calm begins to reclaim these regions. Summers are verdant and lush, and in the mountains, warm (rarely hot) days are the rule, followed by cool nights. Along the coast, ocean breezes keep temperatures down; Cape Cod and the Islands, for example, are generally 10° cooler than the mainland in summer.

The weather in summer is typically decreed by the winds. Southerly winds bring haze, heat, and humidity. Northwest winds bring cool weather and knife-sharp vistas. These systems tend to alternate, often with rain between them, and the change from hot to cool will sometimes occur in a matter of minutes. Rain is never far away—some days it's a quick afternoon thunderstorm, other times it's a steady drizzle that brings a 4-day soaking. Travelers should come prepared.

For most of the region, especially the coastal areas, midsummer is the prime season for travel. Expect to pay premium prices at hotels and restaurants except near the empty ski resorts of northern New England, where you can often find bargains. Also be aware that early summer (generally mid-May through June) brings out voracious black flies and mosquitoes, especially in the north country. Outdoorspeople are best off waiting until July before setting off into the deep woods.

AUTUMN   In northern New England, don't be surprised to smell the tang of fall approaching as early as mid-August, a time when you'll also notice a few leaves turned blaze-orange in otherwise verdant trees at the edges of wetlands. Fall comes early here, puts its feet up on the couch, and stays for some time. The foliage season begins in earnest in the northern part of the region by the third week in September; in the south, it reaches its peak by the middle to end of October. Figure that the change in seasons in southern Connecticut runs three to four weeks behind northern Maine. And the higher elevations of the Green and White mountains likewise start to feel wintry a month or so before coastal locations.

Fall in New England is one of the great natural spectacles in the country, with the rolling hills blanketed with brilliant reds and stunning oranges. Autumn is garish in a way that seems determined to embarrass understated New England. Along winding country roads you'll find heaps of pumpkins for sale beneath blazing red sugar maples, and crisp apples available by the bushel. Take the time to scout out the farm stands, where you'll be amazed at the fertility of this seemingly flinty land.

Keep in mind that this is the most popular time of year to travel—bus tours flock here throughout October. As a result, hotels are invariably booked solid. Reservations are essential; you can also expect to pay a foliage premium $10 or $20 per room at many inns and hotels.

WINTER   New England winters are like wine—some years are good, some are lousy. During a good season, plenty of light, fluffy snow covers the deep woods and ski slopes. A good New England winter offers a profound peace as the muffling qualities of fresh snow bring a thunderous silence to the region. During these winters, exploring the forest on snowshoes or cross-country skis is an experience that borders on the magical.

During the *other* winters, the lousy ones, the weather brings a nasty mélange of rain and sleet. It's bone-numbing cold, and bleak, bleak, bleak. Look into the eyes of the residents on the streets during this time. They are all thinking of the Caribbean.

The higher you go in the mountains, and the further north you head, the better your odds of finding snow and avoiding rain. Winter coastal vacations can be spectacular (nothing beats cross-country skiing at the edge of the pounding surf), but it's a high-risk venture that could definitely yield rain rather than snow.

Ski areas naturally are crowded during the winter months. They're especially so during school vacations, when most resorts tend to jack up their rates.

SPRING   New England is famous for its elusive spring, which some residents claim lasts only a weekend or so, typically around mid-May, but sometimes as late as June. One day the ground is muddy, the trees are barren, and gritty snow is still piled in shady hollows. The next day, temperatures are in the 80s, trees are blooming, and kids are swimming in the lakes. It's weird. Travelers must be very crafty and alert if they want to experience spring in New England. It's also known as the **mud season,** and a time when many innkeepers and restaurateurs close up for a few weeks for either vacation or renovation.

Also be aware that New England is home to a vast number of colleges and universities. As graduation nears (mid- to late May and early June), the region is beset with unusually high hotel occupancy rates in towns near colleges, and even in the city of Boston, which is home to dozens of institutions of higher education. As always, it's best to book rooms in advance.

Burlington, Vermont's Average Temperatures (°F)

	Jan	Feb	Mar	Apr	May	June	July	Aug	Sept	Oct	Nov	Dec
Avg. High	25	27	38	53	66	76	80	78	69	57	44	30
Avg. Low	8	9	21	33	44	54	59	57	49	39	30	15

Boston's Average Temperatures (°F)

	Jan	Feb	Mar	Apr	May	June	July	Aug	Sept	Oct	Nov	Dec
Avg. High	36	38	43	54	67	76	81	79	72	63	49	40
Avg. Low	20	22	29	38	49	58	63	63	56	47	36	25

New England Calendar of Events

January

⚙ **New Year's and First Night Celebrations,** regionwide. Boston, Massachusetts; Portland, Maine; Providence, Rhode Island; Stamford, Connecticut; Portsmouth, New Hampshire; Burlington, Vermont; and many other cities and towns, including on Cape Cod and Martha's Vineyard, celebrate the coming of the New Year with an abundance of festivities. Check with local chambers of commerce for details. New Year's Eve.

February

- **U.S. National Toboggan Championships,** Camden, Maine. Raucous and lively athletic event where being overweight is an advantage. Held at the toboggan chute of the Camden Snow Bowl. Call ☎ **207/236-3438.** Early February.
- **Dartmouth Winter Carnival,** Hanover, New Hampshire. Huge and elaborate ice sculptures grace the village green during this festive celebration of winter, which includes numerous sporting events and other winter-related activities. Call ☎ **603/646-1110.** Midmonth.
- **Stowe Derby,** Stowe, Vermont. The oldest downhill/cross-country ski race in the nation pits racers who scramble from the wintry summit of Mount Mansfield into the village on the Stowe Rec path. Call ☎ **802/253-3423** for details. Late February.

March
- **St. Patrick's Day/Evacuation Day.** Parade, South Boston; Celebration, Faneuil Hall Marketplace. The 5-mile parade salutes the city's Irish heritage and the day British troops left Boston in 1776. Head to Faneuil Hall Marketplace for music, dancing, food, and plenty of Irish spirit. Call ☎ **800/888-5515.** March 17.
- **New England Spring Flower Show,** Dorchester, Massachusetts. This annual harbinger of spring presented by the **Massachusetts Horticultural Society** (☎ **617/536-9280**) draws huge crowds starved for a glimpse of green. Second or third week of the month.
- **Maine Boatbuilders Show,** Portland, Maine. More than 200 exhibitors and 9,000 boat aficionados gather as winter fades to make plans for the coming summer. A great place to meet boatbuilders and get ideas for your dream craft. Call ☎ **207/774-1067.** Mid- to late-March.

April
- ✪ **Patriots Day,** Boston (Paul Revere House, Old North Church, Lexington Green, Concord's North Bridge). The events of April 18 and 19, 1775, which signified the start of the Revolutionary War, are commemorated and reenacted. Participants dressed as Paul Revere and William Dawes ride to Lexington and Concord to warn the Minutemen that "the regulars are out" (not that "the British are coming"—most colonists considered themselves British). Mock battles are fought at Lexington and Concord. Call the **Lexington Visitor Center** at ☎ **781/862-1450,** or the **Concord Chamber of Commerce** at ☎ **978/369-3120.** Third Monday of the month; a state holiday.
- **Boston Marathon,** from Hopkinton, Massachusetts, to Boston. International stars and local amateurs run in the world's oldest and most famous marathon. The noon start means elite runners hit Boston around 2pm; weekend runners stagger across the Boylston Street finish line as many as 4 hours after that. Call the **Boston Athletic Association** at ☎ **617/236-1652.** Always run on Patriots Day, the third Monday of the month.
- **Sugarbush Spring Fling,** Waitsfield, Vermont. Ski-related events herald the coming of spring and the best season for skiing. Special events for kids. Call ☎ **802/ 583-2381.** Mid-April.
- ✪ **Daffodil Festival,** Nantucket. Spring's arrival is heralded with masses of yellow blooms adorning everything in sight, including a cavalcade of antique cars. Call ☎ **508/228-1700.** Late April.

May
- **Annual Basketry Festival,** Stowe, Vermont. A weeklong event with displays and workshops by talented weavers. Call the **Stowe Area Association** at ☎ **800/ 247-8693** or 802/253-7223. Mid-May.
- **Lilac Festival,** Shelburne, Vermont. See the famed lilacs (more than 400 bushes) at the renowned **Shelburne Museum** when they're at their most beautiful. Call ☎ **802/985-3346** for details. Mid- to late May.
- **MooseMainea,** Greenville, Maine. A variety of low-key events, from an antique-car show to a black-fly festival, are staged annually deep in the heart of moose territory. But the real attraction is the possibility of spotting one of the gangly beasts on a woodsy safari. Call ☎ **207/695-2702.** Mid-May to mid-June.
- ✪ **Brimfield Antique Fair,** Brimfield, Massachusetts. Up to 2,000 dealers fill several fields near this central-Massachusetts town, with similar fairs in early July and mid-September. Call ☎ **800/628-8379** or 508/347-2761. Mid-May.

- **Cape Maritime Week,** Cape Cod. A multitude of cultural organizations mount special events—such as lighthouse tours—highlighting the region's nautical history. Call ☎ **508-362-3828.** Mid-May.
- **Lobsterfest,** Mystic, Connecticut. An old-fashioned lobster bake on the banks of the Mystic River. Call ☎ **860/572-5315.** Late May.

June

- **Old Port Festival,** Portland, Maine. A daylong block party in the heart of Portland's historic district with live music, food vendors, and activities for kids. Call ☎ **207/772-2249.** Early June.
- **Yale-Harvard Regatta,** on the Thames River in New London, Connecticut. One of the oldest collegiate rivalries in the country. Call ☎ **617/495-4848.** Early June.
- **Market Square Weekend,** Portsmouth, New Hampshire. This lively street fair attracts hordes from throughout southern New Hampshire and Maine into downtown Portsmouth to dance, listen to music, sample food, and enjoy summer's arrival. Call ☎ **603/431-5388.** Second Saturday in June.
- **Taste of Hartford,** Hartford, Connecticut. One of New England's largest outdoor festivals. Many area restaurants serve up their specialties. You'll also get a "taste" of local music, dance, magic, and comedy. Call ☎ **860/728-3089.** Early June.
- **Convergence International Festival of the Arts,** Providence, Rhode Island. Various Providence arts organizations all pull together for this weeklong citywide event, which includes sculptural installations, musical performances, and other arts events. Call ☎ **401/751-1177.** Mid-June.
- **Motorcycle Week,** Loudon and Weirs Beach, New Hampshire. Tens of thousands of bikers descend on the Lake Winnipesaukee region early each summer to compare their machines and cruise the strip at Weirs Beach. The Gunstock Hill Climb and the Loudon Classic race are the centerpieces of the week's activities. Call ☎ **603/783-4931.** Mid-June.
- *Boston Globe* **Jazz Festival,** Boston. Big names and rising stars of the jazz world appear at lunchtime, after-work, evening, and weekend events, some of which are free. Contact the *Globe* (☎ **617/929-2000**), check the web at **boston.com/ jazzfest,** or pick up a copy of the paper for a schedule when you arrive in town. Some events require tickets purchased in advance. Third week of June.
- **Great Kennebec Whatever Week,** Augusta, Maine. A community celebration to mark the cleaning up of the Kennebec River, culminating in a wacky race involving all manner of watercraft, some more seaworthy than others. Call ☎ **207/623-4559** for details. Late June to early July.
- ✪ **Jacob's Pillow Dance Festival,** Becket, Massachusetts. The oldest dance festival in America features everything from ballet to modern dance and jazz. For a season brochure call ☎ **413/243-0745.** Late June through August.
- **Stowe Flower Festival,** Stowe, Vermont. Nearly three dozen events celebrate the joys of making the earth bloom, with offerings as diverse as garden tours and seminars by the experts. Call ☎ **800/247-8693.** Last week in June.
- **Williamstown Theater Festival,** Williamstown, Massachusetts. This nationally distinguished theater festival presents everything from the classics to uproarious comedies and contemporary works. Scattered among the drama are literary readings and cabarets. Call ☎ **413/597-3399.** Late June through August.

July

- **Prescott Park Arts Festival,** Portsmouth, New Hampshire. Stop by this attractive park for events all summer, including local musical acts on the main stage, kids shows, and lunchtime jazz concerts. The suggested donation is $2. Daily, July and August.

- **Boston Harborfest,** downtown (along Boston Harbor and the Harbor Islands). The city puts on its Sunday best for the Fourth of July, which has become a gigantic weeklong celebration of Boston's maritime history and an excuse to just get out and have fun. Events include concerts, guided tours, cruises, fireworks, the Boston Chowderfest, and the annual turnaround of the USS *Constitution.* Call ☎ **617/227-1528.** First week in July.
- **Boston Pops Concert and Fireworks Display,** Hatch Memorial Shell on the Esplanade. Independence Week culminates in the famous Boston Pops Fourth of July concert. People wait from dawn till dark for the music to start. The program includes Tchaikovsky's *1812 Overture* with actual cannon fire that segues into the fireworks. Call ☎ **617/727-9547,** ext. 555. July 4.
- **Independence Day,** regionwide. Communities throughout New England celebrate the Fourth of July with parades, cook-outs, road races, and fireworks. The bigger the town, the bigger the fireworks. Contact local chambers of commerce for details. July 4.
- **Newport Music Festival,** Newport, Rhode Island. Chamber-music concerts are held inside Newport's opulent mansions. For information call ☎ **401/846-1133.** Second and third weeks of July.
- **Historic Homes Tour,** Litchfield, Connecticut. One day is your only opportunity to tour this beautiful town's historic houses and gardens. Call ☎ **860/567-9423.** Midmonth.
- **Friendship Sloop Days,** Rockland, Maine. This 3-day event is a series of boat races that culminates in a parade of sloops. Call ☎ **207/596-0376.** Midmonth.
- **Wickford Art Festival,** Wickford, Rhode Island. Over 200 artists gather in this quaint village for one of the East Coast's oldest art festivals. Wickford is the ancestral home of author John Updike and is allegedly the setting for his book *The Witches of Eastwick.* Call ☎ **401/295-5566.** Weekend after July 4.
- **Vermont Quilt Festival,** Northfield, Vermont. Displays are only part of the allure of New England's largest quilt festival. You can also attend classes and have your heirlooms appraised. See class and event descriptions at **www.vqf.org** or call ☎ **802/485-7092** for more information. Mid-July.
- **Revolutionary War Days,** Exeter, New Hampshire. Learn all you need to know about the War of Independence during this historic community festival, which features a Revolutionary War encampment and dozens of reenactors. Call ☎ **603/772-2622.** Third weekend in July.
- **Marlboro Music Festival,** Marlboro, Vermont. This is a popular 6-week series of classical concerts featuring talented student musicians performing in the peaceful hills outside of Brattleboro. Call ☎ **802/254-2394** (in winter ☎ **215/569-4690**) for information. Weekends from July to mid-August.
- ❂ **Tanglewood,** near Lenox, Massachusetts. The Boston Symphony Orchestra makes its summer home at this fine estate, bringing symphony, chamber concerts, and solo recitals to the Berkshire Hills. Tickets go on sale in April, and the best seats are usually gone by May or June. Call the **Tanglewood Concert Line** at ☎ **413/637-1666** (July and August only) or **Symphony Hall** at ☎ **617/266-1492.** July to August.
- **Barnstable County Fair,** East Falmouth, Massachusetts (on Cape Cod). An old-time county fair complete with rides, food, and livestock contests. Call ☎ **508/563-3200.** Late July.
- **Maine Lobster Festival,** Rockland, Maine. Fill up on the local harvest at this event marking the importance and delectability of Maine's favorite crustacean. Enjoy a boiled lobster or two, and take in the ample entertainment during this

informal waterfront gala. Call ☎ **800/562-2529** or 207/596-0376. Late July/early August.

August

- **Maine Festival,** Brunswick, Maine. A 3-day festival showcasing Maine-made crafts, music, foods, and performers. It's boisterous, fun, and filling. Call ☎ **207/772-9012.** Early August.
- **Southern Vermont Art and Fine Crafts Fair,** Manchester, Vermont. Nearly 250 artisans show off their fine work at this popular festival, which also features creative food and good music. For more info, call ☎ **802/362-2100.** First weekend in August.
- ✪ **Ben and Jerry Folk Festival & JVC Jazz Festival,** Newport, Rhode Island. Thousands of music-lovers congregate at Fort Adams State Park for a heavy dose of performances on consecutive weekends in August. One of the nation's premier folk festivals is followed by one of the premier jazz venues. Performers have included big names like B. B. King, Suzanne Vega, Ray Charles, and Tony Bennett. For information on schedules and tickets call ☎ **401/847-3700.** Early August.
- **Annual Star Party,** St. Johnsbury, Vermont. The historic Fairbanks Museum and Planetarium hosts special events and shows, including night viewing sessions during the lovely Perseid Meteor Shower. Call ☎ **802/748-2372.** Mid-August.
- **Martha's Vineyard Agricultural Fair,** West Tisbury, Massachusetts. An old-fashioned country fair featuring horse pulls, livestock shows, musician and woodsman contests, and plenty of carnival action. Call ☎ **508/693-4343.** Third weekend in August.
- **Blueberry Festival,** Machias, Maine. A festival marking the harvest of the region's wild blueberries. Eat to your heart's content. Call ☎ **207/794-3543.** Midmonth.
- **Blue Hill Fair,** Blue Hill, Maine. A classic country fair just outside one of Maine's most beautiful villages. Call ☎ **207/374-9976.** Late August to Labor Day.

September

- **Windjammer Weekend,** Camden, Maine. Come visit Maine's impressive fleet of old-time sailing ships, which host open houses throughout the weekend at this scenic harbor. Call ☎ **207/236-4404.** Labor Day weekend.
- **Vermont State Fair,** Rutland, Vermont. All of Vermont seems to show up for this grand event, with a midway, live music, and plenty of agricultural exhibits. Call ☎ **802/775-5200** for details. Early September.
- **Cambridge River Festival,** Cambridge, Massachusetts. A salute to the arts, with music, dancing, children's activities and international food in an outdoor setting. Call ☎ **617/349-4380.** Early September.
- **Providence Waterfront Festival,** Providence, Rhode Island. Musical performances are the highlight of this weekend event, especially the jazz festival on Sunday. A food court and children's tent round out the activities. Call ☎ **401/785-9450.** Weekend after Labor Day.
- **Norwalk Oyster Festival,** Norwalk, Connecticut. This waterfront festival celebrates Long Island Sound's seafaring past. Highlights include oyster-shucking and -slurping contests, harbor cruises, concerts, and fireworks. Call ☎ **203/838-9444.** Weekend after Labor Day.
- **Eastern States Exhibition,** West Springfield, Massachusetts. "The Big E" is New England's largest agricultural fair with a midway, games, rides, rodeo and lumberjack shows, country-music stars, and lots of eats. Call ☎ **413/737-2443** or 413/787-1548. Mid- to late-September.
- **Provincetown Arts Festival,** Provincetown (Cape Cod), Massachusetts. One of the country's oldest art colonies celebrates its past and present with local artists

giving open studios. It's a great opportunity for collecting 20th-century works. Call ☎ **508/487-3424.** Late September.

- **Common Ground Fair,** Unity, Maine. A sprawling old-time state fair with an unusual twist: the emphasis is on organic foods, recycling, and wholesome living. Call ☎ **207/623-5515.** Late September.

October

- **Northeast Kingdom Fall Foliage Festival,** northeast Vermont. A cornucopia of events staged in towns and villages throughout Vermont's northeast corner heralds the arrival of the fall foliage season. Be the first to see colors at their peak. Call ☎ **802/748-3678** for information. Early October.
- **Fryeburg Fair,** Fryeburg, Maine. Cotton candy, tractor pulls, live music, and huge vegetables and barnyard animals are the draw at Maine's largest agricultural fair, which runs for 10 days during the peak of foliage season. There's also harness racing in the evening. Call ☎ **207/985-3278.** Early October.
- **Stowe Art and Fine Crafts Festival,** Stowe, Vermont. Some 180 artisans and craftspeople display their wares for sale beneath a heated tent. Call ☎ **802/253-7321.** Columbus Day weekend.
- **Mystic Chowderfest,** Mystic, Connecticut. A festival of soup served from bubbling cauldrons set on wood fires. Call ☎ **860/572-5315.** Mid-October.
- **Harvest Day,** Canterbury, New Hampshire. A celebration of the harvest season, Shaker-style. Lots of autumnal exhibits and children's games. Call ☎ **603/783-9511.** Mid-October.
- **Cranberry Harvest Festival,** Nantucket. Tour the scenic cranberry bogs and local inns just when foliage is at its burnished prime. Call ☎ **508/228-1700.** Mid-October.
- ✪ **Head of the Charles Regatta,** Boston and Cambridge. High school, college, and postcollegiate rowing teams and individuals—some 4,000 in all—race in front of hordes of fans along the banks of the Charles River. This event always seems to fall on the crispest, most picturesque Sunday of the season. Call the **Metropolitan District Commission Harbor Master** ☎ **617/727-0537** for information. Late October.

November

- **Victorian Holiday,** Portland, Maine. From late November until Christmas, Portland decorates its Old Port in a Victorian Christmas theme. Enjoy the window displays, take a free hayride, and listen to costumed carolers sing. Call ☎ **207/772-6828** for details. Late November.
- **Thanksgiving Celebration,** Plymouth, Massachusetts. The holiday that put Plymouth on the map is observed with a "stroll through the ages," showcasing 17th- and 19th-century Thanksgiving preparations in historic homes. Nearby Plimoth Plantation, where the colony's first years are re-created, wisely offers a Victorian Thanksgiving feast (reservations required). Call the **Plymouth Visitors Center** (☎ **800/872-1620**) or the **Plimoth Plantation** (☎ **508/746-1622**). Thanksgiving Day.
- **Brookfield Holiday Craft Exhibition & Sale,** Brookfield, Connecticut. Thousands of unique, elegant and artful gifts are displayed in gallery settings on three floors of a restored grist mill. Call ☎ **203/775-4526.** Mid-November to end-December.

December

- **Christmas Tree Lighting,** Boston, Prudential Center. Carol singing precedes the lighting of a magnificent tree from Nova Scotia—an annual expression of thanks from the people of Halifax for Bostonians' help in fighting a devastating fire more than 70 years ago. Call the **Greater Boston Convention and Visitors Bureau** at ☎ **617/536-4100.** Early December.

- **Boston Tea Party Reenactment,** Boston, Congress Street Bridge. Chafing under British rule, the colonists rose up on December 16, 1773, to strike a blow where it would cause real pain—in the pocketbook. Call ☎ **617/338-1773.** Mid-December.
- **Candlelight Stroll,** Portsmouth, New Hampshire. Historic Strawbery Banke gets in a Christmas way with old-time decorations and more than 1,000 candles lighting the 10-acre grounds. Call ☎ **603/433-1100** for information. First two weekends of December.
- **Woodstock Wassail Celebration,** Woodstock, Vermont. Enjoy classic English grog, along with parades and dances, at this annual event. Call ☎ **802/457-3555.** Mid-December.
- **Christmas Eve and Christmas Day.** Special festivities throughout New England. In Newport, Rhode Island, several of the great mansions have special tours; Mystic, Connecticut, has a special program of Christmas festivities; Nantucket, Massachusetts, features carolers in Victorian garb, art exhibits, and tours of historic homes. December 24 to 25.

4 The Active Vacation Planner

Don't let New England's outsize reputation for quaint villages and pastoral landscapes obscure another fact: it's also a superb destination for those who like outdoor adventure woven into their vacation itinerary.

Of course, New England isn't the Rockies nor western Canada—you won't find endless acres of unspoiled wilderness populated by grizzlies and bighorn sheep. But you may be surprised at the amount of undeveloped terrain open for backcountry activities. While the three northern states are the least densely populated and offer the best chances for slipping away from the crowds—Maine, for example, has one-third the population of Connecticut living on nearly seven times the land—you'll still find plenty of outdoor opportunities throughout the region, even in the southern reaches.

One bit of advice: If you're truly interested in adventure, plan to stay put. I've seen too many travelers try to bite off too much—biking in the Berkshires, canoeing in the Green Mountains, then maybe a little hiking in the White Mountains to round things off—all in one week. I'd advise adventurers to pick just one area, then settle in for a few days or a week, exploring locally by foot, canoe, or kayak. That way you'll have time to enjoy an extra hour lounging at a remote backcountry lake, or an extra day camping in the backcountry. It takes some time for New England to reveal its best secrets, and travelers in a hurry almost always overlook them.

Guidebooks & Guidance   Guidebooks to New England's trails, lakes, and rivers are plentiful and diverse. L.L. Bean in Freeport, Maine, the Appalachian Mountain Club in Boston, and the Green Mountain Club in Waterbury, Vermont, all have excellent selections of outdoor guidebooks, as do most local bookshops and the chain book stores throughout the region.

To order books in advance, contact the **Appalachian Mountain Club,** 5 Joy St., Boston, MA 02108 (☎ **617/523-0636**) for a brochure listing the guidebooks they publish; **Backcountry Publications,** c/o W. W. Norton & Co., Inc., 500 Fifth Ave,, New York, NY 10110, (☎ **800/233-4830**) also has an extensive catalog. You might also want to check out *Frommer's Great Outdoor Guide to New England.*

On the web, **GORP** has excellent listings for on-line information about New England recreational activities. Head for **www.gorp.com**, then choose from among states or outdoor activities. The site also has links for on-line ordering of outdoor guidebooks.

Local and regional outdoor clubs are also a good source of information, and some open their trips to nonmembers. The most established of the bunch is the Appalachian Mountain Club (see above). AMC regional chapters run group trips almost every weekend throughout the year, with northern New Hampshire especially well represented. Other groups include the **Green Mountain Club,** RR #1, Box 650, Route 100, Waterbury Center, VT 05677 (☎ **802/244-7037**), and the **Maine Outdoor Adventure Club** (☎ **207/828-0918** for a recorded hot line in Portland).

See also the section on recommended reading in the "Getting to Know" chapter for a selection of titles of interest to outdoorspeople.

Outfitter or Solo? New England's compact size and relatively easy access to recreational areas make a self-guided adventure quite easy. But many travelers still find it a great help (and stress reliever) to sign up with an outfitter who takes care of the equipment and planning.

Advantages of hiring an outfitter: You don't have to worry about having all the right equipment, or transporting it from your home to the field. You'll often make new friends, sometimes lasting ones, with like-minded folks in your group. You'll typically learn a lot about the region and its natural history from your guide. And you'll spend less time planning where to go (and second-guessing your trip choices when you arrive) if you leave the itinerary to someone else.

On the downside, you sacrifice some flexibility in choosing areas to visit, and the pace may be slower than you'd like (in groups the pokiest person often sets the pace). And the company you keep is a real crapshoot—you may make friends, but you may find yourself spending days with people you loathe within minutes of meeting.

You can minimize some of the hazards of group travel and reap some of the benefits by signing up for trips that offer outfitter-assisted travel. An outfitter provides you with equipment (for instance, a bike or canoe), an itinerary, vehicle support (such as transfer of luggage), and accommodations, and you can set your own pace and keep your own company. If this interests you, ask about this option when you inquire about trip arrangements.

Reputable outfitters offering New England trips include:

- **Bike Vermont,** P.O. Box 207, Woodstock, VT 05091 (☎ **800/257-2226**), offers weekend, 3-day, 5-day, and 6-day tours to all regions of the state.
- **Battenkill Canoe Ltd.,** Route 7A, Arlington, VT 05250 (☎ **800/421-5268** or 802/362-2800), runs 2- to 6-day canoe and walking trips in Vermont and Maine, with package prices including lodging at inns.
- **Vermont Bicycle Touring,** P.O. Box 711, Bristol, VT 05433 (☎ **800/245-3868** or 802/453-4811), organizes 6-day biking tours in Vermont, Cape Cod and the Islands, and Maine's Penobscot Bay and Acadia National Park.
- **Paddleways,** P.O. Box 65125, Burlington, VT 05406 (☎ **802/660-8606**), offers sea kayak tours on Vermont's Lake Champlain and among the Maine Islands, as well as shorter paddling workshops for beginners and intermediates. Choose from camping or inn-to-inn packages of 3 to 5 nights.
- **North Woods Ways,** RR #2 Box 159A, Guilford, ME 04443 (☎ **207/ 997-3723**), is run by Alexandra and Garrett Conover, who offer multiday canoe trips on several northern Maine rivers (and beyond), and are well versed in North Woods lore.
- **Maine Island Kayak Co.,** 70 Luther St., Peaks Island, ME 04108 (☎ **207/ 766-2373**) arranges multiday sea kayak expeditions along the Maine Coast, with evenings spend camping on islands or ensconced at an inn.

- **Allagash Wilderness Outfitters,** Box 620, Star Route 76, Greenville, ME 04441 (☎ **207/695-2821**), provides a complete canoe-camping gear (canoe, life vests, sleeping bags, tent, saw, ax, shovel, cooking gear, first-aid kit, etc.) and can arrange for a shuttle service for those interested in undertaking a weeklong self-guided canoe trip down Maine's noted Allagash River.

BIKING Small-town New England is synonymous with twisting country lanes, and has long attracted bicyclists in search of lightly traveled routes through pastoral landscapes. You can find superb biking roads in every state—from the Litchfield Hills of Connecticut to far Down East in Maine. The best routes aren't always obvious, and as everywhere, highway departments are afflicted with that mania for widening and straightening roads. The "25 Bicycle Tour" series published by Backcountry Guides (☎ **800/233-4830**) outlines worthy tours in Maine, New Hampshire, Vermont, and on Cape Cod and the Islands. Otherwise, equip yourself with a detailed local map and explore on your own. Bike shops throughout the region are also great spots to inquire about good biking routes.

Mountain bikers will find plenty of dirt roads and backcountry pathways to explore. Several ski areas open their lifts to bikers in summer, and you'll find good choices of trails in the White and Green mountains. **Acadia National Park's carriage roads** are unique and offer a great way to spend a couple of days exploring woods and rocky hills from the saddle.

BIRDING Birding in New England can be extremely rewarding. Serious birders spot 200 or 300 species over the course of a year, ranging from snowy egrets to puffins to bald eagles. During the spring migration, great armies of elusive warblers flit through the forests, and plovers and sandpipers appear along the sea. If you're in the least interested in birding, be sure to pack binoculars and field guides.

There are so many excellent places to view birds that's it's a daunting task to name even a fraction of them. Some spots where you'll never go wrong include Machias Sea Island, Maine (for puffins); Wellfleet Bay Wildlife Sanctuary, Wellfleet, Massachusetts; Monomoy Island, Massachusetts; Umbagog Lake, Errol, New Hampshire; and Acadia National Park, Bar Harbor, Maine.

Each state has one or more birding hot lines, which offer recorded announcements of recent unusual sightings: Connecticut: ☎ **203/254-3665;** Rhode Island: ☎ **401/949-3870;** Cape Cod: ☎ **508/349-9464;** Western Massachusetts: ☎ **413/ 253-2218;** Eastern Massachusetts: ☎ **781/259-8805;** Vermont: ☎ **802/457-2779;** New Hampshire: ☎ **603/224-9900;** and Maine: ☎ **207/781-2332.**

If you'd like to brush up on your spotting skills, consider a week on a Maine island with the **National Audubon Ecology Camp,** 613 Riversville Rd., Greenwich, CT 06831 (☎ **203/869-2017**). The classes are held on beautiful 333-acre Hog Island in Mucongus Bay, just northeast of Pemaquid Point.

CANOEING New England's abundant rivers, lakes, and ponds make it a superb destination for both flat-water and white-water canoeists. In the northern states, hundreds of camping sites occupy the shores and islands, tucked between tall firs and spruces.

Serious canoeists are advised to head for Maine, where the region's best long-distance canoeing is found. The 92-mile Allagash Wilderness Waterway, a series of remote rivers, lakes, and ponds (with a couple of portages), takes between 7 and 10 days to complete. Logging is prohibited within 500 feet of the corridor, and this linear state park has 80 primitive campsites along the route. Most of the trip is flat water, except for two Class II and III stretches known as Chase Rapids and Twin Brook Rapids. A ranger at Churchill Dam will truck you, your equipment, and your canoe around the rapids if you're uncertain of your skills. See the "Canoeing" sections of the Maine chapter for more information.

Outside of Maine, the best overnight canoeing is in Vermont, and the longest journeys are in the northern part of that state. The Winooski, Lamoille, and Missisquoi rivers are all tributaries of Lake Champlain.

The Connecticut River winds 407 miles south from near Canada through Vermont and New Hampshire (it forms the border between the two), then through western Massachusetts to southern Connecticut. It serves as the de facto Old Man River of New England, and offers wonderful day-canoeing options along much of its length.

FISHING   While longtime New Englanders grouse that fishing isn't what it used to be, there are still great opportunities for angling throughout the region. If you're a novice hoping for a quick return on your time, you're probably best off joining a party boat or charter for deep-sea fishing. Point Judith in Rhode Island is the best destination for this. For more information call the **Rhode Island Party & Charterboat Association** (☎ **401/737-5812**).

You can also surf-cast from the shores. Cape Cod and the Islands are to blues and stripers what Montana is to trout. Between late July and October, the bluefish are abundant. Striped bass are a bit more elusive, but still very catchable. Locals start hooking keepers in late May and continue throughout the summer.

The inland lakes and rivers will keep anglers busy throughout the season all through New England, although expect to elbow for casting room early in the season. Fishing licenses are required in all states; contact the local state fish and wildlife department or local sporting goods stores for details.

For a full-immersion fishing vacation, consider a trip to a rustic fishing camp in the Maine woods. Many of these date to the mid–19th century, when urban "sports" first headed en mass to the still forests and pristine lakes of New England's largest state. The **Maine Sporting Camp Association**, P.O. Box 89, Jay, ME 04239, represents some 50 traditional fishing lodges, and offers a fine brochure with brief descriptions of each.

Among the best regarded are **Grant's Kennebago Camps,** P.O. Box 786, Oquossoc, ME 04964 (☎ **800/633-4815** or 207/864-3608), and **Weatherby's**, Grand Lake Stream, ME 04637 (☎ **207/796-5558** summer or 207/237-2911 winter).

If you're looking to develop your skills in fly-fishing you've got a choice of two excellent fishing schools. The **L.L. Bean Fly-Fishing School,** Freeport, ME 04033 (☎ **800/341-4341**), offers various clinics and workshops throughout the year, including a weeklong program at Grand Lake Stream. And **Orvis** in Manchester, VT 05254 (☎ **800/235-9763**), runs one of the top fly-fishing programs in the country.

GOLF   New England has many stupendous golf courses, ranging from simple suburban courses to world-class links. For a serious golf getaway vacation, consider southwestern Vermont's **Equinox** resort (☎ **800/362-4747** or 802/362-4700), with its historic and intricately sculpted course, **The Balsams** (☎ **800/255-0600** or 603/255-3400) in northern New Hampshire, with two golf courses set amid craggy mountains and dense forest, or the **Samoset Resort** (☎ **800/341-1650** outside Maine or 207/594-2511) in Rockland, Maine, with 18 holes laid out along the shores of scenic Penobscot Bay.

Duffers looking to improve their swing might consider **The Golf School** (89 Mountain Rd., Mount Snow, VT 05356; ☎ **800/240-2555**) which offers classes at eight eastern locations, including these in New England: Amherst, New Hampshire; Carrabassett Valley, Maine; and Killington and Mount Snow, Vermont.

HORSEBACK RIDING   For day riders, stables offer lessons and guided trail rides throughout New England. The various sites include the shores of Block Island, the trails of the White Mountains, and the 200-year-old villages of northeastern Connecticut. Consult local chambers of commerce for further information.

The **Kedron Valley Stables,** Route 106, South Woodstock (☎ 802/457-1480), offer 4- to 6-day trips in the Green Mountain National Forest. You'll be guided through secluded woods and historic towns like South Woodstock, Tyson, and Window, staying at inns and eating at wonderful country restaurants.

In a state known for Morgans, the small pony-size horses at **Vermont Icelandic Horse Farm** in Waitsfield (☎ 802/496-7141) are a special treat. Icelandics move at a steady gait without much rocking, much like driving with good shocks. Owner Christina Calabrese offers half-day to 3-day rides for experienced riders only.

SAILING   New England's Atlantic coast deserves its reputation as one of the world's best cruising grounds. Every day in summer, you'll see billowing sails scudding in and out of legendary bays like Narragansett in Rhode Island and Penobscot off the mid-Maine coast. With hundreds of picturesque anchorages and ample services at the dozens of harbors, New England attracts weekend luffers and celebrity yachtsmen alike. If the ocean's a bit intimidating, head to the inland lakes. Champlain, Winnipesaukee, Sebago, and Squam, not to mention many smaller bodies of water, are also justly popular with sailors.

There are a handful of places for bareboat charters (renting a large sailboat for day or overnight trips). Prior sailing experience is necessary for a bareboat charter, especially on the Maine coast where fog, currents, wide tidal range, and a merciless shoreline can wreak havoc. Among the places to reserve a boat are **Hinckley Yacht Charters,** P.O. Box 950, Southwest Harbor, ME 04679 (☎ 800/492-7245), on the southwestern shores of Mount Desert Island (they offer 25 boats, ranging from a 34-ft. Sabre to a 49-ft. Hinckley), and **Winds of Ireland,** P.O. Box 2286, South Burlington, VT 05407 (☎ 802/863-5090), on New England's West Coast, which charters five Hunters, ranging from 28 to 40 feet.

If you lack the experience to charter a sailboat, try the next best thing—a windjammer cruise off the Maine coast. For more information, see the "Penobscot Bay" section of the Maine chapter.

SKIING   New England is the cradle of recreational skiing in the United States—the first ski lift in the country fired up in Vermont in 1933. As such, you'll find dozens of ski resorts, ranging from historic homespun areas perfect for low-key family getaways, to serious modern resorts with enough amenities to keep nonskiers content. Vermont is home to the region's largest ski area (Killington), and is the state where you'll find the best melding of small-town life and good slopes (especially at Stowe, Sugarbush, Okemo). But Maine's two leading ski resorts (Sunday River and Sugarloaf) are fast putting the state on the skier's map. New Hampshire has dozens of inviting slopes in the blustery, hard-edged White Mountains, and even western Massachusetts offers attractive ski areas. See the appropriate sections in each state chapter for more detailed information on alpine ski areas.

New England is also justly famed for its extensive cross-country skiing. A growing number of cross-country ski centers offer professionally groomed trails through a mix of terrain. Among the best destinations in the region are the **Trapp Family Lodge Cross-Country Ski Center** (☎ 800/826-7000 or 802/253-8511) in Stowe, Vermont, and the entire village of **Jackson, New Hampshire,** which is laced with a network of ski trails maintained by the **Jackson Ski Touring Foundation** (☎ 603/383-9355). Many other good choices exist; see the Maine, New Hampshire, and Vermont chapters for further guidance.

Spas for Sybarites

New England's Puritan work ethic and its inhabitants' preference for austere forms of recreation (fly-fishing in April, ice-skiing in January) don't necessarily mean that sybarites will be left out in the cold. Spas have made some inroads in New England, and now offer guests the sort of pampering that the Pilgrims would have found altogether mysterious. Here's a sampling of some reputable spas in New England:

Canyon Ranch, 165 Kemble St., Lenox, MA 01240 (☎ **800/742-9000**), is the region's premier spa. It's located in the Berkshires at the Bellefontaine mansion, an extraordinary 1897 replica of a palace at Versailles. The spa mixes athletic and outdoor endeavors with nutritional dining, and tops it all off with massages and other body work, including mud treatments, reflexology, shiatsu, and herbal wraps. The rates are astronomical (about $350 to $400 per person, per day), but note that this includes treatments and activities that are priced separately at many spas.

Norwich Inn & Spa, 607 W. Thames St., Route 32, Norwich, CT 06369 (☎ **800/ASK-4-SPA**), is an intimate retreat in a brick Georgian mansion not far from Mystic that offers a long list of services like invigorating loofah scrubs, clay wraps, and thalassotherapy, a seawater-based treatment. They also have tennis courts and an 18-hole golf course next door.

Topnotch at Stowe, Mountain Road, Stowe, VT 05672 (☎ **800/451-8686**), has a lovely indoor pool and fitness facility a short drive from the base of Stowe's ski area. There's plenty of hiking and horseback riding, and excellent meals served in the elegant restaurant on premises.

Northern Pines Health Resort, 559 State Rte. 85, Raymond, ME 04071 (☎ **207/655-7624**), is located 40 minutes west of Portland and is less extravagant than other spas. Located on 70 acres on the grounds of a former girl's summer camp, the resort emphasizes a holistic approach to stress control and weight loss. Meals are vegetarian, and tea-time is yoga time.

Kripalu Center for Yoga and Health, P.O. Box 793, Lenox, MA 01240 (☎ **800/967-3577**) is a superb destination for those who use "quest" as a verb. The emphasis is more on spirit and soul, with weekend retreats offering programs such as "The Art of Being Happy in Your Body" and "Taiko Drumming." It's located in the Berkshires on the grounds of a former Jesuit seminary ("Our accommodations are very simple compared to modern hotels."). The center publishes an extensive bulletin of classes and events.

WHITE-WATER RAFTING   In the last two decades whitewater rafting in Maine has grown from the sport of a few reckless adventurers is one of the more popular outdoor attractions. The Kennebec is Maine's most popular rafting river, with big waves in a scenic forested gorge. Trips are also offered on the more technical Penobscot and Dead rivers. Daily water releases from dams ensure enough high water from May into October on the Kennebec and Penobscot; the Dead River is run during several summer and fall releases. For contacts and more information, see the "North Woods" section of the Maine chapter.

Raft Maine (☎ **800/723-8633** or 207/824-3694) is a trade association of whitewater outfitters in Maine. You can also learn more about rafting at their Web site, **www.raftmaine.com**.

5 Health & Insurance

STAYING HEALTHY   New Englanders by and large consider themselves a healthy bunch, which they ascribe to clean living, brisk northern air, vigorous exercise (leaf raking, snow shoveling, etc.), and a sensible diet. Other than picking up a germ or two that might lead to colds or flu, you shouldn't face any serious health risks when traveling the region.

Exceptions? Well, yes—you may find yourself at higher risk when exploring the outdoors, particularly in the back country. A few things to watch for when venturing off the beaten track:

Poison ivy: The shiny, three-leafed plant is common throughout the region. If touched, you may develop a nasty, itchy rash that will seriously erode the enjoyment of your vacation. The reaction tends to be worse in some people than others. It's safest to simply avoid it. If you're unfamiliar with what it looks like, ask at a ranger station or visitor information booth for more information. Many have posters or books to help with identification.

Giardia: That crystal-clear stream coursing down a high backcountry peak may seem as pure as it gets, but consider the possibility that it may be contaminated with animal feces. Gross, yes, and also dangerous. Giardia cysts may be present in some streams and rivers. When ingested by humans, the cysts can result in copious diarrhea and weight loss. Symptoms may not surface until well after you've left the backcountry and returned home. Carry your own water for day trips, or bring a small filter (available at most camping and sporting goods shops) to treat backcountry water. Failing that, at least boil water or treat it with iodine before using it for cooking, drinking, or washing. If you detect symptoms, see a doctor immediately.

Lyme disease: Lyme Disease has been a growing problem in New England since 1975, when the disease was identified in the town of Lyme, Conn. In 1997, some 14,000 cases were reported nationwide. The disease is transmitted by tiny deer ticks—smaller than the more common, relatively harmless wood ticks. Look for a bull's-eye shaped rash (three to eight inches in diameter); it may feel warm but usually doesn't itch. Symptoms include muscle and joint pain, fever, and fatigue. If left untreated, heart damage may occur. It's more easily treated in early phases than later, so it's best to seek medical attention as soon as any symptoms are noted.

Rabies: Since 1989 rabies have been spreading northward from New Jersey into New England. The disease is spread by animal saliva, and is especially prevalent in skunks, raccoons, bats, and foxes. It is always fatal if left untreated in humans. Infected animals tend to display erratic and aggressive behavior. The best advice is to keep a safe distance between yourself and any wild mammal you may encounter. If bitten, wash the wound as soon as you can and immediately seek medical attention. Treatment is no longer as painful as it once was, but still involves a series of shots.

INSURANCE   There are three kinds of travel insurance: trip cancellation, medical, and lost luggage coverage. Trip cancellation insurance is a good idea if you have paid a large portion of your vacation expenses up front. Check your existing policies before you buy any additional coverage. For independent travel health-insurance providers, see below. Your homeowner's insurance should cover stolen luggage. For information on car renter's insurance, see "Getting Around by Car," below.

Some credit cards (American Express and certain gold and platinum Visas and MasterCards, for example) offer automatic flight insurance against death or dismemberment in case of an airplane crash.

Among the reputable issuers of travel insurance are:

- **Access America,** 6600 W. Broad St., Richmond, VA 23230 (☎ 800/284-8300);
- **Travel Guard International,** 1145 Clark St., Stevens Point, WI 54481 (☎ 800/826-1300);
- **Travel Insured International,** Inc., P.O. Box 280568, East Hartford, CT 06128 (☎ 800/243-3174);
- **Travelex Insurance Services,** P.O. Box 9408, Garden City, NY 11530-9408 (☎ 800/228-9792).

A company specializing in accident and medical care is **The Divers Alert Network** (DAN) (☎ 800/446-2671 or 919/684-2948) insures scuba divers.

6 Choosing an Inn or B&B

"The more we travel," said the unhappy couple next to me one morning at a New Hampshire inn, "the more we realize why we go back to our old favorites time and again." The reason for their disgruntlement? They were awake and switching rooms at 2am when rain began dripping on their bed through the ceiling.

New England's inns and bed-and-breakfasts offer a wonderful alternative to the cookie-cutter chain hotels that clutter freeway interchanges. But as that unfortunate couple learned, predictable isn't always a *bad* thing. In a chain hotel you can be reasonably certain that water won't come pouring in through your ceiling late at night. Likewise, you can expect that beds will be firm, that the sink will be relatively new and lacking in interesting sepia-toned stains, that you'll have a TV and telephone and lots of counter space next to the bathroom sink.

The downside is that chain hotels offer nothing for your soul. It's hard to craft a memorable vacation if you wake each morning in a boxy, bland room with a nonopening window that looks out on a parking lot. Throughout New England, you can find eclectic retreats that range from rustic country inns where you prop the window up with a worn piece of wood to let in the sound of crickets and owls at night, to rococo rooms decorated in high style from the high-gloss maple floors to the carved crown moldings. They're not only comfortable, they provide sustenance for the spirit as well.

Where to go? Inns and B&Bs have multiplied astronomically across New England in the past two decades, and figuring out a destination can be overwhelming. With this guide, we hope to point you in the right direction, and provide enough sense of style—from rustic to rococo, from jackets-only formal to feet-on-the-coffee-table informal—to help you narrow your choices and find a place that suits you best.

Keep in mind that the best way to develop a list of favorite places is to abandon caution and take some chances. Occasionally, you'll find yourself at a place that disagrees with you. But with just a bit of luck, you'll stumble into Ralph Waldo Emerson's notion of simple contentment: "Hospitality consists in a little fire, a little food, and an immense quiet."

INN VS. B&B

What's the difference between an inn and a B&B? The difference narrows by the day. Until recently, inns were always full-service affairs, whereas B&Bs consisted of private homes with an extra bedroom or two and a homeowner looking for some extra income. A few of these old-style B&Bs still exist—I once spent an evening sitting in a B&B living room watching Tom Brokaw on TV while being subjected to a lengthy harangue on the wretched state of national affairs by the owner—but they seem to be fading to the margins, in large part driven by the fact that Americans generally don't want to share bathrooms with other guests. (Europeans tend not to be as picky about private bathrooms.)

Today, the only difference between an inn and B&B is often that inns serve dinner (and sometimes lunch), whereas B&Bs provide breakfast only. At least that's the distinction we employ for this guide. Readers shouldn't infer that B&Bs in this guide are necessarily more informal or in any way inferior to a full-service inn. Indeed, many of the B&Bs listed have the air of gracious inns that accidentally overlooked dinner.

B&Bs today are by and large professionally run affairs, where guests have private baths, a common area that's separate from the owner's living quarters, and attentive service. The owners prepare sumptuous breakfasts in the morning, and offer a high level of service. All of the B&Bs in this guide are of the more professionally run variety, although many still have a few rooms that share bathrooms (we note where that's the case).

THE FINE PRINT

As innkeeping evolves into the more complex and demanding "hospitality industry," you're bound to bump up against more restrictions, rules, and regulations at places you're staying. It's always best to ask in advance to avoid unpleasant surprises. A few notes on recent trends:

SMOKING   Smokers looking to light up are being edged out the door to smoke on front lawns and porches. Ten years ago only a handful of places prohibited smoking. Today, I'd wager that the great majority of inns and B&Bs have banned smoking within their buildings entirely, and a number have even exiled smokers from their property, front lawn included.

Travelers should assume that no smoking is allowed at the accommodations listed in this guide, though the larger hotels usually have guest rooms set aside for smokers. If a smoke-free environment is important to you (or, conversely, will have you crawling the walls), be sure to inquire first.

ADDITIONAL GUESTS   The room rates published in this guide are for two people sharing a room. Many places charge $10 or more for each extra guest sharing the room. Don't assume that children traveling with you are free; ask first about extra charges. And don't assume that all places are able to accommodate children or extra guests. The guest rooms at some inns are quite cozy, and lack space for a cot. Ask first if you don't want to end up four to a bed.

MINIMUM STAY   It's become increasingly common for inns to require a minimum of 2 nights or more during busy times. These periods typically include weekends in the summer (or in the winter near ski areas), holidays, and the fall foliage season. These policies are mentioned in the following pages when known, but they're in constant flux, so don't be surprised if you're told you need to reserve an extra day when you make reservations.

Note that minimum-stay policies typically apply only to those making advance reservations. If you stop by an inn on a Saturday night and find a room available, innkeepers won't make you stay a second night.

PETS   Most places don't allow pets. We've noted the ones that do. But it's still good to ask first—in many establishments, pets are permitted only in one or two rooms (often a cottage or room with exterior entrance). Some innkeepers said they will accept pets, provided they can explain the ground rules first, and didn't want to have "pets allowed" mentioned in this guide. It doesn't hurt to inquire.

SERVICE CHARGES   Rather than increase room rates, hotels, inns, and B&Bs are increasingly tacking on unpublicized fees to guests' bills. Most innkeepers will tell you about these when you reserve or check in; the less scrupulous will surprise you at checkout.

The most common surcharge is an involuntary "service charge" of 10% or 15%. Coupled with state lodging taxes (even "sales-tax-free" N.H. hits tourists with an 8% levy), that can bump up the cost of a bed by 20% or 25% (or even more in Conn., which has a 12% lodging tax). Note that the rates listed in this guide don't include service charges or sales tax.

Other charges might include a foliage season surcharge ($10 or more per room), a "resort fee" (there's a 13% to 15% levy at Waterville Valley, N.H., hotels to underwrite guest access at the local athletic club), or a pet fee (as much as $10 per day extra). Other fees are more annoying than financially burdensome. One example: the Radisson Hotel in Burlington has in-room safes, for which guests are billed an additional $1 per day at checkout whether they use them or not.

7 Tips for Travelers with Special Needs

FOR TRAVELERS WITH DISABILITIES   Prodded by the Americans with Disabilities Act, a growing number of inns and hotels are retrofitting some of their rooms for people with special needs. Most innkeepers are quite proud of their improvements. When I arrive for a site visit, they're invariably quick to show me their new rooms with barrier-free entrances, wheelchair-accessible showers, and fire alarms equipped with strobe lights. Outdoor recreation areas, especially on state and federal lands, are also providing more trails and facilities for those who've been effectively barred in the past owing to seemingly small barriers. Accessibility is improving regionwide, but improvements are far from universal. When in doubt, call ahead to ensure that you'll be accommodated.

Wilderness Inquiry, Fifth Street SE, Box 84, Minneapolis, MN 55414 (☎ **800/ 728-0719** or 612/379-3858; **www.wildernessinquiry.org**), is a nonprofit that offers more than 100 adventure travel packages for disabled travelers nationwide, including canoe trips on the Moose and Allagash rivers in Maine.

FOR SENIORS   New England is well suited for older travelers, with a wide array of activities for seniors with discounts often available. It's wise to request a discount at hotels or motels when booking the room, not when you arrive. An identification card from the **American Association of Retired Persons (AARP)**, 601 E St. NW, Washington, DC 20049 (☎ **202/434-2277**), can be invaluable in obtaining discounts.

Excellent programs for seniors are offered by **Elderhostel,** which is based in Boston. These educational programs for people over 55 years old are reasonably priced and include lodging and meals. Participants can study everything from the art of downhill skiing to the art of autobiography. The locations where these classes are held are often intriguing and dramatic. For more information, contact Elderhostel, 75 Federal St., Boston, MA 02110 (☎ **617/426-7788**).

FOR FAMILIES   While New England doesn't have many big and splashy theme-park-style attractions, families shouldn't have any trouble being amused and entertained. The natural world often holds tremendous wonder for the younger set—an afternoon exploring mossy banks and rocky streambeds can be a huge adventure. Older kids may like the challenge of climbing a high mountain peak or learning to paddle a canoe in a straight line. And there's always the beach, which is usually good for hours of diversion.

Be sure to ask about family discounts when visiting attractions. Many places offer a flat family rate that is less than paying for each ticket individually.

Be aware that many inns cater to couples, and kids aren't exactly welcomed with open arms. A number of inns allow children, but only over a certain age. We note this in this guide, but it's still best to ask first just to be safe.

Recommended destinations for families include Cape Cod, with its miles of famous beaches and dunes, and Martha's Vineyard, with bike paths, beaches, and kid-scaled architecture in the cottage section of Oak Bluffs. Other destinations good for kids are Weirs Beach on New Hampshire's Lake Winnipesaukee, and Hampton Beach on New Hampshire's tiny coast, and York Beach and Acadia National Park, Maine.

North Conway, New Hampshire, also makes a good base for exploring with younger kids. The town has lots of motels with pools, and there are nearby train rides, aquaboggans, streams suitable for splashing around, easy hikes, and the always-entertaining StoryLand. Excellent children's museums are located in Mystic (Conn.), Boston, Portsmouth, Portland, and Norwich (Vt.).

Several specialized guides offer more detailed information for families on the go. Try *Best Hikes with Children in Vermont, New Hampshire, & Maine* by Cynthia and Thomas Lewis (Mountaineers, 1991); *Best Hikes with Children in Connecticut, Massachusetts, and Rhode Island,* also by Cynthia and Thomas Lewis (Mountaineers, 1998); *Fun Places to Go with Children in New England* by Pamela Wright and Diane Bair (Chronicle Books, 1998); and *Great Family Vacations North East* by Candyce Stapen (Globe Pequot, 1997).

FOR GAY & LESBIAN TRAVELERS   Provincetown on the tip of Cape Cod, is one of the first and still one of the most famous gay resort communities. Gay entrepreneurs and politicians are well represented in the town's businesses and politics, and much of the nightlife revolves around gay culture. By turns, the town can be wild and flamboyant, and understated and relaxed. For gay travelers somewhat anxious about being *out* in public, Provincetown is a place they can relax and enjoy themselves with aplomb.

Outside of Provincetown, New England isn't exactly a hotbed of gay culture, although there are noted pockets, like Ogunquit, Maine. But the cities, especially Providence, Boston, and Burlington, tend to be very welcoming to alternative lifestyles. For a small city, Portland, Maine, has an active gay population and three or four gay bars and clubs (it tends to fluctuate year to year), attracting many refugees from Boston and New York. Portland also hosts a sizable gay pride festival early each summer that includes a riotous parade and a dance on the city pier.

Outside of the metropolitan areas, attitudes toward homosexuality vary widely, but New Englanders tend to be fairly tolerant of people of all persuasions, provided they're not trying to impose a new tax on them.

In Boston, look for *One-in-Ten* (☎ **617/536-5390**), a monthly publication published by the same folks who put out the Phoenix newspapers in Boston, Worcester, and Providence. It often features groundbreaking articles, and has extensive listings of gay happenings around Boston and beyond. The Web version is at **www.phx.com/ alt1/standard/1in10/**.

Vermont has a fine monthly newsletter covering gay, lesbian, and bisexual issues called *Out in the Mountains* (E-mail: **oitm@together.net,** or write P.O. Box 1078, Richmond, VT 05477). Both the articles and ads will fill you in on gay happenings in the Green Mountain State. The newsletter is available free at many Vermont bookstores and other shops, or for $20 per year by mail from the address above. You can also check out the newsletter's Web site at **www.vtpride.org**.

For a more detailed directory of gay-oriented enterprises in New England, track down a copy of *The Pink Pages,* published by KP Media (66 Charles St., #283, Boston, MA 02114; E-mail: kpmedia@aol.com). The price is $8.95 (plus $11 with shipping and handling). Call ☎ **800/338-6550** or visit the firm's Web site at **www.pinkweb. com**.

More adventurous souls should consider linking up with the **Chiltern Mountain Club,** P.O. Box 407, Boston, MA 02117 (☎ **888-831-3100**). This is an outdoor adventure club for gays and lesbians; about two-thirds of its 1,400 members are men. The club organizes trips to northern New England throughout the year, and its members can help travelers with advice. The club also maintains a helpful Web site at **www.chiltern.org/chiltern**.

8 Getting There

BY CAR   Getting to New England by car doesn't require much special expertise. From the south, I-95 is the major interstate highway serving Connecticut, Rhode Island, Massachusetts, and Maine. The least stressful route (with fewer tractor-trailers) from New York to Boston is via Hartford, Connecticut, using I-84 and the Massachusetts Turnpike. The easiest approach to northern New England from southern New England is along one of the three main interstate highway corridors. I-91 heads more or less due north from Hartford along the Vermont–New Hampshire border, then angles through northern Vermont. Another major interstate is I-93, which departs from I-95 near Boston, then cuts through New Hampshire to connect with I-91 near St. Johnsbury, Vermont. For Maine, take I-95 north; it parallels the southern Maine coast before veering inland.

If scenery is your priority, the most picturesque way to enter New England is from the west. The most dramatic way to arrive in northern Vermont is to drive I-87 to Exit 34 near Port Kent on Lake Champlain, then catch the car ferry across the lake to Burlington. For a more southern route, take any of a half-dozen smaller state highways that cross from New York State into Connecticut and Massachusetts. These routes, while often slow going, take you through rolling hills and farmland and are exceptionally scenic.

Be aware that the interstates leading from Boston can be extremely sluggish on Friday afternoons and evenings in the summer, especially along the routes leading to Cape Cod and Maine. A handful of choke points (particularly the Bourne Bridge to Cape Cod and the Maine tollbooths on I-95) can back up for miles. North Conway, New Hampshire, is also famed for its nightmarish weekend traffic, especially during the foliage season.

BY PLANE   The traditional gateways to New England have been Boston, New York City, and Montreal. In the last few years, however, Providence, Rhode Island, and Manchester, New Hampshire, have grown in prominence thanks to the arrival of Southwest Airlines, which has brought competitive, low-cost airfares and improved service. Manchester in particular has gone from a sleepy backwater airport to a semi-major hub, recently eclipsing Portland in numbers of passengers served. Travelers looking for good deals to the region are advised to first check with Southwest (☎ **800/435-9792**, or on the Web site **www.iflyswa.com**) before pricing other gateways.

Major commercial carriers also serve Hartford, Connecticut (Bradley International); Burlington, Vermont; and Bangor and Portland, Maine. Note also that if you're heading to southwest Vermont (the Bennington or Manchester areas), the closest major airport is Albany, New York.

Several smaller airports in the region are served by feeder airlines and charter companies (see regional chapters for more information). Many of the scheduled flights from Boston to northern New England and Cape Cod and the Islands are aboard smaller prop planes; inquire with the airline or your travel agent if this is an issue for you.

Airlines serving New England include **American** (☎ 800/433-7300), **Comair** (☎ 800/354-9822), **Continental** (☎ 800/525-0280), **Delta** (☎ 800/221-1212), **Northwest** (☎ 800/225-2525), **Southwest** (☎ 800/435-9792), **TWA** (☎ 800/221-2000), **United** (☎ 800/241-6522), and **US Airways** (☎ 800/247-8786).

Carriers to Cape Cod and the Islands include some of the above, plus **Cape Air** (☎ 800/352-0714 or 508/771-6944), **Island Airlines** (☎ 800/248-7779 or 508/775-6606), and **Nantucket Airlines** (☎ 800/635-8787 or 508/790-0300). Charter flights throughout the region are offered by Cape Air and Nantucket Airlines, as well as by **Air New England** (☎ 800/693-8899 or 508/693-8899), **Cape Flight Limited** (☎ 508/775-8171), and **King Air Charters** (☎ 800/247-2427).

BY BUS   **Bonanza** (☎ **800/556-3815** or 617/720-4110) operates largely in Connecticut. **Concord Trailways** (☎ **800/639-3317** or 617/426-8080) serves New Hampshire and Maine, including some smaller towns in the Lake Winnipesaukee and White Mountains areas. **Greyhound** (☎ **800/231-2222** or 617/526-1810) is nationwide. **Peter Pan** (☎ **800/343-9999** or 617/426-7838) serves western Massachusetts and Connecticut. **Plymouth & Brockton** (☎ **508/746-0378**) serves Massachusetts's south shore and out to Cape Cod. And **Vermont Transit** (☎ **800/451-3292**) is affiliated with Greyhound and serves Vermont, New Hampshire, and Maine with frequent departures from Boston.

BY TRAIN   Most passengers who come to New England by train take the Northeast Direct service offered by **Amtrak** (☎ **800/872-7245**). It runs from Newport News, Virginia, to Boston via Washington, Baltimore, Philadelphia, and New York City. North of New Haven, Connecticut, the line divides into two branches, both of which reunite in Boston. Stops along the Hartford branch include Springfield and Worcester; stops on the Providence, Rhode Island branch include New London, Mystic, and Kingston. The route through Providence is about 15 minutes faster.

Train service is very limited in northern New England. Amtrak's *Vermonter* departs Washington, D.C., with stops in Baltimore, Philadelphia, and New York before following the Connecticut River northward. Stops in Vermont include Brattleboro, Bellows Falls, Claremont (N.H.), White River Junction, Randolph, Montpelier, Waterbury, Burlington/Essex Junction, and St. Albans. A bus connection takes passengers on to Montreal.

The *Ethan Allen Express* departs New York and travels north up the Hudson River Valley and into the Adirondacks before veering over to Vermont and terminating at Rutland. Buses continue on to Killington and north to Middlebury and Burlington. For schedule information or reservations call Amtrak's reservation number (listed above) or visit their Web site at **www.amtrak.com**.

The return of rail service from Boston to Portland, Maine, following a hiatus of three decades, has been repeatedly delayed. Service is currently slated to resume sometime in the year 2000, depending on local and national politics and other vagaries. Travelers should contact Amtrak for more information.

For rail service between New York and Connecticut, try cheaper **Metro North** (☎ **800/223-6052** or 212/532-4900), which runs commuter trains connecting many towns from New Haven to New York City.

9 Getting Around

BY CAR   The rise of the car culture doomed New England's once-extraordinary mass transit system. Today you pretty much need a car to do any serious exploring in the area, unless, of course, your trip is confined to the city of Boston.

The major New England airports all host national car-rental chains. Some handy phone numbers are **Avis** (☎ 800/831-2847), **Budget** (☎ 800/527-0700), **Enterprise** (☎ 800/325-8007), **Hertz** (☎ 800/654-3131), **National** (☎ 800/227-7368), **Rent-A-Wreck** (☎ 800/535-1391), and **Thrifty** (☎ 800/367-2277).

Demystifying Renter's Insurance   Before you drive off in a rental car, be sure you're insured. The basic insurance coverage offered by most car rental companies, known as the **Loss/Damage Waiver (LDW)** or **Collision Damage Waiver (CDW)**, can cost as much as $20/day. It usually covers the full value of the vehicle with no deductible if an outside party causes damage to the rental car. In all states but California, you will probably be covered in case of theft as well. Liability coverage varies according to company policy and state law, but the minimum is usually at least $15,000. If you are at fault in an accident, however, you will be covered for the full replacement value of the car but not for liability.

Most **major credit cards** provide some degree of coverage as well—provided they were used to pay for the rental. Terms vary widely, however, so be sure to call your credit card company directly before you rent. The credit card will cover damage or theft of a rental car for the full cost of the vehicle. If you already have insurance, your credit card will provide secondary coverage—which basically covers your deductible. Credit cards will not cover liability.

Arranging Car Rentals on the Web   Internet resources can make comparison shopping easier. **Microsoft Expedia** (**www.expedia.com**) and **Travelocity** (**www.travelocity. com**) help you compare prices and locate car rental bargains from various companies nationwide. They will even make your reservation for you once you've found the best deal.

BY BUS   See "Getting There" for a list of bus companies serving New England. While express bus service to major cities and tourist areas is quite good, and it is possible to travel within the region by bus, quirky schedules and routes between regional destinations may send you miles out of the way, greatly increasing trip time.

Fast Facts: New England

AAA   Members can get help with trip planning, road service, and discount tickets to events and attractions. American Automobile Association also offers excellent free maps to members. Call ☎ **800/564-6222** for more information on membership and branch locations throughout New England.

American Express   AMEX offers travel services, including check cashing and trip planning, through a number of affiliated agencies spread about the region. Call ☎ **800/221-7282.**

Liquor Laws   The legal age to consume alcohol is 21. In Maine, New Hampshire, and Vermont, liquor is sold at government-operated stores only; in Connecticut, Massachusetts, and Rhode Island, liquor is sold privately. Restaurants that don't have liquor licenses sometime allow patrons to bring in their own. Always ask first.

Maps   Maps of the region and individual states are available at convenience stores and supermarkets for $2 or $3. Some states also offer free road maps at their official tourist information centers (they're $1 in Maine). For more detailed coverage, consider purchasing one or more of the **DeLorme** atlases, available for Maine, Massachusetts, New Hampshire, and Vermont. These are sold at most

Driving Distances

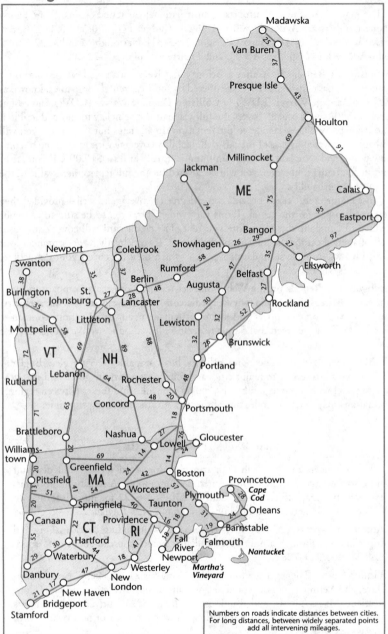

Numbers on roads indicate distances between cities.
For long distances, between widely separated points
add all intervening mileages.

book and outdoor stores around the region. DeLorme's map store is in Yarmouth, Maine (across from the Visitor Information Center at Exit 19).

Newspapers/Magazines   The *Boston Globe* and the *New York Times* are distributed throughout New England, although they can sometimes be hard to come by in smaller, more remote villages. But almost every small town has a daily or weekly newspaper covering local events and happenings. These are good sources of information for local events and specials at down-home restaurants—the day-to-day things that slip through the cracks at the tourist bureaus.

Speed Limits   The speed limit on interstate highways in the region is generally 65 miles per hour, although this is reduced to 55 miles per hour near cities. State highways are a less formal network, and the speed limits (and the conditions of the roads) vary widely. Watch for speed limits to drop in one or two stages as you approach a town; that's where the local constabulary often lurks in search of speeders.

Taxes   The state sales taxes as of 1999 are: Connecticut, 6% (12% on lodging); Maine, 5.5% (7% on meals and lodging); Massachusetts, 5% (5.7% on lodging statewide; local sales taxes may also apply); New Hampshire, no general sales tax but 8% tax on lodging and meals; Rhode Island, 7%; and Vermont, 5% (9% on meals and lodging).

3 For Foreign Visitors

by Wayne Curtis

Most of the information you'll need to ensure a pleasant trip will be found in the preceding introductory chapter. Aspects of U.S. laws, customs, and culture that might be perplexing to guests from overseas are covered in this chapter.

1 Preparing for Your Trip

ENTRY REQUIREMENTS

DOCUMENTS   Canadian citizens have it easiest—they need only to present some form of identification at the U.S. border. A passport isn't necessary unless you plan to stay more than 90 days.

More than two dozen countries are currently participating in the Visa Waiver Pilot program, which allows travelers to enter the United States for up to 90 days with just a valid passport and a visa waiver form. Travelers under this program generally must also have a return ticket and proof of solvency. Check with your travel agency for the current rules. The countries in 1999 were Andorra, Argentina, Austria, Australia, Belgium, Brunei, Denmark, Finland, France, Germany, Iceland, Ireland, Italy, Japan, Liechtenstein, Luxembourg, Monaco, Netherlands, New Zealand, Norway, San Marino, Slovenia, Spain, Sweden, Switzerland, and the United Kingdom.

Other foreign visitors should apply for a U.S. visa at the embassy or consulate with jurisdiction over their permanent residence. You can apply for a visa in any country, but it's generally easier to get one at home. Applicants must have a passport valid for at least 6 months beyond the dates they propose to visit, a passport-size photo (1.5-inch square), and some indication that they have a permanent residence outside the United States. Applicants must also fill out a Form OF-156 (available free at all U.S. embassies and consulates).

Once in the country, foreign visitors come under the jurisdiction of the Immigration and Naturalization Service (INS). If you'd like to change the length or the status of your visa, contact the nearest INS office.

Be sure to carefully check the valid dates on your visa. If you overstay a couple of days, it's probably no big deal, but a longer overstay may hinder efforts to get another visa the next time you apply.

MEDICAL REQUIREMENTS   Unless you've recently been in an area suffering from an epidemic (such as yellow fever or cholera), you don't need any inoculations to enter the United States. Keep in mind not all prescription drugs that are sold overseas are necessarily available in the United States. If you bring your own supplies (especially syringes), it's wise to carry a physician's prescription in case you need to convince customs officials that you're not a smuggler or drug addict.

CUSTOMS REQUIREMENTS   Plane and ship passengers will be asked to fill out a customs form. Visitors planning to spend at least 72 hours in the United States may bring 200 cigarettes, 3 pounds of smoking tobacco, or 100 cigars (but no Cuban cigars), and $100 worth of gifts, without paying any duties. Anything over these amounts will be taxed. No fresh food may be brought into the country, and some restrictions may apply to other foods; live plants are also prohibited. Up to US$10,000 in cash may be brought in or out of the country without any formal notification. If you are carrying more than that amount, you must notify customs officials.

MONEY

The basic unit of U.S. currency is the dollar, which consists of 100 cents. Common coins include a penny (1¢), nickel (5¢), dime (10¢), and quarter (25¢). You may come across a 50¢ or $1 coin, but these are relatively rare. Dollar bills and coins are accepted everywhere, but some smaller shops won't accept larger bills ($50 or up). It's best to travel with a plentiful supply of $10 and $20 bills.

CURRENCY EXCHANGE   Foreign exchange bureaus, which are common in many countries, are rare in the United States. Many banks will exchange foreign currency for dollars, but it's often a time-consuming and expensive process, especially for the less familiar currencies. It's best to plan ahead and obtain dollars or dollar-based traveler's checks in your own country before departure.

Canadian dollars are commonly accepted in the border states of Maine, New Hampshire, and Vermont, although it's harder to use Canadian currency the further you are from the border. Most hotels and many restaurants will accept Canadian currency at a discount close to its current trading value; ask what the rate is before buying to avoid unpleasant surprises.

TRAVELER'S CHECKS   Traveler's checks are considered as good as cash in most U.S. shops and banks. Widely recognized brands include American Express, Barclay's, Thomas Cook, and Visa. With other types of checks, you might meet with some resistance, particularly in smaller towns. Some small shops may resist cashing checks of $100 or more if they have insufficient change; it's best to cash these at hotels or banks. Many banks will cash traveler's checks denominated in U.S. dollars without charge.

ATMS   Check with your bank as to whether you can use automatic teller machines (ATM) in the United States. The most popular U.S. ATM networks are **Cirrus** (☎ 800/424-7787; www.mastercard.com/atm/) and **Plus** (☎ 800/843-7587; www.visa.com/atms).

CREDIT CARDS   It wouldn't be impossible to travel the country without cash, and just a credit card in your back pocket. Among the most commonly accepted credit cards are American Express, Discover, MasterCard, and Visa. Because American Express charges a higher rate for processing its transactions, a number of hotels and restaurants refuse to accept the card. Credit cards are commonly accepted in lieu of deposits when renting a car or a hotel room. Many ATMs (automatic teller machines) will debit your credit card and provide cash on the spot. Don't leave your card as a deposit—the information should be recorded by the person handling the transaction and your card returned to you.

INSURANCE

You are strongly urged to take out a traveler's insurance policy to cover any emergencies that may arise during your stay here. The United States does not offer national medical coverage; medical services must be paid for in cash or by an insurance company. Be aware that hospital and doctors' fees are *extremely* high in the United States, and even a minor medical emergency could result in a huge extra expense.

Comprehensive policies available in your country may also cover other disasters, including bail (in the event you are arrested), automobile accidents, theft or loss of baggage, and emergency evacuation to your country in the event of a dire medical situation.

Check with your local automobile association or insurance company for detailed information on traveler's insurance. Packages such as "European Worldwide Services" in Europe are sold by automobile clubs and travel agencies at attractive rates. Travel Assistance International (TAI) (☎ **800/821-2828** or 202/347-2025) is the agent for European Assistance Worldwide, so holders of this company's policies can contact TAI for assistance while in the United States.

Canadians should check with their provincial health offices or call HealthCanada (☎ **613/957-3025**) to find out the extent of their coverage and what documentation and receipts they must take home in the event they receive medical treatment in the United States.

SAFETY

New England—with the notable exception of parts of Boston—has among the lowest crime rates in the country. The odds of anything untoward happening during your visit here are very slight. But all travelers are advised to take the usual precautions against theft, robbery, and assault.

Travelers should avoid any unnecessary displays of wealth in public. Don't bring fat wads of cash out of your pocket, and save your best jewelry for private occasions. If you are approached by someone who demands money, jewelry, or anything else from you, do what most Americans do: Hand over what the mugger requests. Don't argue. Don't negotiate. Just comply. Afterwards, immediately contact police (see "Emergencies," in "Fast Facts," below).

The crime you're statistically most likely to encounter is theft of items from your automobile. Break-ins can occur any time of the day or night. Don't leave anything of value in plain view; that offers a tempting target for even the casual miscreant. Store your valuables locked securely in your trunk, or better still, keep them with you at all times.

Late at night you should look for a well-lighted area if you need to step out of your car for any reason. Also, it's not advisable to sleep in your car late at night at highway rest areas, which can leave you vulnerable to robbers.

Take the usual precautions against leaving cash or valuables in your hotel room. Many hotels have safe-deposit boxes. Smaller inns and hotels often do not, although it can't hurt to ask to leave small items in the house safe. A good number of small inns in New England don't even have locks on guest-room doors. Don't be alarmed; if anything, this is a good sign, indicating that the staff keeps alert and that there have been no problems in the past.

2 Getting to & Around the United States

GETTING THERE   Most international travelers come into New England either from Canada, or via Boston's Logan Airport or one of the three New York City–area airports. Boston offers the easiest access to northern New England. Portland, the

White Mountains, and the southern Green Mountains are 2 to 3 hours away by car. If you're headed for southern New England, both New York and Boston offer convenient gateways.

Dozens of airlines serve New York and Boston airports from overseas, although New York gets far more air traffic from abroad, and thus the fares are often more competitive. Some helpful numbers include (all numbers in London) **American Airlines** (☎ 0181/572-5555), **British Airways** (☎ 0345/222-111), **Continental** (☎ 4412/9377-6464), **Delta** (☎ 0800/414-767), **United** (☎ 0181/990-9900), and **Virgin Atlantic** (☎ 0293/747-747).

Those coming from Latin America, Asia, Australia, or New Zealand will probably arrive through gateway cities like Miami, Los Angeles, or San Francisco, clearing customs before connecting onward. Airports with regularly scheduled flights into the region include—in addition to Boston—Hartford, Connecticut; Providence, Rhode Island; Portland, Maine; Manchester, New Hampshire; and Burlington, Vermont. Albany, New York, is another option, especially if your destination is southern Vermont.

GETTING AROUND   Most traveling within the United States is by car, and there isn't the extensive inter- or intra-city public transportation that you find in Europe and other parts of the world.

However, throughout the New England region, bus service is fairly extensive, and you can connect to all major cities and many smaller ones through hubs in Boston or New York. Most busses leave Boston from the South Station, 700 Atlantic Ave., and New York from the Port Authority Bus Terminal, Eighth Avenue and 42nd Street. There is frequent train service along the Northeast Corridor from New York to Boston and to most major New England cities.

Travelers seeking to explore the more remote regions like the Litchfield Hills, the Berkshires, northern Maine, or the White Mountains will need to rent a car. Cars may be easily rented at most airports, and in many in-town locations in the larger cities. See the previous chapter for a listing of toll-free phone numbers for car-rental firms.

Fast Facts: For the Foreign Traveler

Abbreviations   On highway signs and publications you'll often see the states of New England abbreviated. Connecticut is "Conn." or "Ct." Massachusetts is "Mass." or "MA," Maine is "Me.," New Hampshire is "N.H.," Rhode Island is "R.I.," and Vermont is "Vt."

Automobile Organizations   Becoming a member of an automobile club is handy for obtaining maps and route suggestions and can be helpful should an emergency arise with your car. The nation's largest automobile club is the American Automobile Association (AAA), which has nearly 1,000 offices nationwide. AAA offers reciprocal arrangements with many overseas automobile clubs; if you're a member of an automobile club at home, find out whether your privileges extend to the United States. For more information on AAA, call ☎ **800/564-6222.**

Business Hours   Businesses are typically open from 9am to 5pm Monday to Friday. Banks typically shut down at 3 or 4pm, although ATM machines operate 24 hours. Most restaurants and some shops stay open until 8 or 9pm. If you need something after hours, head to the nearest mall, which is typically open until 9pm or so.

Climate   See "When to Go," in the previous chapter.

Currency   See "Money," above.

Drinking laws   You must be 21 years old to drink alcohol legally in most of the United States. No matter what your age, state laws in New England are notoriously harsh on those who drive drunk. Know your tolerance. If you plan to exceed that level, allow enough time for the effects to wear off, or imbibe within walking distance of your hotel or inn.

Driving   A current overseas license is valid on U.S. roads. If your license is in a language other than English, it's recommended that you obtain an International Drivers Permit from the American Automobile Association affiliate or other automobile organization in your own country prior to departure. (See "Automobile Organizations," above. Also see "Gasoline" below.)

Electricity   Electrical incompatibility makes it tricky to use in the United States appliances that are manufactured elsewhere. The current here is 110 to 120 volts, 60 cycles, compared to the 220 to 240 volts, 50 cycles used in much of Europe. If you're bringing an electric shaver, camera flash, portable computer, or other gadget that requires electricity, be sure to bring the appropriate converter and plug adapter.

Embassies/Consulates   Embassies are located in Washington, D.C. Call directory assistance (☎ **202/555-1212**) and request the phone number. (Directory assistance calls are free from some pay phones.)

A handful of countries maintain consulates in Boston. Among English-speaking countries, these include **Canada,** 3 Copley Place, Suite 400, Boston, MA 02116 (☎ 617/262-3760); **Great Britain,** Federal Reserve Plaza, 600 Atlantic Ave. (25th floor), Boston, MA 02210 (☎ 617/248-9555); and **Ireland,** 535 Boylston St., Boston, MA 02116 (☎ 617/267-9330). Other consulates are: **France,** Park Square Building, South 750, 31 St. James Ave. Boston, MA 02116 (☎ 617/542-7374); **Germany,** 3 Copley Place, Suite 500, Boston MA 02116 (☎ 617/536-8172); **Israel,** Statler Office Building, 20 Park Plaza, Suite 1020, Boston, MA 02116 (☎ 617/542-0041).

Emergencies   In the event of any type of emergency—whether medical, fire, or if you've been the victim of a crime—simply dial ☎ **911** from any phone. You do not need a coin to make this call. A dispatcher will immediately send medics, police, or the fire department to assist you. If 911 doesn't work, dial "0" and report your situation to the operator. If a hospital is near when a medical emergency arises, look for the emergency entrance, where you will be quickly attended to.

Gasoline (Petrol)   One U.S. gallon equals 3.8 liters. Several grades are available; unleaded gas with the highest octane rating are the most expensive. Most rental cars take "regular" unleaded (only older cars still take leaded gasoline). Gasoline is widely available throughout New England, with the exception of the North Woods region of Maine, where you can travel many miles without seeing a filling station. Gas prices vary throughout the region owing to varied state taxes. In general, you're better off filling up in larger cities or towns before setting off to remote or rural areas.

Holidays   With some important exceptions, national holidays usually fall on Monday to allow workers a 3-day weekend. These are Martin Luther King Day (third Monday in January), Presidents' Day (third Monday in February),

Memorial Day (last Monday in May), Labor Day (first Monday in September), and Columbus Day (second Monday in October). Exceptions are New Year's Day (January 1), Independence Day (July 4), Veterans Day (November 11), Thanksgiving (fourth Thursday in November), and Christmas (December 25). A holiday celebrated in Maine and Massachusetts only, is Patriots' Day, the third Monday in April. On these holidays, banks, government offices, and post offices are closed. Shops are sometimes open and sometimes not on holidays, but assume that virtually everything except for some restaurants will be closed on Thanksgiving and Christmas Day.

Languages   Some of the larger hotels may have multilingual employees, but don't count on it. Outside large cities, English is usually the only language spoken. Along the Canadian border and in some Maine locales (including Old Orchard Beach, Biddeford, Lewiston, and Van Buren), French is commonly spoken or at least understood.

Legal Aid   If a foreign tourist accidentally breaks a law, it's most likely to be for exceeding the posted speed limit on a road (it's also the law U.S. residents most frequently run afoul of). If you are pulled over by a police officer, don't attempt to pay the fine directly—that may be interpreted as a bribe, and you may find yourself in deeper trouble. You'll be issued a summons with a court date and a fine listed on it; if you pay the fine by mail, you won't have to appear in court. If you are arrested for a more serious infraction, you'll be allowed one phone call from jail. It's advisable to contact your embassy or consulate.

Mail   Virtually every small town and village has a post office; ask anyone on the street where it is and you'll be directed there. Mail within the United States (as of 1999) costs 33¢ for a 1-ounce letter, and 22¢ for each additional ounce; postcards are 20¢. A half-ounce letter to Mexico is 40¢; a half-ounce letter to Canada is 46¢. All other countries are 60¢ for a half ounce, $1 for a full ounce. If in doubt about weight or costs, ask the postal clerk. Mail may also be deposited at mailboxes with the inscription U.S. MAIL or UNITED STATES POSTAL SERVICE.

If you need to receive mail during your travels, have your correspondents address it to your name, "c/o General Delivery" at the city or town you are visiting. Go in person to the main post office to collect it; you'll be asked for identification (a passport is ideal) before it's given to you.

Newspapers/Magazines   Foreign newspapers and magazines are commonly found in Boston and Cambridge, but are harder to track down elsewhere in New England. Your best bet is to check in the phone book for one of the larger chain bookstores like Borders or Barnes & Noble. These offer a selection from the overseas press.

Safety   See "Safety" earlier in this chapter.

Taxes   Visitors to the United States are assessed a $10 Customs tax upon entering the country, and a $6 tax on departure. The United States does not have a value-added tax (VAT). Many states have a sales tax (usually 5% to 6%) added on to the price of goods or a tax on services like hotel rooms and restaurant meals. See "Fast Facts: New England" in chapter 2 for a run-down on the New England states.

Telephone & Fax   Pay phones are not hard to find except in the more remote regions. Shops that have public phones inside usually display a blue sign featuring a bell within a circle outside the store. Telephone numbers beginning with "800," "888," or "877" are toll-free. Press "1" before dialing a toll-free number.

Don't confuse these with "900" numbers, which carry a substantial per-minute charge and are often used for phone-sex lines.

Local pay-phone calls typically cost 35¢ for an unlimited amount of time. How far you can call on a local call varies from place to place, and the boundaries will often seem arbitrary. If you're uncertain whether a call is long distance or not, try it as a local call. If a recorded voice comes on telling you to deposit more money for the first 3 minutes, that means it's a long-distance call.

Two kinds of telephone directories are available, the *White Pages*, which list private residences and businesses in alphabetical order, and the *Yellow Pages*, which lists all local services and businesses by type of activity. However, directories are hard to come by outside of hotel rooms and private residences. If you're unsure of a phone number, dial ☎ 411 or the area code and 555-1212; an operator (more and more often an automated voice these days) will tell you the number. There is often (not always) a charge of 75¢ to $1 for this service.

Long-distance calls at pay phones tend to be very expensive, and you'll need a lot of coins. There are other options. At some phones you can use your credit card, and prepaid phone cards are available at many convenience stores and other outlets, typically for $5 or $10. Follow the instructions on the card (you'll call a toll-free number first, then punch in a code and the number you wish to call). Long-distance charges using the cards are usually about 15¢ to 35¢ per minute, which is less expensive and more convenient than feeding coins into a pay phone. Some cards offer generous rates on overseas calls, but rates vary widely; ask before you buy.

Be aware that many hotels (notably the more expensive chain hotels) tack on a surcharge for local and long-distance calls made from your room. Even toll-free calls can cost $1 or more. Ask about these charges when you check in. If your hotel does add a high surcharge and you plan to make a lot of phone calls, you're better off using a pay phone in the lobby.

To charge the phone call to the person receiving your call, dial "0" then the area code and the number you're calling. An operator (or computer) will come on the line and ask your name, and will then call the number to ask if the person you're calling accepts the call.

If you need to send or receive a fax (facsimile), ask at your hotel, or look in the Yellow Pages under "Fax Transmission Service." Many photocopy shops will provide this service for you.

Time   All of New England is in the eastern time zone—the same as New York, and the rest of the Eastern seaboard. All states shift to daylight saving time (1 hour ahead) on the first Sunday in April, and back to standard time on the last Sunday in October. "Spring forward, fall back" is how most Americans remember how to adjust their clocks.

Tipping   Tipping is commonly practiced in the United States. Service charges are never added to bills. Be aware that in restaurants servers depend on tips as part of their wage, and tipping isn't considered optional unless the service is really deplorable. Usually tip 15%; for outstanding or special service, 20%. Bartenders get 10% to 15%; bellhops, $1 per bag; cab drivers, 10% to 15% of the fare; chamber staff $1 per day; checkroom attendants, $1 per garment; hairdressers and barbers, 15% to 20%; parking attendants, $1. No tipping is expected at gasoline stations, at fast-food or other self-service restaurants, or to ushers in cinemas and theaters.

Toilets   Public toilets are commonly called "rest rooms." In U.S. towns and cities facilities are scarce, and where they do exist they're often not fit for use, or, in large cities, may even be unsafe. In Boston, Hartford, or other cities, your best bets are museums, public buildings, or department and other large stores. Malls almost always have decent rest rooms. Restaurants and bars often have signs indicating FOR PATRONS ONLY, but this can sometimes be bypassed by buying a candy bar or a cup of coffee. Fast-food restaurants (like McDonald's or Burger King) are a good bet for reasonably clean toilets. On the major highways, rest stops usually have good facilities.

4

Boston & Cambridge

by Marie Morris

The turn of the century finds Boston where it was at the turn of the other three centuries of its existence: in the middle of a transformation. As the 1700s dawned, the town was growing into a center of colonial commerce; 100 years later, flush with post-Revolutionary prosperity, it was on its way to becoming a city. The end of the 19th century saw the rise of the "Athens of America" and the rich cultural tradition that endures today.

The turn of the millennium finds the city executing a physical change. The elevated expressway that slashes through downtown is moving underground, development is spreading along the waterfront, and Boston is preparing to show off. When the "Big Dig" highway-construction project ends (in 2004, assuming it's on schedule), it will leave behind a mecca of high technology that's also a relentlessly historic destination.

As it has for hundreds of years, Boston offers cosmopolitan sophistication on a comfortable scale, balancing celebration of the past and pursuit of the future. Whether you want to follow in the footsteps of Paul Revere or of Ally McBeal, Boston offers something for everyone, and plenty of it. Throw out your preconceptions about the city's being some sort of open-air history museum (although that's certainly one of the guises it can assume) and allow your interests to dictate where you go.

It's not perfect, of course. Some of its drawbacks are large—the sickening real-estate prices that go hand-in-hand with an economic boom, the construction site that dominates downtown. And some are small—there's almost no late-night scene, the drivers have earned their terrible reputation, and the local accents are as earsplitting as any in Brooklyn or Chicago.

Cambridge and Boston are so closely associated that many people believe they're the same—a notion both cities' residents and politicians are happy to dispel. Cantabrigians are often considered more liberal and better educated than Bostonians, which is another idea that's sure to get you involved in a heated discussion. Harvard dominates Cambridge's history and geography, but there's more to see than just the university.

Take a few days (or weeks) to get to know the Boston area, or use it as a gateway to the rest of New England. Here's hoping your experience is memorable and delightful.

1 Orientation

ARRIVING

BY PLANE   The major domestic carriers flying into Boston are **AirTran** (☎ 800/247-8726), **American** (☎ 800/433-7300), **Continental** (☎ 800/523-3273), **Delta** (☎ 800/221-1212), **Midway** (☎ 800/446-4392), **Northwest** (☎ 800/225-2525), **TWA** (☎ 800/221-2000), **United** (☎ 800/241-6522), and **US Airways** (☎ 800/428-4322). Many major international carriers also serve Boston.

The entry of the discount airline **Southwest** (☎ 800/435-9792) into the market has made viable alternatives of **T. F. Green Airport,** in the Providence suburb of Warwick, R.I. (☎ 888/268-7222; www.pvd-ri.com), and Manchester International Airport in New Hampshire (☎ 603/624-6556; www.flymanchester.com). Several major carriers serve both, and prices often undercut rates for flying to Boston. Providence is a better choice because **Bonanza** (☎ 800/556-3815) offers bus service to Boston's South Station daily 9am to 9pm; the fare is $15 one-way, $27 round-trip. Allow at least 90 minutes. From Manchester, you can arrange to be picked up and dropped off by **Flight Line** (☎ 800/245-2525). The one-way fare is $28, and 24 hours' notice is required.

Boston's **Logan International Airport,** in East Boston at the end of the Sumner, Callahan, and Ted Williams tunnels, is 3 miles across the harbor from downtown. Terminals A, C, and E have information booths; C and E have BankBoston branches that handle currency exchange; and all five terminals have ATMs. An ongoing overhaul called "Logan 2000" looks terrible, but everything is clearly marked.

The Massachusetts Port Authority (☎ 800/23-LOGAN; www.massport.com) coordinates airport transportation. Access to the city is by subway, cab, bus, and boat. The **subway** is fast and cheap—10 minutes to Government Center and 85¢. Free **shuttle buses** run from each terminal to the Airport station on the MBTA Blue Line from 5:30am to 1am every day of the year. The Blue Line stops at Aquarium, then at State Street and Government Center, downtown points where you can exit or transfer (free) to the other lines.

A **cab** from the airport to downtown costs about $18 to $24. The ride into town takes 10 to 45 minutes, depending on traffic and the time of day. If you must travel during rush hour or on Sunday afternoon, allow extra time, or plan to take the subway or water shuttle.

The trip to the downtown waterfront (near cab stands and several hotels) in a weather-protected **boat** takes 7 minutes, dock to dock. Courtesy buses from the airport terminals run to the Logan ferry dock. The **Airport Water Shuttle** (☎ 617/330-8680) runs to Rowes Wharf on Atlantic Avenue from 6am to 8pm Monday to Thursday, until 11pm on Friday, Saturday from 10am to 11pm, and Sunday and national holidays (except January 1, July 4, Thanksgiving, and December 25) from 10am to 8pm. The one-way fare is $10 for adults and children 12 and up, $5 for senior citizens, and free for children under 12.

Harbor Express (☎ 617/376-8417) runs between the airport and Long Wharf 24 times a day Monday to Thursday between 5:30am and 9pm, Friday until 11pm, and less frequently on weekends. There's no service on Thanksgiving and December 25. The one-way fare is $10.

The Massachusetts Port Authority (see above) coordinates **bus service** from the airport to Gate 25 at South Station. The one-way fare is $6, free for children under 12. Some hotels have **limousines** or shuttle vans; ask when you make your reservations. To arrange private service, call ahead for a reservation, especially at busy times. Your hotel can recommend a company, or try **Carey Limousine Boston** (☎ 800/ 336-4646 or 617/623-8700) or **Commonwealth Limousine Service** (☎ 800/ 558-LIMO outside Mass., or 617/787-5575).

BY CAR   Boston is 218 miles from New York; driving time is about 4½ hours. The 992-mile drive from Chicago to Boston should take around 21 hours; from Washington, D.C., it takes about 8 hours to cover the 468 miles.

Driving to Boston is not difficult, but between the cost of parking and the hassle of downtown traffic, the money you save may not be worth the aggravation. The **"Big Dig"** dominates the landscape along the Central Artery, which is being moved underground without being closed. If you're thinking of using the car to get around town, think again.

The major highways that run to and from Boston are **I-90,** the Massachusetts Turnpike (known as the "Mass. Pike"), an east-west toll road that leads to the New York State Thruway; **I-93/U.S. 1,** extending north to Canada and leading to the Northeast Expressway, which enters downtown Boston; **I-93/Route 3,** the Southeast Expressway, which connects Boston with the south, including Cape Cod; and **I-95** (Massachusetts Route 128), which connects to I-93 and to highways in Rhode Island, Connecticut, and New York to the south and New Hampshire and Maine to the north.

The **Mass. Pike** extends into the center of the city and connects with the **Central Artery** (the John F. Fitzgerald Expressway), which meets the Northeast Expressway. To avoid Central Artery construction, exit at Prudential Center in the Back Bay.

To reach Cambridge, take **Storrow Drive** or **Memorial Drive** (on either side of the Charles River). Storrow Drive meets the Mass. Pike's Allston/Brighton exit and has a Harvard Square exit that leads across the Anderson Bridge to John F. Kennedy Street and into the square. Memorial Drive intersects with Kennedy Street; turn away from the bridge to reach the square.

The **American Automobile Association** (☎ 800/AAA-HELP; www.aaa.com) provides members with maps, itineraries, and other travel information, and arranges free towing if you break down. The privately operated Mass. Pike arranges its own towing; if you break down, wait in the car until one of the regular patrols arrives.

BY TRAIN   Boston has three rail centers: **South Station** on Atlantic Avenue, **Back Bay Station** on Dartmouth Street across from the Copley Place mall, and **North Station** on Causeway Street near the FleetCenter. **Amtrak** (☎ 800/USA-RAIL or 617/482-3660; www.amtrak.com) runs to South Station from New York, with stops at Route 128 and Back Bay Station. Express trains make the trip in about 4 hours; others take 4½ to 5 hours or longer. Amtrak is scheduled to institute "high-speed rail" service (3 hours each way) on the New York–Boston route sometime in 2000.

From Washington, D.C., count on 8½ hours; traveling time from Chicago is 22 hours (sleepers are available). During slow times, excursion fares may be available. Discounts are not offered on Friday and Sunday afternoon. Always remember to ask for the discounted rate; also remember that for longer trips, it may be easier than you think to find an airfare that's cheaper than the train.

At South Station you can take the Red Line to Cambridge or to Park Street, the hub of the MBTA **subway** (☎ 617/222-3200; www.mbta.com), where you can make connections to the Green, Blue, and Orange lines. The Orange Line connects Back Bay Station with Downtown Crossing (where there's a walkway to Park Street station) and other points. The MBTA **commuter rail** serves Ipswich, Rockport, and Fitchburg from North Station, and points south of Boston, including Plymouth, from South Station.

BY BUS   The **South Station Transportation Center,** on Atlantic Avenue next to the train station, is the city's bus-service hub. It's served by regional and national lines, including **Greyhound** (☎ **800/231-2222** or 617/526-1801; www.greyhound.com), **Bonanza** (☎ **800/556-3815** or 617/720-4110), and **Peter Pan** (☎ **800/237-8747** or 617/426-8554).

VISITOR INFORMATION

BEFORE YOU LEAVE HOME   Contact the **Greater Boston Convention & Visitors Bureau,** 2 Copley Place, Suite 105, Boston, MA 02116-6501 (☎ **888/ SEE-BOSTON** or 617/536-4100; fax 617/424-7664; www.bostonusa.com). It offers a comprehensive visitor-information kit and a "Kids Love Boston" kit; each costs $5.25 and includes a travel planner, guidebook, map, and coupon book with shopping, dining, attractions, and nightlife discounts. The bureau provides information on attractions, dining, performing arts and nightlife, shopping, and travel services through its **"Boston by Phone"** service, accessible from the main phone numbers.

The **Massachusetts Office of Travel and Tourism,** 100 Cambridge St., 13th Floor, Boston, MA 02202 (☎ **800/227-6277** or 617/727-3201; fax 617/727-6525; www. mass-vacation.com) has a great Web site that even offers a "lobster tutorial." The free *Getaway Guide* magazine includes information about attractions and lodgings, a map, and a seasonal calendar.

The **Cambridge Office for Tourism,** 18 Brattle St., Cambridge, MA 02138 (☎ **800/862-5678** or 617/441-2884; fax 617/441-7736; www.cambridge-usa.org), distributes information about Cambridge.

An excellent source of information for travelers with disabilities is **Very Special Arts Massachusetts,** 2 Boylston St., Boston, MA 02116 (☎ **617/350-7713;** fax 617/ 482-4298; TTY 617/350-6836; www.vsamass.org; E-mail: vsamass@aol.com). It has a comprehensive Web site and publishes *Access Expressed! Massachusetts: A Cultural Resource Directory* ($5), which includes general access information and specifics about more than 200 arts and entertainment facilities in the state.

ON THE WEB   Two **Excite** sites that are packed with information and links are www.city.net/countries/united_states/massachusetts/boston and www.city.net/countries/united_states/massachusetts/cambridge. **Frommer's** Web site (www.frommers. com) has a Boston section, and the **National Park Service** (www.nps.gov) is an excellent resource. The **Massachusetts Port Authority** (www.massport.com) lists many links for visitors, as do the cities of **Boston** (www.ci.boston.ma.us) and **Cambridge** (www.ci.cambridge.ma.us).

Once you're ready to start planning activities, check out ✪ **Boston.com** (www. boston.com). It has links to publications, museums and other arts resources, including the Museum of Fine Arts, and an interactive tour of the Freedom Trail.

IN PERSON   The **Boston National Historic Park Visitor Center,** 15 State St. (☎ **617/242-5642**), across the street from the Old State House and the State Street T, is a good place to start exploring. National Park Service rangers staff the center, dispense information, and lead free tours of the Freedom Trail. The audiovisual show about the trail provides basic information on 16 historic sites. The center is wheelchair accessible and has rest rooms and comfortable chairs. Open daily from 9am to 5pm except January 1, Thanksgiving, and December 25.

The Freedom Trail begins at the **Boston Common Information Center,** 146 Tremont St., on the Common. The center is open Monday to Saturday from 8:30am to 5pm and Sunday from 9am to 5pm. The **Prudential Information Center,** on the main level of the Prudential Center, is open Monday to Saturday from 9am to 8pm, and Sunday from 11am to 6pm. The **Greater Boston Convention & Visitors Bureau** (☎ **888/SEE-BOSTON** or 617/536-4100) operates both centers.

There's a small information booth at **Faneuil Hall Marketplace** between Quincy Market and the South Market Building. It's outdoors and staffed in the spring, summer, and fall from 10am to 6pm Monday to Saturday, noon to 6pm Sunday.

In Cambridge, there's an **information kiosk** (☎ **617/497-1630**) in the heart of Harvard Square, near the T entrance at the intersection of Mass. Ave., John F. Kennedy Street, and Brattle Street. Trained volunteers dispense maps and brochures and answer questions Monday to Saturday from 9am to 5pm and Sunday from 1 to 5pm. Guided tours, offered from mid-June through Labor Day, include the Old Cambridge area. Check at the booth about rates, meeting places, and times, or call ahead.

CITY LAYOUT

Parts of Boston reflect the city's original layout, a seemingly haphazard plan that leaves even longtime residents tearing their hair. Old Boston abounds with alleys, dead ends, one-way streets, streets that change names, and streets named after extinct geographical features. On the plus side, every "wrong" turn **downtown,** in the **North End,** or on **Beacon Hill** is a chance to see something interesting that you might otherwise have missed.

Nineteenth-century landfill projects transformed much of the city's landscape, altering the shoreline and creating the **Back Bay,** where the streets proceed in parallel lines. After some frustrating time in the older part of the city, this simple plan will seem ingenious.

MAIN ARTERIES & STREETS   The most "main" street downtown is **Washington Street.** As a tribute to the first president, most other streets change their names when they cross Washington Street: Bromfield becomes Franklin, Winter becomes Summer, Stuart becomes Kneeland.

The most prominent feature of downtown Boston is **Boston Common.** It's bordered by **Park Street,** which is 1 block long (but looms large in the geography of the T), and four important thoroughfares. **Tremont Street** originates at Government Center and runs through the Theater District into the South End and Roxbury. **Beacon Street** branches off Tremont at School Street and curves around, passing the golden dome of the State House at the apex of Beacon Hill and the Public Garden at the foot, and slicing through the Back Bay and Kenmore Square on its way into Brookline. At the foot of the hill, Beacon crosses **Charles Street,** the fourth side of the Common and the main street of Beacon Hill. (Near Massachusetts General Hospital, Charles crosses **Cambridge Street,** which loops around to Government Center and merges into Tremont Street.)

Boylston Street is the fifth side of the Common. It runs next to the Public Garden, through Copley Square and the Back Bay, and on into the Fenway. To get there it has to cross **Massachusetts Avenue,** or **"Mass. Ave.,"** as it's almost always called (you might as well get into the habit now). Mass. Ave. extends as far as Lexington, 9 miles away, cutting through Arlington and Cambridge before crossing the Charles River into Boston. **Commonwealth Avenue ("Comm. Ave.")** starts at the Public Garden and runs through Kenmore Square, past Boston University, and into the western suburbs.

Parallel to Comm. Ave. is the **Back Bay's** main shopping boulevard, **Newbury Street.** The cross streets in this neighborhood go in alphabetical order, starting at the Public Garden with Arlington, then Berkeley, Clarendon, Dartmouth, Exeter, Fairfield, Gloucester, and Hereford (and then Mass. Ave.). In the **South End,** the grid is less pristine but still pretty logical. Streets change from "West" to "East" when they cross Washington Street.

Before it enters the South End, Mass. Ave. crosses **Huntington Avenue,** which begins at Copley Square and passes Symphony Hall (at Mass. Ave.), Northeastern University, and the Museum of Fine Arts before crossing into Brookline and becoming Mass. Route 9.

Downtown, **I-93** (the Fitzgerald Expressway) separates the North End from the rest of the city. **Hanover Street** is the main street of the North End; at the harbor it intersects with **Commercial Street,** which runs along the waterfront from the North Washington Street bridge (the route to Charlestown, a.k.a. the Charlestown bridge) until it gives way to **Atlantic Avenue** at Fleet Street. Atlantic Avenue completes the loop around the North End and runs more or less along the waterfront past South Station.

FINDING AN ADDRESS   There's no rhyme or reason to the street pattern, compass directions are virtually useless, and there aren't enough street signs. The best way to find an address is to call ahead and ask for directions, including landmarks, or leave extra time for wandering around. If the directions involve a T stop, be sure to ask which exit to use—most stations have more than one.

STREET MAPS   Free maps of downtown Boston and the rapid-transit lines are available at visitor information centers around the city. *Where Boston* and other tourism-oriented magazines available free at most hotels include maps of central Boston and the T.

The **Greater Boston Convention & Visitors Bureau's** kits (see "Visitor Information," above) include a city/subway/Freedom Trail map. Gousha's *Boston Fast Map* ($4.95), *Streetwise Boston* ($5.95), and *Artwise Boston* ($5.95) are sturdy, laminated maps available at most bookstores. Less detailed but more fun is MapEasy's *GuideMap to Boston* ($5.50), a hand-drawn map of the central areas and major attractions.

Boston Neighborhoods in Brief

These are the areas visitors are most likely to frequent. When Bostonians say **"downtown,"** they usually mean the first six neighborhoods defined here.

The Waterfront   This narrow area along Atlantic Avenue and Commercial Street, once filled with wharves and warehouses, now boasts luxury condos, marinas, restaurants, offices, and hotels. Also in this neighborhood are the New England Aquarium and piers where harbor cruises and whale-watching expeditions originate.

The North End   One of the city's oldest neighborhoods has been an immigrant stronghold for much of its history. It's now about half Italian-American and half newcomers, many of them young professionals who walk to work in the Financial District. You'll hear Italian spoken in the streets and find many Italian restaurants, caffès, and shops. Clubs and restaurants dominate the nearby **North Station** area (between North Washington Street and Beacon Hill), but it's not a good place to wander around alone at night.

Faneuil Hall Marketplace & Haymarket   Employees aside, Boston residents tend to be scarce at Faneuil Hall Marketplace (also called Quincy Market). An irresistible draw for out-of-towners and suburbanites, the cluster of restored market buildings across I-93 from the North End is the city's most popular attraction. **Haymarket,** off the Central Artery, is home to an open-air produce market on Friday and Saturday.

Government Center   Here, modern design strays into the red-brick facade of traditional Boston architecture. Across Congress Street from Faneuil Hall, Government Center is home to state and federal office towers and to Boston City Hall.

Financial District   In the city's banking, insurance, and legal center, skyscrapers surround the landmark Custom House Tower. You'll find the area between Faneuil Hall and the Waterfront frantic during the day and practically empty in the evening.

Downtown Crossing   The intersection that gives Downtown Crossing its name is at Washington Street where Winter Street becomes Summer Street. The Freedom Trail runs through this shopping and business district east of the Common, which hops during the day and slows down considerably at night.

Beacon Hill   Narrow, tree-lined streets and architectural showpieces make up this residential area in the shadow of the State House. Louisburg (say "Lewis-burg") Square and Mount Vernon Street, two of the loveliest and most exclusive spots in Boston, are on Beacon Hill. It's also popular with employees of Massachusetts General Hospital, on the nominally less fashionable north side.

Charlestown   One of the oldest areas of Boston is where you'll see the Bunker Hill Monument and USS *Constitution* ("Old Ironsides"), as well as one of the city's best restaurants, Olives (see "Dining," later in this chapter). Off the beaten track, Charlestown is an almost entirely white residential neighborhood with a well-deserved reputation for insularity.

Seaport District   Developers are pushing to make this the name of the new neighborhood on the South Boston waterfront. On the other side of the Fort Point Channel from the downtown waterfront, it's home to the World Trade Center, Seaport Hotel, Fish Pier, federal courthouse, Museum Wharf, and a lot of construction.

Chinatown   The third-largest Chinese community in the country is a small but growing area jammed with Asian restaurants, groceries, and other businesses. As the "Combat Zone," or red-light district, has shrunk, Chinatown has expanded to fill the area between Downtown Crossing and the Mass. Pike extension. The tiny **Theater District** extends about 1½ blocks in each direction from the intersection of Tremont and Stuart streets; be careful there at night after the crowds thin out.

South End   Cross Stuart Street or Huntington Avenue to reach this landmark district packed with Victorian row houses and little parks. Known for its ethnic, economic, and cultural diversity, galleries, and boutiques, the South End has a large gay community and some of the city's best restaurants. *Note:* Don't confuse the South End with South Boston, a predominantly Irish-American residential neighborhood.

Back Bay   A fashionable address since its creation out of landfill a century ago, the Back Bay overflows with gorgeous architecture and chic shops. It extends from the plush area near the Public Garden to the student-dominated sections near Mass. Ave. Newbury Street is largely commercial, Comm. Ave. largely residential; both are great places to walk around.

Huntington Avenue   The honorary "Avenue of the Arts" (or, with a Boston accent, "Otts") is home to a number of landmarks. Not a formal neighborhood, Huntington Avenue is where you'll find Symphony Hall, Northeastern University, and the Museum of Fine Arts.

Kenmore Square   The enormous white-and-red Citgo sign above the intersection of Comm. Ave., Beacon Street, and Brookline Avenue tells you you're approaching Kenmore Square. Boston University students throng its shops, bars, restaurants, and clubs.

The college-town atmosphere goes out the window when the Red Sox are in town and baseball fans flock to Fenway Park, 3 blocks away.

2 Getting Around

It's impossible to say this often enough: When you reach your hotel, *leave your car in the garage and walk or use public transportation.* If you must drive in town, ask at the front desk for a route around or away from the construction area.

BY PUBLIC TRANSPORTATION

The **Massachusetts Bay Transportation Authority,** or **MBTA** (☎ **617/222-3200;** www.mbta.com), is known as the **T,** and its logo is the letter in a circle. It runs subways, trolleys, buses, and ferries in Boston and many suburbs, as well as the commuter rail. The Web site gives you access to maps, schedules, and other information.

Newer stations on the Red, Blue, and Orange lines are wheelchair accessible; the Green Line is in the process of being converted. All MBTA buses have lifts or kneelers. To learn more, call the **Office for Transportation Access** (☎ **800/533-6282** or 617/222-5123; TDD 617/222-5415).

The ✪ **MBTA visitor passport** (☎ **617/222-5218**) includes unlimited travel on all subway lines and local buses, in commuter rail zones 1A and 1B, and on two ferries, plus discounts on attractions. The cost is $5 for 1 day (tokens are cheaper for fewer than six trips), $9 for 3 consecutive days, and $18 for 7 consecutive days. You can buy a pass when you arrive at the Airport T stop, South Station, Back Bay Station, or North Station. They're also for sale at the Government Center and Harvard T stations; the Boston Common, Prudential Center, and Faneuil Hall Marketplace information centers; and some hotels. Wait to buy your passport until you're ready to start sightseeing. Then you can coordinate trips to places that offer discounts within the time period you're eligible.

BY SUBWAY & TROLLEY The subways are color-coded: Red, Green, Blue, and Orange lines. (The commuter rail to the suburbs appears on system maps in purple.) The local fare is **85¢**—you'll need a token—and can be as much as $2.25 for some surface line extensions on the Green and Red lines. Transfers are free. Route and fare information and timetables are available through the Web site and at Park Street station (under the Common), which is the center of the system. Signs reading INBOUND and OUTBOUND refer to service in relation to Park Street.

Service begins around 5:15am and ends between 12:30 and 1am. The only exception is New Year's Eve, when closing time is 2am and service is free after 8pm.

The oldest system in the country, the T dates to 1897. The ancient Green Line is the most unpredictable—leave extra time if you're taking it to a vital appointment. And remember, stops downtown are so close together that walking is often faster.

BY BUS MBTA buses and "trackless trolleys" (identifiable by their electric antennae, but otherwise indistinguishable from buses) provide service crosstown and to and around the suburbs. The local routes you're likeliest to need are **no. 1,** along Mass. Ave. from Dudley Square in Roxbury through the Back Bay and Cambridge to Harvard Square; **nos. 92** and **93,** between Haymarket and Charlestown; and **no. 77,** along Mass. Ave. north of Harvard Square to Porter Square, North Cambridge, and Arlington.

The local bus fare is **60¢**; express buses are $1.50 and up. Exact change is required. You can use a token, but you won't get change.

BY FERRY At press time, two useful ferries (both included in the MBTA visitor passport) run from Lovejoy Wharf, off Causeway Street behind North Station and the

FleetCenter. One goes to Long Wharf (near the Aquarium T stop) and the Charlestown Navy Yard and the Bunker Hill Monument. The other serves the World Trade Center, on Northern Avenue in the Seaport District. The fare is $1. Call ☎ 617/227-4321 for more information.

BY CAR

If you plan to visit only Boston and Cambridge, there's absolutely no reason to have a car. Between the Big Dig and the narrow, one-way streets, Boston in particular is a motorist's nightmare. Leave your car in your hotel garage and use it for day trips. If you don't come by car, you'll probably want to rent one for day trips.

RENTALS The major car-rental firms have offices at Logan Airport and in Boston; some have other area branches. Boston levies a $10 surcharge on car rentals that goes toward the construction of a new convention center. If you're traveling at a busy time, especially during foliage season, reserve well in advance. Most companies set aside cars for nonsmokers, but you have to ask. And be aware that a hefty drop-off charge is usually standard if you rent in one city and return in another. Many car rental agencies offer shuttle service from the airport to their offices.

Companies with offices at the airport include **Alamo** (☎ 800/327-9633), **Avis** (☎ 800/831-2847), **Budget** (☎ 800/527-0700), **Dollar** (☎ 800/800-4000), **Hertz** (☎ 800/654-3131), and **National** (☎ 800/227-7368). **Enterprise** (☎ 800/ 325-8007) and **Thrifty** (☎ 800/367-2277) are nearby but not on the grounds; leave time for the shuttle bus ride.

PARKING It's difficult to find your way around Boston and practically impossible to park in some areas. Most spaces on the street are metered (and patrolled until 6pm on the dot Monday to Saturday), have strict time limits, or both. The penalty is a $25 ticket, but should you blunder into a tow-away zone, retrieving the car will take at least $100 and a lot of running around. Read the sign or meter carefully. In some areas parking is allowed only at certain hours. Rates vary (usually $1 an hour downtown); bring plenty of quarters. Time limits range from 15 minutes to 2 hours.

It's usually best to leave the car in a garage or lot and walk. A full day typically costs no more than $25 (in other words, cheaper than a parking ticket). There's often a lower flat rate if you enter and exit before certain times, if you park in the evening, or patronize an affiliated business, such as a restaurant (ask when you make dining reservations).

The reasonably priced city-run **Boston Common Garage** (☎ 617/954-2096) at Charles Street accepts vehicles less than 6 feet, 3 inches tall. The **Prudential Center Garage** (☎ 617/267-1002) has entrances on Boylston Street, Huntington Avenue, and Exeter Street, and at the Sheraton Boston Hotel. Parking is discounted if you make a purchase at the Shops at Prudential Center. The **Copley Place Garage** (☎ 617/375-4488), off Huntington Avenue, offers a similar deal.

There are good-size garages at **Government Center** off Congress Street (☎ 617/ 227-0385), at the **New England Aquarium** (☎ 617/723-1731), near the Hynes Convention Center on **Dalton Street** (☎ 617/247-8006), at **75 State St.** (☎ 617/742-7275), and at **Zero Post Office Square** in the Financial District (☎ 617/423-1430).

SPECIAL DRIVING RULES When traffic permits, you may turn right at a red light after stopping, unless a sign is posted saying otherwise. Seat belts are mandatory for adults and children, and infants and children under 5 must be in car seats. You can't be stopped just for an unbelted adult, but a youngster on the loose is reason enough to pull you over.

Boston Transit

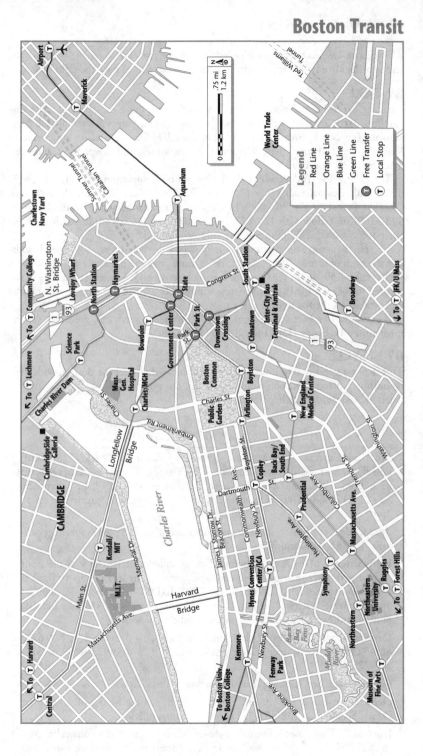

Legend
- Red Line
- Orange Line
- Blue Line
- Green Line
- Ⓣ Free Transfer
- Ⓣ Local Stop

Two state laws to be aware of: Pedestrians in the crosswalk have the right of way, and vehicles already in a rotary (traffic circle or roundabout) have the right of way.

BY TAXI

Taxis are expensive and not always easy to find—seek out a cab stand or call a dispatcher. Stands are usually near hotels. There are also busy ones at Faneuil Hall Marketplace (on North Street), South Station, Back Bay Station, and on either side of Mass. Ave. in Harvard Square in front of BayBank (near the Coop) and Cambridge Trust (near Au Bon Pain).

Try calling the **Independent Taxi Operators Association (ITOA)** (☎ 617/426-8700), **Boston Cab** (☎ 617/536-5010), **Town Taxi** (☎ 617/536-5000), or **Checker Taxi** (☎ 617/536-7000). In Cambridge, call **Ambassador Brattle** (☎ 617/492-1100) or **Yellow Cab** (☎ 617/547-3000). Boston Cab will dispatch a wheelchair-accessible vehicle; advance notice is recommended.

The fare structure: the first quarter-mile (when the flag drops), $1.50; each additional eighth of a mile, 25¢. "Wait time" is extra, and the passenger pays all tolls as well as the $1.50 airport fee (on trips leaving Logan only). Charging a flat rate is not allowed in the city; the Police Department publishes a list of distances to the suburbs that establishes the flat rate for those trips.

If you want to report a problem or have lost something in a cab, the police department runs a **Hackney Hot Line** (☎ **617/536-8294**).

BY BICYCLE

This is not a good option unless you're a real pro—the streets of Boston, with their bloodthirsty drivers and oblivious pedestrians, are notoriously inhospitable to two-wheelers. Cambridge has bike lanes.

Fast Facts: Boston & Cambridge

American Express   The main local office is at 1 Court St. (☎ **617/723-8400**), near the Government Center and State Street T stops. It's open weekdays 8:30am to 5:30pm. The Cambridge office, near Harvard Square at 39 John F. Kennedy St. (☎ **617/868-2600**), is open weekdays 9am to 5pm and Saturday 11am to 3pm.

Area Code   For Boston and the immediate suburbs, it's ☎ **617;** for other suburbs, ☎ **781, 508,** and **978.**

Baby-Sitters   Many hotels maintain lists of reliable sitters; check at the front desk or with the concierge. In an emergency, try Parents in a Pinch, 45 Bartlett Circle, Brookline, MA 02446 (☎ **617/739-KIDS**), weekdays from 8am to 5pm. It charges a referral fee of $30 for an evening or half day, $40 for a full day, plus an hourly wage paid directly to the child-care provider.

Camera Repair   Try Bromfield Camera & Video, 10 Bromfield St. (☎ **617/426-5230**), or the Camera Center, 107 State St. (☎ **800/924-6899** or 617/227-7255).

Car Rentals   See "Getting Around," earlier in this chapter.

Dentists   Ask at the front desk of your hotel or call the Metropolitan District Dental Society (☎ **508/651-3521**) for a recommendation.

Doctors   The Boston Evening Medical Center, 388 Commonwealth Ave. (☎ 617/267-7171), offers walk-in service, honors most insurance plans, and accepts credit cards. Among referral services are Massachusetts General Hospital

Physician Referral Service (☎ **800/711-4MGH**), and New England Medical Center Physician Referral Service (☎ **617/636-9700**).

Embassies/Consulates   See "Fast Facts: For the Foreign Traveler," in chapter 3.

Emergencies   Call ☎ **911** for fire, ambulance, or the police. For the state police, call ☎ **617/523-1212.**

Hospitals   Massachusetts General Hospital, 55 Fruit St. (☎ **617/726-2000,** or 617/726-4100 for children's emergency services), and New England Medical Center, 750 Washington St. (☎ **617/636-5000,** or 617/636-5566 for emergency services), are closest to downtown Boston. In Cambridge are Mount Auburn Hospital, 330 Mt. Auburn St. (☎ **617/492-3500,** or 617/499-5025 for emergency services) and Cambridge **Hospital,** 1493 Cambridge St. (☎ **617/ 498-1000**).

Hot Lines   The AIDS Hot line (☎ **800/235-2331** or 617/536-7733). The Poison Information Center (☎ **800/682-9211** or 617/232-2120). Rape Crisis (☎ **617/492-7273**). The Travelers Aid Society (☎ **617/542-7286**).

Information   See "Visitor Information," earlier in this chapter. For directory assistance, dial ☎ **411.**

Liquor Laws   The legal drinking age is 21. In many bars, particularly near college campuses, you may be asked for ID if you appear to be under 30 or so. At sporting events, everyone buying alcohol must show ID. Some suburban towns, notably Rockport, are "dry."

Newspapers/Magazines   The "Calendar" section of the Thursday *Boston Globe* lists festivals, street fairs, concerts, films, speeches, and dance and theater performances. The Friday *Boston Herald* has a similar, smaller insert called "Scene." Both papers briefly list weekend events in their Saturday editions. The arts-oriented *Boston Phoenix,* published on Thursday, has extensive entertainment and restaurant listings.

   Where Boston, a monthly magazine available free at most hotels, gives information about shopping, nightlife, attractions, and current shows at museums and galleries.

   Newspaper boxes around both cities dispense free copies of the weekly *Tab,* which lists neighborhood-specific events information; the twice-monthly *Improper Bostonian,* with extensive event and club listings; and *Stuff@Night,* an offshoot of the *Phoenix* with selective listings and extensive arts coverage. Available on newsstands, *Boston* magazine is a lifestyle-oriented monthly with cultural and restaurant listings.

Pharmacies (Late-night)   Downtown Boston has no 24-hour drugstore. The pharmacy at the CVS in the Porter Square Shopping Center, off Mass. Ave. in Cambridge (☎ **617/876-5519**), is open 24 hours, 7 days a week. The CVS at 155–157 Charles St. in Boston (☎ **617/523-1028**), next to the Charles/MGH Red Line T stop, is open until midnight. Some emergency rooms can fill your prescription at the hospital's pharmacy.

Police   Call ☎ **911** for emergencies.

Rest Rooms   The visitor center at 15 State St. has public rest rooms, as do most tourist attractions, hotels, department stores, and public buildings. There are rest rooms at the CambridgeSide Galleria, Copley Place, Prudential Center, and Quincy Market shopping areas. One of the few public rest rooms in Harvard Square is in the Harvard Coop.

Safety On the whole, Boston and Cambridge are safe cities for walking. As in any urban area, stay out of parks (including the Esplanade) at night unless you're in a crowd. Areas to avoid at night include Boylston Street between Tremont and Washington, and Tremont Street from Stuart to Boylston. Public transportation is busy and safe, but service stops between 12:30 and 1am.

Taxes The 5% sales tax does not apply to food, prescription drugs, newspapers, or clothing worth less than $175. The lodging tax in Boston and Cambridge is 12.45%; the meal tax (which also applies to takeout food) is 5%.

Taxis See "Getting Around," earlier in this chapter.

Transit Info ☎ **617/222-3200** for the MBTA (subways, local buses, commuter rail). ☎ **800/23-LOGAN** for the Massachusetts Port Authority (airport transportation).

3 Accommodations

Boston has one of the busiest hotel markets in the country, and regularly lands in the top 10 on lists of the most expensive destinations for business travelers. That doesn't mean you have to break the bank, but you do need to do some planning. Rates at most downtown hotels are lower on weekends than on weeknights, when business and convention travelers fill rooms; leisure hotels offer discounts during the week. Bargain hunters who don't mind cold and the possibility of snow can aim for January through March, when some great deals are offered, especially on weekends. It helps to be flexible when you're selecting dates—a hotel that's full of conventioneers one week may be courting business a few days later.

It's always a good idea to make a reservation, especially during the busy spring and fall convention seasons, the vacation months of July and August, and the college graduation season (late May and early June).

Before you rule out a hotel because of its location, consult a map. The neighborhoods, especially downtown, are so small that the borders are somewhat arbitrary. The division to consider is **downtown vs. the Back Bay vs. Cambridge,** and not, say, the Waterfront vs. the Financial District.

The state hotel tax is 5.7%. Boston and Cambridge (as well as Worcester and Springfield) levy a 2.75% convention-center tax on top of the 4% city tax, bringing the total tax to 12.45%.

The Greater Boston Convention and Visitors Bureau has a **Hotel Hot Line** (☎ **800/777-6001**) that can help make reservations even during the busiest times. It's staffed weekdays until 8pm, weekends until 4pm. If you're driving from the west, stop at the Massachusetts Turnpike's Natick rest area and try the **reservation service** at the visitor information center.

BED & BREAKFAST Call as soon as you start planning your trip, especially if you'll be visiting during foliage season. Most places require a minimum stay of at least 2 nights. The following organizations can help you find a B&B:

- **Bed and Breakfast Associates Bay Colony Ltd.,** P.O. Box 57166, Babson Park Branch, Boston, MA 02457 (☎ **800/347-5088** or 781/449-5302; fax 781/449-5958; www.bnbboston.com; E-mail info@bnbboston.com).
- **Bed and Breakfast Agency of Boston,** 47 Commercial Wharf, Boston, MA 02110 (☎ **800/CITY-BNB** or 617/720-3540; fax 617/523-5761; from the U.K., 0800/89-5128; www.boston-bnbagency.com).
- **Bed & Breakfast Reservations North Shore/Greater Boston/Cape Cod,** P.O. Box 600035, Newtonville, MA 02460 (☎ **800/832-2632** outside Mass. or

617/964-1606; fax 617/332-8572; www.bbreserve.com; E-mail info@bbre-serve.com).

- **Host Homes of Boston,** P.O. Box 117, Waban Branch, Boston, MA 02468 (☎ **617/244-1308;** fax 617/244-5156).
- **New England Bed and Breakfast,** P.O. Box 1426, Waltham, MA 02454 (☎ **617/244-2112**).

SERVICES & FACILITIES   Very Expensive and **Expensive** hotels, which generally target business travelers, pile on the amenities. All hotels in those price categories listed here have a concierge, conference rooms, pay-per-view or on-command movies, dry-cleaning and laundry service, express checkout, valet parking, computer data ports, and at least two telephones in each room.

THE WATERFRONT & FANEUIL HALL MARKETPLACE

At all hotels in these neighborhoods, *ask for a room on a high floor*—you'll want to be as far as possible from the noise and disarray of the Big Dig.

VERY EXPENSIVE

The newest hotel near Faneuil Hall Marketplace, on the edge of the Financial District, is the **Wyndham Boston,** 89 Broad St., Boston, MA 02110 (☎ **800/WYN-DHAM** or 617/556-0006; fax 617/556-0053). At press time, the 362-room luxury hotel was scheduled to open in the landmark Batterymarch Building in the summer of 1999.

✪ **Boston Harbor Hotel.** 70 Rowes Wharf (entrance on Atlantic Ave.), Boston, MA 02110. ☎ **800/752-7077** or 617/439-7000. Fax 617/330-9450. www.bhh.com. 230 units. A/C MINIBAR TV TEL. $255–$510 double; from $365 suite. Extra person $50. Children under 18 free in parents' room. Weekend packages available. AE, CB, DC, DISC, MC, V. Valet parking $26; self-parking $22 weekdays, $17 weekends. T: Blue Line to Aquarium or Red Line to South Station. Pets accepted.

The 16-story red-brick Boston Harbor Hotel is one of the finest in town, and certainly the prettiest, with a landmark 6-story-high archway that opens onto the harbor. Near downtown and the waterfront attractions, it offers top-notch service to both business and leisure travelers. Guest rooms, renovated in 1998 and 1999, face the harbor or the skyline (city-view units are less expensive). Each is a luxurious bed- and living-room combination, with an armoire and a desk. Some suites have private terraces. Standard guest room features include windows that open, hair dryers, robes, slippers, and umbrellas. There are 18 rooms for people with disabilities.

   Dining: The excellent Rowes Wharf Restaurant overlooks the harbor, as does Intrigue, the ground-floor cafe, which opens at 5:30am for breakfast (carry-away and sit-down) and has seasonal outdoor seating. The Rowes Wharf Bar serves cocktails and light fare.

   Amenities: Health club and spa with 60-foot lap pool; whirlpool; sauna, steam, and exercise rooms; salon for facials, massage, manicures, pedicures, and spa treatments. State-of-the-art business center with professional staff; 24-hour room service; newspaper delivery; in-room massage; twice-daily maid service; baby-sitting; courtesy car; video rentals.

✪ **Regal Bostonian Hotel.** At Faneuil Hall Marketplace, Boston, MA 02109. ☎ **800/343-0922** or 617/523-3600. Fax 617/523-2454. www.regal-hotels.com/boston. 201 units. A/C MINIBAR TV TEL. $225–$420 double; $255–$450 deluxe; $500–$775 suite. Extra person $20. Children under 18 free in parents' room. Weekend and other packages available. AE, DC, DISC, JCB, MC, V. Parking $30. T: Green or Blue Line to Government Center or Orange Line to State.

Boston Accommodations

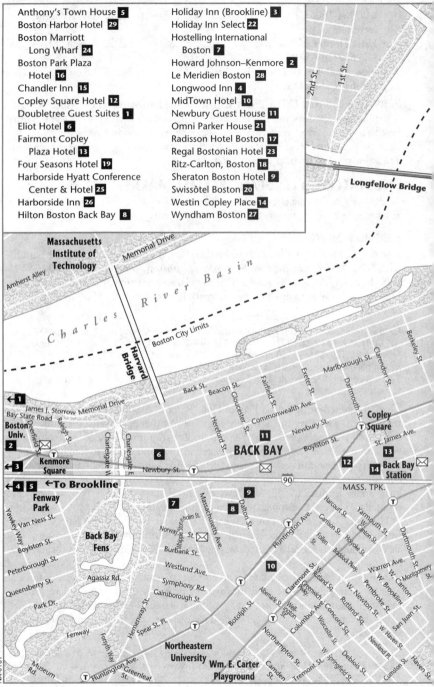

Anthony's Town House 5
Boston Harbor Hotel 29
Boston Marriott
 Long Wharf 24
Boston Park Plaza
 Hotel 16
Chandler Inn 15
Copley Square Hotel 12
Doubletree Guest Suites 1
Eliot Hotel 6
Fairmont Copley
 Plaza Hotel 13
Four Seasons Hotel 19
Harborside Hyatt Conference
 Center & Hotel 25
Harborside Inn 26
Hilton Boston Back Bay 8

Holiday Inn (Brookline) 3
Holiday Inn Select 22
Hostelling International
 Boston 7
Howard Johnson–Kenmore 2
Le Meridien Boston 28
Longwood Inn 4
MidTown Hotel 10
Newbury Guest House 11
Omni Parker House 21
Radisson Hotel Boston 17
Regal Bostonian Hotel 23
Ritz-Carlton, Boston 18
Sheraton Boston Hotel 9
Swissôtel Boston 20
Westin Copley Place 14
Wyndham Boston 27

Longfellow Bridge

Massachusetts
Institute of
Technology

Memorial Drive

Amherst Alley

C h a r l e s   R i v e r   B a s i n

Boston City Limits

Harvard Bridge

James J. Storrow Memorial Drive

Back St.
Beacon St.
Fairfield St.
Cloucester St.
Exeter St.
Marlborough St.
Clarendon St.
Berkeley St.
Dartmouth St.

1

Bay State Road
Raleigh St.
Deerfield St.

Boston Univ.

2

3

Kenmore Square

Charlesgate W.
Charlesgate E.

6

Newbury St.

Hereford St.
Commonwealth Ave.
Newbury St.
Boylston St.

BACK BAY

11

Copley Square

St. James Ave.

12

13

14

Back Bay Station

90

MASS. TPK.

4 5 ←To Brookline

Fenway Park

Yawkey Way
Van Ness St.
Boylston St.

Back Bay Fens

Peterborough St.
Queensberry St.
Park Dr.

Agassiz Rd.

7

Norway St.
Stoneholm St.

8

9

Dalton St.

Massachusetts Ave.

Burbank St.
Westland Ave.
Symphony Rd.
Gainsborough St.

Huntington Ave.

Harcourt St.
Garrison St.
Follen St.
Braddock Pkwy.
Holyoke St.
Yarmouth St.
W. Canton St.

Dartmouth St.

Warren Ave.
W. Canton
W. Brookline
Pembroke St.
W. Newton St.
Rutland Sq.
Montgomery
San Juan St.

10

Claremont Park
Greenwich Park
Greenwich St.
Albemarle St.
Wellington St.
Rutland Sq.
Concord Sq.
Columbus Ave.
Concord St.
Worcester St.

W. Brookline
W. Canton
W. Newton St.
W. Haven St.
Newland Pl.

Museum Rd.

Fenway
Forsyth Way
Hemenway St.
Spear St. Pl.

Huntington Ave.
Greenleaf St.

Northeastern
University

Wm. E. Carter
Playground

Northampton St.
Camden St.
Tremont St.
W. Springfield St.
W. Newton St.
W. Rutland Sq.
W. Brookline
W. Canton St.
W. Dedham St.
Cunston St.
Haven St.

NA-0101

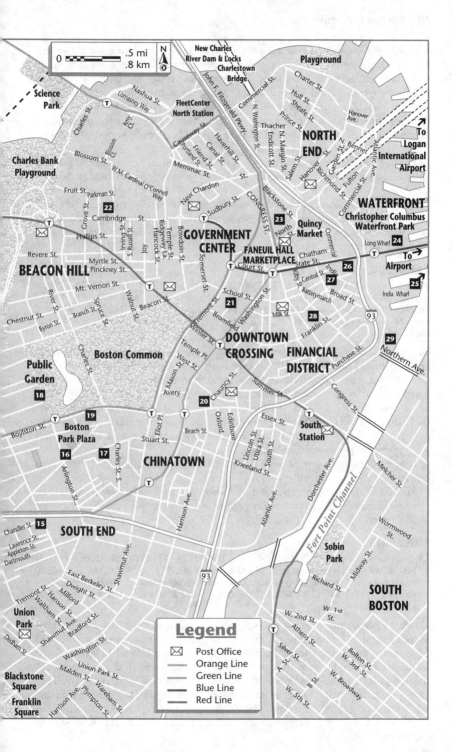

The relatively small Regal Bostonian offers service and features that make it competitive with larger hotels. Guest rooms vary in size; all boast top-of-the-line furnishings and amenities, including robes, safes, hair dryers, heat lamps, and both overhead and European-style handheld shower sprays. Some suites have working fireplaces or Jacuzzis. Half the rooms have French doors that open onto small balconies. Soundproofing throughout the hotel means you can watch the scene at the marketplace, Haymarket, or the Big Dig construction site without hearing all the noise. Rooms for travelers with disabilities are available.

Dining: On the fourth-floor rooftop is the glass-enclosed Seasons restaurant. The Atrium lounge in the glass-walled lobby affords a great view of the scene at the marketplace.

Amenities: 24-hour room service; complimentary health club and swimming pool privileges at the excellent Sky Club, 4 blocks away; newspaper delivery; in-room massage; twice-daily maid service; secretarial services available; complimentary morning limousine service.

EXPENSIVE

Boston Marriott Long Wharf. 296 State St., Boston, MA 02109. ☎ **800/228-9290** or 617/227-0800. Fax 617/227-2867. www.marriott.com/marriott/BOSLW. 400 units. A/C TV TEL. Apr–Nov $265–$350 double; Dec–Mar $190–$265 double; $450–$490 suite. Weekend packages from $145 per night. AE, DC, DISC, JCB, MC, V. Parking $27. T: Blue Line to Aquarium.

The terraced exterior of this seven-story hotel is one of the most recognizable sights on the harbor. The central location on the water is the chief appeal of this otherwise ordinary Marriott. Rooms are large and decor varies; all have coffeemakers, hair dryers, and tables with chairs. Units near the street are just above the Big Dig; ask to be close to the water, and you'll have good views of the wharves and waterfront. Rates for Concierge Level (seventh-floor) rooms include continental breakfast, cocktails, and hors d'oeuvres served in a private lounge, and private exercise facilities. Eighteen units are available for guests with disabilities.

Dining: Oceana Restaurant, with a 180°-expanse of glass wall fronting the harbor; cafe and lounge; bar and grill.

Amenities: Indoor pool with an outdoor terrace; exercise room; whirlpools; saunas; game room; business center; room service until 11pm; newspaper delivery; twice-daily maid service.

MODERATE

✪ **Harborside Inn.** 185 State St., Boston, MA 02109. ☎ **617/723-7500.** Fax 617/670-2010. www.hagopianhotels.com. 54 units. A/C TV TEL. $155–$200 double; $175–$300 suite. Rates include continental breakfast. Rates may be higher during special events. Extra person $15. AE, CB, DC, DISC, MC, V. Parking about $22 at nearby public garages. T: Blue Line to Aquarium.

Under the same management as the Newbury Guest House in the Back Bay, the Harborside Inn offers a similar combination of value, location, and service. The renovated 1858 warehouse is near Faneuil Hall Marketplace and the Financial District. Guest rooms, which have hardwood floors, Oriental rugs, queen-size beds, and Victorian-style furniture, surround an atrium; those with city views are more expensive. They have some features you'd expect at pricier hotels, including free local phone calls and voice mail. Rooms on the top floors of the eight-story building have lower ceilings but better views. On the ground floor are a small exercise room and the cafe, where breakfast is served buffet-style.

AT THE AIRPORT
EXPENSIVE

Harborside Hyatt Conference Center & Hotel. 101 Harborside Dr., Boston, MA 02128. ☎ **800/233-1234** or 617/568-1234. Fax 617/567-8856. www.hyatt.com. 270 units. A/C TV TEL. From $179 double. Children under 12 free in parents' room. AE, CB, DC, DISC, JCB, MC, V. Parking $15. T: Blue Line to Airport, then shuttle bus. By car, follow signs to Logan Airport and take Harborside Dr. past the car-rental area and tunnel entrance.

This striking 14-story waterfront hotel offers unobstructed views of the harbor and city skyline. It caters to the convention trade; sightseers whose transportation budget doesn't include a fair amount of time (on the shuttle bus and subway) or money (ferries, parking, or cabs) will be better off closer to downtown. Guest rooms have all the amenities you'd expect from a deluxe hotel, plus such extras as hair dryers, coffeemakers, irons and ironing boards, luxury bathrooms, and fine wood furnishings. And there's an interesting architectural quirk: The building's tower is a lighthouse (the airport control tower manages the beacon so it doesn't interfere with runway lights). Rooms for people with disabilities are available.

   Dining: The restaurant serves three meals daily and has floor-to-ceiling windows that allow for spectacular views.

   Amenities: Indoor heated pool; health club with sauna; business center; ferries to Rowes Wharf and Long Wharf dock outside; 24-hour airport shuttle service.

FINANCIAL DISTRICT
VERY EXPENSIVE

✪ **Le Meridien Boston.** 250 Franklin St. (at Post Office Sq.), Boston, MA 02110. ☎ **800/543-4300** or 617/451-1900. Fax 617/423-2844. www.lemeridien.com. 326 units. A/C MINIBAR TV TEL. $355–$415 double; $450–$1,300 suite. Weekend rates from $199. Extra person $30. AE, CB, DC, DISC, MC, V. Valet parking $29 Sun–Thurs, $13 Fri–Sat; self-parking $28 Sun–Thurs, $8 Fri–Sat. T: Red Line to Downtown Crossing or South Station, Blue or Orange Line to State. Small pets allowed.

This is the city's premier business hotel. If you're doing a deal, you may not even need to leave the premises—ask for a Business Traveler room (fax machine, oversize desk, halogen lighting, and coffeemaker). Vacationing visitors are near the waterfront and downtown attractions, but not that close to public transportation. The multilingual staff provides superb service. Guest rooms in the 9-story hotel have 153 configurations, including loft suites. All are large and equipped with hair dryers. The glass mansard roof surrounds the top three stories, where a number of rooms have large sloped windows and extraordinary views. Fifteen rooms are equipped for travelers with disabilities.

   Dining/Diversions: Julien serves lunch and dinner daily; the bar features live piano music 6 nights a week. The less formal Café Fleuri serves three meals daily, the Saturday "Chocolate Bar Buffet" (September through May), and Sunday jazz brunch. La Terrasse is the seasonal outdoor cafe.

   Amenities: 40-foot indoor pool; well-equipped health club with whirlpool and sauna; full-service business center with library and full-time staff; 24-hour room service; newspaper delivery; twice-daily maid service; weekend courtesy car to Newbury Street.

DOWNTOWN CROSSING & BEACON HILL

The **Holiday Inn Select Boston Government Center,** 5 Blossom St., at Cambridge St. (☎ **800/HOLIDAY** or 617/742-7630), offers all the features you'd expect at the international chain's business hotels, and has a heated outdoor pool.

VERY EXPENSIVE

Swissôtel Boston. 1 Avenue de Lafayette, Boston, MA 02111. ☎ **800/621-9200** or 617/451-2600. Fax 617/451-0054. www.swissotel.com. 454 units. A/C MINIBAR TV TEL. $315–$405 double; $440–$595 suite or Swiss Butler Executive Level; $2,500 Presidential suite. Extra person $25. Children under 12 free in parents' room. Weekend "Bed & Breakfast" package from $129 per night; other weekend packages available. AE, CB, DC, DISC, JCB, MC, V. Valet parking $28; self-parking $24. T: Red Line to Downtown Crossing, Green Line to Boylston. Small pets accepted.

This centrally located 22-story hotel is a busy convention and business destination during the week, and the excellent weekend packages make it popular with sightseers. Guest rooms cluster around four atriums with semiprivate lobbies, creating the effect of several small hotels in one. Rooms have sitting areas with a desk; suites are either L-shaped rooms with sitting areas or living rooms with connecting bedrooms. All rooms have fax machines and coffeemakers. On the Executive Level, a Swiss butler performs traditional valet functions, acts as a private concierge, and even runs errands.

Dining: Café Suisse serves three meals daily and Sunday brunch. The lounge in the atrium offers cocktails, vintage wines by the glass, and light meals.

Amenities: 52-foot indoor pool; health club; exercise room; saunas; sun terrace; high-tech business center; 24-hour room service; nightly turndown.

EXPENSIVE

✪ Omni Parker House. 60 School St., Boston, MA 02108. ☎ **800/THE-OMNI** or 617/227-8600. Fax 617/742-5729. www.omnihotels.com. 550 units. A/C MINIBAR TV TEL. $185–$325 double; $249–$295 superior room; $279–$369 1-bedroom suite. Children under 18 free in parents' room. Weekend packages available. AE, CB, DC, DISC, MC, V. Valet parking $27; self-parking $20. T: Green Line to Government Center or Red Line to Park Street.

The Parker House offers a great combination of nearly 150 years of history and $60 million in renovations. A massive overhaul completed in 1998 upgraded it throughout and added a business center and exercise facility. Guest rooms now have minibars, hair dryers, irons, and ironing boards. They're not huge, but they are thoughtfully laid out and nicely appointed; many have views of Old City Hall or Government Center. The pattern on the bedspreads—so gaudy that it's elegant—is a reproduction of the 1855 original. Rooms for people with disabilities are available.

Dining/Diversions: Parker's Restaurant serves three meals daily, including Parker House rolls, which were invented here; **Parker's Bar,** open from midday to early morning, has live piano music Monday to Saturday night.

Amenities: Health club; staffed business center; room service until 11pm; newspaper delivery; in-room massage.

CHINATOWN/THEATER DISTRICT
EXPENSIVE

Radisson Hotel Boston. 200 Stuart St. (at Charles St. S.), Boston, MA 02116. ☎ **800/333-3333** or 617/482-1800. Fax 617/451-2750. www.radisson.com. 356 units. A/C TV TEL. $160–$299 double. Extra person or cot $20. Cribs free. Children under 18 free in parents' room. Weekend and theater packages available. AE, DC, DISC, JCB, MC, V. Parking $17. T: Green Line to Boylston, Orange Line to New England Medical Center.

A top-to-bottom renovation completed in 1997 left the centrally located Radisson in great shape. A recent push to attract business travelers has made the 24-story hotel even more appealing. The guest rooms are among the largest in the city. Each has a private balcony, sitting area, hair dryer, coffeemaker, iron, and ironing board. Business-traveler rooms on the top four floors come with upgraded amenities and access to a private lounge.

Dining/Diversions: The 57 Restaurant & Bar serves traditional American food; the Theatre Café is more casual. The 57 Theatre (☎ 800/233-3123) is an intimate venue that lends itself to one-person shows.

Amenities: Heated indoor pool with sundeck and exercise room; staffed business center; room service until 11pm; newspaper delivery.

BACK BAY
VERY EXPENSIVE

✪ **The Fairmont Copley Plaza Hotel.** 138 St. James Ave., Boston, MA 02116. ☎ **800/527-4727** or 617/267-5300. Fax 617/247-6681. www.fairmont.com. E-mail: boston@fairmont.com. 379 units. A/C MINIBAR TV TEL. $289–$409 double; $429–$1,500 suite. Extra person $30. Weekend packages available. AE, CB, DC, JCB, MC, V. Valet parking $26. T: Green Line to Copley, Orange Line to Back Bay. Small pets accepted.

The Fairmont Hotel Group acquired the *grande dame* of Boston hotels in 1996 and has upgraded and renovated it into a true "grand hotel," in line with the chain's most famous property, New York's Plaza. Built in 1912, the six-story hotel faces Copley Square. The large guest rooms, furnished with reproduction Edwardian antiques, echo the opulent public spaces. In-room features include oversize desks, VCRs, coffeemakers, irons, ironing boards, hair dryers, terry robes, and oversize towels. Superb service complements the plush accommodations. Rooms are available for guests with disabilities.

Dining/Diversions: There are two restaurants, the Oak Room and Copley's, and two lounges, the Oak Bar and Copley's Bar.

Amenities: 24-hour room service; fitness center; well-equipped business center; newspaper delivery; in-room massage; twice-daily maid service; baby-sitting; currency exchange; complimentary shoeshine; beauty salon. Guests have access to the nearby coed YWCA, which has a swimming pool.

✪ **Four Seasons Hotel.** 200 Boylston St., Boston, MA 02116. ☎ **800/332-3442** or 617/338-4400. Fax 617/423-0154. www.fourseasons.com. 288 units. A/C MINIBAR TV TEL. $385–$610 double; from $950 suite; from $1,900 2-bedroom suite. Extra person $40. Weekend packages available. AE, CB, DC, DISC, JCB, MC, V. Valet parking $27. T: Green Line to Arlington. Pets accepted.

This is the most luxurious of Boston's luxury hotels. If I were traveling with someone else's credit cards, I'd head straight here. Everything at the 16-story brick-and-glass hotel overlooking the Public Garden is top-of-the-line, from the health club to the legendary service. Each spacious room has a striking view, bay windows that open, a hair dryer, terry robes, and a safe. Children and small pets are treated as generously as their traveling companions. Larger accommodations range from Executive Suites, with alcove areas for entertaining or business meetings, to one-, two-, and three-bedroom deluxe suites. Rooms equipped for people with disabilities are available.

Dining/Diversions: Aujourd'hui is one of Boston's best restaurants (see "Dining," below); the Bristol Lounge offers lunch, afternoon tea, dinner, and Sunday breakfast, and live entertainment nightly (see "The Bar Scene," below).

Amenities: In general, if you want it, you'll get it. Indoor heated 51-foot pool and whirlpool with a view of the Public Garden; spa with fitness equipment, private masseuse, Jacuzzi, and sauna; excellent business center; 24-hour room service; newspaper delivery; in-room massage; twice-daily maid service; baby-sitting; complimentary shoeshine; complimentary limousine service to downtown.

✪ **The Ritz-Carlton, Boston.** 15 Arlington St., Boston, MA 02117. ☎ **800/241-3333** or 617/536-5700. Fax 617/536-1335. www.ritzcarlton.com. 278 units. A/C MINIBAR TV TEL. $285–$495 double; from $545 1-bedroom suite; from $645 2-bedroom suite. Ritz-Carlton

Club $645–$825 1-bedroom suite; from $1,140 2-bedroom suite. Extra person $20. Weekend packages available. AE, CB, DC, DISC, JCB, MC, V. Valet parking $26. T: Green Line to Arlington. Small pets accepted.

This legendary hotel overlooking the Public Garden has attracted the "proper Bostonian" and the celebrated visitor since 1927. The 17-story hotel has the highest staff-to-guest ratio in the city. Although the pricier Four Seasons has better amenities, notably the on-premises pool, the status-conscious consider the Ritz—well, ritzier. Guest rooms have French provincial furnishings, safes, hair dryers, and terry robes; some have windows that open. You'll pay more for rooms with a view. Many suites have wood-burning fireplaces. Guests in Club Level rooms have access to a private lounge, which has its own concierge and serves complimentary food six times a day (including a caviar and champagne hour).

Dining/Diversions: The Dining Room and Bar at the Ritz are as legendary for their clientele as for their food and drink. The Café, though rather cramped, is famous for breakfast. The Lounge serves the city's best afternoon tea, then cognac, cordials, caviar, and desserts. The Roof Restaurant, open seasonally, offers dinner and dancing 17 stories up.

Amenities: Well-equipped fitness center; use of pool at the nearby Candela of Boston spa; 24-hour room service; newspaper delivery; twice-daily maid service; babysitting; secretarial services; complimentary limousine (limited hours); complimentary shoeshine; beauty salon.

EXPENSIVE

Boston Park Plaza Hotel. 64 Arlington St., Boston, MA 02116. ☎ **800/225-2008** or 617/426-2000. Fax 617/423-1708. www.bostonparkplaza.com. 960 units (some with shower only). A/C TV TEL. $175–$265 double; $375–$2,000 suite. Extra person $20. Children under 18 free in parents' room. Senior discount, weekend and family packages available. AE, CB, DC, DISC, MC, V. Valet parking $23; self-parking $19. T: Green Line to Arlington.

A Boston mainstay—it was built as the Statler Hilton in 1927—the Park Plaza Hotel does a hopping convention and function business. It's the antithesis of generic, with an old-fashioned atmosphere, yet offers a full range of modern comforts. Room size and decor vary greatly, and some rooms are quite small. All have hair dryers, and many have coffeemakers. The lobby of the 15-story hotel is a little commercial hub, with a travel agency, currency exchange, Amtrak and airline ticket offices, and pharmacy.

Dining/Diversions: On the ground floor are two restaurants, Finale and Legal C Bar, and two lounges, Swans Court and the cozy Captain's Bar.

Amenities: Health club; business center; room service until 11pm; beauty salon.

Copley Square Hotel. 47 Huntington Ave., Boston, MA 02116. ☎ **800/225-7062** or 617/536-9000. Fax 617/236-0351. www.copleysquarehotel.com. 143 units. A/C TV TEL. $195–$225 double; $345 suite. Children under 18 free in parents' room. Packages and senior discounts available. AE, CB, DC, DISC, JCB, MC, V. Parking $20 (in adjacent garage). T: Green Line to Copley, Orange Line to Back Bay.

The Copley Square Hotel offers a great location along with the advantages and drawbacks of its relatively small size. Built in 1891, the seven-story hotel extends attentive service that's hard to find at the nearby megahotels, without those giants' abundant amenities. Each attractively decorated room has a hair dryer, coffeemaker, and safe; some units are on the small side.

Dining: Afternoon tea is served to guests in the lobby. Speeder & Earl's serves breakfast; Café Budapest and the Original Sports Saloon serve lunch and dinner.

Amenities: Access to health club at the nearby Westin; room service until 11pm; 24-hour currency exchange.

✪ **Eliot Hotel.** 370 Commonwealth Ave. (at Mass. Ave.), Boston, MA 02215. ☎ **800/ 44-ELIOT** or 617/267-1607. Fax 617/536-9114. www.bostbest.com/eliot/. E-mail: HotelEliot@aol.com. 95 units. A/C MINIBAR TV TEL. $255–$325 1-bedroom suite for two; $510–$600 2-bedroom suite. Extra person $20. Children under 12 free in parents' room. AE, DC, MC, V. Valet parking $20. T: Green Line B, C, or D to Hynes/ICA. Small pets accepted.

This exquisite hotel combines the flavor of Yankee Boston with European-style service and amenities that attract tycoons as well as honeymooners. The spacious suites have antique furnishings, French doors between the living rooms and bedrooms, and modern conveniences such as Italian marble bathrooms, personal fax machines, and VCRs. Many suites also have a pantry with a microwave. The hotel is near Boston University and MIT (across the river), and the location on tree-lined Comm. Ave. contrasts pleasantly with the bustle of Newbury Street, a block away. Rooms are available for travelers with disabilities.

Dining: The elegant restaurant, Clio, serves breakfast and, at dinner, contemporary French and American cuisine.

Amenities: Room service until midnight; newspaper delivery; twice-daily maid service; baby-sitting; secretarial services; safe-deposit boxes.

Hilton Boston Back Bay. 40 Dalton St., Boston, MA 02115. ☎ **800/874-0663,** 800/HILTONS, or 617/236-1100. Fax 617/867-6104. www.hilton.com. 385 units (some with shower only). A/C TV TEL. $210–$255 double; $450 minisuite; from $650 suite. Packages and AAA discounts available. Extra person $20. AE, DC, DISC, MC, V. Parking $17. T: Green Line B, C, or D to Hynes/ICA. Small pets allowed.

Across the street from the Prudential Center complex, this hotel recently completed a $10 million expansion and upgrade that added 44 executive rooms. It's a business hotel, and vacationing families will also find it convenient and comfortable. Rooms are large and have modern furnishings, windows that open, coffeemakers, hair dryers, irons, and ironing boards. Rates for executive rooms include continental breakfast and upgraded amenities.

Dining/Diversions: Boodles Restaurant draws businesspeople for grilled steaks and seafood. Also on the premises are Boodles Bar; a lounge; and a nightclub, Club Nicole, which attracts a young crowd.

Amenities: Heated indoor pool; well-equipped 24-hour fitness center; sundeck; business center; room service until midnight; newspaper delivery; currency exchange.

Sheraton Boston Hotel. 39 Dalton St., Boston, MA 02199. ☎ **800/325-3535** or 617/236-2000. Fax 617/236-1702. www.sheraton.com. 1,181 units. A/C TV TEL. $179–$319 double; from $400 suites. Children under 17 free in parents' room. Weekend packages; 25% discount for students, faculty, and retirees with ID (subject to availability). AE, CB, DC, DISC, JCB, MC, V. Valet parking $26; self-parking $24. T: Green Line B, C, or D to Hynes/ICA; E to Prudential. Small pets accepted.

Its central location, range of accommodations, lavish convention facilities, and huge pool make this 29-story hotel one of the most popular in the city. It offers direct access to the Hynes Convention Center and the Prudential Center, and a $65 million renovation project completed in 1999 upgraded the bathrooms and reconfigured the public spaces. A new corporate policy to attract repeat business through improved service—an excellent goal at a hotel this big—seems to be working. Standard rooms are fairly large and contain coffeemakers and hair dryers. Club Level guests get free local calls and admission to a lounge where complimentary continental breakfast and hors d'oeuvres are served. Rooms are available for guests with disabilities.

Dining/Diversions: The lobby restaurant, Apropos, serves three meals daily. The clubby Punch Bar serves after-dinner drinks, cordials, and a breathtaking selection of cigars.

Amenities: Heated indoor/outdoor pool with retractable dome, pavilion, Jacuzzi, and sauna; large, well-equipped health club; room service until late evening; newspaper delivery; in-room massage; courtesy car; car-rental desk.

The Westin Copley Place Boston. 10 Huntington Ave., Boston, MA 02116. ☎ **800/ WESTIN-1** or 617/262-9600. Fax 617/424-7483. www.westin.com. 800 units. A/C MINIBAR TV TEL. $189–$305 double; $350–$1,500 suite. Extra person $25; $20 Guest Office; $30 junior suites and Executive Club Level. Weekend packages available. AE, CB, DC, DISC, JCB, MC, V. Valet parking $24. T: Green Line to Copley, Orange Line to Back Bay. Small pets accepted.

Towering 36 stories above Copley Square, the Westin attracts convention-goers, sightseers, and dedicated shoppers with its great location and multilingual staff. The spacious guest rooms have coffeemakers, hair dryers, safes, and windows that open. You might not notice any of that at first, because of the view—qualms you might have had about choosing a huge chain hotel will fade as you survey the panorama. Executive Club Level guests have private check-in and a lounge that serves complimentary continental breakfast and hors d'oeuvres. There are also 48 guest rooms for people with disabilities.

Dining/Diversions: The Palm, a branch of the famous New York–based chain, serves lunch and dinner—steak, chops, and jumbo lobsters. The excellent seafood restaurant Turner Fisheries features live jazz Tuesday to Saturday after 8pm. The Lobby Lounge offers drinks and great people-watching.

Amenities: Indoor pool; health club with Nautilus equipment and saunas; business center with PC rentals; 24-hour room service; newspaper delivery; twice-daily maid service; baby-sitting; car-rental desk; tour desk; barber shop.

MODERATE

Chandler Inn Hotel. 26 Chandler St. (at Berkeley St.), Boston, MA 02116. ☎ **800/ 842-3450** or 617/482-3450. Fax 617/542-3428. www.chandlerinn.com. E-mail: inn3450@ix. netcom.com. 56 units. A/C TV TEL. Apr to mid-June $89–$109 double; Marathon weekend $150–$160 double; mid-June to mid-Nov $99–$119 double weekdays, $109–$129 double weekends; mid-Nov to Mar $89–$109 double. Rates include continental breakfast. Extra person $10–$20. Children under 12 free in parents' room. AE, CB, DC, DISC, MC, V. No parking available. T: Orange Line to Back Bay.

This is a practical choice for bargain hunters who don't care about a tony address and a lot of extras. The Chandler Inn is in the South End, near the Boston Center for the Arts, but so convenient to the Back Bay and such a good deal that you won't mind the slightly lower-budget address. The guest rooms in the eight-story inn aren't fancy, but if your needs are basic, you'll be fine. And the staff is friendly and helpful.

The MidTown Hotel. 220 Huntington Ave., Boston, MA 02115. ☎ **800/343-1177** or 617/262-1000. Fax 617/262-8739. 159 units. A/C TV TEL. Apr–Aug $149–$209 double, Sept to mid-Dec $159–$219, mid-Dec to Mar $99–$169. Extra person $15. Children under 18 free in parents' room. 10% AARP discount available; government employees' discount subject to availability. AE, DC, DISC, MC, V. Free parking. T: Green Line E to Prudential, or Orange Line to Mass. Ave.

Even without free parking and a pool (open seasonally), this two-story hotel on a busy street would be a good deal for families and budget-conscious businesspeople. The recently renovated rooms are large, bright, and attractively outfitted, though bathrooms are on the small side. All units have coffeemakers and hair dryers, and some have connecting doors that allow families to spread out. Many rooms have two-line phones; photocopying and fax services are available at the front desk. The heated outdoor pool is open from Memorial Day to Labor Day. The restaurant serves breakfast from 7 to 11am.

✪ **Newbury Guest House.** 261 Newbury St. (between Fairfield and Gloucester), Boston, MA 02116. ☎ **617/437-7666.** Fax 617/262-4243. www.hagopianhotels.com. 32 units (some with shower only). A/C TV TEL. $105–$140 double; winter $95–$125 double. Rates include continental breakfast. Rates may be higher during special events. Extra person $10. AE, CB, DC, DISC, MC, V. Parking $15 (reservation required). 2-nights minimum on weekends. T: Green Line to Copley or B, C, or D to Hynes/ICA.

After a little shopping in the Back Bay, you'll appreciate what a find this cozy inn is: a bargain on Newbury Street. In a pair of brick town houses built in the 1880s, it offers comfortable furnishings, a pleasant staff, and a buffet breakfast served in the ground-level dining room, which adjoins a brick patio. Rooms aren't huge but are nicely appointed. The B&B operates near capacity all year, so the only caveat is: Reserve early.

INEXPENSIVE

Hostelling International—Boston. 12 Hemenway St., Boston, MA 02115. ☎ **888/ HOST222** or 617/536-9455. Fax 617/424-6558. www.tiac.net/users/hienec/. E-mail: boston-hostel@juno.com. 205 beds. Members $19 per bed; nonmembers $20 per bed. JCB, MC, V. T: Green Line B, C, or D to Hynes/ICA.

This hostel near the Berklee College of Music and Symphony Hall caters to students, youth groups, and other travelers in search of comfortable, no-frills lodging. It has two full dine-in kitchens, 19 bathrooms, a coin laundry, and a large common room. The recently remodeled public areas contain meeting and workshop space. Accommodations are dorm-style, with 3 to 6 beds per room. The hostel provides a "sheet sleeping sack," or you can bring your own; sleeping bags are not permitted. The staff organizes cultural, educational, and recreational programs on the premises and throughout the Boston area.

Note: To get a bed during the summer season, you must be a member of Hostelling International—American Youth Hostels. For information and an application, contact HI–AYH, P.O. Box 37613, Washington, DC 20013 (☎ **202/783-6161;** www.hiayh. org). If you are not a U.S. citizen, apply to your home country's hosteling association.

OUTSKIRTS & BROOKLINE
EXPENSIVE

✪ **Doubletree Guest Suites.** 400 Soldiers Field Rd., Boston, MA 02134. ☎ **800/ 222-TREE** or 617/783-0090. Fax 617/783-0897. www.doubletreehotels.com. 310 units. A/C MINIBAR TV TEL. $139–$259 double. Extra person $20. Children under 18 free in parents' room. Weekend packages $154–$264. AARP and AAA discounts available. AE, CB, DC, DISC, JCB, MC, V. Parking $15–$18.

This hotel is one of the best deals in town—every unit is a two-room suite. Business travelers can entertain in their rooms, and families can spread out. Overlooking the Charles River at the Allston/Cambridge exit of the Mass. Pike, the hotel is convenient to Cambridge and the bike and jogging path that runs along the river, but isn't in an actual neighborhood. The suites surround a 15-story atrium. Rooms are large, and most bedrooms have king-size beds and a writing desk. Living rooms feature full-size sofa beds, a dining table, a coffeemaker, and a good-size refrigerator. Each floor has suites for people with disabilities.

Dining/Diversions: Scullers Grille and Scullers Lounge serve meals from 6:30am to 11pm. The celebrated Scullers Jazz Club has two nightly shows.

Amenities: Heated indoor pool; exercise room; whirlpool; sauna; room service until 11pm; newspaper delivery; secretarial services; laundry room; game room; complimentary van service to and from attractions and business areas in Boston and Cambridge.

MODERATE

Many options in this price range and area are chain hotels, including the **Holiday Inn Boston Brookline,** 1200 Beacon St., Brookline, MA 02446 (☎ **800/HOLIDAY** or 617/277-1200), and the **Howard Johnson Hotel—Kenmore,** 575 Commonwealth Ave., Boston, MA 02215 (☎ **800/654-2000** or 617/267-3100).

INEXPENSIVE

Anthony's Town House. 1085 Beacon St., Brookline, MA 02446. ☎ **617/566-3972.** Fax 617/232-1085. 12 units (none with private bathroom). A/C TV. $60–$85 double. Extra person $10. Weekly rates and winter discounts available. No credit cards. Free parking. T: Green Line C to Hawes St.

The Anthony family has operated this four-story brownstone guest house since 1944, and a stay here is very much like tagging along with a friend who's spending the night at Grandma's. Each floor has three high-ceilinged rooms furnished in rather ornate Queen Anne or Victorian style, and a shared bathroom with enclosed shower. Smaller rooms (one per floor) have twin beds, and the large front rooms have bay windows. Guests have the use of two refrigerators. The guest house is 1 mile from Boston's Kenmore Square, about 15 minutes from downtown by subway, and 2 blocks from a busy commercial strip. The turn-of-the-century building is listed on the National Register of Historic Places.

Longwood Inn. 123 Longwood Ave., Brookline, MA 02446. ☎ **617/566-8615.** Fax 617/738-1070. www.go.boston.com/longwoodinn. 22 units, 17 with bathroom (some with shower only). A/C TEL. Apr–Nov $71–$81 double; Dec–Mar $61–$71 double. 1-bedroom apt (sleeps 4 plus) $91 summer, $81 winter. Weekly rates available. No credit cards. Free parking. T: Green Line D to Longwood, or C to Coolidge Corner.

In a residential area 3 blocks from Boston, this three-story Victorian guest house offers comfortable accommodations at modest rates. Guests have the use of a fully equipped kitchen and common dining room, coin laundry, and TV lounge. The apartment has a private kitchen and balcony. Tennis courts, a running track, and a playground at the school next door are open to the public. The Longwood Medical Area and Coolidge Corner neighborhood are within walking distance.

CAMBRIDGE
VERY EXPENSIVE

✪ **The Charles Hotel.** 1 Bennett St., Cambridge, MA 02138. ☎ **800/882-1818** outside Mass., or 617/864-1200. Fax 617/864-5715. 293 units. A/C MINIBAR TV TEL. $349–$429 double; $489–$3,000 suite. Extra person $20. Children under 18 free in parents' room. Weekend packages available. AE, CB, DC, JCB, MC, V. Valet parking $18; self-parking $16. T: Red Line to Harvard. Pets accepted.

The Charles Hotel is a phenomenon—an instant classic. The nine-story brick hotel a block from Harvard Square has been *the* place to stay in Cambridge since it opened in 1985. Much of its fame derives from its excellent restaurants, jazz bar, day spa, and service. In the guest rooms, the style is contemporary country, with custom-designed adaptations of Early American Shaker furniture. All rooms have large windows that open, hair dryers, down quilts, scales, and state-of-the-art Bose Wave radios. Twelve units are equipped for people with disabilities, and rooms with special amenities for female travelers are available.

Dining/Diversions: Rialto is one of the best restaurants in Greater Boston. Henrietta's Table offers New England country cooking. The renowned Regattabar features live jazz Tuesday to Saturday nights.

Amenities: 24-hour room service; newspaper delivery; in-room massage; twice-daily maid service; baby-sitting; secretarial services; video rentals; car-rental desk. Glass-enclosed pool, Jacuzzi, sun terrace, and exercise room at the adjacent WellBridge Health and Fitness Center; beauty treatments available at the European-style Le Pli Day Spa.

✪ **Royal Sonesta Hotel.** 5 Cambridge Pkwy., Cambridge, MA 02142. ☎ **800/SONESTA** or 617/806-4200. Fax 617/806-4232. www.sonesta.com. 400 units. A/C MINIBAR TV TEL. $250–$400 double; $400–$600 suite. Children under 18 free in parents' room. AE, CB, DC, DISC, JCB, MC, V. Parking $16. T: Green Line to Lechmere; 10-min. walk.

This luxurious hotel is close to only a few things, but convenient to everything. The CambridgeSide Galleria mall is across the street, the Museum of Science is around the corner on the bridge to Boston (closer than Harvard Square). Most of the spacious rooms have a lovely view of the river or the city, and all have hair dryers. Everything is custom-designed and renovated regularly. There's even cellular phone service linked to your guest-room phone. Travelers with disabilities will find 11 wheelchair-accessible rooms, 16 units equipped for the hearing impaired, and a staff trained in disability awareness.

Dining: Davio's serves three meals daily and has an outdoor patio overlooking the Charles River. The casual Gallery Cafe also has a patio.

Amenities: Heated indoor/outdoor pool with retractable roof; well-equipped health club; Jacuzzi; sauna; sundeck; business center; room service until 1am (2am on weekends); baby-sitting.

EXPENSIVE

The Inn at Harvard. 1201 Mass. Ave. (at Quincy St.), Cambridge, MA 02138. ☎ **800/ 458-5886** or 617/491-2222. Fax 617/491-6520. www.doubletreehotels.com. 109 units (some with shower only). A/C TV TEL. $169–$269 double; $450 presidential suite. Extra person $10. Children under 19 free in parents' room. Packages and senior, AAA, and AARP discounts available. AE, CB, DC, DISC, MC, V. Valet parking $20. T: Red Line to Harvard.

The building looks almost like a Harvard dorm—it's adjacent to Harvard Yard, where its Georgian-style architecture would fit nicely. Inside, it's an elegant hotel, popular with business travelers and university visitors. The four-story skylit atrium holds the "living room," a well-appointed guest lounge. Each elegantly decorated guest room has a work area, windows that open, and an original painting from the Fogg Art Museum. Some have dormer windows and window seats; six are wheelchair accessible.

Dining: The Atrium Dining Room serves seasonal New England fare at breakfast, lunch, dinner, and afternoon tea.

Amenities: Room service; newspaper delivery; secretarial services; safe-deposit boxes.

Sheraton Commander Hotel. 16 Garden St., Cambridge, MA 02138. ☎ **800/325-3535** or 617/547-4800. Fax 617/868-8322. www.sheratoncommander.com. 175 units. A/C TV TEL. $159–$279 double; $330–$550 suite. Extra person $20. Children under 18 free in parents' room. AE, CB, DC, DISC, JCB, MC, V. Free parking. T: Red Line to Harvard.

This six-story hotel in Cambridge's historic district opened in 1927, and it's exactly what you'd expect of a traditional hostelry within sight of the Harvard campus. The guest rooms aren't huge but are attractively furnished in colonial style. Rooms have coffeemakers, hair dryers, irons, and ironing boards. The Club Level offers additional amenities, including in-room fax machines, free local phone calls, and a private lounge. Suites have two TVs, and some have wet bars, refrigerators, and whirlpools.

Dining: The restaurant serves three meals daily and Sunday brunch. The cafe serves lighter fare in the afternoon and evening.

Cambridge Accommodations & Dining

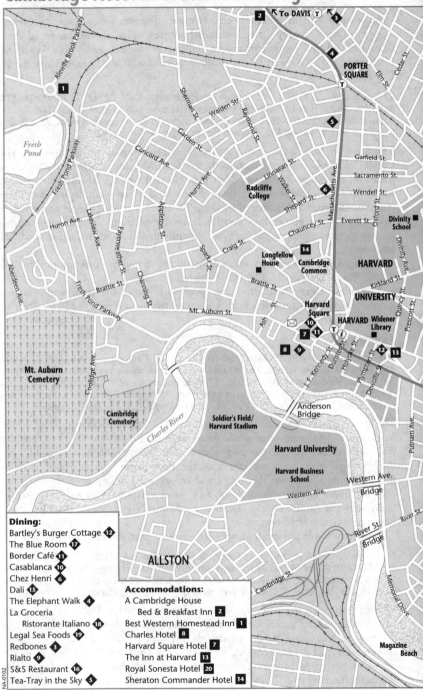

Dining:
Bartley's Burger Cottage 12
The Blue Room 17
Border Café 11
Casablanca 10
Chez Henri 6
Dali 15
The Elephant Walk 4
La Groceria
    Ristorante Italiano 18
Legal Sea Foods 19
Redbones 3
Rialto 9
S&S Restaurant 16
Tea-Tray in the Sky 5

Accommodations:
A Cambridge House
    Bed & Breakfast Inn 2
Best Western Homestead Inn 1
Charles Hotel 8
Harvard Square Hotel 7
The Inn at Harvard 13
Royal Sonesta Hotel 20
Sheraton Commander Hotel 14

NA-0102

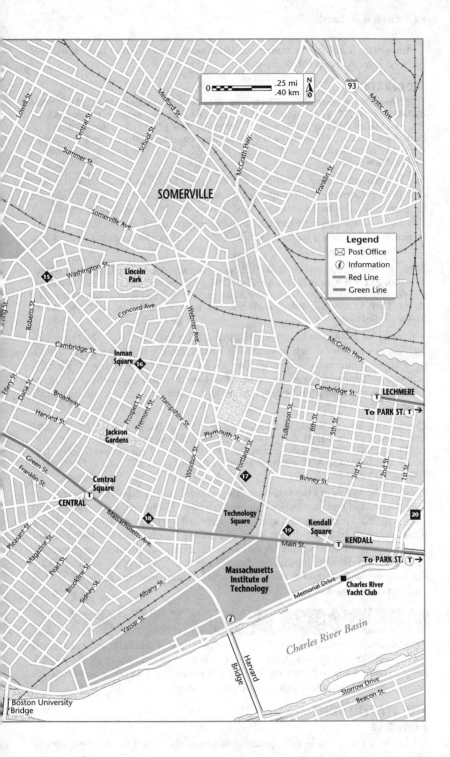

SOMERVILLE

0 ━━━━━ .25 mi
       .40 km

N

93

Legend
⊠ Post Office
ⓘ Information
━ Red Line
━ Green Line

Lincoln
Park

15 Washington St.

Concord Ave.

Cambridge St.

Inman
Square 16

McGrath Hwy.

Cambridge St.

LECHMERE

To PARK ST. ⊤ →

Broadway

Harvard St.

Jackson
Gardens

Plymouth St.

17

Binney St.

Central
Square

CENTRAL ⊤

Massachusetts Ave.

18

Technology
Square

Kendall
Square

19

Main St.

20

KENDALL

To PARK ST. ⊤ →

Massachusetts
Institute of
Technology

Memorial Drive

Charles River
Yacht Club

ⓘ

Vassar St.

Charles River Basin

Harvard
Bridge

Storrow Drive

Beacon St.

Boston University
Bridge

81

Amenities: Small fitness center; sundeck; room service until 11pm; newspaper delivery; laundry room; baby-sitting.

MODERATE

Best Western Homestead Inn. 220 Alewife Brook Pkwy., Cambridge, MA 02138. ☎ **800/ 491-4914** or 617/491-8000. Fax 617/491-4932. www.bwhomestead.com. 69 units. A/C TV TEL. Mid-Mar to Oct $109–$220 double; Nov to mid-Mar $79–$170 double. Rates include continental breakfast. Rates may be higher during special events. Extra person $10. Children under 18 free in parents' room. AE, CB, DC, DISC, JCB, MC, V. Free parking. T: Red Line to Alewife, 10-min. walk.

In a busy commercial neighborhood, this four-story hotel is a comfortable and convenient oasis for motorists. The spacious guest rooms are at least one floor up from the busy street. All have hair dryers, irons, and ironing boards. There's an indoor pool with a Jacuzzi, and a 2½-mile jogging trail around Fresh Pond is across the street. Laundry service (weekdays only), meeting facilities for up to 45 people, and rental-car pickup and drop-off are available.

A Cambridge House Bed & Breakfast Inn. 2218 Mass. Ave., Cambridge, MA 02140. ☎ **800/232-9989** or 617/491-6300; 800/96-2079 in the U.K. Fax 617/868-2848. www.acambridgehouse.com. E-mail: innach@aol.com. 16 units (some with shower only). A/C TV TEL. $139–$275 double. Rates include breakfast. Extra person $35. AE, DISC, MC, V. Free parking. T: Red Line to Porter.

A Cambridge House is a beautifully restored 1892 Victorian home. The three-story building is on a busy stretch of Cambridge's main street, set back from the sidewalk by a lawn. Rooms vary widely in size; all are warmly decorated with Waverly-Schumacher fabrics and period antiques. Most have fireplaces and four-poster canopy beds with down comforters. A generous buffet breakfast and afternoon refreshments are served daily.

✪ **Harvard Square Hotel.** 110 Mount Auburn St., Cambridge, MA 02138. ☎ **800/ 458-5886** or 617/864-5200. Fax 617/864-2409. www.doubletreehotels.com. 73 units. A/C TV TEL. $129–$209 double. Extra person $10. Children under 17 free in parents' room. Corporate rates, AAA, and AARP discounts available. AE, DC, DISC, JCB, MC, V. Parking $18. T: Red Line to Harvard.

Smack in the middle of Harvard Square, this six-story brick hotel is a favorite with visiting parents and budget-conscious business travelers. The unpretentious guest rooms aren't huge but are comfortable and neatly decorated in contemporary style. All have dataports, voice mail, hair dryers, irons, and ironing boards; some overlook Harvard Square. The front desk handles fax and copy services and distributes complimentary newspapers (weekdays only), and dry cleaning and laundry service are available. There are four wheelchair-accessible rooms. Guests have dining privileges at the Inn at Harvard and the Harvard Faculty Club.

4 Dining

Travelers from around the world relish the wide variety of skillfully prepared seafood available in the Boston area. Lunch is an excellent, economical way to check out a fancy restaurant without breaking the bank. At restaurants that take reservations, it's always a good idea to make them, particularly for dinner.

THE WATERFRONT
EXPENSIVE

A branch of **Legal Sea Foods** opened across from the New England Aquarium in 1999; see "Back Bay," below.

MODERATE

Billy Tse Restaurant. 240 Commercial St. ☎ **617/227-9990.** Reservations recommended at dinner on weekends. Main courses $5–$20; lunch specials $5.50–$7.50. AE, DC, DISC, MC, V. Mon–Thurs 11:30am–11:30pm, Fri–Sat 11:30am–midnight, Sun 11:30am–11pm. T: Blue Line to Aquarium or Green or Orange Line to Haymarket. CHINESE/PAN-ASIAN/SUSHI.

This casual, affordable spot on the edge of the Italian North End serves excellent renditions of the usual Chinese dishes and especially good fresh seafood. The Thai- and Vietnamese-influenced pan-Asian selections are just as enjoyable. Main dishes range from seven kinds of fried rice to scallops with garlic sauce to the house special fried noodles, topped with shrimp, calamari, and scallops in a scrumptious sauce. Lunch specials, served until 4pm, include vegetable fried rice or vegetable lo mein.

Daily Catch. 261 Northern Ave. ☎ **617/338-3093.** Reservations accepted only for parties of 8 or more. Main courses $10–$18. AE. Sun–Thurs 11:30am–10:30pm, Fri–Sat 11:30am–11pm. T: Red Line to South Station, 25-min. walk. SOUTHERN ITALIAN/SEAFOOD.

It can take forever to get a table at this Fish Pier institution, and the waitstaff sometimes seems overwhelmed, but the food is terrific. Garlic-lovers will be delighted with the Sicilian-style calamari (squid stuffed with bread crumbs, raisins, pine nuts, parsley, and tons of garlic), freshly shucked clams, mussels in garlic sauce, and broiled and fried fish and shellfish. Try one of the eight or more calamari preparations—even the standard garlic-and-oil pasta sauce has ground-up squid in it.

The other two branches of this minichain don't accept credit cards or reservations. The original Daily Catch, in the **North End** at 323 Hanover St. (☎ **617/523-8567**), keeps the same hours as the Fish Pier location. The **Brookline** restaurant, at 441 Harvard St. (☎ **617/734-5696**), opens at 5pm nightly.

INEXPENSIVE

Jimbo's Fish Shanty. 245 Northern Ave. ☎ **617/542-5600.** Main courses $6–$14. AE, DC, MC, V. Mon–Thurs 11:30am–9:30pm, Fri–Sat 11:30am–10pm, Sun noon–8pm. T: Red Line to South Station, 25-min. walk. SEAFOOD.

Model trains run on tracks suspended from the low ceiling, road signs hang everywhere, and the servers are incredibly informal at this jam-packed restaurant. Under the same management as Jimmy's Harborside across the street, Jimbo's serves decent portions of good, fresh seafood to office workers, tourists, and bargain hunters. The more sophisticated pasta dishes (at dinner only) include a good lobster cream version. The decadent desserts generally involve ice cream and chocolate—save room.

THE NORTH END & CHARLESTOWN

Many North End restaurants don't serve dessert, but you can satisfy your sweet tooth at a *caffè*. Favorites include **Caffè dello Sport,** 308 Hanover St., **Caffè Graffiti,** 307 Hanover St., and **Caffè Vittoria,** 296 Hanover St. There's also table service at **Mike's Pastry,** 300 Hanover St., which is better known for its bustling take-out business.

The **Daily Catch** has a location in the North End; see "The Waterfront," above.

VERY EXPENSIVE

✪ **Mamma Maria.** 3 North Sq. ☎ **617/523-0077.** Reservations recommended. Main courses $18–$29. AE, DC, DISC, MC, V. Sun–Thurs 5–9:30pm, Fri–Sat 5–10:30pm. Valet parking available. T: Green or Orange Line to Haymarket. NORTHERN ITALIAN.

This traditional-looking restaurant offers innovative cuisine and a level of sophistication far removed from the North End's familiar "hey-whaddaya-want" service. The menu changes seasonally; you can usually start with superb risotto or the daily pasta special. The excellent entrees are unlike anything else in this neighborhood, except in their generous size. Fork-tender osso buco is almost enough for two (but you'll want

Boston Dining

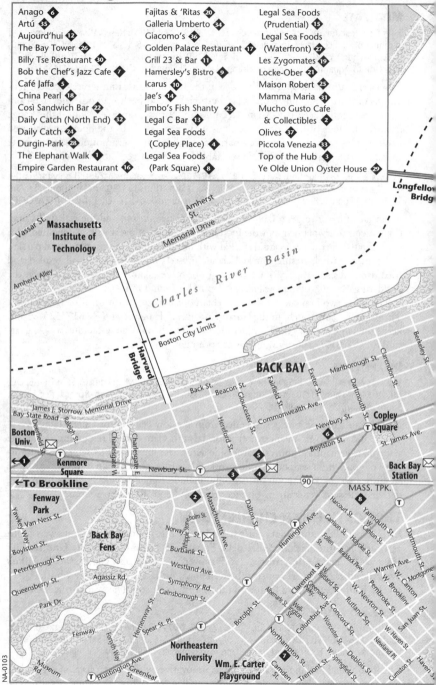

Anago **6**
Artú **35**
Aujourd'hui **12**
The Bay Tower **26**
Billy Tse Restaurant **30**
Bob the Chef's Jazz Cafe **7**
Café Jaffa **5**
China Pearl **18**
Così Sandwich Bar **22**
Daily Catch (North End) **32**
Daily Catch **24**
Durgin-Park **28**
The Elephant Walk **1**
Empire Garden Restaurant **16**

Fajitas & 'Ritas **20**
Galleria Umberto **34**
Giacomo's **36**
Golden Palace Restaurant **17**
Grill 23 & Bar **11**
Hamersley's Bistro **9**
Icarus **10**
Jae's **14**
Jimbo's Fish Shanty **23**
Legal C Bar **13**
Legal Sea Foods
  (Copley Place) **4**
Legal Sea Foods
  (Park Square) **8**

Legal Sea Foods
  (Prudential) **15**
Legal Sea Foods
  (Waterfront) **27**
Les Zygomates **19**
Locke-Ober **21**
Maison Robert **25**
Mamma Maria **31**
Mucho Gusto Cafe
  & Collectibles **2**
Olives **37**
Piccola Venezia **33**
Top of the Hub **3**
Ye Olde Union Oyster House **29**

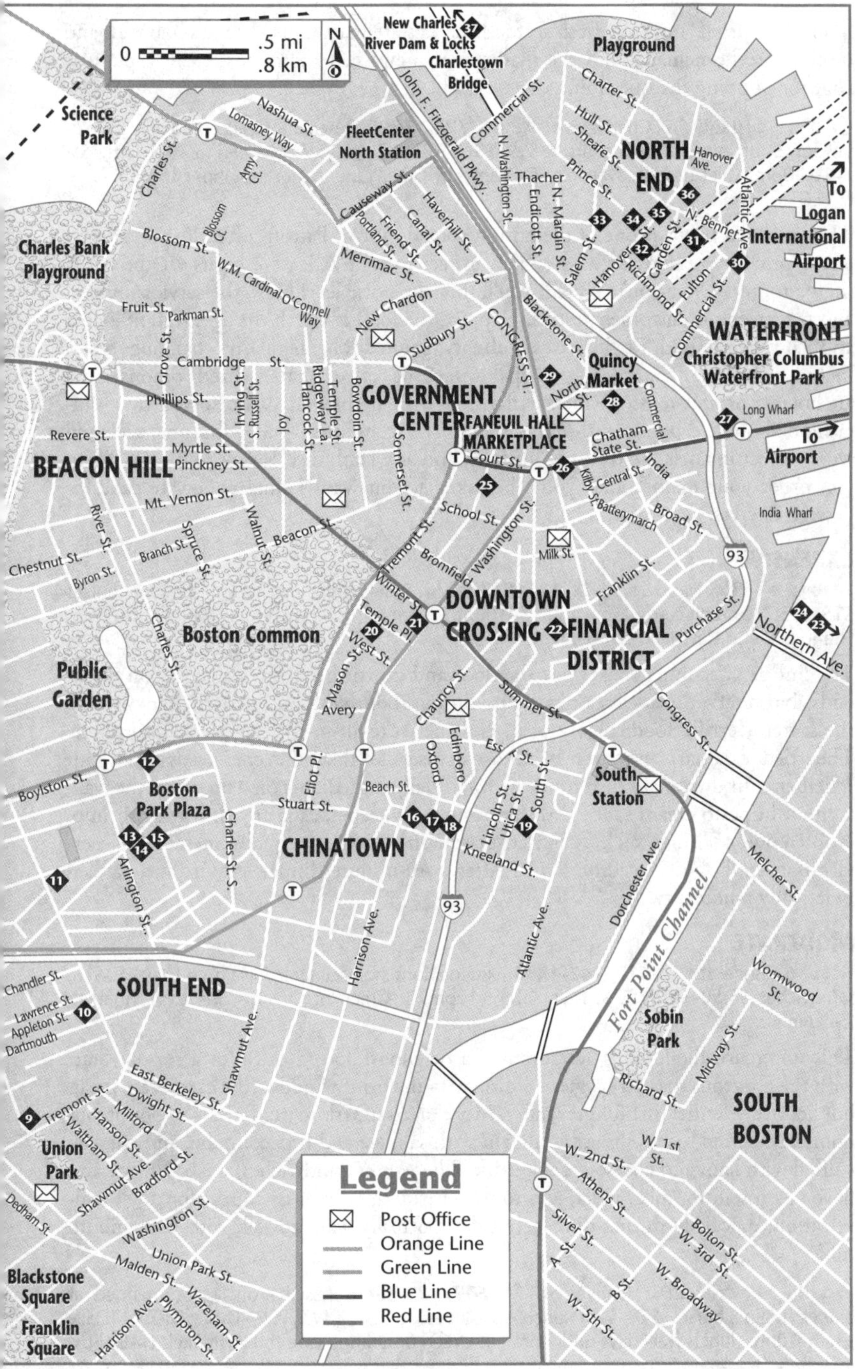

0 .5 mi .8 km
N
New Charles River Dam & Locks
Charlestown Bridge
Playground
Science Park
FleetCenter North Station
NORTH END
To Logan International Airport
Charles Bank Playground
WATERFRONT
Christopher Columbus Waterfront Park
GOVERNMENT CENTER
FANEUIL HALL MARKETPLACE
Quincy Market
BEACON HILL
To Airport
India Wharf
DOWNTOWN CROSSING
FINANCIAL DISTRICT
Boston Common
Public Garden
Boston Park Plaza
CHINATOWN
South Station
SOUTH END
Fort Point Channel
Sobin Park
SOUTH BOSTON
Union Park
Blackstone Square
Franklin Square
Legend
Post Office
Orange Line
Green Line
Blue Line
Red Line

it all for yourself), and the fresh seafood specials are marvelous. The pasta, bread, and desserts are homemade, and the shadowy, whitewashed rooms make this a popular spot for popping the question.

✪ **Olives.** 10 City Sq., Charlestown. ☎ **617/242-1999.** Reservations accepted only for parties of 6 or more. Main courses $19–$32. AE, DC, MC, V. Mon–Fri 5:30–10pm; Sat 5–10:30pm. Valet parking available. T: Orange or Green Line to North Station; 15-min. walk. ECLECTIC.

This informal bistro is one of the hottest spots in town. Patrons often line up shortly after 5pm; if you don't arrive by 5:45, expect to wait at least 2 hours (at the bar if there's room). Once you're seated, you'll find the noise level high, the service uneven, and the ravenous customers festive. Happily, the food is worth the aggravation—chef and co-owner Todd English is a culinary genius. The regularly changing menu includes "Olives Classics"—perhaps a tart of olives, caramelized onions, and anchovies, or spit-roasted chicken flavored with herbs and garlic served over old-fashioned mashed potatoes. Grilling is a favorite technique—yellowfin tuna, accented with perfect mussels, holds up beautifully, and any lamb dish is sure to please. When you order your main course you'll be asked if you want falling chocolate cake for dessert. Say yes.

EXPENSIVE

Giacomo's. 355 Hanover St. ☎ **617/523-9026.** Reservations not accepted. Main courses $15–$25. No credit cards. Mon–Thurs 5–10pm; Fri–Sat 5–10:30pm; Sun 4–10pm. T: Green or Orange Line to Haymarket. ITALIAN/SEAFOOD.

The line at Giacomo's snakes out the door and down the street, especially on weekends. No reservations, cash only, a tiny dining room with an open kitchen—what's the secret? Terrific food, plenty of it, and the we're-all-in-this-together atmosphere. The fried calamari appetizer is almost greaseless. Take the chef's advice or put together your own main dish from the list of daily ingredients on a board on the wall. Salmon in pesto cream sauce with fettuccine is a keeper, as is any dish with shrimp. Nonseafood offerings such as butternut-squash ravioli are equally memorable. Service is friendly but incredibly swift. After a 40-minute dinner, dessert at a caffè is practically a necessity.

MODERATE

Artú. 6 Prince St. ☎ **617/742-4336.** Reservations not accepted. Main courses $9–$18; sandwiches $5.50–$9. MC, V. Daily 11am–10pm. T: Green or Orange Line to Haymarket. ITALIAN.

This unremarkable-looking restaurant is a neighborhood favorite for a reason. Start with the gorgeous roasted veggies on display in the front window (the carrots are great, but licorice-y fennel isn't for everyone). Move on to superb roasted meats or bounteous home-style pasta dishes. Roast lamb, ziti with sausage and broccoli rabe, and chicken stuffed with ham and cheese are all terrific. The *panini* (sandwiches) are big in size and flavor—prosciutto, mozzarella, and tomato is sublime. Artú isn't great for quiet conversation, especially during dinner, but do you really want to talk with your mouth full?

Piccola Venezia. 263 Hanover St. ☎ **617/523-3888.** Reservations recommended at dinner. Main courses $10–$20; lunch specialties $5.25–$8. AE, CB, DISC, MC, V. Daily 11am–10pm (lunch weekdays until 4pm). T: Green or Orange Line to Haymarket. ITALIAN.

Piccola Venezia's glass front wall faces the Freedom Trail—a touristy location with a neighborhood feel. Portions are large and the homey food tends to be heavy on red sauce; more sophisticated dishes are available, often as daily specials. Spaghetti and meatballs, chicken parmigiana, eggplant rolatini, and pasta puttanesca are always available. This is a good place to try traditional Italian-American favorites such as polenta (home-style, not the yuppie croutons available at so many other places), *baccala* (reconstituted salt cod), or the house specialty, tripe.

INEXPENSIVE

Galleria Umberto. 289 Hanover St. ☎ **617/227-5709.** All items less than $3. No credit cards. Mon–Sat 11am–2pm. T: Green or Orange Line to Haymarket. ITALIAN.

The long, fast-moving line of businesspeople and tourists tips you off to the fact that this cafeteria-style spot is a real bargain. The food is good, too. You can fill up on pizza, but if you're feeling adventurous, try the *arancini* (a rice ball filled with ground beef, peas, and cheese). The calzones—ham and cheese, spinach, spinach and cheese, or spinach and sausage—and potato croquettes are also tasty. Study the cases while you wait, and be ready to order at once when you reach the head of the line. Have a quick lunch and get on with your sightseeing.

FANEUIL HALL MARKETPLACE & FINANCIAL DISTRICT

The Quincy Market **food court** at Faneuil Hall Marketplace is a great place to pick up picnic food. Eat there, or cross under the Expressway and pass the Marriott to reach the plaza at the end of Long Wharf. Or go around the hotel to the left and dine in Christopher Columbus Park.

VERY EXPENSIVE

✪ **Maison Robert.** 45 School St. ☎ **617/227-3370.** www.maisonrobert.com. Reservations recommended. Main courses $10–$22 at lunch, $17–$32 at dinner. Le Café fixed-priced menu $18 or $25; à la carte main courses $14–$28. AE, CB, DC, MC, V. Mon–Fri 11:45am–2:30pm; Mon–Sat 5:30–10pm. Valet parking available at dinner. T: Red Line to Park Street, Green Line to Government Center. INNOVATIVE FRENCH.

This world-class French restaurant with a spectacular formal dining room has been a legend in Boston since it opened in Old City Hall in 1971. The food equals the elegant setting, classic but dramatic, with unexpected but welcome Asian influences. You might start with a tender, airy Roquefort soufflé, or smoked lobster cream soup. Entrees include familiar options and pleasant surprises—filet mignon is a meat-lover's delight, and ostrich medallions are marinated in tarragon and served with leek salad.

Sky-High Dining: The Lowdown

First, a disclaimer: This is not to disparage the food at either of these elegant places, which is quite good. But the fact is, you're paying extra for the view at the Bay Tower and Top of the Hub. Make a reservation, and if you can't get a table *by the window* (the odds are better at the Bay Tower), have a drink in the lounge, and eat somewhere else.

The **Bay Tower** (☎ 617/723-1666) is on the 33rd floor of 60 State St., overlooking Faneuil Hall Marketplace, the Waterfront, and the airport. It serves creative American cuisine at dinner Monday to Saturday. The service and desserts are exquisite. Jackets are required for men in the dining room.

Top of the Hub (☎ 617/536-1775) is on the 52nd floor of the Prudential Tower, 800 Boylston St. It serves lunch Monday to Saturday, Sunday brunch, and dinner daily. The contemporary American menu includes excellent clam chowder.

Desserts are impressive, ranging from excellent soufflés to heart-stopping chocolate concoctions to upside-down apple tart.

On the ground floor is the more casual and less expensive—but still thoroughly French—**Ben's Café.** In the summer, cafe seating spills onto the lovely terrace next to the landmark statue of Benjamin Franklin.

EXPENSIVE

✪ **Les Zygomates.** 129 South St. ☎ **617/542-5108.** www.winebar.com. Reservations recommended. Main courses $12–$20. Fixed-price $11 at lunch, $19 at dinner (Mon–Thurs). AE, CB, DC, DISC, MC, V. Mon–Fri 11am–1am (lunch until 2:30pm, dinner until 10:30pm); Sat–Sun 6pm–1am (dinner until 11:30pm). Valet parking available at dinner. T: Red Line to South Station. FRENCH/ECLECTIC.

Pick your way through the construction near South Station to this delightful bistro and wine bar. It offers a great selection of wine by the bottle, glass, and 2-ounce "taste." The efficient staff will guide you to a good accompaniment for chef and co-owner Ian Just's delicious cuisine, which is hearty and filling but not heavy. Pan-fried catfish is flaky and light; flank steak with garlic mashed potatoes and sautéed vegetables is succulent. For dessert, try not to fight over the lemon mousse. Sunday to Thursday nights, you can linger over a glass of wine and listen to live jazz.

Ye Olde Union Oyster House. 41 Union St. (between North and Hanover sts.). ☎ **617/227-2750.** www.unionoysterhouse.com. Reservations recommended. Main courses $9–$19 at lunch, $15–$28 at dinner. AE, CB, DC, DISC, MC, V. Sun–Thurs 11am–9:30pm (lunch until 5); Fri–Sat 11am–10pm (lunch until 6). Union Bar daily 11am–midnight (lunch until 3; supper until 11). T: Green or Orange Line to Haymarket. NEW ENGLAND/SEAFOOD.

America's oldest restaurant in continuous service, the Union Oyster House opened in 1826. Its tasty, traditional New England fare is popular with tourists on the adjacent Freedom Trail. At the crescent-shaped bar on the lower level of the cramped, low-ceilinged building, try the appetizer sampler of hot or cold oysters, clams, and shrimp. Oyster stew makes a good beginning. Follow with a broiled or grilled dish such as scrod or salmon, or perhaps seafood primavera, fried seafood, or grilled pork loin. A shore dinner (chowder, steamers, lobster, salad, corn, and dessert) is an excellent introduction to local favorites. Ask to be seated at John F. Kennedy's favorite booth (no. 18), which is marked with a plaque.

MODERATE

✪ **Durgin-Park.** 340 Faneuil Hall Marketplace. ☎ **617/227-2038.** Reservations not accepted. Main courses $5–$18, specials $16–$25. AE, CB, DC, DISC, MC, V. Mon–Thurs 11:30am–10pm, Fri–Sat 11:30am–10:30pm, Sun 11:30am–9pm. Lunch menu until 2:30pm. T: Green or Blue Line to Government Center, Orange Line to Haymarket. NEW ENGLAND.

For huge portions of delicious food, a rowdy atmosphere where CEOs share tables with students, and famously cranky waitresses who can't seem to bear the sight of any of it, Bostonians have flocked to Durgin-Park since 1827. Politicians rub shoulders with grandmothers, and everyone's disappointed when the waitresses are nice, as they often are. Approximately 2,000 people a day find their way to the line that stretches down a flight of stairs to the first floor of Faneuil Hall Marketplace's North Market building. They come for prime rib the size of a hubcap, giant lamb chops, piles of fried seafood, and bounteous portions of roast turkey. Steaks and chops are broiled on an open fire over wood charcoal. Suppliers deliver fresh seafood twice daily, and fish dinners are broiled to order. Vegetables come à la carte—now is the time to try Boston baked beans. For dessert, the strawberry shortcake is justly celebrated, and hard-core molasses lovers will want to try Indian pudding (molasses and cornmeal baked for hours and served with ice cream).

INEXPENSIVE

Cosí Sandwich Bar. 133 Federal St. ☎ **617/292-2674.** Sandwiches $5.75–$8.25; soups and salads $2.95–$6.50. AE, DC, MC, V. Mon–Fri 6:30am–9pm. T: Red Line to South Station or Orange Line to Downtown Crossing. ITALIAN/ECLECTIC.

Flavorful fillings on delectable bread make Cosí a Financial District hot spot. Tasty Italian flatbread, baked fresh all day, gets split open and filled with your choice of meat, fish, vegetables, cheese, and spreads. The more fillings you choose, the more you pay. Tandoori chicken with caramelized onions is sensational, as is smoked salmon with spinach-artichoke spread. The lunch crowds are more manageable in the summer, when seating extends outdoors, but this is an excellent choice for a detour off the Freedom Trail anytime.

DOWNTOWN CROSSING
VERY EXPENSIVE

Locke–Ober. 3 and 4 Winter Place. ☎ **617/542-1340.** Reservations required. Main courses $8–$24.50 at lunch, $17–$40 at dinner. AE, CB, DC, DISC, MC, V. Mon–Fri 11:30am–10pm; Sat 3–10pm. Valet parking available after 6pm. T: Red or Orange Line to Downtown Crossing. AMERICAN/CONTINENTAL.

"Locke's" is *the* traditional Boston restaurant, a power-broker favorite since 1875. In an alley off Winter Street, this wood-paneled restaurant feels like a men's club. Women won't feel unwelcome, but it's definitely not a "girls' night out" place. For one thing, anyone on a diet will be sorely tempted. This is old-fashioned food: the famous Jonah crab cakes or steak tartare to start, then superb grilled salmon with horseradish sauce, Wiener schnitzel à la Holstein, or an excellent veal chop. The signature dish is lobster Savannah, which calls for the meat of a 3-pound lobster diced with pepper and mushrooms, bound with cheese and sherry sauce, stuffed into the shell, and baked. If your heart doesn't stop on the spot, you won't be hungry again for a long time. The dessert menu lists about two dozen items, and as you might expect, the chocolate mousse is a dish for the ages.

INEXPENSIVE

Fajitas & 'Ritas. 25 West St. (between Washington and Tremont). ☎ **617/426-1222.** Most dishes under $9. AE, DC, DISC, MC, V. Sun–Thurs 11:30am–10pm, Fri–Sat 11:30am–2am. T: Red or Green Line to Park Street or Orange Line to Downtown Crossing. TEX-MEX.

This entertaining storefront restaurant isn't the most authentic in town, but it's one of the most fun. To order, you fill out a slip, checking off fillings and garnishes for your nachos, quesadillas, burritos, and, of course, fajitas. A member of the somewhat harried staff returns with big portions of fresh food—this place is too busy for any ingredient to be sitting around for very long. 'Ritas (margaritas, ordered from a list of about a dozen options using the same check-off system as the food) are a house specialty.

CHINATOWN/THEATER DISTRICT

The best way to sample Chinese food is by trying **dim sum.** It's especially popular with families on weekends, when the variety of offerings is greatest. Three good destinations are **Empire Garden Restaurant,** 690–698 Washington St., second floor (☎ 617/482-8898); **Golden Palace Restaurant,** 14 Tyler St. (☎ 617/423-4565), and **China Pearl,** 9 Tyler St., second floor (☎ 617/426-4338).

EXPENSIVE

Jae's. 212 Stuart St. ☎ **617/451-7788.** Reservations recommended at dinner. Main courses $8.25–$21; sushi from $5.25. AE, DC, MC, V. Mon–Sat 11:30am–4pm; Mon–Wed

5–10:30pm, Thurs–Sat 5pm–1am; Sun noon–10pm. T: Green Line to Arlington, Orange Line to New England Medical Center. KOREAN/SUSHI/PAN-ASIAN.

This fun, frantic restaurant is a three-story food festival, with sushi on the first floor, Korean and pan-Asian dishes on the second, and Korean barbecue on the third. It draws crowds of adventurous food fans, pretheater suburbanites, and hungry businesspeople. The food is even more diverse, ranging from pristine sushi to bountiful noodle dishes (lo mein with tiny clams is a great choice) to traditional Korean fare. Even the crab cakes (not exactly pan-Asian, but so what?) are divine. The service is not quite divine, or at least not always; you'll get better attention earlier in the week.

SOUTH END
VERY EXPENSIVE

Hamersley's Bistro. 553 Tremont St. ☎ **617/423-2700.** Reservations recommended. Main courses $21–$30. Menu degustation varies. AE, DISC, MC, V. Mon–Fri 6–10pm, Sat 5:30–10pm, Sun 5:30–9:30pm. Valet parking available. T: Orange Line to Back Bay. ECLECTIC.

This is the place that put the South End on Boston's culinary map, a pioneering restaurant that's both classic and contemporary. The menu changes seasonally and offers about a dozen carefully considered entrees (always including vegetarian dishes) noted for their emphasis on taste and texture. The signature roast chicken, flavored with garlic, lemon, and parsley, comes with roasted potato and onions, and whole cloves of sweet baked garlic. Salmon au poivre with sorrel, leeks, and fingerling potatoes is delicious, as is grilled fillet of beef with garlic mashed potatoes and delectable red wine sauce. And the wine list is excellent.

✪ **Icarus.** 3 Appleton St. ☎ **617/426-1790.** Reservations recommended. Main courses $19.50–$32.50; "Square Meal" $42. AE, CB, DC, DISC, MC, V. Sun–Thurs 6–10pm, Fri 6–10:30pm, Sat 5:30–10:30pm. Closed Sun July–Aug. Valet parking available at dinner. T: Green Line to Arlington, or Orange Line to Back Bay. ECLECTIC.

This shamelessly romantic subterranean restaurant offers every element of a great dining experience. Chef and co-owner Chris Douglass uses choice local seafood, poultry, meats, and produce to create imaginative dishes that seem more like alchemy than cooking. The menu changes regularly—you might start with grilled shrimp served with mango and jalapeño sorbet, or the daily "pasta whim." Move on to porcini-crusted halibut with Cabernet vinegar sauce, or lemony grilled chicken with garlic mashed potatoes so good you'll want to ask for a plate of them. Don't—save room for one of the unbelievable desserts. The seasonal fruit sorbets are especially delicious.

MODERATE

Bob the Chef's Jazz Cafe. 604 Columbus Ave. ☎ **617/536-6204.** Main courses $9–$15; sandwiches $5–$8. AE, DC, MC, V. Tues–Wed 11:30am–10pm, Thurs–Sat 11:30am–midnight; Sun 11am–9pm (brunch until 3pm). Self-parking ($4) across the street. T: Orange Line to Mass. Ave., 5-min. walk. SOUTHERN/CAJUN.

Bob the Chef's serves generous portions of Southern specialties against a backdrop of jazz. The music is live Thursday to Saturday nights and at Sunday brunch. You'll find dishes such as "glorifried" chicken, served alone or with barbecued ribs; pork chops; "soul fish" (two whole pan-fried porgies), and Cajun specialties such as jambalaya and shrimp étoufée. Side dishes include black-eyed peas, macaroni and cheese, and collard greens. Frying is done in vegetable oil, and everywhere you'd expect bacon for flavoring, there's smoked turkey. For dessert, try the phenomenal sweet-potato pie.

BACK BAY
VERY EXPENSIVE

✪ **Anago.** In the Lenox Hotel, 65 Exeter St. ☎ **617/266-6222.** Reservations recommended at dinner. Main courses $12–$16 at lunch, $10–$32 at dinner. AE, DC, MC, V. Mon–Fri 11:30am–2pm; Sun 11am–2:30pm; Mon–Thurs 5:30–10pm, Fri–Sat 5:30–10:30pm, Sun 5–9pm. Valet parking available. T: Green Line to Copley. CONTEMPORARY AMERICAN.

Anago opened in Boston in 1997 (it had been Anago Bistro in Cambridge), and quickly established itself as one of the city's top restaurants. You can schedule a business lunch, romantic dinner, or family brunch here with equal confidence. Chef and co-owner Bob Calderone makes good use of fresh regional produce, seafood, and meats. Main dishes might include oven-roasted bass with warm potato salad, grilled corn, and heirloom tomato salad, and toothsome rack of lamb with ratatouille, mashed potatoes, and olive tapenade. Desserts are more fanciful than you'd expect— try "chocolate, chocolate, chocolate," when it's available, and be ready to swoon.

✪ **Aujourd'hui.** In the Four Seasons Hotel, 200 Boylston St. ☎ **617/451-1392.** Reservations recommended (required on holidays). Main courses $19–$23.50 at lunch, $32–$45 at dinner; Sun buffet brunch $52. AE, CB, DC, DISC, MC, V. Mon–Fri 6:30–11am, Sat–Sun 7–11am; daily 11:30am–2pm; Mon–Sat 5:30–10:30pm, Sun 6–10pm. Valet parking available. T: Green Line to Arlington. CONTEMPORARY AMERICAN.

On the second floor of the city's premier luxury hotel, the most beautiful restaurant in town offers incredible service and food to a special-occasion and expense-account clientele. Yes, the cost is astronomical, but how often is it true that you get what you pay for? Here, it is. The regularly changing menu encompasses basic offerings you'd expect in a hotel dining room and creations that characterize an inventive kitchen. Executive chef Edward Gannon uses regional products and the freshest ingredients available, and the wine list is excellent. Entrees include rack of lamb served with a timbale of potatoes, goat cheese, mushrooms, and zucchini, and oven-roasted lobster with Thai vinegar sauce and soba noodles. "Alternative Cuisine" offerings slash calories, cholesterol, sodium, and fat, but not flavor. The dessert menu also changes, but always includes picture-perfect soufflés and homemade sorbets.

✪ **Grill 23 & Bar.** 161 Berkeley St. ☎ **617/542-2255.** www.grill23.com. Reservations recommended. Main courses $19–$30. AE, CB, DC, DISC, MC, V. Mon–Thurs 5:30–10:30pm, Fri–Sat 5:30–11pm, Sun 5:30–10pm. Valet parking available. T: Green Line to Arlington. AMERICAN.

This wood-paneled, glass-walled room attracts a briefcase-toting clientele, but it's more than just a steak house. "Grill Classics" such as steak au poivre and lamb chops coexist with bolder "Signature Specials" like inventively updated meat loaf of sirloin and chorizo with roasted-red-pepper relish. If the fish dishes aren't quite as memorable— hey, it's a steak house. The bountiful à la carte side dishes include out-of-this-world garlic mashed potatoes. Desserts, especially crème brûlée, are luscious. The service is exactly right for the setting, helpful but not familiar, but the room does get quite loud.

EXPENSIVE

The Spanish tapas restaurant Dalí has a Back Bay outpost, **Tapéo;** see "Cambridge," below.

✪ **Legal Sea Foods.** 800 Boylston St., in the Prudential Center. ☎ **617/266-6800.** Reservations recommended at lunch, not accepted at dinner. Main courses $7–$13 at lunch, $14– $24 at dinner. AE, CB, DC, DISC, MC, V. Mon–Thurs 11am–10:30pm, Fri–Sat 11am–11:30pm, Sun noon–10pm. T: Green Line B, C, or D to Hynes/ICA; E to Prudential. SEAFOOD.

The food at Legal Sea Foods isn't the fanciest, cheapest, or trendiest. It's the freshest, and management's commitment to that policy has produced a thriving chain. "Legal's" has an international reputation for serving only top-quality fish and shellfish, prepared in every imaginable way. The menu includes regular selections (scrod, haddock, blue-fish, salmon, shrimp, calamari, and lobster, among others) plus whatever looked good at the market that morning, and it's all splendid. The clam chowder is legendary, and the fish chowder equally good.

I suggest the Prudential Center branch because it takes reservations (at lunch only), a deviation from a long tradition. There are about a dozen other locations, including **Copley Place** (☎ 617/266-7775) and **Kendall Square**, 5 Cambridge Center (☎ 617/864-3400). Two new Boston restaurants opened in 1999: Park Square between Columbus Avenue and Stuart Street, opposite the Boston Park Plaza Hotel (☎ 617/426-4444), and the first waterfront location (☎ 617/227-3115), at 255 State St., opposite the New England Aquarium.

MODERATE

Mucho Gusto Cafe & Collectibles. 1124 Boylston St. ☎ **617/236-1020.** Reservations recommended. Main courses $8–$17; tapas $3.50–$8. MC, V. Tues–Wed 4–10pm, Thurs–Sat noon–10pm, Sun noon–4pm. Closed Tues in winter. T: Green Line B, C, or D to Hynes/ICA. CUBAN.

Students and adventurous diners enjoy Mucho Gusto for its Cuban home cooking and its wacky '50s-style decor (much of which is for sale). The rib-sticking food comes in main-dish portions and small plates, or tapas, that are perfect for sharing and go well with the house special sangria. Be sure to try empanadas (flaky turnovers filled with vegetables or meat), picadillo (shredded beef perfectly seasoned and dotted with green olives), and plantain chips fried to slightly greasy perfection. Desserts are on the sweet side, just right with strong Cuban coffee.

INEXPENSIVE

Café Jaffa. 48 Gloucester St. ☎ **617/536-0230.** Main courses $4.25–$10. AE, DC, DISC, MC, V. Mon–Thurs 11am–10:30pm, Fri–Sat 11am–11pm, Sun 1–10pm. T: Green Line B, C, or D to Hynes/ICA. MIDDLE EASTERN.

Glass-fronted Café Jaffa looks more like a snazzy pizza place than the wonderful Middle Eastern restaurant it is. Young people flock here, drawn by the low prices, high quality, and large portions of traditional Middle Eastern offerings such as falafel, baba ghanoush, and hummus, as well as burgers and steak tips. Lamb, beef, and chicken kabobs come with Greek salad, rice pilaf, and pita bread. For dessert, try the baklava if it's fresh.

BROOKLINE & ENVIRONS
MODERATE

The Elephant Walk. 900 Beacon St., Boston. ☎ **617/247-1500.** Reservations recommended at dinner Sun–Thurs, not accepted Fri–Sat. Main courses $6–$18.50 at lunch, $9.50–$18.50 at dinner. AE, DC, DISC, MC, V. Mon–Sat 11:30am–2:30pm; Mon–Thurs 5–10pm, Fri 5–11pm, Sat 4:30–11pm, Sun 4:30–10pm. Valet parking available at dinner. T: Green Line C to St. Mary's St. FRENCH/CAMBODIAN.

France meets Cambodia on the menu here, 4 blocks from Kenmore Square. This madly popular spot has a two-part menu, but the boundary is quite porous. The pleasant staff will help if you need guidance. Many of the Cambodian dishes have part-French names, such as *poulet dhomrei* (chicken with Asian basil, bamboo shoots, fresh pineapple, and kaffir lime leaves) and *curry de crevettes* (shrimp curry). On the

French side, you'll find pan-seared filet mignon with *pommes frites*, and pan-seared tuna with three-peppercorn crust.

There's another Elephant Walk at 2067 Mass. Ave., just north of Cambridge's **Porter Square** (☎ 617/492-6900). It keeps the same hours as the Boston location, except that it opens for dinner at 5pm on Sunday, and offers free parking at the back of the building.

CAMBRIDGE

The MBTA Red Line runs from downtown Boston to the heart of Harvard Square. Many of the restaurants listed here can be reached on foot from there. If inexpensive ethnic food is more your speed, head for Central and Inman squares.

Note: See the "Cambridge Accommodations & Dining" map on pages 80–81 for the locations of the restaurants reviewed below.

VERY EXPENSIVE

✪ **Rialto.** In the Charles Hotel, 1 Bennett St. ☎ **617/661-5050.** Reservations recommended. Main courses $20–$29. AE, CB, DC, MC, V. Sun–Thurs 5:30–10pm, Fri–Sat 5:30–11pm. Bar Sun–Thurs 4:30pm–midnight, Fri–Sat 5pm–1:30am. Valet and validated parking available. T: Red Line to Harvard. MEDITERRANEAN.

If Rialto isn't the best restaurant in the Boston area, it's close. It attracts a chic crowd, but it's not a "scene" in the sense that out-of-towners will feel left behind. It's in a dramatic but comfortable room, with floor-to-ceiling windows overlooking Harvard Square. Chef Jody Adams's menu changes regularly, and main courses are so good that you might as well close your eyes and point. A plate of creamy potato slices and mushrooms is so juicy it's almost like eating meat. Seared duck breast with foie gras, squash raviolis, and quince is wonderful, and anything involving salmon is a guaranteed winner—a perfectly flaky, orange-pink hunk, perhaps with sweet potatoes, dried cranberries, and pine nuts. For dessert, a trio of seasonal sorbets is a great choice, as is the popover served with tangerine cream.

EXPENSIVE

There's a **Legal Sea Foods** branch in Kendall Square; see "Back Bay," above.

✪ **The Blue Room.** 1 Kendall Sq. ☎ **617/494-9034.** Reservations recommended. Main courses $16–$22. AE, DC, DISC, MC, V. Sun–Thurs 5:30–10pm, Fri–Sat 5:30–11pm; Sun brunch 11am–2:30pm. Validated parking available. T: Red Line to Kendall/MIT, 10-min. walk. ECLECTIC.

The Blue Room sits just below plaza level in an office-retail complex, a slice of foodie paradise in high-tech heaven. The cuisine is a rousing combination of top-notch ingredients and layers of aggressive flavors, the service is excellent, and the crowded dining room is not as noisy as you might fear. Main courses tend to be roasted, grilled, or braised, with at least two vegetarian choices. The roast chicken, served with garlic mashed potatoes, is world-class. Grilled tuna appears often, and pork loin with cider glaze will make you think twice the next time you skip over pork on a menu to get to the steak. In warm weather, there's seating on the brick patio.

Casablanca. 40 Brattle St. ☎ **617/876-0999.** Reservations recommended at dinner. Main courses $7–$12 at lunch, $10–$19 at dinner. AE, MC, V. Daily 11:30am–3pm; Sun–Thurs 5:30–10pm, Fri–Sat 5:30–11pm. T: Red Line to Harvard. MEDITERRANEAN.

This old-time Harvard Square favorite is better known for its hopping bar scene, but these days the dining room is where you're sure to get lucky. Casablanca remains true to its reputation for serving tasty Mediterranean cuisine and for rather erratic service (it's better at lunch than at dinner). The walls of the long, skylit dining room and crowded bar sport murals of scenes from the movie. Try the skewered lamb or the grilled chicken, served at dinner with mashed sweet potatoes or as an hors d'oeuvre in wing form, flavored with fiery North African *harissa* spice paste. Just be sure to leave room for dessert—the cookies are a good choice, as is the gingerbread.

Chez Henri. 1 Shepard St. ☎ **617/354-8980.** Reservations accepted only for parties of 6 or more. Main courses $15–$19; 3-course fixed-priced menu $28; bar food $5–$8. AE, DC, MC, V. Mon–Thurs 6–10pm; Fri–Sat 6–11pm; Sun 11am–2pm and 6–9pm. Bar food Mon–Sat to midnight, Sun to 10pm. T: Red Line to Harvard. FRENCH/CUBAN.

In a dark, elegant space off Mass. Ave., Chez Henri is a paragon of fusion cuisine. Under the same ownership as Providence in Brookline, it offers a more focused menu that concentrates on French bistro-style food with Cuban accents. The menu changes regularly; it might include a juicy chicken breast served with black-bean sauce, avocado slaw, and two spicy empanadas (turnovers) filled with potato and cheese; or monkfish with mushrooms, au gratin potatoes, and cinnamon-scented sauce. The prix fixe menu includes one of two appetizers and one of two entrees as well as dessert— the crème brûlée is magnificent. The bar food is Cuban, as are the strong specialty drinks.

☉ Dalí. 415 Washington St., Somerville. ☎ **617/661-3254.** www.dalirestaurant.com. Reservations not accepted. Tapas $2.50–$7.50, main courses $17–$22. AE, DC, MC, V. Daily winter 5:30–11pm, summer 6–11pm. T: Red Line to Harvard; follow Kirkland St. to intersection of Washington and Beacon sts. (20 min.). SPANISH.

Dalí is a festive spot where the bar fills with people cheerfully waiting an hour or more for a table. The payoff is authentic Spanish food, notably tapas, little plates of flavorful hot or cold creations. Entrees include excellent paella, but most people come in a group and explore the three dozen or more tapas offerings, all perfect for sharing. They include delectable garlic potatoes, crunchy-tender saffron-battered shrimp, and rich, light goat cheese baked with tomato and basil. The waitstaff sometimes seems a bit overwhelmed but never fails to supply bread for sopping up juices, and sangria for washing it all down. Finish up with excellent flan, or try the rich *tarta de chocolates.*

The owners of Dalí also run **Tapéo** (☎ 617/267-4799), at 266 Newbury St., between Fairfield and Dartmouth streets in Boston's **Back Bay**.

MODERATE

The **Elephant Walk** (French-Cambodian food), has a Porter Square branch; see "Brookline & Environs," above.

Border Café. 32 Church St. ☎ **617/864-6100.** Reservations not accepted. Main courses $7–$14. AE, MC, V. Mon–Thurs 11am–1am, Fri–Sat 11am–2am, Sun noon–11pm. T: Red Line to Harvard. TEX-MEX/CAJUN.

This unbelievably crowded restaurant has been a favorite Harvard Square hangout for almost 15 years. The presence of patrons loitering at the bar for hours while waiting for a table only enhances the festival atmosphere. The menu features generous portions of Tex-Mex, Cajun, and Caribbean food, and the beleaguered waitstaff keeps the chips and salsa coming. Try the excellent chorizo appetizer, enchiladas, any kind of tacos, or popcorn shrimp. Fajitas for one or two, sizzling noisily in a large iron frying pan, are also popular.

☉ Redbones. 55 Chester St. (off Elm St.), Somerville. ☎ **617/628-2200.** www.red-bonesbbq.com. Reservations accepted only for parties of 11 or more, Sun–Thurs. Main courses $7–$14. No credit cards. Daily 11am–1am (lunch until 4). Valet bicycle parking available seasonally. T: Red Line to Davis. BARBECUE.

Geographically, Redbones is in Somerville, but it's *really* on a back road in Texas or Arkansas or someplace like that—where the sun is hot, the beer is cold, and a big slab of meat is done to a turn. Barbecued ribs (Memphis, Texas, or Arkansas style), smoked beef brisket, fried Louisiana catfish, and grilled chicken come with appropriate side dishes alone or in any combination you want. The chummy staff can help you choose sweet, hot, mild, or vinegar sauce. Portions are enormous, so pace yourself. You'll want to try the wonderful appetizers and sides—catfish "catfingers," buffalo shrimp with blue-cheese sauce, creamy corn pudding—and desserts, especially the pecan pie.

INEXPENSIVE

✪ **Bartley's Burger Cottage.** 1246 Massachusetts Ave. ☎ **617/354-6559.** Most items under $7. No credit cards. Mon–Wed, Sat 11am–9pm; Thurs–Fri 11am–10pm. T: Red Line to Harvard. AMERICAN.

Great burgers and the best onion rings in the world make Bartley's a perennial favorite with Harvard students or regular folks. It's not a cottage, but a high-ceilinged, crowded room plastered with signs and posters (there's also seasonal outdoor seating), where the waitresses might call you "honey." Burgers bear the names of local and national celebrities; the names change, but the ingredients stay the same. Anything you can think of to put on ground beef is available here, from American cheese to béarnaise sauce. There are also some good dishes that don't involve meat, notably turkey or veggie burgers and creamy, garlicky hummus.

✪ **S&S Restaurant.** 1334 Cambridge St., Inman Sq. ☎ **617/354-0777.** Main courses $3–$11. No credit cards. Mon–Sat 7am–midnight; Sun 8am–midnight; brunch Sat–Sun until 4pm. T: Red Line to Harvard, then no. 69 (Harvard–Lechmere) bus to Inman Sq. DELI.

"Es" is Yiddish for "eat," and this Cambridge classic is as straightforward as its name ("eat and eat"). Founded in 1919 by the current owners' great-grandmother, the wildly popular brunch spot draws what seems to be half of Cambridge at busy times on weekends. It looks contemporary, but the kitchen favors traditional pancakes, waffles, fruit salad, and fantastic omelets. After noon, you can order an excellent bloody Mary. You'll find other traditional deli items, and breakfast anytime. Be early for brunch, or plan to spend a good chunk of your Saturday or Sunday standing around people-watching and getting hungry.

Tea-Tray in the Sky. 1796 Massachusetts Ave. ☎ **617/492-8327.** Main courses $4–$10. AE, MC, V. Tues–Wed 10am–10pm, Thurs–Sat 10am–11pm, Sun 10am–9pm. T: Red Line to Porter. AMERICAN/TEAROOM.

Ultrafresh baked goods and a cozy atmosphere make this little storefront a perfect pit stop on a shopping expedition north of Harvard Square. Lavishly decorated with tea-related accessories and original art (much of it for sale), the room seats just 20. The encyclopedic tea menu encompasses the familiar and the exotic—white tea, several kinds of *chai*—and accompanies an extensive food menu. Salads, soups, and sandwiches served on focaccia (including a superb tuna melt) are so delectable that you might forget to save room for the cakes, tarts, scones, and other pastries, all baked in-house. Try anything involving chocolate, and be prepared to share. (The name is a tribute to *Alice's Adventures in Wonderland*—check out the mural at the front of the room.)

5 Seeing the Sights in Boston

If you'll be in town for more than a couple of days, make your first stop a **BosTix** (☎ **617/723-5181;** www.boston.com/artsboston) booth for a coupon book that offers discounts on admission to many area museums and attractions. It's not worth

Boston Attractions

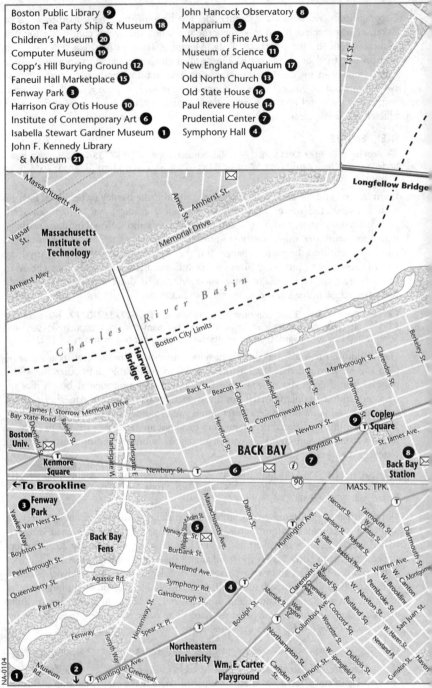

Boston Public Library ⑨
Boston Tea Party Ship & Museum ⑱
Children's Museum ⑳
Computer Museum ⑲
Copp's Hill Burying Ground ⑫
Faneuil Hall Marketplace ⑮
Fenway Park ③
Harrison Gray Otis House ⑩
Institute of Contemporary Art ⑥
Isabella Stewart Gardner Museum ❶
John F. Kennedy Library
  & Museum ㉑

John Hancock Observatory ⑧
Mapparium ⑤
Museum of Fine Arts ❷
Museum of Science ⑪
New England Aquarium ⑰
Old North Church ⑬
Old State House ⑯
Paul Revere House ⑭
Prudential Center ⑦
Symphony Hall ④

Massachusetts Ave.

Amherst St.

Ames St.

Amherst St.

Longfellow Bridge

1st St.

Vassar St.

Massachusetts Institute of Technology

Memorial Drive

Amherst Alley

Charles River Basin

Harvard Bridge

Boston City Limits

James J. Storrow Memorial Drive

Bay State Road

Deerfield St.

Raleigh St.

Back St.

Beacon St.

Gloucester St.

Fairfield St.

Exeter St.

Marlborough St.

Clarendon St.

Berkeley St.

Boston Univ.

Charlesgate W.

Charlesgate E.

Commonwealth Ave.

Hereford St.

Newbury St.

BACK BAY

Boylston St.

Newbury St.

⑨ Ⓣ **Copley Square**

St. James Ave.

Kenmore Square

Newbury St. Ⓣ ⑥ ⓘ ⑦

Back Bay Station ⑧

←To Brookline

90

MASS. TPK.

③ **Fenway Park**

Yawkey Way

Van Ness St.

Boylston St.

Peterborough St.

Queensberry St.

Park Dr.

Back Bay Fens

Agassiz Rd.

Norway St.

Stoneholm St.

⑤

St. Botolph St.

Burbank St.

Westland Ave.

Symphony Rd.

Gainsborough St.

Massachusetts Ave.

Dalton St.

Huntington Ave.

Harcourt St.

Garrison St.

W. Canton St.

Follen St.

Braddock Pkwy.

Holyoke St.

Yarmouth St.

Dartmouth St.

Warren Ave.

W. Canton St.

Pembroke St.

W. Brookline

W. Newton St.

W. Montgome

④ Ⓣ

Claremont St.

Rutland St.

Greenwich

Wellington

Albemarle St.

Concord Sq.

Columbus Ave.

Concord Sq.

Rutland Sq.

San Juan St.

W. Haven St.

Newland Pl.

Hemenway St.

Spear St. Pl.

Forsyth Way

Fenway

Botolph St.

Northampton St.

Worcester Sq.

W. Springfield St.

Deblois St.

Camden St.

Tremont St.

Cunston St.

Northeastern University

Wm. E. Carter Playground

Museum Rd.

❶ ❷ ↓ Ⓣ Huntington Ave. Greenleaf St.

NA-0104

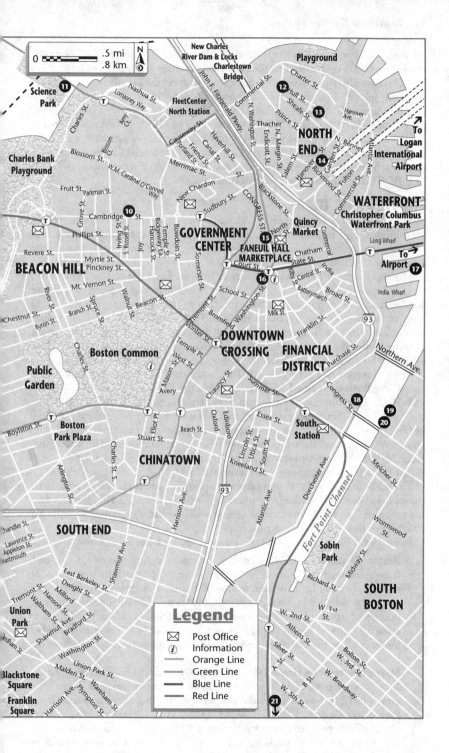

the money (currently $9) for single travelers, because many of the coupons offer two-for-one deals, but couples and families can take advantage of the reduced rates.

A **CityPass** offers great savings—a booklet of tickets to the Isabella Stewart Gardner Museum, John F. Kennedy Library and Museum, John Hancock Observatory, New England Aquarium, Museum of Fine Arts, and Museum of Science. At press time the price (adults, $26.50; seniors, $20.50; youths 13 to 18, $13.50) offers a 50% savings if you visit all six. The passes, good for 9 days from the date of purchase, are on sale at participating attractions, the Boston Common and Prudential Center visitor information centers, through the Greater Boston Convention & Visitors Bureau (☎ 800/SEE-BOSTON), and from **www.citypass.net.ref.**

THE FREEDOM TRAIL

A line of red paint or red brick on the sidewalk, the 3-mile Freedom Trail links 16 historical sights. First painted in 1958, it has undergone a modest transformation over the past few years, with the installation of prominent markers and plaques to make the stops easier to identify.

The trail begins at the **Boston Common Information Center,** 146 Tremont St., on the Common. The center is open Monday to Saturday from 8:30am to 5pm and Sunday from 9am to 5pm, and offers pamphlets to help you along your self-guided tour. You can also explore the **Black Heritage Trail** from here. Sites include stations on the Underground Railroad and homes of famous citizens as well as the African Meeting House, the oldest standing black church in the country. A 2-hour guided tour of this trail starts at the Visitor Center, 46 Joy Street (☎ 617/742-5415).

As you progress along the Freedom Trail, you'll come across another information center, the **Boston National Historic Park Visitor Center,** 15 State St. (☎ 617/242-5642). Pamphlets are available, and from here, you can take a free guided tour of the "heart" of the trail with a park ranger. If you want to start here, take the T (Blue or Orange Line) to State Street; the visitor center is across the street from the Old State House. An audiovisual show provides basic information on the trail. The wheelchair-accessible center has rest rooms and a bookstore. It's open daily from 9am to 5pm except January 1, Thanksgiving, and December 25.

The hard-core history fiend who peers at every artifact and reads every plaque along the trail, will wind up spending four hours or more later at Bunker Hill, feeling weary but rewarded. The family with restless teenagers will probably appreciate the enforced efficiency of the 90-minute ranger-led tour.

Space doesn't permit me to detail every stop on the Trail, but here's a concise listing.

- **Boston Common.** In 1634, when their settlement was just 4 years old, the town fathers paid the Rev. William Blackstone £30 for this property. In 1640 it was set aside as common land. Be sure to stop at Beacon and Park streets to visit the **memorial** designed by Augustus Saint-Gaudens to celebrate the deeds (indeed, the very existence) of Col. Robert Gould Shaw and the Union Army's 54th Massachusetts Colored Regiment, who fought in the Civil War. You may remember the story of the first American army unit made up of free black soldiers from the movie *Glory.*
- **Massachusetts State House** (☎ 617/727-3676). Charles Bulfinch designed the "new" State House, and Gov. Samuel Adams laid the cornerstone of the state capitol in 1795. Free tours (guided and self-guided) leave from the second floor.
- **Park Street Church,** 1 Park St. (☎ 617/523-3383). Consult the plaque at the corner of Tremont Street for a description of this Congregational church's storied past. From late June through August, it's open from 9:30am to 4pm Tuesday to Saturday. Sunday services are at 9 and 10:45am and 5:30pm year-round.

- **Old Granary Burying Ground.** This cemetery, established in 1660, contains the graves of—among other notables—Samuel Adams, Paul Revere, John Hancock, and the wife of Isaac Vergoose, believed to be "Mother Goose" of nursery rhyme fame. It's open daily from 8am to 5pm (3pm in the winter).
- **King's Chapel,** 58 Tremont St. (☎ **617/523-1749**). Completed in 1754, this church was built by erecting the granite edifice around the existing wooden chapel. The **burying ground** (1630), facing Tremont Street, is the oldest in Boston. It's open daily from 8am to 5:30pm (3pm in the winter).
- **Site of the First Public School.** Founded in 1634, the school is commemorated with a colorful mosaic in the sidewalk on (of course) School Street. Inside the fence is the 1856 statue of **Benjamin Franklin,** the first portrait statue erected in Boston.
- **3 School St.** This is the former Old Corner Bookstore. Built in 1712, it's on a plot of land that was once home to the religious reformer Anne Hutchinson.
- **Old South Meeting House,** 310 Washington St. (☎ **617/482-6439**). Originally built in 1670 and replaced by the current structure in 1729, it was the starting point of the Boston Tea Party. It's open daily, April through October from 9am to 5:30pm, November through March weekdays from 10am to 4pm, weekends from 10am to 5pm. Admission is $3 for adults, $2.50 for seniors, $1 for children 6 to 12, free for children under 6.
- ✪ **Old State House,** 206 Washington St. (☎ **617/720-3290**). Built in 1713, it served as the seat of colonial government in Massachusetts before the Revolution, and as the state's capitol until 1797. It houses the Bostonian Society's museum of the city's history, open daily from 9:30am to 5pm. Admission is $3 for adults, $2 for seniors and students, $1 for children 6 to 18, and free for children under 6. Discounted combination tickets are available if you plan to visit the USS *Constitution* Museum during your stay.
- **Boston Massacre Site.** On a traffic island in State Street, across from the T station under the Old State House, a ring of cobblestones marks the location of the skirmish of March 5, 1770.
- ✪ **Faneuil Hall.** Built in 1742 (and enlarged using a Charles Bulfinch design in 1805), it was given to the city by the merchant Peter Faneuil. National Park Service rangers give free 20-minute talks every half hour from 9am to 5pm in the second-floor auditorium.
- ✪ **The Paul Revere House,** 19 North Sq. (☎ **617/523-2338;** www.paulreverehouse.org). The oldest house in downtown Boston (built around 1680) presents history on a human scale. Revere bought it in 1770, and it became a museum in the early 20th century. It's open November 1 to April 14 from 9:30am to 4:15pm, and April 15 to October 31 from 9:30am to 5:15pm; closed Mondays January through March, January 1, Thanksgiving, and December 25. Admission is $2.50 for adults, $2 for seniors and students, $1 for children 5 to 17, and free for children under 5.
- **The Old North Church,** 193 Salem St. (☎ **617/523-6676;** www.oldnorth.com). Paul Revere saw a signal in the steeple when he set out on his "midnight ride." Officially known as Christ Church, this is the oldest church building in Boston; it dates to 1723. It's open daily from 9am to 5pm; Sunday services (Episcopal) are at 9 and 11am and 4pm. The quirky gift shop and museum, in a former chapel, is open daily from 9am to 5pm; all proceeds go to support the church. Donations are appreciated.
- **Copp's Hill Burying Ground,** off Hull Street. The second-oldest cemetery (1659) in the city, it contains the graves of Cotton Mather and his family and of Prince Hall, who established the first black Masonic lodge. It's open daily from 9am to 5pm.

○ **USS** *Constitution* (☎ **617/242-5670**), Charlestown Navy Yard. Active-duty sailors in 1812 dress uniforms give free tours of "Old Ironsides" daily between 9:30am and 3:50pm. The adjacent **USS** *Constitution* **Museum** (☎ **617/426-1812**) is open daily, June 1 to Labor Day from 9am to 6pm; March through May and the day after Labor Day through November from 10am to 5pm; and December to February from 10am to 3pm; it's closed January 1, Thanksgiving, and December 25. Admission is $4 for adults, $3 for seniors, $2 for children 6 to 16, and free for children under 6. Discounted combination tickets are available if you plan to visit the Old State House.

• **Bunker Hill Monument** (☎ **617/242-5644**), Breed's Hill, Charlestown. The 221-foot granite obelisk honors the memory of the men who died in the Battle of Bunker Hill (actually fought on Breed's Hill) on June 17, 1775. The top is 295 stairs up. National Park Service rangers staff the monument, which is open daily from 9am to 4:30pm. Admission is free.

UP, UP & AWAY: GREAT VIEWS

Two of Boston's top attractions are literally *top* attractions. From hundreds of feet in the air, you'll get an unbeatable look at the city and its surroundings. The exhibits at the Prudential are less interesting than those at the Hancock Observatory, but the view is a little better, especially at sunset. The nearest T stops to both are Copley on the Green Line and Back Bay on the Orange Line and commuter rail.

The **John Hancock Observatory,** 200 Clarendon St. (☎ **617/572-6429;** www.cityviewboston.com), would be a good introduction to Boston even if it didn't have a sensational 60th-floor view. The multimedia exhibits include a light-and-sound show that chronicles the events leading to the Revolutionary War and demonstrates how Boston's land mass has changed. There's an illustrated time line, an interactive computer quiz about the city, and a display that generates walking, driving, and public transportation directions to points of interest of your choosing. Powerful binoculars (bring quarters) allow long-distance views, and facsimiles of newspapers give a look at the headlines of the past. Admission is $4.25 for adults and $3.25 for seniors and children ages 5 to 15. Hours are 9am to 11pm Monday to Saturday year-round; Sunday 10am to 11pm from May through October, and noon to 11pm from November to April. The ticket office closes at 10pm.

The **Prudential Center Skywalk,** on the 50th floor of the Prudential Tower, 800 Boylston St. (☎ **617/236-3318**), offers the only 360° view of Boston and beyond. From the enclosed observation deck you can see for miles when it's clear, as far as the mountains of southern New Hampshire or the beaches of Cape Cod. Hours are 10am to 10pm daily. Admission is $4 for adults and $3 for seniors and children ages 2 to 10. On the 52nd floor you can enjoy the view with food and drink at the Top of the Hub restaurant and lounge.

THE TOP ATTRACTIONS

Boston Tea Party Ship & Museum. Congress Street Bridge. ☎ **617/338-1773.** E-mail: bostps@historictours.com. Admission $8 adults, $7 students, $4 children 4–12, free for children under 4. Mar–Nov daily 9am–dusk (about 6pm in summer, 5pm in spring and fall). Closed Thanksgiving, Dec–Feb. T: Red Line to South Station. Walk north on Atlantic Ave. 1 block, past the Federal Reserve Bank, turn right onto Congress St., and walk 1 block.

On December 16, 1773, a public meeting of independent-minded Bostonians led to the symbolic act of resistance commemorated here. The brig *Beaver II* is a full-size replica of one of the three merchant ships loaded with tea that stood at anchor that night. After assembling at the Old South Meeting House, colonists poorly disguised as Indians emptied the vessels' cargo into the harbor. The ship sits alongside a museum

Photo Synthesis

Boston is such a shutterbug magnet that residents have been known to offer to snap a picture of a visiting family before being asked. Arrange Junior and Sis in the lap of one of the area's numerous portrait sculptures, or take a step back and capture the juxtaposition of a 19th-century steeple silhouetted against a 20th-century office tower.

Say "Cheese": At the bronze **teddy bear** in front of FAO Schwarz, 440 Boylston St. (at Berkeley). Arm-in-arm or deep in thought with Mayor **James Michael Curley,** in the park on Union Street across North Street from Faneuil Hall. Pulling the cigar away from Celtics legend **Red Auerbach,** between the South Canopy of Quincy Market and the South Market building, Faneuil Hall Marketplace. Comparing your tiny sneakers to **Larry Bird's** clodhoppers, captured in bronze right next to Red. Falling at the feet of a colonial hero—pedestals support **Benjamin Franklin** (School Street, in front of Old City Hall), **Paul Revere** (Hanover Street at Clark, across from St. Stephen's Church), and **George Washington** (in the Public Garden at the foot of the Comm. Ave. Mall). Perched on Mrs. Mallard (or one of her babies if you fit) of *Make Way for Ducklings* fame, in the Public Garden near the corner of Beacon and Charles streets. Out-distancing the winner (or the runner-up) captured in *The Tortoise and Hare at Copley Square,* in front of Trinity Church. And at a spot so popular that the grass on the area favored by photographers had to be paved over, in front of **John Harvard,** Harvard Yard, Cambridge.

Say "Ooh": Always remember to look up for a quirky perspective. Capture a church against a backdrop of skyscrapers on Tremont Street (with Boston Common at your back, turn left toward Park Street Church) or Boylston Street (in front of the Four Seasons, turn left toward the Arlington Street Church; across from Trinity Church, focus on the Hancock Tower). Kill two birds with one stone: Pointing up at the Paul Revere statue on Hanover Street, you can lock in the **Old North Church** in the background, or walk around the statue for a new perspective on **St. Stephen's Church.** The church crops up all over the North End and Charlestown, as the **Hancock Tower** does throughout the Back Bay. And if your travels take you to the area around the Charles/MGH T stop, wander out onto the **Longfellow Bridge,** especially at twilight—the views of the river are splendid, and if you hit it just right, the moon appears to shine out of the Hancock Tower.

with exhibits on the "tea party." The audio and video displays (including a 15-minute film), dioramas, and information panels tell the story of the uprising. You can dump a bale of tea into Boston Harbor—a museum staffer retrieves it—and drink some complimentary tax-free tea (iced in summer, hot in winter).

The Computer Museum. 300 Congress St. (Museum Wharf). ☎ **617/426-2800.** www.tcm.org. Admission $7 adults, $5 seniors, students, and children 3–18, free for children under 3. July–Aug daily 10am–6pm; Sept–June Tues–Sun and Mon during Boston school holidays and vacations 10am–5pm. T: Red Line to South Station. Walk north on Atlantic Ave. 1 block, past the Federal Reserve Bank, turn right onto Congress St., and walk 1½ blocks.

As computer technology develops, the world's premier computer museum also changes and grows. The exhibits here tell the story of computers from their origins in the 1940s to the latest in PCs and virtual reality. The signature exhibit is the

Walk-Through Computer 2000™, a networked multimedia machine 50 times larger than the real thing. When the computer is as large as a two-story house, the mouse is the size of a car, the CD-ROM drive is 8 feet long, the monitor is 12 feet high, and the humans enjoying the 30 hands-on activities are the equivalent of crayon-size. The exhibit even has a 7-foot-square Pentium processor.

Computers don't exist in a vacuum, of course, and the "Networked Planet" exhibit allows visitors to explore the information superhighway and its offshoots by logging on to real and simulated networks and learning about weather forecasting, financial markets, and air-traffic control. There are also exhibits on robots, the history of the computer, and the practical and recreational uses of the PC—you might compose music or "drive" a race car. The selections in the "Best Software for Kids" gallery change regularly; and there's a "tank" where you can launch "virtual fish" and watch them interact with other visitors' creations. In all, you'll find more than 170 hands-on exhibits, two theaters, and countless ideas to try on your home computer.

✪ **Faneuil Hall Marketplace.** Between North, Congress, and State sts. and I-93. ☎ **617/ 338-2323.** Marketplace Mon–Sat 10am–9pm; Sun noon–6pm. Colonnade food court opens earlier; some restaurants open early for Sun brunch and close at 2am daily. T: Green Line to Government Center, Orange Line to Haymarket or State, Blue Line to State or Aquarium.

It's impossible to overestimate the effect of Faneuil Hall Marketplace on Boston's economy and reputation. A daring idea when it opened in 1976, the festival market— a complex of shops, food stands, restaurants, bars, and public spaces in an urban center—has been widely imitated. Its success with tourists and suburbanites is so great, in fact, that you could be forgiven for thinking that the only Bostonians in the crowd are employees.

The three central buildings of the five-structure complex are listed in the National Register of Historic Places. They're on brick and stone plazas that teem with crowds shopping, eating, performing, watching performers, and just people-watching. **Quincy Market** (you'll hear the whole complex called by that name) is the central 3-level Greek Revival-style building. It reopened after renovations turned it into a festival market on August 26, 1976, 150 years of hard use after Mayor Josiah Quincy opened the original market.

Quincy Market's central corridor, the **Colonnade,** is the food court. You can find anything from a bagel to a full Greek dinner to a cup of chowder to a hunk of fudge. On either side, under glass canopies, pushcarts hold everything from crafts created by New England artisans to hokey souvenirs. In the plaza between the **South Canopy** and the South Market building is an **information kiosk,** and throughout the complex you'll find an enticing mix of chain stores and unique shops. On summer evenings the tables that spill outdoors from the restaurants and bars fill with people. One constant since the year after the market opened—the *original* market, that is—is **Durgin-Park,** a traditional New England restaurant with traditionally crabby waitresses (see "Dining," above).

✪ **Faneuil Hall** itself—nicknamed the "Cradle of Liberty"—sometimes gets overlooked, but it's well worth a visit. National Park Service rangers give **free 20-minute talks** every half hour from 9am to 5pm in the second-floor auditorium.

The Institute of Contemporary Art. 955 Boylston St. ☎ **617/266-5152.** www.culturefinder.com. Admission $6 adults, $4 students and seniors, free for children under 12; free to all Thurs 5–9pm. Wed and Fri–Sun noon–5pm, Thurs noon–9pm. Closed major holidays. T: Green Line B, C, or D to Hynes/ICA.

Across from the Hynes Convention Center, the ICA hosts rotating exhibits of 20th-century art, including painting, sculpture, photography, and video and performance art. The institute also offers films, lectures, music, video, poetry, and educational programs for children and adults.

✪ **Isabella Stewart Gardner Museum.** 280 The Fenway. ☎ **617/566-1401.** www.boston.com/gardner. Admission $11 adults weekends, $10 adults weekdays; $7 seniors, $5 college students with valid ID, $3 college students on Wed, free for children under 18. Tues–Sun, some Mon holidays 11am–5pm. Closed Mon, Jan 1, Thanksgiving, Dec 25. T: Green Line E to Museum.

Isabella Stewart Gardner (1840–1924) was an incorrigible individualist long before such behavior was acceptable for a woman in polite Boston society, and her iconoclasm has paid off for art lovers. "Mrs. Jack" designed her exquisite home in the style of a 15th-century Venetian palace and filled it with European, American, and Asian painting and sculpture, much chosen with the help of her friend and protégé Bernard Berenson. You'll see works by Titian, Botticelli, Raphael, Rembrandt, Matisse, and Mrs. Gardner's friends James McNeill Whistler and John Singer Sargent. Titian's magnificent *Europa*, which many scholars consider his finest work, is one of the most important Renaissance paintings in the nation.

The building, which opened to the public after Mrs. Gardner's death, holds a hodgepodge of furniture and architectural details imported from European churches and palaces. The *pièce de résistance* is the magnificent skylit courtyard, filled year-round with fresh flowers from the museum greenhouse. Although the terms of Mrs. Gardner's will forbid changing the arrangement of the museum's content, there has been some evolution: a special exhibition gallery, which opened in September 1992, features two or three changing shows a year.

✪ **John F. Kennedy Library and Museum.** Columbia Point. ☎ **617/929-4523.** www.cs. umb.edu/jfklibrary. Admission $8 adults, $6 seniors and students with ID, $4 youths 13–17, free for children under 13. Daily 9am–5pm (last film begins at 3:55pm); June–Aug Wed until 8pm. Closed Jan 1, Thanksgiving, Dec 25. T: Red Line to JFK/UMass, then free shuttle bus, which runs every 20 min. By car: Southeast Expressway (I-93/Rte. 3) south to Exit 15 (Morrissey Blvd./JFK Library), left onto Columbia Rd., follow signs to free parking lot.

The Kennedy era springs to life at this dramatic library, museum, and educational research complex overlooking Dorchester Bay. It captures the 35th president's accomplishments and legacy in sound and video recordings and fascinating displays of memorabilia and photos.

Your visit begins with a 17-minute film narrated by John F. Kennedy—a detail that seems eerie for a moment, then perfectly natural. Through skillfully edited audio clips, he discusses his childhood, education, war experience, and early political career. Starting with the 1960 presidential campaign, the exhibits immerse you in the era. The connected galleries hold campaign souvenirs, a film of Kennedy debating Richard Nixon and delivering his inaugural address, a replica of the Oval Office, gifts from foreign dignitaries, letters, documents, and keepsakes. There's a film about the Cuban Missile Crisis, and displays on the civil rights movement, the Peace Corps, the space program, and the Kennedy family. New expanded exhibits focus on First Lady Jacqueline Bouvier Kennedy and on Attorney General Robert F. Kennedy's efforts in the civil rights movement. As the tour winds down, you pass through a darkened chamber where news reports of John Kennedy's assassination and funeral play.

From the final room, the soaring glass-enclosed pavilion that is the heart of the I. M. Pei design, there's a glorious view of the water and the Boston skyline. In the summer, JFK's boyhood sailboat, *Victura*, sits on a strip of dune grass between the library and the harbor.

Mapparium. World Headquarters of the First Church of Christ, Scientist, 250 Massachusetts Ave. (at Huntington Ave.). ☎ **617/450-3793.** www.tfccs.com. Admission free. Mon–Sat

10am–4pm. Mother Church Sun 11:15am–2pm, Mon–Sat 10am–4pm. Bible exhibit Sun 11:15am–2pm, Wed–Sat 10am–4pm. Closed major holidays. MBTA: Green Line E to Symphony, Orange Line to Massachusetts Ave.

One of Boston's most unusual attractions is scheduled to reopen in the fall of 1999. It offers a real insider's view of the world. . . from inside. The unique hollow globe 30 feet across is a work of both art and history. The 608 stained-glass panels are connected by a bronze framework and surrounded by electric lights. Because sound bounces off the nonporous surfaces, the acoustics are as unusual as the aesthetics. As you cross the glass bridge just south of the equator, you'll see the political divisions of the world from 1932 to 1935, when the globe was constructed.

Also in the 14-acre Christian Science complex is the Mother Church. The Romanesque church, opened in 1894, is notable for its stained glass windows; the domed Mother Church Extension (1906), is in Renaissance-Byzantine style and has one of the largest pipe organs in the world. Call for information about tours. A Bible exhibit "A Light Unto My Path" includes a 30-minute film and slide program (shows every hour on the hour), an audiovisual time line, and a sculptured map where 12 journeys of figures from the Bible are illustrated and narrated.

✪ **Museum of Fine Arts.** 465 Huntington Ave. ☎ **617/267-9300.** www.mfa.org. Adults $10, students and seniors $8, when entire museum is open; $8 and $6 respectively when only West Wing is open. Children under 18 free when accompanied by an adult. Voluntary contribution Wed 4–9:45pm. No admission fee for Museum Shop, library, or auditoriums. Entire museum: Mon–Tues 10am–4:45pm, Wed 10am–9:45pm, Thurs–Fri 10am–5pm, Sat–Sun 10am–5:45pm. West Wing only: Thurs–Fri 5–9:45pm. Closed Thanksgiving, Dec 25. T: Green Line E to Museum, Orange Line to Ruggles.

The management team of this great museum works nonstop to make the collections more accessible and interesting. Recent moves to raise the museum's profile have included mounting even more top-notch exhibitions, expanding educational programs, and opening new permanent galleries for the art of Africa, Oceania, and the ancient Americas.

The museum's not-so-secret weapon in its quest is a powerful one: its magnificent collections. Every installation reflects a curatorial attitude that makes even those who go in with a sense of obligation leave with a sense of discovery and wonder. The MFA is especially noted for its Asian and Old Kingdom Egyptian collections, classical art, Buddhist temple, and medieval sculpture and tapestries. The works you might find more familiar are paintings and sculpture by Americans and Europeans, notably the Impressionists. Some favorites: Childe Hassam's *Boston Common at Twilight*, Gilbert Stuart's 1796 portrait of George Washington, John Singleton Copley's 1768 portrait of Paul Revere, a bronze casting of Edgar Degas's sculpture *Little Dancer*, Paul Gauguin's *Where Do We Come From? What Are We? Where Are We Going?*, a wall of Fitz Hugh Lane's Luminist masterpieces, and 43 Monets. There are also magnificent print and photography collections, and that's not even touching on the furnishings and decorative arts, including the finest collection of Paul Revere silver in the world.

Insider Tip

The Huntington Avenue entrance to the Museum of Fine Arts is usually much less busy than the West Wing lobby—and farther from the parking garage, gift shop, restaurants, and access to special exhibits. If you're eager to get started on a lengthy visit (which generally involves lots of walking anyway), walk back along Huntington Avenue when you leave the T and enter from the curved driveway.

Visitors from November 14, 1999, to February 6, 2000, can see the special exhibition "Pharaohs of the Sun: Akhenaten, Nefertiti, Tutankhamen." It will use objects from more than 35 museums and private collections to illustrate the brief but culturally significant Amarna Age (1353 to 1334 b.c.).

I. M. Pei designed the West Wing (1981), the latest addition to the original 1909 structure. It contains the main entrance, an auditorium, and an atrium with a tree-lined "sidewalk" cafe. The excellent Museum Shop expanded in 1997, adding a huge selection of art books. The Fine Arts Restaurant is on the second floor, and there's also a cafeteria. Pick up a floor plan at the information desk, or take a free guided tour (weekdays except Monday holidays at 10:30am and 1:30pm, Wednesday at 6:15pm, Saturday at 10:30am and 1pm).

✪ Museum of Science. Science Park. ☎ **617/723-2500.** www.mos.org. Admission to exhibit halls $9 adults, $7 seniors and children 3–11, free for children under 3. To Mugar Omni Theater, Hayden Planetarium, or laser shows, $7.50 adults, $5.50 seniors and children 3–11, free for children under 3. Discounted tickets to 2 or 3 parts of the complex available. July 5–Labor Day Sat–Thurs 9am–7pm, Fri 9am–9pm. Early Sept to July 4 Sat–Thurs 9am–5pm, Fri 9am–9pm. Closed Thanksgiving, Dec 25. T: Green Line to Science Park; commuter rail to North Station, then 10-min. walk.

For the ultimate pain-free educational experience, head to the Museum of Science. The demonstrations, experiments, and interactive displays introduce facts and concepts so effortlessly that everyone winds up learning something. Take a couple of hours or a whole day to explore the permanent and temporary exhibits, which are dedicated to improving "science literacy."

Among the more than 450 exhibits, you might meet an iguana or a dinosaur, find out how much you'd weigh on the moon, or climb into a space module. Visitors to the activity center **Investigate!** learn to think like scientists, formulating questions, finding evidence, and drawing conclusions through activities such as strapping on a skin sensor to measure reactions to stimuli or sifting through an archaeological dig. In the **Seeing Is Deceiving** section, auditory and visual illusions challenge your belief in what is "real." The **Science in the Park** exhibit introduces the concepts of Newtonian physics—through familiar recreational tools such as playground equipment and skateboards. You can also visit the theater of electricity to see lightning manufactured indoors. And there's a **Discovery Center** especially for preschoolers.

The separate-admission theaters are worth planning for. Even if you're skipping the exhibits, try to see a show. If you're making a day of it, buy all your tickets at once, not only because it's cheaper but because shows sometimes sell out. Tickets for daytime shows must be purchased in person. Evening show tickets, plus a service charge, can be ordered over the phone using a credit card.

The newly renovated **Mugar Omni Theater,** one of only about 150 in the world, is an intense experience. You're bombarded with images on a four-story domed screen, and sounds from a 12-channel sound system with 84 speakers. Even though you know you're not moving, the engulfing sensations and steep pitch of the seating area will have you hanging on for dear life, whether the film you're watching is on whales, Mount Everest, or hurricanes and tornadoes. The films change every four to six months.

The **Charles Hayden Planetarium** takes you into space with daily star shows and shows on special topics that change several times a year. On weekends, rock-music laser shows take over. At the entrance is a hands-on astronomy exhibit, *Welcome to the Universe.*

New England Aquarium. Central Wharf. ☎ **617/973-5200.** www.neaq.org. Admission summer weekends and holidays $13.50 adults, $11.50 seniors, $7 children 3–11; weekdays year-round and off-season weekends $12 adults, $10 seniors, $6 children 3–11. Free for children under 3 and for the outdoor exhibits, cafe, and gift shop. July–Labor Day Mon–Tues and Fri 9am–6pm, Wed–Thurs 9am–8pm, Sat–Sun and holidays 9am–7pm. Early Sept to June Mon–Fri 9am–5pm, Sat–Sun and holidays 9am–6pm. Closed Thanksgiving, Dec 25, and until noon Jan 1. T: Blue Line to Aquarium.

Like a crab molting its outgrown shell, the New England Aquarium has expanded, into a new West Wing building that echoes the waves on adjacent Boston Harbor. The dramatic structure opened in 1998, with an enlarged exhibit space and gift shop, and a new cafe with views of the city and the harbor. In the spring of 2000, the complex is scheduled to gain an IMAX theater; call for admission fees.

Frolicking seals and California sea otters greet you as you approach, the perfect welcome to an entertaining complex that's home to more than 7,000 fish and aquatic mammals. When you head inside, buy an exhibit guide and plan your route as you commune with the penguin colony.

The focal point of the main building is the aptly named Giant Ocean Tank. A four-story spiral ramp encircles the cylindrical glass tank, which contains 187,000 gallons of saltwater, a replica of a Caribbean coral reef, and a conglomeration of sea creatures who seem to coexist amazingly well. Part of the reason for the peace might be that scuba divers feed the sharks five times a day. Other exhibits show off freshwater specimens, denizens of the Amazon, and the ecology of Boston Harbor. At the *Edge of the Sea* exhibit, you're encouraged to touch the sea stars, sea urchins, and horseshoe crabs in the tide pool. Be sure to leave time for a show at the floating marine mammal pavilion, *Discovery*, where sea lions perform every 90 minutes throughout the day.

The aquarium sponsors **whale watches** (☎ **617/973-5281**) daily from May to mid-October and on weekends in April and late October. You'll travel several miles out to sea to Stellwagen Bank, the feeding ground for the whales as they migrate from Newfoundland to Provincetown. Tickets (cash only) are $24 for adults, $19 for senior citizens and college students, $17.50 for youths 12 to 18, and $16.50 for children 3 to 11. Children must be 3 years old and at least 30 inches tall. Reservations are recommended and can be held with a MasterCard or Visa.

ORGANIZED TOURS

WALKING TOURS ✪ **Boston by Foot,** 77 N. Washington St. (☎ **617/367-2345,** or 617/367-3766 for recorded information; www.bostonbyfoot.com), offers excellent tours. From May through October, the nonprofit educational corporation conducts historical and architectural tours that focus on neighborhoods or themes. The rigorously trained volunteer guides encourage questions. Buy tickets ($8) from the guide; reservations are not required. The 90-minute tours take place rain or shine. Call for offerings and schedules.

The **Society for the Preservation of New England Antiquities** (☎ **617/ 227-3956;** www.spnea.org) offers a fascinating tour that describes life in the mansions and garrets of Beacon Hill in 1800. "Magnificent and Modest," a 2-hour program, costs $10 and starts at the Harrison Gray Otis House, 141 Cambridge St., at 11am on Saturday and Sunday from May through October. The price includes a tour of the Otis House, and reservations are recommended.

The **Historic Neighborhoods Foundation,** 99 Bedford St. (☎ **617/426-1885**), offers 90-minute walking tours in several neighborhoods, including Beacon Hill, the North End, Chinatown, the Waterfront, and the Financial District. Schedules change with the season, and the programs highlight points of interest to visitors. Tours usually cost about $6 per person; call for schedules, fees, and meeting places.

The **Boston Park Rangers** (☎ **617/635-7383**) offer free guided walking tours of the Emerald Necklace, a loop of green spaces designed by pioneering American landscape architect Frederick Law Olmsted. You'll see and hear about the city's major parks and gardens, including Boston Common, the Public Garden, the Common-wealth Avenue Mall, the Muddy River in the Fenway, Olmsted Park, Jamaica Pond, the Arnold Arboretum, and Franklin Park. The full 6-hour walk includes a 1-hour tour of any of the sites. Call for schedules.

TROLLEY TOURS Because Boston is so pedestrian-friendly, this isn't the best choice, but if you're short on time, unable to walk long distances, or traveling with small children, a narrated trolley tour can give you an overview of the sights before focusing on specific attractions, or you can use your all-day pass as a way to hit as many places as possible in 8 hours or so.

The various companies cover the major attractions and offer informative narratives and anecdotes in their 90- to 120-minute tours, and most offer free reboarding if you want to visit the sites. Tickets cost $18 to $24 for adults, $12 or less for children. Boarding spots are at hotels, historic sites, and tourist information centers.

Each company paints its cars a different color. Orange-and-green **Old Town Trol-leys** (☎ 617/269-7150) are the most numerous. Minuteman Tours' **Boston Trolley Tours** (☎ 617/269-3626) are blue; **Beantown Trolleys** (☎ 800/343-1328 or 617/236-2148) say "Gray Line" but are red; and **CityView Luxury Trolleys** (☎ 800/525-2489 outside 617, or 617/363-7899) are silver. The **Discover Boston Multilin-gual Trolley Tours** (☎ 617/742-0767) vehicle is white, and conducts tours in Japanese, Spanish, French, German, and Italian.

LITERARY TRAIL This trolley tour of pertinent sites in Boston, Cambridge, and Concord started operating on a trial basis in 1999. The 4-hour, 20-mile trip begins and ends at the Omni Parker House hotel. It explores locations associated with authors and poets such as Emerson, Thoreau, Longfellow, and Louisa May Alcott, among others. The fare at press time was $19 for adults, $17.10 for students and chil-dren under 18; schedules weren't set. For up-to-date information, call the **Boston His-tory Collaborative** (☎ **617/574-5950**).

DUCK TOURS The most unusual way to see Boston is with ✪ **Boston Duck Tours** (☎ **800/226-7442** or 617/723-DUCK; www.bostonducktours.com). The tours are pricey but great fun. Sightseers board a "duck," a reconditioned World War II amphibious landing craft, on the Huntington Avenue side of the Prudential Center. The 80-minute narrated tour begins with a quick but comprehensive jaunt around the city. Then the duck lumbers down a ramp, splashes into the Charles River, and takes a spin around the basin.

Tickets, available at the Prudential Center, are $21 for adults, $18 for seniors and students, $11 for children 4 to 12, and 25¢ for children under 4. Tours run every 30 minutes from 9am to 1 hour before sunset. Reservations are not accepted (except for groups of 16 or more), and tickets usually sell out, especially on weekends. Try to buy same-day tickets early in the day, or plan ahead and ask about the limited number of tickets available 2 days in advance. No tours December through March.

SIGHTSEEING CRUISES The cruise season runs from April through October, with spring and fall offerings often restricted to weekends. If you're prone to seasick-ness, check the size of the vessel before buying tickets; larger boats provide more cush-ioning and comfort than smaller ones.

Boston Harbor Cruises, 1 Long Wharf (☎ **617/227-4321**; www.bostonboats. com), offers narrated trips around the harbor. It runs 30-minute lunchtime cruises on weekdays at 12:15pm; tickets are $2. Ninety-minute **historic sightseeing cruises,** which tour the Inner and Outer harbors, depart daily at 1 and 3pm, at 7pm (the sunset cruise), and at 11am on weekends and holidays. Tickets are $15 for adults, $12 for seniors, $10 for children under 12. The 45-minute *Constitution* cruise takes you around the Inner Harbor and docks at the Charlestown Navy Yard so you can go ashore and visit "Old Ironsides." Tours leave Long Wharf hourly from 10:30am to 4:30pm, and on the hour from the navy yard from 11am to 5pm. The cruise is $8 for adults, $7 for seniors, and $6 for children.

The same company offers service to **Georges Island,** where free water-taxi service to the rest of the Boston Harbor Islands is available (see box, "A Vacation on the Islands," below).

Massachusetts Bay Lines (☎ 617/542-8000; www.massbaylines.com) offers 55-minute harbor tours from Memorial Day to Columbus Day. Cruises leave from Rowes Wharf on the hour from 10am to 6pm; the price is $8 for adults, $5 for children and seniors. The 90-minute sunset cruise, at 7pm, costs $15 for adults, $10 for children and seniors.

The **Charles Riverboat Company** (☎ 617/621-3001) offers 55-minute narrated cruises around the lower Charles River basin and in the opposite direction, through the Charles River locks to Boston Harbor. Boats depart from the CambridgeSide Galleria mall; river tours leave on the hour from noon to 5pm, harbor tours once a day, at 10:30am. Tickets for either tour are $8 for adults, $6 for seniors, and $5 for children 2 to 12.

ON THE CHEAP   You don't have to take a tour to take a cruise. The MBTA, as in the subway, runs a ferry between Long Wharf and the Charlestown Navy Yard. It costs $1 (free if you have a visitor passport) and makes a good final leg of the Freedom Trail.

WHALE WATCHING   The **New England Aquarium** (see listing above) runs its own whale watches. For information on Cape Ann excursions, see "A Whale of an Adventure" in chapter 5.

Boston Harbor Whale Watch (☎ 617/345-9866; www.bostonwhale.com) promises more time watching whales than trying to find them. Tours depart from Rowes Wharf. They operate Friday, Saturday, and Sunday in late June. July to early September, there's service Monday to Friday at 10am and Saturday and Sunday at 9am and 2pm. Expect to spend about 4½ hours at sea. Tickets are $20 for adults, $18 for seniors and children under 13. Reservations are suggested, and discounted parking is available.

KID STUFF

Just about every major destination in the city either is specifically designed to appeal to youngsters or can be easily adapted to do so.

Hands-on exhibits are a big draw at several institutions: The **Boston Tea Party Ship & Museum** (☎ 617/338-1773), the **Computer Museum** (☎ 617/426-2800), and the **New England Aquarium** (☎ 617/973-5200). The **Museum of Science** (☎ 617/723-2500) not only is a hands-on paradise but is also home to the **Charles Hayden Planetarium** and the **Mugar Omni Theater.** See the listings above for full details.

You might get your hands on a baseball at a **Red Sox game,** a sure-fire kid pleaser (see "Spectator Sports," below). For those in the mood to let other people do the work, take in the shows by the street performers at **Faneuil Hall Marketplace** (☎ 617/338-2323).

Admission is free for those under 18 at the **Museum of Fine Arts** (☎ 617/267-9300), which has special weekend and after-school programs.

The allure of seeing people the size of ants draws young visitors to the **John Hancock Observatory** (☎ 617/572-6429) and the **Prudential Center Skywalk** (☎ 617/236-3318). And they can see actual ants—though they might prefer the dinosaurs—at the Museum of Comparative Zoology, part of the **Harvard Museum of Natural History** (☎ **617/495-3045;** see section 6).

Older children who have studied modern American history will enjoy a visit to the **John F. Kennedy Library and Museum** (☎ **617/929-4523**). Young visitors who have read Robert McCloskey's children's classic *Make Way for Ducklings* will relish a visit to the Public Garden, as will fans of E. B. White's *The Trumpet of the Swan,* who certainly will want to ride on the **swan boats** (☎ **617/522-1966** or 617/624-7020). They operate from the Saturday before Patriots Day (the third Monday in April) through September, from 10am to 6pm in summer, 10am to 4pm in spring and fall. The cost is $1.75 for adults and 95¢ for children. Considerably less tame and much longer are **whale watches** (see "Organized Tours," above, and "A Whale of an Adventure," in chapter 5).

The walking tour company **Boston by Foot,** 77 N. Washington St. (☎ **617/ 367-2345,** or 617/367-3766 for recorded information; www.bostonbyfoot.com), has a special program, **Boston by Little Feet,** geared to children 6 to 12 years old. The 60-minute walk gives a child's-eye view of the architecture along the Freedom Trail and of Boston's role in the American Revolution. Children must be accompanied by an adult. Tours ($6 per person) run May through October and meet at the statue of Samuel Adams on the Congress Street side of Faneuil Hall, Saturday at 10am, Sunday at 2pm, and Monday at 10am, rain or shine.

The **Historic Neighborhoods Foundation,** 99 Bedford St. (☎ **617/426-1885**), offers a 90-minute "Make Way for Ducklings" tour ($5 per person age 5 or older). Popular with children and adults, it follows the path of the Mallard family described in Robert McCloskey's famous book, and ends at the Public Garden.

✪ **Children's Museum.** 300 Congress St. (Museum Wharf). ☎ **617/426-8855.** www.bostonkids.org. Admission $7 adults, $6 children 2–15 and seniors, $2 children age 1, free for children under 1; Fri 5–9pm $1 for all. Sept–May Tues–Sun 10am–5pm, Fri until 9pm; June–Aug Mon–Thurs 10am–7pm, Fri 10am–9pm, Sat–Sun 10am–5pm. Closed Jan 1, Thanksgiving, Dec 25, and Mon Sept–June, except Boston school vacations and holidays. T: Red Line to South Station. Walk north on Atlantic Ave. 1 block, past the Federal Reserve Bank, and turn right onto Congress St. Call for information about discounted parking.

No matter how old they are, everyone behaves like a little kid at this delightful museum. You know the museum is near when you see the 40-foot-high red-and-white milk bottle out front. Children can stick with their parents or wander on their own, learning, doing, and role-playing. Some favorites: the **Dress-Up Shop,** a souped-up version of playing in Grandma's closet; **Under the Dock,** an environmental exhibit that teaches young people about the Boston waterfront and allows them to dress up in a crab suit; rooms where children can race golf balls on tracks through various structures and create soap bubbles in water tanks; and **Boats Afloat,** which has an 800-gallon play tank and a replica of the bridge of a working boat.

The **Climbing Sculpture** is a giant maze designed especially for children (adults may get stuck). Another oversize display is a desk with a phone so big it doubles as a slide. You can also explore a Japanese house and subway train from Kyoto, Boston's sister city. Children under 4 and their caregivers have a special room, **Playspace,** that's packed with toys and activities. Call ahead for information about special programs.

6 Exploring Cambridge

Harvard Square is a people-watching paradise of students and instructors, commuters, and sightseers. There are restaurants and stores along the three streets that radiate from the center of the square and the streets that intersect them. On weekend afternoons and evenings year-round, you'll hear music and see street performers. To get away from the urban bustle, stroll down to the paved paths along the Charles River.

From Boston, take the MBTA Red Line toward Alewife. In Cambridge, the subway stops at Kendall/MIT, and Central, Harvard, and Porter squares. If you're staying in or visiting the Back Bay, a longer and more colorful route is the no. 1 bus (Harvard–Dudley), which runs along Mass. Ave.

If you're driving from Boston, follow Mass. Ave., or take Storrow Drive along the south bank of the river to the Harvard Square exit. Memorial Drive runs along the north side of the river to MIT, Central Square, and Harvard. Traffic in and around Harvard Square is almost as bad as in downtown Boston. Once you get to Cambridge, park the car and walk.

HARVARD UNIVERSITY

Harvard is the oldest college in the country, and if you suggest aloud that it's not the best, you may encounter the attitude that inspired the saying "You can always tell a Harvard man, but you can't tell him much." The university encompasses the college and 10 graduate and professional schools located in more than 400 buildings around Boston and Cambridge.

Free, student-led tours of the main campus leave from the **Events & Information Center** in Holyoke Center, 1350 Mass. Ave. (☎ 617/495-1573), during the school year twice a day during the week and once on Saturday, except during vacations, and during the summer four times a day Monday to Saturday and twice on Sunday. Call for exact times; reservations aren't necessary. You're also free to wander on your own. The Events & Information Center has maps, illustrated booklets, and self-guided walking-tour directions. You might want to check out the university's Web site (www.harvard.edu).

Harvard University Art Museums. 32 Quincy St. and 485 Broadway (at Quincy St.). ☎ **617/495-9400.** www.artmuseums.harvard.edu. Admission to all 3 $5 adults, $4 seniors, $3 students, free for children under 18; free to all Wed 10am–5pm, Sat 10am–noon. Mon–Sat 10am–5pm, Sun 1–5pm. Closed major holidays. T: Red Line to Harvard. Cross Harvard Yard diagonally from the T station and cross Quincy St.

The Harvard art museums house a total of about 150,000 works in three collections. The exhibit spaces also serve as teaching and research facilities. You can take a 1-hour guided tour on weekdays August through June, and Wednesdays only in July and August.

The **Fogg Art Museum** (32 Quincy St., near Broadway) centers around an impressive 16th-century Italian stone courtyard. You'll see something different in each of the 19 rooms—17th-century Dutch and Flemish landscapes, 19th-century British and American paintings and drawings, French paintings and drawings from the 18th century through the Impressionist period, contemporary sculpture, and changing exhibits.

The **Busch-Reisinger Museum** in Werner Otto Hall (enter through the Fogg) is the only museum in North America devoted to the painting, sculpture, and decorative art of northern and central Europe, specifically Germany. Its encyclopedic collection also includes prints and illustrated books, and particularly notable early 20th-century collections, including works by Klee, Feininger, Kandinsky, and artists and designers associated with the Bauhaus.

The **Arthur M. Sackler Museum** (485 Broadway, at Quincy Street) houses the university's collections of Asian, ancient, and Islamic art. Included are an assemblage of Chinese jades and cave reliefs that's considered the best in the world, as well as Korean ceramics, Roman sculpture, Greek vases, and Persian miniature paintings and calligraphy.

Harvard Square & Environs

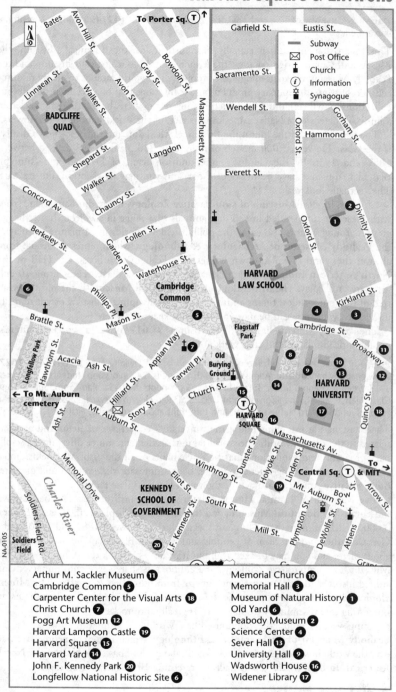

Legend:
- ▬▬ Subway
- ✉ Post Office
- † Church
- ⓘ Information
- ✡ Synagogue

Arthur M. Sackler Museum ⓫
Cambridge Common ❺
Carpenter Center for the Visual Arts ⓲
Christ Church ❼
Fogg Art Museum ⓬
Harvard Lampoon Castle ⓳
Harvard Square ⓯
Harvard Yard ⓮
John F. Kennedy Park ⓴
Longfellow National Historic Site ❻

Memorial Church ❿
Memorial Hall ❸
Museum of Natural History ❶
Old Yard ❻
Peabody Museum ❷
Science Center ❹
Sever Hall ⓭
University Hall ❾
Wadsworth House ⓰
Widener Library ⓱

NA-0105

Harvard Museum of Natural History. 26 Oxford St. ☎ **617/495-3045.** www.hmnh. harvard.edu.

This fascinating museum is actually four institutions: the Botanical Museum, the Museum of Comparative Zoology, the Mineralogical & Geological Museum, and the Peabody Museum of Archaeology & Ethnology. The world-famous scholarly resource center offers interdisciplinary programs and exhibitions that tie in elements of all four collections. You'll certainly find something interesting here, be it a dinosaur skeleton, a hunk of meteorite, a Native American artifact, or the world-famous Glass Flowers.

The best-known of the four is the **Botanical Museum,** and the best-known display is the **Glass Flowers,** 3,000 models of more than 840 plant species devised between 1887 and 1936 by the German father-and-son team of Leopold and Rudolph Blaschka. You may have heard about them, and you may be skeptical, but it's true: They actually look real.

Children love the **Museum of Comparative Zoology,** where dinosaurs share space with preserved and stuffed insects and animals that range in size from butterflies to giraffes. Young visitors also enjoy the dollhouselike "Worlds in Miniature" display at the **Peabody Museum of Archaeology & Ethnology,** which represent people from all over the world in scaled-down homes. The Peabody also boasts the **Hall of the North American Indian,** where 500 native American artifacts representing 10 cultures are on display. The **Mineralogical & Geological Museum** is the most specialized of the four—unless there's an interesting interdisciplinary display or you're really into rocks, your time can be more productively spent elsewhere.

The Peabody Museum has a terrific **gift shop** (☎ 617/495-2248) packed with reasonably priced folk art and craft work.

Peabody Museum of Archaeology & Ethnology. 11 Divinity Ave. ☎ **617/496-1027.** www.peabody.harvard.edu. Admission to both $5 adults, $4 seniors and students, $3 children 3–13, free for children under 3; free to all Sat 9am–noon. Mon–Sat 9am–5pm; Sun 1–5pm. Closed Jan 1, July 4, Thanksgiving, and Dec 25. T: Red Line to Harvard. Cross Harvard Yard, keeping John Harvard statue on right, and turn right at Science Center. First left is Oxford St.

These fascinating museums house the university's collections of items and artifacts related to the natural world. The world-famous academic resource offers interdisciplinary programs and exhibitions that tie in elements of all the associated fields. You'll certainly find something interesting here, be it a dinosaur skeleton, a hunk of meteorite, a Native American artifact, or the world-famous Glass Flowers.

The Museum of Natural History comprises three institutions. The best-known museum is the **Botanical Museum,** and the best-known display is the **Glass Flowers,** 3,000 models of more than 840 plant species devised between 1887 and 1936 by the German father-and-son team of Leopold and Rudolph Blaschka. You may have heard about them, and you may be skeptical, but it's true: They look real. Children love the **Museum of Comparative Zoology,** where dinosaurs share space with preserved and stuffed insects and animals that range in size from butterflies to giraffes. The **Mineralogical & Geological Museum** is the most specialized—hold off unless there's an interesting interdisciplinary display or you're really into rocks.

Young visitors enjoy the dollhouse-like "Worlds in Miniature" display at the **Peabody Museum of Archaeology & Ethnology,** which represent people from all over the world in scaled-down homes. The Peabody also boasts the **Hall of the North American Indian,** where 500 artifacts representing 10 cultures are on display.

A HISTORIC HOUSE
⊙ Longfellow National Historic Site. 105 Brattle St. ☎ **617/876-4491.** www.nps. gov/ long. Guided tour $2 adults, free for seniors and children under 17. Tours June–Oct Wed–Sun and mid-Mar to May and Nov to mid-Dec Sat–Sun 10:45am, 11:45am, 1pm, 2pm, 3pm, 4pm.

Mid-Mar to May and Nov to mid-Dec Wed–Fri 12:30pm, 1:30pm, 2:30pm, 3:30pm. Closed mid-Dec to mid-Mar. T: Red Line to Harvard, then follow Brattle St. about 7 blocks; house is on the right.

By the time you read this, this ravishing yellow mansion should have reopened after a year-long refurbishment. The books and furniture have remained intact since the poet Henry Wadsworth Longfellow died there in 1882. Now a unit of the National Park Service, during the siege of Boston in 1775 to 1776 the house served as the headquarters of Gen. George Washington, with whom Longfellow was fascinated. The poet first lived in the house as a boarder in 1837, and when he and Fanny Appleton married in 1843, her father made it a wedding present. On the absorbing tour—the only way to see the house—you'll learn about the history of the building and its famous occupants.

A CELEBRATED CEMETERY

Dedicated in 1831, **Mount Auburn Cemetery,** 580 Mt. Auburn St. (☎ **617/ 547-7105**), was the first of America's rural, or garden, cemeteries. The establishment of burying places removed from city and town centers reflected practical and philosophical concerns. Development was encroaching on urban graveyards. Also, the ideas associated with the Greek Revival (the word "cemetery" derives from the Greek for "sleeping place") and Transcendentalism dictated that communing with nature take precedence over organized religion. Since the day it opened, Mount Auburn has been a popular place to retreat and reflect—in the 19th century, it was often the first place out-of-town visitors asked to go.

A modern visitor will find history and horticulture coexisting with celebrity. The graves of Henry Wadsworth Longfellow, Oliver Wendell Holmes, Julia Ward Howe, and Mary Baker Eddy are here, as are those of architect Charles Bulfinch, poet and critic James Russell Lowell, painter Winslow Homer, Transcendentalist leader Margaret Fuller, and abolitionist Charles Sumner. In season, you'll see gorgeous flowering trees and shrubs. Stop at the office or front gate to pick up brochures and a map or to rent the 60-minute audiotaped tour ($5; a $12 deposit is required), which you can listen to in your car or on a portable tape player. The **Friends of Mount Auburn Cemetery** (☎ **617/864-9646**) conduct workshops and coordinates walking tours. Call for topics, schedules, and fees.

The cemetery is open daily from 8am to dusk; there is no admission fee. Animals, picnicking, and jogging are not allowed. MBTA bus routes nos. 71 and 73 start at Harvard station and stop near the gates; they run frequently on weekdays, less often on weekends. From Harvard Square by car (5 min.) or on foot (at least 30 min.), take Mount Auburn Street or Brattle Street west; just after they intersect, the gate is on the left.

A STROLL AROUND CAMBRIDGE

To explore Harvard and the surrounding area, begin your walk in **Harvard Square.** Town and gown meet at this lively intersection, where you'll get a taste of the improbable mix of people drawn to the crossroads of Cambridge.

Start at the Harvard T station, with the **Harvard Coop** at your back. Walk half a block, crossing Dunster Street. To your right is **Holyoke Center,** an administration building designed by the Spanish architect Josep Luis Sert, the dean of the university's Graduate School of Design from 1953 to 1969, and a disciple of Le Corbusier.

Across the street is **Wadsworth House,** 1341 Mass. Ave., a yellow wood structure built in 1726 as a residence for Harvard's fourth president. Stop me if you've heard this one: George Washington slept here.

Cross the street, pass through the gate, and walk straight ahead until you see a guardhouse on your left. It's in front of **Johnston Gate,** and you're in the oldest part of **Harvard Yard.** "The Yard" was just a patch of grass with grazing animals when

Harvard College was established in 1636 to train young men for the ministry. It hadn't changed much; the Continental Army spent the winter of 1775–76 here.

With Johnston Gate at your back, to your right is **Massachusetts Hall** (1720), the university's oldest surviving building. It houses the president's office and rooms for first-year students. To your left is **Harvard Hall** (1765), a classroom building. The matching side-by-side buildings behind Harvard Hall are **Hollis** and **Stoughton halls.** Hollis dates to 1763 and has been home to many students who went on to great fame, among them Ralph Waldo Emerson, Henry David Thoreau, and Charles Bulfinch.

Across the Yard is **University Hall,** the college's main administration building, designed by Bulfinch and constructed in 1812 to 1813. It's the backdrop of the **John Harvard statue,** one of the most photographed objects in the Boston area. Designed by Daniel Chester French in 1884, it's known as the "Statue of Three Lies" because the inscription reads "John Harvard—Founder—1638." In fact, the college was established in 1636; Harvard (one of many people involved) wasn't the founder, but donated money and his library; and this isn't John Harvard, anyway. No portraits of him survive, so the model was, according to various accounts, either his nephew or a student. Walk over to the statue and join the throng of tourists posing for pictures with the benevolent-looking gentleman.

Walk around University Hall into the adjoining quadrangle; you're leaving the "Old Yard" for the "New Yard," where commencement and other university-wide ceremonies are held. On your right is **Widener Library,** the centerpiece of the world's largest university library system. It was built in 1913 as a memorial to Harry Elkins Widener, a 1907 Harvard graduate who died when the *Titanic* sank in 1912. Legend has it that he was unable to swim 50 yards to a lifeboat, and his mother donated $2 million for the library on the condition that every undergraduate pass a 50-yard swimming test.

Facing the library is **Memorial Church,** built in 1931 and topped with a tower and weathervane 197 feet tall. You're welcome to look around this Georgian Revival–style edifice unless services are going on. The entrance is on the left. The south wall, toward the Yard, lists the names of the Harvard graduates who died in the world wars, Korea, and Vietnam. One is Joseph P. Kennedy, Jr., the president's brother, class of 1938.

With Memorial Church behind you, turn left toward **Sever Hall,** a classroom building designed by H. H. Richardson (the architect of Boston's Trinity Church) and built from 1878 to 1880. It's noted for its gorgeous brickwork. The front door is set back in the "whispering gallery." Stand on one side of the entrance arch, station a friend or willing passerby on the opposite side, and speak softly into the facade. Someone standing next to you can't hear what you say, but the person at the other side of the arch can.

Walk around Sever Hall and out of the Yard onto Quincy Street. Across the way to the right is the curvilinear **Carpenter Center for the Visual Arts,** 24 Quincy St. It was constructed from 1961 to 1963 and designed by the Swiss-French architect **Le Corbusier,** along with the team of **Sert, Jackson, and Gourley.** It's the only building in North America designed by Le Corbusier.

Reenter the Yard, pass Memorial Church, and turn right. Follow the path out of the Yard to the **Science Center,** Zero Oxford St. The 10-story monolith supposedly resembles a Polaroid camera (Edwin H. Land, founder of Cambridge-based Polaroid Corporation, was one of its main benefactors). Built from 1970 to 1972, it was also designed by Sert.

To your right as you face the Science Center is **Memorial Hall,** a Victorian structure built from 1870 to 1874. The hall of memorials (enter from Kirkland or Cambridge Street) is a transept where you can read the names of the Harvard men who died fighting for the Union during the Civil War—but not those who died for the Confederacy.

With the Science Center behind you and "Mem Hall" to your left, turn right, and follow the walkway for the equivalent of a block and a half as it curves around to the right. The **Harvard Law School** campus is on your right. Carefully cross Mass. Ave. to **Cambridge Common.** Memorials and plaques dot this well-used plot of greenery and bare earth. Turn left and head back toward Harvard Square; after a block or so you'll walk near or over **horseshoes** embedded in the concrete. This is the path William Dawes, Paul Revere's fellow alarm-sounder, took from Boston to Lexington on April 18, 1775.

Turn right onto Garden Street and continue following the Common for 1 block. On your right you'll see a monument marking the place where **Gen. George Washington** took control of the Continental Army on July 3, 1775.

Cross Garden Street and backtrack to **Christ Church,** Zero Garden St. The oldest church in Cambridge, it was designed by Peter Harrison of Newport, Rhode Island (also the architect of King's Chapel in Boston), and opened in 1761. Note the square wooden tower. Inside the vestibule you can still see bullet holes made by British muskets.

With the church at your back, turn right and return to Mass. Ave. Turn right again, walk 2 blocks into the middle of the square and 1 more block on John F. Kennedy Street. Turn left onto Mount Auburn Street. Stay on the left-hand side of the street as you cross Dunster Street, Holyoke Street, and Linden Street.

The corner of Mount Auburn and Linden streets is a good vantage point for viewing the **Harvard Lampoon Castle,** designed by Wheelwright & Haven in 1909. Listed on the National Register of Historic Places, this is the home of Harvard's undergraduate humor magazine, the *Lampoon.* The main tower looks like a face, with windows as the eyes, nose, and mouth, topped by what looks like a miner's hat.

Follow Mount Auburn Street back to John F. Kennedy Street and turn left. Cross the street at some point, and follow it toward the Charles River, almost to Memorial Drive. On your right is **John F. Kennedy Park** and the adjacent Graduate School of Government. Walk away from the street to the fountain, engraved with excerpts from the president's speeches. This is an excellent place to take a break and plan the rest of your day.

7 Spectator Sports & Active Pursuits

SPECTATOR SPORTS

Boston's well-deserved reputation as a great sports town derives in part from the days when at least one of the professional teams was one of the world's best. With the exception of the Patriots, who play in suburban Foxboro (through 2000) and lost the 1997 Super Bowl, none of them has done much lately. Passions still run deep, though. Insult the local teams and be ready to defend yourself. That enthusiasm applies to some extent to college sports as well, particularly hockey, in which the Division I schools are fierce rivals.

The new (as of 1995) **FleetCenter** and **Boston Garden History Center,** 150 Causeway St. (☎ **617/624-1518;** www.fleetcenter.com) are open for tours; call for schedules during your visit. Tickets are $6 for adults, $5 for seniors and students, and $4.50 for children under 12.

BASEBALL   No experience in sports matches watching the **Boston Red Sox** play at **Fenway Park,** which they do from April through September, and later if they make the playoffs. The quirkiness of the oldest park in the major leagues (1912) and the fact that the team last won the World Series in 1918 only add to the mystique. That victory was the team's fifth in the 15-year history of the event, and the ensuing drought is one of the most famous facts in sports history. Many actually believe the Red Sox have been cursed since they sold Babe Ruth to the arch-rival New York Yankees after the 1919 season. The team's four trips to the World Series since then (1946, 1967, 1975, and 1986) have only added to the sense of doom—the Sox lost in the seventh and final game each time.

Fenway has a hand-operated scoreboard built into the Green Monster, or left-field wall (watch carefully during a pitching change—either team's left fielder may suddenly disappear into the darkness to cool off), and the wall itself is such a celebrity that it's often called simply The Wall. It's 37 feet tall, a mere 298 feet from home plate (don't believe the sign), and irresistibly tempting to batters who ought to know better.

Fans wedge themselves into narrow, uncomfortable seats close to the field. A recent fan-relations campaign called "Friendly Fenway" has produced better-mannered employees, a greater variety of concession items, and expanded family-seating sections. You're in an intensely green place that's older than your grandparents, inhaling a Fenway Frank and wishing for a home run—what could be better?

Practical concerns: Compared to its modern brethren, Fenway is tiny. Tickets go on sale in January, and the earlier you order, the better chance you'll have of landing seats during your visit. Forced to choose between tickets for a low-numbered grandstand section (say, 10 or below) and less expensive bleacher seats, go for the bleachers. They can get rowdy during night games, but the view is better from there than from the deep right-field corner. Throughout the season, a limited number of standing-room tickets go on sale the day of the game, and there's always the possibility that tickets will be returned.

The Fenway Park **ticket office** (☎ **617/267-8661** for information, 617/267-1700 for tickets; www.redsox.com) is at 24 Yawkey Way, near the corner of Brookline Avenue. Tickets for people with disabilities and for no-alcohol sections are available. Smoking is not allowed in the park. Games usually begin at 6 or 7pm on weeknights and 1pm on weekends. Take the MBTA Green Line B, C, or D to Kenmore or D to Fenway.

You can also take a **Fenway Park tour** (☎ **617/236-6666**), which includes a walk on the warning track. From May to September, tours begin on weekdays only at 10am, 11am, noon, and 1pm, plus 2pm when the team is away. There are no tours on holidays or before day games. Admission is $5 for adults, $4 for seniors, $3 for children under 16.

BASKETBALL   The 16 NBA championship banners that hang from the ceiling of the FleetCenter, are testimony to the glorious history of the **Boston Celtics.** Unfortunately, the most recent is from 1986. The Celtics play from early October to April or May; when a top contender is visiting, you may have trouble buying tickets. Prices are as low as $10 for some games and top out at $70. For information, call the Fleet-Center (☎ **617/624-1000;** www.bostonceltics.com); for tickets, call Ticketmaster (☎ **617/931-2000**). To reach the FleetCenter, take the MBTA Green or Orange Line or commuter rail to North Station.

The local college teams are competitive but (except for the Harvard women) not world-beaters. The schools and venues: **Boston College,** Conte Forum, Chestnut Hill (☎ **617/552-3000**); **Boston University,** Walter Brown Arena, 285 Babcock St. (☎ **617/353-3838**); **Harvard University,** Lavietes Pavilion, North Harvard Street, Allston (☎ **617/495-2211**); and **Northeastern University,** Matthews Arena, St. Botolph Street. (☎ **617/373-4700**).

FOOTBALL   The **New England Patriots** (☎ **800/543-1776;** www.patriots.com) were playing to sellout crowds even before they won the conference title in 1997 and went to (and lost) the Super Bowl. Plans to move to Hartford, Connecticut, met with the skepticism that such a declaration probably deserves; if it proves true, 2000 will be the team's last season in the Boston area. The Patriots play from August through December (January if they make the playoffs) at Foxboro Stadium on Route 1 in

Foxboro, about a 45-minute drive south of the city. You can drive or catch a bus from the entrance of South Station, the Riverside T station, or Shopper's World in Framingham (west of the city). Tickets ($23 to $60) almost always sell out. Plan as far in advance as you can.

Boston College, another tough ticket, is the only Division I-A college football team in New England. The Eagles play at Alumni Stadium in Chestnut Hill (☎ 617/552-3000). The area's Division I-AA teams are **Harvard University,** Harvard Stadium, North Harvard Street, Allston (☎ 617/495-2211), and **Northeastern University,** Parsons Field, Kent Street, Brookline (☎ 617/373-4700).

HOCKEY The **Boston Bruins** are in roughly the same condition as the Celtics—burdened by history and looking to the future. Their games are exciting, especially if you happen to be in town at the same time as the archrival Montreal Canadiens, but incredibly expensive ($43 to $70)—nevertheless, tickets for many games sell out early. For information, call the FleetCenter (☎ 617/624-1000; www.bostonbruins.com); for tickets, call Ticketmaster (☎ 617/931-2000). To reach the FleetCenter, take the MBTA Green or Orange Line or commuter rail to North Station.

Economical fans who don't have their hearts set on seeing a pro game will be pleasantly surprised by the quality of local ✪ **college hockey.** Even for sold-out games, standing-room tickets are usually available the night of the game. Local teams regularly hit the national rankings; they include **Boston College,** Conte Forum, Chestnut Hill (☎ 617/552-3000); **Boston University,** Walter Brown Arena, 285 Babcock St. (☎ 617/353-3838); **Harvard University,** Bright Hockey Center, North Harvard Street, Allston (☎ 617/495-2211); and **Northeastern University,** Matthews Arena, St. Botolph Street (☎ 617/373-4700). These four men's teams play in the tradition-steeped **Beanpot** tournament on the first two Mondays of February at the FleetCenter.

HORSE RACING **Suffolk Downs,** 111 Waldemar Ave., East Boston (☎ 617/567-3900; www.suffolkdowns.com), is one of the best-run smaller tracks in the country, an excellent family destination (really), sparkling clean, and the home of the Massachusetts Handicap, run in early June. Horse of the Year Cigar won the MassCap in 1995 and 1996, conferring instant cachet on the event and the facility.

The season runs from late September to early June, and there are extensive simulcasting options during and after the live season. The day's entries appear in the *Globe* and the *Herald.* The track is off Route 1A, about a half mile from Logan Airport; the MBTA Blue Line has a Suffolk Downs stop.

THE MARATHON Every year on Patriots Day (the third Monday in April), the ✪ **Boston Marathon** rules the roads from Hopkinton to Copley Square in Boston. Cheering fans line the entire route. An especially nice place to watch is tree-shaded Comm. Ave. between Kenmore Square and Mass. Ave., but you'll be in a crowd wherever you stand, particularly near the finish line in front of the Boston Public Library. For information about qualifying, contact the **Boston Athletic Association** (☎ 617/236-1652; www.bostonmarathon.org).

ROWING In late October, the **Head of the Charles Regatta** (☎ 617/864-8415; www.hocr.org) attracts some 4,000 oarsmen and oarswomen. They race against the clock for 4 miles, from the Charles River basin to the Eliot Bridge in west Cambridge. The largest crew event in the country draws tens of thousands of prepsters who socialize and occasionally even watch the action.

TENNIS The **U.S. Tennis Championship** takes place in August at the Longwood Cricket Club, 564 Hammond St., Brookline (☎ 617/731-4500). Call for tickets and information about the week-long event, sometimes used as a tune-up for the U.S. Open. The finals often sell out early, but demand isn't as high for preliminary matches.

ACTIVE PURSUITS

While you're planning your trip, consult the incredibly helpful site maintained by the ✪ **Metropolitan District Commission** (www.magnet.state.ma.us/mdc/mdc_home.htm). It includes descriptions of properties and activities, and has a planning area to help you make the most of your time.

BEACHES The beaches in Boston proper are decent places to catch a cool breeze and splash around, but for real ocean surf, you'll need to head out of town.

Boston Beaches The **Metropolitan District Commission** (☎ 617/727-9547) is working to restore the run-down beaches under its purview, but the MDC sometimes still has to fly red flags when swimming is not recommended (blue flags mean the water's fine).

Be aware that these are very much neighborhood hangouts. In Dorchester, off Morrissey Boulevard, **Malibu Beach** and **Savin Hill Beach** are within walking distance of the Savin Hill stop on the MBTA Red Line. South Boston beaches are off Day Boulevard and accessible by taking the Red Line to Broadway or Green Line to Copley, then a bus marked "City Point" (routes 9, 10, and 11). Among them are **Castle Island, L Street,** and **Pleasure Bay.**

North Shore Beaches Close to Boston are **Nahant Beach** (follow the signs from the intersection of Routes 1A and 129, near the Lynn–Swampscott border), which is large and extremely popular, and **Revere Beach.** Revere Beach is better known for its pickup scene than its narrow strip of sand, but the cruising crowds are friendly and parking on the boulevard is free. The MBTA Blue Line has a Revere Beach stop; if you're driving, head north for smaller crowds at **Point of Pines,** which has its own exit off Route 1A. Across the street from the water is **Kelly's Roast Beef,** 410 Revere Beach Blvd. (☎ 617/284-9129), a local legend for its onion rings, fried clams, and roast-beef sandwiches (and the double burger from the "sandwich welfare" scene in *Good Will Hunting*). Other North Shore beaches are discussed in chapter 5.

South Shore Beaches Private beaches dominate the southern suburbs, but there are a couple of pleasant public options. In Hull (take Route 3 or 3A to Route 228), **Nantasket Beach** (☎ 617/925-4905) is right in town. It's popular with families for its fairly shallow water and the historic wooden carousel in a building across the street from the main parking lot. Nine-mile-long **Duxbury Beach** (take Route 3A to Route 139 north and go right on Canal Street) makes an enjoyable stop on the way to Plymouth, if that's in your plans. **Plymouth Beach,** off Route 3A south of Plymouth at Warren Avenue, is smaller, with mild surf.

BIKING Even expert cyclists who feel comfortable with Boston's layout will be better off in Cambridge, which has bike lanes. Recreational bikers are better off sticking to Boston's more than 50 miles of marked bike paths. The 17.7-mile **Dr. Paul Dudley White Charles River Bike Path** loops from the Museum of Science to Watertown and back. You can enter and exit at many points along the way. Bikers share the path with lots of pedestrians, joggers, and in-line skaters. On summer Sundays from 11am to 7pm, **Memorial Drive** in Cambridge is closed, giving bikers and skaters a traffic-free ride along the Charles.

Bicycles are forbidden on MBTA buses and the Green Line. You must have a $5 permit (☎ 617/222-5799) to bring your bike on the Blue, Orange, and Red lines and commuter rail, nonrush hours only.

Most rental shops charge around $5 an hour, with a minimum of 2 hours, or a flat daily rate of $20 to $25. They include **Earth Bikes 'n' Blades,** 35 Huntington Ave., near Copley Square (☎ 617/267-4733); **Back Bay Bikes & Boards,** 333 Newbury St., near Mass. Ave. (☎ 617/247-2336); and **Community Bicycle Supply,** 496

A Vacation on the Islands

Majestic ocean views, hiking trails, historic sites, rocky beaches, nature walks, campsites, and picnic areas abound in New England. The **Boston Harbor Islands** (☎ 617/223-8666) weren't widely known until recently. They became a national park in 1997, and summer travelers can now take better advantage of their unspoiled beauty and easy access. For more information, stop at the **kiosk** on Long Wharf or consult the sources below.

There are 30 islands in the Outer Harbor, and at least a half-dozen are open for exploring, camping, or swimming. Bring a sweater or jacket. You can investigate on your own or take a ranger-led tour. Plan a day trip or even an overnight stay, but note that fresh water is not available on any of the islands.

Ferries run to the most popular, **Georges Island,** home of Fort Warren (1834), where Confederate prisoners were kept during the Civil War. Tours are offered periodically. The island has a visitor center, refreshment area, fishing pier, picnic area, and a wonderful view of Boston's skyline. From there, free water taxis run to **Lovell, Gallops, Peddocks, Bumpkin,** and **Grape islands,** which have picnic areas and campsites. Lovell Island also has the remains of a fort (Fort Standish), as well as a sandy beach; it's the only harbor island with supervised swimming in the chilly water.

Administered as a National Park Partnership, the Boston Harbor Islands National Recreation Area (www.nps.gov/boha) is the focus of a public-private project designed to make them more interesting and accessible. **Boston Harbor Cruises** (☎ 617/227-4321; www.bostonboats.com) serves Georges Island from Long Wharf; the trip takes 45 minutes, and tickets are $8 for adults, $7 for seniors, $6 for children under 12. Cruises depart at 10am, noon, and 2pm on spring and fall weekends, and daily on the hour from 10am to 4pm in the summer. Water taxis and admission to the islands themselves are free.

The **Metropolitan District Commission** (☎ 617/727-5290; www.magnet. state.ma.us/mdc/harbor.htm) administers Georges, Lovell, and Peddocks islands; the state **Department of Environmental Management** (☎ 617/740-1605) oversees Gallops, Grape, and Bumpkin islands. For more information, contact the **Friends of the Boston Harbor Islands** (☎ 617/740-4290; www.tiac.net/users/fbhi).

Tremont St., near East Berkeley Street (☎ 617/542-8623). For more information, contact **MassBike** (☎ 617/491-7433; www.massbike.org).

BOATING Riding a pedal-powered **swan boat** *is* boating—not exactly on the high seas, but it's been a classic Boston experience since 1877. The lagoon at the Public Garden turns into a fiberglass swan habitat from the Saturday before Patriots Day (the third Monday in April) through September, from 10am to 6pm in summer, 10am to 4pm in spring and fall. The cost is $1.75 for adults and 95¢ for children (☎ 617/522-1966 or 617/624-7020).

For a less tame option, the **Charles River Canoe and Kayak Center** (☎ 617/965-5110; www.ski-paddle.com) has locations on Soldiers Field Road in Allston and at 2401 Commonwealth Ave. in Newton. Both centers rent canoes and kayaks (the Newton location also rents sculls), and offer lessons. From April through October, they open at 10am on weekdays and 9am on weekends and holidays, and close at dusk.

Noninflatable watercraft are allowed on the Charles River and in the Inner Harbor. If you plan to bring your own boat, call the Metropolitan District Commission **Harbormaster** (☎ 617/727-0537) for information about launches.

GOLF   On weekdays you'll find lower prices and smaller crowds at the area's many courses.

At **Newton Commonwealth Golf Course,** 212 Kenrick St., Newton (☎ 617/ 630-1971), an excellent 18-hole layout designed by Donald Ross, par is 70 and greens fees are $21 on weekdays and $28 on weekends. At 9-hole, par-35 **Fresh Pond Golf Course,** 691 Huron Ave., Cambridge (☎ 617/349-6282), it's $15, or $22 to go around twice, on weekdays, and $18 and $28 on weekends.

Within the city limits there are two 18-hole courses: the par-70 **William J. Devine Golf Course,** in Franklin Park, Dorchester (☎ 617/265-4084), where greens fees are $22 on weekdays and $25 on weekends; and **George Wright Golf Course,** 420 West St., Hyde Park (☎ 617/361-8313), where fees are $21 on weekdays and $24 on weekends.

The **Massachusetts Golf Association,** 175 Highland Ave., Needham, MA 02192 (☎ 781/449-3000; www.mga.org), represents more than 310 golf courses around the state and will send you a list of courses on request.

GYMS   The concierge or front desk staff at your hotel can probably recommend a health club. You'll find the best combination of facilities and value at the **Central Branch YMCA,** 316 Huntington Ave., near Symphony Hall (☎ 617/536-7800). A $10 one-day pass includes the use of the pool, gym, weight room, fitness center, and indoor track. Closer to downtown, **Fitcorp** (☎ 617/375-5600; www.fitcorp.com) charges $12 for a guest pass that includes well-equipped facilities but not a pool. It has locations at 1 Beacon St. (☎ 617/248-9797), near Government Center; 133 Federal St. (☎ 617/542-1010), in the Financial District; and in the Prudential Center (☎ 617/262-2050).

ICE SKATING   The skating rink at the Boston Common **Frog Pond** (☎ 617/ 635-2197) is a popular cold-weather destination. It's an open surface with an ice-making system and a clubhouse where you can rent skates for $5; admission is $3 for adults, free for children under 14.

IN-LINE SKATING   As with biking, unless you're confident of your ability and your knowledge of Boston traffic, stay off the streets. A favorite spot for in-line skaters is the **Esplanade,** between the Back Bay and the Charles River. It continues onto the bike path that runs to Watertown and back, but once you leave the Esplanade, the pavement isn't totally smooth—your best bet is to wait for a Sunday in the summer, when **Memorial Drive** in Cambridge is closed to traffic. It's a perfect surface.

For renters, a former Olympic cyclist and speed skater runs Eric Flaim's Motion Sports, 349 Newbury St. (☎ 617/247-3284). Or try Back Bay Bikes & Boards, 333 Newbury St. (☎ 617/247-2336); the Beacon Hill Skate Shop, 135 Charles St. S. (☎ 617/482-7400); Earth Bikes 'n' Blades, 35 Huntington Ave. (☎ 617/ 267-4733); or Ski Market, 860 Commonwealth Ave. (☎ 617/731-6100).

The **InLine Club of Boston's** Web site (www.sk8net.com/icb) offers up-to-date event and safety information and an extremely clever logo.

JOGGING   Check with the concierge or desk staff at your hotel for a map with suggested routes. The loop around the Charles River (see "Biking") is the area's busiest jogging trail. If you're staying close enough to the river, the bridges allow for circuits of various lengths, but be careful around abutments, where you can't see far ahead. As in any large city, stay out of park areas (including the Esplanade) at night.

In case you want to see the world.

At American Express, we're here to make your journey a smooth one. So we have over 1,700 travel service locations in over 130 countries ready to help. What else would you expect from the world's largest travel agency?

do more AMERICAN EXPRESS

Travel

In case you want to be welcomed there.

We're here to see that you're always welcomed at establishments everywhere. That's why millions of people carry the American Express® Card – for peace of mind, confidence, and security, around the world or just around the corner.

do more AMERICAN EXPRESS

Cards

In case you're running low.

We're here to help with more than 190,000 Express Cash locations around the world. In order to enroll, just call American Express at 1 800 CASH-NOW before you start your vacation.

do more

AMERICAN EXPRESS

Express Cash

And in case you'd rather be safe than sorry.

We're here with American Express® Travelers Cheques. They're the safe way to carry money on your vacation, because if they're ever lost or stolen you can get a refund, practically anywhere or anytime. To find the nearest place to buy Travelers Cheques, call 1 800 495-1153. Another way we help you do more.

do more   AMERICAN EXPRESS®

Travelers Cheques

Other sources of information include the **Metropolitan District Commission** (☎ 617/727-1300), and the **Bill Rodgers Running Center** in Faneuil Hall Marketplace (☎ **617/723-5612**).

SAILING   **Community Boating, Inc.,** 21 Embankment Rd., on the Esplanade (☎ **617/523-1038**), offers sailing lessons and boating programs for children and adults from April through November. It runs on a co-op system; a 30-day adult membership is $65. The **Boston Sailing Center,** 54 Lewis Wharf (☎ **617/227-4198**), offers lessons for sailors of all ability levels. The center is open year-round (even for "frostbite" racing in the winter). Ten classes (five indoors, five outdoors) and a 35-day membership will run you $495. The **Courageous Sailing Center,** Charlestown Navy Yard (☎ **617/242-3821**), offers youth program lessons year-round. A five-lesson program (one in the classroom, four on the water) is $125. And the **Boston Harbor Sailing Club,** 200 High St., at Rowes Wharf (☎ **617/345-9202**), offers rentals and instruction. A package of four classes, 16 hours of on-water instruction, and a 30-day membership is $414. Private lessons (3-hour minimum) are $20 an hour plus the rental of the boat (from $25 an hour) plus tax.

TENNIS   Public courts maintained by the **Metropolitan District Commission** (☎ **617/727-1300**) are available throughout the city at no charge. To find the one nearest you, call the MDC or ask the concierge or desk staff at your hotel. Well-maintained courts near downtown that seldom get busy until after work are at several spots on the Southwest Corridor Park in the South End (there's a nice one near West Newton Street) and off Commercial Street near the North Washington Street bridge in the North End. The courts in Charlesbank Park, overlooking the river next to the State Police barracks on the bridge to the Museum of Science, are more crowded during the day.

8 Shopping

The area's premier shopping area is Boston's **Back Bay.** Dozens of classy galleries, shops, and boutiques make **Newbury Street** a world-famous destination. Nearby, a weatherproof walkway across Huntington Avenue links upscale **Copley Place** (☎ **617/375-4400**) and the **Shops at Prudential Center** (☎ **800/SHOP-PRU;** www.prudentialcenter.com). This is where you'll find **Neiman Marcus, Lord & Taylor,** and **Saks Fifth Avenue.**

Another popular destination is **Faneuil Hall Marketplace** (☎ 617/338-2323). It's the busiest attraction in Boston not only because of its smorgasbord of food outlets, but also for its shops, boutiques, and pushcarts, filled with everything from rubber stamps to costume jewelry, flowers to souvenirs.

If the prospect of the hubbub there is too much for you, stroll over to ✪ **Charles Street,** at the foot of Beacon Hill. It's a short but commercially dense (and picturesque) street noted for its antique and gift shops.

One of Boston's oldest shopping areas is **Downtown Crossing.** Now a traffic-free pedestrian mall along Washington, Winter, and Summer streets near Boston Common, it's home to two major department stores (**Filene's** and **Macy's**) tons of smaller clothing, shoe, and music stores, food and merchandise pushcarts, and outlets of two major bookstore chains, **Barnes & Noble** and **Borders.**

Harvard Square in Cambridge, with its bookstores, boutiques, and T-shirt shops, is about 15 minutes from downtown Boston by subway. An aggressive neighborhood association has attempted to keep the area from being consumed by chain stores. Although the bohemian days of "the Square" are long gone, you'll find a mix of national and regional outlets as well as independent retailers.

The Quintessential Bargain Basement

If one store in Boston deserves to be singled out, it's ✪ **Filene's Basement,** 426 Washington St. (☎ **617/542-2011**). Follow the crowds to this Downtown Crossing institution, which has spoiled New England shoppers for paying retail since 1908. True devotees don't try to conceal their bargains—they boast about them. Here's how it works: After 2 weeks on the selling floor, the already discounted prices automatically fall 25%. Check the dates on the boards hanging from the ceiling against the original sale date (on the back of every price tag). Prices drop until, after 35 days, anything that hasn't sold (for 75% off) goes to charity.

Filene's Basement split off from Filene's, the department store upstairs, in 1988. The independent discount chain has branches throughout the Northeast and Midwest, but the automatic markdown policy applies only at the original store, which attracts 15,000 to 20,000 shoppers a day. The crowds swell for special sales, scheduled when a store is going out of business or a classy designer, retailer, or catalog house (say, Neiman Marcus, Barneys, or Saks Fifth Avenue) finds itself overstocked. You'll see the unpredictable particulars, sometimes including an early opening time, advertised in the newspapers. Four times a year, the legendary $249 wedding-dress sale sparks an alarming display; other featured items include dresses, men's and women's suits, raincoats, dress shirts, lingerie, leather goods, designer shoes, and anything else that looks promising to the store's eagle-eyed buyers. Two weeks later, leftovers wind up on the automatic-markdown racks, and the real hunting begins. Try to beat the lunchtime crowds, but if you can't, don't despair—just be patient.

Tip: If you're not wild about trying on clothes in the open dressing rooms, slip them on over what you're wearing, an acceptable throwback to the days before there were dressing rooms. Or make like the natives and return what doesn't suit you, in person or even by mail.

A walk along **Mass. Ave.** in either direction to the next T stop (**Porter** to the north, **Central** to the southeast) will take an hour or so—time well spent for dedicated shoppers. And if you just can't manage without a trip to a mall, head to East Cambridge or take the Red Line to Kendall/MIT, then the free shuttle bus to the **CambridgeSide Galleria,** 100 CambridgeSide Place (☎ **617/621-8666**).

If you're passionate or just curious about art, try to set aside a couple of hours for strolling along **Newbury Street.** You'll find an infinite variety of styles and media in the dozens of galleries at street level and on the higher floors (remember to look up). Browsers and questions are welcome. Most galleries are open Tuesday to Sunday from 10 or 11am to 5:30 or 6pm.

Bookworms flock to Cambridge; Harvard Square in particular caters to general and specific audiences. Check out the basement of the **Harvard Book Store,** 1256 Mass. Ave. (☎ **800/542-READ** outside 617, or 617/661-1515; www.harvard.com), for great deals on remainders and used books; and **WordsWorth Books,** 30 Brattle St. (☎ **800/899-2202** or 617/354-5201; www.wordsworth.com), for a huge selection, all (except textbooks) discounted. Barnes & Noble runs the book operation at **the Harvard Coop,** 1400 Mass. Ave. (☎ **617/499-2000**), which stocks textbooks, academic works, and a large general selection.

Two excellent Boston stores with huge selections of used merchandise are the **Avenue Victor Hugo Bookshop,** 339 Newbury St. (☎ **617/266-7746**; www.avenuevictorhugobooks.com), in the Back Bay, and the **Brattle Book Store,**

9 West St. (☎ **800/447-9595** or 617/542-0210), near Downtown Crossing. Also near Downtown Crossing are **Barnes & Noble,** 395 Washington St. (☎ **617/ 426-5184;** www.barnesandnoble.com) and **Borders Books & Music,** 24 School St. (☎ **617/557-7188;** www.borders.com).

Note: Massachusetts has no sales tax on clothing priced below $175 or on food. All other items are taxed at 5%, as are restaurant meals and take-out food. The state no longer prohibits stores from opening before noon on Sunday, but many still wait till noon or don't open at all—call ahead before setting out.

9 Boston & Cambridge After Dark

For up-to-date entertainment listings, consult the "Calendar" section of the Thursday *Boston Globe,* the "Scene" section of the Friday *Boston Herald,* and the Sunday arts sections of both papers. The weekly Boston Phoenix (published on Thursday) has especially good club listings, and the twice-monthly *Improper Bostonian* (free at newspaper boxes around town) has extensive live-music listings.

GETTING TICKETS   Ticketmaster (☎ **617/931-2000;** www.ticketmaster.com) **Next Ticketing** (☎ **617/423-NEXT;** www.boston.com/next), and **Tele-charge** (☎ **800/447-7400**), the major agencies that serve Boston, calculate service charges per ticket, not per order. To avoid the charge, visit the venue in person. If you wait until the day before or the day of a performance, you'll sometimes have access to tickets that were held back for one reason or another and have just gone on sale.

DISCOUNT TICKETS   Visit a ✪ **BosTix** (☎ **617/723-5181;** www.boston.com/ artsboston) booth at Faneuil Hall Marketplace (on the south side of Faneuil Hall), in Copley Square (at the corner of Boylston and Dartmouth streets), or in Harvard Square (in the Holyoke Center arcade at 1350 Mass. Ave.). Same-day tickets to musical and theatrical performances are on sale for half price, subject to availability. A coupon book offering discounted and two-for-one admission to many area museums is available, too. Credit cards are not accepted, and there are no refunds or exchanges. Check the board for the day's offerings.

BosTix also offers full-price advance ticket sales; discounts on more than 100 theater, music, and dance events; and tickets to museums, historic sites, and attractions in and around town. The Boston locations are Ticketmaster outlets. The booths are open Tuesday to Saturday from 10am to 6pm (half-price tickets go on sale at 11am), and Sunday from 11am to 4pm. The Copley Square and Harvard Square locations are also open Monday from 10am to 6pm.

THE PERFORMING ARTS

In addition to the companies listed below, **the Boston Lyric Opera (BLO)** mounts three or four annual opera productions in the Schubert Theatre, 265 Tremont Street (☎ **617/542-6772** for tickets; 617/542-6772 for information).

THE MAJOR COMPANIES

✪ **Boston Symphony Orchestra.** Performing at Symphony Hall, 301 Mass. Ave. (at Huntington Ave.). ☎ **617/266-1492,** 617/CONCERT (program information), or 617/266-1200 (SymphonyCharge). www.bso.org. Tickets $24–$75. Rush tickets $8 (on sale 9am Fri; 5pm Tues, Thurs). Rehearsal tickets $14. T: Green Line E to Symphony.

The Boston Symphony Orchestra, one of the world's greatest, was founded in 1881. Plans for 2000 include celebrating the centennial of the BSO's home, acoustically perfect Symphony Hall. Music director Seiji Ozawa is the latest in a line of distinguished conductors of an institution known for contemporary as well as classical music; the 1996 Pulitzer Prize in music was awarded to *Lilacs,* composed for voice and orchestra by George Walker and commissioned by the BSO.

The season runs from October through April, with performances most Tuesday, Thursday, and Saturday evenings, Friday afternoons, and some Friday evenings. Check at the box office 2 hours before show time if you weren't able to buy tickets in advance—returns from subscribers go on sale at full price at that time. A limited number of rush tickets (one per person) are available on the day of the performance for Tuesday and Thursday evening and Friday afternoon. Wednesday evening and Thursday morning rehearsals are sometimes open to the public.

✪ **Boston Pops.** Performing at Symphony Hall, 301 Mass. Ave. (at Huntington Ave.). ☎ **617/266-1492,** 617/CONCERT (program information), or 617/266-1200 (Symphony-Charge). www.bso.org. Tickets $33–$45 for tables, $12.50–$28 for balcony seats. T: Green Line E to Symphony.

From early May to early July, members of the Boston Symphony Orchestra lighten up. Tables and chairs replace the floor seats at Symphony Hall, drinks and light refreshments are served, and the Pops play a range of music from light classical to show tunes to popular music (hence the name), sometimes with celebrity guest stars. Conductor Keith Lockhart is so popular that he could almost give the orchestra its name all by himself. Performances are Tuesday to Sunday evenings. (There's also a week or so of winter holiday performances that usually sell out well in advance.) The season ends with a week of free outdoor concerts at the Hatch Shell on the Charles River Esplanade, including the traditional Fourth of July concert, which features fireworks and a rendition of Tchaikovsky's "1812 Overture" with real cannon fire.

✪ **Boston Ballet.** 19 Clarendon St. ☎ **617/695-6955** or 800/447-7400 (Tele-charge). Performing at Wang Theatre, 270 Tremont St., and Shubert Theatre, 265 Tremont St. (both box offices, Mon–Sat 10am–6pm). Tickets $21–$69. Student rush tickets (1 hr. before curtain) $12.50, except for *The Nutcracker.* T: Green Line to Boylston.

Boston Ballet's reputation seems to jump a notch every time someone says, "So it's not just *The Nutcracker.*" The country's fourth-largest dance company is a holiday staple, and during the rest of the season (October through May), it presents an eclectic mix of classic story ballets and contemporary works.

CONCERT HALLS & LANDMARK VENUES

The city's premier classical performance hall is **Symphony Hall,** 301 Mass. Ave. (☎ **617/266-2492**), which turns 100 in 2000. It plays host to other notable groups and artists when the BSO and the Pops are away.

The ✪ **Hatch Shell** on the Esplanade (☎ **617/727-9547,** ext. 555) is an amphitheater best known as the home of the Boston Pops' Fourth of July concerts. Almost every night in the summer, free music and dance performances and films take over the Hatch Shell stage to the delight of crowds on the lawn.

Other performance spaces that attract big-name visitors and talented local artists include the **Berklee Performance Center,** 136 Mass. Ave. (☎ **617/266-7455**); the five venues at the **Boston Center for the Arts,** 539 Tremont St. (☎ **617/426-7700**); **Jordan Hall,** 30 Gainsborough St. (☎ **617/536-2412**); and **Sanders Theatre,** 45 Quincy St., Cambridge (☎ **617/496-2222;** www.fas.harvard.edu/~memhall).

Rock and pop artists play the **FleetCenter,** 150 Causeway St. (☎ **617/624-1000;** www.fleetcenter.com), when it's not in use by the Bruins (hockey), the Celtics (basketball), the circus (in October) and touring ice shows. Concerts are in the round or on the arena stage.

THEATER & PERFORMANCE ART

Boston is one of the last cities for pre-Broadway tryouts, allowing an early look at a classic (or classic flop) in the making. It's also a popular destination for touring companies of established Broadway hits. You'll find most of the shows headed to or coming from Broadway in the ✪ **Theater District,** at the **Colonial Theatre,** 106 Boylston St. (☎ **617/ 426-9366**); the **Shubert Theatre,** 265 Tremont St. (☎ **617/482-9393**); the **Wang Theatre,** 270 Tremont St. (☎ **617/482-9393;** www.boston.com/wangcenter); and the **Wilbur Theater,** 246 Tremont St. (☎ **617/423-4008**).

The excellent local theater scene boasts the **Huntington Theatre Company,** which performs at the Boston University Theatre, 264 Huntington Ave. (☎ **617/266-0800;** www.bu.edu/huntington), and the **American Repertory Theatre,** which makes its home at Harvard University's Loeb Drama Center, 64 Brattle St., Cambridge (☎ **617/ 547-8300;** www.amrep.org). Some ART projects and independent productions are at the **Hasty Pudding Theatre,** 12 Holyoke St., Cambridge (☎ **617/496-8400**).

The off-Broadway performance-art sensation **Blue Man Group** branched out from New York to Boston in 1995. The troupe of three cobalt-colored entertainers uses music, percussion, food, and audience participants—props include social commentary, Twinkies, marshmallows, breakfast cereal, toilet paper, and lots of blue paint. Older children and teenagers enjoy the mayhem as much as adults. Shows are at the **Charles Playhouse** (☎ **617/426-6912**), 74 Warrenton St. in the Theater District, at 8pm Tuesday to Thursday, 7 and 10pm Friday and Saturday, and 4pm Sunday. Tickets are $39 and $49 at the box office and through Ticketmaster (☎ **617/931-ARTS**).

THE CLUB & MUSIC SCENE
The Boston-area club scene changes constantly, and somewhere out there is a good time for everyone, regardless of age, clothing style, musical taste, and budget. Check the "Calendar" section of the Thursday *Globe,* the *Phoenix,* the *Improper Bostonian,* or the "Scene" section of the Friday *Herald* while you're making plans.

Bars close at 1am, clubs at 2am, and the T shuts down between 12:30 and 1am. The drinking age is 21; a valid driver's license or passport is required as proof of age. The law is strictly enforced, especially near college campuses (in other words, practically everywhere). Be prepared to show ID if you appear to be younger than 35 or so, and try to be patient while the amazed 30-year-old ahead of you fishes out a license.

COMEDY
✪ **Comedy Connection at Faneuil Hall.** Quincy Market, Upper Rotunda. ☎ **617/ 248-9700.** www.go.boston.com/comedyconnection. Cover $8–$30. T: Green or Blue Line to Government Center or Orange Line to Haymarket.

A large room with a clear view from every seat, the oldest original comedy club in town (established in 1978) draws top-notch talent from near and far. Big-name national acts lure enthusiastic crowds, and openers are often just as funny but not as famous—yet. Shows are nightly at 8pm, plus Friday and Saturday at 10:15pm. The cover charge seldom tops $12 during the week, but jumps for a big name appearing on a weekend.

DANCE CLUBS
✪ **Avalon.** 15 Lansdowne St. ☎ **617/262-2424.** Cover $5–$10. T: Green Line B, C, or D to Kenmore.

A cavernous space divided into several levels, with a full concert stage, large dance floors, and a spectacular light show, Avalon is either great fun or sensory overload. When the stage is not in use for the occasional live concert, DJs take over for international music and—particularly on Saturday (suburbanites' night out)—mainstream dance hits. The dress code calls for jackets, shirts with collars, and no jeans or athletic wear. The crowd is slightly older than at Axis; for special events, the connecting doors open to make the two clubs one enormous space. Open Thursday (international night) to Sunday (gay night) from 10pm to 2am.

Axis. 13 Lansdowne St. ☎ **617/262-2437.** Cover $7–$10. T: Green Line B, C, or D to Kenmore.

Progressive rock at bone-rattling volume and "creative dress"—break out the leather— attract a young crowd to Axis. There are special nights for alternative rock, house, techno, soul and funk music, and for international DJs. Open Tuesday to Sunday (gay night with adjoining Avalon) from 10pm to 2am.

The Roxy. 279 Tremont St., in the Tremont Boston hotel. ☎ **617/338-7699.** www.gbcx. com/roxy. Cover $10–$16. No jeans or athletic shoes. T: Green Line to Boylston.

This former hotel ballroom boasts excellent DJs and live music, a huge dance floor, a concert stage, and a balcony (perfect for checking out the action below). The occa- sional concert offerings take good advantage of the acoustics and sight lines. Open 10:30pm to 2am on Thursday (Latin night), Friday (swing night), Saturday (Top 40 night), and some Sundays for special events.

FOLK & ECLECTIC

✪ **Club Passim.** 47 Palmer St., Cambridge. ☎ **617/492-7679.** Cover $5–$22; most shows $12 or less. T: Red Line to Harvard.

Joan Baez, Suzanne Vega, and Tom Rush started out here, in a basement on the street between buildings of the Harvard Coop. Passim is still building on a reputation for more than 30 years of nurturing new talent and showcasing established musicians. Patrons who have been regulars since day one mix with college students. There's live music 4 to 6 nights a week and Sunday afternoons, and coffee and light meals are available all the time. Open Sunday to Thursday from 11am to 11pm, Friday and Sat- urday from 11am to 4am.

✪ **Johnny D's.** 17 Holland St., Davis Sq., Somerville. ☎ **617/776-2004,** or 617/776-9667 (concert line). www.johnnyds.com. Cover $2–$16, usually $5–$10. T: Red Line to Davis.

This family-owned and operated restaurant and music club is one of the best in the area. It draws a congenial crowd for acts on national and international tours, as well as those that haven't been out of eastern Massachusetts. The music ranges from zydeco to rock, rockabilly to jazz, blues to ska. The food's even good. Johnny D's is worth a long trip, but it's only two stops past Harvard Square on the Red Line, about a 15- minute ride at night. Open daily from 11:30am to 1am; dinner Tuesday to Saturday from 4:30 to 9:30pm, with lighter fare until 11pm.

JAZZ & BLUES

On summer Fridays at 6:30pm, the ✪ **Waterfront Jazz Series** (☎ 617/635-3911) brings amateurs and professionals to Christopher Columbus Park, on the waterfront, for a refreshing interlude of free music and cool breezes. The *Boston Globe* **Jazz & Blues Fes- tival** (☎ 617/929-2000) is usually scheduled for the third week of June. Constellations of jazz and blues stars (large and small) appear at lunchtime, after-work, evening, and weekend events, some of them free, many of them outdoors. The festival wraps up with a free Sunday afternoon program at the Hatch Shell.

✪ **House of Blues.** 96 Winthrop St., Cambridge. ☎ **617/491-2583,** or 617/497-2229 for tickets. Dining reservations (☎ 617/491-2100) accepted only for parties of 25 or more.www. hob.com. Cover $7–$30; Sat matinee free. T: Red Line to Harvard.

The original House of Blues packs 'em in every evening and on weekend afternoons. The tourist magnet attracts big names—Junior Brown, Maceo Parker, Koko Taylor, and the Fabulous Thunderbirds have played recently. And there's no telling when one of the legions of out-of-towners in the audience will turn out to be someone famous who winds up on stage jamming. The restaurant is open 11:30am to 11pm Monday to Saturday, 4:30 to 11pm on Sunday; the music hall until 1am Sunday to Wednesday, 2am Thursday to Saturday. Sunday gospel buffet brunch seatings are at 10am, noon, and 2pm; advance tickets ($26) are highly recommended.

Regattabar. In the Charles Hotel, 1 Bennett St., Cambridge. ☎ **617/661-5000,** or 617/876-7777 (Concertix). Tickets $6–$25. T: Red Line to Harvard.

The Regattabar's selection of local and international artists is considered the best in the area—a title Scullers (see below) is happy to dispute. Shirley Horn, Betty Carter, Tito Puente, the Count Basie Orchestra, and Karen Akers have appeared within the past 2 years. The large third-floor room holds about 200 and has a 21-foot picture window overlooking Harvard Square; unfortunately, it sometimes gets a little noisy. Buy tickets in advance from Concertix (there's a $2 per ticket service charge) or try your luck at the door 1 hour before the performance is scheduled to start. Open Tuesday to Saturday and some Sundays with one or two performances per night.

Scullers Jazz Club. In the Doubletree Guest Suites hotel, 400 Soldiers Field Rd. ☎ **617/562-4111** or 617/931-2000 (Ticketmaster). www.scullersjazz.com. Tickets $10–$28.

Overlooking the Charles River, Scullers is a lovely, comfortable room that books top singers and instrumentalists—recent notables include Branford Marsalis, Dave Brubeck, Spyro Gyra, and (quite a coup) Bobby Short. Patrons tend to be more hard-core and quieter than the crowds at the Regattabar, but it really depends on who's performing. There are usually two shows a night Tuesday to Saturday; the box office is open the same days from 11am to 6:30pm. Dinner packages include preferred seating.

ROCK

The Harp. 85 Causeway St. ☎ **617/742-1010.** Cover $5–$7. T: Green or Orange Line to North Station.

Live music on Thursday, Friday, and Saturday nights attracts a young crowd that mills about in long lines along Causeway Street, across from the FleetCenter. Open Monday to Saturday from 11am to 2am, Sunday from noon to midnight.

✪ **Middle East.** 472–480 Mass. Ave., Central Sq., Cambridge. ☎ **617/492-9181.** Cover $3–$16. T: Red Line to Central.

The Middle East books an impressive variety of progressive and alternative rock in two rooms (upstairs and downstairs) every night. Showcasing top local talent as well as bands with international reputations, it's a popular hangout that gets crowded, hot, and *loud.* The bakery next door, under the same management, features acoustic artists most of the time and belly dancers on Wednesday. Most shows are 18-plus (you must be 21 to drink alcohol); some are all ages, but the age of the crowd varies with the performer.

T.T. the Bear's Place. 10 Brookline St., Cambridge. ☎ **617/492-0082,** or 617/492-BEAR (concert line). www.tiac.net/users/ttbears. Cover $3–$15, usually less than $10. T: Red Line to Central.

This no-frills spot admits people 18 and older (you must be 21 to drink alcohol), so the crowd is on the young side, but 30-somethings will feel comfortable, too. Bookings range from cutting-edge alternative rock and roots music to ska and funk shows to up-and-coming pop acts. Monday is Stone Soup Poetry open-mike night. Open Monday 7pm to midnight, Tuesday to Sunday 6pm to 1am.

THE BAR SCENE

The Bay Tower. 60 State St. ☎ **617/723-1666.** www.baytower.com. No cover. T: Green or Orange Line to State or Blue Line to Aquarium.

You'll be mesmerized by the 33rd-floor view from this posh room—the harbor, the airport, and Faneuil Hall Marketplace. There's dancing to live music Monday to Saturday (piano on weeknights, jazz quartet Friday and Saturday). No denim or athletic shoes.

The Big Easy Bar. Boylston Place. ☎ **617/351-7000.** Cover $5. T: Green Line to Boylston.

Buttoned-up Boston meets let-it-all-hangout New Orleans—it could get ugly. Not here, though, in a large, inviting space with a balcony (great for people watching), billiard room, dance floor, and music that runs from soul to alternative rock. No ripped jeans or athletic shoes.

The Black Rose. 160 State St. ☎ **617/742-2286.** www.irishconnection.com. Cover $3–$5. T: Orange or Blue Line to State.

Purists might sneer at the Black Rose's touristy location, but performers don't. Sing along with the authentic entertainment—you might be able to make out the tune on a fiddle over the din—at this jam-packed tavern at the edge of Faneuil Hall Marketplace. Open daily from 11am to 2am.

Boston Beer Works. 61 Brookline Ave. ☎ **617/536-2337.** T: Green Line B, C, or D to Kenmore.

This cavernous, cacophonous microbrewery across the street from Fenway Park has a full food menu and 14 brews on tap, including excellent bitters and ales, seasonal concoctions such as Red Oktoberfest, and especially good cask-conditioned offerings. Try the sweet-potato fries.

✪ **Brew Moon Restaurant & Microbrewery.** 115 Stuart St. ☎ **617/742-BREW.** www.brewmoon.com. T: Green Line to Boylston.

Hand-crafted beer meets tasty edibles at this popular Theater District spot. The Munich Gold won a gold medal at the 1996 Great American Beer Festival; for something lighter, try the Grasshopper IPA or the out-of-this-world house-brewed root beer. There's an equally busy branch in Harvard Square, 50 Church St. (☎ 617/499-BREW). Both have live music at the ✪ **Sunday jazz brunch,** from 11am to 3pm.

✪ **Bristol Lounge.** 200 Boylston St. (in the Four Seasons Hotel). ☎ **617/351-2000.** T: Green Line to Arlington.

An elegant room with soft lounge chairs, a fireplace, and fresh floral arrangements, the Bristol features a fabulous Viennese dessert buffet on weekend evenings. There's live jazz every night. An eclectic menu is available until 11:30pm (12:30am on Friday and Saturday).

Bull & Finch Pub. 84 Beacon St. ☎ **617/227-9605.** www.cheersboston.com. T: Green Line to Arlington.

If you're out to impersonate a native, try not to be shocked when you walk into "the 'Cheers' bar" and realize that it looks nothing like the bar on "Cheers." (The outside does, though.) The Bull & Finch is a neighborhood bar, but today it's far better known for attracting legions of out-of-towners, who find good pub grub, drinks, and plenty of souvenirs. Food is served from 11am to 1:15am.

Casablanca. 40 Brattle St., Cambridge. ☎ **617/876-0999.** T: Red Line to Harvard.

Students and professors jam this legendary Harvard Square watering hole, especially on weekends. You'll find excellent food, an excellent jukebox, and excellent eavesdropping.

Green Street Grill/Charlie's Tap. 280 Green St., Cambridge. ☎ **617/876-1655.** Thurs, Fri, and Sat $4 cover. T: Red Line to Central.

This atmospheric hangout draws a congenial crowd for live blues, rock, and jazz on weekends and, on Tuesdays—we kid you not—magicians. Blues and jazz aficionados will find perhaps the best jukebox on the planet, and there's also excellent Caribbean food.

Hard Rock Cafe. 131 Clarendon St. ☎ **617/424-ROCK.** www.bostondine.com. No cover. T: Orange Line to Back Bay or Green Line to Copley.

This link in the Hard Rock chain is a fun one. The bar is shaped like a guitar, and its stained-glass windows glorify rock stars. Memorabilia of Jimi Hendrix, Elvis Presley, Madonna, local heroes Aerosmith, and others decorate the walls. The restaurant menu favors salads, burgers, and sandwiches (including the legendary "pig sandwich"). There's live acoustic music downstairs on weekends, and T-shirts and other goods for sale.

John Harvard's Brew House. 33 Dunster St., Cambridge. ☎ **617/868-3585.** www.john-harvards.com. No cover. T: Red Line to Harvard.

This subterranean hangout pumps out English-style brews in a clublike setting and prides itself on its food. The regularly changing beer selection might include John Harvard's Pale Ale, Nut Brown Ale, Pilgrim's Porter, and other concoctions.

✪ **Matt Murphy's Pub.** 14 Harvard St., Brookline. ☎ **617/232-0188.** T: Green Line D to Brookline Village.

A long, narrow room that draws a friendly, brogue-intensive crowd, Matt Murphy's has great bartenders, excellent food, live music on weekend nights, and even a traditional pub quiz every other Wednesday. A big plus: no smoking.

Samuel Adams Brew House. In the Lenox Hotel, 710 Boylston St. ☎ **617/536-2739.** T: Green Line to Copley.

This dark, sometimes noisy spot boasts excellent pretzels, friendly service, and the signature local brew, guaranteed to be served fresh. Choose from the dozen beers on tap or order a sampler of four.

Top of the Hub. 800 Boylston St., Prudential Center. ☎ **617/536-1775.** No cover. T: Green Line E to Prudential.

Boasting a 52nd-story panorama of greater Boston, Top of the Hub is especially appealing at sunset. There is music and dancing nightly. Dress is casual but neat.

5

Side Trips from Boston: Lexington & Concord, the North Shore & Plymouth

by Marie Morris

In addition to being, as the saying goes, "the hub of the solar system," Boston is the hub of a network of wonderful day trips and longer excursions. Each is a lively community where you'll find sights and attractions of great beauty and historical significance that offer enough diversions to fill several days.

If you have a few days to spend exploring eastern Massachusetts and history is your main motivation, consider approaching the area in roughly chronological order. Start in Plymouth with the Pilgrims, then move on to Lexington and Concord to learn about the rebellious colonists. Finally, acquaint yourself with the North Shore and Cape Ann and the prosperity of the post-Revolutionary era.

WEST OF BOSTON   If time is short, combine a visit to Cambridge (see chapter 4) with a trip to **Lexington** and **Concord** for a hefty dose of American history. The route Paul Revere took out of Boston on April 18, 1775, is tough to follow—he started by crossing the harbor in a rowboat, for one thing. But his fellow rider William Dawes cut through Cambridge at Harvard Square. Both proceeded to warn the colonists that British troops were on the march, a story you'll soon know well.

MBTA buses serve Lexington from North Cambridge, and the commuter rail runs to Concord from Boston and from Cambridge's Porter Square, north of Harvard Square.

NORTH OF BOSTON   The years immediately following the Revolution brought great prosperity to eastern Massachusetts as the new nation took advantage of the lifting of British trade barriers. The spoils of the China trade adorn mansions and public edifices in the seaside towns and cities from Boston all the way to New Hampshire. Fishing is still an important industry, but today this area caters more to commuters and tourists than to those who make their living from the sea.

The MBTA commuter rail and a network of bus lines run to and around the **North Shore** and **Cape Ann,** but this area is best approached by private auto.

SOUTH OF BOSTON   The communities between Boston and Cape Cod are mostly commuter suburbs. A town that's famous in its own right is **Plymouth**, one of the oldest permanent European settlements in North America. It's a lovely town where you can walk in the footsteps of the Pilgrims—and of the countless out-of-towners who make it a popular destination in the summer and at Thanksgiving.

Farther south, the old whaling port of **New Bedford** and the textile-industry center of **Fall River** make interesting detours.

The commuter rail from Boston runs to Plymouth, and all three cities are accessible by bus.

1 Lexington

The shooting phase of the Revolutionary War started here with the skirmish on the Town Green, which began when British troops clashed with local militia members, who were known as "Minutemen" for their ability to assemble on short notice.

Tensions with the royal government had risen throughout the early 1770s. Soldiers were quartered in colonists' homes, and the "Intolerable Acts" of 1774 imposed new taxes. Mutual distrust ran high—Paul Revere wrote of helping form "a committee for the purpose of watching the movements of the British troops." When the commander in Boston, General Gage, learned that the colonists were accumulating arms and ammunition, he dispatched men to destroy the stockpiles.

Troops marched from Boston to Lexington late on April 18, 1775 (no need to memorize the date; you'll hear it everywhere), preceded by Revere and William Dawes, who sounded the warning. They did their job so well that the alarm came far ahead of the advancing forces.

The Lexington Minutemen, under the command of Capt. John Parker, got the word shortly after midnight, but the redcoats had taken so long to get out of Boston that they were still several hours away. The colonists repaired to their homes and the Buckman Tavern (see below). Five hours later, some 700 British troops under Major Pitcairn arrived.

A tense standoff ensued. Three times Pitcairn ordered them to disperse, but the patriots—fewer than 100, and some accounts say 77—refused. Parker called: "Stand your ground. Don't fire unless fired upon, but if they mean to have a war, let it begin here!" Finally, the captain, perhaps realizing as the sky grew light just how badly out-numbered his men were, gave the order to fall back.

As the Minutemen began to scatter, a shot rang out. One British company charged into the fray, and the colonists attempted to regroup at the same time that Pitcairn tried unsuccessfully to call off his troops. Nobody knows who started the shooting, but when it was over, 8 militia members were dead, including a drummer boy, and 10 wounded.

Today, the country village turned Boston suburb takes great pride in its history. The **Battle Green,** next to a bustling business district, is an open common where you can see the famous Minuteman statue and several other memorials.

Before you set out, you might want to read "Paul Revere's Ride," Henry Wadsworth Longfellow's classic but historically questionable poem about the events of April 18 and 19, 1775.

ESSENTIALS

GETTING THERE   Route 2A approximates Paul Revere's path, but if you attempt to follow it during rush hour, you'll wish you had a horse of your own. Instead, take Route 2 from Cambridge through Belmont, and follow signs for Route 4/225 into the center of Lexington. Or take Route 128 (I-95) to Exit 31, and follow signs. Mass. Ave. (the same street you might have seen in Boston and Cambridge) runs through the center of town. Lexington is 6 miles northwest of Cambridge, 9 miles northwest of downtown Boston, and 6 miles east of Concord.

The **MBTA** (☎ **617/222-3200;** www.mbta.com) runs bus routes no. 62 (Bedford) and 76 (Hanscom) to Lexington from Alewife station, the last stop on the Red Line.

Around Boston

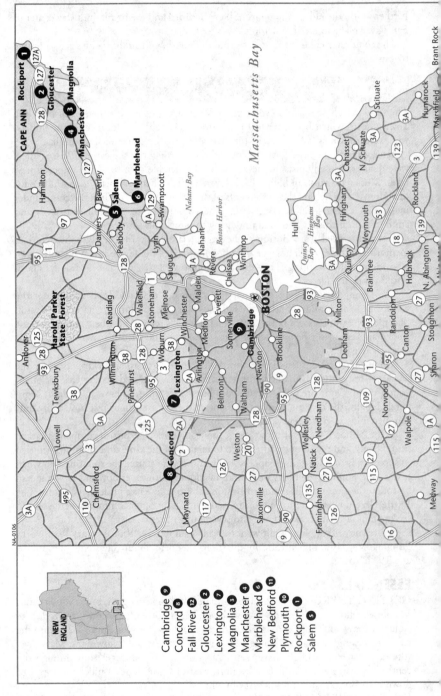

NA-0106

Cambridge **9**
Concord **8**
Fall River **12**
Gloucester **2**
Lexington **7**
Magnolia **3**
Manchester **4**
Marblehead **6**
New Bedford **11**
Plymouth **10**
Rockport **1**
Salem **5**

NEW ENGLAND

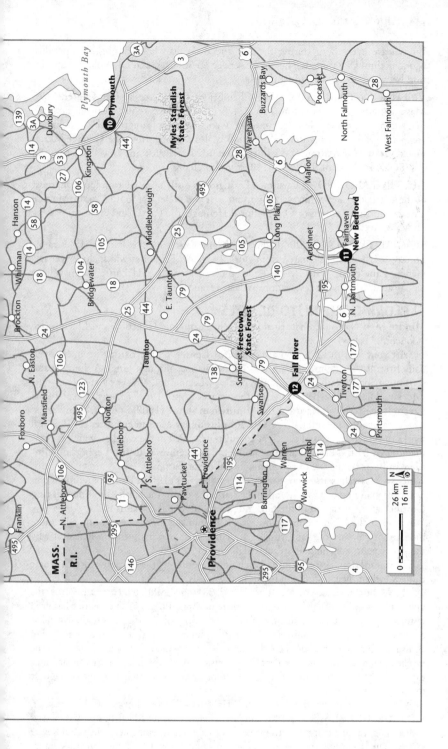

Buses leave every hour during the day and every half hour during rush periods, Monday through Saturday. There is no service on Sundays, and no public transportation between Lexington and Concord.

VISITOR INFORMATION   The Chamber of Commerce **Visitor Center,** 1875 Massachusetts Ave., Lexington, MA 02473 (☎ **781/862-1450**), distributes sketch maps and information. The community Web site (www.lexingtonweb.com) has an area with visitor information. Information is also available from the **Greater Merrimack Valley Convention & Visitors Bureau,** 22 Shattuck St., Lowell, MA 01582 (☎ **800/443-3332** or 978/459-6150; www.lowell.org).

GETTING AROUND   Downtown Lexington is easily negotiable on foot, and most of the attractions are within walking distance. If you prefer not to walk to the Munroe Tavern and the Museum of Our National Heritage, the no. 62 and 76 buses pass by on Mass. Ave.

SPECIAL EVENTS   In 2000, the 225th anniversary of the start of the Revolutionary War will be celebrated from April 14 to 17. Festivities will include reenactments of the battle, Paul Revere's ride, and other events, and Battle Green will be rededicated. Make your reservations well in advance.

EXPLORING THE HISTORIC SITES
Minute Man National Historical Park is in Lexington, Concord, and Lincoln (see "Concord," below).

Start your visit to Lexington at the **Visitor Center,** on the Battle Green. It's open daily from 9am to 5pm (9:30am to 3:30pm October through June). A diorama and accompanying narrative illustrate the Battle of Lexington. When you step back outside, you'll have a new perspective on the events of April 19, 1775, as you explore the Green. Its best-known feature is the **Minuteman statue** (1900) of Capt. John Parker, who commanded the militia. The **Old Revolutionary Monument** dates to 1799 and marks the grave of seven of the eight colonists who died in the conflict, which is commemorated by the **Line of Battle Boulder.** The **Memorial to the Lexington Minutemen** bears the names of the men who fell in the battle.

Across Massachusetts Avenue, near Clarke Street, is the **Old Belfry,** a reproduction of the freestanding bell that sounded the alarm the day of the battle. **Ye Olde Burying Ground,** at the west end of the Green, dates to 1690 and contains Parker's grave.

A stop at the Visitor Center and a walk around the monuments won't take more than about half an hour, and you'll get a good sense of what went on here and why the participants are still held in such high esteem.

Three important destinations in Lexington were among the country's first **"historic houses"** when their restoration began in the 1920s.

The ✪ **Buckman Tavern,** 1 Bedford St. (☎ 781/862-5598), built around 1710, is the only building still on the Green that was there on April 19, 1775. The interior has been restored to its appearance on that day. You'll see the original bar and front door, which has a hole in it from a British musket ball. Here the Minutemen gathered to wait for word of British troop movements, and here they brought their wounded after the conflict. In the excellent tour, costumed guides describe the history of the building and its inhabitants, explain the battle, and discuss colonial life. If time is short and you have to pick one house to visit, this is the one.

Within easy walking distance, is the **Hancock–Clarke House,** 36 Hancock St. (☎ 781/861-0928). Samuel Adams and John Hancock, who had left Boston several days earlier upon learning that the British were after them, were sleeping here when Paul Revere arrived. They were evacuated to nearby Woburn. Built around 1698 by Hancock's grandfather and lavishly improved by his uncle, Thomas Hancock, the house was the Rev. Jonas

Lexington

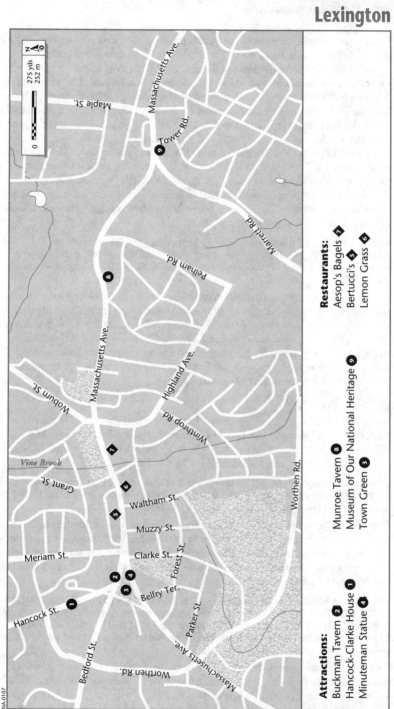

Attractions:
Buckman Tavern **2**
Hancock-Clarke House **1**
Minuteman Statue **4**
Munroe Tavern **8**
Museum of Our National Heritage **9**
Town Green **3**

Restaurants:
Aesop's Bagels **7**
Bertucci's **5**
Lemon Grass **6**

NA-0107

135

Clarke's parsonage at the time of the Revolution. The 1698 structure, restored and furnished in colonial style, contains the Historical Society's museum of the Revolution.

The British took over the **Munroe Tavern,** 1332 Mass. Ave. (about 1 mile from the Green), to use as their headquarters and, after the battle, field hospital. The taproom ceiling still has a bullet hole made by a careless soldier. The building (1690) is packed with fascinating artifacts and furniture carefully preserved by the Munroe family, including the table and chair where President Washington dined in 1789. The grounds are beautifully planted and maintained.

All three houses are open for **guided tours** Monday to Saturday from 10am to 5pm and Sunday from 1 to 5pm, April through October. Admission for adults is $4 per house, $10 for all three; for children 6 to 16, $2 per house, $4 for all three. The last tour starts at 4:30pm; tours take 30 to 45 minutes. Call for information about group tours, which are offered by appointment. The Munroe Tavern houses the **Lexington Historical Society** (☎ **781/862-1703**), which operates all three.

Museum of Our National Heritage. 33 Marrett Rd., Rte. 2A (at Mass. Ave.). ☎ **781/ 861-6559** or 781/861-9638. www.mnh.org. Free admission. Mon–Sat 10am–5pm, Sun noon–5pm. Closed Jan 1, Thanksgiving, Dec 25. T: No. 62 or 76 bus from downtown Lexington to Rte. 2A.

This museum mounts fascinating, accessible exhibits that explore history through popular culture. The installations in the six exhibition spaces change regularly; you can start with another dose of the Revolution, the permanent exhibit *Lexington Alarm'd.* Other topics have ranged from George Washington to Frank Lloyd Wright, American circus posters to quilting. It's great fun, especially for children tired of nonstop colonial lore. Lectures, concerts, and family programs are also offered. The museum is sponsored by the Scottish Rite of Freemasonry.

WHERE TO STAY

Bedford is 15 minutes from downtown Lexington along Route 4/225 on the other side of I-95. The **Ramada Inn Bedford Boston,** 340 Great Rd., Bedford, MA 01730 (☎ **800/2-RAMADA** or 781/275-6700), is a pleasant motor inn with an indoor pool. The high-season rate for a double is about $110.

Sheraton Lexington Inn. 727 Marrett Rd. (Exit 30B off I-95), Lexington, MA 02173. ☎ **800/325-3535** or 781/862-8700. Fax 781/863-0404. 119 units. A/C TV TEL. $129–$234 double; $199–$250 suite. Extra person $10. AE, DC, DISC, MC, V.

Overlooking the interstate, but sheltered from the noise by a stand of trees, this two-story hotel is 5 minutes from downtown by car. It offers the usual chain amenities—reliable, if generic. Rooms have coffeemakers and hair dryers and are large enough to hold a wing chair or couch. Some have balconies. On the premises are an outdoor pool (open seasonally) and an exercise room.

Renaissance Bedford Hotel. 44 Middlesex Tpk., Bedford, MA 01730. ☎ **800/HOTELS-1** or 781/275-5500. Fax 781/275-3042. www.renaissancehotels.com/BOSSB. 284 units. A/C MINIBAR TV TEL. Sun–Thurs $170–$200 double; Fri–Sat $125–$155 double. Extra person $15. Children under 19 stay free in parents' room. Weekend packages and senior discount available. AE, CB, DC, DISC, JCB, MC, V.

The sights in Lexington and Concord are convenient to this three-story hotel, which neatly makes the transition from a primarily business destination during the week to a family resort on weekends. There's also plenty to do without leaving the property. The country lodge-style building on wooded grounds has a business center, recently renovated meeting space, a fitness center, an indoor pool, a whirlpool, a sauna, and indoor and outdoor tennis courts. A restaurant and lounge are in the hotel; there is also 24-hour room service. A complimentary shuttle transports guests to destinations within 5 miles, including the Burlington Mall. Larger rooms have king-size beds; a few units have twin beds; all have hair dryers. Several suites have sofas and conference tables. A newspaper and coffee arrive at your room with your wake-up call. There are 11 rooms for people with disabilities.

WHERE TO DINE

Bertucci's, 1777 Mass. Ave. (☎ **781/860-9000**), is a branch of the family-friendly pizzeria chain. It also serves a great selection of salads and pasta dishes. **Aesop's Bagels,** 1666 Mass. Ave. (☎ **781/674-2990**), is a good place to pick up a light meal.

Lemon Grass. 1710 Mass. Ave. ☎ **781/862-3530.** Main courses $5.50–$8.25 at lunch, $7–$15.50 at dinner. AE, DISC, MC, V. Mon–Fri 11:30am–3pm; Mon–Thurs 5–9:30pm, Fri–Sat 5–10pm, Sun 4–9pm. THAI.

A welcome break: The space is a former coffee shop disguised with bamboo decorations and the aromas of Asian spices. You might start with satay (skewers of meat served with a delectable peanut sauce) or chicken coconut soup, with a kick of pepper and plenty of poultry. Entrees include a tasty rendition of traditional pad Thai and excellent curry dishes. The accommodating staff will adjust the heat and spice to suit your taste.

2 Concord

✪ **Concord** (say "conquered") revels in its legacy as a center of groundbreaking thought and its role in the country's political and intellectual history. After just a little time in this charming town, you may find yourself adopting the local attitude toward two of its most famous former residents: Ralph Waldo Emerson, who comes across as a well-respected uncle figure, and Henry David Thoreau, everyone's favorite eccentric cousin.

Long before they wandered the countryside, the first official battle of the Revolutionary War took place at the North Bridge, now part of Minute Man National Historical Park. By the middle of the 19th century, Concord was the center of the Transcendentalist movement. Homes of Emerson, Thoreau, Nathaniel Hawthorne, and Louisa May Alcott are open to visitors, as is the authors' final resting place, Sleepy Hollow Cemetery. Consider starting your visit at the Concord Museum, which offers an excellent overview.

ESSENTIALS

GETTING THERE   From Lexington, take Route 2A west from Mass. Ave. (Route 4/225) at the Museum of Our National Heritage; follow the BATTLE ROAD signs. From Boston and Cambridge, take Route 2 into Lincoln and stay in the right lane. Where the main road makes a sharp left, go straight onto Cambridge Turnpike, and follow signs to HISTORIC CONCORD. Concord is 18 miles northwest of Boston, 15 miles northwest of Cambridge, and 6 miles west of Lexington.

The MBTA **commuter rail** (☎ 617/222-3200; www.mbta.com) takes about 45 minutes from North Station in Boston, with a stop at Porter Square in Cambridge. There is no bus service from Boston to Concord, and no public transportation between Lexington and Concord. The station is about three-quarters of a mile over flat terrain from the town center.

VISITOR INFORMATION   The **Chamber of Commerce,** 2 Lexington Rd., Concord, MA 01742 (☎ **978/369-3120**), maintains an information booth on Heywood Street, 1 block southeast of Monument Square; open weekends in April and daily May through October, 9:30am to 4:30pm. One-hour tours are available starting in May on Saturday, Sunday, and Monday holidays, or on weekdays by appointment. Group tours are available by appointment. Concord's community Web site (www.concordma.com) has an area for visitors. Information is available from the **Greater Merrimack Valley Convention & Visitors Bureau,** 22 Shattuck St., Lowell, MA 01582 (☎ **800/443-3332** or 978/459-6150; www.lowell.org).

GETTING AROUND   Major attractions are within walking distance of downtown. If you're trying to stop everywhere in a day or are visiting Walden Pond or Great Meadows, you'll need a car.

SEEING THE SIGHTS

The **Concord Museum** sells a brochure ($1) that describes an excellent driving-walking tour of the town.

The **Wright Tavern** (1747), 2 Lexington Rd., served as headquarters twice on April 19, 1775—for the Minutemen in the morning and the British in the afternoon. Today, it plays the same role for the Chamber of Commerce and several businesses and is open to the public during business hours.

Also overlooking the square is the 1716 **Colonial Inn** (see "Where to Stay," below). **Longfellow's Wayside Inn,** 30 to 40 minutes away in Sudbury, makes an entertaining side trip (see "A Historic Inn Nearby," below).

LITERARY LANDMARKS & HISTORIC ATTRACTIONS

✪ **Concord Museum.** Lexington Rd. and Cambridge Tpk. ☎ **978/369-9763.** www.concordmuseum.org. Admission $6 adults, $5 seniors, $4 students, $3 children under 16, $12 families. Apr–Dec Mon–Sat 9am–5pm, Sun noon–5pm. Jan–Mar Mon–Sat 11am–4pm, Sun 1–4pm. Parking on road allowed. Follow Lexington Rd. from Concord Center; bear right at museum onto Cambridge Tpk.; entrance on left.

A visit to this superb museum is a great way to start your visit to the town. In the History Galleries, you'll explore the question "Why Concord?" Artifacts, murals, films, maps, documents, and other presentations illustrate the town's role as a Native American settlement, Revolutionary War battleground, 19th-century intellectual center, and focal point of the 20th-century historic preservation movement. Displays include archaeological artifacts, silver from colonial churches, a fascinating collection of embroidery samplers, and rooms furnished with period furniture. Explanatory text places the exhibits in context. You'll see one of the lanterns that signaled Paul Revere from the Old North Church, the contents of Ralph Waldo Emerson's study arranged as it was at his death in 1882, and a large collection of Henry David Thoreau's belongings. The New Wing holds changing exhibits.

On the front lawn, what appears to be a shed is a replica of the cabin Thoreau lived in at Walden Pond from 1845 to 1847. The furnishings are in the museum.

The Old Manse. 269 Monument St. (at North Bridge). ☎ **978/369-3909.** Guided tour $5 adults, $4 students and seniors, $3.50 children 6–12, $13 families (3–5 people). Mid-Apr to Oct Mon–Sat 10am–5pm, Sun and holidays noon–5pm. Closed Nov to mid-Apr. From Concord Center, follow Monument St. to North Bridge parking lot (on right); Old Manse is on left.

The Rev. William Emerson built the Old Manse in 1770 and watched the Battle of Concord from the yard. He died during the Revolutionary War, and the house was occupied for almost 170 years by his widow, her second husband, their descendants, and two famous friends: Nathaniel Hawthorne and Sophia Peabody moved in after their marriage in 1842 and stayed for 3 years. As a wedding present, Henry David Thoreau sowed a vegetable garden for them (in 1997 cultivation resumed after a 49-year break). This is also where William's grandson Ralph Waldo Emerson wrote the essay "Nature." Today, you'll see mementos and memorabilia of the Emerson and Ripley families and of the Hawthornes, who scratched notes on two windows with Sophia's diamond ring.

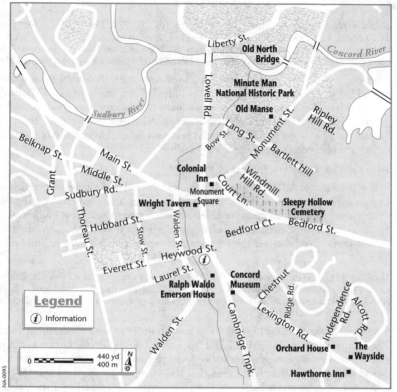

Orchard House. 399 Lexington Rd. ☎ **978/369-4118.** www.louisamayalcott.org. Guided tours $5.50 adults, $4.50 seniors and students, $3.50 children 6–17, $16 families (up to 2 adults and 4 children). Apr–Oct Mon–Sat 10am–4:30pm, Sun 1–4:30pm. Nov–Mar Mon–Fri 11am–3pm, Sat 10am–4:30pm, Sun 1–4:30pm. Closed Jan 1–15, Easter, Thanksgiving, Dec 25. Follow Lexington Rd. from Concord Center; bear left at Concord Museum; house is on the left. Overflow parking lot across street.

With the release of the 1994 movie *Little Women* (filmed elsewhere), Louisa May Alcott's best-known and most popular work moved into the modern mainstream. The 1868 book was written and set at Orchard House, though most of the actual events took place earlier—Louisa was in her mid-30s when *Little Women* was published. Fans won't want to miss the excellent tour, copiously illustrated with heirlooms. (Serious buffs can call ahead for information on holiday programs and other special events, some of which require reservations.)

Louisa's father, Amos Bronson Alcott, was a writer, educator, philosopher, and leader in the Transcendentalist movement. The family lived here from 1858 to 1877, socializing in the same circles as Emerson, Thoreau, and Hawthorne. The Alcotts were known for artistic and cultural achievements. The Alcott daughters were models for the characters in *Little Women:* Anna ("Meg"), the eldest, was an amateur actress, and May ("Amy") a talented artist. Elizabeth ("Beth"), a gifted musician, died before the family moved to this house. Their mother, the social activist Abigail May Alcott, frequently assumed the role of family breadwinner—Bronson, as Louisa wrote in her journal, had "no gift for money making."

Ralph Waldo Emerson House. 28 Cambridge Tpk. ☎ **978/369-2236.** Guided tours $4.50 adults, $3 seniors and children 7–17. Call to arrange group tours (10 people or more). Mid-Apr to Oct Thurs–Sat 10am–4:30pm, Sun 2–4:30pm. Closed Nov to mid-Apr. Follow Cambridge Tpk. out of Concord Center; just before Concord Museum, house is on the right.

Emerson, philosopher, essayist, and poet, lived here from 1835 until his death in 1882. He had just married his second wife, Lydia Jackson, whom he called "Lydian"; she called him "Mr. Emerson," as the staff still does. The tour gives a good look at his personal side and at the fashionably ornate interior decoration of the time. You'll see original furnishings and some of Emerson's personal effects. (The contents of his study at the time of his death are in the Concord Museum.)

Sleepy Hollow Cemetery. Entrance on Rte. 62 W.

Follow the signs for AUTHOR'S RIDGE and climb the hill to the graves of the Alcotts, Emerson, Hawthorne, and Thoreau. Emerson's grave, fittingly, bears no religious symbols, just an uncarved quartz boulder. Thoreau's grave is nearby; at his funeral in 1862, his old friend Emerson concluded his eulogy with these words: ". . . wherever there is knowledge, wherever there is virtue, wherever there is beauty, he will find a home."

The Wayside. 455 Lexington Rd. ☎ **978/369-6975.** www.nps.gov/mima/wayside. Guided tours $4 adults, free for children under 17. May–Oct Thurs–Tues 10am–4:30pm. Closed Nov–Apr. Follow Lexington Rd. from Concord Center past Concord Museum and Orchard House; Wayside is on the left.

The Wayside was Nathaniel Hawthorne's home from 1852 until his death, in 1864. The Alcotts lived here (the girls called it "the yellow house"), as did Harriett Lothrop, who wrote the *Five Little Peppers* books under the pen name Margaret Sidney and owned most of the current furnishings. The interesting ranger tour (the house is part of Minute Man National Historical Park) illuminates the occupants' lives and the house's crazy-quilt architecture.

MINUTE MAN NATIONAL HISTORICAL PARK

This 900-acre park preserves the scene of the first Revolutionary War battle on April 19, 1775. A visit can take as little as half an hour for a jaunt to the ✪ **North Bridge,** to half a day or more for stops at both visitor centers and perhaps a ranger-led program.

From Concord Center, follow Monument Street until you see the parking lot on the right. Walk a short distance to the bridge (a reproduction), stopping along the unpaved path to read the narratives and hear the audio presentations.

You can also start at the **North Bridge Visitor Center,** 174 Liberty St., off Monument Street (☎ **978/369-6993;** www.nps.gov/mima), that overlooks the Concord River and the bridge. A diorama and video program illustrate the Battle of Concord, and exhibits include uniforms, weapons, and tools of colonial and British soldiers. Park rangers on duty lead programs and answer questions. Outside, picnicking is allowed, and the scenery (especially the fall foliage) is lovely. The bridge isn't far; you'll want to see the exhibits there, too. The center is open daily from 9am to 5:30pm (until 4pm in winter), and closed January 1 and December 25.

Encouraged by their victory in Lexington, the British moved on to Concord in search of stockpiled arms, which the militiamen had already moved. Warned of the troops' advance, the colonists were preparing for a confrontation. The Minutemen crossed the North Bridge, evading the "regulars" standing guard, and awaited reinforcements on a nearby hilltop. In Concord the British were searching homes and burning any guns they found. The Minutemen saw the smoke and, mistakenly thinking the British were burning the town, advanced against the men standing guard at the bridge. The redcoats opened fire and the colonists retaliated. At the North Bridge, the Minutemen fired what Ralph Waldo Emerson called "the shot heard around the world."

On one side of the bridge you'll find a plaque commemorating the British soldiers who died in the Revolutionary War; on the other is Daniel Chester French's **Minute Man** statue, engraved with a stanza of the poem Emerson wrote for the dedication ceremony in 1876.

The park is open daily, year-round. At the Lexington end of the park, the **Minute Man Visitor Center,** off Route 2A, one-half mile west of I-95 (☎ **781/862-7753;** www.nps.gov/mima) is open daily from 9am to 5pm (until 4pm in winter), and closed January 1 and December 25.

The park includes the first 4 miles of the **Battle Road,** the route the defeated British troops took as they left Concord on the afternoon of April 19, 1775. They were harassed by colonial fire almost all the way back to Boston. Although this area is pretty built up, you'll still get a sense of how demoralizing the retreat must have been. At the visitor center, you'll see informational displays, a new multimedia program about the Revolution, and a new 40-foot mural illustrating the battle. On summer weekends, rangers lead tours of the park—call ahead for times. The new 5.5-mile **Battle Road Interpretive Trail** permits pedestrian, wheelchair, and bicycle traffic. Exhibit panels and granite markers bear information about the area's military, social, and natural history and point the way along the trail.

Also on the park grounds, on Old Bedford Road, is the **Hartwell Tavern.** Costumed interpreters demonstrate daily life on a farm and tavern in colonial days. It's not Disney, but it is interesting. It's open daily June through August and on weekends in April, May, September, and October, from 9:30am to 5pm. Admission is free.

NEARBY SIGHTS

DeCordova Museum and Sculpture Park. 51 Sandy Pond Rd., Lincoln. ☎ **781/259-8355.** www.decordova.org. Museum $6 adults, $4 seniors, students, and children 6–12. Tues–Sun and Mon holidays 11am–5pm. Sculpture park admission free. Daily 8am–10pm. Closed Jan 1, July 4, Thanksgiving, Dec 25. From Rte. 2 E., take Rte. 126 to Baker Bridge Rd. (1st left after Walden Pond). When it ends, go right onto Sandy Pond Rd.; museum is on the left. From Rte. 2 W., take I-95 to Exit 28B, follow Trapelo Rd. 2.5 miles to Sandy Pond Rd., then follow signs.

Indoors and out, the DeCordova shows the work of American contemporary and modern artists, with an emphasis on living New England residents. The main building, on a leafy hilltop, overlooks a pond and the area's only outdoor public sculpture park. Recent renovations have added several galleries, room for interactive exhibits, a video space, a roof garden, and a sculpture terrace, which displays the work of one sculptor per year. Picnicking is allowed in the sculpture park; bring lunch, or buy it at the cafe (open 11am to 4pm, Wednesday through Sunday).

Gropius House. 68 Baker Bridge Rd., Lincoln. ☎ **781/259-8843** or 617/227-3957, ext. 300. www.spnea.org. Guided tours $5. Tours on the hour June–Oct 15 Wed–Sun 11am–4pm; Oct 16–May Sat–Sun 11am–4pm. Take Rte. 2 to Rte. 126 south to left on Baker Bridge Rd.; house is on the right. From I-95 Exit 28B, follow Trapelo Rd. to Sandy Pond Rd., go left onto Baker Bridge Rd.; house is on the left.

Architect Walter Gropius (1883–1969), founder of the Bauhaus, built this home for his family in the prosperous suburb of Lincoln in 1937. Having accepted an appointment to teach at the Harvard Graduate School of Design, he worked with Marcel Breuer to design the hilltop house, now maintained by the Society for the Preservation of New England Antiquities. They used traditional materials such as clapboard, brick, and fieldstone, with components then seldom used in domestic architecture, including glass blocks and welded steel. Breuer designed many of the furnishings, which were made for the family at the Bauhaus. Decorated as it was in the last decade of Gropius's life, the house affords a revealing look at his life, career, and philosophy. Call for information on special tours and workshops.

WILDERNESS RETREATS

The titles of Henry David Thoreau's first two published works can serve as starting points: *A Week on the Concord and Merrimack Rivers* (1849) and *Walden* (1854).

To see the area from water level, there's no need to take a week; 2 hours or so should suffice. Rent a canoe at the **South Bridge Boathouse,** 496 Main St. (☎ **978/ 369-9438**; www.sbridge.qpg.com), west of the center of town, and paddle to the Old North Bridge and back. Rates are about $10 per hour on weekends, less on weekdays.

At the ✪ **Walden Pond State Reservation,** Route 126 (☎ **978/369-3254;** www.state. ma.us/dem/parks/wldn.htm), a pile of stones marks the site of the cabin where Thoreau lived from 1845 to 1847. Today, the picturesque reservation is an extremely popular destination for hiking (a path circles the pond), swimming, and fishing. Call for the schedule of interpretive programs. Take Walden Street (Route 126) south, away from Concord Center, cross Route 2, and follow signs to the parking lot. From Memorial Day through Labor Day, a daily parking fee is charged and the lot still fills early every day—call before setting out to make sure there's room.

Another Thoreau haunt, an especially popular destination for birders, is **Great Meadows National Wildlife Refuge** (☎ **978/443-4661;** www.fws.gov/r5fws/ma/grm. htm). The Concord portion of the 3,400-acre refuge includes 2½ miles of walking trails around man-made ponds that attract abundant wildlife. More than 200 species of native and migratory birds have been recorded. The refuge is open daily, sunrise to sunset, and admission is free. Don't forget your camera and sunscreen. Follow Route 62 (Bedford Street) east out of Concord Center for 1.3 miles, then turn left onto Monsen Road.

WHERE TO STAY

About 2 miles from the center of town, the **Best Western at Historic Concord,** 740 Elm St., Concord, MA 01742 (☎ **800/528-1234** or 978/369-6100), is just off Route 2. It's a two-story motel with a fitness room and a seasonal outdoor pool. The high-season rate for a double is about $110.

Colonial Inn. 48 Monument Sq., Concord, MA 01742. ☎ **800/370-9200** or 978/ 369-9200. Fax 978/369-2170. www.concordscolonialinn.com. 45 units (some with shower only). A/C TV TEL. Apr–Oct $169–$195 main inn, $125–$189 Prescott wing, $230–$295 cottage. Nov–Mar $139–$145 main inn, $125–$145 Prescott wing, $200–$235 cottage. AE, CB, DC, DISC, MC, V.

The main building of the Colonial Inn has overlooked Monument Square since 1716. Additions have left the inn large enough to offer modern conveniences and small enough to feel friendly. The 12 original guest rooms—one is supposedly haunted— are in great demand, so reserve early if you want to stay in the main inn. Rooms in the three-story Prescott wing are a bit larger and have country-style decor. The public areas, including a sitting room and front porch, are decorated in colonial style. Dry-cleaning and laundry service are available, as are conference rooms. The inn has two lounges that serve drinks and bar food, and a lovely restaurant that offers salads, sandwiches, and pasta at lunch and traditional American fare at dinner. Afternoon tea is served Wednesday through Sunday; reservations (☎ **978/369-2373**) are required.

✪ **Hawthorne Inn.** 462 Lexington Rd., Concord, MA 01742. ☎ **978/369-5610.** Fax 978/287-4949. www.concordmass.com. 7 units (some with shower only). A/C TV. $150–$215 double. Extra person $15. Rates include continental breakfast. AE, DISC, MC, V. From Concord Center, take Lexington Rd. ¾ miles east; inn is on right.

This is the quintessential country inn, built around 1870, a tree-shaded property across the street from Nathaniel Hawthorne's home, the Wayside. Antiques and hand-made quilts decorate the rooms, and original art is on display. Outside, there's a small pond in the peaceful garden. Gregory Burch and Marilyn Mudry, who have operated the inn for more than 20 years, will acquaint interested guests with the philosophical, spiritual, military, and literary aspects of Concord's history.

A HISTORIC INN NEARBY

✪ Longfellow's Wayside Inn. Wayside Inn Rd., Sudbury, MA 01776. ☎ **800/339-1776** or 978/443-1776. Fax 978/443-8041. www.wayside.org. 10 units (some with shower only). A/C TEL. Summer $110–$130 double; off-season $80–$110 double. Extra person $15. Rates include full breakfast. AE, CB, DC, DISC, MC, V. Closed July 4, Dec 25. From Main St. in Concord, follow Sudbury Rd. to Rte. 20 west; 11 miles after passing I-95, bear right onto Wayside Inn Rd. The inn is on the right.

Worth a visit even if you're not spending the night or dining, this local institution dates to 1716 and got its name in 1863, when Henry Wadsworth Longfellow's *Tales of a Wayside Inn* was published. Henry Ford bought the property in 1923, and it has evolved into a private, nonprofit educational and charitable trust. Today, it claims to be the country's oldest operating inn. Ask at the information desk for a pamphlet that describes the self-guided tour of the public rooms and historical artifacts. All 10 guest rooms are attractively decorated and furnished with antiques, but only two (the most popular, of course) are in the original building. Make your reservations as early as possible, especially for those rooms.

In addition to being a popular wedding and honeymoon destination, the inn is the centerpiece of what amounts to a tiny theme park. On the 106 acres that surround it are a restored barn, the Redstone School of "Mary Had a Little Lamb" fame (built in Sterling, Massachusetts, in 1798 and moved to Sudbury in 1926), a wedding chapel, and a working grist mill. The mill, a reproduction built by Ford in 1929, stone-grinds the wheat flour and cornmeal used in the inn's baked goods (they're also for sale at the gift shop). Old grindstones dot the lawn, a pleasant spot for sunbathing.

Dining: In the inn's rambling dining rooms, costumed staff members dish up generous portions of traditional New England fare. It often incorporates produce grown on the inn's property. The menu changes daily; favorite choices include prime rib, lobster casserole, and, for dessert, strawberry shortcake. You'll see lots of families—this seems to be *the* place for grandparents' birthdays. Food is served Monday through Saturday from 11:30am to 3pm and 5 to 9pm, and Sunday from noon to 8pm (dinner menu only). Main courses at lunch are $8 to $14.50, at dinner $15 to $27. Reservations are recommended, especially on weekends.

WHERE TO DINE

For basic to lavish picnic provisions, stop in downtown Concord at the **Cheese Shop,** 25–31 Walden St. (☎ **978/369-5778**), before setting out. See also the Colonial Inn and Longfellow's Wayside Inn, above.

✪ Guida's Coast Cuisine. 84 Thoreau St. (Rte. 126), at Concord Depot. ☎ **978/371-1333.** Reservations recommended. Main courses $7–$14 at lunch, $16–$25 at dinner. AE, DC, DISC, MC, V. Daily 11:30am–2:30pm; Sun–Thurs 5:30–9:30pm, Fri–Sat 5:30–10pm. PORTUGUESE/SEAFOOD.

Concord isn't exactly on a coast, but don't let that keep you away from this excellent restaurant. Guida Ponte, a native of the Azores and a veteran of Legal Sea Foods, works wonders with all manner of fish and shellfish. Her clam chowder is world-class—maybe even better than the version at Legal's, and that's exalted company. A special of mussels one day recently was a huge portion swimming in flavorful broth meant to be sopped up with fluffy (another neat trick) gnocchi. The home-style Portuguese fish cakes, served with greens, potatoes, and roasted vegetables, are less sophisticated and equally delectable. We couldn't believe the desserts could be as good as the food, but they are—if flourless chocolate cake is available, don't think twice.

3 Marblehead

Scenery, history, architecture, and shopping combine to make ✪ **Marblehead** a won-derful place to spend a few hours or a few days. The narrow streets of the historic district, known as "Old Town," lead down to the magnificent harbor that helps make this the self-proclaimed "Yachting Capital of America." The homes along the way have plaques bearing the dates of construction as well as the names of the builders and original occupants—a history lesson without any studying.

Many of the houses have stood since before the Revolutionary War, when Marblehead was a center of merchant shipping. Two historic homes are open for tours, and you can shop for antiques, jewelry, clothing, and boating paraphernalia, just for starters.

ESSENTIALS

GETTING THERE   From Boston, take Route 1A north until you see signs in Lynn for Swampscott and Marblehead. Take Lynn Shore Drive to Route 129, and follow it into Marblehead. Or take I-93 or Route 1 to Route 128, then Route 114 through Salem into Marblehead. It's 15 miles northeast of Boston, 4 miles southeast of Salem.

MBTA (☎ **617/222-3200;** www.mbta.com) bus route no. 441/442 runs from Haymarket (Orange or Green Line) in Boston to downtown Marblehead. During rush periods on weekdays, the no. 448/449 connects Marblehead to Downtown Crossing. The trip takes about an hour.

VISITOR INFORMATION   The **Marblehead Chamber of Commerce,** 62 Pleasant St., P.O. Box 76, Marblehead, MA 01945 (☎ **781/631-2868;** www.marble-headchamber.org), is open weekdays from 9am to 3pm. It operates an **information booth** (daily in season, 10am to 5:30pm) on Pleasant Street near Spring Street. It also publishes a visitor's guide; pamphlets that list dining, shopping, and accommodations options and marine services; and a map of the historic district with two well-plotted walking tours. Marblehead has a community Web site (www.marblehead.com).

GETTING AROUND   Wear your good walking shoes—the car or bus can get you to Marblehead, but it can't negotiate many of the narrow streets of Old Town. The downtown area is fairly compact and moderately hilly.

SPECIAL EVENTS   There's sailboat racing all summer, highlighted at the end of July by Marblehead Race Week (which draws competitors from across the country), and a Christmas celebration in early December.

EXPLORING THE TOWN

A stroll through the winding streets of Old Town invariably leads to shopping, snacking, or gazing at something picturesque, be it the harbor or a beautiful home. If you prefer more structure, follow the Chamber of Commerce's 1- or 2-mile walking tour. Even if you don't, pass by the **Lafayette House,** a private home at the corner of Hooper and Union streets. Legend has it that one corner of the first floor was chopped off in 1824 to allow Lafayette's carriage to negotiate the corner. In Market Square on Washington Street, near the corner of State Street, is the **Old Town House,** a public meeting and gathering place since 1727.

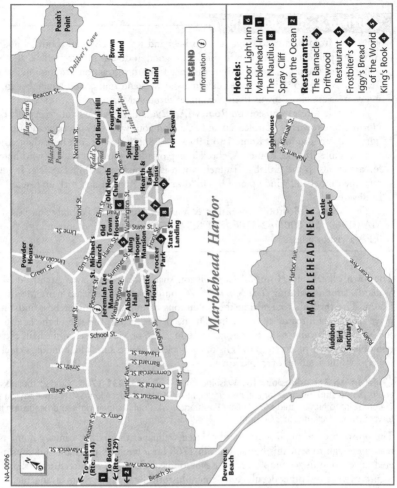

Hotels:
- Harbor Light Inn 6
- Marblehead Inn 1
- The Nautilus 8
- Spray Cliff on the Ocean 2

Restaurants:
- The Barnacle 9
- Driftwood 3
- Frostbiter's 7
- Iggy's Bread of the World 5
- King's Rook 4

LEGEND
Information (i)

Be sure to spend some time in **Crocker Park,** on the harbor off Front Street. Especially in the warmer months, when boats jam the water nearly as far as the eye can see, the view is breathtaking. There are benches and a swing, and picnicking is allowed. You may not want to leave, but snap out of it—the view from **Fort Sewall,** at the other end of Front Street, is just as mesmerizing. The ruins of the fort, built in the 17th century and rebuilt late in the 18th, are another excellent picnic spot.

By car or bicycle, the swanky residential community of **Marblehead Neck** is worth a look. Follow Ocean Avenue across the causeway and visit the **Audubon Bird Sanctuary** (look for the tiny sign at the corner of Risley Avenue) or continue to **Castle Rock** for another eyeful of scenery. At the end of "the Neck," at Harbor and Ocean avenues, is **Chandler Hovey Park,** which has a (closed) lighthouse and a panoramic view.

Abbot Hall. Washington Sq. ☎ **781/631-0528.** Free admission. Year-round Mon–Tues, Thurs 8am–5pm, Wed 7:30am–7:30pm, Fri 8am–1pm; May–Oct Fri 8am–5pm, Sat 9am–6pm, Sun 11am–6pm. From the historic district, follow Washington St. up the hill.

North of Boston: Road Tips

The drive from Boston to Cape Ann on I-93 and Route 128 takes about an hour. Although public transportation in this area is good, it doesn't go everywhere, and in many towns the train station is some distance from the attractions, so driving is the best option. Try to visit on a weekday to avoid weekend traffic, and remember that many areas are ghost towns from November through March.

A more leisurely excursion on Routes 1A, 129, and 114 allows you to explore the North Shore towns of Marblehead and Salem on your way to Gloucester and Rockport. You can also follow Route 1 to I-95 and 128, but during rush hour the traffic is unbearable. To take Route 1A, check a map or ask at the front desk of your hotel for directions to the Callahan Tunnel, which is at the heart of the Big Dig. If you miss the tunnel and wind up on I-93, follow signs to Route 1 and pick up Route 1A in Revere.

The **North of Boston Convention & Visitors Bureau,** 17 Peabody Sq., Peabody, MA 01960 (☎ **800/742-5306** or 978/977-7760; www.northofboston.org), publishes a visitor guide.

The town offices and Historical Commission share Abbot Hall with Archibald M. Willard's famous painting *The Spirit of '76,* on display in the Selectmen's Meeting Room. The thrill of recognizing the ubiquitous drummer, drummer boy, and fife player is the main reason to stop here. The deed that records the sale of the land by the Native Americans to the Europeans in 1684 is also on view. Cases in the halls contain objects and artifacts from the Historical Society's collections. The building's clock tower is visible from all over Old Town.

✪ **Jeremiah Lee Mansion.** 161 Washington St. ☎ **781/631-1768.** Guided tours $4 adults, $3.50 students, free for children under 11. Mid-May to Oct Mon–Sat 10am–4pm, Sun 1–4pm. Closed Nov to mid-May. Follow Washington St. until it curves right and heads uphill toward Abbot Hall; house is on right.

The prospect of seeing original hand-painted wallpaper in an 18th-century home is reason enough to visit this house, built in 1768 for a wealthy merchant and considered an outstanding example of pre-Revolutionary Georgian architecture. Original rococo carving and other details complement historically accurate room arrangements, and ongoing restoration and interpretation by the Marblehead Historical Society place the 18th- and 19th-century furnishings and artifacts in context. The friendly guides welcome questions and are well versed in the history of the home. The lawn and gardens are open to the public.

The Historical Society's headquarters, across the street at 170 Washington St., house the **J. O. J. Frost Folk Art Gallery** and a changing exhibition gallery. Frost, a noted primitivist painter, was a Marblehead native. The building is open 10am to 4pm, weekdays year-round, and on weekends mid-May through October. Admission is $2 ($1 with admission to the mansion). The society occasionally offers candlelight tours of the house and sponsors walking tours of Marblehead on Thursdays in July, Sundays in August, and Saturdays in September. Call ahead to see if your schedules match.

Tip: On the hill between the Lee Mansion and Abbot Hall, the private homes at 185, 181, and 175 Washington St. are other good examples of the architecture of this period.

King Hooper Mansion. 8 Hooper St. ☎ **781/631-2608.** Donation requested for tour. Mon–Sat 10am–4pm, Sun 1–5pm. Call ahead; no tours during private parties. Where Washington St. curves at foot of hill near Lee Mansion, look for the colorful sign.

Shipping tycoon Robert Hooper got his nickname because he treated his sailors so well, but it's easy to think he was called "King" because he lived like royalty. Around the corner from the home of Jeremiah Lee (whose sister was the second of Hooper's four wives), the 1728 King Hooper Mansion gained a Georgian addition in 1747. The period furnishings, though not original, give a sense of the life of an 18th-century merchant prince, from the wine cellar to the third-floor ballroom. The building houses the headquarters of the Marblehead Arts Association, which stages monthly exhibits and runs a gift shop where members' work is for sale. The mansion also has a lovely garden; enter through the gate at the right of the house.

SHOPPING

Your own piece of history (contemporary or otherwise) may be waiting for you in one of Marblehead's galleries or antiques, clothing, and jewelry shops. Old Town is the favored destination for shoppers, but don't forget that Atlantic Avenue and the south end of Pleasant Street are home to more mainstream businesses. This is just a selection—part of the fun of shopping, of course, is the thrill of discovery.

Along the square around the Old Town House are any number of delightful shops. Poke around in **Heeltappers Antiques,** 134 Washington St. (☎ **781/631-7722**); the **Old Town Antique Co-op,** 108 Washington St. (☎ **781/631-8777**), with four dealers under one roof; and **Cargo Unlimited,** 82 Washington St. (☎ **781/631-1112**). **Calico,** 92 Washington St. (☎ **781/631-3607**), stocks casual vintage home and garden furnishings. **O'Rama's,** 148 Washington St. (☎ **781/631-0894**), sells "miscellaneous elegancies"—jewelry, lingerie, accessories, and other high-end girl stuff.

At the **Marblehead Kite Company,** 1 Pleasant St. (☎ **781/631-7166**), kites share space with souvenirs, greeting cards, T-shirts, toys, and stuffed animals. The town's toy emporium, **Hector's Pup,** 84 Washington St. (☎ **781/631-5860**), is best approached from State Street, where the corner windows overflow with dollhouse furniture.

At the other end of State Street, **Antiquewear,** 82 Front St. (☎ **781/639-0070;** www.shore.net/~antiquew/; E-mail: antiquew@shore.net), sells 19th-century buttons ingeniously fashioned into women's and men's jewelry of all descriptions; and **Brass 'n Bounty,** 68 Front St. (☎ **781/631-3864**), specializes in marine antiques and antique lighting.

Up the hill you'll find the **Art Guild Gallery,** 78 Washington St. (☎ **781/631-3791**), the oldest (since 1957) artists' cooperative gallery in the country. **Arnould Gallery and Framery,** 111 Washington St. (☎ **781/631-6366**), which emphasizes Marblehead and New England themes, and **Concetta's Gallery,** 11 Pleasant St. (☎ **781/639-2113**), are worth a visit to see what the local artists are up to.

WHERE TO STAY

The Chamber of Commerce accommodations listings include many of the town's inns and bed-and-breakfasts. Call or write for a pamphlet (see "Visitor Information," above). Or consult one of the agencies listed in chapter 4.

Harbor Light Inn. 58 Washington St., Marblehead, MA 01945. ☎ **781/631-2186.** Fax 781/631-2216. www.harborlightinn.com. 21 units (some with shower only). A/C TV TEL. $105–$155 double; $160–$275 suite. Rates include continental breakfast. Corporate rate available midweek. 2-night minimum stay weekends, 3-night minimum holiday weekends. AE, MC, V. Free parking.

A stone's throw from the Old Town House, the Harbor Light Inn combines two Federal-era mansions into one gracious lodging. From the wood floors to the 1729 beams (in a third-floor room) to the heated outdoor pool, the inn is both historical and relaxing. Rooms are comfortably furnished in period style, with some antiques, and most have canopy or four-poster beds. Eleven have working fireplaces, and 5 of those have double Jacuzzis. VCRs and free video rentals are available. Rooms at the back overlook the lawn, sundeck, and pool (open seasonally). There are gorgeous harbor views from some rooms and from the rooftop observation deck, which is open to all guests.

✪ **Marblehead Inn.** 264 Pleasant St. (Rte. 114), Marblehead, MA 01945. ☎ **800/ 399-5843** or 781/639-9999. Fax 781/639-9996. www.marbleheadinn.com. 10 units. A/C TV TEL. $129–$189 double. Rates include continental breakfast. Winter discounts and long-term rates available. Extra person $15. 2-night minimum stay weekends, 3-night minimum holiday weekends. AE, MC, V. Free parking.

This three-story Victorian mansion just outside the historic district underwent extensive restoration and reopened in 1998 as an all-suite inn. Each attractively decorated unit has a living room, bedroom, workstation, and self-catering kitchenette (the inn supplies breakfast provisions). This is a good choice for families traveling with children or businesspeople making an extended stay. Some suites in the 1872 building, which has been an inn since 1923, have working fireplaces, and some have small patios.

The Nautilus. 68 Front St., Marblehead, MA 01945. ☎ **781/631-1703.** 4 units, none with private bathroom. $65–$75 double. No credit cards. Ask for parking suggestions when you call for reservations.

This little guest house is as close to the harbor as you can get without being drenched. Rooms are on the second floor of a plain but comfortable private home and have semi-private bathroom facilities. Reserve well in advance, because the combination of location and cheerful, homey service makes the Nautilus a popular destination.

Spray Cliff on the Ocean. 25 Spray Ave., Marblehead, MA 01945. ☎ **800/626-1530** or 781/631-6789. Fax 781/639-4563. www.marbleheadchamber.org/spraycliff. E-mail: spray-cliff@aol.com. 7 units (some with shower only). May–Oct $180–$215 double. Off-season discounts available. Extra person $25. Rates include continental breakfast, evening refreshments, and use of bicycles. 2-night minimum stay weekends, 3-night minimum busy holiday weekends. AE, MC, V. Free parking. Take Atlantic Ave. (Rte. 129) to traffic light at Clifton Ave. and turn east (right from north, left from south); parking area at end of street. No children accepted.

Spray Cliff, a three-story Victorian Tudor built in 1910 on a cliff overlooking the ocean, is 5 minutes from town and a world away. Five of the large, sunny rooms face the water, three have fireplaces, and all are luxuriously decorated in contemporary style with bright accents. Roger and Sally Plauché have run their romantic inn on a quiet residential street 1 minute from the beach since 1994.

A SEASIDE INN NEARBY

Diamond District Bed and Breakfast. 142 Ocean St., Lynn, MA 01902. ☎ **800/ 666-3076** or 781/599-4470. Fax 781/599-5122. www.bbhost.com/diamonddistrict. 11 units, 7 with bathroom (1 with shower only). A/C TV TEL. $100–$245 double. Winter discounts available. Extra person $20. Rates include full breakfast. 2-night minimum stay holiday, summer, and fall weekends. AE, DC, DISC, MC, V. Take Rte. 1A north to signs for Swampscott/Marblehead; after rotary, take Lynn Shore Dr. north 9/10 of a mile, past 2 traffic lights and Christian Science Church (brick building with white pillars). Turn left onto Wolcott Rd., then right onto Ocean Ave.; inn is on the right.

Travelers stopping in Lynn can take advantage of the same attribute that draws property buyers: good value. The ocean views are as breathtaking as those elsewhere on the North Shore, without the breathtaking expense of those posh communities. Downtown Marblehead is about 15 minutes away.

This comfortable B&B is a three-story Georgian-style mansion built in 1911 as a private home, and innkeepers Jerry and Sandra Caron court both business and leisure travelers. The Atlantic is a block away; the 3-mile public beach (a good place to burn off the inn's generous breakfast) is popular for jogging, skating, and biking, as well as swimming. It's visible from many of the good-size, tastefully decorated rooms. All have down comforters and two-line phones with data ports, and two have alcohol-burning fireplaces. The four third-floor rooms, which share two bathrooms and a modest living room, are smaller but quite pleasant and make a good choice for families. Guests have the use of a large heated whirlpool spa on the back lawn.

WHERE TO DINE

At a number of places in Old Town, you can stock up for a picnic along the water. **Frostbiter's,** 78 Front St. (☎ 781/631-6222), sells excellent deli sandwiches, soups, and ice cream. **Iggy's Bread of the World,** 5 Pleasant St. (☎ 781/639-4717), offers fabulous gourmet baked goods and coffee. Both also have small seating areas, but really, go outside.

The Barnacle. 141 Front St. ☎ **781/631-4236.** Reservations not accepted. Main courses $4–$13 at lunch, $11–$17 at dinner. No credit cards. Daily 11:30am–4pm and 5–10pm. SEAFOOD.

This unassuming spot doesn't look like much from the street, but at the end of the gang-plank-like entrance is a front-row seat for the action on the water. You'll have a shore-bird's-eye view of the mouth of the harbor and the ocean from the jam-packed dining room or the deck. The food isn't much of a distraction, but it's tasty, plentiful and fresh—the restaurant's lobster boat delivers daily. The chowder and fried seafood, especially clams, are terrific. This is an ideal place to quaff a beer and watch the boats sail by.

Driftwood Restaurant. 63 Front St., Marblehead. ☎ **781/631-1145.** Main courses $2–$9.50. No credit cards. Summer daily 6:30am–5pm; winter daily 6:30am–2pm. DINER/ SEAFOOD.

At the foot of State Street next to Clark Landing (the town pier) is an honest-to-good-ness local hangout. Whether you're in the mood for pancakes and hash or chowder and a seafood "roll" (a hot-dog bun filled with, say, fried clams or lobster salad), join the crowd. The house specialty, served on weekends and holidays, is fried dough, which is exactly as delicious and indigestible as it sounds.

King's Rook. 12 State St. ☎ **781/631-9838.** Reservations not accepted. Main courses $5–$9. MC, V. Mon–Fri noon–2:30pm; Tues–Fri 5:30–11:30pm, Sat–Sun noon–11:30pm. CAFE/WINE BAR.

This cozy spot was a favorite long before coffeehouses ruled prime-time television. It serves coffees, teas, hot chocolates, soft drinks, and more than two dozen wines by the glass, and the food has a sophisticated flair. The intimate side-street atmosphere and racks of newspapers and magazines make it a great place to linger over a pesto pizza, a salad, or a sinfully rich dessert.

4 Salem

Settled in 1626 (4 years before Boston) and later known around the world as a center of merchant shipping, ✪ **Salem** is internationally famous today for an episode that happened in 1692. The Salem witchcraft trials led to 20 deaths, 3 centuries of notoriety, countless lessons on the evils of prejudice, and countless bad puns ("Stop by for a spell" is a favorite slogan). Unable to live down the association, Salem has embraced it. The high school sports teams are the Witches, and the logo of the *Salem Evening News* is a silhouette of a sorceress.

Visitors expecting wall-to-wall witches won't be disappointed, but they will miss another important part of the city's history. Salem flourished in the 17th and 18th centuries as its merchant vessels circled the globe, returning with treasures and artifacts that can be seen today. Its dominance peaked between the Revolutionary War and the War of 1812, with the opening of the China trade—many overseas trading partners even believed that Salem was an independent country. One reminder of that era, a replica of the 1797 East Indiaman tall ship *Friendship,* is anchored near the Salem Maritime National Historic Site.

The shipping trade was in decline by the 1840s when Salem native Nathaniel Hawthorne worked in the Custom House, where he found a scarlet "A" that sparked his imagination.

ESSENTIALS

GETTING THERE　From Marblehead, take Route 114 west into downtown Salem. From Boston, take Route 1A north to Salem, being careful in Lynn, where the road turns left and immediately right. If it's not rush hour, take I-93 or Route 1 to Route 128, then Route 114 east. There's plenty of metered street parking, and a reasonably priced garage opposite the visitor center. Salem is 16 miles northeast of Boston, and 4 miles northwest of Marblehead.

From Boston, the **MBTA** (☎ **617/222-3200;** www.mbta.com) runs commuter trains from North Station and bus route no. 450 from Haymarket (Orange or Green Line). The train takes 30 to 35 minutes, the bus about an hour. An experimental program that started in 1998 instituted ferry service from Boston. It runs from July through October and takes about an hour. For more information, contact **Massport** (☎ **800/23LOGAN;** www.massport.com) or **Harbor Express** (☎ **978/741-3442**).

VISITOR INFORMATION　An excellent place to start is the **National Park Service Visitor Center,** 2 New Liberty St. (☎ **978/740-1650;** www.nps.gov/sama), open daily 9am to 5pm. Exhibits highlight early settlement, maritime history, and the leather and textiles industries. The center distributes brochures and pamphlets, including one that describes a **walking tour** of the historic district, and has an auditorium where a free film on Essex County provides a good overview.

The **Salem Chamber of Commerce,** 32 Derby Sq., Salem, MA 01970 (☎ **978/744-0004**), maintains an information booth in Old Town Hall that's open weekdays from 9am to 5pm. The chamber collaborates with the **Salem Office of Tourism & Cultural Affairs,** 93 Washington St., Salem, MA 01970 (☎ **800/777-6848;** E-mail: SalemMA@cove.com), to publish a free visitor's guide. Salem has an excellent community Web site (www.salemweb.com).

GETTING AROUND　In the congested downtown area, walking is the way to go. If you plan to visit more than three or four places, you might prefer to ride. At the Essex Street side of the Visitor Center, you can board the **Salem Trolley** (☎ **508/744-5469**) for a 1-hour narrated tour. It operates from 10am to 5pm, daily April through October, weekends in March and November. Tickets ($8 adults, $7 students, $4 children 5 to 12, $20 family of two adults and two or more children) are good all day, and you can reboard as many times as you like at any of the 15 stops. It's a good deal if you're spending the day and don't want to keep moving the car or carrying leg-weary children.

SPECIAL EVENTS　Should you find yourself in town in late October, you won't be able to miss **Haunted Happenings,** the city's 2-week Halloween celebration. Parades, parties, and tours lead up to a ceremony on the big day.

During **Heritage Days,** a weeklong event in mid-August, the city celebrates its multicultural history with musical and theatrical performances, a parade, and fireworks.

Salem

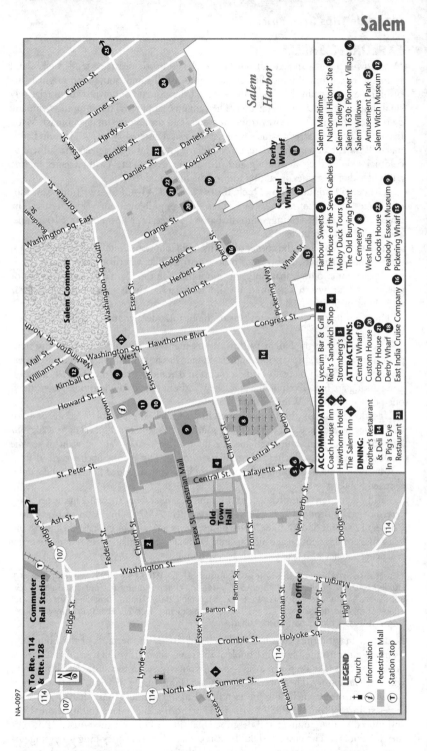

ACCOMMODATIONS:
Coach House Inn **7**
Hawthorne Hotel **3**
The Salem Inn **1**

DINING:
Brother's Restaurant & Deli **14**
In a Pig's Eye Restaurant **23**
Lyceum Bar & Grill **2**
Red's Sandwich Shop **7**
Stromberg's **3**

ATTRACTIONS:
Central Wharf **17**
Custom House **20**
Derby House **21**
Derby Wharf **18**
East India Cruise Company **16**
Harbour Sweets **5**
The House of the Seven Gables **11**
Moby Duck Tours **8**
The Old Burying Point Cemetery **8**
West India Goods House **22**
Peabody Essex Museum **15**
Pickering Wharf **16**
Salem Maritime National Historic Site **19**
Salem Trolley **10**
Salem 1630: Pioneer Village **6**
Salem Willows Amusement Park **25**
Salem Witch Museum **12**

LEGEND
✝ Church
ⓘ Information
Pedestrian Mall
Ⓣ Station stop

NA-0097

151

EXPLORING SALEM

Downtown Salem is spread out but flat, and the historic district extends well inland from the waterfront. Many 18th-century houses still stand, some with original furnishings. Ship captains lived near the water, at the east end of downtown, in relatively small houses crowded close together. The captains' employers, the shipping-company owners, built their homes away from the water (and the accompanying aromas). Many lived on **Chestnut Street,** which is preserved as a registered National Historic Landmark. Residents along the grand thoroughfare must, by legal agreement, adhere to colonial style in their decorating and furnishings. Ask at the Visitor Center for the pamphlet that describes a walking tour of the historic district.

Narrated 50-minute **Moby Duck Tours** (☎ 508/741-4386) leave from New Liberty Street in front of the Visitor Center. The amphibious tour vehicle cruises the streets of the city, then plunges into the harbor. Tickets are $12 for adults, $10 seniors, and $8 for children under 12.

Pickering Wharf, at the corner of Derby and Congress streets, is a cluster of shops, boutiques, restaurants, and condos near a marina. The waterfront setting makes it a good place for strolling, snacking, and shopping. You can also take a harbor cruise or go on a whale watch organized by the **East India Cruise Company** (☎ 800/745-9594 or 508/741-0434).

Three destinations on the outskirts of the historic district are worth the trip if you have time.

By car or trolley, the **Salem Willows** amusements are 5 minutes away; many signs point the way. The strip of rides and snack bars has a honky-tonk air, but the waterfront park is a good place to bring a picnic and wander along the shore. Admission and parking are free. To enjoy the great view without the arcades and rides, have lunch one peninsula over at **Winter Island Park.**

Upscale gift shops throughout New England sell the chocolate confections of ✪ **Harbor Sweets,** and you can go to the source at Palmer Cove, 85 Leavitt St. (☎ 508/745-7648). The retail store overlooks the floor of the factory—if you want to see the machinery in action, call ahead to see if it's running. The shop is open weekdays from 8:30am to 4:30pm and Saturday from 9am to 3pm, with extended hours around candy-centered holidays.

Finally, if you can't get witchcraft off your mind, several shops specialize in the necessary accessories. The **Broom Closet,** 3–5 Central St. (☎ 978/741-3669), and **Crow Haven Corner,** 125 Essex St. (☎ 978/745-8763), sell everything from crystals to clothing and cast a modern-day light on age-old customs. Do bear in mind that Salem is home to many practicing witches who take their beliefs very seriously.

The House of the Seven Gables. 54 Turner St. ☎ **978/744-0991.** www.7gables.org. Guided tours $7 adults, $4 children 6–17, free for children under 6. Tour and Salem 1630 admission $10 adults, $6 children 6–17. May–Nov daily 10am–5pm; Dec–Apr Mon–Sat 10am–5pm, Sun noon–5pm. Closed Jan 1, Thanksgiving, Dec 25. From downtown, follow Derby St. east 3 blocks past Derby Wharf.

Nathaniel Hawthorne's cousin lived here, and stories and legends of the house and its inhabitants inspired his 1851 book of the same name. If you haven't read the eerie novel, don't let that keep you away—begin your visit with the audiovisual program, which tells the story. The house, built by Capt. John Turner in 1668, holds six rooms of period furniture, including pieces referred to in the book, and a narrow, twisting secret staircase. Tours include a visit to Hawthorne's birthplace (built before 1750 and moved to the grounds) and describe what life was like for the house's 18th-century inhabitants. The costumed guides can get a little silly as they mug for young visitors, but they're well versed in the history of the buildings and artifacts, and eager to answer questions. Also on the grounds, overlooking Salem Harbor, are period gardens, the **Retire Beckett House** (1655), the **Hooper–Hathaway House** (1682), and a **counting house** (1830).

✪ **Peabody Essex Museum.** E. India Sq. ☎ **800/745-4054** or 978/745-9500. www.pem.org. Admission (good on 2 consecutive days) $8.50 adults, $7.50 seniors and students with ID, $5 children 6–16, $20 family (2 adults, 1 or more children). Tues–Sat and Mon Memorial Day–Oct 10am–5pm, Sun noon–5pm. Closed Jan 1, Thanksgiving, Dec 25, Mon Nov–Memorial Day. Take Hawthorne Blvd. to Essex St., following signs for Visitor Center. Enter on Essex St. or New Liberty St.

The Peabody Essex Museum celebrated its bicentennial in 1999, seven years after the merger of the Peabody Museum and the Essex Institute. Its fascinating collections illustrate Salem's international adventures and domestic development. In 1799 the East India Marine Society founded the Peabody Museum, now the nation's oldest in continuous operation. The sea captains and merchants provided for a "museum in which to house the natural and artificial curiosities" brought back from their travels. The collections of the Essex Institute (1821), the county's historical society, encompass American art, crafts, furniture, and architecture (including nine historic houses), as well as dolls, toys, and games.

It all adds up to the impression that you're in Salem's attic, but instead of opening dusty trunks and musty closets, you find the treasures arranged in well-planned displays that help you understand the significance of each artifact. Trace the history of the port of Salem and the whaling trade, learn about the witchcraft trials, and study figureheads of ships or portraits of area residents (including Charles Osgood's omnipresent rendering of Nathaniel Hawthorne). One wing displays decorative art pieces made in Asia for Western use from the 14th to the 19th century. Sign up for a tour of one or more houses—the **Gardner–Pingree House** (1804), a magnificent Federal mansion has been gorgeously restored. You can also take a gallery tour or select from about a dozen pamphlets for self-guided tours on various topics.

Salem Maritime National Historic Site. 174 Derby St. ☎ **978/740-1660.** www.nps. gov/sama. Free admission. Guided tours $3 adults, $2 seniors and children 6–16, $10 family. Daily 9am–5pm. Closed Jan 1, Thanksgiving, Dec 25. Take Derby St. east; just past Pickering Wharf, orientation center is on right.

With the decline of the shipping trade in the early 19th century, Salem's wharves fell into disrepair, a state the National Park Service began to remedy in 1938 when it took over a small piece of the waterfront. **Derby Wharf** is now a finger of parkland extending into the harbor, part of the 9 acres dotted with explanatory markers that make up the historic site. An exciting addition is a full-size replica of a 1797 East Indiaman merchant vessel, the *Friendship,* a three-masted 171-footer. The hull was laid in Albany, New York, and moved (using motors) to Salem, where construction was completed. The tall ship is a faithful replica with some concessions to the modern era, such as diesel engines and accessibility for people with disabilities. Fees for visitors were not set at press time.

On adjacent **Central Wharf** is a warehouse (circa 1800) that houses the orientation center. Ranger-led tours, which vary seasonally, expand on Salem's maritime history. Yours might include the **Derby House** (1762), a wedding gift to shipping magnate Elias Hasket Derby from his father, and the **Custom House** (1819), where Nathaniel Hawthorne was working when he found an embroidered scarlet "A." If you prefer to explore on your own, you can see the free film at the orientation center and wander around **Derby Wharf,** the **West India Goods Store,** the **Bonded Warehouse,** the **Scale House,** and **Central Wharf.**

Trying Times: The Salem Witch Hysteria

The Salem Witch Trials took place in 1692, a product of superstition brought to the New World from Europe, religious control of government, and plain old boredom.

The events that led to the trials began in the winter of 1691–92 in Salem Village (now the town of Danvers). The household of Rev. Samuel Parris included his 9-year-old daughter, Elizabeth, her cousin Abigail, and a West Indian slave named Tituba who told stories to amuse the girls and their friends during the long, harsh winter. Entertained by tales of witchcraft, sorcery, and fortune-telling, the girls and their friends, notably Ann Putnam, began to act out the stories, claiming to be under a spell, rolling on the ground and wailing. The settlers—aware that thousands of people in Europe had been executed as witches in the previous centuries—took the behavior seriously. A doctor diagnosed the girls as bewitched.

At first only Tituba and two other local women were accused of casting the spells. Soon, though, the infighting that characterized the Puritan theocracy came to the fore, and an accusation of witchcraft became a handy way to settle a score. Anyone considered "different" was a potential target, from the elderly to the deaf to the poor. A special court convened in Salem proper, and even though the girls soon recanted, the trials began. Defendants had no counsel, and pleading not guilty or objecting to the proceedings was considered the equivalent of a confession. Between March 1 and September 22, 27 of the more than 150 people accused were convicted.

In the end, 19 people went to the gallows, and one man who refused to plead, Giles Corey, was pressed to death by stones piled on a board on his chest (under English law, a person who refused to plead could not have his property confiscated). Finally, cooler heads prevailed. Leading cleric Cotton Mather and his father, Harvard president Increase Mather, led the call for tolerance. With the jails overflowing, the trials were called off and the remaining prisoners, including Tituba, were freed.

This tale's lessons about open-mindedness and tolerance have been absorbed with varying degrees of success in the years since. Salem was the backdrop for Arthur Miller's play *The Crucible* (you might have seen the 1996 film version). The 1953 play is both a story about the witch trials and an allegory about the McCarthy Senate hearings of the 1950s—another kind of witch hunt in a time when those lessons needed to be taught again.

Salem 1630: Pioneer Village. Forest River Park, off West Ave. ☎ **978/744-0991.** www.7gables.org. Admission $5 adults, $3 seniors and children 6–17. Admission and House of the Seven Gables tour $10 adults, $6 children 6–17. Mid-May to Oct Mon–Sat 10am–5pm, Sun noon–5pm. Closed Nov–early May. Take Lafayette St. (Routes 114 and 1A) south from downtown to West Ave., turn left and follow signs.

A re-creation of life in Salem just a few years after European settlement, this Puritan village is staffed by costumed interpreters who lead tours, demonstrate crafts, and tend farm animals. They escort visitors around the various dwellings—wear sneakers, because the village isn't paved—and explain their activities. As with any undertaking of this nature, it takes a while to get used to the atmosphere, but once you do, it can be great fun.

✪ **Salem Witch Museum.** 19½ Washington Sq. ☎ **978/744-1692.** www.salemwitch-museum.com. Admission $6 adults, $5.50 seniors, $3.75 children 6–14. July–Aug daily 10am–7pm, Sept–June daily 10am–5pm. Closed Jan 1, Thanksgiving, and Dec 25. Follow Hawthorne Blvd. to the northwest corner of Salem Common.

This is one of the most memorable attractions in eastern Massachusetts—it's both interesting and scary. The main draw of the museum (a former church) is a three-dimensional audiovisual presentation with life-size figures. The show takes place in a huge room lined with displays that are lighted in sequence. The 30-minute narration dramatically but accurately tells the story of the witchcraft trials and the accompanying hysteria (you may need to remind smaller children that the man being pressed to death by rocks piled on his chest isn't real). The narration is available in French, German, Italian, Japanese, and Spanish. There's also a new exhibit that traces the history of witches, witchcraft, and witch hunts.

On the traffic island across from the entrance is a statue that's easily mistaken for a witch. It's really Roger Conant, who founded Salem in 1626.

WHERE TO STAY

Danvers is about 20 minutes west of Salem, convenient to other destinations north of Boston. Near Route 1, three-quarters of a mile north of Route 114, is the **Comfort Inn Danvers,** 50 Dayton St., Danvers, MA 01923 (☎ **800/228-5150** or 978/777-1700). The comfortable five-story motel has an indoor-outdoor pool. A double in the high season runs $100 to $130, and rates include continental breakfast.

Coach House Inn. 284 Lafayette St. (Rtes. 1A and 114), Salem, MA 01970. ☎ **800/688-8689** or 978/744-4092. Fax 978/745-8031. www.salemweb.com/biz/coachhouse. E-mail: coachhse@star.net. 11 units, 9 with bathroom (1 with shower only). A/C TV. $71–$85 double with shared bathroom; $78–$105 double with private bathroom; $95–$155 suite. Extra person $20. Rates include continental breakfast. 2- or 3-night minimum stay weekends and holidays. AE, DISC, MC, V. Free parking.

Built in 1879 for a ship's captain, the Coach House Inn is 2 blocks from the harbor. It's a good choice if you don't mind the 20-minute walk or 5-minute drive from downtown Salem. The pleasant, high-ceilinged rooms in the three-story mansion were redecorated in 1998. They have coffeemakers and elegant furnishings, and most have (nonworking) fireplaces. Breakfast arrives at your door in a basket.

Hawthorne Hotel. 18 Washington Sq. (at Salem Common), Salem, MA 01970. ☎ **800/729-7829** or 978/744-4080. Fax 978/745-9842. www.hawthornehotel.com. 83 units (some with shower only). A/C TV TEL. $99–$182 double, $150–$275 suite. Off-season discounts available. Extra person $12. Children under 16 stay free in parents' room. Senior discount, weekend and other packages available. 2-night minimum stay holiday weekends. AE, CB, DC, DISC, MC, V. Parking $5. Small pets allowed; $15 charge.

This historic hotel, built in 1925, is both convenient and comfortable. The six-story building is centrally located and well maintained—the lobby was remodeled in 1995, the guest rooms renovated from 1997 to 1999. The attractively furnished rooms are adequate in size; some overlook Salem Common. Ask to be as high up as possible, because the neighborhood is a busy one. Guests have the use of an exercise room, and there are two restaurants on the ground floor, room service until 11pm, and dry-cleaning and laundry service.

Salem Inn. 7 Summer St. (Rte. 114), Salem, MA 01970. ☎ **800/446-2995** or 978/741-0680. Fax 978/744-8924. www.salemweb.com/biz/saleminn. E-mail: saleminn@earthlink.net. 39 units (some with shower only). A/C TV TEL. Mid-Apr to Sept $129–$229 double; Oct $160–$280 double; Nov to mid-Apr $109–$209 double. Rates include continental breakfast. 2-night minimum stay during special events and holidays. AE, DC, DISC, JCB, MC, V. Free parking.

The Salem Inn—a good compromise between too-big hotel and too-small B&B—consists of three properties. The 1834 West House and the 1854 Curwen House, former homes of ship captains, are listed on the National Register of Historic Places. The 1874 Peabody House is a newly restored mansion divided into luxury and family suites. The large, tastefully decorated guest rooms all have coffeemakers, and some have fireplaces, canopy beds, and whirlpool baths. Suites have kitchenettes. A peaceful rose garden and brick patio are at the rear of the main building, which also holds a meeting space. The lower-level restaurant, Cuvée, serves dinner Tuesday through Sunday from 6 to 10:30pm.

Sheraton Ferncroft Resort. 50 Ferncroft Rd., Danvers, MA 01923. ☎ **800/325-3535** or 978/777-2500. Fax 978/750-7959. www.sheraton.com. 367 units. A/C TV TEL. $119–$249 double; from $250 suite. Extra person $15. Children under 12 stay free in parents' room. Weekend packages and AARP, AAA, and government employees' discount available. AE, CB, DC, DISC, MC, V.

This popular business destination is a great spot for a golf vacation. Robert Trent Jones designed the 18-hole championship course, and the rooms high above Route 1 (at I-95) look out on the course or the surrounding countryside. Nongolfers will find tennis, racquetball, basketball, and cross-country skiing facilities; an indoor and an outdoor pool; and a health and fitness center with cardiovascular room, Nautilus room, aerobics studio, sauna, and masseuse. The eight-story resort has a concierge, a staffed business center, and meeting and function space. All rooms have a sofa, desk, heat controls, coffeemaker, hair dryer, iron, and ironing board. The property has four restaurants, and room service until midnight. There are 23 rooms for people with disabilities.

WHERE TO DINE

Pickering Wharf has a food court as well as a link in the **Victoria Station** chain (☎ 978/745-3400), where the deck has a great view of the marina. For a quick bite, try **Brothers Restaurant & Deli,** 283 Derby St. (☎ 978/741-4648), an inexpensive cafeteria-style family spot with home-cooked Greek meals that serves breakfast all day.

The **Rockmore Restaurant** (☎ 978/740-1001 or 781/639-0600), is on a float in the middle of Salem Harbor. It's open daily from 11am to 10pm from Memorial Day weekend to Labor Day weekend, weather permitting. Main courses run $7 to $15 (MasterCard and Visa are accepted). If you're not traveling by boat, ferry service is available at Pickering Wharf or at Village Street Pier on the west side of Marblehead.

In a Pig's Eye. 148 Derby St. ☎ **978/741-4436.** www.inapigseye.com. Reservations recommended at dinner. Sandwiches and salads $4–$7.50; main courses $10–$15 at dinner Wed–Sat, $6–$11 at dinner Mon–Tues. AE, MC, V. Mon–Sat 11:30am–3pm and 6–10pm; Sun 11:30am–4pm. AMERICAN/MEXICAN.

Although it appears to be just a neighborhood bar near the House of the Seven Gables, it's much more—the food is wonderful. The lunch menu offers bar fare that's a step up from basic, with several vegetarian options, and Mexican food. Mexican nights are Monday and Tuesday—Mexican pizza (mounds of vegetables and salsa on flour tortillas) is terrific, as are the gigantic burritos. The regular menu offers creative pasta dishes, beef, chicken, and at least half a dozen seafood choices. There's live music Monday and Thursday beginning at 9pm.

✪ **Lyceum Bar & Grill.** 43 Church St. (at Washington St.). ☎ **978/745-7665.** Reservations recommended. Main courses $6–$10 at lunch, $14–$19 at dinner. AE, DISC, MC, V. Mon–Fri 11:30am–3pm; Sun brunch 11am–3pm; daily 5:30–10pm. CONTEMPORARY AMERICAN.

The elegance of the high-ceilinged front rooms and glass-walled back rooms at the Lyceum—in the building where Alexander Graham Bell made the first long-distance telephone call—matches the quality of the food. Be sure to try the marinated, grilled portobello mushrooms. They're available as an appetizer and scattered throughout the menu, in a delectable pasta with chicken, red peppers, and Swiss chard in wine sauce, or with beef tenderloin, red-pepper sauce, and garlic mashed potatoes. Spicy vegetable lasagna is also tasty. Try to save room for a traditional yet sophisticated dessert—the brownie sundae is out of this world.

Red's Sandwich Shop. 15 Central St. ☎ **508/745-3527.** Most items under $6. No credit cards. Mon–Sat 5am–3pm, Sun 6am–1pm. DINER.

Locals and visitors feel equally comfortable at this no-frills spot. Hunker down at the counter or a table and be ready for your waitress to call you "dear" as she brings you pancakes and eggs at breakfast, or soup (opt for chicken over chowder) and a burger at lunch. **Red's Winter Island Grille** (☎ **508/744-0203**), under the same management, is open seasonally at Winter Island Park.

Stromberg's. 2 Bridge St. (Rte. 1A). ☎ **508/744-1863.** Reservations recommended at dinner. Main courses $10–$15; lobster priced daily; children's menu $3–$5. AE, DISC, MC, V. Sun, Tues–Thurs 11am–9pm; Fri–Sat 11am–10pm. Closed Tues after long holiday weekends. SEAFOOD.

For generous portions of well-prepared seafood and a view of the water, head to this popular spot. Beverly Harbor isn't the most exciting spot, but you won't mind, especially if it's summer and you're out on the deck enjoying the live entertainment (weekends only). The fish and clam chowders are excellent, daily specials are numerous, and there are more chicken, beef, and pasta options than you might expect. Crustacean-lovers in the mood to splurge will fall for the world-class lobster roll.

5 Cape Ann

Gloucester, Rockport, Essex, and Manchester-by-the-Sea make up Cape Ann, a rocky peninsula so enchantingly beautiful that when you hear the slogan "Massachusetts's *other* Cape," you may forget what the first one was. Cape Ann and Cape Cod do share some attributes—scenery, shopping, seafood, traffic. The smaller cape's proximity to Boston and manageable scale make it a wonderful day trip as well as a good choice for a longer stay. With the decline of the fishing industry that brought great prosperity to the area in the 19th century, Cape Ann has played up its long-standing reputation as a haven for artists. Along with galleries and crafts shops, you'll find historical attractions, beaches—and oh, that scenery!

Be aware that this is anything but a four-season destination. Many attractions are closed from fall or early winter through April or May. Rockport in particular shuts up tighter than an Essex clam.

The **Cape Ann Transportation Authority,** or CATA (☎ **978/283-7916**) runs buses from town to town on Cape Ann.

The **Cape Ann Chamber of Commerce,** 33 Commercial St., Gloucester, MA 01930 (☎ **800/321-0133** or 978/283-1601; www.cape-ann.com/cacc), can be helpful.

MANCHESTER-BY-THE-SEA

The scenic route to Gloucester from points south is Route 127, which runs through Manchester-by-the-Sea, a lovely village incorporated in 1645. Now a prosperous suburb of Boston, Manchester is probably best known for **Singing Beach** (see box,

Life's a Beach

Paradoxically, Cape Ann is almost as well known for its sandy beaches as for its rocky coastline. Two caveats: It's not Florida, so don't expect 70° water (the operative word is "refreshing"). And parking can be scarce, especially on weekends, and pricey—as much as $15 per car. If you can't set out early, wait till midafternoon and hope that the people who beat you to the beach in the morning have had enough. During the summer, lifeguards are on duty from 9am to 5pm at larger public beaches. Surfing is generally permitted outside of those hours.

Probably the best-known North Shore beach is **Singing Beach,** off Masconomo Street in Manchester-by-the-Sea. It's named for the sound the sand makes under your feet. The legions of people walking six-tenths of a mile on Beach Street from the train station attest to both the beach's reputation and the difficulty and expense of parking. Save some cash and aggravation by taking the MBTA **commuter rail** (☎ **617/222-3200;** www.mbta.com) from Boston's North Station. **White Beach,** off Ocean Street, is another public beach in town.

Nearly as famous as Singing Beach and equally popular is **Crane Beach,** off Argilla Road in Ipswich. It's part of a 1,400-acre barrier beach reservation whose expanses of white sand and fragile dunes lead down to Ipswich Bay. The surf is calmer than that at less sheltered Singing Beach, but still quite chilly. Also on Ipswich Bay is Gloucester's **Wingaersheek Beach,** on Atlantic Street off Route 133. From Exit 13 off Route 128, the beach is about 15 minutes away (mind the speed limits). When you finally arrive, you'll find beautiful white sand, a glorious view, and more dunes. Across the bay, there's a beach at **Plum Island** that's part of the **Parker River National Wildlife Refuge** (see "Newburyport, Ipswich & Plum Island").

Watch out for the greenhead flies at North Shore beaches in late July and early August. They don't sting—they take little bites of flesh. Plan to bring or buy insect repellent.

Other good beaches in Gloucester are **Good Harbor Beach,** off Route 127A at Thatcher Road in East Gloucester; **Coffin Beach,** just northwest of Wingaersheek; and **Half Moon Beach** and **Cressy's Beach,** at Stage Fort Park, off Route 127 near Route 133 and downtown. The park also contains a visitor information office (summer only), playgrounds, picnic and cookout areas, and the ruins of a Revolutionary War fort.

In Rockport, **Front Beach** and **Back Beach** are on Beach Street just north of downtown, and **Old Garden Beach** is on Old Garden Road east of downtown. Heading south on Route 127A toward Gloucester, you can detour to **Pebble Beach,** off Penzance Road, **Cape Hedge Beach,** off South Street, and **Long Beach,** off Thatcher Road.

below). The MBTA **commuter rail** (☎ **617/222-3200;** www.mbta.com) stops in the center of the compact downtown area, where there are many shops and restaurants. Nearby **Masconomo Park** overlooks the harbor.

The home of the Manchester Historical Society is the **Trask House,** 10 Union St. (☎ **978/526-7230**), a 19th-century sea captain's home. Tours show off the period furnishings and the society's costume collections. It's open from late June to August, Saturday from 10am to 4pm, Sunday noon to 4pm, and by appointment. A donation is requested.

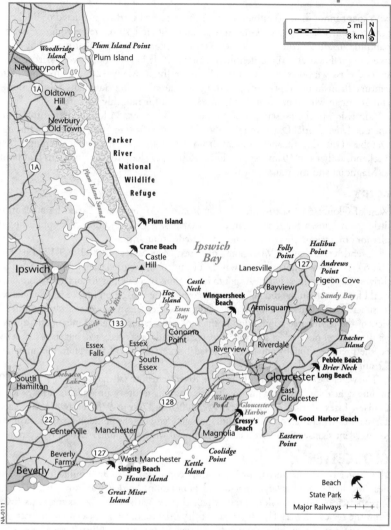

0 | 5 mi
0 | 8 km
N

Woodbridge Island
Plum Island Point
Plum Island
Newburyport

(1A) Oldtown Hill ▲

Newbury Old Town

(1A)

Plum Island Sound

Parker River National Wildlife Refuge

🏖 Plum Island

🏖 Crane Beach
Castle Hill ▲

Ipswich

Ipswich Bay

Folly Point
Halibut Point
Andrews Point
Lanesville
Pigeon Cove

Castle Neck

Bayview

Sandy Bay

Hog Island

🏖 Wingaersheek Beach

Atmisquam

Essex Bay

Castle Neck River

(133)

Conomo Point

Riverview

Riverdale

Rockport

Thacher Island

Essex Falls
Essex
South Essex

Castle River

🏖 Pebble Beach
Brier Neck
Long Beach

South Hamilton

Chebacco Lake

Gloucester

East Gloucester

(128)

Walnut Pond

Gloucester Harbor

🏖 Cressy's Beach

🏖 Good Harbor Beach

(22)

Centerville   Manchester

Magnolia

Eastern Point

Beverly Farms

(127)

West Manchester

🏖 Singing Beach

House Island

Coolidge Point

Kettle Island

Beverly

Great Miser Island

Beach 🏖
State Park 🌲
Major Railways ┣━━┫

NA-0111

MAGNOLIA

Pay close attention as you head north from Manchester or south from Gloucester on Route 127—the signs for Magnolia are small and easy to miss, but the village (which is technically part of Gloucester) is well worth a detour. Notable for its lack of water-front commercial property, the village center is small and unremarkable, but the homes surrounding it, many of them once summer residences now occupied through the winter, are magnificent.

Less than a mile up the coast are two notable geological formations. **Rafe's Chasm** is a huge cleft in the shoreline rock, opposite the reef of **Norman's Woe,** which figures in Henry Wadsworth Longfellow's scary poem "The Wreck of the Hesperus."

And then there's the **Hammond Castle Museum,** 80 Hesperus Ave. (☎ **978/ 283-7673,** or 978/283-2080 for recorded information; www1.shore.net/ ~hammond). It was the brainchild of eccentric inventor John Hays Hammond, Jr., who spent more than $6 million to have the medieval castle constructed of Rockport granite from 1926 to 1929. Guided tours aren't offered, so you're on your own with a pamphlet to direct you—not the best way to explore such a peculiar place, but if you like the medieval era, you'll definitely enjoy this. It has 85-foot towers, battlements, stained-glass windows, and a great hall 60 feet high. Many 12th-, 13th-, and 14th-century furnishings, tapestries, paintings, and architectural fragments fill the rooms, and an organ with more than 8,200 pipes is used for monthly concerts.

Admission to the museum is $6 for adults, $5 seniors, $4 for children 4 to 12. It's open daily Memorial Day through Labor Day from 10am to 5pm, Labor Day through October Thursday through Sunday from 10am to 4pm, November through May weekends only from 10am to 4pm. From Route 127, look for the tiny signs that point to Magnolia and the museum.

ESSEX

West of Gloucester (past Route 128) on Route 133, you'll find **Essex.** It's a beautiful little town known for Essex clams, salt marshes, a long tradition of shipbuilding, a plethora of antique shops, and one celebrated restaurant.

Legend has it that ✪ **Woodman's of Essex,** Main Street (☎ **800/649-1773** or 978/768-6451; www.woodmans.com), was the birthplace of the fried clam in 1916. Today, the thriving family business is a great spot to join legions of locals and visitors from around the world for lobster "in the rough," steamers, corn on the cob, onion rings, and (you guessed it) superb fried clams. The line is long, even in winter, but it moves quickly and offers a view of the regimented commotion in the food-preparation area. Eat in a booth, upstairs on the deck, or out back at a picnic table. Credit cards aren't accepted, but there's an ATM on the premises. You'll want to be well fed before you set off to explore the numerous ✪ **antique shops** along Main Street.

The water views in town are of the Essex River, actually a saltwater estuary. Narrated 90-minute sightseeing tours that put you in prime birding territory are available at **Essex River Cruises,** Essex Marina, 35 Dodge St. (☎ **800/748-3706** or 978/768-6981; www.cape-ann.com/es-riv-cruise), daily from April through October. The pontoon boat, which allows for excellent sightseeing, is screened and equipped with rest rooms. Call for reservations.

GLOUCESTER

Gloucester is the most urban of Cape Ann's communities, with a built-up downtown near the harbor and a large year-round population. Settled by Europeans in 1623, 7 years before Boston, Gloucester (which rhymes with "roster") has made its living from the sea ever since. The depletion of the Atlantic fishing stock in recent years has left a void now partly filled by the thriving whale-watching industry (see below).

ESSENTIALS
Getting There

From Boston, the quickest route is I-93 (or Route 1, if it's not rush hour) to Route 128, which ends at Gloucester. The slower but prettier approach is to take Route 1A—all the way from East Boston, or from downtown Salem—across the bridge at Beverly and pick up Route 127. It runs through Manchester to Gloucester. Route 128 exits for Manchester allow access to Route 127. Gloucester is 33 miles northeast of Boston, 16 miles northeast of Salem, and 7 miles south of Rockport.

The MBTA **commuter rail** (☎ 617/222-3200; www.mbta.com) runs from Boston's North Station. The trip takes about an hour. The station is across town from downtown, so allow time for getting to the waterfront area. The **Cape Ann Transportation Authority,** or CATA (☎ 978/283-7916) runs buses from town to town on Cape Ann.

Visitor Information

The **Gloucester Tourism Commission,** 22 Poplar St., Gloucester, MA 01930 (☎ **800/649-6839** or 978/281-8865; www1.shore.net/~nya/gloucester.html), operates an excellent **Visitors Welcoming Center** at Stage Fort Park, off Route 127 near the intersection with Route 133. It's open during the summer daily from 9am to 5pm. Ask for a copy of the Tourism Commission's guide to the Gloucester Maritime Trail, a pamphlet that describes four walking tours.

The information center run by the **Cape Ann Chamber of Commerce,** 33 Commercial St., Gloucester, MA 01930 (☎ **800/321-0133** or 978/283-1601; www.cape-ann.com/cacc), is open year-round (summer, weekdays from 8am to 6pm, Saturday 10am to 6pm, Sunday 10am to 4pm; winter, weekdays from 8am to 5pm) and has a helpful staff. Call or write for the chamber's four-color map and brochure.

The **North of Boston Convention & Visitors Bureau,** 17 Peabody Sq., Peabody, MA 01960 (☎ **800/742-5306** or 978/977-7760; www.northofboston.org), publishes a visitor's guide. And Gloucester has a page on the Cape Ann Web site (www.cape-ann.com).

Before you go, you might want to read *The Perfect Storm,* by Sebastian Junger. It's a thrilling but tragic nonfiction account of the travails of the Gloucester fishing fleet during the no-name hurricane of 1991.

Getting Around

The **Cape Ann Transportation Authority** (see above) serves most of Gloucester on its regular routes and operates special loops during the summer. If you can manage it, try to travel by car. You'll be able to make the best use of your time, especially if you plan several stops.

Special Events

The fishing fleet enjoys some divine intervention every year during **St. Peter's Fiesta,** a colorful 4-day event at the end of June. The Italian-American fishing colony's enormous festival has more in common with a carnival midway than a religious observation, but it's great fun. There are parades, rides, music, food, sporting events, and, on Sunday, the blessing of the fleet.

On summer Sunday nights, the **Concerts in the Park** (☎ **978/281-0543**) series brings live jazz, country, and traditional music to Stage Fort Park.

EXPLORING THE TOWN

Start at the water, the city's lifeblood since long before the first European settlement in 1623. The French explorer Samuel de Champlain called the harbor "Le Beauport" in 1604—some 600 years after the Vikings first visited here—and its configuration and proximity to good fishing gave it the reputation it enjoys to this day. Follow one or more of the Tourism Commission's walking tours, or explore on your own.

On Stacy Boulevard west of downtown (which has a sensational view of the harbor and the Eastern Point lighthouse) is a reminder of the sea's danger. Leonard Craske's bronze statue of the Gloucester Fisherman, known as *The Man at the Wheel,* bears the inscription "They That Go Down to the Sea in Ships 1623–1923." More than 10,000 fishermen lost their lives during the city's first 300 years, and a statue honoring the women and children who waited for them is in the works.

To reach **East Gloucester,** follow signs as you leave downtown or go directly from Route 128, Exit 9. On East Main Street, you'll see signs for the world-famous **Rocky Neck Art Colony,** the oldest continuously operating art colony in the country. Park in the lot on the tiny causeway and walk 2 blocks west to Rocky Neck Avenue. In the summer it's jammed with studios, galleries, restaurants, and people. The attraction is the presence of working artists, not just shops that happen to sell art. Most galleries are open daily in the summer from 10am to 10pm. Another place to see local artists' creations is the **North Shore Arts Association,** 197 E. Main St. (☎ 978/283-1857), founded in 1923. It's open June through September, Monday to Saturday from 10am to 5pm and Sunday from 1 to 5pm, and admission is free.

Moby Duck Tours (☎ 978/281-3825) are 50-minute sightseeing expeditions that travel on land before plunging into the water. The amphibious vehicles leave from **Harbor Loop** downtown, where tickets ($12 adults, $10 seniors, $8 children under 12) are available. Plan to take a tour if you have children along; as soon as they see the vessels, they'll want a ride.

Also at Harbor Loop, you can tour the two-masted schooner *Adventure* (☎ 978/281-8079; www.cape-ann.com/adventure.html), a 121-foot fishing vessel built in Essex in 1926. The "living museum," a National Historic Landmark under continual restoration, is open to visitors Memorial Day to Labor Day, Thursday to Sunday from 10am to 4pm. (Suggested donation $5 adults, $4 children.)

Stage Fort Park (off Route 127 near the intersection with Route 133) offers an excellent view of the harbor and is a good spot for a picnic, swimming, or just playing on the cannons in the Revolutionary War fort.

✪ **Beauport (Sleeper-McCann House).** 75 Eastern Point Blvd. ☎ **978/283-0800.** www.spnea.org. Guided tours $6 adults, $5.50 seniors, $3 children 6–12. Tours on the hour mid-May to mid-Oct Mon–Fri 10am–4pm; mid-Sept to mid-Oct daily 10am–4pm. Closed mid-Oct to mid-May, summer weekends. Take E. Main St. south to Eastern Point Blvd. (a private road), drive ½ mile to the house, park on left.

The Society for the Preservation of New England Antiquities, which operates Beauport, describes it as a "fantasy house," and that's putting it mildly. Interior designer Henry Davis Sleeper used his summer residence as a retreat and a repository for his vast collections of American and European decorative arts and antiques. From 1907 to 1934, he adorned the 40 rooms (26 are open to the public) to illustrate literary and historical themes. The entertaining tour concentrates more on the house and rooms in general than on the countless objects on display. You'll see architectural details rescued from other buildings, magnificent arrangements of colored glassware, an early American kitchen, the "Red Indian Room" (with a majestic view of the harbor), and "Strawberry Hill," the master bedroom. Call ahead to see if a special event (afternoon tea, twilight tour, or evening concert) is being offered while you're in town. Note that the house is closed on summer weekends.

Cape Ann Historical Museum. 27 Pleasant St. ☎ **978/283-0455.** Admission $4 adults, $3.50 seniors, $2.50 students, free for children under 6. March–Jan Tues–Sat 10am–5pm. Closed Feb. Follow Main St. west through downtown and turn right onto Pleasant St.; the museum is 1 block up on the right. Metered parking on street or in lot across street.

This meticulously curated museum makes an excellent introduction to Cape Ann's history and artists. It devotes an entire gallery to the extraordinary work of ✪ **Fitz Hugh Lane,** the Luminist painter whose light-flooded canvases show off the best of his native Gloucester. The nation's single largest collection of his paintings and drawings is here. Other galleries feature works on paper by 20th-century artists such as Maurice Prendergast and Milton Avery, work by other contemporary artists, and granite-quarrying tools and equipment. On display in the **maritime and fisheries galleries** are entire vessels (including one about the size of a station wagon that actually crossed the Atlantic), exhibits on the fishing industry, ship models, and historic photographs and models of the Gloucester waterfront. The **Capt. Elias Davis House** (1804), decorated and furnished in Federal style with furniture, silver, and porcelains, is part of the museum.

A WHALE OF AN ADVENTURE

The waters off the coast of Massachusetts are prime **whale-watching** territory, and Gloucester is a center of whale-watching cruises. **Stellwagen Bank,** which runs from Gloucester to Provincetown about 27 miles east of Boston, is a rich feeding ground for the magnificent mammals, who dine on sand eels and other fish that gather along the ridge. The most commonly sighted species in this area are baleen whales, the finback and the humpback, and you might also see minke whales and rare right whales. They often perform for their audience by jumping out of the water, and dolphins occasionally join the show.

Once the novelty of putting out to sea is behind them, children tend not to be thrilled with the time it takes to reach the bank, which makes their reaction to a sighting all the more gratifying. This is not the most time- or cost-effective way to spend half a day, but it is an "only in New England" experience kids (and adults) will remember for a long time.

Dress warmly, because it's much cooler at sea than in town, and take sunglasses, sunscreen, a hat, rubber-soled shoes, and a camera with plenty of film. If you're prone to motion sickness, take appropriate precautions, because you'll be out on the open sea for 4 to 6 hours.

Check the local marinas for sailing times, prices ($23 to $26 for adults, less for children and seniors), and reservations, which are always a good idea. It's an extremely competitive business—most companies guarantee sightings, offer AARP and AAA discounts, honor other firms' coupons, and offer a morning and an afternoon cruise as well as deep-sea fishing excursions. Naturalists on board narrate the trip for the companies listed here, pointing out the whales and describing the birds and fish that may cross your path.

In downtown Gloucester, **Cape Ann Whale Watch,** 415 Main St., at Rose's Wharf (☎ 800/877-5110 or 978/283-5110; www.caww.com), is the oldest and best-known operation. Or try **Captain Bill's Whale Watch,** 33 Harbor Loop (☎ 800/ 33-WHALE or 978/283-6995; www.cape-ann.com/captbill.html), and **Seven Seas Whale Watch,** at Seven Seas Wharf (☎ 800/238-1776 or 978/283-1776; www.cape-ann.com/whalewatch.html). At the Cape Ann Marina, off Route 133, you'll find **Yankee Whale Watch** (☎ 800/WHALING or 978/283-0313; www.yankee-fleet.com/whale.htm).

WHERE TO STAY

Atlantis Oceanfront Motor Inn. 125 Atlantic Rd., Gloucester, MA 01930. ☎ **978/ 283-0014.** Fax 978/281-8994. www.cape-ann.com/atlantis.html. 40 units (some with shower only). TV TEL. Late June to Labor Day $120–$140 double; spring and fall $80–$115 double. Extra person $8. Closed Nov to mid-Apr. 2-night minimum stay spring and fall weekends, 3-night minimum summer and holiday weekends. AE, MC, V. Follow Rte. 128 to the end (Exit 9, E. Gloucester), turn left onto Bass Ave. (Rte. 127A), and follow ½ mile. Turn right and follow Atlantic Rd.

The stunning views from every window of this motor inn across the street from the water would almost be enough to recommend it, but it also has a heated outdoor pool and a friendly staff. The good-size guest rooms are decorated in comfortable, contemporary style. Every room has a terrace or balcony and a small table and chairs. The coffee shop on the premises serves breakfast until 11am.

Best Western Bass Rocks Ocean Inn. 107 Atlantic Rd., Gloucester, MA 01930. ☎ **800/ 528-1234** or 978/283-7600. Fax 978/281-6489. 48 units. A/C TV TEL. Late Apr to late May $105–$135 double; Memorial Day to late June and early Sept to Oct $120–$160 double; late June to Labor Day $125–$170 double. Extra person $8. Rollaway $12. AE, CB, DC, DISC, MC, V. Rates include continental breakfast. Children under 12 stay free in parents' room. 3-night minimum stay summer weekends, some spring and fall weekends. Closed Nov to late

Apr. Follow Rte. 128 to the end (Exit 9, E. Gloucester), turn left onto Bass Ave. (Rte. 127A) and follow ½ mile. Turn right and follow Atlantic Rd.

A family operation since 1946, the Bass Rocks Ocean Inn offers modern accommodations in a traditional setting. The spacious guest rooms overlook the ocean from a sprawling, comfortable two-story motel across the road from the rocky shore. A Colonial Revival mansion built in 1899 and known as the "wedding-cake house" holds the office and public areas. The rooftop sundeck, balconies, and heated outdoor pool offer excellent views of the surf. Each guest room has a refrigerator, a balcony or patio, and a king bed or two double beds. In the afternoon coffee, tea, lemonade, and chocolate-chip cookies are offered. Bicycles, a billiard room, and the library are at the disposal of the guests.

WHERE TO DINE

See "Essex," above, for information about **Woodman's of Essex,** which is about 20 minutes from downtown Gloucester.

Boulevard Oceanview Restaurant. 25 Western Ave. (Stacy Blvd.). ☎ **978/281-2949.** Reservations recommended at dinner in summer. Sandwiches $3–$7; main courses $6.50–$15; lobster priced daily. DISC, MC, V. Summer daily 11am–10pm; winter daily 11am–9:30pm. PORTUGUESE/SEAFOOD.

This is a friendly, unassuming neighborhood place in a high-tourist-traffic location. Across the street from the waterfront promenade just outside downtown, it's a dinerlike spot with water views from the front windows and the small deck. It serves ultrafresh seafood (crane your neck and you can almost see the processing plants) as well as lunch-counter sandwiches. Try "Seafood Portuguese style"—shrimp *a la plancha* (in an irresistible lemon-butter sauce) and *sao* style (in garlic and wine sauce), and several unusual casseroles. The hostess and I were chatting about where to send visitors to eat in Gloucester when a waitress chimed in: "Send 'em here, dear," she said. "It's the best food they'll ever eat." Even if that's not strictly true, it's good to know an employee thinks so.

The Gull. 75 Essex Ave. (Rte. 133), at Cape Ann Marina. ☎ **978/281-6060.** Reservations recommended for parties of 8 or more. Main courses $6–$12 at lunch, $8–$22 at dinner. DISC, MC, V. Daily 6am–9pm. Closed Nov to late Apr. Take Rte. 133 west from intersection with Rte. 127, or take Rte. 133 east from Rte. 128. SEAFOOD.

Floor-to-ceiling windows show off the Annisquam River from almost every seat at the Gull. This big, friendly seafood restaurant is also known for prime rib. It draws locals, visitors, boaters, and families for large portions at reasonable prices. The seafood chowder is famous (with good reason), appetizers tend toward bar food, and fish is available in just about any variety and style—ask about the daily specials. At lunch, there's an extensive sandwich menu.

The Rudder Restaurant. 73 Rocky Neck Ave., E. Gloucester. ☎ **978/283-7967.** Reservations required on weekends. Main courses $13–$20; children's menu $8. DISC, MC, V. Memorial Day to Labor Day daily noon–10:30pm; call for spring and fall hours. Closed Dec to mid-Apr. SEAFOOD/INTERNATIONAL.

A meal at the Rudder (also known as Evie's Rudder) isn't just a meal—it's a party. Overlooking Smith Cove, in the heart of the Rocky Neck Art Colony, the 40-year-old restaurant is packed with gadgets, colored lights, antiques, photos, menus from around the world, and other collectibles. Ask for a seat on the deck (if it's not low tide) and be prepared for "spontaneous entertainment." You might hear live piano music or see Susan's invisible flaming baton twirling act. Yes, it's pricey, but you're also paying for the floor show. The chefs are creative, too—try the shrimp farcis appetizer. Main course offerings run the gamut from shrimp scampi over fresh linguine to chicken piccata.

ROCKPORT

This lovely little town at the tip of Cape Ann was settled in 1690. Over the years it has been an active fishing port, a center of granite excavation and cutting, and a thriving summer community whose specialty seems to be selling fudge and refrigerator magnets to out-of-towners. There's more to Rockport than gift shops—you just have to look. For every year-round resident who seems genuinely startled when people with cameras around their necks flock here each summer, there are dozens who are proud to show off their town.

Take a little time to explore beyond the immediate downtown area, and you'll see what Winslow Homer, Fitz Hugh Lane, Childe Hassam, and other artists were getting at when they captured Rockport in magnificent seascapes. Peer down the alleyways between the waterfront buildings or walk out to a spot with a clear view of the ocean to get your own perspective. The views from **Halibut Point State Park** (see below) are particularly dramatic. The town is still popular with painters, photographers, sculptors, and jewelry designers, and the Rockport Art Association is active all year. Many galleries show the work of local artists.

ESSENTIALS
Getting There
Rockport is north of Gloucester along Route 127 or 127A. At the end of Route 128, turn left at the signs for Rockport to take 127. Or continue until you see the sign for East Gloucester and turn left onto Route 127A, which runs along the east coast of Cape Ann. Rockport is 40 miles northeast of Boston, 7 miles north of Gloucester.

The MBTA **commuter rail** (☎ **617/222-3200;** www.mbta.com) runs from Boston's North Station. The trip takes 60 to 70 minutes. The **Cape Ann Transportation Authority,** or CATA (☎ **978/283-7916**) runs buses from town to town on Cape Ann.

Visitor Information
The **Rockport Chamber of Commerce and Board of Trade,** 3 Main St. (☎ **978/ 546-6575;** www.rockportusa.com), is open daily in summer from 9am to 5pm, and winter weekdays from 10am to 4pm. The chamber also operates an information booth from mid-May to mid-October on Upper Main Street (Route 127), about a mile from downtown—look for the WELCOME TO ROCKPORT sign. At either location, ask for the pamphlet "Rockport: A Walking Guide," which has a good map and descriptions of three short walking tours.

Getting Around
For traffic and congestion, downtown Boston has nothing on Rockport on a summer Saturday afternoon. If you can schedule only one weekday trip, make it this one. When you arrive, park and walk, especially downtown. If there's no place to park, use the parking lot on Upper Main Street (Route 127) on weekends. Parking from 11am to 6pm costs $6 to $7, and a free shuttle takes you downtown and back. The Cape Ann Transportation Authority (see above) also runs within the town.

EXPLORING THE TOWN
The most famous example of what to see in ✪ **Rockport** has something of an "Emperor's New Clothes" aura—it's a wooden fish warehouse on the town wharf, or T-Wharf, in the harbor. The barn-red shack known as **Motif No. 1** is the most frequently painted and photographed object in a town filled with lovely buildings and surrounded by rocky coastline. The color certainly catches the eye in the neutrals of the surrounding seascape. Originally constructed in 1884 and destroyed during the blizzard of 1978, Motif No. 1 was rebuilt using donations from the local community and

visitors. It stands again on the same pier, duplicated in every detail, and reinforced to withstand storms. Walk to the end of T-Wharf and look to the left so you can say you saw it, then move on.

Nearby is **Bearskin Neck,** named after an unfortunate ursine visitor who drowned and washed ashore in 1800. It has perhaps the highest concentration of gift shops anywhere. It's a narrow peninsula with one main street (South Road) and several alleys lined—crammed, really—with galleries, snack bars, antiques shops, and ancient houses. You'll find dozens of little shops carrying clothes, gifts, toys, inexpensive novelties, and expensive handmade crafts and paintings. Walk all the way to the end of the peninsula for a magnif-icent water view.

More than two dozen art galleries display the work of local and nationally known artists. The **Rockport Art Association,** 12 Main St. (☎ **978/546-6604**), open daily year-round, sponsors major exhibitions and special shows throughout the year. Chamber music fans can contact the Chamber of Commerce for information about the **Rockport Chamber Music Festival,** an early summer highlight.

If the mansions of Gloucester were too plush for you, or you want some recycling tips, visit the **Paper House,** 52 Pigeon Hill St., Pigeon Cove (☎ **978/546-2629**). It was built in 1922 entirely out of 100,000 newspapers—walls, furniture, even a piano. Every item of furniture is made from papers of a different period. It's open daily mid-April through October from 10am to 5pm. Admission is $1.50 for adults and $1 for children. Follow Route 127 north out of downtown until you see signs pointing to the left.

Don't fight the craving for fudge that inexplicably overwhelms otherwise mild-mannered travelers when they get their first whiff of salt water. Give in to temptation, then watch taffy being made at **Tuck's Candy Factory,** 7 Dock Sq. (☎ **800/569-2767** or 978/546-6352), a local landmark since the 1920s.

A TRIP TO THE EDGE OF THE SEA

The very tip of Cape Ann is accessible to the public, and worth the 2½-mile trip north on Route 127 to ✪ **Halibut Point State Park** (☎ **978/546-2997**). The surf-battered point got its name not from the fish, but because sailing ships heading for Rockport and Gloucester must "haul about" when they reach the jutting promontory.

About 10 minutes from the parking area you'll come to a huge water-filled quarry next to a visitor center, where staffers dispense information, brochures, and bird lists. Swimming in the quarry is absolutely forbidden. There are walking trails, tidal pools, a Second World War observation tower that's open to visitors, and a rocky beach where you can climb around on giant boulders. Swimming is not forbidden but not encouraged—the surf is rough and dangerous, and there are no lifeguards. Guided tours ($2.50 per person) are available on Saturday mornings in the summer, and there are also bird, wildflower, and tidal-pool tours; call the park or write **Friends of Halibut Point State Park,** P.O. Box 710, Rockport, MA 01966, for information and schedules. This is a great place just to wander around and admire the scenery. On a clear day, you can see Maine.

WHERE TO STAY

When Rockport is busy, it's *very* busy, and when it's not, it's practically empty. If you haven't made summer reservations well in advance, cross your fingers and call the Chamber of Commerce to ask about cancellations.

On Route 127 between Route 128 and downtown is the **Sandy Bay Motor Inn,** 173 Main St., Rockport, MA 01966 (☎ **800/437-7155** or 978/546-7155; fax 978/546-9131). A modern, two-story building overlooking the road, it has an indoor pool and accepts pets with payment of a $50 deposit. Prices for a double in the summer start at about $100.

In Town

Addison Choate Inn. 49 Broadway, Rockport, MA 01966. ☎ **800/245-7543** or 978/ 546-7543. Fax 978/546-7638. www.cape-ann.com/addison-choate. 8 units, 2 apts (some with shower only). Mid-June to mid-Sept $115–$140 double; $850 per week suite. Spring and fall $95–$115 double; $110 suite. Extra person $25. Rates include continental breakfast and afternoon refreshments. 2-night minimum stay summer weekends, 3-night minimum July 4th weekend. DISC, MC, V. Children under 12 not accepted.

Long known as Rockport's most charming place to stay, the Addison Choate Inn is a Greek Revival–style house built in 1851 and beautifully restored. The nicely appointed rooms have a mix of period antiques and more modern furnishings, and innkeepers Shirley and Knox Johnson redecorate one room each year. Some have canopied beds, and all but one unit is air-conditioned. The rooms range from comfortable to downright plush—the third-floor "Celebrations Suite" has a sitting room and a view of the harbor, and the apartment units in the stable house at the back of the property have loft bedrooms, kitchenettes, and phones. Guests have the use of a TV room and the outdoor pool. The suite and apartments have cable TV.

Captain's Bounty Motor Inn. 1 Beach St., Rockport, MA 01966. ☎ **978/546-9557.** www.cape-ann.com/capt-bounty. 24 units. TV TEL. May to mid-June $78 double, $82 efficiency, $88 efficiency suite; mid-June to early Sept $100 double, $115 efficiency, $125 efficiency suite; mid-Sept to Oct $85 double, $90 efficiency, $95 efficiency suite. Extra person $10; each child over 5 years old $5. Rates based on double occupancy. 2-night minimum stay weekends, 3-night minimum holiday weekends. DISC, MC, V. Closed Nov–Apr.

This modern, well-maintained motor inn is on the water. In fact, it's almost in the water, and close to the town center. Each rather plain room in the three-story building overlooks the water and has its own balcony and sliding glass door. Ocean breezes provide natural air-conditioning. Although it's hardly plush, and the pricing structure is a bit peculiar (note the charge for children), you can't beat the location. Rooms are spacious and soundproofed, and kitchenette units are available.

Inn on Cove Hill. 37 Mt. Pleasant St., Rockport, MA 01966. ☎ **888/546-2701** or 978/ 546-2701. www.cape-ann.com/covehill. 11 units, 9 with bathroom (4 with shower only, 1 with tub only). A/C TV. $68–$115 double with private bathroom, $50 with shared bathroom. Extra person $25. Rates include continental breakfast. 3-night minimum stay July–Aug weekends, 2-night minimum June, Sept–Oct weekends. MC, V. Closed Nov to mid-Apr. No children under 11 accepted.

This three-story inn was built in 1791 using the proceeds of pirates' gold found nearby. It's an attractive Federal-style home just 2 blocks from the head of the town wharf. Although it's close to downtown, the inn is set back from the road and has a delightful hideaway feel. Innkeepers Marjorie and John Pratt have decorated the guest rooms in period style, with at least one antique piece in each room. Most rooms have colonial furnishings and handmade quilts, and some have canopy beds. In warm weather, breakfast (with home-baked breads and muffins) is served on china at the garden tables; in inclement weather, breakfast in bed is served on individual trays.

Peg Leg Inn. 2 King St., Rockport, MA 01966. ☎ **800/346-2352** or 978/546-2352. www.cape-ann.com/pegleg. 33 units (some with shower only). TV. Mid-June to Labor Day plus holiday and fall weekends $90–$145 double; $160 2-bedroom unit. Off-season discounts available. Extra person $10. Rates include continental breakfast. 2-night minimum stay weekends, 3-night minimum holiday weekends. AE, MC, V. Closed Nov–Mar.

The Peg Leg Inn consists of five early American houses with front porches, attractive living rooms, and well-kept flower-bordered lawns that run down to a gazebo at the ocean's edge. It's not luxurious, but it is convenient and comfortable. Rooms are good size and neatly furnished in colonial style, and some have excellent ocean views. Guests may use the sandy beach across the road.

On the Outskirts

✪ **Old Farm Inn.** 291 Granite St. (Rte. 127), Rockport, MA 01966. ☎ **800/233-6828** or 978/546-3237. Fax 978/546-9308. 10 units (some with shower only), 1 cottage. A/C TV TEL. July–Oct $88–$130 double; mid-Apr to June and Nov $78–$125 double. Room with kitchenette $120, 2-room suite $130. 2-bedroom housekeeping cottage $1,125 per week July–Aug. Extra person $15. Rollaway $20. Room rates include buffet breakfast. 3-night minimum stay holiday and summer weekends. AE, MC, V. Closed Dec to mid-Apr. Follow Rte. 127 north from center of town until signs point to right for Halibut Point State Park; inn is in front of you.

This gorgeous bed-and-breakfast is a 1799 farm with antiques-furnished rooms in the Inn, the Barn Guesthouse, and the Fieldside Cottage. Each room is individually decorated with country-style furnishings (many have beautiful quilts on the beds), refrigerator, and coffeemaker. Innkeepers Susan and William Balzarini will make you feel at home. They serve a generous buffet breakfast in the first-floor sunroom. About 2½ miles from the center of town, the inn is in a beautiful location a stone's throw from Halibut Point State Park.

Ralph Waldo Emerson Inn. 1 Cathedral Ave., P.O. Box 2369, Rockport, MA 01966. ☎ **800/964-5550** or 978/546-6321. Fax 978/546-7043. www.ralphwaldoemersoninn.com. E-mail: emerson@cove.com. 34 units (some with shower only). A/C TEL. Spring–fall $115–$195 double; winter $85–$145 double. Extra person $15. Crib or cot $15. Rates include full breakfast spring to fall, continental breakfast in winter. Weekly rates available. 2-night minimum stay summer weekends. AE, CB, DC, DISC, MC, V. Follow Rte. 127 north from the center of town for 2 miles and watch for sign; turn right at Phillips Ave.

Somewhere in an old guest register you might find the name of Emerson himself—the philosopher was a guest in the original (1840) inn. The oceanfront building was expanded in 1912 and still has an old-fashioned feel, with the enjoyable modern convenience of a heated outdoor saltwater pool. Furnishings such as spool beds and four-posters grace the rooms, which are nicely appointed but not terribly large. There's no elevator; rooms that require a climb and face the street or have indirect water views are less expensive than more accessible accommodations. If you can manage the stairs, the view from the top-floor rooms is worth the exertion and expense. Recreation rooms include areas for playing cards or table tennis, or watching the wide-screen TV. The indoor whirlpool and sauna is available for a fee, and there are coin laundry facilities.

Yankee Clipper Inn (Romantik Hotel). 96 Granite St. (Rte. 127), P.O. Box 2399, Rockport, MA 01966. ☎ **800/545-3699** or 978/546-3407. Fax 978/546-9730. www.yankeeclipperinn.com. E-mail: info@yankeeclipperinn.com. 29 units. A/C TEL. Memorial Day to mid-Oct $139–$289 double; spring and fall weekends $115–$157 double, weeknights $109–$139 double. Extra person $26. Rates include full breakfast in summer, continental breakfast spring and fall. 2-night minimum stay weekends. AE, DISC, MC, V. Closed mid-Dec to mid-Mar.

Just north of town, this luxurious lodging sits on extensive lawns overlooking the sea. The three-story main inn—with its Georgian architecture, outdoor heated saltwater pool, and rooms with private balconies—is the most beautiful of the hotel's four buildings. Rooms are attractively furnished, with plenty of ruffles and florals; most are large, and many have views of the water. The least expensive offer neither, but you might not mind feeling like a poor relation at a place this nice. Many common rooms, notably the Veranda restaurant, face the water. Reservations (☎ **978/546-7795**) are required of guests as well as the public.

WHERE TO DINE

Rockport is a "dry" community where the law prevents restaurants from serving alcohol—but you can bring your own bottle. There are liquor stores nearby in Gloucester and the village of Annisquam (on the west side of the peninsula off Route 127).

For deli sandwiches during the day and sit-down service of Italian specialties Wednesday through Saturday evenings, **LoGrasso's,** 13 Railroad Ave., Route 127 (☎ **978/546-7977**), is a good choice.

Brackett's Oceanview Restaurant. 29 Main St. ☎ **978/546-2797.** Reservations recommended at dinner. Main courses $6–$15. AE, DC, DISC, MC, V. Mid-Apr to Memorial Day Thurs–Sun 11:30am–8pm. Memorial Day–Oct Sun–Fri 11:30am–8pm, Sat 11:30am–9pm. Closed Nov to mid-Apr. SEAFOOD/AMERICAN.

From the dining room at Brackett's, there's a gorgeous view of the water you glimpsed as you walked along Main Street. The nautical decor suits the seafood-intensive menu, which offers enough variety to make this a good choice for families—burgers are always available. The service is friendly, and the fresh seafood quite good, if not particularly innovative. Try the codfish cakes if you're looking for a traditional New England dish, or something with Cajun spices for a little variety. The most exciting offerings are on the extensive dessert menu, where anything homemade is a great choice.

✪ The Greenery. 15 Dock Sq. ☎ **978/546-9593.** Reservations recommended at dinner. Main courses $6.25–$12 at lunch, $9.25–$22 at dinner; breakfast items $1.25–$7. DISC, MC, V. Mid-Apr to Oct Mon–Fri 9am–10pm, Sat–Sun 8am–10pm. Closed Nov to mid-Apr. SEAFOOD/AMERICAN.

This is the best restaurant in Rockport, a place that could (but doesn't) get away with serving so-so food because of its great location at the head of Bearskin Neck. The cafe at the front gives no hint that the rear dining room boasts a great view of the harbor. The terrific food ranges from crab salad quiche at lunch to lobster at dinner to steamers anytime, and the huge salad bar is available on its own or with many entrees. Breakfast is served on weekends. All baking is done in-house. This is a good place to launch a picnic lunch on the beach, and an equally good spot for lingering over coffee and a delectable dessert and watching the action on and near the harbor.

My Place By-the-Sea. 68 South Rd., Bearskin Neck. ☎ **978/546-9667.** Reservations recommended at dinner. Main courses $5–$13 at lunch, $14–$22 at dinner. AE, CB, DC, DISC, JCB, MC, V. Apr–Nov daily 11:30am–9:30pm. Closed Dec–Mar. SEAFOOD.

The lure here is the location at the very end of Bearskin Neck, where you'll find Rockport's only outdoor oceanfront deck. There are excellent views of Sandy Bay from the two decks and shaded patio. The menu is reliable, with many options dictated by the daily catch. The baked fish and seafood pasta entrees are good choices, and you can also have chicken or beef. The dessert menu includes excellent homemade fruit pies.

Peg Leg. 18 Beach St. ☎ **978/546-3038.** Reservations recommended. Main courses $7–$19; children's menu $7. AE, MC, V. In season, daily 5:30–9pm. AMERICAN/SEAFOOD.

This pleasant restaurant serves tasty, uncomplicated food in a gardenlike setting, with plants and flowers all around. The romantic greenhouse, with recessed spotlights and candles, is behind the cozy main restaurant. Entrees include the house special chicken pie, seafood "pies" (casseroles), fresh fish, steaks, and lobster. All baking is done on the premises, and bread baskets always include sweet rolls.

Portside Chowder House. Bearskin Neck. ☎ **978/546-7045.** Reservations not accepted. Most menu items less than $8. No credit cards. Late June to Labor Day daily 11am–8pm; Labor Day to late June daily 11am–3pm. Closed Thanksgiving, Dec 25. CHOWDER.

Look left as you set out along Bearskin Neck; the crowds in front of the small house on the first cross street are waiting for chowder—clam and whatever else looked good that day. It comes by the cup, pint, and quart, to go or to eat in the tiny, low-ceilinged dining room with partial water views. You can also get seafood platters and surprisingly good burgers, but the real reason to come here is for tasty chowder to carry to the edge of the sea for a picnic.

6 Newburyport, Ipswich & Plum Island

The area between Cape Ann and the New Hampshire border is magnificent, with outdoor sights and sounds that can only be described as natural wonders, and enough impressive architecture to keep any city slicker happy.

In a part of the world where the word "charming" is used almost as often as "hello," **Newburyport** is a singular example of a picturesque waterfront city. Downtown Newburyport is on the Merrimack River. On the town's Atlantic coast, **Plum Island** contains one of the country's top nature preserves. On the other side of Ipswich Bay, **Ipswich** is a lovely little town that's home to **Crane Beach,** on another wildlife reservation.

NEWBURYPORT

To go directly from Boston, take I-93 (or Route 1 if it's not rush hour) to I-95— *not* Route 128, as for most other destinations in this chapter—and follow it to Exit 57, a solid 45-minute ride. Signs point to downtown, where you can park on the street or in a lot (there's one on the waterfront at the foot of Green Street) and explore. The MBTA **commuter rail** (☎ **617/222-3200;** www.mbta.com) instituted service from Boston's North Station in 1998. The trip takes about 1 hour, 15 minutes.

Perhaps because its distance from Boston makes the commute onerous (though not impossible), Newburyport has a substantial year-round population that lends it a less touristy atmosphere than its appearance might suggest. Start your visit at the **Greater Newburyport Chamber of Commerce and Industry,** 29 State St., Newburyport, MA 01950 (☎ **978/462-6680;** www.newburyportchamber.org), in the heart of the red-brick downtown shopping district. It also runs a seasonal information booth on Merrimac Street near Green Street. You can pick up maps, brochures, and shopping and accommodations directories.

Market Square, at the foot of State Street near the waterfront, is the center of a neighborhood packed with boutiques, gift shops, plain and fancy restaurants, and many antiques stores. You can also wander over to the water, take a stroll on the boardwalk, and enjoy the action on the river. Architecture buffs will want to climb the hill to High Street, where the Charles Bulfinch–designed building that houses the Superior Court (1805) is only one of several Federal-era treasures. Ask at the Chamber of Commerce for the walking-tour map.

If you haven't gone out to sea yet, now is a good time, and here's a good place: **Newburyport Whale Watch,** Hilton's Dock, 54 Merrimac St. (☎ **800/848-1111** or 978/465-9885; www.newburyportwhalewatch.com), offers 4½-hour cruises on a 100-foot boat with professional marine biologists on board as guides. Tickets are $25 for adults, $20 for senior citizens, and $17 for children 4 to 16; reservations are suggested. (See "A Whale of an Adventure," above, for more information.)

Or head to the ocean using an inland route. From downtown, take Water Street south until it becomes Plum Island Turnpike and follow it to the Parker River National Wildlife Refuge.

PARKER RIVER NATIONAL WILDLIFE REFUGE

The 4,662-acre refuge (☎ 978/465-5753; www.fws.gov/r5fws/ma/pkr.htm) on ✪ Plum Island is a complex of barrier beaches, dunes, and salt marshes, one of the few remaining in the Northeast. There's an entrance fee for motorists, bikers, and pedestrians. The refuge is flat-out breathtaking, whether you're exploring the marshes or the seashore. More than 800 species of plants and animals (including more than 300 bird species) visit or make their home on the narrow finger of land between Broad Sound and the Atlantic Ocean. The seven parking lots fill up quickly on weekends when the weather is good. Plan to arrive early. South of lot 4 (Hellcat Swamp), the access road isn't paved; although it's flat and well maintained and the speed limit is low, this isn't the place for your brand-new sports car.

The refuge offers some of the best ✪ birding anywhere, and observation of mammals and plants, too. Wooden boardwalks wind through marshes and along the shore—most don't have hand rails, so this isn't an activity for rambunctious children. You might see native and migratory species such as owls, hawks, martins, geese, warblers, ducks, snowy egrets, swallows, monarch butterflies, Canada geese, foxes, beavers, and harbor seals.

The ocean beach closes April 1 to allow piping plovers, listed by the federal government as a threatened species, to nest. The areas not being used for nesting reopen July 1; the rest open in August when the birds are through. The currents are strong and can be dangerous, and there are no lifeguards—you may prefer to stick to surf fishing. Striped bass and bluefish are found in the area. A permit is required for night fishing and vehicle access to the beach.

IPSWICH

Across Ipswich Bay from Plum Island is the town of Ipswich. It's accessible from Route 1A (which you can pick up in Newburyport or at Route 128 in Hamilton) and from Route 133 (which intersects with Route 128 in Gloucester and I-95 in Georgetown). The **visitor center** in the Hall Haskell House on South Main Street (Route 133) is open daily in the summer, and visitor information is also available from the **Ipswich Community Chamber of Commerce,** 46 Newmarch St., Ipswich, MA 01938 (☎ 978/356-3231) and the community Web site www.ipswichma.com.

Settled in 1630, Ipswich is dotted with 17th-century houses but better known for two more contemporary structures. The **Clam Box,** 206 High St., Route 1A/133 (☎ 978/356-5019), is a restaurant shaped like—you guessed it—a red-and-white-striped take-out clam box. This is a great place to try Ipswich clams, and not an easy place to sneak past if you have children in the car. Heading south from Newburyport, it's on the right.

South of Ipswich Center, near the intersection of Routes 1A and 133, look carefully for the Argilla Road sign (on the east side of the street). If you're traveling west on Route 133 from Gloucester and Essex, watch for a sign on the right pointing to Northgate Road, which intersects with Argilla Road. Follow it east to the end, where you'll find the 1,400-acre **Crane Memorial Reservation.** The property is home to **Crane Beach** (see box, "Life's a Beach"), a network of hiking trails, and **Castle Hill.** One of the Boston area's most popular wedding locations, the exquisite Stuart-style seaside mansion known as the Great House was built by Richard Teller Crane, Jr., who made his fortune in plumbing and bathroom fixtures early in this century.

If you can't wangle an invitation to a wedding, tours of the house ($7 adults, $5 seniors and children) are given on Wednesday and Thursday in the summer and

2 Sundays a year, spring and fall. They're also offered with a themed tea on the last Thursday of the month from May through October. Call for reservations.

From late May to October, you can ride in a hay wagon for a tour of the Crane Wildlife Refuge on Hog and Long islands, reached by boat across the Castle Neck River. The 90-minute **Crane Islands Tour** ($12 adults, $5 children under 12) is offered daily at 10am and 2pm. For more information, contact Castle Hill/Crane Memorial Reservation, 290 Argilla Rd., P.O. Box 563, Ipswich, MA 01938 (☎ **978/ 356-4351;** www.ttor.org).

Children (and adults) who can't get excited about a tour can be sent on to the beach, or they might be pacified by a stop just before Castle Hill. **Goodale Orchards Store and Winery,** 143 Argilla Rd. (☎ **978/356-5366**), is open weekends in April and daily from May to Christmas Eve. There are a picnic area, farm animals to visit, and an excellent country store where apples and baked goods are always available. Depending on the season, you might go on a hayride or participate in a fruit-wine tasting. Whatever the season, be sure to try some cider and doughnuts.

7 Plymouth

Everyone educated in the United States knows at least a little about Plymouth—about how the Pilgrims, fleeing religious persecution, left England on the *Mayflower* and landed at **Plymouth Rock** in 1620. Many also know that the Pilgrims endured disease and privation, and that just 51 people from the original group of 102 celebrated the first Thanksgiving in 1621 with Squanto, a Pawtuxet Indian associated with the Wampanoags, and his cohorts.

What you won't know until you visit is how small everything was. The *Mayflower* (a replica) seems perilously tiny, and when you contemplate how dangerous life was at the time, it's hard not to be impressed by the settlers' accomplishments.

Capt. John Smith sailed along the coast of what he named "New England" in 1614, calling the mainland opposite Cape Cod "Plimoth." The *Mayflower* passengers had contracted with the London Virginia Company for a tract of land near the mouth of the Hudson River in "Northern Virginia." In exchange for their passage to the New World, they promised to work the land for the company for 7 years. However, on November 11, 1620, rough weather and high seas forced them to make for Cape Cod Bay and anchor there, at Provincetown. The captain then announced that they had found a safe harbor, and he refused to continue to their original destination. On December 16, Provincetown having proven an unsatisfactory location, the weary travelers landed at Plymouth. They had no option but to settle in New England, and with no one to command them, their contract with the London Virginia Company became void. They were on their own to begin life in a new world.

Today, Plymouth is a manageable day-trip destination, and particularly enjoyable if you're traveling with children. It also makes a good stop between Boston and Cape Cod.

ESSENTIALS

GETTING THERE   By car, follow the Southeast Expressway (I-93) from Boston to Route 3. From Cape Cod, take Route 3 north. Take Exit 6A to Route 44 east, and follow signs to the historic attractions. The 40-mile trip from Boston takes about 45 minutes if it's not rush hour. Take Exit 5 for the **Regional Information Complex,** where you can pick up maps, brochures, and information about Plymouth and the rest of eastern Massachusetts. Take Exit 4 to go directly to **Plimoth Plantation.**

Plymouth

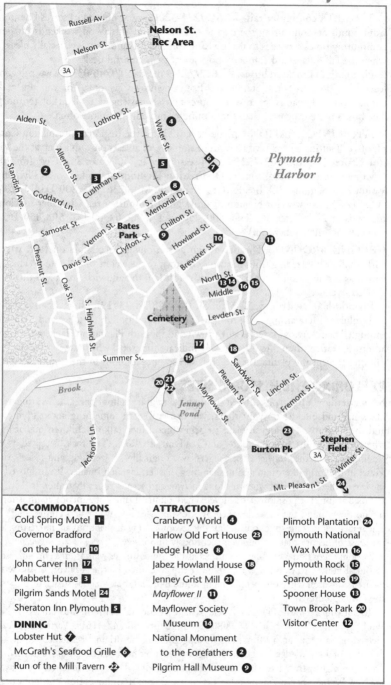

Plymouth Harbor

Nelson St. Rec Area

Plymouth Harbor

Bates Park

Cemetery

Jenney Pond

Brook

Burton Pk

Stephen Field

ACCOMMODATIONS
Cold Spring Motel **1**
Governor Bradford
  on the Harbour **10**
John Carver Inn **17**
Mabbett House **3**
Pilgrim Sands Motel **24**
Sheraton Inn Plymouth **5**

DINING
Lobster Hut **7**
McGrath's Seafood Grille **6**
Run of the Mill Tavern **22**

ATTRACTIONS
Cranberry World **4**
Harlow Old Fort House **23**
Hedge House **8**
Jabez Howland House **18**
Jenney Grist Mill **21**
Mayflower II **11**
Mayflower Society
  Museum **14**
National Monument
  to the Forefathers **2**
Pilgrim Hall Museum **9**

Plimoth Plantation **24**
Plymouth National
  Wax Museum **16**
Plymouth Rock **15**
Sparrow House **19**
Spooner House **13**
Town Brook Park **20**
Visitor Center **12**

NA-00XX

The MBTA **commuter rail** (☎ 617/222-3200; www.mbta.com) serves Plymouth from South Station during the day on weekdays and all day on weekends (at peak commuting times service is to nearby Kingston). The 1-hour trip is especially pleasant when the fall foliage and cranberry bogs are at their colorful peak.

Plymouth & Brockton **buses** (☎ 617/773-9401 or 508/746-0378; www.p-b.com) leave from Boston's South Station and from downtown Hyannis. You can also make connections at Logan Airport, where buses take on passengers at all airline terminals. The bus is more expensive than the commuter rail but runs more often.

VISITOR INFORMATION   If you haven't visited the Regional Information Complex (see "Getting There"), you'll want to stop in and at least pick up a map at the **Visitor Center** (☎ 508/747-7525), open seasonally at 130 Water St., across from the town pier. To plan ahead, contact **Destination Plymouth** (also known as Plymouth Visitor Information), P.O. Box ROCK, Plymouth, MA 02361 (☎ 800/USA-1620 or 508/747-7525; www.visit-plymouth.com). The **Plymouth Area Chamber of Commerce** is at 225 Water St., Suite 500, Plymouth, MA 02360 (☎ 508/830-1620; www.plymouthchamber.com).

GETTING AROUND   The downtown attractions are accessible on foot, with a fairly shallow hill leading from the center of town to the waterfront. Route 3A changes names as it runs through town, from Court to Main to Sandwich Street and finally to Warren Avenue.

Plymouth Rock Trolley, 22 Main St. (☎ 508/747-3419), offers a narrated tour and unlimited reboarding daily from Memorial Day through October and weekends through Thanksgiving. It serves downtown and Plimoth Plantation. Tickets are $7 for adults, $3 for children 3 to 12. Markers indicate the stops, which are served every 20 minutes (except the plantation, which is served once an hour in the summer).

EXPLORING THE HISTORIC SITES

No matter how often you suffered through elementary school pageants wearing a big black hat and buckles on your shoes, you can still learn something about Plymouth and the Pilgrims. The logical place to begin (good luck talking children out of it) is where the Pilgrims first set foot—at ✪ **Plymouth Rock.** The rock, accepted as the landing place of the *Mayflower* passengers, was originally 15 feet long and 3 feet wide. Time, in the form of erosion and mishandling, has left it much smaller. It was moved on the eve of the Revolution, when it broke in two, and several times thereafter. In 1867, it assumed its present position at tide level. The Colonial Dames of America commissioned the portico around the rock, designed by McKim, Mead & White and erected in 1920. The rock itself isn't much to look at, but the accompanying descriptions are interesting and the sense of history that surrounds it is curiously impressive.

At 6pm every Friday in August, citizens in Pilgrim costumes walk from Plymouth Rock to Burial Hill at Town Square, reenacting a trip to church by the survivors of the settlement's first winter. Fifty-one people might sound like a lot, but you'll be struck by the small size of the group.

To put yourself in the Pilgrims' footsteps, take a **Colonial Lantern Tour** offered by New World Tours, 98 Water St. (☎ 800/698-5636 or 508/747-4161). Participants carry pierced-tin lanterns on a 90-minute walking tour of the original settlement under the direction of a knowledgeable guide. It might seem a bit hokey at first, but it's fascinating. Tours run nightly from late March through Thanksgiving. The standard history tour leaves the New World office at 7:30pm; the "Legends and Lore" tour leaves from the lobby of the John Carver Inn, 25 Summer St., at 9pm. Tickets are $9 for adults and $7 for children. The same company offers a 2-hour "Lunch on Burial Hill" tour at noon daily in July and

August. The price ($15 adults, $10 children) includes a picnic lunch, and reservations are required.

A 40-minute harbor tour is another good introduction to Plymouth and a nice break from walking. You'll get a new perspective on Plymouth Rock and the *Mayflower II* and learn about maritime history. **Cape Cod Cruises** (☎ 508/747-2400) runs tours on the hour from 11am to 7pm, June through September. They leave from State Pier, near the *Mayflower II*. Tickets are $5 for adults, $4 for seniors, $3 for children under 12.

To get away from the bustle of the waterfront, make your way to **Town Brook Park,** at Jenney Pond, across Summer Street from the John Carver Inn. Across from the tree-bordered pond is the **Jenney Grist Mill,** 6 Spring Lane (☎ 508/747-3715; admission $2.50 adults, $2 children 5 to 12). It's a working museum where you can see a reconstructed water-powered mill that operates in the summer, daily from 10am to 5pm. The specialty shops in the complex, including the ice cream shop, are open daily year-round, from 10am to 6pm. There is plenty of parking.

Also removed from the waterfront is the **National Monument to the Forefathers** (☎ 508/746-1790), a granite behemoth inscribed with the names of the *Mayflower* passengers. Heading away from the harbor on Route 44, look carefully on the right for the turn onto Allerton Street, and climb the hill. The 81-foot-high monument is elaborately decorated with figures representing moral and political virtues and scenes of Pilgrim history—a style of public statuary so unfashionable that it seems quite rebellious. The monument is incongruous in its little park in a residential neighborhood, but it's also quite impressive. The view from the hilltop is excellent.

Mayflower II. State Pier. ☎ 508/746-1622. www.plimoth.org/mayflowe.htm. Admission $5.75 adults, $3.75 children 6–12. *Mayflower II* and Plimoth Plantation admission $18.50 adults, $16.50 seniors, $11 children 6–12. Both free for children under 6. Apr–Nov daily 9am–5pm.

Berthed a few steps from Plymouth Rock, *Mayflower II* is a full-scale reproduction of the type of ship that brought the Pilgrims from England to America in 1620. Even at full scale, the 106½-foot vessel, constructed in England from 1955 to 1957, seems remarkably small. Although little technical information about the original *Mayflower* survives, William A. Baker, designer of the replica, incorporated the few references in Governor Bradford's account of the voyage with other research to re-create the ship as closely as possible. In 1997, up to 3 years of extensive reconstruction and renovation began. The exhibit changes regularly the work proceeds, incorporating the workers' explanations and interpretations of their efforts. (Ordinarily, costumed guides provide first-person narratives about the vessel and voyage.)

Other displays describe and illustrate the trip and the Pilgrims' experience, including 17th-century navigation techniques and the history of the *Mayflower II*. Plimoth Plantation, which is 3 miles south of the ship, owns and maintains the vessel.

Pilgrim Hall Museum. 75 Court St. ☎ 508/746-1620. www.pilgrimhall.org. Admission $5 adults, $4.50 seniors and AAA members, $3 children. Feb–Dec daily 9:30am–4:30pm. From Plymouth Rock, walk north on Water St. and up the hill on Chilton St.

This is a great place to get a sense of the day-to-day lives of Plymouth's first European residents. Many original possessions of the early Pilgrims and their descendants are on display, including an uncomfortable chair that belonged to William Brewster (alongside a replica—that's how you can tell it's uncomfortable), one of Myles Standish's swords, and Governor Bradford's Bible. Regularly changing exhibits explore aspects of the settlers' lives, such as home construction or the history of prominent families. Among the permanent exhibits is the skeleton of the *Sparrow-Hawk,* a ship wrecked on Cape Cod in 1626 that lay buried in the sand until 1863. It's even smaller than the

Mayflower II. Built in 1824, the Pilgrim Hall Museum is the oldest public museum in the United States.

Plimoth Plantation. Rte. 3. ☎ **508/746-1622.** www.plimoth.org. Admission $15 adults, $9 children 6–12. Plimoth Plantation and *Mayflower II* admission $18.50 adults, $16.50 seniors, $11 children 6–17. Both free for children under 6. Apr–Nov daily 9am–5pm. From Rte. 3, take Exit 4, Plimoth Plantation Hwy. From downtown, take Rte. 3A south 2½ miles.

Allow at least half a day to explore this re-creation of the 1627 Pilgrim village, which children and adults find equally interesting. You enter by the hilltop fort that protects the villagers and walk down the hill to the farm area, visiting homes and gardens constructed with careful attention to historic detail. Once you get over the feeling that the whole operation is a bit strange—we heard someone mention Pompeii—it's great fun to talk to the "Pilgrims." They're actors who, in speech, dress, and manner, assume the personalities of members of the original community. You can watch them framing a house, splitting wood, shearing sheep, preserving foodstuffs, or cooking a pot of fish stew over an open hearth, all as it was done in the 1600s. They use only the tools and cookware available then. Sometimes you can join the activities. Wear comfortable shoes, because you'll be walking a lot, and the plantation isn't paved.

The community is as accurate as research can make it. Accounts of the original Pilgrim colony were combined with archaeological research, old records, and the history written by the Pilgrims' leader, William Bradford (who often used the spelling "Plimoth" for the settlement). There are daily militia drills with matchlock muskets that are fired to demonstrate the community's defense system. In fact, little defense was needed, because the Indians were friendly. Local tribes included the Wampanoags, who are represented at a homesite near the village (included in plantation admission), where members of the museum staff show off native foodstuffs, agricultural practices, and crafts.

At the main entrance, you'll find two modern buildings with an interesting orientation show, exhibits, gift shop, crafts center, bookstore, and cafeteria. There's a picnic area nearby.

✪ **Plymouth National Wax Museum.** 16 Carver St. ☎ **508/746-6468.** Admission $5.50 adults, $5 seniors, $2.25 children 5–12, free for children under 5 accompanied by parents. Mar–June and Sept–Nov daily 9am–5pm; July–Aug daily 9am–9pm. Closed Dec–Feb. From Plymouth Rock, turn around and walk up the hill or the steps.

Across New England (and probably across the country), adults who visited this museum as children can still tell you all about the Pilgrims. The galleries hold more than 180 life-size figures arranged in scenes. Dramatic soundtracks tell the story of the move to Holland to escape persecution in England, the harrowing trip across the ocean, the first Thanksgiving, and even the tale of Myles Standish, Priscilla Mullins, and John Alden. This museum is a must if children are in your party, and adults will enjoy it, too. On the hill outside is a monument at the gravesite of the Pilgrims who died during the settlement's first winter.

Cranberry World. 225 Water St. ☎ **508/747-2350.** Free admission. May–Nov daily 9:30am–5pm. Guided tours available; call for reservations. From Plymouth Rock, walk north for 10 min. along the waterfront.

Cranberries aren't just for Thanksgiving dinner, as Ocean Spray's interesting visitor center will remind you. Displays include outdoor demonstration bogs, antique harvesting tools, a scale model of a cranberry farm, and interactive exhibits. There are cooking demonstrations and free cranberry refreshments. September and October are harvest time.

THE HISTORIC HOUSES

You can't stay in Plymouth's historic houses, but they're worth a visit to see the changing styles of architecture and furnishings since the 1600s. Costumed guides explain the homemaking and crafts of earlier generations. Most of the houses are open from Memorial Day through Columbus Day and during Thanksgiving celebrations; call for schedules.

Especially if you're sightseeing with children, pretend the next sentence is written in capital letters: Unless all of you have a sky-high tolerance for house tours, pick just one or two from eras that you find particularly interesting. The Sparrow and Howland houses are most engaging for those curious about the original settlers.

The 1640 **Sparrow House,** 42 Summer St. (☎ **508/747-1240;** admission $1), is believed to be the oldest house still standing in Plymouth. It provides a fascinating look at the early residents' home life. Pottery made on the premises is for sale in the gallery. The house is near Town Brook Park. It's open Thursday through Tuesday from 10am to 5pm.

The 1666 **Jabez Howland House,** 33 Sandwich St. (☎ **508/746-9590;** guided tour $3 adults, 75¢ children 6 to 12), is the only house in Plymouth known to have been lived in by *Mayflower* passengers—Elizabeth Tilley and John Howland. The tour tells about them and gives another good look at the Pilgrims' lives. The house is near the corner of Sandwich and Water streets and is open daily from 10am to 4:30pm.

The next three houses are operated by the **Plymouth Antiquarian Society** (☎ **508/746-0012**). Call ahead before you visit to make sure they're open. At each house, admission is $3 for adults, 75¢ for children 6 to 12.

The 1677 **Harlow Old Fort House,** 119 Sandwich St., is staffed by costumed interpreters who demonstrate domestic crafts such as spinning and weaving amid period furnishings. By this time, the Pilgrims were settled, and you'll get a sense of life once mere survival stopped being a daily struggle. The house is about 4 blocks south of the center of town; open hours are usually 10am to 4pm, Thursday through Saturday in July and August, and Friday and Saturday in June and September through mid-October.

The 1749 **Spooner House,** 27 North St., was a family residence for more than 2 centuries and is furnished with a wealth of heirlooms that illustrate the changes in daily life over that period. The house is a few steps up the hill from Plymouth Rock. It's usually open from noon to 4pm, Tuesday to Sunday in July and August, and Wednesday to Saturday in June and September through mid-October.

The 1809 **Hedge House,** 126 Water St., is a Federal-style mansion next door to the visitor center and near the Town Wharf. It has period furnishings as well as a gallery with regularly changing exhibits drawn from the Antiquarian Society's collections of textiles and decorative arts. The hours are the same as those of the Spooner House.

The 1754 (with an 1898 addition) **Mayflower Society Museum,** 4 Winslow St. (☎ **508/746-2590;** admission $2.50 adults, 75¢ children 6 to 12), was originally the home of Edward Winslow, a great-grandson of the Pilgrim of the same name who served as governor of Massachusetts. Today, the furnishings span the 17th, 18th, and 19th centuries, plus there's a "flying" staircase that appears to defy gravity, and the formal gardens are a peaceful place to stroll. The museum is open from 10am to 4:15pm daily in July and August, Friday through Sunday in June, September through mid-October, and Thanksgiving weekend. From Plymouth Rock, turn around, walk 1 short block up North Street, and turn right onto Winslow Street.

WHERE TO STAY

On busy summer weekends, it's not unusual for every room in town to be taken. Make reservations well in advance.

If you're planning a longer stay, the lodgings listed here (and a number of others) participate in Destination Plymouth's **Historic Value Vacation Package** program. Three- and four-night packages (2 nights in April, May, or November) include a good deal on a room and free admission to a variety of attractions. Prices start at $100 per person, double occupancy. Ask about availability when you call for reservations.

A block and a half from the water, the **Mabbett House,** 7 Cushman St., Plymouth, MA 02360 (☎ **800/572-7829** or 508/830-1911; fax 508/830-9775; www.mabbet-thouse.com), is a gracious bed-and-breakfast with a double room ($99) and a two-bedroom suite ($170). Each unit in the turn-of-the-century colonial has a private bathroom and fireplace.

Cold Spring Motel. 188 Court St. (Rte. 3A), Plymouth, MA 02360. ☎ **800/678-8667** or 508/746-2222. Fax 508/746-2744. www.coldspringmotel.com. 31 units (some with shower only), 2 two-bedroom cottages. A/C TV TEL. Mid-May to Oct (including continental breakfast) $59–$99 double; $99–$139 suite; $79–$109 cottage. Off-season discounts available. Extra person $5. Closed Dec–Mar. AE, DISC, MC, V.

Convenient to downtown and the historic sights, this pleasant, well-maintained motel and the adjacent cottages surround a nicely landscaped lawn. Its location, a bit removed from the water, makes it a great deal. The two-story building is 2 blocks inland, not far from Cranberry World, and set back from the street in a quiet part of town.

Governor Bradford on the Harbour. 98 Water St., Plymouth, MA 02360. ☎ **800/332-1620** or 508/746-6200. Fax 508/747-3032. www.governorbradford.com. 94 units (some with shower only). A/C TV TEL. $89–$124 double. Extra person $10. Off-season and AAA discounts available. Children under 16 stay free in parents' room. AE, CB, DC, DISC, MC, V.

This three-story motor inn is across the street from the waterfront and 1 block from Plymouth Rock, the *Mayflower II,* and the center of town. Each attractively decorated room has two double beds, modern furnishings, a refrigerator, and a coffeemaker. More expensive units are higher up and have clearer views of the water. There are a small heated outdoor pool and coin laundry facilities.

✪ **John Carver Inn.** 25 Summer St., Plymouth, MA 02360. ☎ **800/274-1620** or 508/746-7100. Fax 508/746-8299. www.johncarverinn.com. 79 units (some with shower only). A/C TV TEL. Mid-Apr to mid-June and mid-Oct to Nov $79–$109 double, $159–$169 suite; mid-June to mid-Oct $99–$129 double, $179 suite; Dec to mid-Apr $69–$89 double, $149 suite. Extra person $10. Rollaway $10. Cribs free. Children under 19 stay free in parents' room. Passport to History package rates change seasonally. Senior and AAA discounts available. AE, CB, DC, DISC, MC, V.

A three-story colonial-style building with a landmark portico, this hotel offers comfortable, modern accommodations, a large outdoor pool, room service, and conference rooms. The good-size guest rooms are regularly renovated and decorated in colonial style. Children will enjoy the indoor "theme pool," with a water slide and Pilgrim ship model. The inn is within walking distance of the main attractions, and the staff is friendly and helpful. There's a Hearth 'n' Kettle restaurant on the premises. The Passport to History package includes a 2-night, 3-day stay for two, four breakfast tickets and two $10 discount dinner tickets for the restaurant, two Plimoth Plantation or whale-watch tickets, and two tickets to the trolley or Wax Museum.

Pilgrim Sands Motel. 150 Warren Ave. (Rte. 3A), Plymouth, MA 02360. ☎ **800/729-SANDS** or 508/747-0900. Fax 508/746-8066. www.pilgrimsands.com. E-mail:

thebeach@pilgrimsands.com. 66 units. A/C TV TEL. Summer $98–$130 double, spring and early fall $85–$110 double, Apr and late fall $65–$85 double, Dec–Mar $55–$85 double; $100–$200 2-bedroom suite year-round. 2-night minimum stay for holiday weekends. Rates may be higher on holiday weekends. Extra person $6–$8. AE, CB, DC, DISC, MC, V.

This attractive motel is on a private beach 3 miles south of town, within walking distance of Plimoth Plantation. If you want to avoid the bustle of downtown and still be near the water, it's a fine choice. The good-size, modern units have individual climate control and tasteful furnishings; three are accessible for travelers with disabilities. If you can swing it, book a beachfront room—the view is worth the money. In the summer, guests have access to the sundeck, whirlpool spa, and outdoor and indoor swimming pools. Most rooms have two double or queen beds, and many have refrigerators. They're divided into smoking and no-smoking wings. There's a coffee shop on the premises.

Sheraton Inn Plymouth. 180 Water St., Plymouth, MA 02360. ☎ **800/325-3535** or 508/747-4900. Fax 508/746-2609. www.sheratonplymouth.com. 175 units. A/C TV TEL. Apr–Oct $115–$225 double, Nov–Mar $100–$175 double. Children under 18 stay free in parents' room. Extra person $15. AE, CB, DC, DISC, JCB, MC, V.

If you need the amenities of a chain and want to be near the historic sights, this is your only choice—happily, it's a good one. The four-story hotel sits on a hill across the street from the waterfront. Rooms are tastefully furnished in contemporary style and have climate control and in-room movies. Some rooms have small balconies that overlook the indoor swimming pool and whirlpool. The first floor (41 rooms) was renovated in 1998. The hotel also has an exercise room, a business center and conference rooms, room service until 11pm, weekday newspaper delivery and dry cleaning, a laundry room, baby-sitting, a restaurant, and a pub. Rooms for travelers with disabilities are available.

WHERE TO DINE

Lobster Hut. Town Wharf. ☎ **508/746-2270.** Fax 508/746-5655. Reservations not accepted. Luncheon specials $5–$8; main courses $6–$14; sandwiches $3–$7; lobster priced daily. MC, V. Summer daily 11am–9pm; winter daily 11am–7pm. SEAFOOD.

The Lobster Hut is a self-service restaurant with a great view. Order and pick up at the counter, then take your food to an indoor table or out on the large deck that overlooks the bay. For starters, have some clam chowder or lobster bisque. The seafood "rolls" (hot-dog buns with your choice of filling) are excellent. The long list of fried seafood includes clams, scallops, shrimp, and haddock. There are also boiled and steamed items, burgers, chicken tenders—and lobster. Beer and wine are served, but only with meals.

McGrath's Seafood Grille. Town Wharf. ☎ **508/746-9751.** Reservations recommended at dinner. Main courses $10–$15. AE, DC, DISC, MC, V. Daily 11:30–9pm. Closed Mon in winter. SEAFOOD.

McGrath's is a big, busy place, the choice of many families, local businesspeople, and tour groups. Besides fish and seafood dinners, the extensive menu features poultry (including turkey, of course), prime rib, and sandwiches. Ask for a table overlooking the water, because the room facing inland is on the gloomy side, and be sure you're in good company, because service can be slow.

Run of the Mill Tavern. Jenney Grist Mill Village, off Summer Street. ☎ **508/830-1262.** Reservations recommended at dinner. Main courses $7–$12; children's menu $2.75–$3.25. AE, MC, V. Mon–Sat 11:30am–10pm; Sun noon–10pm. AMERICAN.

This friendly restaurant is near the water wheel at Jenney Grist Mill Village in Town Brook Park. It's an attractive setting, surrounded by trees, and the wood-paneled tavern offers good, inexpensive meals. The clam chowder is fantastic. Other appetizers include nachos, potato skins, buffalo wings, and mushrooms. Entrees are standard meat, chicken, and fish, and there are also seafood specials.

8 New Bedford & Fall River

New Bedford's history is inextricably bound to the whaling trade, as Fall River's is to the textile industry. Their decline in the 19th and early 20th centuries led to the cities' deterioration. Recently both have pushed to make themselves more attractive to the tourist trade, but it's a tough market. Almost anywhere else in the country, they would probably be rousing successes. In southeastern Massachusetts, about an hour from Boston and even closer to Plymouth, Cape Cod, and Newport, they're better known for outlet shopping than for historic attractions.

In New Bedford, at least, change is in the air. In 1997, the National Park Service created the **New Bedford Whaling National Historical Park.** The park, which encompasses the downtown historic district, commemorates the city's past as the world's leading whaling port.

New Bedford and Fall River are 15 miles apart on I-195 and Route 6. From Boston, take the Southeast Expressway south to I-93 (Route 128), then Route 24 south. It runs directly to Fall River, where you can pick up I-195 or Route 6 east to New Bedford. To go straight to New Bedford, take Route 24 to Route 140 south to I-195. From Plymouth, take Route 44 west to Route 24 south.

To get information before you go, contact the **Bristol County Convention & Visitors Bureau,** 70 N. Second St., P.O. Box 976, New Bedford, MA 02741 (☎ **800/ 288-6263** or 508/997-1250; www.bristol-county.org), which distributes a vacation guide with a section on outlet shopping. Also contact the **Office of Tourism,** Wharfinger Building, Pier No. 3, New Bedford, MA 02740 (☎ **800/508-5353** or 508/979-1745; www.ci.new-bedford.ma.us); the **New Bedford Area Chamber of Commerce,** 794 Purchase St., P.O. Box 8827, New Bedford, MA 02742 (☎ **508/ 999-5231;** www.nbchamber.com); or the **Fall River Area Chamber of Commerce,** 200 Pocasset St., P.O. Box 1871, Fall River, MA 02722 (☎ **508/676-8226;** www. frchamber.com).

NEW BEDFORD

The masses that flock to eastern Massachusetts aren't yet swarming the cobblestoned streets of historic New Bedford, which makes it a good destination for families on the verge of crowd-phobia. The attractions are reasonably close together, and there's a lot to be said for the fact that the residents genuinely welcome visitors.

The downtown area near the waterfront has been nicely restored. Start your visit at the **National Park Service Visitor Center,** 33 William St. (☎ **508/991-6200;** www.nps.gov/nebe), which is open daily from 9am to 4pm, except January 1, Thanksgiving, and December 25. Take a guided walking tour (daily in the summer, weekends in the off-season), or pick up a brochure that describes self-guided excursions around the historic district.

The centerpiece of the Historic Park is the ✪ **New Bedford Whaling Museum,** 18 Johnny Cake Hill (☎ **508/997-0046;** www.whalingmuseum.org). It's the world's premier whaling museum, which sounds terribly specialized but is actually quite absorbing. Children love the half-scale model of the whaling bark *Lagoda,* the world's largest ship model, and there are exhibits of the Old Dartmouth Historical Society's extensive art and maritime collections.

The newest display is the skeleton of a 65-foot juvenile blue whale. It was killed in a collision with a tanker in 1998, and the process of preparing it for show is as interesting as the skeleton eventually (by the fall of 2000) will be. The museum is open daily from 9am to 5pm, until 8pm on Thursdays in the summer. Admission is $4.50 for adults, $3.50 seniors, $3 children 6 to 14, free for children under 6.

The **Seamen's Bethel,** 15 Johnny Cake Hill (☎ **508-992-3295**), a nondenominational chapel described in Herman Melville's classic novel *Moby Dick,* is across the street from the museum. Up the hill from the water, the **Rotch–Duff–Jones House & Garden Museum,** 396 County St. (☎ **508/997-1401**), is an 1834 Greek Revival mansion with magnificent formal gardens.

FALL RIVER

On the waterfront, **Battleship Massachusetts,** Battleship Cove (☎ **800/533-3194** or 508/678-1100), is a five-vessel complex where you can see and board the 680-foot battleship USS *Massachusetts,* a destroyer, a submarine, and two PT boats. Also at Battleship Cove is the fully restored **Fall River Carousel** (☎ **508/324-4300**), built in 1920 and moved here from a nearby park in 1992.

The **Marine Museum,** 70 Water St. (☎ **508/674-3533**), became even more popular with its connection to movie history—it contains a 1-ton model of the *Titanic,* as well as many other models and exhibits about maritime history.

Lest you think Fall River emphasizes its seafaring legacy over its ties to the textile industry, don't forget the **factory outlets.** Clustered near I-195 (start at Exit 8A) in restored mill buildings, the outlets offer great prices on just about anything that can be manufactured from thread, including clothing, outerwear, linens, and curtains. And, of course, you'll also need accessories, hats, housewares, books, shoes, and more. Wear comfortable shoes.

Fall River's most famous former resident wasn't a sailor but a teacher—and an accused murderer. Although Lizzie Borden was acquitted in 1893 of killing her father and stepmother the previous year, she is remembered because of the verse: *Lizzie Borden took an ax / And gave her mother forty whacks. / When she saw what she had done / She gave her father forty-one.*

After many years as a private residence, the Borden house (where Lizzie continued to live) has been painstakingly restored as a B&B. Tours are offered if you don't want to spend the night—or if you're afraid to. As you might imagine, the building is reputed to be haunted. The family bedrooms (including the one where Mrs. Borden's body was found) are on the second floor. Breakfast (served to overnight guests only) includes some of the same dishes that were served on the fateful morning: johnny-cakes, bananas, sugar cookies, and coffee.

The **Lizzie Borden Bed & Breakfast,** 92 Second St., Fall River, MA 02720 (☎ **800/00-9549** for room reservations, or 508/675-7333; fax 508/675-7333; www.lizzie-borden.com); 30-minute tours leave every half-hour, daily from 11am to 3pm in summer (call for winter schedules), and cost $7.50 for adults, $3.50 for children 7 to 12. Overnight rates are $220 per night on the second floor and $165 per night on the third floor. Children under 12 are allowed overnight.

6 Cape Cod

by Laura M. Reckford

Only 70 miles long, Cape Cod is a curling peninsula encompassing miles of beaches, hundreds of freshwater ponds, more than a dozen richly historic New England villages, scores of classic clam shacks and ice cream shops—and it's just about everyone's idea of the perfect summer vacation.

More than 13 million visitors flock to the Cape from around the world to enjoy summertime's nonstop carnival. The Cape is, if anything, perhaps a bit too popular at full swing. Connoisseurs are beginning to discover the subtler appeal of off-season, when prices plummet along with the population. For some select travelers, the prospect of sunbathing en masse on sizzling sand can't hold a candle to a long, solitary stroll on a windswept beach with only the gulls as company. Come Labor Day, the crowds clear out—even the stragglers are gone by Columbus Day—and the whole place hibernates till Memorial Day weekend, the official start of "the season."

We've listed mostly **summer rates** for the accommodations in this chapter since that's when the vast majority of travelers plan their trips, but if you do want to explore the Cape off-season, you'll get the added benefit of lower hotel rates everywhere you go.

The **Cape Cod Chamber of Commerce,** Routes 6 and 132, Hyannis, MA 02601 (☎ **888/332-2732** or 508/362-3225; fax 508/362-3698; www.capecodchamber.org; E-mail: info@capecodchamber.org), is a clearinghouse of information about vacationing here. Stop in at their Information Center (seasonal) at the Sagamore Bridge rotary.

1 The Upper Cape

Because the Upper Cape towns are so close to Boston by car (just over an hour), they've become bedroom as well as summer communities. They may not have the let-the-good-times-roll feel of more seasonal towns farther out on the Cape, but then again they're spared some of the fly-by-night qualities that come with a transient populace. Shops and restaurants—many catering to an older, affluent crowd—tend to stay open year-round.

SANDWICH

The oldest town in this corner of the Cape (it was founded in 1637 by a contingent of Puritans who considered the environs north of Boston a mite crowded), Sandwich serves as a crash course in quaintness. A 1640 grist mill churns away at the mouth of a quiet pond frequented by swans, geese, ducks, and canoeists, while two early-19th-century churches and the columned Greek Revival Town Hall, in service since 1834, preside over the town square. On the whole, the pleasures that this region offers tend to be considerably quieter and more refined than the thrills offered elsewhere on the Cape; hence it tends to attract a more sedate, settled crowd. Older visitors, as well as young children, will find plenty to intrigue them. Those in-between, however, may get restless and yearn for livelier climes.

ESSENTIALS

GETTING THERE   Cross the Cape Cod Canal on either the Bourne or Sagamore bridges. At the Bourne Bridge rotary, take Sandwich Road along the canal; it turns into Route 6A as it nears Sandwich Center. If you cross the Sagamore Bridge, take exit 1 or 2, and follow Sandwich Road/Route 6A or Route 130, respectively, to Sandwich Center. It's 3 miles east of Sagamore, 16 miles northwest of Hyannis.

VISITOR INFORMATION   The **Cape Cod Canal Region Chamber of Commerce,** 70 Main St., Buzzards Bay (☎ **508/759-6000;** fax 508/759-6965; www. capecodcanalchamber.org; E-mail: canalreg@capecod.net), can provide literature on both Sandwich and Bourne. A consortium of Sandwich businesses has put together an excellent walking guide (with map). For a copy, contact the Summer House inn at ☎ **508/888-4991.**

BEACHES & OUTDOOR PURSUITS

BEACHES   For the Sandwich beaches listed below, nonresident parking stickers—$20 for the length of your stay—are available at Sandwich Town Hall Annex, 145 Main St. (☎ **508/833-8012**). There's no swimming allowed within the Cape Cod Canal—currents are much too swift and dangerous.

- ✪ **Sandy Neck Beach,** off Sandy Neck Road in East Sandwich. This 6-mile stretch of silken barrier beach with hummocky dunes is popular with endangered piping plovers—and, unfortunately, their nemesis, off-road vehicles. ORV permits ($80 per season for nonresidents) can be purchased at the gatehouse (☎ **508/ 362-8300**) as long as it's not nesting season. But do this fragile environment a favor and walk. ORV drivers must be equipped with supplies like spare tire, jack, shovel, and tire pressure gauge. Parking costs $10 per day in season, and up to 3 days of camping in self-contained vehicles is permitted at $10 per night.
- **Town Neck Beach,** off Town Neck Road in Sandwich. A bit rocky but ruggedly pretty, this narrow beach offers a busy view of passing ships, plus rest rooms and a snack bar. Parking costs $4 per day, or you can hike from town (about 1½ miles) via the community-built boardwalk spanning the salt marsh.
- **Wakeby Pond,** Ryder Conservation Area, John Ewer Road (off South Sandwich Road on the Mashpee border). The beach, on the Cape's largest freshwater pond, has lifeguards, rest rooms, and parking ($4 per day).

BICYCLING   The Army Corps of Engineers (☎ **508/759-5991**) maintains a ✪ **flat 14-mile loop** along the Cape Cod Canal equally suited to bicyclists and skaters, runners and strollers. Park (free) at the Bourne Recreation Area, north of the Bourne Bridge, on the Cape side. The closest bike rentals are available at **Cape Cod Bike Rental,** 40 Rte. 6A, Sandwich(☎ **508/833-2453,** which rents hybrid, mountain, and tandem bikes at around $22 per day. You can also park at the Sandcatcher Recreation Area at the end of Freezer Road in Sandwich.

BOATING   Cape Cod Coastal Canoe & Kayak (☎ **888/226-6393** or 508/564-4051; www.capecod.net/canoe; E-mail: cccanoe@capecod.net)runs naturalist-guided trips throughout the Cape. If you want to explore on your own by canoe, you can rent one in

Cape Cod

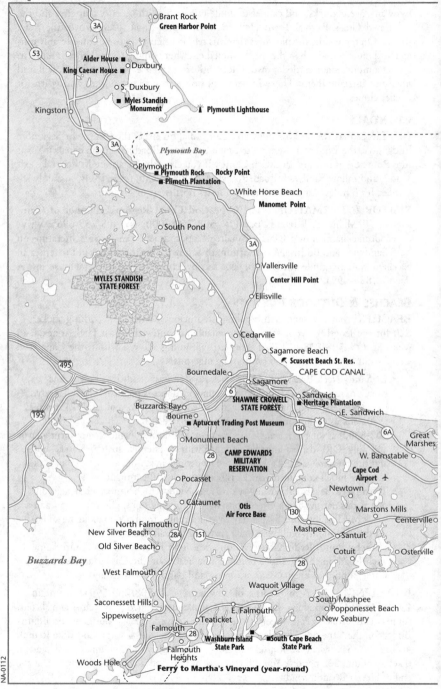

Brant Rock
Green Harbor Point

3A

53

Alder House ■
King Caesar House ■ ○ Duxbury

○ S. Duxbury

Kingston ○ ■ **Myles Standish Monument**

✝ **Plymouth Lighthouse**

3 3A

Plymouth Bay

○ Plymouth
■ **Plymouth Rock** — **Rocky Point**
■ **Plimoth Plantation**
○ White Horse Beach
Manomet Point

○ South Pond

MYLES STANDISH STATE FOREST

3A

○ Vallersville
Center Hill Point
○ Ellisville

○ Cedarville

3 ○ Sagamore Beach
↖ **Scussett Beach St. Res.**
CAPE COD CANAL

495

Bournedale ○ ○ Sagamore
6
Buzzards Bay ○ **SHAWME CROWELL STATE FOREST**
○ Sandwich
■ **Heritage Plantation**
○ E. Sandwich

195

Bourne ○
■ **Aptucxet Trading Post Museum**

130 6 6A

Great Marshes

○ Monument Beach

CAMP EDWARDS MILITARY RESERVATION

W. Barnstable ○

Cape Cod Airport ✈

28

○ Pocasset

Newtown ○

Marstons Mills ○

Centerville ○

○ Cataumet

Otis Air Force Base

130

North Falmouth ○
New Silver Beach
Old Silver Beach ○

28A 151

Mashpee ○ ○ Santuit

Cotuit ○ ○ Osterville

Buzzards Bay

West Falmouth ○

28

Waquoit Village ○

○ South Mashpee
○ Popponesset Beach
○ New Seabury

Saconessett Hills ○
Sippewissett ○

E. Falmouth ○
○ Teaticket

Falmouth ○ 28
■ **Washburn Island State Park**
■ **South Cape Beach State Park**

Falmouth Heights

Woods Hole ○

Ferry to Martha's Vineyard (year-round)

NA-0112

184

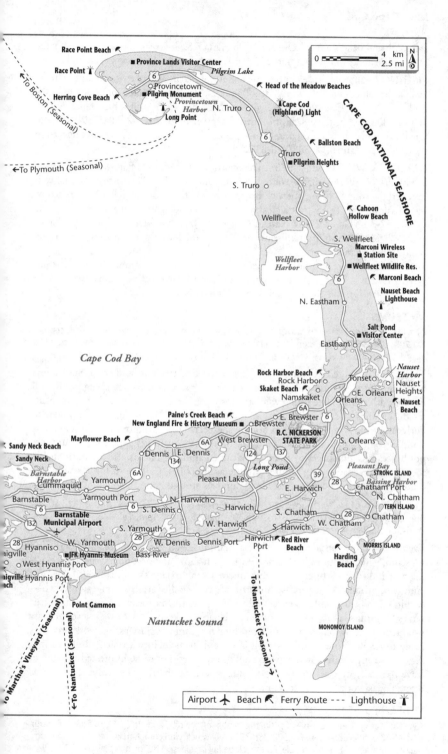

Race Point Beach
Race Point
Province Lands Visitor Center
To Boston (Seasonal)
Herring Cove Beach
Pilgrim Lake
6
Provincetown
Pilgrim Monument
Provincetown Harbor
Long Point
N. Truro
Head of the Meadow Beaches
Cape Cod (Highland) Light

CAPE COD NATIONAL SEASHORE

←To Plymouth (Seasonal)
6
Ballston Beach
Truro
Pilgrim Heights
S. Truro

Wellfleet
Cahoon Hollow Beach
S. Wellfleet
Marconi Wireless Station Site
Wellfleet Harbor
Wellfleet Wildlife Res.
Marconi Beach
Nauset Beach Lighthouse
N. Eastham
Salt Pond Visitor Center
Eastham

Cape Cod Bay

Rock Harbor Beach
Rock Harbor
Skaket Beach
Namskaket
Tonset
Nauset Harbor
Nauset Heights
E. Orleans
Orleans
Nauset Beach

6A
Paine's Creek Beach
New England Fire & History Museum
Mayflower Beach
Brewster
E. Brewster
R.C. NICKERSON STATE PARK
S. Orleans
Pleasant Bay
STRONG ISLAND

Sandy Neck Beach
Sandy Neck
Barnstable Harbor
Cummaquid
Barnstable
132
Yarmouth
Yarmouth Port
6A
6
Dennis
134
E. Dennis
West Brewster
124
137
Long Pond
Pleasant Lake
39
E. Harwich
28
Bassing Harbor
Chatham Port
N. Chatham
TERN ISLAND
Chatham

Barnstable Municipal Airport
S. Dennis
N. Harwich
Harwich
S. Chatham
28
W. Chatham

28
Hyannis
S. Yarmouth
aigville
West Hyannis Port
aigville Hyannis Port
ach
JFK Hyannis Museum
Bass River
W. Yarmouth
28
W. Dennis
W. Harwich
Dennis Port
Harwich Port
S. Harwich
Red River Beach
MORRIS ISLAND
Harding Beach

Point Gammon

Nantucket Sound

To Nantucket (Seasonal)

MONOMOY ISLAND

To Martha's Vineyard (Seasonal)
To Nantucket (Seasonal)
To Nantucket (Seasonal)

Airport ✈   Beach ☈   Ferry Route - - -   Lighthouse ⚓

0   4 km
     2.5 mi
N

185

Falmouth and paddle around Old Sandwich Harbor, Sandy Neck, or the salt-marsh maze of Scorton Creek, which leads out to Talbot Point, a wooded spit of conservation land.

FISHING   Sandwich has eight fishable ponds; for details and a license, inquire at Town Hall in the center of town (☎ **508/888-0340**). No permit is required for fishing from the banks of the Cape Cod Canal. Here your catch might include striped bass, bluefish, cod, pollock, flounder, or fluke. Call **the Army Corps of Engineers** (☎ **508/759-5991**) for Canal tide and fishing info. Local deep-water charters include the *Tigger Two*, docked in the Sandwich Marina (☎ **508/888-8372**).

NATURE & WILDLIFE AREAS   The **Shawme-Crowell State Forest,** off Rte. 130 in Sandwich (☎ **508/888-0351**), offers 285 campsites and 742 acres to roam. Entrance is free; parking costs $2. The Sandwich Boardwalk links the town and Town Neck Beach by way of salt marshes that attract a great many birds, including great blue herons.

The 57-acre **Green Briar Nature Center & Jam Kitchen** off Route 6A, Sandwich(☎ **508/888-6870;** admission free) has a mile-long path crossing marsh and stands of white pine.

To obtain a map of other conservation areas in Sandwich (some 16 sites encompassing nearly 1,300 acres), stop by the **Sandwich Conservation Commission** at 16 Jan Sebastian Dr. (off Route 130; ☎ **508/888-4200**).

MUSEUMS

✪ **Heritage Plantation of Sandwich.** Grove and Pine sts. (about ½ mile SW of town center). ☎ **508/888-3300.** Admission $9 adults, $8 seniors, $4.50 children 6–18. Mid-May to mid-Oct daily 10am–5pm; no tickets sold after 4:15pm. DISC, MC, V. Closed late Oct to mid-May.

This is one of those rare museums equally appealing to adults and children. All ages have the run of 76 beautifully landscaped acres, crisscrossed with walking paths, and riotous with color in late spring when the towering rhododendrons are in bloom. Scattered buildings offer a wide variety of collections, from Native American artifacts to Early American weapons. The art holdings, especially the primitive portraits, are outstanding. The high point for kids is a ride on the 1912 carousel, where the mounts are not horses but a menagerie of fancifully carved animals. There's also a replica Shaker round barn packed with gleaming antique automobiles. Call ahead for a schedule of outdoor summer concerts, usually held Sundays around 2pm, included in admission.

✪ **Sandwich Glass Museum.** 129 Main St. (center of town). ☎ **508/888-0251.** Admission $3.50 adults, $1 children 6–16. Apr–Oct daily 9:30am–5pm; Feb–Mar and Nov–Dec Wed–Sun 9:30am–4pm. Closed Jan.

Even if you don't consider yourself a glass fan, make an exception for this fascinating museum, which captures the history of the town above and beyond its legendary glass-making industry. A brief video introduces Deming Jarves's brilliant 19th-century endeavor: bringing glassware—a hitherto rare commodity available only to the rich—within reach of the middle classes. All went well until Midwestern factories undercut Jarves by using coal to fire their furnaces. Unable to keep up with their level of mass production, he switched back to hand-blown techniques just as his workforce was ready to revolt. None of this turmoil is evident in the dainty artifacts displayed in a series of sunny rooms. Anyone who goes in expecting not to be impressed is liable to leave dazzled. An excellent little gift shop stocks Sandwich glass replicas, as well as original glassworks by area artisans.

WHERE TO STAY

✪ **The Belfry Inne.** 8 Jarves St. (in the center of town), Sandwich, MA 02563. ☎ **800/ 844-4542** or 508/888-8550. Fax 508/888-3922. www.belfryinn.com. E-mail: info@belfryinn.com. 9 units. Summer $95–$165 double. Rates include full breakfast. MAP plan available. AE, MC, V.

You can't miss it: It's the gaudiest "painted lady" in town, restored to its original flamboyant glory after skulking for decades under three layers of siding. This turreted 1879 rectory has turned its fancy to romance, with queen-size retrofitted antique beds, a claw-foot tub (or Jacuzzi) in every room, and a scattering of fireplaces and private balconies. The third floor, with its single attic rooms and its delightful Alice-in-Wonderland mural leading up to the belfry, is perfect for families with children. The newest addition to the inn property is the 1902 church next door, which has 6 more rooms, all upscale.

Dining: The Belfry Bistro is an elegant choice for romantic fine dining in the cozy confines of the inn's several common rooms (see "Where to Dine," below).

The Dan'l Webster Inn. 149 Main St. (in the center of town), Sandwich, MA 02563. ☎ **800/444-3566** or 508/888-3622. Fax 508/888-5156. www.danlwebsterinn.com. 47 units. A/C TV TEL. Summer $139–$179 double, $209 suites. AE, CB, DISC, MC, V.

On this site once stood a colonial tavern favored by the famous orator, who came to these parts to go fishing. The tavern burned to the ground in 1971, but the modern replacement suits modern travelers perfectly. All the rooms are ample and nicely furnished with reproductions. The suites, located two historic houses across the street, are especially appealing; they feature fireplaces and canopied beds. The inn's common spaces are convivial, if bustling. This is a very popular place, among locals as well as travelers.

Dining: The restaurant here turns out surprisingly sophisticated fare, especially considering the high volume (see "Where to Dine," below).

Amenities: A small heated pool; access to a local health club.

Captain Ezra Nye House. 152 Main St. (in the center of town), Sandwich, MA 02563. ☎ **800/388-2278** or 508/888-6142. Fax 508/833-2897. www.captainezranyehouse.com. E-mail: captnye@aol.com. 7 units. Summer $85–$110 double. Rates include full breakfast. AE, DISC, JCB, MC, V.

A handsome federal manse, graced by a fanlight and twin chimneys, this B&B is not so forbidding that you can't kick off your shoes to enjoy a board game in the den. Rooms, if not ultra luxurious, are nicely appointed with eclectic antiques. Rates are a bargain, and breakfast tends to be quite substantial, along the lines of goat-cheese soufflé or upside-down apple French toast.

Spring Garden Motel. 578 Rte. 6A/P.O. Box 867 (about 5 miles E of town center), E. Sandwich, MA 02537. ☎ **800/303-1751** or 508/888-0710. Fax 508/833-2849. www.springgarden.com. E-mail: springg@capecod.net. 11 units. A/C TV TEL. Summer $83 double, $99 efficiency. Rates include continental breakfast. AE, DISC, MC, V. Closed Dec–Mar.

Looking like an elongated rose-covered cottage, this pretty double-decker motel overlooks the Great Sandwich Salt Marsh, and every room comes with a southern-oriented patio or porch that takes in the lush green landscape. With its spacious, tree-shaded backyard and pool, the motel is understandably popular with families.

✪ **The Village Inn at Sandwich.** 4 Jarves St. (in the center of town), Sandwich, MA 02563. ☎ **800/922-9989** or 508/833-0363. Fax 508/833-2063. www.capecodinn.com. E-mail: capecodinn@aol.com. 8 units, 2 with shared bathroom. Summer $85–$105 double. Rates include full breakfast. AE, DISC, MC, V.

Why envy the guests relaxing in rockers on the wraparound porch of this gracious 1837 Federal house when you could be among them? Better yet, you'll enjoy surprisingly light and airy sleeping quarters, with gleaming bleached floors, California-like splashes of colorful fabrics, and fluffy duvets. From the French country-style dining room to the cozy dormered attic, the mood is one of carefree comfort. Innkeeper Susan Fehlinger, an artist, also runs a program called "Sandwich

Artworks" out of the inn, with workshops by well-known Cape Cod artists. Packages are available.

WHERE TO DINE

✪ **The Bee-Hive Tavern.** 406 Rte. 6A (about ½ mile E of town center), E. Sandwich.
☎ **508/833-1184.** Main courses $5–$18. MC, V. Late May to early Sept Mon–Fri 11:30am–3pm, 5–9pm, Sat–Sun 8am–3pm, 5–9pm. Call for off-season hrs. AMERICAN.

A cut above the rather characterless restaurants clustered along this stretch of road, this modern-day tavern employs some atmospheric old-timey touches without going overboard. Dark wooden booths, green-shaded banker's lamps, and vintage prints and paintings convey a clubby feel. The food is good, and well priced for what it is. Straightforward steaks, chops, and fresh-caught fish are among the pricier choices, while burgers, sandwiches, and salads cater to lighter appetites (and wallets). This is a great option for lunch, when you should try the lobster roll, one of the Cape's best.

The Belfry Bistro. 8 Jarves St. (in the center of town). ☎ **508/888-8550.** Reservations recommended. Main courses $19–$25. AE, MC, V. April–Oct Tues–Sat 5:30–10pm; Oct–Mar Thurs–Sat 5:30–9pm. NEW AMERICAN.

This bistro is perhaps the most romantic choice in Sandwich, with its snowy, dense linens, intimate rooms, and ingratiating menu geared to grazers. Portions are generous and elegantly presented. Selections change with the seasons, but among the appetizers, you might find a lobster, scallop, and leek strudel wrapped in phyllo dough, baked golden brown and served on a bed of sautéed leeks and scallions with a Chardonnay cream sauce. The entrees run the gamut from the delicate Thai shrimp scampi in a red curry and lemongrass sauce; to the hearty filet mignon served with scallion and potato rosti wedges, baby carrots, and a medley of spinach, tomato and onion with a red-wine demi-glace. Desserts here are clearly a specialty, with choices like the white-chocolate cheesecake with morsels of meringue in a pool of raspberry coulis.

The Dan'l Webster Inn. 149 Main St. (in the center of town). ☎ **508/888-3623.** Reservations recommended. Main courses $15–$25. AE, CB, DC, DISC, MC, V. Daily 8am–9pm. INTERNATIONAL.

You have a choice of four main dining rooms—from a casual, colonial-motif tavern to a skylight-topped conservatory fronting a splendid garden. All of the dining rooms are served by the same kitchen, under the masterful hand of chef/co-owner Robert Catania. Try a classic dish like the fruits de mer (seafood) in white wine, or entrust your palate to a seasonal highlight (the specials menu changes monthly). The desserts are also superb.

FALMOUTH & WOODS HOLE

Often overlooked in the rush to catch the island ferries, Falmouth is a classic New England town, complete with 19th-century houses and churches encircling the town green. In fact, the area around the historic Village Green is a veritable hotbed of B&Bs, each vying in providing the most elaborate breakfasts and solicitous advice.

Officially a village within Falmouth (one of nine), tiny Woods Hole has been a world-renowned oceanic research center since 1871, when the U.S. Commission of Fish and Fisheries set up a primitive seasonal collection station. Today, the various scientific institutes crowded around the harbor—principally, the National Marine Fisheries Service, the Marine Biological Laboratory, and the Woods Hole Oceanographic Institute—employ thousands of scientists. Woods Hole's scientific institutions offer a unique opportunity to get in-depth—and often hands-on—exposure to marine biology.

Belying stereotype, the community is far from uptight and nerdy; in fact, it's one of the hip communities on the Cape. In the past few decades, a number of agreeable restaurants and shops have cropped up, making the small, crowded gauntlet of Water Street—don't even think about parking here in summer—a very pleasant place to stroll.

Falmouth Heights, a cluster of shingled Victorian summerhouses on a bluff east of Falmouth's harbor, is as popular as it is picturesque; its narrow ribbon of beach is a magnet, especially for the younger crowd. The Waquoit Bay area, a few miles east of town, has so far eluded the overcommercialization that blights most of Route 28. Several thousand acres of this vital estuarine ecosystem are now in federal custody.

ESSENTIALS

GETTING THERE   After crossing the Bourne Bridge, take Route 28 south. It's 18 miles south of Sagamore, 20 miles southwest of Hyannis.

The **Sea Line bus service** (☎ 800/352-7155) connects Woods Hole, Falmouth, and Mashpee with Hyannis year-round (except Sundays and holidays); the fare ranges from $1 to $3.50, depending on distance, and children under 5 ride free.

VISITOR INFORMATION   Contact the **Falmouth Chamber of Commerce,** Academy Lane, Falmouth, MA 02541 (☎ 800/526-8532 or 508/548-8500; fax 508/540-4724; Web site Falmouth/capecod.com).

BEACHES & OUTDOOR PURSUITS

BEACHES   While Old Silver Beach, Surf Drive Beach, and Menauhaut Beach sell a 1-day parking pass for $10, most other Falmouth public beaches require a weekly or seasonal parking sticker. Renters can obtain temporary beach parking stickers for $50 per week, $75 per month—at Falmouth Town Hall, 59 Town Hall Sq. (☎ 508/548-8623), or at the Surf Drive Beach Bathhouse in season ☎ 508/548-8623. The town beaches all have rest rooms and a concession stand.

- ✪ **Falmouth Heights Beach,** off Grand Avenue in Falmouth Heights. Acknowledged college-kid turf, this is where teens and twentysomethings tend to congregate. Parking is sticker-only.
- **Menauhant Beach,** off Central Avenue in East Falmouth. A bit off the beaten track, Menauhant is a little less mobbed than Surf Drive Beach, and better protected from the winds. Parking costs $10 per day.
- **Old Silver Beach,** off Route 28A in North Falmouth. Western-facing (great for sunsets) and relatively calm, this warm Buzzards Bay beach is a popular, often crowded choice. Mothers and their young charges cluster on the opposite side of the street where a shallow pool, formed by a sandbar, is perfect for toddlers. Parking costs $10 per day.
- **Surf Drive Beach,** off Shore Street in Falmouth. About a mile from downtown, and appealing to families, this is an easy-to-get-to choice with limited parking. Parking costs $10 per day.

BIKING   The ✪ **Shining Sea Bicycle Path** (☎ 508/548-8500) is a 3.6-mile beauty skirting the Bay from Falmouth to Woods Hole, with plenty of swimmable beach along the way; it also connects with a 23-mile scenic-road loop through pretty Sippewissett. You can park at the trailhead on Locust Street in Falmouth, or any spot in town (parking in Woods Hole is scarce). The closest bike shop—convenient to the main cluster of B&Bs, some of which offer "loaners"—is **Corner Cycle** at Palmer Avenue and North Main Street (☎ 508/540-4195).

BOATING   **Patriot Party Boats,** 227 Clinton Ave. (at Scranton Avenue on the harbor), Falmouth (☎ 800/734-0088 or 508/548-2626), offers scenic cruises past the Elizabeth

Islands on a sleek replica 1750s Pinky schooner, the *Liberte* (2-hr. sails; $20 adults, $14 children 12 and under).

Cape Cod Kayak (☎ 508/540-9377) rents kayaks (free delivery) by the day or week, and offers lessons and eco-tours on local waterways. If you want to explore on your own, **Edward's Boat Yard,** 1209 E. Falmouth Hwy., East Falmouth (☎ 408/548-2216), rents out canoes and kayaks for exploring Waquoit Bay; and **Cape Cod Coastal Canoe & Kayak** (☎ 888/226-6393 or 508/564-4051) runs naturalist-guided trips throughout the Cape (see "Nature & Wildlife Areas," below).

FISHING   Falmouth has six ponds. Licenses can be obtained at Falmouth Town Hall, 59 Town Hall Sq. (☎ 508/548-7611, ext. 219). Surf Drive Beach is a great spot for surf casting, once the crowds have dispersed. To go after bigger prey, head out on one of the **Patriot Party Boats** based in Falmouth's Inner Harbor (☎ 800/734-0088 or 508/548-2626). The clunky *Patriot Too,* with an enclosed deck, is ideal for family-style "bottom fishing," (half-day sails $20 adults, $14 children; equipment provided), and the zippy *Minuteman* (sportfishing for $75 per person) is geared to pros.

For serious fishing, go gunkholing with 30-year veteran Capt. John Christian on his Aquasport *Susan Jean* (☎ 508/548-6901), moored in Woods Hole's Eel Pond; he hunts for trophy bass among the neighboring Elizabeth Islands.

NATURE & WILDLIFE AREAS   Right in the town of Falmouth (just follow Depot Road to the end) is the 650-acre **Beebe Woods,** equally appealing to hikers and mountain-bikers. The 2,250-acre **Waquoit Bay National Estuarine Research Reserve (WBNERR),** at 149 Waquoit Hwy. in East Falmouth (☎ 508/457-0495), maintains a 1-mile, self-guiding nature trail. The reserve offers a number of interpretive programs, including the popular "Evenings on the Bluff," geared to families. Also inquire about its half-hour canoe trip over to **Washburn Island** on Saturday in season, by reservation. It has 11 primitive campsites—permits cost a mere $4 a night.

Though hardly in its natural state, the ✪ **Ashumet Holly and Wildlife Sanctuary,** operated by the Massachusetts Audubon Society at 186 Ashumet Rd., off Route 151 (☎ 508/563-6390), is an intriguing 49-acre collection of more than 1,000 holly trees, along with over 130 species of birds, and a kettle pond that's covered with a carpet of oriental lotus blossoms in summer. The trail fee is $3 for adults, $2 for seniors and children under 16.

WATER SPORTS   Falmouth is something of a sailboarding mecca, prized for its unflagging southwesterly winds. Both boards and boats can be rented at **Cape Cod Windsurfing Academy & Watersports Rentals** (☎ 508/495-0008), located at the Surfside Resort in Falmouth Heights; they also offer windsurfing lessons by appointment. Windsurfers can be rented for $15 an hour, $40 for a half day, or $50 for a full day. Kayaks rent for $15 an hour, $25 for a half day, or $35 for a full day. Sunfish sailboats rent for $30 an hour, $50 for a half day, and $90 for a full day.

SEA SCIENCE

National Marine Fisheries Service Aquarium. Albatross St. (off the western end of Water St.), Woods Hole. ☎ **508/495-2001**. Free admission. Mid-June to mid-Sept daily 10am–4pm; mid-Sept to mid-June Mon–Fri 10am–4pm.

A little beat up after 1¼ centuries of service and endless streams of eager school-children, this aquarium—the first such institution in the country—is no longer what you'd call state of the art, but is a treasure nonetheless. The displays, focusing on local waters, might make you think twice before taking a dip. Children show no hesitation, though, in getting up to their elbows in the "touch tanks." A key exhibit that everyone should see concerns the effect of plastic trash on the marine environment. You might time your visit to coincide with the feeding of two seals that summer here: The fish fly at 11am and 3pm.

○ **Woods Hole Oceanographic Institution's Exhibit Center.** 15 School St. (off Water St.), Woods Hole. ☎ **508/289-2252.** Donation suggested: $2, adults. Late May to early Sept Mon–Sat 10am–4:30pm, Sun noon–4:30pm; call for off-season hrs. Closed Jan–Mar.

This world-class research organization—locally referred to by its acronym, WHOI, pronounced "Hooey"—is dedicated to the study of marine science. And with some $80 million in annual funding at stake, there's some serious science going on here. The visitor center shows revolving videos about the institution's scientific work, including WHOI's discovery of the Titanic. One hour walking tours are offered twice a day in season; reservations are required.

WHERE TO STAY
Expensive
Coonamessett Inn. Jones Rd. and Gifford St. (about ½ mile N of Main St.), Falmouth, MA 02540. ☎ **508/548-2300.** Fax 508/540-9831. www.capecodtravel.com/coonamessett. E-mail: cmi.cathi@aol.com. 25 units, 1 cottage. A/C TV TEL. Summer $160–$235 double. Rates include continental breakfast. AE, MC, V.

A gracious, traditional inn built around the core of a 1796 homestead, The Coonamessett Inn is Falmouth's most established lodging choice. Set on seven lushly landscaped acres overlooking a pond, it has the feel of a country club where all comers are welcome. Some of the rooms, decorated in reproduction antiques, can be a bit somber, so try to get one with good light. Most have a separate sitting room attached. All have coffeemakers and hair dryers.

   Dining/Diversions: The Coonamessett Inn Dining Room is unabashedly formal, and fairly good, though the quality of the food can be inconsistent. A better choice is the adjoining Eli's, a clubby tavern, where a mellow jazz combo holds forth on weekends.

Moderate
○ **Grafton Inn.** 261 Grand Ave. S., Falmouth Heights, MA 02540. ☎ **800/642-4069** or 508/540-8688. Fax 508/540-1861. www.sunsol.com/graftoninn. 10 units. A/C TV. Summer $129–$174 double. Rates include full breakfast. AE, MC, V. Closed mid-Dec to mid-Feb.

Reminiscent of a more leisurely age, this turreted Victorian *grande dame* has a front-row seat on Falmouth Heights's lively beach. View-seekers will be delighted with the vista of Martha's Vineyard glimmering across the Sound. All rooms have extra touches like hair dryers, extra pillows, homemade chocolates, and fresh flowers—as well as coveted ocean views. Breakfast is served at individual tables on the screen porch overlooking the beach. The alternating, elaborate breakfast menu might include Sonoma Eggs (with sun-dried tomato, basil, chives, and salsa), Belgian waffles, or Hawaiian toast. In the afternoon, wine and cheese is served. The ferry to Martha's Vineyard, leaving from Falmouth Harbor, is only a 10-minute walk away.

○ **Inn on the Sound.** 313 Grand Ave., Falmouth Heights, MA 02540. ☎ **800/564-9668** or 508/457-9666. Fax 508/457-9631. www.falmouth-capecod/fww/inn.on.the.sound/. 10 units. TV. Summer $95–$175 double. Rates include full breakfast. AE, DISC, MC, V.

The ambience here is as breezy as the setting, high on a bluff beside Falmouth's premier sunning beach, with a sweeping view of Nantucket Sound from the new large front deck. Innkeeper Renee Ross is an interior decorator, and it shows. There's none of the usual frilly/cutesy stuff in these well-appointed guest rooms, most of which have ocean views and several with their own private decks. Many of the bathrooms have been newly renovated with large, luxurious tiled showers. The focal point of the living room is a handsome boulder hearth. The breakfasts served, especially the surprise French toast (baked and stuffed with cream cheese and berries) and the crab-and-cream-cheese soufflé, offer incentive to dawdle.

✪ **Mostly Hall.** 27 W. Main St. (W of the Village Green), Falmouth, MA 02540. ☎ **800/ 682-0565** or 508/548-3786. Fax 508/457-1572. www.mostlyhall.com. E-mail: mostlyhl@ cape.com. 6 units. A/C. Summer $135–$145 double. Rates include full breakfast. AE, DISC, MC, V. Closed Jan to mid-Feb.

Built by a sea captain to please his New Orleans–born bride, this plantation-style house exudes Southern graciousness and style. Longtime innkeepers Caroline and Jim Lloyd have pretty much mastered the art, providing memorable breakfasts (for example, eggs Benedict soufflé), loaner bikes, and plenty of valuable advice. Each of the six stately, high-ceilinged corner bedrooms boasts a canopied four-poster and cheery floral wallpaper. The mature gardens are particularly lovely in spring when the dogwoods, azaleas, and cherry trees are in bloom. The gazebo makes a pleasant retreat—as does the house's cupola, which is perfect for watching videos or reading.

Sands of Time Motor Inn & Harbor House. 549 Woods Hole Rd. (about ½ mile W of town), Woods Hole, MA 02543. ☎ **800/841-0114** or 508/548-6300. Fax 508/457-0160. www.sandsoftime.com. E-mail: reservations@sandsoftime.com. 35 units. A/C TV TEL. Summer $105–$150 double. Rates include continental breakfast. AE, CB, DC, DISC, MC, V. Closed Nov–Mar.

It's two facilities in one: a two-story block of motel rooms (with crisp, above-average decor, plus private porches) and, next door, a shingled 1879 Victorian manse, where the quarters tend to be more lavish and romantic—some with four-posters, working fireplaces, wicker furnishings, the works. Both types of accommodation, though, afford the same charming harbor views and share the well-kept grounds and small pool.

Inexpensive

Coppage Inn. 224 Waquoit Hwy. (Rte. 28, about 3 miles SW of the Mashpee rotary), Waquoit, MA 02536. ☎ **508/548-3228.** Fax 508/540-0814. 5 units, 2 with shared bathroom. Summer $85–$135 double. Rates include continental breakfast. MC, V.

This bargain-priced B&B may be the only small inn on the Cape with its own good-sized heated indoor swimming pool and sauna. The inn itself is a handsome, meandering 1800 colonial, with a beautiful large lawn dotted with flower gardens. Nearby is Waquoit Bay, perfect for canoeing, and a few miles away is Mashpee's South Cape Beach, one of the best in the area. Your hosts Bill and Elberta Warburton are models of hospitality. Several of the rooms are quite spacious and charmingly decorated, some with fireplaces and four-poster beds on painted wideboard floors. Elberta, a local caterer, bakes all the goodies for the continental breakfast which, weather permitting, is served on individual tables outside on the patio. Otherwise, you can enjoy breakfast poolside in the sunroom or even in the privacy of your room. The inn also has an unusual number of commons rooms (seven), so you're sure to find a comfy spot to curl up with a good book or to plan the day's activities.

WHERE TO DINE

Very Expensive

✪ **Regatta at Falmouth by-the-Sea.** 217 Clinton Ave. (off Scranton Ave., about 1 mile S of Main St.). ☎ **508/548-5400.** Reservations recommended. Main courses $23–$34. AE, MC, V. Late May to mid-Sept daily 4:30–10pm. Closed mid-Sept to Apr. INTERNATIONAL.

This place has it all: harbor views, polished yet innovative cuisine, and superb service. You're likely to find owner Brantz Bryan affably circulating: He's the one who seems to have wandered in off a golf course. His wife and partner, Wendy Bryan, designed the decor, from the rose-petal pale walls to the custom Limoges china on which two roses entwine. Chef Kenneth Biggs continues the innovative excellence in the kitchen. Menu favorites include a native scallop bisque with leeks and fresh tarragon, and the medallions of lamb tenderloin, herb-encrusted with a rosemary red wine sauce, served with basil risotto, oven-roasted tomatoes and grilled eggplant. If the dessert decision throws you into a tizzy, abandon all caution and order the "dessert for two"—a sampling of their four best desserts and sauces.

Moderate

Chapaquoit Grill. 410 Rte. 28A, W. Falmouth. ☎ **508/540-7794.** Reservations not accepted. Main courses $8–$18. MC, V. Daily 5–10pm. NEW AMERICAN.

The only dining spot in sleepy West Falmouth, this little roadside bistro has Californian aspirations—and attains them, with wood-grilled slabs of fish accompanied by trendy salsas, and crispy personal pizzas delivered straight from the brick oven. People drive from miles around for this flavorful food, and no reservations means long waits nightly in season and weekends year-round.

Fishmonger's Cafe. 56 Water St. (at the Eel Pond drawbridge), Woods Hole. ☎ **508/540-5376.** Main courses $10–$19. AE, MC, V. Mid-June to mid-Oct daily 7am–10:30pm. Call for off-season hrs. Closed Dec to mid-Feb. NATURAL.

A cherished carryover from the early 1970s, this sunny cafe attracts local young people and execs as well as Bermuda-shorted tourists, with an ever-changing array of imaginatively prepared dishes. Chef Harold Broadstock changes the dinner menu every couple of weeks and has added some Thai entrees to the varied menu. Regulars sit at the counter to enjoy a bowl of the Fisherman's Stew, while schmoozing with staff bustling about the open kitchen. Newcomers usually go for the tables by the window, where you can watch the Eel Pond boats come and go. Lunch could be a tempeh burger made with fermented soybeans, or an ordinary beef burger.

Landfall. Luscombe Ave. (half a block S of Water St.), Woods Hole. ☎ **508/548-1758.** Reservations recommended. Main courses $15–$21. AE, MC, V. Mid-Apr to Oct daily noon–11pm. Closed Nov to mid-Apr. AMERICAN.

A terrific setting overshadows the middling cuisine and ho-hum entertainment. Come for a drink, at least, to enjoy this massive wooden building constructed of salvage, both marine and terrestrial. The "ship's knees" on the ceiling are the ribs of an old schooner which broke up on the shores of Cuttyhunk Island; the big stained-glass window came from a mansion on nearby Penzance Point. A large bank of windows looks out onto the harbor, and the Martha's Vineyard ferry, when docking, appears to be making a beeline straight for your table.

The Quarterdeck Restaurant. 164 Main St. (opposite Town Hall Sq.). ☎ **508/548-9900.** Main courses $10–$17. AE, CB, DC, DISC, MC, V. June–Sept daily 11:30am–10pm; call for off-season hrs. REGIONAL.

Chef Keith Pacheco is amazingly versatile. He'll turn out Portuguese pork chops, Cajun-spiced barbecue, and veal meunière all in the course of an ordinary evening. Despite the standard-issue nautical trappings, this civilized spot is a definite cut above other look-alikes.

Inexpensive

Betsy's Diner. 457 Main St. (in the center of town). ☎ **508/540-0060.** Main courses $4–$10. AE, MC, V. May–Aug Mon–Sat 6am–10pm, Sun 6am–8pm; call for off-season hrs. AMERICAN.

Nothing could be finer than a resurrected diner—especially one offering hearty comfort food. Turkey dinner, breakfast all day, homemade pies—now, these are traditions worth maintaining. The original aluminum features dazzle as they did back then, and the jukebox is primed with oldies.

The Clam Shack. 227 Clinton Ave. (off Scranton Ave., about 1 mile S of Main St.). ☎ **508/540-7758.** Main courses $5–$11. No credit cards. Daily 11:30am–7:45pm. Closed mid-Sept to late May. SEAFOOD.

"Shack" is the appropriate term. This tumble-down shanty clings to its pier like a barnacle, having weathered three decades of nor'easters, not to mention the occasional hurricane. The fare has withstood the test of time, too: your basic fried clams (with belly intact, the sign of a joint that knows clams) and whatever else the nets have tossed up. Sitting at a postage-stamp table hinged to the wall, you can soak up a truly magnificent view.

FALMOUTH AFTER DARK

DRINKS   God knows whom you'll meet in the rough-and-tumble old Cap'n Kidd, 77 Water St., in Woods Hole (☎ 508/548-9206): maybe a lobster woman, maybe a Nobel Prize winner. Good grub, too.

The **Dry Dock Bar** (a.k.a. The Casino), at 281 Grand Ave., beneath the Wharf Restaurant (☎ 508/548-0777), is essentially a dance hall catering to twentysomethings. The fun spills over from the sand; locally bred bands provide the beat. There's a $5 cover. Closed October through April.

Everyone heads to **Liam McGuire's Irish Pub** on 273 Main St. in Falmouth (☎ 508/548-0285) for a taste of the Emerald Isle. Liam's the jolly, back-slapping guy with a touch of the blarney.

An alternative to rowdy bars is **Coffee Obsession,** 110 Palmer Ave. at the corner of North Main Street (☎ 508/540-2233), a hip yet friendly coffee bar.

2 The Mid-Cape

If the Cape could be said to have a capital, Hyannis would have to be it. It's a sprawling monstrosity, a concrete jungle of strip malls and chain stores, where the Kennedy mystique of the 1960s had the unfortunate side effect of spurring heedless development over the next several decades—a period during which the Cape's year-round population nearly doubled to approximately 200,000. The summer resident population is about three times that, and you'd swear every single person had daily errands to run in Hyannis. And yet this overrun town still has pockets of charm, especially the waterfront area and Main Street.

But the real beauty of the Mid-Cape is in its smaller places: old-money hideaways like Osterville to the west, and charming villages like West Barnstable and Yarmouthport, which can be found along the ✪ **Old King's Highway** (Rte. 6A) on the bay side of the Cape. A drive along this winding two-lane road, a former stagecoach route, reveals the early architectural history of the region, from humble colonial saltboxes to ostentatious captains' mansions. Scores of intriguing antiques shops subtly compete to draw a closer look, and each village seems a throwback to a kinder, gentler era.

HYANNIS & ENVIRONS

Many visitors experience post-Camelot letdown the first time they venture into Hyannis. But the downtown area, sapped by the strip development that proliferated at the edges of town after the Cape Cod Mall was built in 1970, is making a valiant comeback, with attractive banners and a pretty public park flanking the wharf where frequent ferries depart for the islands. If you were to confine your visit to this one town, however, you'd get a warped view of the Cape. Along Routes 132 and 28 you

Hyannis

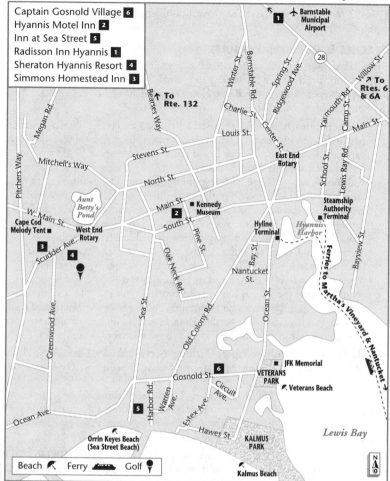

Captain Gosnold Village **6**
Hyannis Motel Inn **2**
Inn at Sea Street **5**
Radisson Inn Hyannis **1**
Sheraton Hyannis Resort **4**
Simmons Homestead Inn **3**

Beach — Ferry — Golf

could be visiting Anywhere, USA: They're lined with the standard chain stores, restaurants, and hotels, and mired with maddening traffic. While Hyannis's huge, impersonal hotels and motels have more beds at better prices than anywhere else on the Cape, there's little reason for choosing them, unless you happen to have missed the last ferry out. I'd recommend staying in Hyannisport, or heading over to Barnstable Village, due north. There you'll find a myriad charming B&Bs in historic houses along the scenic Old King's Highway. Once settled in, you can visit Hyannis to sample some of the area's best restaurants and nightlife. See below for details on Barnstable Village and environs.

ESSENTIALS

GETTING THERE After crossing either the Bourne or Sagamore bridges, head east on Route 6 or 6A. The latter passes through Barnstable Village; Route 132 south of Route 6A leads to Hyannis.

VISITOR INFORMATION For information, contact the **Hyannis Area Chamber of Commerce,** 1481 Rte. 132, Hyannis, MA 02601 (☎ **800/449-6647,**

877/492-6647, or 508/362-5230; www.hyannischamber.com; E-mail: chamber@ capecod.net).

Beaches & Outdoor Pursuits

BEACHES   Most of the sound's beaches are fairly protected and thus not big in terms of surf. Beach parking costs $8 a day, usually payable at the lot; for a weeklong parking sticker ($35), visit the **Recreation Department** at 141 Basset Lane, behind the Kennedy Memorial Skating Rink (☎ **508/790-6345**).

- **Craigville Beach,** off Craigville Beach Road in Centerville: Once a magnet for Methodist "camp" meetings (conference centers still line the shore), this broad expanse of sand boasts lifeguards and rest rooms. A magnet for the bronzed and buffed, it's known as "Muscle Beach."
- **Kalmus Beach,** off Gosnold Street in Hyannisport: This 800-foot spit of sand stretching toward the mouth of the harbor makes an ideal launching site for windsurfers, who sometimes seem to play chicken with the steady parade of ferries. The surf is tame, the slope shallow—the conditions are ideal for little kids. Lifeguards, a snack bar, and rest rooms facilitate family outings.
- **Orrin Keyes Beach** (a.k.a. Sea Beach), at the end of Sea Street in Hyannis: This little beach at the end of a residential road is popular with families.
- **Veterans Beach,** off Ocean Street in Hyannis: A small stretch of harborside sand adjoining the John F. Kennedy Memorial (a moving tribute from the town), this spot is not tops for swimming, unless you're very young and easily wowed. Parking is usually available, though, and it's walkable from town. The snack bar, rest rooms, and playground will see to a family's needs.

FISHING   The **Tightlines Sport Fishing Service** at 65 Camp St., Hyannis (☎ **508/790-8600**), conducts saltwater fly-fishing expeditions. **Hy-Line Cruises** offers seasonal sonar-aided "bottom" or blues fishing from its Ocean Street dock in Hyannis (☎ **508/790-0696**). **Helen H Deep-Sea Fishing** at 137 Pleasant St., Hyannis (☎ **508/790-0660**), offers year-round expeditions aboard a 100-foot boat with a heated cabin and full galley. For a smaller, more personalized expedition, get in touch with Capt. Ron Murphy of **Stray Cat Charters** (☎ **508/428-8628**).

GOLF   Open year-round, the **Hyannis Golf Club,** Rte. 132 (☎ **508/362-2606**), offers a 46-station driving range, as well as an 18-hole championship course. Smaller, but scenic, is the 9-hole **Cotuit High Ground Country Club,** 31 Crockers Neck Rd., Cotuit (☎ **508/428-9863**).

WATER SPORTS   **Eastern Mountain Sports,** 1513 Iyanough Rd./Route 132 (☎ **508/362-8690**), offers rental kayaks—tents and sleeping bags, too—and sponsors occasional overnights to Washburn Island in Waquoit Bay, as well as free clinics.

Touring by Steamer & Sloop

The Hesperus. Pier 16, Ocean St. Dock, Hyannis. ☎ **508/790-0077.** Rates $25 adults, $20 seniors and children 12 and under. Late May to mid-Oct daily 12:30, 3, and 5:30pm; call for off-season schedule. Closed Nov–Apr.

Offering an elegant means of exploring the harbor (while sneaking a peak at the Kennedy compound), the 50-foot, U.S. Coast Guard–certified John Alden sloop accommodates only 22 passengers, who are welcome to help trim the sails or even steer. Most opt to luxuriate in the sparkling sun and cooling breezes. The sporadic moonlight sails are especially romantic.

Hyannisport Harbor Cruises. Ocean St. Dock, Hyannis. ☎ **508/790-0696.** Tickets $10–$14 adults, free–$7 children 12 and under. Late June–Aug, 16 departures daily; call for schedule. Closed Nov to early Apr.

For a fun and informative introduction to the harbor and its residents, take a leisurely—1- to 2-hour—narrated tour aboard the Hy-Line's 1911 steamer replicas *Patience* and *Prudence*. Five family trips a day in season offer free passage for children under 12, but for a real treat take them on the Sunday 3:30pm "Ice Cream Float," which includes a design-your-own Ben & Jerry's sundae, or the Thursday 9pm "Jazz Boat," accompanied by a Dixieland band. There is also a lobster luncheon cruise, which leaves at 12:15pm on Mondays and Wednesdays.

THE KENNEDY LEGACY

For a lovely sightseeing drive, mosey around the moneyed Sound shore to the west. Don't even bother tracking down the Kennedy Compound in Hyannisport; it's effectively screened from view, and you'll see more at the John F. Kennedy Hyannis Museum in town. Or if you absolutely have to satisfy your curiosity, take a harbor cruise (see above).

John F. Kennedy Hyannis Museum. 397 Main St. (in the center of town), Hyannis. ☎ **508/790-3077.** Admission $3 adults, children under 16 free. Mid-April to mid-Oct Mon–Sat 10am–4pm, Sun 1–4pm (no admittance after 3:30pm); call for off-season hrs.

This primarily photographic display—supplemented by a brief video program narrated by Walter Cronkite—captures the Kennedys during the glory days of 1934 to 1963. Most of us have seen some of these photos before, but here they are all blown up, mounted, and neatly labeled; if you get confused about lineage, consult the family tree on the wall at the end of the exhibit.

SHOPPING

Although Hyannis is undoubtedly the commercial center of the Cape, the stores you'll find there are fairly standard for the most part. Head for the wealthy enclaves west of Hyannis, and along the antiquated Old King's Highway (Rte. 6A) to the north, where you're likely to find the real gems.

The Farmhouse, 1340 Main St. (about 1 mile south of Rte. 28), Osterville (☎ **508/420-2400**), Carolyn and Barry Crawford's 1742 farmhouse, is set up like an adult-scale dollhouse, and the "lifelike" settings should lend decorative inspiration. Self-confident sorts will go wild in the barn; it's packed with intriguing architectural salvage.

Ex-Nantucketer Bob Marks fashions the only authentic Nantucket lightship baskets, crafted off-island, and as aficionados know, they don't come cheap (a mere handbag typically runs in the thousands). You'll find them at **Oak and Ivory,** 1112 Main St. (about 1 mile south of Rte. 28), Osterville (☎ **508/428-9425**).

If you like potato chips, don't miss **Cape Cod Potato Chips,** Breed's Hill Road (at Independence Way, off Rte. 132), Hyannis (☎ **508/775-7253**)—they really are the world's best. Free factory tours are offered Monday through Friday from 9am to 5pm and Saturday from 10am to 4pm in July and August. The **Country Store,** 877 Main St., in the center of Osterville (☎ **508/428-2097**), is an old-fashioned general store, scarcely touched by time.

WHERE TO STAY

In Hyannis, Hyannisport, and Marstons Mills

There are a variety of large, generic, but convenient hotels and motels in Hyannis.

Right smack on Main Street within strolling distance of restaurants, shopping, and the ferries is the **Hyannis Motel Inn,** 473 Main St., Hyannis (☎ **800/922-8993** or 508/775-0255). Summer rates are $97 to $135 double. During the Kennedy administration, this motel served as the press headquarters. It has an indoor pool, a breakfast restaurant (not included with room rates), and a cocktail lounge.

A more upscale alternative is the **Radisson Inn Hyannis,** 287 Iyanough Rd. (Rte. 28), Hyannis, just east of the airport rotary (☎ **800/333-3333** or 508/771-1700), which features a full health club (a branch of Gold's Gym) and a bistro/pizzeria. Summer rates are $139 to $149 double, $159 to $189 suites. You'll have to overlook the uninspiring location in strip-mall hell, but it's within spitting distance of the airport. Rooms are clean and comfortable with attractive blond-wood furniture and plush carpeting.

If you prefer more amenities, there's the **Sheraton Hyannis Resort** at the West End Circle just off Main Street (☎ **800/598-4559** or 508/775-7775). Summer rates are $209 to $219 double. Out the back door is an 18-hole, par-3 executive golf course. There are also four tennis courts, an indoor and an outdoor pool, two restaurants, and a fitness center.

Inn at Sea Street. 358–363 Sea St., Hyannis, MA 02601. ☎ **508/775-8030.** Fax 508/ 771-0878. www.capecod.net/innonsea. E-mail: innonsea@capecod.net. 10 units (2 with shared bathroom), 1 cottage. Summer $90–$135 double; $145 cottage; $175 carriage-house suite. Rates include full breakfast. AE, DC, DISC, MC, V.

Just a short walk from Sea Street beach, this establishment is comprised of two well-maintained historic houses across the street from each other, with a tiny cottage nestled behind one. The main house is more formally decorated in a Victorian style with interesting antiques, and has high ceilings throughout. Some of the rooms have four-poster or canopied beds and claw-foot tubs. The house across the street has larger rooms, decorated with English country antiques. All rooms in this house have TVs and air-conditioning. The cute little cottage in back, with kitchen and sitting room, is a delight.

Inn at the Mills. 71 Rte. 149 (at the intersection of Rte. 28), Marstons Mills, MA 02648. ☎ **508/428-2967.** Fax 508/420-0075. 6 units. A/C. Summer $75–$125 double. Rates include continental breakfast. No credit cards. No children.

Unheralded by so much as a sign, this 1780 inn looks more like someone's enviable private estate—an illusion maintained once you venture indoors and step into a rustic, beamed kitchen. A sun porch harboring a white baby grand and comfy wicker couches overlooks both a small pool and a good-sized pond, occupied by gliding waterfowl and flanked by an inviting gazebo. The rooms are the picture of tasteful primness, with the exception of the cathedral-ceiling "hayloft" room that has dimensions fit for a medieval dining hall. This is where the honeymooners usually end up after a picture-perfect gazebo wedding.

✪ **Simmons Homestead Inn.** 288 Scudder Ave. (about ¼ mile W of the West End Rotary), Hyannisport, MA 02647. ☎ **800/637-1649** or 508/778-4999. Fax 508/790-1342. www. capecodtravel.com/simmonsinn. E-mail: simmonsinn@aol.com. 14 units. Summer $150–$200 double; $300 2-bedroom suite. Rates include full breakfast. AE, DISC, MC, V. Dogs welcome.

A former ad exec and race-car driver, innkeeper Bill Putman has a silly side and isn't afraid to show it. He started collecting animal artifacts—stuffed toys, sculptures, even needlepoint and wallpaper—to differentiate the rather traditional rooms in this rambling 1820s captain's manse, and kind of got carried away. The animal kingdom, plus his general friendliness, serve as an icebreaker. This is an inn where you'll find everyone mulling around the hearth sipping complementary wine (served at "6-ish") while they compare dinner plans. Guests who prefer privacy may book the spiffily updated "servants' quarters," a spacious, airy wing with its own private deck. Rooms vary in size, but all have extras like irons and hair dryers. Guests have access to a fleet of loaner bikes and a billiard room. In accordance with the permissive (i.e., fun) atmosphere here, dogs are allowed, and so is smoking in the commons room.

WHERE TO DINE
Very Expensive
✪ **The Regatta of Cotuit at the Crocker House.** 4631 Rte. 28 (near the intersection of Rte. 130), Cotuit. ☎ **508/428-5715.** Reservations recommended. Main courses $22–$35. AE, MC, V. June–Aug daily 5–10pm, Sept–May Tues–Sun 5–10pm. NEW AMERICAN.

One of the best restaurants on Cape Cod, this year-round cousin of the Regatta at Falmouth-by-the-Sea serves many of the same signature dishes—such as the stellar lamb en chemise—in a suite of charmingly decorated Federal-era rooms. Nightly specials might include hearty offerings like buffalo tenderloin or perhaps a 12-oz. veal chop. The cuisine is at once exquisitely prepared and presented, fortified by herbs and vegetables plucked fresh from the kitchen garden, and the mood is invariably festive. You're likely to experience the best service on Cape Cod here.

Expensive
Penguin SeaGrill. 331 Main St. (in the center of town), Hyannis. ☎ **508/775-2023.** Reservations recommended. Main courses $15–$24. AE, DISC, MC, V. Sun–Thurs 5–10pm, Fri–Sat 5–11pm; call for off-season hrs. Closed Jan to mid-Feb. INTERNATIONAL.

Chef/owner Bob Gold is one of those restless types who, having mastered one style of cuisine (Italian), can't wait to take on another. Hence the versatile menu, which bounces from Asian influences like "Thai Jumpin' Squid," to mussels Portuguese style. The specialty here is definitely seafood; pay attention to the specials and you can't go wrong. Large lobsters are served nightly; meats and fish are wood-grilled. The setting is handsome and contemporary, with brick walls, mirrored accents, and mammoth carved fish. There's live jazz weekend nights in season.

✪ **Ristorante Barolo.** 1 Financial Place (297 North St., just off the W. End Rotary), Hyannis. ☎ **508/778-2878.** Main courses $9–$22. AE, DC, MC, V. June–Sept Sun–Thurs 4–11pm, Fri–Sat 4pm–midnight; call for off-season hrs. NORTHERN ITALIAN.

This is the best Italian restaurant in town, part of a smart-looking brick office complex. A thoroughly up-to-date establishment, it does everything right, from the extravirgin olive oil for dunking its crusty bread to those perfectly al dente pastas. Appetizers perfect for sharing are *polpette gartinate alla Romana* (homemade meatballs in a tomato and basil sauce) and *gamberi al martini* (shrimp sautéed with fresh scallions and martini wine sauce). Entrees include a number of tempting veal choices, like *vitello alla Sorrentina* (provimi veal, mozzarella and basil with plum tomato sauce), as well as such favorites as linguine al frutti di mare, with littlenecks, mussels, shrimp and calamari. The desserts are brought in daily from Boston's famed North End.

✪ **Roadhouse Cafe.** 488 South St. (off Main St., near the W. End Rotary), Hyannis. ☎ **508/775-2386.** Main courses $12–$24. AE, CB, DC, DISC, MC, V. Daily 4pm–11pm. AMERICAN/NORTHERN ITALIAN.

The humble name belies the culinary caliber of this intimate but ambitious restaurant. This is not the hybrid "Italian-American" fare that so poorly represents both. Instead, the extensive menu is pretty much split between American standards such as steak (not to mention oysters Rockefeller or casino) and real Italian cooking, unstinting on the garlic. There's also a less expensive lighter-fare menu, including what some have called "the best burger in the world," served in the snazzy bistro in back. Among the appetizers are such delicacies as beef carpaccio with fresh-shaved Parmesan, and vineripened tomatoes and buffalo mozzarella drizzled with balsamic vinaigrette. The latter also makes a tasty marinade for native swordfish headed for the grill. The signature dessert, a distinctly non-Italian cheesecake infused with Bailey's Irish Creme, is itself an excuse to come check out the live jazz in the bistro (see "Hyannis & Environs After Dark," below).

Moderate

The Black Cat. 165 Ocean St. (opposite the Ocean St. dock), Hyannis. ☎ **508/778-1233.** Main courses $11–$24. AE, DC, DISC, MC, V. Apr–Oct daily 11:30am–10pm; call for off-season hrs. NEW AMERICAN.

Conveniently located less than a block from the Hy-Line ferries, this is a fine place to catch a quick bite or full meal while you wait for your boat to come in. The menu is pretty basic—steak, pasta, and, of course, fish—but attention is paid to the details; the onion rings, for instance, are made fresh. The dining room, with its bar of gleaming mahogany and brass, will appeal to chilled travelers on a blustery day; in fine weather, you might prefer the porch. There's live jazz weekend nights in season.

Tugboats. 21 Arlington St. (at the Hyannis Marina, off Willow St.), Hyannis. ☎ **508/775-6433.** Main courses $11–$17. AE, DC, DISC, MC, V. July–Sept daily 11:30am–10:00pm; call for off-season hrs. Closed Nov–Mar. AMERICAN.

Yet another harborside perch for munching and ogling, this one's especially appealing: The two spacious outdoor decks are angled just right for you to catch the sunset with cocktails in hand. Forget fancy dining and chow down on blackened-swordfish bites (topping a Caesar salad, perhaps) or lobster fritters, or the double-duty Steak Neptune, topped with scallops and shrimp. For dessert, try the shortbread-crusted Bourbon pecan pie, or a Key lime pie purportedly lifted straight from Papa's of Key West.

Inexpensive

Baxter's Boat House. 177 Pleasant St. (near Steamship Authority ferry), Hyannis. ☎ **508/775-7040.** Main courses $8–$14. AE, MC, V. Late May–early Sept Mon–Sat 11:30am–10pm, Sun 11:30am–9pm; call for off-season hrs. Closed mid-Oct to mid-Apr. SEAFOOD.

A shingled shack on a jetty jutting out into the harbor, Baxter's has catered to the boating crowd since the mid-1950s, with Cape classics such as fried clams and fish virtually any way you like it, from baked to blackened, served on paper plates.

The Egg & I. 521 Main St. (in the center of town), Hyannis. ☎ **508/771-1596.** All items under $10. AE, CB, DC, DISC, MC, V. April–Oct daily 11pm–1pm. Mar and Nov, weekends only. Closed Dec–Feb. AMERICAN.

Yes, those are the correct hours. This Tudor-storefront diner opens at 11 at night, then serves past noon. A town with this many bars needs a place where patrons and staff alike can unwind and/or sober up after last call; a wholesome meal wouldn't hurt either. Breakfast is usually the meal of choice, especially the "create an omelet" option, but the pancakes—from chocolate-chip to fruit-loaded Swedish—are strong contenders. Children go gaga over the Mickey Mouse waffle (only $3, with bacon or sausage), and those who feel silly having breakfast before bed can order sandwiches or one of a dozen or so daily specials that change with the season.

HYANNIS & ENVIRONS AFTER DARK

From July to early September, try to catch a show at ✪ **The Cape Cod Melody Tent,** West End Rotary, Hyannis (☎ 508/775-9100). Built as a summer theater in 1950, this billowy blue big top proved even better suited to variety shows. A nonprofit venture since 1990 (proceeds fund other cultural initiatives Cape-wide), the Melody Tent hosted the major performers of the past half century, from jazz greats to comedians, crooners to rockers. Every seat is a winner in this grand oval, only 20 banked aisles deep. There's also a children's theater program Wednesday mornings at 11am.

Everyone's glowing with the day's exertions as they cram onto the deck at **Steamers Grill & Bar,** 235 Ocean St., Hyannis (☎ 508/778-0818) to enjoy liberal libations, a lingering sunset and, on weekends, live bands. Upstairs, it's a young, sporty crowd for the most part, and by 9pm on Fridays and Saturdays in season, it's packed. No cover.

A good place for after-dinner entertainment is the ✪ **Roadhouse Cafe,** 488 South St. (see "Where to Dine," above), Hyannis (☎ 508/775-2386), a dark-paneled bar, decorated in burgundy leather like an English gentlemen's club. The bar stocks 48 boutique beers, in addition to all the usual hard, soft, and sweet liquors, and you won't go hoarse trying to converse over the soft jazz.

At **Baxter's Boat House,** 177 Pleasant St. (see "Where to Dine," above), Hyannis (☎ 508/775-7040), the congenial little lounge, with map-topped tables and low-key blues piano, draws an attractive crowd, including the occasional vacationing celebrity.

Roo Bar, 586 Main St., Hyannis (☎ 508/778-6515) feels very Manhattan, with ultra-cool servers, a long sleek bar area, and lots of attitude. The bistro food is good too. Cigar smoking starts after 10pm.

The cramped dance floor makes for instant camaraderie at **Harry's,** 700 Main St., Hyannis (☎ 508/778-4188). The classic blues music heard here really demands to be absorbed in such an intimate space. On Thursday and Saturday nights, there's a $3 to $4 cover.

Both the whimsically decorated setting and the solicitous staff contrive to ensure a good time at **Starbuck's,** 645 Rte. 132, Hyannis (☎ 508/778-6767). There is no cover for the acoustic acts and soft-rock bands featured here, and the drinks range from silly (for example, Grape Crush) to serious (27-oz. margaritas).

BARNSTABLE VILLAGE & ENVIRONS

Just a couple miles from hectic Hyannis, the bucolic village of Barnstable houses the county courthouse and government offices for the region. In this peaceful setting are some of the most charming and well-managed B&Bs around. The bay area along historic Route 6A unfolds in a blur of greenery and well-kept colonial houses. I'd suggest staying here and venturing into Hyannis for restaurants and nightlife.

OUTDOOR PURSUITS

BEACHES   Barnstable's primary Bay beach is Sandy Neck, accessed through East Sandwich (see "Beaches" under the Sandwich section above).

BOATING   Cape Cod Coastal Canoe & Kayak (☎ 888/226-6393 or 508/564-4051) runs naturalist-guided trips throughout the Cape. Trips (2, 4, and 6 hr.) are offered daily, weather-permitting, April through September, and weekends through October.

If you want to explore on your own, you can rent a kayak from Eastern Mountain Sports (see "Watersports" above) and paddle around Scorton Creek, Sandy Neck, and Barnstable Harbor. For experienced paddlers, Barnstable's **Great Marsh**—one of the largest in New England—offers beautiful waterways out to Sandy Neck.

FISHING   The township of Barnstable has 11 ponds for freshwater fishing; for information and permits, visit **Town Hall** at 367 Main St., Hyannis (☎ 508/790-6240) or **Sports Port,** 149 West Main Street, Hyannis (☎ 508/775-3096). Shellfishing permits are available from the **Department of Natural Resources** at 1189 Phinneys Lane, Centerville (☎ 508/790-6272). Surf casting, without a license, is permitted on Sandy Neck. Among the charter boats berthed in **Barnstable Harbor** is the *Drifter* (☎ 508/398-2061), a 35-foot boat offering half- and full-day trips.

WHALE WATCHING   Better whale-watching tours leave from Provincetown at the tip of the Cape, but if you'd rather spend the extra hour on a boat than in a car, hop aboard at **Hyannis Whale-Watch Cruises,** Barnstable Harbor (about ½ mile north of Rte. 6A on Mill Way), Barnstable (☎ 888/942-5392 or 508/362-6088), for a

3½-to-4-hour voyage on a 100-foot high-speed cruiser. Naturalists provide the narration, and should you fail to spot a whale, your next trek is free. Tickets $24 adults, $20 seniors, $15 children 4 to 12 from April through October; call for schedule and off-season rates. No outings are offered November through March.

Shoppin7g

Of the hundreds of antiques shops scattered through the region, perhaps a dozen qualify as destinations for well-schooled collectors. ✪ **Harden Studios,** 3264 Rte. 6A (in the center of town), Barnstable Village (☎ 508/362-7711), is one of them. Some items, such as the primitive portraits and mourning embroidery, are all but extinct outside of museums.

Richard Kiusalas and Steven Whittlesey salvage antique lumber and turn it into cupboards, tables, and chairs at **West Barnstable Tables,** 2454 Meetinghouse Way (off Rte. 149 near the intersection of Rte. 6A), West Barnstable (☎ 508/362-2676). When the wood still bears interesting traces of its former life, it's turned into folk-art furniture.

Town pooh-bahs fussed and fumed when Barre Pinske constructed a giant mailbox right on historically correct Route 6A. But he'd found a legal loophole: There are no local laws (as yet) that dictate mailbox size. All his stuff has a sense of humor, from the couch he carved out of paper bags to his "Post-Industrial Expressionist" chain-saw art. It can all be seen at the **Pinske Art Center,** 1989 Rte. 6A (about ¼ mile east of Rte. 132), West Barnstable (☎ 508/362-5311).

WHERE TO STAY

✪ **The Acworth Inn.** 4352 Rte. 6A (near the Yarmouth Port border), Cummaquid, MA 02637. ☎ **800/362-6363** or 508/362-3330. Fax 508/375-0304. www.acworthinn.com. 5 units. Summer $105–$125 double; $185 suite. Rates include full breakfast. AE, DISC, MC, V.

Cheryl and Jack Ferrell know that it's the small touches that make a stay memorable, and anyone lucky enough to land in this sunnily rehabbed house is sure to remember every last one, from the cranberry spritzer offered on arrival to the handmade chocolates on the pillow each night. Cheryl even grinds the whole grains that go into her home-baked breakfasts in the form of cranberry-orange rolls or whole-wheat pancakes. Anyone looking to avoid the excess of Victorian furnishings in many B&Bs will delight in the simple, fresh, immaculate decor here, mainly in shades of white and beige. The inn is close to charming Barnstable Village and popular Cape Cod Bay beaches, so the complimentary bikes may be all you need in the way of wheels.

Ashley Manor Inn. 3660 Rte. 6A (just E of Hyannis Rd.), Barnstable, MA 02630. ☎ **888/535-2246** or 508/362-8044. Fax 508/362-9927. www.capecod.net/ashleymn. E-mail: shleymn@capecod.net. 6 units. A/C. Summer $130–145 double; $165–$180 suite. Rates include full breakfast. DC, DISC, MC, V.

This delightful country inn is a much-modified 1699 colonial mansion that still retains many of its original features, including a hearth with beehive oven (the perfect place to sip port on a blustery evening), built-in corner cupboards in the wainscoted dining room, and wide-board floors, many of them brightened with Nantucket-style splatter-paint. The rooms (all but one boast working fireplaces) are spacious and inviting: a true retreat. The 2-acre property itself is shielded from the road by an enormous privet hedge, and fragrant boxwood camouflages a Har-Tru tennis court. You'll find loaner bikes beside it, ready to roll. Romantics can sequester themselves in the flower-fringed gazebo. Breakfast on the brick patio is worth waking up for: You wouldn't want to miss the homemade granola, much less the main event—quiche, perhaps, or crepes.

✪ **Beechwood Inn.** 2839 Rte. 6A (about 1½ miles E of Rte. 132), Barnstable, MA 02630. ☎ **800/609-6618** or 508/362-6618. Fax 508/362-0298. www.virtualcapecod.com/market/

beechwood. E-mail: bwdinn@virtualcapecod.com. 6 units. A/C. Summer $135–$170 double. Rates include full breakfast. AE, DISC, MC, V.

Look for a butterscotch-colored 1853 Queen Anne Victorian all but enshrouded in weeping beeches. The interior remains dark and rich, with a red-velvet parlor and tin-ceiling dining room where innkeeper Debbie Traugot serves a three-course breakfast that features home-baked delights such as applesauce pancakes and raspberry bread. Two of the upstairs bedrooms embody distinctive period styles: The Cottage Room contains furniture painted in an 1860s mode, and Eastlake Room is in 1880s William Morris style. Each affords a distant view of the sparkling bay. The Traugots are always making improvements; most recently they've added new Sealy Posturepedic Plush mattresses. Rooms range from quite spacious (Lilac) to romantically snug (Garret). Loaner bikes are available.

WHERE TO DINE
Moderate

Barnstable Tavern & Grille. 3176 Main St., Barnstable. ☎ **508/362-2355.** Main courses $12–$22. AE, DISC, MC, V. Sun–Thurs 11:30am–10pm, Fri–Sat 11:30am–11pm. REGIONAL.

From the outside, this restaurant—a former stagecoach stop smack dab in the middle of Barnstable Village—feels like it's been here forever. Inside has been cheerfully revamped. The tavern area is now separate from the main dining room, so diners have a smoke-free experience. But in season, you'll want one of the tables outside in the courtyard with views of the majestic courthouse across the street. The entire restaurant serves 38 wines by the glass and serves food till midnight. Specialties here include Black Angus sirloin and fresh grilled swordfish. Off-season there's a large brunch buffet on Sundays.

Mattakeese Wharf. 271 Mill Way (about ½ mile N of Rte. 6A), Barnstable. ☎ **508/ 362-4511.** Reservations recommended. Main courses $12–$25. AE, MC, V. June–Oct daily 11:30am–10pm; call for off-season hrs. Closed Nov–Apr. SEAFOOD.

This waterview fish house, its broad decks jutting out into the harbor, gets packed in season; don't even bother on summer weekends. The outdoor seating fills up first, and no wonder, with Sandy Neck sunsets to marvel over and fish so fresh it could have flopped on deck. There's a Mediterranean subtext to the extensive menu. The bouill-abaisse is worthy of the name, and the varied combinations of pasta, seafood, and sauce—from Alfredo to fra diavolo—invite return visits. There's live piano music most nights in season. Just 50 yards from the whale-watching boat, this is also a good choice for lunch.

YARMOUTH

This cross-section represents the Cape at its best—and worst. Yarmouth Port, on Cape Cod Bay, is an enchanting village with interesting shops and architectural pearls, while the sound-side villages of West and South Yarmouth are an object lesson in unbridled development run amuck. This section along Route 28 is a nightmarish gauntlet of ticky-tacky accommodations and "attractions." Yet even here you'll find a few choice spots. You've got the north shore for culture and refinement, the south shore for kitsch. Take your pick, or ricochet back and forth, enjoying the best of both worlds.

ESSENTIALS

GETTING THERE   After crossing either the Bourne Bridge or the Sagamore Bridge, head east on Route 6 or 6A. Route 6A (north of Rte. 6's Exit 7) passes through the village of Yarmouth Port. The villages of West Yarmouth, Bass River, and South Yarmouth are located along Route 28, east of Hyannis; to reach them from Route 6, take Exit 7 south (Yarmouth Road), or Exit 8 south (Station Street).

VISITOR INFORMATION   Contact the **Yarmouth Area Chamber of Commerce,** 657 Rte. 28, West Yarmouth, MA 02673 (☎ **508/778-1008**).

BEACHES & OUTDOOR PURSUITS

BEACHES   Yarmouth boasts 11 saltwater and 2 pond beaches open to the public. The body-per-square-yard ratio can be pretty intense along the sound, but so is the social scene, so no one seems to mind. The beachside parking lots charge $8 a day and sell weeklong stickers ($30).

- **Bass River Beach,** off South Shore Drive in Bass River (South Yarmouth). Located at the mouth of the largest tidal river on the eastern seaboard, this sound beach offers bathroom facilities and a snack bar, plus a bonus—a wheelchair-accessible fishing pier. The beaches along the south shore (Nantucket Sound) tend to be clean and sandy with comfortable water temps (kids will want to stay in all day). You'll need a beach sticker to park here.
- **Grays Beach,** off Centre Street in Yarmouth Port. This tiny beach has tame waters excellent for children. Though the view is lovely, the sand here is dark and dense. This beach adjoins the Callery-Darling Conservation Area (see "Nature & Wildlife Areas," below). The Bass Hole boardwalk next to the beach offers one of the most scenic walks in the Mid-Cape. Parking is free here, and there's a picnic area with grills.
- **Parker's River Beach,** off South Shore Drive in Bass River. The usual amenities like rest rooms and a snack bar, plus a 20-foot gazebo for the sun-shy.
- **Seagull Beach,** off South Sea Avenue in West Yarmouth. Rolling dunes, a boardwalk, and all the necessary facilities, like rest rooms and a snack bar, attract a young crowd. Bring bug spray, though: Greenhead flies get the munchies in July.

FISHING   Of the five fishing ponds in the Yarmouth area, Long Pond near South Yarmouth is known for its largemouth bass and pickerel; for details and a license (shellfishing is another option), visit **Town Hall** at 1146 Rte. 28 in South Yarmouth (☎ **508/398-2231**) or **Riverview Bait and Tackle** at 1273 Rte. 28 in South Yarmouth (☎ **508/394-1036**). Full-season licenses for Massachusetts residents cost $28.50; for out-of-staters, $38.50. You can cast for striped bass and bluefish off the pier at Bass River Beach.

NATURE & WILDLIFE AREAS   In Yarmouth Port, follow Centre Street about a mile north and bear northeast on Homers Dock Road; from here a 2½-mile trail through the **Callery-Darling Conservation Area** leads to Grays Beach, where you can continue across the Bass Hole Boardwalk for a lovely view of the marsh.

A HISTORIC MUST-SEE

✪ **Winslow Crocker House.** 250 Rte. 6A (about ½ mile E of town center), Yarmouth Port. ☎ **508/362-4385.** Admission $4 adults, $3.50 seniors, $2 children 6–12. June to mid-Oct hourly tours Sat–Sun 11am–5pm (last tour at 4pm). Closed mid-Oct to May.

The only property on the Cape currently preserved by the prestigious Society for the Preservation of New England Antiquities, this house, built around 1780, deserves every honor. Not only is it a lovely example of the shingled Georgian style, it's packed with outstanding antiques—Jacobean to Chippendale—collected in the 1930s by Mary Thacher, a descendant of the town's first land grantee. Anthony Thacher and his family had a rougher crossing than most: Their ship foundered off Cape Ann in 1635 (near an island that now bears their name), and though their four children drowned, Thacher and his wife were able to make it to shore, clinging to the family cradle. You'll come across a 1690 replica in the parlor. The Thachers later begat a son, John, who built the house next door in around 1680, and raised a total of 21 children between two wives. All the museum-worthy objects in the Winslow Crocker House would seem to have similar stories to tell.

Kid Stuff

ZooQuarium. 674 Rte. 28 (midway between W. Yarmouth and Bass River), W. Yarmouth. ☎ **508/775-8883**. Admission $7.50 adults, $5 children 2–9. Late June to early Sept daily 9:30am–6pm; off-season 9:30am–5pm. Closed late Nov to mid-Feb.

This slightly scruffy wildlife museum has made great strides in recent years toward blending entertainment with education. It's a little easier to enjoy the sea-lion show once you've been assured that the stars like performing, have been trained with positive reinforcement only, and, furthermore, arrived here with injuries that precluded their survival in the wild. The aquarium is arranged in realistic habitats, and the "zoo" consists primarily of indigenous fauna, both domesticated and wild (the pacing bobcat is liable to give you pause). The zoorific theater (a live animal education program) and the children's discovery center with hands-on activities will entrance children. The new exhibit, "A Walk Through the Cape Cod Woods" features some of the little creatures that inhabit the woodland floor. In addition, a very creditable effort is made to convey the need for ecological preservation.

Shopping

Route 6A through Yarmouth Port remains a rich vein of antiques shops. Check them all out, if you're so inclined and have the time. Most Cape antiques stores offer plenty of decorative items such as glass, china, and silver but scant big pieces of centuries-old furniture. However, there's plenty of the latter at **Nickerson Antiques,** 162 Rte. 6A (in the center of town), Yarmouth Port (☎ **508/362-6426**), some imported from Great Britain.

The most colorful bookshop on the Cape (if not the whole East Coast) is ✪ **Parnassus Books,** 220 Rte. 6A (about ¼ mile east of town center), Yarmouth Port (☎ **508/362-6420**). This jam-packed repository—housed in an 1858 Swedenborgian church—is the creation of Ben Muse, who has been collecting and selling vintage tomes since the 1960s. Relevant new stock, including the Cape-related reissues published by Parnassus Imprints, is offered alongside the older treasures. Don't expect much hand-holding on the part of the gruff proprietor. The outdoor racks, maintained on an honor system, are open 24 hours a day.

Where to Stay

There are so many hotels and motels lining Route 28 and along the shore in West and South Yarmouth that it may be hard to make sense of the choices. The following are some that offer clean rooms and cater to families looking for a reasonably priced beach vacation. All are within a few miles of the beach or right on the beach. For those staying on Route 28, the town runs frequent beach shuttles in season.

The Tidewater Motor Lodge, 135 Main St. (Rte. 28), West Yarmouth (☎ **800/338-6322**); www.tidewaterml.com; E-mail:tidewater@tidewaterml.com), is a short walk (half a mile) from a small beach on Lewis Bay, and a not-so-short walk (about a mile) from Hyannis' Main Street and the ferries to Nantucket. Summer rates are $89 to $99 double. One of the more attractive motels along this strip, it's a white clapboard double-decker motel with green shutters and doors. The Tidewater also has an indoor pool, an outdoor pool, and a breakfast restaurant.

All Seasons Motor Inn, 1199 Main St. (Rte. 28), South Yarmouth (☎ **800/527-0359** or 508/394-7600; www.allseasons.com), is popular with families. Summer rates are $99 to $125 double. It has indoor and outdoor pools, a breakfast restaurant, and exercise and game rooms.

The Cove at Yarmouth, 183 Main St. (Rte. 28), West Yarmouth (☎ **800/ 228-2968**), offers suites and town-house accommodations for $165 a night on summer weekends. The most popular rooms are in the atrium overlooking the indoor pools. There's also an outdoor pool, two indoor tennis courts, a fitness room, and a restaurant.

Ocean Mist, 97 S. Shore Dr., South Yarmouth (☎ **800/248-MIST** or 508/ 398-2968), is a large motel right on the beach. There's also an indoor pool, just in case it rains. Summer rates are $179 to $189 double, $229 to $259 suites.

Captain Farris House. 308 Old Main St. (about just W of the Bass River Bridge), Bass River, MA 02664-4530. ☎ **800/350-9477** or 508/760-2818. Fax 508/398-1262. www.inn.to. 8 units. A/C TV TEL. Summer $95–$140 double; $150–$185 suite. Rates include full breakfast. AE, MC, V.

Sumptuous is the only way to describe this 1845 inn, improbably set amid a peaceful garden, a block off bustling Route 28. A skilled interior decorator has combined fine antiques and striking contemporary touches to lift this inn's interiors way above the average home-y (if homely) B&B decor. Some suites are apartment-size with fireplaces in the sitting rooms and whirlpool-tubs in the bathrooms bigger than the average bedroom. Next door, the 1825 Elisha Jenkins House contains an additional large suite with its own sundeck. Welcoming touches in rooms include chocolates, fresh flowers, and plush robes. All rooms are equipped with irons, hair dryers, and dataports; VCRs are available upon request. Breakfast consists of three courses served in the formal dining room or the sunny courtyard.

Red Jacket. S. Shore Dr. (Box 88), S. Yarmouth, MA 02664. ☎ **800/672-0500** or 508/ 398-6941. Fax 508/398-1214. www.redjacketinns.com/redjacket. 150 units, 13 cottages. A/C TV TEL. Summer $175–$275 double; $350–$475 cottages. MC, V. Closed Nov to mid-Apr.

Of the huge resort motels lining Nantucket Sound in Yarmouth, Red Jacket has the best location. It is the last hotel at the end of the road and borders Parker's River on the west, so sunsets are particularly fine. Families who want all the fixings will find them here, though the atmosphere may be a bit impersonal. All rooms have balconies or private porches; you'll want one overlooking the private beach on Nantucket Sound or looking out towards Parker's River. Also, all rooms have fridges and some have Jacuzzis. Off-season, rooms can be as cheap as $85 a night.

Dining/Diversions: The dining room, serving breakfast, lunch, and dinner in season, may come in handy in the morning, though you'll probably want to try something more inspiring for dinner. There's a lounge/bar area open for cocktails nightly.

Amenities: Full concierge service. Daily summertime children's program of supervised sports and activities, which may take advantage of the playground, minigolf, shuffleboard, horseshoes, and badminton. Tennis, basketball, and volleyball courts (one of each), as well as a putting green. Indoor and outdoor heated pools, plus whirlpool, sauna, and exercise rooms. Water sports include parasailing, sailboat rentals, kayaking, paddleboats, and catamaran cruises.

✪ **Wedgewood Inn.** 83 Main Street/Rte. 6A (in the center of town), Yarmouth Port, MA 02675. ☎ **508/362-5157** or 508/362-9178. Fax 508/362-5851. www.virtualcapecod.com/ market/wedgewoodinn. 9 units. A/C. Summer $125–$195 double. Rates include full breakfast. AE, DC, MC, V.

This elegant 1812 Federal house sits atop its undulating lawn with unabashed pride. Innkeeper Gerrie Graham provides a warm welcome, complete with tea delivered to your room. In the main house, the four formal and spacious front rooms all have cherry-wood pencil-post beds, Oriental rugs, antique quilts, and wood-burning fireplaces, and two downstairs ones have private screened porches. All have ample bathrooms. The two romantic hideaways under the eaves are decorated in a cheerful country casual style. The picturesque barn in back includes three very private, spacious suites, with canopied beds, fireplaces, decks, and sparkling contemporary bathrooms. These barn suites also include telephones and televisions cleverly tucked into painted cabinets.

WHERE TO DINE

Don't miss **Hallet's,** 139 Rte. 6A, Yarmouth Port (☎ **508/362-3362**): Unsuspecting passersby invariably do a double-take when they happen upon this 1889 drugstore. Mary Hallet Clark, the granddaughter of town pharmacist (and postmaster and justice-of-the-peace) Thacher Taylor Hallet, is now the one dishing out frappes and floats from the original marble soda fountain. Rumor has it that some years ago a couple of honchos from Walt Disney offered to buy the entire interior for their "Main Street USA" at Disney Land; fortunately, the generous offer was declined. Visit the display area upstairs for a look at old apothecary knickknacks and historic photos.

Aardvark. 134 Rte 6A (in the village center), Yarmouth Port. ☎ **508/362-9866.** Reservations recommended. Main courses $11–$18. AE, DC, MC, V. June–Oct Mon 7–11:30am, Tues–Sat 8am–3pm, 5–9:30, Sun 9am–3pm; call for off-season hours. INTERNATIONAL.

Set in a whimsical Victorian "painted lady," this sweet little place evolved from a terrific coffee bar. Now it serves three meals. The menu is small but select, with ethnic influences ranging from Italian to Far Eastern to Caribbean. For dinner, choose between the catch of the night, the steak of the night, or the chicken of the night. Everything is served with either smashers (garlic mashed potatoes) or herb risotto. Or you could have the popular spicy Thai noodles stir-fried with your choice of veggies and chicken, tofu, sirloin, shrimp, or Thai (chicken and turkey) sausage. There's a small children's menu, and outdoor seating in season. And they still serve the best coffee in town.

✪ **abbicci.** 43 Main St. (Rte. 6A, near the Cummaquid border), Yarmouth Port. ☎ **508/362-3501.** Reservations recommended. Main courses $16–$28. AE, DC, DISC, MC, V. Daily 11:30am–2:30pm and 5–10pm. NORTHERN ITALIAN.

Many consider this sophisticated venue the place to eat on Cape Cod these days. While the exterior is that of a modest mustard-colored 18th-century Cape, the interior features mosaic floors and muralled walls in several cozy dining rooms. The knowledgeable and efficient wait staff deliver delicious dishes, artfully prepared and presented. In fact, the whole setup seems almost out of place in folksy Yarmouth Port. New chef Frank Delebois specializes in seafood dishes, but veal, lamb, and, of course, pasta are also favorably represented, all in a delicate Northern Italian style. A taste of the veal *nocciole* (with toasted hazelnuts and a splash of balsamic vinegar), and you'll be transported straight to Tuscany. This small restaurant can get overburdened on weekends; expect a wait even with a reservation.

✪ **Inaho.** 157 Main St./Rte. 6A (in the village center), Yarmouth Port. ☎ **508/362-5522.** Reservations recommended. Main courses $12–$23. MC, V. Tues–Sun 5–10pm. JAPANESE.

What better place than the Cape to enjoy fresh-off-the-boat sushi? You can sit at the sushi bar to watch chef/owner Yuji Watanabe perform his wizardry or enjoy the privacy afforded by a gleaming wooden booth. From the front, Inaho is a typical Cape Cod cottage, but park in the back so you can enter through the Japanese garden. Inside, it's a veritable shibui sanctuary, with minimalist decor (the traditional shoji screens and crisp navy-and-white banners) softened by tranquil music and service.

Lobster Boat. 681 Rte. 28 (midway between W. Yarmouth and Bass River), W. Yarmouth. ☎ **508/775-0486.** Main courses $10–$18. AE, DISC, MC, V. May–Oct daily 4–10pm. SEAFOOD.

Just about every town seems to have one of these barnlike restaurants plastered with flotsam and serving the usual array of seafood in the usual manner, from deep-fried to boiled or broiled. True to its sound-side setting, this tourist magnet advertises itself rather flamboyantly with a facade that features the hull of a ship grafted onto a shingled shack.

Jack's Outback. 161 Main St./Rte. 6A (behind Main St. buildings, in the center of town), Yarmouth Port. ☎ **508/362-6690.** Most items under $5. No credit cards. Daily 6:30am–2pm. AMERICAN.

This is a neighborhood cafe as Dr. Seuss might have imagined it: hyperactive and full of fun. Chef/owner Jack Braginton-Smith makes a point of dishing out good-natured insults along with the home-style grub, which you bus yourself from the open kitchen, thereby saving big bucks as well as time. This is a perfect place for impatient children, who'll find lots of familiar dishes on the hand-scrawled posters that serve as a communal menu.

DENNIS

In Dennis, as in Yarmouth, virtually all the good stuff—pretty drives, inviting shops, restaurants with real personality—are in the north, along Route 6A. Route 28 is chockablock with more typical tourist attractions, RV parks, and family-oriented motels—some with fairly sophisticated facilities, but nonetheless undistinguished enough to warrant even a drive by (the few exceptions are noted below). In budgeting your time, I'd allocate the lion's share to Dennis itself and not its southern offshoots.

ESSENTIALS

GETTING THERE   After crossing either the Bourne Bridge or the Sagamore bridge, head east on Route 6 or 6A. Route 6A passes through the villages of Dennis and East Dennis (which can also be reached via northbound Rte. 134 from Rte. 6's Exit 9). Route 134 south leads to the village of South Dennis; if you follow Route 134 all the way to Route 28, the village of West Dennis will be a couple of miles to your west, and Dennisport a couple of miles east.

VISITOR INFORMATION   Contact the **Dennis Chamber of Commerce,** 242 Swan River Rd., West Dennis, MA 02670 (☎ **800/243-9920** or 508/398-3568, www.dennischamber.com).

BEACHES & OUTDOOR PURSUITS

BEACHES   Dennis harbors more than a dozen saltwater and two freshwater beaches open to nonresidents. The bay beaches are charming and a big hit with families, who prize the easygoing surf, so soft it won't bring toddlers to their knees. The beaches on the sound tend to attract wall-to-wall families, but the parking lots are usually not too crowded since so many beachgoers choose accommodations within walking distance. The lots charge $9 per day; for a weeklong permit ($28), visit **Town Hall** on Main Street in South Dennis (☎ **508/760-6159**).

- **Chapin Beach,** off Rout 6A in Dennis. A nice, long bay beach pocked with occasional boulders and surrounded by dunes. No lifeguard, but there are rest rooms.
- **Corporation Beach,** off Route 6A in Dennis. This bay beach offers wheelchair-accessible boardwalk, lifeguards, snack bar, rest rooms, and a children's play area.
- **Mayflower Beach,** off Route 6A in Dennis. This 1,200-foot bay beach has the necessary amenities, plus an accessible boardwalk. The tidal pools attract lots of children.

- **Scargo Lake in Dennis.** This large kettle-hole pond (formed by a melting fragment of a glacier) has two pleasant beaches: Scargo Beach, accessible right off Route 6A, and Princess Beach, off Scargo Hill Road, where there are rest rooms and a picnic area.
- **West Dennis Beach,** off Route 28 in West Dennis. This long (1½-mile) but narrow beach along the sound has lifeguards, a playground, a snack bar, rest rooms, and a special kite-flying area. The eastern end is reserved for residents, but that's okay because the western end tends to be less packed.

BIKING   The 25-mile ✪ **Cape Cod Rail Trail** (☎ **508/896-3491**) starts here, on Route 134, ½ mile south of Route 6's Exit 9. Once a Penn-Central track, this 8-foot-wide paved bikeway extends all the way to Wellfleet (with a few on-road lapses), passing through woods, marshes, and dunes. Sustenance is never too far off-trail, and plenty of bike shops dot the course. At the trailhead is Barbara's Bike and Sports Equipment, 430 Rte. 134, South Dennis (☎ **508/760-4723**), which rents bikes and in-line skates and does repairs. Rates are $8 for a couple hours and up to $18 for the full day.

FISHING   Fishing is allowed in Fresh Pond and Scargo Lake, where the catch includes trout and smallmouth bass; for a license (shellfishing is also permitted), visit **Town Hall** on Main Street in South Dennis (☎ **508/394-8300**) or **Riverview Bait and Tackle** at 1273 Rte. 28 in South Yarmouth (☎ **508/394-1036**). Plenty of people drop a line off the Bass River Bridge along Route 28 in West Dennis.

Several charter boats operate out of the Northside Marina in East Dennis's Sesuit Harbor, including the Albatross (☎ **508/385-3244**).

NATURE & WILDLIFE AREAS   Behind the Town Hall parking lot on Main Street in South Dennis, a half-mile walk along the Indian Lands Conservation Trail leads to the Bass River, where blue herons and kingfishers often take shelter. Dirt roads off South Street in East Dennis, beyond the Quivet Cemetery, lead to Crow's Pasture, a patchwork of marshes and dunes bordering the bay; this circular trail is about a 2½-mile round-trip.

WATER SPORTS   Located on the small and placid Swan River, **Cape Cod Waterways,** 16 Rte. 28, Dennisport (☎ **508/398-0080**), rents canoes, kayaks, and paddleboats for exploring 200-acre Swan Pond (less than a mile north) or Nantucket Sound (2 miles south). A full day canoe or kayak rental costs $35.

AN ART MUSEUM

Cape Museum of Fine Arts. 60 Hope Lane (off Rte. 6A in the center of town). ☎ **508/385-4477.** Admission $5 adults, free for children under 16; free admission Sat 10am–1pm. June–Sept Mon–Wed and Fri–Sat 10am–5pm, Thurs 10am–7:30pm, Sun 1–5pm; call for off-season hrs.

Part of the prettily landscaped Cape Playhouse complex, this small museum has done a great job of acquiring hundreds of works by representative area artists dating back to the turn of the century.

KID STUFF

Dennisport boasts the best rainy-day—or any-day—destination for little kids on the entire Cape, the nonprofit **Cape Cod Discovery Museum & Toy Shop,** at 444 Rte. 28 (☎ **508/398-1600**). Hours are 9:30am to 7:30pm daily in season; 9:30am to 5:30pm (except Thanksgiving, Christmas, and Easter) off-season. For a nominal admission fee ($2.50 adults, $4.50 children 1 to 15, $2 seniors), whole families can amuse themselves amid a vast educational play space equipped with a frozen-shadow wall, a transparent piano, a pretend diner, a dress-up puppet theater, a veterinary shop, and all sorts of other fun stuff. Special workshops, including reptiles shows, are offered daily. On Friday mornings in season, at 9:30 and 11:30am, the **Cape Playhouse** at 36 Hope Lane in Dennis (☎ 508/385-3911) hosts various visiting companies that mount musicals geared to children 4 and up; at only $6, tickets go fast.

SHOPPING

There's a growing cluster of antiques shops in Dennisport, but the stock is flea-market level. Save your time, and money, for the better shops along Route 6A, where you'll also find fine contemporary crafts. More than 136 dealers stock the co-op **Antiques Center of Cape Cod,** 243 Rte. 6A (about 1 mile south of Dennis Village center), Dennis (☎ 508/385-6400); it's the largest such enterprise on the Cape. You'll find all the usual "smalls" on the first floor; the big stuff—from blanket chests to copper bathtubs—beckons above.

The premier place for antique wicker furniture on the Cape is **Leslie Curtis Antiques** at two locations in Dennis Village, 776 Main St./Rte. 6A and 838 Main St./Rte. 6A) (☎ 508/385-2921). Her wicker selection includes Victorian pieces and Bar Harbor wicker of the 1920s. She also specializes in French Quimper pottery, as well as an eclectic stock of other antiques.

Dennis Village along Route 6A has become a magnet for terrific small galleries. Certainly among the finest is the magical ✪ **Scargo Stoneware Pottery and Art Gallery,** 30 Dr. Lord's Rd. S. (off Rte. 6A, about 1 mile east of town center), Dennis (☎ 508/385-3894). Harry Holl set up his glass-ceiling studio here in 1952; today his work, and the output of his four daughters, fills a sylvan glade overlooking Scargo Lake.

WHERE TO STAY

Of the many impersonal megamotels lining the Sound, the **Corsair and Cross Rip Resort Motels** are among the nicest, and you can't beat the location: right on the beach. They are at 41 Chase Ave. (off Depot Street, a mile southeast of Rte. 28), Dennisport (☎ 800/345-5140 or 508/398-2279. Fax 508/760-6681). Summer rates are $95 to $105 double, $135 to $185 efficiencies.

The Four Chimneys Inn. 946 Rte. 6A (about ½ mile E of town center), Dennis, MA 02638. ☎ 800/874-5502 or 508/385-6317. Fax 508/385-6285. www.virtualcapecod.com/ fourchimneys. E-mail: chimneys4@aol.com. 8 units. TV. Summer $90–$150 double; $125 suite. Rates include continental breakfast. AE, MC, V. Closed mid-Dec to mid-Feb.

Scargo Lake is directly across the street and the village is a brief walk away from this imposing 1880 Victorian, former home to the town doctor. Opulent tastes are evident in the high ceilings and marble fireplace of the front parlor. Rooms vary in size, but new innkeeper Kathy Clough has rendered them all quite appealing, with hand-painted stenciling and summery wicker furnishings. The breakfasts are knockouts, featuring such inspirations as orange ricotta French toast.

✪ **Isaiah Hall B&B Inn.** 152 Whig St. (1 block NW of the Cape Playhouse), Dennis, MA 02638. ☎ 800/736-0160 or 508/385-9928. Fax 508/385-5879. www.virtualcapecod.com/ isaiahhall. E-mail: isaiah@capecod.net. 10 units. A/C TV. Summer $93–$128 double; $156 suite. Rates include continental breakfast. AE, MC, V. Closed mid-Oct to mid-Apr. No children under age 7.

Many stars from the nearby Cape Playhouse have stayed here over the past half century, and if you're lucky, you'll find a few sharing the space. Your animated hostess, Marie Brophy, has been entertaining the entertainers for over 15 years. The "great room" in the carriage-house annex is a virtual green room: It seems to foment late-night discussions to be continued over home-baked breakfasts at the long plank table that dominates the 1857 country kitchen. Room styles range from 1940s knotty pine to spacious and spiffy. They are quaint, countrified, and spotlessly clean; several have balconies. Most rooms, including the spacious suite, have VCRs. The inn's location on a quiet side street in a residential neighborhood bodes well for a good night's sleep. But the central location means a short walk to restaurants, entertainment options, and Corporation Beach on Cape Cod Bay.

✪ **Lighthouse Inn.** 4 Lighthouse Rd. (off Lower County Rd., ½ mile S. of Rte. 28). W. Dennis, MA 02670. ☎ **508/398-2244.** Fax 508/398-5658. www.lighthouseinn.com. 34 units, 27 cottages. TV TEL. Summer $200–$225 double, $230–$285 2-bedroom cottage. Rates include full breakfast and all gratuities. MC, V. Closed mid-Oct to mid-May.

Set smack dab on placid West Dennis Beach on Nantucket Sound, this popular resort has been welcoming families for over 60 years. In 1938, Everett Stone acquired a decommissioned 1885 lighthouse and built a charming inn and a 9-acre cottage colony around it. Today, his grandsons run the show, pretty much as he envisioned it. Families still gather at group tables in the large dining room; many coordinate their vacations so that they can catch up with the same group of friends year after year. The rooms aren't what you'd call fancy, but some have great Nantucket Sound views. Also, they're stocked with conveniences like a hair dryer, VCR, in-room safe, and minifridge. This is one of the few places on Cape Cod where single occupancy is half price.

Dining/Diversions: Serving three meals, the huge dining room is open to the general public, and the prices are quite reasonable (entrees, for example, rarely exceed $17). Lunch is served under umbrellas on the deck overlooking Nantucket Sound, a delightful setting to enjoy a club sandwich. Down the road, at the entrance to the complex, The Sand Bar, a classic bar with cabaret-style entertainment, serves as an on-site nightspot (see "Dennis After Dark," below).

Amenities: Private beach, outdoor heated pool, and tennis court. Though "InnKids," the supervised play program, is free of charge, children's rates are $40 to $64 per day, depending on the child's age. There's also a game room, shuffleboard, volleyball, and mini-golf.

WHERE TO DINE

The best ice cream parlor in these parts is Sundae School, 387 Lower County Rd. at Sea Street, about ⅓ mile S of Route. 28, Dennisport ☎ **508/394-9122,** which features a turn-of-the-century marble soda fountain and other artifacts from the golden age of ice cream.

✪ **Bob Briggs' Wee Packet Restaurant and Bakery.** 79 Depot St. (at Lower County Rd., about ⅓ mile S of town center), Dennisport. ☎ **508/398-2181.** Main courses $6–$12. MC, V. July–August daily 8am–8:30pm; May, June and Sept daily 11:30am–8:30pm. Closed Oct–Apr. SEAFOOD.

It's been Bob Briggs's place since 1949; otherwise, the name that might leap to mind would be "Mom's." This tiny joint serves exemplary diner fare, plus all the requisite seafood staples, fried and broiled. Five generations have been known to commandeer a couple of the Formica tables for a traditional summer feast topped off by a timeless dessert such as blueberry shortcake.

✪ **Gina's by the Sea.** 134 Taunton Ave. (about 1½ miles NW of Rte. 6A, off New Boston and Beach sts.). ☎ **508/385-3213.** Reservations not accepted. Main courses $10–$19. AE, MC, V. June–Aug daily 5–10pm; April–May, Sept–Nov Thurs–Sun 5–10pm. Closed Dec–Mar. ITALIAN.

A landmark amid Dennis's "Little Italy" beach community since 1938, this intimate little restaurant has a few nuovo tricks up its sleeve, such as homemade ravioli stuffed with smoked mozzarella. Most of the fare here is the traditional Italian food of our youth, but nonetheless tasty: The ultra-garlicky shrimp scampi, for instance, needs no updating. Save room for Mrs. Riley's chocolate rum cake made daily by owner Larry Riley's mother; it's scrumptious. This small, popular place fills up fast, and no reservations accepted means a long waiting list; if you want to eat before 8:30pm, arrive before 5:30. Take a sunset or moonlight walk on the beach (just over the dune) to round off the evening.

The Marshside. 28 Bridge St. (at the junction of Rte. 134 and 6A), East Dennis. ☎ **508/ 385-4010.** Main courses $7–$15. AE, DC, DISC, MC, V. Daily 7am–9pm. AMERICAN.

This is one of the Cape's best diners: it's a clean, well-run establishment overlooking a picturesque marsh and, in the distance, Sesuit Harbor. There's a relaxed atmosphere here that comes from having a year-round waitstaff that know what they're doing. The food is fresh, tasty, and cheap, be it a fried fish platter, a cheeseburger with french fries, or a veggie melt. Save room for homemade desserts.

✪ **The Red Pheasant Inn.** 905 Main St. (about ½ mile E of town center), Dennis. ☎ **508/ 385-2133.** Reservations recommended. Main courses $16–$29. DISC, MC, V. Mid-April to Dec daily 5–10pm; Jan to mid-April Wed–Sun 5–10pm. NEW AMERICAN.

An enduring Cape favorite since 1977, this handsome space—an 18th-century barn turned chandlery—has managed not only to keep pace with contemporary trends, but to remain a front-runner. Chef/owner Bill Atwood has a way with local victuals. He transforms the ubiquitous zucchini of late summer, for instance, into homemade ravioli enfolding tasty chèvre, and his signature cherrystone-and-scallop chowder gets its zip from fresh-plucked thyme. Influences are international, like the appetizer, cassoulet of escargot with tomato, garlic and Swiss chard; or the entrée, sesame-crusted Atlantic halibut with marinated cucumbers, bijiki and tobikko Thai curry and tamarind sauce. Two massive brick fireplaces tend to be the focal point in the off-season, drawing in the weary—and delighted—wanderer. In fine weather you'll want a table in the garden room.

Scargo Cafe. 799 Main St./Rte. 6A (opposite the Cape Playhouse). ☎ **508/385-8200.** Main courses $13–$19. AE, DISC, MC, V. Mid-June to mid-Sept 11am–11pm; call for off-season hrs. INTERNATIONAL.

A richly paneled captain's house given a modernist reworking, this lively bistro—named for Dennis's scenic lake—deftly spans old and new with a menu neatly split into "traditional" and "adventurous" categories. For traditional, you'll find surf-and-turf, and the popular grilled lamb loins served with mint jelly (talk about traditional!); adventurous dishes include the likes of "wildcat chicken" (a sauté with sausage, mushrooms, and raisins, flambéed with apricot brandy). Lighter nibbles, such as burgers or "Scallop Harpoon"—a bacon-wrapped skewerful, served over rice—are available throughout the day, a boon for beachgoers who tend to return ravenous. A kitchen that's open until 11pm makes this the perfect—and only—place in town to go after a show at the Cape Playhouse, which is across the street.

DENNIS AFTER DARK

The oldest continuously active straw hat theater in the country and still one of the best, **The Cape Playhouse,** 36 Hope Lane on Route 6A, in the center of Dennis Village (☎ **508/385-3911**) was the 1927 brainstorm of Raymond Moore, who'd spent a few summers as a playwright in Provincetown and quickly tired of the strictures of "little theater." Salvaging an 1838 meetinghouse, he plunked it down amid a meadow, and got his New York buddy, designer Cleon Throckmorton, to turn it into a proper theater. Even with a roof that leaked, it was an immediate success, and a parade of stars, both established and budding, trod the boards in the coming decades, from

Humphrey Bogart to Tab Hunter, from Ginger Rogers to Jane Fonda (her dad spent his salad days there, too, playing opposite Bette Davis in her stage debut). Not all of today's headliners are quite as impressive (many hail from the netherworld of TV reruns), but the theater—the only Equity enterprise on the Cape—can be counted on for a varied season of polished work. Performances run from mid-June to early Sept; tickets are $15 to $28.

The Sand Bar at the Lighthouse Inn (☎ 508/398-2244; see "Where to Stay," above), was built the very year Dennis went "wet." Rock King, a combination boogie-woogie pianist and comedian, still rules the evening and wows the crowd.

The ✪ **Cape Cinema,** 36 Hope Lane, off Route 6A, in the center of Dennis (☎ 508/385-2503 for a recording or 508/385-5644) part of the Cape Playhouse complex, is an art-deco surprise, with a Prometheus-thumbed ceiling mural and folding curtain designed by artist Rockwell Kent and Broadway set designer Jo Mielziner. Independent-film maven George Mansour, curator of the Harvard Film Archive, sees to the art-house programming. That, plus the setting and seating—black leather armchairs—may spoil you forever for what passes for cinemas today. Closed mid-November to early April.

3 The Lower Cape

Occupying the easternmost portion of historic Route 6A, Brewster still enjoys much the same cachet that it boasted as a high roller in the maritime trade. Except for a relatively recent incursion of condos and, of course, the car traffic, it looks much as it might have in the late–19th century, with its general store still serving as a social center point. Perhaps because excellence breeds competition, Brewster has spawned several fine restaurants in recent years and has become something of a magnet for gourmands.

Chatham, a larger, more prosperous community, is being touted by local Realtors as "the Nantucket of the Cape." Its Main Street, a gamut of appealing shops and eateries, approaches an all-American small-town ideal—complemented nicely by a scenic lighthouse and plentiful beaches nearby.

As the gateway to the Outer Cape, where all roads merge, Orleans is a bit too frantic to offer the peace most vacationers seek. Its nearby cousin, East Orleans, is on the upswing as a destination, offering a couple of fun restaurants and—best of all—a goodly chunk of magnificent, unspoiled Cape Cod National Seashore.

BREWSTER

Brewster somehow sets itself apart. Mostly free of the commercial encroachments that have plagued the southern shore, this thriving community seems to go about its business as if nothing were amiss. It has even managed to absorb an intrusively huge development within its own borders, the 380-acre condo complex known as Ocean Edge, on what was once a huge private estate. The dust settled, the trees grew back, the buildings started to blend in, and it's life as usual, if a bit more closely packed. Brewster also welcomes the tens of thousands of transient campers and day-trippers who arrive each summer to enjoy the nearly 2,000 wooded acres of Nickerson State Park. And the town's stretch of Route 6A offers the best antiquing on the entire Cape.

ESSENTIALS

GETTING THERE   After crossing either the Bourne Bridge or the Sagamore bridge, head east on Route 6 or 6A. Route 6A passes through the villages of West Brewster, Brewster, and East Brewster. You can also reach Brewster by taking Route 6's Exit 10 north, along Route 124.

VISITOR INFORMATION   Contact the **Brewster Visitor Center** behind Brewster Town Hall, 2198 Main St./Route 6A, East Brewster (☎ **508/896-3500;** fax 508/896-1086; www.capecod.com/brewster; E-mail: infobrew@capecod.com).

BEACHES & OUTDOOR PURSUITS

BEACHES   Brewster's eight bay beaches have minimal facilities, which make for a more natural experience. When the tide is out, the "beach" extends as much as 2 miles, leaving behind tide pools to splash in and explore, and vast stretches of rippled, reddish "garnet" sand. On a good day, you can see the whole curve of the Cape, from Sandwich to Provincetown. You can purchase a beach parking sticker ($8 per day, $25 per week) at the Visitor Center behind Town Hall at 2198 Main St., (Rte. 6A; ☎ **508/896-4511**).

- **Breakwater Beach,** off Breakwater Road, Brewster. Only a brief walk from the center of town, this calm, shallow beach (the only one with rest rooms) is ideal for young children.
- **Flax Pond** in Nickerson State Park (see "Nature & Wildlife Areas," below). This large freshwater pond, surrounded by pines, has a bathhouse and offers water-sports rentals. The park contains two more ponds with beaches—Cliff and Little Cliff. Access and parking are free.
- **Linnell Landing Beach,** on Linnell Road in East Brewster. This is a half-mile, wheelchair-accessible bay beach.
- **Paine's Creek Beach,** off Paines Creek Road, West Brewster. With 1½ miles to stretch out in, this bay beach has something to offer sun-lovers and nature-lovers alike.

BIKING   The Cape Cod Rail Trail intersects with the 8-mile Nickerson State Park trail system at the park entrance, where there's plenty of free parking; you could follow the Rail Trail back to Dennis (about 12 miles) or onward toward Wellfleet (13 miles).

Idle Times (☎ **508/255-8281**) provides rentals within the park, in season. Another good place to jump in is on Underpass Road about ½ mile south of Route 6A. Here you'll find **Brewster Bicycle Rental,** 442 Underpass Rd. (☎ **508/896-8149**). Just up the hill is the well-equipped Rail Trail **Bike & Blade,** 302 Underpass Rd.(☎ **508/896-8200**), next door to Pizza and More.

BOATING   **Cape Cod Coastal Canoe & Kayak** (☎ **888/226-6393** or 508/564-4051) runs naturalist-guided trips throughout the Cape. Trips (2, 4, and 6 hr.)—daily, weather-permitting, April through September, weekends through October.

FISHING   Brewster offers more ponds for fishing than any other town: 14 in all. Among the most popular are Cliff and Higgins ponds within Nickerson State Park, which are regularly stocked. For a license, visit the **Town Clerk** at Town Hall at 2198 Rte. 6A (☎ **508/896-4506**).

GOLF   Part of a large resort, the 18-hole championship **Ocean Edge Golf Course** at 832 Villages Dr. (☎ **508/896-5911**) is the most challenging in Brewster, followed closely by **Captain's Golf Course** at 1000 Freemans Way (☎ **508/896-5100**). In season, a round at the Ocean Edge course will run you about $75 (including mandatory cart).

NATURE & WILDLIFE AREAS   Admission is free to the two trails maintained by the Cape Cod Museum of Natural History (see below). The **South Trail,** covering a ¾-mile round-trip south of Route 6A, crosses a natural cranberry bog beside Paine's Creek to reach a hardwood forest of beeches and tupelos; toward the end of the loop, you'll come upon a "glacial erratic," a huge boulder dropped by a receding glacier. Before heading out on the ¼ mile **North Trail,** stop in at the museum for a free guide describing the local flora, including wild roses, cattails, and sumacs.

Also accessible from the museum parking lot is the **John Wing Trail,** a 1½-mile network traversing 140 acres of preservation land, including upland, salt marsh, and beach. (*Note:* This can be a soggy trip. Be sure to heed the posted warnings about high tides, especially in spring, or you might very well find yourself stranded.) Keep an eye out for marsh hawks and blue herons.

As it crosses Route 6A, Paine's Creek Road becomes Run Hill Road. Follow it to the end to reach **Punkhorn Park Lands,** an undeveloped 800-acre tract popular with mountain bikers; it features several kettle ponds, a "quaking bog," and 45 miles of dirt paths comprising three marked trails (you'll find trail guides at the trailheads).

The small **Spruce Hill Conservation Area** behind the Brewster Historical Society Museum includes a 600-foot stretch of beach, reached by a former carriage road reportedly favored by Prohibition bootleggers.

Just east of the museum is the 1,955-acre **Nickerson State Park** at Route 6 and Crosby Lane (☎ **508/896-3491**), the legacy of a vast, self-sustaining private estate that once generated its own electricity (with a horse-powered plant) and attracted notable guests, such as President Grover Cleveland. It has its own golf course and game preserve. Today, it's a back-to-nature preserve encompassing 418 campsites (reservations pour in a year in advance, but some are held open for new arrivals willing to wait a day or two), 8 kettle ponds, and 8 miles of bicycle paths. The rest is trees—some 88,000 evergreens, planted by the Civilian Conservation Corps.

WATER SPORTS   Various small sailboats, kayaks, canoes, and even aqua bikes (a.k.a., sea cycles) are available seasonally at **Jack's Boat Rentals** (☎ **508/896-8556**), located on Flax Pond within Nickerson State Park.

A NATURAL HISTORY MUSEUM

✪ **Cape Cod Museum of Natural History.** 869 Rte. 6A (about 2 miles W of Brewster center). ☎ **508/896-3867.** Admission $5 adults, $4.50 seniors, $2 children 5–12. Mon–Sat 9:30am–4:30pm, Sun 11am–4:30pm; extended evening hours until 7:30pm Wed July–August. Closed major holidays.

Long before "ecology" had become a buzzword, noted naturalist writer John Hay helped to found a museum that celebrates and helps to preserve Cape Cod's unique landscape. Open since 1954, the museum was one of the first to present interactive exhibits. The display on whales, for instance, invites the viewer to press a button to hear eerie whale songs; the children's exhibits include an animal-puppet theater. All ages are intrigued by the "live hive"—set up like an ant farm, only with busy bees. Four new marine room tanks (one 125-gallon tank and three 55-gallon tanks) contain freshwater and saltwater fish, turtles, frogs, crabs, lobster, starfish, and a variety of mollusks. The bulk of the museum is outdoors, where 85 acres invite exploration (see "Nature & Wildlife Areas," above). Visitors are encouraged to log their bird and animal sightings upon their return. The museum features an on-site archaeology lab on Wing Island, thought to have sheltered one of Brewster's first settlers—the Quaker John Wing, driven from Sandwich in the mid–17th century by religious persecution—and before him, summering native tribes dating back 10 millennia or more. A true force in fostering environmental appreciation, the museum sponsors all sorts of activities from lectures and concerts to marsh cruises and "eco-treks"—including a sleep-over on uninhabited Monomoy Island off Chatham.

ANTIQUING

Brewster's stretch of Route 6A offers the best antiquing on the entire Cape. Diehards would do well to stop at every intriguing-looking shop; you never know what you might find. There are several consistent standouts.

Serious collectors with bankrolls to match will want to make a beeline to ○ **William M. Baxter Antiques,** 3439 Main St. (Rte. 6A), about 1 mile east of the town center (☎ **508/896-3998**). Mr. Baxter has been in the business for decades, first on Charles Street (Boston's antiques mecca), then here in the boondocks, where fans gladly followed. There aren't too many colonial highboys still bobbing about, but he's got several, along with a dazzling array of mirrors and much distinguished Orientalia. Closed late November to late May.

The artifacts gathered at **Kingsland Manor Antiques,** 440 Rte. 6A, about 1 mile east of the Dennis border (☎ **800/486-2305** or 508/385-9741), tend to be on the flamboyant side, accent pieces rather than serviceable, retiring classics—which makes browsing all the more fun. There's always an interesting variety of items at **Monomoy Antiques,** 3425 Rte. 6A (☎ **508/896-6570**) including many fascinating finds from local estate sales. Specialties include rare books, English china, Native American artifacts, sterling silver, and decoys.

Imagine a town dump full of treasures all meticulously arranged, and you'll get an idea of what's in store at **Diane Vetromile's Antiques** at 3884 Rte. 6A in Brewster (no phone). If the sign that reads ANTIQUES is out, it's open; if not, it's closed. This place is a tad kooky, but any junk aficionado will be thrilled by the pickings: hubcaps, wooden nails, iron rakes, wood shutters—the more peeled paint the better. Owner Diane Vetromile is herself a sculptor, who works with (surprise) found objects, and you'll find her work on view at Jacob Fanning Gallery and Farmhouse Antiques, both in Wellfleet.

WHERE TO STAY

Beechcroft Inn. 1360 Rte. 6A (about 1 mile W of town center), Brewster, MA 02631. ☎ **877/233-2446** or 508/896-9534. Fax 508/896-8812. www.beechcroftinn.com. 10 units. Summer $75–$155 double. Rates include full breakfast. AE, CB, DC, DISC, MC, V.

Though it looks every inch the gracious summer home, this 1828 building, an inn since 1852, began as a meetinghouse. Subtract one steeple, relocate atop a little hillock crowned with magnificent beeches (people seem to have moved houses in those days the way we change jobs), and presto—a made-to-order country retreat. The rooms, none terribly grand, are nevertheless sweet as can be, with fresh country accents. The in-house bistro, though up against some stiff local competition, can hold its own and is certainly convenient.

○ **Captain Freeman Inn.** 15 Breakwater Rd. (off Rte. 6A, in town center), Brewster, MA 02631. ☎ **800/843-4664** or 508/896-7481. Fax 508/896-5618. www.captainfreemaninn.com. E-mail: visitus@capecod.net. 12 units. Summer $130–$250 double. Rates include full breakfast and afternoon tea. AE, MC, V. No children under age 10.

The creation of an exemplary country inn is part business, part art, and Carol Covitz Edmondson—the ex-marketing director behind this beauty—poured plenty of both into her mint-green 1866 Victorian. The "luxury rooms"—each complete with fireplace and a private porch with a 2-person hot tub—boast lots of extras: a canopied, four-poster queen-size bed, a love seat facing the cable TV/VCR (she has a store's worth of tapes available for loan), telephone with answering machine, even a little fridge prestocked with cold soda. The plainer rooms are just as pretty. Delectable yet healthy breakfasts (Edmondson, a culinary maven, hosts weekend cooking courses off-season) are served in the elegant parlor or on a screened porch overlooking the solar-heated outdoor pool and a lush lawn set up for badminton and croquet. Breakwater Landing is a bucolic 5-minute walk, or just moments away, if you avail yourself of a loaner bike.

○ **Old Sea Pines Inn.** 2553 Main St. (about 1 mile E of town center), Brewster, MA 02631. ☎ **508/896-6114.** Fax 508/896-7387. www.oldseapinesinn.com. E-mail: seapines@c4.net. 23 units, 5 with shared bathroom. Summer $70–$125 double; $125–$155 suite. Rates include full breakfast and afternoon tea. AE, CB, DC, DISC, MC, V. Closed Jan–Mar.

This reasonably priced large historic inn is a great spot for families. In the early part of the century, the grand 1907 shingle-style mansion was the site of the Sea Pines School of Charm and Personality for Young Women. A great deal of that charm is still evident. In fact, the hosts, Michele and Steve Rowan, have done their best to recreate the gracious ambience of days gone by. The parlor and expansive porch lined with rockers are just as the young ladies might have found them, as are a handful of rather minuscule boarding-school–scale rooms on the second floor. This is one of the few places on the Cape where solo travelers can find a single room and pay no surcharge. These bargain rooms with shared bathrooms are also the only ones in the house without air-conditioning, but at $55/night in season, who cares? There is also an added annex that's fully wheelchair-accessible. While the main house has an air of exuberance muted by gentility, the annex rooms are outright playful, with colorful accoutrements, including pink TVs. Steve does double duty as the breakfast chef and prepares good old-fashioned food. Sunday evenings in season, Old Sea Pines is the site of a dinner/theater performance by the Cape Cod Repertory Theatre.

WHERE TO DINE
Very Expensive

✪ **The Bramble Inn Restaurant.** 2019 Main St. (about ⅓ mile E of Rte. 124). ☎ **508/ 896-7644.** Reservations required. Fixed-price $42–$55. AE, DISC, MC, V. June to mid-Oct Tues–Sun 6–9pm; call for off-season hrs. Closed Nov to mid-May. INTERNATIONAL.

Often named among the best on Cape Cod, there's an impromptu feel to this intimate restaurant, which is comprised of five small dining rooms each with its own personality, from sporting (the Tack Room) to Sunday best (the Elegant Parlor). One-of-a-kind antique table settings add to the charm. Such niceties fade to mere backdrop, though, beside Ruth Manchester's extraordinary cuisine. A four-course menu that evolves every few weeks gives her free rein to follow fresh enthusiasms, as well as seasonal delicacies. She has a solid grounding in Mediterranean cuisine and a gift for improvisation. Her assorted seafood curry (with lobster, cod, scallops, and shrimp in a light curry sauce with grilled banana, toasted almonds, coconut and chutney) and her rack of lamb (with deep-fried beet and fontina polenta, pan-seared zucchini and mustard port cream) were written up in the *New York Times*.

Chillingsworth. 2449 Main St. (about 1 mile E of town center). ☎ **800/430-3640** or 508/ 896-3640. Reservations required. Jacket requested. Fixed-price $48–$62. AE, DC, MC, V. July to early Sept daily 11:30am–2:30pm and 6–9:30pm; Mid to late June and early Sept to mid-Oct Tues–Sun 11:30am–2:30pm and 6–9:30pm; call for off-season hrs. Closed Dec to mid-May. FRENCH.

A longtime contender for the title of best restaurant on the Cape, Chillingsworth is certainly the fanciest, what with antique appointments reaching back several centuries and a six-course Francophiliac table d'hôte menu that will challenge the most shameless gourmands. Don't be distracted by the crystal and Limoges china as you dine on grilled pheasant with soft polenta, chanterelles and French beans. Or perhaps you'd prefer the roasted tenderloin of buffalo with dauphine potato, roasted shallots and truffle sauce. For a sampling, drop by the Bistro (you don't need a reservation) where the menu is à la carte.

✪ **High Brewster.** 964 Satucket Rd. (off Rte. 6A, about 2 miles SW of town center). ☎ **508/896-3636.** Reservations required. Fixed-price $34–$58. AE, MC, V. Late May to mid-Sept daily 5:30–9pm; call for off-season hrs. Closed Dec–Mar. CLASSIC AMERICAN.

By candlelight, the close yet cozy keeping rooms and paneled parlors of this 1738 colonial are irresistibly romantic. It's difficult to decide between the Rooster Room, with its whimsical wallpaper, or the Front Room, with its clever hand-painted murals.

Stephen Arden's sensual, sophisticated cuisine only serves to intensify the mood. Dishes tend to be bold and modern—lobster-filled ravioli, for instance, with tomato-tarragon cream sauce, or pan-seared salmon with homemade malted chili catsup—yet Arden's good at adapting local ingredients and traditional preparations. Celebrate the harvest with apple crisp topped with homemade apple-rum ice cream.

Moderate
The Brewster Fish House. 2208 Main St. (about ½ mile E of town center). ☎ 508/896-7867. Reservations not accepted. Main courses $14–$22. MC, V. June to early Sept Tues–Sat 11:30am–3pm and 5–10pm, Sun noon–3pm and 5–9:30pm; call for off-season hrs. Closed mid-Dec to mid-Apr. NEW AMERICAN.

Spare and handsome, this small restaurant bills itself as "nonconforming" and delivers on the promise. The approach to seafood borders on genius: Consider squid delectably tenderized in a marinade of soy and ginger, or silky-tender walnut-crusted ocean catfish accompanied by kale sautéed in marsala. Better get there early if you want to get in.

Brewster Inn & Chowder House. 1993 Rte. 6A (in the center of town). ☎ 508/896-7771. Main courses $12–$16. AE, DISC, MC, V. Late May to mid-Oct daily 11:30am–4pm; Sun–Thurs 5–9:30pm, Fri–Sat 5–10pm; call for off-season hrs. ECLECTIC.

To really get the gist of the expression "chow down," just observe the early-evening crowd happily doing so at this plainish century-old restaurant known mostly by word of mouth. The draw is hearty, predictable staples—the homemade chowder, various fried, broiled, or baked fish—at prices geared to ordinary people rather than splurging tourists. Check the blackboard for some interesting variations—maybe mussels steamed in cream and curry. If you like to indulge in a martini before your meal, this place makes the best ones in town. There's also a good old bar, The Woodshed, out back.

Inexpensive
Cobie's. 3260 Rte. 6A (about 2 miles E of Brewster center). ☎ 508/896-7021. Most items under $10. No credit cards. Late May to mid-Sept daily 11am–9pm. Closed mid-Sept to late May. AMERICAN.

This picture-perfect clam shack has been dishing out exemplary fried clams, lobster rolls, foot-long hot dogs, black-and-white frappes, and all the other beloved staples of summer, since 1948.

CHATHAM
Sticking out like a sore elbow, ✪ **Chatham** (say it "Chatt-um," the way the natives do) was one of the first spots to attract early explorers. Samuel de Champlain stopped by in 1606 but got into a tussle with the prior occupants over some copper cooking pots and had to leave in a hurry. The first colonist to stick around was William Nickerson, from Yarmouth, who befriended a local *sachem* (tribal leader) and built a house beside his friend's wigwam in 1656. One prospered; the other—for obvious reasons—didn't. To this day, listings for Nickersons occupy a half-page in the Cape Cod phone book.

Chatham, along with Provincetown, is the only area on the Cape to support a commercial fishing fleet—against increasing odds. Overfishing has resulted in closely monitored limits, to give the stock time to bounce back. Boats must now go out as far as 100 miles to catch their fill. Despite the difficulties, it's a way of life few locals would willingly relinquish.

As in Provincetown, there's surprisingly little animosity between the hard-working residents and summerers at play, perhaps because it's clear that discerning tourist dollars are helping to preserve this lovely town for all.

ESSENTIALS

GETTING THERE After crossing either the Bourne Bridge or the Sagamore Bridge, head east on Route 6 and take Exit 11 (Rte. 137) south to Route 28. From this intersection, the village of South Chatham is about ½ mile west, and West Chatham is about 1½ miles east. Chatham itself is about 2 miles farther east on Route 28. The town lies 32 miles east of Sandwich, 24 miles south of Provincetown.

VISITOR INFORMATION Contact the **Chatham Chamber of Commerce,** 533 Main St., Chatham, MA 02633 (☎ **800/715-5567** or 508/945-5199).

BEACHES & OUTDOOR PURSUITS

BEACHES Chatham has an unusual array of beach styles, from the peaceful shores of the Nantucket Sound to the treacherous, shifting shoals along the Atlantic. For information on beach stickers ($8 per day, $35 per week), call the **Permit Department** on George Ryder Road in West Chatham (☎ **508/945-5180**).

- **Chatham Light Beach.** Located directly below the lighthouse parking lot (where stopovers are limited to 30 min.), this narrow stretch of sand is easy to get to: Just walk down the stairs. Currents here can be tricky and swift, though, so swimming is discouraged.
- **Cockle Cove Beach, Ridgevale Beach, and Hardings Beach.** Lined up along the sound, each at the end of its namesake road south of Route 28, these family-pleasing beaches offer gentle surf suitable for all ages, as well as full facilities.
- **Forest Beach.** No longer an officially recognized town beach (so there's no lifeguard), this sound landing near the Harwich border is still popular, especially among surfboarders.
- **North Beach.** Extending all the way south from Orleans, this 5-mile barrier beach is accessible from Chatham only by boat; if you don't have your own, you can take the *Beachcomber,* a water taxi, which leaves from the fish pier. Call ☎ **508/945-5265** to schedule your trip. The round-trip cost is $15 adults, $8 children 5 to 16, under 5 free. Inquire about other possible drop-off points if you'd like to beach around. They also do sunset cruises and seal watches.
- **Oyster Pond Beach,** off Rte. 28. Only a block from Chatham's Main Street, this sheltered saltwater pond (with rest rooms) swarms with children.
- **South Beach.** A former island jutting out slightly to the south of the Chatham Light, this glorified sandbar can be equally dangerous, so heed posted warnings and content yourself with strolling or, at most, wading.

BIKING Though Chatham has no separate recreational paths per se, a demarcated bike/blading lane makes a scenic, 8-mile circuit of town, heading south onto "The Neck," east to the Chatham Light, up Shore Road all the way to North Chatham, and back to the center of town. A descriptive brochure prepared by the **Chatham Chamber of Commerce** (☎ **800/715-5567** or 508/945-5199) shows the suggested route, and there are lots of lightly trafficked detours worth taking. Rentals are available at **Bikes & Blades,** 195 Crowell Rd., Chatham (☎ **508/945-7600**).

FISHING Chatham has five ponds and lakes that permit fishing; Goose Pond off Fisherman's Landing is among the top spots. For saltwater fishing from land, try the fishing bridge on Bridge Street at the southern end of Mill Pond. First, though, get a license at **Town Hall** at 549 Main St. in Chatham (☎ **508/945-5101**). Shellfishing licenses are available at the **Permit Department** on George Ryder Road in West Chatham (☎ **508/945-5180**). If you hear the deep sea calling, sign on with the *Booby Hatch* (☎ **508/430-2312**), a 33-foot sportfisherman out of Chatham. The

31-foot *Banshee* (☎ **508/945-0403**) and *Tiger Too* (☎ **508/945-9215**), are sport-fishing boats berthed in Stage Harbor.

NATURE & WILDLIFE AREAS   Heading southeast from the Harding's Beach parking lot, the 2-mile, round-trip **Seaside Trail** offers beautiful parallel panoramas of Nantucket Sound and Oyster Pond River; keep an eye out for nesting pairs of horned lark. Access to 40-acre **Morris Island,** southwest of the Chatham Light, is easy: You can walk or drive across and start right in on a marked ¾-mile trail. Heed the high tides, as advised, though—they can come in surprisingly quickly, leaving you stranded. The *Beachcomber* (**508/945-5265**) runs seal-watching cruises out of Stage Harbor. There is a free pick up service from the A&P parking lot or anywhere else in Chatham. The cruises cost $20 adults, $12 children 5 to 12, under 5 free.

Chatham's natural bonanza lies southward: The uninhabited ✪ **Monomoy Islands,** 2,750 acres of brush-covered sand favored by some 285 species of migrating birds, is the perfect pit stop along the Atlantic Flyway. Harbor and gray seals are catching on, too: Hundreds now carpet the coastline from late November through May. At that time, you won't have any trouble seeing them—they're practically unavoidable. Shuttle service to South Island is available aboard the *Rip Ryder* out of the **Stage Harbor Marina** (☎ **508/945-5450**), but you'll get a lot more out of the trip—and probably leave this unspoiled landscape in better shape—if you let a naturalist lead the way. Both the **Wellfleet Bay Wildlife Sanctuary** operated by the Audubon Society (☎ **508/349-2615**) and Brewster's **Cape Cod Museum of Natural History** (☎ **508/896-3867**) offer guided trips. The Audubon's 3, 4, or 7-hour trips take place April through November, and they cost $25 to $55 per person. The boat to Monomoy leaves from Chatham and the trip includes a naturalist-guided nature hike. About a dozen times each summer, the Museum organizes sleepovers in the island's only surviving structure, a clapboard "keeper's house" flanked by an 1849 lighthouse.

WATER SPORTS   Seaworthy vessels, from surf- and sailboards to paddle craft and Sunfish, can be rented from **Monomoy Sail and Cycle** at 275 Rte. 28 in North Chatham (☎ **508/945-0811**). Pleasant Bay is the best place to play for those with sufficient experience; if the winds don't seem to be going your way, try Forest Beach on the South Chatham shore.

SHOPPING

Chatham, its tree-shaded Main Street lined with specialty stores, offers a terrific opportunity to shop and stroll. The goods tend to be on the conservative side, but ever so often you'll happen upon something unusual. One of the best nautical antiques shops in the region is **The Spyglass,** 618 Main St. in the center of town (☎ **508/945-9686**), which stocks antique telescopes, sextants, barometers, captains' desks, and maps and charts. The **Artful Hand Gallery**, 459 Main St., in the center of town (☎ **508/945-4933**) is always worth a visit for colorful and intriguing fine crafts and gifts.

Also of note, **Chatham Glass,** 758 Main St., just west of the Chatham rotary (☎ **508/945-5547**), with outstanding handblown glassworks; and **Chatham Pottery,** 2058 Rte. 28, east of intersection with Route 137 (☎ **508/430-2191**), where Gill Wilson (potter) and Margaret Wilson-Grey (glazer) make and display their striking stoneware.

WHERE TO STAY

Chatham's lodging choices tend to be more expensive than those of neighboring towns, because it's considered a chichi place to vacation. But for those allergic to fussy, fancy B&Bs and inns, Chatham has several good motel options.

Practically across the street from the Chatham Bars Inn, **The Hawthorne,** 196 Shore Rd. (☎ **508/945-0372**) is a very basic, no-frills motel with one of the best locations in town: right on the water, with striking views of Chatham Harbor, Pleasant Bay and the Atlantic Ocean. Rates are $130 to $150 double.

Another option is **The Chatham Motel,** 1487 Main St./Route 28, Chatham (☎ **800/770-5545** or 508/945-2630), 1½ miles from Hardings Beach. Look for the shingled motel with yellow shutters. There's an outdoor pool, shuffleboard, and plenty of barbecue grills. Summer rates are $115 double, $145 suite.

Very Expensive

✪ **Chatham Bars Inn.** Shore Rd. (off Seaview St., about ½ mile NW of town center), Chatham, MA 02633. ☎ **800/527-4884** or 508/945-0096. Fax 508/945-5491. E-mail: resrvcbi@chathambarsinn.com. 173 units. A/C TV TEL. Summer $190–$400 double; $405–$480 1-bedrm suite, $570–$1,100 2-bedrm suite. AE, CB, DC, MC, V.

Set majestically on the beach in Chatham, commanding views out to a barrier beach and the Atlantic Ocean beyond, the grand old Chatham Bars Inn is simply the premier hotel on Cape Cod. A private hunting lodge built for a Boston family in 1914, this curved and colonnaded brick building—surrounded by 26 shingled cottages on 20 acres—has regained its glory days with recent renovations. The large and cushy lobby clearly invites lingering, as the professional staff bustle around fluffing pillows and tending to guests every whim. The best spot to take in the grandeur—as well as the sweeping ocean views—is the breezy veranda, from whence you can order a drink (make mine an old fashioned) and recline in an adirondack chair. All rooms have VCRs (borrow classics and some new selections gratis), iron/ironing boards, and hair dryers; many have private balconies with views of the beach or the prettily landscaped grounds. Cottage rooms are cheery with painted furniture and Waverly fabrics.

Dining/Diversions: Options include the formal Main Dining Room (see "Where to Dine," below); the new fireplaced Tavern; and the seasonal Beach House Grill located right on the beach, which, in addition to offering a breakfast buffet and lunch, puts on a prix-fixe theme feast with live bands 3 evenings a week.

Amenities: There is an outdoor heated pool beside ¼ mile private beach, where you can also catch a complimentary launch to Nauset Beach; four all-weather tennis courts and a putting green (Seaside Links, a nine-hole course open to the public, adjoins the resort), plus shuffleboard, croquet, and volleyball. There is also a basic fitness room. "Beach Buddies," a complimentary children's program for ages 3½ and up; and babysitting. Room service is available from 7am to 9pm.

✪ **Pleasant Bay Village.** 1191 Orleans Rd./Rte. 28 (about 3 miles N of Chatham center), Chathamport, MA 02633. ☎ **800/547-1011** or 508/945-1133. Fax 508/945-9701. 58 units. A/C TV TEL. Summer $195–$245 double; $395–$455 1- or 2-bedrm suite (for 4 occupants). AE, MC, V. Closed Nov–Apr.

Set across the street from Pleasant Bay, this is one fancy motel (with prices set accordingly). Owner Howard Gamsey is a prodigious gardener: Over the past quarter-century, he has transformed this property into a playful Zen paradise, where waterfalls (seven) cascade through colorful rock gardens into a stone-edged pool dotted with lily pads and flashing koi. Actually, he has poured that kind of attention into the entire 6-acre complex. The rooms and cottages, done up in restful pastels, are unusually pleasant. All rooms have hair dryers and refrigerators; suites have kitchenettes. The breakfast room features antique kilims, crewel curtains, and antique tables. In summer, you can order lunch from the grill without having to leave your place at the heated pool. In July and August, dinner is also served.

Wequassett Inn. 178 Rte. 28 (about 5 miles NW of town center, on Pleasant Bay), Chatham, MA 02633. ☎ **800/225-7125** or 508/432-5400. Fax 508/432-1915. 104 units. A/C MINIBAR TV TEL. Summer $280–$515 double. AE, DC, DISC, MC, V. Closed late Nov to Mar.

A virtual village occupying its own little beachfront cove, this low-key, 22-acre complex should quash any preconceived notions of what constitutes a cottage colony. Tucked amid the woods along the shore, 15 modest dwellings, built in the 1940s, harbor roomy quarters done up in an opulent country style: They cost a bit more than the 56 more modern "villa" rooms but, with their picturesque settings, are definitely worth the surcharge. This is one of those places where—well housed, well fed, and pleasantly occupied indeed—you're assured of a temporary respite from the "real" world.

Dining: The 18th-century Eben Ryder House is home to an elegant and very expensive restaurant with lovely Pleasant Bay views. Three meals a day are served here, and jackets are required for gentlemen in the evenings. Lighter fare is served at the Pool Bar & Grille from 10am to 6pm for guests only.

Amenities: Guests have access (for a fee) to four all-weather Plexipave tennis courts, plus a pro shop. Bikes and water crafts may be rented on-site. Croquet and volleyball equipment may be borrowed gratis. A fitness room adjoins the heated pear-shaped pool set at the neck of Clam Point, a calm beach. Nauset Beach is a 15-minute ride via the inn's Power Skiff. Instruction is available in tennis (there are three pros on-site), sailing (coordinated by Cape Water Sports), and saltwater fly-fishing (a branch of the Orvis School). Complimentary van service is offered to two public golf courses, and to the private and exclusive new Cape Cod National Golf Club, a challenging course with waterviews. Van service is also available to Chatham and Orleans villages for shopping.

Expensive

✪ **Captain's House Inn.** 369-377 Old Harbor Rd. (about ½ mile N of the rotary), Chatham, MA 02633. ☎ **800/315-0728** or 508/945-0127. Fax 508/945-0866. www.captainshouseinn.com. E-mail: capthous@capecod.net. 19 units. A/C TEL. Summer $160–$350 double. Rates include full breakfast and afternoon tea. AE, DISC, MC, V.

This 1839 Greek Revival house, along with a cottage and carriage house set on 2 meticulously maintained acres, is a shining example of its era and style. The rooms, named for clipper ships, are richly furnished, with a preponderance of canopied four-posters, beamed ceilings, and, in some cases, brick hearths. All rooms have hair dryers, robes, and slippers, and some are equipped with Jacuzzis and TV/VCRs. Bikes are available. Breakfast is served at individual tables, and the window-walled breakfast room is also the site of a traditional tea—presided over by innkeeper Jan McMasters, formerly of Bournemouth in Great Britain, who knows how to pour a proper cuppa.

Moderate

The Dolphin of Chatham Inn & Motel. 352 Main St. (at the west end of Main St.), Chatham, MA 02633-2428. ☎ **800/688-5900** or 508/945-0070. Fax 508/945-5945. www.dolphininn.com. E-mail: romance@dolphininn.com. 34 units, 3 cottages. A/C TEL TV. Summer $139–$199 double, $199–$269 2-bedroom suites, $1,500/week cottage. AE, DC, MC, V.

With an 1805 main inn building, motel units, and several cottages, The Dolphin offers a wide range of lodging options in the heart of Chatham. Even on Chatham's exquisitely groomed Main Street, this property's landscaping stands out with its extensive and colorful gardens. The 1805 main inn has seven individually decorated rooms with romantic touches like beamed ceilings, canopied beds, and lacy curtains. The rest of the units are standard motel rooms, except for the honeymoon suite, which is housed in a whimsical windmill. All rooms have minifridges and hair dryers, and several have Jacuzzis. In the center of the complex is a heated outdoor pool and hot tub with a pool bar that serves lunch and drinks. The inn's restaurant serves three meals a day.

Moses Nickerson House. 364 Old Harbor Rd. (about ½ mile N of Main St.), Chatham, MA 02633. ☎ **800/628-6972** or 508/945-5859. Fax 508/945-7087. www.capecod.net/moses-nickersonhouse. E-mail: tmnhi@capecod.net. 7 units. A/C TEL. Summer $129–$189 double. Rates include full breakfast and tea. AE, DISC, MC, V.

Your host George "I am not Moses" Watts and his wife Linda, run this gem of a B&B with a sense of humor mixed with gracious hospitality. A grand captain's home in the classicist style, this 1839 manse is every inch devoted to stylish comfort. Whether you opt for a canopied bed with freshly scented linens or a ruggedly handsome, hunt-club–style room, rest assured you'll be pampered—with a home-baked breakfast in the garden-view solarium, and later a late-afternoon pick-me-up in the dazzling parlor, which is mostly white, with glints of vintage cranberry glass. Your hosts are most accommodating—if you are so inclined, a TV will be provided upon request.

WHERE TO DINE
Very Expensive
✪ **The Main Dining Room.** Chatham Bars Inn, Shore Rd. (about ⅓ mile NW of town center). ☎ **508/945-0096.** Reservations recommended. Main courses $21–$35. AE, DC, MC, V. June to Nov daily 7:30–11am; 6:30–9:30pm; call for off-season hrs. NEW AMERICAN.

If it's grandeur you're after, this setting supplies a surplus. The dining room is vast, with ballroom dimensions all but lost in the modern age, and the view is of the million-dollar variety—the Atlantic Ocean in all its splendor. Your fellow diners are decked out in their summer finery, and in the background, a live pianist tickles the ivories. Chef Al Hynes serves hearty traditional New England fare like roasted duckling with orange mandarin ginger sauce and wild rice; roasted quail stuffed with foie gras and raisins with an Armagnac sauce and sautéed green grapes; and fillet of haddock with lobster stuffing and a Newburg sauce. This is not delicate food, but it is delicious. In fact, the clam chowder may be the best on Cape Cod. Dessert choices are equally dense, like hot fudge sundae. Unusual on the Cape, a 17% service charge (gratuity) is added on to your check here. Though there's no dress requirement, a lot of people dress up for this one.

Moderate
Chatham Wayside Inn. 512 Main St. (in the center of town). ☎ **508/945-5550.** Reservations accepted. Main courses $13–$22. AE, DISC, MC, V. Daily 8–11am, 11:30am–4pm, 5–10pm. NEW AMERICAN.

The Wayside's central location on Main Street makes it a good spot for a reasonably priced meal in Chatham. Diners have several seating choices depending on their mood (and the weather): the clubby tavern with gleaming wood tables surrounded by comfy Windsor chairs; the front room with cozy booths; or the large screened terrace, perfect during summer's dog days. Chef Shane Coughlin brings his own flair to basic Wayside specialties like crab cakes, or entrees like rack of lamb, and pesto cod. For something a little different, try the chowder; it's prepared Portuguese style with double-smoked bacon, fresh quahogs, and red bliss potatoes. Whether summer or winter, you'll want to end your meal with the apple-and-cranberry crisp; the secret is the oatmeal and brown-sugar crust.

The Impudent Oyster. 15 Chatham Bars Ave. (off Main St., in the center of town). ☎ **508/ 945-3545.** Reservations suggested. Main courses $8–$20. AE, DC, MC, V. Mon–Sat 11:30am–3pm, Sun noon–3pm; daily 5–10pm. INTERNATIONAL.

All but hidden off the main drag, this perennially popular 1970s-era eatery—complete with decorative stained glass—continues to cook up fabulous fish in exotic guises, ranging from Mexican to Szechuan, but mostly continental. There is also a children's menu here for the little ones.

Two Turtles at the Chatham Townhouse Inn. 11 Library Lane (just past the rotary on Main St.). ☎ **508/945-1234.** Reservations recommended. Main courses $15–$22. AE, CB, DC, DISC, MC, V. Tues–Sun 5:30pm–close. Closed Jan to mid-May. NEW AMERICAN.

On a clear night, try to get one of the two tables out on the porch of this undiscovered gem, and you may enjoy one of the best meal deals in town. Because the inn sits above Main Street, the tables set up on the porch have a great view of the strolling scene. Meanwhile in the kitchen, Chef David Peterson, makes the best seafood paella in town. His concoction includes mussels, clams, shrimp, salmon, squid, chicken, and chorizo sausage and is served over saffron rice. The menu is weighted with wonderful seafood dishes, but there are also fine meat and fowl choices, including a pan-seared breast of duck festively served with cranberry sauce and garlic mashed potatoes. The three intimate, candlelit dining rooms are somewhat generic, though the SS *United States* room displays the famous ship's set of dinnerware that was coveted by none other than Malcolm Forbes.

CHATHAM AFTER DARK

Chatham's free **band concerts**—40 players strong—are arguably the best on the Cape and attract crowds in the thousands. This is small-town America at its most nostalgic, as the band, made up mostly of local folks, plays those standards of yesteryear that never go out of style. Held in Kate Gould Park (off Chatham Bars Avenue, in the center of town) from July through early September, it kicks off at 8pm every Friday. Better come early to claim your square of lawn, and be prepared to sing—or dance—along. Call ☎ **508/945-5199** for more information.

A great leveler, **The Chatham Squire,** 487 Main St. (☎ **508/945-0945**) is a local institution that attracts all the social strata in town. CEOs, seafarers, and collegiates alike convene over the roar of a jukebox or band. Cover varies.

Beloved by an upscale local crowd, **Upstairs at Christian's,** 443 Main St. (☎ **508/945-3362**) is a piano bar with the air of a vintage frat house with scuffed leather couches and movie posters. The live music is offered nightly in season and weekends year-round. Cinematically themed nibbles are always available to offset the generous movie-motif drinks. There's no cover.

ORLEANS

Orleans is where the "Narrow Land" (the early Algonquian name for the Cape) starts to get very narrow indeed: From here on up—or "down," in local parlance—it's never more than a few miles wide from coast to coast. This is also where the ocean-side beaches open up into a glorious expanse some 40 miles long, framed by dramatic dunes and serious surf.

The Cape's three main roads (Rtes. 6, 6A, and 28) converge here, so on summer weekends this spot acts as a rather frustrating funnel. Nevertheless, Main Street Orleans's center boasts a number of appealing restaurants and shops. Nearby, East Orleans is fast emerging as a sweet little beach village with allure for both families and singles. About 2 miles east is seemingly endless (nearly 10-mile-long) Nauset Beach, the southernmost stretch of the Cape Cod National Seashore preserve, and a magnet for the young and the buff.

ESSENTIALS

GETTING THERE After crossing either the Bourne Bridge or the Sagamore Bridge, head east on Route 6 or 6A (the long but scenic route); both converge with

Route 28 in Orleans. The town is 31 miles east of Sandwich, 25 miles south of Provincetown.

VISITOR INFORMATION   Contact the **Orleans Chamber of Commerce,** 44 Main St. (Box 153), Orleans, MA 02653 (☎ **800/865-1386** or 508/255-1386; www.capecod-orleans.com; E-mail: visit@capecod-orleans.com). There's also an **information booth** at the corner of Route 6A and Eldredge Parkway (☎ **508/ 240-2484**).

BEACHES & OUTDOOR PURSUITS

BEACHES   From here all the way to Provincetown, on the eastern side you're dealing with the wild and whimsical. Current conditions are clearly posted at the beach entrances. Weeklong parking permits ($25 for renters, $30 for transients) may be obtained from **Town Hall** on School Road (☎ **508/240-3775**). Day-trippers who arrive early enough—better make that before 9am—can pay at the gate (☎ **508/ 240-3780**).

- **Crystal Lake,** off Monument Road about ¾ mile south of Main Street. Parking—if you can find a space—is free, but there are no facilities.
- ✪ **Nauset Beach,** in East Orleans (☎ **508/240-3780**). Stretching southward all the way past Chatham, this 10-mile-long barrier beach is part of the Cape Cod National Seashore, but is managed by the town. It's long been one of the Cape's more gonzo beach scenes—good surf, big crowds, lots of young people. Full facilities can be found within the 1,000-car parking lot; the in-season fee is $8 per car, which is also good for same-day parking at Skaket Beach (see below). Substantial waves make for good surfing in the special section reserved for that purpose, and boogie boards are ubiquitous. In July and August, there are concerts from 7 to 9pm in the gazebo.
- **Pilgrim Lake,** off Monument Road about 1 mile south of Main Street. This small freshwater beach is covered by a lifeguard in season, You must have a beach parking sticker.
- **Skaket Beach,** off Skaket Beach Road to the west of town (☎ **508/255-0572**). This peaceful bay beach is a better choice for families with young children. When the tide recedes (as much as a mile), little kids will enjoy splashing about in the tide pools left behind. Parking costs $8, and you'd better turn up early.

BIKING   Orleans presents the one slight gap in the 25-mile off-road **Cape Cod Rail Trail** (☎ **508/896-3491**): Just east of the Brewster border, the trail merges with town roads for about 1½ miles. The best way to avoid vehicular aggravation and breathing fumes is to zigzag west to scenic Rock Harbor. Bike rentals are available at **Orleans Cycle** at 26 Main St. in the center of town (☎ **508/255-9115**).

BOATING   **Arey's Pond Boat Yard,** off Rte. 28 in South Orleans (☎ **508/ 255-7900**), offers sailing lessons on daysailers, Catboats, and Rhode 19s in season on Little Pleasant Bay. The **Goose Hummock Outdoor Center** at 15 Rte. 6A, south of the rotary (☎ **508/255-2620**; www.goose.com), rents out canoes, kayaks, and more, and the northern half of Pleasant Bay is the perfect place to use them; inquire about guided excursions.

FISHING   Fishing is allowed in Baker Pond, Pilgrim Lake, and Crystal Lake; the third is a likely spot to reel in trout and perch. For details and a license, visit **Town Hall** at Post Office Square in the center of town (☎ **508/240-3700,** ext. 305) or Goose Hummock (see above). Surf casting—no license needed—is permitted on Nauset Beach South, off Beach Road.

✪ **Rock Harbor,** a former packet landing on the bay (about 1¼ miles northwest of the town center) shelters New England's largest sportfishing fleet: some 18 boats at last count. One call (☎ **800/287-1771** (only in MA) or 508/255-9757) will get you information on them all. Or go look them over; the sunsets are sublime.

NATURE & WILDLIFE AREAS　Inland there's not much, but on the Atlantic shore is a biggie, **Nauset Beach.** Once you get past the swarms of people near the parking lot, you'll have about 9 miles of beach mostly to yourself. You'll see lots of birds (take a field guide) and perhaps some harbor seals off-season.

WATER SPORTS　The **Pump House Surf Co.** at 9 Cranberry Hwy./Route 6A (☎ **508/240-2226**) rents and sells wetsuits, bodyboards and surfboards, while providing up-to-date reports on where to find the best waves. **Nauset Sports** at Jeremiah Square (Rte. 6A at the rotary; ☎ **508/255-4742**) also rents surfboards, bodyboards, skimboards, and wetsuits.

Shopping

Though shops are somewhat scattered, Orleans is full of great finds for browsers.

Continuum Antiques, 7 S. Orleans Rd. (Rte. 28), south of the junction of Route 6A (☎ **508/255-8513**), has some 400 vintage light fixtures, from Victorian on down, along with a smattering of old advertising signs and venerable duck decoys. **Pleasant Bay Antiques,** 540 S. Orleans Rd. (Rte. 28), about ½ mile south of town center in South Orleans (☎ **508/255-0930**) has one of the finest Early American collections in the region.

Addison Holmes Gallery, 43 Rte. 28 north of Main Street (☎ **508/255-6200**), represents such diverse artists as Lois Griffel of Provincetown, whose luminous oils and watercolors typify "Cape Cod Impressionism," and Gary Gilmartin of Truro, a realist working in egg tempera and watercolor, who paints Cape-inspired subjects.

Tree's Place, Route 6A at the intersection of Route 28, Orleans (☎ **888/255-1330** or 508/255-1330), is considered the premier gallery for contemporary realist work in the region. There is also an extensive fine craft, gift, and tile shop here.

Birders will love ✪ **Bird Watcher's General Store,** 36 Rte. 6A (south of the rotary; ☎ **800/562-1512** or 508/255-6974). It stocks virtually every bird-watching accessory under the sun, from basic binoculars to costly telescopes, modest birdhouses to birdbaths fit for a tiny Roman emperor.

Where to Stay

Moderate

The Barley Neck Inn Lodge. 5 Beach Rd. (in the center of town), E. Orleans, MA 02643. ☎ **800/281-7505** or 508/255-8484. Fax 508/255-3626. www.barleyneck.com. E-mail: reservations@barleyneck.com. 18 units. A/C TV TEL. Summer $115–$149. Rates include continental breakfast in season. AE, DC, MC, V.

Every room in this well-managed motel is a little different, but all boast fluffy designer comforters, minifridges, and stylish appointments. There's a little pool within the complex, and Nauset Beach is a mile down the road.

The Cove. 13 S. Orleans Rd. (Rte. 28, N of Main St.), Orleans, MA 02653. ☎ **800/ 343-2233** or 508/255-1203. Fax 508/255-7736. www.thecoveorleans.com. E-mail: thecove@c4.net. 47 units. A/C TV TEL. Summer $99–$169 double; $159–$179 suite or efficiency. AE, CB, DC, DISC, MC, V.

Sensibly turning its back on busy Route 28, this well-camouflaged motel complex focuses instead on placid Town Cove, where guests are offered a free minicruise in season. The interiors are adequate, if not dazzling, and a small heated pool and a restful gazebo overlook the waterfront. All rooms have hair dryers, VCRs, and minifridges; some have kitchenettes, and balconies with cove views.

✪ Kadee's Gray Elephant. 212 Main St., East Orleans, MA 02643. ☎ **508/255-7608.** Fax 508/240-2976. E-mail: kadees@capecod.net. 6 units. A/C TV TEL. Summer $95–$120 double. Weekly rates available. MC, V.

Available short- or long-term, these exuberantly decorated studios, all with fully-equipped kitchens, are extremely cheery and ideal for families. Nauset Beach is a few miles down the road; meanwhile, everything you'll need is right in town—or on the grounds. There's a friendly restaurant/snack bar right next door (see "Where to Dine," below), and the little minigolf course out back is just right for minigolfers.

✪ Nauset House Inn. 143 Beach Rd. (about 1 mile E of village center), East Orleans, MA 02643. ☎ **508/255-2195.** www.nausethouseinn.com. E-mail: jvessell@capecod.net. 14 units, 6 with shared bathroom. Summer $65–$135 double. Rates include full breakfast. DISC, MC, V. Closed Nov–Mar. No children under 12.

Heathcliff would have loved this place, or at least the surrounding moors. Modern nature-lovers with a taste for creature comforts will, too. Several of the rooms in greenery-draped outbuildings feature such romantic extras as a sunken bath or private deck. The most romantic hideaway here, though, is a 1907 conservatory appended to the 1810 farmhouse inn. It's the perfect place to lounge with a novel or lover (or both) as the rain pounds down. Breakfast would seem relatively workaday, were it not for the setting—a pared-down, rustic refectory—and innkeeper Diane Johnson's memorable muffins and pastries.

Nauset Knoll Motor Lodge. 237 Beach Rd. (at Nauset Beach, about 2 miles E of town center), E. Orleans, MA 02643. ☎ **508/255-2364.** 12 units. TV. Summer $135 double. MC, V. Closed late Oct to mid-Apr.

If you're the type who's determined to keep the sea within sight at all times—past a very busy beach, in this case—this nothing-fancy motel with picture windows should suit you to a T. By staying here, you'll save on daily parking charges at Nauset Beach (one of the most popular on Cape Cod), and the simple, clean rooms are well maintained.

The Parsonage Inn. 202 Main St., Box 1501, East Orleans, MA 02643. ☎ **888/422-8217** or 508/255-8217. Fax 508/255-8216. www.parsonageinn.com. E-mail: innkeeper@parsonageinn.com. 8 units. A/C. Summer $95–$125 double. Rates include full breakfast. AE, MC, V.

Blessed with charming British innkeepers, this 1770 full Cape—whose name describes its original function—offers the kind of personalized experience especially prized by "innies" (the country-inn counterpart to foodies). Elizabeth Browne is an accomplished pianist who might, if the evening mood is right, take flight in a Chopin mazurka or Mozart sonata. All rooms have fixings for coffee and tea, and several rooms have minifridges and TVs. The studio has a separate entrance and a full kitchen. Breakfast on the brick patio, in the dining room, or in the privacy of your room.

WHERE TO DINE

Fancy's Farm, 199 Main St., in the center of East Orleans (☎ **508/255-1949**), features particularly appealing produce, whether domestic or imported from halfway across the world. The charming barnlike setting also houses extras like fresh breads, pastries, juices, and exotic salads and soups to go.

The Arbor. 20 S. Orleans Rd. (Rte. 28, N of Main St.). ☎ **508/255-4847.** Reservations recommended. Main courses $14–$22. AE, MC, V. Mid-May to mid-Oct daily 5–10pm; mid-Oct to mid-May Fri–Sun 5–10pm. Closed Jan. ECLECTIC.

With every spare inch crammed with junque—including intentionally mismatched crockery—this place is a visual maelstrom, but all the more fun for it. The cuisine tends toward the saucy continental. If you'd like to just take a look around and dine more simply—not to mention cheaply—try the adjoining and equally interesting Binnacle Tavern, which specializes in pizza.

✪ **The Barley Neck Inn.** 5 Beach Rd. (about ½ mile E of town center). ☎ **800/281-7505** or 508/255-0212. Reservations recommended. Main courses $14–$24. AE, MC, V. June to early Sept daily 5–10pm; call for off-season hrs. FRENCH.

Tastefully restored, this 1857 captain's house boasts a superb chef in Franck Champely, who came from Taillevent and Maxim's by way of New York's Four Seasons. His classical background shines in straightforward yet subtle dishes such as grilled Atlantic salmon fillet with a red-pepper coulis and basil vinaigrette, or sautéed shrimp in a sauce of sweet garlic and Chablis atop lemon angel-hair pasta and shiitake mushrooms. The cuisine may be high-brow—the wine list a connoisseur's delight—but the ambience is festive, verging on boisterous. For a less expensive menu operating out of the same kitchen, you can go to Joe's Beach Road Bar and Grille next door. Joe's keeps serving till 11pm and on summer weekends till midnight.

Kadee's Lobster & Clam Bar. 212 Main St., East Orleans. ☎ **508/255-6184.** Fax 508/240-2926. Reservations not accepted. Main courses $7–$24. MC, V. Late June to early Sept daily 11:30am–9:30pm; late May to late June Fri–Sun 11:30am–9:30pm. Closed early Sept to late May. SEAFOOD.

This atmospheric sea shanty has been rigged to improve on the climate. When the sun's out, the brightly-colored umbrellas pop up on the patio; as soon as the chilly seaborne fog moves in, a curtained awning drops down. The menu is equally adaptable: There's nothing like the classic chowders and stews or a healthy seafood kabob to take the chill off; fine weather, on the other hand, calls for a lobster roll, or perhaps the obligatory (at least once a summer) Fisherman's Feed combo platter splurge. There is also a raw bar with oysters, clams, and shrimp. Due to meticulous management, the staff is a particularly sunny gang here.

The Lobster Claw Restaurant. Rte. 6A (just S of the rotary), Orleans. ☎ **508/255-1800.** Main courses $10–$19. AE, CB, DISC, MC, V. Daily 11:30am–9pm. Closed Nov–Apr. SEAFOOD.

This family-owned and -operated business has been serving up quality seafood for almost 30 years. There's plenty of room for everyone in this sprawling restaurant, where booths spill over with boisterous families, and the usual flotsam and jetsam hang artfully from the ceiling. Get the baked stuffed lobster here with all the fixings. There's a children's menu, as well as early-bird specials served daily from 4 to 5:30pm.

Nauset Beach Club. 222 Main St. (about ½ mile E of town center). ☎ **508/255-8547.** Reservations not accepted. Main courses $14–$19. AE, DISC, MC, V. Late May to mid-Oct daily 5–10pm, Fri–Sat; mid-Oct to May Tues–Sat 5–9:30pm. NORTHERN ITALIAN.

The first thing you may notice about this peachy roadside trattoria (once a duck-hunter's cottage) is the tantalizing aromas. Unfortunately, the next impression is apt to be a surfeit of attitude, when, for example, the maître d' informs you, unbidden, that each person in your party must order an entree—no exceptions made for young diners or small appetites. If you're willing to play by the rules, the reward is worth it: lusciously sauced, perfectly al dente pastas and other Italian-accented regional fare.

ORLEANS AFTER DARK

Joe's Beach Road Bar & Grille at the Barley Neck Inn, 5 Beach Rd., East Orleans (☎ 508/255-0212) is a big old barn of a bar that might as well be town hall. It's where you'll find all the locals exchanging juicy gossip and jokes. On Sunday evenings in season, the weekend warriors who survived in style can enjoy live "Jazz at Joe's." Other nights there's Jim Turner, a blind piano player, who entertains with show tunes and boogie-woogie. There's never a cover charge.

There's live music on weekends off-season at the **Land Ho!** (☎ **508/255-5165**), the best pub in town. There's no cover charge.

4 The Outer Cape

It's only on the ✪ **Outer Cape** that the landscape, even the air, feel really beachy. You can smell the seashore just over the horizon—in fact, everywhere you go, because you're never more than a mile or two away from sand and surf. You won't find any high-rise hotels here or tacky amusement arcades. In fact, there's not a whole lot of anything along this coastline, other than dune grass rippling in the wind. That's because in the early 1960s, 27,000 acres here became the federally-protected Cape Cod National Seashore.

WELLFLEET

Wellfleet—with the well-tended look of a classic New England town—is the perfect destination for artists, writers, off-duty psychiatrists, and other contemplative types who hope to find more in the landscape than mere quaintness or rusticity. Distinguished literati such as Edna St. Vincent Millay and Edmund Wilson put this rural village on the map in the 1920s, in the wake of Provincetown's bohemian heyday.

Wellfleet remains remarkably unspoiled. Once you depart from Route 6, commercialism is kept to a minimum, though the town boasts plenty of appealing shops—including a number of distinguished galleries—and a couple of excellent New American restaurants. It's hard to imagine any other community on the Cape supporting as sophisticated an undertaking as the Wellfleet Harbor Actors' Theatre, or hosting such a wholesome event as public square-dancing on the adjacent Town Pier. And where else could you find a thriving drive-in movie theater right next door to an outstanding nature preserve?

ESSENTIALS

GETTING THERE   After crossing either the Bourne Bridge or the Sagamore Bridge, head east on Route 6 or 6A (the long but scenic route) to Orleans, and continue north on Route 6. Wellfleet is 42 miles northeast of Sandwich, 14 miles south of Provincetown.

VISITOR INFORMATION   Contact the **Wellfleet Chamber of Commerce,** off Route 6, Wellfleet, MA 02663 (☎ **508/349-2510;** fax 508/349-3740; www.capecod. net/wellfleetcc; E-mail: wellfleet@capecod.net).

BEACHES & OUTDOOR PURSUITS

BEACHES   Wellfleet's fabulous ocean beaches tend to sort themselves demographically: **LeCount Hollow** is popular with families, **Newcomb Hollow** with highschoolers, White Crest with the college crowd (including surfers and off-hour hang gliders), and Cahoon with thirtysomethings. Alas, only the latter two beaches permit parking by nonresidents ($10/day). To enjoy the other two, as well as Burton Baker Beach on the harbor and Duck Harbor on the bay, plus three freshwater ponds, you'll have to walk or bike in, or see if you qualify for a sticker ($25 per week). Bring proof of residency to the seasonal **Beach Sticker Booth** on the Town Pier, or call the Wellfleet Recreation Department (☎ **508/349-9818**).

- **Marconi Beach,** off Marconi Beach Road in South Wellfleet. A National Seashore property, this cliff-lined beach (with rest rooms) charges an entry fee

Biking the Cape Cod Rail Trail

The 25-mile Cape Cod Rail Trail (☎ **508/896-3491**) is one of New England's longest and most popular bike paths. Once a bed of the Penn Central Railroad, the trail is relatively flat and straight. On weekends in summer months, you'll have to contend with dogs, in-line skaters, young families, and bikers who whip by you on their way to becoming the next Greg LeMond. Yet, if you want to venture away from the coast and see some of the Cape's countryside without having to deal with motorized traffic, this is one of the few ways to do it.

The trail starts in South Wellfleet on Lecount Hollow Road or in South Dennis on Mass. Rt. 134, depending on which way you want to ride. Beginning in South Wellfleet, the path cruises by purple wildflowers, flowering dogwood, and small maples where red-winged blackbirds and goldfinches nest. In Orleans, you'll have to ride on Rock Harbor and West Roads until the City Council decides to complete the trail. At least you get a good view of the boats lining Rock Harbor. Clearly marked signs lead back to the Rail Trail. You'll soon enter the Nickerson State Park bike trails, or you can continue straight through Brewster to a series of swimming holes—Seymour, Long, and Hinckleys ponds. A favorite picnic spot is the Pleasant Lake General Store in Harwich. Shortly afterwards, you cross over U.S. 6 on Mass. Rt. 124 before veering right through farmland, soon ending in South Dennis.

—by Stephen Jermanok

of $7 per day, or only $20 for the season. *Note:* The bluffs are so high that the beach lies in shadow by late afternoon.

- **Mayo Beach,** Kendrick Avenue (near the Town Pier). Right by the harbor, facing south, this beach (with rest rooms) is hardly secluded but will please young waders and splashers. And the price is right; parking is free. You could grab a bite (and a paperback) at **The Bookstore Restaurant** across the street, which serves three meals a day and sells used books around back.
- **White Crest and ✪ Cahoon Hollow beaches,** off Ocean View Drive in Wellfleet. These two town-run ocean beaches—big with surfers—are open to all. Both have snack bars and rest rooms. Parking costs $10 per day.

BIKING   To date, the terminus of the 25-mile—and growing—**Cape Cod Rail Trail** (see above), Wellfleet is also among its more desirable destinations: A country road off the bike path leads right to LeCount Hollow Beach. Located at the current terminus, the **Black Duck Sports Shop** at 1446 Rte. 6 in Wellfleet (at the corner of LeCount's Hollow Road; ☎ 508/349-9801) stocks everything from rental bikes to "belly boards" and inflatable boats; the deli at the adjoining South Wellfleet General Store (☎ 508/349-2335) can see to your snacking needs.

BOATING   **Jack's Boat Rentals,** located on Gull Pond off Gull Pond Road, about ½ mile south of the Truro border (☎ 508/349-9808), rents out canoes, kayaks, sailboards, Sunfish, as well as sea cycles and surf bikes. Gull Pond connects to Higgins Pond by way of a placid, narrow channel lined with red maples and choked with yellow water lilies. Needless to say, it's a great place to paddle. If you'd like a canoe for a few days, you'll need to go to Jack's Boat Rentals location on Route 6 in Wellfleet (next to the Cumberland Farms).

In addition to watercraft to go, Jack's is also the place for information about **Eric Gustavson's guided kayak tours** (☎ 508/349-1429) of nearby kettle ponds and tidal rivers.

The Chequessett Yacht & Country Club on Chequessett Neck Road in Wellfleet (☎ 508/349-3704) offers sailing lessons for approximately $30 an hour. For those who already know how, **Wellfleet Marine Corp.** on the Town Pier (☎ 508/349-2233) rents 14- to 20-foot sailboats in season.

FISHING   For a license to fish at Long Pond, Great Pond, or Gull Pond (all stocked with trout and full of native perch, pickerel, and sunfish), visit **Town Hall** at 300 Main St. (☎ 508/349-0301) or the Town Pier (☎ 508/349-9818). Surf casting, which doesn't require a license, is permitted at the town beaches.

Shellfishing licenses—Wellfleet's oysters are world-famous—can be obtained from the **Shellfish Department** on the Town Pier off Kendrick Avenue (☎ 508/349-0325).

Also heading out from here, in season, is the 60-foot party fishing boat *Navigator* (☎ 508/349-6003), and three smaller sports-fishermen: the *Erin-H* (☎ 508/349-9663), *Jac's Mate* (☎ 508/255-2978), and *Snooper* (☎ 508/349-6113).

NATURE & WILDLIFE AREAS   You'll find 6 miles of very scenic trails lined with lupines and bayberries—Goose Pond, Silver Spring, and Bay View—within the Wellfleet Bay Wildlife Sanctuary in South Wellfleet (see below).

Right in town, the short, picturesque boardwalk known as **Uncle Tim's Bridge,** off East Commercial Street, crosses Duck Creek to access a tiny island crisscrossed by paths. The Cape Cod National Seashore maintains two spectacular self-guided trails. The 1¼-mile **Atlantic White Cedar Swamp Trail,** off the parking area for the Marconi Wireless Station, shelters a rare stand of the light-weight white cedars prized by Native Americans as wood for canoes; red maples are slowly crowding out the cedars, but meanwhile the tea-tinted, moss-choked swamp is a magical place, refreshingly cool even at the height of summer. A boardwalk will see you over the muck (these peat bogs are 7 feet deep in places), but the return trip does entail a calf-testing ½-mile trek through deep sand. Consider it a warm-up for magnificent **Great Island,** jutting 4 miles into the bay (off the western end of Chequessett Neck Road) to cup Wellfleet Harbor. It is uninhabited and a true refuge for those strong enough to go the distance. Just be sure to cover up, wear sturdy shoes, bring water, and venture to Jeremy Point—the very tip—only if you're sure the tide is going out.

WATER SPORTS   Surfing is restricted to White Crest Beach, and sailboarding to Burton Baker Beach at Indian Neck during certain tide conditions; ask for a copy of the regulations at the Beach Sticker Booth on the Town Pier.

Wellfleet Bay Wildlife Sanctuary—A spiffy new eco-friendly visitor center serves as both introduction and gate-way to this 1,000-acre refuge maintained by the Massachusetts Audubon Society. Passive solar heat and composting toilets are just a few of the waste-cutting elements incorporated in the seemingly simple $1.6 million building, which nestles into its wooded site. You'll see plenty of wildlife—especially lyrical redwing blackbirds and circling osprey—as you follow 5 miles of looping trails through pine forests, salt marsh, and moors. To hone your observation skills, avail yourself of the naturalist-guided tours during the day. Also inquire about special workshops for children and about canoeing, birding, and off-season seal-watching excursions. The center is located off Route 6, a couple hundred yards north of the Eastham border, in South Wellfleet (☎ 508/349-2615; fax 508/349-2632). Trail use is free for Massachusetts Audubon Society members; the trail fee for nonmembers is $3 adults, $2 seniors and children. Trails are open July through August from 8am to 8pm, and September through June from 8am to dusk. The visitor center is open Memorial Day to Columbus Day daily from 8:30am to 5pm; during the off-season, it's closed Mondays.

SHOPPING

Wellfleet calls itself "the art-gallery town." Though it may lag behind Provincetown in terms of quantity, the quality is comparable. Crafts make a strong showing, too, as do contemporary women's clothing and eclectic home furnishings. Unlike Provincetown, which has something to offer virtually year-round, Wellfleet pretty much closes up come Columbus Day.

Cherry Stone Gallery, 70 E. Commercial St. (about ⅛ mile south of East Main Street; ☎ **508/349-3026**), is probably more influential than all the others put together. It got a head start, opening in 1972 and showing such luminaries as Rauschenberg, Motherwell, and, more recently, Wellfleet resident Helen Miranda Wilson.

The Cove Gallery, 15 Commercial St. (by Duck Creek; ☎ **508/349-2530**) carries the paintings and prints of many well-known artists, including Barry Moser and Leonard Baskin. John Grillo's work astounds every summer during his annual show, which recently featured boldly painted tango-themed paintings, watercolors, and prints.

Crafts make a stronger stand than art **at ۞ Left Bank Gallery,** 25 Commercial St. (by Duck Creek; ☎ **508/349-9451**). The **Left Bank Small Works & Jewelry Gallery,** 3 W. Main St. (in the center of town; ☎ **508/439-7939**) features an irresistible sampling of new-wave jewelry designs.

WHERE TO STAY

Even'tide. 650 Rte. 6 (about 1 mile N of Eastham border), S. Wellfleet, MA 02663. ☎ **800/ 368-0007** in MA only, or 508/349-3410. Fax 508/349-7804. www.capecod.net/eventide. E-mail: eventide@capecod.net. 31 units. A/C TV TEL. Summer $79–$110 double; $115 efficiency. AE, CB, DC, DISC, MC, V.

Set back from the road in its own roomy compound complete with playground, this motel feels more like a friendly village centered around a large, heated indoor pool— a godsend in inclement weather. The Rail Trail goes right by the motel, and a ¾-mile footpath through the woods leads to Marconi Beach.

The Inn at Duck Creeke. 70 Main St., Box 364, Wellfleet, MA 02667. ☎ **508/349-9333.** Fax 508/349-0234. www.capecod.net/duckinn. E-mail: duckinn@capecod.net. 25 units (8 with shared bath). Summer $65–$100 double. Rates include continental breakfast. AE, MC, V.

This historic complex consists of four buildings set on 5 woodsy acres overlooking a tidal creek and salt marsh. Three lodging buildings include the main building, an 1880's captain's house with wideboard floors and charming but basic rooms, many with shared bath; the carriage house with a few light and airy cabinlike rooms; and the saltworks building with smaller cottagey rooms with antique decor. In the main building, the shared bathrooms adjoin two rooms, so there's an intimacy here that shyer types might not desire. And if the adjoining room houses a family of four, it might be a rough night. The rooms in the carriage house and saltworks building are quieter and can be downright romantic. But there's definitely a no-frills quality to this lodging option: towels are thin, and so are walls. Even the continental breakfast is very basic: a buffet of tiny muffins on paper plates. A big plus is that there are two good restaurants (see "Where to Dine," below) on site: Sweet Seasons, the more expensive, and the Tavern, with a publike atmosphere and live entertainment in season.

Surfside Cottages. Ocean View Dr. (at LeCount Hollow Rd.), Box 937, S. Wellfleet, MA 02663. ☎ **508/349-3959.** www.capecod.net/surfside/. E-mail: surfside@capecod.net. 18 cottages. TEL. Summer $750–$1,350 weekly; off-season $70–$125 per day. MC, V. Pets allowed off-season.

This is where you want to be: smack dab on a spectacular beach with 50-foot dunes, biking distance to Wellfleet Center, a short drive to Provincetown for dinner. These cottages, fun and modern in a 1960s way, have one, two, or three bedrooms. All cottages have kitchens, fireplaces, barbecues, and screened porches. Reserve early.

WHERE TO DINE

A former fishing shack, **Hatch's Fish & Produce Market,** 310 Main St. behind Town Hall (☎ **508/349-2810**), is the unofficial heart of Wellfleet. You'll find the best of local bounty from fresh-picked corn and fruit-juice popsicles to steaming lobsters and home-smoked local mussels and pâté. Virtually no one passes through without picking up a little something, along with the latest talk of the town. Closed late September to late May.

Aesop's Tables. 316 Main St. (in the center of town). ☎ **508/349-6450.** Reservations recommended. Main courses $16–$23. AE, CB, DC, MC, V. July–Aug Wed–Sun noon–3pm; daily 5:30–9:30pm. Call for off-season hrs. Closed mid-Oct to mid-May. INTERNATIONAL.

This delightful restaurant is offbeat and avant-garde enough to stay interesting year after year. Since 1965, it has reliably and artistically turned out delectable food in a handsome, historic setting with a relaxed and festive atmosphere. Brian Dunne is at once owner and host; he sets the mood and even grows some of the edible flowers and delicate greens that go into the "Monet's Garden" salad. His wife, Kim Kettler, is the artist behind the handmade paper collages decorating the walls. The scallops (served whole) and oysters come straight from the bay to be imaginatively treated. For dessert, don't miss "Clementine's Citrus Tart," a rich pastry offset by a white chocolate and fruit mousse. Lunch on the front lawn overlooking Wellfleet's Main Street is a summertime treat, and the kid's menu is particularly good here.

The Lighthouse. 317 Main St. (in the center of town). ☎ **508/349-3681.** Main courses $9–$18. DISC, MC, V. Daily 6:30am–10pm. AMERICAN.

Nothing special in and of itself, this bustling year-round institution is an off-season haven for locals and a beacon to passing tourists year-round. Except on Thursday's "Mexican Night," the menu is all-American normal, from the steak-and-eggs breakfast to the native seafood dinners. Appreciative patrons usually keep up a dull roar throughout the day, revving up to a deafening roar as the Bass and Guinness flow from the tap.

Moby Dick's Restaurant. Rte. 6, Wellfleet. ☎ **508/349-9795.** Reservations not accepted. Main courses $6–$16. MC, V. June–Sept 11:30am–10pm; call for off-season hrs. Closed mid-Oct to April. SEAFOOD.

This is your typical clam shack, with netting and buoys hanging from the ceiling. Order your meal at the register, sit at a picnic table, and a cheerful college student brings it to you. Fried fish, clams, scallops, and shrimp are all good here; get the Moby's Seafood Special, a heaping platter of all of the above plus coleslaw and fries. Then there's the clambake special with lobster, steamers, and corn on the cob. Portions are huge; bring the family and chow down.

✪ **Painter's Restaurant and Studio Bar.** 50 Main St. (near Rte. 6). ☎ **508/349-3003.** Main courses $8–$23. AE, MC, V. Late May to mid-Oct daily 6–10pm; mid-Oct to late May Wed–Sat 6–10pm. NEW AMERICAN/ASIAN.

Kate Painter trained at some pretty fancy establishments: San Francisco's world-famous Stars, Boston top spot Biba, and Cape Cod's own Chillingsworth. Still, if she had her druthers—and now she does—she'd prefer, in the words of her motto and mission statement, "simple food in a funky place." The setting, a wood-beamed bistro dressed up with friends' artwork, is indeed funky, but her kitchen is turning out very hip food. On the appetizer list, the crackling Asian Cellophane Shrimp served with tomato coulis is a flavorful delight. The entrees include such dishes as Painter's Tuna, seared with sesame and mustard seed, served with a lovely orange-ginger Asian dipping sauce and wasabi. Painter's sense of humor shows up in the desserts: "Something Chocolate" and "Something Lemon" are just that, an intriguing cross between cake and soufflé.

Sweet Seasons Restaurant. At the Inn at Duck Creeke, 70 Main St. (about ⅛ mile W of Rte. 6). ☎ **508/349-6535.** Reservations recommended. Main courses $16–$22. AE, MC, V. Late June to mid-Sept daily 5:30–10pm. Closed mid-Sept to late June. NEW AMERICAN.

The competition has grown heated of late, but chef-owner Judith Pihl's Mediterranean-influenced fare is still appealing after 20-plus years, as is this dining room's peaceful marsh view. Some of the dishes can be a bit heavy by contemporary standards, but there's usually a healthy alternative, like *scallops Josephine*: pan-seared scallops served with a chilled oriental cucumber salad and sesame noodles. Lighter fare is served in the adjoining Duck Creeke Tavern.

WELLFLEET AFTER DARK

Arguably the best dance club on Cape Cod, **The Beachcomber,** 1220 Old Cahoon Hollow Rd., off Ocean View Drive (☎ **508/349-6055**) is definitely the most scenic, and not just in terms of the barely legal-age clientele. The 'Comber is right on Cahoon Hollow Beach—so close, in fact, that late beachgoers on summer weekends can count on a free concert: reggae, perhaps, or the homegrown "Toots and the Maytalls." Other nights, you might run into blues, ska, or rock, and often some very big names playing mostly for the fun of it. The cover varies.

Three restaurants become evening roosts as the hour grows later: **Duck Creeke Tavern,** 70 Main St. (☎ **508/349-7369**) hosts local talent to go with its light fare; **Painter's Upstairs,** 50 Main St. (☎ **508/349-3003**) features an artsy crowd, a pool table, and an oyster hour from 5 to 6pm daily; locally spawned blues and jazz usually inhabit the cozy attic at the **Upstairs Bar** at Aesop's Tables, 316 Main St. (☎ **508/ 349-6450**). Wednesday nights in summer, Wellfleet's workaday fishing pier (off Kendricks Avenue) resounds to the footfalls of avid amateur square dancers of every age. Call ☎ **508/349-0330** for more information.

The **Wellfleet Drive-In Theater,** 51 Rte. 6, just north of the Eastham border, (☎ **800/696-3532** or 508/349-2520), clearly deserves National Landmark status: Built in 1957, it's the only drive-in left on Cape Cod and one of a scant half-dozen surviving in the state. The rituals are as endearing as ever: the playtime preceding the cartoons, the countdown plugging the allures of the snack bar, and finally, two full first-run features. Open daily from late May through mid-September; show time is at dusk. Call for off-season hours. Admission is $6 adults, $3.50 seniors and children 5 to 11.

5 Provincetown

You made it! To one of the most interesting, rewarding spots on the eastern seaboard. Explorer Bartholomew Gosnold must have felt much the same thrill in 1602 when he and his crew happened upon a "great stoare of codfysshes" here (it wasn't quite the gold they were seeking, but valuable enough to warrant changing the peninsula's name). The Pilgrims, of course, were overjoyed when they slogged into the harbor 18 years later: Never mind that they'd landed several hundred miles off course—it was a miracle they'd made it 'round the treacherous Outer Cape at all.

And much later on in the late 1890s, Charles Hawthorne, the painter who "discovered" this near-derelict fishing town and introduced it to the Greenwich Village intelligentsia, was besotted by this "jumble of color in the intense sunlight accentuated by the brilliant blue of the harbor." He'd probably be aghast at the commercial circus his enthusiasm has wrought—though he'd be proud, perhaps, to find the Provincetown Art Association & Museum, which he helped found in 1914, still going strong. The town is wholeheartedly dedicated to creative expression, both visual and verbal, and right now it's on a roll. Maybe the inspiration comes from the quality of the light (and it is particularly lovely—soft and diffuse) or the solitude afforded by long, lonely winters. The general atmosphere of open-mindedness plays a pivotal role, allowing a very varied assortment of individuals to explore their creative urges.

That same open-mindedness may account for Provincetown's ascendancy as a gay and lesbian resort. During peak season, Provincetown's streets are a celebration of the individual's freedom to be as "out" as imagination allows. The term "family values" enjoy a very broad definition here. "Family" encompasses all the populace in its glorious diversity. Those who've settled here know they've found a very special place, and in that they have something precious in common.

ESSENTIALS

GETTING THERE   After crossing either the Bourne Bridge or Sagamore Bridge, head east on Route 6 or 6A (the long but scenic route) to Orleans, then north on Route 6. Provincetown is 56 miles north of Sandwich, 42 miles northeast of Hyannis.

Bay State Cruises (☎ 617/457-1428) makes round-trips from Boston, daily from late June to early September and weekends in the shoulder seasons. **Cape Cod Cruises** (☎ 508/747-2400) connects Plymouth and Provincetown in summer.

VISITOR INFORMATION   Contact the **Provincetown Chamber of Commerce,** 307 Commercial St., Provincetown, MA 02657 (☎ 508/487-3424; fax 508/487-8966; www.ptownchamber.com; E-mail: info@ptownchamber.com); or the gay-oriented **Provincetown Business Guild,** 115 Bradford St., Box 421, Province-town, MA 02657 (☎ 800/637-8696 or 508/487-2313; fax 508/487-1252; www.ptown.org; E-mail: pbguild@capecod.net).

BEACHES & OUTDOOR PURSUITS

BEACHES   With nine-tenths of its territory (basically, all but the "downtown" area) protected by the Cape Cod National Seashore, Provincetown has miles of beaches. The 3-mile bay beach that lines the harbor, though certainly swimmable, is not all that inviting compared to the magnificent ocean beaches overseen by the National Seashore. The two official access areas (see below) tend to be crowded; however, you can always find a less densely populated stretch if you're willing to hike. *Note:* Local beachgoers have been lobbying for "clothing-optional" beaches for years, but the rangers—fearful of voyeurs trampling the dune grass—are firmly opposed and routinely issue tickets, so stand forewarned (and fully clothed).

- **Herring Cove and Race Point:** Both National Seashore beaches are known for their spectacular sunsets; observers often applaud. Race Point, on the ocean side, is rougher, and you might actually spot whales en route to Stellwagen Bank. Calmer Herring Cove is a haven for same-sex couples, who tend to sort themselves by gender. Parking costs $7 per day, $20 per season.
- **Long Point:** Trek out over the breakwater and beyond, or catch a water shuttle—$10 round-trip—from Flyer's Boat Rental (see "Boating," below) to visit this very last spit of land, capped by an 1827 lighthouse. Locals call it "the end of the Earth."

BIKING   North of town, nestled amid the Cape Cod National Seashore preserve, is one of the more spectacular bike paths in New England, the 7-mile ✪ **Province Lands Trail,** a heady swirl of steep dunes (watch out for sand drifts on the path) anchored by wind-stunted scrub pines. With its free parking, the Province Lands Visitor Center (☎ 508/487-1256) is a good place to start: You can survey the landscape from the observation tower to try to get your bearings before setting off amid the dizzying maze. With any luck, you'll find a spur path leading to one of the beaches—Race Point or Herring Cove—lining the shore. Bike rentals are offered seasonally, practically on-site, by **Nelson's Bike Shop** at 43 Race Point Rd. (☎ 508/487-4335). It's also an easy jaunt from town, where you'll find plenty of good bike shops—such as the centrally located **Ptown Bikes** at 42 Bradford St. (☎ 508/487-TREK; reserve several days in advance).

BOATING   In addition to operating a Long Point shuttle from its own dock (see "Beaches," above), **Flyer's Boat Rental** at 131 Commercial St. in the West End (☎ 508/487-0898)—established in 1945—offers all sorts of craft, from kayaks and dinghies to sailboats of varying sizes; they also give sailing lessons and organize fishing trips.

FISHING   Surf casting is permitted at New Beach (off Rte. 6) and Race Point Beach (near the Race Point Coast Guard Station); also, many people drop a hand-line or light tackle right off the West End breakwater. For low-cost deep-sea fishing via party boat, board the *Cee Jay* (☎ 800/675-6723 or 508/487-4330). For serious sportfishing, sign on for the *Shady Lady II* (☎ 508/487-0182). Both depart from MacMillan Wharf.

HORSEBACK RIDING   **Nelson's Riding Stable** on Race Point Road (☎ 508/487-1112) offers slow, guided, 1-hour trail rides through the dunes daily at 10am, noon, 2, and 4 from April through October; in the summer, there is also a 6pm trip. In the spring and fall, equestrians can make a reservation for a sunset sprint along the beach.

NATURE TRAILS   Within the Province Lands (off Race Point Road, ½ mile north of Rte. 6), the National Seashore maintains the 1-mile, self-guided Beech Forest Trail, a shaded path that circles a shallow freshwater pond blanketed with water lilies before heading into the woods. You can see the shifting dunes (much of this terrain is soft sand) gradually encroaching on the forest.

Another wonderful walk is along the West End breakwater out to the end of Long Point, about 3 miles round-trip. The breakwater is located at the end of Commercial Street, next to the Provincetown Inn. It's about a 20-minute walk across the wide breakwater; then it's soft sand for the remainder of the hike. Wood End Lighthouse is directly across the spit of sand near the breakwater. It will take about another 40 minutes to reach Long Point Light at the very tip of Cape Cod. Hikers determined to reach the end of Long Point will want to bring a hat, water, and sunscreen for this intense trek along the beach. The outside of the arm tends to be the more scenic route for contemplative hikers; the inside coast can be crowded with picnicking families and surf casters.

WHALE WATCHING   ✪ **Stellwagen Bank,** 8 miles off Provincetown, is a rich feeding ground for whales, and the **Dolphin Fleet,** on MacMillan Wharf (☎ 800/826-9300 or 508/349-1900), was the first, and by most accounts still the best, outfit running whale-watching trips to Stellwagen. Most cruises carry a naturalist (a very vague term) to provide running commentary; on the *Dolphin*, scientists from the Center for Coastal Studies are out there doing research crucial to the whales' survival, and part of the proceeds goes to further their worthwhile efforts.

Some tips for first-timers: Dress very warmly, in layers (it's cold out on the water), and definitely take along a waterproof windbreaker, if you've got one (maybe your innkeeper can offer a spare). And last but not least, if you're prone to seasickness, you'd better take a motion-sickness pill one hour before boarding the vessel. It gets rough out there. Tickets are $17 to $18 for adults, $16 for seniors, $15 for children 7 to 12, and free for children 6 and under. From April through October there are three 3½-hour trips daily; in July and August there are nine trips daily. Call for a schedule and reservations (required). Closed November to mid-April.

Provincetown

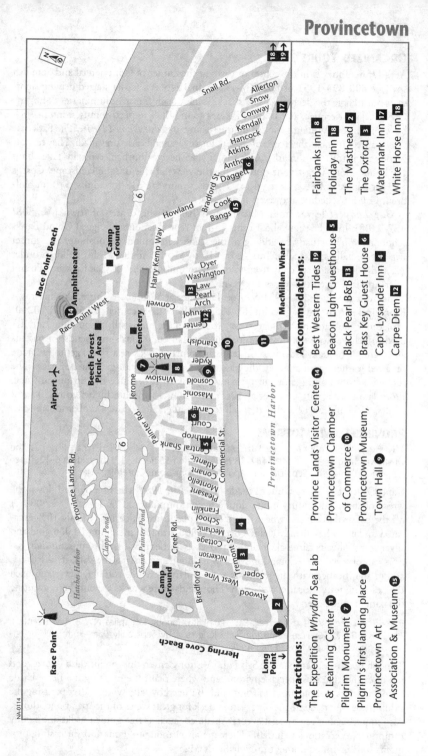

Attractions:

The Expedition *Whydah* Sea Lab & Learning Center **11**

Pilgrim Monument **7**

Pilgrim's first landing place **1**

Provincetown Art Association & Museum **15**

Province Lands Visitor Center **14**

Provincetown Chamber of Commerce **10**

Provincetown Museum, Town Hall **9**

Accommodations:

Best Western Tides **19**

Beacon Light Guesthouse **5**

Black Pearl B&B **13**

Brass Key Guest House **6**

Capt. Lysander Inn **4**

Carpe Diem **12**

Fairbanks Inn **8**

Holiday Inn **18**

The Masthead **2**

The Oxford **3**

Watermark Inn **17**

White Horse Inn **18**

NA-0314

237

ORGANIZED TOURS

Art's Dune Tours is in the center of town at the corner of Commercial and Standish sts. (☎ **800/894-1951** or 508/487-1950). In 1946, Art Costa started driving sightseers out to ogle the decrepit "dune shacks" where such transient luminaries as Eugene O'Neill, Jack Kerouac, and Jackson Pollock found their respective muses; in one such hovel, Tennessee Williams cooked up the steamy *Streetcar Named Desire.* The Park Service wanted to raze these eyesores, but luckily saner heads prevailed: They're now National Historic Landmarks. Art's tours, via Chevy Suburban, typically take about 1¼ hours. Don't forget your cameras for the views of this unique landscape. Cost is $10 for adults and $8 children 4 to 11; sunset tours are $12 for adults, $10 for children. Call for schedule and reservations.

Bay Lady II leaves from MacMillan Wharf in the center of town (☎ **508/487-9308**). In sightseeing aboard this 73-foot reproduction gaff-rigged Grand Banks schooner, you'll actually be adding to the scenery for onlookers onshore. The sunset trip is especially spectacular. Tours cost $10 to $15 for adults, $6 for children under 12, and 2-hour sails are daily from mid-May to mid-October 4. Call for schedule and reservations. Closed the rest of the year.

Board a cheery yellow 1931 Stinson Detroiter at **Willie Air Tours,** Provincetown Municipal Airport on Race Point Rd. 2 miles NW of town center (☎ **508/487-0240**) for a quick look around. It's a great way to fathom the forces still shaping the land. It's hard to believe from the tiny exterior, but you can cram four slim friends (or parents and a couple of lucky kids) into this adorable biplane. Back-seat riders get to luxuriate on a red leather banquette, but the passenger next to the pilot gets the best view. The flight is smooth and gentle, an intoxicating way to experience the tip of the Cape. From late May to late October at 10am and 6pm, 15-minute flights cost $50 for 2 adults, $15 children 12 and under; call for schedule. Closed late October to late May.

PROVINCETOWN MUSEUMS

The Expedition Whydah Sea Lab & Learning Center. MacMillan Wharf (just past the whale-watching fleet). ☎ **508/487-8899.** Admission $5 adults, $3.50 children 6–12. June–Aug daily 10am–7pm; Sept–Dec and April–May 10am–5pm. Closed Jan–Mar.

Cape Cod native Barry Clifford made headlines in 1984 when he tracked down the wreck of the 17th-century pirate ship Whydah (pronounced "Wid-dah,") 1,500 feet off the coast of Wellfleet, where it had lain undisturbed since 1717. Only 10% excavated to date, it has already yielded over 100,000 artifacts, including 10,000 gold and silver coins, plus its namesake bell that proves its authenticity. In this museum/lab, visitors can observe the reclamation work as it's done and discuss the ship, its discovery, and its significance with the scientists and scholars on hand. You may never approach the beach in quite the same way again: Thousands more wrecks are out there, awaiting the patient and clever.

Province Lands Visitor Center. Race Point Rd. (about 1½ miles NW of town center). ☎ **508/487-1256.** Free admission. Late June to early Sept daily 9am–5pm; call for off-season hrs. Closed late Nov to mid-April.

Though much smaller than the Salt Pond Visitor Center, this satellite also does a good job of explicating this special environment, where plant life must fight a fierce battle to maintain its toehold amid shifting sands buffeted by salty winds. After perusing the exhibits, be sure to circle the observation deck for great views of the "parabolic" dunes. Also inquire about any special events scheduled, such as free guided walks and family campfires (reservations required). There are also canoe programs and surfcasting programs (both with equipment provided cost $12).

Pilgrim Monument & Provincetown Museum. High Pole Hill Rd. (off Winslow St., N of Bradford St.). ☎ **800/247-1620** or 508/487-1310. Admission $5 adults, $3 children 4–12 (includes 2-hr. free parking). July–Aug daily 9am–7pm; off-season daily 9am–5pm. Last admission 45 min. before closing. Closed Dec–Mar.

You can't miss it: Anywhere you go in town, this granite tower looms, ever ready to restore your bearings. Climb up the 60 gradual ramps interspersed with 116 steps—a surprisingly easy lope—and you'll get a gargoyle's-eye view of the spiraling coast and, in the distance, Boston against a backdrop of New Hampshire mountains. Definitely devote some time to the curious exhibits in the museum at the monument's foot, chronicling Provincetown's checkered past as both fishing port and arts nexus. Among the memorabilia you'll find polar bears brought back from MacMillan's expeditions and early programs for the Provincetown Players.

✪ **Provincetown Art Association & Museum.** 460 Commercial St. (in the E. End). ☎ **508/487-1750.** Suggested donation $3 adults, $1 seniors and children under 12. May–Sept daily noon–5pm and 8–10pm; call for off-season hrs.

This extraordinary cache of 20th-century American art began with five paintings donated by local artists, including Charles Hawthorne, the charismatic teacher who first "discovered" this picturesque outpost. Founded in 1914, only a year after New York's revolutionary Armory Show, the museum was the site of innumerable "space wars," as classicists and modernists vied for square footage; an uneasy truce was finally struck in 1927, when each camp was accorded its own show. In today's less competitive atmosphere, it's not unusual to see a tame still life hanging alongside a statement of twentysomething angst or an acknowledged master sharing space with a less-skilled upstart. Juried members' shows usually accompany the in-depth retrospectives, so there are always new discoveries to be made. Fulfilling its charter to promote "social intercourse between artists and laymen," the museum sponsors a full schedule of concerts, lectures, readings, and classes.

SHOPPING

ART GALLERIES   Of the several dozen art galleries in town, only the handful noted below are reliably worthwhile. (For in-depth coverage of the local arts scene, look to *Provincetown Arts,* a glossy annual sold at the Provincetown Art Association & Museum shop.) In season, most of the galleries and even some of the shops take a suppertime siesta so as to reopen later and greet visitors as late as 10 or 11pm. Shows usually open Friday evening, prompting a "stroll" tradition spanning the many receptions.

Berta Walker is a force to be reckoned with, having nurtured many top artists before opening her own gallery in 1990. Her historic holdings, displayed at the ✪ **Berta Walker Gallery,** 208 Bradford St. (in the East End; ☎ **508/487-6411**), span Charles Hawthorne, Milton Avery, and Robert Motherwell. Whoever has her current attention—such as figurative sculptor Romolo Del Deo—warrants watching. Closed late October to late May.

✪ **DNA (Definitive New Art) Gallery,** 288 Bradford St. (in the East End; ☎ **508/ 487-7700**), an airy loft over the Provincetown Tennis Club, quickly rose to the top tier. It has attracted such talents as photographer Joel Meyerowitz (Provincetown's favorite portraitist, known for such tomes as *Cape Light*); and sculptor Conrad Malicoat, whose free-form brick chimneys and hearths can be seen and admired about town. Another contributor is local conceptualist/provocateur Jay Critchley, whose ongoing cause célèbre is to see the town declared a "cultural sanctuary." It's a very lively bunch, appropriately grouped under the rubric "definitive new art," and readings by cutting-edge authors add to the buzz. Closed mid-October to late May.

Julie Heller started collecting early Provincetown paintings as a child—and a tourist at that. She chose so incredibly well, her roster, shown at the **Julie Heller Gallery,** 2 Gosnold St. (☎ 508/487-2169), now reads like a who's who of local art. Hawthorne, Avery, Hofmann, Lazzell, Hensche—all the big names are here, as well as some contemporary artists who, in her view, "continue to carry on the tradition." Closed weekdays January through April. Open winter weekends by chance or appointment.

The art shown at **Rice/Polak Gallery,** 430 Commercial St. (in the East End; ☎ 508/487-1052), has a decorative bent, which is not to say that it will match anyone's sofa, only that it has a certain stylish snap to it. Several gallery artists have fun with dimensions, including painter Tom Seghi with his mammoth pears. Photographer Karin Rosenthal's sculptural female nudes blend humor with utmost beauty. Closed December through April.

The new kid on the block is the **Schoolhouse Center for Art and Design,** 494 Commercial St. (in the East End; ☎ 508/487-4800). This is an impressive set-up, with two galleries, arts programs, studios, and an events series. The Driskel Gallery features photography and fine objects. The Silas-Kenyon Gallery shows contemporary fine arts. You won't want to miss any showing of the work of William Oscar Johnson who does enchanting primitive-style paintings of the old lifesavers of Cape Cod. Also strong is the work of Kathi Smith, whose colorful woodcuts of the Provincetown skyline are descended from the early 20th century group called the Provincetown Printers, who invented the art of white-line woodcuts.

DISCOUNT SHOPPING   **Adams' Pharmacy,** 254 Commercial St. (in the center of town; ☎ 508/487-0069), is Provincetown's oldest business (est. 1868), complete with an old-fashioned soda fountain. We—and apparently, a great many drag queens—like it for the cheapo makeup (two-for-$1 lipsticks) in outrageous colors.

Want to make a fast buck? Dare someone to go into the jam-packed **Marine Specialties** at 235 Commercial St. (in the center of town; ☎ 508/487-1730), and come out empty-handed. There's just too much useful stuff, from discounted Doc Martens to cut-rate Swiss Army knives and all sorts of odd nautical surplus whose uses will suggest themselves to you eventually. Be sure to look up: Hung among the rafters are some real antiques, including several carillon's worth of ship's bells.

FASHION   Want to try on new identity? **Mad Hatter,** 360 Commercial St. (in the center of town; ☎ 508/487-4063), may be the next best thing, with hats to suit every style and inclination, from folksy to downright diva-esque. Closed January through mid-February. Check out **No. 5,** 199 Commercial St. (in the West End; ☎ 508/487-1594), an ultrastylish men's shop, for a glimpse of what tomorrow's best-dressed males will be wearing.

Perfect examples of the art of understatement, Jerry Giardelli's unstructured clothing elements—shells, shifts, palazzo pants—come in vibrant colors and inviting textures; they demand to be mixed and matched and perhaps offset by Diana Antonelli's statement jewelry. You'll find it all at **Giardelli/Antonelli Studio Showroom,** 417 Commercial St. (in the East End; ☎ 508/487-3016).

GIFTS/HOME DECOR   The animal-themed **City Zoo,** 371 Commercial St. (at Pepe's Wharf in the center of town; ☎ 508/487-2032) is a shop with a sense of humor. Featuring boldly-colored folk art (including Haitian metal sculpture), home accessories, clothing, and even kids stuff, there's something here for the wild beast in all of us. Now that Provincetown's fishing fleet is basically history, respected columnist and fisherwoman Molly Benjamin has opened **Something Fishy,** 3 Standish St. (in the center of town; ☎ 508/487-5996), which is filled with gifts made by local fishermen and women. This is a perfect place to get a unique souvenir of your trip.

WHERE TO STAY

Very Expensive

✪ The Brass Key Guesthouse. 67 Bradford St. (in the center of town), Provincetown, MA 02657. ☎ **800/842-9858** or 508/487-9005. Fax 508/487-9020. www.brasskey.com. E-mail: ptown@brasskey.com. 29 units, 4 cottages. A/C TV TEL. Summer $195–$365 double; $275–$365 cottage. Rates include continental breakfast. AE, DISC, MC, V. Closed Dec–March.

After a multimillion-dollar expansion, the Brass Key Guesthouse, has become the place to stay in Provincetown. It's now a compound consisting of four buildings. With Ritz-Carlton–style amenities and service in mind, Michael MacIntyre and Bob Anderson have created a paean to luxury. These are the kind of innkeepers who think of everything: pillows are goose down, showers have wall jets, and free iced tea is delivered poolside in season. While all rooms share top-notch amenities like Boze radios, minifridges, hair dryers, safes, and VCRs, there is a range of decorative styles according to building. The original 1828 Federal-style house and the Gatehouse are decorated in a more playful country style, while rooms in the Victorian-era building are classically elegant, with materials like mahogany, walnut, and marble. Most deluxe guest rooms have gas fireplaces and oversized whirlpool tubs. Fortunately those bathrooms also include telephones and some have TVs so that you can be entertained while soaking.

Amenities: An extensively landscaped multileveled patio area with outdoor heated pool and large (17 ft.) whirlpool.

Expensive

The Beacon Light Guesthouse. 12 Winthrop St. (in the W. End), Provincetown, MA 02657. ☎ **800/696-9603** or ☎/fax 508/487-9603. www.capecod.net/beaconlight/. E-mail: beaconlite@capecod.net. 10 units. A/C TV TEL. Summer $100–$165 double; $180–$200 suites. Rates include continental breakfast. AE, MC, V.

British innkeepers Stephen Mascilo and Trevor Pinker have decorated this 1850 home in an exuberant English country style. These are detail-oriented hosts, and you can be sure no pillow is left unfluffed. Walls are painted striking colors to coordinate with exquisite fabrics on beds, chairs, and windows. The elegant drawing room features overstuffed sofas in front of a fireplace, and a fully tuned grand piano welcomes those with a classical repertoire. While most of the rooms are exceptionally light, airy, and spacious, there are also smaller rooms at less expensive rates. All rooms have minifridges and some have VCRs. Telephones have dataports and voice mail. Breakfast is served on the old pine refectory table in the sunny kitchen or out on the patio. There are large decks on all floors where lounge chairs await. The first floor deck has a new 8-person hot tub, and the third floor deck is perhaps the largest in town with panoramic views of Provincetown and the bay.

Best Western Tides Beachfront. 837 Commercial St. (near the Truro border), Provincetown, MA 02657. ☎ **800/528-1234** or 508/487-1045. Fax 508/487-1621. www.bwprovincetown.com. 64 units. A/C TV TEL. Summer $139–$199 double; $249–$269 suite. AE, CB, DC, DISC, MC, V. Closed Nov–Apr.

Located on a peaceful 6-acre parcel well removed both from Provincetown's bustle, this surprise oasis boasts every feature you might require of a beachfront retreat, including a nice wide beach you can literally flop onto from the ground-level units. Most of the rooms overlook Provincetown's quirky skyline, as does the generously proportioned outdoor pool. Every inch of this complex has been groomed to the max, including the ultragreen grounds, the Wedgwood-blue breakfast room which seems to have been lifted whole from an elegant country inn, and the spotless rooms decorated in a soothing ivory and pale pastels. All rooms have minifridges. And the only sound you'll hear at night is the mournful refrain of a foghorn.

The Masthead. 31-41 Commercial St. (in the W. End), Provincetown, MA 02657. ☎ **800/ 395-5095** or 508/487-0523. Fax 508/487-9251. www.capecod.com/masthead. 20 units (2 with shared bath), 4 cottages. A/C TV TEL. Summer $79–$188 double; $158–$263 efficiency; $218 apt; cottages $1,405–$1,815/weekly. Off-season $60–$103 double; $72–$116 efficiency; $99–$120 apt; $97–$160 cottage. AE, CB, DC, DISC, MC, V.

In its late-1950s heyday, glam types like Helena Rubenstein came to this funky resort at the far west end of Commercial Street to rough it. These days, it's one of the few places in town, other than the impersonal motels, that actively welcomes families, and the placid 450-foot private beach will delight young splashers. Many rooms are individually and creatively decorated, and all have minifridges and coffeemakers with complimentary tea and coffee. The cottages are fun, some with net stair railings, wicker furniture, and hand-painted antique furniture by Peter Hunt, as well as full (if tiny) kitchens. In-season the cottage units rent weekly, but the rather generic motel units rent nightly. In some waterview rooms perched above the surf, with their 7-foot picture windows overlooking the Bay and Long Point, you may feel like you are on board a ship. Rates here off-season are a steal, considering the waterfront locale. The yachting crowd can take advantage of free deep-water moorings and launch service.

✪ **Watermark Inn.** 603 Commercial St. (in the E. End), Provincetown, MA 02657. ☎ **508/ 487-0165.** Fax 508/487-2383. 10 units. TV TEL. Summer $140–$300 suite. AE, MC, V.

If you'd like to experience Provincetown without being stuck in the thick of it (the carnival atmosphere can get tiring at times), this contemporary inn at the peaceful edge of town is the perfect choice. Resident innkeeper/architect Kevin Shea carved this beachfront manor into 10 dazzling suites: The prize ones, on the top floor, have peaked picture windows and sweeping views from their decks. All have kitchenettes that include dishwashers. Innkeeper/designer Judy Richland, Shea's wife, saw to the interior decoration—pastel handmade quilts brighten up clean, monochromatic rooms.

Moderate

Carpe Diem. 8 Johnson St. (in the center of town), Provincetown, MA 02657. ☎ **888/ 847-7926** or ☎/fax 508/487-4242. www.capecod.net/carpediem. E-mail: carpediem@ capecod.net. 10 units, 5 with shared bathroom. AC TV TEL. Summer $80–$85 shared bath double, $120–$150 private bath double. Rates include continental breakfast. AE, MC, V.

Rainer, Jurgen, and Johannes, three young, urbane Germans, have recently purchased this formerly down-on-its-luck boarding house and transformed it into a modestly priced, stylish lodging option, whose devil-may-care theme is "seize the day." The location, a quiet side street right in the center of town, would suit most Provincetown habitués to a T. Most of the rooms here are small, yet exquisitely decorated with European antiques and brightly painted walls and wallpapers, and many have bay views. The telephones have voice mail and dataports. All rooms have VCRs, and most have minifridges. The third floor has single rooms with shared baths, but even these possess exceptional elan. Continental breakfast features homemade German bread and muffins washed down with Carpe Diem coffee from Maine (a guest clued them in to the namesake brand). On clear days, sun worshipers choose between the decks or the brick patio overlooking a tiny goldfish pond.

✪ **The Fairbanks Inn.** 90 Bradford St. (near the center of town), Provincetown, MA 02657. ☎ **800/324-7265** or 508/487-0386. Fax 508/487-3540. www.capecod.net/fairbank. E-mail: fairbank@capecod.net. 14 units, 2 with shared bathroom. Summer $95–$149 double; $175 efficiency. Rates include continental breakfast. AE, MC, V.

This colonial mansion (built in 1776) looks its era without looking its age. Beautifully maintained, it boasts gleaming wooden floors softened by rich Oriental rugs and romantic bedding—sleigh beds and four-posters. Most of the rooms have fireplaces. A patio, porch, and rooftop sundeck lend themselves to pleasant socializing. The attention to detail throughout the inn makes this one of the top places to stay in town.

Holiday Inn. 698 Commercial St. (at Rte. 6A, in the E. End), Provincetown, MA 02657. ☎ **800/422-4224** or 508/487-1711. Fax 508/487-3929. www.capecod.net/hiptown. 78 units. A/C TV TEL. Summer $140 double. AE, CB, DC, DISC, MC, V. Closed Nov–Apr.

A good choice for first-timers not quite sure what they're getting into, this no-surprises motel-with-pool at the eastern edge of town is a bit far from the action but congenial enough. Guests get a nice view of town, along with cable TV in the rooms and free movies in the restaurant/lounge. All rooms have minifridges, coffeemakers, irons, and hair dryers. A free shuttle to town center and to the beach operates in season.

The Oxford. 8 Cottage St. (in the W. End), Provincetown, MA 02657. ☎ **888/456-9103** or 508/487-9103. Fax 508/487-9603. www.capecod.net/oxford/. E-mail: oxford@capecod.net. 6 units, 3 with shared bathroom. AC TV TEL. Summer $100–$185 double. Rates include continental breakfast. AE, MC, V.

Stephen Mascilo and Trevor Pinker, the exceptionally stylish British owners of the Beacon Light Guesthouse, have recently restored and refurbished this 1853 house in the far West End, adding yet another posh address to the town. This is truly affordable elegance. All rooms have upscale amenities like down comforters, bathrobes, hair dryers, telephones with voice mail and dataports, minifridges, VCRs, and radio/CD players. One downstairs room is quite large, with 8-foot windows overlooking the landscaped grounds. Rooms with shared baths are smaller. The drawing room is especially cozy with big down sofas and arm chairs in front of a fireplace above which a TV is cleverly hidden. An extensive continental breakfast is served in the morning when the inn fills with the scrumptious aroma of home-baked breads and coffee cake. You may want to take your coffee outside on the veranda overlooking the courtyard's fountain and pond.

Inexpensive

✪ **The Black Pearl Bed & Breakfast.** 11 Pearl St. (off Commercial St., near the center of town), Provincetown, MA 02657. ☎ **508/487-6405.** Fax 508/487-7412. www.provincetown.com/blackpearl/index.html. E-mail: blkpearl@capecod.net. 5 units, 1 cottage. Summer $80–$95 double, $175 suite; $150 cottage. Rates include continental breakfast. MC, V. Closed Jan to mid-Mar.

Every room in this cheerily updated captain's house has a look all its own, from bold Southwestern to fanciful Micronesian, and several boast skylights and private decks. The fully muralled Connemara Cottage takes the cake, with an antique bedstead, wood-burning fireplace, and double Jacuzzi, plus such niceties as air-conditioning, telephone, and a cable TV with VCR. The Lullwater suite consists of two rooms with TV/VCR, telephone, air-conditioning, minifridge, microwave, fireplace, and a separate entrance with French doors to a private deck.

Captain Lysander Inn. 96 Commercial St. (in the W. End), Provincetown, MA 02657. ☎ **508/487-2253.** Fax 508/487-7579. 13 units (6 with shared bath), 1 cottage. Summer $95 shared bath double, $105 private bath double; $125 efficiency; $1,200/weekly, $200/daily apt; $1400/weekly, $250/daily cottage. Rates include continental breakfast. MC, V.

This 1840 captain's house has definite curb appeal: Set back a bit from the street in the quiet West End, it's fronted by a flower-lined path leading to a sunny patio. The conservatively furnished rooms are quite nice for the price, and some have lovely water views. Tall windows and ceiling fans make these rooms light and airy; they're also spotlessly clean. Rooms with shared baths share with just one other room. The whole gang can fit in either the apartment or the cottage, both of which sleep six.

✪ **White Horse Inn.** 500 Commercial St. (in the E. End), Provincetown, MA 02657. ☎ **508/487-1790.** 18 units (9 with shared bathroom), 6 efficiencies. Summer $70–$75 double; $100–$125 efficiency. No credit cards.

Look for the house with the bright yellow door with the oval window in the far East End of town. The rates are a literal steal, especially given the fact that this inn is the very embodiment of Provincetown's bohemian mystique. In addition to doubles, there are singles with shared bathroom for only $50. Frank Schaefer has been tinkering with this late–18th-century house since 1963; the rooms may be a bit austere, but each is enlivened by the paintings by local artists that he has collected over the decades. A number of his fellow artists helped him out in cobbling together the studio apartments out of salvage: There's an aura of Beatnik improv about them still. This is where cult filmmaker John Waters stays every summer when he comes to town.

WHERE TO DINE

You absolutely have to peruse the cases of pasteis (meat pies) and pastries at ✪ **Provincetown Portuguese Bakery,** 299 Commercial St. (in the center of town; ☎ 508/487-1803). Point to a few and take your surprise package out on the pier for delectation. It's the best way to sample the scrumptious international output of this beloved institution. Closed November through March.

A local landmark, **Spiritus**, 190 Commercial St. (in the center of town; ☎ 508/487-2808), is an extravagant pizza parlor known for after-hours cruising: It's open until 2am. The pizza's good, as are the fruit drinks, specialty coffees, and four brands of premium ice cream, from Emack & Bolio's to Coconut Joe's. For a peaceful morning repast—and perhaps a relaxed round of bocce—check out the little garden in back. Closed November through March.

Very Expensive

✪ **Chester.** 404 Commercial St. ☎ **508/487-8200.** Reservations recommended. Main courses $20–$29. AE, MC, V. July to early Sept daily 6–10pm; May, June, mid-Sept to Dec Thurs-Tues 6–10pm. Closed Jan–April. NEW AMERICAN.

This newest entry in Provincetown's fine dining scene specializes in local seafoods, meats, and vegetables prepared simply and with a Mediterranean flourish by Chef Chris Christman. The restaurant is named after the owners' Airedale terrier whose regal profile serves as their logo. The candlelit dining room, painted a summery yellow, is decorated with brightly-colored paintings by local artists; you'll want to sit at the comfy banquets lining the edges of the room. There's a crispness to the decor without the formality. As to be expected, service is exceptional here. The food is beautifully presented, and portions are hearty. Your meal may begin with an *amuse bouche*, like smoked mackerel. Starters like oyster stew in the shell; and tomato and fennel risotto with mussels take advantage of local provender, as does the succulent Chatham Cod with kale and chourico. Though I'm reluctant to order meat when I can see the ocean out the window, the rack of medium rare lamb (4 beautiful chops) with Moroccan sauce and rosewater couscous, melted off the bone. For dessert, look no further than the grilled pineapple with vanilla butterscotch.

✪ **Martin House.** 157 Commercial St. ☎ **508/487-1327.** Reservations recommended. Main courses $14–$30. AE, CB, DC, DISC, MC, V. June–Oct daily 6–11pm; Nov–May Thurs–Mon 6–10pm. Closed mid-Dec. FUSION.

Easily one of the most charming restaurants on the Cape, this snuggery of rustic rooms also just happens to contain one of the Cape's most forward-thinking kitchens. Co-owners Glen and Gary Martin are the conceptualizers behind the inspired regional menu, and chef Alex Mazzocca the gifted creator. The team favors regional delicacies, such as the Thai crab-and-shrimp soup with green curry and crispy rice noodles, or the local littlenecks that appear in a kaffir lime-tamarind broth with Asian noodles. Main courses might include local lobster–stuffed squash blossoms with a warm porcini-saffron vinaigrette, or grilled rack of pork with mango salsa and cactus-pear demi-glace on spicy masa. The dinners, pleasantly delivered, exceed every expectation and the peaceful, softly lit rooms make an optimal setting for exploring new tastes. In season, there's also seating in the rose-choked garden terrace beside the small fountain.

Expensive

The Commons Bistro & Bar. 386 Commercial St. ☎ **508/487-7800.** Reservations recommended. Main courses $14–$23. AE, MC, V. Late June to early Sept daily 8:30–1am; call for off-season hrs. Closed Jan. ECLECTIC/FRENCH BISTRO.

It's a toss-up: The sidewalk cafe provides an optimal opportunity for studying Provincetown's inimitable street life, whereas the plum-colored dining room inside affords a refuge adorned with the owners' extraordinary collection of original Toulouse-Lautrec prints. Either way, you'll get to partake of Chach Breseno's (formerly of Front Street) tasty and creative fare. At lunchtime, her overstuffed "lobster club" sandwich on country bread is nonpareil, and the smoked chicken and avocado salad is the ultimate summertime refresher. The Commons boasts the only wood-fired oven in town to date, which comes in handy in preparing the popular gourmet pizzas with combos like smoked salmon, crème fraîche, and golden caviar. Dinner appetizers include root vegetable cake with smoked trout; and wood-oven roasted mussels with yellow Thai curry. As a main course, you must try the gingered and smoked salmon with scallion basmati rice and orange-soy vinaigrette. For dessert, choose the crème brûlée.

The Dancing Lobster Cafe/Trattoria. 463 Commercial St. (in the E. End). ☎ **508/487-0900.** Reservations recommended. Main courses $13–$20. MC, V. July–Sept Tues–Sun 5:30–11pm; April–June and Oct–Nov 6–10pm. Closed Dec–Apr. MEDITERRANEAN.

It seems apropos that native son Nils "Pepe" Berg should open a dining establishment on the site of Provincetown's oldest restaurant, where literati like Gertrude Stein and Anaïs Nin flocked after its early-1930s debut. This is a popular place, and you should expect to wait a half-hour, even with a reservation. Still, the food is excellent. Start with the grilled-squid bruschetta, the saffrony Venetian fish soup, the crab ravioli, or perhaps the steamed mussels with a basil aïoli. Main courses may include steak al "Pepe" with green and black peppercorns, brandy, demi-glace and cream; or Basque stew with littleneck clams, chicken, shrimp, linguiça, squid and mussels steamed with white beans.

The Mews Restaurant & Cafe Mews. 429 Commercial St. ☎ **508/487-1500.** Reservations recommended. Main courses $18–$24. AE, CB, DC, DISC, MC, V. Mid-June to mid-Sept daily 11am–2:30pm and 5:30pm–1am; Jan to mid-June and mid-Sept to late Dec Thurs–Mon 11am–2:30pm and 5:30–1am. Closed for 2 weeks in late Dec. FUSION.

Here's an enduring favorite where you can always bank on fine food and suave service. The formal dining room downstairs is right on the beach—practically of the beach, with its sand-toned walls warmed by toffee-colored Tiffany table lamps. Perennial pleasures include the sublime oysters mignonette, featuring Wellfleet oysters with tarragon vinegar, shallot and jalapeño sauce; and crespelle alla Fiorentina, which are Italian pancakes filled with spinach, prosciutto and Parmesan, topped with béchamel sauce. I'd travel for miles for a bowl of the Parisian bouillabaisse: a blend of white fish, shrimp, scallops, mussels, littleneck clams and calamari in a seasoned broth. Desserts and coffees are delectable. You might take them upstairs in the cafe to the accompaniment of improvisatory soft-jazz piano.

Moderate

Bubala's by the Bay. 183 Commercial St. (in the W. End). ☎ **508/487-0773.** Main courses $9–$19. AE, DISC, MC, V. Apr–Oct daily 8am–1am. Closed Nov–Mar. ECLECTIC.

Once a nothing-special seaside restaurant, this trendy bistro—miraculously transformed with a gaudy yellow paint job and Picassoesque wall murals—promises "serious food at sensible prices." That's what it delivers, all day long—from buttermilk waffles with real maple syrup to lobster tarragon salad and creative focaccia sandwiches to fajitas, Cajun calamari, and pad Thai. In season, there's entertainment nightly from 10pm to 1am.

Cafe Heaven. 199 Commercial St. (in the center of town). ☎ **508/487-9639.** Reservations not accepted. Most items under $11–$18. No credit cards. June–Sept daily 8am–3pm and 6–10pm; April, May, and Oct–Jan daily 8am–3pm. Closed Feb and March. AMERICAN.

Prized for its leisurely country breakfasts (served till midafternoon, for you reluctant risers), this modernist storefront—adorned with big, bold paintings by acclaimed Wellfleet artist John Grillo—also turns out substantive sandwiches, such as avocado and goat cheese on a French baguette. The salads are appealing as well—especially the "special shrimp," lightly doused with dilled sour cream and tossed with tomatoes and grapes. New chef Alan Cullinane has expanded the dinner choices to include local seafoods, steaks, chops, and poultry and well as create-your-own-pasta options, plus "heavenly" burgers with a choice of internationally inspired toppings. The no-reservations policy means long lines in July and August.

Ciro & Sal's. 4 Kiley Ct. (at Commercial St.). ☎ **508/487-0049.** Reservations recommended. Main courses $11–$22. MC, V. Late May to Sept daily 6–10pm; call for off-season hrs. NORTHERN ITALIAN.

Having evolved from a 1951 cafe, Ciro Cozzi's cozy trattoria is retro in setting only—the usual raffia-wrapped Chianti bottles, an operatic sound track, etc. But the preparations, adapted from Italy's regional cuisines, can pack an unexpected punch, as in the horseradish sauce accompanying the fried calamari. Though pasta prevails, local fish and hand-cut veal get equal play, with treatments varying night to night. The seafood risotto here is excellent. Though decades of diners have enjoyed the chowing down in the brick basement, the recently renovated upstairs is light and airy and perhaps preferable (though decidedly less moody and romantic).

The Lobster Pot. 321 Commercial St. (in the center of town). ☎ **508/487-0842.** Reservations not accepted. Main courses $14–$21. AE, CB, DC, DISC, MC, V. Mid-June to mid-Sept daily 11:30am–10:30pm; mid-Sept to mid-June daily 11:30am–9:30pm. SEAFOOD.

Snobbish foodies might turn their noses up at a venue so flagrantly Olde Cape Coddish, but for Provincetown regulars, no season seems complete without at least one pilgrimage. You may feel like a long-suffering pilgrim waiting to get in: The line, which starts near the aromatic albeit frantic kitchen, often snakes into the street. While waiting, check out the hand-painted bar stools which provide an architectural history of Provincetown. A lucky few will make it all the way to the outdoor deck; however, most tables, indoors and out, afford nice views of MacMillan Wharf. Spring for a jumbo lobster, by all means—boiled or broiled, sauced or simple. And definitely start off with the chowder, a perennial award-winner.

Lorraine's. 229R Commercial St. (in the center of town). ☎ **508/487-6074.** Main courses $13–$20. MC, V. April–Dec 6–10pm. Closed Jan–Mar. MEXICAN/NEW AMERICAN.

There's a twilight-of-Havana look to this deco-accented cafe, and chef/owner Lorraine Najar brings a certain daring to bear on the cuisine she learned at her grandmother's knee. Consider duckling taquitos, chunks of marinated breast enrobed in corn tortillas, then deep-fried, or a dish like *viere verde*—sea scallops sautéed with tomatillos, flambéed in tequila, and cloaked in a green-chili sauce.

The Moors. 5 Bradford St. (at Province Lands Rd.). ☎ **800/843-0840** or 508/487-0840. Reservations recommended. Main courses $9–$20. AE, MC, V. May to mid-Oct daily 5:30–10pm; call for off-season hrs. Closed Nov–Mar. PORTUGUESE.

A salty classic since 1939, this ramshackle restaurant, composed primarily of nautical salvage, serves traditional Azorean fare, such as *espada cozida* (flash-broiled swordfish marinated in lemon juice, olive oil, parsley, and garlic) and *galinha à moda da Madeira* (chicken breast baked Madeira style). The standout is *porco em pau*, a Brazilian casserole of fork-tender pork tenderloin cubes in a spicy marinade.

Napi's. 5 Freeman St. (at Bradford St.). ☎ 800/571-6274 or **508/487-1145.** Reservations recommended. Main courses $12–$23. AE, CB, DC, DISC, MC, V. May–Oct daily 5–11pm; Nov–April daily 11:30am–4pm, 5–10pm. INTERNATIONAL.

Restaurateur Napi Van Dereck can be credited with bringing Provincetown's restaurant scene up to speed—back in the early 1970s. His namesake restaurant still reflects that zeitgeist, with its rococo carpentry, select outtakes from his sideline in antiques, and some rather outstanding native art, including a crazy quilt of a brick wall by local sculptor Conrad Malicoat. Hearty peasant fare never really goes out of style. And these peasants really get around, culling dumplings from China, falafel from Syria, and, from Greece, shrimp feta flambéed with ouzo and Metaxa. The lower priced tavern menu available weeknights ranges from $5 to $11.

Sal's Place. 99 Commercial St. (in the W. End). ☎ **508/487-1279.** Reservations recommended. Main courses $10–$20. MC, V. July–Aug daily 6–10pm; May, June, Sept, Oct Fri–Mon 6–10pm. Closed Nov–Apr. SOUTHERN ITALIAN.

Sal spun off from Ciro (see Ciro & Sal's, above) back in 1963, and his place is a little looser. The kitchen's right out in the open, for one thing, so you can see those shrimp Adriatico (with calamari and pesto) jumping in the pan, and see that someone's tending to the spaghettini alla foriana (with pine nuts, raisins, walnuts, and anchovies) so that it will arrive perfectly al dente. The nostalgic dining rooms, festooned with old posters, are great for blustery days, but on a fine evening nothing beats the harborside arbor.

PROVINCETOWN AFTER DARK

There's so much going on in season on any given night that you might want to simplify your search by calling or stopping in at the **Provincetown Reservations System** office at 293 Commercial St., in the center of town (☎ **508/487-6400**).

THE CLUB SCENE—Perhaps the nation's premier gay bar, **The Atlantic House,** 6 Masonic Place (off Commercial St., 2 blocks W of Town Hall ☎ **508/487-3821**) is open year-round. The "A-house" also welcomes straight folks, except in the leather-oriented Macho Bar upstairs. Late in the evening, there's usually plenty going on in the Big Room dance bar, where the cover is $5 to $10. In the little fireplaced bar downstairs, check out the Tennessee Williams memorabilia, including a portrait au naturel.

Come late afternoon, if you wonder where all the beachgoers went, it's a safe guess that a goodly number are attending the gay-lesbian tea dance held daily in season from 3:30 to 6:30pm on the pool deck at the **Boatslip Beach Club,** 161 Commercial St. (☎ **508/487-1669**). The action then shifts to the Pied Piper (see below), but returns here later in the evening for some disco or two-stepping. Cover varies.

In season, a "parade" of gay revelers descends in early evening from the Boatslip to the **Pied Piper,** 193A Commercial St. (☎ **508/487-1527**) for its After Tea T-Dance from 6:30 to 10pm. The late-night wave consists of a fair number of women, or fairly convincing simulacra thereof. For a glimpse of stars-in-the-making, check out "Putting on the Hits," a sampling of local talent held Tuesday nights at 10pm. Cover varies; call for schedule.

Crown & Anchor, 247 Commercial St. (☎ **508/487-1430**) has been completely rebuilt since a fire in the winter of 1998 made national headlines. It's pretty much back the way it was. The specialty bars span leather (in "The Vault"), disco, comedy, drag shows, and cabaret. Facilities include a pool bar and game room. Cover varies; call for schedule.

THE BAR SCENE—Governor Bradford, 312 Commercial St. (in the center of town ☎ 508/487-9618) is a good old bar, featuring karaoke and (yes, it's back) disco. Cover varies.

6 Cape Cod National Seashore

No trip to Cape Cod would be complete without a visit to the Cape Cod National Seashore on the Outer Cape. Take a late-afternoon barefoot stroll along "The Great Beach" and see why the Cape is filled with artists and poets. On August 7, 1961, President John F. Kennedy signed a bill designating 27,000 acres in the 40 miles from Chatham to Provincetown as **The Cape Cod National Seashore,** a new national park. However, as early as the 1930s, the National Park Service had been interested in Cape Cod's Great Beach; back then, the land would have cost taxpayers about $10 an acre! Unusual in a national park, the Seashore includes 500 private residences, the owners of which "lease" land from the park service. Convincing residents that a National Seashore would be a good thing for Cape Cod was an arduous task back then, and Provincetown still grapples with Seashore officials over town land issues.

ESSENTIALS
GETTING THERE   Take Route 6, the Mid-Cape Highway to Eastham (about 45 miles).

VISITOR INFORMATION   Pick up a map of the Cape Cod National Seashore at the **Salt Pond Visitor Center** in Eastham (☎ **508/255-3421**). It's open daily from late May to early Sept 9am to 5pm; early Sept to late May 9am to 4:30pm. There is another visitor center at Race Point. Both centers offer free admission and have ranger activities, maps, gift shops, and bathrooms. Seashore beaches are all off Route 6 and are clearly marked. Additional beaches along this stretch are run by individual towns, and you must have a sticker or pay a fee.

RECOMMENDED READING   Henry David Thoreau's *Cape Cod* (Penguin, 1987), an entertaining account of Thoreau's journeys on the Cape in the late–19th century. The writer/naturalist walked along the beach from Eastham to Provincetown, and you can follow in his footsteps. Henry Beston's *The Outermost House* (Henry Holt & Co., 1992) describes a year of living on the beach in Eastham in a simple one-room dune shack. The shack washed out to sea about 20 years ago, but "The Great Beach" remains.

BEACHES & OTHER PURSUITS
BEACHES   The Seashore's claim to fame is its spectacular beaches—in reality, one long beach—with dunes 50 to 150 feet high. This is the Atlantic Ocean, so the surf is rough (and cold), but a number of the beaches have lifeguards. A $20 pass will get you into all of them for the season, or you can pay a daily rate of $7. Most of the Seashore beaches have large parking lots, but you'll need to get there early (before 10am) on

busy summer weekends. If the beach you want to go to is full, try the one next door—most of the beaches are 5 to 10 miles apart. Don't forget your beach umbrella; the sun exposure here can get intense. Seashore beaches include:

- **Coast Guard Beach** and **Nauset Light Beach,** off Ocean View Drive, Eastham. Connected to outlying parking lots by a free shuttle, these pristine National Seashore beaches have lifeguards and rest rooms.
- **Marconi Beach,** off Marconi Beach Road in South Wellfleet. A National Seashore property, this beach is cliff-lined (it has rest rooms). *Note:* The bluffs are so high that the beach lies in shadows by late afternoon.
- **Head of the Meadow Beach,** head of the Meadow Road, off Route 6, Truro. Among the more remote National Seashore beaches, this spot (equipped with rest rooms) is known for its excellent surf.
- **Race Point** and **Herring Cove Beaches,** in Provincetown. Race Point has rough surf; it's a good place to watch spectacular sunsets, and you might even spot a whale. Herring Cove, with much calmer waters, is popular with same-sex couples.

BIKING   The best bike path on Cape Cod is the **Province Lands Trail,** 5 swooping and invigorating miles at Race Point Beach. If that's not enough in the way of sports, surf fishing is allowed from the ocean beaches—Race Point is a popular spot.

WALKING TRAILS   The Seashore also has a number of walking trails—all free, all picturesque, and all worth a trip. In Eastham, ✪ **Fort Hill** (off Rte. 6) has one of the best scenic views on Cape Cod, and a popular boardwalked trail through a red maple swamp. Following the trail markers around Fort Hill, you'll pass "Indian Rock" (bearing the marks of untold generations who used it to sharpen their tools) and enjoy scenic vantage points overlooking the channel-carved marsh—keep an eye out for egrets and great blue herons—and out to sea. The Fort Hill Trail hooks up with the ½-mile **Red Cedar Swamp Trail,** offering boardwalk views of an ecology otherwise inaccessible.

The **Nauset Marsh Trail** is accessed from the Salt Pond Visitor Center on Route 6 in Eastham. **Great Island** on the bay side in Wellfleet is surely one of the finest places to have a picnic; you could spend the day hiking the trails. On **Pamet Cranberry Bog Trail** off North Pamet Road in Truro, hikers pass the decrepit old cranberry-bog building (restoration is in the works) after a boardwalked romp over the bog itself. **Atlantic White Cedar Swamp Trail** is located at the Marconi Station site (see "Wellfleet, above). **Small Swamp** and **Pilgrim Spring** trails are found at Pilgrim Heights Beach, and **Beech Forest Trail** is located at Race Point in Provincetown.

SEASHORE SIGHTS

The Seashore includes several historic sites that tell their part of the region's history.

The **Old Harbor Life-saving Museum,** Race Point Beach (off Race Point Road), Provincetown (☎ **508/487-1256**) was one of 13 life-saving stations mandated by Congress in the late 19th century—this shingled shelter with a look-out tower was part of a network responsible for saving some 100,000 lives. Before the U.S. Lifesaving Service was founded in 1872 (it became part of the Coast Guard in 1915), shipwreck victims lucky enough to be washed ashore were still doomed unless they could find a "charity shed"—a hut supplied with firewood—maintained by the Massachusetts Humane Society. The six valiant "Surfmen" manning each life-saving station took a more active approach, patrolling the beach at all hours, sending up flares at the first sign of a ship in distress, and rowing out into the surf to save all they could. All the old equipment is on view at this museum. Free admission; parking fee for Race Point Beach (see "Beaches," above). It's open July through August, daily 3 to 5pm; call for off-season hours. Closed November and April.

The **Marconi Wireless Station**, on Marconi Park Site Rd. (off Route 6), South Wellfleet (☎ **508/349-3785**) tells the story of the first international telegraphic communication. It's from this bleak spot that Italian inventor Guglielmo Marconi sent, via a complex of 210-foot cable towers, the world's first wireless communique: "cordial greetings from President Theadore [sic] Roosevelt to King Edward VII in Poldhu, Wales." It was also here in 1912 that news of the troubled Titanic first reached these shores. There's scarcely a trace left of this extraordinary feat of technology (the station was dismantled in 1920); still, the outdoor displays convey the leap of imagination that was required.

The Captain **Edward Penniman House,** at Fort Hill off Route 6 in Eastham, is a grandly ornate multicolored 1868 Second Empire mansion maintained by the National Seashore. The house is open daily from 1 to 4pm in season (or call the Visitor Center at ☎**508/255-3421**), but the exterior far outshines the interior, and more interesting sights await outside.

Five lighthouses dot the Seashore. **Nauset Light** in Eastham, with its cheerful red stripe (a "day mark"), was moved from Chatham in 1923. The lighthouse flashes an alternating red-and-white light every 10 seconds and can be seen for 23 miles. Nauset and Highland Light were both recently moved back from precarious positions on the edge of dunes.

Highland Light, also known as Cape Cod Light, in Truro, is the site of the first light in this area, dating back to 1798. The present structure was built in 1857. Follow signs from Route 6 in North Truro, to the end of Highland Road. This lighthouse, set high on a cliff, was the first light seen by ships traveling from Europe.

Race Point Light in Provincetown was first established in 1816, and the current structure was built in 1876. The light is accessible by boat or by foot, a 2-mile walk over soft sand from Race Point beach.

Wood End Light on Long Point in Provincetown is an unusual square lighthouse, built as a "twin" to Long Point Light in 1873. Hearty souls can hike first across the breakwater at the west end of Commercial Street and then about half a mile over soft sand to see this lighthouse. Its beacon is now powered by solar energy.

Long Point Light in Provincetown, established in 1827, is isolated at the very tip of Cape Cod. It's about an hour's walk from the breakwater, or a short boat ride the center of town. Its fixed green light can be seen for 8 miles. This lighthouse was once the center of a thriving fishing community in the 1800s. Storms and erosion led the community to float their houses across the bay to Provincetown's west end, where a couple of the houses, some of the oldest in town, are still standing

Martha's Vineyard & Nantucket

By Laura M. Reckford

Martha's Vineyard and Nantucket, two distinctly different islands off the coast of Cape Cod, have much to offer both vacationing families and couples seeking a romantic getaway. But the popularity of these islands means that if you must go in the middle of summer, expect crowds and even—yikes!—traffic.

Megastars and CEOs, middle-class families and penniless students all seek refuge on these naturally isolated islands. Their fame as summer resorts doesn't begin to take into account their historic roots, diverse communities, and artistic traditions.

Though geographically similar, each island has a separate personality. Martha's Vineyard, large enough to support a year-round population spanning a broad socioeconomic spectrum, is not quite so rarefied as is Nantucket. Vineyarders pride themselves on their liberal Democratic stance. True, a prime ocean-side estate might fetch millions here, but the residents still dicker over the price of zucchini at the local farmers market. Nantucket, flash-frozen in the mid–19th century through zealous zoning, has long been considered a Republican haven. It's rich and traditional, as the stereotype goes, and if your great-grandparents didn't summer here, you might as well not bother: You'll just be roundly ignored. The younger generation, however, many of whom did indeed grow up summering here among the old guard, tend to be more welcoming. In fact, there's a small creative buzz that's making itself heard on Nantucket in the form of brave new enterprises, especially shops and restaurants. In other words, there's something for everyone on both islands, and it's fun to keep exploring and comparing until you happen upon a niche that feels just right.

1 Martha's Vineyard

With 100 square miles, Martha's Vineyard is New England's largest island, yet each of its six small towns are blessed with endearing and historic charm. Lately, the First Family has made a habit of vacationing here, and locals joke that the President tests their reputed nonchalance toward famous faces. But don't visit the Vineyard for the celebrities. Instead, savor the decidedly laid-back pace of this unique place.

Most visitors never take the time to explore the entire island, staying in the down-island towns of Vineyard Haven (officially called Tisbury), Edgartown, and Oak Bluffs. The "up-island" towns—West Tisbury, Chilmark (including the fishing village of Menemsha), and Gay Head—tend to be far less touristy.

Ferry Reservations Policy for Cars

Vehicle reservations are required to bring your car to Martha's Vineyard on Friday, Saturday, Sunday, and Monday from mid-June to mid-September. During these times, standby is in effect only on Tuesdays, Wednesdays, and Thursdays. Vehicle reservations are also required to bring your car to Martha's Vineyard on Memorial Day Weekend. There will be no standby service available during these dates. Although technically, reservations can be made up to 1 hour in advance of ferry departure, ferries in season are almost always full, and you certainly cannot depend on a cancellation during the summer months. Also be aware that your space may be forfeited if you have not checked into the ferry terminal 30 minutes prior to sailing time. Reservations may be changed to another date and time with at least 24 hours notice; otherwise you will have to pay for an additional ticket for your vehicle.

If you arrive without a reservation on a day that allows standby, come early and be prepared to wait in the standby line for hours. The Steamship Authority guarantees your passage if you're in line by 2pm on designated standby days only. For up-to-date Steamship Authority information, check out their Web site (**www.islandferry.com**).

By all means, admire the regal sea captain's houses in Edgartown. Stroll down Circuit Avenue in Oak Bluffs with a Mad Martha's ice-cream cone, then ride the Flying Horses Carousel, said to be the oldest working carousel in the country. Check out the cheerful "gingerbread" cottages behind Circuit Avenue, where the echoes of 19th-century revival meetings still ring out from the imposing tabernacle.

But don't forget to journey "up-island" to marvel at the red clay cliffs of Gay Head, a national historic landmark. Or bike the country roads of West Tisbury and Chilmark. Buy a lobster roll in the fishing village of Menemsha. There's a surprising degree of diversity here, for those who take the time to discover it.

ESSENTIALS
GETTING THERE

BY FERRY   Most visitors take ferries from the mainland to the Vineyard. You'll most likely catch a boat from Woods Hole on Cape Cod; however, boats do run from Falmouth, Hyannis, New Bedford, and Nantucket. It's easy to get a passenger ticket on almost any of the ferries, but space for cars is extremely limited, especially on summer weekends, when reservations must be made months in advance. Unless you absolutely must have your car with you, you'll probably want to leave it on the mainland, especially if you're going to stick to the down-island towns. Traffic and parking on the island can be brutal in summer and, it's easy to take the shuttle buses (see below) from town to town or simply bike your way around.

From Woods Hole   The state-run **Steamship Authority** (☎ **508/477-8600** mid-April to mid-Sept daily 6am to 9pm; or 508/693-9130 daily 7:30am to 9pm; off-season office hours vary; www.islandferry.com) operates daily, year-round, weather permitting. It maintains the only ferries that accommodate cars, in addition to passengers. These large ferries make the 45-minute trip to Vineyard Haven throughout the year; some boats go to Oak Bluffs from late May to late October (call for seasonal schedules). The cost of a round-trip car passage from mid-May to mid-October is $94; in the off-season it drops to $42.

Martha's Vineyard

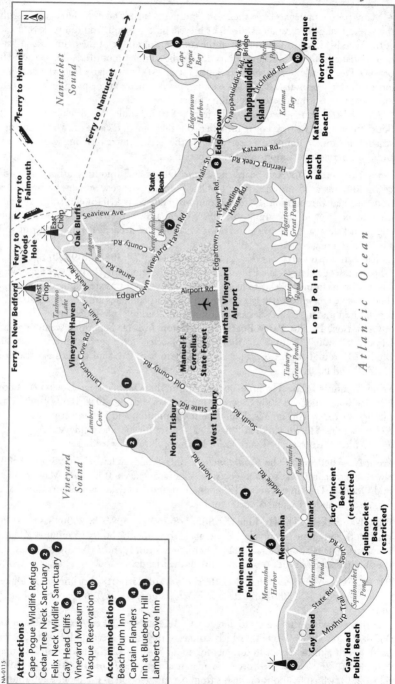

Attractions
Cape Pogue Wildlife Refuge ⑨
Cedar Tree Neck Sanctuary ②
Felix Neck Wildlife Sanctuary ⑦
Gay Head Cliffs ⑥
Vineyard Museum ⑧
Wasque Reservation ⑩

Accommodations
Beach Plum Inn ⑤
Captain Flanders ④
Inn at Blueberry Hill ③
Lambers Cove Inn ①

Many people prefer to leave their cars on the mainland, take the ferry (often with their bikes), and then rent a car, jeep, or bicycle on the island. You can park your car at the Woods Hole lots (always full in the summer) or at one of the many lots in Falmouth that absorb the overflow of cars during the summer months. Parking costs $10 per day. Free shuttle buses (some equipped for bikes) run regularly from the outlying lots to the ferry terminal. If you are parking, plan to arrive at the parking lots in Falmouth at least 45 minutes before sailing time.

A round-trip passenger ticket on the ferry is $10 for adults, $5 for children 5 to 12 (kids under 5 ride free). If you're bringing your bike along, it's an extra $6 round-trip, year-round. You do not need a reservation on the ferry if you're traveling without a car, and there are no reservations needed for parking.

From Falmouth You can board the *Island Queen* at Falmouth Harbor (☎ 508/ 548-4800) for a 35-minute cruise to Oak Bluffs (passengers only). The boat runs from late May through mid-October; round-trip fare costs $10 for adults, $5 for children under 13, and an extra $6 for bikes. There are seven crossings a day in season (eight on Friday and Sunday), and no reservations are needed. Parking will run you $10 or $12 a day.

The **Falmouth Ferry Service** (278 Scranton Ave.; ☎ 508/548-9400) operates a 1-hour passenger ferry, called the *Pied Piper,* from Falmouth Harbor to Edgartown. The boat runs from late May to mid-October, and reservations are required. In season, there are five crossings a day (six on Fridays). Round-trip fares are $22 for adults, $16 for children under 12. Bicycles are $6 round-trip. Parking is $10 per day.

Off-season, **Patriot Party Boats,** 227 Clinton Ave. (at Scranton Avenue on the harbor; ☎ 800/734-0088 or 508/548-2626) offers ferry service directly to Oak Bluffs ($10 round-trip). Boats operate Monday to Saturday, four times a day; call for schedule and hours.

From Hyannis The **Hy-Line** operates from the Ocean Street Dock (☎ 888/ 778-2600 or 508/778-2600, www.hy-line cruises.com) to Oak Bluffs from May through October. Trip time is about 1 hour 45 minutes, and a round-trip ticket costs $22 for adults, $11 for children 5 to 12 ($10 extra for bikes). In July and August it's a good idea to reserve a parking spot in Hyannis; the all-day fee is $10.

From New Bedford The *Schamonchi* at Billy Woods Wharf (☎ 508/997-1688; www.mvferry.com) takes island-goers to Vineyard Haven from mid-May through mid-October. Trip time is about 1½ hours. A round-trip ticket is $19 for adults, $10 for children under 13, and $5 extra for bikes.

From Nantucket The **Hy-Line** (☎ 888/778-2600 or 508/778-2600) has ferries to Oak Bluff, early June through late September. Trip time is 2 hours 15 minutes and the round-trip fare is $22 for adults, $11 for children 5 to 11, and $10 extra for bikes. It's the only passenger service (no cars) between the islands.

BY PLANE You can fly into **Martha's Vineyard Airport,** also known as Dukes County Airport (☎ 508/693-7022) in West Tisbury, about 5 miles outside Edgartown.

Airlines serving the Vineyard include **Cape Air/Nantucket Airlines** (☎ 800/ 352-0714 or 508/771-6944), which connects the island year-round with Boston (with hourly shuttle service in summer for about $140 to $225 round-trip), Hyannis, Nantucket, and New Bedford; **Continental Express/Colgan Air** (☎ 800/ 525-0280), which has nonstop flights from Newark (seasonal) for about $240 round-trip; and **US Airways Express** (☎ 800/428-4322), which flies from Boston for about $100 round-trip and also has seasonal weekend service from La Guardia, which costs approximately $170–$190 round-trip.

Two companies offering year-round charter service are: **Air New England** (☎ 508/693-8899) and **Direct Flight** (☎ 508/693-6688).

BY BUS   **Bonanza Bus Lines** (☎ 800/556-3815) have service to the Woods Hole ferry port from Boston (new South Station), New York City, and Providence, Rhode Island. The trip from Boston takes about 1 hour 35 minutes and costs about $15 one-way; from New York, it's about a 6-hour trip to Hyannis or Woods Hole and costs approximately $45 each way.

BY LIMO   **Cape Cod Livery** (☎ 800/235-5669 or 508/563-5669) will pick you up at Boston's Logan Airport and take you to meet your ferry in Woods Hole (or anywhere else in the Upper Cape area). The trip takes about 1 hour 45 minutes depending on traffic, and costs about $105 each way for a car-load or a van-load of people. You'll need to book the service a couple of days in advance.

GETTING AROUND

BY BICYCLE & MOPED   The best way to explore the Vineyard is on two wheels. There's a little of everything for cyclists, from paved cycle paths to hilly country roads (see "Exploring the Vineyard on Two Wheels," below for details on where to ride).

Mopeds are also a popular way to navigate Vineyard roads, but remember that some roads tend to be narrow and rough—the number of accidents involving mopeds seems to rise every year. You'll need a driver's license to rent a moped. Bike, scooter, and moped rental shops are clustered throughout all three down-island towns. Bike rentals cost about $10 to $25 a day, scooters and mopeds $30 to $80. In Vineyard Haven, try **Martha's Vineyard Bikes** on Union Street (☎ 508/693-0782). In Oak Bluffs, there's **Anderson's** (☎ 508/693-9346), which rents bikes only; or **DeBettencourt's Bike Shop** (☎ 508/693-0011) both on Circuit Avenue Extension. In Edgartown, try **Edgartown Bicycles** at 190 Upper Main St.(☎ 508/627-9008).

BY CAR   If you're staying for a long visit, or want to do some exploring up-island, you may want to bring your car or rent one on the island. Keep in mind that car-rental rates can soar during peak season, and gas is also much more expensive on the island. There are representatives of the national car-rental chains at the airport and in Vineyard Haven and Oak Bluffs. Local agencies also operate out of all three port towns and many of them also rent jeeps, mopeds, and bikes.

National chains include: Alamo (☎ 800/327-9633); Budget (☎ 800/527-0700); Hertz (☎ 800/654-3131); and Thrifty (☎ 800/FOR-CARS). Local agencies are Adventure Rentals (☎ 508/693-1959) and Atlantic (☎ 508/693-0480), both on Beach Road in Vineyard Haven. There's also AAA Island Rentals at 141 Main St. in Edgartown (☎ 508/627-6800) or at Five Corners in Vineyard Haven (☎ 508/696-5300). Another recommendable Island company that operates out of the airport is All Island Rent-a-Car (☎ 508/693-6868).

BY SHUTTLE BUS & TROLLEY   Low-cost ($1.50 to $4, depending on distance) shuttle buses make the circuit around the down-island towns in season (from late June to early September) from 6am to midnight; for information and a schedule, call **Island Transport** (☎ 508/693-1589 or 508/693-0058). Hours are reduced in spring and fall. From late June through August, the buses go out to Gay Head (via the airport, West Tisbury, and Chilmark), leaving every couple of hours from down-island towns.

The **Martha's Vineyard Transit Authority** (☎ 508/627-7448 or 508/627-9663) operates several shuttle buses in season (white buses with a purple come ride with us logo). The **Edgartown Downtown Shuttle** and the **South Beach buses** circle throughout town or out to South Beach, every 20 minutes in season. They also stop at the free parking lots just north of the town center. Parking here and shuttling into town is a great way to avoid circling the streets in search of a vacant spot on busy weekends. A one-way trip in town is just 50¢; a trip to South Beach (leaving from Edgartown's Church Street Visitor Center) is $1.50.

BY TAXI   Upon arrival, you'll find taxis at all ferry terminals and at the airport, and there are permanent taxi stands in Oak Bluffs (at the Flying Horses Carousel) and Edgartown (next to the Town Wharf). Most taxi outfits operate cars as well as vans for larger groups and travelers with bikes. Cab companies on the island include: Adam Cab (☎ **800/281-4462** or 508/693-3332); All Island Taxi (☎ **800/693-TAXI** or 508/693-2929); Martha's Vineyard Taxi (☎ **508/693-9611** or 508/693-8660); and Marlene's Taxi (☎ **508/693-0037**). Rates from town to town in summer are generally flat fees based on where you're headed and the number of passengers on board. A trip from Vineyard Haven to Edgartown would probably cost around $10 for two people. Keep in mind that rates double after midnight.

THE CHAPPAQUIDDICK FERRY   The **On Time** ferry (☎ **508/627-9427**) runs the 5-minute trip from Memorial Wharf on Dock Street in Edgartown to Chappaquiddick Island from June to mid-October, 7am to midnight. Passengers, bikes, mopeds, dogs, and cars (three at a time) are all welcome. The one-way cost is $1 per person, $4 for one car/one driver, $2.50 for one bike/one person, and $3.50 for one moped or motorcycle/one person.

VISITOR INFORMATION

Contact the **Martha's Vineyard Chamber of Commerce** at Beach Road, Vineyard Haven, MA 02568 (☎ **508/693-0085;** fax 508/693-7589; E-mail mvcc@mvy.com) or visit their Web site at www.mvy.com. Their office is just 2 blocks up from the ferry terminal in Vineyard Haven. There are also information booths at the ferry terminal in Vineyard Haven, across from the Flying Horses Carousel in Oak Bluffs, and on Church Street in Edgartown.

For **information on current events,** always check the two local newspapers, the *Vineyard Gazette* and the *Martha's Vineyard Times*. In case of an **emergency,** call ☎ 911 and/or head for the Martha's Vineyard Hospital, which has a 24-hour emergency room, on Linton Lane in Oak Bluffs (☎ **508/693-0410**).

BEACHES

Most down-island beaches in Vineyard Haven, Oak Bluffs, and Edgartown are open to the public and just a walk or a short bike ride from town. In season, shuttle buses make stops at State Beach between Oak Buffs and Edgartown. Most of the Vineyard's magnificent up-island shoreline, alas, is privately owned or restricted to residents, and thus off-limits to visitors. Renters in up-island communities, however, can obtain beach stickers (around $35–$50 for a season sticker) for those private beaches by applying with a lease at the relevant **town hall:** West Tisbury, ☎ **508/696-0148;** Chilmark, ☎ **508/645-2113** or 508/645-2100; Gay Head, ☎ **508/645-2300.** Also, many up-island inns offer the perk of temporary passes to the beautiful up-island beaches. In addition to the public beaches listed below, you might also track down a few hidden coves by requesting a map of conservation properties from the **Martha's Vineyard Land Bank** (☎ **508/627-7141**). Below is a list of visitor-friendly beaches.

- **East Beach,** Wasque (pronounced Way-squee) Reservation, Chappaquiddick. Relatively few people go to the bother of biking or hiking (or four-wheel driving) this far, so you should be able to find all the privacy you crave. Because of its exposure on the east shore of the island, the surf is rough here. It's one of the

Vineyard's best-kept secrets and an ideal spot for bird watching. There are no facilities, so pack a picnic before you go.

- **Gay Head Beach (Moshup Beach)**, off Moshup Trail. Parking costs $15 a day (in season) at this peaceful ½-mile beach just east of the colorful cliffs. Because of rapid erosion, climbing the cliffs or stealing clay for a souvenir here is against the law. Rest rooms are near the parking lot; lifeguards patrol the beach.
- **Joseph A. Sylvia State Beach,** midway between Oak Bluffs and Edgartown. Stretching a mile and flanked by a paved bike path, this placid beach has views of Cape Cod and Nantucket Sound and is prized for its gentle and (relatively) warm waves, which make it perfect for swimming. The wooden drawbridge is a local landmark, and visitors and islanders alike have been jumping off it for years. State Beach is one of the Vineyard's most popular spots and by mid-summer it's packed. The shuttle bus stops here, and roadside parking is also available—but it fills up fast, so stake your claim early. There are no rest rooms, and only the Edgartown end of the beach, known as *Bend-in-the-Road Beach,* has lifeguards.
- **Lake Tashmoo Town Beach,** off Herring Creek Road, Vineyard Haven. The only spot on the island where lake meets the ocean, this tiny strip of sand is good for swimming and surf casting, but is somewhat marred by limited parking and often brackish waters.
- **Menemsha Beach,** next to Dutchers Dock in Menemsha Harbor. Despite its rough surface, this small but well-trafficked strand—with lifeguards and rest rooms—is quite popular with families. Nearby food vendors in Menemsha—selling everything from ice cream and hot dogs to steamers and shrimp cock-tails—are also a plus here.
- **Oak Bluffs Town Beach,** Seaview Avenue. This sandy strip extends from both sides of the ferry wharf, which makes it a convenient place to linger while waiting for the next boat. The surf is consistently calm and the sand smooth, so it's also ideal for families with small children. Public rest rooms are available at the ferry dock, but there are no lifeguards.
- **Owen Park Beach,** off Main Street in Vineyard Haven. A tiny strip of harbor-side beach adjoining a town green with swings and a bandstand will suffice for young children. Lifeguards yes, rest rooms no.
- **South Beach (Katama Beach),** about 4 miles south of Edgartown on Katama Road. If you only have time for one trip to the beach and you can't get up-island, I'd go with this popular, 3-mile barrier strand that boasts heavy wave action (check with lifeguards for swimming conditions), sweeping dunes, and most important, relatively ample parking space. It's also accessible by bike path or shuttle. Lifeguards patrol some sections of the beach, and there are sparsely scat-tered toilet facilities. The rough surf here is popular with surfers. *Tip:* Families tend to head to the left, college kids to the right.
- **Wasque Beach,** Wasque Reservation, Chappaquiddick. Surprisingly easy to get to (via the On-Time ferry and a bike or car), this ½-mile-long beach has all the amenities—lifeguards, parking, rest rooms—without the crowds. Wasque Beach is a Trustees of Reservations property, and if you are not a member of this land preservation organization, you must pay at the gatehouse ($3 per car and $3 per person) for access in season.

OUTDOOR PURSUITS

FISHING   For shellfishing, you'll need to get information and a permit from the appropriate town hall (for the telephone numbers, see "Beaches," above). Popular

Exploring the Vineyard on Two Wheels

Biking on the Vineyard is a memorable experience, not just for the smooth, well-maintained bike paths, but also for the long stretches of virtually untrafficked roads that reveal breathtaking country landscapes and sweeping ocean views.

A triangle of paved bike paths, roughly 8 miles on each side, links the down-island towns of Oak Bluffs, Edgartown, and Vineyard Haven. The Sound portion along Beach Road, flanked by water on both sides, is especially enjoyable. From Edgartown, you can also follow the bike path to South Beach. For a more woodsy ride, there are paved paths and mountain biking trails in the **Manuel E. Correllus State Forest** (☎ 508/693-2540), a vast spread of scrub oak and pine smack dab in the middle of the island. The bike paths are accessible off Edgartown–West Tisbury Road in Oak Bluffs, West Tisbury, and Edgartown.

The up-island roads leading to West Tisbury, Chilmark, Menemsha, and Gay Head are a cyclist's paradise, with sprawling, unspoiled pastureland, old farmhouses, and brilliant sea views reminiscent of Ireland's countryside. But keep in mind that the terrain is often hilly, and the roads are narrow and a little rough around the edges. From West Tisbury to Chilmark Center, try South Road—about 5 miles—where you'll pass stone walls rolling over moors, clumps of pine and wildflowers, verdant marshes and tidal pools, and, every once in awhile, an Old Vineyard farmhouse. Middle Road is another lovely ride with a country feel, and will also get you from West Tisbury to Chilmark (it's usually less trafficked, too).

My favorite up-island route is the 6-mile stretch from Chilmark Center out to Gay Head via State Road and ✪ **Moshup Trail.** The ocean views along this route are nothing less than spectacular. Don't miss the Quitsa Pond Lookout, about 2 miles down State Road, which provides a panoramic vista of Nashaquitsa and Menemsha ponds, beyond which you can see Menemsha, the Vineyard Sound, and the Elizabeth Islands—it's an amazing place to watch the sunset on a clear evening. A bit farther, just over the Gay Head town line, is the Gay Head spring, a roadside iron pipe where you can refill your water bottle with the freshest and coldest water on the island. At the fork after the spring, turn left on Moshup Trail—which is in fact a regular road—and follow the coast, which offers gorgeous views of the water and the sweeping sand dunes. You'll soon wind up in Gay Head, where you can explore the red-clay cliffs and pristine beaches. On the return trip, you can take the handy bike ferry ($7 round-trip) from Gay Head to Menemsha. It runs daily in summer and weekends in May.

There are lots of bike-rental operations near the ferry landings in Vineyard Haven and Oak Bluffs, and there are also a few outfits in Edgartown. For information on bike rental shops, see "Getting Around," above.

A very good outfit out of Boston called **Bike Riders** (☎ 800/473-7040; www.bikeriderstours.com; E-mail: info@bikeriderstours.com) runs 3-day biking trips of Martha's Vineyard. The cost is $380 per person plus $60 if you need to borrow one of their bikes. It's a great way to experience the island.

spots for surf casting include Wasque Point on Chappaquiddick (see "Nature Trails," below), South Beach, and the jetty at Menemsha Pond.

The party boat *Skipper* (☎ 508/693-1238) offers half-day trips out of Oak Bluffs harbor in season. The cost is $25 for adults, $15 for children 12 and under. Bring your own poles and bait. Deep-sea excursions can be arranged aboard the *Slapshot II* (☎ 508/627-8087) out of Edgartown, which charges $375 for up to six people.

Other charter boats include Big Eye Charters (☎ 508/627-3649) out of Edgartown, and **Summer's Lease** (☎ 508/693-2880) out of Oak Bluffs. Up-island, there are **Conomo Charters** (☎ 508/645-9278) out of Gay Head; and **North Shore Charters** (☎ 508/645-2993) and **Flashy Lady Charters** (☎ 508/645-2462) out of Menemsha, locus of the island's commercial fishing fleet.

IGFA world-record holder Capt. Leslie S. Smith operates **Backlash Charters** (☎ 508/627-5894; E-mail: backlash@tiac.net), specializing in light tackle and fly-fishing, out of Edgartown. Cooper Gilkes III, proprietor of **Coop's Bait & Tackle** at 147 W. Tisbury Rd. in Edgartown (☎ 508/627-3909), that offers rentals as well as supplies, is another acknowledged authority. He's available as an instructor or charter guide.

GOLF President Clinton helped to publicize the 9-hole **Mink Meadows Golf Course** off Franklin Street in Vineyard Haven (☎ 508/693-0600), which occupies a top-dollar chunk of real estate but is open to the general public, as well as the semi-private, championship-level 18-hole **Farm Neck Golf Club** off Farm Neck Road in Oak Bluffs (☎ 508/693-3057).

IN-LINE SKATING In-line skaters are everywhere on the island's paved paths. You'll find rentals at **Jamaikan Jam,** 47 Circuit Ave. (☎ 508/693-5003) in Oak Bluffs. Other sources include **Sports Haven,** 5 Beach St., Vineyard Haven (☎ 508/696-0456) and the **Vineyard Sports Center** at the Triangle in Edgartown (☎ 508/627-3933). Rates are about $15–$25 per day, including pads.

NATURE TRAILS About a fifth of the Vineyard's land mass has been set aside for conservation. The **West Chop Woods,** off Franklin Street in Vineyard Haven, comprise 85 acres with marked walking trails. Midway between Vineyard Haven and Edgartown, the **Felix Neck Wildlife Sanctuary** includes a 6-mile network of trails over varying terrain, from woodland to beach.

Accessible by ferry from Edgartown, quiet Chappaquiddick is home to two sizable preserves: The **Cape Pogue Wildlife Refuge** and **Wasque Reservation** (gatehouse ☎ 508/627-7260), covering much of the island's eastern barrier beach, have 709 acres that draw flocks of nesting or resting shorebirds. The 4,000-acre **Manuel F. Correllus Vineyard State Forest** occupies a sizable, if not especially scenic, chunk of midisland property; it's riddled with mountain-bike paths and riding trails.

The **Cedar Tree Neck Sanctuary,** off Indian Hill Road southwest of Vineyard Haven (☎ 508/693-5207), offers some 300 forested acres that end in a stony beach, where, alas, swimming and sunbathing are prohibited.

WATER SPORTS Wind's Up at 95 Beach Rd. in Vineyard Haven (☎ 508/693-4252) rents out canoes, kayaks, and various sailing craft, including Windsurfers, and offers instruction on-site, on a placid pond; they also rent surfboards and boogie boards. Rank beginners may enjoy towing privileges at **M.V. Parasail** and **M.V. Ski** at Pier 44 off Beach Road in Vineyard Haven (☎ 508/693-2838): For the former you're airborne by parachute, for the latter you straddle water skis, a knee board, a wake board, or an inner tube.

A STROLL AROUND EDGARTOWN

A good way to get acclimated to the pace and flavor of the Vineyard is to walk the streets of ✪ **Edgartown.** This walk starts at the Dr. Daniel Fisher House and meanders along for about a mile; depending on how long you linger at each stop, it should take about 2 to 3 hours. If you're driving, park at the free lots at the edge of town (you'll see signs on the roads from Vineyard Haven and West Tisbury) and bike or take the shuttle bus (it only costs 50¢) to the Edgartown Visitor Center on Church Street.

The **Dr. Daniel Fisher House,** 99 Main St. (☎ **508/627-8017**), is a prime example of Edgartown's trademark Greek Revival opulence. A key player in the 19th-century whaling trade, Dr. Fisher amassed a fortune sufficient to found the Martha's Vineyard National Bank. Built in 1840, his prosperous and proud mansion boasts such classical elements as colonnaded porticos, as well as a delicate roof-walk.

Note: The only way to view the interior (now headquarters for the Martha's Vineyard Preservation Trust) is with a guide from **Vineyard History Tours** (☎ **508/627-8619**). This tour, which also takes in the neighboring Old Whaling Church, originates next door at the Vincent House Museum. Tours are offered June to September Monday to Saturday from 10:30 to 3pm, and cost $6 to $8 for adults, free for children 12 and under.

The **Vincent House Museum,** off Main Street between Planting Field Way and Church Street, a transplanted 1672 full Cape is considered to be the oldest surviving dwelling on the island. The **Old Whaling Church,** 89 Main St. (☎ **508/627-4442**), a magnificent 1843 Greek Revival edifice designed by local architect Frederick Baylies, Jr., is built as a whaleboat would have been, out of massive pine beams. With its 27-foot windows and 92-foot tower (a landmark easily spotted from the sea), this is a building that knows its place in the community: central. Maintained by the Preservation Trust and still supporting a Methodist parish, the building is now primarily used as a performance site.

Continuing down Main Street and turning right onto School Street, you'll pass another Baylies monument, the 1839 **Baptist Church,** which, having lost its spire, was converted into a private home with a rather grand, column-fronted facade.

Two blocks farther, on your left, is **The Vineyard Museum,** 59 School St. (☎ **508/627-4441**), a fascinating complex assembled by the Dukes County Historical Society. A palimpsest of island history, this cluster of buildings contains exhibits of early Native American crafts; an entire 1765 house; an extraordinary array of maritime art, from whalers' logs to WPA-era studies by Thomas Hart Benton; a carriage house to catch odds and ends; and the Gay Head Lighthouse's decommissioned Fresnel lens.

Give yourself enough time to explore the museum's curiosities before heading south 1 block on Cooke Street. Catty-corner across South Summer Street, you'll spot the 1828 **Federated Church.** One block left are the offices of the *Vineyard Gazette,* 34 S. Summer St. (☎ **508/627-4311**). Operating out of a 1760 house, this exemplary small-town newspaper (circulation 14,000) has been going strong since 1846.

Heading toward Main Street, you'll happen upon the **Charlotte Inn,** 27 S. Summer St. (☎ **508/627-4751**), among the most charming on the entire East Coast (see "Where to Stay," below). You don't have to be a guest here to appreciate the English gardens, and in fact, the in-house **Edgartown Art Gallery** provides a good excuse to explore the common rooms.

Head down Main Street toward the water, stopping in at any inviting shops along the way. Veer left on Dock Street to reach the **Old Sculpin Gallery,** 58 Dock St. (☎ **508/627-4881**). The output of the Martha's Vineyard Art Association displayed here tends to be amateurish, but you might happen upon a find. The real draw is the stark old building itself, which started out as a granary (part of Dr. Fisher's vast holdings) and spent the better part of the 20th century as a boatbuilding shop.

Cross the street to survey the harbor from the deck at **Town Wharf.** It's from here that the tiny On-Time ferry makes its 5-minute crossing to Chappaquiddick Island. (Don't bother looking for the infamous Dyke Bridge, scene of the Kennedy/Kopechne debacle; it's been dismantled and, at long last, replaced.)

Stroll down North Water Street to admire many formidable captain's homes, several of which have been converted into inns. Each has a tale to tell. The 1750 **Daggett House** (no. 59), for instance, expanded upon a 1660 tavern, and the original beehive oven is flanked by a "secret" passageway. Nathaniel Hawthorne holed up at the **Edgartown Inn** (no. 56)

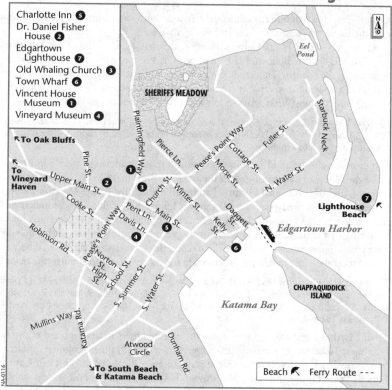

Charlotte Inn ❺
Dr. Daniel Fisher House ❷
Edgartown Lighthouse ❼
Old Whaling Church ❸
Town Wharf ❻
Vincent House Museum ❶
Vineyard Museum ❹

↖To Oak Bluffs

↖ To Vineyard Haven

SHERIFFS MEADOW

Eel Pond

Starbuck Neck

Plaintingfield Way
Pierce Ln.
Pease's Point Way
Cottage St.
Morse St.
Fuller St.
N. Water St.
Pine St.
Upper Main St.
Church St.
Winter St.
Daggett St.
Kelly St.

Lighthouse Beach ❼ ↖

Cooke St.
Pent Ln.
Main St.
Robinson Rd.
Pease's Point Way
Davis Ln.

Edgartown Harbor

Norton St.
High St.
School St.
S. Summer St.
S. Water St.

CHAPPAQUIDDICK ISLAND

Mullins Way
Katama Rd.

Katama Bay

Atwood Circle

Dunham Rd.

↘To South Beach & Katama Beach

Beach ↖   Ferry Route ---

NA-0116

for nearly a year in 1789 while writing *Twice Told Tales*—and, it is rumored, romancing a local maiden who inspired *The Scarlet Letter*. On your way back to Main Street, you'll pass the **Gardner-Colby Gallery** (no. 27), filled with beautiful island-inspired paintings.

After all that walking, you'll need a refreshment at **Espresso Love,** at 2 South Water St. (☎ **508/627-9211**), whose muffins and pastries are legendary.

MUSEUMS & HISTORIC LANDMARKS

Cottage Museum. 1 Trinity Park (within the Camp Meeting Grounds), Oak Bluffs. ☎ **508/693-7784.** Admission $1 (donation). Mid-June to Sept Mon–Sat 10am–4pm. Closed Oct to mid-June.

Oak Bluffs' famous "Camp Ground"—a 34-acre circle with more than 300 multicolored, elaborately trimmed Gothic carpenter's cottages, looks very much the way it might have more than 100years ago. These adorable little houses, loosely modeled on the revivalists' canvas tents that inspired them, have been handed down through generations. Unless you happen to know a lucky camper, your best chance of getting inside one is to visit this homey little museum.

The compact architecture is at once practical and symbolic. The Gothic-arched French doors off the peak-roofed second-story bedroom, for instance, lead to a tiny balcony used for keeping tabs on community doings. The daily schedule was, in fact, rather hectic. In 1867, when this cottage was built, campers typically attended three lengthy prayer services daily. Today's denizens tend to blend in with the visiting tourists, though opportunities for worship remain at the 1878 Trinity Methodist Church within the park, or just outside, on Samoset Avenue, at the nonsectarian 1870

Union Chapel, a magnificent octagonal structure with superb acoustics (posted signs give the lineup of guest preachers and musicians).

At the very center of the Camp Ground is the striking ✪ **Trinity Park Tabernacle** (☎ **508/693-0525**). Built in 1879, the open-sided chapel is the largest wrought-iron structure in the country. Thousands can be accommodated on its long wooden benches, which are usually filled to capacity for the Sunday-morning services in summer, as well as for community sings (Wednesdays in July and August) and occasional concerts.

✪ **Flying Horses Carousel.** 33 Circuit Ave. (at Lake Ave.), Oak Bluffs. ☎ **508/693-9481.** Tickets $1 per ride, or $8 for 10. Late May to early Sept daily 9:30am–10pm; call for off-season hrs. Closed mid-Oct to mid-Apr.

You don't have to be a kid to enjoy the colorful mounts adorning what is considered to be the oldest working carousel in the country. Built in 1876 at New York's fabled Coney Island, this National Historic Landmark maintained by the Martha's Vineyard Preservation Trust predates the era of carousel horses that "gallop." These merely glide smoothly in place to the joyful strains of a calliope. The challenge lies in going for the brass ring that entitles the lucky winner to a free ride. Some regulars, adults included, have grown rather adept—you'll see them scoop up several in a single pass. In between rides, take a moment to admire the intricate hand-carving and real horsehair manes.

The Martha's Vineyard Historical Society/Vineyard Museum. 59 School St. (2 blocks SW of Main St.), Edgartown. ☎ **508/627-4441.** Fax 508/627-4436. Admission in season $6 adults, $4 children 6–15. Mid-July to mid-Oct Tues–Sat 10am–5pm; off-season Wed–Fri 1–4pm, Sat 10am–4pm.

All of Martha's Vineyard's colorful history is captured here, in a compound of historic buildings. To acclimate yourself chronologically, start with the precolonial artifacts—from arrowheads to colorful Gay Head clay pottery—displayed in the 1845 **Captain Francis Pease House.** The Gale Huntington Reference Library houses rare documentation of the island's history, from genealogical records to whale-ship logs. There's also some extraordinary memorabilia, including scrimshaw and portraiture, on view in the adjoining **Francis Foster Museum.**

To get a sense of daily life during the era when the waters of the East Coast were the equivalent of a modern highway, visit the **Thomas Cooke House,** a shipwright-built Colonial, built in 1765, where the customs collector lived and worked. The Fresnel lens on display outside the museum was lifted from the Gay Head Lighthouse in 1952, after nearly a century of service. Though it no longer serves to warn ships of dangerous shoals (that light is automated now), it still lights up the night every evening in summer, just for show.

CRUISES

Hugh Taylor (James's equally musical brother) alternates with a couple of other captains in taking the helm of the ✪ *Arabella*, at North Road, Menemsha Harbor (☎ **508/645-3511**). This swift 50-foot catamaran makes daily trips to Cuttyhunk and sunset cruises around the Gay Head cliffs. Zipping along at 15 knots, it's a great way to see lovely coves and vistas otherwise denied the ordinary tourist. Evening sails are $40 adults, $20 children under 12. Day sails are $60 adults, $30 children under 12. Departures are mid-June to mid-Sept daily 10:30am and 6pm. Reservations are required.

Black Dog owner Robert Douglas's prized 108-foot square topsail schooner *The Shenandoah*, Beach Street Extension, Vineyard Haven. (☎ **508/693-1699**), is modeled on an 1849 revenue cutter and fitted out with period furnishings. It spends most of the summer doing windjammer duty, transporting some 26 lucky children (ages 11 to 14) wherever the wind happens to take them in the course of a week. Day sails are offered for one week at the height of the season—a great way for adults to experience the cruise.

Douglas's newest vessel is *The Alabama*—a 90-foot ex-pilot modeled after a Grand Banks fishing schooner—which also provides kids cruises and occasional day sails.

SHOPPING

ANTIQUES/COLLECTIBLES You don't have to be a bona fide collector to marvel over the museum-quality marine antiques at **C. W. Morgan Marine Antiques,** Beach Road, just east of town center, Vineyard Haven (☎ 508/693-3622). Frank Rapoza's collection encompasses paintings and prints, intricate ship models, nautical instruments, sea chests, and scrimshaw.

ARTS & CRAFTS No visit to Edgartown would be complete without a peek at the wares of scrimshander Thomas J. DeMont Jr. at ✪ **Edgartown Scrimshaw Gallery** on Main St. (☎ 508/627-9439). In addition to DeMont's work, the shop carries the work of a number of the country's top scrimshaw artists. All the scrimshaw in the gallery is hand-carved using ancient mammoth ivory or antique fossil ivory.

In the center of Edgartown, stop in at **Gardner Colby Gallery** on 27 N. Water St. (☎ 888/969-9500 or 508/627-6002), a soothing and sophisticated art showroom filled with Vineyard-inspired paintings. The **Chilmark Pottery,** off State Road (about 4 miles southwest of Vineyard Haven), West Tisbury (☎ 508/693-6476), features tableware fashioned to suit its setting. Geoffrey Borr takes his palette from the sea and sky and produces highly serviceable stoneware with clean lines and a long life span.

The **Field Gallery,** State Road (in the center of town), West Tisbury (☎ 508/693-5595), set in a rural pasture, is where Marc Chagall meets Henry Moore and where Tom Maley's playful figures have enchanted locals and passersby for decades. You'll also find paintings by Albert Alcalay, and drawings and cartoons by Jules Feiffer. The Sunday-evening openings are high points of the summer social season.

Don't miss the **Granary Gallery** at the Red Barn, Old County Road (off Edgartown–West Tisbury Road, about ¼ mile north of the intersection), West Tisbury (☎ 800/472-6279 or 508/693-0455), which displays astounding prints by Alfred Eisenstaedt, dazzling color photos by local luminary Alison Shaw, and a changing roster of fine artists.

World-renowned master glassblowers sometimes lend a hand at **Martha's Vineyard Glass Works,** State Road, North Tisbury (☎ 508/693-6026), just for the fun of it. The three resident artists—Andrew Magdanz, Susan Shapiro, and Mark Weiner—are no slouches themselves, having shown nationwide to considerable acclaim.

FASHION **Jamaikan Jam,** 47 Circuit Ave. (in the center of town), Oak Bluffs (☎ 508/693-5003), is one of the best ethnic shops along Circuit Avenue, carrying colorful and comfortable clothes and island tchotchkes. You can also buy or rent in-line skates here.

Treading a comfortable middle ground between functional and fashionable, the varied women's and men's labels at **LeRoux,** 89 Main St. (in the center of town), Vineyard Haven (☎ 508/693-6463), include some nationally known names, like Patagonia.

GIFTS/HOME DECOR The owners of **Bramhall & Dunn,** 23 Main St., Vineyard Haven (☎ 508/693-6437), have a great eye for the kind of chunky, eclectic extras that lend character to country homes. Expect to find the requisite rag rugs, rustic pottery, English country antiques, bed linens, and a large selection of sweaters.

Carly Simon's venture in Vineyard Haven is called **Midnight Farm,** 18 Water-Cromwell Lane, Vineyard Haven (☎ 508/693-1997), after her popular children's book. This home store offers a world of high-end, carefully selected and imaginative gift items starting with soaps and candles and including children's clothes and toys, rugs, furniture, books, and glassware.

WHERE TO STAY

When deciding where to stay on Martha's Vineyard, you'll need to consider the type of vacation you prefer. The down-island towns of Vineyard Haven, Oak Bluffs, and Edgartown provide shops, restaurants, beaches, and harbors all within walking distance and frequent shuttles to get you all over the island. But all three can be overly crowded on busy summer weekends. Vineyard Haven is the gateway for most of the ferry traffic. Oak Bluffs is a raucous town with most of the Vineyard's bars and nightclubs. And many visitors make a beeline to Edgartown's manicured Main Street. Up-island inns provide more peace and quiet, but you will probably need a car to get around. Also, you may not be within walking distance of the beach (and, after all, isn't that why you came?).

I've given mostly summer rates below, since that's when most visitors head to the Vineyard. If you do choose to come in the off-season, you'll not only avoid crowds, but you'll find much more reasonable rates at any of the hotels that remain open.

EDGARTOWN

Very Expensive

✪ **Charlotte Inn.** 27 S. Summer St. (in the center of town), Edgartown, MA 02539. ☎ **508/627-4751.** Fax 508/627-4652. 25 units. A/C. Summer $295–$495 double; $495–$750 suite. Rates include continental breakfast. AE, MC, V. Open year-round.

Ask anyone to recommend the best inn on the island, and this is the name you're most likely to hear. This is the only Relais & Chateaux property on the Cape and Islands—a world-class distinction that designates excellence in hospitality. Owners Gery and Paula Conover have been tirelessly fine-tuning this cluster of 18th- and 19th-century houses (five in all, counting the Carriage House, a Gery-built replica) since 1971. Linked by formal gardens, each house has a distinctive look and feel—though the predominant mode is English country house. All rooms have hair dryers. Most have telephones and television, and some have VCRs. Bathrooms are luxurious, and some are also enormous (bigger than most hotel rooms).

Dining: However sterling the accommodations at the Charlotte Inn, the restaurant may actually gather more laurels: L'Eetoile is one of the island's finest. See "Where to Dine," below, for more information.

Amenities: Turndown service in the evenings; newspapers available at breakfast every morning.

Harbor View Hotel. 131 N. Water St. (about ½ mile NW of Main St.), Edgartown, MA 02539. ☎ **800/255-6005** or 508/627-7000. Fax 508/627-7845. www.harbor-view.com. 124 units. A/C TV TEL. Summer $285–$475 double; $485–$675 suite. AE, DC, MC, V. Open year-round.

With an exterior that is grander than grand, this shingle-style complex started out as two Gilded Age hotels, ultimately joined by a 300-foot veranda. Treated to a massive centennial makeover in 1991, the interior is rather generic except for the lobby that's right out of an Adirondack lodge. Front rooms overlook little Lighthouse Beach; in back, there's a large pool surrounded by newer annexes, where some rooms and suites have kitchenettes. All rooms have minifridges and hair dryers. The hotel is located just far enough from "downtown" to avoid the traffic hassles, but close enough for a pleasant walk past impressive captain's houses.

Dining/Diversions: The casual Breezes restaurant, stationed in a vintage bar, is open daily for breakfast, lunch, and dinner; you can ask to be served on the veranda or by the pool, if you like. the recently renovated Coach House (see "Where to Dine," below) serves more formal meals in an elegant setting.

Amenities: Heated outdoor pool, two tennis courts, concierge, room service, overnight laundry, baby-sitting. Guests enjoy privileges at the Farm Neck Golf Club (see "Beaches & Outdoor Pursuits," above).

✪ **Tuscany Inn.** 22 N. Water St. (in the center of town), Edgartown, MA 02539. ☎ **508/627-5999** or 508/627-8999. Fax 508/627-6605. www.mvweb.com/tuscany. E-mail: tuscany@vineyard.net. 8 units. A/C TV on request. Summer $200–$375 double. Rates include full breakfast in season. AE, DC, DISC, MC, V. Closed Jan–Mar.

Innkeepers Rusty and Laura Scheuer have transformed a derelict captain's house into a winning little inn. The interior decor is straight from sunny Italy, with warm colors and an abundance of fine old paintings—a far cry from the usual Yankee austerity. Past a little library lined with leather-backed books is Laura's open kitchen, where she gives cooking classes off-season (she's from Florence, and leads a 1-week cooking class trip to Tuscany and Rome every fall). Lavish breakfasts (blueberry buttermilk pancakes or frittata with focaccia) are served here when the weather precludes a patio feast. Each of the eight rooms is a gem, with toile wallpaper, hand-painted antique armoires, and fanciful beds—and, in some cases, skylights, marble whirlpools, and harbor views. All rooms have comfortable sitting areas and bathrooms with hair dryers and luxurious toiletries. TV is available on request.

Expensive

Colonial Inn of Martha's Vineyard. 38 N. Water St., Edgartown, MA 02539. ☎ **800/627-4701** or 508/627-4711. Fax 508/627-5904. 43 units. A/C TV TEL. Summer $150–$215 double; $260 suite or efficiency. Rates include continental breakfast. AE, MC, V. Closed Jan–Mar.

Somewhat big and impersonal, this 1911 inn has been transformed into a fine modern hotel. It's been the unofficial center of town since its doors opened, and its lobby also serves as a conduit to the Nevins Square shops beyond. The lobby has a somewhat transient feel, hardly enhanced by a self-service breakfast cart—but the lack of ceremony is a plus if, like most tourists, you're bursting to get out and about. The 43 rooms, decorated in soothing, contemporary tones (with pine furniture, pastel fabrics, and brass beds), offer all one could want in the way of conveniences. All rooms have hair dryers and telephones with dataports; some have harbor views. Suites have VCRs (complimentary videos) and kitchenettes. Be sure to visit the roof deck, ideally around sunset.

✪ **Hob Knob Inn.** 128 Main St. (on upper Main St., in the center of town), Edgartown, MA 02539. ☎ **800/696-2723** or 508/627-9510. Fax 508/627-4560. www.hobknob.com. E-mail: hobknob@vineyard.net. 16 units. TV TEL. Summer $185–$375 double. Rates include full breakfast and afternoon tea. AE, MC, V. Open year-round.

Owner Maggie White has reinvented this 19th-century Gothic Revival inn as an exquisite destination now vying for top honors as one of the Vineyard's best places to stay. Her style is peppy/preppy, with crisp floral fabrics and striped patterns creating a clean and comfortable look. The full farm breakfast is a delight and is served at beautifully appointed individual tables in the sunny, brightly painted dining rooms.

Amenities: The inn has fitness equipment; massages and facials are available on the premises (for an extra charge). Maggie and her attentive staff will pack a splendid picnic basket for a day at the beach or plan a charter fishing trip on Maggie's 27-foot Boston Whaler.

The Jonathan Monroe House. 100 Main St., Edgartown, MA 02539. ☎ **508/627-5536.** 7 units, 1 cottage. A/C. Summer $175–$225 double; $300 cottage. Rates include full breakfast. AE, MC, V. No children under 12.

With its lovely wraparound, colonnaded front porch, the Jonathan Monroe House stands out from the other inns and captain's homes on this stretch of upper Main Street. Inside, the formal parlor has been transformed into a comfortable gathering room with a European flair. Guest rooms are immaculate, antique-filled, and dotted with clever details. Many rooms have fireplaces and baths with whirlpool jets. All have sitting areas, perfect for curling up with an antiquarian book (provided) or for matching wits over a game of chess (also provided). At breakfast, don't miss the home-made waffles and pancakes, served on the screened-in porch. Guests will immediately feel relaxed in the presence of genial host Chip Yerkes, an enthusiastic athlete, who will gladly assist guests with daily excursions that could include a trip around Sengekon-tacket Pond in one of his three canoes, a game of tennis, a bike ride, or a sail around Edgartown Harbor on his friend's sloop. Request the garden cottage, with its flowering window boxes, if you are in a honeymooning mood.

✪ **Victorian Inn.** 24 S. Water St. (in the center of town), Edgartown, MA 02539. ☎ **508/ 627-4784.** 14 units. Summer $145–$325 double. Rates include full breakfast and afternoon tea. MC, V. Open year-round. Pets allowed off-season.

Do you ever long to stay at a quaint, reasonably priced inn that is bigger than a B&B but smaller than a Marriott? In the center of Edgartown, the Victorian Inn is a freshened-up version of those old-style hotels that used to exist in the center of every New England town. There are enough rooms here so you don't feel like you are tres-passing in someone's home, yet there's a personal touch. With three floors of long, graceful corridors, the Victorian could serve as a stage set for a 1930s romance. Sev-eral rooms have canopied beds and a balcony with a harbor view. Bring your kids (and off-season, your dog) for a perfect family vacation.

Moderate

Edgartown Inn. 56 N. Water St., Edgartown, MA 02539. ☎ **508/627-4794.** www.vine-yard.net/biz/edgartowninn. 20 units, 4 with shared bathroom. A/C. Summer $90–$185 double. No credit cards. Closed Nov–Mar.

Nathaniel Hawthorne holed up here for nearly a year while secretly courting a Wampanoag maiden who, it is rumored, inspired *The Scarlet Letter*. It's also where a young and feckless Ted Kennedy sweated out that shameful, post-Chappaquiddick night. Questionable karma aside, it's a lovely 1798 Federal manse, a showplace even here on captain's row, and the rooms are traditional but not overdone. Rooms here are no frills but pleasant; some have TVs. Breakfast, which costs extra for guests, is served in the dining room. Some rooms in the front of the house have harbor views. Mod-ernists might prefer the two cathedral-ceilinged quarters in the annex out back, which offer lovely light and a sense of seclusion.

OAK BLUFFS

Moderate

The Dockside Inn. Circuit Ave. Ext., Box 1206, Oak Bluffs, MA 02557. ☎ **800/245-5979** or 508/693-2966. Fax 508/696-7293. www.vineyard.net/inns. E-mail: inns@vineyard.net. 22 units. A/C TV TEL. Summer $130–$175 double; $240–$350 suite. Rates include continental breakfast. AE, DISC, MC, V. Closed Nov–Mar.

Set close to the harbor, the Dockside is perfectly located for exploring the town of Oak Bluffs. The welcoming exterior, with its colonnaded porch and balconies, replicates the inns of yesteryear. Most of the standard-size rooms have either a garden or harbor view; they're decorated cheerfully in pinks and greens. All rooms have hair dryers. Suites have kitchenettes, and some have private decks. There are two handicap-accessible rooms here. Location, charm, and flair mean this is a popular place, so book early.

✪ **The Oak House.** Seaview Ave. (on the sound), Oak Bluffs, MA 02557. ☎ **800/245-5979** or 508/693-4187. Fax 508/696-7385. www.vineyard.net/inns. E-mail: inns@vineyard.net. 10 units. A/C TV TEL. Summer $150–$190 double; $260 suite. Rates include continental breakfast and afternoon tea. AE, DISC, MC, V. Closed Nov to mid-May.

An 1872 Queen Anne bay-front beauty, this one-time home of former Massachusetts governor William Claflin has preserved all the luxury and leisure of the Victorian age. The rooms toward the back are quieter, but those in front have Nantucket Sound views. The common rooms, like the bedrooms, are furnished in an opulent Victorian mode. Innkeeper Betsi Convery-Luce serves fabulous home-baked pastries at breakfast and teatime.

Inexpensive

Attleboro House. 42 Lake Ave. (on the harbor), Oak Bluffs, MA 02557. ☎ **508/693-4346.** 11 units, all with shared bathroom. Summer $65–$95 double, $95–$175 suite. Rates include continental breakfast. MC, V. Closed Oct–May.

As old-fashioned as the afghans that proprietor Estelle Reagan crochets for every bed, this harborside guest house—serving Camp Meeting visitors since 1874—epitomizes the simple, timeless joys of summer. None of the 11 rooms is graced with a private bath, but the rates are so retro that you may not mind.

VINEYARD HAVEN (TISBURY)
Expensive

The Lothrop Merry House. Owen Park (off Main St.), Vineyard Haven, MA 02568. ☎ **508/693-1646.** www.tiac.net/users/lothmer. E-mail: lothmer@tiac.net. 7 units, 3 with shared bathroom. A/C. Summer $149–$215 double. Rates include continental breakfast. MC, V.

You'll get more than the superficial Vineyard experience by opting to stay at this nicely weathered 1790s B&B. It overlooks the harbor, with its own little stretch of beach and a canoe and Sunfish to take out at your leisure. Innkeepers Mary and John Clarke run a quaint establishment; it's a little like going to visit grandma. A few of the simply furnished rooms have fireplaces, and the two rooms without water views compensate by having air-conditioning.

✪ **Martha's Place.** 114 Main St. (across from Owen Park, in the center of town), Vineyard Haven, MA 02568. ☎ **508/693-0253.** Fax 508/693-1890. www.marthasplace.com. E-mail: martha@vineyard.net. 6 units. A/C. Summer $175–$325 double. Rates include continental breakfast and afternoon tea. MC, V. Open year-round.

Martha's Place is exceptional for its elegance in the heart of this bustling port town. Owners Richard Alcott and Martin Hicks have lovingly restored and refurbished this stately Greek Revival home and surrounded it with rose bushes. Now swags and jabots line the windows; every knob has a tassel, every fabric, a trim. If you enjoy admiring a neoclassical armoire or an antique bed draped in blue velvet, Martha's is the place. The bathrooms here are quite luxurious: Ever seen one with a fireplace? Most rooms have harbor views; TVs are available on request. Breakfast is served in the sunlit dining room on a long table set with china and silver. There are loaner bikes and a little Owen Park Beach is across the street. There is one limited handicap-accessible room.

CHILMARK (INCLUDING MENEMSHA), WEST TISBURY & GAY HEAD
Expensive

Beach Plum Inn. Beach Plum Lane (off North Rd., ½ mile NE of the harbor), Menemsha, MA 02552. ☎ **508/645-9454.** Fax 508/645-2801. www.beachpluminn.com. 5 units, 4 cottages. A/C TV TEL. Summer $200–$350 double or cottage. Rates include full breakfast. AE, DC, DISC, MC, V. Closed late Oct to Apr.

It's the ideal hideaway: a prettified farmhouse on 8 verdant acres, with a lawn sloping graciously down to the water. There's a croquet course and Nova Grass tennis court on the grounds, and bikes to take exploring. The decor is predominantly white—all the better to set off a bounty of flowers, outdoors and in. All of the comfortable rooms are equipped with hair dryers, irons, and ironing boards. Some, with canopied beds, are quite romantic. The honeymoon suite has a whirlpool bath. Most rooms have decks, some with views of Menemsha Harbor.

Dining: The inn's restaurant is popular for its continental flair. The full breakfast served daily includes such hearty fare as steak and eggs, as well as a jogger's special (grapefruit, two poached eggs, and dry toast). Dinners are cooked to order and must be ordered several days in advance. The menu changes nightly but may include Tournedos Rossini prepared classically with foie gras and served atop a rich demi-glace; or salmon en papillote with a saffron, mint, and orange butter.

Amenities: There is a concierge, laundry service, and twice daily maid service. Arrangements can be made for baby-sitting, secretarial services, and in-room massage. On the grounds are a tennis courts, a croquet court, and an exercise room.

The Inn at Blueberry Hill. North Rd. (about 4 miles NE of Menemsha), Chilmark, MA 02535. ☎ **800/356-3322** or 508/645-3322. Fax 508/645-3799. www.blueberryinn.com. 25 units. TEL. Summer $210–$235 double; $280–$650 suite. Rates include continental breakfast. AE, MC, V. Closed Nov–May. No children under 12.

Energetic owners Bob and Carolyn Burgess bought this one-time white elephant while on their honeymoon, which may partly explain its runaway romanticism. Their goal was to create a spalike retreat of the utmost luxury without in any way compromising the lovely natural setting—56 acres of former farmland, surrounded by vast tracts of conservation forest. They've succeeded splendidly. The 1792 farmhouse has been spruced up to suit a more modern aesthetic—still simple, in the neo-Shaker mode, but suffused with light. The same is true of the scattered cottages (some tucked under towering spruces), where the decor has been kept intentionally minimal, so as to play up the natural beauty all around. Tasteful, handcrafted furnishings and such gentle touches as fluffy comforters. One room is wheelchair-accessible. TVs are available on request at an extra charge.

Dining: Local ingredients are showcased at Theo's (see "Where to Dine," below).

Amenities: The renovated barn contains a full-scale Cybex fitness center overlooking a solar-heated outdoor lap pool and hot tub. Equipment is provided for croquet, horseshoes, and volleyball. Beyond the tennis court, miles of walking paths branch out through the woods. Carolyn Burgess, a personal trainer, can fashion a custom fitness program on request and oversee workouts, or arrange for massages and facials. Inn guests may avail themselves of complimentary passes and shuttles to Lucy Vincent and Squibnocket beaches.

Moderate

The Captain R. Flanders House. North Rd. (about 1 mile NE of Menemsha), Chilmark, MA 02535. ☎ **508/645-3123.** 5 units (2 with shared bath), 2 cottages. Summer $150 double; $205 cottage. Rates include continental breakfast. AE, DISC, MC, V.

Set amid 60 acres of rolling meadows crisscrossed by stone walls, this late-18th-century farmhouse built by a whaling captain has remained much the same for 2 centuries. The living room, with its broad plank floors, is full of astonishing antiques, but there's no self-conscious showiness. This is a working farm, so there's no time for posing (even if it was featured in Martha Stewart's Weddings). Two countrified cottages overlooking the pond have living rooms but not kitchenettes. After fortifying themselves with homemade muffins, honey, and jam at breakfast, guests can use the inn's coveted pass to nearby Lucy Vincent Beach.

Lambert's Cove Country Inn. Lambert's Cove Rd. (off State Rd., about 3 miles W of Vineyard Haven), W. Tisbury, MA 02568. ☎ **508/693-2298.** Fax 508/693-7890. www.vineyard.net/biz/lambertscoveinn. 15 units. A/C. Summer $145–$185 double. AE, MC, V. Rates include full breakfast. Open year-round.

Set far off the main road and surrounded by apple trees and lilacs, this secluded estate is the perfect place to relax. A dedicated horticulturist created this haven in the 1920s, expanding on a 1790 farmstead. You can see the old beams in some of the upstairs bedrooms. Among his more prized additions is the Greenhouse Room, a bedroom with its own conservatory. You'll find an all-weather tennis court on the grounds, and the namesake beach nearby. Brunch on the patio is a beloved island tradition, as are the skilled New American dinners (see "Where to Dine," below).

WHERE TO DINE

Outside Oak Bluffs and Edgartown, all of Martha's Vineyard is "dry," including Vineyard Haven, so bring your own bottle; some restaurants charge a small fee for uncorking.

EDGARTOWN
Very Expensive

✪ **l'etoile.** Charlotte Inn, 27 S. Summer St. (off Main St.). ☎ **508/627-5187.** Reservations required. Jacket recommended. Fixed-price $65 and up. AE, MC, V. July–Aug daily 6:30–9:45pm; call for off-season hrs. Closed Jan to mid-Feb. FRENCH.

Every signal (starting with the price) tells you that this is going to be one very special meal. Having passed through a pair of sitting rooms that double as the Edgartown Art Gallery, you'll come upon a conservatory sparkling with the light of antique brass sconces and fresh with the scent of potted citrus trees. Everything is remarkable, from the table settings (gold-rimmed Villeroy & Boch) to a nouvelle-cuisine menu that varies seasonally. Chef Michael Brisson continually dazzles, with an ever-evolving menu of delicacies flown in from the four corners of the earth. Sevruga usually makes an appearance—perhaps as a garnish for chilled leek soup. An étouffée of lobster with champagne sauce might come with flying-fish-roe ravioli, or warm Mission figs might offset seared pheasant breast in an Armagnac-sage sauce.

Expensive

The Coach House. At the Harbor View Hotel (see "Where to Stay," above), 131 N. Water St. ☎ **508/627-7000.** Reservations recommended. Main courses $19–$31. AE, MC, V. Mon–Sat 7–11am and noon–2pm, Sun 8am–2pm; daily 6–10pm. NEW AMERICAN.

A major makeover has opened up and transformed this restaurant from a stuffy room to a terrific place to dine with a perfect view of Edgartown Harbor and the lighthouse. The new long and elegant bar is particularly smashing, making this the swanky-est place to have a drink in town. The menu is simple but stylish—hip even. You'll want to start with a salad of smoky bluefish, lil' beets and frisée with horseradish crème fraîche; or just the Thimble Farm tomato-and-bread salad with a balsamic vinaigrette. As a main course, the seared rare tuna with soy and ginger is lovely but served, oddly, in an Asian-style bowl. The crusty barbecued striped bass with black-eyed peas and Georgia "peanut" sauce, is certainly one of the more original preparations for this noble fish. Service here is excellent; these are trained waiters, not your usual college surfer dude. At the end of your meal, you may want to sit on the rockers on the Harborview Hotel's wraparound porch and just watch the lights twinkling in the harbor.

✪ **La Cucina Ristorante at the Tuscany Inn.** 22 N. Water St. (in the center of town). ☎ **508/627-8161.** Reservations recommended. Main courses $25–$30. MC, V. May–Sept Wed–Mon 6–9pm. Closed Oct–May. NORTHERN ITALIAN.

Laura Sbrana, a native of Tuscany and a formidable chef, has brought European panache and sophistication to this sometimes dowdy little town. Her restaurant, with her son Marco installed as chef, is sensational. Seating is outdoors under a verdant arbor with candles twinkling or indoors in the tiled dining rooms. Specialties of the house are a bit more refined than at most local venues: marinated quail salad; roasted salmon with fennel, red onion and mint salad, ginger-infused fig and port compote; or rosemary- and lavender-marinated lamb chops with cannellini beans, oven-dried tomatoes, sage, and lamb jus. If you are unable to pop over to Tuscany this year, La Cucina will tide you over just fine.

✪ **Savoir Fare.** 14 Church St. (Old Post Office Sq., off Main St. in the center of town). ☎ **508/627-9864.** Reservations recommended. Main courses $27–$32. AE, MC, V. Apr–Oct daily 5:30–10pm; call for off-season hrs. Closed Nov–Mar. NEW AMERICAN.

Scott Caskey initially opened this stylish cathedral-ceiling space as a gourmet deli/catering concern. Spurred by a rumor of impending competition (which never did materialize), he switched to haute restaurateur and has no regrets. Some of the prettiest seating is outside, under the graceful pergola (you'd never guess you were surrounded by a parking lot), where champagne and shellfish are always on ice. Savor an appetizer of garlicky marinated frogs legs on roasted eggplant risotto with marinated tomatoes and tarragon before a main course of Sicilian-style grilled breaded quail with favas, roast shiitakes, and mustard thyme jus. To top it off, Scott has a winning way with unusual desserts.

Moderate

Among the Flowers Cafe. Mayhew Lane. ☎ **508/627-3233.** Main courses $5–$24. DC, MC, V. July–Aug daily 8am–10pm; May, June, Sept, and Oct 8am–4pm. Closed Nov–Apr. AMERICAN.

Everything's fresh and appealing at this outdoor cafe near the dock. Sit under the awning and you'll just catch a glimpse of the harbor. The breakfasts are the best around, and all the crepes, waffles, and eggs are also available at lunch. The comfort-food dinners (chicken and black pepper sauté served over pasta; butter- and crumb-crusted baked haddock with a sautéed lobster and shallot butter cream) are among the most affordable options in this pricey town. There's almost always a wait, not just because it's so picturesque, but because the food is homey, hearty, and kind on the wallet.

Chesca's. At the Colonial Inn, 38 N. Water St. ☎ **508/627-1234.** Main courses $13–$32. AE, MC, V. Reservations not accepted. Late June to early Sept daily 5:30–10pm; call for off-season hrs. Closed Nov–Mar. ITALIAN.

Chesca's is a solid entry in the yummy-food-at-reasonable-prices category, and you're sure to find all your Italian favorites here: paella (with roasted lobster and other choice seafoods), risotto (with roasted vegetables), and ravioli (with portobello mushrooms and asparagus). Smaller appetites can fill up on homemade soup and salad.

The Newes from America. At The Kelley House, 23 Kelley St. ☎ **508/627-4397.** Main courses $7–$10. AE, DC, MC, V. Daily 11am–11pm. PUB GRUB.

The pub grub is better than average at this subterranean tavern, built in 1742 and only recently resurrected. The decor may be more Edwardian than colonial, but those who come to quaff don't seem to care. Try a "rack" of five esoteric brews, or select a single brew to complement your meal, which might be a wood-smoked oyster "Island Poor Boy" sandwich with linguica relish, or an 18-ounce porterhouse steak.

Inexpensive

Main Street Diner, Old Post Office Square, off Main St. in the center of town (☎ **508/627-9337**), is open daily from 7am to 9pm year-round, and is a solid choice for a cheap breakfast or lunch, with no-nonsense selections that seem straight out of the 1950s.

OAK BLUFFS

Few can resist the two dozen enticing flavors of homemade ice cream at Mad Martha's, 117 Circuit Ave. (☎ **508/693-9151**) in the center of Oak Bluffs. President Clinton opted for a relatively restrained mango sorbet, which isn't to say you shouldn't go for a good old-fashioned hot fudge sundae.

Expensive

✪ **Sweet Life Cafe.** 63 Circuit Ave. ☎ **508/696-0200.** Reservations recommended. Main courses $19–$30. AE, DISC, MC, V. Mid-May to mid-Sept daily 5:30–10pm; call for off-season hrs. Closed Jan–Mar. NEW AMERICAN.

Locals are crazy about this new restaurant set in a restored Victorian house on upper Circuit Avenue. In season, the most popular seating is outside in the gaily lit garden. Fresh island produce is featured here, and seafood specials are an enticing draw. You can't go wrong with the roasted lobster with potato Parmesan risotto, roasted yellow beets, and smoked-salmon chive fondue.

Moderate

Jimmy Seas Pan Pasta Restaurant. 32 Kennebec Ave. ☎ **508/696-8550.** Reservations not accepted. Main courses $16–$23. No credit cards. May to mid-Oct daily 5–10pm; call for off-season hrs. MEDITERRANEAN.

If you're wondering why the luncheonette-level decor at this restaurant doesn't quite match up with menu prices, it's because chef Jimmy Cipolla gives his all to his one-pot pasta dishes, served right in the pan. Pasta comes in such intriguing guises as pumpkin tortellini in a creamy sage sauce. Everything's fair game for toppings, from chicken and shrimp with fresh pesto to swordfish in a balsamic vinaigrette. Portions are enormous.

Zapotec. 14 Kennebec Ave. (in the center of town). ☎ **508/693-6800.** Reservations not accepted. Main courses $14–$18. AE, MC, V. May–Oct daily 11:30am–2pm and 5–10pm. Closed Nov–Apr. MEXICAN/SOUTHWESTERN.

Look for the chili-pepper lights entwining the porch of this clapboard cottage: They're a beacon leading to tasty regional Mexican cuisine, from Mussels Oaxaca (with chipotle peppers, cilantro, lime, and cream) to Crab cakes Tulum (mixed with codfish and grilled peppers, and served with dual salsas), plus the standard chicken and beef burritos. Fish tacos are surprisingly tasty. There's also a small children's menu. A good mole is hard to find this far north; here you can accompany it with Mexico's unbeatable beers (including several rarely spotted north of the border).

Inexpensive

Papa's Pizza. 158 Circuit Ave. ☎ **508/693-1400.** Most items under $8. MC, V. June–Aug 11am–10pm; call for off-season hrs. PIZZA.

The pizza at this vintage-look parlor is on the tame side (so you won't have to pick off the arugula). Nevertheless, some say this is the best pizza on the Vineyard. For families with kids, it's ideal.

VINEYARD HAVEN (TISBURY)

Just around the corner from the Black Dog Tavern, on Water Street near the ferry terminal, is the **Black Dog Bakery** (☎ **508/693-4786**). The doors to this bakery open at 5:30am, and from midmorning on, it's elbow-room only as customers line up for freshly baked breads, muffins, and desserts. Don't forget some homemade doggie biscuits for your pooch.

The Quintessential Lobster Dinner

When the basics—a huge lobster and a sunset—are what you crave, visitors and locals alike head to **The Home Port** on North Road in Menemsha (☎ **508/645-2679**). At first glance, prices for the lobster dinners may seem a bit high, but note that they include an appetizer of your choice—go with the stuffed quahog—salad, amazing fresh-baked breads, a nonalcoholic beverage (remember, it's BYOB in these parts), and dessert. The decor is on the simple side, but who really cares? It's the scintillating harbor views that have drawn the faithful hordes to this family-friendly place for over 60 years. Locals not keen on summer crowds prefer to order their lobster dinners for pickup (half-price) at the restaurant door, then mosey on down to Menemsha Beach for a private sunset supper. Reservations are highly recommended and the fixed-price platters range from $20 to $36 (AE, MC, and V are accepted). The Home Port is open June through September, daily from 6 to 10pm; call for off-season hours. Closed mid-October through mid-April.

Expensive

Le Grenier. 96 Main St. (in the center of town), Vineyard Haven. ☎ **508/693-4906.** Reservations suggested. Main courses $19–$30. AE, DC, MC, V. July–Aug daily 5:30–10pm; call for off-season hrs. Closed Jan–Feb. FRENCH.

If Paris is the heart of France, Lyons is the belly—and that's where chef-owner Jean Dupon grew up on his Mama's hearty cuisine (she now helps out here, cooking lunch). Dupon has the moves down, as evidenced in such classics as steak au poivre, calf's brains Grenobloise with beurre noir and capers, or lobster Normande flambéed with calvados, apples, and cream. For an attic (the literal translation and the actual location), the restaurant is quite romantic, especially when aglow with hurricane lamps.

Moderate

✪ **Black Dog Tavern.** Beach St. Ext. (on the harbor), Vineyard Haven. ☎ **508/693-9223.** Reservations not accepted. Main courses $14–$25. AE, MC, V. June to early Sept Mon–Sat 7–11am, 11:30am–2:30pm, and 5–10pm; Sun 7am–1pm and 5–10pm; call for off-season hrs. NEW AMERICAN.

How does a humble harbor shack come to be a national icon? Location helps. So do cool T-shirts. Soon after *Shenandoah* captain, Robert Douglas, decided in 1971 that this hard-working port could use a good restaurant, influential vacationers, stuck waiting for the ferry, began to wander in to this saltbox to tide themselves over with a bit of "blackout cake" or peanut-butter pie. The rest is history, as smart marketing followed good word of mouth. The smartest of these was the invention of the signature "Martha's Vineyard whitefoot," a black Lab whose stalwart profile now adorns everything from baby's overalls to doggy bandannas. Still, visitors love this rough-hewn tavern, and it's not just hype that keeps them happy. The food is still home-cooking good—heavy on the seafood, of course (including grilled swordfish with banana, basil, and lime, and bluefish with mustard soufflé sauce). Though the lines grow ever longer (there can be a wait to get on the wait list!), nothing much has changed at this beloved spot. Eggs Galveston for breakfast at the Black Dog Tavern is still one of the ultimate Vineyard experiences.

WEST TISBURY, CHILMARK (INCLUDING MENEMSHA) & GAY HEAD

You might want to check out **Alley's General Store** on State Road in the center of West Tisbury (☎ **508/693-0088**), which has been in business since 1858, for picnic fixings and a bulletin board that offers a local view of noteworthy activities and events. Its neighbor, **Back Alley's Bakery & Deli,** has the best sandwiches in this neck of the woods.

Very Expensive

✪ **Red Cat Restaurant.** 688 State Rd., W. Tisbury. ☎ **508/693-9599.** Reservations recommended. Main courses $27–$32. MC, V. April–Oct daily 5–9:30pm; Nov–Mar Fri–Sun 6–9pm. NEW AMERICAN.

Chef Benjamin deForest may have honed his skills at Boston's formidable and sophisticated Four Seasons, but his laid-back island style comes naturally. From the exterior, this is a humble roadside shack, but inside you're likely to find Vineyard celebrities like Carly Simon. The menu varies weekly depending on available island-grown produce, locally raised lamb, and locally caught fish and shellfish. Try a tasty "fresca" of tomatoes, corn, and basil, for instance, or a showy dish involving a hefty 14-ounce pork chop sauced with calvados, pears, and blond raisins and topped with crispy sweet-potato curls. Come early—and midweek, if you can manage it. August is booked here 3 weeks in advance.

Theo's. At the Inn at Blueberry Hill, North Rd. (about 4 miles NE of Menemsha), Chilmark. ☎ 508/645-3322. Reservations required. Fixed-price $45–$70. AE, MC, V. late June–early Sept daily 6–9:30pm; May to late June and early Sept to Oct Thurs–Sun 6–9:30pm. Closed Nov–Apr. NEW AMERICAN.

Theo's is quite a combination: sufficiently formal yet soothing and relaxed, satisfying to all the senses, yet still health-conscious. Renowned local chef Robin Ledoux-Forte plucks each tender vegetable herself from the inn garden; her husband often hauls in the catch of the day. And while her preparations may be minimalist, she's awfully good at finding delicious combinations—surrounding noisettes of Menemsha swordfish, for instance, with sesame aïoli and a spicy Asian slaw. The lighting, cast by candles in blue goblets across rag-painted walls, creates an aura of unhurried comfort and a pervasive sense that all is as it should be, here in the unspoiled countryside.

Expensive

Lambert's Cove Country Inn. Lambert's Cove Rd. (off State Rd., about 3 miles W of Vineyard Haven), W. Tisbury. ☎ 508/693-2298. Reservations recommended. Main courses $24–$28. AE, MC, V. July–Aug daily 6–9pm; call for off-season hrs. NEW AMERICAN.

Whether you choose to dine on the wisteria-canopied outdoor patio, or indoors on candlelit lace tablecloths, the setting here is sheer romance. The country-house cuisine shows just enough quirks to tickle the tired palate. The domestic rack of lamb, for instance, is dressed with raspberry-blackberry mint vinegar; and the peppered pork tenderloin is garnished with green apple chutney and cabernet roasted red pepper cream.

Inexpensive

✪ **The Menemsha Bite.** Basin Rd. (off North Rd., about ¼ mile NE of the harbor), Menemsha. ☎ 508/645-9239. Most items under $15. No credit cards. June to mid-Sept daily 11am–9pm. Closed mid-Oct to June. SEAFOOD.

It's usually places like "The Bite" that we crave when we think of New England. This is your quintessential "chowdah" and clam shack, flanked by picnic tables. Run by two sisters employing their grandmother's recipes, this place makes superlative chowder, potato salad, fried fish, and so forth.

MARTHA'S VINEYARD AFTER DARK

BARS & CLUBS   All towns except for Oak Bluffs and Edgartown are dry and last call at bars and nighhtclubs is at midnight. Hit Oak Bluffs for the rowdiest bar scene and best nighttime street life. In Edgartown, you may have to hop around before you find the evening's most happening spot; for instance, you could happen upon an impromptu performance by Vineyard Sound, a grooving all male a cappella group.

The Vineyard's first and only brew pub, **Offshore Ale Company**, 30 Kennebec Ave., Oak Bluffs (☎ **508/693-2626**), is an attractively rustic place with a high ceiling, oak booths lining the walls, and peanut shells strewn on the floor. The beers range from crisp lagers and pale ales to sturdy stouts. Local acoustic performers entertain several nights a week in season, and there's no cover.

People have been known to dance on the tables at **David Ryans,** 11 N. Water St., Edgartown (☎ **508/627-4100**). You can hear the music blaring from Main Street. The bartender decides the canned tunes, from Sinatra to Smashing Pumpkins. There is no cover.

Located at Martha's Vineyard Airport, ✪ **Hot Tin Roof,** Airport Rd., Edgartown (☎ **508/693-1137**) is a nightclub in a hangar, first opened by Carly Simon in the 1970s. Over the years, Carly lost interest, and the club lost its cache. Now with backing from a handful of high-rollers, it's hip again. Notoriously stage-shy, Carly will sometimes take the mike herself, but is mostly content to attract an eclectic roster including such notables as Jimmy Cliff, Peter Wolf, and the Bacon Brothers (Kevin Bacon's band). Comedians command the stage on Tuesday. Cover varies. It's closed Nov–May.

Locals and visitors alike flock to **The Ritz Cafe,** 1 Circuit Ave. in the center of Oak Bluffs (☎ **508/693-9851**), a down-and-dirty blues club that features live music every night in season and on weekends year-round. The cover hovers around $2.

PERFORMING ARTS   Attend a concert, play, or lecture at the **Old Whaling Church,** 89 Main St., Edgartown (☎ **508/627-4442**). This magnificent 1843 Greek Revival church functions primarily as a 500-seat performing-arts center offering lectures and symposia, films, plays, and concerts. Such Vineyard luminaries as the actress Patricia Neal and the late Life photographer Alfred Eisenstaedt have taken their place at the pulpit, not to mention Livingston Taylor and Andre Previn, whose annual gigs here always sell out. Ticket prices vary; call for schedule.

The Vineyard Playhouse, 24 Church St., Vineyard Haven (☎ **508/696-6300** or 508/693-6450) is an intimate (112-seat) black-box theater, where Equity professionals put on a rich season of old favorites and challenging new work—followed, on summer weekends, by musical or comedic cabaret in the gallery/lounge. Children's theater selections are Saturdays at 10am. Townspeople often get involved in the outdoor Shakespeare production, a 3-week run starting in mid-July at the Tashmoo Overlook Amphitheatre about 1 mile west of town. June–Sept Tues–Sun at 8pm; call for off-season hrs.

The Wintertide Coffeehouse, Five Corners, Vineyard Haven (☎ **508/693-8830**) is a great hangout. It's a community-run, alcohol-free folkie haven that not only helps keep the natives entertained through the long, lonely winters, it has been hailed by Billboard as one of the country's top 10 coffeehouses. Lunch and dinner are served here, while some big names on the folk, blues, and jazz circuits (like Patti Larkin, Cheryl Wheeler, John Gorka) contribute the live soundtrack. You'll also catch an occasional comic, including the homegrown troupe W.I.M.P. (as in Wintertide Improv), as well as poetry and theater. Cover varies; call for schedule. Closed Mondays.

2 Nantucket

Once the whaling capital of the world, this tiny island, 30 miles off the coast of Cape Cod, still counts its isolation as a defining characteristic. Only 3½ by 14 miles, Nantucket is smaller and more insular than Martha's Vineyard. But charm-wise,

Nantucket stands alone, providing 20th-century luxury and amenities wrapped in an elegant 19th-century package.

Sophisticated Nantucket Town features bountiful stores, quaint inns, cobblestoned streets, interesting historic sites, and pristine beaches. The rest of the island is mainly residential, but for a couple of notable villages. Siasconset (nicknamed 'Sconset), on the east side of the island, is a tranquil community with picturesque, rose-covered cottages and a handful of businesses, including a *très cher* French restaurant. Sunset aficionados head to Madaket, on the west coast of the island, for evening splendor.

The lay of the land on Nantucket is rolling moors, heathlands, cranberry bogs, and miles of exquisite public beaches. The vistas are honeymoon-romantic: an operating windmill, three lighthouses, and a skyline dotted with church steeples. (And dog owners, rejoice: Nantucket is a very dog-friendly place where Fido can romp on the beach. The chamber of commerce, listed below can supply the names of several lodgings that accept pets.)

ESSENTIALS
GETTING THERE

BY FERRY   Ferry service to Nantucket is frequent and uncrowded, unless you're bringing a car in summer. But first-time visitors to the island will find a car more of a nuisance than a convenience, unless they're staying outside of Nantucket Town.

From Hyannis (South Street Dock), the **Steamship Authority** (☎ **508/477-8600;** from Nantucket, 508/228-3274) operates year-round ferry service (including cars, passengers, and bicycles) to Steamship Wharf in Nantucket. No advance reservations are required for passengers. But if you bring your car in summer, you must reserve months in advance—only six boats make the trip daily and they fill up fast. If you arrive without a reservation, there's no guarantee you'll get to the island that day. Arrive at least one hour before departure to avoid having your space being released to standbys. There is a $10 processing fee for cancelling reservations with two weeks notice. Total trip time is 2 hours 15 minutes. A round-trip fare with car costs $230 from mid-May to mid-October; $162 mid-March to mid-May and mid-October through December; and $118 from January to mid-March. For passengers, a round-trip ticket is $24 for adults, $12 for children 5 to 12, and $10 extra for bikes. Remember that parking at the ferry dock costs $8–$10 per day; you do not need to make parking reservations.

The Steamship Authority's new **Fast Ferry** (☎ **508/495-3278**) to Nantucket for passengers only takes one hour and runs 4 times a day in season. Unfortunately, this ride is not as smooth as Hy-line's 1-hour ferry; insiders have dubbed it the "vomit comet." But it is cheaper at $22 one-way ($40 round-trip) for adults, $16.50 one-way ($30 round-trip) for children 5 to 12. Parking costs $8 to $10. Passenger reservations are highly recommended.

Hy-Line Cruises (Ocean Street Dock; ☎ **888/778-2600** or 508/778-2600) also runs two types of passenger ferries from the Ocean Street Dock in Hyannis to Nantucket's Straight Wharf. The *Grey Lady II,* a year-round high-speed passenger catamaran, cuts trip time from 2 hours to 1, but costs significantly more. The one-way fare is $29 for adults ($52 round-trip), $23 for children 1 to 12 ($39 round-trip), and $5 extra for bicycles. The boat seats 70 and makes six round-trips daily to Nantucket in season—reserve in advance. From early May through October, Hy-Line runs its standard, 2-hour ferry service. A one-way ticket is $11 for adults, $5.50 for children ages 4 to 12, and $5 extra for bikes. On busy holiday weekends, the slow ferry fills up too, so you may want to order tickets in advance. Either way, you should buy or pick up your tickets at least half an hour before your boat leaves the dock. For all Hy-Line ferry service, it's also a good idea to reserve a parking spot in Hyannis in July and August; the all-day fee is $10.

Three of the six standard crossings (on the MV *Great Point*) have a first-class section with a private lounge, bathrooms, bar, and snack bar. One-way fare is $21 for adults and children. If you are taking the slow boat, you should definitely spend the extra $10 on first class at least one-way. The large, comfortable, cozy seats in first class are a far cry from the unforgiving benches otherwise available.

Hy-line's "Around the Sound" cruise, is a 1-day, round-trip excursion from Hyannis with stops in Nantucket and Martha's Vineyard that runs from early June to late September. The price is $33 for adults, $16.50 for children 1 to 12, and $15 extra for bikes.

From Martha's Vineyard, Hy-Line runs passenger-only ferries to Nantucket from early June to late September (there is no car-ferry service between the islands). The trip time from Oak Bluffs is 2 hours 15 minutes. The one-way fare is $11 for adults, $5.50 for children 1 to 12, and $5 extra for bikes.

From Harwich Port, you can avoid the summer crowds in Hyannis and board one of **Freedom Cruise Line**'s (☎ 508/432-8999) passenger-only ferries to Nantucket. From mid-May to mid-October, boats leave from Saquatucket Harbor in Harwich Port; the trip takes 1½ hours. A round-trip ticket is $34 for adults, $28 for children under 12, and $10 extra for bikes. Parking is free for the first 24 hours; $10 each day thereafter. Advance reservations are recommended.

BY AIR   You can fly into Nantucket Memorial Airport (☎ 508/325-5300), which is about 3 miles south of Nantucket Road on Old South Road. The airport's call letters, "ACK," are ubiquitous—they appear everywhere on T-shirts and bumper stickers. Flight time from Boston to Nantucket is about 35 minutes, about 15 minutes from Hyannis, and a little more than an hour from New York City airports.

Airlines providing service to Nantucket include: Business Express/Delta Connection (☎ 800/345-3400) from Boston (year-round) and New York (seasonally); Cape Air/Nantucket Air (☎ 800/352-0714) year-round from Hyannis, Boston, Martha's Vineyard, and New Bedford; Colgan Air (☎ 800/272-5488) year-round from La Guardia and Hyannis; Continental Express (☎ 800/525-0280) from Newark; Island Airlines (☎ 508/228-7575) year-round from Hyannis; and US Airways Express (☎ 800/428-4322) year-round from Boston.

Island Airlines and Nantucket Airlines (see above) both offer year-round charter service to the island.

GETTING AROUND

Nantucket is easily navigated on bike, moped, or foot, and also by shuttle buses or taxis. The chamber of commerce strongly suggests that visitors opt not to bring cars, in order to minimize congestion and environmental impact. If you're staying outside of Nantucket Town, however, or if you plan to explore the outer reaches of the island, you might want to bring your car or rent one here. Keep in mind, in-town traffic can reach gridlock in the peak season, and parking can be a nightmare.

BY BIKE & MOPED   When I head to Nantucket for a few days, I prefer to get around by bike. The island itself is relatively flat, and paved bike paths abound—they'll get you from Nantucket Town to Siasconset, Surfside, and Madaket. There are also many unpaved back roads to explore, which make mountain bikes a wise choice when pedaling around the island. Mopeds are also available, but be aware that local rules and regulations do exist and are strictly enforced. Mopeds are not allowed on sidewalks or bike paths. You'll need a driver's license to rent a moped, and state law requires that you wear a helmet.

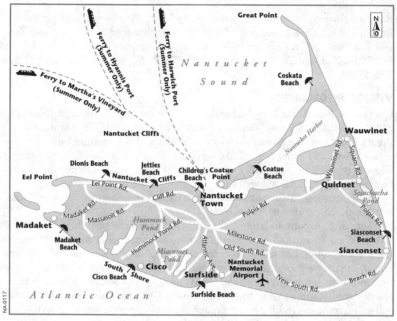

You can bring your own bike over on the ferries for a small additional charge. Otherwise, here's a list of shops that rent bikes and mopeds (all are within walking distance of the ferries): **Cook's Cycle Shop, Inc.,** 6 S. Beach St. (☎ **508/228-0800**); **Holiday Cycle,** 4 Chester St. (☎ **508/228-3644;** rents bikes only); **Nantucket Bike Shops,** at Steamboat Wharf and Straight Wharf (☎ **508/228-1999**); and **Young's Bicycle Shop** at Steamboat Wharf (☎ **508/228-1151;** also does repairs).

BY SHUTTLE BUS From June through September, inexpensive shuttle buses, with bike racks and wheelchair lifts, make a loop through Nantucket Town and to a few outlying spots; for routes and stops, contact the **Nantucket Regional Transit Authority** (☎ **508/228-7025;** www.nantucket.net/trans/nrta) or pick up a map and schedule at the **Visitors Service Center** on Federal Street or the **Chamber of Commerce Office** on Main Street. The cost is 50¢–$1.00, and exact change is required. A 3-day pass can be purchased at the Visitors Center for $10. Dogs are allowed on the bus as long as they are relatively clean and dry.

BY CAR I'd recommend a car only if you'll be here for more than a week, are staying outside Nantucket Town, or are unable to bike. Remember, though, that there are no in-town parking lots; parking is free but limited.

Here's a list of rental agencies on the island: Affordable Rentals of Nantucket, 6 S. Beach Rd. (☎ **508/228-3501**); Budget, at the airport (☎ **800/527-0700** or 508/228-5666); Hertz, at the airport (☎ **800/654-3131** or 508/228-9421); Nantucket Windmill Auto Rental, at the airport (☎ **800/228-1227** or 508/228-1227); Thrifty Car Rental, at the airport (☎ **508/325-4616**); and Young's 4 × 4 & Car Rental, Steamboat Wharf (☎ **508/228-1151**). A four-wheel-drive rental car will run you about $135–$170 per day (including oversand permits).

BY TAXI You'll find taxis (many are vans that can accommodate large groups or those traveling with bikes) waiting at the airport and at all ferry ports. During the summer, I recommend reserving a taxi in advance to avoid a long wait upon arrival.

Rates are flat fees, based on one person riding before 1am, with surcharges for additional passengers, bikes, and dogs. A taxi from the airport to Nantucket Town hotels will cost about $8. Recommendable cab companies on the island include: A-1 Taxi (☎ **508/228-3330**), Aardvark Cab (☎ **508/728-9999**), and All Point Taxi (☎ **508/228-5779**).

VISITOR INFORMATION

Contact the **Nantucket Island Chamber of Commerce** at 48 Main St., Nantucket, MA 02554 (☎ **508/228-1700;** www.nantucketchamber.org). When you arrive, you should also stop by the **Nantucket Visitors Service and Information Bureau** in Nantucket Town at 25 Federal St. (☎ **508/228-0925**), which is open daily July through Labor Day; weekdays Labor Day through June. There are also information booths at Steamboat Wharf and Straight Wharf.

For information on **current events and activities** around town, check the island's newspaper, the *Inquirer & Mirror.*

Nantucket Accommodations, Box 217, Nantucket, MA 02554 (☎ **508/228-9559**), a 26-year-old private service, arranges advance reservations for inns, cottages, guest houses, bed-and-breakfasts, and hotels. You can call up until the day of arrival, and they will arrange a booking based on your preferences. Nantucket Accommodations has access to 95% of the island's lodging facilities, in addition to houses and cottages available to rent by the night or week (as opposed to most realtors who will only handle rentals for 2 weeks or more). The charge for the service is $15—a fee assessed only when a reservation is made. The customer pays Nantucket Accommodations with any major credit card or check, and the service then pays the inn or hotel. Last-minute travelers should keep in mind that the **visitor's center** (see above) has a daily referral service for available rooms (not a booking service). They always have the most updated list of accommodations availability and cancellations.

ATMs can be difficult to locate on Nantucket. Nantucket **Bank** (☎ **508/228-0580**) has three locations: 2 Orange St., 104 Pleasant St., and the Airport lobby, all open 24 hours. **Pacific National Bank** has four locations: A&P Supermarket (next to the wharves), the Stop & Shop (open 24 hours seasonally), the Steamship Wharf Terminal, and the Pacific National Bank lobby (open during bank hours only).

For **emergencies,** Nantucket Cottage Hospital, 57 Prospect St. (☎ **508/228-1200**), is open 24 hours.

BEACHES

In distinct contrast to Martha's Vineyard, virtually all of Nantucket's 110-mile coastline is open to the public—on purpose.

- ♻ **Children's Beach.** This small beach is a protected cove just west of busy Steamship Wharf. Appealing to families, it has a park, playground, rest rooms, lifeguards, snack bar, and even a bandstand for free weekend concerts.
- **Cisco Beach.** About 4 miles from town, in the southwestern quadrant of the island (from Main Street, turn onto Milk Street, which becomes Hummock Pond Road), Cisco enjoys vigorous surf—great for the surfers who flock here, not so great for the waterfront homeowners. Rest rooms and lifeguards are available.
- **Coatue.** This fishhook-shaped barrier beach, on the northeastern side of the island at Wauwinet, is Nantucket's outback, accessible only by four-wheel–drive vehicles, water craft, or the very strong-legged. Swimming is strongly discouraged because of fierce tides.
- **Dionis Beach.** About 3 miles out of town (take the Madaket bike path to Eel Point Road), is Dionis, which enjoys the gentle sound surf and steep, picturesque

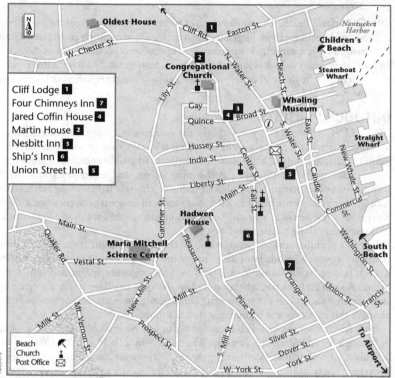

Beach
Church
Post Office

Cliff Lodge **1**
Four Chimneys Inn **7**
Jared Coffin House **4**
Martin House **2**
Nesbitt Inn **3**
Ship's Inn **6**
Union Street Inn **5**

bluffs. It's a great spot for swimming, picnicking, and shelling. Stick to the established paths to prevent further erosion. Lifeguards patrol here and rest rooms are available.

- **Jetties Beach.** Located about ½ mile west of Children's Beach on North Beach Street, Jetties is about a 20-minute walk, or even shorter bike or shuttle bus ride, or drive from town. There's a large parking lot, but it fills up early on summer weekends. It's another family favorite, for its mild waves, lifeguards, bathhouse and rest rooms, and relatively affordable restaurant, the Jetties Cafe & Grille. Facilities include the town tennis courts, volleyball nets, a skate park, and a playground; water-sports equipment and chairs are also available to rent. Every August, Jetties hosts an intense sandcastle competition, and the 4th of July fireworks are held here.

- **Madaket Beach.** Accessible by Madaket Road, the 6-mile bike path that runs parallel to it, and by shuttle bus, this westerly beach is narrow and subject to pounding surf and sometimes serious cross-currents. Unless it's a fairly tame day, you might content yourself with wading. It's the best spot on the island for admiring the sunset. Facilities include rest rooms, lifeguards, and mobile food service.

- **Siasconset Beach.** The easterly coast of 'Sconset is as pretty as the town itself and rarely, if ever, crowded, perhaps because of the water's strong sideways tow. You can reach it by car, shuttle bus, or by a less scenic and somewhat hilly (at least for Nantucket) 7-mile bike path. There are usually lifeguards on duty, but the closest facilities (rest rooms, grocery store, cafe) are back in the center of the village.

- ✪ **Surfside Beach.** Three miles south of town via a popular bike/skate path, broad Surfside—equipped with lifeguards, rest rooms, and a surprisingly accomplished little snack bar—is appropriately named and commensurately popular. It draws thousands of visitors a day in high season from college students to families, but the free-parking lot can only fit about 60 cars—you do the math, or better yet, ride your bike or take the shuttle bus.

OUTDOOR PURSUITS

BICYCLING   Several lovely, paved bike paths radiate out from the center of town to outlying beaches. The main paths run about 6.2 miles west to Madaket, 3.5 miles south to Surfside, and 8.2 miles east to Siasconset. To avoid backtracking from Siasconset, continue north through the charming village, and return on Polpis Road. Polpis does not yet have a bike path, but traffic is relatively light. Strong riders could do a whole circuit of the island in a day, but most will be content to combine a single route with a few hours at a beach. You'll find picnic benches and water fountains at strategic points along all the paths.

Lighthouse enthusiasts will want to stop by **Brant Point Light** at the end of Easton Street. It's a quick bike ride from the center of town. Located next to the Coast Guard station, this squat lighthouse is still used by boats maneuvering in and out of the harbor. A scenic spot to take a break and enjoy the view, you'll see ferries chugging by, and immense yachts competing for prize berths along the wharves. For newlyweds, a photo at this romantic and picturesque spot is a must.

For a free map of the island's bike paths (it also lists Nantucket's bicycle rules), stop by **Young's Bicycle Shop** at Steamship Wharf (☎ **508/228-1151**). It's definitely the best place for bike rentals. See "Getting Around," above for more bike-rental shops.

FISHING   For shellfishing, you'll need a permit from the **harbormaster's office** at 38 Washington St. (☎ **508/228-7260**). You'll see surf casters all over the island (no permit is required); for a guided trip, try Mike Mont of **Surf & Fly Fishing Trips** (☎ **508/228-0529**). Deep-sea charters heading out of Straight Wharf include Captain Robert DeCosta's *The Albacore* (☎ **508/228-5074**), Captain Josh Eldridge's *Monomoy* (☎ **508/228-6867**), and Captain David Martin's *Flicka* (☎ **508/325-4000**).

NATURE TRAILS   Through preservationist foresight, about one-third of Nantucket's 42 square miles are protected from development. Contact the **Nantucket Conservation Foundation** at 118 Cliff Rd. (☎ **508/228-2884**) for a $3 map of their holdings, which include the 205-acre Windswept Cranberry Bog (off Polpis Road), where bogs are interspersed amid hardwood forests, and a portion of the 1,100-acre Coskata-Coatue Wildlife Refuge, comprising the barrier beaches beyond Wauwinet. The **Trustees of the Reservations** (☎ **508/228-6799**), who oversee the bulk of this tract, offer 3-hour naturalist-guided tours via Ford Expedition out to the Great Point Lighthouse. The Maria Mitchell Association (see "Museums & Historic Landmarks," below) also sponsors guided birding and wildflower walks in season.

WATER SPORTS   **Nantucket Community Sailing** manages the concession at Jetties Beach (☎ **508/228-5358**), which offers lessons and rents out kayaks, sailboards, sailboats, and more. **Sea Nantucket,** on tiny Francis Street Beach off Washington Street (☎ **508/228-7499**), also rents kayaks; it's a quick sprint across the harbor to beautiful Coatue.

MUSEUMS & HISTORIC LANDMARKS

Jethro Coffin House. Sunset Hill Rd. (off W. Chester Rd., about ½ mile NW of town center). ☎ **508/228-1894.** Admission $3 adults, $2 children 5–14; also included in Nantucket

Historical Association pass ($10 adults, $5 children). June–Sept daily 10am–5pm; call for off-season hrs. Closed mid-Oct to Apr.

Built around 1696, this saltbox is the oldest building left on the island. A National Historical Landmark, it is also known as "The Horseshoe House" for the brick design on its central chimney. It was struck by lightning and severely damaged (in fact, nearly cut in two) in 1987, prompting a long-overdue restoration. Dimly lit by leaded glass diamond-pane windows, it's filled with period furniture such as latched ladder-back chairs and a clever trundle bed on wooden wheels. Nantucket Historical Association docents will fill you in on all the related lore.

Hadwen House. 96 Main St. (at Pleasant St., a few blocks SW of town center). ☎ **508/228-1894.** Admission $3 adults, $2 children 5–14; also included in Nantucket Historical Association pass ($10 adults, $5 children). June–Sept daily 10am–5pm; call for off-season hrs. Closed mid-Oct to Apr.

During Nantucket's most prosperous years, whaling merchant Joseph Starbuck built the "Three Bricks" (nos. 93, 95, and 97 Main St.) for his three sons. His daughter married successful businessman William Hadwen, owner of the candle factory that is now the Whaling Museum, and Hadwen built this grand Greek Revival home across the street from his brothers-in-law in 1845. Although locals (mostly Quakers) were scandalized by the opulence, the local outrage spurred Hadwen on, and he decided to make the home even grander than he had at first intended. The home soon became a showplace for entertaining the Hadwens many wealthy friends. Soon after, Hadwen built the matching home next door for his niece, and it is assumed that he enjoyed using its grand ballroom for his parties too. The Historical Association has done a magnificent job restoring the home and furnishing it with period furniture, fabrics, porcelains, wallpapers, and other decorative accessories that were thought to be in the home when the Hadwens lived there. The gardens are maintained in period style by the Nantucket Garden Club.

The Maria Mitchell Science Center. 2 Vestal St. (at Milk St., about ½ mile SW of town center). ☎ **508/228-9198.** www.mmo.org. Admission $7 adults, $4 children 6 to 14, $5 seniors. Early June to late Aug Tues–Sat 10am–4pm; call for off-season hrs.

This is a group of buildings organized and maintained in honor of distinguished astronomer, Vassar professor, and Nantucket native Maria Mitchell (1818–89). The science center consists of astronomical observatories, with a lecture series, children's science seminars, and stellar observation opportunities (when the sky is clear).

The Hinchman House at 7 Milk St. is home to the Museum of Natural Science, and offers evening lectures, bird watching, wildflower and nature walks, and children's nature classes. The Mitchell House at 1 Vestal St., the astronomer's birthplace, features a children's history series and adult-artisan seminars, and has wildflower and herb gardens. The Science Library is at 2 Vestal St. and the tiny, child-oriented aquarium is at 28 Washington St. The Loines Observatory on Milk Street Extension has open nights when skies are clear.

Nantucket Lifesaving Museum. Polpis Rd. ☎ **508/228-1855.** Admission $3 adults, $2 children. Mid-June to mid-Oct daily 9:30am–4:30pm.

Housed in a replica of the Nantucket Lifesaving station (the original serves as a youth hostel), the museum has loads of interesting exhibits, including historic photos and newspaper clippings, as well as one of the last remaining Massachusetts Humane Society surfboats and its horse-drawn carriage.

✪ **Whaling Museum.** 13 Broad St. (in the center of town). ☎ **508/228-1894.** Admission $5 adults, $3 children 5–14; also included in the Nantucket Historical Association pass ($10 adults, $5 children). June to Sept daily 10am–5pm; call for off-season hrs.

Housed in a former spermaceti (a waxy fluid extracted from sperm whales) candle factory, this museum is a must-visit; if not for the awe-inspiring skeleton of a 43-foot finback whale (stranded in the 1960s), then for the exceptional collections of scrimshaw and nautical art. Check out the action painting, *Ship* Spermo *of Nantucket in a Heavy Thunder-Squall on the Coast of California 1876,* executed by a captain who survived the storm. The price of admission includes daily lectures on the brief and colorful history of the industry, like the beachside "whalebecue" feasts that natives and settlers once enjoyed.

CRUISES

Built in 1926, the *Christina* at Slip 19, Straight Wharf (☎ 508/325-4000) is a classic solid mahogany catboat. The boat makes seven 1½-hour trips daily in season, and the sunset trips tend to sell out a day or two in advance. Catboats were invented on the waters of Nantucket Sound by the Crosbys of Osterville, who still run a thriving boatyard across the Sound in that village. The sturdy sailboat was said to come about "quick like a cat," thus the sobriquet. Pricewise, a sail around the harbor on the *Christina* ($15 per person; $20 per person for sunset sails) is probably the best entertainment bargain on Nantucket. Reservations are recommended. No sailings November through April.

The *Endeavor* (Nantucket Whaleboat Adventures) at Slip 15, Straight Wharf (☎ 508/228-5585) is a spirited 31-foot replica Friendship sloop, ideal for jaunts across the harbor into Nantucket Sound. Skipper James Genthner will gladly drop you off for a bit of sunbathing or beachcombing. New to his fleet is a faithfully re-created whaleboat, *The Wanderer*—crews of six can recapture the arduous experience of chasing a whale—minus the target, of course. Rates start at $15 for a 1-hour sail; reservations are recommended. No sailings from November through April.

In summer, **Nantucket Harbor Cruises** at Slip 11, Straight Wharf (☎ 508/228-1444) offers lobstering demos on the *Anna W. II,* a lobster-boat-turned-pleasure-barge, and passengers sometimes get to take home the proceeds. There's also a 1-hour ice-cream cruise leaving at 3:30pm daily. In winter, the boat runs seal-sighting cruises along the jetty. In between seasons, Capt. Bruce Cowan takes groups out just to view the lovely shoreline. Rates are $15 to $25 adults, $10 to $20 for children 4 to 12; call for reservations. Closed May.

SHOPPING

All of the shops listed below are located right in the center of Nantucket Town.

ANTIQUES/COLLECTIBLES　**Tonkin of Nantucket,** 33 Main St. (☎ 508/228-9697), is a perennially well-stocked antique store specializing in brass and silver knickknacks and antique Nantucket lightship baskets—those peculiar woven purses you see dangling from tanned, moneyed arms.

ART & CRAFTS　The **Artists' Association of Nantucket** has the widest selection of work by locals, and their gallery at 19 Washington St. (☎ 508/228-0294) is quite impressive. Like many seaside resort communities, Nantucket tends to foster pretty imagery more than serious art; however, **Main Street Gallery,** 2 S. Water St. (☎ 508/228-2252), offers more substantial work to savor. Poke your head in **Sailor's Valentine** in the Macy Warehouse on lower Main Street (☎ 508/228-2011) for a surprising mix of "outsider art" and new versions of the namesake craft, a boxed design of colorful shells, which 19th-century sailors used to bring back from the Caribbean for their sweethearts at home.

FASHION　Martha's Vineyard may have spawned "Black Dog" fever, but this island boasts the inimitable "Nantucket reds"—cotton clothing that starts out tomato-red and washes out to salmon-pink. The fashion originated at **Murray's Toggery Shop,** 62 Main St. (☎ **800/368-2134** or 508/228-0437). Roland Hussey Macy, founder of Macy's, got his start here in the 1830s.

GIFTS/HOME DECOR   A casual counterpart to its Madison Avenue boutique, **Erica Wilson Needle Works,** 25-27 Main St.(☎ **508/228-9881**), spills over with needlepoint kits, richly textured sweaters, sweet-smocked baby clothes, and home accessories. Resembling an old-fashioned pharmacy, The **Fragrance Bar,** 5 Centre St. (☎ **800/223-8660** or 508/325-4740), stocks some 400 essential oils with which they can duplicate designer scents or customize blends. Centrally located **Nantucket Looms,** 16 Main St. (☎ **508/228-1908**), is an elegant shop featuring beautifully textured woven items as well as fine furniture and gifts.

TOYS   **The Toy Boat,** Straight Wharf (☎ **508/228-4552**), is keen on creative toys that are also educational (delighted beneficiaries will never suspect).

WHERE TO STAY

As with the Cape and the Vineyard, I've only given summer rates here, since Nantucket is so seasonal. However, if you do visit in the off-season, you can find substantial discounts on hotel rates at any of the places that remain open. But lodging rates on Nantucket are at high season levels during the popular Christmas Stroll in December and Daffodil Festival in April.

VERY EXPENSIVE

✪ **Cliffside Beach Club.** Jefferson Ave. (off Spring St.), Nantucket, MA 02554. ☎ **508/ 228-0618.** Fax 508/325-4735. www.cliffsidebeach.com. 27 units, 1 cottage. TV TEL. Summer $310–$500 double; $630–$1,200 suites; $610 apt; $800 cottage. Rates include continental breakfast. AE. Closed mid-Oct to late May.

Located right on the beach and within walking distance (about a mile) from town, this is surely the premier lodging on the island. It may not be fancy as some, but there's a sublime beachy-ness to the whole setup, from the simply decorated rooms, the cheerful, youthful staff, the sea of antique wicker in the clubhouse and, of course, the blue, yellow, and green umbrellas lined up on the beach. All rooms have such luxuries as French milled soaps, large, thick towels, and exceptional linens. Each room has a minifridge; most have air-conditioning. Turndown service is provided. Guests receive an umbrella, chairs and beach towels. A very good continental breakfast is served in the large clubhouse room, its beamed ceilings draped with colorful quilts. Lucky guests on the fourth of July get a front-row seat for the fireworks staged at Jetties Beach nearby.

   Dining/Diversions: The Galley Restaurant is an elegant French bistro specializing in seafood and sunsets.

   Amenities: There is a new exercise facility with Cybex equipment and an trainer on staff. There's also an indoor hydrotherapy spa, steam saunas, and a climate controlled massage room. These services are complimentary to guests.

Summer House. 17 Ocean Ave., Siasconset, MA 02564. ☎ **508/257-4577.** Fax 508/ 257-4590. 10 units. A/C TEL. Summer $325–$525 double. Rates include continental breakfast. AE, MC, V. Closed Nov–Apr.

Romance incarnate, these former fishing shacks, entwined with roses, fragrant honeysuckle, and ivy, hug a bluff overlooking the sea. The cottages encircle a lush, shady lawn, dotted with Adirondack chairs. At the bottom of the bluff is a sparkling pool, where lunch is served; beyond it are miles of scarcely populated beach. The cottages are outfitted with charming English country antiques and luxurious linens, and bathrooms in all but one unit have a marble Jacuzzi. All rooms have hair dryers and minifridges; some have kitchenettes.

Dining/Diversions: On the premises is a celebrated restaurant of the same name serving cutting-edge cuisine (see "Where to Dine," below) with live piano music nightly and a hopping bar scene. Lunch is served by the pool and under the tent overlooking the ocean. From 3–6pm, there's a sushi bar set up by the pool in season.

Amenities: The concierge can arrange for services like in-room massage and babysitting. There's also turndown service.

✪ **The Wauwinet.** 120 Wauwinet Rd. (about 8 miles E of Nantucket center), Wauwinet, MA 02554. ☎ **800/426-8718** or 508/228-0145. Fax 508/228-6712. www.wauwinet.com. E-mail: email@wauwinet.com. 25 units, 5 cottages. A/C TV TEL. Summer $330–$790 double; $610–$1,290 cottage. Rates include full breakfast and afternoon port. AE, DC, MC, V. Closed Nov to mid-Apr.

In 1988, Stephen and Jill Karp renovated this ultra-deluxe retreat for roughly $3 million, and it has earned several nicknames, including "The Ultimate," or, as the staff has been known to joke, the "We Want It." With 25 rooms in the main building (which started out as a restaurant in 1850) and 10 more in 5 modest-looking shingled cottages, the complex can only hold about 80 spoiled guests, tended to by 100 staffers. Each of the lovely rooms—all provided with a cozy nook from which to gaze out across the water—has an individual decorating scheme, with pine armoires, plenty of wicker, exquisite Audubon prints, handsome fabrics, and antique accessories. Extras include hair dryers, irons/ironing boards, Egyptian cotton bathrobes, and bottled water. An additional perk is a personalized set of engraved notecards. All rooms have CD players and VCRs, and if you order up a video from the extensive (500 videos) library, it is delivered on a tray by a steward in a 1930s usher outfit with a couple of boxes of complimentary hot popcorn. That's service.

Dining: Guests can dine in the highly acclaimed Topper's restaurant (see "Where to Dine," below).

Amenities: The staff goes to great lengths to please, ferrying you into town, for instance, in a 1936 "Woody," or dispatching you on a 21-foot launch across the bay to your own private strip of beach. The inn is the last stop on an 8-mile road to nowhere (actually, a wildlife sanctuary), and it boasts several clay tennis courts with a pro shop and teaching pro, a croquet lawn, a platform for nearly life-size "beach chess," and plenty of boats and bikes to borrow.

EXPENSIVE

✪ **Four Chimneys.** 38 Orange St. (about ¼ mile E of Main St.), Nantucket, MA 02554. ☎ **508/228-1912.** Fax 508/325-4864. 10 units. A/C. Summer $165–$275 double. Rates include continental breakfast. AE, MC, V. Closed Nov to mid-Apr.

The Four Chimneys is a bed-and-breakfast of rare charm, stylishly outfitted with a grand piano in the front parlor and a crystal-chandelier in the dining room. For privacy-seekers, there's a beautiful little Japanese garden in back. Authentic antiques, including some stunning colonial chests, adorn the bedrooms, where beds have down comforters. Some rooms have fireplaces and/or terraces. There's nightly turndown service, when a Godiva chocolate is placed on your pillow. The elaborate continental breakfast is served outside on the porch, in the double drawing room, or cheerfully delivered to your room.

Jared Coffin House. 29 Broad St. (at Centre St.), Nantucket, MA 02554. ☎ **800/248-2405** or 508/228-2400. Fax 508/228-8549. www.jaredcoffinhouse.com. E-mail: jchouse@nantucket.net. 60 units. TV TEL. Summer $160–$225 double. Rates include full breakfast. AE, CB, DC, DISC, MC, V. Dogs allowed.

Built to the specs of the social-climbing Mrs. Coffin in 1845, this grand brick manse was renovated to its original splendor by the Nantucket Historical Trust. It is now the social center of town, as well as a mecca for visitors. Accommodations range from well-priced singles (rare in these parts) to roomy suites. Rooms in the neighboring annex houses are equally grand (but the front rooms can be quite noisy). The staff is extremely helpful and gracious. At breakfast, the cranberry pancakes are worth the wait, which can be substantial.

Union Street Inn. 7 Union St. (in the center of town), Nantucket, MA 02554. ☎ **800/ 225-5116** or 508/228-9222. www.union-street-inn.com. E-mail: unioninn@nantucket.net. 12 units. A/C TV. Summer $145–$210 double; $245 suite. Rates include full breakfast. AE, MC, V. Open year-round.

Sophisticated innkeepers Deborah & Ken Withrow have a terrific location for their historic property, just steps from Main Street but in a quiet, residential section of town. Ken's experience in big hotels shows in the amenities (like hair dryers) and full concierge service offered here. Over the past few years, the Union Street Inn has been completely restored, highlighting its period charms. Many rooms have canopied or four-poster beds; some have working fireplaces. Don't miss the superb full breakfast, served on the garden patio.

MODERATE

✪ **Cliff Lodge.** 9 Cliff Rd. (a few blocks from the center of town), Nantucket, MA 02554. ☎ **508/228-9480.** Fax 508/228-6308. 11 units, 1 apt. A/C TV TEL. Summer $130–$170 double; $255 apt. Rates include continental breakfast. MC, V. Open year-round.

Debby and John Bennett have freshened up this popular inn with their own countri-fied style. The result is a charmer: sunny, cheerful rooms with colorful quilts and splatter-painted floors. Though the inn is vintage 18th century, there is not a cobweb to be found in this immaculate setting. For continental breakfast, there are home-baked breads and muffins, which are served in the sunny garden. Chat with Debby for a wealth of island info and the latest goings-on, then climb up to the roof walk for a bird's-eye view of the town and harbor.

Martin House Inn. 61 Centre St. (between Broad and Chester sts.), Nantucket, MA 02554. ☎ **508/228-0678.** Fax 508/325-4798. www.nantucket.net/lodging/martinn. E-mail: martinn@nantucket.net. 13 units, 5 with shared bathroom. Summer $85–$195 double. Rates include continental breakfast. AE, MC, V.

This is one of the most affordable B&Bs in town, but also one of the most stylish, with a formal parlor and dining rooms and a spacious side porch, complete with hammock. The garret single rooms with a shared bath are a real deal. Other higher priced rooms have four-posters and fireplaces.

The Ship's Inn. 13 Fair St., Nantucket, MA 02554. ☎ **508/228-0040.** 12 units, 2 with shared bathroom. TV TEL. Summer $125–$150 double. Rates include continental breakfast. AE, DISC, MC, V. Closed mid-Oct to late May.

This pretty historic inn is on a quiet side street, just slightly removed from Nantucket's center. Rooms are comfortable, spacious, and charming. There is also a good variety of bedding situations here, like single rooms and twin beds. The restaurant downstairs holds its own.

INEXPENSIVE

The Nesbitt Inn. 21 Broad St., Box 1019, Nantucket, MA 02554. ☎ **508/228-0156** or 508/228-2446. 13 units (all with shared bathroom), 2 apts. Summer $65 single, $80–$105 double; apts $1,000 weekly. Rates include continental breakfast. MC, V.

This Victorian-style inn in the center of town has been run by the same family for 95 years. Though a bit tired, this place is certainly a bargain for Nantucket. Rooms have sinks, while common bathrooms are in the hall. There's a friendly, family-oriented atmosphere to the inn, and beloved innkeepers Dolly and Nobby Noblit are salt-of-the-earth Nantucketers, who will cheerfully fill you in on Island lore.

WHERE TO DINE
VERY EXPENSIVE

Chanticleer Inn. 9 New St., Siasconset. ☎ **508/257-6231.** Reservations recommended. Jacket required. Main courses $32–$40; fixed-price dinner $70. AE, MC, V. Mid-May to mid-Oct Tues–Sun noon–2pm and 6:30–9:30pm. Closed mid-Oct to mid-May. FRENCH.

A contender for the priciest restaurant on the Cape and Islands, this rose-covered cottage-turned-French-auberge has fans who don't begrudge a penny and who insist they'd have to cross an ocean to savor the likes of the classic cuisine that has been served here since the mid-1970s. Just to highlight a few glamorous options on the prix-fixe menu: **gâteau de grenouilles aux pommes de terre** (a frog's legs "cake" in a potato crust); *tournedos de lotte marinée au gingembre, sauce au rhum, croquettes d'ail* (a gingered monkfish scaloppini with a lemon-rum sauce and sweet garlic fritters); and *pain perdu, glace au chocolat blanc, coulis d'abricots secs* (a very classy bread pudding with white-chocolate ice cream and apricot sauce). The restaurant also has a stellar wine cellar stocked with 38,000 bottles.

✪ **Club Car.** 1 Main St. ☎ **508/228-1101.** Reservations recommended. Main courses $27–$36. MC, V. July–Aug daily 11am–3pm and 6–10pm; call for off-season hrs. Closed Jan–May. CONTINENTAL.

For decades one of the top restaurants on Nantucket, this posh venue is also popular with locals, many of whom particularly enjoy beef-Wellington night on autumn Sundays. Executive chef Michael Shannon is chummy with Julia Child, and the menu has classic French influences. Interesting offerings include a first course of Japanese octopus in the style of Bangkok (with mixed hot peppers, tiparos fish sauce, mint, cilantro, lime, and tomato concassé) and a main course of roast rack of lamb Club Car (with fresh herbs, honey mustard glaze, minted Madeira sauce). Some nights, seven-course tasting menus are available at a fixed price of $65 per person. The lounge area is within an antique first-class car from the old Nantucket railroad; you'll want to have a drink while cuddled in the red leather banquets before or after dinner. Lunch at the Club Car is a great deal for those on a budget; all that atmosphere and hearty food arrive without the soaring prices.

✪ **The Summer House.** 17 Ocean Ave., Siasconset. ☎ **508/257-9976.** Reservations recommended. Main courses $28–$42. AE, MC, V. July–Aug daily 12:30–3:30pm and 6–10pm; Closed mid-Oct to Apr. NEW AMERICAN.

The classic Nantucket atmosphere, 'Sconset-style, distinguishes this fine dining experience from the many others on the island: wicker and wrought iron, roses and honeysuckle. A pianist plays nightly—often Gershwin standards. The pounding Atlantic Ocean is just over the bluff. Service is wonderful, and the food is excellent, though expensive. Chef Carl Keller has taken over the reigns of the kitchen here, but the signature dishes remain. Specialties of the house include fresh, locally caught seafood with island vegetables delicately prepared and stylishly presented. Tempting appetizers include the grilled portobello mushrooms served with a pungent Stilton basil terrine; and the house smoked salmon frisée with avocado salsa. The distinctive main courses are roast saddle of lamb with rosemary caponatina port and feta mashed potatoes; the unusual and tasty lobster cutlets with coconut jasmine risotto timbale and mint tomato relish; and the grilled rib-eye with wild mushrooms, foie gras, and cabernet. Desserts are bountiful. Order the blueberry pie if it's in season.

✪ **Topper's.** At The Wauwinet, 120 Wauwinet Rd. (off Squam Rd.), Wauwinet. ☎ **508/228-8768.** Reservations recommended. Jacket requested. Main courses $29–$52. AE, DC, MC, V. May–Oct Mon–Sat noon–2pm and 6–9:30pm, Sun 11am–2pm and 6–9:30pm. Closed Nov–Apr. REGIONAL/NEW AMERICAN.

This 1850s restaurant—part of a secluded resort—is a tastefully subdued knockout, with wicker armchairs, splashes of chintz, and a two-tailed mermaid to oversee a chill-chasing fire. Try to sit at one of the cozy banquets if you can. New chef Chris Freeman continues a tradition of the finest regional cuisine: In his hands, lobster becomes a major event (it's often sautéed with champagne beurre blanc), and he also has a knack for unusual delicacies such as arctic char. Those are Gruyère and chive biscuits in the bread basket, and you need to try one. Other recommendable house specialties include the lobster and crab cakes appetizer and the roasted muscovy duck breast. Desserts are fanciful and fabulous: Consider the toasted brioche with poached pears and caramel sauce. The Wauwinet runs a complimentary launch service to the restaurant for lunch and dinner; it leaves from Straight Wharf at 11am and 5pm, takes 1 hour, and also makes the return trip.

EXPENSIVE

DeMarco. 9 India St. (between Federal and Centre sts.). ☎ **508/228-1836.** Reservations recommended. Main courses $18–$30. AE, MC, V. June to mid-Oct daily 6–10pm; call for off-season hrs. Closed mid-Oct to mid-May. NORTHERN ITALIAN.

This frame house carved into a cafe/bar and loft pioneered haute northern Italian cuisine on the island. A forward-thinking menu and attentive service ensure a superior meal, which might include *antipasto di salmone* (house smoked salmon rollantini, lemon herb cream cheese, cucumber and endive salad with chive vinaigrette) and the delicate *capellini con scampi* (capellini with rock shrimp, tomato, black olives, capers, and hot pepper).

✪ **India House Restaurant.** 37 India St. (about ⅛ mile W of Centre St.). ☎ **508/228-9043.** Reservations recommended. Main courses $17–$35. AE, DISC, MC, V. Late May to Nov, daily seatings at 6:30 and 9:30pm; call for off-season hrs. Closed Jan–Mar. NEW AMERICAN.

Three small dining rooms, with listing floors and low-slung ceilings, make a lovely, intimate setting for superb candlelit dinners. A longtime favorite dish is lamb India House, enrobed in rosemary-studded breading and cloaked in béarnaise sauce. However, new influences have recently surfaced: for example, Asian (as demonstrated in the 12-spice salmon sashimi with garlic and mint soy oil) and Southwestern (Texas wildboar ribs with grilled pineapple barbecue sauce). The menu changes biweekly, so you can be sure that this wonderful restaurant won't be resting on its well-deserved laurels.

✪ **Òran Mór.** 2 S. Beach St. (in the center of town). ☎ **508/228-8655.** Reservations recommended. Main courses $18–$38. AE, MC, V. May–Dec daily 6–10pm, Sun 10am–2pm; call for off-season hrs. INTERNATIONAL.

Chef Peter Wallace, formerly of Topper's at the Wauwinet, has taken over at this second-floor waterfront venue, long a beloved neighborhood restaurant. The unusual name is Gaelic and means "great song," which is the name of Wallace's favorite single-malt scotch. Climb up the stairs of this historic building and prepare yourself for a somewhat extravagant dining experience. (There's a seven-course fixed-price tasting menu here for $50, $80 with wine.) The menu changes nightly and there are always some surprising and unusual choices. Appetizers like carpaccio and tartare of beef with truffle oil are fancy even by Nantucket standards. I wasn't there the night baby moose leg was on the menu but a friend reported that it was tender and delicious. Some other winning entrees are grilled yellowfin tuna with a chipotle tomato broth; and grilled breast and long cooked leg of duck with black barley, which some say is the best duck dish on the island. An excellent sommelier is on hand to assist wine lovers.

21 Federal. 21 Federal St. (in the center of town). ☎ **508/228-2121.** Reservations recommended. Main courses $24–$34. MC, V. June–Oct daily 11:30am–2pm and 6–10pm; call for off-season hrs. Closed Jan–Mar. NEW AMERICAN.

Your agreeable host Chick Walsh has created an institution popular with locals, particularly for the happening bar scene. With 4 years of *Wine Spectator* awards to their credit, each night about 11 carefully selected wines available by the glass are featured. Chef Russell Jaehnig seems to get better and more refined every year. Don't fill up on the cheddar-cheese bread sticks: There's a lot of good food to come. Try the melt-in-your-mouth appetizer, tuna tartare with wasabi crackers and cilantro aïoli. Order a side of mashed potatoes if they don't come with your main course. Not that you'll need more food; portions are generous. The fish entrees are most popular here, although you might opt for the fine breast of duck accompanied by pecan wild rice and shiitake mushrooms. I prefer the pan-crisped salmon with champagne cabbage and beet butter sauce or the pepper-seared yellowfin tuna with cucumber and tamari butter, which have been staples on the menu for years. The small selection of desserts are tantalizing and sinful.

MODERATE

Black-Eyed Susans. 10 India St. (in the center of town). ☎ **508/325-0308.** Reservations accepted for 6pm seating only. Main courses $14–$19. No credit cards. Apr–Nov daily 7am–1pm and Mon–Sat 6–10pm. ETHNIC ECLECTIC.

This is supremely exciting food in a funky bistro atmosphere. It's a small venue and popular with locals, so it's packed. Reservations are accepted for the 6pm seating only, and these go fast. Others must line up outside the restaurant (the line starts forming around 5:30pm), and the hostess will assign you a time to dine; you'll have a better choice if you don't mind sitting at the counter. Inside, it may seem a bit overly cozy, but that's all part of the charm. If you want to watch adventurous Chef Jeff Worster from the counter in front of the open kitchen, beware of flying spices. The menu is in constant flux, as the chef's mood and influences change biweekly. I was last there during an Indian and Southern–inspired moment, and we relished tandoori chicken on khichuri with pineapple mint raita; and Dos Equis beer–battered catfish quesadilla with mango slaw, hoppin' johns, and jalapeño. We mopped it up with the delectable organic sourdough bread. Black-Eyed Susans has no liquor license, so you must BYOB.

Kendrick's. 5 Chestnut St. ☎ **508/228-9156.** Reservations recommended. Main courses $16–$29. AE, DISC, MC, V. June–Sept Mon–Fri Mon–Sat 7:30–11:30am, Sun 9am–2pm; daily 6–10pm; call for off-season hours. Closed Jan to late Apr. NEW AMERICAN.

Owners Kendrick Anderson and Stephanie Silva's restaurant concentrates on high quality, fresh ingredients, simple preparations, and ample portions. The menu is small but diverse; a mixed vegetarian-carnivore couple will be satisfied here. Every night there is a tofu vegetarian dish, a steak dish, and a few fish specials, in addition to other choices. Dishes tend to have strong international influences: Grilled rare tuna is served with bok choy and udon noodle cake, and rack of lamb comes with eggplant turbans, feta, and couscous. In one of Nantucket's shingled historic inns in the center of town, Kendrick's has three small dining rooms. The bar menu served till 11pm (with prices under $15) is popular with the late-night crowd.

Le Languedoc Cafe. 24 Broad St. ☎ **508/228-2552.** Reservations not accepted for cafe; reservations recommended for main dining room. Main courses $9–$19. AE, MC, V. Daily 6–10pm; Tues–Sun noon–2pm. Closed Jan–Mar. NEW AMERICAN.

There's also an expensive dining room upstairs but I prefer the casual bistro atmosphere downstairs and out on the terrace. There's a clubby feel here—locals come and go, greeting one another and enjoying themselves. Soups are superb, as are Angus-steak burgers. More elaborate dishes include the roasted tenderloin of pork stuffed with figs and pancetta, berlotti bean stew, and the napoleon of grilled tuna, tapenade, and roasted vegetables, with pesto sauce.

Obadiah's. 2 India St. (between Federal and Centre sts.). ☎ **508/228-4430.** Main courses $15–$32. AE, MC, V. Mid-June to mid-Oct daily 5:30–10pm. Closed late Sept to mid-June. REGIONAL AMERICAN.

Finding a reasonably priced restaurant in Nantucket is no mean feat. But this one is a gem. You can eat outdoors, on a lantern-lit patio, or in the atmospheric brick-walled basement of the 1840s house. The cuisine is not all that daring, but reliably and substantially good. Portions are generous; service is swift and friendly. Favorites on the menu include the unique lobster chowder, Jonah crab cakes, and native lobster stuffed with shrimp, scallops, and served with a white-wine cream sauce. For the finale, try Obadiah's big, bad dessert, a dark-chocolate cake with mocha frosting topped with walnuts, coconut, and whipped cream.

INEXPENSIVE

Arno's. 41 Main St. ☎ **508/228-7001.** Reservations recommended. Main courses $12–$19. AE, DISC, MC, V. Apr–Dec 8am–9pm; call for off-season hrs. Closed Jan–Mar. ECLECTIC.

A storefront facing the passing parade of Main Street, this institution packs surprising style between its bare-brick walls. The internationally influenced menu yields tasty, bountiful platters for breakfast, lunch, and dinner. Specialties include grilled sirloin steaks and fresh grilled fish. Generous servings of specialty pasta dishes like chicken and linguiça radiatore are featured nightly.

Espresso Cafe. 40 Main St. ☎ **508/228-6930.** Most items under $10. No credit cards. Late May to Nov daily 7:30am–10pm; Nov–May 7:30am–4:30pm. INTERNATIONAL.

This reliable self-service cafe is in the heart of town. Pastries, sandwiches, and international dishes are affordably priced and delicious, and the cafe has some of the best coffee in town (the "Nantucket" and "Harvard" blends are perennial favorites). In good weather, enjoy a leisurely snack on the sunny patio out back.

Fog Island Cafe. 7 S. Water St. ☎ **508/228-1818.** Most items under $8. MC, V. Mon–Sat 7am–2pm, Sun 7am–1pm. Open year-round. NEW AMERICAN.

You'll be wowed by the creative breakfasts and lunches at this sassy cafe; they're reasonably priced, with superfresh ingredients. Homemade soups and salads are healthy and yummy. This local joint also has their cookbook for sale on site.

TAKE-OUT & PICNIC FARE

You can get fresh-picked produce right in town from **Bartlett's traveling market** (there's a truck parked on Main Street in season), or head out to **Bartlett's Ocean View Farm,** 33 Bartlett Farm Rd. (☎ **508/228-9403**), where, in June, you can pick your own strawberries. Before you bike out of town to the beach, stop by Provisions, Harbor Square, Straight Wharf (☎ **508/228-3258**) for picnic staples like sandwiches, salads, soups, and muffins. Open year-round.

✪ **The Juice Bar,** 12 Broad St. (☎ **508/228-5799**) is a humble hole-in-the-wall that scoops up some of the best homemade ice cream and frozen yogurt around, complemented by superb homemade hot fudge. The pastries are also excellent, and yes, you can get juice—from refreshing lime rickeys to healthful carrot cocktails. Closed mid-October to May.

NANTUCKET AFTER DARK

Acoustic performers from all over the country hold forth in **The Brotherhood of Thieves,** 23 Broad St. (in the center of Nantucket Town; no phone) an atmospheric pub where you'll find live folk music just about every night in season, when lines tend to form out the door. It's closed February; no cover. **The Chicken Box,** 12 Dave St. (☎ **508/228-9717**), is the rocking spot for the twentysomething crowd. Depending on the band or theme (disco nights rule), it sometimes seems like the entire population of the island is shoving their way in here. Jimmy Buffett shows up late night about once a summer, unannounced, and jams with the band. Cover varies.

The **Hearth Pub and Patio** at the Harbor House, 23 S. Water St. (☎ **508/228-1500**), is a handsome, beamed hall with elegant appointments. There's live music most nights in season from 5pm to midnight. The performers range from P. J. Moody on acoustic guitar to jazz by Richard Sylvester and Friends. The Smitty Trio, a premier jazz and cabaret act, plays in July and August. There's no cover. The **Rose & Crown,** 23 S. Water St. (☎ **508/228-2595**) features live, loud music for dancing, and all ages show up for the fun. Closed January through March.

The **Nantucket Arts Alliance** (☎ **800/228-8118** or 508/228-8118) operates Box Office Nantucket, offering tickets for all sorts of cultural events around town. They operate out of the Macy Warehouse on Straight Wharf in season, daily 10am–4pm.

Theater buffs will want to spend an evening at the **Actors' Theatre of Nantucket,** Methodist Church, 2 Centre St. (☎ **508/228-6325**). Drawing on some considerable local talent of all ages, this shoebox theater assays thought-provoking plays as readily as summery farces. Tickets are $15, and the theater is open late May to mid-September, Monday to Saturday at 8:30pm; call for off-season hrs. You can catch the children's productions (tickets $10) from mid-July to mid-August, Tuesday to Saturday at 5pm.

Central & Western Massachusetts

by Herbert Bailey Livesey

8

While Boston and its maritime appendages of Cape Ann and Cape Cod face the sea and gingerly embrace it, inland Massachusetts turns in upon itself. Countless ponds and lakes shimmer in its folds and hollows, often hidden by deep forests and granite outcroppings. Farming and industry grew along the north-south valleys of the Connecticut and Housatonic rivers.

The heartland Pioneer Valley, bordering the Connecticut River, earned its name in the early–18th century, when European trappers and farmers first began to push west from the colonies clinging to the edges of Massachusetts Bay. They were followed by visionary capitalists who erected redbrick mills along the river for the manufacture of textiles and paper. Most of those enterprises failed or faded in the post–World War II movement to the milder climate and cheaper labor of the South, leaving a miasma of economic hardship that has yet to be remedied. But those industrialists also helped fund several distinguished colleges for which the valley is now known, whose educated populations provide much energy and a rich cultural life.

Roughly the same pattern applied in the Berkshires, the twin ranges of rumpled hills that define the western band of the state. There is only one college of note here, however, and development of this region in the 19th century owed most to its accessibility by railroad from New York and Boston. Artistic and literary folk made a favored summer retreat of it, followed by wealthy urbanites attracted by the region's reputation for creativity and bohemianism. Many of their extravagant mansions, dubbed "Berkshire Cottages," still survive, and to this day the region attracts the Town-and-Country crowd, who support a vibrant summer schedule of the arts, then steal away as the crimson leaves fall and the Berkshires grow quiet beneath six months of snow.

1 Sturbridge & Old Sturbridge Village

First things first. Sturbridge and Old Sturbridge Village aren't a single entity. The former is an organic community, populated by working people with real lives. But why so many motels and restaurants in a town of fewer than 8,000 residents? That's due to the latter, a fabricated early-19th-century village composed of authentic buildings moved here from other locations and peopled by docents pretending to follow the pursuits of 170 years past. It is deservedly popular, one of the two most prominent tourist destinations in central Massachusetts.

ESSENTIALS

GETTING THERE   Take the east-west Massachusetts Turnpike (I-90) to Exit 9, or take I-84 to Exit 3B. Sturbridge is 18 miles southwest of Worcester, and 32 miles east of Springfield.

VISITOR INFORMATION   The **Sturbridge Area Visitors Center,** 380 Main St., Sturbridge, MA 01566 (☎ **508/347-2761**), is open weekdays during regular business hours.

SPECIAL EVENTS   Highly popular annual occasions are the ✪ **Brimfield Antique and Collectible Shows,** when at least 3,000 dealers gather along a mile-long strip for up to 6 days (Tuesday to Sunday) in mid-May, mid-July, and early September. Call ☎ **413/283-2418** for details. Brimfield is an otherwise sleepy village adjoining Sturbridge on the west. Since it has so few hotels, most of the dealers and seekers stay in Sturbridge, so you'll need to reserve your own room half a year or more in advance during show periods.

Thanksgiving and Christmas weeks at Old Sturbridge Village are particularly special. Traditional New England dinners, concerts, and candlelit nights are only a few of the events brightening the calendar. Call ☎ **800/733-1830** or 508/347-3362 for details.

EXPLORING A 19TH-CENTURY VILLAGE

There is only one sight of significance in this otherwise pleasantly unremarkable town. Expect crowds on long holiday weekends in summer and during the October foliage season.

✪ **Old Sturbridge Village.** 1 Old Sturbridge Rd. ☎ **800/733-1830** or 508/347-3362. Fax 508/347-5375. www.osv.org. E-mail: osv@osv.org. Admission (2-day pass) $16 adults, $15 seniors, $8 children 6–15, free for children under 6. Apr–Oct daily 9am–5pm; Nov–Dec and Mar daily 10am–4pm; schedule varies Jan–Feb, call ahead. Take Exit 3B off I-84 or Exit 9 off I-90, drive west on Rte. 20, and bear right into the turnaround just before the entrance to the village.

Only one of the more than 40 restored structures in the complex stands on its original site—the Oliver Wight House, now part of the OSV Lodges, beside the entrance road. The rest were transported here from as far away as Maine, starting 50 years ago. All are authentic buildings, not re-creations, and they represent the living quarters and places of trade and commerce of a settlement of the 1830s. Among these are a Quaker meetinghouse, a sawmill, a bank, a store, and a school.

Costumed docents perform carefully researched demonstrations of blacksmithing, hearth cooking, sheep shearing, maple sugaring, musketry, printing, basket weaving, carpentry, and more. Visitors are welcome to question them as they go about their tasks. "Residents" include children who roll hoops and play games true to the period. These change with the seasons, and special events and activities mark such dates as Washington's Birthday, Mother's Day, Thanksgiving, Christmas, and the Fourth of July. Town meetings, weddings, militia drills, and a harvest fair are staged. A new 20-minute boat ride on the adjacent Quinebaug River has proved popular.

Cafeteria meals are available in Bullard Tavern, and a gift shop and bookstore are open during museum hours. You can see and do everything here in 2 to 3 hours, but given the relatively high cost of admission, consider making a day of it.

WHERE TO STAY

When the choices below are full, try the **EconoLodge,** 262 Main St. (☎ **508/347-2324**), the **Colonial Quality Inn,** on Route 20 (☎ **508/347-3306**), or the

Central & Western Massachusetts

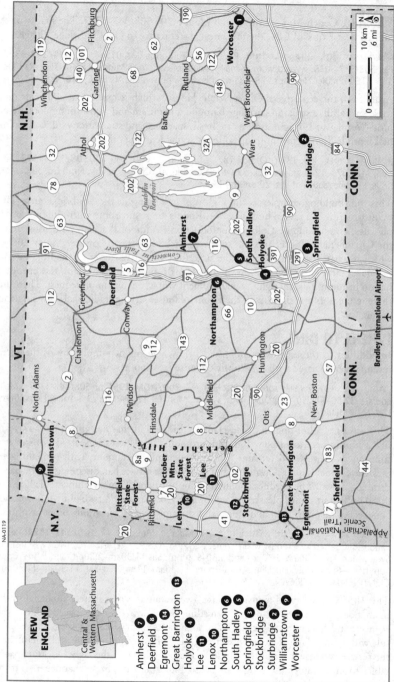

Sturbridge Coach Motor Lodge. 408 Main St. ☎ **508/347-7327.** The first two are located near Exit 9 of I-84, the third near the entrance to Old Sturbridge Village.

Old Sturbridge Village Lodges. Rte. 20 E., Sturbridge, MA 01566. ☎ **508/347-3327.** Fax 508/347-3018. www.osv.org. E-mail: osvlodge@osv.org. 59 units. A/C TV TEL. May–Oct $85–$130 double; Nov–Apr $75–$95 double. Extra person $5. AE, DISC, MC, V.

Apart from the centerpiece Oliver Wight House, which is more than 200 years old, these six barnlike structures arranged around a common and a swimming pool are of post–World War II origin. Rooms are fresh, spacious, and straightforward, with colonial reproductions. Free morning coffee is available in the office.

Publick House. Rte. 131 (P.O. Box 187), Sturbridge, MA 01566. ☎ **508/347-3313.** Fax 508/347-5073. 17 units. A/C TEL. $90–$155 double. AE, CB, DC, MC, V. From Exit 3B of I-84, drive 1.5 miles south of Rte. 20 on Rte. 131.

This four-building complex is the high-profile lodging in the Sturbridge area. The main structure is a tavern built in 1771. Rooms are rustic, some with canopied beds, rag rugs, and farmhouse Colonial reproductions. Additional accommodations are in the Chamberlain House, adjacent to the Publick House; the Country Motor Lodge, which is what it sounds like; and the peaceful Colonel Ebenezer Crafts Inn, a 1786 Federalist farmhouse a mile from the hotel. A B&B with its own pool, the Ebenezer has no in-room TVs, though the management will wheel one in on request. There are three restaurants associated with the Publick House, serving traditional New England dishes.

WHERE TO DINE

In addition to the establishments listed below, you might sample any of the three restaurants associated with the **Publick House** (see above).

Rom's. Rte. 131 (2 miles south of Rte. 20). ☎ **800/ROM-1952** or 508/347-3349 . Main courses $7.50–$12.50. AE, DISC, DC, MC, V. Mon–Fri 11am–9pm, Sat–Sun 11am–10pm. ITALIAN/AMERICAN.

This was once a hot-dog and fried-clam roadside stand that has grown over 47 years like a multigenerational New England farmhouse. Today, it can seat 750 diners at a time on two levels and remains a near-ideal family restaurant, with something to please everyone. Liquor is available, but only from a service bar, discouraging the hard-drinking crowd. The Wednesday night (5 to 9pm) and Thursday lunch (11:30am to 2pm) buffets are crowd pleasers, as are the always-low prices. A take-out window ladles "buckets of rigatoni," fish-and-chips, and shrimp in a basket, among other favorites.

The Whistling Swan/Ugly Duckling. 502 Main St. (Rte. 20). ☎ **508/347-2321.** Reservations suggested weekends. Main courses $12.95–$23.95. AE, CB, DC, MC, V. Whistling Swan: Mon–Fri 11:30am–2:30pm and 5:30–9:30pm, Sat 11:30am–2:30pm and 5:30–10pm, Sun noon–8pm. Ugly Duckling: Tues–Thurs 11:30am–11pm, Fri–Sat 11:30am–11:30pm. CONTINENTAL/AMERICAN.

This 1855 Greek Revival mansion houses two restaurants that share a kitchen. On the main floor are the rooms of the Whistling Swan, with widely spaced tables, wall sconces, and Sheraton-style chairs. The menu lists dishes like frog's legs Provençale, sole with orange-lime sauce, even surf-and-turf. The execution is safe and careful, and the service is efficient if not terribly sophisticated. Upstairs, the Ugly Duckling packs tables together under the rough-cut board roof and a big brass chandelier. Patrons strive to be heard over the live piano—it's loud, even boisterous. The food is simple and hearty.

Which venue to choose? I'd mount the stairs, in a New York minute.

2 Springfield

Times have been tough in this once-prosperous manufacturing city on the east bank of the Connecticut River. But its loyal citizens haven't given in to the consequences of job flight and high unemployment, and there is evidence of redevelopment throughout the downtown district, with recycled loft and factory buildings standing beside modern glass towers. Springfield remains the most important city in western Massachusetts and has succeeded in attracting new enterprises, notably in plastics, toolmaking, and electronic equipment.

ESSENTIALS

GETTING THERE   Springfield is located near the juncture of the east-west Massachusetts Turnpike (I-90), a toll highway, and north-south I-91, and is readily accessible from every city in the Northeast. It's 89 miles west of Boston, and 32 miles north of Hartford.

Bradley International (☎ 203/627-3000) in Windsor Locks, Connecticut, is the nearest major airport, about 20 miles to the south. Rent a car there from any of the major companies or catch a bus, cab, or limo into Springfield. Major airlines serving Bradley include **American** (☎ 800/433-7300), **Continental** (☎ 800/525-0280), **Delta** (☎ 800/221-1212), **Northwest** (☎ 800/225-2525), **United** (☎ 800/241-6522), and **US Airways** (☎ 800/247-8786).

Several **Amtrak** trains stop daily both ways in Springfield on their routes between Boston and Chicago; Boston and Washington, D.C.; and New York and St. Albans, VT (where there are connecting buses from Montréal, Québec), with intermediate stops in Philadelphia, New York, and Hartford, among others. Schedules change often, however, so call ☎800/USA-RAIL for up-to-date information and reservations.

VISITOR INFORMATION   The Greater Springfield Convention and Visitors Bureau (☎ 413/787-1548) is at 1500 Main St., Springfield, MA 01103.

SPECIAL EVENTS   A highlight of the annual calendar is the **Eastern States Exposition,** a huge old-fashioned agricultural fair with games, rides, a midway, and entertainment. It's held on a fairground on the opposite side of the Connecticut River in West Springfield in mid-September. Call ☎ 413/737-2443 for details. Also on the grounds is the **Old Storrowtown Village,** a collection of restored colonial buildings, accessible by guided tour Monday to Saturday from June to Labor Day, and by appointment the rest of the year.

MUSEUMS & HISTORIC SITES

Springfield has enjoyed its share of wealthy benefactors, and enough of them gave back to their community to produce a number of museums of varying levels of interest. The more conventional are the four clustered around the grassy quadrangle behind the Springfield Library. In addition, there are three specialized museums that do their duty well but can easily be skipped by those who don't share those interests, including the Basketball Hall of Fame, described below. Bikers devout and fantasizing will want to check out the **Indian Motorcycle Museum,** 33 Hendee St. (☎ 413/737-2624), while gun enthusiasts will be intrigued by the 1840s **Springfield Armory,** 1 Armory Sq. (☎ 413/734-8551), now a museum tracing the evolution of weapons once made here.

Basketball Hall of Fame. W. Columbus Ave. (at Union St.). ☎ **413/781-6500.** Fax 413/781-1939. Admission $16 adults over 16, $5 seniors and children 7–15, free for children under 7. Daily 9am–6pm.

Dr. James Naismith invented basketball in Springfield in 1891, providing the logic for this memorial and entertainment center. A must for fans, it is painless even for those who regard the game as a blur of 7-foot armpits.

Take the elevator to the third floor and work your way down. Up there are the inductees and displays recalling the history of the game. Remember the Waterloo Hawks? The Indianapolis Kautskys? Or the Philadelphia Hebrews? The Hall covers every aspect of the game, from high school to the NBA to the Olympics, as well as such offshoots as wheelchair leagues and the Harlem Globetrotters. A map of the United States announces the latest boys' and girls' champs in every state. No aspect of the sport is too small, attested to by the collections of Topps cards and sneakers.

On the ground floor is a shooting court with baskets at various heights, and next to it a virtual-reality display, in which visitors can insert themselves on a large viewing screen and play against the pros. A brand-new facility is under construction on the other side of the parking lot, expected to open sometime in 2001.

Springfield Museums at the Quadrangle. 220 State St. (corner of Chestnut St.). ☎ **413/263-6800.** www.quadrangle.com. Admission for all 4 museums $4 adults, $1 ages 6–18, free for children under 6. $1 more for the planetarium. Wed–Sun noon–4pm.

Four museums and a library surrounding a single inner quadrangle constitute this worthwhile resource, much of it built by the generosity of industrialists who flourished in Springfield during the 19th and early–20th centuries.

Begin a tour by entering the library from State Street and walking through to the back. On the right is the first museum, and the others around the quad make a counterclockwise circuit. Before setting out, note the limited hours above.

The **George Walter Vincent Smith Art Museum**'s eponymous donor, a wealthy carriage manufacturer, assembled the eclectic collection he installed in this 1896 Italian Renaissance–style mansion. Proceeding upstairs, find a gallery of largely sentimental pastoral scenes, with a few small landscapes by George Inness, Thomas Cole, and Albert Bierstadt. Subsequent rooms house substantial numbers of Apulian red-figured vases and Chinese cloisonné, a form of pottery that employs metal, glass, and enamel. On the main floor are cases of Japanese samurai armor and weaponry surrounding a heavily carved Shinto shrine dating from 1805.

Likely to be the biggest winner with children, the **Science Museum** contains a planetarium (show time at 2:45pm), dioramas of large African animals, and downstairs, the Monsato Eco-Center. This new section strives for cohesion with some interactive devices, aquariums with native and tropical fish, a boa and poisonous frogs, and scattered other exhibits.

Enter the **Connecticut River Valley Historical Museum** through a gateway that is a representation of the headgear worn by Dr. Seuss's famous Cat in the Hat. (The children's author grew up in Springfield.) Inside are examples of weapons made by the city's firearms manufacturers, including a blunderbuss and an unusual 1838 rifle with a revolving cartridge chamber.

The strongest and most professionally organized repository of the lot is the ✪ **Museum of Fine Arts,** which has 20 galleries with canvases by European and American artists. The latter are the most interesting, with examples of colonial paintings through Gilbert Stuart and John Copley to early-20th-century realists George Bellows and Reginald Marsh, culminating with both magic realists and abstract expressionists of recent decades—Frank Stella, Helen Frankenthaler, Don Eddy, and George Sugarman. Make a particular effort to view the remarkable serigraph of lower Manhattan by Richard Estes.

WHERE TO STAY

Directly across the street from the Sheraton (described below) is the comparable **Marriott Springfield,** Boland and Columbus aves., Springfield, MA 01105 (☎ **413/781-7111;** fax 413/731-8932), with similar prices and amenities.

Sheraton Springfield Monarch. One Monarch Place, Springfield, MA 01114. ☎ **800/325-3535** or 413/781-1010. Fax 413/734-3249. 310 units. A/C TV TEL. $139–$169 double. AE, DC, DISC, MC, V.

Easy to find, just off the Springfield Center exit of I-91, this can be a real treat after a few nights in idiosyncratic New England bed-and-breakfasts. Predictable, yes, but curl up in a room with cable TV with hit movies on order, a hair dryer, coffeemaker, and phone with dataport, and lack of charm can suddenly seem unimportant—especially when it's combined with room service, a parking garage, indoor pool, exercise room, friendly bar, and a capable restaurant, Peter's Grill. The executive "Club" floor has a private lounge that lays out a continental breakfast in the morning and hors d'oeuvres in the evening (Monday to Friday). Due to quirks in pricing and season, Club rooms, with whirlpool tubs, are sometimes cheaper than standard units, so ask.

WHERE TO DINE

Pioneer Valley Brew Pub. 51-59 Taylor St. (near Dwight St.). ☎ **413/732-2739.** Main courses $11.95–$17.95. Tues–Fri 11:30am–9pm, Sat 5–10pm. AE, CB, DC, MC, V. ECLECTIC AMERICAN.

This "deco diner" is a welcome exception to the largely forlorn local dining scene. The main room is spacious, and a second one in the back adjoins a dining terrace. In addition to a regular slate of ales and lagers on tap (try Armory Amber), there are seasonal special brews to wash down such tasty dishes as grilled pork loin with apple-raisin chutney and sautéed duck breast with wild rice pancakes and warm fruit compote. Main courses come with bread, vegetable, and a salad that has stayed too long in the fridge. Subtlety isn't a strong suit, not with flavors and portions this big.

Student Prince and The Fort. 8 Fort St. (west of Main St.). ☎ **413/734-7475.** Main courses $7.50–$14.25. Daily noon–10pm. AE, CB, DC, DISC, MC, V. GERMAN/AMERICAN.

In 1935, German immigrants opened a cafe they called the Student Prince and began serving beer in steins with schnitzels, sauerbraten, and hasenpfeffer. That might not have seemed the precise historical moment to ensure the success of such an enterprise, but it thrived. In 1946, they added a large dining room next door, which they chose to call The Fort. The result is the most popular place in town. Waitresses rush about in sensible shoes, slapping plates down and tolerating no lip from playful patrons. Monster portions are the rule, with veal shanks as thick as a linebacker's forearm and plates heaped high with sausages, boiled potatoes, and sauerkraut. Check out the enormous stein collection at the bar. On draft are seven German brews.

SPRINGFIELD AFTER DARK

Springfield Symphony Hall, Court St. & East Columbus Ave. (☎413/787-6600) is the principal facility for one-night stands of touring solo performers and bus-and-truck musicals, as well as productions meant for children. Think *Fiddler on the Roof* and *Cinderella.*

A strip of beer-and-pool joints, music bars, and hip eateries is developing along downtown Worthington Street. Check out the food and weekend live jazz at **Caffeine's** (☎ 413/788-6646) or puff an hour away in its adjacent cigar lounge, **Nicotine's** (☎ 413/781-0386). They are at 54 Worthington.

3 The Pioneer Valley

Low billowing hills and quilted fields channel the Connecticut River as it runs south toward Long Island Sound, forming the Pioneer Valley. The earliest European settlers came here for what proved to be uncommonly fertile soil and were followed in the 19th century by men who harnessed the power of the river and became wealthy textile and paper manufacturers.

These industrialists took the lead in funding the institutions of higher learning that are now the pride of the region. Prestigious Smith, Mount Holyoke, and Amherst are here, as are innovative Hampshire College and the sprawling main campus of the University of Massachusetts, with its enrollment of more than 25,000 students. All five contribute mightily to the cultural life of the valley, and the towns of **Northampton, Amherst,** and **South Hadley** are invigorated by the vitality of thousands of college-age young people.

In the north, near Vermont, the living village of ✪ **Deerfield** preserves the architecture and atmosphere of colonial New England, but without the whiff of sterility that often afflicts artificial gatherings of old buildings with costumed docents.

Interstate 91 and Route 5 both traverse the valley from south to north. The trip from edge to edge on the Interstate takes less than an hour, while Route 5 tenders more of the flavor of pastoral vistas and colorful mill towns.

There are ample numbers of motels along the way, but if you're looking for lodgings more representative of the character of the region, you might contact the **Folkstone Bed & Breakfast Reservation Service** (☎ **800/762-2751** or 508/480-0380). They have listings throughout central Massachusetts with rates of $50 to $150 a night; all accept MasterCard and Visa.

ESSENTIALS

GETTING THERE   From Boston and upstate New York, take the Massachusetts Turnpike (I-90), a toll highway, to Springfield, then follow I-91 or Route 5 north. While there are local buses, you'll want a car.

The nearest major airport is **Bradley International** (☎ **203/627-3000**), just south of Springfield, in Windsor Locks, Connecticut. (See the "Springfield" above section of this chapter for a list of airlines that serve Bradley.) A private service called **Valley Transporter** (☎ **800/872-8752** or 413/549-1350) offers van shuttles between the airport and Amherst, Northampton, Hadley, Holyoke, and Deerfield.

Amtrak *Vermonter* trains stop in Amherst and Northampton on their route between Burlington, Vermont, and Washington, D.C., but schedules change at least twice yearly, so call ☎ **800/USA-RAIL** (872-7245) for up-to-date information and reservations.

VISITOR INFORMATION   The **Pioneer Valley Tourist Information Center** (☎ 413/665-7333) is at the intersection of Routes 5 and 10 in South Deerfield, at Exit 24 of I-91.

HOLYOKE

Once an important paper-manufacturing center, Holyoke, which lies 8 miles north of Springfield and 88 miles west of Boston, has suffered a long economic slide since World War II. Abandoned factories and the dissolute air of the commercial center don't bolster first impressions. Still, there are a couple of modestly worthwhile sights and a pleasant inn for a meal or an overnight stay.

SIGHTS & ACTIVITIES

Canals dug during the city's heyday as a paper-manufacturing center still cut through the downtown area (they were intended to allow access to the mills and bypass a dam in the Connecticut River). Long and narrow **Heritage State Park,** with its entrance at 221 Appleton St. (☎ 413/534-1723), runs beside one of the canals, and has an interpretive center that offers walking tours and exhibits revisiting the industrial glory days. On most Sundays from mid-June to late August, the ancient locomotive of the **Heritage Park Railroad** pulls three cars of train buffs on a 2-hour, 5-mile trip down-river from the park to Holyoke Mall at Ingleside. Times and fares vary, since demand and funds fluctuate. Call Heritage State Park for more information.

Next to the park is the **Volleyball Hall of Fame,** 444 Dwight St. (☎ 413/536-0926), a specialized museum of the sort that abounds in the Valley. The game was invented in Holyoke in 1895. Passionate fans are the only travelers likely to find it of more than passing interest.

For skiing, hit **Mount Tom,** 2 miles north of the city center off Route 5 (☎ 800/545-7163). At 1,150 feet, it won't remind anyone of the Jungfrau, but still, there are 17 mostly intermediate trails and a long run of 3,600 feet. They are lighted for night skiing, and snowmaking equipment is at hand. Rentals are available. All-day lift tickets are $30 for adults, $26 for seniors and children ages 9 to 12. Summer recreational facilities include an artificial-wave pool, water slide, and water tube ride, as well as hiking trails.

WHERE TO STAY & DINE

Yankee Pedlar Inn. 1866 Northampton St. (Rte. 5), Holyoke, MA 01040. ☎ 413/532-9494. Fax 413/536-8877. www.yankeepedlar.com. E-mail: info@yankeepedlar.com. 28 units. A/C TV TEL. $70–$130 double. Rates include breakfast. AE, CB, DC, DISC, MC, V. Take Exit 16 off I-91 and head east for 5 blocks.

If you're looking for a sedate, tranquil country inn, this isn't it. Business is thriving, and it bristles with weddings, tour group luncheons, and corporate get-togethers. Of the five buildings in the largely Victorian complex, the 1850 House has the most modern rooms, and the Carriage House has the least expensive. Some rooms have canopied beds and/or kitchenettes.

Dining/Diversions: The main dining room, with its breezy menu and lively bar, is popular with locals as well as travelers. Closed Mondays. Live musical entertainment is presented on weekends.

SOUTH HADLEY

Pioneer educator Mary Lyon founded Mount Holyoke Female Seminary here in 1836 and presided over it for 12 years. One of the Seven Sisters group of prestigious women's colleges, it emphasizes liberal arts and preparation for the service professions, including law, medicine, teaching, and social work.

Strung along the eastern side of Route 116 (College Street), the college is the essential reason for the existence of this small town (population 13,600), although it was settled in the late–17th century. It lies 15 miles north of Springfield and 7 miles south of Amherst.

On the campus is a worthy **Art Museum** (☎ 413/538-2245), which focuses on art of the Orient, Egypt, and the Mediterranean, but also mounts temporary exhibits on a considerable range of topics. Hours are Tuesday to Friday from 11am to 5pm, Saturday and Sunday from 1 to 5pm. Admission is free. It's closed during school holidays, but not in summer. To find it, take Park Street from the east side of the Y intersection in the center of town and follow the signs.

Joseph Skinner State Park (☎ 413/586-0350) straddles the border between South Hadley and Hadley. On its 390 acres are miles of walking trails, picnic grounds, and the historic Summit House. The building (open weekends only from May through October) was erected in a single day in 1821 by a group of energetic male friends who wanted a place to party with copious quantities of gin, rum, cigars, and panoramic views of the valley.

A tastefully designed mall called **The Village Commons** (☎ **413/532-3600**) stands alongside Route 116 opposite the Mount Holyoke campus. More than 30 shops, including a movie theater, three restaurants, and the **Odyssey Bookshop,** are clustered in white clapboard buildings suggesting a classic New England village.

NORTHAMPTON

Smith College, with its campus sprawling along Main Street slightly west of the commercial center, is Northampton's dominating physical and spiritual presence. One of the original Seven Sisters (before that informal league of women's colleges was broken up by coeducation), Smith is the largest female liberal-arts college in the United States.

Northampton was long the home of Calvin Coolidge, who pursued his law practice here before and after his monosyllabic occupancy of the Oval Office. (At a White House dinner, Silent Cal was seated next to a woman who said she had made a bet she could get three words out of him. "You lose," he said.) He lived in houses at 21 Massasoit St. and on Hampton Terrace, but the homes are privately owned and not open to the public. A room containing many of his papers is maintained by the **Forbes Library,** 20 West St. (☎ **413/584-6037**).

SEEING THE SIGHTS

Historic Northampton. 46 Bridge St. (east of the railroad bridge). ☎ **413/584-6011.** Admission $3 adults, $1 children 7–12, free for children under 7. Tours Mar–Dec Thurs–Sun noon–4pm.

Among Northampton's most popular attractions are the Museum Houses, three historic homes still standing on their original sites (although lately looking in need of maintenance). They are the 1730 Parsons House, the 1796 Shepherd House, and the 1812 Isaac Damon House, which contains a furnished parlor true to 1820.

Smith College.

To a considerable extent, the campus buildings that line Elm Street are a testament to the excesses of late-19th-century architecture. Their often egregious admixtures of Gothic, Greco-Roman, Renaissance, and medieval esthetic notions lend a Teutonic sobriety to the west end of town.

That aside, one of those ponderous brown monoliths boasts a worthwhile **Museum of Art,** 76 Elm St. at Bedford Terrace (☎ **413/585-2760**). Included in its permanent holdings of more than 24,000 works of the late–19th- and 20th-centuries are paintings by Degas, Monet, Seurat, Picasso, and Winslow Homer. Admission is free. It's open September through June, Tuesday, Friday, and Saturday from 9:30am to 4pm, Wednesday and Sunday from noon to 4pm, and Thursday from noon to 8pm; in July and August hours are Tuesday through Sunday from noon to 4pm.

Words & Pictures Museum. 140 Main St. ☎ **413/586-8545.** Admission $3 adults, $2 seniors and students, $1 children under 18. Tues–Thurs noon–8pm, Fri noon–8pm, Sat 10am–8pm, Sun noon–5pm.

Funding is provided in part by a creator of the Teenage Mutant Ninja Turtles, but this repository of comic-book illustrations ("sequential art" is the loftier term) may not be the place to take the kiddies. Most of the work on display, while expertly rendered, is of the decidedly adult variety, with action characters demonstrating a predilection for violence as well as for costumes of an S&M persuasion displaying more than a few bared breasts and buttocks. If you've brought your kids this far, though, escort them through the mock "cave" entrance onto the elevator and go directly to the second floor, where there are interactive computer games and a replica of a Ninja Turtles movie set. An addition is being built to display a Batmobile.

OUTDOOR PURSUITS

Three miles southwest of town on Route 10 in Easthampton is **Arcadia Nature Center and Wildlife Sanctuary,** 127 Combs Rd. (☎ **413/584-3009**), a 700-acre preserve operated by the Massachusetts Audubon Society. It contains a mixed ecology of marshes and woods bordering the Connecticut River. Over 5 miles of trails provide access to a variety of flora and fauna. The sanctuary is open from dawn to dusk, Tuesday to Sunday. Admission is $3 for nonmember adults, $2 for seniors and ages 3 to 15, and free for children under 3.

Cyclists make good use of the **Norwottuck Trail Bike Path,** an 8½-mile trail that follows a former railroad bed running between Northampton and Amherst, reached by an old bridge across the river. Access is via Damon Road and at Mount Farms Mall. Bikes can be rented at **Valley Bicycles,** 319 Main St. (☎ **413/256-0880**), across the river in Amherst.

Look Memorial Park, 300 N. Main St. (☎ **413/584-5457**), is northwest of town off Route 9, with 157 acres of woods, a 5-acre lake, picnic grounds, and a small zoo of native animals. Boats are available for rent. There are musical and theatrical events, including puppet shows, in summer.

SHOPPING

One of the pleasures of college towns for browsing bibliophiles is the larger than usual number of bookstores, often dealing in exotica not found in the big national chains. Northampton has those, in abundance, but also enjoys the most diverse shopping in the valley. Most of the following stores are open 7 days a week.

CDs, greeting cards, and stationery supplement the extensive stock of the deep, two-level **Beyond Words Bookshop,** 189 Main St. (☎ **413/586-6304**), which has a good children's section and a second-floor cafe that's open late. The store motto is "Book lovers never go to bed alone."

The **Antiques Center of Northampton,** 9½ Market St. (☎ **413/584-3600**), contains the stalls of more than 60 independent dealers on three floors. Closed Wednesday. **Ferrin Gallery and Pinch Pottery,** 179 Main St. (☎ **413/586-4509**), offers quality contemporary jewelry, glassware, and ceramics, and represents elite craftspeople whose works are found in the White House Collection. There are no bargains, but there are affordable pieces. A former department store has been reconfigured into **Thorne's Marketplace,** 150 Main St. (☎ **413/584-5582**), which now contains more than 30 specialty boutiques on four floors. Goods and services include furniture, clothing, folk art, records, toys, candy, jewelry, books, a coffee shop and a box office for upcoming theatrical and music events.

WHERE TO STAY

This is a college town, with frequent influxes of parents and alumnae during graduations, homecomings, and other events, so anticipate higher rates and limited vacancies at those times, in addition to the usual holiday weekends.

Autumn Inn. 259 Elm St., Northampton, MA 01060. ☎ **413/584-7660.** Fax 413/586-4808. 30 units. A/C TV TEL. Apr–Nov $86–$108 double; $120–$140 suite. Dec–Mar $78–$88; $105 suite. AE, CB, DC, MC, V.

A genteel motel with a vaguely Georgian style, the Autumn is conveniently situated opposite the quieter northern end of the Smith campus. There is a restaurant with a huge wood-burning fireplace serving breakfast and lunch (not dinner). In summer, an unheated pool is available. Rates listed above are for April to November, and are substantially lower December to March.

Hotel Northampton. 36 King St., Northampton, MA 01060. ☎ **413/584-3100.** Fax 413/584-9455. www.hotelnorthampton.com. 99 units. A/C TV TEL. $95–$195 double. AE, DC, DISC, MC, V.

Built in 1927, this five-story brick building at the center of town looks older. Recent restoration and modernization have brought it up to date, with rooms containing lots of wicker and colonial reproductions, feather duvets, and assorted Victoriana. Another 18 rooms and suites were added last year. Many front rooms have balconies overlooking King Street; some have canopied beds, and a few have Jacuzzis.

Dining/Diversions: Service in the hotel's Coolidge Park Cafe is pleasant enough, but glacial. Downstairs, Wiggins Tavern is an authentic colonial watering hole that predates the hotel by a couple of centuries, with dark beams and stone fireplaces.

Inn at Northampton. Rte. 5 and I-91 (just west of Exit 18), Northampton, MA 01060. ☎ **800/582-2929** or 413/586-1211. Fax 413/586-1723. www.virtual-valley.com/innatnoho. 124 units. A/C TV TEL. $129–$139 double; $149 suite. AE, CB, DC, DISC, MC, V.

The entrance isn't clearly marked, and the inn is hidden behind a Mobil gas station. Renovations have elevated it from a standard motel to something closer to a modest resort and conference center, with a lighted tennis court and two swimming pools, one of them indoors. The restaurant has been done over as *Montana's*, a steakhouse with pseudo-western trappings. A free continental breakfast is provided Monday to Friday, replaced by a $7.95 buffet Saturday to Sunday.

WHERE TO DINE

Eastside Grill. 19 Strong Ave. (1 block south of Main St.). ☎ **413/586-3347.** Main courses $9.95–$14.95. AE, MC, V. Mon–Thurs 4:30–9:30pm, Fri 4:30–10:30pm, Sat 4–10:30pm, Sun 4–9pm. REGIONAL AMERICAN.

The consensus choice for tops in town, this white clapboard building with a nautical look is a retreat for the 40-plus set from the prevailing collegiate tone of Northampton. The far-reaching menu has bayou riffs, such as duck étouffée and shrimp and andouille jambalaya. But while the Cajun/Creole dishes obviously absorb much of the kitchen's attention, there are ample alternatives. Seafood is impressive, and the "cowboy steak" has an herb-chipolte rub and is served with red pepper salsa butter and roasted garlic potatoes. Singles might wish to eat at the bar, attended by the droll chaps who man the bottles and taps. Note that they no longer serve lunch.

Fitzwilly's. 21 Main St. (near Pleasant St.). ☎ **413/584-8666.** Main courses $9.25–$14.95. AE, CB, DC, DISC, MC, V. Daily 11:30am–1am. AMERICAN.

Occupying a building constructed in 1898, this ingratiating pub makes the most of its high stamped-tin ceilings and ample space. Big copper brewing kettles signal an intriguing selection of beers, some from regional microbreweries, including draft Smuttynose Lager and Berkshire Porter. Beyond the two long bars are curtained booths where patrons dive into grilled pizzas, ribs, pastas, and such pub faves as blooming onion, Buffalo shrimp, and fried calamari.

La Cazuela. 7 Old South St. (down the hill from Main St.). ☎ **413/586-0400.** Main courses $9.25–$12.95. AE, DISC, MC, V. Sun–Thurs 5–9pm, Fri–Sat 5–10pm. SOUTHWESTERN/MEXICAN.

The menu at this restaurant mixes recipes of the American Southwest with those of Mexico, and the kitchen takes its job quite seriously. In addition to the predictable flautas, enchiladas, and chimichangas, dinner specials explore lesser-known regional cuisines with such dishes as *pollo en pipian:* chicken chunks fried in cilantro pesto then simmered in a sauce of ground pumpkin and sesame seeds, chiles, garlic, cloves, and cinnamon. With rice, veggie, salad, and tortilla, it's only $11.75. La Cazuela is in a rustic 1850 building, with folkloric artifacts and adobe-red walls that give the interior a Santa Fe look.

Vermont Country Deli & Cafe. 48 Main St. (near Pleasant St.). ☎ **413/586-7114.** Main courses $5.50–$7.95. MC, V. Sun–Wed 7am–7pm, Thurs–Sat 7am–8pm. ECLECTIC.

Appetizing sights glimpsed through the window drag people inside. On the right is a long case crowded with platters of tantalizing salads and main courses, like Hunan orange chicken, sesame noodles, grilled vegetables, Vietnamese pasta salad, and spinach knishes. Fat focaccia sandwiches are made to order, including one with "Cajun" turkey and coriander horseradish dressing. On the opposite side of the room are plump sticky buns, lemon muffins, sourdough baguettes, and several urns of various coffees. Eat at one of the tables in back, or keep it in mind for a take-out picnic.

Northampton After Dark

The presence of Smith College only partially accounts for the large number of music bars and clubs in town, making Northampton the nightlife magnet of the valley. In April, the **Loud Music Festival** rattles walls with more than 250 alternative rock bands from around the country. For a rundown of what's happening, pick up a copy of the weekly handout, *The Valley Advocate* (www.valleyadvocate.com).

Still thriving after 105 years, the **Academy of Music,** 74 Main St. (☎ 413/584-8453), serves several functions, and has done so since the first acting Barrymores came through town. It shows big-screen films as well as providing a venue for opera, ballet, and pop performers on tour. The hall operates irregularly, and the acts and prices vary, so call ahead for details.

Another old favorite, the **Iron Horse Music Hall,** 20 Center St. (☎ 413/584-0610), has played host to an enormous variety of artists, from Bonnie Raitt and Livingston Taylor to jazzmen Dave Brubeck and Pat Metheny to Celtic fiddlers, blues belters, and grunge rockers. It's open nightly from 5:30pm to 1am, usually with 7 and 9pm shows. All ages are welcome, but covers vary, so call ahead.

Live bluegrass, jam rock, and soul-funk alternate with DJ dance parties at the two-floor **Pearl Street Nightclub,** 10 Pearl St. (☎ 413/584-0610). There are often dance-party nights targeted at teenagers as well as gay nights (usually Wednesday). Call ahead for details on specific events. Closed on Mondays.

The **Calvin Theatre and Performing Arts Center,** 19 King St. (☎ 401/586-8686) treads a different road, offering touring performers and groups as diverse as Sonny Rollins, the Kronos String Quartet, James Galway, flamenco troupes, and children's musicals.

AMHERST

Yet another Pioneer Valley town defined by its educational institutions, this one has an even bigger student population than most, with distinguished Amherst College occupying much of its center, the large University of Massachusetts campus to its immediate northwest, and Hampshire College off South Pleasant Street.

On the edge of the town green is a seasonal **information booth.** Its hours vary, and when it is closed, visitors can call the **Chamber of Commerce** office (☎ 413/253-0700).

Historic Homes & Colleges

Most of the historic homes are within a few blocks of the Amity/Main/Pleasant street crossing. **Amherst College,** which has two museums of interest, lies mostly along the east side of the town common. At the northeast corner of the green is the **Town Hall,** another fortress-like Romanesque Revival creation of Boston's H. H. Richardson.

Amherst College. S. Pleasant and College sts. ☎ **413/542-2000.**

Named for Baron Jefferey Amherst, a British general during the last of the French and Indian Wars, the illustrious liberal-arts college maintains a cooperative relationship with Smith, Mount Holyoke, the University of Massachusetts, and the experimental Hampshire College. It was founded in 1821, with Noah Webster on its first board of trustees. Robert Frost was a member of the faculty for more than a decade.

Its large campus cuts through the heart of the town and contains two museums open to the public. The **Pratt Museum of Natural History** (☎ 413/542-2165), at the southeast corner of the main quadrangle, contains dinosaur tracks collected from sedimentary rocks of the Valley, as well as fossils, a mastodon skeleton, and indigenous rocks and minerals. The **Mead Art Museum** (☎ 413/542-2335), at the intersection of Routes 116 and 9, displays varied collections of sculptures, paintings, photographs, and antiquities. Its strengths lie in the works of 19th- and 20th-century American artists and French Impressionists. Admission to both museums is free.

Dickinson Homestead. 280 Main St. (2 blocks east of the Town Hall). ☎ **413/542-8161.** Admission $4 adults, $3 students, $2 children 6–11, free for children under 6 and students from the 5 area colleges. Guided tours only, Mar, Nov to mid-Dec Wed and Sat on the hour 1–4pm; Apr–May and Sept–Oct Wed–Sat on the hour 1–4pm; June–Aug Wed–Sun on the half-hour at 1–4pm, Sat also 10:30 and 11:30am. Reservations recommended.

Designated a National Historic Monument, this is the house where Emily Dickinson was born in 1830 and where she lived until her family moved in 1840. They returned in 1855, and the famous poet stayed here from then until her death 31 years later. The "Belle of Amherst" was the granddaughter and daughter of local movers and shakers, the source of her support while she produced the poetry that was to be increasingly celebrated even as she withdrew into near-total seclusion.

University of Massachusetts. Rte. 116. Tour info **413/545-4237.** Campus tours are available daily at 11am and 1:15pm, except weekends in June–July, Mar break, and most holidays.

Though the university was founded in 1863, this sprawling 1,200-acre campus north of the town center dates only from the 1960s. Several of its buildings top out at over 20 stories. Its 25,000 students study for degrees in 90 academic fields. The university's sporadic success in basketball has provoked the enthusiasm of sports fans all over the state.

Art is given a high priority by the administration, with six galleries scattered around the campus. Foremost among these is the University Gallery in the **Fine Arts Center,** beside the pond in the quadrangle. It focuses on works of 20th-century artists. The center also mounts productions in dance, music, and theater. Call the box office at ☎ 413/545-2511 for information about current and upcoming performances.

OUTDOOR PURSUITS

An 8½-mile bicycle trail following an old railroad bed between Amherst and Northampton is well used by residents of both towns. Bicycles can be rented at **Valley Bicycles,** 319 Main St. (☎ 800/831-5437 or 413/256-0880), in Amherst.

SHOPPING

Atticus/Albion Bookstore, 8 Main St. (☎ 413/256-1547), has a rumpled aspect that is catnip for readers who like to poke among the piles of books and take a seat on the window sofa to skim their finds. The nearby **Jefferey Amherst Bookshop,** 55 S. Pleasant St. (☎ 413/253-3381), is tidier, emphasizing paperbacks and specializing in Emily Dickinson and academic texts.

WHERE TO STAY

Allen House Victorian Inn. 599 Main St. (5 blocks east of Town Hall), Amherst, MA 01002.
☎ **413/253-5000.** www.allenhouse.com. 7 units. A/C TEL. $45–$135 double. Rates include
breakfast. DISC, MC, V. No children under 10.

The colorful exterior paint job makes this Queen Anne–style Victorian, built in 1886,
easy to spot. The interior is fitted out in the manner of the eye-blink moment of the
Aesthetic artistic movement, which had Oscar Wilde as a booster but barely lasted 10
years. In any event, the parlor and bedrooms are lovingly decorated and highly visual,
embellished with tracery and curlicues that are somehow Arabic in feel. The Eastlake
Room is the prize. Free pickup service from the Amtrak station is provided.

WHERE TO STAY & DINE

Lord Jefferey Inn. 30 Boltwood Ave. (next to the Town Hall), Amherst, MA 01002. ☎ **800/**
742-0358 or 413/253-2576. Fax 413/256-6152. www.pinnacle-inns.com/lordjefferyinn. 48
units. A/C TV TEL. $79–$173 double. AE, DC, MC, V.

It's a running battle to keep the principal lodging in a college town from looking a
little battered. At the moment, the Lord Jeff is winning, thanks to almost constant renovation and redecorating, lately with new fabrics and rugs. So despite the wear and
tear of more than 70 years of graduations, homecomings, and conferences, the inn
offers an environment that is as warm as its several working fireplaces. Robert Frost
stayed here for two of his last years as an English professor at the college.

   Dining: A new chef with credentials has turned *The Windowed Hearth* into
Amherst's event restaurant, open for dinner and Sunday brunch, and the casual Boltwood's Tavern, also updated, serves sprightly pub food from 7 to 10am and 11:30am
to 10pm.

WHERE TO DINE

Judie's. 51 N. Pleasant St. (north of Amity and Main sts.). ☎ **413/253-3491.** Main courses
$6.50–$15.25. AE, DISC, MC, V. Sun–Thurs 11:30am–10pm; Fri–Sat 11:30am–11pm.
ECLECTIC AMERICAN.

Judie's does its best to suit every taste. Just to keep things ticking, for example, there's
a "Munchie Madness" period from 3 to 6pm, with a half-price snacks menu.
Throughout the day, folks drop by for just a cup of seafood bisque and one of the
trademark popovers. A glass-enclosed porch fronts the converted house, which has
several interior rooms. Typical of the lunch specials is swordfish cakes with red Thai
curried sour cream, followed, perhaps, by white chocolate bread pudding with a
brown sugar rum sauce.

AMHERST AFTER DARK

Students and other young adults tend to gravitate toward the livelier music scene
in Northampton, but Amherst itself does offer some nighttime entertainment.
Close at hand is the **Black Sheep Cafe,** 79 Main St. (☎ 413/253-3492), which is
active nightly, with folk and blues singers, poetry readings, chamber music—a broad,
unpredictable selection. Entrance is usually free. The beer is good, the food indifferent, and the music varied at the **Amherst Brewing Company,** 36 N. Pleasant St.
(☎413/253-4400). Reggae, soul, and r&b are some of the forms on stage, usually at
least Thursday through Saturday nights at 10pm.

   Throughout the school year, Amherst College's **Buckley Recital Hall** (☎ 413/
542-2195) and **The Mullins Center** (☎ 413/733-2500) at UMass mount a variety
of pop, classical, dance, and theatrical performances that might include, for example,
the Cincinnati Symphony, Mummenschantz, or Elton John.

DEERFIELD

Meadows cleared and plowed more than 300 years ago still surround this historic town between the Connecticut and Deerfield rivers. Every morning tobacco and dairy farmers leave houses fronting the main street to work their land nearby. Students attend the distinguished prep school, Deerfield Academy, founded in 1797. Lawyers maintain offices here, while other residents commute to jobs elsewhere. Deerfield is an invaluable fragment of American history, and it isn't one of those New England village exhibits with costumed performers who go home to their condos at night.

A town still exists here, 16 miles north of Northampton and 16 miles northwest of Amherst, because the earliest English settlers were determined to thrive despite their status as a frontier pressure point in the wars that tormented colonial America. Massacres of Deerfield's settlers by the French and Indian enemies of the British nearly wiped out the town in 1675 and again in 1704. In the latter raid, 47 people were killed and another 112 were taken prisoner and marched to French Quebec.

The main thoroughfare, simply called "The Street," is lined with more than 80 houses built in the 17th, 18th, and 19th centuries. Most are private, but 14 of them can be visited through tours conducted by **Historic Deerfield,** a local tourism organization (see below).

MUSEUMS & HISTORIC HOMES

"The Street" is a mile long, with most of the museum houses concentrated along the long block north of the central town common. There are two buildings operated by organizations other than Historic Deerfield. One is Memorial Hall Museum, east of the town common on Memorial Street, for which a separate admission is charged. (For the slightly larger fee of $12 adults, $5 children 6 to 21, tours of the 14 museum houses can be combined with a visit to Memorial Hall through Historic Deerfield.) The other is the Indian House Memorial, north of the Deerfield Inn, also maintained by a separate organization. Since it is only a 1929 reproduction of an earlier house, it is of less interest than the other structures.

Special celebrations in the town are held on Patriots' Day (the third Monday in April), Washington's Birthday, Thanksgiving, and over the Christmas holidays. In summer there is an antique and classic car show; call the information center (☎ 413/774-5581; see below) for details.

✪ **Historic Deerfield.** Information Center, Hall Tavern, The Street. ☎ **413/774-5581.** Admission to all museum houses (good for 1 week) $12 adults, $6 children 6–21, free for children under 6; admission to one museum house or the walking tour $6 adults, $3 children 6–21. Daily 9:30am–4:30pm.

Begin with a visit to the Hall Tavern, opposite the post office, where tickets are sold and maps and brochures are available. A particularly useful booklet provides a walking tour of 88 historic locations in the village. This is also the departure point for guided tours, which customarily leave on the half hour during busier seasons (April through October), and according to demand during the slower months. While there are no charges for simply strolling The Street, the only way to get inside the museum houses is by tour.

The 14 houses on the tour were constructed between 1720 and 1850. They contain more than 20,000 furnishings, silver and pewter pieces, textiles, ceramics, and implements used from the early–17th century to 1900. Included are imports from China and Europe as well as items made in the Connecticut River valley during its prominence as an industrial center. The objects are all tidily arranged and displayed to good effect, and the tour guides provide interesting descriptions and background.

Historic Deerfield's **Museum Store** (☎ **413/774-5581**) is in a weathered shack between the post office and the Deerfield Inn. Apart from a few T-shirts, its judicious selections include weather vanes, hand-dipped candles, books, fruit preserves, and reproductions of light fixtures found in the village houses. It's open during museum hours.

A large stone building behind the Dwight House contains the new **Flynt Center of Early American Life.** Opened in 1998, it has extensive galleries for changing exhibitions of paintings, textiles, and decorative arts relevant to the local history. Entrance is included in the general admission fee.

A free attraction is the **Channing Blake Meadow Walk.** Open from 8am to 6pm in good weather, the trail begins beside the Rev. John Farwell Moors House, a Historic Deerfield holding on the west side of The Street. The walk is marked by interpretive tablets and goes through a working farm, past the playing fields of Deerfield Academy, and through pastures beside the Deerfield River. Along the trail you can see sheep and cattle up close (which delight the kids), but for that reason, dogs aren't allowed on the trail.

Memorial Hall Museum. 8 Memorial St. (between The Street and Routes 5 and 10). ☎ **413/774-3768.** Admission $6 adults, $3 children 6–21, free for children under 6. May–Oct daily 9:30am–4:30pm.

Deerfield Academy's original 1798 classroom building was converted into this museum of village history in 1880. A popular, if suggestively grisly, exhibit is the preserved door of a 1698 home that shows the gashes made by weapons of the French and Indian raiders in 1704. Should the point be too muted, a hatchet is also imbedded in the door.

Five period rooms are also on view, and other exhibitions display collections of colonial furniture, vintage clothing, quilts, paintings, pottery, and pewter, as well as examples of Native American weapons and tools.

WHERE TO STAY & DINE

✪ **Deerfield Inn.** 81 Old Main St., Deerfield, MA 01342. ☎ **800/926-3865** or 413/774-5587. Fax 413/773-8712. www.deerfieldinn.com. 23 units. A/C TV TEL. $140–$206.50 double. Rates include breakfast and afternoon tea. AE, DC, MC, V, personal check.

Even if it had any significant competition, this inn would attract more than its share of guests. Built in 1884, it's located in the middle of The Street and is one of the stellar stopping places in the valley. The innkeepers restlessly scour their establishment, over the last few years replacing all the bathroom fixtures, refinishing the older furniture, and installing new carpeting. Six of the bedrooms, named after people who lived in the village, have four-posters, while others have various combinations of beds and fold-out sofas to accommodate different family configurations. On premises are both a full-service dining room and an informal cafeteria. Midweek discounts are available.

4 The Berkshires

They are more than hills, but less than mountains, so the Taconic and Hoosac ranges that define this region at the western end of the state go by the collective name of "The Berkshires." The hamlets, villages, and two small cities that have long drawn energy and sustenance from the region's kindly Housatonic River and its tranquil tributaries are as New England as New England can be.

Mohawks and Mohegans lived and hunted here, and while white missionaries established settlements at Stockbridge and elsewhere in an attempt to Christianize the native tribes, the Indians eventually moved on west. Farmers, drawn to the narrow but fertile floodplains of the Housatonic, were supplanted in the 19th century by manufacturers, who erected the brick mills that drew their power from the river. Many of these factories survive, but they are largely abandoned or converted to other functions.

At the same time, artists and writers came here for the mild summers and seclusion that these hills and many lakes offered. Nathaniel Hawthorne, Herman Melville, and Edith Wharton were among those who put down temporary roots. By the last decades of the 19th century and the arrival of the railroad, wealthy New Yorkers and Bostonians had discovered the region and began to erect extravagant summer "cottages" with dozens of bedrooms on scores of tailored wooded acres. With their support, culture and the performing arts found a hospitable reception. By the 1930s, theater, dance, and concerts had established themselves as regular summer fixtures. Tanglewood, Jacob's Pillow, and the Berkshire and Williamstown Theatre festivals are events that draw tens of thousands of visitors every July and August.

When making reservations, note that the many inns in the region routinely stipulate minimum 2- or 3-night stays in summer and over holiday weekends and often require advance deposits.

ESSENTIALS

GETTING THERE The Massachusetts Turnpike (I-90) runs east-west from Boston to the Berkshires, with an exit near Lee and Stockbridge. From New York City, the scenic Taconic State Parkway connects with I-90 not far from Pittsfield.

Amtrak operates several trains daily between Boston and Chicago, stopping in Pittsfield each way. Call ☎ **800/USA-RAIL** (872-7245) for details on schedules and fares.

VISITOR INFORMATION Pittsfield's **Berkshire Visitors Bureau,** Berkshire Common (off South Street, near the entrance to the Hilton), Pittsfield, MA 01201 (☎ **800/237-5747** or 413/443-9186), provides brochures and answers questions for the entire region. In addition, local chambers of commerce and other civic groups maintain information booths at central locations in Great Barrington, Lee, Lenox, Pittsfield, Stockbridge, and Williamstown (details are found in the sections that follow). Internet surfers can find on-line information on what's happening in Berkshire County at: **http://berkcon.com.**

SHEFFIELD

The first settlement of any size encountered when approaching from Connecticut on Route 7, is ✪ **Sheffield,** known as the "Antiques Capital of the Berkshires." It occupies a floodplain beside the Housatonic River, 11 miles south of Great Barrington, with the Berkshires rising to the west.

Agriculture has been the principal occupation of its residents, and still is to a large degree. Everyone else sells antiques, or so it might seem driving along Route 7 (a.k.a., Main Street or Sheffield Plain). The wide road and generously spaced, meticulously maintained houses cultivate an impression of prosperous tranquillity.

A PIONEER'S HOME

May through October, make a short excursion to see the **Colonel Ashley House,** Cooper Hill Road (☎ 413/229-8600), in Ashley Falls. Built in 1735, this small, gray, modified saltbox is believed to be the oldest house in Berkshire County. Its builder, Colonel Ashley, was a person of considerable repute in colonial western Massachusetts, a pioneer settler, an officer in one of the French and Indian Wars, and later a lawyer and a judge. Furnishings and farm tools appropriate to the period inform the interior.

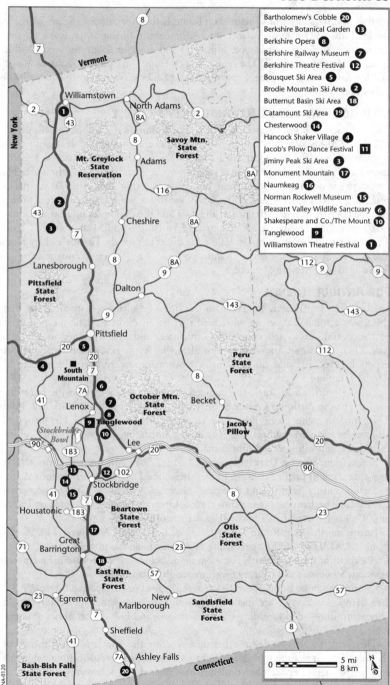

The Berkshires

Bartholomew's Cobble **20**
Berkshire Botanical Garden **13**
Berkshire Opera **8**
Berkshire Railway Museum **7**
Berkshire Theatre Festival **12**
Bousquet Ski Area **5**
Brodie Mountain Ski Area **2**
Butternut Basin Ski Area **18**
Catamount Ski Area **19**
Chesterwood **14**
Hancock Shaker Village **4**
Jacob's Pilow Dance Festival **11**
Jiminy Peak Ski Area **3**
Monument Mountain **17**
Naumkeag **16**
Norman Rockwell Museum **15**
Pleasant Valley Wildlife Sanctuary **6**
Shakespeare and Co./The Mount **10**
Tanglewood **9**
Williamstown Theatre Festival **1**

NA-0120

To find it, drive south from Sheffield on Route 7, then veer off onto Route 7A toward Ashley Falls. After a short distance on 7A, bear right on Rannappo Road. At the Y intersection, turn right on Cooper Hill Road and drive for about 200 yards. Visiting times are sharply restricted. The house is open from 1 to 5pm on Saturday, Sunday, and holiday Mondays in June, September, and October; Wednesday to Sunday July to Labor Day.

OUTDOOR PURSUITS AT BARTHOLOMEW'S COBBLE

The 278-acre nature reservation called **Bartholomew's Cobble,** on Route 7A (☎ 413/229-8600), lies beside an oxbow bend in the Housatonic. It is latticed with 6 miles of trails for hiking or cross-country skiing. They cross pastures, penetrate forests, and provide vistas of the river valley from the area's high point, Hurlburt's Hill. Picnicking is permitted. A sign near the entrance claims there are 700 varieties of plants, 125 types of trees, and 450 kinds of wildflowers. Birders should take binoculars, for many species are attracted to the flora and the feeders set up near the administrative cabin. The requested donations are $3 for adults and $1 for children 6 to 12. To get to Bartholomew's Cobble, follow the directions for the Colonel Ashley House (see above), except at the end of Rannappo Road, bear left on Weatogue Road and follow it to the reservation entrance.

FOR ANTIQUE HOUNDS

Sheffield can legitimately lay claim to the title of "Antiques Capital of the Berkshires"—no small feat, given what seems to be an effort by half the population of the Berkshires to sell collectibles, treasures, and near-antiques to the other half. These are canny, knowledgeable dealers who know exactly what they have, so expect high quality and no bargains. Of the many, many possibilities, here is a slender sampling.

Driving north on Route 7, the jumbled display of birdhouses on the right drags your eye to the **Antiques Center of Sheffield,** 33 S. Main St. (☎ 413/229-3400). The garrulous owner claims it has been an antiques store since 1860. His stock is not afflicted by excessive tidiness, but it is diverse, including railroad lanterns, military mementos, and wildly varied Americana.

Across Main Street is **Darr Antiques** (☎ 413/229-7773), two well-ordered buildings that stand in pristine contrast to their neighbor. Darr specializes in formal 18th- and 19th-century English and American furniture, with some Chinese accessories, accumulated on frequent buying trips abroad. Open year-round, it's closed on Tuesday and Wednesday in winter, Tuesday only the rest of the year.

Farther north along Route 7, on the right, is **Dovetail Antiques,** 440 Sheffield Plain (☎ 413/229-2628), specializing in American clocks, primarily those made in Connecticut in the last century. Some have gears, cogs, and other internal parts made of wood. Stoneware and country furniture are also available.

Continuing along Route 7, on the left at the edge of town, is **Susan Silver** (☎ 413/229-8169). On display are meticulously restored 18th- and 19th-century English library furniture—desks, reading stands, cabinets—and French accessories of comparable age.

There are at least two dozen other dealers along this route. Most of them stock the **free directory** of the Berkshire County Antiques Dealers Association, which lists and briefly describes member dealers from Sheffield to Cheshire and across the border in Connecticut and New York. Look, too, for the pamphlet called *The Antique Hunter's Guide to Route 7,* covering 81 dealers along that road in both Massachusetts and Vermont.

WHERE TO STAY

Ivanhoe Country House. 254 S. Undermountain Rd. (Rte. 41), Sheffield, MA 01257.
☎ **413/229-2143.** 9 units. Summer $95–$125 double; winter $75–$95 double. Rates
include breakfast. No credit cards, but personal checks accepted. Dogs allowed ($10 extra).

A stay at this inn feels like a visit to a gregarious country aunt, the one who has her
rules. No decorator had a hand in assembling the stolid, comfortable furnishings.
Rooms have either double beds or twins (no queens) and each has a refrigerator for
guests' beverages. Three have working fireplaces and access to porches. Tray breakfasts
are left outside guests' doors each morning. The only TV is in the common room, and
there's an unheated pool out back.

   Rules? No children under 15 on weekends in July and August; dogs must be leashed
at all times and cannot be left alone in guests' rooms.

SOUTH EGREMONT

If you're coming to the Berkshires from the Taconic Parkway in New York, you can't
help but drive through the town of Egremont. Its larger, busier half is South Egremont, a diverting village that was once a stop on the stagecoach route between Hartford and Albany. It retains many structures from that era, including mills that utilized
the stream that still rushes by. Those circumstances make it a magnet for antiques
dealers, restaurateurs, and refugee urban professionals who have made the precarious
leap into innkeeping and retailing.

OUTDOOR PURSUITS

HIKING   In warmer months, scenic ✪ **Bash Bish Falls State Park,** on Route 23
(☎ 413/528-0330), makes a rewarding day outing for hiking, birding, and fishing. (No
camping or picnicking, though.)

   To get there, drive west on Route 23 from the town center, turning south on Route
41, and immediately right on Mount Washington Road. Keep alert for signs directing
the way to Mount Washington State Forest and Bash Bish Falls. After 8 miles, past
fallow fields, summer houses, and groves of white birch bright against the deep green
of dense pine, a sign indicates a right turn toward the falls. Look for it opposite a
board-and-batten church with an unusual steeple. The road begins to follow the
course of a mountain stream, going downhill. In about 3 miles, on the left, is a large
parking place next to a craggy promontory and a sign prohibiting alcohol, camping,
and fires.

   The sign also points off to a trail down to the falls, which should only be negoti-
ated by reasonably fit adults. First, mount the promontory for a splendid view across
the plains of the Hudson Valley to the pale-blue ridgeline of the Catskill Mountains,
between two rounded peaks off to the west. The falls can be heard, but not yet seen,
down to the left. If this trail seems too steep, continue driving down the road to
another parking area, on the left. From here, a gentler trail a little over a mile long
leads to the falls. The falls themselves are quite impressive, crashing down from
more than 50 feet into a deep pool. The park is open from dawn to dusk. Admission is free.

SKIING   At the western edge of the township, touching the New York border, is the
Catamount Ski Area, on Route 23 (☎ 413/528-1262, www.catamountski.com).
About 2 hours from Manhattan, it is understandably popular with New Yorkers, who
must drive twice as long to get to Vermont's higher peaks. It has 24 trails, including
the daunting "Catapult," the steepest run in the Berkshires (experts only), and four
double chairlifts. There is also night skiing on 13 of the area's trails.

SHOPPING

Fans of 19th-century weathervanes and museum-quality folk arts or of painted country furniture from America, Quebec, and Bavaria, are delighted by the offerings of **The Splendid Peasant,** on Route 23 (☎ 413/528-5755). Evidently, they have much company, for the owners have expanded their galleries into a second building.

Kenver, a ¼-mile west on Route 23, is a ski shop in a handsome 18th-century brick building. Its comprehensive stock includes wide selections of skis, boots, helmets, parkas and related clothing. They install and test bindings as well as sharpen and wax skis. Open daily September through March.

WHERE TO STAY

Egremont Inn. Old Sheffield Rd. (1 block off Rte. 23), S. Egremont, MA 01258. ☎ **413/528-2111.** Fax 413/528-3284. www.egremontinn.com. E-mail: egremontinn@taconic.net. 21 units. A/C TEL. Summer/autumn $90–$170 double; winter/spring $80–$165 double. Rates include breakfast. Weekend packages available. AE, DISC, MC, V, personal checks.

Slip into this friendly former stagecoach stop as easily as into a favorite old flannel robe. Tens of thousands of travelers have preceded you, for the Egremont has been a tavern and inn since 1780. That longevity shows, in tilting floors and lintels and a grand brick fireplace constructed over an ancient blacksmith hearth. Ongoing renovations have included the merging of smaller bedrooms to create five suites, and two now have whirlpool baths. The only TV is the satellite-fed set in one of the common rooms.

Dining/Diversions: Dinner is served Wednesday to Sunday year-round, with entrees from $16 to $20.50 in the dining room and $10 to $14.50 for the casual menu in the tavern. A singer-guitarist performs Thursday nights, a jazz ensemble Saturday evenings.

Amenities: There are two tennis courts and a pool out back.

Weathervane Inn. Rte. 23, S. Egremont, MA 01258. ☎ **800/528-9580** or 413/528-9580. Fax 413/528-1713. www.weathervaneinn.com. E-mail: innkeeper@weathervaneinn.com. 13 units. A/C. $125–$165 double; $150–$175 suite. Rates include breakfast and afternoon tea. AE, MC, V, personal checks. Children over 7 welcome.

An affectionate cat welcomes new arrivals to a building that began as a 1735 farmhouse, but was renovated in Greek Revival style in 1835. Many of the bedrooms have four-poster beds with quilts; fireplaces have been added to two rooms, and a whirlpool bath is to be added to one of the suites. An unheated pool is available, and there is a public golf course next door. So far, the new innkeepers, who took over in 1998, haven't made too many changes.

WHERE TO DINE

✪ **John Andrew's.** Rte. 23. ☎ **413/528-3469.** Reservations recommended on weekends. Main courses $13–$24. MC, V. June–Aug Mon–Sat 5:30–10pm; Sun 11am–3pm and 4–10pm. Sept–May Thurs–Tues 5–10pm. ECLECTIC AMERICAN.

The exalted standing of this superior farmhouse restaurant hasn't dipped an inch, even though the owners are now also behind the new Union Bar & Grill in Great Barrington. A fertile imagination is at work behind the kitchen doors, one that conjures such refreshing departures as seared sea scallops with couscous and sweet-pea mint coulis. A variety of breads—rosemary focaccia, pita, and sourdough, for example—arrives with the generous cocktails. Rows of windows in the rear dining room let in the fading summer light, which falls on Parsons chairs, wood floors, and sponged walls of dusky rose. All is very near countrified faultlessness.

Mom's Cafe. Main St. ☎ **413/528-2414.** Main courses $8.95–$9.95. MC, V. Daily 6:30am–10pm. ECLECTIC.

This informal drop-in place perks from early breakfast to late cappuccino seven days a week. That and its low prices are the cafe's greatest virtues in an area where most chefs are intent on working only five evenings a week. Mom's menu runs from omelets and pancakes to pastas and pizzas with toppings as diverse as avocado and pineapple. In good weather, eat on the deck over the stream that runs behind the building.

GREAT BARRINGTON

Even with a population well under 8,000, this pleasant commercial and retail center, 7 miles south of Stockbridge, is the largest town in the southernmost part of the county. Rapids in the Housatonic provided power for a number of mills in centuries past, most of which are now gone, and in 1886 it was one of the first communities in the world to have electricity on its streets and in its homes. More recently, it was spared by the killer tornado of Memorial Day 1995 that hopped over Great Barrington only to touch down again a few miles east around Monterey, tearing off hundreds of trees halfway up their trunks. That devastation will be seen along Route 23 for years to come.

Great Barrington has no sights of particular significance, leaving time to browse its many antiques galleries and growing number of specialty shops. Convenient as a home base for excursions to such nearby attractions as Monument Mountain, Bash Bish Falls, Butternut Basin, Tanglewood concerts, and the museums and historic houses of Stockbridge, it has a number of unremarkable but entirely adequate motels along or near Route 7 that tend to fill up more slowly on weekends than the better-known inns in the area. It is something of a dining center, too, compared to other Berkshire towns.

The **Southern Berkshire Chamber of Commerce** maintains an information booth at 362 Main St. (☎ **413/528-1510**), near the town hall. It's open Monday to Thursday from 9:30am to 4:30pm, Friday from 9:30am to 5pm, and Saturday from 9:30am to 3:30pm.

OUTDOOR PURSUITS

The **Egremont Country Club,** on Route 23 (☎ **413/528-4222**), is open to the public. Its facilities include an 18-hole golf course, tennis courts, and an Olympic-size pool.

Butternut Basin, also on Route 23, 2 miles east of town (☎ **413/528-2000,** www.butternutbasin.com), is known for its strong family ski programs. A children's center provides day care for kids ages 2½ to 6 daily from December 23 until the end of the season, and the SKIwee program offers full- and half-day programs for children 4 to 12 that include lunch, ski instruction, and a lift ticket. Six double and quad chair-lifts provide access to 22 trails, the longest of which is a 1½-mile run. There are also 5 miles of cross-country trails. Midday grooming of the trails is a recent innovation.

A little over 4 miles north of town, west of Route 7, is **Monument Mountain,** with two hiking trails to the summit. The easier route is called the Indian Monument Trail, about an hour's hike to the top; the more difficult one, the Hickey Trail, isn't much longer but takes the steep way up, and should probably be avoided by novice hikers. The summit, called Squaw Peak for an Indian maiden who allegedly leapt to her death from the spot, offers splendid panoramic views. Nathaniel Hawthorne and Herman Melville, two members of the remarkable mid-19th-century literary set that summered in the Berkshires, first met here on a hiking trip.

SHOPPING

Head straight for **Railroad Street,** the town's best shopping strip. Start on the corner with Main Street, at **T. P. Saddle Blanket & Trading Co.,** 304 Main St. (☎ **413/ 528-6500**), an unlikely emporium that looks as if it had been lifted whole from the Colorado Rockies. Packed with country furniture and Western gear—boots, hats, plates, Indian jewelry, pitchers, jars of salsa, rugs, and blankets—it's open every day.

Down the left side of Railroad Street is **Mistral's,** (☎ 413/528-1618), whose French-Canadian owner parades her good taste with a stock of Gallic tableware, bed linens, fancy foods, furniture, and night wear. It's open daily. Nearby, at no. 9, **Nahuál** (☎ 413/528-2423) offers colorful and imaginative folk arts and handicrafts, primarily from Africa and Latin America.

Across the street at no. 4 is the **Church Street Trading Company** (☎413/ 528-6120). It defies easy categorization, what with walking sticks, feather dusters, dog collars, and aromatic candles all on display, but the primary wares are sturdily stylish north country sweaters, shirts, and pants for men and women.

Around the corner, at 290 Main Street, is **The Chef's Shop** (☎413/528-0135). Along with a bounty of kitchen gadgets, cookware, and cookbooks, chefs from several of the restaurants recommended in these pages conduct periodic 3-hour cooking classes.

Several antiques and art galleries and other enterprises mingle kitsch and class at **Jennifer House Commons** (☎ 413/528-2690), north of town on Route 7.

In town, just before Route 7 turns right across a short bridge, Route 41 goes straight, toward the village of Housatonic. In about 4 miles you'll see a long shed that houses the kiln and workrooms of **The Great Barrington Pottery** (☎ 413/ 274-6259). Owner/master Richard Bennett has been throwing pots according to ancient Japanese techniques for over 30 years. His separate showroom is open year-round.

WHERE TO STAY

North of town on U.S. 7 is economical **Monument Mountain,** 249 Stockbridge Rd. (☎ 413/528-3272), which has a pool, tennis courts, and a riverside location.

The Old Inn on the Green & Gedney Farm. Rte. 57, New Marlborough, MA 01230. ☎ 800/286-3139 or 413/229-3131. Fax 413/229-8236. www.oldinn.com. 26 units. TEL. $135–$225 double, $245–$285 suite, $300–$350 Thayer House rooms. 25% discount Mon–Wed. Rates include breakfast. AE, MC, V. Take Rte. 23 east from Great Barrington, picking up Rte. 57 after 3.4 miles. After 5.7 miles, the Old Inn is on the left. Continue another ¼ mile to the barns on the left. Registration is on the ground floor of the gray barn.

This three-part establishment is comprised of a former 1760 tavern/general store and the newly renovated 18th-century Thayer House, both on the village green, and a pair of converted dairy barns down the road. The most desirable rooms are the five luxury guest rooms in Thayer House, some with fireplaces, and in the barn, where contemporary furnishings and accessories are combined with Oriental rugs. Given the steep prices, guests might reasonably expect TVs and air-conditioning. They don't get them; there is a pool, though.

Dining: The restaurant, which has built a reputation based on the pronounced creativity of its kitchen, is in the Old Inn, open only for dinner.

Windflower Inn. 684 S. Egremont Rd. (P.O. Box 25), Great Barrington, MA 01230. ☎ 800/ 992-1993 or 413/528-2720. Fax 413/528-5147. www.windflowerinn.com. 13 units. A/C TV. $100–$180 double. Rates include breakfast and afternoon tea. AE.

A roadside lodging for decades, the Windflower has attained its highest order of quality under the current owners, a two-generation family that has operated it since 1980. Built in the middle of the last century in Federal style, it commands a large plot of land opposite the Egremont Country Club on Route 23 between Great Barrington and South Egremont. All rooms have small black-and-white TVs, six have fireplaces, and four have canopied beds. Out back is an unheated pool. Children are welcome (for another $25 each).

WHERE TO DINE

In addition to the places listed below, you might check out the restaurant at the **Old Inn on the Green & Gedney Farm** (see "Where to Stay," above).

Barrington Brewery. Rte. 7 (in the Jennifer House complex, north of town). ☎ **413/528-8282.** Main courses $9.95–$14.95. AE, DISC, MC, V. Daily 11:30am–10 or 11pm (depending on business). ECLECTIC AMERICAN.

Nothing detracts from the primary function of this brewery in a converted barn. All its beers and ales are made upstairs and funneled directly to the taps in the tavern. They are good enough to distract even devoted oenophiles (although interesting wines are also available). A fun gimmick is the "Brewer's Taste," a selection of five shot glasses filled with samples of current beers. Grub, of the burger and nacho variety, is secondary but tasty enough to serve as foil for the brews. They bake their own breads and desserts. The ground floor is all no-smoking, even at the bar.

✪ **Castle Street Cafe.** 10 Castle St. (near the Town Hall). ☎ **413/528-5244.** Main courses $9–$21. AE, DISC, MC, V. Wed–Mon 5–9pm, (until 10pm Fri–Sat). NEW AMERICAN.

This storefront bistro has ruled the Great Barrington roost for some time now, and recently expanded into the next building, installing what it calls a "Celestial Bar," with live jazz on weekends. While a Francophilic inclination is apparent in the main room, it isn't overpowering, not with sole stuffed with smoked salmon mousse among the possibilities. Pasta servings are so large that half portions are available. There's a short bar in the new room to have a drink while checking out the night's menu. Stay there for such casual eats as burritos, burgers, and pâtés. An award-winning wine list is another reason to stop in. It's smoke-free until 9pm, at which time addicts light up in the bar area.

Union Bar & Grill. 293 Main St. ☎413/528-6228. Main courses $14.95–18.95. MC, V. Thurs–Tues 11:30am–11pm (bar until 1am). ECLECTIC.

A sculptor designed the industrial-chic interior, with the exposed ceiling ducts, rows of hanging bulbs, and brushed metal trim that are associated with New York's TriBeCa. The menu might have been transplanted, too, given, for one example, the herb-crusted snowy halibut and its accompanying scallion pancake with tomato-ginger jam. Even the usually prosaic steak sandwich at lunch turns out to be a grilled pita wrapped around caramelized red onion, beef slices, melted cheese, and a piquant sauce. The owners also created the admirable John Andrew's, described above.

GREAT BARRINGTON AFTER DARK

The **Aston Magna Festival** features baroque and classical music performed on period instruments. Concerts are held on five Sundays in July and August at the St. James Church, Main Street and Taconic Avenue (☎ 413/528-3595) at 6pm. The **Berkshire Opera Company** (☎ 413/528-4420) offers several performances of two operas, sung in English, in July and August. They are usually presented in the theater of the Monument Mountain Regional High School on U.S. 7. Call for a schedule.

The fairly small **Triplex Cinema**, at 70 Railroad St. (☎413/528-8885), a block west of Main St., shows a mixed bag of independent and foreign flicks as well as major studio releases.

STOCKBRIDGE

Stockbridge's ready accessibility to Boston and New York (about 2½ hours away from both and reachable by rail since the second half of the 19th century) transformed the original frontier settlement into a Gilded Age summer retreat for the super-rich and the merely wealthy. The town has long been popular with artists and writers as well. Norman Rockwell, who lived here for 25 years, rendered the Main Street of his adopted town in a famous painting. Along and near Main Street are a number of historic homes and other attractions, enough to fill up a long weekend, even without the Tanglewood concert season in nearby Lenox.

✪ **Stockbridge** lies 7 miles north of Great Barrington and 6 miles south of Lenox. The chamber of commerce maintains a seasonal **information booth** opposite the row of stores depicted by Rockwell. It's open, often with an attendant, from May through October, with stocks of pamphlets and notices about area attractions and lodgings.

SEEING THE SIGHTS

✪ **Norman Rockwell Museum.** Rte. 183. ☎ **413/298-4100.** www.nrm.org. Admission $9 adults, $2 children 6–18, $20 family. May–Oct daily 10am–5pm. Nov–Apr Mon–Fri 10am–4pm; Sat–Sun 10am–5pm. Take Main St. (Rte. 102) west to the junction with Rte. 183, then turn left (south) at the traffic signal. In about ½ mile, you'll see the entrance to the museum on the left.

This striking, generously proportioned building opened in 1993, at a cost of $4.4 million, to house the works of Stockbridge's favorite son. The beloved illustrator used both his neighbors and the town where he lived for the last third of his life to tell stories about an America rapidly fading from memory. Most of Rockwell's paintings adorned covers of the weekly *Saturday Evening Post:* warm and often humorous depictions of homecomings, first proms, and visits to the doctor and the marriage-license bureau. He addressed serious concerns, too, notably with his series *The Four Freedoms* and his poignant portrait of a little African-American girl in a white dress being escorted by U.S. marshals into a previously segregated school. Art critics regarded his work as saccharine and sentimental, but the self-effacing artist didn't fire back; instead he professed his admiration for the work of the Abstract Expressionists.

Selections of his illustrations are rotated into view from the large permanent collection, the pity being that none of his ingenious *April Fool's* covers are included.

The lovely 36-acre grounds also contain Rockwell's last studio, moved here to a point overlooking a bend in the Housatonic. Picnic tables are provided.

Chesterwood. 4 Williamsville Rd. ☎ **413/298-3579.** Admission $7.50 adults ($5.50 for grounds only), $4 ages 13–18, $2 children 6–12, free for children under 6. May 1–Oct 31 daily 10am–5pm. Drive west on Main St., south on Rte. 183 about 1 mile to the Chesterwood sign.

Sculptor Daniel Chester French, best known for the Abraham Lincoln Memorial in Washington, D.C., used this estate as his summer home and studio for over 30 years. His *Minute Man* statue at the Old North Bridge in Concord, completed in 1875 at the age of 25, launched his highly successful career. His house and studio here were designed by his friend and collaborator, Henry Bacon. The grounds of the 122-acre estate are used for an annual show of contemporary sculpture. A visit here can easily be combined with one to the Rockwell Museum, which is less than a mile away.

Naumkeag. Prospect Hill. ☎ **413/298-3239.** Admission $7 adults, $2.50 children. Daily Memorial Day to Columbus Day 10am–5pm. From the Cat & Dog Fountain in the intersection next to the Red Lion Inn, drive north on Pine St. to Prospect Hill Rd. about ½ mile on the left.

Architect Stanford White of the celebrated firm of McKim, Mead & White designed this 26-room house for Joseph Hodge Choate in 1886. His client dubbed the classic Berkshire cottage "Naumkeag," an Amerindian name for Salem, Massachusetts, his childhood home. Choate was a lawyer and served as U.S. ambassador to the Court of St. James's. His many-gabled-and-chimneyed house is largely of the New England Shingle style, surrounded by impressive gardens. Admission is by guided tour only, but worth it for the glimpses of the rich interior, fully furnished and decorated in the manner of the period, including an extensive collection of Chinese export porcelain.

Berkshire Botanical Garden. Routes 102 and 183. ☎ **413/298-3926.** Admission $5 adults, $4 seniors, free for children under 12. May–Oct daily 10am–5pm. Drive west from downtown Stockbridge on Main St., picking up Church St. (Rte. 102) northwest for about 2 miles.

These 15 acres of flower beds, shrubs, ponds, and raised vegetable and herb gardens are an inviting destination for strollers and picnickers. The first weekend in October is devoted to a harvest festival, which features jugs of cider, displays of pumpkins, and hayrides. A new shade perennial display garden was installed in Spring 1999. Tours are offered on weekends from June through August.

Children's Chime Bell Tower. Main St. No phone. Free admission.

West of the town center, the Greek Revival Town Hall and a mid-19th-century red-brick Congregational church face the old village green. The campanile out front is the 1878 Children's Chime Bell Tower. Its bells are tolled every evening from "apple blossom time until frost."

Merwin House. 14 Main St. ☎ **413/298-4703.** Admission $4 adults, $3.50 seniors, $2 children 6–12, free for children under 6. Tours June 1–Oct Sat–Sun 11am–4pm on the hour.

A small brick Federalist house with a later wood-frame extension, this 1825 residence contains furnishings true to the period. The lawn runs down to the Housatonic.

Mission House. Main and Sergeant sts. (Rte. 102). ☎ **413/298-3239.** Admission $5 adults, $2.50 children. Memorial Day to Columbus Day daily 10am–5pm.

The Rev. John Sergeant had the most benevolent, if paternalistic, of intentions: he sought to build a house among the members of the Housatonic tribe, hoping to convert them to civilized (i.e., English) ways through proximity to his godly self and his small band of settlers. The weathered Mission House, built in 1739, was the site of this Christianizing process, and it was moved to its current location in 1928. Visits are by guided tour and include a stroll around the herb garden.

✪ THE BERKSHIRE THEATRE FESTIVAL

From June to late August, and occasionally at other times during the year, the Berkshire Theatre Festival, P.O. Box 797, Main St. (☎ **413/298-5576**), holds its summer season of classic and new plays, often with marquee names starring or directing. Dianne Wiest and Joanne Woodward were recent participants. Its venue is a "casino" built in 1887 to plans by architect Stanford White of McKim, Mead & White. A second theater, the Unicorn Stage, opened in 1996. Tickets are $21 to $36 for the main stage, less for the Unicorn, and are usually pretty easy to get, unless you're trying for a weekend night or a performance with a name star.

WHERE TO STAY

✪ **Inn at Stockbridge.** 30 East St. (Rte. 7; Box 618), Stockbridge, MA 01262. ☎ **888/ 466-7865** or 413/298-3337. Fax 413/298-3406. www.stockbridgeinn.com. E-mail: innkeeper@stckbridgeinn.com. 12 units. A/C TV TEL. June–Oct $125–$275 double; Nov–May $115–$205 double. Rates include breakfast. AE, DISC, MC, V. No children under 12.

A mile north of Stockbridge center, this 1906 building with a grandly columned porch is set well back from the road on 12 landscaped acres. The former New Yorkers who own and run the inn are eager to please, serving full breakfasts by candlelight and afternoon spreads of cheese and wine (hot cider in cold weather). They have added another four attractively decorated bedrooms in a new annex, most desirable for guests who prefer more space. The four have VCRs. Greater charm is enjoyed in the older accommodations, however, especially the Terrace Room, with a deck, a private entrance, and Jacuzzi. There is also an outdoor pool. Totally no-smoking.

The Red Lion. Main St., Stockbridge, MA 01262. ☎ **413/298-5545.** Fax 413/298-5130. www.redlioninn.com. 111 units, 18 share bathrooms. A/C TEL. Late Apr to late Oct $115–$165 double; $185–$355 suite. Late Oct to late Apr $87–$140 double; $165–$325 suite. AE, CB, DC, DISC, MC, V.

So well known that it serves as an all-inclusive symbol of the Berkshires, this eternally busy inn had its origins as a stagecoach tavern in 1773. That original building is long gone, and the summer hotel that grew up on the site burned to the ground in 1896. It was quickly rebuilt into what is essentially the structure extant today. Many of the antiques arranged in both public and private rooms survived the fire, including a collection of colonial table china. Most, but not all, rooms have TVs, some have VCRs. Make reservations even further in advance than is recommended for other Berkshire inns. The rocking chairs on the long porch are the perfect place to while away an hour reading or people-watching. Unending renovations recently brought heat to the outdoor pool.

   Dining/Diversions: Guests may choose among the main dining room (jackets required for men at dinner), the casual Widow Bingham Tavern, the basement Lion's Den, and, in good weather, the courtyard out back. The **Lion's Den** also has nightly live entertainment, usually of the folk-rock variety, and never a cover charge.

Taggart House. Main St., Stockbridge, MA 01262. ☎ and fax **413/298-4303.** 4 units. A/C. July–Oct $235–$355 double; Nov–June $175–$255 double. Rates include breakfast. 2- or 3-day minimum stays summer and fall weekends. AE, CB, DC, DISC, MC, V. Inquire about children.

Ordinarily, an inn with only four guest rooms wouldn't merit space here. But what rooms! The decor and furnishings of this outwardly sedate 1850 Victorian/colonial mansion, a block west of the Red Lion, are breathtaking. Start with the theatrical main floor—the dining room, perhaps. The inlaid mahogany table was once a centerpiece in an Argentine palace and is now the site of candlelight breakfasts that more nearly resemble brunch. Wallpapers and fabrics are mostly of the complex arts-and-crafts variety. A birch-bark canoe hangs above the billiard table, the largest item of a collection of Native American artifacts. There is a paneled library, a ballroom, a harpsichord, and nine beguiling fireplaces. And upstairs, beds with fur throws or East Indian silk coverlets or velvet canopies and chests painted with turtle-shell effects . . . it would take many more pages than are available to describe this immersion in the Gilded Age.

WHERE TO DINE

Michael's. Elm St. (off Main St.). ☎ **413/298-3530.** Main courses 12.95–$15.95. AE, CB, DC, MC, V. Mon–Sat 11:30am–9pm, Sun noon–10pm (bar until 1am). ITALIAN/AMERICAN.

This tavern with a sports tilt is one of the few nearby alternatives to the Red Lion Inn. Bar snacks served around the 60-inch TV are of the nachos variety, while dinner entrees in the dining room run to steaks, chicken dijon and scallops marinara. The food is pretty good, the greeting friendly, and the place stays open throughout the day. Upstairs are pool tables and video games.

WEST STOCKBRIDGE

The hills around this Stockbridge satellite (it's just 5 miles northwest) are alive with creativity. Potters, painters, writers, sculptors, weavers, and glassblowers pursue their compulsions summers or year-round, selling the results from their studios and several galleries. A pamphlet called *The Art of West Stockbridge* is available in display racks throughout the area and describes the work of some of the more important artisans and where it can be found.

One of the most ambitious new creative enterprises is the **Berkshire Center for Contemporary Glass,** 6 Harris St. (☎ **413/232-4666**). The spanking new building has space for both a showroom and a large work area. Kids find the process fascinating and are even allowed to participate. Classes and workshops are scheduled. The center, located in the heart of the village, is open daily from 10am to 10pm May through October, 10am to 6pm November through April.

WHERE TO STAY & DINE

Williamsville Inn. Rte. 41 (about 5 miles south of town), West Stockbridge, MA 01266. ☎ **413/274-6118.** Fax 413/274-3539. www.williamsvilleinn.com. E-mail: williamsville@ taconic.net. 16 units. A/C. July–Oct $120–$185 double; Nov–June $120–$160 double. AE, MC, V.

Rooms are in the 1797 main house, the converted barn, or in the no-frills cottages. Some have woodstoves or fireplaces, full bathrooms or shower stalls, and some are more expensive than they should be.

Dining/Diversions: The kitchen has received good notices for its "eclectic country cuisine," and the two dining rooms are open for dinner from 6 to 9pm—Wednesday to Monday from June through October, Thursday to Sunday from November through May. A popular storytelling-and-dinner series is held Sunday nights from November through April.

Amenities: On the grounds are a clay tennis court, a pool, and a summer sculpture garden.

WHERE TO DINE

La Bruschetta. 1 Harris St. ☎ **413/232-7141.** Reservations advised. Main courses $17.50–$20. AE, MC, V. July–Oct daily 5–9pm; May–June Thurs–Mon 5–9pm; Nov–Apr Thurs–Sat 5–9pm. NEW ITALIAN.

Forgive them their too-brief hours, for the chef-owners create splendidly aromatic dishes that require care and advanced technique. *Pre*-appetizers are *bruschettas,* grilled slices of bread piled with a variety of fragrant toppings. A basket of warm bread and a saucer of olive oil follow, so you might want to skip first courses. Rich, long-simmered sauces characterize the main courses, whether pasta, meat, or fowl, demanding to be sopped up to the last drop. Wines are as carefully selected as the ingredients. Just make sure the place is open before making the trip.

✪ **Truc Orient Express.** 2 Harris St. ☎ **413/232-4204.** Main courses $7.50–$12. AE, MC, V. Daily 11am–3pm and 5–10pm. Closed Tues in winter. VIETNAMESE.

If La Bruschetta is closed, as is often the case, just walk across the yard to Truc, in a rambling onetime warehouse. The menu is full of revelatory taste sensations. *Mai tuyet nhi* is a soup adrift with snow mushrooms and lobster meat, a suitable lead-in to the extravaganza called *lauthap cam-chap pin loo,* a hot pot crowded with meatballs, shrimp, squid, scallops, and assorted veggies simmered tableside in a shiny brass pot and ladled over rice noodles.

LEE

While Stockbridge and Lenox were developing into luxurious recreational centers for the upper crust of Boston and New York, Lee was a thriving paper-mill town. That meant it was shunned by the wealthy summer people and thus remained essentially a town of workers and merchants. It has a somewhat raffish, although not unappealing, aspect, its center bunched with shops and offices and few of the stately homes and broad lawns that characterize its neighboring communities.

The town's contribution to the Berkshire cultural calendar is the Jacob's Pillow Dance Festival, which first thrived as "Denishawn," a fabled alliance between founders Ted Shawn and Ruth St. Denis.

Lee is located 5 miles southeast of Lenox. The Lee Chamber of Commerce operates an **information center** during summer and early fall on the Town Common, Route 20 (☎ **413/243-0852**).

✪ THE JACOB'S PILLOW DANCE FESTIVAL

Jacob's Pillow, George Carter Road, Becket (☎ **413/243-0745**), is to dance what Tanglewood is to classical music. Once a regular summer venue for famed dancer and choreographer Martha Graham, the theater has long welcomed troupes of international reputation, of late including the Mark Morris Dance Group, the Merce Cunningham Dance Company, and the Paul Taylor Dance Company, as well as companies whose work is based on jazz, flamenco, and Indian and Asian music. The season is from late June to late August, and tickets go on sale May 1 (the summer's program is usually announced by February; call the number above to request a schedule by mail). The more prominent companies are seen in the main Ted Shawn Theatre, where tickets are in the $27-to-$45 range; other troupes are assigned to the Studio/Theatre, where tickets are $12 to $16. Tickets are usually readily available, unless the performance in question is a big-name event, or you've decided to go at the last minute. They can be ordered any time at **www.jacobspillow.org.**

A BERKSHIRE ART GALLERY

With no immediate obligatory historic homes or museums to see, visitors often make the short excursion to the hamlet of Tyringham. To get there, take Route 20 south to Route 102, near the no. 2 interchange of the Massachusetts Turnpike. Following the signs through the complicated intersection, pick up Tyringham Road and drive south about 4 miles.

You'll know when you get there. It's on the left, an odd fairy-tale structure called **Santarella** (☎ **413/243-3260**), but known by most people simply as Tyringham's "Gingerbread House." At the front wall are jagged limestone outcroppings, in back are conical turrets topping towers, and the shingled roof rolls like waves on the ocean. Erected at the turn of the century, it served as a studio for sculptor Henry Hudson Kitson from 1930 to 1947. It now houses art galleries showcasing the works of Berkshire artists. Open daily from 10am to 4:30pm, May through October. Admission is $3.75 adults; free for children.

OUTDOOR ACTIVITIES

October Mountain State Forest offers 50 campsites (with showers) and more than 16,000 acres for hiking and walking, canoeing and other nonmotorized boating, cross-country skiing, and snowmobiling. To get there, drive northwest on Route 20 into town, turn right on Center Street, and follow the signs.

WHERE TO STAY

The **Lee Chamber of Commerce,** which operates an information center during summer and early fall on the Town Common, Route 20 (☎ **413/243-0852**), can help you find lodging in the area, often in modest guest houses and B&Bs—rarely as grand as those in Lenox (see below), but nearly always significantly cheaper. That's something to remember when every other place near Tanglewood seems to be either fully booked or quoting prices of $200 a night or more.

A lakeside motel on the road to Lenox, the **Black Swan,** 435 Laurel St., Mass. 20 (☎ **413/243-2700**), has a pool and sauna.

✪ **Applegate.** 279 W. Park St., Lee, MA 01238. ☎ **800/691-9012** or 413/243-4451. www.applegateinn.com. 6 units. A/C. June–Oct $115–$230 double; Nov–May $95–$195 double. MC, V. From Stockbridge, drive north on Rte. 7. In about a ½ mile, take a right on Lee Rd. The inn is 2¼ miles ahead, on the right. No children under 12.

This paragon of the B&B trade utilizes a gracious 1920s Georgian colonial manse to full advantage. The most desirable lodging has a huge canopied bed with a puffy comforter, Queen Anne reproductions, sunlight filtering through gauzy curtains, a walk-around steam shower, and a fireplace (with real wood). Robes hang ready for guests' use, and a carafe of brandy is waiting. Wing chairs have good reading lights. Other rooms are similar, albeit somewhat smaller. The two-bedroom carriage-house suite has a Jacuzzi and a kitchenette. No room TVs, but there's a large set with VCR on the sunporch.

Breakfast is by candlelight, and the innkeepers set out wine and cheese in the afternoon. There's a swimming pool, and across the street is a nine-hole golf course. Five cats call Applegate home, so drive in carefully.

Chambéry Inn. 199 Main St., Lee, MA 01238. ☎ **413/243-2221.** Fax 413/243-0039. 9 units. A/C TV TEL. July–Aug and 1st 2 weeks in Oct $99–$160 double; $135–$275 suite. Sept and last 2 weeks in June $85–$150 double; $129–$220 suite. Nov to mid-June $85–$135 double; $119–$220 suite. Rates include breakfast. AE, DC, DISC, MC, V. No children under 18.

This was the Berkshires' first parochial school (1885), named for the French hometown of the nuns who ran it. That accounts for the extra-large bedrooms, which were formerly classrooms. Seven of them, with 13-foot ceilings and the original woodwork and blackboards, are equipped with whirlpool baths and gas fireplaces. Room-service dinners are provided by the Sullivan Station restaurant in back, itself a converted train depot. Rates kick up another $25 to $65 for certain Tanglewood concerts and foliage weekends.

Federal House. Main St. (Rte. 102), South Lee, MA 01260. ☎ **800/243-1824** or 413/243-1824. www.berkshireweb.com. 10 units. A/C. Memorial Day to Oct $85–$185 double; Nov–May $75–$125 double. Rates include full breakfast. AE, MC, V.

Built in 1824 in the Federalist style, including a portico with fluted columns, this distinguished little inn still sports antiques belonging to the original family in its upstairs bedrooms, which are perfectly nice if a bit pricey. Four have TVs. Three new bedrooms have been created.

Dining: The Federal House made a name for itself with sumptuous "event" and holiday meals. The understated elegance was fashioned by the owners, who learned their craft in prestigious restaurants in the New York area. Both dining rooms have fireplaces, the one in the front parlor carved from black marble. Food is contemporary French, but with excursions farther afield. It is complemented by an impressive wine cellar. Dinner is served from 5:30 to 9:30pm Friday to Sunday from November through April, nightly from May through October. Reservations are recommended. Dinner for two, before wine and tip, should be under $80.

WHERE TO DINE

The Federal House (see "Where to Stay," above) offers the best dining in town. Here's a more casual alternative.

Cactus Café. 54 Main St. ☎ **413/243-4300.** Main courses $6.50–$17.50. AE, DISC, MC, V. Thurs–Mon noon–2:30pm and 5–9pm. MEXICAN.

What must have been a 1930s luncheonette has had a few coats of pastel paint slapped on the walls and stamped-tin ceiling, with serapes and sombreros hung from nails. The food is as artlessly homemade, heaped on thick white china. It's filling and tastes good, from quesadillas and enchiladas to the more ambitious stew, *caldo Quintanaroo*, with tuna, scallops, mussels, shrimp, and white fish in a chile-charged broth. An adjoining room, **Y Mas!**, serves espresso and pastries.

LENOX & TANGLEWOOD

Stately homes and fabulous mansions mushroomed in this former agricultural settlement from the 1890s until 1913, when the 16th Amendment, authorizing income taxes, put a severe crimp in that impulse. But Lenox remains a repository of extravagant domestic architecture surpassed only in such fabled resorts of the wealthy as Newport and Palm Beach. And since many of the cottages have been converted into inns and hotels, it is possible to get inside some of these beautiful buildings, if only for a cocktail or a meal.

The reason for so many lodgings in a town with a permanent population of barely 5,000 (more than two dozen buildings post signs and others take in guests through B&B networks) is Tanglewood, a nearby estate where a series of concerts by the Boston Symphony Orchestra is held every summer. While the weekend performances of the BSO are the big draw, there are also solo recitals, chamber concerts, and appearances by the privileged young musicians who study at the prestigious Tanglewood Music Center.

Lenox lies 7 miles south of Pittsfield. The **Lenox Chamber of Commerce** has operated an information center in the Lenox Academy Building, 75 Main St. (☎ **413/ 637-3646**), but a recent fire closed down the operation. They can still answer questions on the telephone, and you might ask if a new location has been found.

✪ TANGLEWOOD MUSIC FESTIVAL

Lenox is filled with music every July and August, and the undisputed headliners are the Boston Symphony Orchestra and its music director, Seiji Ozawa. Controversy attended the redirection of policy and programs of the Tanglewood Music Center demanded by Mr. Ozawa in 1997 and the turmoil it created with a shakeout of unhappy administrators. The Center and the summer festival landed on their feet over the following year, however, and consensus has pronounced them stronger than ever. Symphony concerts are given at the famous **Tanglewood** estate, usually beginning the last weekend in June and ending the weekend before Labor Day. The estate is on West Street (actually in Stockbridge township, although it's always associated with Lenox). From Lenox, take Route 183 1½ miles southwest of town.

While the BSO is Tanglewood's 800-pound cultural gorilla, the program features a menagerie of other performers and musical idioms. These run the gamut from popular artists (past performers have included Jackson Browne, Tony Bennett, and Bonnie Raitt) and jazz vocalists and combos (including Dave Brubeck, Chick Corea, and Sonny Rollins), to such guest soloists and conductors as André Previn, Isaac Stern, Jessye Norman, and Yo-Yo Ma.

The Koussevitzky Music Shed is an open-ended auditorium that seats 5,000, supplemented by a surrounding lawn where an outdoor audience lounges on folding chairs and blankets. This is the venue for orchestral and other large concerts. Chamber groups and solo performers appear in the smaller Ozawa Hall. Seats in the Shed range from $14 to $79, while lawn tickets are usually $13 to $16. (Higher prices apply for some special appearances.) Major performances are on Friday and Saturday nights and Sunday afternoon.

For recorded **information on concert programs,** call ☎ 617/266-1492 from September to June 10 (note that the recorded message in Boston will not have information about upcoming Tanglewood concerts until the program is announced in March or April). Or go to the Web site after January: **www.bso.org**. To order tickets by mail before June, write the Tanglewood Ticket Office at Symphony Hall, Boston, MA 02115. After June 5th, write the Tanglewood Ticket Office, Lenox, MA 01240. Tickets can be charged to a credit card by phone through **SymphonyCharge** (☎ **800/274-8499** outside Boston, or 617/266-1200 in Boston) or purchased on the Net at www.bso.org. For tickets to the Popular Artists Series, call **Ticketmaster** (☎ **800/347-0808** outside Mass., 212/307-7171 in N.Y., 617/931-2000 in Boston), or 800/274-8499 in other areas. Tentative programs are available after the New Year; the summer schedule is usually locked in by March. *Note:* Tickets, especially to the most popular performances, can sell out quickly, so it's a good idea to get yours as far in advance as possible. If you do decide to go at the last minute, take a blanket or lawn chairs and get tickets for the lawn, which are almost always available. Lawn tickets for children under 12 are free; children under 5 aren't allowed in the Shed or Ozawa Hall during concerts. You can also attend open rehearsals during the week, and the rehearsal for the Sunday concert on Saturday morning.

The estate itself (☎ **413/637-5165** June through August), with more than 500 gorgeous acres of manicured lawns, gardens, and groves of ancient trees, much of it overlooking the lake called Stockbridge Bowl, was put together starting in 1849 by William Aspinwall Tappan. Admission to the grounds is free.

At the outset, the only structure on the property was a modest something referred to as the Little Red Shanty. In 1851, it was rented to Nathaniel Hawthorne and his wife Sophia. The author of *The Scarlet Letter* and *The House of the Seven Gables* stayed there long enough to write a children's book, *Tanglewood Tales,* and meet Herman Melville, who lived in nearby Dalton and became a close friend. The existing Hawthorne Cottage is a replica, now serving as practice studios. (It isn't open to the public.) On the grounds is the original Tappan mansion, with fine views.

A Literary Landmark & Performing Arts Center

The Mount, Edith Wharton Restoration. Plunkett St. (at the intersection of Rtes. 7 and 7A). ☎ **413/637-1899.** www.edithwharton.org. Guided tours given weekends in May and daily from Memorial Day through Oct 9am–2pm. Admission $6 adults, $5.50 seniors, $4.50 children 13–18, free for children under 13.

Wharton, who won a Pulitzer Prize for her novel *The Age of Innocence,* was singularly equipped to write that subtle and deftly detailed examination of the upper classes of the Gilded Age and the first decades of this century. She was born into that stratum of society in 1862 and traveled in the circles that made the Berkshires a regular stop on their restless movements between New York, Florida, Newport, and the Continent.

She had her own villa built on this 130-acre lakeside property in 1902 and lived there 10 years before leaving for France, never to return. Wharton took an active hand in the creation of The Mount and the execution of its details; the mansion is a notable rarity—one of the few designated National Historic Landmarks designed by a woman. She was, after all, the author of an upscale 1897 how-to guide called *The Decoration of Houses.* Grand by today's standards, the house wasn't especially large for the time.

A $2-million restoration of the exterior was completed in 1999, only the first stage in a planned $15-million overall campaign to rescue the interior, the terrace, and extensive gardens. Tours continue while work proceeds.

✪ **Shakespeare & Company** uses buildings and outdoor amphitheaters on the grounds of The Mount to stage its late-May-to-late-October season of plays by the Bard, works by Edith Wharton and George Bernard Shaw, and new American playwrights. Performances by dance troupes, student actors, and even puppets flesh out the schedule. The venues are the outdoor amphitheaters, Mainstage and Oxford Court, and two indoor stages, Stables and Wharton. According to a recent agreement put together after years of contention between opposing parties, the theatrical company's lease will expire in 2003.

Staggered performances take place Tuesday to Sunday (weekends only after Labor Day), usually at 3, 5, or 8pm. Tickets range from $15 to $32 and are generally easy to get, since the theater rarely draws name actors. Call the box office at ☎ **413/637-3353;** the summer's schedule is announced by February or March. Lunch and dinner picnic baskets can be purchased on site.

A SITE FOR TRAIN BUFFS

Berkshire Scenic Railway Museum. Housatonic St. and Willow Creek Rd. ☎ **413/637-2210.** Train rides $2 adults, $1 under 14. Guided tours given Memorial Day weekend through Oct on weekends and holidays 10am–4pm (last train run at 3:30).

Housed in a deactivated and restored train station, the Berkshire Scenic Railway Museum has displays of model railroads, a gift shop, and a real caboose. Fifteen-minute shuttle train rides are also offered. This is one of the few attractions in Lenox likely to appeal to children.

OUTDOOR PURSUITS

Pleasant Valley Wildlife Sanctuary, West Mountain Road (☎ **413/637-0320**), has a small museum and 7 miles of hiking and snowshoeing trails crossing its 1,500 acres. Beaver lodges and dams can be glimpsed from a distance and waterfowl and other birds are found in abundance, rewarding targets for those who come equipped with binoculars. Open Tuesday to Sunday, dawn to sunset, admission is $3 for adults and $2 for children 3 to 15. To get there, drive north 6.6 miles on Routes 7 and 20 and turn left on West Dugway Road.

In town, **Main Street Sports & Leisure,** 48 Main St. (☎ **413/637-4407**), rents bicycles, canoes, in-line skates, snowshoes, cross-country skis, tennis rackets, and related equipment. They can also advise on routes and trails, give you preprinted driving directions to several area state parks and forests, and even provide guided outdoor trips. **Kennedy Park,** right down the street from the store, is a favorite spot for cross-country skiing in winter, or for a ramble in any season. Dogs are allowed off-leash throughout the 12 miles of trails.

More extensive hiking trails can be found at **October Mountain State Forest** (see "Outdoor Activities" under "Lee," above) or at **Beartown State Forest,** in nearby Monterey. The Appalachian Trail, which runs from Maine to Georgia, connects with a loop trail around a small pond with a nice swimming area. To get there, take Route 7 South for 3½ miles, then turn left onto West Road. After 2½ miles, turn left at the T intersection onto Route 102 East. After about ¹/₁₀ mile, turn right over the bridge onto Meadow Street. After another ¹/₁₀ mile, turn right onto Pine Street and follow the signs from there.

Those who enjoy mildly strenuous organized outings might want to contact **Greylock Discovery Tours,** based in Lenox (☎ **800/877-9656** or 413/637-4442), which organizes **hikes** and **canoe trips** from May through October.

WHERE TO STAY

The long list of lodgings below is only partial—most can accommodate only small numbers. The Tanglewood concert season is a powerful draw, so prices are highest in summer and the brief fall foliage season, usually occurring the two weeks around Columbus Day. Rate schedules are of Byzantine complexity, with tariffs set according to wildly varying combinations of seasons and days of the week as well as facilities offered. Minimum 2- or 3-night stays are usually required during the Tanglewood weeks, October foliage, and long holiday weekends. *Note:* If you're hoping to book a room during the Tanglewood concert season, be sure to make your reservations well in advance.

Given the substantial numbers of lodging places and limited space to describe them, admittedly arbitrary judgments have been made to winnow the list. Some inns, for example, are so rule-ridden and facility-free they come off as crabby—no children, no pets, no phones, no TV, no credit cards, no breakfast before 9am, shared bathrooms, checkout at 11am, check-in after 3pm—and they cost twice as much as nearby motels that have all those conveniences. Let them seek clients elsewhere.

Others are open only 6 or 7 months a year and charge the world for a bed or a meal. In this latter category, though, one place demands at least a mention: **Blantyre,** 16 Blantyre Rd. (☎ **413/637-3556** in summer; 413/298-3806 in winter), in its 1902 Tudor-Norman mansion, cossets its guests with a soak in undeniable luxury, both in the dining room and bedchamber.

When all the area's inns are fully booked or if you want to be assured the full quota of 20th-century comforts and gadgets, Routes 7 and 20 north and south of town harbor a number of conventional motels. Among the possibilities are the **Mayflower Motor Inn** (☎ **413/443-4468**), the **Susse Chalet** (☎ **413/637-3560**), and the **Lenox Motel** (☎ **413/499-0324**).

Very Expensive

Canyon Ranch in the Berkshires. 165 Kemble St., Lenox, MA 01240. ☎ **800/726-9900** or 413/637-4100. Fax 413/637-0057. www.canyonranch.com. 127 units. A/C TV TEL. 4-night packages $2,030 double; 7-night packages $3,230 double. Rates include all meals. Taxes and 18% service charge extra. AE, DISC, MC, V.

Welding turn-of-the-century opulence to contemporary impulses for dietary deprivation and masochistic physicality isn't the way most people choose to spend their leisure time—at least not at these prices. But for the too-rich and too-thin set or for those who'd like to splurge just once, this is the place.

A polite but firm security guard turns away the unconfirmed at the gate, so there's no popping in for a look around. The core facility is the 1897 extravaganza of a mansion, Bellefontaine, said to be modeled after Le Petit Trianon at Versailles. Unfortunately, a fire in 1949 left only the magnificent library untouched. That loss has been offset by two major renovations since the current owners took over, including a massive $6 million project just completed. Bedrooms are in "contemporary New England style," equipped with video players and hair dryers (but no minibars).

Dining: After being steamed, exhausted, massaged, and showered, the real events of each day are mealtimes: "nutritionally balanced gourmet," natch.

Amenities: Sweat away the pounds in the huge spa complex, with 40 exercise classes a day, weights, an indoor running track, racquetball, squash, indoor and outdoor pools, tennis, and cycling, canoeing, and hiking outings. But first have a consultation with a staff member who "can help you enhance your wellness opportunities."

✪ **Cranwell Resort & Golf Club.** 55 Lee Rd. (Rte. 183), Lenox, MA 01240. ☎ **800/272-6935** or 413/637-1364. Fax 413/637-4364. www.cranwell.com. E-mail:infr@cranwell.com. 95 units. A/C TV TEL. July–Aug $199–$439 double; Sept–Oct $129–$409 double; Nov–Mar $89–$229 double; Apr–May $129–$329 double; June $169–$359 double. 3-night minimum stay July–Aug. AE, CB, DC, DISC, MC, V. From Lenox Center, go north to Rte. 20 E. The resort is on the left.

The main building looks like a castle in the Scottish Highlands, but no 17th-century laird lived this well. It stands at the center of a 380-acre resort, ringed by unobstructed views of the surrounding hills. That's where the most expensive rooms are; the rest are in a number of smaller buildings. Some have wet bars or kitchenettes. Rooms are less concerned with adherence to a particular style than with surrounding guests in immediate comfort. They are equipped with coffeemakers and hair dryers, and robes wait in closets.

Spa, golf, and ski themes dominate the roster of packages. A 1-night weekend stay including breakfast and dinner for two, for example, costs $279 *per room*, and adds a massage and facial for one guest.

Dining/Diversions: Three dining rooms range from formal to pubby, and there is live jazz Friday and Saturday nights.

Amenities: In addition to the lovely grounds and the 18-hole, par 71 golf course, there are two tennis courts, a new fitness center, a large heated pool, and a 60-acre golf school with sessions throughout the year. In winter, the gentle slopes serve as cross-country ski trails.

✪ **Wheatleigh.** Hawthorne Rd., Lenox, MA 01240. ☎ **413/637-0610.** Fax 413/637-4507. 19 units. A/C TV TEL. $175–$625 double. AE, CB, DC, MC, V.

Glamorous young New Yorkers and Europeans drape themselves in Gatsbyesque poses around the lavishly appointed great hall. Much of the time, they look elaborately bored, no easy feat in this persuasive 1893 replica of a 16th-century Italian palazzo, which matches the highest standards of the moneyed Berkshires. Wheatleigh has always been very expensive and still is. But other places are catching up, and the French manager is striving to give requisite value. All rooms have VCRs, fax machines, and hair dryers. Paradoxically, the cheapest units—they average only 11 by 13 ft—are too expensive, while the priciest rooms are almost reasonable, at least by these rarefied standards.

Dining: The dining room gratifyingly rounds out the experience, with immaculate floral arrangements on white napery, original contemporary art on the walls, muted chamber music playing just below recognition level. The year-round fixed-price menu is $75; reservations recommended on weekends.

Amenities: Concierge, dry cleaning/laundry service, newspaper delivery, in-room massage, twice-daily maid service, baby-sitting, valet parking, exercise room, heated pool, tennis court, bicycle rental.

Expensive

Brook Farm Inn. 15 Hawthorne St., Lenox, MA 01240. ☎ **800/285-7638** or 413/637-3013. Fax 413/637-4751. www.brookfarm.com. E-mail: innkeeper@brookfarm.com. 12 units. A/C TEL. July to Labor Day $125–$210 double; Labor Day to Oct $105–$165 double; Nov–June $90–$140 double. Rates include breakfast and afternoon tea. DC, DISC, MC, V. From the town center, go south 1 block on Old Stockbridge Rd. Turn right. No children under 15.

"There is poetry here," insist the owners of this picture-pretty 1870 farmhouse, and an afternoon idle in the hammock overlooking the pool or a curled-up read by the fireplace will have you agreeing. Breakfast is an ample buffet. Six rooms have wood-burning fireplaces, and those on the top floor have just been redecorated. There is an outdoor pool.

Cliffwood Inn. 25 Cliffwood St., Lenox, MA 01240. ☎ **413/637-3330.** www.cliffwood.com. 7 units. A/C. July to Labor Day and foliage season $209–$240 double; May 15–June 30 and Sept after Labor Day $109–$182 double; Nov–May 14 $87–$141. Rates include breakfast daily in high season, weekends only in shoulder season, Sun and holiday weekends in low season. No credit cards. Children over 10 welcome.

One of the relatively compact manses of the Vanderbilt era, this has a long veranda in back overlooking the outdoor pool. Antiques and convincing reproductions of many styles and periods fill the common and private spaces. Six of the seven bedrooms have working fireplaces (including one in a bathroom!). Only one unit has a TV. The owners will loan beach chairs to use on the lawn at Tanglewood.

Amenities: Outdoor pool and an indoor counter-current workout pool and whirlpool.

Gateways Inn. 51 Walker St., Lenox, MA 01240. ☎ **800/492-9466** or 413/637-2532. Fax 413/637-1432. www.gatewaysinn.com. E-mail: gateways@berkshire.net. 12 units. A/C TV TEL. June–Oct $100–$400 double; Nov–May $80–$315 double. Rates include breakfast. AE, DC, DISC, MC, V.

Harley Procter, who hitched up with a man called Gamble and made a bundle, had this house, christened "Orleton," built as his summer home in 1912. Its most impressive feature is the eye-catching staircase that winds down into the lobby. An oft-repeated myth contends that it was designed by Stanford White, but that would have been quite a trick—White died in 1906. Still, whoever did it, it's a stunner, just the thing for a grand entrance. Equally impressive is the suite named for conductor Arthur Fiedler, with not one but two fireplaces, a big four-poster on the sunporch, and a Jacuzzi in the bathroom. A new common room has been created for guests, seven bathrooms have been redone, replacement beds and antiques have been purchased, and eight rooms now have working fireplaces.

Dining: Dining here is one of Lenox's greater pleasures. Dinner reservations are recommended on weekends; entrees run $17 to $27.

Whistler's Inn. 5 Greenwood St., Lenox, MA 01240. ☎ **413/637-0975.** Fax 413/637-2190. E-mail: rmears3246@aol.com. 14 units. A/C TV TEL. July–Oct $100–$225 double; Nov–June $90–$180 double. Rates include breakfast. AE, DISC, MC, V.

Both innkeepers are compulsive travelers, with particular fondness for India and Africa. They bring things back from every trip, filling the cavernous rooms of their Tudor mansion with clusters of cut glass, painted screens, assorted Victoriana, grandfather clocks, Persian rugs, ormolu candelabras, a grand piano, and shelf after shelf of books (both of them are writers). The result: rooms that are not so much decorated as gathered, without a single boring corner. Breakfast is suitably proportioned and a bottle of sherry or port is kept in the library for guests to pour themselves a drink to sip with tea and cookies. Facilities for children are limited.

Moderate

Amadeus House. 15 Cliffwood St. (near the corner of Main St.), Lenox, MA 01240. ☎ **800/205-4770** or 413/637-4770. Fax 413/637-4484. www.amadeushouse.com. E-mail: info@amadeushouse.com. 8 units, 6 with private bathroom. July to Labor Day $70–$225 double; mid-May to June and Sept–Oct $65–$190 double; Nov to mid-May $65–$160 double. Rates include breakfast. AE, DISC, MC, V. Children over 10 are welcome.

The owners are lovers of classical music, made clear by the names of the guest rooms—Bach, Brahms, and Mozart are the largest—and the fact that the usual common-room TV is replaced by a stereo and stacks of CDs. "Beethoven" is a two-bedroom suite with a sitting area and fully stocked kitchen. Only one room has air-conditioning; most of the rest have ceiling fans. The central part of the house dates from 1820. Breakfast incorporates a hot entree and afternoon tea is served. A black Lab named Bravo is the only pet permitted here.

Candlelight Inn. 53 Walker St., Lenox, MA 01240. ☎ **800/428-0560** or 413/637-1555. www.candlelightinn-lenox.com. E-mail: innkeeper@candlelightinn-lenox.com. 8 units. A/C. $65–$175 double. Rates include breakfast. AE, MC, V. No children under 10.

A folksy gathering place for locals as well as guests, the bar at the end of the center hall in this 1885 Victorian enjoys a convivial nightly trade, and the four dining rooms are often full. In winter, clink glasses beside a crackling fire; in summer, reserve a table in the courtyard beneath Campari umbrellas. Lunch is served from Memorial Day to late October, dinner year-round (with entrees from $16 to $24). While the Candlelight does most of its business on the restaurant side, the upstairs rooms are homey and unpretentious. They often close for a week or so in January for renovations.

Gables Inn. 81 Walker St., Lenox, MA 01240. ☎ **800/382-9401** or ☎ /fax 413/637-3416. www.gableslenox.com. 20 units. A/C TV. $80–$160 double; $160–$210 suite. Rates include breakfast. DISC, MC, V. No children under 12.

Edith Wharton, who spent more than two decades in Lenox, made this Queen Anne mansion her home for two years while her house, The Mount, was being built. That may be enough to interest fans of the novelist, but there is much more to appeal to potential guests, including the canopied four-poster and working fireplace in Edith's bedroom. Meticulously maintained Victoriana and related antiques are found in every corner, notably in the eight-sided library. No rooms have phones, but suites have VCRs and refrigerators. An outdoor pool and tennis court are available.

Village Inn. 16 Church St., Lenox, MA 01240. ☎ **800/253-0917** or 413/637-0020. Fax 413/637-9756. www.villageinn-lenox.com. 33 units. A/C TEL. Summer–fall $80–$210 double; $330–$395 suite. Winter–spring $65–$165 double; $240–$310 suite. AE, DC, DISC, MC, V. No children under 6.

An inn since 1775, apart from occasional periods when it was put to other uses, this place hasn't a whiff of pretense. Its unusually large number of rooms come in considerable variety and are categorized as "Superior," "Standard," or "Economy." That means four-posters in the high-end rooms, some of which have fireplaces and/or whirlpool baths, and constricted quarters with double beds at the lower prices. Clawfoot tubs are common in rooms in all categories.

Afternoon tea and dinner are served June through October in the restaurant, light meals in the tavern (the only room where smoking is allowed).

WHERE TO DINE

See also "Where to Stay," above, since many of the local inns have dining rooms. In particular, **Blantyre** (☎ **413/637-3556**) is worth a splurge.

✪ **Church Street Cafe.** 65 Church St. ☎ **413/637-2745.** Reservations recommended on weekends. Main courses $17.95–$25.95. MC, V. Daily 11:30am–2pm and 5:30–9pm. Closed Sun–Mon in winter. ECLECTIC AMERICAN.

The most popular place in town got that way by delivering fanciful combinations that please the eye and pique the taste buds. Creative appearances on the seasonally changing menu have included a pizza extravagantly topped with lobster and mascarpone drizzled with white truffle oil and a dinner plate of grilled miso-marinated salmon on Asian eggplant with braised greens and scallion rice. The unembellished surroundings are plain wood chairs and tables and crocks of flowers. A large dining deck fills up whenever the weather allows.

Lenox 218. 218 Main St. (Rte. 7A). ☎ **413/637-4218.** Main courses $12.95–$24.50. AE, DC, DISC, MC, V. Mon–Sat 11:30am–2:30pm and 5–10pm, Sun 11:30am–9pm. ITALIAN/AMERICAN.

Largely black and white, with hanging pots of ivy, the decor falls short of the urban sophistication it seeks. So does the food, which mainly consists of such familiar fare as veal piccata, chicken cacciatora, and meat loaf with mashed potatoes. But that's OK. It's cooked and assembled well enough, and the service is pleasant. Lunch might be the better time, when prices are much lower. The bar in front gets lively in the evening, and its own menu offers snacks and light meals from hot wings to half orders of pasta.

Roseborough Grill. 71 Church St. ☎ **413/637-2700.** Main courses $16–$26. AE, CB, DC, DISC, MC, V. Thurs–Mon 11:30am–3pm and 5–9pm (until 10pm weekends). CREATIVE AMERICAN.

Inside the rambling old farmhouse are plain wooden tables and chairs unadorned at lunch but dressed with linen and candles at night. Serious jazz drifts out of the stereo and often surprising food issues from the kitchen. Mains like chicken osso bucco sound ordinary until it is recalled that the Italian original is made of veal shanks, while this is wine-braised poultry over vegetables and pappardelle. Thai shrimp linguini and Asian braised short ribs further demonstrate that the chef gambles in many scented fields, usually emerging with dignity intact. Polish off with such amusing concoctions as caramelized banana spring rolls or the towering chocolate mousse Napoleon. Remember that they serve lunch, in an area where most restaurants and inns don't open until evening.

✪ **Spigalina.** 86 Main St. (Rte. 7A). ☎ **413/637-4455**. Reservations suggested weekends. Main courses $14–$20. AE, DC, DISC, MC, V. July–Aug Sat–Sun noon–3pm, daily 5–9pm; Sept–June Thurs–Mon 5–9pm. CREATIVE MEDITERRANEAN.

Don't take the above stated hours too seriously. The newly married Swiss-French host and Italian chef just opened here in spring 1997, and they're still feeling their way. About hours, that is. She, the whirlwind who tends the skillets, is as sure handed as they come. Her imaginative renderings of standard recipes of the Mediterranean Rim constitute a virtually new cuisine. Take her version of Portuguese *cataplana*, the classic pork and clam stew: she sends it out as three properly pink slices of the tenderloin draped over a timbale of cilantro-scented rice, three delicate little clams positioned around the edges. Service can be forgetful, admittedly, but this is the new flaming star of the Berkshire dining scene. Get there. Just call first. Who knows when they might be open? They actually held their wedding on Super Bowl Sunday.

PITTSFIELD

Berkshire County's largest city (population 48,000) gets little attention in most tourist literature, and there's good reason. A commercial and industrial center—Martin Marietta is the largest employer—it presents little of the charm that marks such popular destinations as Stockbridge and Lenox. Still, it is a convenient base for day excursions to attractions elsewhere in the region, including several ski centers, the summer concert season at Tanglewood, and Hancock Shaker Village, a few miles to the west. In summer the Pittsfield Mets play minor-league baseball at Wahconah Park, a 1919 stadium with real wooden box seats. Pittsfield is also home to the house where Herman Melville wrote *Moby Dick* and to an eccentric little museum with a theater showing art films much of the year.

The **Berkshire Visitors Bureau** (☎ 800/237-5747 or 413/443-9186) is located in the same block of buildings as the Crowne Plaza Hotel, on Berkshire Common. Pittsfield lies 137 miles west of Boston, and 7 miles north of Lenox.

SEEING THE SIGHTS

Arrowhead. 780 Holmes Rd. ☎ 413/442-1793. Admission $5 adults, $4.50 seniors, $3 children 6–16, $15 for families, free for children under 6. Open daily from Memorial Day Fri to Oct 31st 9:30am–5pm, rest of year by appointment only. Drive east from Park Sq. on East St., turn right on Elm St. and right again on Holmes Rd.

Herman Melville, just one prominent member of the literary and artistic community that kept summer homes in the Berkshires, bought this 18th-century house in 1850 and lived here until 1863. It was during this time that he wrote his masterpiece, *Moby Dick*. He dedicated his seventh novel, *Pierre*, to Greylock Mountain, which he viewed every day from his study. One of his best friends was Nathaniel Hawthorne, and they conversed regularly at a table beside the large fireplace in the kitchen. In truth, however, the house is of limited interest to visitors other than literature students and avid readers. Visits are by guided tour only, leaving every hour on the hour starting at 10am and ending at 4pm.

Berkshire Museum. 39 South St. (Rte. 7, 1 block south of Park Sq.). ☎ **413/443-7171.** www.berkshireweb.com/berkshiremuseum. Admission $6 adults, $5 seniors and students, $4 children 3–18. Tues–Sat 10am–5pm, Sun 1–5pm (open daily in July–Aug).

It began in 1903 as the "Museum of Natural History and Art," words chiseled in stone above the entrance. The holdings bounce from Babylonian cuneiform tablets to stuffed birds to mineral displays to tanks of live fish in the basement aquarium. An auditorium seating 300 serves as the "Little Cinema," which has a season of art and foreign films during the warmer months.

Apart from the aquarium, the greatest interest may be generated by the art and archaeological artifacts assembled on the second floor. A sculpture gallery has full-size casts of important 16th-century Italian sculptures and a 19th-century *Diana* by American Augustus Saint-Gaudens. While those looking for name artists will generally be disappointed, there are a number of canvases and sculptures by contemporary artists that deserve attention, and here and there are minor Alexander Calders, a Reginald Marsh, and a couple of landscapes by Albert Bierstadt. Among cases of 2nd-century Mediterranean glassware and Roman funerary busts are pieces of ancient Egyptian jewelry and pottery and a delicate necklace from Thebes dating to at least 1500 b.c. Kids will love the mummy, of course, and the tropical and native fish and amphibians in the basement.

✪ **Hancock Shaker Village.** Rtes. 20 and 41, Pittsfield. ☎ **800/817-1137** or 413/443-0188. Admission Memorial Day to late Oct $13.50 adults, $5.50 children 6–17, $33 families (2 adults and children under 18); Apr to Memorial Day and late Oct to Nov $10 adults, $5 children 6–17, $25 families, free for children under 6. Apr to Memorial Day and late Oct to late Nov daily 10am–3pm (guided tours); Memorial Day to 3rd week in Oct daily 9:30am–5pm. Call ahead for open hours and events other times of the year.

Of the 20 restored buildings that make up the village, its signature structure is easily the 1826 round stone barn. The Shaker preoccupation with functionalism joined with purity of line and respect for materials has never been clearer than it is in the design of this building—its round shape expedited the chores of feeding and milking livestock by arranging cows in a circle, and the precise joinery of the roof beams and support pillars is a joy to see.

The second "must-see" on the grounds is the brick dwelling that contained the communal dining room, kitchens, and upstairs sleeping quarters. Sexes were separated at meals, work, and religious services, and equality was served by such features as the opposing staircases leading to male and female "retiring rooms."

Other buildings of note include the Meeting House, where religious services were held, and the recently restored 1792 laundry and machine shop, where a working reproduction of a 19th-century water turbine has been installed.

While artisans and docents labor in herb and vegetable gardens and in shops demonstrating Shaker crafts and techniques, they are not in costume, nor do they pretend to be Shaker inhabitants. They are knowledgeable about their subject, though, and dispense such nuggets as explanations of the Shaker discipline that required members to dress the right side first, to button from right to left, and to step with the right foot first. A new dairy program has been initiated, allowing visitors to watch cows being milked and to assist in making butter and cheese. Crafts demonstrations begin in May.

The museum shop is excellent, and a cafe serves lunches in summer and fall, with some dishes based on Shaker recipes. On Saturday nights from July through October,

Movers & Shakers

Mother Ann arrived in 1774 with eight disciples just as the disgruntled American colonies were about to burst into open rebellion. The former Ann Lee, once imprisoned in England for her excess of religious zeal, had anointed herself leader of the United Society of Believers in Christ's Second Coming. The austere Protestant sect was dedicated to simplicity, equality, and celibacy. They were popularly known as "The Shakers" for their spastic movements when in the throes of religious ecstasy. By the time of her death in 1784, Mother Ann had made many converts, who then fanned out across the country to form communal settlements from Maine to Indiana. One of the most important Shaker communities, Hancock, edged the Massachusetts–New York border, near Pittsfield.

Shaker society produced dedicated, highly disciplined farmers and craftspeople whose products were much in demand in the outside world. They sold seeds, invented early agricultural machinery and hand tools, and erected large buildings of several stories and exquisite simplicity. Their spare, clean-lined furniture and accessories anticipated the so-called Danish Modern style by a century and in recent years have drawn astonishingly high prices at auction.

All of these accomplishments required a verve owed at least in part to sublimation of sexual energy, for a fundamental Shaker tenet was total celibacy for its adherents. They kept going with converts and adoption of orphans (who were free to leave, if they wished). But by the 1970s the inevitable result of this policy left the movement with a bare handful of believers. The string of Shaker settlements and museums that remain is testament to their dictum, "Hands to work, hearts to God."

the village presents tours and Shaker four-course dinners by candlelight at a cost of about $40 per person. Reservations for these are essential (☎ 413/443-0188).

OUTDOOR PURSUITS

A useful Pittsfield store is **Plaine's Bike Golf Ski,** 55 W. Housatonic St. (☎ 413/499-0294), which rents bikes by the day and week and carries equipment for all the sports its name suggests. Open daily, it's on Route 20, west of downtown, at the corner of Center Street.

A prime recreational preserve is **Pittsfield State Forest,** entered on Cascade Street (☎ 413/442-8992), a little over 3 miles west of the center of town, on West Street. Its 10,000 acres have 31 campsites, boat ramps, streams for canoeing and fishing, and trails for hiking, horseback riding, and cross-country skiing. Open daily from 8am to 8pm. Admission is $2 per car.

BOATING   Onota Boat Livery, 463 Peck Rd. (☎ 413/442-1724), rents canoes and motorboats for use on Onota Lake, conveniently located at the western edge of the city.

SKIING   South of the city center, off Route 7 near the Pittsfield city limits, is the **Bousquet Ski Area,** Dan Fox Drive (☎ 413/442-8316 business office, 413/442-2436 snow phone). Bousquet (pronounced "Bos-kay") has 21 trails, the longest over a mile long with a vertical drop of 750 feet, with two double chairlifts and two rope tows. Night skiing is available Monday to Saturday, when trails are open until 10pm; equipment can be rented. Tickets are only $20 all day, every day, $15 at night.

About 10 miles north of Pittsfield on Route 7 in the town of New Ashford, is **Brodie Mountain Ski Area** (☎ 413/443-4752), with a vertical drop of 1,250 feet and a long run of 2½ miles. Midweek ski-school packages are attractive, there is night skiing, and in summer they offer racquetball, tennis, and campsites.

Alternatively, turn west a mile short of Brodie Mountain on Brodie Mountain Road and continue about 2 miles to ✪ **Jiminy Peak,** Hancock, MA 01237 (☎ 413/ 738-5500, or 413/738-7325 for 24-hour ski reports). This expanding resort aspires to four-season activity, so skiing on 28 trails (18 are open at night) with seven lifts is supplemented the rest of the year with horseback riding, trapshooting, fishing in a stocked pond, six tennis courts, mountain biking, pools, and golf at the nearby Waubeeka Springs course. Ample lodging is available.

WHERE TO STAY

The Country Inn at Jiminy Peak. Brodie Mountain Rd. (near Rte. 43), Hancock, MA 01237. ☎ **800/882-8859** or 413/738-5500. Fax 413/738-5513. www.jiminypeak.com. 105 suites. A/C TV TEL. $138–$330 suite. Rates include breakfast. AE, DC, DISC, MC, V.

The "Jiminy Peak" moniker might suggest a mock-Alpine enclave with rapacious singles and indefatigable social directors in Tyrolean pants. On the contrary, this is one of the better lodging deals in the Berkshires, if your idea of luxury is space. All units are one-bedroom suites with full kitchens and pullout sofas, suitable for families or two couples traveling together. A buffet breakfast is served in the Founders' Grill from late June to mid-October and mid-December through April. The furnishings are a bit worn, and guests could probably live without the constant reminders that they, too, "could be part of the Jiminy Peak family" by buying a condo. But these shortcomings pale beside the two pools and abundant recreational facilities (see "Outdoor Pursuits," above), and Tanglewood is less than 30 minutes away.

Crowne Plaza Pittsfield-Berkshires. West St., Pittsfield, MA 01201. ☎ **800/227-6963** or 413/499-2000. Fax 413/442-0449. www.crowneplaza.com/hotels/ptfma/index.html. E-mail: crplaza@berkshire.net. 175 units. A/C TV TEL. Summer $140–$210 double; fall–spring $119–$159 double. Children under 18 stay free in parents' room. AE, CB, DC, DISC, MC, V.

The tallest building in town at 14 stories, this former Hilton isn't hard to find, although it takes a little round-the-block maneuvering to get to the front door. It has the bells and whistles expected of upper-middle chain hotels and is more family-friendly than many lodgings in the region. With this many rooms, there's a pretty good chance of copping a bed on Tanglewood weekends. All units have hair dryers, robes, radios, coffeemakers, free delivery of *USA Today*, phones with dataports and voice mail, playstations, and dozens of pay-per-view movies; some have fold-out sofa beds and stocked minibars. Free self-parking is available in the adjacent garage.

Dining: There are two restaurants, Rockwell's and the informal Park Square Grill.

Amenities: A fitness room with Jacuzzi and sauna serves adults, and a heated indoor pool keeps the kids occupied.

WILLIAMSTOWN

This community and its prestigious liberal-arts college were both named for Col. Ephraim Williams, who was killed in 1755 in one of the French and Indian Wars. He bequeathed the land for creation of a school and a town. His college grew, spreading east from the central common along both sides of Main Street (Route 2). Over the town's 200-year history, buildings have been erected in several styles of the times. That makes Main Street a virtual museum of institutional architecture, with representatives of the Georgian, Federalist, Gothic Revival, Romanesque, and Victorian modes and a few that are yet to be labeled. They stand at dignified distances from one another, so what might have been a tumultuous visual hodgepodge is a stately lesson in historical design.

A free weekly newspaper, the *Advocate,* produces useful guides to both the northern and southern Berkshires. For a copy, send a check for $3.50 to The Advocate, P.O. Box 95, 38 Spring St., Williamstown, MA 01267. An unattended information booth at the corner of North Street (Route 7) and Main Street (Route 2) has an abundance of pamphlets and brochures free for the taking.

✪ The Williamstown Theatre Festival

The festival is Williamstown's premier attraction each summer. It performs in the Adams Memorial Theatre, Main Street, P.O. Box 517, Williamstown, MA 01267 (☎ **413/597-3400**). Staging classic and new plays during its season (late June through August), the festival attracts many top actors and directors (Frank Langella has been a regular). The Main Stage presents works by major playwrights, while the Other Stage often features more experimental productions. Ticket prices range from $14 to $32, depending upon venue and performance date. The summer's schedule is usually announced by March. It's not too difficult to get tickets, except at the last minute.

ART MUSEUMS

✪ **Sterling and Francine Clark Art Institute.** 225 South St. ☎ **413/458-9545.** Admission July–Oct $5 adults, free students and under age 18; free to all Tues and Nov–June. Sept–June Tues–Sun 10am–5pm; July–Aug Tues–Sun 10am–5pm (until 8pm Tues).

Mr. Clark was an heir to the Singer fortune, which allowed him to pursue his love of art and bestow this remarkable repository upon this community. Clark's endowment funded the modern wing added to the original white marble neoclassical building and has covered all acquisitions, upkeep, and recent renovations. His stipulation that there be no admission fee was breached last year, but it only applies to adults, four months a year, and Tuesdays are always free.

Clark's gift was remarkable, for this is not the collection of an undisciplined, self-absorbed millionaire. Within these walls are canvases by Renoir (34 of them), Degas, Gauguin, Toulouse-Lautrec, Pisarro, and their predecessor, Corot. While they are the stars, there are also 15th- and 16th-century Dutch portraitists, English and European genre and landscape painters, and Americans Sargent and Homer, as well as fine porcelain, silverware, and antique furnishings. This qualifies as one of the great cultural resources of the Berkshires and the state. Temporary exhibitions of scholarly intent are mounted throughout the year.

Massachusetts Museum of Contemporary Art. 87 Marshall St., North Adams. ☎ **413/664-4481.** www.massmoca.org. Call for admission fees and hours.

A lot of excitement and anticipation is being invested in this ambitious project, the conversion of an abandoned 27-building textile factory complex into a center for the visual and performing arts. Even before its official opening, it had a nickname—MASS MoCA—and hosted performances by David Byrne and the Williamstown Theatre Festival. Its creators and the residents of North Adams nurture fervent hopes that it will be an attraction to reverse the slide of the depressed mill town and enhance the touristic and commercial desirability of the northern Berkshires. It is too soon to tell whether those ambitions will be fulfilled, but the museum is certainly worth the short detour east from neighboring Williamstown.

Williams College Museum of Art. Main St. ☎ **413/597-2429.** www.williams.edu/wcma. Admission free. Tues–Sat (and some Mon holidays) 10am–5pm, Sun 1–5pm.

The second, lesser leg of Williamstown's two prominent art repositories exists in large part due to the college's collection of almost 400 paintings by the American modernists Maurice and Charles Prendergast. Some of their works are always rotated into view, and while they are of moderate interest, visitors are more likely to be drawn to such names as Juan Gris, Fernand Léger, Giorgio De Chirico, James Whistler, and Pablo Picasso. These are salted with more contemporary pieces by Andy Warhol and Edward Hopper. The striking three-story entrance atrium was designed by prominent architect Charles Moore.

OUTDOOR PURSUITS

Waubeeka Golf Links, Routes 7 and 43, South Williamstown, MA 01267 (☎ **413/ 458-5869**), is open to the public, with highest weekend greens fees of $35. The clubhouse can seat 150 people in three dining rooms.

Mount Greylock State Reservation contains the highest peak (3,487 ft.) in Massachusetts and a section of the Appalachian Trail. A road allows cars almost to the summit, where War Memorial Tower affords even the most sedentary visitor 360° vistas of the Taconic and Hoosac ranges, far into Vermont and New York.

More active people will find hiking trails radiating from the parking lot near **Bascom Lodge,** P.O. Box 1800, Lanesboro, MA 01237 (☎ **413/743-1591** or 413/443-0011), a grandly rustic creation of the Civilian Conservation Corps in the New Deal 1930s. Simple dormitory beds and four private rooms are available by the night from mid-May to late October. Rates on Friday and Saturday and all of August are $20 to $25 for adults in bunkrooms, $62 for private rooms. Members of the Appalachian Mountain Club receive discounts. Dinners are available by reservation. Look for North Main Street off Route 7 in Lanesboro.

SHOPPING

At 70 Spring St., in the small downtown shopping district, **The Library** (☎ **413/ 458-3436**) fills three adjoining storefronts with a wealth of English chess sets, African carvings and jewelry, Peruvian alpaca sweaters, Turkish kilim, and antique American fishing lures and creels. **Saddleback Antiques,** 1395 Cold Spring Rd. (☎ **413/ 458-5852**), features country, wicker, and Victorian furniture and a variety of collectibles, while **Collectors Warehouse,** 105 North St. (☎ **413/458-9686**), has a little bit of everything— jewelry, books, dolls, furniture, and glassware. Both are on Route 7, the first to the south of the town center, the second slightly to the north.

In South Williamstown, the white frame building on the right (if you are going north on Route 7) looks like a recycled general store, and it is. **The Store at Five Corners,** Routes 7 and 43 (☎ **413/458-3176**), now stocks "gourmet" gifts and selections of sandwiches, salads, pumpkin fudge, pies, and wines for takeout. It's open daily.

WHERE TO STAY

This is a college town, so in addition to the usual peak periods of July, August, and the October foliage season, lodgings fill up during graduation (late May to early June) and on football weekends. The largest facility in town is the 100-unit **Williams Inn,** 1090 Main St. (**800/828-0133** or 413/458-9371). Despite the name, it is a standard motel, containing the conveniences most travelers expect, including a dining room, informal tavern, and indoor pool. Three miles south of town at the juncture of Routes 2 and 7 is the brookside **Berkshire Hills Motel** (☎413/458-3950), which has a heated pool and includes a buffet breakfast in its economical rates.

Blackinton Manor. 1391 Massachusetts Ave., North Adams, MA 01247. ☎800/795-8613 or 413/663-5795. www.blackinton-manor.com. E-mail:epsteind@bcn.net. 5 units. A/C TV. $105–$125 double. MC, V. Children over 7 welcome. Follow Rte. 2 east from Williamstown into North Adams, left on Ashton, then right after railroad bridge, ¼ mile to the inn, on the left.

Music informs this converted 1849 Greek Revival house, hardly surprising since one of the owner-managers is the pianist of the Raphael Trio and his wife is an opera singer and invested cantor. They hold a number of chamber concerts and musicales at irregular intervals throughout the year, many of them to benefit favorite causes. They don't neglect their hospitality functions for a minute, be assured, and this may be the most gracious of inn experiences to be enjoyed in the northern Berkshires. Pass an evening in the living room with a complimentary glass of sherry in front of the fire (other beverages are $3 to $6). All of the rooms are grandly furnished with rich linens on queen or king beds, but ask for the lavishly appointed ground-floor Music Room, spacious enough to contain its own piano. A typical breakfast consists of a fresh fruit plate, an herbed omelet, and freshly baked pastries. There is an unheated outdoor pool. Smoking is confined to the porch.

Field Farm Guesthouse. 554 Sloan Rd., Williamstown, MA 01262. ☎ and fax **413/458-3135.** 5 units. TEL. $125 double. DISC, MC, V. Follow Rte. 7 to Rte. 43 and turn west, then make an immediate right turn on Sloan Rd. Continue 1 mile to the Field Farm entrance, on the right.

After an extended vacation of B&B hopping, there may come a time when one more tilted floor or wobbly Windsor chair will send even a devout inn-lover over the edge. Here's an antidote. This pristine example of postwar modern architecture rose in 1948 in the middle of a spectacularly scenic 296-acre estate. Most rooms look over meadows to Mount Greylock. The living room is equipped with a telescope to view the beavers and waterfowl on the lake a hundred yards away. Most of the Scandinavian Modern furniture was made to order for the house. Rooms are spare, in muted colors. Three have decks; two have fireplaces. A heated pool, tennis court, and 4 miles of nature trails are available to guests. Breakfasts are hearty meals of waffles and five-cheese omelets utilizing fruits, herbs, and vegetables grown on the property. Well-behaved children are welcome.

Orchards. 222 Adams Rd. (corner Main St.), Williamstown, MA 01267. ☎ 800/225-1517 (outside Mass.) or 413/458-9611. Fax 413/458-3273. 47 units. Summer $165–$230 double; winter $135–$185 double. AE, CB, DC, MC, V.

Most guests seem satisfied with this small hotel at the eastern edge of town, although little about it will quicken heartbeats. The management tries hard, though. Rooms have reproductions of English furniture, with fewer antiques than claimed in the brochures. Room fridges are stocked with soft drinks, the TVs have VCRs, and many rooms have working fireplaces. Terry-cloth robes are also provided. The restaurant kitchen seeks no new frontiers (main courses $16.50 to $23).

There's an exercise room with Jacuzzi and sauna, an outdoor pool, and access to nearby tennis and golf.

WHERE TO DINE

Main Street Café. 16 Water St. ☎413/458-3210. Main courses $15.95–$20.95. AE, DC, MC, V. Daily 5–10pm (until 11pm weekends). CREATIVE ITALIAN.

The owner's previous establishment was on Main Street in another town and he kept the name for good luck when he opened here in 1998. On the evidence, he won't need help from Fate. This is a sparkling addition to a largely woebegone local dining scene, with a determination to meet a variety of needs and wants. The bar, more for eating than drinking, has a tasting menu of snacks. There are five pizzas from the brick oven, and special risottos and raviolis (maybe porcini with Marsala sauce) every day. Twenty wines are available by the glass. Cigar dinners are held. Meals are served on the deck, beside the flourishing garden. All these options mean that the waitstaff is burdened with long recitations of specials.

Mezze. 84 Water St. ☎ **413/458-0123.** Main courses $12–$15. AE, MC, V. Mon–Fri 5:30pm–1am, Sat 5:30pm–2am, Sun 5:30pm–midnight. ECLECTIC.

Sheathed in blond wood, this looks like a sushi bar, but traffics in such edibles as Asian salmon cakes with wasabi cream and chicken breast on couscous with coconut chutney. That venturesome menu, changed monthly, combined with live music of all genres on weekends, often for dancing, attracts hip gays and grad students in black and young profs in tweed. A terrace in back hangs over the Green River.

Wild Amber Grill. 101 North St. ☎ **413/458-4000.** Reservations suggested weekends. Main courses $15–$33. AE, MC, V. Mon–Sat 5:30–10pm (until 9:30pm Sun). ECLECTIC AMERICAN.

Handy walking distance from the Williamstown Theatre Festival is one draw, dining on the screened porch another, live music weekend nights yet another. The long low building is being reconfigured, so a pool table, burgers, and comfort foods will enforce the informal mood of one large room, and more ambitious meals in the other are expected to appeal to gourmands. The French-trained chef executes twists on continental classics, as with the frenched rack of lamb, osso bucco on a bed of sauce-slippery linguini, and scallop and smoked mozzarella ravioli with pepper sauce and pesto.

WILLIAMSTOWN AFTER DARK

In addition to the Williamstown Theatre Festival (see above), the Williams College Department of Music sponsors diverse concerts and recitals, from choral groups to jazz ensembles. Call their 24-hour recorded **Concertline** at ☎ **413/597-3146** to learn of upcoming events. In addition, the Sterling and Francine Clark Art Institute (see "Art Museums," above) hosts frequent classical-music events.

Connecticut 9

by Herbert Bailey Livesey

Connecticut resists generalization and confounds spinners of superlatives. It doesn't rank at the top or bottom of any important chart of virtues or liabilities, which makes it impossible to stuff into pigeonholes. The nation's second-smallest state is certainly compact—only 90 miles wide and 55 miles top to bottom—but it is still three times the size of the most diminutive of all, which happens to lie right next door. While parts of it are clogged with humanity (only three states are more congested), some corners of Connecticut are as empty and undeveloped as inland Maine.

By many measures, Connecticut's citizens are as wealthy as any in the country, but dozens of its cities and large towns are only shells of their prosperous 19th-century selves, beset by crime and poverty as intractable as it gets. It can boast no dramatic geographical feature—no Smuggler's Notch, no Cape Cod—and its highest elevation is only 2,380 feet, a hill so far north it almost tips into Massachusetts. Established in 1635 by disgruntled English settlers who didn't like the way things were going at Plymouth Colony, it has long seemed spiritually divorced from the rest of New England—an appendage of New York, or a place to be traversed on the way from there to Boston.

All this might appear to constitute an identity crisis and hardly makes Connecticut seem an appealing vacation destination. But a closer look reveals an abundance of reasons to slow down, to linger there.

To a great extent, the state owes its existence to the presence of water. In addition to having Long Island Sound along its entire southern coast, several significant rivers and their tributaries slice through the hills and coastal plain—the Housatonic, Naugatuck, Quinnipiac, Connecticut, and Thames. They provided power for the mills along their courses and the towns and cities that grew around them. Industry still drives most of the economy, despite the bucolic image that mention of the state often conjures. But the water pollution that industry has caused is now being cleaned up, both in the rivers and the Sound.

Development, too, has slowed, helping to preserve for a little longer Connecticut's scores of classic colonial villages, from the Litchfield Hills to the Mystic coast. They are as placid and timeless as they have been for more than three centuries, or as polished and sophisticated as transplanted urbanites can make them.

And the state's salty maritime heritage is palpable in the old boat building and fishing villages at the mouths of its rivers, especially those east of New Haven.

Connecticut is New England's front porch. Pull up a chair and stay awhile.

1 The Gold Coast

Mansions, marinas, and apartment blocks elbow for space right up to the deeply indented Long Island Sound shoreline in the southwestern corner of the state. This is one of the most heavily developed stretches of the coast, and, in terms of family income, one of the wealthiest (hence the name "Gold Coast"). As the land rises slowly inland from the water's edge, woods thicken, roads narrow, and pockets of New England unfold. Yacht country becomes horse country.

The first suburbs began to form in the middle of the last century, when train rails started radiating north and east from New York's Grand Central Terminal into the countryside. This part of the state was made accessible for summertime refugees from the big city, and eventually—inevitably—weekend houses became permanent dwellings. Corporate executives liked the life of the gentry, so after World War II, they started moving their companies closer to their new homes. Stamford became a city; Greenwich, New Canaan, Darien, and Westport were the bedrooms of choice—pricey, haughty, redolent of the good life. (Of course, Fairfield County also contains Bridgeport, a depressed city that once considered filing for bankruptcy.)

But for visitors, the fashionable exurbs are the draw, along with the villages farther north, especially Ridgefield, that hint of Vermont, within an hour and a half of Times Square.

ESSENTIALS

GETTING THERE   From New York and points south, take I-95 or, preferably, the Hutchinson and Merritt parkways. From eastern Massachusetts and northern Connecticut, take I-84 south to Danbury, then Route 7 south into Fairfield County.

The **Metro North** commuter line (☎ **800/223-6052** or 212/532-4900) has many trains daily to and from New York's Grand Central Terminal, with stops at Greenwich, Stamford, Darien, Norwalk, Westport, and additional stations all the way to New Haven. Less frequent trains connect Danbury with Norwalk.

VISITOR INFORMATION   An information booklet for the northern part of the county is available from the **Housatonic Valley Tourism District,** P.O. Box 406, Danbury, CT 06813 (☎ **800/841-4488**), while the **Coastal Fairfield County Convention and Visitor Bureau,** 383 Main Ave., Norwalk, CT 06851 (☎ **800/ 473-4868**), can provide informative materials about the Gold Coast itself.

STAMFORD

A trickle of corporations started moving their headquarters from New York 38 miles northeast to Stamford in the 1960s. That flow became a steady stream, if not exactly a flood, by the 1980s. The trend was cut short by the recession at the end of that decade, but recovery is evident in much new construction, and more than a dozen Fortune 500 companies continue to direct their operations from here. They have erected shiny mid-rise towers that give the city of 108,000 residents an appearance more like the new urban centers of the Sun Belt than those of the Snow Belt.

One result is a lively downtown that other, weaker Connecticut cities surely envy. Roughly contained by Greylock Place, Tresser Boulevard, and Atlantic and Main streets, it has two theaters offering live entertainment, tree-lined streets with many viable shops and a large mall, pocket parks and plazas, and a number of stylish restaurants, sidewalk cafes, and nightclubs.

Connecticut

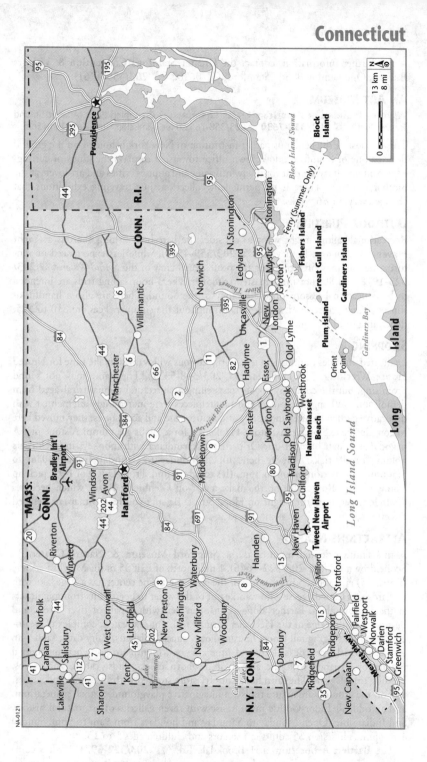

NA-0121

For further information, contact the **Greater Stamford Convention & Visitors Bureau,** One Landmark Sq., Stamford, CT 06902 (☎ **203/359-4761**).

AN ART MUSEUM

Whitney Museum of American Art at Champion. 1 Champion Plaza (Atlantic St. and Tresser Blvd.). ☎ **203/358-7630** or 203/358-7652. Free admission. Tues–Sat 11am–5pm.

This outpost of the generous parent institution in New York is housed on the ground floor of one of Stamford's downtown office towers. It displays the kinds of cutting-edge contemporary art that routinely infuriates and amuses critics and art-lovers at the mother museum. There is no permanent collection; just traveling exhibitions that change every 5 or 6 weeks.

OUTDOOR PURSUITS

Recreational sailors might want to consider the bare boat fishing charters at **Yacht Haven,** Washington Boulevard (☎ 203/359-4500), while less experienced or venturesome folk may prefer joining the professional crew of the *Sound Waters* (☎ 203/323-1978), an 80-foot three-masted schooner. The 3-hour sailing trips are intended to be educational lessons on the ecology of the Sound. There are also a handful of sunset dinner cruises and singles sails throughout the summer. Fees are $10 to $25, depending on the event.

SHOPPING

Dedicated antiques hounds and the simply curious will want to make time for **United House Wrecking,** 535 Hope St. (☎ 203/348-5371). The name may not sound promising, but the company got its start selling architectural remnants salvaged from demolitions. When these pillars and mantelpieces were increasingly augmented with decorative garden fixtures and used antique furniture and accessories, they moved here to contain the exploding inventory. Hankering for a 1930s gas pump? A stone pig? A pagoda? A funfair bumper car? Or perhaps a chandelier with monkeys in frock coats holding candlesticks? They're here. Open Monday to Saturday from 9:30am to 5:30pm, Sunday from noon to 5pm. (It's tough to find. From Exit 9 of I-95, pick up Route 1, then Route 106 north, make a left on Glenbrook Road, which becomes Church Street, then turn right on Hope Street. Be sure you have a map, or detailed directions.)

ATTRACTIONS NEARBY

A fine family-oriented resource is the **Stamford Museum & Nature Center,** 39 Scofieldtown Rd. (☎ 203/322-1646), 1 mile north of Exit 35 of the Merritt Parkway (Route 15) and about 5 miles north of the city center. The center has a large lake with mallards and Canada geese who waddle out of the water to beg tidbits from picnickers at the nearby tables. Farther along is an open pen with a pair of river otters, and beyond that, the edge of the Hecksher Farm, a real, not re-created, complex of weathered barns and zigzag rail fences housing goats, sheep, chickens, dairy cattle, and—an exotic surprise!—peacocks. May and June are good months to go, when the animal population expands with the arrival of newborn chicks, kids, calves, and lambs. Feeding time is 9am. The farm has a country store stocked with souvenirs and snacks, and on the grounds are nature trails, an imaginative playground, a small planetarium, and an oddball Tudor-Gothic main house with seven galleries of art, natural history, and Indian lore. Open Monday to Saturday and holidays from 9am to 5pm, Sunday 1 to 5pm. Admission $5 adults, $4 seniors and children ages 5 to 13.

The **Bartlett Arboretum,** 151 Brookdale Rd. (☎ 203/322-6971), is less compelling, perhaps, but quieter and as soothing as only a garden in the woods can be.

Operated by the University of Connecticut, which has an adjoining campus, the horticultural preserve has several walking trails, none of them strenuous. Gardeners working with their blossoming charges are happy to chat with visitors about techniques and choices. The grounds are open daily from 8:30am to sunset year-round. Admission is free.

WHERE TO DINE

Buster's. 1308 East Main St. (Rte. 1). ☎ **203/961-0799**. Main courses $9.50–$23.95. AE, DC, MC, V. Mon–Thurs 11:30am–2pm and 4:30–9pm, Fri–Sat 11:30am–10pm, Sun 11:30am–9pm (bar until 1am Sun–Thurs, until 2am Fri–Sat). BARBECUE.

This ramshackle roadhouse smack on the Stamford/Darien line wouldn't pass an Amarillo authenticity test, but it's close enough, here in the clutch of Megalopolis Bowash. Upstairs is a down-and-dirty sports bar patronized by large men in hooded sweatshirts and fingerless gloves who linger long over their after-work beers. Downstairs is a classic BBQ joint. Select from the confusing lists of ribs, brisket, pulled pork, sausage, and birds and try to convey your choices to the people behind the cafeteria line, who seem to be speaking an alien tongue. Don't expect a glass for your beer or even a plate for your food. The aliens simply lay a piece of butcher paper in the tray and plop your selections directly thereon. Sauces of varying hotness are pumped nearby, and ravenous eaters then retire to oilcloth-covered picnic tables to gorge.

La Hacienda. 222 Summer St. (north of Main St.). ☎ **203/324-0577**. Reservations suggested weekends. Main courses $11.95–$18.95. AE, CB, DC, DISC, MC, V. Mon–Thurs 11:30am–2:30pm and 5–10pm, Fri 11:30am–2:30pm and 5–11pm, Sat noon–11pm; Sun 1–9pm. TEX-MEX/MEXICAN.

There aren't any surprises on the menu, but aficionados of mainstream Mexican cookery aren't necessarily looking for invention. Specialties are the *camarones en salsa bruja* (shrimp in a spicy "witch's" sauce) and *puerco en salsa chipotle* (pork in a smoked jalapeño sauce). A tantalizing starter is *ceviche del día* (marinated fish of the day). Skip the ordinary combination plates.

The owners have opened an adjoining Argentine steakhouse, **La Estancia**. The short menu lists three grilled fish and six slabs of charred beef as entrees. For $22.95, try the *parrillada*, a platter comprised of no less than short ribs, pork loin, chorizo, sweetbreads, and morcilla (blood sausage).

Kathleen's. 25 Bank St. (between Summer and Atlantic sts.). ☎ **203/323-7785**. Reservations recommended. Main courses $15.50–$22. AE, CB, DC, DISC, MC, V. Mon–Fri 11:30am–3pm; Mon–Thurs 5:30–9:45pm; Fri–Sat 5:30–10:45pm, Sun 11am–9pm. NEW AMERICAN.

In warm weather, tables on the sidewalk face a leafy triangular plaza across the street. When the snow flies, the interior has a clubby atmosphere, with a paneled ceiling above the bar and baskets of flowers. Shirt-sleeved regulars occupy the bar, while garden-club ladies mingle with executives in the back. The menu ranges around the hemisphere. Jamaican jerk tuna with mango salsa shares menu space with a fiery seafood gumbo, crowded with whole clams and plump shrimp. With the Palace Theatre, Rich Forum, and a new cineplex nearby, Kathleen's does brisk business at night, too, and they've added a gourmet deli and takeout shop next door.

STAMFORD AFTER DARK

Community and corporate leaders have long supported the cultural and popular performing arts in the city, which also gives rise to commercial performance spaces and nightclubs. The **Rich Forum** of the **Stamford Center for the Arts,** Atlantic Street and Tresser Boulevard (☎ **203/325-4466**), presents professional productions, with name actors, of successful Broadway and off-Broadway plays, while the **Palace Theatre,** 61 Atlantic St. (☎ **203/325-4466**), offers musicals, rotating appearances by the Stamford Symphony Orchestra, the Connecticut Grand Opera and Orchestra, and the Connecticut Ballet, as well as one-night stands by solo acts and traveling troupes like George Carlin, the Beach Boys, and the Alvin Ailey Dance Theater.

Among the handful of downtown clubs is the **Art Bar,** 84 W. Park Place (☎ **203/973-0300**), which has DJ rock for dancing. The **Terrace Club,** 1938 W. Main St. (☎ **203/961-9770**), alternately features live acts and DJ dance nights. The aptly named **Next Door Cafe,** 1990 W. Main St. (☎**203/961-9770**) has deejays most nights, spiced with open mike and special one-time events, like male strippers on Super Bowl Sunday.

NORWALK

Given the despair that grips many New England cities, the improvement of this city's once notorious South Norwalk neighborhood gladdens the heart. The rehabilitation of several blocks of 19th-century row houses is transforming the waterfront district into a trendy precinct that has come to be called, inevitably, "SoNo." The transformation is far from complete, and decay still festers around the edges, but new shops, restaurants, and nightspots open weekly, a process that looks to be self-generating. The opening of the Maritime Aquarium was a prime motivation, and the district, bounded roughly by Washington, Water, and North and South Main streets, is readily accessible from the South Norwalk railroad station.

SEEING THE SIGHTS

✪ **The Maritime Aquarium at Norwalk.** 10 N. Water St. ☎ **203/852-0700.** Admission $7.75 adults, $7 seniors, $6.50 children 2–12; IMAX $6.50 adults, $5.50 seniors, $4.75 children; combination packages $12 adults, $10.50 seniors, $9.50 children. July to Labor Day daily 10am–6pm; early Sept to June 10am–5pm.

This facility remains the centerpiece of revitalized SoNo. The present name isn't inclusive, since part of the complex includes a section of boat builders at work as well as exhibits of model ships and full-size vessels, including the *Tango,* which was *pedaled* across the Atlantic Ocean.

The main attractions, though, are the marine creatures and mammals on view. On the ground floor is an indoor-outdoor tank of five harbor seals, which are found in adjacent Long Island Sound. They are fed at 11:45am, 1:45 and 3:45pm, when they wriggle up on the rocks and all but rest their heads in their handler's lap.

Additional exhibits include a pair of river otters, an open pool of cow-nosed rays, and tanks alive with fish and sea creatures found in Sound waters, from monster lobsters, flounder, and pollock to the more exotic sea robin, skate, and bristling sea ravens. And to make sure no one's expectations are unmet, there is a large tank of tiger sand sharks, swimming silently and eerily in unending circles, their fearsome mouths inches away from onlookers. A long-term exhibition is "Aliens From The Sea," with tanks of flamboyant lionfish, scary moray eels, and spidery Hawaiian ghost shrimp. The installation remains until April 30, 2000.

A giant IMAX screen shows nature films that aren't necessarily confined to the seven seas. Two recent shows were *Everest* and *T-Rex: Back to the Cretaceous.*

Lockwood-Mathews Mansion Museum. 295 West Ave. ☎ **203/838-1434.** Admission $5 adults, $3 seniors and children 12 and under. Mar to mid-Dec Tues–Fri 11am–3pm, Sun 1–4pm. From I-95 southbound, take Exit 15; from I-95 northbound, take Exit 14.

Erected in 1864 for a financier by the name of LeGrand Lockwood, this four-story granite mansion covered with peaked and mansard slate roofs has 50 rooms arranged around a stunning skylit octagonal rotunda. Marble, gilt, intricately carved wood, marquetry, etched glass, and frescoes were commissioned and incorporated with abandon. It cost $1.2 million (real money back then). Visits are by 1-hour guided tour only.

CRUISES

Excursions to **Sheffield Island** and its historic lighthouse are offered by the *M/V Island Girl* (☎ 203/838-9444), a 60-passenger vessel that departs from Hope Dock, near the Maritime Aquarium at Washington and North Water streets. Weather permitting, the boat sets out two to four times daily, weekends from late May to late September and weekdays from late June to Labor Day. The round-trip takes about 1½ hours, with a 15-minute layover on the island. Fares are $9 for adults, $8 for seniors, and $7 for children under 12. Special outings at extra cost include Thursday evening clambakes and occasional Sunday picnics. Call ahead.

Similarly, the oyster sloop *Hope* has "creature cruises" in winter to spot seals and bird life, and marine study cruises at other times, a service of the Maritime Aquarium. Fares are $15 per person. Inquire and reserve ahead at ☎ **203/852-0700,** ext. 206.

SHOPPING

Don't make a special trip, but **Stew Leonard's,** 100 Westport Ave. at Route 1 (☎ **203/847-7213**), isn't your average grocery store and is worth a quick look in passing. They say so themselves, with humongous signs reading WORLD'S LARGEST DAIRY STORE AS FEATURED IN RIPLEY'S BELIEVE IT OR NOT. The store's general jokey tone is established by a sign at the door, RULE 1: THE CUSTOMER IS ALWAYS RIGHT. RULE 2: IF THE CUSTOMER IS EVER WRONG, RE-READ RULE 1. Inside, there's a wall of signed photos of celebrity visitors and model trains run around the walls. Otherwise, those expecting a Disneyland of dairy and produce will be disappointed (talking, singing barnyard figures notwithstanding). Bulk quantities rather than wide selection is the name of the game, and most shoppers will find less variety than they expect of their neighborhood supermarket, despite the hoopla.

Serious shoppers have several choices, primarily among the boutiques and galleries along Washington and Main streets. One shop that may produce a bargain or at least a surprise is **Saga,** 119 Washington St. (☎ **203/855-1900**). It specializes in folk arts and crafts as well as jewelry and furnishings, from the southwestern United States, Mexico, and points south. Prices are fair.

WHERE TO DINE

✪ **Amberjacks Coastal Grill.** 99 Washington St. (between Broad and Main sts.). ☎ **203/ 853-4332.** Main courses $18–$24. AE, DC, MC, V. Mon–Fri noon–3pm and 5:30–10pm, Sat–Sun 12:30–4pm and 5:30–11pm. CONTEMPORARY AMERICAN.

The owner/chef used to run a restaurant in Key West, and this room looks as if he trucked it up intact from Duval Street. The bar is shaped like the prow of a boat, maritime paintings adorn the walls, and wiry Italianate lights dangle overhead. His food is boldly flavored, with liberal use of tropical and Asian fruits and spices. Examples are the yellowfin tuna burger with ginger and mango-papaya "ketchup" on a Portuguese onion roll at lunch and the dinnertime pan-seared black tip shark with sautéed sweet lotus, bok choy, and Chinese pesto topped with tempura watercress. Also offered are "small plates"—essentially large appetizers costing $6.95 to $11.95—perfect for a light lunch or as side orders to be shared at dinner. Jazz combos, blues, and local bands appear Thursday, Friday, and some Saturdays. The lively Friday happy hour draws thirty-ish singles who move out onto the outdoor deck in summer.

Barcelona. 63 N. Main St. (east of Washington St.). ☎ **203/899-0088** or 203/854-9088. Tapas $3.50–$8. Main courses $16–$22. AE, MC, V. Sun–Thurs 5pm–midnight, Fri–Sat 5pm–1am. MEDITERRANEAN.

Tapas are the featured attraction here, which is dressed up to look like a designer bar from Barcelona's tony Eixample district, but larger appetizers and entrees are also available. The kitchen isn't doctrinaire about recipes, which range all over the Mediterranean for inspiration, from antipasti to meze. The back bar is lined with platters of the night's delectables. They might include empanadas of spiced beef, *boquerones* (marinated anchovies), or calamari with smoked tomato aïoli.

WESTPORT

After World War II, the housing crunch had young couples scouring the metropolitan area for affordable housing lying along the three main routes of what is now known as the Metro North transit system. Some of them wound up in this pretty village beside the Saugatuck River, several miles inland from Long Island Sound (47 miles northeast of New York City, 29 miles southwest of New Haven). Most of the new commuter class found Westport to be too far away from Manhattan (an hour to an hour and a half each way on the train), and it was deemed the archetype of the far-out bedroom communities that were dubbed the "exurbs"—beyond suburban. Notable for its large contingent of people in the creative crafts, primarily commercial artists, advertising copywriters, art directors, and their fellows, the town was also appealing to CEOs and higher-level executives, many of whom solved their commuting problem by moving their offices to nearby Stamford. The result is a bustling community with surviving elements of its rural New England past wrapped in a sheen of Big Apple panache.

For further information, contact the **Westport Chamber of Commerce,** 180 Post Rd. E., Westport, CT 06881 (☎ **203/227-9234**).

OUTDOOR PURSUITS

One of several state parks making the most of their Sound-side locations, **Sherwood Island State Park,** Green Farms (☎ **203/226-6983**), has two long swimming beaches separated by a grove of trees sheltering dozens of picnic tables with grills. Surf fishing is a possibility from designated areas, and the park has concession stands, rest rooms, and an amateurish "nature center." The park is open from 8am to sunset. Pets aren't allowed from April 15 to September 30. Get there from Exit 18 of I-95 or U.S. 1, following the road called the Sherwood Island Connector. Admission is $8 for out-of-state cars.

West of the town center is **The Nature Center for Environmental Activities,** 10 Woodside Lane (☎ **203/227-7253**). Its 62 acres have several walking trails, a wildlife rehab center, and a building with live animals and an aquarium. Admission is $1 for adults, 50¢ for children 3 to 14. Open Monday to Saturday from 9am to 5pm, Sunday from 1 to 4pm.

Rent a sailboat or arrange a lesson at the **Longshore Sailing School,** Longshore Club Park, 260 S. Compo Rd. (☎ **203/226-4646**), about 2 miles south of the Boston Post Road (U.S. 1).

SHOPPING

Window-shopping along Main Street is diverting, although stores increasingly are outlets of the chains seen in malls, including **Brooks Brothers, Talbots, The Gap, Eddie Bauer, J. Crew, Banana Republic, Williams-Sonoma, Crabtree & Evelyn,** and **Ann**

Taylor. Less conventional is **Lillian August,** 17 Main St. (☎ 203/629-1539), with a large collection on two floors of paintings, rugs, overstuffed chairs and sofas, and related accessories. Owing allegiance to no specific style, it looks as if it was conceived by Laura Ashley on speed.

WHERE TO STAY

✪ **Inn at National Hall.** 2 Post Rd. (at the west end of the Saugatuck Bridge), Westport, CT 06880. ☎ **800/628-4255** or 203/221-1351. Fax 203/221-0276. 15 units. A/C MINIBAR TV TEL. $200–$425 double; $425–$600 suite. Rates include breakfast. AE, DC, MC, V.

It's nearly impossible to go wrong choosing a member of Relais & Châteaux for a night's stay. This riverside hotel was offered virtually instant membership into that association and, if anything, stands above its already high standards. You know something special is going on as soon as you enter the elevator, which turns out to be a *trompe l'oeil* representation of an estate library, complete with a skulker betwixt the volumes. That playful elegance is on display throughout. Space doesn't allow detailed description of the voluptuous furnishings, baroque canopied beds, and the antiques that fill the public rooms and bilevel suites, but it's improbable that you've seen anything like this elsewhere. The inn's 1873 brick building was a furniture store, bank, town hall, and office building before it finally realized its destiny as an exquisitely decorated and furnished hotel.

Dining/Diversions: Boston superchef Todd English has taken over the restaurant, renamed Miramar. His cuisine is highly creative and largely Mediterranean in inspiration, notably his famed pizzas and paella "Olivacious." Main courses are $19 to $29.

Amenities: Concierge, 24-hour room service, dry cleaning/laundry, newspaper, nightly turndown, in-room massages, twice-daily maid service, baby-sitting, secretarial services, express checkout, valet parking.

WHERE TO DINE

Also recommended is Miramar in the Inn at National Hall, above.

Acqua. 43 Main St. (near east end of Saugatuck Bridge). ☎ **203/222-8899.** Reservations recommended weekends. Main courses $15–$28. AE, DC, MC, V. Mon–Thurs noon–2:30pm and 5:30–9:30pm, Fri–Sat noon–2:30pm and 5:30–10:30pm. MEDITERRANEAN/SEAFOOD.

Chef Bernard put in long years at New York's Lutèce and Ridgefield's Stonehenge before alighting here. He's come to conclusions about what he wants to put out and what to avoid. So . . . anticipate food prepared with a lightened French touch, techniques and sensibilities that do wonders with such immaculately fresh ingredients as sea bass, crab, skate and thimble-size clams. His presentations are marvelously inviting, yet without the appearance of excessive pushing and prodding in the kitchen, and in manageable portions that can be consumed by a normal person. A great deal of money has been put into the bilevel establishment, with murals depicting cherubim and Renaissance musicians, aged-looking decorative tiles, and a bar arching around the wood-burning brick oven, used for pizzas and a customer favorite, roasted chicken. Prices are reasonable for the quality provided and for pricey Westport, especially at lunch.

WESTPORT AFTER DARK

One of the oldest theaters on the straw hat circuit, the **Westport Playhouse,** 25 Powers Ct. (☎ 203/227-4177), is entering its 70th year. Outdoor musical performances are offered at **Levitt Pavilion,** off Jesup Green (☎ 203/226-7600). Both are near the center of town. The local movie house, on the scene since 1916, has succumbed to video technology.

RIDGEFIELD

No town in Connecticut has a more imposing main street. Ridgefield's main avenue is almost 100 feet wide, lined with ancient towering elms, maples, and oaks, and bordered by massive 19th-century houses set well back on plush carpets of lawn. Impressive at any time of the year, it is in its glory during the brief blaze of October foliage season. Only a little over an hour from New York City (58 miles northeast, to be exact), the town is nonetheless a true evocation of the New England character, and a popular weekend getaway for stressed Manhattanites.

There was a settlement here as early as 1709—at least one building, the Keeler Tavern, survives from those years. In 1777, Benedict Arnold, who was to cause mischief all over this state and nearby New York, was still on the side of the rebels. That April he commanded American troops against a British force retreating from Danbury. After a fierce skirmish, the Redcoats smashed through Arnold's barricades and escaped to the coast. It remains known as the Battle of Ridgefield.

SEEING THE SIGHTS

Aldrich Museum of Contemporary Art. 258 Main St. (near the intersection of Routes 35 and 33 at the south end of Main St.). ☎ **203/438-4519.** Admission $5 adults, $2 seniors and students, free for children under 12. Tues–Sun noon–5pm (until 8pm Fri).

This superb collection of paintings and sculptures from the second half of the 20th century was begun by the eponymous founder decades ago and continues to grow. The original white clapboard structure has more than doubled in size with a harmonious addition, and a professional curator now oversees the permanent holdings and organizes three major exhibitions a year, as well as jazz concerts, films, lectures, and other events. The outdoor sculptures set up in the side- and backyards can be viewed even when the museum itself is closed (which may happen, as hours fluctuate with the season and current exhibitions).

Keeler Tavern. 132 Main St. ☎ **203/438-5485.** Admission $4 adults, $2 seniors, $1 children. Wed and Sat–Sun 1–4pm.

This 1715 stagecoach inn was providing sustenance to travelers between Boston and New York long before the Revolutionary War, but that conflict provided it with its object of greatest note. A British cannonball is imbedded in one of its walls, presumably fired during the Battle of Ridgefield in 1777. Since 1966, it has been a museum of colonial life. Period furnishings have been installed to set the tone, and costumed guides tell the story.

And the tavern has another claim to fame: It was long the summer home of architect Cass Gilbert (1849–1934), who designed the Supreme Court Building in Washington, D.C., and was a key figure in the construction of the George Washington Bridge in New York.

SHOPPING

Apart from the usual antiques shops and the funk of strip malls and franchise enterprises north of the town center on Route 35, one of the most interesting stops for devoted foodies is the **Hay Day Market,** 21 Governor St. (☎ **203/431-4400**), in a shopping center behind the shops that line Main Street. Open daily, it is about as upscale a food market as exists outside of Manhattan, with sections devoted to excellent produce, prepared foods, baked goods, charcuterie, cheeses, and fresh flowers. Check out items like Camembert en brioche and platters of pasta primavera.

WHERE TO STAY & DINE

The Elms. 500 Main St. (Rte. 35, at the north end of town), Ridgefield, CT 06877. ☎ and fax **203/438-2541.** www.elmsinn.com. 20 units. A/C TV. $130–$185 double. Rates include breakfast. AE, CB, DC, MC, V.

This pair of buildings constitutes Ridgefield's oldest (1799) operating inn. As you face them from the street, the one on the right has the reception desk and most of the rooms. Inside, it has the ambience of a contemporary small hotel with the conveniences many travelers desire, as well as newly decorated rooms with canopied four-poster beds.

Dining: The dining areas (☎ **203/438-9206**), now in the hands of a celebrated Manhattan chef, are in the other building, where a 1996 renovation has freshened the restaurant and lower-priced tavern without masking its 18th-century origins. Food is of the Creative American variety, utilizing regional ingredients. Reservations are essential on weekends. A dining porch is inviting in good weather.

West Lane Inn. 22 West Lane (off Rte. 35), Ridgefield, CT 06877. ☎ **203/438-7323.** Fax 203/438-7325. 20 units. A/C TV TEL. $110–$180 double. Rates include breakfast. AE, CB, DC, MC, V. Driving north from Wilton on Rte. 33, turn west on Rte. 35 at the edge of town.

An inn to fit most images of a romantic country getaway, this also works for businesspeople, since it offers modem jacks and voice mail in every room, as well as laundry service and express checkout. Some rooms have fireplaces, and all have queen-size four-poster beds, VCRs, hair dryers, and coffeemakers. The 1849 house sports a fine oak staircase and stands on a property blessed with giant shade trees.

There is no formal dining room, but the **Inn at Ridgefield** (☎ **203/438-8282**), next door, serves lunch and dinner daily. Reservations are required on weekends, and men are expected to wear jackets at dinner.

2 The Litchfield Hills

When the Hamptons got too pricey, too visible, and too chichi back in the 1980s, a lot of stockbrokers, CEOs, and celebs started discovering the ✪ **Litchfield Hills,** arguably the most fetchingly rustic yet sophisticated part of Connecticut.

The topography and, to an extent, the microculture of the region are defined by the river that runs through it, the Housatonic. Broad but not deep enough for vessels larger than canoes, it waters farms and villages and forests along its course, provides opportunities for recreational angling and float trips, and, over the millennia, has helped to shape these foothills, which merge with the Massachusetts Berkshires.

Men in overalls and CAT caps still stand on the porches of general stores, their breath steaming in the bracing autumn air. Others wade into the river, working the riffs and rills with long looping casts of trout flies hand-tied over the winter. Churches hold pancake-breakfast fund-raisers; neighbors squabble about development. That's one side of these bucolic hills, less than two hours from Times Square.

Increasingly, the other side is fashioned by refugees, permanent and temporary, from New York and its workaholic suburbs. These chic seekers of tranquillity and real estate fled to pre-Revolutionary saltboxes and Georgian colonials on Litchfield's warren of back roads and brought Manhattan-bred expectations with them. Boutiques fragrant with designer coffees and cachets opened in spaces once occupied by luncheonettes and feed stores. The *New York Times* and *Wall Street Journal* appeared on racks next to local weeklies. Restaurants discovered sushi and sun-dried tomatoes and just how much money they could get away with charging the newcomers.

Compromises and city-country conflicts aside, the Litchfield Hills remain a satisfying all-season destination for day trips and overnights from metropolitan New York and Connecticut.

ESSENTIALS

GETTING THERE   From New York City, take the Hutchinson River Parkway to I-684 north to I-84 east, taking Exit 7 onto Route 7 north. Continue on Route 7 for New Milford, Kent, West Cornwall, and Canaan. For Washington Depot, New Preston, and Litchfield, branch off onto Route 202 at New Milford.

An especially attractive entrance into the region is Route 44 from the Taconic Parkway, through Millerton and into Lakeville and Salisbury.

From Boston, take the Massachusetts Turnpike west to the Lee exit, picking up Route 7 south from nearby Stockbridge.

VISITOR INFORMATION   A useful 40-page *Unwind* brochure is produced by the **Litchfield Hills Visitors Bureau,** P.O. Box 968, Litchfield, CT 06759 (☎ **860/ 567-4506,** fax 860/567-5214, www.litchfieldhills.com).

NEW MILFORD

A gateway to the Litchfield Hills, this town was founded in 1703 by immigrants from the older Milford, down on the coast. It functions as a commercial center for the smaller villages that surround it—Roxbury, Bridgewater, Washington, and Brookfield—and as host for such industrial entities as Kimberly-Clark and Nestlé. Several rivers and streams run through it, and dammed Candlewood Lake (notorious for daredevil water-skiers and speedboats) is nearby. It is also at the high end of a long stretch of overdeveloped Route 7, which is clogged with minimalls, auto dealerships, and ill-conceived enterprises dealing in hubcaps and plastic lawn ornaments.

For those reasons, New Milford is a welcome stop on the drive north, if only for lunch and a short stroll. Turn right on Route 202 where it splits from Route 7 and crosses the Housatonic River and a railroad track. Up on the left is one end of the long town green, marked by an early–World War II tank and a bandstand. A fire in 1902 destroyed many of the buildings around the green, so this isn't one of those picture-book New England settings. Rather, it is a mix of late Victoriana, early Greek Revival, and Eisenhower-era architecture, not to ignore the requisite First Congregational Church.

Otherwise, there are no obligatory sights, so a walk down Bank Street, west of the green and along Railroad Street, with its crafts shops, a bookstore, and an art-moderne movie house, won't take long. There are also almost a dozen family-friendly restaurants of various levels of accomplishment.

CANDLEWOOD LAKE

Candlewood Lake (☎ 860/354-6928) is the third-largest man-made lake in the eastern United States. It has a finger that pokes into New Milford, but the area with the most recreational facilities is a few miles to the east. From New Milford, drive north on Route 7 about 2½ miles, turn west on Route 37 toward and through Sherman, then south on Route 39 to the unfortunately named **Squantz Pond State Park** (☎ **860/424-3200**). With over 170 acres along the lakeshore, it offers swimming, ice skating, fishing, hiking and cycling trails, picnic grounds, rental canoes, and a boat launch.

SHOPPING

When conductor Skitch Henderson and his wife Ruth decided to put together **The Silo,** 44 Upland Rd. (☎ **860/355-0300**), they didn't allow themselves to be hemmed in by conventional categories. Housed in their old farm buildings are an arts-and-crafts gallery, a store selling kitchen implements and packaged food products, and a cooking school where noted chefs and food critics give classes most weekends. Open

The Litchfield Hills

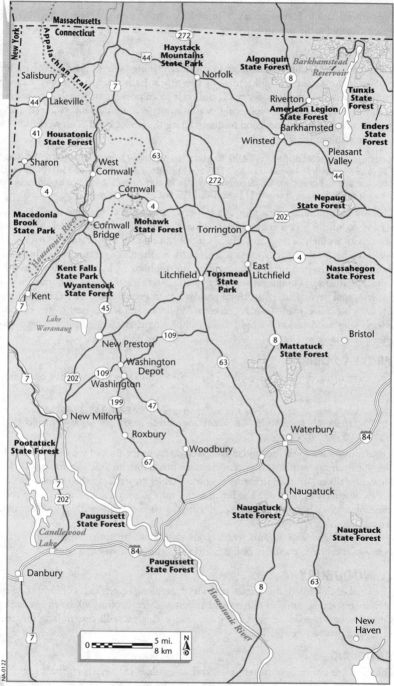

daily from 10am to 5pm. Find it off Route 202, 4 miles north of New Milford center; watch closely for the unobtrusive sign on the right.

WHERE TO STAY

There are good reasons for families to consider making New Milford their base for exploring the Litchfield Hills. Inns in the towns farther north typically exclude smokers, pets, and children under 12, and their room rates fluctuate wildly according to day and season. But the following establishment is more tolerant, relatively inexpensive, and because it does good business during the week as well as on weekends, its rates are stable.

Heritage Inn. 34 Bridge St. (opposite Railroad Station), New Milford, CT 06776. ☎ **800/311-6294** or 860/354-8883. Fax 860/350-5543. 20 units. A/C TV TEL. $85–$100 double. Rates include full breakfast. Children under 5 stay free in parents' room; older kids sharing their parents' room are charged $15. AE, DC, DISC, MC, V. Pets allowed.

This sky-blue building started life as a tobacco warehouse in 1870, but after the conversion to an inn over a century later, it looks more like a railroad hotel in the Old West, with its high ceilings and a long central hall that runs from front to back. The heavy old beams were left exposed, a nice touch, for the decor is otherwise uninspired, though perfectly comfortable and hardly claustrophobic. The somewhat more spacious upstairs rooms pull together better visually, and several have sitting areas. Breakfast goes well beyond the continental standard, with French toast, pancakes, and eggs any way, including made-to-order omelets. While the inn stands next to the railroad tracks, only an occasional freight train rumbles past, since commuter service was ended years ago.

WHERE TO DINE

There are many dining choices along Bank and Railroad streets and out on nearby Route 7.

The Bistro Café. 31 Bank St. (west of the town green). ☎ **860/355-3266.** Main courses $13.95–$18.95. AE, MC, V. Mon–Sat 11am–3pm and 5–10pm, Sun noon–4pm and 4:30–10pm. NEW AMERICAN.

Consensus points to this redundantly named eatery as the pick of the local litter. The late-19th-century structure has served many functions, including a funeral parlor. Now, its walls are stripped to the brick and the tables are dark polished wood, each set with a blue flask of olive oil. The lunch menu runs to soups, salads, and sandwiches, most of it given interesting twists, as with the chicken club with spicy andouille sausage.

Upstairs is the **Tap Room,** with a convivial bar at its center, open only in the evenings and offering a menu of light dishes. It's closed Sunday and Monday.

✪ WOODBURY

The chief distinction of this attractive town strung along several miles of Route 6, west of Waterbury, is its number of high-end antiques stores—at least 40, by rough count. On weekends in good weather, the main road is clogged with cars trolling for treasures, and progress can be slow.

ANTIQUING

Shoppers are drawn here for antiques and collectibles of every sort, from funky to obscure to elegant, with a few contemporary crafts thrown in. Pick up a copy of the directory of shops produced by the **Woodbury Antiques Dealers Association** at one of the member stores to winnow down the list.

Start slowly in the building at the intersection of Routes 6 and 317 that contains **Nancy Fierberg Antiques** (☎ 203/263-4957), carrying American country furniture and folk art such as weather vanes and barbershop poles; **Rosebush Farm** (☎203/266-9114), with "statement" pieces that are catnip to interior decorators; and **Des Jardins** (☎203/263-0075), with antique and new oriental rugs.

Then drive south on Main St. (Route 6) and move up in breadth and quality at **Wayne Pratt Antiques,** 346 Main St. (☎203/263-5676), which specializes in 18th-century American furniture, much of it Chippendale and Queen Anne with original finishes. Here are museum-level pieces that cost from the low five figures to nearly half a million dollars. They get a lot of just-lookers, obviously, but there are items within reach of the rest of us, including keepsake Chinese porcelain boxes for $12 each.

Of similar high order are the offerings of **Country Loft Antiques,** 567 Main St. (☎203/266-4500), which utilizes a fine old barn to display its largely French furnishings and *objets*. Wares run from biscuit tins to deeply carved armoires, bolts of fabric to 18th-century dining tables, boar's-tusk corkscrews to grape-gathering baskets.

Back at the north end of the strip is **British Country Antiques,** 50 Main St. (☎203/263-5100), which fills two floors of a 1790 house as well as the barn in back with 18th- and 19th-century pine furniture from England, Wales, and Scotland, and a few French fruitwood pieces for leavening. Prices are less startling than those at the two emporia described immediately above.

A variation on the prevailing menu is **A Merry-Go-Round of Fine Crafts,** 319 Main St. (☎ 203/263-2920), with six rooms of traditional crafts of every sort, all by Connecticut artisans. Among the items on display are wheat weavings, handmade picture and mirror frames, dolls, samplers, and stenciled floor cloths.

On most Saturdays in decent weather, the **Woodbury Antiques & Flea Market** (☎203/263-2841) sets up in a parking lot at the south end of town.

SEEING THE SIGHTS

About the only scrap of surviving history worth mentioning is the 1750 **Glebe House,** on Hollow Road (☎ 203/263-2855), a quarter mile west of Route 6 on a street of fine 18th-century houses. A *glebe* was a property given to a preacher, in this case an Episcopal bishop, as partial compensation for his services. Inside are furnishings true to the period; outside is the **Gertrude Jekyll Garden,** named for a prominent English landscape gardener of this century. Open April through November, Wednesday to Sunday from 1 to 4pm. Admission is $4 for adults, $1 for children under 12.

North of Woodbury on Route 6, watch for Flanders Road forking to the left. Three miles along, on the right, is the office building for **Flanders Nature Center** (☎ 203/263-3711). The organization that runs it is also a land trust, keeping its 1,300 acres in four different towns out of the hands of developers. Trail maps of the various properties are available in the office, which is open Monday to Friday from 9am to 5pm; the trails, dawn to dusk.

WHERE TO STAY

Merryvale. 1204 Main St. (Rte. 6), Woodbury, CT 06798. ☎ **203/266-0800.** Fax 203/263-4479. www.litchfieldcty.com/lodging/merryvale. 4 units (8 more to be added). A/C TV TEL. $110–$150 double. Rates include full breakfast. AE, DC, MC, V.

South of the town center, this 2-century-old house was converted into a B&B back in 1951, but the present owners took over only a few years ago. A focal point is an original wall painting of an American eagle, revealed during the renovation process. One of the owners is an architect and the other worked in fashion, accounting for the spare good taste evident throughout. They are adding eight more rooms in a new building on the 4-acre property and are expanding their dining room into a 48-seat restaurant; call about availability and rates. Breakfasts are "historic," featuring dishes from the colonial and Federal periods.

WHERE TO DINE

Good News Café. 694 Main St. (Rte. 6). ☎ **203/266-4663.** Reservations recommended on weekends. Main courses $14–$27.50. AE, DC, MC, V. Wed–Mon 11:30am–10pm. NEW AMERICAN.

Owner Carole Peck used to have a restaurant in New Milford, where she packed a scrapbook with glowing reviews. She's doing the same at this location. Part of the secret is that she doesn't see her work as nuclear fission. It's a fun place, with a cheery young staff, a constantly changing menu, and rooms doused in blazing primary colors. The paintings on the walls are all for sale.

And the food? Make it Europe meets Asia, touching down in various parts of the Americas along the way, the resulting concoctions often deployed on the same plate. Examples: pecan-crusted fresh oysters with cranberry tomatillo salsa and Cuban cassoulet with smoked duck, pork, and sausage in a black-bean casserole. Most of the entrees qualify as heart-healthy. Desserts, however, tend to the rich, gooey, and caloric. Saturday nights they have live jazz, and there is outdoor dining in summer.

WASHINGTON & WASHINGTON DEPOT

Settled in 1734, its name changed in 1779 to honor the first American president, ○ **Washington** occupies the crown of a hill beside Route 47. Its village green, with the impressive 1802 Congregational Meeting House surrounded by uniformly white buildings with black shutters and sheltered by towering shade trees, is an example of a municipal arrangement found all over New England but rarely to such near-perfection. The village is home to the exclusive Gunnery School and the renowned Mayflower Inn.

Adjacent Washington Depot, down the hill beside the Shepaug River, serves as the commercial center, with a small cluster of mostly upscale shops.

EXPLORING THE AREA

Nearby **Steep Rock Reservation** is a lovely spot for hiking, fly-fishing, or cross-country skiing. (Dogs are allowed here off-leash.)

The traveling series of musical events known as the **Armstrong Chamber Concerts** usually alights in Washington on four Sunday afternoons in spring and fall (other appearances are in Greenwich, Conn., and Lenox, Mass.). Performances are in the Congregational Church.

A worthwhile detour takes drivers down Curtis Road, past the private Gunnery School to the **Institute for American Indian Studies,** on Route 199 (☎ **860/868-0518**). The small repository of Native American crafts and artifacts is presented with sensitivity and, for the most part, without polemics. A sound track of birdsong and running water plays in the galleries of permanent and temporary exhibits. These baskets, pots, tools, and artworks are used to tell the story of American Indians past and present, mostly of those who lived and still live in this region. Displays are supplemented by workshops, performances, films, and storytelling sessions. Down a nearby path is a re-creation of an Algonquian village. Open Monday to Saturday from 10am to 5pm, Sunday noon to 5pm (closed Monday and Tuesday from January through March). Admission is $4 adults, $2 children 6 to 16.

In Washington Depot, consider putting together a picnic from the delectable array of quiches, pizzas, and salads at **The Pantry,** 5 Titus Rd. (☎ **860/868-0258**). Or, eat there, at tables surrounded by an abundance of cookware and other kitchen gizmos and necessities. Nearby is the beguiling **Hickory Stick Bookshop,** 2 Greenhill Rd. (☎ 860/868-0525), with far-ranging book choices, gifts, and a small CD section.

WHERE TO DINE

G.W. Tavern. Rte. 47 (north of Washington Depot shopping center). ☎**860/868-6633.** Main courses $10.75–$22.50. AE, MC, V. Daily 11:30am–2:30pm and 5:30–10pm (Fri until 11pm). ECLECTIC AMERICAN.

The atmospheric bar in front has booths, tables, and a working fireplace, offering comfort on a rainy winter day, while the simulated barn attached is airier, with an outdoor deck that looks down on Bee Brook. This place used to be named for the waterway until it was transformed a few years ago. Multiple images of the first President justify the current name. Apart from an occasional digression like mulligatawny, the kitchen is dedicated to interpretations of such robust Americana as cobb salad and burgers. There are spins on convention, though, in the roasted garlic mashed potatoes that join the meat loaf, in the snap of cayenne in the black-bean soup, in the sourdough used for the clam fritters. There are vegetable burritos and grilled portobello sandwiches for the flesh-adverse and calming new-age music on the stereo.

WHERE TO STAY & DINE

✪ **Mayflower Inn.** 118 Woodbury Rd. (Rte. 47), Washington, CT 06793. ☎ **860/868-9466.** Fax 860/868-1497. 25 units. A/C TV TEL. $250–$415 double. AE, MC, V. Take Rte. 202 north 2 miles past New Preston, turn south on Rte. 47 through Washington Depot and up the hill past Washington Common. The entrance is on the left. Children over 12 welcome.

These words can do little to burnish the reputation of one of Connecticut's courtliest (and most expensive) manor inns. Galaxies of stars, diamonds, and flags have already been showered upon it by the usual arbiters of taste.

While the main building is almost entirely new, some elements survive from the original 1894 structure, the most delightful of which is the richly paneled library. Porches look out across manicured lawns and flower beds to deep woods. Furnishings throughout reflect a knowledge of sumptuous English country houses and French provincial *auberges*, a sensibility that brought the Tabriz carpets and the genuine Joshua Reynolds portrait to the parlor.

Unlike lesser inns that cut corners on modern conveniences, the Mayflower makes available everything that a superior urban hotel might offer. That includes minibars in all rooms and gas fireplaces in most, bathrooms done with tapestry rugs and mahogany wainscoting, and two-line phones with voice mail and dataports. All is as close to perfection as such an enterprise is likely to be, *almost* justifying the breathtaking prices and occasional excesses of pretension. The fact that the clientele is largely drawn from the generation that remembers the last World War may not endear it to affluent younger people who aren't on honeymoons.

Dining: Three dining rooms of differing styles present dishes created by a chef who manages to transform humble tapioca into something rivaling crème brûlée. Service is intelligent and alert.

Amenities: Heated outdoor pool, tennis court, and a fitness center equipped with saunas, weights, Stairmasters, treadmills, and classes. Massages can be booked at the fitness center.

NEW PRESTON & LAKE WARAMAUG

Never more than a few houses and retailers at the junction of two country roads, this hamlet long served primarily as a supplier for local residents and, starting in the middle of the 19th century, the large families who summered each year on nearby

Lake Waramaug (named for a Chief Waramaug, whose daughter Lillinoah was one of the countless Indian maidens alleged to have leapt off ledges across North America). More recently, New Preston's small grocery and hardware stores have been converted to antiques emporia of high order, and they find themselves surrounded on weekends by BMWs and Volvos.

Exploring the Lake Waramaug Area

At the northwest tip of the L-shaped lake, the 95-acre **Lake Waramaug State Park,** Lake Waramaug Road (☎ 860/868-0220), gives the public access to a beautiful body of water that is otherwise monopolized by the private homes and inns that border it. Canoes and paddleboats are for rent, there is a swimming beach as well as picnic tables, food concessions, and a total of almost 80 camping and RV sites.

A former dairy farm on a promontory above Lake Waramaug was converted in 1979 into the **Hopkins Vineyard,** Hopkins Road (☎ 860/868-7954). Headquartered in a 19th-century barn across the street from the Hopkins Inn (see "Where to Stay & Dine," below), it produces 10 or so bottlings ranging from a sparkling white to hard cider, with Chardonnays and a Pinot Noir in between. They won't make anyone forget the Napa Valley, but prices are fair. A wine bar overlooks the lake and serves pâté and cheese. The tasting and sales rooms are open in January and February, Friday to Saturday from 10am to 5pm, Sunday from 11am to 5pm; March and April, Wednesday to Saturday from 10am to 5pm, Sunday from 11am to 5pm; and May through December, Monday to Saturday from 10am to 5pm, Sunday 11am to 5pm.

Shopping

In no time, the intersecting streets that form the center of the village have gone from sleepy to spiffy, catering to nouveau Nutmeg Staters from Manhattan and weekenders from all over the Northeast. Especially notable among the shops are **J. Seitz & Co.,** Main Street/East Shore Road (☎ 860/868-0119), featuring Indian blankets, clothing, and furniture. Next door is a new, much smaller shop, **Del Mediterraneo** (☎ 860/868-8070), selling pottery from the Catalonia region of Spain, and across the street is **The Trumpeter** (☎ 860/868-9090), specializing in English antiques, including silver desk sets and candlesticks, leather frames and valises, and huge model sailboats.

Where to Stay & Dine

Enthusiastic reviews were lavished upon the latest resurrection of the restaurant of **The Birches Inn,** 233 West Shore Rd. (☎ 860/868-1735). Trouble is, it has only been open for dinner five nights a week and has been closed from New Year's Day to mid-March. That might change—call ahead to find out. There are eight bedrooms, available year-round.

The Boulders. E. Shore Rd. (Rte. 45), New Preston, CT 06777. ☎ 800/552-6853 or 860/868-0541. Fax 860/868-1925. www.bouldersinn.com. 17 units. A/C TEL. $225–$275 double. Rates are $50 lower midweek Nov–Apr, $50 higher Fri–Sat Memorial Day to Oct. Rates include breakfast. MAP is $50 more than B&B rate. AE, MC, V. Drive north from New Preston about 2 miles on Rte. 45.

This once rustic lakeside inn has scrambled steadily upward in both price and quality. Part of the improvement lies with the outlying "guest houses," four new buildings with two spacious units each. All enjoy private decks, fireplaces, whirlpool tubs, and refrigerators. These have contemporary furnishings, while the tone of the rooms in the 1895 main house is set by antiques and reproductions of country styles. Plates of cookies await arriving guests, and the *New York Times* is provided daily.

Dining: Great views are bonuses of the sitting and dining rooms. A serious wine cellar complements the acclaimed cuisine. Guests are encouraged to take the MAP rates; they're a bargain.

Amenities: Down by the shore is a private boathouse with canoes, rowboats, and paddleboats available free to guests. Tennis court.

Hopkins Inn. 22 Hopkins Rd., New Preston, CT 06777. ☎ **860/868-7295.** Fax 860/868-7464. 13 units, 11 with private bathroom. $69–$150 double. AE, MC, V. Closed Jan to late Mar. From New Preston, take Rte. 45 north about 2½ miles and look for the sign on the left.

A family named Hopkins started farming this land in 1787, and its descendants were still around in 1979, when they turned the farm into a vineyard and winery. The yellow frame farmhouse with black shutters that is now the inn sits atop a hill with the best views of Lake Waramaug. Food is the main event at the inn, since most of the guest rooms are on the spartan side, with phones and TV only in the two-bedroom suite in the annex.

Dining: A dining terrace takes maximum advantage of the lake view. Dishes from the Swiss and Austrian Alps, like backhendl with lingonberries, are served in hefty portions by waitresses in uniforms hinting of the Tyrol. Lighter possibilities are *trout bleu* or *meunière*. Entrees run from $17.25 to $21.75. Breakfast, lunch, and dinner are served Tuesday to Sunday, May through October, but only breakfast, dinner, and Saturday lunch are offered in April, November, and December. Reservations are requested for both lunch and dinner.

LITCHFIELD

Possessed of a long common with stately trees reconfigured around the turn of the century by the Frederick Law Olmsted landscaping firm (designers of New York's Central Park), Litchfield is testimony to the taste and affluence of the Yankee entrepreneurs who built it up in the late–18th and early–19th centuries from a colonial farm community to an industrial center. The factories and mills were dismantled toward the end of the 19th century, and the men who built them settled back to enjoy their riches.

Their uncommonly large homes, either authentic Federalists and Greek Revivals or later remodeled to look that way, are set well back from the streets. The commercial district is a block of late-19th-century houses facing the common, with gaudier enterprises kept to the outskirts.

Litchfield has produced its share of notables, including Harriet Beecher Stowe, author of *Uncle Tom's Cabin,* and her abolitionist preacher brother, Henry Ward Beecher.

In recent decades, the town was discovered by fashionable New Yorkers, who find it less frenetic than the Long Island Hamptons. Their influence is seen both in the quality of store merchandise and restaurant fare and the lofty prices houses command.

A WALK THROUGH HISTORY

Litchfield's houses and broad tree-lined streets reward leisurely strolls, whether kicking through piles of fallen leaves in autumn or passing through shafts of summer sunlight piercing the canopy of arching trees.

From the stores and restaurants along West Street, walk east (that's to the right when you're facing the common), then turn right on South Street. On the opposite corner is the **Litchfield Historical Society,** at South and East streets (☎ 860/567-4501), containing exhibits outlining life in the area during the late-colonial and post-Revolution periods, with paintings, furniture, and household utensils. Inquire here about tours of private homes conducted every July. It's open April to mid-November, Tuesday to Saturday from 11am to 5pm, Sunday from 1 to 5pm. Admission is $5.

Walking down South Street, on the right behind a white picket fence is one of the few historic houses regularly open to the public, the 1773 **Tapping Reeve House** and adjacent 1784 **Law School** (☎ 860/567-4501). This was the earliest American law school, established before independence. It counted among its students Aaron Burr, Noah Webster, and three Supreme Court justices. The house belonged to Mr. Reeve, who taught his classes in the small building to the left. Hours are the same as those of the Litchfield Historical Society, which maintains it.

When the street starts to peter out into more modern houses, walk back toward the common and cross over to the north side. Over there on the right is the magisterial **First Congregational Church,** built in 1828. Turn left, then right on North Street, where the domestic architecture matches the quiet splendor of South Street.

OUTDOOR PURSUITS

The **White Memorial Foundation,** Route 202 (☎ 860/567-0857), is a 4,000-acre wildlife sanctuary and nature conservancy about 3 miles southwest of Litchfield. It has campsites and 35 miles of trails for hiking, cross-country skiing, and horseback riding. On the grounds is a small museum of natural history with nature exhibits, stuffed native animals, and a gift shop, and the nearby Holbrook Bird Observatory looks out on a landscape specially planted to attract birds.

This is horse country, so consider a canter across the meadows and along the wooded trails of **Topsmead State Park** (☎ 860/567-5694). The park has a wildlife preserve and a Tudor-style mansion that can be toured in the summer. Follow Route 118 for a mile east of town. Horses can be hired nearby at **Lee's Riding Stables** (☎ 860/567-0785).

SHOPPING

Most of the interesting shops are in the row of late-19th-century brick buildings on the south side of the town green. In the front of **Barnidge & McEnroe,** 7 West St. (☎ 860/567-4670), is a coffee bar for muffins and lattes, which will keep you going as you browse through its entertaining three floors of books, gifts, and ceramics. It's open daily.

Women who share the owner's taste for clothes by Zanella, Ann Freedberg, and hats by Eric Javits will want to check out **Hayseed** (☎ 860/567-8777), a couple of stores away. She also stocks antique and reproduction Indian and Afghan necklaces, jewelry by Connecticut craftswoman Amy Kahn Russell, and striking handbags by Rafael Sanchez. **Kitchenworks,** 23 West St. (☎ 860/567-5011), moved here from a less prominent location, continues to purvey its wide assortment of cooking utensils, glassware, kitchen gadgets, and related items.

ATTRACTIONS NEARBY

It isn't often that a commercial nursery becomes a tourist attraction, but **White Flower Farm,** Route 63 (☎ 860/567-8789), is special. For avid gardeners across the country, this is the L.L. Bean of the mail-order plant and seedling trade. The four main sections strung out along Route 63 (3 miles south of Litchfield center) display perennials, flats of seedlings, bulbs, herbs, florals, potted plants, and shrubs. A featured attraction is the greenhouse full of rare tuberous begonias. The visitor center has informative attendants and rest rooms. The Farm is open April through October 9am to 6pm, November through March 10am to 5pm.

Chardonnays and Rieslings don't spring to mind as likely Connecticut products, but the **Haight Vineyard,** 29 Chestnut Hill Rd. (☎ 860/567-4045), corrects that impression. Established in 1978, it has grown and prospered, presently offering 11 drinkable bottlings, including a respectable Riesling, a couple of sturdy picnic-style reds, and a traditional apple wine. They range in price from $7 to $13 per bottle. The tasting room is open year-round Monday to Saturday from 10:30am to 5pm, Sunday from noon to 5pm. There is a second winery in Mystic.

WHERE TO STAY

✪ **Tollgate Hill Inn.** Rte. 202 (Tollgate Rd., 2½ miles northeast of Litchfield), Litchfield, CT 06759. ☎ **800/445-3903**, 860/567-4545, or 860/567-3821. Fax 860/567-8397. 21 units. A/C TV TEL. Mid-May to Dec $110–$175 double; Jan to mid-May $90–$150 double. Rates include breakfast. AE, CB, DC, DISC, MC, V.

Three barn-red buildings on 10 wooded acres, including the 1745 tavern that is the main house, constitute the liveliest, most atmospheric lodging in Litchfield, and tariffs remain reasonable. The bedrooms are comfortable, with most of the electronic conveniences that might be needed. Morning coffee is free for the pouring at the registration desk, next to the parrot.

Dining/Diversions: The busy restaurant may have wavy wide-board floors and high-backed wooden booths in its oldest room, but the food is of the contemporary-French persuasion (main courses $18 to $25). A Bloody Mary at the table in front of the fireplace in the bar is a treat on a frosty afternoon. From mid-June through October, jazz combos perform on Saturday nights in the cellar or for Sunday brunch.

WHERE TO DINE

The County Seat Café. 3 West St. (on the green). ☎ **860/567-8069.** Main courses $6–$15. AE, MC, V. Mon–Thurs 7am–9pm (until 11pm in summer), Fri 7am–midnight, Sat 8am–midnight, Sun 8am–9pm (until 11pm in summer). ECLECTIC.

Not easy to describe, but a pleasure to experience, the County Seat has a store in front selling kitchenware, coffee beans, baskets, and espresso machines. In back is a soda fountain, and in between is a coffee bar/lunch counter/dining room offering soups, sandwiches, salads, and light meals. One featured sandwich is a smoked-mozzarella quesadilla with mixed greens and olive mayonnaise. There is table service, and upholstered chairs and sofas are available for lounging and chatting. Live music of many kinds is on tap Friday and Saturday nights, with a modest cover charge.

West Street Grill. 43 West St. (on the green). ☎ **860/567-3885.** Reservations necessary for dinner, essential for weekends. Main courses $17.95–$23.95. AE, MC, V. Mon–Thurs 11:30am–2:30pm and 5:30–9pm, Fri–Sun 11:30am–4pm and 5:30–10pm. NEW AMERICAN.

Known as an incubator for some of Connecticut's best chefs, several of whom have gone off to open their own places, this sprightly contemporary bistro hasn't lost a step, despite the frequent changes. Entrees tend toward Cal-Ital renditions of meats, fowl, and grilled fish, little of which knocks your socks off. It just looks and tastes good. The trendiest spot for miles, it attracts the weekend celebrity set, with vaguely familiar faces exchanging confidences across tables. Their usual dress falls somewhere between Ralph Lauren and Eddie Bauer.

LITCHFIELD AFTER DARK

No one goes to Litchfield for its pounding nightlife, but movie-lovers might consider the **Bantam Cinema** (☎ **860/567-0006**) in the otherwise unremarkable village of Bantam, about 3 miles southeast on Route 209. Don't expect the latest Schwarzenegger action flick, since the managers concentrate on art and foreign films that don't get wide distribution. Otherwise, drop by **The County Seat** (see above) for one of its weekend musicales.

KENT

A prominent prep school of the same name, a history as an iron-smelting center, and a continuing reputation as a gathering place of artists and writers define this town of fewer than 2,000. Noted 19th-century landscape painter George Inness helped establish that assessment, and several galleries represent the works of his creative descendants. They are joined by a multiplicity of antiques shops and bookstores, most of them strung along Route 7. South of town on the same road is the hamlet of Bull's Bridge, named for one of the two remaining covered bridges in the state that can be crossed by cars.

North of Kent center, near Kent Falls, is the double-duty **Sloane-Stanley Museum & Kent Furnace,** on Route 7 (☎ 860/927-3849). Fans of the books of illustrator-author Eric Sloane, who celebrated the work and crafts of rural America, will enjoy this replica of his studio, exhibits of tools he depicted, and the drawings and paintings that adorn the walls. On the grounds are the ruins of an iron furnace that was in operation for much of the 19th century, one of many once active ironworks in the Kent area. Open mid-May through October, Wednesday to Sunday from 10am to 4pm. Admission is $3 adults, $1.50 seniors and children.

Four miles north of Kent is the handily accessible **Kent Falls State Park,** on Route 7 (☎ 860/927-3238). Its centerpiece, a 250-foot cascade, is clearly visible from the road, and picnic tables are set about the grounds. A path mounts the hill beside the falls, and there are a total of 295 wooded acres to explore. Rest rooms are available. A parking fee of $8 per car is charged on weekends and holidays from June through October. Serious hikers have a greater challenge nearby, should they choose to undertake it: on the opposite side of Route 7, the Appalachian Trail follows a stretch of the Housatonic River north toward Cornwall Bridge and West Cornwall and all the way into Massachusetts.

WEST CORNWALL

Not to be confused with Cornwall, about 4 miles to the southeast, nor Cornwall Bridge, about 7 miles to the south, this tiny village is best known for its picturesque covered bridge, one of only two in the state that still permit the passage of cars. The bridge connects Routes 7 and 128, crossing the Housatonic. With a state forest to the north and a state park to its immediate south, West Cornwall, a cluster of houses and a handful of commercial enterprises, enjoys a piney seclusion that remains welcoming to passersby.

EXPLORING THE AREA

Housatonic Meadows State Park, on Route 7 (☎ 860/672-6772 in summer, 860/927-3238 the rest of the year), is comprised of 452 acres bordering both sides of the Housatonic River immediately south of West Cornwall and provides access to fishing, canoeing, and picnicking.

A couple of local organizations offer equipment and guidance. One is **Housatonic Anglers** (☎ 860/672-4457), whose owners offer float trips, weekend fly-fishing schools, lodging in two streamside cottages, and guided fishing trips ($100 for a half day, $150 for a full day, both with lunch). All day float trips by canoe cost $175. The other firm is **Clarke Outdoors,** 163 Rte. 7, Cornwall (☎ 860/672-6365), which provides rentals of river craft, including kayaks and rafts, as well as instruction and guided white-water trips.

Just outside Cornwall proper, off Route 4, is **Mohawk Mountain Ski Area,** 46 Great Hollow Rd. (☎ 800/895-5222 or 860/672-6100). "Mountain" is an overstatement, but this is the state's oldest ski resort, with five chairlifts, 23 trails, and snowmakers. The main base lodge has a fireplace and outdoor deck. Rentals and instruction are provided.

Shoppers are drawn to **The Cornwall Bridge Pottery Store,** Route 128 (☎ **860/672-6545**), which features handmade and manufactured ceramics as well as counters and shelves of lamps, copper pots, wind chimes, kitchen gadgets, and even knitwear.

SHARON

Early on, this attractive hamlet near the New York border established a reputation for its manufactures, which included mousetraps and cannon shells. Those industries no longer exist, and Sharon is now primarily residential, a picturesque village with many houses made of brick or fieldstone in a region where wood-frame houses prevail.

The **Sharon Audubon Center,** Route 4 (☎ **860/364-0520**), is a 758-acre nature preserve with herb and flower gardens, a shop and interpretive center, and 11 miles of hiking and nature trails. Injured birds are brought to the center for rehabilitation, and there are usually several raptors (birds of prey) recuperating in house. The grounds are open dusk to dawn, the main building Monday to Saturday from 9am to 5pm and Sunday from 1 to 5pm. Admission to trails is $3 for adults, $1.50 for seniors and children.

WHERE TO DINE

West Main Cafe. 13 W. Main St. ☎ **860/364-9888.** Main courses $16.50–$19.95. AE, MC, V. Mon, Wed–Thurs 5:30–9pm, Fri–Sun 11:30am–2pm and 5:30–9pm. ELECTIC MULTINATIONAL.

Another chef who passed through Litchfield's West Street Grill took a flier a few years ago on this once-scorned eatery. There aren't a dozen tables in the dining room of the frame house, and calling the decor minimalist would be kind. That leaves the spotlight on the food, which handily surpasses anything that can be found within miles in any direction. Matthew Fahrner's fancies bound around the culinary map, his menu changing at least once a month. What results is inevitably appetizing and often nearly indescribable, but playing with and merging Southwestern, Asian, and Mediterranean themes. Partner Susan Miller covers the front and performs as pastry chef. Praline cheesecake with carmel sauce, anyone?

LAKEVILLE & SALISBURY

These two attractive villages share a common history and a main street lined with 19th-century houses stretching along Route 44. The "lake" in question is called Wononscopomuc, slightly south of the town center, its shoreline dotted with summer homes.

The discovery in the area of a particularly pure iron ore led to the development of mines and forges as early as the mid-1700s. One of the ironworkers was the eccentric Ethan Allen, later to become the leader of the Green Mountain Boys and a hero for his capture of Fort Ticonderoga from the British in 1775. The forges of the area supplied Washington's army with many cannons in the critical early years of the Revolution.

EXPLORING THE AREA

One wealthy forge owner and manufacturer, John Milton Holley, bought a 1768 mansion and doubled its size in 1808. The result is the **Holley House,** 15 Millerton Rd., Route 44 (☎ **860/435-2878**), a Federalist and Greek Revival architectural mix. One of the few historic houses in the area open to the public, it contains furnishings and collections of china, silverware, and glass collected by Holley and his descendants over the continuous 173 years the family lived there. Open mid-June to mid-October, Saturday and Sunday from noon to 5pm. Admission is free, but guided tours cost $3 for adults, $2 for seniors and students, free under 5.

Not far from Lakeville center (south on Route 41, then east on Route 112) is **Lime Rock Park** (☎ 860/435-2571), one of the premier auto-racing courses in the Northeast. It garnered even greater attention when Paul Newman, a Connecticut resident, started piloting his own car around the turns. While sports cars are the central attraction, there are special races with vintage vehicles and NASCAR stock cars, and the famous **Skip Barber Racing School** (☎ 800/221-1131) is located here. Races are held late April to early November, Saturdays and Monday holidays.

In Salisbury, the **Salisbury Antiques Center,** 46 Library St. (☎ 860/435-0424), deals in exalted forms of English and American furniture and accessories.

WHERE TO STAY & DINE

White Hart. The Village Green (P.O. Box 545), Salisbury, CT 06068. ☎ 860/435-0030. Fax 860/435-0040. www.whitehartinn.com. 26 units. A/C TV TEL. Mid-Apr to Nov 14 $95–$195 double; Nov 15 to mid-Apr $75–$155 double. AE, CB, DC, MC, V. Pets allowed.

Its fortunes have fluctuated in the White Hart's 180-plus years, but lately this white clapboard inn at the end of Salisbury's main street is on the rise. The front porch, with its voluptuously curved wicker furniture, is the prime summertime site. A front parlor with fireplace long ago replaced a cheesy gift shop. Apart from the three suites and the large Ford Room, most of the rooms are on the small side.

Dining: The creative main restaurant, the American Grill, has gathered its share of kudos. Informal meals and snacks are served in the Tap Room and Garden Room. Duos perform Wednesday nights in the Tap Room.

NORFOLK

Founded in 1758, Norfolk was long popular as a summer vacation destination for industrialists who owned mills and factories along Connecticut's rivers. At the least, drive into the center for a look at the village green. It is highlighted by a monument that involved the participation of two of the late–19th century's most celebrated creative people—sculptor Augustus Saint-Gaudens and architect Stanford White.

At the opposite corner is the 90-year-old "Music Shed," a closed auditorium on the Ellen Battell Stoeckel Estate that is the venue for an eagerly awaited series of summer events, the ✪ **Norfolk Chamber Music Festival**. Held from July to late August, it hosts evening performances by such luminaries as the Tokyo String Quartet and the Vermeer Quartet. These are augmented by morning recitals by young professional musicians. From June through August, call ☎ 860/542-3000 or write to the Ellen Battell Stoeckel Estate, Routes 44 & 272, Box 545, Norfolk, CT 06058-0545; from September through May, call ☎ 203/432-1966 or write to 435 College St., P.O. Box 208246, New Haven, CT 06520-8246.

Two prime recreational areas are near each other on Route 272, north of town. One mile from the village green is **Haystack Mountain State Park** (☎ 860/482-1817). Its chief feature is a short trail leading up from the parking lot to a stone tower at the 1,715-foot crest. On clear days, the views from the top take in a panorama stretching from the Catskill Mountains in New York to the Long Island Sound. Picnicking is allowed.

Another 5 miles farther north, on the Massachusetts border, is **Campbell Falls** (☎ 860/482-1817), which enjoys an abundance of streams, rapids, and cascades. Fishing is a possibility, as are hiking and picnicking.

WHERE TO STAY

Greenwoods Gate. 105 Greenwoods Rd. E., Norfolk, CT 06058. ☎ 860/542-5439. Fax 860/542-5697. www.greenwoodsgate.com. E-mail: greenwoodsgate@snet.net. 6 units. A/C.

June–Oct $175–$250 double; Nov–May 10% less. Rates include breakfast and afternoon tea. MC, V. Children over 12 welcome.

This 1797 hideaway is routinely described as "romantic." Some, however, may see instead a clutter of objects, perfumed soaps, candy dishes, books, and the like that borders on cute. Whatever your take, the inn's pampering comforts are undeniable, as is the sumptuousness of the breakfast, which starts with a buffet of pastries and fruits and continues to eggs any way and cranberry/raspberry/apple pancakes. Arrivals are greeted with wine and hors d'oeuvres.

3 New Haven

The approach to New Haven via Interstate 95 isn't a paean to positive urban planning. At the waterfront are acres of railroad switchyards, storage tanks, and warehouses. Inland are a few half-hearted mid-rise office buildings reached by streets that radiate a sense of hopes unfulfilled. It is easy to decide to drive on by.

That would be shortchanging both the city and yourself. For while New Haven suffers the afflictions of most of Connecticut's cities—nearly a quarter of its citizens live at or below the poverty line—it also has a great deal to offer the leisure traveler. Ready and waiting to fill out a rewarding weekend are four active performing-arts centers and theaters with September-to-June seasons of first-rate professional caliber, three outstanding small museums, autumn renewals of college football rivalries that date back over 120 years, and a variety of ethnic restaurants that will drive foodies mad with choices.

Much of what is worthwhile about New Haven can be credited to the presence of one of the world's most prestigious universities. Yale both enriches its community and exacerbates the usual town-grown conflicts—a paradox with which the institution and civic authorities have struggled since the colonial period. But there can be no denying that the city would be reduced to a lump of queasy urban malaise were the university to disappear.

Relatively little serious history has happened here, but there are a number of amusing "firsts" that boosters love to trumpet. Yale awarded the first Doctor of Medicine degree in 1729 to a man who never practiced medicine. The first hamburger was allegedly made and sold here, as was—even less certainly—the first pizza. Noah Webster compiled his first dictionary in New Haven, and Eli Whitney perfected his cotton gin here. A resident invented the corkscrew in 1860, and a candy company came up with the name "lollipop" for one of its products. The first telephone switchboard was made here, necessitated by a Rev. John E. Todd, who was the first person in the world to request telephone service. Charles Goodyear of New Haven came up with a way to vulcanize rubber, and a local man named Colt invented a revolver in 1836.

ESSENTIALS

GETTING THERE   Interstate 95 between New York and Providence skirts the shoreline of New Haven; I-91 from Boston and Hartford ends there. Connections can also be made from the south along the Merritt and Wilbur Cross parkways.

Tweed–New Haven Airport receives feeder flights connecting with several major airlines, including **Continental** (☎ 800/525-0280), **US Airways** (☎ 800/428-4322), and **United** (☎ 800/241-6522). It's located southeast of the city, near Exits 50 and 51 of I-95.

Amtrak (☎ **800/523-8760** for Metroliners, 800/USA-RAIL for all other trains) has several trains daily that run between Boston and New York and stop in New Haven.

Metro North (☎ 800/METRO-INFO) commuter trains make many daily trips between New Haven and New York. To or from New York takes 1½ hours; to or from Boston, about 3 hours. Metro-North tickets are much cheaper than Amtrak's, but their trains take longer.

PARKING   Downtown traffic isn't too congested, except at the usual rush hours, and there are ample parking lots and garages near the green and Yale University, where most visitors spend their time. Even on-street spots aren't difficult to find most of the day.

VISITOR INFORMATION   The Greater New Haven Convention & Visitors Bureau maintains an attended office at 1 Long Wharf Drive, New Haven, CT 06511 (☎ 203/777-8550), visible and easily reached from Exit 46 of I-95. It's open from Memorial Day to Labor Day. An especially useful detailed map of New Haven that even points out restaurants and store locations is *Professor Pathfinder's Yale University & New Haven,* available in bookstores.

SPECIAL EVENTS   Important seasonal events are the new **International Festival of Arts & Ideas,** held at many sites around the city in late June, and a free **jazz festival** on the green from late July through early August. Call the visitors bureau at ☎ 203/777-8550 for additional details.

EXPLORING YALE & NEW HAVEN

The major attractions are all associated with Yale University, and except for the Peabody Museum, are within walking distance of each other near the **New Haven Green,** which is bounded by Elm, Church, Chapel, and College streets.

The flat green, about one-third the size of Boston Common, is divided into two unequal parts by north-south Temple Street. It was set aside by town elders in the earliest colonial days as a place for citizens to graze their livestock, bury their dead, and spend leisure hours strolling its footpaths. Government and bank buildings, including the Gothic Revival City Hall, border it on the east, a retail district on the south, and some older sections of the vast Yale campus to the north and west.

Facing Temple Street are three historic churches, all dating from the early–19th century. Next to Chapel Street is **Trinity Episcopal,** a brownstone Gothic Revival structure, the Georgian **First Church of Christ/Center Congregational,** and the essentially Federalist **United Congregational.** The First Church of Christ is of the greatest interest, built atop a crypt with tombstones inscribed as early as 1687. Tours are conducted Tuesday to Friday between 10:30am and 2:30pm.

The oldest house in New Haven is now the **Yale University Visitor Information Center,** a white colonial facing the north side of the green at 149 Elm St., near College Street (☎ 203/432-2300). While its primary mission is to familiarize prospective students and their parents with the hour-long **guided walking tour** (Monday to Friday 10:30am and 2pm, Saturday and Sunday at 1:30pm), the center has an introductory video and maps for self-guided tours. It's open Monday to Friday from 9am to 4:45pm, Saturday and Sunday from 10am to 4pm. Guided tours are available Monday through Friday at 10:30am and 2pm, Saturday and Sunday at 1:30pm.

It is impossible to imagine New Haven without Yale, so pervasive is its physical and cultural presence. After all, it helped educate our last two presidents, as well as Gerald Ford, William Howard Taft, Noah Webster, Nathan Hale, and Eli Whitney. Established in 1702 in the shoreline town now known as Clinton, the young college was eventually moved here in 1718 and named for Elihu Yale, who made a major finan-

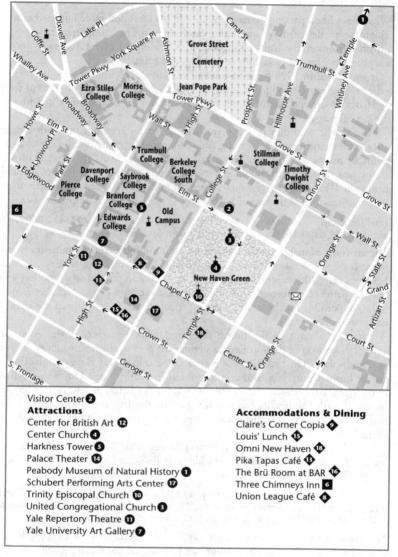

Visitor Center ❷
Attractions
Center for British Art ⓬
Center Church ❹
Harkness Tower ❺
Palace Theater ⓮
Peabody Museum of Natural History ❶
Schubert Performing Arts Center ⓱
Trinity Episcopal Church ❿
United Congregational Church ❸
Yale Repertory Theatre ⓫
Yale University Art Gallery ❼

Accommodations & Dining
Claire's Corner Copia ❾
Louis' Lunch ⓯
Omni New Haven ⓲
Pika Tapas Café ⓭
The Brü Room at BAR ⓰
Three Chimneys Inn ❻
Union League Café ❽

cial contribution. It has many prestigious schools and divisions, including those devoted to medicine, law, theology, architecture, and engineering.

The most evocative quadrangle of the sprawling institution is the **Old Campus,** which can be entered from College, High, or Chapel streets. Inside, the mottled green is enclosed by Federalist and Victorian Gothic buildings and dominated by **Harkness Tower,** a 1920 Gothic Revival campanile that looks much older. Sculptures of notable Yale alumni constitute much of the exterior ornamentation.

Yale Center for British Art. 1080 Chapel St. (at High St.). ☎ **203/432-2800.** Free admission. Tues–Sat 10am–5pm, Sun noon–5pm.

What looks like a parking garage from outside is a great deal more impressive inside. The museum, designed by Louis Kahn, claims to be the most important repository of British art outside the United Kingdom with holdings of over 1,400 paintings and sculptures and tens of thousands of drawings and prints.

It was closed in 1998 for a $3-million renovation, reopening a year later with a major retrospective of 60 paintings by Francis Bacon and lesser exhibitions of works by Henry Moore and Lucian Freud, arguably Britain's three most influential artists of the last 50 years.

Most of the paintings in the permanent collection are from the 16th through early–19th centuries, carefully hung and illuminated by many translucent skylights, primarily on the fourth floor. It's a dazzling array, with about 250 canvases on view at any one time, by such luminaries as Hogarth, Gainsborough, Joshua Reynolds, Benjamin West, and the glorious Turner, from his early realistic seascapes to the lyrical visions toward the end of his life (1851) that anticipated impressionism.

Yale University Art Gallery. 1111 Chapel St. (at York St.). ☎ **203/432-0600.** Free admission ($5 suggested donation). Tues–Sat 10am–5pm, Sun 1–6pm.

The artworks of many epochs and regions are on display, but the museum is most noted for its collections of French impressionists and American realists of the late 19th and early 20th centuries. It's a satisfying collection for connoisseurs, and won't test the patience of teenagers or other irregular museum-goers. Architect Louis I. Kahn, responsible for the nearby Center for British Art, also designed the larger of these two buildings.

Take the elevator to the fourth floor and work your way down. Asian arts and crafts command the top floor, a permanent core of them surrounded by temporary displays. The tiny Netsuke ivories at the center bear close examination, as do the bronze, porcelain, and ceramic vessels in nearby cases. On the third floor, to the right, are 14th- to 18th-century Gothic ecclesiastical panels, mainly tempera on wood with prodigious amounts of gilt. To the left are 16th-century Italian and Dutch portraits and allegorical scenes, among them paintings by Rubens and Frans Hals.

In sharp contrast are adjoining galleries of avant-garde 20th-century Americans of the abstract expressionist school—Rothko and Rauschenberg as well as Europeans Braque, Picasso, Mondrian, and Miró.

Peabody Museum of Natural History. 170 Whitney Ave. (at Sachem St.). ☎ **203/432-5050** (recording). Admission $5 adults, $3 seniors and children 3–15, free for children under 3. Mon–Sat 10am–5pm, Sun noon–5pm. Closed major holidays.

Head to the third floor and work your way down, especially if a school group has just entered—the assault on adult eardrums can be fearsome, for this is probably the most popular field-trip destination in town.

Up there are dioramas with stuffed animals in various environments, abetted by effective backdrop paintings. There are Bighorn sheep, Alaskan brown bears, Southwestern javelina, bison, musk oxen, and the assorted birds, snakes, and rodents with which they share their natural settings. An adjoining gallery has mounted birds representing every species found in Connecticut. On the same floor is a small but illuminating collection of ancient Egyptian artifacts.

The second floor doesn't hold much of general interest, but down on the first is a "bestiary" of large stuffed animals, which leads logically into the Great Hall of Dinosaurs. Its assembled fossils range from a pea-brained stegosaurus and mastodons to the fearsome brontosaurus.

Remaining galleries deal with animal and human evolution, including displays of the weapons, headdresses, clothing, and body ornaments of Polynesian, Plains Indian, and pre-Columbian cultures.

SHOPPING

A retail time machine, **Group W Bench,** 1171 Chapel St. (☎ **203/624-0683**), celebrates an eye-blink epoch that lasted about three years in real time but has continued to reverberate through the terms of six presidents. Started in 1968, the store is packed with beads, chimes, peace emblems, peacock feathers, Mexican yo-yos, rubber chickens, and bumper stickers reading "Thank You, Jerry" (Garcia). You can get a nostalgia contact high just walking in the door. The bearded founder also owns the **Gallery Raffael,** 1177 Chapel St. (☎ **203/772-2258**), next door, which showcases mostly African masks and sculptures, with American arts and crafts, including jewelry and small water fountains.

Farther east on the opposite side of the same street is **News Haven,** 1058 Chapel St. (☎**203/624-1121**), which stocks more magazine titles that you knew existed, as well as newspapers from many foreign cities. Nearby is **WAVE,** 1046 Chapel St. (☎ **203/782-6212**), an upscale operation with a wealth of handblown glassware, brightly colored ceramics, candles, fragrances, toiletries, and mirrors with hand-painted frames.

Atticus Bookstore & Cafe, 1082 Chapel St. (☎ **203/776-4040**), might as easily be listed under "Where to Dine," for half of the store consists of an always-occupied lunch counter and take-out section. Famous for its scones, the cafe also sells delectable pastries, crusty loaves of bread, soups, and hero sandwiches stuffed with meat, cheeses, and vegetables. The New Orleans–style muffuletta is especially good. The rest of the space is devoted to what many call the best bookstore in town. It's open daily from 8am to midnight.

WHERE TO STAY

New Haven lodgings are both limited and, with one notable exception, devoid of either charm or distinctiveness. Still, its motels and hotels fill up far in advance for football weekends, alumni reunions, and graduation. One hotel reports reservations for graduation week into the next century.

Among the national chains represented in town are the **Holiday Inn,** 30 Whalley Rd. (☎ 203/777-6221); **Grand Chalet Inn & Suites,** 400 Sargent Dr. (☎ 203/562-1111); and the **Residence Inn,** 3 Long Wharf Dr. (☎ 203/777-5337). The visitors bureau has a **hotel reservation service** (☎ 800/332-7829).

Omni New Haven. 155 Temple St. (south of Chapel St.), New Haven, CT 06510. ☎ **800/ THE-OMNI** or 203/772-6664. Fax 203/974-6780. www.omnihotels.com. 306 units. A/C MINIBAR TV TEL. $99–$199 double. AE, CB, DC, DISC, MC, V.

A conventional entry in the reliable chain, this came about after extensive renovation of a hotel that had been derelict for years. Its location couldn't be improved, next to the Green, in walking distance of the theaters, much of the University campus, business and government offices, and two of the Yale museums. Prices jump for special-event days at Yale, true of all local lodgings. Over two-thirds of rooms are no-smoking.

Dining/Diversions: Galileo's, the 19th-floor restaurant, serves decent food and fine views of the Green and surrounding cityscape.

Amenities: Concierge, room service, hair dryers, phones with dataports, fitness center, express checkout, business center.

✪ **Three Chimneys Inn.** 1201 Chapel St. (between Park and Howe sts.), New Haven, CT 06511. ☎ **800/443-1554** (out-of-state) or 203/789-1201. Fax 203/776-7363. www.threechimneysinn.com. E-mail: chimneysnh@aol.com. 10 units. A/C TV TEL. $165 double. Rates include full breakfast and afternoon tea. AE, DC, DISC, MC, V. Children over 6 welcome.

This 1870 mansion long did business as the Inn at Chapel West. After a long decline, energetic management resurrected this favorite inn of Yalies and their parents. A new roof was added and all rooms were retrofitted with custom-made armoires to hide the TVs, and mahogany four-poster kings and queens, three of which have drapes that can be completely drawn. Many rooms have stuffed chaises, and all have at least two reading chairs, as well as hair dryers and two-line phones with dataports. The decor has a strongly masculine flavor. Smoking isn't allowed.

In the morning, a selection of newspapers waits outside the dining room. Gas fires burn there and in the parlor in winter. A full breakfast and afternoon tea are served, and in the parlor, a tray of cordials is set out for guests to pour themselves. Businesspeople are more in evidence than is usual at an inn, many of them here to interview Yale students for jobs. Meeting rooms are in the basement.

WHERE TO DINE

✪ **The Brü Rm at BAR.** 254 Crown St. (between High and College sts.). ☎ **203/495-1111.** Pizzas $5–$11. MC, V. Mon–Tues 5pm–1am, Wed 11:30am–2:30pm and 5pm–1am, Thurs–Fri 11:30am–1am, Sat 5pm–2am, Sun 2pm–1am. PIZZA.

Yes, those spellings and capitalizations are correct. This is a 1996 brew pub tacked onto a slightly older nightclub ("BAR"). It's also a naked challenge in the eternal New Haven pizza wars. If Frank Pepe's is the champ, as consensus insists, this whippersnapper is a leading contender. This assumes that you share the conviction that the thinner the crust the better. The pizzas here easily meet that requirement—if they were any thinner, you could read this page through them.

Basic categories are red, red with cheese, and white (cheese only), with 20 additional toppings to choose from. The smallest size can feed two people, especially if they start with the house salad, a concoction of pears and pecans atop mixed greens with crumbled blue cheese scattered over all. The shiny chrome and copper vats on the ground floor and open mezzanine produce five beers and ales, from the BAR Blonde to the Damn Good Stout. They are drawn as half-pints, pints, and pitchers.

Claire's Corner Copia. 100 Chapel St. (at College St.). ☎ **203/562-3888.** Main courses $5.25–$8.50. No credit cards. Daily 8am–10pm. VEGETARIAN.

Few college towns are without at least one low-cost vegetarian restaurant. This one has ruled in New Haven since 1975, more than enough time for the founder to produce three cookbooks, all available for purchase. Dining options include curried couscous, eggplant rollatini, and a number of Mexican entrees, but the stars might well be the veggie burgers and pizzettes. The operators aren't vegans, to be sure, offering lox platters and albacore melt sandwiches. Breakfast brings a bounty of plump scones and massive muffins. A big blackboard lists many choices for all three meals and in-between snacks. All this, and the kitchen keeps kosher, too.

✪ **Frank Pepe's.** 157 Wooster St. (between Olive and Brown sts.). ☎ **203/865-5762.** Pizzas $4.95–$10. No credit cards. Mon and Wed–Thurs 4–10:30pm, Fri–Sat 11:30am–midnight, Sun 2:30–10:30pm. PIZZA.

On the scene for most of this century, Pepe's has long claimed the local pizza crown while fighting off perpetual challenges. In exchange for super, almost unimaginably thin-crusted pies, pilgrims put up with long lines, a nothing decor, and a sullen staff that brooks no hesitancy or questioning from the paying supplicants.

If the wait looks to be especially long, you can do about as well at ✪ **Sally's,** 237 Wooster St. (☎ **203/624-5271**), just down the street.

✪ **Louis' Lunch.** 261–263 Crown St. (between High and College sts.). ☎ **203/562-5507.** Burgers $3–$4.50. No credit cards. Mon–Wed 11am–4:30pm, Thurs–Sat 11am–2am. AMERICAN.

Here's history on a shingle. The claim, unprovable but gaining strength as the decades roll on, is that America's very first hamburger was sold in 1900 at this boxy little brick luncheonette with the shuttered windows.

Louis' Lunch moved from its original location a few years ago to escape demolition, but not much else has changed. The tiny wooden counter and tables are carved with the initials of a century of patrons. The beef is freshly ground each day, thrust into gas-fired ovens almost as old as the building, and then served (medium rare, usually) on two slices of white toast. The only allowable garnishes are slices of tomato, onion, or cheese (all three constitute "the works"). There's no mustard and no ketchup, so don't even ask. And no fries, either, just potato chips. They usually have three or four kinds of pie, though, and if they have time, they might make a tuna or steak sandwich.

Pika Tapas Café. 39 High St. (south of Chapel St.). ☎ **203/865-1933.** Main courses $8.75–$15.75, tapas $4.75–$8.75. AE, MC, V. Sun–Tues 5–10pm; Wed–Sat 11:30am–2:30pm and 5–10pm (until 11am Fri–Sat). SPANISH.

Tapas, for those still uninitiated, are the tasty snacks served in Spanish taverns as accompaniments to wine or beer. Comparable to hors d'oeuvres or antipasti, they come in an infinite variety of tastes and combinations. Among the most common are the *tortilla,* a firm potato-and-onion omelet; *pan Catalan,* thick slices of bread rubbed with tomato pulp and draped with Serrano ham and manchego cheese; and *gambas al ajillo,* shrimp sautéed with garlic. These and another dozen or so are set out at the big semicircular bar in front of the Miró-like mural at this sprightly enterprise. Keep it in mind for light meals before or after curtains at the nearby theaters. There are also larger portions of such classics as paella and lamb stew.

✪ **Union League Café.** 1032 Chapel St. (between High and College sts.). ☎ **203/562-4299.** Main courses $14.50–$21.75. AE, MC, V. Mon–Fri 11:30am–2:30pm; Mon–Thurs 5:30–9:30pm, Fri–Sat 5:30–10pm, Sun 4–8:30pm. CREATIVE FRENCH.

These grand salons with high arched windows opening onto Chapel Street retain an air of their aristocratic origins, which date back to 1854. Even the name fairly shrieks of its former status as a bastion of WASP privilege, the Union League Club. It has loosened up considerably, and jeans-clad Yalies, their doting parents, philosophizing profs, and deal-making execs are all equally comfortable. The atmosphere is now closer to updated Provençal brasserie than to that of a gentlemen's sanctuary, with waiters in aprons and tables with butcher paper. Dinner entrees routinely tinker with tradition, as with the *medaillons de lotte en croute de pomme terre* (monkfish in potato crust) or *poulet grillé aux éspices* (grilled marinated chicken with curry, ginger, and cumin over a basmati risotto). The bar in back offers light snacks.

NEW HAVEN AFTER DARK

The presence of Yale and a highly educated faction of the general population ensures a cultural life equal to that in many larger places. A reliable source of information about cultural events and nightlife is the free weekly newspaper, the *New Haven Advocate,* widely available at hotels, bookstores, and restaurants.

Within a couple of blocks of the Green are the **Shubert Performing Arts Center,** 247 College St. (☎ **800/228-6622** or 203/562-5666), which presents such touring troupes as the Bolshoi Ballet and the Alvin Ailey Dance Theater, musical plays, opera, cabaret, and miscellaneous concerts; and the **Palace Performing Arts Center,** 248 College St. (☎ **203/789-2120**), with a more erratic schedule of pop singers and bands.

A deconsecrated church is the home of the **Yale Repertory Theatre,** Chapel and York streets (☎ **203/432-1234**), west of the Green, which mounts an October-through-May season of mixed productions as fresh as tomorrow and as classic as plays by Shakespeare and George Bernard Shaw. Away from downtown, but worth the taxi fare, is the prestigious **Long Wharf Theatre,** 222 Sargent Dr. (☎ **203/787-4282**), known for its success in producing new plays (October through June) that often make the jump to off-Broadway and even Broadway.

Several additional venues on the Yale campus, including **Sprague Memorial Hall,** 470 College St. (☎ **203/432-4157**), and **Woolsey Hall,** College and Grove streets, host the performances of many resident organizations, including the New Haven Symphony Orchestra, the New Haven Civic Orchestra, the Yale Concert Band, the Yale Glee Club, Yale Philharmonia, and Yale Symphony Orchestra. For upcoming events, call the **Yale Concert Information Line** at ☎ **203/432-4157.**

Bars and clubs also thrive, in considerable variety. The biggest and best venue for live rock and pop is **Toad's Place,** 300 York St. (☎ **203/621-TOAD**), which has welcomed the likes of the Rolling Stones, U2, Phoebe Snow, Bob Dylan, and Johnny Winter. Admission charges can get up to $15 or more for the top acts, but are much lower most of the time. The club usually features live music Wednesday to Sunday, with dancing (to a band or DJ) on most Saturday nights.

A less frenetic evening of music and conversation can be spent at **Xando,** 338 Elm St. (☎ **203/495-7166**). A bilevel postmodernist environment with brick walls and track lighting, it has an espresso bar and a pizzeria and less crowded tables on the upper level, where folk singers often perform.

For something in between, there's **BAR,** 254 Crown St. (☎ **203/495-1111**), which has a lounge in front—open to the street on warm nights—and a pool table, a terrace, and a dance floor with another bar in back. Connected to BAR is the Brü Rm, described above under "Where to Dine."

4 Hartford

Connecticut's capital and second-largest city endures a drooping uneasiness it hasn't been able to shake. There was hope for revival last year when it appeared that the Governor had persuaded the New England Patriots to move to downtown Hartford. A proposed new stadium was to have been the centerpiece of a $1 billion 35-acre riverfront development called Adriaen's Landing, a project that would include a hotel, apartments, a convention center, and a 35,000-seat sports center to house the frequently top-ranked University of Connecticut men's and women's basketball teams.

At the last contractual minute, the Patriots exercised an escape clause, choosing to remain in the Boston area. While it is possible that parts of the ambitious plan will yet

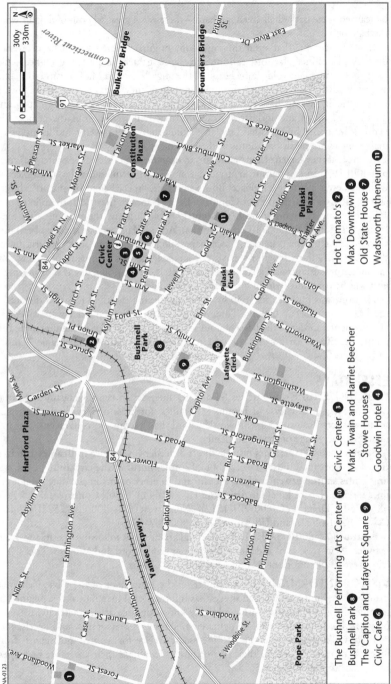

Hartford

Hot Tomato's ❷
Max Downtown ❺
Old State House ❼
Wadsworth Atheneum ⓫

Civic Center ❸
Mark Twain and Harriet Beecher
Stowe Houses ❶
Goodwin Hotel ❹

The Bushnell Performing Arts Center ❿
Bushnell Park ❽
The Capitol and Lafayette Square ❾
Civic Cafe ❻

be realized—the basketball arena, perhaps—there was a great whoosh of despair when the balloon burst.

It was uncertain that even the ambitious original scheme would have reversed decades of decline. Hartford continues to point gamely to its grand edifices—the divinely overwrought gold-domed capitol, the High Victorian Mark Twain House, the august Wadsworth Atheneum. Worthwhile though they certainly are, many visitors have difficulty seeing past the miles of distressed housing, weed-strewn lots, and hollow-eyed office and industrial structures that radiate out from the center. The bedrock insurance business has been in the doldrums, and poverty and its attendant malignancies are persistent thorns in the civic hide.

It isn't as if they haven't tried before this to heal the wounds. A civic center was completed in 1975 in an attempt to attract business downtown, and a flyway connects it with the newer 39-story CityPlace. Both venues offer special concerts and art exhibits, and the 489-seat Hartford Stage Company has a 10-month theatrical season in its own 1977 building catercorner from the center. A block away, the gracious Old State House has reopened after a 4-year renovation. Across Main Street a shed has been provided for a daily farmers market; a local paper sponsors noontime rock concerts during the summer. All these efforts have encouraged the establishment of a few cosmopolitan restaurants and a couple of good hotels, so most of a day trip or overnight visit will be contained within only a few square blocks.

Hartford was founded in 1636 by dissidents fleeing the rigid religious dictates of the Massachusetts Bay Colony. Three years later, they drafted what were called the "Fundamental Orders," the basis of a subsequent claim that Connecticut was the first political entity on earth to have a written constitution, hence the nickname "Constitution State."

ESSENTIALS

GETTING THERE Interstates 84 and 91 intersect in central Hartford, halfway between New York City and Boston (115 miles northeast of New York, 103 miles southwest of Boston). Downtown Hartford has plenty of convenient parking, including the garage of the Civic Center.

Several major U.S. airlines provide direct or feeder-line service to **Bradley International Airport** in Windsor Locks, about 12 miles north of the city. Buses, cabs, and limousines shuttle passengers into the city and to other points in the state. Major airlines serving Hartford include **American** (☎ 800/433-7300), **Continental** (☎ 800/525-0280), **Delta** (☎ 800/221-1212), **Northwest** (☎ 800/225-2525), **United** (☎ 800/241-6522), and **US Airways** (☎ 800/247-8786).

Amtrak (☎ **800/USA-RAIL**) has several trains daily following the inland route between New York City and Boston, stopping at Hartford and Windsor Locks. The trip to either New York or Boston takes about 2½ hours.

VISITOR INFORMATION A counter on the main floor of the Civic Center, at Trumbull, Asylum, and Church streets, has informational materials and is manned by members of the **Hartford Guides.** Highly knowledgeable about their city, they not only provide information about sightseeing, shopping, restaurants, and hotels, they conduct walking tours and can provide escort service for women and seniors from lodgings or eating places to their cars or buses. To obtain their assistance or suggestions, call ☎ **860/293-8105.**

SPECIAL EVENTS Hartford makes the most of its association with one of America's most beloved authors, Mark Twain. His image is seen everywhere, and the city puts on three "Mark Twain Days" in mid-August, with such relevant events as frog jumping, fence painting, riverboat rides, and performances of plays based on Twain's life or works. Most activities are free.

In late July, there is a **Festival of Jazz** with free performances at the pavilion in Bushnell Park.

SEEING THE SIGHTS

The Old State House. 800 Main St. (at Asylum Ave.). ☎ **860/522-6766.** Free admission. Mon–Fri 10am–4pm, Sat 11am–4pm.

After a 4-year $12-million restoration, the 1796 State House opened in time to celebrate its bicentennial. Costumed "interpreters" stand ready, even eager, to answer questions. Upstairs on the right is the Senate chamber, with a full-length painting of the first president by the indefatigable Washington portraitist, Gilbert Stuart. Across the hall is the room that housed the city council after the state government moved to a larger facility. These days, the building is used for temporary art exhibitions, changed two or three times yearly.

✪ **Mark Twain House.** 351 Farmington Ave. ☎ **860/247-0998.** Admission $9 adults, $8 seniors, $5 children 6–12. Memorial Day to Oct 15 and Dec Mon–Sat 9:30am–5pm, Sun 11am–5pm. Rest of the year, Sun noon–5pm, closed Tues. Visits by guided tour only; last tour begins at 4pm. Take Exit 46 off I-84, turn right onto Sisson Ave., then right onto Farmington Ave. The house is on the right, in less than a ½ mile. From downtown, drive west on Asylum St., bearing left on Farmington Ave. The house is on the left.

This 19-room house is a fascinating example of the late-19th-century style sometimes known as "Picturesque Gothic," with several steeply peaked gables and brick walls whose varying patterns are highlighted by black or orange paint.

Samuel Clemens, whose pseudonym was a term used by Mississippi River pilots to indicate a water depth of 2 fathoms, lived here with his wife, Olivia, and three daughters from 1873 to 1897. The high-Victorian decor of the interior was the work of distinguished designers of the time, including Louis Comfort Tiffany, who provided advice and stained glass. Twain's enthusiasm for newfangled gadgets—*Tom Sawyer* is said to be the first novel written on a typewriter—led to the installation of a primitive telephone in the entrance hall.

The guided tour takes about an hour and proceeds through the drawing room, dining room, and library (which has a magnificent carved mantelpiece), and then up through the bedrooms on the second floor. On the top floor is the writer's main workroom, a large space that also has a pool table. Twain would often walk across the hall in the middle of the night and wake up his butler to play a few games.

✪ **Harriet Beecher Stowe House.** 73 Forest St. (☎ **860/525-9317**). Admission $9 adults, $8 seniors, $5 children 6–12. Memorial Day to Oct 15 and Dec Mon–Sat 9:30am–5pm, Sun 11am–5pm. Rest of the year, Sun noon–5pm, closed Tues. Visits by guided tour only; last tour begins at 4pm.

On the adjacent property, about 60 yards across the lawn from the Twain residence, this is a smaller version of its neighbor, built in 1871. Stowe lived there for most of the time Twain resided in his. The author of *Uncle Tom's Cabin* was hardly a great writer, despite the fact that her antislavery novel is probably the first international bestseller. Perhaps that is why Twain regarded the older woman with neighborly equanimity. (He was not so disposed toward many of his contemporary and earlier rivals—of an acclaimed novel by Henry James, Twain expressed the sentiments of countless university students when he commented that "Once you put it down, it isn't possible to pick it up again.")

The competence of the guides here depends greatly on the luck of the draw. Most are admirably well versed, but others are lost outside the bounds of their rehearsed spiels.

✪ **Wadsworth Atheneum.** 600 Main St. (one block west of the Old State House). ☎ **860/278-2670.** Admission $7 adults, $5 seniors and students, $3 children 6–17, free for children under 6 (free Thurs and 11am–noon on Sat); surcharges for some special exhibitions. Tues–Sun 11am–5pm (until 8pm 1st Thurs of month).

Opened in 1842, this was the first public art museum in the United States. It looks its age from the outside, its wings and additions a hodgepodge of ineptly executed Gothic, Renaissance, and Victorian styles. The refurbished interior is another story, with its soaring atrium courts ringed with open galleries and balconies, although a confusion of varying levels and frequent temporary exhibitions often make movement difficult from one part of the second floor to the other.

Persevere, for this is a repository with few equals in New England. The strength of the collection lies primarily in its American paintings, spanning the period from land-scapists of the first half of the 19th century through luminaries of the New York School of the mid-20th to the provocative work of today's young artists. Some space is also devoted to 17th- and 18th-century European artworks of lesser magnitude.

For an overview, proceed by elevator to the top floor. In a far corner is a room devoted to Thomas Cole, a leader among artists of the Hudson River School. In the next gallery are works by Frederick Church, a Hartford native, and the flamboyant Albert Bierstadt, who fashioned huge, sumptuous portrayals of the Rocky Mountains and the West. On the balcony outside are more Americans—Frederic Remington, Andrew Wyeth, Ben Shahn, Reginald Marsh, Milton Avery, even Norman Rockwell. Watch for the shadow box by Joseph Cornell. These lead naturally to a gallery of the so-called American impressionists.

Second floor highlights are rooms of early Connecticut furniture, most of it elabo-rately carved in a form of utilitarian folk art. On the first floor is the MATRIX Gallery, full of rule-bending multimedia works, as well as rooms of large canvases by abstract expressionists and pop and op artists of the 1950s and 1960s like de Kooning, Rauschenberg, Albers, and Kline. Also on this floor is the **Museum Cafe,** which has surprisingly good light items and tables out on the terrace in fair weather.

WHERE TO STAY

The Hartford Sheraton recently became a **Hilton,** 315 Trumbull St., Hartford, CT 06103 (☎ **860/728-5151,** fax 860/522-3356). It couldn't be properly evaluated while in transition, but the 22-story slab can be assumed to offer the advantages expected of either chain. Renovations are underway while the hotel continues in operation.

The Goodwin Hotel. 1 Haynes St. (at Asylum St.), Hartford, CT 06103. ☎ **800/922-5006** or 860/246-7500. Fax 860/244-2669. www.goodwinhotel.com. 124 units. A/C TV TEL. $99–$247 double; $250–$750 suite. AE, CB, DC, DISC, MC, V. Valet parking $15.

This quiet hostelry opposite the Civic Center is housed in a Queen Anne–style Vic-torian built in 1881 as a residence for J.P. Morgan, 19th-century industrialist and railway tycoon. Its understated public areas are attractive, the cautiously decorated bedrooms neither special nor mean. Each has bathrobes, a hair dryer, iron and ironing board, and a phone with dataport. VCRs are available on request. Valet parking, often slow at checkout time, is still a blessing along this crowded block. Friday-to-Saturday packages constitute substantial discounts.

Dining: Pierpont's is the in-house restaurant, with a decidedly erratic reputation.

Amenities: Concierge, room service (6am to midnight), secretarial services, modest health club.

WHERE TO DINE

Civic Café. 150 Trumbull St. (near Asylum St.). ☎ **860/493-7412.** Main courses $17.95–$24.95. AE, DC, DISC, MC, V. Mon–Fri 11am–1am, Sat 5–2am. ECLECTIC.

The self-satisfied young execs and lawyers who frequent this restaurant, who would be at ease in Boston or New York, have found a place that looks like it belongs in a hipper city. Air-conditioning is glacial, and so, sometimes, is the service. No one seems to mind, so busy are they watching the collision of egos. Suits dominate at lunch, when the raw bar near the front is a big draw, and at happy hour, when patrons down fruit-colored martinis around the rectangular bar. The food itself gets your attention, not least for the gobs of salsas and dustings of herbs cast over each plate. T-shirts and shorts are no-nos.

Hot Tomato's. 1 Union Place (corner of Asylum St.). ☎ **860/249-5100.** Main courses $13.95–$21.95. AE, CB, DC, MC, V. Sun–Mon 5:30–9:30pm, Tues–Thurs 5:30–10pm, Fri–Sat 5:30–11pm. ITALIAN.

The renovation of Union Station spawned this popular trattoria in one wing. Walk from the host's podium past the ordered frenzy of the open kitchen and down into a large glass-sided dining room or out onto the dining terrace. A casually dressed crowd tucks into big black bowls of garlicky pasta, which they are usually unable to finish. Especially spicy dishes are marked with a star, and one such is ziti tossed with grilled chicken strips and bitter broccoli rabe. Main courses come with a house salad.

✪ **Max Downtown.** 185 Asylum St. (opposite City Center). ☎ **860/522-2530.** Main courses $15.95–$28.95. AE, CB, DC, MC, V. Mon–Fri 11:30am–2:30pm and 5–10:30pm (Fri until 11:30pm), Sat 5–11:30pm, Sun 5–10pm. CONTEMPORARY AMERICAN.

Hartford's prime-time power and event epicenter has a crowd that looks essentially interchangeable with the one that frequents the Civic Café (above), albeit with a few more suits and fading hairlines at midday and a lot of air-kissing at night. The tavern is jump-off for office parties and deals-in-progress. Too bad no one seems to pay much attention to the bar menu, for its treats are along the lines of mulligatawny and mahimahi with mango-papaya sauce. Over 12 wines are available by the glass, generously poured and served with a warm baguette. The main room has padded banquettes and booths arrayed behind expanses of glass, with a flashy mural on the back wall. Patrons there are indulged with chophouse favorites—thick veal chops and strip steaks—and flightier efforts, such as coconut-crusted shrimp and peppered yellowfin tuna with red-wine broth and gnocchi. Service is anticipatory and without a hint of hauteur. There's a separate cigar bar for those who haven't gotten over that fad yet.

HARTFORD AFTER DARK

A widely available free weekly paper, the *Hartford Advocate,* provides useful information on cultural, sports, and musical events.

The Bushnell Performing Arts Center, 166 Capitol Ave. (☎ **860/246-6807**), is the venue for the **Hartford Ballet,** a classical and contemporary troupe that doesn't neglect to stage its version of the obligatory Christmas *Nutcracker.* It is also home to the **Hartford Symphony,** the **Connecticut Opera,** and the **Hartford Pops,** when it isn't hosting visiting orchestras or road companies of Broadway plays like *Miss Saigon.*

The **Hartford Stage,** 50 Church St. (☎ **860/527-5151**), mounts a variety of mainstream plays, occasionally introducing new productions, while **Theatreworks,** 233 Pearl St. (☎ **860/527-7838**), explores new frontiers.

Several downtown clubs and bars put on live bands, usually Thursday to Saturday. Assuming they're still in operation (never something to be assumed), check out the **bar with no name,** 115 Asylum St. (☎ **860/522-4646**), **The Russian Lady,** 191 Ann St. (☎ **860/525-3003**), and **Arch Street Tavern,** 85 Arch St. (☎ **860/246-7610**).

For beer by the pint or pitcher along with Monday Night Football, where better than **Coach's,** 187 Allyn St. (☎ **860/522-6224**)? It has 32 TVs and serves bar snacks like chili in scooped-out loaves of bread. A similar sports bar is **Finn's**, 93 Church St. 9 (☎**860/240-7293**), open daily 5pm to midnight.

5 The Way East: Guilford to Old Saybrook

Usually ignored by vacationers anxious to get on to Mystic and Essex and the new casinos, the stretch of coast between New Haven and the Connecticut River, known simply as the Shoreline, has its gentle pleasures, enough to justify a short detour for lunch, a walk on a beach, a spell of shopping, or even a proper British high tea (in Madison). When lodgings are difficult to find at the better-known destinations, Shoreline's inns and resorts are logical alternatives within easy driving distance.

ESSENTIALS

GETTING THERE   The Shoreline can be reached from Exit 57 of I-95. Pick up Route 1 (a.k.a., Boston Post Road), which serves as the main street of several Shoreline towns.

Several daily **Amtrak** trains stop at Old Saybrook, and the **Shoreline East** (☎ **800/255-7433**) commuter line uses the same tracks to service towns between there and New Haven, but only Monday to Friday.

VISITOR INFORMATION   Informational materials can be obtained in advance from the **Connecticut River Valley and Shoreline Visitors Council,** 393 Main St., Middletown, CT 06457 (☎ **800/486-3346** or 860/347-0028).

GUILFORD

One of the state's oldest colonial settlements (1639), this village, 13 miles east of New Haven, is embraced by the West and East rivers and has an uncommonly large green bordered by churches, shops, and public buildings.

SEEING THE SIGHTS

There are dozens of historic houses to see in town, most of them privately owned and a few others open to the public on a limited seasonal basis, typically Memorial Day weekend to Labor Day or Columbus Day. **Hyland House,** 84 Boston St. (☎ **203/453-9477**), built around 1660, and the **Thomas Griswold House,** 171 Boston St. (☎ **203/453-3176**), from 1774, are two of these.

Henry Whitfield State Museum. 248 Old Whitfield St. ☎ **203/453-2457.** Admission $3 adults, $1.50 seniors and children 6–17, free for children under 6. Feb 1 to Dec 14 Wed–Sun 10am–4:30pm; Dec 15–Jan 30 by appointment only.

The Whitfield Museum's billing as the "oldest house in Connecticut and the oldest stone house in New England" is misleading. Apart from undergoing frequent alterations over the years, the house was devastated by a major fire in 1860 that left little more than the granite walls. It was reconstructed and occupied until the turn of the century, but by the 1930s had deteriorated from neglect and had to be rebuilt once again.

Most of what you see now, including the leaded windows, dates from the second reconstruction and not from the mid-1600s. It is presented as a museum, not a historic home. The furnishings are authentic to the period, and there are displays of powder horns, flintlock rifles, spinning wheels, and a loom.

The Puritan settlers of Guilford were fearful of hostile action from nearby English and Dutch colonies. The original building was one of four that served as part of a fortification system. Look for the unusual corner window on the second floor that would have been used as a lookout over the Long Island Sound (now concealed by tree growth).

WHERE TO DINE

The Bistro on the Green. 25 Whitfield St. ☎ **203/458-9059.** Dinner main courses $12–$21. MC, V. Mon–Thurs 11am–9pm, Fri 11am–10pm, Sat 11am–10pm, Sun 10am–9pm. CONTINENTAL.

This popular spot hews to the conventions that the word "bistro" suggests. Butcher paper is laid over white tablecloths under vases of fresh flowers; escargot and cassoulet are among frequent offerings. But the new chef is pushing the edges, so there is a *bruschetta du jour,* as well as various pastas and loosely "New American" dishes like pistachio-crusted salmon. No smoking.

MADISON

Madison, 19 miles east of New Haven, is home to a historic architectural district that stretches west of the business district along the Boston Post Road, from the main green to the town line, and contains many examples of 18th- and 19th-century domestic styles and few commercial intrusions.

EXPLORING THE TOWN

Well-to-do Madison has completed the transition from colony to seaside resort to year-round community, a process begun when the first house was built in 1651. Today there are two dwellings from the early years that can be visited on limited summer schedules. **Deacon John Grave House,** 581 Boston Post Rd. (☎ 203/245-4798), dates from 1685, and the **Allis-Bushnell House,** 853 Boston Post Rd. (☎ **203/ 245-4567),** from 1785.

Off the Boston Post Road east of the town center, also reached from Exit 62 off I-95, is **Hammonasset Beach State Park** (☎ 203/245-1817), a more-than-900-acre peninsula jutting into the Long Island Sound that has the only public swimming beach in the area. The park also has a nature center, picnic areas, and campgrounds, and offers boating, too. Cars with Connecticut license plates get in for $5 Monday to Thursday and $7 weekends; out-of-state plates cost $8 and $12, respectively.

SHOPPING

Madison's central commercial district may look ordinary at first glance, but several specialty shops along Boston Post Road and intersecting Wall Street provide entertaining browsing. They are the remaining holdouts against the magnetic pull of the monster outlet malls recently opened in neighboring Clinton and Westbrook.

One of the most active stores in the community is **R. J. Julia Booksellers,** 768 Boston Post Rd. (☎ 203/245-3959), which holds frequent author readings and poetry slams. Many books on the store's two levels have annotation cards offering the specific observations of obviously well-read staff members. There is a large, separate children's section.

A few steps east is **Walker-Loden,** 788 Boston Post Rd. (☎ 203/245-8663), which inadequately describes its wares as "gifts, antiques, and artwork." On hand are diverse souvenir and household items, such as straw hats, cookbooks, nonmechanical toys, greeting cards, pillboxes, prayer rugs, silk ties and scarves, and much more.

Cross the street and head north, and you'll come across several other stores. One of them, in a plum-colored 1690 saltbox, is **The British Shoppe,** 45 Wall St. (☎ 203/ 245-4521), which stocks such English favorites as kippers, bangers, pork pies, boxes of various teas, and several sublime cheeses, all imported from Blighty. Gifts and housewares of British origin are on sale, and lunches and afternoon teas are served in the "Front Parlor." Classic ploughman's lunches of cheese, bread, tomato, lettuce, and pickled onions recall those in English pubs (unfortunately, without pints of English beer, licensing requirements being too tough to meet). Lunch is served from 11:30am to 1:30pm Monday to Saturday, and afternoon teas are served Monday to Saturday from 2 to 4pm and Sunday from 12:30 to 4pm, offering properly brewed loose teas with finger sandwiches and cakes.

WHERE TO STAY & DINE

A useful B&B a few blocks east of the business center is the **Tidewater Inn**, 949 Boston Post Rd., Madison 06443 (☎ **203/245-8457**, fax 203/318-0265). All 9 units have air-conditioning, TV, and phones, and breakfast is substantial.

The Inn at Lafayette/Cafe Allegre. 725 Boston Post Rd., Madison, CT 06443. ☎ **203/245-7773.** Fax 203/245-6256. 5 units. A/C TV TEL. Late May to mid-Oct $125–$175 double; mid-Oct to mid-May $95–$150 double. Rates include breakfast. AE, MC, V. Children over age 12 welcome.

The stately Greek Revival portico in the middle of the business district promises a touch of elegance, and the interior delivers. Since June 1998, the ground floor restaurant has housed Cafe Allegre. Its sponged beige walls and soft carpeting the soothing setting for northern Italian food of considerable accomplishment. No thin tomato sauces or high-rise architectural presentations here. Food arrangements are pretty but subdued, flavors full but exquisitely balanced. The bar in front is low-keyed gathering place, popular for lunch, with a piano player on Thursday and Friday nights. The new owners (including the chef) haven't done much with the rooms upstairs, but they are already comfortable enough, with marble baths, cable TV, and phones with dataports. They all have king- or queen-size beds, and one has a whirlpool bath. The rooms are no-smoking.

WESTBROOK

In Westbrook, a roadside sprawl more plebeian in character than Guilford and Madison, intermittent houses share space with strip malls, fish shanties, cookie-cutter franchises, marinas, and enterprises dedicated to boating services. Only the town center, 28 miles east of New Haven, preserves a touch of its New England character.

Giving a boost to the local economy is the new outlet mall, **Westbrook Factory Stores,** 314 Flat Rock Place (☎ 860/399-8656), north of town at Exit 65 of I-95. Housing over 80 outlets, the complex observes an architectural style that might be described as Rural Railroad Revival, actually a pleasant change from the cell-block design common to many malls. Name dealers include Reebok, Timberland, Dockers, Bugle Boy, Olga/Warner's, Haggar, Corning/Revere, American Tourister, Nordic Track, Springmaid/Wamsutta, J. Crew, Jockey, and Oshkosh B'Gosh. Open daily.

WHERE TO STAY

Water's Edge. 1525 Boston Post Rd. (Rte. 1), Westbrook, CT 06498. ☎ **800/222-5901** or 860/399-5901. Fax 860/399-6172. 32 units. A/C TV TEL. Memorial Day to Labor Day $165–$300 double; Labor Day to Nov and mid-Apr to Memorial Day $150–285 double; Dec to mid-Apr $110–$225 double. AE, CB, DC, DISC, MC, V.

The Water's Edge started out as Bill Hahn's Resort, a shambling family getaway spot that had the feel of a Catskills resort transplanted to the Connecticut coast. It grew and grew into what is now a full-service hotel, which also has time-share condo units. Used for corporate conferences as well as by families and couples, it has sacrificed a former coziness in favor of efficiency and a measure of gloss. Families may want to inquire about renting one of the unoccupied villas instead of the standard hotel rooms.

Dining/Diversions: The restaurant is a pink-and-buff affair with terraces overlooking the lawn and the wide sandy beach. While the kitchen is capable, the best deal is the generous Sunday brunch. There's live music and dancing on weekends.

Amenities: Supervised summer play program for kids. All manner of recreational facilities are available, including two pools (one indoor), paddleboats and sailboats, a fitness center, and tennis courts.

WHERE TO DINE

Lenny & Joe's Fish Tale. 86 Boston Post Rd. (Rte. 1). ☎ **860/669-0767.** Main courses $6.95–$14.95. MC, V. Sun–Thurs 11am–9pm, Fri–Sat 11am–10pm (open an hour later in summer). SEAFOOD.

This is a rough-and-ready fish shack with low ceilings, few pretenses to decor, and waitresses in shorts, aprons, and sneakers. On each bare table is ketchup and sea salt. Fish is the thing, of course, most of it fried. And while it is sure to elevate triglyceride counts, the nutty, crunchy coating on superfresh whole clams, oysters, shrimp, or calamari is hard to resist, especially on a summer evening when the air carries the scent of oceans and distant islands. The menu is printed daily to reflect market prices and availability.

Families are more likely to be encountered at the even more informal **Fish Tale in Madison,** 1301 Boston Post Rd. (☎ **203/245-7289**), especially since a new carousel was installed. No credit cards there.

OLD SAYBROOK

Its location at the mouth of the Connecticut River (35 miles east of New Haven, 26 miles west of Mystic) is this otherwise nondescript town's principal lure. Get off Route 1 to see it at its best. Pick up Route 153 south at the western edge, following its nearly circular route as it touches the shore and passes through the hamlets of Knollwood and Fenwick and across the causeway to Saybrook Point before ending up back in the main business district.

Movie buffs will get a kick out of cruises on *The African Queen,* moored at the River Landing Marina, Ferry Road (☎ **860/388-2007**), the actual steam-powered launch from the 1951 film starring Humphrey Bogart and Katharine Hepburn. It makes voyages May through October, Wednesday to Sunday from 11am to 6:30pm. The fare for the half-hour trip is $15.

WHERE TO DINE

Cuckoo's Nest. 1712 Boston Post Rd. (Rte. 1). ☎ **860/399-9060.** Main courses $10.95–$15.95. AE, DC, DISC, MC, V. Mon–Thurs 11:30am–10pm, Fri–Sat 11:30am–11pm, Sun 11am–10pm. MEXICAN/CAJUN/CREOLE.

Sticklers for gastronomic verisimilitude can look elsewhere. The rest of us can have a good time at moderate cost at this raffish roadhouse, which comes with beat-up wooden chairs and tables on site since the 1976 opening. On the walls are old advertising signs and English street markers; pierced-tin lamps hang over some of the tables, and fans rotate lazily overhead. A jazz duo performs Thursday nights, a pianist on Sundays.

As for the food, roast duckling jambalaya may not be truly Creole, nor the tuna marinated in soy-sherry pepper sauce strictly Mexican, but they taste mighty good. So do the beef fajitas, topped with shredded cheese and *pico de gallo,* not to mention the popcorn shrimp or the catfish fingers. A little gumbo couldn't hurt, either. Sunday brunch is all you can eat for only $9.95. Begin your visit with a mango margarita, out on the expanded terrace if it's a warm night.

6 The Connecticut River Valley

New England's longest river originates in the far north near the Canadian border, 407 miles from Long Island Sound. It separates Vermont from New Hampshire, splits Massachusetts in half, then takes a 45° turn at Middletown, south of Hartford, to make its final run to the sea.

Native Americans of the region called the river *Quinnehtukqut,* which, to the tin ears of the English settlers, sounded like "Connecticut." The colonists encroached upon Indian territory as far north as present-day Windsor, which ignited a brief war with the Pequot, who occupied the land.

Since the river was navigable by relatively large ships as far as Hartford, the sheltered lower Connecticut became important for boat building and industries associated with the international clipper trade. The Connecticut River retains that nautical flavor, and the valley has miraculously avoided the industrialization, development, and decay that afflicts most of the state's other rivers.

ESSENTIALS

GETTING THERE   Limited-access state highway 9 runs parallel to the river, along the west side of the valley, connecting I-91 south of Hartford with I-95 near Old Saybrook. The lower valley is therefore readily accessible from all points in New England and from the New York metropolitan area and points south.

Amtrak (☎ **800/USA-RAIL**) trains stop at Old Saybrook, at the mouth of the river, several times daily on their runs between New York and Boston. In addition, **Shoreline East** (☎ **800/255-7433**) commuter trains operate Monday to Friday between New Haven and Old Saybrook.

VISITOR INFORMATION   The **Connecticut River Valley and Shoreline Visitors Council,** 393 Main St., Middletown, CT 06457 (☎ **800/486-3346** or 860/347-0028), is a source of pamphlets, maps, and related materials.

A NOTE ON LODGINGS   There aren't a great many motels between Haddam and Old Lyme, the southernmost segment of the valley that is of greatest interest to tourists, but there are several excellent full-service inns and many bed-and-breakfasts, some of which can only be found through referral agencies. Two such companies are **Bed & Breakfast, Ltd.,** P.O. Box 216, New Haven, CT 06513 (☎ **203/469-3260**), and **Nutmeg Bed & Breakfast Agency,** P.O. Box 1117, West Hartford, CT 06127 (☎ **800/727-7592** or 860/236-6698).

OLD LYME

As quiet a town as the coast can claim, with tree-lined streets largely free of traffic, Old Lyme (40 miles east of New Haven, 21 miles west of Mystic) was the favored residence of generations of seafarers and ship captains. Many of their 18th- and 19th-century homes have survived, some as summer residences of the artists who established a colony here around the turn of the century, a few as inns and museums.

A MANSION OF ART

Florence Griswold Museum. 96 Lyme St. (Rte. 1). ☎ **860/434-5542.** Admission $4 adults, $3 seniors and students, free for children under 12. June–Dec Tues–Sat 10am–5pm, Sun 1–5pm. Jan–May Wed–Sun 1–5pm.

Once the shipbuilding and merchant trade had all but flickered out at the end of the last century, artists who came to be known as the "American Impressionists" took a fancy to this area. They received encouragement, patronage, and even food and shelter from Ms. Griswold, the wealthy daughter of a sea captain. Her 1817 Federalist mansion was the temporary home for a number of painters, most of whom left samples of their work in gratitude, sometimes painting directly on the walls of the dining room. Visitors can walk across the mansion's 6 acres to the Lieutenant River, a brief course that flows slightly to the west of the Connecticut.

Rotating temporary exhibits are held on the first and second floors. The restored studio of Impressionist William Chadwick is also on view.

OUTDOOR PURSUITS

One of several state parks located at the edge of the Long Island Sound, **Rocky Neck State Park,** Route 156 (☎ 860/739-5471), east of Old Lyme, has a half-mile crescent-shaped beach and over 560 acres for camping, picnicking, fishing, and hiking. Take I-95 to Exit 72 and follow Route 156 south. Open daily from 8am to sunset.

Although headquartered in New York's Hudson Valley, **Atlantic Kayak Tours,** 320 W. Saugerties Rd., Saugerties, NY 12477 (☎ 914/246-2187), conducts many tours along Connecticut's rivers and shoreline, as well as crossings to Long Island. Most excursions are in the 6- to 14-mile range, with levels of difficulty ranging from beginner to highly advanced. With some exceptions, tours are $80, including kayak use.

WHERE TO STAY & DINE

Bee and Thistle Inn. 100 Lyme St. (Rte. 1), Old Lyme, CT 06371. ☎ **800/622-4946** or 860/434-1667. Fax 860/434-3402. www.beeandthistleinn.com. E-mail: info@bee-andthistleinn.com. 11 units, 1 cottage. A/C TEL. $75–$155 double; $210 cottage. AE, DC, DISC, MC, V. Approaching from the south, take Exit 70 from I-95; turn left, then right on Rte. 1 (Hall Rd.) north. Children over 12 welcome.

On over 5 acres beside the Lieutenant River, the core structure of the inn dates from 1756, with the usual wings and additions. Every corner of the place is an enjoyable jumble of antiques and collectibles. A small detached cottage is the best lodging, with the only room TV and a fireplace. Year after year, the inn is voted "best overall" and "most romantic" in the state according to reader polls.

Dining/Diversions: A skilled professional kitchen staff prepares three creative meals a day, served on tables near fireplaces by an eager-to-please waitstaff. Entrees range from $19.95 to $28.95. Musicians are on hand weekend evenings. Jackets requested for men.

Old Lyme Inn. 85 Lyme St. (Rte. 1), Old Lyme, CT 06371. ☎ **800/434-5352** or 860/ 434-2600. Fax 860/434-5352. www.oldlymeinn.com. E-mail: olinn@aol.com. 13 units. A/C TV TEL. $99–$158 double. Rates include breakfast. AE, CB, DC, DISC, MC, V. To get there, follow the directions for the Bee and Thistle, above.

Most of the spacious bedrooms in this 1850s farmhouse are furnished in part with attractive Victorian pieces, including love seats and four-poster or "cannonball" beds. Pets are accepted, a rare policy among New England inns.

Dining/Diversions: The dining rooms are even more impressive, especially the Grill, which features an entire antique bar and marble-mantled fireplace. Admirers of Victorian taverns might not want to leave. The Grill offers a light dinner menu, with live music on weekends. The other dining rooms are more formal (but not stuffy) and serve more substantial creative American meals prepared by competent chefs. Entrees in the main rooms are $19.95 to $32, about 25% less in the Grill.

ESSEX

It is hard to imagine what improvements might be made to bring to ✪ **Essex,** this dream of a New England town close to perfection. In fact, a published survey, *The 100 Best*

Small Towns in America, ranks this waterside village number one. Among the criteria were low crime rates (residents insist they can still leave their doors unlocked), per-capita income, proportion of college-educated residents, and numbers of physicians.

Tree-bordered streets are lined with shops and homes that retain an early-18th-century flavor without the unreal frozen-in-amber quality that often afflicts other towns as postcard-pretty as this. People live and work and play here, and bustle busily along a Main Street that runs down to Steamboat Dock and its flotilla of working vessels and pleasure craft.

SEEING THE SIGHTS

Clustered along the harbor end of Main Street are three historic houses that can be visited on limited schedules. No. 40 is the **Richard Hayden House,** an 1814 brick Federalist that was home to the namesake merchant and shipbuilder. During the War of 1812, British raiders burned Hayden's entire fleet. He was ruined and died soon after, still a young man. Next door, at no. 42, is the **Noah Tooker House,** an 18th-century center-hall colonial that was also the home of a boatbuilder. And at no. 51 is the **Robert Lay House,** completed around 1730 and thought to be the oldest original structure in town.

Connecticut River Museum. Steamboat Dock (at the foot of Main St.). ☎ **860/ 767-8269.** $4 adults, $3 seniors, $2 children 6–12, free for children under 6. Tues–Sun 10am–5pm.

Anglers cast lines from the dock while gulls and ducks hang around hoping for a discarded tidbit. Steamboat service was fully operational here from 1823, and the existing dock dates from 1879. Designated a National Historic Site, the museum proper is a converted warehouse, with two floors of intricately detailed model ships, marine paintings, and related artifacts. Exhibits are changed three or four times a year. They relate the story of shipbuilding in the valley, which began in 1733 and helped make this a center of world trade far into the 19th century. Essex had as many as nine boat-yards, and the first American warship constructed for the War of Independence, the *Oliver Cromwell,* was finished here in 1775. Also in the museum is a replica of the first submersible vessel deployed in wartime, the *Turtle.* The museum usually has walking-tour maps ($1) of Essex, making this a good first stop on a visit.

Essex Steam Train. Railroad Ave. (Rte. 154). ☎ **860/767-0103.** Train and boat $15 adults, $7.50 children 3–11; train only $10 adults, $5 children 3–11, free for children under 3. Daily trips mid-June to Labor Day, less frequently Sept–Apr.

Steam locomotives from the 1920s chug along a route from this station on the road between Essex center and Ivoryton to a boat landing in the hamlet of Deep River, a mildly engrossing excursion of about an hour. It can be combined with an optional cruise on the river, for a total of 2½ to 3 hours. Special events include a Halloween "ghost" train, a Christmas express with Santa Claus, a jazz festival in June, and dinner trains.

WHERE TO STAY & DINE

✪ **Griswold Inn.** 36 Main St. (center of town), Essex, CT 06426. ☎ **860/767-1776.** Fax 860/767-0481. www.originalinns.com. E-mail: griswoldinn@snet.net. 30 units. A/C TEL. $90–$185 double. Rates include breakfast. AE, MC, V.

Gloss over the assertion that "the Griz" is the oldest inn in America (there are other claimants). What's more important to locals and regular guests from out of town is that the inn has been rescued by three brothers who grew up with it as a focal part of their lives. Managing partner Doug Paul vows that there will be no dramatic changes, and maintenance and modest alterations proceed at a measured pace. That's a relief, for it is difficult to imagine this corner of New England without the Griz. Rumpled, cluttered, folksy, and forever besieged by drop-in yachtspeople, anglers, locals, guests, and tourists, the main building dates to 1776. The brothers are now upgrading the too-often plain and unadorned bedrooms scattered through six buildings. Several new suites are now available. Viva Griz!

Dining/Diversions: The atmospheric taproom started life as a schoolhouse and was moved here in 1800. Its vaulted ceiling is said to be made of crushed shells and horsehair, seemingly held up there by the centuries of wafting nicotine that turned it a deep tobacco brown. The walls are layered with nautical memorabilia, as are most of the public rooms. There is live entertainment every night, be it a Dixieland band or only a man with a banjo. The several dining rooms are nearly as colorful, named for their displays of books, antique weapons, or marine paintings. The food is hearty, no-foolin' victuals—turkey with stuffing, roast loin of pork, mixed grill with sauerkraut. Creative risks are restricted to the menu's descriptive prose, which employs titles like "The Awful Awful NY Sirloin: awful big and awful good." Some lighter dishes have been added.

IVORYTON

Once a center for the ivory trade, where factories fabricated piano keys and hair combs, Ivoryton has since subsided into a residential quietude. A virtual suburb of the only slightly larger Essex, a few miles east, the town perks up a bit in the summer, when the **Ivoryton Playhouse** (☎ 860/767-3075) opens its June-to-August theatrical season. The playhouse's repertoire runs to revivals of Broadway and off-Broadway comedies and mysteries.

WHERE TO STAY & DINE

✪ **Copper Beech Inn.** 46 Main St., Ivoryton, CT 06442. ☎ **888/809-2056** or 860/767-0330. www.copperbeachinn.com. 13 units. A/C TV TEL. $105–$180 double. Rates include breakfast. AE, CB, DC, MC, V. Take Exit 3 from Rte. 9 and head west on Main St. Children over 10 are welcome.

Despite comparisons with the Griswold Inn in nearby Essex, these are two very different animals. Where the Griz is decidedly populist and perennially busy, the stately Copper Beech has much less traffic, without a single figurative hair out of place. Previous owners rescued this 19th-century house hours before its destruction, gutting it and rebuilding from the studs out, and the present innkeepers have expanded on the earlier effort. The nine rooms in the converted barn they call the "Carriage House" have ample elbow room, cushy chairs, expensive reproductions of 19th-century furniture styles, whirlpool tubs, sundecks, phones, and TVs. The four rooms in the main building have most of the character, with original turn-of-the-century bathroom fixtures and plenty of antiques. They have phones but no TVs, and staying there can be as nostalgic as a visit to Aunt Edna's. No smoking.

Dining: The Copper Beech is home to one of the most honored kitchens in the region. "New Traditionalist" might describe the chef's take on French recipes and techniques as applied to his high-quality ingredients. Service is seamless in the three formal dining areas, with rolled napkins in the water glasses standing as alert as rabbit ears in a meadow. The restaurant is closed Monday from April through December, and Monday and Tuesday from January through March. Dinner entrees run from $22.75 to $28.75.

CHESTER

Hardly more than a 3-block business center with a few side streets that straggle off past stone fences into the countryside, Chester can be dismissed easily enough. But pause a moment, for this is a riverside hamlet that deserves savoring. Along Main Street are antiques shops and art galleries, the post office, a library, and several eating places that range from sandal informal to dressy casual. The two small streams that once provided power for early grist- and sawmills are canalized and all but hidden.

Downtown Chester doesn't have much room for shops, but it squeezes in at least a couple that deserve a closer look. At **Naturally, Books and Coffee,** 16 Main St. (☎ 860/526-3212), a small selection of books occupies the front of the store, and there's an espresso bar in the back. They have outdoor tables on warm days and live acoustic jazz, folk, and pop performers on weekends. **Ceramica,** 36–38 Main St. (☎ 860/526-9978), an outlet of a small chain with branches in SoHo (Manhattan), West Hartford, Westport, and Scarsdale, New York, carries a line of mostly Italian and uniformly gorgeous hand-painted platters, bowls, pitchers, vases, cups, tureens, and teapots. It's open daily.

WHERE TO DINE

Fiddlers. 4 Water St. (behind Main St.). ☎ **860/526-3210.** Main courses $10.95–$15.95. DC, MC, V. Tues–Thurs 11:30am–2pm and 5:30–9pm, Fri 11:30am–2pm and 5:30–9:30pm; Sat 5:30–10pm, Sun 4–9pm. SEAFOOD.

Have your fish any way you want—poached, sautéed, broiled, baked, or grilled over mesquite—or leave it up to the skillful kitchen, for they can come up with some eye-openers. If "lobster au pêché" (fat chunks of lobster meat married to peach nubbins, shallots, mushrooms, cream, and peach brandy) is still on the menu, go for it. Not for lobster purists, certainly, but a revelatory example of what an imaginative chef can do. All entrees come with a starch, vegetable, and salad. The dining rooms are cheerfully unremarkable, with bentwood chairs, marine prints, and ruffled curtains.

The Wheatmarket. 4 Water St. ☎ **860/526-9347.** Soups, salads, and sandwiches $3.99–$6.99. MC, V. Mon–Sat 9am–6pm. DELI.

Eat out or in at this upwardly mobile country delicatessen, next door to Fiddlers. The staff will serve you there or make up picnic baskets for $9.50 to $16 per person. "The Gourmet" version includes smoked salmon with capers, cream cheese, and red onion; mousse truffée with toast points, chicken-and-grape salad, Caesar salad, cheesecake, and sparkling cider. Or put together your own from the appetizing array of breads, cheeses, pâtés, cold cuts, soups, salads, and sandwiches. Shelves are stocked with packaged "gourmet" items.

EAST HADDAM

Hardly more than a wide spot in a country road surrounded by woods and meadows, Hadlyme (a jurisdiction of the town of East Haddam) wouldn't attract much attention at all if a wealthy thespian hadn't decided to build his hilltop redoubt here.

To get there, take the **Chester-Hadlyme Ferry,** at the end of Route 148, slightly less than 2 miles from Chester. A ferry has operated here since 1769, and the current version takes both cars and pedestrians ($2.25 for vehicles plus $1.50 for trailers, 75¢ for walk-on passengers). It operates (when it feels like it) from 7am to 6:45pm in the warmer months. If it's closed down, there will be a sign posted out at the intersection of Routes 148 and 154, in which case you have to drive north on 154 to Haddam and take the bridge.

AN ECCENTRIC'S CASTLE

Gillette Castle State Park. 67 River Rd. ☎ **860/526-2336.** Admission $4 adults, $2 children 6–11, free for children under 6. Grounds open daily 8am–sunset; castle Memorial Day to Labor Day Fri–Sun 10am–6pm.

William Gillette was a successful actor and playwright known primarily for his the-atrical portrayals of Sherlock Holmes. He took the money and ran to this hill rearing above the Connecticut River, where he had his castle built.

It's difficult to believe that he really thought the result resembled the Norman fortresses that allegedly were his inspiration. Rock gardens by roadside eccentrics in South Dakota or Death Valley are closer relations. Gillette felt it necessary, for one example, to design a dining-room table that slid into the wall, an inexplicable space-saving effort by a bachelor rattling around in 24 oddly shaped rooms.

But whatever Gillette's deficiencies as an architect and designer, no one can argue with his choice of location. The castle sits atop a hill above the east bank, with superlative vistas upriver and down. Nowhere else is the blessed underdevelopment of the estuary more apparent.

Since the terrace of the "castle" can be entered for free, many visitors just come to take in those views and avoid the fees for entering the interior. The 184-acre grounds have picnic areas, nature trails, and fishing sites.

RIVER CRUISES

A voyage on the river is an irresistible outing. Cruises of a variety of lengths, times, and themes are offered by **Camelot Cruises,** 1 Marine Park (☎ **800/522-7463**). The pride of their fleet is the M/V *Camelot,* a 160-foot vessel carrying as many as 500 passengers. In addition to dinner and mystery cruises (in which the passengers solve a staged "murder"), there are summer and fall excursions to Sag Harbor, Long Island.

EAST HADDAM AFTER DARK

From Gillette State Park, turn north on Route 82 and make the short drive to East Haddam proper. The dominant building is a restored six-story Victorian of splendid proportions that opened in 1877 and is now the **Goodspeed Opera House,** Goodspeed Landing (☎ **860/873-8668**). A century ago, it presented such productions as *All is Not Gold that Glitters* and *Factory Girl.* Now it mostly stages revivals of Broadway musicals on the order of *Sweeney Todd* and *Annie,* but has made room for more experimental shows that have eventually made it all the way to the Big Apple. The Goodspeed's season is usually from April through December.

7 Mystic & the Southeastern Coast

If a whirlwind driving tour of New England leaves only 2 or 3 days for all of Connecticut, spend them in this section of the coast that segues into the mainland beach resorts of Rhode Island. And go soon, because it's impossible to predict the eventual effects that the gushers of money produced by two new and immensely successful gambling casinos will have on the character of this region.

The town of Mystic and its singular attraction, the living, working museum that is Mystic Seaport, are the prime reasons for a stay—the Seaport alone can easily occupy most of a day and the two-part town itself sustains a delightful nautical air, with fun shops and restaurants to suit most tastes and every budget.

But that's not a complete list of the region's charms. The tranquil neighboring village of Stonington is home to an active commercial fishing fleet, the last in the state; nearby Groton, on the Thames River, offers tours of the world's first nuclear submarine; there are several enchanting inns in the area; many companies and individuals offer their vessels for whale watching, dinner cruises, and deep-sea fishing excursions. And yes, for those with a taste for the adrenaline rush of a winning streak, there are those two casinos.

If at all possible, avoid July and August, when the crowds are oppressive, restaurants are packed, and rooms are booked months in advance at very high rates.

ESSENTIALS

GETTING THERE   From New York City, take I-95 to Exit 84 (New London), 86 (Groton), 90 (Mystic), or 91 (Stonington). Or, to avoid the heavy truck and commercial traffic of the western segment of I-95, use the Hutchinson River Parkway, which becomes the Merritt Parkway (Route 15) and merges with the Wilbur Cross Parkway. Continue to Exit 54, connecting with I-95 for the rest of the trip. From Boston, take the Massachusetts Turnpike to I-395 south to Exit 75, then south on Route 32 to New London and I-95.

Amtrak (☎ 800/USA-RAIL) has six trains daily (three each way) on its Northeast Direct route between New York, Providence, and Boston, with intermediate stops at New Haven, Old Saybrook, New London, and Mystic. New high-speed trains are to be phased in throughout the coming year.

The regional bus company, **SEAT** (☎ 860/886-2631), connects the more important towns and villages of the district, except for North Stonington.

An exciting new way to get from the metropolitan New York-New Jersey region to New London, and from there to the Foxwoods complex, is the super-fast tri-catamaran **ferry** operated by **Fox Navigation** (☎888-724-5369). The trip takes about 2 hours 45 minutes, at speeds approaching 50 miles an hour and passed on reclining airline-type seats with on-board movies and food service. Liberty State Park on the Jersey shore is the departure point, which can be reached by car or by water taxi from the World Financial Center in lower Manhattan. Passengers debark at the State Pier in New London. There are three classes of service, with introductory round-trip fares starting at $80.

VISITOR INFORMATION   The **Mystic & More Convention and Visitors Bureau,** P.O. Box 89, 470 Bank St., New London, CT 06320 (☎ 860/444-2206, fax 860/442-4257; www.mysticmore.com), can provide free vacation kits.

A NOTE ON LODGINGS   Motels abound, especially in clusters around the several exits off I-95, and can handle the load most of the year (though it's tight in July and August). But travelers who seek lodgings of a more intimate and sometimes less expensive sort can contact the Southeastern Connecticut Tourism District to request a folder describing the loosely affiliated **Bed & Breakfasts of Mystic Coast,** which lists 23 establishments in the area, including four just across the Rhode Island state line. Most are in the $60-to-$120 range and accept credit cards.

NEW LONDON

Founded in 1646 and first known by the Pequot name *Nameaug,* New London's protected deep-draft harbor at the mouth of the Thames River was responsible for its long and influential history as a whaling port. That heritage lingers, but its years of great prosperity are behind it.

Possessed of an architecturally interesting but somnolent downtown district, New London, which lies 46 miles east of New Haven and 45 miles southeast of Hartford, is of note to travelers primarily because it's a transit point for three ferry lines connecting Block Island, Rhode Island, and Long Island, New York, with the mainland, as well as the new high-speed ferries connecting with Martha's Vineyard and the Port of New York. **Connecticut College** has a large campus at the northern edge of the city, along Route 32 and Williams Street. The **U.S. Coast Guard Academy** is also here, but while it welcomes visitors, it is of interest primarily to alumni and prospective students and their parents.

Note: In July 2000, New London is one of the ports for **Op Sail,** a voyage of tall ships expected to recall the similar event that celebrated America's Bicentennial. Exact dates of arrival and departure are uncertain at this writing, so contact the **Mystic & More Convention and Visitors Bureau,** detailed above.

An attended **information booth** is located in downtown New London at the corner of Eugene O'Neill Drive and Golden Street (no phone). It's open June through August daily from 10am to 4pm; May, September, and October, Friday to Sunday from 10am to 4pm.

SEEING THE SIGHTS

Coast Guard Academy. 15 Mohegan Ave. (off Williams St., north of Exit 84 of I-95). ☎ **860/444-8611.** Free admission. Grounds daily 9am–5pm; Visitors Pavilion May–Oct daily 10am–5pm; Apr Sat–Sun 10am–5pm. Pavilion closed Nov–Mar.

Visitors to the base are directed to a pavilion overlooking the Thames. It doesn't offer much except views of the river and shores. A full-rigged sailing vessel, the *Eagle,* is the academy's principal attraction, with boarding allowed on a very limited basis, usually only in April and May. The latest in a line of Coast Guard cutters that goes back to 1792, it was built as a training ship for German Naval cadets in 1936 and taken as a war prize after World War II. Renamed, the barque continues that instructional function at the academy. On some Fridays in spring or early fall, there are dress parades by the corps of cadets.

Lyman Allyn Art Museum. 625 Williams St. ☎ **860/443-2545.** Admission $4 adults, $3 seniors and students, free for children under 6. Tues–Sat 10am–5pm; Sun 1–5pm. From Exit 83 of I-95, follow brown signs to the museum.

This neoclassical granite pile stands on a hill looking across Route 32 toward the Coast Guard Academy. Its holdings are the results of the enthusiasms of private collectors and therefore hold to no specific curatorial or scholarly vision. The various parts are interesting, however, even if they don't belong to a harmonious whole.

The basement contains detailed room settings of Victorian dollhouse furniture, right down to tiny ladles on the kitchen counter and buttonhooks on the bureau. On the main floor are American paintings and furnishings dating to the colonial period, including landscapes by Hudson River School artists Frederic Edwin Church, George Inness, and Albert Bierstadt. Upstairs are galleries with exhibits as diverse as Asian temple castings, African carvings, Japanese lacquerware, and paintings related to New London's past.

OUTDOOR PURSUITS

Not far from downtown is **Ocean Beach Park,** at the south end of Ocean Avenue (☎ **800/510-7263** or 860/447-3031), a 40-acre recreational facility with a broad sand beach, a boardwalk, a 50-meter-long freshwater pool, a miniature-golf course, and a triple water slide. Also available are a bathhouse with lockers and showers, concession stands, and a lounge. Live entertainment is scheduled throughout the summer. Open Memorial Day weekend through Labor Day, daily from 9am to 10pm. The parking fee also covers admission for all occupants of the car.

From June through September, waterborne excursions run by **Thames River Cruises** (☎ **860/444-7827**) carry passengers up past the *Nautilus* submarine base (see "Groton," below). Daily departures are made hourly from 9am to 5pm; home dock is the City Pier at the foot of State Street, behind the railroad station. The fare is $10 for adults, $6 for children 6 to 13.

The ferries that ply the Long Island Sound from New London have a recreational aspect, as well as simply serving as transport between Block Island and Long Island.

Year-round service to Orient Point on Long Island is provided by **Cross Sound Ferry** (☎ 860/443-5281). Departures are every hour or two during the day, and the one-way voyage takes about an hour and 20 minutes. Call ahead both to confirm departure times and make reservations, especially when taking a car. The **Fishers Island Ferry** (☎ 860/443-6851) also has daily departures for Long Island. **Nelseco Navigation Co.** (☎ 860/442-7891 or 860/442-9553) operates its ferry once a day (with an extra trip Friday evenings) from mid-June to early September between New London and the Old Harbor on Block Island. The one-way trip takes about 2 hours. An advance reservation for cars is essential, but a call ahead is also important to determine fares and current sailing times.

WHERE TO STAY

Queen Anne Inn. 265 Williams St. (east of Rte. 32), New London, CT 06320. ☎ 800/347-8818 or 860/447-2600. Fax 860/443-0857. www.queen-anne.com. E-mail: queen-anne@snet.net. 10 units, 8 with private bathroom. A/C. $89–$185 double. Rates include full breakfast and afternoon tea. AE, DISC, DC, MC, V.

Parents visiting their kids at the area colleges are frequent guests at the 1903 Queen Anne, as are businesspeople who prefer to avoid the anonymity of motels. As a result, rates don't fluctuate as much from season to season as they do at many area inns. An oak staircase reaches up three floors (there's no elevator) to the Tower Room, the best of the lot. It is equipped with a TV and phone as well as a kitchen with stove, fridge, and coffeemaker. Not every room has such appointments—two rooms share a bathroom, and only some have phones and TVs—so make your needs known when reserving. A couple of rooms have fireplaces or fax machines. A 30% discount is often available midweek.

Breakfast is an extravaganza of quiches, chocolate waffles, and citrus French toast, and that treat is complemented with high teas (3 to 9pm) of coffee cakes and delicate sandwiches.

GROTON

The future is uncertain for this naval-industrial town on the opposite side of the Thames from New London, for it has long been dependent on the presence of the Electric Boat division of General Dynamics and the Navy's Submarine Base. And cutbacks in military budgets, which have adversely affected Groton, show no signs of reversal. Whatever happens, the principal tourist attraction remains the USS *Nautilus,* the world's first nuclear-powered vessel.

SEEING THE SIGHTS

After a visit to the submarine museum, history buffs may wish to stop for a stroll around **Fort Griswold Battlefield State Park,** Monument Street and Park Avenue (☎ 860/445-1729 or 860/449-6877). It was here, in 1781, that the traitor Benedict Arnold led a British force against American defenders, ruthlessly ordering the massacre of his 88 prisoners after they had surrendered. The museum is open Memorial Day to Labor Day daily from 10am to 5pm and Labor Day to Columbus Day, Saturday and Sunday from 10am to 5pm. Free admission.

Submarine Force Museum. Submarine Base. ☎ 800/343-0079 or 860/449-3174. Free admission. May 15 to Oct 31 Wed–Mon 9am–5pm, Tues 1–5pm. Nov 1 to May 14 Wed–Mon 9am–4pm. Take Exit 86 from I-95, drive north on Rte. 12, then follow signs to the USS *Nautilus.*

Outside the museum are battered minisubs used by the Axis powers in World War II. The entry hall and adjoining galleries display models of submarines, torpedoes, missiles, deck guns, hands-on periscopes, and a full-scale cross-section of Bushnell's

Turtle, the "first submersible ever used in a military conflict" in 1776—unsuccessfully, as it happens.

Continuing out the back and across a set of railroad tracks, the USS *Nautilus* itself stands at its mooring, ready for inspection. Before descending into the sub, keep in mind that large people or those with arthritis or similar afflictions might find it difficult to negotiate some of the hatchways and steep staircases. The somewhat claustrophobic walk through the control rooms, attack center, galley, and sleeping quarters is aided by listening devices handed out to each visitor that click on with audio descriptions at appropriate points along the tour. The self-guided tour only takes about 10 minutes.

FISHING TRIPS

A number of companies offer full- and half-day fishing trips. Typical of the party boats is the 114-foot *Hel-Cat II,* 181 Thames St. (☎ **860/535-2066** or 860/535-3200), operating from its own pier about 2 miles south of Exit 85N or 86S of I-95.

Both charter and party boats are available from the **Sunbeam Fleet** based at **Captain John's Sport Fishing Center,** 15 First St., Waterford (☎ **860/443-7259**). Fishing party boats sail twice daily in June, Friday to Sunday; July to Labor Day, Thursday to Tuesday. The same firm has daylong whale-watching voyages Sunday, Tuesday, and Thursday in July and August. Nature cruises go eagle watching in February and March and search for harbor seals from March through May. A substantial variety of fishing trips is offered. The whale-watch boat has a galley and bar. Waterford is the town immediately south of New London; the dock is next to the Niantic River Bridge.

MYSTIC

The spirit and texture of the maritime life and history of New England are captured in many ports along its indented coast, but nowhere more cogently than beside the Mystic River estuary with its harbor, nearly stoppered by Mason Island. This was a furiously active whaling and shipbuilding center during the colonial period and into the last century, but the discontinuation of the first industry and the decline of the second haven't adversely affected the community. No derelict barge nor rotting pier degrade the views and waterways (or at least not many).

Mystic and West Mystic are stitched together by a drawbridge, the raising of which, mostly for sailboats, causes traffic stoppages at a quarter past every hour but rarely shortens tempers, except for visitors who don't leave their urban impatience behind. There are complaints by some that the two-part town has been commercialized, but the incidence of T-shirt shops and related tackiness is limited, and the more garish motels and attractions have been restricted to the periphery, especially up near Exit 90 of I-95.

The town is home to one of New England's most singular attractions, the Mystic Seaport museum village. Far more than the single building the name might suggest, it is a re-created seaport of the mid-1800s, with dozens of buildings and watercraft of that romantic era of clipper ships and the China Trade. The spidery webs of full-rigged sailing ships beckon visitors almost as soon as they leave the highway, and the briny tang of the ocean air draws them on.

A **visitor information center** is located in the Olde Mistick Village shopping center, at Route 27 and Coogan Boulevard, near the Interstate (☎ **860/536-1641**). Mystic is 55 miles east of New Haven.

SEEING THE SIGHTS

✪ **Mystic Seaport.** 75 Greenmanville Ave. (Rte. 27). ☎ **888/9SEAPORT** or 860/ 572-5315. www.mysticseaport.org. Admission $16 adults, $8 children 6–12, free for children under 6 (2nd day included with validation). AE, MC, V. Apr–Oct 9am–5pm, Nov–Mar 10am–4pm. Take Exit 90 from I-95, driving about 1 mile south on Rte. 27 toward Mystic. Parking lots are on the left, the entrance on the right.

Few visitors fail to be enthralled by this evocative museum village. It encompasses an entire waterfront settlement, more than 60 buildings on and near a 17-acre peninsula poking into the Mystic River. With all there is to see and do, and considering the hefty admission charges, plan to set aside at least 2 or 3 hours for a visit. In fact, you could easily fill an entire day here, especially if you're one of those people who thrill at the sight of full-rigged tall ships standing at their wharves as if readying for voyages to the Spice Islands. A useful guide map is available at the ticket counter in the visitor center in the building opposite the Museum Stores (which can be saved for later, since they stay open later than the village most of the year).

A recommended route, exiting the visitor center, is to bear right along the path leading between the Galley Restaurant and the village green. It bends to the left, intersecting with a street of shops, public buildings, and houses. At that corner is an 1870s hardware and dry-goods store.

Turning right there, pass a one-room schoolhouse, a chapel, a furnished 1830s home, and stop at the children's museum, which invites youngsters to play games characteristic of the seafaring era. It faces a small square that is the starting point for horse-drawn wagon tours of the village.

From there, the three-masted barque *Charles W. Morgan,* one of the proudest possessions of the seaport fleet of over 400 craft, is only a few steps away. It was built in 1841, a whaler that called New Bedford home.

If you're a fan of scrimshaw and intricate ship models, continue along the waterfront to the right until you reach the Stillman Building, which contains fascinating exhibits of both. Otherwise, head left toward the lighthouse. Along the way, you'll encounter a tavern (nonfunctional), an 1833 bank with an upstairs shipping office, a house with a garden, a cooperage (where barrels and casks were made), a print shop, and other shops and services that did business with the whalers and clipper ships that put in at ports such as this.

The friendly docents in the village are highly competent at the crafts they demonstrate and are always ready to impart as much information as visitors care to absorb. The fact that they aren't dressed in period costumes, paradoxically enhances the village's feeling of authenticity by avoiding the contrived air of many such enterprises.

The next vessel encountered is the iron-hulled square-rigger *Joseph Conrad,* which dates from 1881 and has spent most of its life as a training ship. Up ahead is a small lighthouse at the point of the peninsula, which looks out across the water toward the large riverside houses that line the opposite shore. Round the horn, go past the boat sheds, fishing shacks, and the ketches and sloops that are moored along here in season until you come to the dock for the perky 1908 SS *Sabino.* This working ship gives half-hour river rides from mid-May to early October daily from 11am to 4pm ($3.50 adults, $2.50 children 6 to 15) and 1½-hour evening excursions Monday to Thursday leaving at 5pm ($8.50 adults, $7 children), Friday and Saturday at 7pm. A few steps away is the 1921 fishing schooner, *L.A. Dunton.*

And still the village isn't exhausted. A few steps south is the Henry B. Du Pont Preservation Shipyard, where the hundreds of boats in the collection are painstakingly restored and the work can be observed in progress. One of its recent projects is a schooner to be named *Amistad,* scheduled to be completed in May 2000.

When you exit for the day, ask the gatekeeper to validate your ticket so you can come back the next day for free.

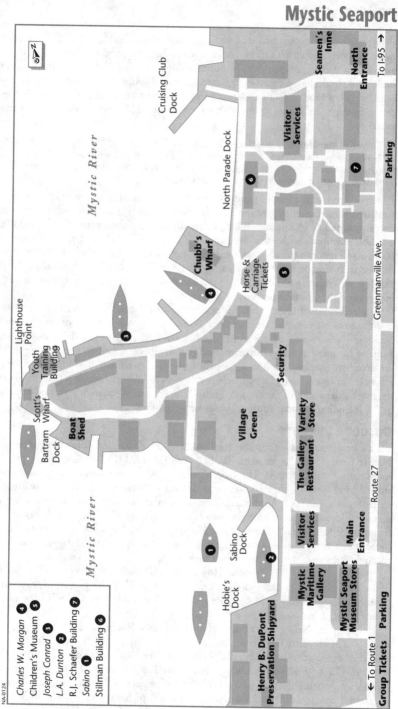

Mystic Seaport

Charles W. Morgan ❹
Children's Museum ❺
Joseph Conrad ❸
L.A. Dunton ❷
R.J. Schaefer Building ❼
Sabino ❶
Stillman Building ❻

NA-0124

Mystic River

Lighthouse Point

Scott's Wharf

Youth Training Building

Bartram Dock

Boat Shed

Chubb's Wharf ❹

❸

Cruising Club Dock

North Parade Dock

Visitor Services

❻

❼

Seamen's Inne

North Entrance

To I-95 →

Parking

Horse & Carriage Tickets

❺

Security

Village Green

The Galley Restaurant

Variety Store

Greenmanville Ave.

Mystic River

Hobie's Dock

Sabino Dock

❶

❷

Visitor Services

Main Entrance

Henry B. DuPont Preservation Shipyard

Mystic Maritime Gallery

Mystic Seaport Museum Stores

Route 27

← To Route 1

Group Tickets   Parking

Across the brick courtyard with the giant anchor is a building containing several museum stores and an art gallery. These superior shops stock books dealing with every aspect of seafaring; kitchenware, including enameled metal plates and cups that are perfect for the deck or picnics; fresh-baked goods and coffee; nautical prints and paintings; and ship models, both crude and inexpensive or exquisite and costly. (At this point, it might be useful to know that there is an ATM next to the visitor center entrance.)

✪ **Mystic Marinelife Aquarium.** 55 Coogan Blvd. (at Exit 90 of I-95). ☎ **860/ 572-5955.** www.mysticaquarium.org. Admission $13 adults, $12 seniors, $8 children 3–12, free for children under 3. July to Labor Day daily 9am–6pm; Labor Day to June daily 9am–5pm. Closed major holidays and last week in Jan.

If you've never seen a dolphin and whale show, this is the place. Less gimmicky than similar commercial enterprises in Florida and California, the show illuminates as it entertains, and at 15 minutes in length, doesn't test very young attention spans. The adorable mammals with their permanent grins squawk, click, and make thumping sounds, roll up onto the apron of their pool, tail walk, joyously splash the nearer rows of spectators, and pick out variously shaped toys in the water when blindfolded. All of this is at the command of their trainers, who vary the show depending upon their preferences and the animals currently in residence.

While the rest of the exhibits necessarily fall in the shadow of the stars, they are enough to occupy at least another hour. Near the entrance is a tank of fur seals, out back are sea lions and a flock of African black-footed penguins, and in between are some of the most remarkable marine creatures you'll ever see eye to eye. Among them are scorpion fish and sea horses propelled on gossamer fins; billowing, translucent jellyfish; sea ravens; and the pugnacious yellow-head jaw fish, which spends its hours digging fortifications in the sand. A $52-million expansion program was completed in 1999, including a 1-acre outdoor beluga whale exhibit.

OUTDOOR PURSUITS

For a change from salt air and ship riggings, drive inland to the **Denison Pequotsepos Nature Center,** 109 Pequotsepos Rd. (☎ 860/536-1216), a 125-acre property with more than 7 miles of trails. The center building has a thrown-together quality, with stuffed birds next to plaster snakes and dog-eared books next to the live boa constrictor and worm farm. Younger children are nonetheless fascinated, and outside are picnic tables and cages of raptors—two horned owls, last time we looked. There are five marked nature trails. Admission is $3 for adults, $1 for children. Open Monday to Saturday from 9am to 5pm, Sunday from 1 to 5pm (closed Sunday January through April and Monday September through April).

Across the road is the **Denison Homestead** (☎ 860/536-9248), a 1717 farmhouse that sheltered 11 generations of Denisons and is filled with that family's antique furnishings. Admission is $4 for adults, $1 children under 16. Open Thursday to Sunday from 1 to 5pm.

To get to the Nature Center and Homestead, take Route 27 north from Mystic, make a right on Mistuxet Avenue, then turn left on Pequotsepos Road.

Several operators offer **sailing and fishing cruises.** One of the most convenient is the *Argia* (☎ 860/536-0416), which docks only 100 feet south of the drawbridge in downtown Mystic. Morning sails on this 81-foot replica of a 19th-century schooner are from 10am to 1pm, afternoon sails are from 2 to 5pm, and evening cruises are from 6 to 8pm. Refreshments are served. Fares are $30 to $35 for adults, $20 children under 18. Longer sailing possibilities are the outings of the windjammer *Mystic Whaler* (☎ 800/697-8420 or fax 860/536-4219), which offers 3-hour lobster dinner sails, day trips, and extended cruises that can last 2, 3, or 5 days. Corresponding rates go from as little as $55 per passenger to $695. Voyages set out from a pier at 7 Holmes St., off Route 27, 1 mile south of Mystic Seaport.

SHOPPING

Olde Mistick Village, Route 27 and Coogan Boulevard (☎ 860/536-4941), is a conventional mall, but is housed in buildings that simulate a colonial village. More than 60 shops and restaurants are on site, including two banks, cinemas, and a winery. The village is open daily, year-round.

Downtown Mystic has limited shopping. One of the most engaging choices is **Bank Square Books,** 53 W. Main St. (☎ 860/536-3795). Maybe they don't actually have any volume you want in their jumble of shelves and racks, but it's fun looking anyway.

WHERE TO STAY

There are plenty of ho-hum but adequate motels in the area that can soak up the traffic at all but peak periods, meaning weekends from late spring to early fall and high season weekdays in July and August, when it is necessary to have reservations. Pick of the litter may be the **Best Western Sovereign** (☎800/528-1234), immediately north of Exit 90. With hair dryers and fridges in its rooms, and a pool, sauna, and restaurant on the premises, it's as comprehensive in its offerings as any in the immediate neighborhood.

Nearby competitors with similar facilities are the **Comfort Inn** (☎ 800/228-5150 or 860/572-8531), **Days Inn** (☎ 800/325-2525 or 860/572-0574), and **Residence Inn** (☎ 800/331-3131 or 860/536-5150). For more distinctive accommodations, try one of the inns listed below.

The Inn at Mystic. Rtes. 1 and 27, Mystic, CT 06355. ☎ 800/237-2415 or 860/536-9604. www.innatmystic.com. 67 units. A/C TV TEL. $65–$220 motel double; $135–$275 mansion and gatehouse doubles. Packages available. AE, DC, DISC, MC, V.

A variety of lodgings and prices are on offer at this inn occupying 13 hillside acres overlooking Long Island Sound. The complex also incorporates one of the area's best restaurants. At the crest of the hill is the impressive inn, a 1904 classical-revival mansion with rooms as grand as the exterior, enhanced by whirlpool baths, fireplaces, and canopied beds. Bogart and Bacall spent part of their honeymoon here. Down the hill a way is the intimate Gatehouse, similarly accoutred, and furnished with a scattering of antiques. Some of the rooms in the new motel sections are equally well appointed, including a few with balconies; others are modest and conventional. All rooms have hair dryers and clock radios.

Dining: See "Where to Dine," below, for a review of Flood Tide, the inn's restaurant. Don't miss the bounteous breakfasts, featuring stuffed crepes, Belgian waffles, and eggs Benedict . . . with lobster! A complimentary afternoon tea is served as well.

Amenities: A tennis court and an outdoor pool are on the premises; guests have access to a nearby health club and to paddleboats and canoes down on the water.

Mystic Hilton. 20 Coogan Blvd., Mystic, CT 06355. ☎ 800/445-8667 or 860/572-0731. Fax 860/572-0328. 184 units. A/C TV TEL. $90–$250 double. AE, CB, DC, DISC, MC, V. Take Exit 90 off I-95 and drive south, following signs to the Aquarium. The hotel is opposite.

Unlike the motels clustered around the I-95 interchange, this is a full-service hotel, providing the facilities and services expected of its big-city cousins. As a Hilton, that means crisp efficiency, if not much personality, plus all the useful room amenities such as room service, OnCommand in-room movies, phones with dataports, coffeemakers, and hair dryers—you get the picture. The front desk is often willing to negotiate prices according to season and demand (give it a try). The hotel is owned by the Pequot tribe, so it's no surprise that there are posters announcing coming attractions and a shuttle van to take you there.

Dining/Diversions: An above-average restaurant called The Moorings is on site, and a piano player entertains many evenings in the fireplace lounge.

Amenities: Room service until 1am. Fitness room, indoor pool, and a new outdoor pool.

✪ **Steamboat Inn.** 73 Steamboat Wharf, Mystic, CT 06355. ☎ **860/536-8300.** Fax 860/536-9258. www.visitmystic.com/steamboat. 10 units. A/C TV TEL. Late May to Nov $150–$275 double, Dec to late May $110–$225 double. Rates include breakfast. AE, DISC, MC, V. Look for the inn sign pointing down an alley on the west bank of the Mystic River, just before the drawbridge. Children over 9 welcome.

Mystic's most appealing lodging is easily overlooked from land, but readily apparent from the river. Perched on the riverbank, the yellow clapboard structure first served as a warehouse in the early part of this century and was converted to a luxury bed-and-breakfast only a few years ago. Its four downstairs rooms are larger, with double whirlpool baths, wet bars, and some kitchen facilities, while the upstairs six have smaller whirlpools and wood-burning fireplaces; all have hair dryers. While every room is decorated differently, they are uniformly attractive—Laura Ashley must have been a muse—and all but one have water views. Antique armoires hide the TVs. Totally no smoking.

Breakfast in the common room is "hearty continental," with ample quantities of plump homemade muffins, fresh bagels, granola, and fruit compote. Sherry is left out all day for guests to pour themselves.

Taber Inne. 66 Williams Ave. (Rte. 1; 2 blocks east of the intersection with Rte. 27), Mystic, CT 06355. ☎ **860/536-4904.** Fax 860/572-9140. www.taberinne.com. 25 units. A/C TV TEL. Mid-Apr to Nov $95–$135 double; $195–$320 suite. Nov to mid-Apr $85–$125 double; $145–$310 suite. AE, MC, V.

Not quite an inn but more than a motel, this has something to suit most tastes and budgets, with seven immaculate buildings containing both simple units and hedonistic two-bedroom suites with whirlpool baths, decks, and fireplaces. The homey "Little House" has two bedrooms, a sitting room, and a kitchen with dishwasher, sleeping up to six for only $195 in high season. Some accommodations have porches, others have fireplaces and/or canopied beds. There's a coffeepot waiting in the reception area, and the manager hands out discount coupons for village restaurants.

Amenities: Guests have access to a community center with indoor pool, tennis, racquetball, and a fitness room.

Whaler's Inn. 20 E. Main St., Mystic, CT 06355. ☎ **800/243-2588** or 860/536-1506. Fax 860/572-1250. www.whalersinnmystic.com. E-mail: whalers.inn@riconnect.com. 41 units, all with bathroom (20 with shower only). A/C TV TEL. Early May to Sept 6 $99–$149 double; Sept 7 to late May $89–$135. Children under 16 stay free in parents' room. AE, MC, V.

The most commendable aspects of this downtown inn are its restaurant and its relatively low rates. Its reception staff could still display a touch more warmth, and decor slides from bleakly old-fashioned to faux Victorian, which they're attempting to erase with the introduction of new furnishings. Rooms are deployed in four adjacent buildings, one of which is a house constructed in 1865, another a three-story building dating from 1917 that was once the "U.S. Hotel." They're comfortable enough and can be useful to businesspeople on tight budgets as well as leisure travelers. Phones have dataports, hair dryers and clock radios are at hand, and beds are queens or doubles. Coffee is set out in the lobby.

Dining: See "Where to Dine," below, for a review of the hotel's restaurant, Bravo Bravo.

WHERE TO DINE

☼ Abbott's Lobster in the Rough. 117 Pearl St., Noank. ☎ **860/536-7719.** Main courses $15–$23. AE, MC, V. First Fri in May to Labor Day daily noon–9pm; Labor Day to Columbus Day Fri–Sun noon–7pm. Drive south from downtown Mystic on Rte. 215, alert for signs to Noank, and cross a railroad bridge. At Main St. in Noank, turn left, then take an immediate right on Pearl St. Be prepared to ask for directions anyway. SEAFOOD.

It's as if a wedge of the Maine coast had been punched into the Connecticut shore. This is a nitty-gritty lobster shack with plenty of indoor and outdoor picnic tables and not a frill to be found. While there are many options and combinations, including hot dogs and chicken for the crustaceanphobic, the classic shore dinner rules. That means clam chowder, a mess of boiled shrimp in the shell, a bowl of steamed mussels, and a small but tasty lobster. That'll be $21.95 (or thereabouts, subject to market fluctuations), with coleslaw, potato chips, and drawn butter thrown in. Dessert can be cheese- or carrot cake. Bring your own beer or wine.

Bravo Bravo. In the Whaler's Inn, 20 E. Main St. ☎ **860/536-3228.** Main courses $14.95–$27.95. AE, MC, V. Sun and Tues–Thurs 5–9pm, Fri–Sat 5–10pm. NEW ITALIAN/AMERICAN.

Ask locals about the best restaurant in town, and as often as not they'll send you here. In warm weather, it adds a tented deck, and the resulting combination is a money machine for the owners, even on a nondescript Tuesday evening. Both are filled with families, couples, and men in suits or polo shirts and khakis. As the night wears on, it can get as noisy as a disco, and the waitstaff can get a little scattered.

A basket of foccacia arrives with drinks, along with a ramekin of a white beans and roasted garlic spread. That will have to keep you happy until someone shows up for your order. Keep it simple, for some dishes sound appealing but are overloaded with ingredients. Daily specials are apt to be better choices–grilled ostrich with fried angel hair pasta and lightly fried oysters with a spicy remoulade were two recent possibilities. Otherwise, pastas reign. Prices out on the deck are lower for less complicated dishes.

Flood Tide. In The Inn at Mystic, Rtes. 1 and 27. ☎ **860/536-8140.** Reservations recommended. Main courses $16.95–$27.95. AE, DC, DISC, MC, V. Mon–Thurs 7–10:30am, 11:30am–2:30pm, and 5:30–9:30pm; Fri–Sat 7–10:30am, 11:30am–2:30pm, and 5:30–10pm; Sun 11am–2:30pm and 5:30–9:30pm. CONTINENTAL.

Peel back about three decades. They still do tableside preparations here, especially Caesar salad and fettuccine Alfredo, but also beef Wellington and rack of lamb, carved showily before your eyes. The retro performance reminds us why we used to relish this celebratory stuff in the days before Nouvelle-Pan-Asian-Italo-Fusion firecracker pseudo food was invented. Flood Tide even has a pianist plinking at the baby grand nightly and at Sunday brunch. The two dining rooms look out over the Sound, so ask for a window table. Lunch is cheaper and less fussy, and breakfast is a particular treat.

Go Fish. In Olde Mystic Village at Exit 90 off I-95. ☎ **860/536-2662.** Reservations suggested for dinner. Main courses $14.95–$21.95. AE, DC, DISC, MC, V. Sun–Thurs 11:30am–9:30pm, Fri–Sat 11:30am–10:30pm. SEAFOOD.

Brash, vast, and boisterous, this brassy newcomer has a floor plan dominated by a sprawling square bar of black granite with a sea of tables filling the perimeter spaces, some of them designated for nonsmokers. At the bar, choose from a generous list of sushi or from a menu of bar noshes. Otherwise, ask for fish cooked just about any way it can be–baked, roasted, grilled, deep-fried, and pan-blackened. Entrees are abundant and preceded by salads, so you might wish to skip appetizers, enticing though they are (the creamy bisque, for one). Stick to the less complex dishes, preferable to the festive amalgams of several kinds of fish composed by the black-clad chefs in the far open kitchen.

PizzaWorks. 12 Water St. (Rte. 215, south of Main St.) ☎ **860/572-5775.** Pizzas and pastas $6–$13.95. MC, V. Daily 4–9 or 10pm. ITALIAN.

Mystic Pizza is still on Main Street, gussied up since Julia Roberts made her debut there in the movie of the same name. But if good pizza is more important to you than dimly reflected Hollywood glory, get yourself here. In appearance, it's your basic pizza parlor, with neon signs and oilcloth on the tables. Pizzas are "red" (with tomato sauce) or "white" (without). Toppings are inventive but well short of gimmicky, and the regular recipes stand alone. Any combination of the 25 possible toppings make eyeballs roll in pleasure. Quality is uneven, presumably due to frequent staff changes, but find no better place east of New Haven. The long beer list includes Old Speckled Hen, Shipyard, and Cottrell Ale (made down the road in Pawcatuck).

STONINGTON & NORTH STONINGTON

Not much seems to happen in these slumbering villages, only lightly brushed by the 20th century despite all the thrashing about over in heavily touristed Mystic. That suits the residents just fine, explaining why most of them are not thrilled by the possibility that a giant Six Flags theme park might be erected in their midst. It is difficult to imagine what that will do to inland North Stonington, as peaceful a New England retreat as can be found, with hardly any commercialization beyond a couple of inns. Soundside Stonington has a pronounced maritime flavor, sustained by the presence of the state's only remaining (albeit dwindling) fishing fleet. Its two lengthwise streets are lined with well-preserved Federalist and Greek Revival homes.

EXPLORING THE AREA

For an introduction, drive south to **Cannon Square** along Stonington's **Water Street,** which has most of the town's shops and restaurants. Standing in the raised grassy main square are two 18-pound cannons that were used to fight off an attack by British warships during the War of 1812. Opposite is a lovely old granite house, and on the corner, a neoclassical bank.

Continue south to the end of Water Street, where there is a parking lot and the small **town beach** (admission $2 to $3 per person, $5 to $6 per family). The misty blue headland directly south across the Sound is Montauk Point, the eastern extremity of New York's Long Island. Return along Main Street, which is almost exclusively residential except for a few government buildings.

You might also check out the **Old Lighthouse Museum,** 7 Water St. (☎ **860/ 535-1440**). Built of stone in 1823, this two-story lighthouse with its short tower was moved here from a hundred yards away and deactivated. Most of the exhibits inside relate to the maritime past of the area, with scrimshaw tusks, a whalebone wool-winding wheel, a tortoise-shell serving dish, and the export porcelain that constituted much of the 19th-century China Trade. There are also weapons and relics of the Revolutionary period and the War of 1812, but the most interesting item is the carved ivory pagoda. Climb the tower for a view of coast and sea. Admission is $4 for adults, $2 for children 6 to 12; free for children under 6. Open May through October, Tuesday to Sunday from 11am to 5pm.

Duffers who feel overwhelmed by all the nautical talk and activity of the area can retreat to the fairway familiarity of their favorite game at the **Pequot Golf Club,** on Wheeler Road in Stonington (☎ **860/535-1898**). It has a par 70, 18-hole course and is fully open to the public, including the restaurant. Cart and club rentals are available. Call ahead to make reservations for weekend tee times. Take Exit 91 from I-95 north to Taugwonk Road, turn west on Summers Lane, and south on Wheeler Road.

One of the Nutmeg State's handful of earnest wineries, **Stonington Vineyards,** 523 Taugwonk Rd., Stonington (☎ **860/535-1222**), has a tasting room in a barn beside its vineyard. There are usually six or seven pressings to be sampled, from a blush to a Riesling, with a Chardonnay leading the pack. Bottles cost from $8 to $17. Open daily from 11am to 5pm, with a cellar tour at 2pm. To get there, take Exit 91 from I-95 and drive north 2½ miles.

WHERE TO STAY

Antiques & Accommodations. 32 Main St., N. Stonington, CT 06359. ☎ **800/554-7829** or 860/535-1736. Fax 860/535-2613. www.visitmystic.com/antiques. 7 units. A/C TV. May 1 to Jan 1 $129–$199 double; $149–$229 suite. Jan 2 to Apr $99–$169 double; $129–$199 suite. Rates include full breakfast. MC, V. Take Exit 92 of I-95, drive west on Rte. 2 for 2½ miles, then turn right onto Main St. at the sign.

Gardens, porches, and patios invite lounging and ambling at this converted 1820 farmhouse and 1861 Victorian. Rooms and suites vary substantially in dimension and fixtures. One has two bedrooms sharing a kitchen and sitting room, while the "bridal suite" has a canopied queen-size bed. Three units have working fireplaces, but none have phones, so make your needs and wishes known at the outset. Everyone shares the four-course candlelit breakfast, with such surprises as cantaloupe soup and walnut-and-banana waffles. Guests who take a liking to any of the antique silver or crystal pieces or furnishings will be pleased to know that just about everything is for sale. A formal herb and edible flower garden has been planted behind the carriage house.

Randall's Ordinary. Rte. 2, N. Stonington, CT 06359. ☎ **860/599-4540.** Fax 860/599-3308. www.randallsordinary.com. 15 units. A/C. $75–$195 double. Rates include breakfast. AE, MC, V. Take Exit 92 from I-95, head north on Rte. 2.

The oldest structure on this 27-acre estate dates from 1685. The three bedrooms upstairs have fireplaces and are charmingly furnished with four-poster and canopied beds, but have no phones or TVs. Those amenities are found in most of the rooms of the nearby barn, moved here from upstate New York and converted for this purpose. While the barn interior is dramatic, with heavy hand-cut beams and banisters made of stripped logs, the furnishings are, well, ordinary, and on bare floors. Coffee is set out in the lobby, near the parrot. Randall's Ordinary is now owned by the Pequot tribal organization, but that affiliation isn't noticeable.

Dining: Dinners are cooked at an open hearth and served by a staff in period costumes. Considering the primitive circumstances under which the food is prepared, it is hearty and tasty, if simple. Waits between courses are lengthy. Reservations are recommended, especially for the $30 fixed-price dinner. This takes place in the farmhouse that was occupied continuously by members of the Randall family for over 200 years.

WHERE TO DINE

Boom. At the Dodson Boatyard, 194 Water St. ☎860/535-2588. Main courses $13.50–$18. AE, MC, V. Mon–Sat 11:30am–3pm, Sun 10am–3pm, and daily 5:30–9:30pm.and 5:30–9:30pm. ECLECTIC.

With Stonington restaurants closing unexpectedly over the last few years due to retirement, moves, bankruptcies, and fire, a travel writer can get gun-shy. But okay: this one looks to have the necessaries to survive, barring calamity. It's a companionable, under-decorated little room with segregated bar looking over a marina of working and pleasure boats. The chef demonstrates interesting takes on current culinary enthusiasms. There's an amusing mussel bruschetta among the appetizers and entrees of sweet-potato

A Casino in the Woods

What has been wrought in the woodlands north of the Mystic coast is nothing less than astonishing. There was very little there when the Mashantucket Pequot tribe received clearance to open a gambling casino on their ancestral lands in rural **Ledyard.** Virtually overnight, the tribal bingo parlor was expanded into a full-fledged casino, and a hotel was built.

That was in 1992. Within three years, it had become the single most profitable gambling operation in the world, with a reported 40,000 visitors a day. Money cascaded over the Pequot (pronounced *Pee*-kwat) in a seemingly endless torrent. Expansion was immediate—another hotel, then a third, more casinos, golf courses, a possible monorail, and the new $139-million **Mashantucket Pequot Museum and Research Center** devoted to Native American arts and culture. The tribe bought up adjacent lands, at least four nearby inns and hotels, and opened a shipworks to build high-speed ferries. All that hasn't sopped up the floods of profit, and the tribe has made major contributions to the Mystic Aquarium and Smithsonian Museum of the American Indian.

All this prosperity came to a tribe of fewer than 520 acknowledged members, nearly all of them of mixed ethnicity. Residents of surrounding communities were ambivalent, to put the best face on it. When it was learned that one of the tribe's corporate entities was to be called "Two Trees Limited Partnership," a predictable query was, "Is that all you're going to leave us? Two trees?"

But while there is a continuing danger of damage to the fragile character of this most authentically picturesque corner of Connecticut, it is also a fact that due to the recent development, thousands of non-Pequots have found employment at a time of corporate and military downsizing.

The complex is reached through forested countryside of quiet hamlets that give little hint of the behemoth rising above the trees in Ledyard township. There are no signs screaming "Foxwoods." Instead, watch for plaques with the symbols of tree, wolf, and fire above the word RESERVATION. As you enter the property,

ravioli with sliced chicken and sage cream sauce or scallops with red pepper curry sauce on Jasmine rice. Local purveyors are employed for seafood only hours from the nets, and the restaurant moves a lot of lobster in summer. Help keep it around a while.

FOXWOODS RESORT CASINO

This casino-hotel complex (☎ 860/885-3000) is a moving target, forever changing, adding, renovating, expanding. There are, in fact, several cavernous gambling rooms, one of the most popular being the hall containing 4,500 slot machines. A high-tech horse parlor, with tote boards and live feeds from tracks around the country, is an impressive newcomer. All the usual methods of depleting wallets are at hand—blackjack, bingo, chuck-a-luck, keno, craps, baccarat, roulette, acey-deucy, money wheel, and several variations of poker. To keep players at tables, there is food service in the poker parlor and complimentary drinks are served at craps and blackjack tables.

SEEING THE SIGHTS

A $135 million trickle of the floods of cash washing over southeastern Connecticut and its resurgent Indian Nation has been diverted to create the **Mashantucket Pequot Museum & Research Center,** 110 Pequot Trail (☎ 860-396-6800). Opened in 1998 to substantial fanfare, it has justified the hoopla with a carefully conceived mix of film, platoons of attendants point the way to parking and hotels. Ongoing construction surrounds the glassy, turquoise-and-violet towers of the hotels and sprawling casino. Though busy and bustling, it doesn't look like Vegas from the outside—happily, there are no sphinxes, no pyramids, and no 20-story neon palm trees.

Inside, the glitz gap narrows, but it is still relatively restrained as such temples to chance go. The gambling rooms have windows, for example, when the prevailing wisdom among casino designers is that they should not give customers any idea of what time of day or night it is.

And no one is allowed to forget that this whole eye-popping affair is owned and operated by Native Americans. Prominently placed around the main buildings are larger-than-life sculptures by artists of Chiricahua and Chippewa descent, depicting Amerindians in a variety of poses and artistic styles. One other Indian-oriented display is *The Rainmaker,* a glass statue of an archer shooting an arrow into the air. Every hour on the hour, he is the focus of artificial thunder, wind-whipped rain, and lasers pretending to be lightning bolts, the action described in murky prose by a booming voice-of-Manitou narrator. That's as close as the chest thumping gets to going over the top, although some visitors might reflect upon the political correctness of the non-Indian cocktail waitresses outfitted in skimpy Pocahontas minidresses with feathers in their hair.

The pace of all this might be slowing, at least temporarily. The Pequots are watching closely as the new Mohegan Sun Resort, barely 6 miles away as the crow flies, continues to crowd in on their territory. There's talk that competition between the two casino complexes will force room rates down.

Two dozen bus companies provide daily service to Foxwoods from Boston, Hartford, Providence, New York, Philadelphia, and Albany, among many other cities—too many to list here. For information about **transit** from particular destinations, call ☎ **860/885-3000.**

murals, models, dioramas, and re-creations of scenes of Native American life before and after the arrival of European settlers, most of the displays augmented with computerized sounds of the woodland settlements.

A 175-foot **observation tower** supplies views of the forested Pequot reservation. Lunches and snacks are served from 11am to 5:30pm in the large restaurant, and there is a museum shop with books, jewelry, crafts, and related items. Admission is $10 for ages 16 to 54, $8 ages 55 and over, $6 ages 6 to 15, free under age 6. It's open daily 10am to 7pm; closed major holidays.

WHERE TO STAY

The resort has three hotels, the newest and most luxurious of which became operational in 1998, more than doubling the resort's housing capacity to 1,400 rooms. Unlike Las Vegas and other gambling centers, room rates aren't kept artificially low as an inducement to gamblers, although that policy may change depending upon competitive pressures from the rival Mohegan Sun Resort.

To get to the resort from Boston, take I-95 south to Exit 92 onto Route 2 west. From New Haven and New York, take I-95 to I-395 north to Exit 79A onto Route 2A east, picking up Route 2 east. Don't bother trying to park your car in the huge garage. It takes forever, and the valet parking at the front door is free.

✪ **Grand Pequot Tower.** Rte. 2, Ledyard, CT 06339. ☎ **800/369-9663** or 860/ 885-3000. Fax 860/312-7474. www.foxwoods.com. 800 units. A/C TV TEL. July –Labor Day $220–$295 double, from $400 suite; Sept –June $195–$270 double, from $400 suite. AE, CB, DC, DISC, MC, V.

The newest of Foxwoods' hotels (so far) is the grandest in space and concept, yet it is also the most tasteful of the three. Polished granite and imported woods and marbles feature extensively in the handsome lobby. It handily takes its place among New England's elite resort hotels.

Dining/Diversions: The tower's main restaurants, seafood Fox Harbour and Italian Al Dente, surpass all the resort competition. Live piano music accompanies cocktails in the lobby lounge.

Amenities: In back is a 50,000-square-foot casino, containing a plush Club Newport International open only to big-money players. The spa and fitness center in the Great Cedar are available to guests. There is a concierge, 24-hour room service, laundry/cleaning, express checkout.

Great Cedar Hotel. Rte. 2, Ledyard, CT 06339. ☎ **800/369-9663** or 860/885-3000. Fax 860/885-4040. www.foxwoods.com. 312 units. A/C TV TEL. July to Labor Day $195–$265 double; $500 suite. Sept– June $170–$222 double; $500 suite. AE, CB, DC, DISC, MC, V.

Well maintained despite the heavy foot traffic, this hotel has eight floors adjoining the casinos. Rooms are colorful, but not too gaudy (except for the suites for high rollers on the top floor), and are provided with the usual amenities. There are no premium channels or in-room movies on the TV, though; the management doesn't want you lolling around your room watching the tube when you could be downstairs losing money.

Amenities: There's a fitness center as well as a spa and indoor pool to relax those neck muscles knotted from hours spent hunched over a card table.

Two Trees Inn. 240 Lantern Hill Rd. (off Rte. 2), Ledyard, CT 06339. ☎ **800/369-9663** or 860/312-3000. Fax 860/885-4050. www.foxwoods.com. 280 units. A/C TV TEL. July–Nov $160–$195 double; $185–$220 suite. Sept–June $135–$160 double; $160–$185 suite. AE, CB, DC, DISC, MC, V.

This was the first Foxwoods hotel, built in less than three months, now a short shuttle-bus ride or 10-minute walk from the casino complex. A conventional motor hotel, it attracts large numbers of bus tours. Free coffee and juice in the small lobby provides the opportunity to contemplate your fellow guests' taste in white pants and hot pastel tops . . . in January.

Dining: There is a busy middling restaurant called Branches.

Amenities: Heated indoor pool, sauna, fitness room.

WHERE TO DINE

Twelve sit-down restaurants and numerous fast-food operations situated throughout the casino complex cover the most popular options. Only a couple aspire to even moderately serious culinary achievement.

Cedars Steak House (☎ **860/885-3000,** ext. 4252) grills beef and seafood that are supplemented by a raw bar, **Al Dente** (ext. 4090) does designer pizzas and pastas, and **Fox Harbour** (ext. 2445) specializes in seafood. All three expect their guests to be dressed at least a notch better than tank tops and shorts. They are the only ones that accept reservations.

The most popular dining room is the **Festival Buffet** (ext. 3172), which charges $10 for an all-you-can-eat spread that usually includes five or six main courses plus soups, salads, sides of vegetables and starches, and desserts.

Other self-explanatory possibilities are **Han Garden** (ext. 4093), **Pequot Grill** (ext. 2690), and **The Deli** (ext. 5481).

FOXWOODS AFTER DARK

Just as in Vegas and Atlantic City, big showbiz names are whisked onto the premises, usually on weekends. Even Wayne Newton makes the scene, as do the likes of Diana Ross, Tony Bennett, Paul Anka, Reba McEntire, Bill Cosby, Liza Minnelli, and Jay Leno. For information about current headliners, call ☎ **800/200-2882.**

For a break from the whirring of the slots and the insistent chatter of the croupiers, or simply to occupy underage kids, Foxwoods has created Cinetropolis, an entertainment center that looks like a cleaned-up futuristic Gotham. This is the electronic age at its most playfully frantic. **Turbo Ride** lets you pretend you are experiencing the rumbling takeoffs and powerful G-forces of jets taking off, this by way of giant films and machinery that makes your seat rock and roll as if in a cockpit. **Fox Giant Screen Theatre** is an IMAX-like production that features front-row rock concerts and exploding volcanoes, and **Virtual Adventures** lets you take control of an undersea vessel slipping past the dangers of the ocean depths. Once all that is exhausted, the **Fox Arcade** has pinball and video games that might seem a little pallid after the rest of these diversions.

UNCASVILLE & THE MOHEGAN SUN CASINO

About halfway between New London and Norwich, this blue-collar town once hardly provided sufficient reason even to downshift your car. That's changed, for good.

In October 1996, the barely extant Mohegan tribe opened its gambling casino, **Mohegan Sun,** Mohegan Sun Boulevard (☎ **888/226-7711**). Sitting in the middle of a potential $1-billion annual market, it was drawing 20,000 gamblers a day away from Foxwoods within a few weeks of opening. Obviously, the initial outlay of over $300 million for land and construction paid off handsomely, for the tribe announced only a year after inauguration that it was committing another $400 million for new hotels, a marina, and nongambling entertainment facilities to be completed by the year 2000.

The central building is circular, with four entrances named for the seasons. The core of 150,000 square feet is devoted to the games, everything from blackjack and baccarat to craps and Pai Gow poker, supplemented by 3,000 slot machines. In the center is a nightclub featuring weekend headliners on the order of George Benson and nightly entertainers unlikely to rise above lounge-act stature. Overhead are simulated log constructions meant to suggest ancient lodge houses. It is an esthetically pleasing space, as casinos go, although few of the avid players seem to notice. They can even park their kids in the child-care center.

Of the several dining places circling the gambling, the relatively ambitious **Longhouse** proffers mostly prime beef and seafood, while other eateries feature Asian, Italian, deli, and just-about-everything-else chow.

The casino is right off Exit 79A of I-395, which makes for easy on/off access for gamblers who don't want to deal with that onerous 20-minute drive to Foxwoods before emptying their bank accounts.

NORWICH

There is tourist potential here, where the Yantic and Shetucket rivers converge to form the Thames. Blocks of Broadway and Union Street are lined with substantial mansions in styles ranging from the Federalist and Classical Revival of the first half of the 19th century to the Italianate, French Second Empire, and eclectic Victorian conceits of the second. They survive from the city's golden era, when the abolitionist preacher Henry Ward Beecher was inspired to compare the hills of Norwich to the petals of a rose, prompting the oft-repeated reference to the city as the "Rose of New England."

There is no pretending, however, that this historic old mill town isn't in the doldrums, and so far, the presence of the nearby Mohegan Sun casino hasn't had much spillover effect. Until efforts to reverse that decline take hold, the principal reason for a visit is the wonderful lodging described below.

WHERE TO STAY & DINE

✪ **Norwich Inn & Spa.** 607 W. Thames St. (Rte. 32), Norwich, CT 06360. ☎ **800/267-4772** or 860/886-2401. Fax 860/886-9483. E-mail: wersd@connect.reach.net. 140 units. A/C TV TEL. May–Oct $130–$185 double; $200–$245 suite. Nov–Apr $115–$170 double; $185–$230 suite. AE, DC, MC, V. From New Haven, take Exit 76 off I-95 onto I-395 north, Exit 79A onto Rte. 2A east, then exit onto Rte. 32 north and drive 1.5 miles to the inn entrance.

You could spend a week here without experiencing a whiff of deprivation, for the Norwich Inn & Spa has none of that tone of rigidly enforced self-denial that exists at other places that call themselves "spas." The property is owned by the Pequot tribal organization, but that association isn't noticeable. Foxwoods Casino is about 15 minutes away, making this a soothing and convenient respite from the glitz.

The complex is set among woods on a 40-acre property, the main building augmented by outlying "villas" with 160 condo units, about half of which are suites available to overnight guests. A typical suite has a fully equipped kitchen, a large sitting area with logs and paper laid in the fireplace, two double beds in the separate bedroom, and a deck overlooking the woods and a pond. Inn rooms aren't as expansive and don't have fireplaces, but they are hardly spartan.

Dining: The Prince of Wales dining room has a versatile kitchen staff capable of producing meals either conventional or fitness-minded, both satisfying.

Amenities: Everyone has access to two outdoor pools, an indoor pool, a golf course, and a gym with stationary bikes, treadmills, StairMasters, and weight machines, as well as steam rooms and saunas. Massages are available, too.

Rhode Island

10

by Herbert Bailey Livesey

Water defines "Little Rhody" as much as mountain peaks characterize Colorado. The Atlantic thrusts all the way to the Massachusetts border, cleaving the state into unequal halves and filling the geological basin that is Narragansett Bay. That leaves 400 miles of coastline and several large islands.

A string of coastal towns runs in a northeasterly arc from the Connecticut border up to Providence, the government and business capital, which lies at the point of the bay, 30 miles from the open ocean. It was here that Roger Williams, banned from the Massachusetts Bay Colony in 1635 for his outspoken views on religious freedom, established his colony. Little survives from that first century, but a large section of the city's East Side is composed almost entirely of 18th- and 19th-century dwellings and public buildings.

Another group of Puritan exiles established their settlement a couple of years after Providence, on an island known to the Narragansett as "Aquidneck." Settlers thought their new home resembled the Isle of Rhodes in the Aegean, so the official name became "Rhode Island and Providence Plantations," a moniker that was subsequently applied to the entire state, and remains the official name.

The most important town on Aquidneck is ✪ **Newport,** and it's the best reason for an extended visit to the state. Its first era of prosperity was during the colonial period, when its ships not only plied the new mercantile routes to China but engaged in the reprehensible "Triangular Trade" of West Indies molasses for New England rum for African slaves. Additional skills at smuggling and evading taxes brought Newport into conflict with its British rulers, whose occupying army all but destroyed the town during the Revolution. After the Civil War, the town began its transformation from commercial outpost to resort, with the arrival of the millionaires of what Mark Twain sneeringly described as the "Gilded Age." They built astonishingly extravagant mansions, their contribution to Newport's bountiful architectural heritage.

With Newport's winning of the America's Cup and with its subsequent defense of yachting's most famous trophy, the town became a recreational sailing center with a packed summer cultural calendar. As a result, travelers who want nothing more than a deep tan by Monday can coexist with history buffs and music-lovers, who come to attend concerts held against a backdrop of waves hissing across packed sand.

Finally, there is Block Island, an hour's ferry ride from Point Judith. A classic summer resort, Block Island has avoided the imposition of both

Vineyard chic and Provincetown clutter. It has also sidestepped history (even though it was first settled in 1661), so there are few mandatory sights. Visitors are free simply to explore its lighthouses, hike its cliff-side trails, and hit the beach.

1 Providence

Providence is moving up, counter to the downward trend of so many small and mid-size New England cities. Revival is in the air and prosperity is returning. This is especially evident in the resurgent "downcity" business district. Rivers have been uncovered to form canals and waterside walkways, kayaks and a gondola glide beneath graceful bridges, distressed buildings of the last century have been reclaimed, and continued new construction includes Providence Place, a monster mall that brings national department stores to town for the first time. Much of the credit for this, grudging or exuberant, goes to the ebullient four-terms-and-counting mayor, Vincent A. Cianci, Jr., who even peddles bottles of his own marinara sauce.

This is a city of manageable size—the population is about 170,000—that can easily occupy two or three days of a Rhode Island vacation. Locals are proud of the burgeoning reputation of the city's dining scene, pointing to ambitious new restaurants that are nearly always less expensive than their counterparts in Boston and New York. College Hill is only one of 26 National Historic Districts, the calendar is full of concerts and special events, and the presence of so many young people guarantees a lively nightlife.

Roger Williams obviously had good instincts for town building. He planted the seeds of his settlement on a steep rise overlooking a swift-flowing river at the point where it widened into a large protected harbor. That part of the city, called "East Side" and dominated by the ridge now known as College Hill, remains the most attractive city district in New England, second only to Boston in the breadth of its cultural life and rich architectural heritage.

College Hill is so named because it is the site of Brown University, which started life in 1764 as a small college. Also on the Hill is the highly regarded Rhode Island School of Design, whose buildings are wrapped around the Brown campus. In and around these institutions are several square miles of 18th- and 19th-century houses, from colonial to Victorian, lining streets that are often gaslit. At the back of the Brown campus is the funky shopping district along Thayer Street, while at the foot of the Hill is the largely commercial Main Street.

While most points of interest are found on the East Side, the far larger collection of neighborhoods west of the river has its own attractions. The level downtown area is the center for business, government, and entertainment, with City Hall, a new convention center, the two best large hotels, some small parks and historic buildings, and several theaters. To its north, across the Woonasquatucket River, is the imposing State House and the Amtrak railroad station. And to its west, on the other side of Interstate 95 (I-95), is Federal Hill, a residential area with a strong ethnic identity, primarily Italian, but increasingly leavened by numbers of more recent immigrant groups.

ESSENTIALS

GETTING THERE I-95, which connects Boston and New York, runs right through the city, which lies 45 miles south of Boston and 55 miles northeast of New London. From Cape Cod, pick up I-195 west.

T. F. Green/Providence Airport (☎ 401/737-8222) in Warwick, south of Providence (Exit 13, I-95), handles all national flights. Major airlines serving this airport include: **American** (☎ 800/433-7300), **Continental** (☎ 800/525-0280), **Delta** (☎ 800/221-1212), **Northwest** (☎ 800/225-2525), **United** (☎ 800/241-6522),

Rhode Island & South County

and **US Airways** (☎ 800/247-8786). The Rhode Island Public Transit Authority (RIPTA) provides transportation between the airport and the city center. Taxis are also available, costing about $20 for the 20-minute trip.

Amtrak (☎ **800/USA-RAIL**) runs several trains daily along the shore route between Boston and New York, stopping at the attractive new station at 100 Gaspee St., near the State House.

VISITOR INFORMATION   Before your visit, contact the **Greater Providence Convention and Visitors Bureau** of the Chamber of Commerce, 30 Exchange Terrace, Providence, RI 02903 (☎ **401/274-1636**). Once in Providence, you can consult the visitor information center at that address, or check with the helpful park rangers at the visitor center of the Roger Williams National Park at the corner of Smith and North Main streets, open daily from 9am to 4:30pm.

GETTING AROUND   Traffic on local streets isn't bad, even at rush hour, so by all means drive. Taxis are not easy to come by, with few to be found outside even the largest hotels. They can take 15 minutes or more when called from restaurants.

EXPLORING PROVIDENCE
STROLLING AROUND THE HISTORIC NEIGHBORHOODS

Two leisurely walks, one short, another longer, pass most of the prominent attractions and offer a palpable sense of the city's evolution from a colony of dissidents to a contemporary center of commerce and government.

Downtown, chart a route from the 1878 City Hall on Kennedy Plaza along Dorrance Street and walk 1 block to Westminster and turn left. Walk 1 block, make a right, and go past The Arcade (see "Quick Bites," below), then left on Weybosset. Follow Weybosset until it joins Westminster and continue across the Providence River. Turn right on the other side, walking along South Water Street as far as James Street, just before the I-195 overpass. Turn left, cross South Main, then make a left on Benefit Street. This is one end of the so-called **Mile of History,** lined with restored or carefully preserved 18th- and 19th-century houses. The street is a feast for aficionados of Early American domestic architecture, enhanced by gas street lamps and sections of brick herringbone sidewalk. Along the way are opportunities to visit, in sequence, the 1786 **John Brown House,** the **First Unitarian Church** (1816), the **Providence Athenaeum,** and the **Museum of Art, Rhode Island School of Design.** Two of our recommended inns are also on this lovely street, and an uphill detour on College Street leads to the handsome campus of Brown University.

For a shorter walk, begin in the same way. After you pass The Arcade, turn left on Weybosset and walk to Westminster.

Those who prefer expert direction to haphazard rambling may want to take advantage of the walking tours provided by the **Providence Preservation Society,** 21 Meeting St. (☎ **401/831-7440**). Two 90-minute audiocassette tours are available, in addition to booklets describing several historic neighborhoods. The cassettes can be rented (with your driver's license as hostage), the booklets purchased. The office is open Monday to Friday from 9am to 5pm.

SEEING THE SIGHTS

Boosters are proud of their new **Waterplace Park and Riverwalk,** which encircles a tidal basin and borders the Woonasquatucket River down past where it joins the Moshassuck to become the Providence River. It incorporates an amphitheater, boat landings, landscaped walkways with benches and trees, and vaguely Venetian bridges that cross to the East Side. Summer concerts and other special events are held here. Among these are the increasingly popular Waterfires, when dozens of bonfires are set

Providence

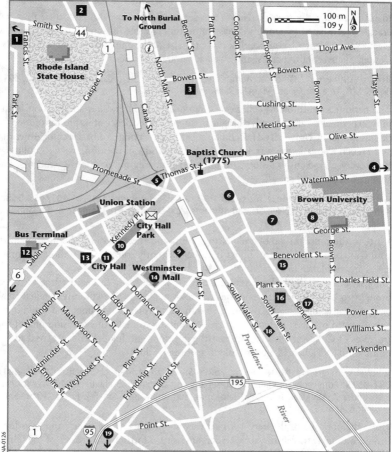

NEW ENGLAND

Providence ★

Legend
Church ✝
Information ⓘ
Post Office ✉

Attractions
The Arcade ⑭
City Hall ⑪
First Unitarian Church ⑮
Gov. Henry Lippitt
  House Museum ④
John Brown House ⑰
Kennedy Plaza ⑩
Museum of Art,
  Rhode Island
  School of Design ⑥
Providence Athenaeum ⑦
Roger Williams Park Zoo ⑲
University Hall ⑧

Accommodations
C.C. Ledbetter ⑯
Marriott ❷
The Old Court ❸
Providence Biltmore ⑬
State House Inn ❶
Westin Providence ⑫

Dining
Amicus ⑱
Café Nuovo ❺
Pot au Feu ❾

to blazing along the river on New Year's Eve and summer Saturdays, their roar and crackle accentuated by amplified classical music. Nearby, in Kennedy Plaza, the new Fleet Skating Center has an ice rink twice the size of the one in New York's Rockefeller Center. Skate rentals, lockers, and a snack bar are available.

Brown University. Office of Admissions, 45 Prospect St. (near Angell St.). ☎ **401/ 863-2378.** Free admission. Mon–Fri 9am–5pm.

The nation's seventh-oldest college was founded in 1764 and has a reputation as the most experimental among its Ivy League brethren. The evidence of its pre-Revolutionary origins is seen in **University Hall,** built in 1771 and serving as a barracks for American and French troops in the war against the British. Tours of the campus, with buildings from every period in its history, are intended primarily for prospective students, but anyone can join (call ahead).

Gov. Henry Lippitt House Museum. 199 Hope St. (at Angell St.). ☎ **401/453-0688.** Admission $4 adults, $2 seniors and students. Apr–Dec Tues–Fri 11am–3pm; Sat–Sun and Jan–Mar by appointment only.

Visits to the museum are by guided tour only, and these leave on the hour, so plan your trip accordingly, for this house is as magnificently true to its grandiose Victorian era as any residence in the country.

Its style is technically Renaissance Revival—which really means that the architect brought to bear any motif or notion that took his fancy. Meticulously detailed stenciling, expanses of stained glass, ornately framed mirrors, inlaid floors, and wood intricately carved or made to look like marble combine to make this mansion one of the treasures of College Hill. The fact that the governor and his descendants lived in the house until 1981 helped enormously in its preservation.

John Brown House Museum. 52 Power St. (at the corner of Benefit St.). ☎ **401/ 331-8575.** Admission $6 adults, $4.50 seniors and students, $3 children 7–17, free for children under 7. Mar–Dec Tues–Sat 10am–5pm, Sun noon–4pm. Jan–Feb Fri–Sat 10am–5pm, Sun noon–4pm.

Quite the opposite of the fiery 19th-century abolitionist of the same name, *this* John Brown was an 18th-century slave trader, amassing a fortune as a master of the China Trade. He and his descendants contributed much of that fortune to the university that bears the family name. Brown is said to have been responsible for the burning of a British warship, the *Gaspee,* four years before the start of the Revolution.

The style of his three-story 1786 brick mansion is Georgian, although he no doubt preferred to think of it as Federalist after the Revolution. Brown's widow, children, and grandchildren lived here until 1846. Subsequent owners made additions and redecorated in the Victorian fashion. Their efforts were reversed after the house was bequeathed to the Rhode Island Historical Society in 1941, which restored it to its original condition.

Museum of Art, Rhode Island School of Design. 224 Benefit St. (between Waterman and College sts.). ☎ **401/454-6100.** Admission $5 adults, $4 seniors, $2 college students with ID, $1 children 5–18, free for children under 5. Wed–Sun 10am–5pm, until 8pm Fri.

Prestigious RISD (pronounced *Riz*-dee) supports this ingratiating center that houses the 65,000 artworks of the permanent collection and frequent temporary exhibitions, including biennial shows of the work of RISD faculty. A broad collection includes Chinese terra-cotta sculptures, Greek statuary, French Impressionist paintings, and Early American decorative arts. Probably of greatest general interest are the rooms of works by such masters as Monet, Cézanne, Rodin, Picasso, and Matisse. But allow time for the American wing, which contains not only fine antique furnishings and accessories but paintings by Gilbert Stuart, John Singleton Copley, and John Singer Sargent.

The Providence Athenaeum. 251 Benefit St. (at College St.). ☎ **401/421-6970.** Free admission. Mon–Thurs 10am–8pm, Fri–Sat 10am–5pm, Sun 1–5pm. Closed Sat–Sun in summer.

The Providence Athenaeum, a learned society founded in 1753, commissioned this granite 1838 Greek Revival building to house its lending library. The fourth oldest such library in the United States, it was an innovative concept at the time.

Edgar Allan Poe courted Sarah Whitman, his "Annabel Lee," between these shelves. Random glances through the old card catalog reveal handwritten cards dating well back into the 1800s. It has a large and active children's section and is a marvelous place in which bibliophiles can lose themselves. Rotating exhibits of rare books and works by local artists are additional attractions.

Roger Williams Park Zoo. 950 Elmwood Ave. (at Exit 17 off I-95). ☎ **401/785-3510.** Admission $6 adults, $3.50 seniors and children 3–12, free for children under 3. Apr–Oct Mon–Fri 9am–5pm, Sat–Sun 9am–6pm. Nov–Mar daily 9am–4pm. Driving south on I-95, take exit 17; driving north, take exit 16.

In a 430-acre park that also contains a museum of natural history and a planetarium, the zoo is divided into three habitats: Tropical America, the Farmyard, and the Plains of Africa. Of the more than 150 species on view, the most popular are the polar bears, giraffes, penguins, the birds of the walk-through rain forest, and the cuddly critters of the petting zoo. Ongoing renovations have removed the prisonlike structures of the Victorian era, replacing them with concealed moats and hidden fences so that the animals can be viewed with less obvious barriers. Also in the park are a museum of natural history with a planetarium, a carousel, and a boathouse. Every 20 minutes a trolley carries passengers (at $1 each) on a circuit of those attractions. An all-day pass including all the sites and the trolley costs $10.25 for adults, $8.25 for seniors, and $6.75 for children.

You can also treat your kids to rides on the carousel, a little train, on real ponies, and in paddleboats on the lake. Families might want to take a picnic and make a day of it.

Rhode Island State House. 82 Smith St. (between Francis and Hayes sts.). ☎ **401/277-2357.** Free admission. Tours Mon–Fri 8:30am–noon.

Constructed of Georgian marble that blazes in the sun, the 1900 capitol building dominates the city center by virtue of its hilltop location and superior aesthetic. This near-flawless example of neoclassical governmental architecture (McKim, Mead & White, 1891–92) has room to flaunt itself, with open spaces all around. Its self-supported golden dome is one of the largest in the world, reminding many viewers of St. Peter's Cathedral in Rome. The gilded figure on top represents *Independent Man*, the state symbol. Inside, a full-length portrait of George Washington is given pride of place, one of the many depictions of the father of his country by Gilbert Stuart, who was Rhode Island's own. Guided tours by appointment.

SHOPPING

Thayer Street, the main commercial district for the university, has the official **Brown Bookstore** at no. 244 (corner of Olive Street), open daily, but not in the evenings, as well as the **College Hill Bookstore** at no. 252, funkier and wider-ranging in its selections and open daily until midnight. Also in the vicinity are **Urban Cargo** (at no. 224), with casual clothes and jewelry for college-age women, and **Hillhouse** (no. 135), long in the business of providing male Brownies with Ivy dress-up clothes for interview weeks and parent days.

WHERE TO STAY

Assuming that charm and character aren't paramount criteria in lodging, the clusters of motels around most of the exits from I-95 and I-195 are routinely comfortable and offer decent value, especially since you're not likely to stay more than a night or two. Among possibilities are the **Ramada Inn,** 940 Fall River Ave., Seekonk, MA 02771 (☎ **508/336-7300**), and the **Days Hotel**, 220 India St., Providence, RI (☎ **401/ 272-5577**.

Alternatives are provided by B&B referral agencies, such as **Bed & Breakfast of Rhode Island,** P.O. Box 3291, Newport, RI 02840 (☎ **800/828-0000** or 401/ 849-1298). These are rooms in private homes, so sometimes quirky rules and limitations apply. Remember, too, that they are rarely as inexpensive as local branches of motel chains.

Lodgings in the historic districts are required to provide off-street parking. Rates at most area inns and motels go up on alumni and parents' weekends and graduation weeks.

C. C. Ledbetter. 326 Benefit St. (between Charlesfield and Power), Providence, RI 02903. ☎ andfax **401/351-4699.** 5 units, 3 with private bathroom. A/C TV. $75–$125 double. Rates include breakfast. DISC, MC, V. Free parking.

There's no sign out front, because Ms. Ledbetter doesn't want to bother her neighbors. Look for the 1780 clapboard building with the olive-green exterior. Things are more colorful inside (repainted last year) with lots of books and a substantial collection of contemporary artworks. Two rooms share a bath; another might be the only one in the state to contain a rowing machine. A hearty continental breakfast is served around a common table downstairs, where the two resident dogs usually linger. While the owner isn't enthusiastic about accepting children and pets, she'll consider either. Since it's only a couple of blocks from Brown and RISD, graduation weekends are already booked through the end of the century.

Marriott. 1 Orms St., Providence, RI 02904. ☎ **800/937-7768** or 401/272-2400. www.marriott.com. 345 units. A/C TV TEL. $99–$154 double. AE, CB, DC, DISC, MC, V. Free parking.

This busy, popular stop for both business and leisure travelers is north of downtown, but within a 10-minute drive of most of the city's attractions. There is an indoor-outdoor pool adjoined by a modest exercise room with whirlpool. The serviceable Bluefin Grille gets mostly favorable notices. A 24-hour shuttle service to and from the airport and the bus and train stations can be arranged when booking. At off-times, bargaining often results in a lower rate.

The Old Court. 144 Benefit St., Providence, RI 02903. ☎ **401/751-2002** or 401/ 351-0747. Fax 401/272-4830. www.oldcourt.com. E-mail: reserve@loa.com. 10 units. A/C TV TEL. $95–$145 double. Rates include breakfast. AE, DISC, MC, V. Free parking.

This was built in 1863 as a rectory, and the furnishings reflect that period. There are examples of Rococo-Revival and Eastlake styles, secretaries embellished with marquetry, and oriental rugs on bare floors, as well as more familiar Victoriana. Most traces of its tenure as a boardinghouse for college students have been expunged. Breakfast is a production, always with a hot entree.

Families or longer-term visitors may be interested in the apartment across the street. Admittedly a little dowdy, it's nonetheless spacious, with a separate bedroom, living room, and full kitchen with dining nook.

Providence Biltmore. Kennedy Plaza, Providence, RI 02903. ☎ **800/294-7709** or 401/421-0700. Fax 401/455-3050. 244 units. A/C TV TEL. $120–$160 double. AE, CB, DC, MC, V. Parking $10.

A grand staircase beneath the stunning Deco bronze ceiling dates the centrally located building to the 1920s, and a plaque in the lobby shows the nearly 7-foot-high water level of the villainous 1938 hurricane. A dramatic glass elevator starts in the lobby and exits outdoors to scoot up the side of the building. In the large rooms are pay-per-view movies and phone service that includes voice mail and modem ports; some suites have kitchenettes. Signs of wear indicate overdue maintenance, however.

Dining: Davio's is the streetside cafe, a popular meeting place; room service is available from 6:30am to 11pm.

Amenities: Concierge, dry cleaning/laundry, newspaper delivery, nightly turn-down, baby-sitting, express checkout, valet parking, free coffee in the lobby, fitness center with 24-hour access, telephone with voice mail and dataports, business center, conference rooms.

State House Inn. 43 Jewett St., Providence, RI 02908. ☎ **401/785-1235.** www.providence-inn.com. 10 units. A/C TV TEL. $99–$139 double. Children welcome. Rates include breakfast. Lower weekday corporate rates. AE, DISC, MC, V. Free parking. From the easily identified State House, drive west on Smith St., over I-95, then left on Holden and right on Jewett.

The neighborhood isn't the best (though downtown restaurants are only minutes away), but the owners compensate with lower rates and hotel conveniences, including hair dryers and clock radios; guests also have access to a fax and copier. Some rooms have canopy beds or fireplaces, and new and antique furnishings have been added in the last year. Breakfast is substantial, with at least one hot dish, and there is an honor snack area the rest of the day. Children are welcome.

✪ Westin Providence. 1 W. Exchange St., Providence, RI 02903. ☎ **800/228-3000** or 401/598-8000. Fax 401/598-8200. www.westin.com. 363 units. A/C MINIBAR TV TEL. $140–$205 double. AE, DC, MC, V. Parking $10.

The city's best hotel by far, this place does nothing to diminish the strong reputation of the Westin chain, And even with its luxurious interior and downtown location, its rates are considerably lower than siblings in Boston and New York. Bedrooms have dozens of pay-per-view movies, Nintendo play stations, hair dryers, coffeemakers, and phones with dataports and voice mail. A skyway connects the hotel with the convention center and another is planned to the new Providence Place mall. The architectural grandeur of the lobby rotunda and other public spaces doesn't dampen the sunny dispositions of the staff.

Dining/Diversions: Off the lobby rotunda is a lounge with the buffed glow of an exclusive men's club, and on the second floor is the newly upgraded IYAC sports bar and a cafe. On the same floor is the posh main restaurant.

Amenities: Concierge, room service (6:30am to midnight), dry cleaning/laundry, free newspaper delivery, baby-sitting, express checkout, valet parking, courtesy limo, two-level health club with separate aerobics and free weights rooms, massage, heated indoor pool, Jacuzzi, sauna, business center, valet parking.

WHERE TO DINE

Providence has a sturdy Italian heritage, resulting in a profusion of tomato sauce and pizza joints, especially on Federal Hill, the district west of downtown and I-95. Since they are so numerous and so obvious, the suggestions below focus, perhaps a bit perversely, on restaurants that have broken away from the red-gravy imperative.

One fruitful strip to explore for dining options is that part of **Thayer Street** that borders the Brown University campus, counting Thai, Tex-Mex, barbecue, Indian, and even Egyptian restaurants among its possibilities.

Amicus. 345 S. Water St. ☎ **401/521-7722.** Main courses $15–$22. AE, DC, MC, V. Tues–Fri 11:30am–3pm; Tues–Sun 5–11pm. MEDITERRANEAN FUSION.

This is a young undertaking run by eager-to-please brothers who've yet to see their 30th birthdays. A fine mahogany bar occupies center stage with tables up a few steps. While Italy is a primary inspiration, the chef doesn't hesitate to borrow from other cuisines, with bouillabaisse, blackened mahimahi, and lobster and scallop sausages with red-onion confit among the notables. All breads and desserts are made in-house. There are outdoor tables.

Atomic Café. 99 Chestnut St. (corner of Clifford St.) ☎ **401/621-8888.** Main courses $12.50–$16.95. AE, CB, DC, DISC, MC, V. Mon–Fri 11:30am–midnight, Sat–Sun 5pm–midnight. ECLECTIC.

This is one of a growing number of enterprises looking to transform the distressed Jewelry District into Providence's SoHo. The high ceilings and big beams of the old loft building look down on walls painted lime green and furniture that looks to have been remaindered in 1948. Blackboards announce the day's specials and the nightly entertainment (live music Tuesday, Wednesday, and Saturday). Its hyperkinetic owner has filled his kitchen with grads of the nearby Johnson and Wales University, known for its programs in the culinary arts. They aren't timid, and nothing that arrives at the table looks or tastes exactly as it does anywhere else. That's a positive, as with the delectable wood-fired appetizer pizzas and such main dishes as grilled sea bass with Tuscan bread, fava bean salad, and sautéed winter vegetables with citrus-chive aïoli.

CAV. 14 Imperial Place (near corner of Basset St.) ☎ **401/751-9164.** Main courses $11.50–$20.95. DISC, MC, V. Mon–Sat 11:30am–1am, Sun 11:30am–10pm. ECLECTIC.

No corporate design drudge had a hand in *this* warehouse interior, another Jewelry District pioneer. CAV is an acronym for "Coffee/Antiques/Victuals," and patrons are surrounded by tribal rugs, primitive carvings, and assorted antiques and old stuff (most for sale.) Your self-announced server is likely to be a Leonardo look-alike between auditions. He brings dishes prepared by folks more accomplished at their craft than he—such strenuous menu swings as wild mushroom strudel, prodigious portions of spinach gnocchi and pastas, or "kavakia," a simmered stew of salmon, shrimp, scallops, mussels, and littlenecks. The small stage has an open mike on Mondays, live jazz or blues Friday and Saturday nights. The bill is presented before you ask.

✪ **Cafe Nuovo.** 1 Citizens Plaza (access is from the Steeple St. bridge). ☎ **401/421-2525.** Main courses $14.50–$24.95. AE, DC, DISC, MC, V. Mon–Fri 11:30am–3pm; Mon–Thurs 5–10:30pm, Fri–Sat 5–11pm. MEDITERRANEAN FUSION.

This spacious room of glass, marble, and burnished wood occupies part of the ground floor of a postmodernist office tower that looks out at the confluence of the Moshassuck and Woonasquatucket rivers. Its reputation as a place to see-and-be-seen shortchanges the skill of its capable chefs. They are grounded in the Italian repertoire but skip lightly among other inspirations—Thai, Greek, and Portuguese among them. That restlessness brings them to dishes like lamb shank baked in a clay pot with orzo and rosemary, or cioppino of lobster chunks, shrimp, littlenecks, calamari, and whitefish. Afterward, go for the remarkable crème brûlée confection, tiered and spiky with spun sugar. There are tables outside in warm weather, and music on weekends.

✪ **The Gatehouse.** 4 Richmond Sq. (east end of Pitman St.) ☎ **401/521-9229.** Reservations recommended on weekends. Main courses $18.95–$25.95. AE, DC, MC, V. Mon–Fri noon–2:30pm, Sun 11am–2pm; daily 5:30–10pm. NEW AMERICAN.

If you can only have one meal in Providence, have it here. Step inside a refined taproom with a green marble bar on the left, a working fireplace and elegantly set tables over to the right. Downstairs is a candlelit lounge and an outdoor deck perched above the Seekonk River. Jazz pianists or duos perform down there Wednesday to Saturday, and a pub menu offers burgers and pastas.

Service and cuisine are more polished on the main floor. Imagine the signature appetizer: a fig wrapped in a phyllo husk combines with tastes of Stilton cheese, toasted pine nuts, prosciutto, cream, and port with a balsamic glaze. It's a perfect marriage, unlikely as it may sound. Most of the entrees are grilled, at least in part, as with roasted tomato polenta, portobello mushrooms, and julienned vegetables cooked over hickory and rolled into a warm tortilla. Presentation is careful but not fussy.

Pot au Feu. 44 Custom St. (off Weybosset St.) ☎ **401/273-8953.** Main courses: salon $22–$29; bistro $9.95–$19.95. AE, CB, DC, MC, V. Salon Tues–Fri noon–1:30pm and 6–9pm, Sat 6–9:30pm. Bistro Mon–Fri 11:30am–2pm; Mon–Thurs 5:30–9pm, Fri–Sat 5:30–10pm, Sun 4–9pm. TRADITIONAL FRENCH.

If English wasn't being spoken all around, you'd think the restaurant was on a village square in Provence. Dishes like steak au poivre and *choucroute garni* are exactly as they should be, remembrances of what made Gallic cooking memorable long before the excesses of the food revolution set in.

Unless someone else is paying or you simply must have a tablecloth, there's no reason not to head straight downstairs, especially at dinner, when the price gap widens between the salon and the basement bistro. The brick floors and overhead pipes do nothing to muffle the din down there, but that earthy food comes from the same kitchen.

QUICK BITES

A bona fide National Historic Landmark is an unlikely venue for snaffling up cookies, salads, souvlaki, doughnuts, and egg rolls. But **The Arcade,** 65 Weybosset St. (☎ **401/456-5403**), is a 19th-century progenitor of 20th-century shopping malls, an 1828 Greek Revival structure that runs between Weybosset and Westminster streets. Its main floor is given over largely to fast-food stands and snack counters of the usual kind—yes, the Golden Arches, too—while the upper floor is primarily clothing and jewelry boutiques and toy and souvenir shops. It's open daily.

Another local culinary institution arrives in Kennedy Plaza on wheels every afternoon around 4:30pm. The grungy aluminum-sided **Haven Bros.** (☎ **401/ 861-7777**) is a food tractor-trailer with stools inside and good deals on decent burgers and better fries from its parking space next to City Hall. No new frontiers here, except that it hangs around until way past midnight to dampen the hunger pangs of club-goers, lawyers, night people, and workaholic pols (the mayor is a regular).

PROVIDENCE AFTER DARK

This being a college town, there is no end of music bars, small concert halls, and pool pubs. A good source of information about who's appearing where is the free weekly, *The Providence Phoenix* or its Web site, **www.providencephoenix.com.**

The **Rhode Island Philharmonic** (☎ **401/831-3123**) usually appears at the **Providence Performing Arts Center, 220 Weybosset St**. The **Ocean State Lyric Opera** (☎ **401/331-6060**) stages two or three productions a season at various locations, including the Lincoln School Theatre and Veterans Memorial Auditorium. Big-ticket touring musicals on the order of *Phantom of the Opera,* as well as traveling dance companies, comedians, and other attractions, are also showcased at the **PPAC** (☎**401/421-2787**), while new plays share space with Ibsen and Shakespeare at the **Trinity Repertory Company,** 201 Washington St. (☎**401/351-4242**).

The southern end of Water and Main streets, known as India Point, has several bar/restaurants functioning essentially as nightspots. **The Hot Club,** 575 S. Water St. (☎ 401/861-9007) sits out over the water, with two bars and two terraces. They have views of a marina, a power plant, and the Fox Point Hurricane Barrier, all incorporated into scenes for the movie, *There's Something About Mary.* It's open from noon until well past midnight. Other nearby South Water Street possibilities, last I looked, are **Steam Alley,** a sports bar with pool tables and 14 beers on tap, **Fish Company,** popular with twentysomethings, and **Grappa.**

South of downtown, in the Jewelry District, **The Complex** (☎ 401/751-4263) has four dance clubs for only one cover charge: retro disco **Polly Esta's,** top 40 **Algiers,** the **Slick Willies** piano bar, and **Swingers,** serving the current swing-dance fad. Not far away, sharing a building with the Atomic Café (see above), is **Snooker's** (☎ 401/351-7665), a pool hall with live music Friday and Saturday nights in its **Green Room.** Rooms behind the restaurant house **Fusion,** where a DJ pushes a Latin beat, geared to an older crowd. **Lupo's Heartbreak Hotel** is at 239 Westminster St. (☎ 401/272-5876), with live concerts five or six nights a week by tribute bands and alternative, hip hop, techno, and house groups. Tickets are sold at the **Met Café,** around the corner at 130 Union St.. At the **Trinity Brewhouse,** 186 Fountain St. (☎ 401/453-2337) live jazz and blues share attention with boutique beers, a pool table, and a warm-weather deck.

Star acts like Steve Winwood and Jon Bon Jovi, as well as mainstream and alternative bands, appear at **The Strand,** 79 Washington St. (☎ 401/272-0444). **The Call,** 15 Elbow St. (☎ 401/751-2255), promotes a similar card, with fewer familiar names but as energetically presented.

For art-house films and midnight cult movies, there is the **Avon Repertory Cinema,** on Thayer Street, near Meeting Street.

2 A Bucolic Detour to Sakonnet Point

As a break from the rushed urbanity of Providence or the concentration of sights and activities that is Newport, a side trip down the length of the oddly isolated southeastern corner of the state is a soothing excursion.

No one has thought to throw a bridge or run a ferry across the water between Newport and Sakonnet Point, prospects the reclusive residents would no doubt resist to the last lawsuit (they have been known to steal away with road signs to discourage summer visitors). There are almost no enterprises geared to attract tourists. Things are quiet in these parts, and the locals intend to keep it that way.

GETTING THERE   To get there from Providence or Boston, pick up I-195 east, then Route 24 south, toward Newport. Take Exit 4 for Route 77 south, just before the Sakonnet River Bridge. From Newport, take Route 138 toward Fall River, and exit on Route 77 south immediately after crossing the bridge.

EXPLORING THE AREA

After a welter of small businesses, most of them involved in some way with the ocean, Route 77 smoothes out into a pastoral Brigadoon, not quite rural, but more rustic than suburban. Colonial farmhouses, real or replicated, bear sidings and roofs of weathered shakes the color of wood smoke. They are centered in tidy lawns, with fruit trees and firs as sentinels, and bordered by miles and miles of low stone walls assembled with a sculptural sense of balanced shapes and textures. No plastic deer, no tomato plants in front yards, none of those cute little banners hung from porches to herald seasons and holidays. It is as if a requirement of residence was attendance at a school of good taste.

There are a few antiques shops and roadside farm stands of both the permanent and card-table variety as well as a snack shop or two and a garden store, but nothing even remotely intrusive to sour the serenity.

One of the rare good reasons to pull off the road is **Sakonnet Vineyards,** 162 W. Main Rd. (☎ **401/635-8486**), with an entrance road on the left, about 3 miles south of the traffic light in Tiverton Four Corners. In operation for over 20 years, it is one of New England's oldest wineries, and produces 50,000 cases of creditable wines annually. Types range from a popular Pinot Noir to a dry Gewürztraminer, abetted by such whimsical bottlings as their Eye of the Storm blush, that commemorates the 1985 arrival of Hurricane Gloria. Those with the foresight to bring along a picnic lunch can buy a bottle or two and retire to one of the tables beside the pond near the tasting room. The hospitality center is open daily from 10am to 6pm in summer, 11am to 5pm in winter.

Continuing south on Route 77, the road skirts Little Compton and heads on to **Sakonnet Point,** where the inland terrain gives way to stony beaches and coastal marshes. There's a wetlands wildlife refuge (where you might glimpse snowy egrets and herons), a small harbor with working boats, and not much else.

Now head back north on Route 77, watching for the green-and-white sign pointing toward Adamsville (if the natives haven't made off with it). Take the right turn at the triangular traffic island just beyond, onto a road that seems to have neither name nor number. Shortly it arrives at a T intersection surrounded by a Congregational church, some small shops, a post office, and the Common's Restaurant (see below). That's downtown **Little Compton.** Turn left (north) and you're back in the country before you shift into third gear. In about 4 miles, the road ends at Peckham Road. Turn right, in the faith that you are heading toward **Adamsville;** you'll arrive there in about 8 miles. It's here that you'll come across Abraham Manchester's (see below).

From Adamsville, return to Route 77 via Route 179 to Tiverton Four Corners to get back to Newport, or take Route 81 to Route 24 if returning to Providence or Boston.

WHERE TO STAY ALONG THE WAY

Stone House Club. 122 Sakonnet Point Rd., Little Compton, RI 02837. ☎ **401/635-2222.** Fax 401/635-2822. www.stonehouseclub.com. 14 units, 4 with shared bathroom. Summer and holidays $58–$110 double; $125–$225 suite. Nov–Apr $48–$80 double; $90 suite. Rates include breakfast. *Note:* Additional membership fee as noted below. MC, V.

From the last stop in Sakonnet Point, return along Route 77, and you'll shortly note the entrance to this restaurant/tavern/inn. It's open to the public, but it must observe the wink-wink subterfuge of being a private club because it serves spirits and there is a church next door. That means a $20 membership fee for individuals and $36 for couples in addition to the room rates. Furnishings are worn and unstylish, but look oddly right for their location. Two private swimming beaches are available to guests.

Dining: The cellar Tap Room and more formal dining room upstairs traipse all over the gastronomic map—traditional, nouvelle, Italian, Asian—with an emphasis on seafood. They are open Tuesday to Sunday in summer, Friday to Sunday November through April.

WHERE TO DINE ALONG THE WAY

Abraham Manchester's. Main Rd. ☎ **401/635-2700.** Main courses $6.85–$21.95. MC, V. Daily 11:30am–10pm. ECLECTIC.

Adamsville, birthplace of the Rhode Island Red breed of chicken, is a less pristine hamlet than Little Compton, with a disheveled aspect and more pickup trucks than

SUVs. At its center is Abraham Manchester's, which serves as much as the town's social center as a restaurant. The gregarious owner and her staff greet almost everyone by name, bantering as old friends do. The building is a former general store, but not much attention is paid the niceties of historic preservation. A mounted stag head and wagon wheel are typical of the decor.

The menu is unexpectedly imaginative, with, for example, a smoked chicken Alfredo over spinach fettuccine, and a production called the "Manchester Medley Platter." That's a jumble of shrimp marinated in red wine, blackened swordfish, barbecued chicken, and a slab of tenderloin. Portions are daunting.

Before 11:30am the owner's daughter runs **The Barn** on the other side of the parking lot, offering elaborate breakfasts with freshly baked breads and pastries.

Common's. On the Little Compton Commons. ☎**401/635-4388.** Main courses $5.75–$11.95. No credit cards. Daily 5am–6pm (until 7pm Fri–Sat). REGIONAL AMERICAN.

The apostrophe in the name is theirs—no one seems to know whether it's a mistake or a joke. Never mind. This is the place to sample a few Rhode Island specialities. There are *johnnycakes*, lacy pancakes of stoneground cornmeal as thin as playing cards, and *stuffies*, chopped Quahog (KWAH-og or KOH-hog) clams mixed with minced bell peppers and bread crumbs and packed into both halves of the shell for baking. A satisfying lunch is the chock-full lobster roll, which comes with Quahog chowder, fries, and fritters for $10.95. Everyone here knows everyone else, filling the place with joshing and laughter.

3 Newport

"City by the Sea" is the singularly unimaginative nickname an early resident unloaded on Newport. At least it was accurate, since for a time during the colonial period it rivaled Boston and even New York as a center of New World trade and prosperity. Newport occupies the southern tip of Aquidneck Island in Narragansett Bay, and is connected to the mainland by three bridges and a ferry.

Wealthy industrialists, railroad tycoons, coal magnates, financiers, and robber barons made respectable by political connections and vast fortunes were drawn to the area, especially between the mid–19th century and World War I. They bought up property at the ocean's rim, building summer mansions, patterned after European palaces, that they jokingly referred to as summer "cottages."

Their toys were equally extravagant pleasure yachts, and competitions among them established Newport's reputation as a sailing center. In 1851, the sporting schooner *America* defeated a British ship in a race around the Isle of Wight. The prize trophy became known as the America's Cup, which remained in possession of the New York Yacht Club (with an outpost in Newport) until 1983. In that shocking summer, *Australia II* snatched the Cup away from *Liberty* in the last race of a four-out-of-seven series. An American team regained the cup in 1987, but in 1995, a New Zealand crew snatched it back down under. The strong U.S. yachting tradition has endured despite the loss of the Cup, and Newport continues as a center of world sailing and a destination for long-distance races.

The perimeter of the city resembles a heeled boot, its toe pointing west, not unlike Italy. About where the laces of the boot would be is the downtown business and residential district. Several wharves push into the bay, providing support and mooring for flotillas of pleasure craft, from stubby little inboards and character boats to graceful sloops and visiting tall ships. Much of the strolling, shopping, eating, quaffing, and gawking is done along this waterfront and its parallel streets: America's Cup Avenue

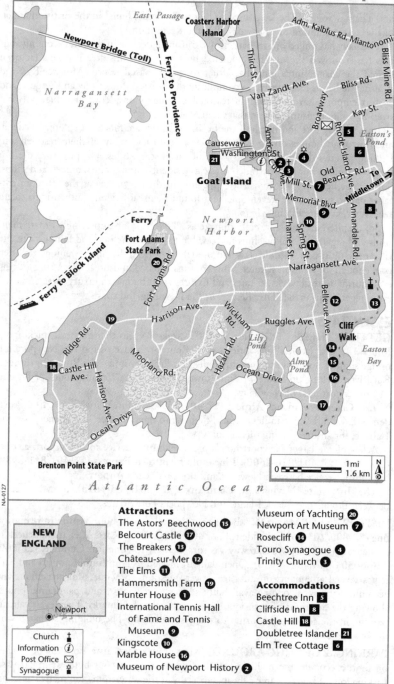

Newport

East Passage

Coasters Harbor Island

Newport Bridge (Toll)

Ferry to Providence

Narragansett Bay

Third St.

Adm. Kalbfus Rd. Miantonomi

Van Zandt Ave.

Bliss Rd.

Bliss Mine Rd.

Kay St.

Causeway

Washington St.

①

㉑

America's Cup Ave.

Easton's Pond

⑤

⑥

②

④

Broadway

Rhode Island Ave.

③

Goat Island

Mill St.

Old Beach Ave.

⑦

To Middletown

Memorial Blvd.

⑨

⑩

Newport Harbor

Ferry

Fort Adams State Park

Spring St.

Thames St.

Annandale Rd.

⑧

⑪

Ferry to Block Island

⑳

Fort Adams Rd.

Narragansett Ave.

Harrison Ave.

Wickham Rd.

Hazard Rd.

Ruggles Ave.

Bellevue Ave.

⑫

⑬

Cliff Walk

⑲

Ridge Rd.

Moorland Rd.

Lily Pond

Almy Pond

Ocean Drive

⑭

Easton Bay

⑱

Castle Hill Ave.

Harrison Ave.

Ocean Drive

⑮

⑯

⑰

0   1mi
     1.6 km

N

Brenton Point State Park

Atlantic Ocean

NA-0127

NEW ENGLAND

Newport

Church ✝
Information ⓘ
Post Office ✉
Synagogue ✡

Attractions

The Astors' Beechwood **⑮**
Belcourt Castle **⑰**
The Breakers **⑬**
Château-sur-Mer **⑫**
The Elms **⑪**
Hammersmith Farm **⑲**
Hunter House **①**
International Tennis Hall of Fame and Tennis Museum **⑨**
Kingscote **⑩**
Marble House **⑯**
Museum of Newport History **②**

Museum of Yachting **⑳**
Newport Art Museum **⑦**
Rosecliff **⑭**
Touro Synagogue **④**
Trinity Church **③**

Accommodations

Beechtree Inn **⑤**
Cliffside Inn **⑧**
Castle Hill **⑱**
Doubletree Islander **㉑**
Elm Tree Cottage **⑥**

and Thames Street. (The latter used to be pronounced "Tems" in the British manner, but was Americanized to "Thaymz" after the Revolution.)

The navy has pulled out its battleships, causing a decline in the local economy, but this hasn't proved the disaster predicted by some. And this area has thus far been spared the coarser intrusions that afflict so many coastal resorts. Monster RVs and motorcycle bands rarely arrive to complicate the heavy traffic of July and August, and T-shirt emporia have kept within reasonable limits. Considering that Newport has over 3.7 million visitors a year, that's remarkable.

Immediately east and north of the business district are blocks of colonial, Federal, and Victorian houses of the 18th and 19th centuries, many of them restored and bearing plaques designating them as National Historic Sites. Happily, they are not frozen in amber, but are very much in use as residences, restaurants, offices, and shops. Taken together, they are as visually appealing in their own way as the 40-room cottages of the super-rich. Steven Spielberg found them sufficiently authentic to spend several weeks there filming *Amistad*.

So, despite Newport's prevailing image as a collection of stupefyingly ornate mansions and regattas of sailing ships inaccessible to all but the rich and famous, the city is, for the most part, middle class and moderately priced. Summer evenings are often cool enough for a cotton sweater. Scores of inns and bed-and-breakfasts assure lodging even during festival weeks, at rates and fixtures from budget to luxury level. In nearly every regard, this is the "First Resort" of the New England coast.

ESSENTIALS

GETTING THERE   From New York City, take I-95 to the third exit, picking up Route 138 east (which joins briefly with Route 4) and crossing the Newport toll bridge slightly north of the downtown district. From Boston, take Route 24 through Fall River, picking up Route 114 into town. Newport lies 75 miles south of Boston, 115 miles northeast of New Haven.

T. F. Green/Providence Airport (☎ 401/737-8222) in Warwick, south of Providence (Exit 13, I-95), handles national flights into the state. See "Providence," section 1 above, for airlines serving this airport.

A few of the larger Newport hotels provide shuttle service to the airport, as does **Cozy Cab** (☎ 401/846-2500). **Pineapple Beantown Express** (☎ 401/841-8989) has shuttle service between Newport and Boston's Logan Airport.

The **Interstate Navigation Company** (☎ 401/783-4613) provides ferries between Providence, Block Island, and Newport's Fort Adams.

VISITOR INFORMATION   Before a visit, call the 24-hour **visitor information** line (☎ 800/263-4636 outside R.I., or 401/848-2000 in R.I.). After arrival, check in at the excellent **Newport Gateway Visitors Center,** 23 America's Cup Ave. (☎ 800/326-6030 or 401/849-8040). Open daily from 9am to 5pm (until 6pm Fri and Sat), it has several attendants on duty to answer questions, brochures for attractions and accommodations, a lodging-availability service, rest rooms, and panoramic photos showing the locations of mansions, parks, and other landmarks. They even validate parking in the adjacent lot for up to the first half hour. The building is shared with the bus station.

PARKING & GETTING AROUND   Most of Newport's attractions can be reached on foot, except for the mansions, so leaving your car at your hotel or inn is wise. Parking lots and garages aren't cheap, especially at the waterfront, and many streets are very narrow. The metered parking slots along Thames Street are closely monitored by police and fines are steep (although in the off-season, the meters are hooded and parking is free for up to 3 hr.). Renting or bringing a bicycle is an attractive option (see "Outdoor Pursuits," below for a list of bike rental places).

The **Rhode Island Public Transit Authority** (RIPTA; ☎ **401/781-9400**) has a free shuttle bus that follows a roughly circular route through town, making stops at major sights.

SPECIAL EVENTS   Arrive any day between Memorial Day and Labor Day and expect to find at least a half-dozen ✪ **festivals** and competitions in progress. Following is only a partial list of some of the more prominent events. (Specific dates often change from year to year, so call ahead to confirm; ☎ **800/263-4636** outside R.I., or 401/848-2000 in R.I.).

While there are a few substantive events in the off-season months—notably the **February Winter Festival** (☎ **401/849-8048** for details), which focuses on food and winter sports—the pace ratchets up in June, starting with the annual **Great Chowder Cook-Off** at the Newport Yachting Center (☎ **401/845-1600** for details). In the third week of June is the 3-day **Secret Garden Tour** (☎ **401/847-0514**), when the gardens of the Point section of town are open to visitors.

In July, the principal music events are the ✪ **Newport Music Festival** (☎ **401/846-1133**), which offers three classical music concerts daily at various venues during the middle two weeks of the month, and the **Rhythm and Blues Festival** (☎ **401/847-3700**), held outdoors in Fort Adams Park for two days at the end of the month. The second week of July sees the **Hall of Fame Tennis Tournament** (☎ **401/849-6053**), the only U.S. men's ATP tournament held on grass, overlapping the days of the pro women's **Hall of Fame Invitational.** In the third week of the month is the **Black Ships Festival** (☎ **401/847-3700**), a celebration of all aspects of Japanese culture.

August brings the 2-day **Ben & Jerry's Folk Festival** and the 3-day **JVC Jazz Festival** (☎ **401/847-3700** for both), both held at Fort Adams Park. Things wind down after Labor Day, though there's still the 2-day **Irish Music Festival** (☎ **401/849-2028**) toward the end of September and the annual **Bowen's Wharf Waterfront Seafood Festival** (☎ **401/849-2243**) in the third week of October.

The rosters of scheduled performers for the blues, folk, and jazz festivals are usually released by May. While tickets are often available near concert time, it's wise to purchase them at least a month in advance for the best-known groups and soloists. Newport somehow absorbs the throngs that descend upon it for these events, but lodgings for weekends from Memorial Day to Labor Day should be secured at least two months in advance, and sooner is better.

THE COTTAGES

That's what wealthy summer people called the almost unimaginably sumptuous mansions they had built in Newport in the last decades before the 16th Amendment to the Constitution permitted an income tax.

Say this for the wealthy of the Gilded Age, many of whom obtained their fortunes by less than honorable means: they knew a good place to put down roots when they saw it. These are the same people who developed Palm Beach in winter, the Hudson Valley in spring, the Berkshires in autumn, and, of course, Newport in summer, sweeping from luxurious house to luxurious house with the insouciance of a bejeweled matron dragging her sable down a grand staircase. They were Vanderbilts and Astors and their chums and rivals, and they rarely stayed in any one of their mansions for more than a few weeks a year.

When driving or biking through the cottage district (walking its length is impractical for most people), consider the fact that most of these astonishing residences are still privately owned. That's almost as remarkable as the grounds and interiors of the nine that are open to the public.

Before you set out, ask if Rough Point, the fabled 1887 Tudor mansion of the late Doris Duke (still protected by high walls topped with barbed wire at this writing), has begun to welcome visitors; it is slated to open in the near future. To find it, continue south on Bellevue from Belcourt Castle. It's on the left, just before a sharp turn west along what becomes **Ocean Drive.**

Also, resolve to visit only one or two homes per day. The sheer opulence of the mansions can soon become numbing, an effect not unlike touching down in five European countries in a week and touring the most lavish palaces in each.

Each residence requires 45 minutes to an hour for its guided tour. The aptitude and personality of individual docents is generally good, apart from their understandable tendency to take on a robotic tone. If at all possible, go during the week. Weekend foot and vehicular traffic can resemble Times Square at curtain time.

Six of the mansions are maintained by the **Preservation Society of Newport County,** 424 Bellevue Ave. (☎ **401/847-1000**), which also operates the 1748 Hunter House and the Green Animals Topiary Gardens in Portsmouth (www.newportmansions.org). They sell a **combination ticket,** good for a year, to eight properties; it's $35.50 for adults, $14 for children 6 to 11. Individual tickets for The Breakers are $10 for adults, $6 for students, and $4 for children 6 to 11. Individual tickets for Kingscote, The Elms, Château-sur-Mer, Marble House, Hunter House, and Rosecliff are $8 for adults, $5 for students, and $3.50 for children. Strip tickets for two to eight mansions are also available. They can be purchased at any of the properties. Credit cards are accepted at most, but not all, of the cottages.

The mansions that aren't operated by the Preservation Society but are open to the public are Belcourt Castle and Beechwood.

Following are descriptions of the nine in the order they are encountered when driving south from Memorial Boulevard along Bellevue Avenue, then west on Ocean Avenue.

Kingscote. Bowery St. (west of Bellevue Ave.). Mar 21 to Apr 30 Sat–Sun 10am–5pm, May to Columbus Day daily 10am–5pm. See above for admission details.

This mansion (on the right-hand side of the avenue) is a reminder that well-to-do Southern families often had second homes north of the Mason-Dixon line to avoid the sultry summers of the deep South. Kingscote was built in 1839, nearly 40 years before the Gilded Age (usually regarded as the era between the end of the Civil War and the beginning of World War I). But it is considered one of the Newport Cottages because it was acquired in 1864 by the sea merchant William Henry King, who furnished it with porcelains and textiles accumulated in the China Trade. Architect Richard Upjohn designed the mansion in the same Gothic Revival style he used for Trinity Church in New York. The New York architectural firm of McKim, Mead & White was commissioned to design the 1881 dining room, notable for its Tiffany glass panels.

The Elms. Bellevue Ave. Late Mar to Apr daily 10am–5pm, May–Oct daily 10am–5pm, Nov 1–15 and late Nov to early Jan daily 10am–4pm. See above for admission details.

Architect Horace Trumbauer is said to have been inspired by the Château d'Asniéres outside Paris, and a first look at the ornate dining room of the Elms, suitable for at least a marquis, buttresses that claim. So, too, do the sunken gardens (currently under renovation), laid out and maintained in the formal French manner.

The owner was a first-generation millionaire, a coal tycoon named Edward J. Berwind. His cottage was completed in 1901, and he filled it with genuine Louis XIV and XV furniture and paintings and accessories true to the late–18th century.

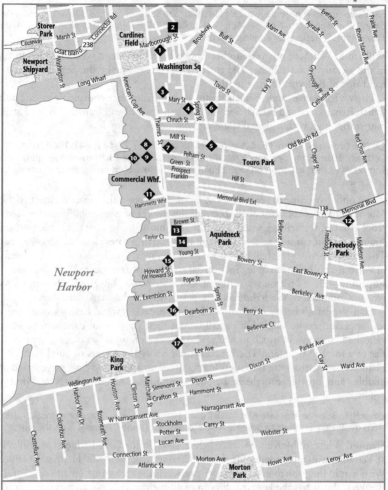

Accommodations & Dining

Admiral Fitzroy Inn **14**

Asterix & Obelix ◆**17**

Black Pearl ◆**10**

Bouchard ◆**16**

Brick Alley Pub ◆**3**

Cheeky Monkey ◆**11**

Clarke Cook House ◆**9**

Francis Malbone Inn **13**

Jailhouse Inn ◆**1**

Le Bistro ◆**8**

Mill Street Inn ◆**5**

Music Hall Café ◆**7**

Pilgrim House ◆**4**

Scales & Shells ◆**15**

The Victorian Ladies ◆**12**

Vanderbilt Hall ◆**6**

White Horse Tavern **2**

Château-sur-Mer. Bellevue Ave. Late Jan to Apr Sat–Sun and holidays 10am–5pm, May–Sept daily 10am–5pm, Oct–Nov Sat–Sun and holidays 10am–4pm, late Nov to Jan 3 daily 10am–4pm. See above for admission details.

William S. Wetmore was yet another Rhode Island merchant who made his fortune in the lucrative China Trade. The entrance to this "Castle by the Sea" is on the left-hand side of Bellevue, driving south.

High Victorian in style, which means it drew from many inspirations (including Italian Renaissance and French Second Empire), the Château features a central atrium four stories high with a glass skylight and balconies at every level.

✪ **The Breakers.** Ochre Point Ave. (east of Bellevue Ave.) ☎ **401/847-1000.** Late Mar to Oct daily 10am–5pm. See above for admission details. After Château-sur-Mer, turn left on Ruggles Ave., then left again on Ochre Point Ave. The Breakers is on the right; a parking lot is on the left.

If you only have time to see one of the Cottages, make it this one. Architect Richard Morris Hunt was commissioned to create this replica of a generic Florentine Renaissance palazzo, replacing a wood structure that burned down in 1892. He was unrestrained by cost considerations. The high iron entrance gates alone weigh over 7 tons. The 50-by-50-foot great hall has 50-foot-high ceilings, forming a giant cube sheathed in African and Italian marble. Such mind-numbing extravagance shouldn't really be surprising—Hunt's patron was, after all, Cornelius Vanderbilt II, grandson of railroad tycoon Commodore Vanderbilt and a superstar spender of the Gilded Age.

Had Vanderbilt been European royalty, The Breakers would have provided motive for a peasant revolt. Vanderbilt's small family, their guests, and their staff of 40 servants had 70 rooms in which to roam. The mansion's foundation is approximately the size of a football field, and The Breakers took nearly three years to build (1892–95). Platoons of artisans were imported from Europe to apply gold leaf, carve wood and marble, and provide mural-size baroque paintings. The furnishings on view are original.

Rosecliff. Bellevue Ave. Late Mar to Oct daily 10am–5pm. See above for admission details. From the Breakers, return to Bellevue Ave. and turn left (south). Rosecliff is on the left.

Stanford White, of McKim, Mead & White, thought the Grand Trianon of Louis XVI at Versailles a suitable model for this 1902 commission for Mr. Hermann Oelrichs. With a middling 40 rooms, it doesn't overwhelm, at least not on the scale of The Breakers. But it has the largest ballroom of all the cottages, not to mention a storied heart-shaped grand staircase. All this was made possible by one James Fair, an immigrant who made his fortune after he unearthed the thickest gold and silver vein of Nevada's Comstock Lode and bought this property for his daughters, Theresa and Virginia (a.k.a., Tessie and Birdie).

In 1941, the mansion and its contents were sold for $21,000. It was used as a setting for some scenes in the Robert Redford movie of Fitzgerald's *The Great Gatsby* and for a ballroom scene in Arnold Schwarzenegger's *True Lies.*

The Astors' Beechwood. 580 Bellevue Ave. ☎ **401/846-3772.** Admission $9 adults, $7 seniors and children 5–12, free for children under 5, $25 family rate. Mid-May to Nov 7 daily 10am–5pm (every 20 minutes); Christmas tours Nov 10 to Dec 16 Wed–Sun (on the hour); Feb 5 to mid-May Fri–Sun 10am–4pm (every 30 minutes).

Mrs. William Backhouse Astor—*the* Mrs. Astor, as every brochure and guide feels compelled to observe—was, during her active life, the arbiter of exactly who constituted New York and Newport society. "The 400" list of socially acceptable folk was influenced or perhaps even drawn up by her, and that roster bore meaning, in some quarters, well into the second half of the 20th century. Being invited to Beechwood was absolutely critical to a social pretender's sense of self-worth, and elaborate machinations were set in motion to achieve that goal. (It may be of some comfort to the descendants of the failed supplicants that Mrs. Astor spent her last few years at the cottage greeting imaginary guests.)

Rebuilt in 1857 after a fire destroyed the original version, the mansion isn't as large or impressive as some of its neighbors. But unlike those managed by the Preservation Society, it provides a little theatrical pizzazz with a corps of actors who pretend to be friends, children, and servants of Mrs. Astor. Frequent special events are held, often replicating those that took place when she held court, including costume balls and specially decorated banquets with Victorian music and dancing.

✪ **Marble House.** Bellevue Ave. Late Mar to Oct daily 10am–5pm, Nov Sat–Sun 10am–4pm, late Nov to Jan 3 daily 10am–4pm, Jan–Mar Sat–Sun 10am–4pm. See above for admission details.

Architect Richard Morris Hunt, another favorite of the cottage builders, outdid himself for his clients William and Alva Vanderbilt. Several types of marble were used both outside and inside with a lavish hand that rivals the palaces of the Sun King, especially Le Petit Trianon at Versailles. It reaches its apogee in the ballroom, which is encrusted with three kinds of gold.

It cost William $11 million to build and decorate Marble House, but Alva divorced him four years after the project was finished. She got the house, which she soon closed after marrying William's friend and neighbor. When her second husband died, Alva discovered the cause of female suffrage, and reopened Marble House in 1913 to hold a benefit for the campaign for women's right to vote. (Dishes in the scullery bear the legend, "Votes for Women.")

Belcourt Castle. Bellevue Ave. (at Lakeview Ave.) ☎ **401/846-0669.** Admission $7.50 adults, $6 seniors and college students, $5 children 13–18, $3 children 6–12, free for children under 6. Feb–May Sat–Sun and holidays 10am–3pm; Memorial Day to mid-Oct daily 9am–5pm; mid-Oct to Nov daily 10am–4pm; Dec (special tours) 10am–3pm. Closed Jan.

This was the (only slightly) less grand mansion to which Alva Vanderbilt repaired after her second marriage. While the Vanderbilts were avid yachtsmen, her new husband, Oliver Hazard Perry Belmont, was a fanatical horseman. His 62-room house, also a design by Richard Morris Hunt, actually contained stables on the ground floor, where his beloved steeds slept under monogrammed blankets (the Belmonts were instrumental in building New York's famed Belmont Racetrack).

Alva and Oliver entertained frequently, and counted among their guests Kaiser Wilhelm and the Duke of Windsor. The castle, meant to resemble a royal hunting lodge, contains a collection of European stained glass, scores of Oriental carpets, and French Renaissance furniture and artifacts. Thomas Edison designed the lighting.

Hammersmith Farm. Ocean Dr. (past Castle Hill Ave.)

Built for John W. Auchincloss in 1887, this house was used for the wedding reception of one of his descendants, Jacqueline Bouvier, in 1953. Set on a rise with an unimpeded view of Narragansett Bay across 50 acres of lawns and gardens, it subsequently became the unofficial summer White House of the short Kennedy presidency. There is irony in that identity, for a building on the adjoining Fort Adams State Park was the Dwight D. Eisenhower summer White House. It makes concrete the symbolism mentioned by Kennedy in his inaugural address, the passing of power from men born in the last century to those born in this one.

Hammersmith has been sold for a rumored $9 million. The buyer plans to use it as a private residence and it will no longer be open to the public. The date of that closing

Camelot Summers

There comes a moment in every tour of **Hammersmith Farm** when the group lets loose an involuntary sound that is part starstruck gasp, part sad sigh. That's when the guide pauses at the foot of the main staircase.

Up there at the top, on September 12, 1953, she says, Jacqueline Bouvier Kennedy stood in her ivory silk wedding gown and tossed her bouquet to the single women at her reception. It was the first day of her 10 years as the wife of America's youngest elected president.

Jack Kennedy had wasted no time after his service in the navy in World War II, either in ascending the political ladder or in sowing wild oats. At the arranged dinner where he first met Jackie, an erstwhile deb queen and inquiring photographer, Washington's most eligible bachelor "reached across the asparagus and asked her for a date." It was time for a man of high ambition to take a politically acceptable wife, and, soon after, he did.

Jack won the presidency seven years after his marriage to Jackie. The shingled Victorian mansion on a hill overlooking Narragansett Bay became his summer White House. Despite its 28 rooms and the extensive gardens designed by Frederick Law Olmsted, the designer of New York's Central Park, it seems a relatively modest residence, compared to Newport's other mansions.

But here is a history we remember. The president, Jacqueline, and their children lived and worked and played here. The presidential yacht, *Honey Fitz,* used to be moored down at the dock.

John Auchincloss built the cottage in 1887. His son Hugh married Janet Lee Bouvier, Jackie's mother. Yet another Auchincloss—Louis—is the lawyer and novelist who chronicled the lives and times of the well-bred and well-heeled of New York and New England. It is the whispers of those lives that lend the cottage at Hammersmith an air of profound purpose and loss.

is still vague, although expected in late 1999, so check at the **Newport Gateway Visitors Center** (☎ 800/326-6030 or (☎ 401/849-8040) for an update. At least the house can still be seen from the road.

A HISTORIC HOME

Hunter House. 54 Washington St. (at Elm St.). ☎ **401/847-1000.** See above for admission details. May–Sept daily 10am–5pm; Apr and Oct Sat–Sun 10am–5pm. Closed Nov–Mar.

Another property of the Preservation Society, this 1754 colonial with its gambrel roof and widow's walk is one of the most impressive dwellings in the lightly touristed neighborhood known as the Point, north of downtown.

Above the doorway, within the broken pediment, is a carved wooden pineapple. This symbol of welcome derived from the practice of placing a real pineapple at the door to announce that the sea-captain owner had returned from his long voyage and was ready to receive guests. The interior displays furniture crafted by Newport's famed 18th-century cabinetmakers, Townsend and Goddard.

OTHER SIGHTS

In addition to checking out the attractions described below, you might want to stroll along **Spring Street** between Memorial Boulevard and Touro Street. **Historic Hill** is the large district of colonial Newport that rises from America's Cup Avenue, along the waterfront, to Bellevue Avenue, the beginning of Victorian Newport. Spring Street serves as the Hill's main drag, and it's a treasure trove of colonial, Georgian, and Federal structures serving as residences, inns, and antiques and other shops. There are no 20th-century architectural intrusions.

Chief among its visual delights is the 1725 **Trinity Church,** at the corner of Church Street. Said to be fashioned in the manner of the legendary British architect Christopher Wren, it certainly reflects that inspiration in its belfry and distinctive spire, seen from all over downtown Newport and dominating Queen Anne Square, a greensward that runs down to the waterfront. The church is sheathed in beige clapboard and has two stained-glass windows by Tiffany.

International Tennis Hall of Fame. 194 Bellevue Ave. (at the corner of Memorial Blvd.). ☎ **401/849-3990.** Admission $8 adults, $6 seniors, $4 children under 13, $20 family. Daily 9:30am–5pm (except during tournaments).

On Bellevue Avenue, there was (and is) an exclusive men's club, the Newport Reading Room. One member was James Gordon Bennett, Jr., the wealthy publisher of the *New York Herald.* He persuaded a friend to ride a horse into the club. The outraged members reprimanded Bennett, who had an instant snit that they hadn't enjoyed his little jest. He went right out and bought a property on the other side of Memorial Boulevard, and ordered a structure built for his own social and sports club.

The New York architectural firm of McKim, Mead & White produced a shingle-style edifice of lavish proportions with turrets and verandas and an interior piazza for lawn games, equestrian shows, concerts, and a new game called tennis. It is now given to a permanent grass court cropped down to a thick emerald nap. As Bennett hoped, his Newport Casino swiftly became the premier gathering place of his privileged compatriots.

Now the pavilion hosts professional tournaments and its courts are open to the public for play (phone ahead to make reservations, May through October). The building itself houses the Tennis Hall of Fame, recently renovated at a cost of $6 million, containing trophies, memorabilia, and computerized interactive exhibits. The Hall is of interest primarily to fans of the game, but has photographic highlights recognizable to casual observers. An in-house restaurant (☎ **401/847-0418**) serves lunch, sunset dinners, and weekend brunch.

Museum of Newport History. Washington Sq. (at Thames and Touro sts.). ☎ **401/841-8770.** Admission $5 adults, $4 seniors, $3 children 6–18, free for children under 6. Mid-May to Oct Mon and Wed–Sat 10am–5pm; Sun 1–5pm. Nov to mid-May Fri–Sat 10am–4pm.

One of five properties maintained by the Newport Historical Society, this museum is in the refurbished 1772 Brick Market (not to be confused with the nearby shopping mall, Brick Marketplace). The architect was Peter Harrison, also responsible for the Touro Synagogue (see below). The market has been refurbished and reconfigured to contain this professionally installed illumination of the city's history. It houses boat models, paintings, antique silverware, old photos, and a ship figurehead, and features videos and occasional audio commentaries on Newport history. A printing press used by Benjamin Franklin's brother, James, is also on display.

Newport Art Museum. 76 Bellevue Ave. (at the corner of Beach Rd.) ☎ **401/848-8200.** Admission $4 adults, $3 seniors, $2 students, free for children under 6. Only a voluntary donation charged for entrance Sat 10am–noon. Memorial Day to Labor Day Mon–Tues, Thurs–Sat 10am–5pm, Sun noon–5pm; Labor Day to Memorial Day Mon–Tues, Thurs–Sat 10am–4pm, Sun noon–4pm.

Across the avenue from Touro Park, this was the first Newport commission of Richard Morris Hunt, who went on to design many of the cottages along Bellevue Avenue.

Unlike most of his later Newport houses, this 1862 structure, the former Griswold Mansion, is in the Victorian stick style, a wood construction that had origins in earlier Carpenter Gothic. Now a museum and headquarters of the local art association, it mounts exhibitions of the works of Newport artists, offers classes and lectures, and frequently serves as a venue for concerts.

Touro Park. Bellevue Ave. (between Pelham and Mill sts.).

Opposite the Newport Art Museum, this small park provides a shaded respite from shopping. Its center is the Old Stone Mill. Dreamers like to believe that the eight columns of the roughly circular structure were erected by Vikings. Realists say it was built by Benedict Arnold, a governor of the colony long before his great-great-grandson committed his infamous act of treason during the War for American Independence.

Touro Synagogue. 72 Touro St. (Spring St.) ☎ **401/847-4794.** Free admission. July 4–Labor Day, Sun–Fri 10am–5pm; Labor Day–Columbus Day and Memorial Day–July 4, Mon–Sun 11am–3pm. Columbus Day to Memorial Day Sun 1–3pm, Mon–Fri at 2pm (by appointment only); Sun 1–3pm. Guided tours only.

This is the oldest existing synagogue in the United States, dating from 1763. A Sephardic Jewish community existed in Newport from the mid–17th century (largely refugees from Portugal)—100 years before this building was erected. It was designed by Peter Harrison, who was also responsible for the Brick Market (see "Museum of Newport History," above). The synagogue was closed at the end of its first century for lack of an adequate congregation. It came back into use 100 years later, and was designated a National Historic Site in 1946. On display inside is a 500-year-old Torah.

Next door is the **Newport Historical Society,** 82 Touro St. (☎ **401/846-0813**). In addition to its displays of colonial Newport furnishings and decorative arts, the Society sponsors walking tours (details in "Tours & Cruises," below).

OUTDOOR PURSUITS

✪ **Cliff Walk** skirts the edge of the southern section of town where most of the cottages were built, and provides better views of many of them than can be seen from the street. Traversing its length, high above the crashing surf, is more than a stroll, but less than an arduous hike. It is lined with marine flora, including rose hip, wild roses, goldenrod, and morning glories. For the full 3½-mile length, start at the access point near the intersection of Memorial Boulevard and Eustis Avenue. For a shorter walk, start at the Forty Steps, at the end of Narragansett Avenue, off Bellevue. Leave the walk at Ledge Road and return via Bellevue Ave. Figure 2 to 3 hours for the round-trip, and be warned that there are some mildly rugged sections to negotiate. The walk is open from 9am to 9pm.

Fort Adams State Park, Harrison Ave. (☎ **401/847-2400**), is on the thumb of land that partially encloses Newport Harbor. It can be reached by driving or biking south on Thames Street and west on Wellington Avenue (a section of Ocean Drive, which becomes Harrison Avenue). The 1820s fort for which the park is named is being restored. Boating, ocean swimming, fishing, and sailing are all available on its 105 acres. Open Memorial Day to Labor Day; admission is $4 per car ($2 for Rhode Islanders and seniors). Tours are conducted from the visitor center during summer, daily from 10am to 4pm. Also on the grounds is the **Museum of Yachting** (☎ **401/847-1018**), housed in a stone barracks of the early–19th century. Photographs, videos, paintings, and models chart the history of competitive sailing. Open mid-May to October 31 daily from 10am to 5pm, by appointment the rest of the year. Admission is $3 for adults, $6 for families, $2.50 for seniors, and free for children under 12.

Farther along Ocean Drive, past Hammersmith Farm, is **Brenton Point State Park,** a dramatically scenic preserve that borders the Atlantic, with nothing to impede the waves rolling in and collapsing on the rock-strewn beach. Scuba divers surface offshore and anglers cast from the long breakwater. These breakers are usually high enough for rather sedate surfing.

There are other beaches more appropriate for swimming. The longest (over a mile long) and most popular is **Easton's Beach,** which lies along Route 138A, the extension of Memorial Boulevard, east of town. It's the best choice for families, since the breakers are usually gentle, and there are plenty of facilities, including a bathhouse, eating places, picnic areas, lifeguards, a carousel, and the **Newport Aquarium** (☎ 401/849-8430). On Ocean Drive, less than 2 miles from the south end of Bellevue Avenue, is **Gooseberry Beach,** which is privately owned but open to the public.

Biking is one of the best ways to get around town, especially out to the mansions and along Ocean Drive. Among several rental shops are **Firehouse Bicycle,** 25 Mill St. (☎ 401/847-5700); **Ten Speed Spokes,** 18 Elm St. (☎ 401/847-5609); and **Fun Rentals,** 1 Commercial Wharf (☎ 401/846-3474). The last firm also rents mopeds. **Adventure Sports Rentals,** at the Inn on Long Wharf, 142 Long Wharf (☎ 401/849-4820), not only rents bikes and mopeds, but outboard boats, kayaks, and sailboats, and arranges parasailing outings.

Guided fly-fishing trips and fly-casting instruction are offered by **The Saltwater Edge,** 561 Lower Thames St. (☎ 401/842-0062). Captain Weatherby takes anglers out in his Boston Whaler on half- and full-day quests for yellowfin tuna, blue shark, white marlin, and dorado. He also sells topflight gear in his pro shop, which is open daily.

TOURS & CRUISES

Several organizations conduct tours of the mansions and the downtown historic district. In summer, the **Newport Historical Society,** 82 Touro St. (☎ 401/846-0813), has two itineraries. Tours of Historic Hill leave at 10am and 3pm Thursday and Friday and 10am Saturday, and tours of Cliff Walk at 10am and 3pm on Saturday. Prices are $5 and $7, respectively. **Newport on Foot** leaves the Gateway Visitors Center twice daily on 90-minute tours.

If your car has a cassette deck, a company called **CCInc Auto Tape Tours** produces a 90-minute recorded tour of the mansions. It has an intelligent narration backed by music and sound effects, although it takes a little while to get the hang of when to turn it on and off. The tapes are available at a booth in the Gateway Visitors Center for $12.95 each or directly from the company at P.O. Box 227, 2 Elbrook Dr., Allendale, NJ 07401 (☎ 201/236-1666).

Viking Tours, based at the Gateway Visitors Center (☎ 401/847-6921) has narrated bus tours of the mansions and 1- and 2½-hour harbor cruises on the excursion boat *Viking Queen.*

Yankee Boat Peddlers, Bannister's Wharf (☎ 401/847-0299), schedules narrated cruises of its 72-foot schooner *Madeleine* and its classic powerboat *RumRunner II,* daily in summer, weekends in spring and fall.

One-and-a-half-hour cruises of the bay and harbor are given by **Newport Navigation** on its *Spirit of Newport,* which leaves from Newport Harbor Hotel & Marina (☎ 401/849-3575) twice daily Monday to Friday, three times on weekends. Another possibility is the *Adirondack,* a 78-foot schooner that makes 2-hour cruises from the Newport Yachting Center (☎401/846-1600). Its ticket booth is on America's Cup Boulevard at Commercial Wharf; payment and reservations must be made in advance.

And the **Old Newport Scenic Railway,** 19 America's Cup Ave. (☎ 401/624-6951), has 3-hour excursions in vintage trains along the edge of the bay to the Green Animals Topiary Gardens in Portsmouth, at the northerly end of the island.

SHOPPING

At the heart of the downtown waterfront, **Bannister's Wharf, Bowen's Wharf,** and **Brick Marketplace** have about 60 stores between them, none of them especially compelling.

More interesting, if only for their quirky individuality, are the shops along **Lower Thames Street.** For example, **Aardvark Antiques** (no. 475) specializes in salvaged architectural components and larger items rescued from old houses. Books, nautical charts, and sailing videos are offered at **Armchair Sailor** (no. 543), and for vintage clothing, visit **Cabbage Rose** (no. 493).

Spring Street is noted for its antiques shops, but purveyors of crafts, jewelry, and folk art are here. One of these is **MacDowell Pottery** (no. 140), a studio and retail shop selling ceramics and gifts by Rhode Island artisans; another, the nearby **J. H. Breakell & Co.** (no. 135), is a good source for handcrafted sterling and gold jewelry. Antique boat models, including mounted half-hulls and miniatures in bottles, are displayed along with charts and navigational instruments at **The Nautical Nook** (no. 86). For a pricey memento of Newport's history, check out **The Drawing Room/The Zsolnay Store** (no. 152–154), which stocks 19th-century estate furnishings and specializes in Hungarian Zsolnay ceramics. Folk art and furniture are primary goods at **Liberty Tree** (no. 104).

Spring intersects with **Franklin Street,** which harbors even more antiques shops in its short length, alongside the post office. **Newport China Trade Co.** (no. 8) deals in export porcelain and objects associated with 19th-century China. Take a fat wallet to **The John Gidley House** (no. 22) for European antiques of high order. **Patina** (no. 32) is another dealer in Americana and folk art.

Note that most of these dealers have their own notions about what are appropriate operating hours and may not be open when other stores are.

WHERE TO STAY

The **Gateway Visitors Center** (☎ **800/326-6030** or 401/849-8040) provides a useful service to those who arrive in town without reservations. Motels, hotels, and inns that have vacancies that night are listed on a frequently updated board. Most have a number next to their names, to be called from the free direct-line phones located nearby. With dozens of possibilities, there is nearly always something available, even in summer, but less impulsive travelers will want to make reservations in advance to be certain of getting what they want, especially on summer weekends.

Newport Reservations (☎ **800/842-0102** or 401/842-0102; fax 401/842-0104) is one free service representing a number of hotels, motels, inns, and B&Bs. **Anna's Victorian Connection** (☎ 401/849-2489) is similar, but charges a fee and doesn't represent hotels or motels. They both accept credit cards.

The better motels are located in Middletown, about 3 miles north of downtown Newport. Possibilities include **Courtyard by Marriott,** 9 Commerce Dr. (☎ **401/ 849-8000**), **Quality Inn Suites,** 936 W. Main Rd. (☎ **401/846-7600**), the **Newport Gateway Hotel,** 31 West Main Rd. (☎ 401/847-2735), and the **Howard Johnson Lodge,** 351 W. Main Rd. (☎ **401/849-2000**).

The rates given below generally have very wide ranges. Newport hotel rates shift dramatically to meet seasonal demand, so a room with a $200 price tag on weekends in July might be half that price in the spring. The summer season is usually defined as Memorial Day to Columbus Day, with lower prices in effect the rest of the year.

VERY EXPENSIVE

Castle Hill. Ocean Dr., Newport, RI 02840. ☎ **888/466-1355** or 401/849-3800. Fax 401/849-3838. 40 units, 6 harbor houses, 17 beach cottages. TEL. Summer $225–$250 double; $250–$325 suite. Fall–spring $95–$165 double; $125–325 suite. Weekly cottage rentals $900–$1,100. Rates include breakfast. AE, MC, V. Open weekends only Nov–Apr. Closed Jan. Limited accommodations for children under 12.

The setting, with 40 beautiful oceanfront acres on a near island, is the overwhelming attraction of this venerable resort. But now that a sorely needed renovation of the 1874 Victorian mansion and its outbuildings is bearing fruit, even a visit in foul weather is a treat. The former summer-camp dowdiness of the bedrooms is fast becoming a memory, and new marble bathrooms, TVs, and air conditioners in most units now help to justify the high summer rates. Best value is the Harbor Houses, which have been gutted and completely overhauled, with new furniture, TVs, whirlpools, and porches overlooking the bay. But many guests still like the more basic, separate Beach Cottages down by the entrance road. With only functional furnishings and no central heating, they are available only in summer. Renovations are underway, however, and children are accepted in the cottages, though not in the main house.

Dining: Meals in the revived dining room keep guests on the premises to sample the earnest young chef's inventive cuisine. Use of native produce is paramount. The handsome taproom is sheathed in wood, with a riveting view (shared by the dining room, deck, and many of the bedrooms) of sailing ships on Narragansett Bay. Breakfast buffets are expansive, with daily hot entrees. Main courses at dinner cost $18 to $27. Live jazz is performed on Sundays.

✪ **Cliffside Inn.** 2 Seaview Ave. (near Cliff Ave.), Newport, RI 02840. ☎ **800/845-1811** or 401/847-1811. Fax 401/848-5850. www.cliffsideinn.com. 15 units. A/C TV TEL. $195–$285 double; $285–$475 suite. Rates include breakfast. AE, CB, DC, DISC, MC, V.

Assuming that money is no object, there are really only two places to stay in Newport—this and the Francis Malbone House (see below).

It is difficult to imagine what further improvements might be made in these accommodations, although they keep tinkering and upgrading. Eleven of the fifteen units have whirlpool baths and working fireplaces; all have nightly turndown service and terry-cloth robes. Antiques and admirable reproductions are generously deployed, including Eastlake originals and Victorian fancies that include (room 11) an amusing "birdcage" shower from 1890. Favorite units are the Garden Suite, a duplex with private garden and a big double bath with radiant heat beneath the Peruvian tile floors, and the Tower Suite, with a green marble bath, a fireplace, and a cedar-lined steeple above the bed. Coffee, juice, and the newspaper of your choice are delivered to your room even before the full breakfast. A showy afternoon tea of sweets and savories is an additional enticement.

✪ **Francis Malbone House.** 392 Thames St. (south of Memorial Blvd.), Newport, RI 02840. ☎ **800/846-0392** or 401/846-0392. Fax 401/848-5956. www.malbone.com. 18 units. A/C TEL. Summer $175–$375 double; winter $155–$295 double. Rates include breakfast. AE, MC, V. No children under 12.

Nine new rooms have been added in a wing of the original 1760 colonial house. Very nice they are, with king-size beds, working fireplaces, and excellent reproductions of period furniture. Four of them share two sunken gardens, and three have whirlpool baths built for two. But given a choice, take a room in the old section. There, antiques outnumber repros, glowing Oriental rugs lie upon buffed wide-board floors, and silks and linens are deployed unsparingly. There are no TVs in the main building, though—they'd destroy the effect. In the front hall is a print of a painting by Gilbert Stuart of shipping merchant Francis Malbone and his brother. A full breakfast is served, and afternoon refreshments are set out. The most interesting part of the waterfront is right outside the door.

Vanderbilt Hall. 41 Mary St. (west of Bellevue), Newport, RI 02840. ☎**401/846-6200**. Fax 401/846-0701. www.vanderbilthall.com. 50 units. A/C TV TEL. Summer $195–$520 double, $445–$720 suite. Fall–spring $155–395, $335–$565 suite. Winter $95–$310 double, $225–$460 suite. Rates include afternoon tea. AE, DC, DISC, MC, V.

After its $10 million dormer-to-cellar renovation, this 1908 Georgian Revival mansion gives no hint of its origin as a YMCA. Built with a donation by Alfred Vanderbilt, it would now suit its benefactor as one of his residences. The many varied public rooms are marked by the serenity fostered by judiciously placed antiques, paintings, artful reproductions, and Oriental carpets laid on wall-to-wall carpeting. The reception desk is hidden off to one side to heighten the illusion of a private club or home. Bedrooms and suites extend the mood, with armoires instead of closets and period patterns on draperies, beds, and sofas. In the older wing, the ceilings are 18 feet high. Discreet modernity is provided with hair dryers, TV cable, and dataports on the phones. If you hope to impress someone, though, spring for the grand duplex Lighthouse Suite.

Dining: Four dining rooms set the tone with Rosenthal crystal and Wedgwood china in one and a less formal glass conservatory with plants and adjoining terrace where three daily meals and tea are served. The already acclaimed menu can be inadequately described as "eclectic American," with a five-course prix fixe of $50.

Amenities: Small fitness room, indoor pool, whirlpool, steam and sauna.

EXPENSIVE

Admiral Fitzroy. 398 Thames St. (south of Memorial Blvd.), Newport, RI 02840. ☎ **800/343-2863** or 401/848-8000. Fax 401/848-8006. www.admiralsinns.com. E-mail: 5star@admiralsinns.com. 17 units. A/C TV TEL. Summer $140–$225 double; winter $85–$125 double. Rates include breakfast. AE, DISC, MC, V.

The largest of a group of three local inns, the Admiral Fitzroy attracts many Europeans and Australians drawn to the international yachting events held here. Despite the current name, the antique barometers, and the ship model at the end of the reception desk, this used to be a nunnery. That doesn't mean Spartan gloom. Rehabilitating old buildings is a central interest of the owners, whose attention to detail is seen in the hand-painted floral renderings found in every room. Many rooms have "peek" harbor views, but you'll get a better look from the roof deck, which offers a 360° panorama. In addition to the breakfast buffet, the kitchen serves a choice of hot dishes each morning. The staff is unfailingly pleasant. Since they accept children, as many inns do not, lots of families make this home base.

If the 1854 Fitzroy is full, reservations can be made through the same telephone numbers for the similar **Admiral Benbow,** at 93 Pelham St., and the **Admiral Farragut,** at 31 Clarke St. These places rotate 2- to 4-week closings each winter.

✪ **Beech Tree.** 34 Rhode Island Ave., Newport, RI 02840. ☎ **800/748-6565** or 401/847-9794. Fax 401/847-6824. www.beechtreeinn.com. 15 units. A/C TV TEL. May 1 to mid-Nov $109–$275 double; late Nov to April $89–$195 double. Rates include breakfast. AE, DC, MC, V. Drive north on Broadway from downtown and turn right on Rhode Island Ave. It's the eighth house on the left.

Arrive here on a Friday evening and the avuncular owner sits you down to a bowl of chowder and a glass of wine. After that, a lot of guests skip dinner and go straight upstairs to soak in a whirlpool bath. The other big event of the day is the most elaborate breakfast served by any B&B in Newport. There are bagels, muffins, pastries, fruit bowls, and five juices to pave the way for plates heaped with eggs, waffles, pancakes, sausages, and/or bacon. Lunch becomes irrelevant. The owners even leave out brandy and cordials and invite guests to help themselves. Rooms have king- or queen-size beds and good reading chairs. The four newest rooms are especially striking, ideal for romantic overnights, with working fireplaces and big whirlpool baths sharing space with king-size beds. In public areas, a chatty family atmosphere prevails.

Doubletree Islander. Goat Island, Newport, RI 02840. ☎ **800/222-8733** or 401/849-2600. Fax 401/846-7210. 264 units. A/C TV TEL. Summer $160–$289 double; winter $99–$175 double. AE, CB, DC, DISC, MC, V.

More than 25 years old (previously a Hilton and then a Sheraton), the Doubletree is notable primarily for its full hotel services and its location on an island at the northern end of Newport Harbor. You might expect such a place to be impersonal, but most of the staff endeavors to be pleasant. There are delightful views of the harbor and town from most of the guest rooms.

Dining/Diversions: Both formal and casual restaurants are on the premises, along with a lounge.

Amenities: Fitness center with sauna and spa with massage, facials, and wraps; indoor and outdoor pools, two tennis courts.

Elm Tree Cottage. 336 Gibbs Ave., Newport, RI 02840. ☎ **888/356-8733** or 401/849-1610. Fax 401/849-2084. www.elmtreebnb.com. 6 units. A/C. July–Oct $185–$250 double; $350 suite. Nov–Apr $135–$195 double; $235–$295 suite. May–June $150–$250 double; $275–$350 suite. Rates include breakfast. AE, MC, V. No children under 14.

Only a couple of blocks from the beach, this B&B is placed among Newport's best-loved inns. The flamboyant Victorian manse is a pleasure to behold, inside and out. In an agreeable deviation from local convention, many of the furnishings are French, though they do reflect the Victorian time period, with Louis XV as a central inspiration. All but one of the rooms have fireplaces. One of the owners creates stained-glass panels and plays musical instruments in the spare time that only innkeepers seem to be able to find. Look for the bar with silver dollars embedded in its surface in the sitting room, where she has two pianos and puts out refreshments in the afternoon. Breakfasts are ample.

The Victorian Ladies. 63 Memorial Blvd. (east of Bellevue Ave.), Newport, RI 02840. ☎ and fax **401/849-9960.** www.victorianladies.com. E-mail: info@victorianladies.com. 11 units. A/C TV. Summer $145–$195 double; winter $95–$145 double. Rates include breakfast. MC, V,. Closed Jan. No children under 10.

The owners of this little compound of four small buildings tirelessly add new rooms, fixtures, and comforts. They have chosen a version of Victorian decor in keeping with the age of the main house, but updated to suit contemporary tastes. Every guest room is different, but most have queen-size beds, often four-posters. Pocket gardens extend an added welcome for chats and idles. Six rooms have phones. Full breakfasts include homemade breads and hot entrees. Newport's main shopping district is nearby.

MODERATE

Mill Street. 75 Mill St., Newport, RI 02840 (2 blocks east of Thames). ☎ **800/392-1316** or 401/849-9500. Fax 401/848-5131. 23 units. A/C TV TEL. June–Sept $115–$325 suite; Oct–May $65–$235 suite. Rates include breakfast and afternoon tea. Children under 16 stay free in parents' room. AE, CB, DC, MC, V.

Something different from most Newport inns, this turn-of-the-century sawmill was scooped out and rebuilt from the walls in. Apart from exposed expanses of brick and an occasional wood beam, all of it is new. An all-suite facility, even the smallest unit has a queen-size bed in the bedroom and a convertible sofa in the sitting room, making it a good deal for families. Bagged snacks and soft drinks are provided in every suite. The more expensive duplexes have private balconies, but everyone can use the rooftop deck, where breakfast is served on warm days. Coffee and cookies are set out in the lobby in the afternoon. During quiet times, rates dip as low as $59 a night.

INEXPENSIVE

Jailhouse. 13 Marlborough St. (east of Thames St., on the same block as the White Horse Tavern), Newport, RI 02840. ☎ **800/427-9444** or 401/847-4638. Fax 401/849-0605. 22 units. A/C TV TEL. Summer $85–$250 double; winter $55–$215 double. Rates include breakfast and afternoon tea. AE, MC, V.

They claim that this was once a colonial jail, although it doesn't look as if it's that old or served that purpose. In any case, the management has toned down the incarceration theme and minimized references to its "prison staff" and the "cell block" rooms. What remains, including the caged reception desk, isn't as cute as someone thinks, but there are compensations—the rates, primarily. Even during a festival week in July, a room can be had here for as little as $85 (the high rate noted above is for a two-bedroom suite). And that includes motel conveniences like cable TV with HBO and a fridge in every room. Listless efforts at decor have pegboards instead of closets, but also new bathrooms and carpeting.

Pilgrim House. 123 Spring St. (between Mary and Church sts.), Newport, RI 02840. ☎ **800/525-8373** or 401/846-0040. Fax 401/838-0547. 11 units, 2 with shared bathroom. A/C. Summer $65–$175 double; winter $55–$125 double. Rates include breakfast. MC, V.. Often closed in Jan. No children under 12.

This narrow, four-story, elevatorless mid-Victorian has a rooftop deck with unobstructed harbor views, its top selling point. On good days, you can have your "enhanced" continental breakfast there. Afternoon refreshments might be sherry and shortbread. The rooms don't have phones or TVs, they do have clock radios, and the common room has a fireplace, and TV/VCR. The two cheapest rooms share a bath, logical for a family of three or four.

WHERE TO DINE

There are far too many restaurants in Newport to give full treatment even to only the best among them. Equal in many ways to those recommended below are **Canfield House,** 5 Memorial Blvd. (☎ 401/847-0416); **Yesterday's & The Place,** 28 Washington Sq. (☎ 401/847-0116); and **The West Deck,** 1 Waites Wharf (☎ 401/847-3610).

VERY EXPENSIVE

Asterix & Obelix. 599 Lower Thames St. ☎ 401/841-8833. Reservations recommended on summer weekends. Main courses $19.25–$29.75. MC, V. Daily 5pm–10pm (until 11pm Sat–Sun). CONTEMPORARY/FRENCH.

Named for the famous French cartoon characters, for no obvious reason, this cheerful place does render classic Gallic bistro dishes. Come and remember how delectable escargot à la Bourguignonne, lobster navarin, steak au poivre, and sole meunière can be. To add a note of authenticity, bluepoints, Wellfleets, and littlenecks are opened to order as starters. Daily specials, on the other hand, are considerably more venturesome, blending ingredients and techniques of many cuisines. What was once a car-repair shop has been given great splashes of color, with a bar installed on the left and an open kitchen in back. Sunday dinners are served to live jazz from 7pm. Breads are provided by the owner-chef's **Boulangerie Obelix,** at 382 Spring St.

Bouchard. 505 Lower Thames St. ☎ 401/846-0123. Reservations recommended in season. Main courses $18.75–$26. AE, DISC, MC, V. Wed–Mon 6–9pm (until 10pm Sat–Sun). Closed first 10 days in Jan. FRENCH.

Settle in for the evening on comfortable Empire chairs that make that indulgence possible. The ebullient headwaiter fairly dances between the widely spaced tables to take your coat and your cocktail order, recite the night's specials, record your selections, and pour your wine. It is a polished performance, and what issues from the kitchen validates that promise. Presentations are thoughtfully conceived, attractive without voguish excesses. Here come pheasant redolent with lavishly applied truffles and puff pastries with lobster nuggets, split asparagus spears, and a lemony light white sauce— typical of the dishes long relished by a clientele who started learning about classic French cooking when Julia Child was still in black-and-white. This is dining in a grand tradition.

EXPENSIVE

Black Pearl. Bannister's Wharf. ☎ **401/846-5264.** Reservations and jackets required for dinner in Commodore's Room. Main courses $13–$23 in the Tavern, $17.50–$28.50 in the Commodore's Room. AE, MC, V. Tavern daily 11am–11pm; Commodore daily 11:30am–2:30pm and 6–11pm. Closed 6 weeks in winter. SEAFOOD/AMERICAN.

This long building near the end of the wharf is divided into two sections. The Tavern has an atmospheric bar and a room painted mostly in black with marine charts on the walls. The Commodore's Room is more formal, and a 2-pound lobster goes for $35, with trimmings. The simpler preparations of fish, duck, and beef are the ones to order. In the Tavern, don't miss the definitive Newport chowder, followed by a Pearlburger or one of the other overstuffed sandwiches. And in summer, the menu is similar at the dining patio and an open-air bar out on the wharf.

✪ **Cheeky Monkey.** 14 Perry Mill Wharf. ☎ **401/845-9494.** Reservations recommended in season. Main courses $12.95–$25. AE, DC, MC, V. June–Sept Sun–Thurs 5:30–10pm, Fri–Sat 5:30–11pm. Oct–May Tues–Sat 5:30–10pm. ECLECTIC.

In a town blessed with more than its share of outstanding chefs, James Maxwell is a star. The canny owners of the Gatehouse in Providence brought him on board for this new enterprise in 1997. Every one of his creations is an explosion of flavor—his spicy fried calamari redefines that now-common appetizer—and even his seemingly odd ideas work. Witness Caesar salad with fried oysters. You can make a meal of the appetizers (be sure to include the sensational smoky quesadilla). Decor is of the frisky sort: water glasses bear female nudes in relief, and there are leopard-print dadoes and paintings of anthropomorphic simians bearing resemblances to George Burns and Diana Vreeland. Someone stole the stuffed gorilla that used to occupy a seat in the bar.

✪ **Clarke Cooke House.** Bannister's Wharf. ☎ **401/849-2900.** Reservations recommended on summer weekends. Main courses $14.95–$21.95 in the Candy Store and Grill, $22–$30 in the Dining Room. AE, DC, DISC, MC, V. Candy Store and Grill daily 11:30am–10:30pm in summer; Fri–Sun 11:30am–10:30pm in winter. Dining Room daily 6–10pm in summer; Wed–Sun 6–10pm in winter. ECLECTIC.

For many, this is the quintessential Newport restaurant. Most of its several levels are open to the air in summer and glassed-in in winter, with overhead fans dispersing the sea breezes. Several bars lubricate conversation. The one on the main floor has a 5-foot model of a schooner on the back wall and the real thing straining at hawsers right outside. The 19th-century structure was moved to the wharf from America's Cup Avenue in the 1970s.

Up on the formal third floor, they sauté your lobster out of the shell while you put away appetizers of wild mushrooms with leeks and morels bound with mushroom butter ($9.50) or duck foie-gras terrine with Black Mission fig compote ($17.50). If that seems too rich for wallet or liver, spare the walk upstairs and opt for swordfish with red-pepper coulis or the Thai-style whole-wheat spaghetti with jalapeño, shrimp, cilantro, and peanuts. At one side is an espresso bar, and people stop in throughout the day for a latte, a beer, or a sandwich.

Le Bistro. Bowen's Wharf (near America's Cup Ave.). ☎ **401/849-7778.** Reservations recommended on summer weekends. Main courses $12.95–$23.95 ($34.95 for a 2-lb. lobster). AE, DC, DISC, MC, V. Daily 11:30am–11pm. FRENCH.

This kitchen is among the most capable in town, assembling lightened versions of French country standards. A rough country pâté is worth the wait—nibble at crusty bread while checking out the congenial lot that frequents the place. Eventually comes the excellent bouillabaisse, the Black Angus tenderloin with Saga sauce, the creamy lobster fettuccine tossed with snow peas and sweet peppers. The last three months of the year, a sub-menu of game is introduced, followed by another three months of classic bistro recipes. The second-floor dining room is somewhat more formal than the third floor, which contains the bar and a few tables.

MODERATE

☼ **Scales & Shells.** 527 Lower Thames St. ☎ **401/846-3474.** Reservations accepted May–Sept. Main courses $9.95–$18.95. No credit cards. Sun–Thurs 5–10pm, Fri–Sat 5–11pm. SEAFOOD.

That graceless name reflects the uncompromising character of this clangorous fish house. Diners who insist upon a modicum of elegance should head for the less boisterous upstairs room, called "Upscales." A waiting list lengthens at the door as the evening wears on.

Lots of different fish and shellfish are listed on the big blackboard in back. An open kitchen with a low counter starts almost at the door—no secrets there. They put together ingredients in guileless preparations that allow the natural tastes to prevail. Substantial, too: the "large" appetizer of fried calamari is enough for four eaters. Bluefish with black olives and grilled yellow peppers is typical. Also in front, the stressed bartender not only pours every drink, but opens every clam and oyster served. Smoking isn't permitted.

☼ **White Horse Tavern.** Marlborough and Farewell sts. ☎ **401/849-3600.** Reservations recommended. Jackets required for men at dinner. Main courses $14–$19. AE, DC, DISC, MC, V. Wed–Mon noon–3pm; daily 6–10pm. NEW AMERICAN.

Still going strong after 325 years, the White Horse claims to be the oldest operating tavern in America. Once the residence of a pirate-turned-tavern-keeper, it has undergone many alterations, but retains its authenticity. On the ground floor are a bar and two dining rooms, with a big fireplace once used for cooking. The upstairs has a similar arrangement.

Given the setting, the kitchen could have chosen to coast on Indian pudding and boiled dinners. But the food is quite good, from the daily soup-and-sandwich lunch specials ($9 to $10) to the mesquite-grilled veal chop with an ancho rub and applejack reduction sauce. About a third of the dishes involve seafood. Prices are significantly lower at lunch and at Sunday brunch. Smoke-free.

Brick Alley Pub. 140 Thames St. ☎ **401/849-6334.** Reservations recommended for dinner. Main courses $8.95–$21.95. AE, CB, DC, DISC, MC, V. Mon–Fri 11:30am–midnight, Sat–Sun 11am–midnight. ECLECTIC.

Just so you know what you're getting into, the cab of a red Chevy pickup truck is next to the soup-and-salad bar. Walls are covered with old advertising posters and a room in back has a pool table, pinball machine, and video games. Families, tourists, working stiffs, and yachtsmen squeeze through the doors into the thronged front dining rooms, the bar in the middle, and out onto the tree-shaded terrace in back. They're big on frozen daiquiris. The voluminous menu doesn't leave out much: stuffed clams, six Caesar salads, hot cherry peppers stuffed with prosciutto and provolone, Cajun catfish, nachos, 20 kinds of burgers, seven pizzas, chicken teriyaki, and "triple hot buf-falo shrimp pasta" (whatever that might be)—with the admonition, "No crybabies!" It's loud and good-natured and prices are palatable if you avoid lobster.

INEXPENSIVE

Flo's Clam Shack. 4 Wave Ave. ☎ **401/847-8141**. Platters $6.95–$12.95. No credit cards. March to late Sept, daily 11am–10pm, late Sept to Feb Wed–Sun 11am–9pm. SEAFOOD.

Located just past Easton's Beach over the Newport/Middletown line, this old-timer is more than a lopsided strand-side shanty—but not *much* more. Step up to the order window (inside or outside), choose from the handwritten menu, and receive a stone with a number painted on it. They'll call you. What you'll get, if you're wise, is clams, on a plate or on a roll. Cooked swiftly to order, they are as tender as any to which you might have set your teeth. All the fish is that way, as if it were netted that morning from the bay out front. You can get beef here, but why? Upstairs are a raw bar and deck even more happily ramshackle than below.

Music Hall Café. 250 Thames St. ☎ **401/848-2330**. Main courses $9.75–$16.75. AE, DISC, MC, V. Daily noon–10pm. SOUTHWESTERN.

Named for the 1894 building in which it is located, this restaurant looks straight out of Santa Fe. There are carvings of howling coyotes, a kiva ladder, bleached skulls, and hand-painted Mexican tiles on the bar. Under the tricolored awning out front is a row of green tables, ideal for evaluating the Thames Street scene. While fajitas and que-sadillas are still available, the menu is moving away from Tex-Mex conventions to pastas and barbecued items. Even when every chair is occupied, the place isn't crowded.

NEWPORT AFTER DARK

The most likely places to spend an evening of elbow bending, conversation, or lis-tening to music lie along **Thames Street.** Bars are unthreatening and casual. The **Candy Store** (☎ 401/849-2900) of Cooke House, at Bannister's Wharf, has a classic waterside bar. Nearby, two of the most obvious possibilities are **The Red Parrot** (☎ 401/847-3140), at Memorial Boulevard and Thames Street, which has the look of an Irish saloon and features jazz combos Thursday to Sunday year-round, and **One Pelham East** (no phone), at Thames and Pelham streets, with a cafe to one side, a small dance floor, and a stage for rockers at the front. **Park Place Tavern** (☎ 401/847-1767) at the corner of Thames and Church streets, above a Starbucks, makes room for jazz duos Thursday to Sunday.

A full schedule of live music is on the plate at the **Newport Blues Café,** at Thames and Green streets (☎ 401/841-5110), with bands and shouters Monday to Saturday evenings in season (Thursday to Saturday off-season) and a Sunday gospel brunch. With its fireplace, much dark wood, and the massive steel door in back that used to guard the safe of this former bank, this has a lot more class than most of the town's music bars. Meals are available Thursday through Sunday from 5 to 10pm.

Attracting a younger crowd less attuned to its surroundings is **Sully's Pub,** 108 Williams St. (☎ 401/849-4747). Folk and rock duos play for an under-35 singles more interested in each other than in music or the event of the moment shown on eight TV sets. The pool table stays busy. Upstairs is **Señor Frogg's,** a disco with a rudi-mentary light show and a talkative DJ.

David's, 28 Prospect Hill St. (☎ 401/847-9697), north of Thames, is Newport's only gay and lesbian bar, with an old-fashioned taproom and an adjoining disco right out of the 1970s.

While the Basque sport of jai alai is proclaimed the fastest in the world, the real reason for the existence of **Newport Jai Alai,** 150 Admiral Kalbfus Rd. (☎ **401/849-5000**), is gambling. In addition to the game itself, and its highly complicated scoring and odds systems, there are over 400 video slot machines and simulcasts of horse and dog races from around the country. Slots are open daily from 10am until 1am. Jai alai games, held from May through October, start at 7pm Wednesday to Friday, at noon Monday and Saturday, and at 1pm on Sunday.

4 South County: From Wickford to Watch Hill

Travelers rushing along the Boston–New York corridor inevitably choose I-95 to get from Providence to the Connecticut border. They either do not have the time for a detour or don't know that the nearby shore has some of the best beaches and most congenial fishing and resort villages in New England. This is called "South County," a designation that has no official status, but refers to the coast that is the southerly edge of Bristol County. It has escaped much of the commercial development that besets most of the New England coast and preserves not only long beaches but many small-boat harbors, wetlands, and small state parks.

Rhode Islanders certainly know about the beguilements of South County, though, so try to avoid weekends in July and August, when the crush of day-trippers can turn these two-lane roads into parking lots. Worst of all is arriving on a Friday afternoon and departing on a Sunday evening. If those are your only options, however, lock in lodging reservations well in advance.

Definitions are fuzzy, but for our purposes, South County runs from Wickford, near Providence, to Westerly, nudging Connecticut.

ESSENTIALS

GETTING THERE From Providence or Boston, take I-95 south, leaving it at Exit 9 to pick up Route 4, also a limited-access highway. In about 7 miles, exit onto Route 102 east, and you'll soon arrive in Wickford. From Newport, cross the Newport and Jamestown bridges on Route 138 to Route 1A north, and follow it to Wickford. Narragansett, at the center of South County's beach country, is 32 miles southwest of Providence and 14 miles west of Newport.

VISITOR INFORMATION The **chamber of commerce** sponsors the tourist information office in the landmark Towers on Route 1A in Narragansett (☎ **401/783-7121**). The **South County Tourism Council** at 4808 Tower Hill Rd. in Wakefield (☎ **800/548-4662** or 401/789-4422) is a good information source, and on request will mail a useful 48-page brochure, *South County Style.*

WICKFORD

Apart from those crowded summer weekends, a day or two in South County is as stress-free and laid back as an outing can be. There is nothing that can be regarded as a must-see sight, hardly any museums to speak of, and only a couple of historic houses to divert from serious cafe-sitting, sunbathing, and shopping—and these are the chief pursuits in Wickford, a tidy village that crowds the cusp of a compact harbor.

Sailors and fishermen, artists and craftspeople are among the residents, all of them evident within a block on either side of the **Brown Street** bridge that crosses the narrow neck of the waterway connecting Academy Cove with the harbor, where both working and pleasure boats share the crowded waters of the port. Most of the shopping of interest clusters there, slipping over to adjoining **Main Street.** Buildings in the area are largely survivors from the 18th and 19th centuries. Parking is usually easy to find, for this is the quiet end of South County.

One place that catches the eye is **The Shaker Shop,** 16 W. Main St. (☎ **401/ 294-7779**), which features handcrafted replicas of the clean-limbed furniture of the eponymous religious sect. Quilts, baskets, and boxes are also displayed, and cooking and crafts demonstrations are often staged on weekends. Next to the shop, at the same street address, is **Seaport Tavern** (☎ **401/294-5771**). Its deck is just the spot for a snack, a light meal, or a glass of iced tea.

Proceed south on Route 1A, known through here as Boston Neck Road. About a mile south of Hamilton, watch for the side street on the right with a marker for the **Gilbert Stuart Birthplace,** 815 Gilbert Stuart Rd. (☎ **401/294-3001**). This may be the one historic homestead in South County that is worth a detour, and not because the painter, famous for his portraits of George Washington, was born here. (After all, he left for good in young adulthood, and none of his original art is on display.) It is the setting and the two preserved buildings that reward a visit. First is a weathered gristmill dating from the late 1600s; second, the Stuart birthplace itself, built over his father's snuff mill. The undershot waterwheel and millstones still work, powered by controlled discharges from the adjacent pond. Admission is $3 for adults, $1 for children 6 to 12, free for children under 6, and you have to go on the guided tour. Open from April through October, Thursday to Monday from 11am to 4:30pm.

Still on Route 1A, on the right, south of Saunderstown, is the **Casey Farm** (☎ **401/295-1030**). Owned by the Society for the Preservation of New England Antiquities, the working 300-acre farmstead is a handsome 18th-century complex of barns and houses. Free-range chickens hop along the carefully laid stone walls that section the fields. The farm is only open to visitors June 1 to October 15, Tuesday, Thursday, and Saturday from 1 to 5pm. Admission for adults is $3, children $1.50.

NARRAGANSETT & THE BEACHES

Continuing south on 1A from the Casey Farm, the pace quickens, at least from late spring to foliage season. After crossing the Narrow River Inlet, the road bends around toward **Narragansett Pier**—its name derives from a 19th-century amusement wharf that no longer exists. Along here, and several miles on south to Port Judith and Jerusalem, are some of the most desirable beaches in New England. They are made so by their swaths of fine sand, relatively clean waters, and summer water temperatures that average about 70°. Also, shops and food stands facing the water generally avoid honky-tonk excesses.

After a few blocks, Route 1A makes a sharp right turn (west), but stick to the shore, proceeding south on Ocean Road. Straight ahead is **The Towers,** a massive stone structure that spans the road between cylindrical towers with conical roofs. It is all that remains of the Gilded Age Narragansett Casino, which was designed by the New York firm of McKim, Mead & White, but was lost in a 1900 fire. In the seaward tower is the **Narragansett Tourist Information Office** (☎ **401/783-7121**), run by the local chamber of commerce, whose attendants can help find lodging for visitors without reservations.

WHERE TO STAY

There are several inns and hotels in the vicinity, many of them looking out over the water across wide lawns. Those who prefer the predictability of a motel might consider the **Village Motel,** 1 Beach St., Narragansett, RI 02882 (☎ **800/843-7437** or 401/783-6767), across the street from the strand.

Stone Lea. 40 Newton Ave., Narragansett, RI 02882. ☎ **401/783-9546.** www.webitor. com. 8 units. $150–$225. Rates include breakfast. MC, V. Weekends only Apr–May and Oct–Nov; closed Dec–Mar.

Situated near the crest of a cliff that falls into the ocean, this McKim, Mead & White 1884 commission is an antique-filled delight to wander through, if a bit formal in tone. The terrace overlooking the sea is a special treat at sunset. Lawn croquet and the mock-antique pool table are other diversions; there's a TV in the sitting room. Fresh paint and wallpaper have been applied recently, and all beds and linens replaced. Breakfasts are substantial, often including pancakes or quiche.

WHERE TO DINE

Coast Guard House. 40 Ocean Rd. ☎ **401/789-0700.** Main courses $13.50–$22.95. AE, DC, DISC, MC, V. Mon–Thurs 11:30am–3pm and 5–10pm, Fri 11:30am–3pm and 5–11pm, Sat 5–11pm, Sun 10am–2pm and 4–10pm. Closed first 2 weeks in Jan. SEAFOOD/AMERICAN.

Adjacent to The Towers is this 1888 former Coast Guard headquarters, now a highly regarded restaurant. It has recovered from a devastating 1991 hurricane, and enjoys unobstructed views of the beach and breakers crashing a few feet below its wraparound picture windows. Despite the location, the menu features more meat dishes than seafood, but all are executed with a measure of sophistication. Do sample the Rhode Island clam chowder, prepared with broth, not the traditional milk. There is another bar on the covered deck upstairs. On summer weekends a pop duo plays for dancing.

✪ A SIDE TRIP TO POINT JUDITH

Follow scenic Ocean Road south from The Towers, soon arriving at **Scarborough State Beach.** Noticeably well kept, with a row of modern pavilions for picnicking and changing, it has ample parking and surroundings unsullied by brash commercial enterprises. The beach is largely hard-packed sand, pebbly in streaks and fairly narrow at high tide. While it has a mild surf that makes it good for families with young children, sections of it are often also jammed with frolicking young people.

Continuing on Ocean Road to the end, you'll reach the **Point Judith Lighthouse,** 1460 Ocean Rd. (☎ **401/789-0444**). Built in 1816, the brick beacon is a photo op that can be approached but not entered.

GALILEE

Backtrack along Ocean Road, turning left on Route 108, then left again on Sand Hill Cove Road, past the dock of the only year-round ferries to Block Island, and into the Port of Galilee. At the end, past a cluster of restaurants beside the channel connecting Point Judith Pond with the ocean, is the redundantly named **Salty Brine State Beach.** Though small, it is protected by a long breakwater that blunts the waves produced by the passing vessels and is a good choice for families with younger children. On the opposite side of the channel is popular **East Matunuck State Beach,** where waves break upon the sand at an angle, producing enough action to permit decent surfing on some summer days.

To get a better sense of the area from the water, consider the 1¾-hour tour on the *Southland,* which departs from State Pier in Galilee (☎ **401/783-2954**). It's a renovated Mississippi riverboat that hugs the coast as it moves past fishing villages and beaches. Prices are $6 for adults, $4 for children 4 to 12. Reservations aren't necessary and there's a bar and snack counter on board.

Another possible excursion is a **whale-watching cruise** on one of the three boats of the **Frances Fleet,** 2 State St., Point Judith (☎ **800/662-2824** or 401/783-4988). Cruises are made July 1 to Labor Day, Monday to Saturday from 1pm to about 6pm, depending on the location of the whales. It isn't cheap, at $30 for adults, $27 for seniors, and $20 for children under 12; but the sight of a monster humpback leaping from the water is unforgettable. Numerous party and charter boats leave for fishing expeditions from Point Judith.

WHERE TO DINE

George's of Galilee. 250 Sand Hill Cove Rd. ☎ **401/783-2306.** Main courses $9.75–$18.95 (market prices for lobster). AE, DISC, MC, V. May–Oct daily noon–10pm; Nov–Apr Thurs–Sun noon–2:30pm and 6–9:30pm. SEAFOOD/AMERICAN.

The impulse to drive as far as you can without winding up in the drink may account for the popularity of George's. It can't be the food, which is mostly ordinary. Anyway, prices aren't exorbitant, and while it can be brassy on weekends, its decks give good vantage to watch the boat and ferry traffic on the adjacent channel. As for food, give the fried clams and the stuffies a thought, maybe picking them up at the take-out window and carrying them over to the picnic tables by the beach.

WESTERLY

Although much of the 30-square-mile township remains peacefully semirural, it contains over a dozen villages, notably the land's-end resort of Watch Hill, and several contiguous public beaches on slender barrier islands enclosing large saltwater ponds. The village of Westerly presses up against the Pawcatuck River delineating the Connecticut border, making the area an attractive lodging alternative within short drives of Mystic Seaport and the Foxwoods casino complex.

Westerly found fame and profit in its extensive granite quarries, a product used for monuments and buildings throughout the Northeast. Shipping the granite and the textiles that were manufactured in the township in the 19th century called for a railroad, and Amtrak trains still stop here.

Stretching from the eastern edge of the township to the southwesternmost tip of the state at Watch Hill are **Dunes Park Beach, Atlantic Beach, Misquamicut State Beach,** and **Napatree Point Barrier Beach.** Most are noted for their fine-grained sand and swimming in gentle surf with slow drop-offs, explaining their popularity with families. While its beach is unremarkable, **Napatree Point** is special for its abundance of protected seabirds.

From Connecticut, take I-95 to Exit 92 south, following Route 2 south to U.S. 1, then west across the border into Westerly center. From Providence and points north, drive south on U.S. 1, toward Connecticut. **Amtrak** trains from Boston and New York stop in Westerly several times daily. There is a pull-over information office on I-95 near the Connecticut border, and a **chamber of commerce** office at 74 Post Rd. in Westerly (☎ **800/732-7636**).

WHERE TO STAY & DINE

Shelter Harbor Inn. 10 Wagner Rd., Westerly, RI 02891. ☎ **800/468-8883** or 401/322-8883. Fax 401/322-7907. 23 units. TV. May–Oct $95–$136 double; Nov–Apr $72–$115 double. Rates include breakfast. AE, CB, DC, DISC, MC, V.

If it's time to stop for the night, for dinner, or simply a spectacular Sunday brunch (reservations essential), watch for the entrance to this venerable inn off U.S. 1, about 6 miles east of Westerly town center. Parts of the main building date to 1810, and a genteel tone prevails. Several of the rooms in three buildings have fireplaces, decks, or both. A rooftop whirlpool, two paddle-tennis courts, and a croquet green are available, and a shuttle takes guests to the private beach a mile away. A creative restaurant and honored wine cellar round out the picture.

WATCH HILL

A beautiful land's-end village that achieved its resort status during the post–Civil War period, Watch Hill has retained it ever since. Many grand shingled summer mansions and Queen Anne gingerbread houses remain from that time. The north side of the point occupied by the village is the harbor, packed with pleasure boats. Along the south shore is the west end of long but often crowded **Misquamicut State Beach,** and jutting out into the water is hook-shaped **Napatree Point,** a protected wildlife preserve.

To get to Watch Hill from the north, take Exit 1 off I-95, south on Route 3, which passes through the village of Westerly and continues to Watch Hill. From Connecticut, take Exit 92 from I-95, going south briefly on Route 2, picking up Route 78 (the Westerly Bypass) down along Airport Road into Watch Hill.

SEEING THE SIGHTS

At the small **Watch Hill Beach,** younger kids get a kick out of the nearby **Flying Horse Carousel,** which dates to 1867 and recently was the beneficiary of a 3-year restoration. The meticulously carved horses have leather saddles and horsehair manes, and rather than just pumping up and down, they "fly" out to the sides from overhead cables. There's even a brass ring to catch. Only kids are allowed to ride; tickets are 50¢. The carousel is open daily from mid-June to early September. Parents will have to settle for the more than 50 boutiques that fill the town's commercial blocks. And for a rare East Coast treat, find a seat to watch the sun drop into the ocean.

South of town on Watch Hill Road is the picturesque 1856 **Watch Hill Lighthouse.** Open only from 1 to 3pm Tuesday and Thursday, it is otherwise viewable only from outside.

WHERE TO STAY

If you arrive during season without reservations, you might want to check with **The Inn at Watch Hill,** 118 Bay St. in Westerly (☎ **401/596-0665**). Inconspicuously installed above the long row of shops directly opposite the water, it provides motel comforts and convenience.

The Villa. 190 Shore Rd., Westerly, RI 02891. ☎ **800/722-9240** or 401/596-1054. Fax 401/596-6268. www.thevillaatwesterly.com. E-mail: villa@riconnect.com. 6 suites. A/C TV TEL. Memorial Day to Columbus Day $75–$105 suite. Columbus Day to Memorial Day $120–$135 suite. Rates include breakfast. AE, DISC, MC, V. Pets allowed, with limitations.

A Dutch colonial manor with many Italianate overlays on Route 1A outside of town, The Villa is most often recommended for its extensive gardens and warm hospitality. Substantial renovations to both public areas and suites in the last year or two have made it still more desirable. Early risers can have coffee delivered to their rooms at 6am to tide them over until breakfast; there's a complimentary dinner buffet by the outdoor pool on summer Thursdays. All the suites have refrigerators, three have Jacuzzi tubs, and a couple have fireplaces.

Watch Hill Inn. 38 Bay St., Watch Hill, RI 02891. ☎ **800/356-9314** or 401/348-8912. Fax 401/546-9410. www.digiworld.com/watchillinn. 16 units. A/C TV TEL. Mid-June to early Sept $130–$195 double; late Mar to mid-June and early Sept to Dec 1 $95–$145 double; Dec 2 to late Mar $75–$130 double. Rates include breakfast. MC, V.

Savor sunsets from the veranda of this big white century-old clapboard lodge. Bedrooms are mostly of good size, with nothing special by way of decor, apart from the four-posters and occasional antiques. All meals are served, largely in the current seafood-and-pasta tradition, but with superb views. There is access to a beach.

WHERE TO DINE

Olympia Tea Room. 74 Bay St. ☎ **401/348-8211.** Reservations not accepted. Main courses $9.95–$17.95. AE, MC, V. June 1 to Columbus Day daily 8am–10pm, mid-Oct to Nov and Apr–May Fri–Sun 11am–9pm. Closed Dec–Easter. NEW AMERICAN.

The genteel tone of Watch Hill is undergirded by the Olympia, everyone's favorite meet-and-eat retreat. This version of a still older restaurant opened in 1939, and retains its old-timey soda fountains and high-backed wooden booths. Even the wait-resses are dressed in yesterday's uniforms. The kitchen cranks out pretty imaginative food, with a predilection for fish. Jump for the appetizer of plump, lightly fried oys-ters on wilted spinach and corn salsa, and the lobster roll is as good as you're ever likely to taste in all of coastal New England. Everyone loves the Key lime pie and raspberry bread pudding. Don't take the hours listed above too literally—weather, business, and simple whim can change them unexpectedly.

✪ **Three Fish.** 37 Main St., Westerly. ☎ **401/348-9700.** Reservations recommended for dinner. Main courses $14–$24. AE, DISC, MC, V. Mon–Fri 11:30am–2:30pm and 5:30–9pm (until 9:30pm Fri), Sat 5:30–9:30pm. ECLECTIC.

Lively, ramshackle downtown Westerly is an unlikely place to find what is arguably one of the state's top five dining places. But there it is, pushed up next to a gas station and cantilevered out over the rushing Pawcatuck, a converted old woolen mill. Inside, a homey pub precedes the large dining room, two-tiered to allow water views through the tall glassed wall. It has a north woods look, with bare wideboard floors and touches of green and blue on chairs and cupboards. That's diverting enough until the food arrives. Eyes widen with each course, for sophistication and creativity inform every last dish. First, warm, crusty, chewy bread; then, perhaps, fish chowder in an outsize pasta bowl—cubes of potatoes and nuggets of salmon wrapped in wonton leaves afloat in a smooth leek broth that owes nothing to the usual milky New England "chowda." Follow with three crab and seafood cakes the size of baby fists settled on a remoulade puddle spiked with chipolte and abetted by pickled vegetable slaw. Absolutely nothing disappoints, and meat-eaters needn't be concerned—more than half the selections use land-based flesh. Wine is generously poured. Don't deny yourself this experience.

5 Block Island

Viewed from above or on a map, Block Island resembles a pork chop with a big bite out of the middle. Only 7 miles long and 3 miles wide, it is edged with long stretches of beach lifting at points into dramatic bluffs. The interior is dimpled with undulating hills, only rarely reaching above 150 feet in elevation. Its hollows and clefts cradle 365 sweet-water ponds, some no larger than a backyard swimming pool. That "bite" out of the western edge of the "chop" is **Great Salt Pond,** which almost succeeds in cut-ting the island in two, but, as it is, serves as a fine protected harbor for fleets of plea-sure boats.

The only significant concentration of houses, businesses, hotels, and people is at **Old Harbor,** on the lower eastern shore, where the ferries from the mainland arrive and most of the remaining commercial fishing boats moor.

Named for Adrian Block, a Dutch explorer who briefly stepped ashore in 1641, the island's earliest European settlement was in 1661, and it has since attracted the kind of people who nurture a fierce conviction of independence, fueled in part by the streak of paranoia that leads them to live on a speck of land with no physical connection to the mainland. That has meant farmers, pirates, fishermen, smugglers, scavengers, and entrepreneurs, all of them willing to deal with the realities of isolation, lonely winters, and occasional killer hurricanes. Today, it means about 875 permanent residents who tough it out nine months a year waiting for the sun to stay a while.

The challenges of island living aren't readily apparent to the tens of thousands of visitors who arrive every summer for a day or a season. Visitors are wont to describe this as "paradise," a commendation that seems to be assigned only to islands. And they are correct, at least if sun and sea and zephyrs are paramount considerations. These ele-ments transformed the island from an offshore afterthought into an accessible summer retreat for the urban middle class after the Civil War, in America's first taste of mass tourism.

Unlike other such regions throughout the country that have lost their sprawling Victorian hotels to fire or demolition, Block Island has preserved many such buildings from that time. They crowd around Old Harbor, providing most of the lodging base. Smaller inns and bed-and-breakfasts add tourist rooms, most in converted houses built at the same time as the great hotels. There are only a handful of establishments that even look like motels, and building stock is marked, with few exceptions, by tasteful Yankee understatement. Angular structures covered in weathered gray shingles prevail. Despite the ominous presence of a few houses that resemble those plunked down in potato fields in hyper-chic precincts of New York's Long Island, development so far remains under control.

It's an island of peaceful pleasures and gentle observations. Police officers wear Bermuda shorts. Children tend lemonade stands in front of picket fences. Old-timers work their morning route along Water Street, barely making it to the other end in time for lunch, so many are the opportunities to exchange views and news.

ESSENTIALS

GETTING THERE **The Interstate Navigation Company,** P.O. Box 482, New London, CT 06320 (☎ **401/783-4613**), provides most of the surface service, including passenger-only ferries on daily triangular routes between Providence, Newport, and Block Island from June 22 to September 2. Bicycles may be taken on board for a small extra fee. While reservations aren't required for passengers, get to the dock early, because the boats fill up quickly.

Getting a car to Block Island is something of a hassle and considerably more expensive. Car ferries of the **Nelseco Navigation Company** (same address, telephone, and management as above) depart from the Port of Galilee at Point Judith, Rhode Island. Apart from blacked-out days from Christmas to New Year's Day, there are daily departures year-round—as few as one or two a day in winter to as many as ten a day from early June to late August. Sailing time on the new, larger, vessel is usually about 55 minutes. Drivers, be prepared: you are expected to *back* your car into the close quarters of the ferry's main deck.

Additional ferries leave New London, Connecticut, daily from early June to Labor Day at 9am (extra trips at 7:15pm Friday) and return daily at 4:30pm. Sailing time is a little over 2 hours. Since the round-trip fare for a 2- or 3-day weekend for a car and a driver can total nearly $80—more, with additional passengers—consider parking in one of the nearby garages at Point Judith or New London. Block Island is small, rental bicycles and mopeds are readily available, there are cabs for longer distances, and most hotels and inns are within a few blocks of the docks. If you intend to take a car anyway, understand that it is important to make ferry reservations well in advance—a month or two isn't too early for weekend departures.

Service is also provided between Block Island and Montauk, at the eastern end of New York's Long Island, by **Viking Ferry Lines,** R.D. #1 (P.O. Box 159), West Lake Drive, Montauk, NY 11954 (☎ **516/668-5700**). From late May to mid-October, there are daily departures at 9am, returning from Block Island at 4:30pm. Trips take about 1 hour 45 minutes. Only passengers and bicycles can be accommodated; parking is available in Montauk. Advance reservations are advised.

Westerly State Airport, near the Connecticut border, is the base for over a dozen regular daily flights to and from Block Island by **New England Airlines** (☎ **800/ 243-2460,** 401/596-2460 in Westerly, or 401/466-5881 on Block Island). Flights take 12 minutes, and are more frequent in the summer. They are supplemented by the

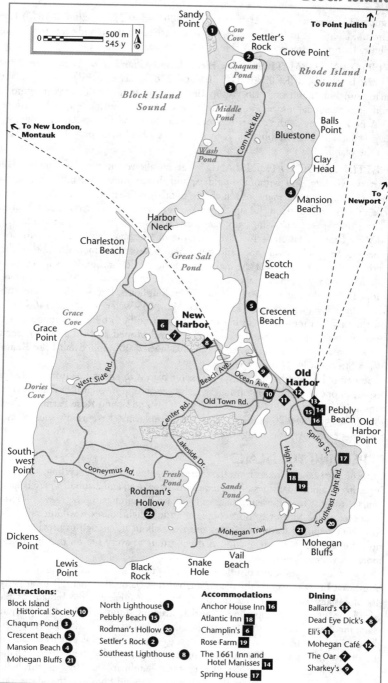

Block Island

To Point Judith

Sandy Point

Cow Cove

Settler's Rock

Grove Point

Chaqum Pond

Rhode Island Sound

Block Island Sound

Middle Pond

Balls Point

Bluestone

Clay Head

To New London, Montauk

Corn Neck Rd.

Wash Pond

Mansion Beach

To Newport

Harbor Neck

Charleston Beach

Great Salt Pond

Scotch Beach

Grace Cove

New Harbor

Crescent Beach

Grace Point

Dories Cove

West Side Rd.

Beach Ave.

Ocean Ave.

Old Harbor

Old Town Rd.

Pebbly Beach

Old Harbor Point

Center Rd.

Lakeside Dr.

Spring St.

South-west Point

Cooneymus Rd.

Fresh Pond

Sands Pond

High St.

Southeast Light Rd.

Rodman's Hollow

Dickens Point

Mohegan Trail

Mohegan Bluffs

Lewis Point

Black Rock

Snake Hole

Vail Beach

0   500 m   545 y

N

NA-0128

Attractions:
Block Island Historical Society 10
Chaqum Pond 3
Crescent Beach 5
Mansion Beach 4
Mohegan Bluffs 21
North Lighthouse 1
Pebbly Beach 15
Rodman's Hollow 20
Settler's Rock 2
Southeast Lighthouse 8

Accommodations
Anchor House Inn 16
Atlantic Inn 18
Champlin's 6
Rose Farm 19
The 1661 Inn and Hotel Manisses 14
Spring House 17

Dining
Ballard's 13
Dead Eye Dick's 8
Eli's 11
Mohegan Café 12
The Oar 7
Sharkey's 9

June-to-October service of **Action Air** (☎ **800/243-8623** or 860/448-1646) from Groton, Connecticut. In either case, make advance reservations and allow for the possibility that not-infrequent coastal fogs will delay or cancel flights.

VISITOR INFORMATION   The **Block Island Chamber of Commerce,** Water Street, Block Island, RI 02807 (☎ **401/466-2982**), has knowledgeable attendants, many brochures, and can help visitors find lodging. It is open daily year-round. In addition, a seasonal information booth at the dock opens during ferry debarkations.

A new building at the corner of Corn Neck Road and Ocean Avenue contains a bagel shop and The Washington Trust Company, a bank with one of the few ATMs on the island.

GETTING AROUND THE ISLAND   Cars are allowed on the island, but roads are narrow, winding, and without shoulders, and drivers must contend with flocks of bicycles and mopeds, many of which are piloted by inexperienced riders. If you're taking a car to the island, fill up the tank before boarding the ferry. There is only a rudimentary gas station—no signs, nameless pumps—behind Sharky's restaurant.

My recommendation is to leave your car on the mainland and join the two-wheelers. Several in-town shops and stands rent bikes and/or mopeds, most of them within a couple of blocks of the main ferry dock at Old Harbor. Rates for cruiser or mountain bikes are typically about $28 a day, with widely available discount coupons. Moped rates vary, but are usually about $50 for four hours. Prices are lower after Labor Day. One convenient source is **The Moped Man,** 435 Water St. (☎ **401/466-5011**), on the main business street facing the dock, renting both bikes and mopeds at the prices mentioned above. Similar outlets are **Island Moped and Bike Rental,** behind the Harborside Inn on Water Street (☎ **401/466-2700**), and **Esta's Bike Rentals,** Water Street (☎ **401/466-2651**).

Several inns also rent bicycles, so a possible plan is to take a taxi from the ferry or airport to one of them, drop off luggage, and get around by bike after that. Two such inns are the **Seacrest,** 207 High St. (☎ **401/466-2882**), and **Rose Farm,** on Roslyn Road (☎ **401/466-2034**), but most hotels and inns have ready sources about rentals—inquire when making room reservations.

EXPLORING THE ISLAND

Little on the island distracts from the central missions of sunning, cycling, lolling, and ingesting copious quantities of lobster, clams, chowders, and alcohol. There is no golf course, and the lone museum takes only about 20 minutes to cover, even for those enamored of local history. Add a couple of antique lighthouses, a wildlife refuge, and three topographical features of note, and that's about it, enough to provide destinations for a few leisurely bike trips. A driving tour of every site on that list takes no more than about 2 hours.

A couple of miles south of Old Harbor on what starts out as Spring Street is the **Southeast Lighthouse.** By the road is a tablet that claims that in 1590 a war party of 40 Mohegans was driven over the bluffs by the Manisseans, the Indians of Block Island. An undeniably appealing Victorian structure, built in 1874, the lighthouse's claim for attention lies primarily in the fact that it had to be moved 245 feet back from the eroding precipice a couple of years ago to save it. That was expensive, and now they must raise another $1 million for desperately needed renovation. That the building was designated a National Historic Landmark in 1997 might help in fundraising. There is a free small exhibit on the ground floor, but the admission fee to the top is as steep as the stairs ($5).

Continuing a hundred feet or so along the same road to the **Edward S. Payne Overlook,** paths from the small parking lot lead out to a promontory with views of the 160-foot-high **Mohegan Bluffs,** cliffs plunging down to the ocean. Pretty, yes; stunning, no.

Continuing in the same direction along the same road, which goes through other names and soon makes a sharp right turn inland, watch for the left (west) turn onto Cooneymus Road. In a few hundred yards, pull over near the sign for **Rodman's Hollow,** a geological dent formed by a passing glacier. Claims of its magnificence pale before the reality of undeveloped acres of low trees laced with walking trails.

Back in Old Harbor, proceed north on Corn Neck Road, skirting Crescent Beach, on the right. The paved road ends at **Settler's Rock,** with a plaque naming the English pioneers who landed here in 1661. This is one of the loveliest spots on the island, with mirrored **Chaqum Pond** (suitable for swimming) behind the Rock and a scimitar beach curving out to **North Lighthouse,** erected in 1867. In between is a **National Wildlife Refuge** that is of particular interest to birders. The lighthouse, best reached by foot along the rocky beach, is now an interpretive center of local ecology and history, open late June to Labor Day daily from 10am to 5pm.

Back in Old Harbor, the **Block Island Historical Society Museum,** Old Town Road and Ocean Avenue (☎ **401/466-2481**), was an 1871 inn converted to this use in 1945. The ground floor contains a miscellany of photos, ship models, a World War I uniform, a wicker baby carriage, tools, and an old cash register. Upstairs is a room set up to reflect the Victorian period.

Apart from sunbathing, the island's most popular pursuit is cycling. The ferries allow visitors to bring their own bicycles (for a small fee) but several local agencies rent multispeed cruiser and mountain bikes (see "Getting Around the Island," above).

Use your bike to get to the many beaches. The longest (about 3 miles long) and most popular strand is **Crescent Beach,** which runs over 2 miles along the shore north of Old Harbor and has a pavilion halfway along the beach. (It changes names, to Scotch Beach and then Mansion Beach as you head farther north from Old Harbor.) Mostly sand, if a little rocky in places, it is lifeguarded and family-oriented, with a bathhouse. The sections nearest Old Harbor are the most crowded, but the more northerly stretches are more secluded, even on July weekends.

Parasailing has become popular here, and striped chutes can be seen lifting riders up to 600 feet above the ocean. Athletic ability isn't necessary, and participants take off and land on the deck of the tractor boat. Contact **Block Island Parasail,** Old Harbor (☎ **401/466-2474**).

Other beaches on the island, such as the aptly named **Pebbly Beach** (which is also very crowded because it is just south of the main harbor), are shorter and rockier.

Fishing, kayaking, and canoeing are hugely popular, and the name to know is **Oceans & Ponds,** at Ocean and Connecticut avenues (☎ **800/678-4701** or 401/466-5131). Loquacious owner Bruce Johnson possesses an encyclopedic knowledge of his island and doesn't stint on sharing it. His quality stock features Orvis clothing, duffels, and fishing gear. Kayaks and canoes are available for rent, and he can arrange charter trips on three sport fishing boats. Twice a summer, he hosts 1-day fly-fishing schools with Orvis instructors.

WHERE TO STAY

Getting off the ferry at Old Harbor, you'll be facing Water Street and its row of Victorian hotels. Reading from left to right, they are the **Harborside Inn,** the **New Shoreham House,** the **Water Street Inn,** the **National,** and the **Surf.** Their accommodations range from barely adequate to satisfactory, and they are a logical option for people who arrive without reservations (not a good idea on weekends).

High cost can't be equated with luxury on the island. Just because your room costs $225 for a Saturday night in July, don't expect 24-hour room service, a fitness center, or even a TV. That doesn't happen. Even in a low-end B&B, a midweek night in high season is likely to cost at least $90. High season is short, roughly Memorial Day to Labor Day, and most inns and hotels are closed from Columbus Day to May. Also keep in mind that very few island lodgings have air-conditioning, but sea breezes make it unnecessary on all but a few days each summer. Two- or three-day minimum stays apply on weekends. If you don't have reservations, here's a tip: show up at an inn an hour or so after the last ferry has departed and they will often lower their quoted rates if they still have rooms left.

For help in finding lodging, try the Chamber of Commerce on Water Street, to the left and around the corner from the dock. They stay in touch with the island's inns and B&Bs and can offer suggestions. Another, more limited, option is the **Block Island Reservations** office (☎ 800/825-6254) in the middle of Water Street. Open daily in season, it represents five inns under single ownership.

Anchor House Inn. 253 Spring St., Block Island, RI 02807. ☎ **800/730-0181** or 401/466-5021. Fax 401/466-8887. 4 units. TV TEL. $99 double Oct to late May $99, $120–$150 double late May to mid-Oct. Rates include breakfast. AE, MC, V. No children under 12.

A huge anchor out front marks this former eyesore, transformed into a B&B in 1996. Two more rooms will probably have been added by the time you call; they won't have as many steep stairs to negotiate. Room decor is spare and restful, avoiding froufrou: quilts on the beds and a few pictures by island artists are about it. All rooms have ceiling fans. Breakfasts are of the hearty continental variety, including fruit, juices, bagels, and fresh muffins. Take your coffee out to one of the rocking chairs lined up on the porch. Parking is limited.

✪ **Atlantic Inn.** High St., Box 188, Block Island, RI 02807. ☎ **800/224-7422** or 401/466-5883. Fax 401/466-5678. 21 units. TEL. Mid-June to Labor Day and weekends Sept–Nov $125–$210 double; mid-Apr to mid-June and Labor Day to Nov $115–$160 double. Rates include breakfast. DISC, MC, V. Closed late Oct to mid-Apr.

Perched upon 6 rolling acres south of downtown, this 1879 Victorian hotel beguiles with its long veranda. Drawn by the promise of spectacular sunsets and a menu of Mediterranean nibbles joined with the most diverse beer and wine selection on the island, people start assembling from 4:00pm on. The flowers that brighten the public and private rooms are grown on the property. Bedrooms are decorated mostly with antiques, not just reproductions. Note, for example, the magnificent grandfather clock in the lobby.

Dining: The Atlantic shines most in its dining room, a fact that drew President Clinton and his family to an unannounced but long dinner a summer ago. Only four-course fixed-price dinners ($39) are offered, and they change often. Ingredients are the freshest available and presentations are as eye-pleasing as the food is gratifying. The Culinary Institute–trained chef might decide on a Thai stew of monkfish, littlenecks, and mussels in a lemongrass broth with wheat noodles one night, then move on to a rack of lamb made memorable by carrot polenta, Swiss chard, and a balsamic red wine jus the next. The staff does its own smoking of fish, fowl, and vegetables. Reservations are essential from June to September, especially on weekends.

Amenities: Two all-weather tennis courts.

✪ **Champlin's.** Great Salt Pond, P.O. Box J, Block Island, RI 02807. ☎ **800/762-4541** or 401/466-2641. Fax 401/466-2638. www.blockisland.com/champlins.com. 30 units. A/C TV. Summer $135–$250 double; spring and fall $85–$200 double. AE, MC, V. Closed mid-Oct to early May. From Old Harbor, drive west on Ocean Ave. and turn left on West Side Rd. The entrance road to Champlin's is on the right. The ferry from Long Island docks nearby.

Families with kids are welcome at this all-inclusive resort, with 220 transient slips in the marina for visiting yachtspeople (for reservations, call ☎ **800/762-4541**). Those who can live without the tilted floors and idiosyncratic adornments of the Victorian inns will be pleased by the clean lines and muted fabrics of the bedrooms and the standard microwave ovens and compact fridges. Once you've unpacked, there isn't much to compel you to leave.

Dining/Diversions: Restaurant, pool bar, snack shop, game rooms, and even a theater showing first-run movies. There's live music on weekends.

Amenities: A shuttle van is provided for trips to other parts of the island. On the premises are a large freshwater pool, a beach, two tennis courts, a minimart, and a Laundromat. Cars, mopeds, bicycles, kayaks, and paddleboats are all available for rent.

Rose Farm. Roslyn Rd., Box E, Block Island, RI 02807. ☎ **401/466-2034.** Fax 401/466-2053. 19 units. TEL. $99–$195 double. Rates include breakfast. AE, DISC, MC, V. Closed at least 2 months in winter. From Old Harbor, drive west on High St. and turn left on the paved driveway past the Atlantic Inn to Rose Farm. No children under 12.

The remodeled 1897 farmhouse that was the original inn has now been joined by an additional house across the driveway. Four of the rooms in the new building have large whirlpool baths and decks. Some have canopied beds, most have ocean views, and all have Victorian reproduction furnishings with a few antiques, including a handsome Eastlake bedstead. The inn rents 21-speed mountain bikes, and the self-service laundry room is useful. Afternoon refreshments are served, usually iced tea and pastries.

The 1661 Inn & Hotel Manisses. 1 Spring St., Block Island, RI 02807. ☎ **800/626-4773** or 401/466-2421/2063. Fax 401/466-3162. E-mail: biresorts@aol.com. 25 units (some with shared bathroom) in main inn, plus 23 in satellite buildings. TEL. $65–$335 double. Rates include breakfast. MC, V.

Pulling into the parking space up the hill from Old Harbor, many guests are delighted to see llamas grazing in the meadow down to the left. There are emus, goats, geese, black swans, and a Scottish Highland ox down there, too. They belong to the Manisses, which itself is only the most visible of a small hospitality empire. Other properties include the 1661 Inn, farther up the hill, and the Dodge, Sherman, and Nicholas Ball cottages. (Children are welcome in four of the five buildings.) Reception personnel at the hotel are helpful and are kept aware of vacancies at the other houses.

Upstairs guest rooms in the hotel use oak antiques and lots of wicker. Their size varies widely; the corner rooms are largest, and have whirlpool tubs. (The $335 room called "Edwards" has a king-size canopied bed, a loft with a spa tub, and a deck with ocean view.) Each room has a tray of soft drinks, cordials, and snacks next to a carafe of sherry.

Dining/Diversions: All meals are served, eliciting frequent superlatives from guests. Choices are breakfast at the 1661 Inn, with other meals in the informal Gatsby Room, next to the oak bar downstairs at the Manisses, or in the more formal adjacent dining room. In either, the median age is noticeably grayer than in the brew 'n' burger joints scattered around the island. Menus and prices are essentially the same in the latter two, with main dinner courses going for $9 to $17. Next to the front desk are two rooms that serve a dessert parlor in evening, where flaming coffees are featured.

Spring House. 902 Spring St., P.O. Box 902, Block Island, RI 02807. ☎ **800/234-9263** or 401/466-5844. 63 units. TEL. Summer $145–$250 double; $175–$250 suite. Spring and fall $99–$149 double; $155–$185 suite. Rates include breakfast. AE, MC, V. Closed mid-Oct to mid-June.

Marked by its red mansard roof and wraparound porch, the island's oldest hotel (1852) has hosted the Kennedy clan, Mark Twain, Ulysses S. Grant . . . and Billy Joel. The young staff is congenial, if occasionally a bit scattered. Swimming is allowed in the freshwater pond on the property. There are three styles of bedrooms, most of good size, with dusky-rose carpeting, queen-size beds, and pullout sofas. They don't have TVs or air-conditioning, but wet bars are standard.

Dining/Diversions: A considerable attraction is the all-you-can-eat barbecue lunch next to the bar on the veranda. Alert to trends, the management has a portable humidor that it trots out in the spacious lounge, Victoria's Parlor. In the lobby is a sitting area with a fireplace, and from there stretches the bright white dining room, with a menu that's executed quite competently.

WHERE TO DINE

Apart from a couple of kitchens that aspire to more rarefied levels of achievement, expect boiled or broiled lobsters, lots of fried and grilled fish and chicken, and the routine varieties of burgers and beef cuts. Chowders are usually surefire, especially but not exclusively the creamy New England version. Clam cakes are ubiquitous. (Actually deep-fried fritters containing more dough than clams, they are still fun eating, especially when dipped in tartar sauce.)

Several inns and hotels on the island have dining rooms worth noting (see "Where to Stay," above), especially the Atlantic and the Manisses. Even there, nether jackets nor ties are required.

Ballard's. Old Harbor. ☎ **401/466-2231.** Main courses $9.50–$21.95. AE, MC, V. Daily 11:30am–11pm. Closed Oct 1 to mid-May. AMERICAN/SEAFOOD.

Sooner rather than later, everyone winds up at Ballard's. Behind the long porch is a warehouse-like hall hung with nautical flags, and beyond that is a terrace with resin furniture beside a crowded beach. Several bars fuel the late-evening crowd that piles in for frequent live entertainment, much of which was in style 50 years ago.

The menu is all over the map, with something for everyone. Execution is usually ordinary, but one surprising appetizer is Ballard's Clam Cake Special, comprised of a bowl of chowder, six clam cakes, and a wedge of watermelon. At under $7, it makes an ample and inexpensive lunch.

Dead Eye Dick's. Payne's Dock, New Harbor. ☎ **401/466-2654.** Main courses $13.95–$19.95. AE, MC, V. Daily noon–3pm and 5pm–midnight. Closed mid-Sept to Memorial Day. SEAFOOD/AMERICAN.

Its name and logo—a shark with an eye patch—suggest a joint that sponsors wet T-shirt contests. But Dead Eye Dick's doesn't. Feel free to take either kids or grandparents. Appetizers include clams casino and crab cakes, along with designer pizzas and bruschettas. Follow with grilled or blackened fish steaks, often accompanied by jalapeño jelly. Salads come with good crusty bread. While seafood is the kitchen's focus, they also do well by beef and pork cuts. This positive assessment might change up or down with rumored new ownership.

✪ Eli's. 456 Chapel St. ☎**401/466-5230.** Main courses $13–$23. MC, V. May–Oct daily 5–10pm, Nov–Dec Sat–Sun 5–10pm. Closed Jan–April. Reservations essential. ITALIAN/AMERICAN.

Eli was a black Lab, and the place named for him used to be just a spaghetti-and-grinders drop-in. It's evolved into one of the island's most desirable eating places, thronged with mainlanders and natives lusting for its huge servings of quality fish, pasta, and meats. Problem is, they can only serve 50 voracious diners at a time, and if you put your name on the hostess' list, it can be 90 minutes before you get a shot at a seat, even at the bar. The kitchen doesn't concern itself overmuch with presentation, albeit every offering is appetizing and immensely flavorful. Immense portions defy anyone to finish, and it helps if your room at the inn has a microwave to zap the leftovers. Ciderhouse pork tenderloin tops a lot of lists, but some find the sauce cloying, and might prefer an alternative—the baked flounder roulade wrapped around a lobster-scallop mixture and drizzled with a lemon beurre blanc, perhaps. Wine and beer only.

Ernie's. Water St. ☎ **401/466-2473.** Breakfasts $2.95–$5.50; main courses $3–$20.45. AE, MC, V. Daily 6:30am–noon. Closed Columbus Day to Memorial Day. AMERICAN.

Breakfast, and nothing but, is what they've been doing at street-level Ernie's for more than 35 years. That means an early crowd of anglers and insomniacs and, later, stumbling late sleepers so relaxed they can barely move. They have choices of low-fat plates of scrambled egg substitutes and turkey sausages or thick dipped-in-batter French toast drenched with maple syrup and heaped with hash browns and rashers of bacon. (Guess which breakfast most people pick?)

Mohegan Café. Water St. ☎ **401/466-5911.** Main courses $16.95–$21.95. No credit cards. Summer Sun–Thurs 11:30am–9pm, Fri–Sat 11am–10pm. AMERICAN.

Walk straight across from the ferry landing into this ever-filled tavern—everyone does, sooner or later. Featured microbrews and ales are listed on the blackboard next to the bar, and most of the daytime menu is standard pub fare, with chowder, burgers, and fried clams among the most ordered. At night, offerings are more ambitious, such as grilled jerk-seasoned mahimahi topped with cranberry mango citrus compote. Faded photos of old Island scenes, trophies, antique rental signs, and a big model sailboat constitute the haphazard decor. Music on the stereo runs from Louis Armstrong to Metallica at the whim of the bartender.

The Oar. West Side Rd. ☎ **401/466-8820.** Sandwiches and salads $2.75–$11.75, fried chicken $7–$20. AE, MC, V. Daily 6:30–midnight. Closed late Oct to May. AMERICAN.

The Oar is more good-time bar than eating place. Locals drop in partly because off-islanders are less likely to find it (at the Block Island Marina), but mostly for the dramatic views of storms over the mainland and of the Great Salt Pond and its fleet of pleasure boats. Take it in from either the deck or the cool bar, with its wide picture window. The restaurant's name should be plural, since the ceiling and walls are hung with scores of oars—all of them painted with cartoons, graffiti, names, and assorted messages of obscure or ribald intent. Commemorating races, anniversaries, important events, or simply some really good parties, they provide such idle diversions as "find the oldest" (1965). Buffalo wings, fried calamari, burgers, lobster rolls, and plates and buckets of fried chicken comprise much of the menu. Drinks are served until 1am.

Sharky's. Cornet St. ☎ **401/466-9900.** Main courses $6.95–$17.95. MC, V. Summer daily 11:30am–10pm, winter Mon–Fri 11:30am–2:30pm and 5–9pm, Sat–Sun 11:30am–10pm. AMERICAN.

With its kicked-back atmosphere and pubby menu, this two-year-old entry has a clear kinship with at least a dozen casual eateries on the island. The useful distinction for off-season visitors is the fact that it keeps the grill fired up all year, unlike most of the others. Apart from the expected burger variations and Philly cheesesteak pretenders, lunch items get as inventive as "black-and-blue" chicken—blackened with Cajun seasonings and topped with blue cheese. Dinner entrees run to fettuccine Alfredo, mussels scampi, prime ribs and their mates.

BLOCK ISLAND AFTER DARK

Nightlife isn't of the rollicking south Florida variety, but they don't close the bars at sunset either. Prime candidates for a potential rockin' good time are **Captain Nick's** on Ocean Avenue (☎ **401/466-5670**), with pool tables and live bands supplemented by disco, and the year-round **Yellow Kittens,** on Corn Neck Road (☎ **401/466-5855**), also presenting live bands four or five nights a week in high season, with darts, two pool tables, and Ping-Pong to help fill the winter nights.

Ballard's (see "Where to Dine," above) has music nightly in season, often of the accordion or "big band" variety. Pitchers of beer, pool tables, pinball, and foosball are the attractions at **Club Soda,** on Connecticut Avenue (☎ **401/466-5912**), but there is live music once or twice a week. Find it under the Highview Inn, up a hill off Ocean Avenue. Another occasional live-music venue is the lounge of the **National Hotel,** on Water Street (☎ **401/466-2901**).

Two cinemas show current films: **Oceanwest,** Champlin's Marina, New Harbor (☎ **401/466-2971**), and the **Empire,** Water Street, Old Harbor (☎ **401/466-2555**), which also has a video-game room.

Vermont

by Wayne Curtis

A pair of East Coast academics raised some dust a few years back with a proposal to turn much of the Great Plains into a national park and let the buffalo roam free again.

With all due respect, if there's any place that should be turned wholesale into a national park, it's Vermont. Such a move would preserve a classic American landscape of rolling hills punctuated with slender white church spires and covered bridges (Vermont has more than 100). It would preserve the perfectly scaled main streets in towns like Woodstock and Bennington and Middlebury and Montpelier. It would save the dairy farms that sprawl across the shoulders of verdant ridges. But most of all, it would preserve a way of life that, one day, America will wish it had done much more to save.

Without feeling in the least like a theme park, Vermont captures a sense of America as it once was. Vermonters still share a strong sense of community, and they still respect the ideals of thrift and parsimony. They prize their small villages and towns, and they understand what makes them special. Gov. Howard Dean once said that one of Vermont's special traits was in knowing "where our towns begin and end." It seems a simple notion, but that speaks volumes when one considers the erosion of identity that has afflicted many small towns swallowed up by one creeping megalopolis or another.

Of course, it's not likely that Vermont residents would greet a national-park proposal with much enthusiasm. Meddlesome outsiders and federal bureaucrats don't rank high on their list of folks to invite to Sunday supper. At any rate, such a preservation effort would ultimately be doomed to failure: Vermont's impeccable sense of place is tied to its autonomy and independence, and any effort to control it from above would certainly cause the state as we know it to perish.

Happily for travelers exploring the state, it's not hard to get a taste of Vermont's way of life. You'll find it in almost all of the small towns and villages. And they are small—let the numbers tell the story: Burlington, Vermont's largest city, has just 39,127 residents; Montpelier, the state capital, 8,247; Brattleboro, 8,612; Bennington, 9,532; Woodstock, 1,037; Newfane, 164. (All these figures are from the 1990 census.) The state's entire population is just 560,000—making it one of a handful of states with more senators than representatives in Congress.

Of course, numbers don't tell the whole story. You have to let the people do that. One of Vermont's better-known residents, Nobel

Prize–winning author Sinclair Lewis, wrote 70 years ago: "I like Vermont because it is quiet, because you have a population that is solid and not driven mad by the American mania—that mania which considers a town of four thousand twice as good as a town of two thousand. . . . Following that reasoning, one would get the charming paradox that Chicago would be 10 times better than the entire state of Vermont, but I have been in Chicago and not found it so."

With all respect to readers from Chicago, that still holds true today.

1 Enjoying the Great Outdoors

BACKPACKING   The **Long Trail** runs 270 miles from Massachusetts to the Canadian border. The nation's first long-distance hiking path, it remains one of the best. This high-elevation trail follows Vermont's gusty ridges and dips into shady cols, crossing federal, state, and private lands. Open-sided shelters are located about a day's hike apart. To hike the entire length requires stamina and experience. The best source of information about backcountry opportunities is the **Green Mountain Club** (4711 Waterbury-Stowe Rd., Waterbury Center, VT 05677; ☎ **802/244-7037;** www.green-mountainclub.org; E-mail: gmc@sover.net), which publishes the *Long Trail Guide.* Club headquarters is on Route 100 between Waterbury and Stowe, and the information center and bookstore is open weekdays usually until about 4:30pm. Annual membership dues, which will get you a newsletter and discounts on guides, are $27 for an individual, or $35 for a family.

BIKING   Vermont's back roads offer some of the most appealing biking in the Northeast. Even Route 100—the main north-south thoroughfare up the middle of the state—is inviting along many stretches, especially from Killington to Sugarbush. While steep hills on some back roads can be excruciating for those who've spent too much time behind a desk, close scrutiny of a map should reveal routes that follow rivers and offer less grueling pedaling.

Vermont also lends itself to superb mountain biking. Abandoned county and town roads offer superior backcountry cruising. Most Green Mountain National Forest trails are also open to mountain bikers (but not the Appalachian or Long trails). Mountain bikes are prohibited from state-park and state-forest hiking trails, but are allowed on gravel roads. Mount Snow and Jay Peak ski areas, among others, will bring you and your bike to blustery ridges via lift or gondola, allowing you to work with gravity on your way down. The Craftsbury Center is your best bet if you're looking for back-road cruising through farmland rather than forest.

Organized inn-to-inn bike tours are a great way to see the countryside by day while relaxing in luxury at night. Tours are typically self-guided, with luggage transferred for you each day by vehicle. Try **Vermont Bicycle Touring** (☎ 800/245-3868), **Country Inns Along the Trail** (☎ 800/838-3301 or 802/247-3300; E-mail: rciatt@ sover.net), **Bike Vermont** (☎ 800/257-2226; E-mail: bikevermont@bikevermont. com), and **Cycle-Inn-Vermont** (☎ 802/228-8799).

CANOEING   Good paddling rivers include the Battenkill in southwest Vermont, the Lamoille near Jeffersonville, the Winooski near Waterbury, and the Missisquoi from Highgate Center to Swanton Dam. The whole of the historic Connecticut River, while frequently interrupted by dams, offers uncommonly scenic paddling through rural farmlands. Especially beautiful is the 7-mile stretch between Moore and Comerford dams near Waterford. Rentals are easy to come by near Vermont's major waterways; just check the local Yellow Pages.

For inn-to-inn canoe touring packages (2 to 6 days), contact **Battenkill Canoe Ltd.,** Route 7A, Arlington, VT 05250 (☎ 800/421-5268 or 802/362-2800).

Vermont

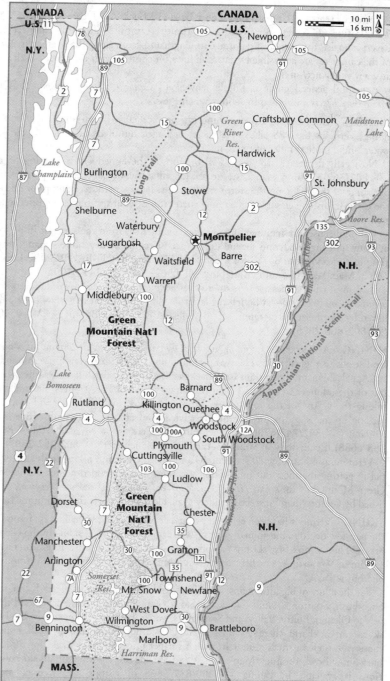

In recent years the **Upper Valley Land Trust** (19 Buck Rd., Hanover, NH 03755; ☎ 603/643-6626) set up a network of primitive campsites along the Connecticut River; canoeists can paddle and portage its length and camp along the riverbanks. Two of the campsites are accessible by car. Call for a brochure or visit the group's Web site at **www.valley.net/~uvlt**.

A helpful general guide is Roioli Schweiker's *Canoe Camping Vermont & New Hampshire Rivers,* published by Countryman Press.

FISHING   Both lake and river fishing can be excellent—if you know what you're doing. Vermont has 288 lakes of 20 acres or larger, hundreds of smaller bodies of water, and countless miles of rivers and streams.

Novice fly-fishermen would do well to stop by the famed **Orvis Catalog Store** (☎ 802/362-3750) in Manchester to ask for some friendly advice, then perhaps try out some of the tackle on the store's small ponds. If time permits, sign up for one of the Orvis fly-fishing classes and have an expert critique your technique and offer some pointers.

Fishing licenses are required and are available by mail from the state, or in person at many sporting-goods and general stores. License requirements and fees change from time to time, so write or call for a complete list: **Vermont Fish & Wildlife Dept.,** 103 S. Main St., #10 South, Waterbury, VT 05671 (☎ 802/241-3700).

Two invaluable guides are *The Atlas of Vermont Trout Ponds* ($14.95) and *Vermont Trout Streams* ($24.95)—although the latter may be out of print in 1999—both published by Northern Cartographic, 4050 Williston Rd., South Burlington, VT 05403 (☎ 802/860-2886).

HIKING   A spectacular range of hiking trails are here, from undemanding woodland strolls to rugged treks. The two premier long-distance pathways in Vermont are the Appalachian and Long trails (see "Backpacking" above); day hikes are easily carved out of these longer treks. The Green Mountain National Forest offers 500 miles of hiking trails. Any of the four Green Mountain offices will make a good stop for picking up maps and requesting hiking advice from rangers. The **main office** is in Rutland (☎ 802/747-6700). District **ranger offices** are in Middlebury (☎ 802/388-6688), Rochester (☎ 802/767-4261), and Manchester (☎ 802/362-2307).

Vermont also has some 80 state forests and parks. Guides to hiking trails are essential to getting the most out of a hiking vacation. Recommended guides include the Green Mountain Club's *Day Hiker's Guide to Vermont* and *50 Hikes in Vermont,* published by Countryman Press, both widely available in bookstores throughout the state.

SKIING   Vermont has been eclipsed by upscale Western and Canadian ski resorts in the past few decades, but to many, it's *still* the capital of downhill skiing in the United States. The nation's first ski lift—a rope tow—was rigged up off a Buick engine in 1933 near Woodstock. The first lodge to accommodate skiers was built in Vermont at Sherburne Pass.

For the allure of big mountains, steep faces, and a lively ski scene, there's Killington, Sugarbush, Stratton, Mount Snow, and Stowe. Families and intermediates find their way to Okemo, Bolton Valley, and Smuggler's Notch. For old-fashioned New England ski-mountain charm, there's Mad River Glen, Ascutney, Burke, and Jay Peak. Finally, those who prefer a small mountain with a smaller price tag make tracks for Middlebury Snow Bowl, Bromley, Maple Valley, and Suicide Six. Information on **ski conditions** is available by calling ☎ 800/837-6668 or visiting the Web at **www. skivermont.com.** Note that lift-ticket prices listed in this guide don't include a 5% Vermont sales tax.

Vermont is also blessed with about 50 cross-country ski areas. These range from modest mom-and-pop operations to elaborate destination resorts with snowmaking. Many of these are connected by the 200-mile Catamount Trail, which runs the length of the state parallel to, but at lower elevations than the Long Trail. For more information, contact the **Catamount Trail Association**, P.O. Box 1235, Burlington, VT 05402 (☎ **802/864-5794;** E-mail: ctamail@aol.com). For a free brochure listing all the cross-country facilities, contact the **Vermont Department of Travel and Tourism** (☎ **800/837-6668**). The state updates a recorded cross-country ski report every Thursday (☎ **802/828-3239**). A fax of the report is available by calling **800/ 833-9756.**

2 Bennington, Manchester & Southwestern Vermont

Southwestern Vermont is the turf of Ethan Allen, Robert Frost, Grandma Moses, and Norman Rockwell. As such, it may very well feel familiar to you even if you've never been here before. Over the decades, it has subtly managed to work itself into America's cultural consciousness.

The region is sandwiched between the Green Mountains to the east and the rolling hills along the Vermont–New York border to the west. If you're coming from Albany or the southwest, the first town you're likely to hit is Bennington—a commercial center that offers up low-key diversions for residents and tourists alike. Northward toward Rutland, the terrain is more intimate than intimidating, with towns clustered in broad and gentle valleys along rivers and streams. Former 19th-century summer colonies and erstwhile lumber-and-marble towns exist side by side, offering pleasant accommodations, delightful food, and—in the case of Manchester Center—world-class shopping.

BENNINGTON

Bennington owes its fame (such as it is) to a handful of eponymous moments, places, and things. Like the Battle of Bennington, fought in 1777 during the American War of Independence. And Bennington College, a small but prestigious liberal-arts school that produced a bumper crop of prominent young novelists in the 1980s (including Donna Tartt, Brett Easton Ellis, and Jill Eisenstadt). And Bennington pottery, which traces its ancestry back to the first factory here in 1793, and is today prized by collectors for its superb quality.

Today, visitors will find two Benningtons. Historic Bennington with its white clapboard homes sits atop a hill just west of town off Route 9. (Look for the mini–Washington Monument.) Modern downtown Bennington is a pleasant if no-frills commercial center with restaurants and stores that still sell things that people actually need. It's not so much a tourist destination as a handy supply depot. (It's actually Vermont's third largest city.) The downtown is home to a number of handsome commercial buildings.

ESSENTIALS

GETTING THERE   Bennington is located at the intersection of Routes 9 and 7. If you're coming from the south, the nearest interstate access is via the New York Thruway at Albany, New York, about 35 miles away. From the east, I-91 is about 40 miles away at Brattleboro.

Vermont Transit (☎ **800/451-3292** or 802/442-4808) offers bus service to Bennington from Albany, Burlington, and other points. Buses arrive and depart from 126 Washington St.

Southern Vermont

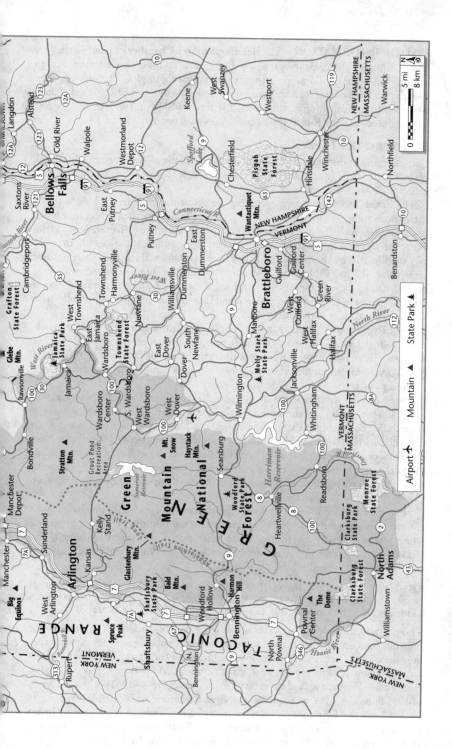

VISITOR INFORMATION   The **Bennington Area Chamber of Commerce,** Veterans Memorial Drive, Bennington, VT 05201 (☎ **802/447-3311**), maintains an information office on Route 7 north near the veterans complex. The office is open Monday to Friday from 9am to 5pm year-round; in summer and fall it's also open weekends from 9am to 4pm. Information is also available on the Internet at www. bennington.com or by E-mail from benncham@sover.net.

EXPLORING THE TOWN

One of Bennington's claims to history is the fabled Battle of Bennington, which took place August 16, 1777. A relatively minor skirmish, it had major implications for the outcome of the American Revolution.

The British had devised a grand strategy to defeat the impudent colonists: divide the colonies from the Hudson River through Lake Champlain, then concentrate forces to defeat first one half and then the other. As part of the strategy, British general John Burgoyne was ordered to attack the settlement of Bennington and capture the military supplies that had been squirreled away by the Continental militias. There he came upon colonial forces led by Gen. John Stark, a veteran of Bunker Hill. After a couple of days playing cat and mouse, Stark ordered the attack on the afternoon of August 16, proclaiming, "There are the redcoats, and they are ours, or this night Molly Stark sleeps a widow!" (Or so the story goes.)

The battle was over in less than two hours —the British and their Hessian mercenaries were defeated, with more than 200 enemy troops killed; the colonials lost but 30 men. This cleared the way for another vital colonial victory at the Battle of Saratoga, that ended the British strategy of divide and conquer, and set the stage for colonial victory.

That battle is commemorated by northern New England's most imposing monument. You can't miss the **Bennington Battle Monument** if you're passing through the surrounding countryside. This 306-foot obelisk of blue limestone atop a low rise was dedicated in 1891. It resembles a shorter, paunchier Washington Monument. Note also that it's actually about 6 miles from the site of the actual battle; the monument marks the spot where the munitions were stored. The monument's viewing platform, which is reached by elevator, is open from 9am to 5pm daily from April through October. A fee of $1 is charged.

Near the monument you'll find distinguished old homes lushly overarched with ancient trees. Be sure to spend a few moments exploring the old burying ground, where several Vermont governors and the noted poet Robert Frost are buried. The chamber of commerce (see above) offers a walking tour brochure that will help you make sense of the neighborhood's vibrant past.

Bennington Museum. W. Main St. (Rte. 9 between Old Bennington and the current town center). ☎ **802/447-1571.** $6 adults, $5 students and seniors, free for children under 12, $13 family (with children under 18). Daily 9am–6pm (until 5pm Nov 1 to May 31).

This eclectic and vastly intriguing collection traces its roots back to 1875, although the museum has occupied the current stone-and-column building overlooking the valley only since 1928. Nine galleries (and growing) feature a wide range of exhibits on local arts and industry, including furniture, glass, paintings, and pottery. Of special interest are the colorful primitive landscapes by Grandma Moses (1860–1961), who lived much of her life nearby. (The museum has the largest collection of Moses paintings in the world.) Look also for the glorious luxury car called the Wasp, 16 of which were handcrafted in Bennington between 1920 and 1925. A $2 million expansion is underway in 1999, so expect new exhibits and attractions as the construction dust settles.

WHERE TO STAY

Four Chimneys. 21 West Rd., Bennington, VT 05201. ☎ **802/447-3500.** Fax 802/
447-3500. www.fourchimneys.com. 11 units. TV. Weekends, holidays, summer midweek,
$125–$185 double; winter midweek $100–$160. Rates include breakfast. 2-night minimum
stay foliage and holiday weekends. AE, CB, DC, DISC, MC, V. No children under 12.

This striking colonial-revival building will be among the first to catch your eye as you
arrive in Bennington from the west. Set off Route 7 on an 11-acre, nicely landscaped
lot, it's an imposing white, three-story structure with—no surprise—four prominent
chimneys. (Local secret: The third chimney's a fake, added for the purpose of symmetry.) The inn, built in 1912, is at the edge of Historic Bennington; the towering
Bennington Monument looms over the backyard. The carpeted guest rooms are
inviting and homey.

   Dining: The well-regarded dining room offers meals with a continental flair. It's
open Tuesday to Sunday for lunch and dinner; dinner is fixed-price at $32.50.

South Shire Inn. 124 Elm St., Bennington, VT 05201. ☎ **802/447-3839.** Fax 802/
442-3547. E-mail: sshire@sover.net. 9 units. A/C TEL. $105–$160 double; foliage season
$125–$180 double. Rates include full breakfast. AE, MC, V. No children under 12.

A locally prominent banking family hired architect William Bull to design and build
this impressive Victorian home in 1880. The downstairs is spacious and open, with
detailing including leaded glass on the bookshelves and intricate plasterwork in the
dining room. The guest rooms are richly hued, and most have canopied beds and
working fireplaces (Duraflame-style logs only). The best of the bunch is the old master
bedroom, which has a king-size canopied bed, a tile-hearth fireplace, and a beautiful
bathroom with hand-painted tile. Four more modern guest rooms are in the old carriage house. The carriage house's downstairs rooms are slightly more formal; the
upstairs rooms are more intimate with low eaves and skylights over the tubs.

WHERE TO DINE

Alldays & Onion. 519 Main St. ☎ **802/447-0043.** Reservations accepted for dinner, but
not often needed. Breakfast $2–$6; sandwiches $2.25–$6.95; dinner $10.95–$19.95.
AE, DISC, MC, V. Mon–Tues 7:30am–5pm, Wed–Sat 7:30am–8:30pm. ECLECTIC.

First off, the name: This eminently casual place is named after a turn-of-the-century
British automobile manufacturer. Locals flock here to enjoy the wholesome, tasty
sandwiches, the filling deli salads, and tasty soups. More ambitious dinners are served
later in the week, with entrees changing frequently but including the likes of Southwest cowboy steak with skillet corn sauce and soba and stir-fried vegetables. The
atmosphere is that of a small-town restaurant gussied up for a big night out—the flu-
orescent lights are a bit bright, but the dark hues of the walls knock down the inten-
sity a notch, and folk-rock background music mellows it further still.

✪ **Blue Benn Diner.** North St. (Rte. 7). ☎ **802/442-5140.** Breakfast $1.50–$5.95; sandwiches and entrees $1.95–$5.75; dinner $7.95. No credit cards. Mon–Tues 6am–5pm,
Wed–Fri 6am–8pm, Sat 6am–4pm, Sun 7am–4pm. DINER.

Diner aficionados make pilgrimages here to enjoy the ambience of this 1945 Silk City
classic, with barrel ceiling and copious amounts of stainless steel. Blue stools line the
laminate counter, on which you see plain evidence that more people are right-handed
than left-handed by the wear marks. But even folks who don't give a fig for diners flock
here for the tremendous value on food. The printed menu is vast, but don't overlook
the specials scrawled on paper and taped all over the walls. Blue-plate dinner specials
are $7.95 or $8.95 and include vegetables, rice, soup or salad, rolls, and rice pudding
for dessert. A bit incongruously, fancier and vegetarian fare is also available; especially

good is the grilled portobello on sourdough. There's also a great selection of pies, like blackberry, pumpkin, and chocolate cream, which start at $2.75 a slice.

ARLINGTON, MANCHESTER & DORSET

The rolling Green Mountains are rarely out of view from this cluster of hamlets. And in midsummer the lush green hereabouts gives Ireland a good run for its money—verdant hues are found in the forests blanketing the hills, the valley meadows, and the mosses along the tumbling streams, making it obvious how these mountains earned their name.

These quintessential Vermont villages make ideal destinations for romantic getaways, aggressive antiquing, and serious outlet shopping. Each of the towns is worth visiting, and each has its own peculiar charm. Arlington has a town center that borders on microscopic; with its auto-body shops and redemption center (remnants of a time when the main arterial passed through town), it gleams a bit less than its sibling towns to the north, and has a slightly less refined character.

To the north, Manchester and Manchester Center share a blurred town line, but maintain distinct characters. The more southerly Manchester has an old-world, old-money elegance with a campus-like town centered around the resplendently columned Equinox Hotel. Just to the north, Manchester Center is a major mercantile center with dozens of national outlets offering discounts on brand-name clothing, accessories, and housewares. A worthy detour off the beaten track is Dorset, an exquisitely preserved town of white clapboard architecture and marble sidewalks.

ESSENTIALS

GETTING THERE   Arlington, Manchester, and Manchester Center are located north of Bennington on Historic Route 7A, which runs parallel to and west of the more modern, less scenic Route 7. Dorset is north of Manchester Center on Route 30, which departs from Route 7A in Manchester Center. Vermont Transit bus lines (☎ 800/451-3292 or 802-362-1226) offers service to Manchester.

VISITOR INFORMATION   The **Manchester and the Mountains Chamber of Commerce,** 5046 Main St., Suite 1, Manchester Center, VT 05255 (☎ 802/362-2100), maintains a year-round information center in Manchester Center approx. 2 blocks north of the blinking light. Look for the white house on Adam Park Green. Hours are 9am to 5pm Monday to Saturday (from Memorial Day weekend through Oct it's also open Sunday 9am to 5pm).

For information about outdoor recreation, the Green Mountain National Forest maintains a district **ranger office** (☎ 802/362-2307) in Manchester on Routes 11 and 30, east of Route 7. It's open from 8am to 4:30pm Monday to Friday.

EXPLORING THE AREA

Arlington has long been associated with painter and illustrator Norman Rockwell, who resided here from 1939 to 1953. Arlington residents were regularly featured in Rockwell covers for the *Saturday Evening Post.* "Moving to Arlington had given my work a terrific boost. I'd met one or two hundred people I wanted to paint . . . the sincere, honest, homespun types that I love to paint," Rockwell wrote in his autobiography.

Visitors can catch a glimpse of this long relationship in a 19th-century Carpenter Gothic–style church in the middle of town, **The Norman Rockwell Exhibition** (☎ 802/375-6423). This small museum features a variety of displays, including many of those famous covers, along with photographs of the original models. Sometimes you'll find the models working as volunteers. Reproductions are available at the gift shop. It's open from 9am to 5pm daily in summer; open in the off-season from 10am to 4pm weekdays and 10am to 5pm weekends (closed January). Admission is $1. (For the major Rockwell museum, see chapter 8, section 4, under "Stockbridge.")

Manchester has long been one of Vermont's more moneyed resorts, attracting prominent summer residents like Mary Todd Lincoln and Julia Boggs Dent, the wife of Ulysses S. Grant. This town is well worth visiting just to wander its quiet streets, bordered with distinguished homes dating from the early Federal period. It feels a bit like you've entered a time warp here, and the cars driving past the green seem strangely out of place. Be sure to note the sidewalks made of irregular marble slabs. The town is said to have 17 miles of such sidewalks, made from the castoffs of Vermont's marble quarries.

On Route 30, 7 miles north of Manchester is the village of **Dorset.** Fans of American architecture owe themselves a visit. While not as grand as Manchester, this quiet town of white clapboard and black and green shutters has a quiet and appealing grace. The elliptical green is fronted by early homes that are modest by Manchester standards, but nonetheless are imbued with a subtle elegance. In the right light, Dorset feels more like a Norman Rockwell painting than many Norman Rockwell paintings.

Museums & Historic Homes

American Museum of Fly-Fishing. Rte. 7A (a block north of the Equinox Hotel), Manchester. ☎ **802/362-3300.** Admission $3 adults; free for children under 12 and students. Daily 10am–4pm. Closed major holidays.

This is the place for serious anglers interested in the rich history and delicate art of fly-fishing. The museum includes exhibits on the evolution of the fly-fishing reel, paintings and sculptures of fish and anglers, displays of creels, and dioramas depicting fishing at its best. You can see the fly-fishing tackle of some of the nation's more notable anglers, including Herbert Hoover, Andrew Carnegie, and Ernest Hemingway. And, naturally, there are extensive exhibits of beautifully tied flies, displayed in oak and glass cases.

✪ **Hildene.** Rte. 7A, Manchester. ☎ **802/362-1788.** Admission $8 adults, $4 children 6–14, free for children under 6. Tours given daily mid-May through Oct 9:30am–4pm; grounds close at 5:30pm. Special holiday tours Dec 27–29.

Robert Todd Lincoln was the only son of Abraham and Mary Todd Lincoln to survive to maturity. But he's also noted for his own achievements: He earned millions as a prominent corporate attorney and served as secretary of war and ambassador to Britain under three presidents. He also was president of the Pullman Company (makers of deluxe train cars) from 1897 to 1911, stepping in after the death of company founder George Pullman.

What did one do with millions of dollars in an era when a million bucks was more than chump change? Build lavish summer homes, for the most part. And Lincoln was no exception. He summered in this stately, 24-room Georgian Revival mansion between 1905 and 1926 and delighted in showing off its remarkable features, including a sweeping staircase and a 1908 Aeolian organ with its 1,000 pipes (you'll hear it played). It's more regal than ostentatious, and made with an eye to quality. And what summer home would be complete without formal gardens? Lincoln had gardens designed after the patterns in a stained-glass window and planted on a gentle promontory with outstanding views of the flanking mountains. The home is viewed on group tours that start at an informative visitor's center; allow time following the tour to explore the grounds.

Southern Vermont Art Center. West Rd. (P.O. Box 617), Manchester. ☎ **802/362-1405.**
$3 adult, 50¢ students, free Sat 10am–noon. Tues 10am–8:30pm, Wed–Sat 10am–5pm, Sun
noon–5pm. Closed late Oct to March.

This outstanding art center is well worth the short detour from town. Located in a
striking Georgian Revival home surrounded by nearly 400 pastoral hillside acres (it
overlooks land that once belonged to Charles Orvis), the center features a series of galleries in which it displays works from its 700-piece permanent collection, as well as
frequently changing exhibits of contemporary Vermont artists. Check the schedule;
you may be able to take in a concert, or sign up for a class while you're in town. At
least leave time to enjoy a light lunch at the Garden Cafe, and to wander the grounds,
exploring both the sculpture garden and the fields and woods beyond. One word of
caution: plans call for aggressively expanding the museum with new construction in
the coming years, so the pastoral quality may be missing while the work is underway.

SHOPPING

Manchester Center is one of several upscale factory-outlet meccas in New England,
and it may be the most upscale of the bunch. Retailers include (take a deep breath)
Christian Dior, Mikasa, Boston Traders, Brooks Brothers, Coach, Cole-Haan, J. Crew,
Seiko, Giorgio Armani, and Dansk. The shops conveniently cluster along a T intersection in the heart of Manchester Center. Most are readily accessible on foot, while
others are a bit farther afield, requiring scuttling from one to the next by car.

One hometown favorite is worth seeking out if your interests include fishing or rustic,
outdoorsy fashion: Orvis, which has crafted a worldwide reputation for manufacturing
topflight fly-fishing equipment, happens to be based in Manchester. The **Orvis Catalog
Store** (☎ **802/362-3750**) is located between Manchester and Manchester Center and
offers housewares, sturdy outdoor clothing, and—of course—fly-fishing equipment.
Two small ponds just outside the shop allow prospective customers to try before they
buy.

OUTDOOR PURSUITS

HIKING & BIKING   Scenic hiking trails ranging from challenging to relaxing can
be found in the hills a short drive from town. At the Green Mountain District Ranger
Station (see "Visitor Information," above), ask for the free brochure *Day Hikes on the
Manchester Ranger District.*

The Long Trail and Appalachian Trail overlap in southern Vermont. They run just
east of Manchester; a popular day trek is along these trails to **Spruce Peak.** Five miles
east of Manchester Center on Routes 11 and 30, look for parking where the two trails
cross the road. Strike out southward on foot over rocky terrain for 2.2 miles to the
peak, looking for the blue-blazed side trail to the open summit with its breathtaking
views of the Manchester Valley.

ON THE WATER   For a duck's-eye view of the rolling hills, stop by **Battenkill
Canoe Ltd.** in Arlington (☎ **800/421-5268** or 802/362-2800; www.battenkill.com;
E-mail: info@battenkill.com). This friendly outfit offers daily canoe rentals on the
scenic Battenkill and surrounding areas. Trips range from 2 hours to a whole day ($45
including shuttle), and multiday inn-to-inn canoe packages are also available. The
shop is open daily in season (May through October) from 9am to 5:30pm; limited
hours the remainder of the year.

Aspiring anglers can sign up for fly-fishing classes taught by skilled instructors affiliated with **Orvis** (☎ **800/548-9548**), the noted fly-fishing supplier and manufacturer. The 2½-day classes include instruction in knot tying and casting; students
practice catch-and-release fishing on the company pond and the Battenkill River.
Classes are held from mid-April to Labor Day.

SKIING

Bromley. P.O. Box 1130, Manchester Center, VT 05255. ☎ **800/865-4786** for lodging, or 802/824-5522. www.bromley.com. Vertical drop: 1,334 ft. Lifts: 6 chairlifts (including 1 high-speed detachable quad), 3 surface lifts. Skiable acreage: 175. Lift tickets: $46 weekends, $35 weekdays.

Bromley is a great place to learn to ski. Gentle and forgiving, the mountain also features long, looping intermediate runs that are tremendously popular with families. The slopes are mostly south-facing, which means they receive the warmth of the sun and some protection from the harshest winter winds. The base lodge scene is more mellow than at many resorts, and your experience is almost guaranteed to be relaxing.

Stratton. Stratton Mountain, VT 05155. ☎ **800/843-6867** for lodging or 802/297-2200. www.stratton.com. Vertical drop: 2,003 ft. Lifts: 1 gondola, 9 chairlifts (including one 6-person high-speed), 2 surface lifts. Skiable acreage: 583. Lift tickets: $52 weekends and holidays, $48 weekdays.

Founded in the 1960s, Stratton labored in its early days under the belief that Vermont ski areas had to be Tyrolean to be successful. Hence Swiss chalet nightmare architecture, and the overall feel of being Vail's younger, less affluent sibling. In recent years, Stratton has worked to leave the image of Alpine quaintness behind in a bid to attract a younger, edgier set. New owners added $25 million in improvements, mostly in snowmaking, with coverage now up over 80 percent The slopes are especially popular with snowboarders, a sport that was invented here when bartender Jake Burton slapped a big plank on his feet and aimed down the mountain. The mountain expanded its glade skiing in 1998. Expert skiers should seek out Upper Middlebrook, a fine, twisting run off the summit.

WHERE TO STAY

In addition to the inns listed below, two motels offer sanctuary to the harried traveler. The **Four Winds,** Route 7A (2 miles north of Manchester Center), ☎ **888/368-7946** or 802/362-1105, is a colonial-style country motel with an outdoor pool and Hitchcock furnishings; a golf course is just across the road.

Nearby on Route 7A is the **Aspen Motel,** ☎ **802/362-2450,** located on nine leafy acres and home to a pool and shuffleboard court. It's a mile north of the village center.

Arlington Inn. Rte. 7A (P.O. Box 369), Arlington, VT 05250. ☎ **800/443-9442** or 802/375-6532. Fax 802/375-6534. www.arlingtoninn.com. E-mail: arlinn@sover.net. 17 units. A/C TV. $110–$215 double. Rates include breakfast. 2-night minimum stay most weekends. AE, DC, DISC, MC, V.

This stout, cream-colored, multicolumned Greek Revival home, built in 1848, would be perfectly at home in the Virginia countryside. But it anchors this village well, set back from the Historic Route 7A on a lawn bordered with sturdy maples. Inside, the inn boasts a similarly courtly feel, with unique wooden ceilings adorning the first-floor rooms and a tavern that borrows its atmosphere from an English hunt club. If you prefer modern comforts, ask for a room in the 1830 parsonage next door, where you'll find telephones and TVs. The quietest rooms are in the detached carriage house, which is at a remove from the sounds of the highway. New innkeepers Sherrie and Bill Noonan are taking steps to upgrade the inn (they already turned three rooms into two suites), and give it a more Victorian feel.

Dining: The chef strives to use local produce and other Vermont products wherever possible. Depending on the season, options may include chicken breast stuffed with goat cheese, or grilled salmon with a lobster beurre blanc sauce. Entrees are priced from $18.50 to $24.

Amenities: Tennis court, municipal golf course nearby, baby-sitting.

Barrows House. Rte. 30, Dorset, VT 05251. ☎ **800/639-1620** or 802/867-4455. Fax 802/
867-0132. www.barrowshouse.com. E-mail: barhouse@vermontel.com. 28 units. A/C. $155–
$250 double. Rates include breakfast and dinner. B&B rates also available. Discounts available
in the off-season and midweek. 2-night minimum stay weekends and some holidays. AE, DISC,
MC, V. Pets allowed in 2 cottages.

Within easy strolling distance of the village of Dorset stands this compound of eight
early American buildings set on nicely landscaped grounds studded with birches, firs,
and maples. The main house was built in 1784, and it's been an inn since 1900. The
rooms are more comfortable than elegant; some have gas or wood fireplaces. A few
rooms have telephones—ask in advance if that's important. Innkeepers Linda and Jim
McGinnis are very cordial and helpful, especially in planning day trips around the
region.

Dining: Enjoy a before-dinner drink in the casual and cozy tavern with the trompe-
l'oeil bookshelves. The main dining area offers a choice: traditional country-inn room
or a modern greenhouse addition. The cuisine is contemporary New England, with
entrees like Chesapeake-style Maine crab cakes, or strip steak with caramelized onions
and roasted shiitake mushrooms. Entrees range from $9.95 to $22.95.

Amenities: Outdoor heated pool, bicycle rental, game room, sauna, two tennis
courts.

Dorset Inn. Church and Main sts., Dorset, VT 05251. ☎ **802/867-5500.** Fax 802/
867-5542. 31 units. $150– double; $200–$240 suite; foliage season $200 double, $220–$260
suite. Rates include breakfast. AE, MC, V. No children under 5.

Set in the center of genteel Dorset, this former stagecoach stop was built in 1796 and
claims to be the oldest continuously operating inn in Vermont. With 31 rooms, the
Dorset Inn is fairly large by Vermont standards, but far more intimate than compa-
rably sized places. The carpeted guest rooms, some of which are in a well-crafted addition built in the 1940s, are furnished in an upscale country style, with a mix of
reproductions and antiques, including canopied and sleigh beds. All but two rooms
have air-conditioning, and only the two suites have TVs and telephones.

Dining: The tavern is wonderfully casual and pubby, paneled in dark wood with a
stamped-tin ceiling. The dining room is a bit more formal, although the menu is anything but stuffy. Dinner options range from an oversize burger with red-wine sauce to
blackened tuna with a mango-papaya salsa. Entrees range from $12.50 to $20.

✪ **1811 House.** Rte. 7A, Manchester Village, VT 05254. ☎ **800/432-1811** or 802/
362-1811. Fax 802/362-2443. www.1811house.com. E-mail: info@1811house.com. 14 units.
A/C. $180–$230 double. Rates include full breakfast. AE, DISC, MC, V.

This historic Manchester Village home, the first part of which was built in the mid-
1770s, started taking in guests in 1811 (hence the name). And it often seems that not
much has changed here in the intervening centuries. The warrenlike downstairs
common rooms are rich with history—the pine floors are uneven, the doors out of
true, and everything is painted in earthy, colonial tones. Even the exterior is painted a
pheasant-brown color. The antique furniture re-creates the feel of the house during the
Federal period, and a delightful English-style pub lies off the entryway, complete with
tankards hanging from the beams. The rooms are comfortably sized—you won't feel
that you're lost in them, but neither will you feel cramped. Among my favorites: the
Robinson Room, with a private deck, great view, and unique tub-shower combo. The
chocolate-chip cookies offered each afternoon are most memorable.

The Equinox. Rte. 7A (P.O. Box 46), Manchester Village, VT 05245. ☎ **800/362-4747** or
802/362-4700. Fax 802/362-1595. www.equinoxresort.com. E-mail: reservations@
equinoxresort.com. 183 units. A/C TV TEL. $189–$329 double; $489–$579 suite. Ask about
package rates. AE, DC, DISC, MC, V.

A blue-blood favorite, the Equinox faces the village green and dominates Manchester Village with its gleaming white clapboard and trim rows of columns. The resort's roots extend back to 1769, when the Marsh Tavern was established (today the structure serves as an informal restaurant within the resort). But make no mistake, this is a full-blown modern resort, its historic lineage notwithstanding. You'll find extensive sports facilities spread about its 2,300 acres, four dining rooms, and all the expected in-room amenities. Guest rooms are by and large decorated similarly in a country pine motif, although the suites are a bit richer hued. Room prices vary based on size, but in truth there's not a huge difference between the largest and smallest rooms. In any event, guests are likely to spend much of their time living large around the resort, both within the buildings and when availing themselves of the numerous amenities, which includes falconry lessons and a Land Rover off-road driving school.

Next door to the inn is the grand **Charles Orvis Inn,** an 1812 home renovated and managed by the Equinox. It offers nine elegantly appointed suites for $569 to $899 per night, including breakfast. It's quite nice, but not really worth the super-premium price.

Dining: Choose the dining room to fit your mood: There's the continental elegance of the Colonnade, where it's suggested that men wear jackets at dinner, or the more relaxed, clubby comfort of Marsh Tavern.

Amenities: Golf course, indoor and outdoor pools, three tennis courts, nature trails, croquet court, health club, sauna, sundeck, limited room service, concierge, valet parking, baby-sitting, dry-cleaning and laundry services, express checkout, safe-deposit boxes, valet parking, nightly turndown, beauty salon, boutiques, and a falconry school. In winter, there's ice-skating on the grounds and cross-country skiing and snowshoeing nearby.

✪ Inn at Ormsby Hill. Rte. 7A (near Hildene, south of Manchester Village), Manchester Center, VT 05255. ☎ **800/670-2841** or 802/362-1163. Fax 802/362-5176. www.ormsby-hill.com. E-mail: ormsby@vermontel.com. 10 units. A/C TEL. $215–$255 double weekends; $165–$205 double weekdays; $265–$305 double during foliage season. Rates include full breakfast. Discounts midweek and off-season. 2-night minimum stay weekends. DISC, MC, V. Closed briefly in Apr. No children under 14.

The oldest part of the striking Inn at Ormsby Hill dates to 1764 (the revolutionary, Ethan Allen, was rumored to have hidden out here). Today, it's a harmonious medley of eras and styles, with inspiring views out toward the Green Mountains, and wonderful hospitality offered by veteran innkeepers Chris and Ted Sprague. The common rooms are comfortable and spacious; the most intriguing is the dining room, built by prominent 19th-century attorney Edward Isham to resemble the interior of a sumptuous steamship. This is now the inn's dining room, where guests enjoy Chris's otherworldly breakfasts as they admire the views. Among the best guest rooms are the Taft Room, with its vaulted wood ceiling, and the first-floor Library, with many of Isham's books still lining the shelves. New for 1998 is the Tower Room, which features an extraordinary Jacuzzi-steam shower combination on the top floor of the home's compact tower. Nine of the ten rooms feature two-person Jacuzzis and fireplaces.

Dining: Chris offers guests a light supper upon arrival on Friday nights at $30 per couple.

The Reluctant Panther. 1 West Rd. (P.O. Box 678), Manchester Village, VT 05254. ☎ **800/822-2331** or 802/362-2568. Fax 802/362-2586. www.reluctantpanther.com. E-mail: panther@sover.net. 22 units, 1 with detached private bathroom. A/C TV TEL. Weekends $198–$395 double year-round; $235–$450 double during foliage and holiday weekends; $168–$298 midweek (summer). Rates include breakfast and dinner. Winter midweek rates ($120–$250) include breakfast only. AE, MC, V. No children under 14.

The Reluctant Panther, located a short walk from the Equinox, is easy to spot: It's painted a pale eggplant color and has faded yellow shutters, making it stand out in this staid village of white clapboard. It's run with couples in mind. This 1850s home is elegantly furnished throughout (as are guest rooms in an adjacent building, built in 1910) and features nice touches, including goose-down duvets in every room. Twelve of the rooms have fireplaces (some more than one), and the Mark Skinner suite even features a wood-burning fireplace and a double Jacuzzi in the bathroom.

Dining: The first-floor dining room, decorated with floral prints, achieves the feat of being intimate without feeling crowded. The cuisine is European, prepared by Swiss-German chef Robert Bachofen, a former director at the Plaza Hotel in New York. The menu changes frequently, but expect entrees like veal sautéed with mushrooms in a Chardonnay cream. Entree prices range from $21 to $27.

West Mountain Inn. River Rd., Arlington, VT 05250. ☎ **802/375-6516.** Fax 802/375-6553. www.westmountaininn.com. E-mail: info@westmountaininn.com. 18 units (including 6 suites). A/C. Spring & winter weekends, summer, $176–$224 double; spring & winter midweek $145 double; foliage season $196–$244 double. Rates include breakfast and dinner. 2-night minimum stay weekends. AE, DISC, MC, V.

Sitting atop a grassy bluff at the end of a dirt road a half mile from Arlington center, the West Mountain Inn's rambling, white-clapboard building dates back a century and a half. It's a perfect place for travelers seeking to get away from the irksome hum of modern life. The guest rooms, named after famous Vermonters, are nicely furnished with country antiques and Victorian reproductions. The rooms vary widely in size and shape, but even the smallest has plenty of charm and character. Several rooms in outlying cottages feature kitchenettes.

Dining: Dinners feature regional fare and prepared and served with flair; seasonal menus are augmented with nightly specials. Typical entrees might include filet mignon and shrimp on smoked morel ragout, and citrus poached halibut with grilled eggplant. Dinner for nonguests is $35 fixed price; reservations requested.

Amenities: Conference rooms, nature trails, nearby health club; in-room massage and baby-sitting by prior arrangement.

Wilburton Inn. River Rd., Manchester Village, VT 05254. ☎ **800/648-4944** or 802/362-2500. www.wilburton.com. E-mail: wilbuinn@sover.net. 36 units (1 with private hall bath). A/C TV TEL. Weekends $140–$205 double, midweek $120–$185, holidays & foliage $160–$235. Rates include full breakfast. 2-night minimum weekends, 3-night minimum holidays. AE, MC, V.

This is the sort of inn where you find yourself involuntarily muttering, "My, my!" You arrive at this vast country estate built in 1902 via a driveway that ascends a knoll theatrically up a broad curve and under spreading maples. The brick Tudor-style manor is sumptuously appointed, the common spaces filled with European antiques, Persian carpets, and even a baby grand.

Throughout the manor you'll find works from the eclectic modern art collection amassed by the inn's owners, Albert and Georgette Levis (he's a Greek psychiatrist; she's sister of playwright Wendy Wasserstein). The guest rooms, which aren't as lavishly appointed as the common rooms, are divided between the main house (11 rooms) and several outbuildings of various vintages. They vary in size and style. Room No. 15 is the smallest and would be suitable for one person. The second floor contains mostly spacious suites, some with great valley views. In the outbuildings, my favorite is No. 24, with plenty of room and a private deck with views of Mount Equinox and quirky outdoor sculpture. Three rooms have fireplaces. One note: The inn hosts weddings virtually every weekend in summer, so travelers looking for quiet may be best off booking midweek.

Dining: The two dining rooms—the dusky Billiard Room and the Formal Dining Room—are wonderful settings for elegant meals. Entrees change seasonally; look for dishes along the lines of cornmeal-crusted trout with a brown hazelnut butter, or sirloin prepared with a peppercorn demi-glace. Main courses are priced $17.50 to $24. Dinner is served nightly except Tuesday; outside diners should call for reservations.

Amenities: Access to the lush 20-acre estate studded with modern sculpture is almost worth the price of the room. Other amenities include three tennis courts and an outdoor pool. Golf is nearby.

WHERE TO DINE

Note that most of the inns listed above offer excellent dining, often in romantic settings.

✪ **Chantecleer**. Rte. 7A (3½ miles north of Manchester Center). ☎ **802/362-1616.** Reservations recommended. Main courses $25–$35. AE, DC, MC, V. Wed–Mon 6–9:30pm. Closed Mon in winter and for 2–3 weeks in Nov and Apr. CONTINENTAL.

If you like superbly prepared continental fare but are put off by the stuffiness of highbrow Euro–wanna-be restaurants, this is the place. Rustic elegance is the best description for the dining experience in this century-old dairy barn. The oddly slick exterior, which looks as if it could house a Ponderosa-style chain restaurant, doesn't offer a clue to the pleasantly romantic interior. Heavy beams define the soaring space overhead, the walls are appropriately of barn board, and the small bar is crafted of a slab of pine. A rooster motif predominates (*chantecleer* is French for rooster), fresh flowers decorate the tables, and, when the weather's right, a fire blazes in the arched fieldstone fireplace. Swiss-born chef Michel Baumann, who's owned and operated the inn since 1981, changes his menu every 3 weeks, but his selections might feature veal sweetbreads in a Madeira morel sauce, rack of lamb, Dover sole, or filet mignon. Arrive expecting an excellent meal; few are disappointed.

Little Rooster Cafe. Rte. 7A S., Manchester Center. ☎ **802/362-3496.** Breakfast items $4.95–$7.25, lunch $6.95–$8.95. No credit cards. Thurs–Tues 7am–2:30pm. CREATIVE BREAKFAST/LUNCH.

This appealing spot near the outlets is partly owned by the same folks at the decidedly creative Chantecleer (see above), and their inclination to serve good food creatively even applies at these budget prices. The place has more of a feel of a restaurant than a diner, with cloth napkins and jams served nobly in ramekins rather than ignobly in vexing plastic tubs with peel-off tops. Breakfasts include smoked salmon and bagels, Belgian waffles, and a luscious corned beef hash (go ahead—your doctor won't know). Lunches feature a creative sandwich selection, like roast beef with pickled red cabbage and a horseradish dill sauce.

Mistral's at Toll Gate. Toll Gate Rd. (east of Manchester off Rte. 11). ☎ **802/362-1779.** Reservations recommended. Main courses $19–$27. AE, MC, V. Thurs–Tues 6–9pm (from May–Nov also closed Wed). FRENCH.

The best tables at Mistral's are along the windows, which overlook a lovely New England bedrock creek that's spotlit at night. Located in a tollhouse of a long-since-bypassed byway, the restaurant is a mix of modern and old, blended together in a way that invites romance. The menu changes seasonally and is exceptionally inviting, with dishes like salmon cannelloni stuffed with lobster, or grilled filet mignon with Roquefort ravioli. The kitchen is run with great aplomb by chef-owner Dana Markey, who does an admirable job ensuring consistent quality. (That's his wife, Cheryl, who seated you.) The couple has been in business here since 1988, and they understand both food and hospitality. The service is just right, neither too aloof nor too folksy.

3 Brattleboro & the Southern Green Mountains

The southern Green Mountains are New England writ large. If you've developed a notion in your head of what New England looks like but haven't ever been there, this may be the place you're thinking of. You half expect to walk into an inn and bump into Bob Newhart.

The hills and valleys around the bustling town of Brattleboro in Vermont's southeast corner contain some of the state's best-hidden treasures. Driving along the main valley floors—on roads along the West or the Connecticut rivers, or on Route 100—tends to be fast and only moderately interesting. To really soak up the region's flavor, turn off the main roads and wander up and over rolling ridges, and into the narrow folds in the mountains that hide peaceful villages. If it seems to you that the landscape hasn't changed all that much in the past two centuries, well, you're right. It hasn't.

The single best source of regional travel information on the region is the **state visitor center** (☎ 802/254-4593) on I-91 in Guilford, south of Brattleboro.

BRATTLEBORO

Deeply set in a scenic river valley, Brattleboro is not only a good spot for last-minute provisioning, but it also has a funky, slightly dated charm that's part 19th century, part 1960s. The rough brick texture of this compact, hilly city has aged nicely, its flavor only enhanced since it was adopted by "feral hippies" (as a friend of mine calls them), who live in and around town and operate many of the best local enterprises.

Brattleboro is the commercial hub of southeastern Vermont, located at the junction of I-89, Routes 5 and 9, and the Connecticut River. It's also the most convenient jumping off point for those arriving from the south via the interstate. If you're looking to resupply with basics, a strip-mall area with grocery stores and the like is just north of town on Route 5.

Brattleboro has long seemed immune from the vexations of modern life, but one modern inconvenience has made a belated appearance: traffic jams. Lower Main Street (near the bridge from New Hampshire) can back up heading into town, leading to horns and frustration. It's the source of considerable local grousing.

ESSENTIALS

GETTING THERE   From the north or south, Brattleboro is easily accessible by car via Exit 1 or 2 on I-91. From the east or west, Brattleboro is best reached via Route 9. Brattleboro is also a stop on the **Amtrak** (☎ 800/872-7245) line from Boston to northern Vermont.

VISITOR INFORMATION   The **Brattleboro Chamber of Commerce,** 180 Main St., Brattleboro, VT 05301 (☎ 802/254-4565) dispenses travel information year-round between 8:30am and 5pm weekdays. Or request information via E-mail at **bratchmb@sover.net;** the Web address is **www.sover.net/~bratchmb.**

EXPLORING THE TOWN

The commercially vibrant downtown is blessedly compact, and strolling around on foot is the best way to appreciate its human scale and handsome commercial architecture. It's a town of cafes, bookstores, antiques stores, and outdoor recreation shops, and it invites browsing. Even if you're en route to a destination up north, it's well worth a stop for a bite to eat and some light shopping.

Enjoyable for kids and curious adults is the **Brattleboro Museum & Art Center** (☎ 802/257-0124) at the Union Railroad Station. Founded in 1972, the center offers wonderful exhibits highlighting the history of the town and the Connecticut

River valley, along with paintings and sculpture by artists of local and international repute. The museum is open Tuesday to Sunday from noon to 6pm, mid-May through October. It's located downtown near the bridge to New Hampshire. Admission is $3 for adults, $2 for seniors and college students, free for children under 18.

OUTDOOR PURSUITS

A soaring aerial view of Brattleboro can be found atop **Wantastiquet Mountain,** which is just across the Connecticut River in New Hampshire (figure on a round-trip of about 3 hours). To reach the base of the "mountain" (a term that's just slightly grandiose), cross the river on the two green steel bridges, then turn left on the first dirt road; go two-tenths of a mile to a parking area on your right. The trail begins here via a carriage road (stick to the main trail and avoid the side trails) that winds about 2 miles through forest and past open ledges to the summit, which is marked by a monument dating from 1908. From here, you'll be rewarded with sweeping views of the river, the town, and the landscape beyond.

Serious canoeists and dabbling paddlers alike will find contentment at **Vermont Canoe Touring Center** (☎ **802/257-5008** or 802/254-3908), where Route 5 spans the West River north of town. Located in a shady riverside glen, this is a fine spot to rent a canoe or kayak to poke around for a couple of hours ($10 for two people), a half day ($15), or a full day ($20). Explore locally, or arrange for a shuttle upriver or down. The owners are exceedingly helpful about providing information and maps to keep you on track. Among the best spots, especially for birders, are the marshy areas along the lower West River and a detour off the Connecticut River locally called "the Everglades." Get a lunch to go at the Brattleboro Food Co-op (see below) and make a day of it.

Bike rentals and good advice on day-trip destinations are both available at the **Brattleboro Bicycle Shop,** at 165 Main St. (☎ **800/272-8245** or 802/254-8644). Bikes can be rented by the day ($20) or week ($100).

WHERE TO STAY

The Artist's Loft (103 Main St.; ☎ **802/257-5181;** www.theartistsloft.com) features one—count it—one accommodation, but if it's available it's a good deal. It's a spacious and bright third-floor suite with two rooms, smack in the middle of downtown. It faces east, away from traffic and toward the river. It's run by Patricia Long and William Hays, who also operate the art gallery next door. (Hays' paintings adorn the guest room). One funky thing: the shared bathroom is in the Hays' adjacent apartment. Get beyond that, though, and you'll find good value at $78 double ($88 weekends, $120 foliage season).

Latchis Hotel. 50 Main St., Brattleboro, VT 05301. ☎ **802/254-6300.** Fax 802/254-6304. 30 units. A/C TV TEL. $75–$115 double. AE, MC, V.

This downtown hotel fairly leaps out in Victorian-brick Brattleboro. Built in 1938 in an understated art-deco style, the Latchis was once the cornerstone for a tiny chain of hotels and theaters. It no longer has its own orchestra or commanding dining room (although the theater remains), but it's still owned by the Latchis family and has an authentic if slightly dated flair. For the most part, the guest rooms are compact and comfortable, but not luxurious, with simple maple furniture and old-time radiators that keep the place toasty in winter. About two-thirds of the rooms have limited views of the river, but those come with the sounds of cars on Main Street. If you want quiet, you can sacrifice a view and ask for a room in the back. From the hotel, it's easy to explore the town on foot, or you can wander the first-floor hallways to take in a first-run movie at the Latchis Theatre or quaff a fresh pint at the Windham Brewery. See the listing for the Latchis Grille & Windham Brewery, below.

40 Putney Rd. 40 Putney Rd., Brattleboro, VT 05301. ☎ **800/941-2413** or 802/254-6268. Fax 802/258-2673. www.putney.net/40putneyrd/. E-mail: frtyptny@sover.net. 4 units. A/C TV TEL. $110–$175 double. Rates include breakfast. 2-night minimum stay first 3 Oct weekends. AE, DISC, MC, V. No children under 12.

Built in the early 1930s, this compact French château–style home features four guest rooms that are attractively appointed with a mix of modern country furnishings and reproductions. (Plans call for adding several rooms within the next five years). Two feature gas fireplaces; all rooms have VCRs (free videos from downstairs) and modem hookups. The best of the bunch is Room 4, a spacious minisuite with built-in bureaus and an old-fashioned tiled bathroom. It's close enough to town that you can stroll there within a few minutes. The one downside: it's situated along a busy road, which diminishes the pastoral qualities somewhat. The new innkeepers are Gwen and Dan Pasco, who bought the B&B in late 1998.

WHERE TO DINE

Brattleboro Food Co-op. Brookside Plaza, 2 Main St.. ☎ **802/257-0236.** Sandwiches $3.50–$5.50, salads $3.25/pound, prepared foods around $4–$5/pound. Mon–Wed, Sat 9am–8pm, Thurs–Fri 9am–9pm, Sun 10am–6pm. DELI.

The Co-op has been selling wholesome foods since 1975, and its location, downtown near the New Hampshire bridge with plenty of parking, features a deli counter and seating area. It's a great spot for a quick, filling lunch. The emphasis is on natural foods, although it's not all tofu and sprouts—you can get a smoked turkey and Swiss cheese sandwich, or opt for a crunchy salad (priced by the pound) or something like a plate of steamed cold broccoli with a garlic black-bean sauce. Before you leave, check out the eclectic wine selection and the cheeses, especially the award-winning Vermont Shepherd cheeses, made nearby in Putney.

✪ **The Common Ground.** 25 Eliot St. ☎ **802/257-0855.** Reservations not accepted. Lunch $3–$7.50; dinner $3.50–$8. No credit cards. Summer Mon–Thurs 11:30am–8pm, Fri–Sat 11:30am–9pm, Sun 11am–2pm and 5–8pm. Fall–spring Thurs–Sun 5–8pm, plus Sun 11am–2pm. VEGETARIAN.

The Common Ground opened 2 years after the Woodstock Music Festival, which establishes it both chronologically and spiritually. This culinary landmark occupies a funky, sometimes chaotic space on the second floor of a downtown building. At the top of the stairs, diners choose from a well-worn dining room with flea-market tables or a pleasant greenhouse addition overlooking the street. The Common Ground is operated as a worker-owned cooperative, and service is cordial if not always brisk. A meal might include grilled tofu with tahini, brown rice with tamari ginger sauce, or a marinated sea-vegetable salad. There's often live music on the weekends, usually of the folk variety.

Curtis Bar-B-Q. Rte. 5, Putney. ☎ **802/387-5474.** Main courses $4–$20. No credit cards. Wed–Sun 10am–dark. Closed Nov–spring. BARBECUE.

Just uphill from Exit 4 off I-91 (about 9 miles north of Brattleboro) you suddenly smell the delicious aroma of barbecue sizzling over flaming pits. Do not pass this place by, because you *will* change your mind later and waste a lot of time and gasoline backtracking. This classic roadside food joint, situated on a scruffy lot next to a gas station, has a heap of charm despite itself. This self-serve restaurant consists of two blue school buses and a tin-roofed cooking shed; guests take their booty to a smattering of picnic tables scattered about the lot. Place your order, grab a seat, dig in, and enjoy.

Latchis Grille & Windham Brewery. 6 Flat St., Brattleboro. ☎ **802/254-4747.** Reservations for parties of 6 or more only. Cafe items $6–$10; main courses $13–$18. AE, DISC, MC, V. June–Dec Wed–Mon 5–9pm, Jan–May Wed–Sun 5–9pm; also open for lunch Fri–Sun 11:30am–3pm. INTERNATIONAL.

The Latchis Grille is situated beneath the Latchis Theatre and Latchis Hotel. And it's well worth venturing downstairs, both for the international flair of the food and to sample the excellent homemade ales, stouts, and lagers made on-site by the Windham Brewery. The Latchis Grille, while subterranean, is comfortably decorated with paintings and old lithographs. The rectangular dining room has soft lighting and upbeat jazz; enclosed at one end is an informal, tile-floored bar great for sipping the local stuff. Appetizers include delectable Tibetan *momos* (steamed lamb and pork dumplings); entrees feature chicken breast stuffed with cheese, pears, and watercress and grilled filet mignon with sherried wild mushrooms. The "Vermont Favorites" section of the menu offers cheaper, more basic fare, like baked scrod and grilled pork chops.

✪ **T. J. Buckley's.** 132 Eliot St. ☎ **802/257-4922.** Reservations usually essential. Main courses $25. No credit cards. Wed–Sun 6–9pm, open later on busy nights. NEW AMERICAN.

This is Brattleboro's best restaurant. The Lilliputian T. J. Buckley's is housed in a classic old diner on a dim side street. It's been renovated with slate floors and golden lighting into an intimate restaurant that seats about 20. There are no secrets between you, the chef, the sous chef, and the server, all of whom remain within a couple dozen feet of one another throughout the meal. The entire restaurant is smaller than just the kitchen at many other restaurants. The menu is limited, with just four entrees each night—beef, poultry, shellfish, and fish—but the food has absolutely nothing in common with simple diner fare. The ingredients are fresh and select; the preparation more concerned with melding the tastes just right rather than dazzling with architectural flourishes. The beef is typically left alone in all its goodness; if you want to sample chef Michael Fuller's inventiveness, try the fish or shellfish. Vegetarians can ask for the special veggie platter.

THE WILMINGTON/MOUNT SNOW REGION

Set high in the hills on the winding mountain highway midway between Bennington and Brattleboro, Wilmington has managed to retain its charm as an attractive crossroads village despite its location on two busy roads. It's definitely a town for tourists— if you want to get a lightbulb or haircut, you're better off in Bennington or Brattleboro, but Wilmington has a nice selection of antiques shops, boutiques, and pizza joints. Except on busy holiday weekends, when it's inundated by visitors (especially from the N.Y. metro area), Wilmington still manages to feel like a gracious mountain village untroubled by the times.

From Wilmington, the ski resort of Mount Snow/Haystack is easily accessible to the north via Route 100, which is brisk, busy, and close to impassable on sunny weekends in early October. Heading north, you'll first pass through West Dover, an attractive, classically New England town with a prominent steeple and acres of white clapboard.

ESSENTIALS

GETTING THERE   Wilmington is located at the junction of Routes 9 and 100. Route 9 offers the most direct access. The Mount Snow area is located north of Wilmington on Route 100. No buses connect to Wilmington, although plans are underway to establish a connection.

VISITOR INFORMATION   The **Mount Snow/Haystack Region Chamber of Commerce,** P.O. Box 3, Wilmington, VT 05363 (☎ **802/464-8092**), maintains a visitor's center on West Main Street in Wilmington. It's open year-round from 10am to 5pm daily. Information may also be requested via E-mail at **info@visitvermont. com.** The chamber offers a room booking service, which is especially for smaller inns and B&Bs; call ☎ **800/887-6884.** For on-mountain accommodations, check with **Mount Snow Lodging Bureau and Vacation Service** (☎ **800/245-7669**).

THE MARLBORO MUSIC FESTIVAL

The renowned ✪ **Marlboro Music Festival** offers classical concerts performed by accomplished masters as well as highly talented younger musicians on weekends from mid-July to mid-August in the agreeable town of Marlboro, east of Wilmington on Route 9. The retreat was founded in 1951 and has hosted countless noted musicians, including Pablo Casals, who participated between 1960 and 1973. Concerts take place in the 700-seat auditorium at Marlboro College, and advance ticket purchases are strongly recommended. Call or write for a schedule and a ticket order form. Ticket prices range from $5 to $25. Between September and June, contact the festival's winter office at **Marlboro Music,** 135 S. 18th St., Philadelphia, PA 19103 (☎ **215/569-4690**). In summer, write Marlboro Music, Marlboro, VT 05344, or call the box office (☎ **802/254-2394**).

MOUNTAIN BIKING

Mount Snow was one of the first resorts to foresee the growing appeal of mountain biking, and the region remains one of the leading destinations for those whose vehicle of choice has knobby tires. Mount Snow established the first mountain-bike school in the country. The **Mountain Bike Center** (☎ **800/245-7669**) at the base of the mountain offers equipment rentals, maps, and advice. Independent mountain bikers can also explore some 140 miles of trails and abandoned roads that lace the region. For a small fee, you can take your bike to the mountaintop by chairlift and coast your way down along marked trails or earn the ride by pumping out the vertical rise to the top. Fanning out from the mountain are numerous abandoned town roads that make for less challenging but no less pleasant excursions.

SKIING
Alpine Skiing

Mount Snow/Haystack. Mount Snow, VT 05356. ☎ **800/245-7669** for lodging, or 802/ 464-3333. www.mountsnow.com. E-mail: info@mountsnow.com. Vertical drop: 1,700 ft. Lifts: 21 chairlifts (3 high-speed), 4 surface lifts. Skiable acreage: 768. Lift tickets: $53 weekends/ holidays, $50 midweek. Haystack only: $40 weekend/holiday, $28 midweek.

These two former ski resorts, once competitors, are now both owned by American Skiing Company, which also owns Killington and numerous other ski resorts. The main mountain is noted for its widely cut runs on the front face (disparaged by some as "vertical golf courses"), yet remains an excellent destination for intermediates and advanced intermediates. More advanced skiers can migrate to the North Face, which is its own little world of bumps and glades.

Because it's the closest Vermont ski area to Boston and New York (it's a 4-hour drive from Manhattan), the mountain can get crowded, especially on weekends. A new high-speed quad opened in 1997 and helped put a dent in some of those lines. Don't overlook Haystack, which is 10 miles distant by car (it's much closer if you're a crow), a classic older New England ski mountain, with challenging, narrow runs. Lift lines are typically much shorter at Haystack.

Mount Snow's village is attractively arrayed along the base of the mountain. The most imposing structure is the balconied hotel overlooking a small pond, but the overall character is shaped more by the unobtrusive smaller lodges and homes. Once famed for its groovy singles scene, Mount Snow's postskiing activities have mellowed somewhat and embraced the family market, although twentysomethings will still find a good selection of après-ski activities.

Cross-Country Skiing

The Mount Snow area offers excellent cross-country ski centers. The 9 miles of groomed trail at **Timber Creek Cross-Country Touring Center** (☎ 802/464-0999) in West Dover near the Mount Snow access road is a popular area with beginners and holds snow nicely thanks to its high elevation. Ticket price is $14. The **Hermitage Ski Touring Center** (☎ 802/464-3511) attracts more advanced skiers to its varied terrain and 30 miles of trails. A trail pass is $14. The **White House Ski Touring Center** (☎ 800/541-2135 or 802/464-2135), at the inn by the same name on Route 100, has the easiest access to the Vermont woods, a good range of terrain, and 25 miles of trails ($12). The center also maintains extensive snowshoe trails and offers rentals.

WHERE TO STAY

The Hermitage. Coldbrook Rd. (P.O. Box 457), Wilmington, VT 05363. ☎ **802/464-3511.** Fax 802/464-2688. www.hermitageinn.com. E-mail: hermitage@sover.net. 15 units. TV TEL. $225–$250 double Rates include breakfast and dinner. 2- or 3-night minimum stay weekends/holidays in winter. AE, DC, MC, V.

I love this place not so much for its unpretentious sense of style—the 19th century as interpreted by the 1940s—but for the way it combines the stately with the quirky. The inn is located on 25 acres of meadow and woodland, and feels a bit like one of those British summer estates that P. G. Wodehouse wrote about. Out back are cages filled with game birds, some quite exotic, that are raised for eating, hunting, and show. There's the new 15-station sporting clays area for shotgun enthusiasts. The walls are obsessively covered with the busy, happy lithographs of Michael Delacroix. And you'll find an extensive wine shop in the basement, where Californian and French wines are well-represented, especially burgundies. The guest rooms are designed for comfort more than for elegance, and are a bit past their prime. But that's part of the charm—it's still far from shabby. I prefer the four older rooms in the main inn to seven rooms in the adjacent Wine House rooms, that are a bit lacking in character, or the four rooms in the nearby carriage house.

Dining: The two handsome dining rooms are best known for their wines (some 40,000 bottles age quietly in the cellar), but the continental cuisine carries its own quite nicely. For a special treat, opt for one of the game birds raised on the premises. Entrees for outside guests are $14 to $25 (mostly $19 and up).

Amenities: Cross-country ski center on premises; sporting clays ($45 per 100), stocked trout pond, private hunting preserve, access to clay tennis court and pool (1 mile away).

Inn at Quail Run. 106 Smith Rd. Wilmington VT 05363. ☎ **800/343-7227.** E-mail: quailrunvt@aol.com. 13 units. TV. Summer $120–$160 double, foliage $165–$200, ski season $135–$180. Rates include full breakfast. 3-night minimum holiday weekends, 2-night minimum foliage season. AE, DISC, MC, V. Pets allowed (limited rooms), $15 per night.

Quail Run is a hybrid of the sort New England could use more of: an intimate B&B that welcomes families (and even pets). Set on 13 acres a short distance off Route 100, the converted ski lodge was renovated and expanded in 1997, with guest rooms done up in a contemporary country style. Family accommodations include king and bunk beds; the standard rooms are motel-size, and four have gas fireplaces. Other amenities include a kid's playroom with Ping-Pong and video games, a heated pool, sauna, and a nine-person Jacuzzi.

Trail's End. 5 Trail's End Lane (look for turn between Haystack and Mt. Snow), Wilmington, VT 05363. ☎ **800/859-2585** or 802/464-2727. www.trailsendvt.com. E-mail: trailsend@ together.net. 15 units. Summer $105–$155 double; fall $115–$175 double; winter $115– $175 double. Rates include full breakfast. 2-night minimum stay weekends, 3-night minimum holidays. AE, DISC, MC, V. Children over 7 are welcome.

Trail's End, located a short drive off Route 100 on 10 nicely tended acres, is located in an updated vintage 1960s ski lodge with attractive rooms and plenty of common space. The carpeted guest rooms that are spotlessly clean, styled in a modern country fashion with pine and wicker furniture. Six feature fireplaces, and two have Jacuzzis. The two suites are fit for cocooning, with microwaves, refrigerators, and VCRs. My favorite? Number 6, with a lovely fireplace and nice oak accents. Other good places to hang out include the main common room with 22-foot stone fireplace, the stone-floored library and game room, and the informal second-floor loft.

Amenities: Heated outdoor pool (summer only), clay tennis court, Jacuzzi, game rooms, sundeck, free videos.

WHERE TO DINE

Dot's. West Main St. Wilmington. ☎ **802/464-7284.** Breakfast $2.95–$7.25, lunch $2.75– $7.50, dinner $2.75–$10.95. DISC, MC, V. Daily 5:30am–8pm. DINER.

Wilmington is justly proud of Dot's, an institution that has stubbornly remained loyal to its longtime clientele, offering good, cheap food in the face of creeping boutique-ification elsewhere in town. Located right in the village, Dot's is a classic, with pine paneling, swivel stools at the counter, and checkerboard linoleum tile. It's famous for its chili and pancakes, but don't overlook other breakfast fare, like the Cajun skillet—a medley of sausage, peppers, onions, and home fries sautéed and served with eggs and melted jack cheese (although they certainly don't call it a medley here).The budget-priced blue-plate specials include New England fare like roast turkey and gravy served with fries and coleslaw.

✪ **Inn at Sawmill Farm.** Rte. 100, W. Dover. ☎ **802/464-8131.** Reservations recommended. Main courses $27–$38. AE, MC, V. Daily 6–9:30pm. Closed Apr and first 2 weeks in May. CONTINENTAL.

More than 30,000 bottles of wine lurk in the inn's custom-made wine cellar, and in part that's what garnered it a coveted "Grand Award" from *Wine Spectator* magazine. You can order uncommonly excellent wines by the glass, and if you feel like splurging on a $400 bottle of wine, this is your place.

But the wine is only one of the reasons the inn consistently attracts well-heeled diners. The food is deftly prepared by innkeeper/chef Brill Williams (son of founding innkeepers Ione and Rodney Williams), with entrees ranging from breast and roasted leg of duck with saffron rice and spicy black beans, to loin of venison with peppercorn sauce and wild mushroom duxelle. The converted barn-and-farmhouse atmosphere is romantic and the service superb, although the formality of the servers (one waiter will lavish grated cheese on your salad while another simultaneously proffers pepper) may put some folks on edge.

Le Petit Chef. Rte. 100, Wilmington. ☎ **802/464-8437.** Reservations recommended. Main courses $17–$28 (mostly $22–$24). AE, MC, V. Wed–Thurs and Sun–Mon 6–9pm; Fri–Sat 6–10pm. Closed late fall and early spring. FRENCH.

Situated in an old Cape Cod–style farmhouse on Route 100, Le Petit Chef has attracted legions of satisfied customers who flock here to sample Betty Hillman's creative fare. The interior has been updated and modernized at the expense of some historic character, but the quality of the food usually makes diners overlook the made-for-ski-crowds ambience. By all means, start with the signature "Bird's Nest," an innovative mélange of shiitake mushrooms and onions cooked in a cream sauce and served in a basket of deep-fried potato. The main courses are equally succulent, with selections like a fillet of salmon baked in a horseradish crust, loin of venison with red onion marmalade and poached pears, and fillet of beef with Merlot sauce and morels.

Piero's Trattoria. Rte. 100, Wilmington. ☎ **802/464-7147.** Reservations recommended. Main courses $10.95–$16.95. AE, MC, V. Thurs–Sun 5:30–9:30pm. ITALIAN.

This isn't the sort of place you'd ordinarily notice as you speed by on Route 100, but it's worth slowing down to seek out. The styleless dining room is small and dim, with just seven tables, located off the lobby to the upstairs B&B. Not a promising appearance, but note that both chefs come from the central Italian province of Le Marche. The pastas are homemade, and include a fine smoked salmon and capers tagliatelle. The other entrees are largely restricted to chicken and veal dishes (including a unique veal ravioli). Some evenings (generally on weekends) a six-course meal is offered for $25.95.

✪ NEWFANE & TOWNSHEND

These two villages, about 5 miles apart on Route 30, are the picture-perfect epitome of Vermont. Both are set deeply within the serpentine West River valley, and both are built around open town greens. Both towns consist of impressive white clapboard homes and public buildings that share the grace and scale of the surrounding homes. Both boast striking examples of Early American architecture, notably Greek Revival.

Don't bother looking for strip malls, McDonald's, or garish video outlets hereabouts. Newfane and Townshend have a feel of having been idled on a sidetrack for decades while the rest of American society steamed blithely ahead. But these villages certainly don't have the somber feel of a mausoleum. On one visit during a breezy autumn afternoon, a swarm of teenagers skateboarded off the steps of the courthouse in Newfane, and a lively basketball game was underway at the edge of the green in Townshend. There is life here.

ESSENTIALS

GETTING THERE Newfane and Townshend are located on Route 30 northwest of Brattleboro. The nearest interstate access is off Exit 3 from I-91.

VISITOR INFORMATION There's no formal information center serving these towns. Brochures are available at the **state visitor center** (☎ 802/254-4593) on I-91 in Guilford, south of Brattleboro.

EXPLORING THE AREA

Newfane was originally founded on a hill a few miles from the current village in 1774; in 1825 it was moved to its present location on a valley floor. Some of the original buildings were dismantled and rebuilt, but most date from the early to mid-19th century. The **National Historic District** is comprised of some 60 buildings around the green and on nearby side streets. You'll find styles ranging from Federal through colonial revival, although Greek Revival appears to carry the day. A strikingly handsome courthouse—where cases are still heard, as they have been for nearly two centuries—dominates the shady green. This structure was originally built in 1825; the imposing portico was added in 1853. For more detailed information on area buildings, obtain a copy of the free walking-tour brochure at the Moore Free Library on West Street.

Hard-core treasure hunters should time their visit to hit the **Newfane Flea Market** (☎ 802/365-4000), that features 100-plus tables of assorted stuff. The flea market is held Sunday from May through October on Route 30 just north of Newfane village.

OUTDOOR PURSUITS

Townshend State Park (☎ 802/365-7500) and **Townshend State Forest** are located at the foot of Bald Mountain, 3 miles outside Townshend. The park consists of a solidly built campground constructed by the Civilian Conservation Corps in the 1930s. You can park here to hike **Bald Mountain,** one of the better short hikes in the region. A 3.1-mile loop trail begins behind the ranger station, following a bridle path along a brook. The ascent soon steepens, and at 1.7 miles you'll arrive at the 1,680-foot summit, that turns out not to be bald at all. Open ledges afford views toward Mount Monadnock to the east and Bromley and Stratton mountains to the west. The descent is via a steeper 1.4-mile trail that ends behind the campground. The park is open early May to Columbus Day; a small day-use fee is charged. Ask for trail maps at the park office. The park is reached by crossing the Townshend Dam (off Route 30), then turning left and continuing to the park sign.

WHERE TO STAY

Four Columns Inn. West St. (P.O. Box 278), Newfane, VT 05345. ☎ **800/767-6633** or 802/365-7713. Fax 802/365-0022. www.fourcolumnsinn.com. E-mail: frcolinn@sover.net. 15 units. A/C TEL. $100–$255 double. Rates include continental breakfast. AE, CB, DC, DISC, MC, V. Pets allowed.

You can't help but notice the Four Columns Inn in Newfane: It's the regal white clapboard building with four Ionic columns just off the green. This perfect village setting hides a near-perfect inn within. Pam and Gorton Baldwin, who bought the inn in 1996, have retained the best parts of the inn (the chef, for instance, who has been here for more than two decades), while improving those areas where quality had slipped over the years. Rooms in the Main House and Garden Wing are larger (and more expensive) than those above the restaurant. Four of the fifteen rooms have been made over as luxury suites, with double Jacuzzis. Among the best rooms is No. 18, with its handsome cherry sleigh bed.

Dining: There's a pleasing atmosphere with low beams and white damask tablecloths, but the place isn't quite as atmospheric or romantic as other dining rooms in the region (Windham Hill and the Old Tavern both come to mind). Main courses feature delectable New American cooking, with entrees like seared tuna in coconut, lemongrass, and lime leaves, or grilled beef with portobello mushrooms and a sweet-and-sour dipping sauce. Entree prices range from $21 to $26.

Amenities: Outdoor pool, hiking trails on 150 private acres, sundeck, baby-sitting.

West River Lodge. R.R. #1 (P.O. Box 693), Newfane, VT 05345. ☎ **802/365-7745.** E-mail: wrlodge@sover.net. 8 units (2 with private bathroom; 6 others share 3 bathrooms). $80–$90 double. Rates include full breakfast. Closed during mud season. DISC, MC, V.

This is as close as you'll come to a dude-ranch vacation in the East. Situated in a beautiful, broad valley with views of farmland and countryside, the West River Lodge caters to equestrians in the summer and cross-country skiers in the winter. This is not the place to be if you prefer to be left alone on your vacation. Guests become part of the family here, with everyone sitting down to eat at 7pm and sharing stories in cluttered and cozy common rooms after the meal. The adjacent West River Stables have been offering English riding instruction since 1948, and the staff knows well the hidden bridle trails. If you're not a horse person, you can just enjoy farm life (there are also dogs, cats, and cows) or walk down the dirt lane to a quiet swimming hole.

✪ **Windham Hill Inn.** Windham Hill Rd., W. Townshend, VT 05359. ☎ **800/944-4080** or 802/874-4080. Fax 802/874-4702. www.windhamhill.com. E-mail: windham@sover.net.

21 units. A/C TEL. $245–$370 double. Rates include breakfast and dinner. 2-night minimum stay weekends. AE, DISC, MC, V. Closed the week prior to Dec 27. Turn uphill across from the country store in W. Townshend and climb 1¼ miles to a marked dirt road; turn right and continue to end. No children under 12.

The Windham Hill Inn is about as perfect as an inn gets, especially if you're looking for a romantic getaway. Situated on 160 acres at the end of a dirt road in a high upland valley, the inn was originally built in 1823 as a farmhouse and remained in the same family until the 1950s, when it was converted to an inn. Under the ownership of innkeepers Pat and Grigs Markham, the Windham Hill has ratcheted up several notches in quality as extensive renovations have managed to meld the best of the old and the new. The guest rooms are wonderfully appointed in an elegant country style; a half dozen have Jacuzzis or soaking tubs, nine have balconies or decks, thirteen have gas fireplaces, and all feature views. Especially nice is Jesse's Room on the third floor, with soaking tub, gas woodstove, a large bathroom, and lustrous pine floors; and Forget-Me-Not, with soaking tub and four-poster bed. The common areas, like the guest rooms, are appointed in a restrained country fashion that's more refined than rustic.

Dining: The dining room, which is open to the public, features exceptionally creative cooking with a strong emphasis on local and seasonal ingredients. Recent entrees have included cashew-crusted salmon with a peach-fig compote, and beef tenderloin with a balsamic glaze and a rosemary-Merlot sauce. The prix-fixe five-course dinner is $40, and offers good value at that.

Amenities: Hiking trails, outdoor heated pool, clay tennis court, game alcove, conference rooms, 6 miles of groomed cross-country ski trails.

GRAFTON & CHESTER

When I first visited ✪ **Grafton,** I was fully prepared to dislike it. I'd heard from others that it was pristine and quaint, the result of an ambitious preservation plan by wealthy benefactors. I figured it would be too precious, too fussy, too much an overwrought picture-book re-creation of New England, as envisioned by the D.A.R. But it only took me about half an hour of aimless wandering to come away a serious booster of the place. It's not a museum like Sturbridge Village or Colonial Williamsburg, but an active town with around 600 residents. It just happens to have dozens of museum-quality homes and buildings.

To the north, more commercial **Chester** is less pristine and seems more lived in. The downtown area has a pleasant neighborly feel to it, along with a handful of intriguing boutiques and shops along the main road. Chester is a great destination for antiquing, with several good dealers in the area. When heading north of town on Route 103, be sure to go slow enough to enjoy the Stone Village, a neighborhood of well-spaced, austere stone homes that line the roadway. Many of these are said to be major stopping points on the Underground Railroad.

ESSENTIALS

GETTING THERE   Take I-91 to Bellows Falls (Exit 5 or 6), and follow signs to town via Route 5. From there, take Route 121 west for 12 miles to Grafton. For a more scenic route, take Route 35 north from Townshend.

VISITOR INFORMATION   The **Grafton Information Center,** Grafton, VT 05146 (☎ 802/843-2255), is located in the Daniels House on Townshend Road (look for "visitor information" sign). For information about Chester, contact the **Chester Area Chamber of Commerce,** P.O. Box 623, Chester, VT 05143 (☎ 802/875-2939).

EXPLORING GRAFTON

Grafton is best seen at a languorous pace, on foot, when the weather is welcoming. Don't expect to be overwhelmed with grandeur. Instead, keep a keen eye out for telling historical details. Start at the **Grafton Information Center** (see above), which offers parking and access to the rest of the village. Exhibits in the main center provide some background on the village's history. Barns nearby house other informative exhibits.

From here, follow a footpath past the barns and through a small covered bridge to the **Grafton Village Cheese Co.** (☎ **800/472-3866**), a small, modern building where you can buy a snack of award-winning cheese and peer through plate-glass windows to observe the cheese-making process. (Outwardly, cheese-making is neither very complicated nor interesting.) It's open Monday to Friday 8am to 4pm, weekends 10am to 4pm.

Cross back over the covered bridge and bear right on the footpath along the cow pasture to the **Kidder Covered Bridge,** then head into town via Water Street, continuing on to Main Street. Toward the village center, white clapboard homes and shade trees abound. This is about as New England as New England gets.

If you're visiting in winter, Grafton offers superb cross-country skiing at the **Grafton Ponds Cross-Country Ski Center** (☎ **802/843-2400**), located just south of the cheese factory on Route 35. Managed by the Old Tavern, Grafton Ponds has 18 miles of groomed trails and a warming hut near the ponds where you can sit by a woodstove and enjoy a steaming bowl of soup. The Big Bear loop runs high up the flanks of a hill and is especially appealing; travel counterclockwise so that you walk up the steep hill and enjoy the rolling descent. Ski and snowshoe rentals are available; a trail pass costs $14 for adults and $6 for children 12 and under (6 and under ski free). Half-day passes are also available at noon.

WHERE TO STAY & DINE

Hugging Bear Inn. 244 Main St., Chester, VT 05143. ☎ **802/875-2412.** 6 units. www. huggingbear.com. E-mail: inn@huggingbear.com. $85–$115 double. Rates include full breakfast. AE, DISC, MC, V.

Little kids love this place. It's an old Queen Anne–style home on Chester's Main Street that's absolutely filled with teddy bears. And I mean filled. There's a 5-foot teddy in the living room and some 250 of them scattered about the inn. ("A teddy bear in every bed.") And that's just the tip of the iceberg. In the attached barn there's another about, oh, *six thousand* teddy bears for sale at the Hugging Bear Shoppe, which attracts collectors from around the world. The guest rooms are themed around—no surprise here—teddy bears. Expect bear sheets, bear light-switch plates, bear shower curtains, etc. "Panadamonium" has a panda theme; the "Winnie the Pooh Room" is all Winnie all the time.

✪ **The Old Tavern at Grafton.** Rtes. 35 and 121, Grafton, VT 05146. ☎ **800/843-1801** or 802/843-2231. www.old-tavern.com. E-mail: tavern@sover.net. 65 units. $145–$280 double year-round. Rates include full breakfast. Discounts available May–June and midweek in summer. 2- or 3-day minimum stay on winter weekends, some holidays, and during foliage season. MC, V. Closed Apr. No children under 8.

Countless New England inns seek to replicate the service and gracious style of a far larger resort, but fall short because of understaffing and a lack of capital. But the Old Tavern at Grafton succeeds, and wildly so. It should be noted that this is called Old Tavern, not "Ye Olde Taverne," a good reflection of the understated quality and professional service that has long pervaded the establishment. The inn, the main part of which was built in 1801, seems much more intimate than its 66 guest rooms would suggest, since the rooms are spread throughout the town.

Dining/Diversions: "Appropriate dinner attire" is requested, but there's still a fairly relaxed air to the three dining rooms in the evening. Dinner features adaptations of traditional New England fare, including gulf shrimp with a Ritz cracker stuffing, and double lamp chops with a rosemary and roasted garlic sauce; dinner prices from $14 to $26. Live music is offered some evenings in a rustic pub.

Amenities: Sand-bottomed pond, bicycle rentals, game room, nature trails, laundry facility, Jacuzzi, two tennis courts, platform tennis (night-lit in winter), cross-country skiing, and conference rooms.

LUDLOW & OKEMO

Ludlow is home to Okemo Mountain, a once-sleepy ski resort that's been nicely upgraded in the past decade. Ludlow is also notable as one of the few ski towns that didn't go through an unfortunate Tyrolean identity crisis, as did many winter resorts in New England.

Centered around a former mill that produced fabrics and, later, aircraft parts, Ludlow has an unpretentious made-in-mill-town-Vermont character that seems quite distant from the prim grace of white-clapboard Grafton. Low-key and unassuming, it draws skiers by the busload in winter (it's especially popular with travelers from the N.Y. area); in summer, it's a good place to slouch down in a comfortable chair and watch the clouds float over the mountaintops.

ESSENTIALS

GETTING THERE   Ludlow is situated at the intersection of Routes 193 and 100. The most direct route from an interstate is Exit 6 off I-91; follow Route 103 west to Ludlow. **Vermont Transit** (☎ 800/451-3292) bus lines offers service to Ludlow.

VISITOR INFORMATION   The **Ludlow Area Chamber of Commerce,** P.O. Box 333, Ludlow, VT 05149 (☎ 802/228-5830), staffs a helpful information booth at the Okemo Marketplace, at the foot of Mountain Road. It's generally open 10am to 4pm daily except Monday, with some seasonal variations. Information can be had on-line from **www.vacationinvermont.com,** or by e-mailing heartovt@tds.net.

SKIING

Okemo. Ludlow, VT 05149. ☎ **800/786-5366** for lodging or 802/228-4041. www.okemo. com. E-mail: info@okemo.com. Vertical drop: 2,150 ft. Lifts: 10 chairlifts (3 high-speed), 3 surface lifts. Skiable acreage: 500. Lift tickets: $52 weekend, $48 weekday.

Okemo fans like to point out a couple of things. First, this is one of the few family-owned mountains remaining in Vermont (it's been owned by Tim and Diane Mueller since 1982). Second, it now features more varied terrain, including challenging advanced trails on the south face, ridding it of the charges that it's only a mountain for intermediates. It's also put considerable effort into making it more welcoming and challenging for young snowboarders. Fans also point out that Okemo doesn't attract as many yahoos as does Killington to the north. As such, it's first and foremost a mountain for families, who not only like the varied terrain but the friendly base area whose scale isn't too intimidating for kids. Families should note also that the mountain offers three levels of ticket prices, with discounts for young adults (ages 13 to 18) and juniors (7 to 12). Children 6 and under ski free.

WHERE TO STAY

During ski season, contact the **Okemo Mountain Lodging Service** (☎ 800/786-5366 or 802/228-5571) for reservations in slope-side condos.

The Castle. Rte. 103 (P.O. Box 207), Proctorsville, VT 05153. ☎ **800/697-7222** or 802/226-7222. Fax 802/226-7853. www.thecastle-vt.com. E-mail: castlevt@luld.tds.net. 10 units.

Winter weekends $160–$210 double; summer weekends $116–$170 double. Rates include breakfast. 2-night minimum year-round, midweek, and weekends. AE, MC, V. Closed 2 weeks in Apr.

The original owner of this stone mansion, situated on a rise overlooking Route 103 (at Rte. 301), had an obvious thing for wood. The 1901 home is opulent, but its dark, chocolatey woodworking can make the house a little gloomy during the day. Not to worry, though, because at night it glows with a golden luster, warmly lit by logs burning in the fireplaces. The mansion has come a long way since Boston corporate refugees Erica and Richard Hart bought the place in early 1995. Some of the old details are nice, like the spherical glass doorknobs. Be forewarned that some of the bathrooms are quite small. On the other hand, six of the guest rooms feature wood-burning fireplaces, that are wonderful in the winter.

Dining: The kitchen produces tasty meals with a classical French touch. You might start with crab-stuffed prawns or a baked Roquefort-and-pear tart, then graduate to crispy sautéed salmon with a red-pepper-and-fennel sauce or the house specialty, rack of lamb. Leave some room for desserts, which might include a chocolate velvet terrine or the homemade fresh fruit sorbet. Entrees range in price from $16 to $24.

Amenities: Outdoor swimming pool, tennis court.

The Governor's Inn. 86 Main St., Ludlow, VT 05149. ☎ **800/468-3766** or 802/228-8830. 8 units. $95–$160 double; $265 suite. Add $10 during peak periods. Rates include full breakfast. MC, V.

This attractive village home was built in 1890 by Vermont governor William W. Stickney (hence the name) and is the very picture of Victorian elegance. The downstairs lobby and common room (both with gas fireplaces) are richly hued with time-worn hardwood, and the walls are filled with photos and mementos of the innkeeper's ancestors. The rooms vary in size (some are quite small), but each is comfortably appointed with antiques. Nice touches abound, like a turndown service with chocolates and a shot of Bénédictine and brandy delivered before bedtime.

Dining: Chef-innkeeper Deedy Marble is proud of her culinary accomplishments, and rightly so. The noted six-course dinners (by advance reservation only) are served in the handsome Victorian dining room, and the fare might be described as New England Deluxe, with entrees like polenta-crusted native game birds, or scallops in a brandied cream sauce. Just one entree is offered each night, so ask when you make reservations to ensure it's a good match with your appetite. The fixed-price meal varies from $45 to $50.

WHERE TO DINE

Harry's Cafe. Rte. 103 (5 miles north of Ludlow), Mt. Holly. ☎ **802/259-2996.** Reservations recommended on weekends. Main courses $10.95–$16.95. AE, MC, V. Wed–Sun 5–10pm. ECLECTIC.

Along a dark stretch of road north of Ludlow you'll pass a brightly lit roadside cafe with a red neon "Harry's" over the door. This isn't a hamburger joint, as you might initially assume, but an appealing family restaurant with a menu that spans the globe. Entrees are a veritable culinary United Nations, with New York sirloin, jerk pork, flautas, spicy Thai curry, fish-and-chips, Portuguese seafood stew, and chicken breast stuffed with ricotta cheese, basil, and sun-dried tomatoes. ("An oasis for the passionate appetite" is their slogan.) You may be most content with the Thai fare, which is the house specialty. On the downside, the interior is more blandly efficient than cozy, and the service can bog down on busy nights.

Nikki's. Rte. 103, Ludlow. ☎ **802/228-7797.** Reservations not accepted. Main courses $12.95–$24.95. MC, V. Daily, spring & summer 5:30–9:30pm, fall and winter 5–9pm (until 10pm weekends). REGIONAL.

Nikki's is a popular and friendly local spot that's been serving up filling meals since 1976. It's divided between the older section with a crackling fireplace, and the new addition that's bright and sleekly modern. Think of the fare as modern comfort food, with familiar favorites like ravioli and Black Angus steak, along with a few more adventurous dishes like Jamaican jerk chicken, and lobster served with a lemon-leek beurre-blanc sauce. The wine selection is good and popularly priced.

4 Woodstock

For more than a century, the resort community of ✪ **Woodstock** has been considered one of New England's most exquisite villages, and its attractiveness has benefited from the largess of some of the country's affluent citizens. Even the surrounding countryside is by and large unsullied—you simply can't drive to Woodstock on a route that *isn't* pastoral and scenic, putting one in mind of an earlier, more peaceful era. Few other New England villages can top Woodstock for sheer grace and elegance. The tidy downtown is compact and neat, populated largely by galleries and boutiques. The superb village green is surrounded by handsome homes, creating what amounts to a comprehensive review of architectural styles of the 19th and early 20th centuries.

Much of the town is on the National Register of Historic Places, and 500 acres surrounding Mount Tom (see below) has been deeded to the National Park Service by the Rockefeller family. In fact, locals sometimes joke that the whole of downtown Woodstock could be renamed Rockefeller National Park, given the attention and cash the Rockefeller family has lavished upon the town in the interest of preservation. (For starters, Rockefeller money built the faux-historic Woodstock Inn and paid to bury the unsightly utility lines around town.)

Woodstock is also a historic center for winter recreation. The nation's first ski tow (a rope tow fashioned from an old Buick motor) was built in 1933 at the Woodstock Ski Hill near today's Suicide Six ski area. While no longer the skiing center of Vermont, Woodstock remains a worthy destination during the winter months for skating, low-key downhill skiing, ambitious cross-country skiing, and snowshoeing.

ESSENTIALS

GETTING THERE   Woodstock is 13 miles west of White River Junction on Route 4 (take Exit 1 off I-89). From the west, Woodstock is 20 miles east of Killington on Route 4. Vermont Transit ☎ **800/451-3292** offers daily bus service to Woodstock, with connections to Boston and Burlington.

VISITOR INFORMATION   The **Woodstock Area Chamber of Commerce,** 18 Central St., Woodstock, VT 05091 (☎ **802/457-3555**), staffs an information booth daily from 9:30am to 5:30pm on the green from June through October.

EXPLORING THE AREA

The heart of the town is the shady, elliptical Woodstock Green. Admiral George Dewey spent his later years in Woodstock, and locals may tell you that the Green was laid out in the shape of Dewey's flagship. This is such a fine and believable explanation for the odd, cigar-shaped green that it distresses me to note that the Green was in place by 1830, seven years before Dewey was born.

To put local history in perspective, stop by the **Woodstock Historical Society,** 26 Elm St. (☎ **802/457-1822**). Housed in the 1807 Charles Dana House, this beautiful home has rooms furnished in Federal, Empire, and Victorian styles, and offers displays of dolls, costumes, and examples of early silver and glass. The Dana House and adjoining buildings featuring more exhibits are open from late May through

October, plus weekends in December. Hours are 10am to 5pm Monday to Saturday and Sunday from noon to 4pm. Admission is $1.

Billings Farm and Museum. Elm St. (about ½ mile north of town on Rte. 12). ☎ **802/ 457-2355.** $7 adult, $6 senior, $5.50 children 13–17, $3.50 children 5–12, $1 children 3–4. Daily May–Oct 10am–5pm.

You needn't be a farm or history buff to enjoy a trip to the nearby Billings Farm and Museum, a working farm worth visiting for a glimpse of life in a grander era as well as an introduction to the history of scientific farming techniques. This extraordinary spot, now operated by a nonprofit foundation, was the creation of Frederick Billings, who is credited with completing the Northern Pacific Railroad. (Billings, Montana, is named after him.) This 19th-century state-of-the-art dairy farm was once renowned for its scientific breeding of Jersey cows and its fine architecture, especially the gabled 1890 Victorian farm house. A tour of the farm includes hands-on demonstrations of farm activities, exhibits of farm life, a look at an heirloom kitchen garden, and a visit to active milking barns.

Marsh-Billings National Historic Park. P.O. Box 178, Woodstock, VT 05091. ☎ **802/ 457-3368.** Free admission to grounds; mansion tour $6 adult, $3 for 16 and under. Daily May–October 10am–5pm.

The Billings Farm and the National Park Service have teamed up to manage the new Marsh-Billings National Historic Park. This is the first and only national park that focuses on the history of conservation. You'll learn about the life of George Perkins Marsh, the author of *Man and Nature* (1864), which is considered one of the first and most influential books in the history of the environmental movement. You'll also learn how Woodstock native and rail tycoon Frederick Billings, who read *Man and Nature,* eventually returned and purchased Marsh's boyhood farm, putting into practice many of the principles of good stewardship that Marsh espoused. The property was subsequently purchased by Mary and Laurance Rockefeller, who in 1982 established the nonprofit farm; a decade later they donated more than 500 acres of forest land and their mansion, filled with exceptional 19th-century landscape art, to the National Park Service. Visitors can tour the elaborate Victorian mansion, walk the graceful carriage roads surrounding Mount Tom, and view one of the oldest professionally managed woodlands in the nation. Tours of the mansion can accommodate only a limited number of people; advance reservations are highly recommended (☎ **802/457-3368,** ext. 22).

SIGHTS NEARBY

Birders and other wildlife aficionados will enjoy a trip to the **Vermont Institute of Natural Science** (☎ **802/457-2779**), which also houses the Vermont Raptor Center. The center is home to 25 species of birds of prey that have been injured and can no longer survive in the wild. The winged residents change from time to time, but typically range from majestic bald eagles to the diminutive saw-whet owl. Serious birders might also choose to spend some time in the institute's Pettingill Ornithological Library. Other attractions include an herbarium, nature trails, and exhibits of live animals, including snakes, bees, and tarantulas. The institute is located 1.5 miles south of the village on Church Hill Road. From May through October it's open daily from 9am to 5pm; November through April open Monday to Saturday 10am to 4pm. Admission is for $6 adult, $3 for students 12 to 18, $2 for children 5 to 11, under 5 free.

About 5 miles east of Woodstock is the riverside village of **Quechee.** The small village, with a handful of boutiques and restaurants, still revolves spiritually and economically around the restored brick mill building along the falls. **Simon Pearce Glass**

(☎ 802/295-2711), which makes exceptionally fine glassware and pottery, occupies the former Downer's Mill, where it houses a glassmaking operation, retail store, and well-regarded restaurant (see "Where to Dine," below). Visitors can watch glass-blowing take place weekdays and on summer weekends from a downstairs viewing gallery. It's open daily from 9am to 9pm.

OUTDOOR PURSUITS

Outdoor activities in the Woodstock area aren't as rugged as those you'll find in the Green Mountains to the west, but they'll easily occupy travelers for an afternoon or two.

HIKING MOUNT TOM   Don't leave the village without climbing Mount Tom, the prominent hill that overlooks Woodstock. (It's part of the Marsh-Billings National Historic Park; see above.) Start your ascent from Faulkner Park, named after Mrs. Edward Faulkner, who created the park and had the mountain trail built to encourage healthful exercise. (To reach the trailhead from the Woodstock Green, cross Middle Covered Bridge and continue straight on Mountain Avenue. The road bends left and soon arrives at the grassy park at the base of Mount Tom.)

The trail winds up the hill, employing one of the most lugubrious sets of switch-backs I've ever experienced. Designed after the once-popular "cardiac walks" in Europe, the trail appears to require you to walk miles only to gain a few feet in eleva-tion. But persevere. This gentle trail eventually arrives at a clearing overlooking the town. A steeper, rockier, and more demanding trail continues 100 yards or so to the summit. At the top, a carriage path encircles the summit like a friar's fringe of hair, offering fine views of the town and the Green Mountains to the west. You can follow the carriage path down to Billings Farm or retrace your steps back to the park.

HORSEBACK RIDING   Experienced and aspiring equestrians should head to the **Kedron Valley Stables** (☎ 802/457-1480), about 4.5 miles south of Woodstock on Route 106. A full menu of riding options is available, ranging from a 1-hour beginner ride ($35, or $30 per person for parties of two or more) to a 5-night inn-to-inn excur-sion ($1,420 per person including all meals and lodging, double occupancy). The sta-bles rent horses to experienced riders for local trail rides, offer sleigh and carriage rides, and have an indoor riding ring for inclement weather. It's open every day except Thanksgiving and Christmas.

QUECHEE GORGE   Five miles east of town, Route 4 crosses Quechee Gorge, a venerable if somewhat overrated tourist attraction. The sheer power of the glacial runoff that carved the gorge some 13,000 years ago must have been dramatic, but the 165-foot gorge itself isn't all that impressive today. More impressive is its engineering history. This chasm was first spanned in 1875 by a wooden rail trestle, when 3,000 people gathered along the gorge to celebrate the achievement. The current steel bridge was constructed in 1911 for the railroad, but the tracks were torn up in 1933 and replaced by Route 4.

The best view of the bridge is from the bottom of the gorge, which is accessible by a well-graded gravel path that descends south from the parking area on the gorge's east rim. The round-trip requires no more than a half hour. If the day is warm enough, you might also follow the path northward, then descend to the river to splash around in the rocky swimming hole near the spillway.

SKIING   The area's best cross-country skiing is at the **Woodstock Ski Touring Center** (☎ 800/448-7900 or 802/457-6674) at the Woodstock Country Club, just south of town on Route 106. The center maintains 36 miles of trails, including 12 miles of trails groomed for skate-skiing. And it's not all flat; the high and low points along the trail system vary by 750 feet in elevation. There's a lounge and restaurant at the ski center and a large health and fitness center accessible via ski trail. Lessons and picnic tours are available. The full-day trail fee is $12 for adults and $8 for children under 14.

Suicide Six ski area (☎ 802/457-6661) has an intimidating name, but at just 650 vertical feet it doesn't pose much of a threat to either life or limb. Owned and operated by the Woodstock Inn, this venerable family ski resort (it first opened in 1934) has two double chairs, a complimentary J-bar for beginners, and a modern base lodge. Beginners, intermediates, and young families will be content here. Weekend lift tickets are $38 for adults, $24 for seniors and children under 14; midweek it's $21 and $17, respectively. The ski area is located 2 miles north of Woodstock on Pomfret Road.

WHERE TO STAY

Jackson House Inn. 37 Old Rte. 4 W., Woodstock, VT 05091. ☎ **800/448-1890** or 802/457-2065. www.jacksonhouse.com. E-mail: innkeepers@jacksonhouse.com. 15 units. A/C. $180–$290 double. Rates include full breakfast. 2-night minimum stay most weekends. AE, MC, V. No children under 14.

Antiques buffs will be at home in the Jackson House Inn, located just west of Woodstock en route to Killington. The furnishings in this yellow 1890 Victorian are perfectly chosen, from the Oriental rugs to the antique chests. The home was built by a lumber baron who hoarded the best wood for himself; the cherry and maple floors are so beautiful you'll feel guilty for not taking off your shoes. The guest rooms are equally well appointed, although some of the older rooms are rather small. A sympathetic 1997 addition added four "one-room suites" with fireplaces and Jacuzzis. The inn welcomes guests with a series of nice surprises, including complimentary evening hors d'oeuvres and champagne, a small basement fitness room with steam room, and a 3-acre backyard with formal English gardens. Only its location, a stone's throw off a busy stretch of Route 4 detracts from the graceful tranquillity the innkeepers have succeeded in creating.

Dining: In 1997 the inn opened a restaurant in a graceful addition facing the gardens. The fare is regional gourmet, with entrees like cider poached salmon, and roasted loin of rabbit with a parsnip puree. A five-course fixed-price meal is $45. Open nightly in season 6 to 9pm.

✪ **Kedron Valley Inn.** Rte. 106, S. Woodstock, VT 05071. ☎ **800/836-1193** or 802/457-1473. Fax 802/457-4469. E-mail: kedroninn@aol.com. 26 units (2 with shower only). TV. $120–$230 double; foliage season and Christmas week $150–$260 double. Rates include full breakfast. Discounts available spring and midweek. AE, DISC, MC, V. Closed Apr and briefly prior to Thanksgiving. Pets allowed with advance approval.

This is a stand-out inn. Located in a complex of Greek Revival buildings at a country crossroads about 5 miles south of Woodstock, the inn is run by Max and Merrily Comins, a cordial couple who offer guests a bit of history, a bit of country style, and a whole lot of good food and wine. The attractive guest rooms in all three buildings are furnished with a mix of antiques and reproductions, and all have heirloom quilts from Merrily's collection; 15 feature wood-burning fireplaces, and two have double Jacuzzis. Don't be alarmed if you're put in the newer, motel-like log building by the river. The rooms are equally well furnished, with canopied beds, custom oak woodwork, and fireplaces. And they're less expensive. Room 37 even has a private streamside terrace.

Dining: The menu is contemporary American cooking built on a classical French foundation. You might start with fresh tomatoes and chèvre, or shrimp cocktail with anchos and lime. Then it's on to sea scallops with a shiitake and sherry sauce, or sautéed chicken with asparagus and tomato. There are also vegetarian courses and a lighter tavern menu. The main entrees are priced from $16.50 to $24.

Amenities: Baby-sitting (extra charge), safe, private swimming pond with two beaches, health club nearby ($10 extra).

✪ **Twin Farms.** Barnard, VT 05031. ☎ **800/894-6327** or 802/234-9999. Fax 802/234-9990. 14 units and cottages. A/C MINIBAR TV TEL. $800–$950 double; $950–$1,500 cottage. Rates include all meals, liquor, and many amenities. AE, MC, V. Closed Apr. No children under 18.

Twin Farms offers uncommon luxury at an uncommon price. Housed on a 300-acre farm that was once home to Nobel Prize–winning novelist Sinclair Lewis and his wife, journalist Dorothy Thompson, Twin Farms has carved out an international reputation as a very private, exceptionally tasteful small resort. The clientele includes royalty and corporate chieftains looking for simplicity and willing to pay for it. The compound consists of the main inn with four guest rooms, and 10 outlying cottages. The inn is owned by the Twigg-Smith family, who are noted art collectors in Hawaii. Some of the work on display at the inn and in guest rooms includes originals by David Hockney, Roy Lichtenstein, Milton Avery, and William Wegman. Rates include everything, including open bar and use of all recreational equipment.

Dining: Meals are understatedly sumptuous affairs served at locations of your choosing—at your cottage, along a stream, or in one of the dining areas around the estate. Don't bother looking for a menu; the gourmet chefs serve what's fresh, and your meal is likely to include ingredients from the organic vegetable and herb gardens on the property. If you have any special requests, don't hesitate to make them.

Amenities: Lake swimming, bicycle and car rentals, game rooms, Jacuzzi, two tennis courts, nature trails, conference rooms, fitness center, canoes, fishing pond, croquet, concierge, limited room service, newspaper delivery, in-room massage, twice-daily maid service, valet parking, free shuttle to rail or plane, guest safe.

Woodstock Inn & Resort. 14 The Green, Woodstock, VT 05091. ☎ **800/448-7900** or 802/457-1100. www.woodstockinn.com. E-mail: email@woodstockinn.com. 141 units, 3 town houses. A/C TV TEL. $165–$325 double; $425–$535 suite. Ask about packages and off-season rates. AE, MC, V.

The Woodstock Inn, an imposing brick structure set behind a garden off the Woodstock Green, appears a venerable and long-established institution at first glance. But it's not—at least not *this* building; it wasn't built until 1969. Happily, the inn shunned the unfortunate trends in 1960s architecture for the more dignified look suitable for Woodstock. Everyone's the better for it. Inside, guests are greeted by a broad stone fireplace, and sitting areas are tucked throughout the lobby in the manner of a 1940s-era resort. Guest rooms are tastefully decorated in either country pine or a Shaker-inspired style. The best rooms are in the new wing (built 1991) and feature lush carpeting, refrigerators, fireplaces, and built-in bookshelves.

Dining: The dining room is classy and semiformal, with continental and American dishes served on elegant green-bordered custom china. Entrees are in the $19-to-$29 price range. The more casual Eagle Cafe is open for three meals, with dinner priced from $9 to $18.

Amenities: Robert Trent Jones–designed golf course (at the inn-owned Woodstock Country Club), two swimming pools (indoor and outdoor), nature trails, putting greens, fitness center with tennis, squash, racquetball, and steam rooms. In winter, 36 miles of groomed cross-country ski trails.

WHERE TO DINE

Woodstock is prime picnicking territory. A great place to provision for an excursion is the **Woodstock Farmers Market** (☎ **802/457-3658**), open daily on Route 4 just west of Woodstock Village. (It's on your left if you're headed west.) You'll find plenty of fresh produce and gourmet goods, along with a great deli counter.

✪ **The Prince and the Pauper.** 24 Elm St. ☎ **802/457-1818.** Reservations recommended. Dinner (appetizer, salad, entree) $35. AE, DISC, MC, V. Sun–Thurs 6–9pm; Fri–Sat 6–9:30pm. Lounge opens at 5pm. NEW AMERICAN/CONTINENTAL.

It takes a bit of sleuthing to find the Prince and the Pauper, located down Dana Alley (next to the Woodstock Historical Society's Dana House). But it's worth the effort. This is one of Woodstock's finest restaurants, with an intimate but informal setting. Ease into the evening with a libation in the taproom (it's open an hour before the restaurant), then move over to the rustic-but-elegant dining room. The menu changes daily, but you might start with an appetizer of ravioli with roasted artichoke or a curried broccoli soup, then move on to filet mignon with a green peppercorn sauce, or seared tuna with a Thai ginger sauce. The fixed-price dinner offers good value (although desserts are extra, at $4 to $5.50 additional), but if that's out of your budget, head to the lounge and order off the bistro menu ($12 to $16), with selections like barbecue pork, Maryland crab cakes, and Indonesian curried lamb. There's also a selection of tasty pizzas.

Simon Pearce Restaurant. The Mill, Quechee. ☎ **802/295-1470.** Reservations recommended for dinner. Lunch items $8.50–$11.50; dinner main courses $18–$25. AE, CB, DC, DISC, MC, V. Daily 11:30am–2:45pm and 6–9pm. AMERICAN/CONTINENTAL.

The setting can't be beat. Housed in a restored 19th-century woolen mill with wonderful views of a waterfall (it's spotlit at night), Simon Pearce is a collage of exposed brick, buttery-yellow pine floorboards, and handsome wooden tables and chairs. Meals are served on Simon Pearce pottery and glassware—if you like your setting, you can buy it afterward at the sprawling retail shop in the mill. The restaurant atmosphere is a wonderful concoction of formal and informal, ensuring that everybody feels comfortable here whether in white shirt and tie or (neatly pressed) jeans. Lunches features dishes like crispy calamari with field greens and crab-and-cod-cakes with a red pepper coulis. At dinner, look for dishes like crispy roast duck with mango chutney, or salmon baked in phyllo with roast shiitakes and spinach.

Wild Grass. Rte. 4 (east of the village), Woodstock. ☎ **802/457-1917.** Reservations recommended during peak season. Main courses $11.75–$18.50. DC, DISC, MC, V. Sun–Thurs 6–9pm; Fri–Sat 6–9:30pm. ECLECTIC.

Wild Grass is located in one of the few charmless parts of town, and the interior has an unfortunate chain-bistro kind of feel to it, with painted grapevines and plate-glass windows. But the food rises above the prosaic surroundings, and the menu contains genuinely creative offerings. Especially appealing are the unique crispy sage leaves with tangy dipping sauces as an appetizer. Fish is grilled to perfection here, and sauces are pleasantly zesty and piquant.

5 Killington

In 1937, a travel writer described the town near Killington Peak as "a small village of a church and a few undistinguished houses built on a highway three corners." The area was rugged and remote, isolated from the commercial center of Rutland to the west by imposing mountains and accessible only through daunting Sherburne Pass.

That was before Vermont's second highest mountain was developed as the Northeast's largest ski area. And before a wide, 5-mile-long access road was slashed through the forest to the mountain's base. And before Route 4 was widened and improved, easing access to Rutland. In fact, that early travel writer would be hard-pressed to recognize the region today.

Killington is definitely not the Vermont pictured on calendars and place mats. It's more like a satellite of Anywhere, USA strip-mall suburb. But Killington boasts Vermont's most lively winter scene, with loads of distractions both on and off the mountain. The area has a frenetic, where-it's-happening feel in winter. (That's not the case in summer, when empty parking lots can trigger mild melancholia.) Those most content here are skiers who like their skiing BIG, singles in search of aggressive mingling, and travelers who want a wide selection of amenities and are willing to sacrifice the quintessential New England charm in exchange for a broader choice of diversions.

ESSENTIALS

GETTING THERE   Killington Road extends southward from Routes 4 and 100 (marked on some maps as Sherburne). It's about 12 miles east of Rutland on Route 4. Many of the inns offer shuttles to the Rutland airport. **Amtrak** (☎ **800/USA-RAIL**) offers frequent service from New York to Rutland, with connecting shuttles to the mountain and various resorts.

The **Marble Valley Regional Transit District** (☎ **802/773-3244**) operates the **Skibus,** offering service between Rutland and Killington ($1), as well as up and down the access road (free during the day, $1 evenings).

VISITOR INFORMATION   The **Killington & Pico Areas Association,** P.O. Box 114, Killington, VT 05751 (☎ **802/773-4181**), supplies lodging and travel package information. For information about accommodations in the area and travel to Killington, contact the **Killington Lodging and Travel Service** (☎ **800/621-6867**).

SKIING
ALPINE SKIING
Killington. Killington, VT 05751. ☎ **800/621-6867** for lodging, or 802/422-3261. Vertical drop: 3,150 ft. Lifts: 2 gondolas, 30 chairlifts (6 high-speed), 2 surface lifts. Skiable acreage: 1,200. Lift tickets: $52.

Killington is by far New England's largest, most bustling ski area, and offers more vertical drop than any other New England mountain. It's the skier's equivalent of the Mall of America: huge and run with a certain efficiency but not offering much of a personal touch. That said, Killington has a broad selection of slopes, with trails ranging from long, old-fashioned narrow runs with almost no discernible downhill angle, to killer bumps high on its flanks. Thanks to this diversity, it has long been the destination of choice for serious skiers.

In 1996, Killington's owner—the American Skiing Company—acquired struggling Pico, a middling but respected ski area just over the ridge. Plans call for connecting the two areas with ski trails and lifts, making Killington even more gargantuan. (Environmental permitting has made the timetable for this hard to predict, but the link may be completed by the 1999–2000 ski season.)

It's already a huge mountain and easy to get lost on, double-sided maps notwithstanding. My advice: Ask about the free tours of the mountain, led by the ski ambassadors based at Snowshed. Alternatively, at the outset focus on one lift and follow the lift signs—don't even try to figure out the trail signs. After a couple of runs, the layout of that part of the mountain will start to make sense. Then move on to another lift.

CROSS-COUNTRY SKIING
Nearest to the ski area (just east of the Killington Road on Route 100/Route 4) is **Mountain Meadows Cross Country Ski Resort** (☎ **800/221-0598** or 802/775-7077), with

34 miles of trails groomed for both skating and classic skiing. The trails are largely divided into three pods, with beginning skiing trails closest to the lodge, an intermediate area a bit farther along, and an advanced 6-mile loop farthest away. Rentals and lessons are available at the lodge. A full day pass is $13, or $10 for half-day.

The intricate network of trails at the **Mountain Top Inn** (☎ 800/445-2100 or 802/483-2311) has had a loyal local following for years, but it's now attracting considerable attention from far-flung skiers as well. The 66-mile trail network runs through mixed terrain with pastoral views and is groomed for both traditional and skate-skiing. The area is often deep with snow owing to its high ridge-top location in the hills east of Rutland, and snowmaking along key portions of the trail ensure that you won't have to walk across bare spots during snow droughts. The resort maintains three warming huts along the way, and lessons and ski rentals are available. The trails have a combined elevation gain of 670 feet. Trail passes are $15 for adults, $12 for children.

SUMMER OUTDOOR PURSUITS

MOUNTAIN BIKING   Mountain bikers challenge themselves on Killington's five mountains as they explore 50 miles of trails. One gondola is equipped to haul bikes and riders to the summit, delivering spectacular views. Riders then give their forearms a workout applying brakes with some vigor and frequency while bumping down the slopes. Explore on your own, or sign up for a full- or half-day tour.

The **Mountain Bike Shop** (☎ 802/422-6232) is located at the Killington Base Lodge and is open from June to mid-October from 9am to 6pm daily. A trail pass is $8; trail pass with a two-time gondola ride is $20; unlimited gondola rides are $30 per day. Bike rentals are also available, starting at $20 for 2 hours, or $32 for a day. Helmets are required ($3 per day).

Also at the base lodge—and of note to families with teens—are an in-line skate park, BMX course (rentals available), and waterslide. Call Killington ☎ 800/621-6867 or 802/422-3261 for more information.

HIKING   In summer, Killington provides ample opportunities for hiking. Novices unsure of themselves in the woods or less than thrilled with the idea of actually climbing a towering hill should head for the **Killington Hiking Center** (☎ 802/422-6708), at the Killington base lodge. The center's staff can offer helpful recommendations on area trails based on your abilities. For $15 per person ($19 during foliage) you get a map, pocket field guide, and a gondola ride to the summit.

Area hikers often have their sights on **Deer Leap Mountain** and its popular 3-hour loop to the summit and back. The trail departs from the Inn at Long Trail off Route 4 at Sherburne Pass. Park across from the inn, then head north through the inn's parking lot onto the Long Trail/Appalachian Trail and into the forest. Follow the white blazes (you'll return on the blue-blazed trail you'll see entering on the left). In a half mile you'll arrive at a crossroads. The Appalachian Trail veers right to New Hampshire's White Mountains and Mount Katahdin in Maine; Vermont's Long Trail runs to the left. Follow the Long Trail, and, after some hiking through forest and rock slab over the next half mile or so, turn left at the signs for Deer Leap Height. Great views of Pico and the Killington area await you in four-tenths of a mile. After a snack break here, continue down the steep, blue-blazed descent back to Route 4 and your car. The entire loop is about 2.5 miles.

A HISTORIC SITE

✪ **President Calvin Coolidge State Historic Site.** Rte. 100A, Plymouth. ☎ **802/672-3773.** Admission $5 adults, free for children 14 and under. Daily 9:30am–5pm. Closed mid-Oct to late May.

When told that Calvin Coolidge had died, literary wit Dorothy Parker is said to have responded, "How can they tell?" Even in his death, the nation's most taciturn president had to fight for respect. A trip to the Coolidge Historic District should at least raise Silent Cal's reputation among visitors, who'll get a strong sense of the president reared in this mountain village, a man shaped by harsh weather, unrelieved isolation, and a strong sense of community and family.

Situated in a high upland valley, the historic district consists of a group of about a dozen unspoiled buildings open to the public and a number of other private residences that may be observed from the outside only. It was at the Coolidge Homestead (open for tours) that in August 1923 Vice President Coolidge, on a vacation from Washington, was awakened in the middle of the night and informed that President Warren Harding had died. His father, a notary public, administered the presidential oath of office.

Be sure to stop by the **Plymouth Cheese Factory** (☎ 802/672-3650), in a trim white shop just uphill from the Coolidge Homestead. Founded in the late 1800s as a farmer's cooperative by President Coolidge's father, the business is still owned by the president's son, now in his nineties, who continues to stop by daily in summer. Excellent cheeses are available here, including a spicy pepper cheddar. "It's got some authority," the clerk warned me, and she was right. It's open June through November daily from 8am to 5:30pm; from December through May, weekdays from 8am to 4:30pm.

WHERE TO STAY

Rutland has a selection of basic roadside motels and chain hotels, mostly clustered along Route 7 south of town. Rooms at the **Comfort Inn at Trolley Square** (☎ 800/228-5150 or 802/775-2200) include a free continental breakfast. The **Holiday Inn** (☎ 800/462-4810 or 802/775-1911) has an indoor pool, hot tub, and sauna. Likewise, the **Howard Johnson Rutland** (☎ 800/446-4656 or 802/775-4303) features an indoor pool and sauna, with the familiar orange-roofed restaurant next door. The **Best Western Hogge Penny Inn** (☎ 800/828-3334 or 802/773-3200), which is on Route 4, offers individual rooms and suites, along with a swimming pool and tennis court. Rates vary widely at these chains, depending on season and whether you're traveling midweek or on a weekend, but figure on a range of $59 to $129 double.

Skiers headed to Killington for a week or so of skiing should consider the condo option. A number of condo developments spill down the hillside and along the low ridges flanking the access road. These vary in elegance, convenience, and size. **Highridge** features units with saunas and two-person Jacuzzis, along with access to a compact health club. **Sunrise Village** has a more remote setting, along with a health club and easy access to the Bear Mountain lifts. **The Woods at Killington** are farthest from the slopes (free shuttle), but offer access to the finest health club and the access road's best restaurant. Rates fluctuate widely, depending on time of year, number of bedrooms, and number of days you plan to stay. Prices typically range from $95 to $121 per person per day, which includes lift tickets.

You can line up a vacation—or request more information—with a phone call to the **Killington Lodging and Travel Bureau** (☎ 800/621-6867), which also arranges stays at area inns and motels.

Butternut on the Mountain Motor Inn. Killington Rd., Killington, VT 05751. ☎ **800/524-7654** or 802/422-2000. Fax 802/422-3937. E-mail: butternt@together.net. 18 units. TV TEL. Winter $70–$120 double. Rates lower off-season. AE, DISC, MC, V.

Butternut is a short remove from the access road, just enough to lend a little quiet. It's not an especially noteworthy spot, but a recommended budget choice. The rooms are motel-size with motel decor, but a few extras (like a tiny indoor pool, a small whirlpool, and coin-operated laundry) make it an attractive option. There's a lounge area with fireplace on the second floor and a restaurant with full bar and darts on the first floor. Eleven rooms have air-conditioning.

Inn at Long Trail. Rte. 4, Killington, VT 05751. ☎ **800/325-2540** or 802/775-7181. www. innatlongtrail.com. E-mail: ilt@vermontel.com. 19 units. Midweek $84–$104 double. Rates include full breakfast. 2-night minimum stay weekends and during foliage season at $320–$408 double, including 2 dinners, and 2 breakfasts. AE, MC, V. Closed late Apr to late June. Pets allowed by advance arrangement (with damage deposit).

The Inn at Long Trail is situated in an architecturally undistinguished building at the intersection of Route 4 and the Long and Appalachian trails (about a 10-min. drive from Killington's ski slopes). The interior of this rustic inn is far more charming than the exterior. Tree trunks support the beams in the lobby, that sports log furniture and banisters of yellow birch along the stairway. The older rooms in this three-floor hotel (built in 1938 as an annex to a long-gone lodge), are furnished simply in ski-lodge style. Comfortable, more modern suites with fireplaces, telephones, and TVs are offered in a motel-like addition.

Dining/Diversions: The dining room maintains the Keebler-elf theme, with a stone ledge that juts through the wall from the mountain behind. The menu features a selection of hearty meals, including the inn's famed Guinness stew, corned beef and cabbage, and chicken pot pie (entrees $11.95 to $16.95). There's live Irish music in the pub on weekends during the busy seasons.

Killington Grand. 228 E. Mountain Rd. (near Snowshed base area), Killington, VT 05751. ☎ **802/422-5001.** Fax 802/422-6881. www.killington.com. E-mail: killingtongrand@ killington.com. 200 units. A/C TV TEL. Spring–fall $176–$195 double; ski season $250 mid-week, $302 weekend, $347 holiday. 5-night minimum stay during Christmas and school holidays; 2-night minimum on weekends. AE, DISC, MC, V.

This is the newest addition to the vast hotel pool along the access road (it opened in 1998), and it's a good if pricey choice for travelers seeking contemporary accommodations on the mountain. More than half (133 units) feature kitchen facilities, and most are quite spacious if decorated in a blandly generic country-condo style. Some units can sleep up to six people (priced higher), and the resort has placed an emphasis on attracting families. You pay a premium for convenience compared to other spots near the mountain, but that convenience is hard to top during ski season. The common area is nicely designed in an understated mission style, and the helpful service is a step above that typically experienced at large ski hotels.

Dining: The hotel has two restaurants: Ovations is open daily for breakfast and dinner, with dinner entrees divided between a bistro menu (pasta and pizza, mostly, price $12.95 to $17.95) and a fine dining menu, with entrees like veal and lobster tail in a sun-dried tomato cream ($13.95 to $27.50.) The Alpine Cafe is open daily for lunch and offers sandwiches, salads, and create-your-own pizzas ($5.75 to $7.95).

Amenities: Fitness center, heated outdoor pool (year-round), 2 tennis courts, hot tub, sauna, on-site day care and summer day camp, business center and conference rooms, limited room service, valet parking, massage, concierge, washer-dryer, same-day dry cleaning, and safe deposit boxes.

Mountain Top Inn. Mountain Top Rd., Chittenden, VT 05737. ☎ **800/445-2100** or 802/483-2311. Fax 802/483-6373. 55 units (20 have 1–4 bedrooms). A/C TEL. Summer and fall $176–$226 double. Winter $176–$226 double midweek; $196–$268 double weekends and holidays. Off-season $168–$268 double. AE, MC, V.

The Mountain Top Inn was carved out of a former turnip farm in the 1940s, but has left its root-vegetable heritage long behind. Situated on 1,300 ridge-top acres with expansive views of the rolling Vermont countryside, the inn has the feel of a classic, small Pocono resort hotel, where the hosts make sure you've got something to do every waking minute. Overall, the Mountain Top doesn't offer much value to travelers simply looking for room and board. But those who like to be active outdoors and who prefer to stay put during their vacation can keep busy for their money. The inn is located about a 25-minute drive from Killington's slopes.

Dining: The pleasant dining room, with heavy beams and rustic, rawhide-laced chairs, features regional American cuisine with a continental flair. Entrees, which range from $13.95 to $22.95, might include pork tenderloin served with apples and an applejack brandy sauce or New England seafood pie. Breakfast and dinner are available to guests for $42 per person per day.

Amenities: 66 miles of cross-country ski trails, horseback riding.

The Summit. Killington Rd. (P.O. Box 119), Killington, VT 05751. ☎ **800/635-6343** or 802/422-3535, or 0800/89-7627 in the U.K. Fax 802/422-3536. 45 units. TV TEL. Summer $88 double (no meals); winter $90–$175 double, including breakfast. AE, DC, MC, V.

Think plaid carpeting and Saint Bernards. Those two motifs seem to set the tone at this inviting spot on a knoll just off the access road. The inn has the big dogs and photos and illustrations of Saint Bernards throughout. Although built only in the 1960s, it has a surprisingly historic character, with much of the common space constructed of salvaged barn timbers. The guest rooms are less distinguished, with clunky pine furniture and little ambience, although all have balconies or terraces. You may not spend all that much time in your rooms, however, since the numerous common spaces are so inviting. Read some of the *Reader's Digest* condensed books filling the bookshelves, or play a game of Twister! The Summit has more character than most self-styled resorts along the access road, and offers good value for the price.

Dining: Maxwell's Restaurant is spacious and rustic, with wide boards and terra-cotta floors. Expect standard resort fare, with entrees like grilled pork chop, chicken parmigiana, and prime rib. Entrees range from $15.95 to $20.

Amenities: A circular tiled hot tub in the basement seats about a dozen. The tiny heated outdoor pool can accommodate about the same number in winter; the summer pool is larger. There's also virtual indoor golf on the property, five clay tennis courts, limited room service, coin laundry, massage, and a game room.

WHERE TO DINE

The mere mention of the restaurants along Killington's access road no doubt strikes fear into the faint hearts of poultry across the nation, because it's my impression that *every* Killington restaurant serves up chicken wings, and plenty of them. If you love wings, especially free wings, you'll be in heaven. Alas, if you're looking for something more adventurous, the access road is home to an astonishing level of culinary mediocrity—bland pasta, tired pizza, soggy nachos—capped off with indifferent, harried service. Most restaurants are OK spots to carboload for a day on the slopes or hiking the mountains, and if you're with a group of friends you may not mind the middling quality and relatively high-prices. But for the most part you shouldn't expect much of a dining adventure.

A handful of happy exceptions exist:

Choices. Killington Rd. (at Glazebook Center). ☎ **802/422-4030.** Main courses $11.95–$21.75 (mostly $14–$19). AE, DC, MC, V. Sun–Thurs 5–10pm, Fri–Sat 5–11pm, Sun brunch 11am– 2:30pm. BISTRO.

One of the locally favored spots for consistently good, unpretentious fare is Choices, located on the access road across from the Outback and Peppers. Full dinners come complete with salad or soup and bread and will amply restore calories lost on the slopes or the trail. Fresh pastas are a specialty (try the Cajun green peppercorn fettuccine); other inviting entrees include meats from the rotisserie. The atmosphere is nothing special, and the prices are higher than at most nearby burger joints, but the better quality of the food makes up for it.

✪ **Hemingway's.** Rte. 4 (between Rte. 100 N and Rte. 100 S). ☎ **802/422-3886.** Reservations strongly recommended. Fixed-price menu $50; vegetarian menu $45; tasting menu $72 (with wines). AE, MC, V. Open daily during ski and foliage seasons; closed Mon-Tues other seasons. Weekends 6-10pm, weekdays 6-9pm. Closed mid-Apr to mid-May and early Nov. NEW AMERICAN.

Hemingway's is an uncommonly elegant spot and ranks among the half-dozen best restaurants in New England (that's including Boston). Located in the 1860 Asa Briggs House, a former stagecoach stop now fronting a busy stretch of highway between Killington and Woodstock, Hemingway's seats guests in three formal areas. The wine cellar has an old-world intimacy and is suited for groups out for a celebration; the two upstairs rooms are elegant with damask linen, silver flatware, crystal goblets, fresh flowers, and contemporary art on the walls. Fellow diners tend to be dressed causally but neatly (no shorts or T-shirts). The food is expertly prepared, and the three- or four-course dinner (including extras like bread, canapés, and coffee) is offered at a price that turns out to be rather reasonable given the quality of the kitchen and the unassailable service.

The menu changes frequently to reflect available stock. A typical meal might start with a cured salmon on a crispy potato waffle or duck strudel with hazelnuts and orange. Then it's on to the splendid main course: perhaps Vermont venison with pumpkin sage pudding in fall, or cod prepared with lobster, corn and vanilla in summer. For sheer architectural bravado, little tops the caged desserts, like the pumpkin crème brûlée with apple-cider sauce. New for 1999: an à la carte menu will be offered midweek in the summer, with entree prices ranging from $24 to $32.

Mother Shapiro's. Killington Rd. ☎ **802/422-9933.** Reservations not accepted. Breakfast $2.99–$8.95; sandwiches $4.95–$7.95; dinner entrees $10.95–$18.95. AE, DISC, MC, V. Daily 7am–3pm and 4:30–10pm. PUB FARE.

Mother's is the place for breakfast or brunch. You'll find omelets, lox, corned beef hash, and pancakes (served with real maple syrup, with "first pitcher on us"). At Sunday brunch there's a unique Bloody Mary bar—you get a glass with vodka and formulate your own spicy concoction from a lineup of ingredients. It's a fun place that kids adore—it's done up in a comic-book Victorian vaudeville/brothel look, and the menu nags ("No whining," "Don't make a mess," "No substitutions concerning this menu unless it's not too busy, then we'll talk"). Although it's open for lunch and late for bar food, the quality of the food and service seems to slip as the day progresses.

✪ **Panache.** Killington Access Rd., Killington. ☎ **802/422-8622.** Reservations recommended. Main courses $20–$29. AE, CB, DC, DISC, MC, V. Sun–Thurs 6–9pm, Fri–Sat 6–10pm. EXOTIC GAME.

Panache's isn't for everyone. For starters, the restaurant—located at The Woods condo complex—offers giraffe and camel and cobra and other fare that I'll bet won't show up any time soon on the McDonald's menu. The exotic offerings attract adventurous gourmands in search of new flavors, but there's also a good selection of more traditional fare, like bison, elk, filet mignon, and veal. And once you get beyond the eye-popping menu, you'll discover a superior restaurant with a deft touch and a creative flair. The service is good, the decor is colorful and modern, and the food presentation is excellent. As an added bonus, parents who make reservations can drop off their kids (no infants or toddlers) at a wonderful adjacent game room with air hockey and video games; the staff will keep an eye on them and feed them free pizza.

KILLINGTON AFTER DARK

Killington has more going on after dark than any other Vermont ski resort, with a variety of dance clubs and live-music venues along the access road. The **Wobbly Barn,** Killington Road (☎ **802/422-3392;** www.wobblybarn.com), is best known for its popular happy hour, but also packs in the crowds for dancing and mingling until late in the evening. Expect bands that play good, hard-driving rock.

Killington's largest and loudest nightclub, the **Pickle Barrel,** Killington Road (☎ **802/422-3035**), lures in touring acts with cover charge ranging from a couple of bucks to nearly $20. The music tends to be mellower at **Outback/Nightspot,** also on Killington Road (☎ **802/422-9885**), with acoustic musicians often heading the lineup. It's the place to go if you want to chat with friends while enjoying music and wood-fired pizza. Note the curious beer-mug cooling system.

6 Middlebury

Middlebury is a gracious college town set amid rolling hills and pastoral countryside. The town center is idyllic in a New-England-as-envisioned-by-Hollywood sort of way. All that's lacking is Jimmy Stewart wandering around, muttering confusedly to himself.

The town centers on an irregular sloping green; above the green is the commanding Middlebury Inn. Shops line the downhill sides. In the midst of the green is a handsome chapel, and the whole scene is lorded over by a fine, white-steepled Congregational church, built between 1806 and 1809. Otter Creek tumbles dramatically through the middle of town and is flanked by a historic district where you can see the intriguing vestiges of former industry. In fact, Middlebury has 300 buildings listed on the National Register of Historic Places. About the only disruption to the historical perfection is the growl of trucks downshifting as they drive along the main routes through town.

Middlebury College, which is within walking distance of downtown, doesn't so much dominate the village as coexist nicely alongside it. The college has a sterling reputation for its liberal-arts education, but may be best known for its intensive summer language programs. Don't be surprised if you hear folks gobbling in exotic tongues while walking through town in summer. Students commit to total immersion, which means no lapsing by speaking in English while they're enrolled in the program.

ESSENTIALS

GETTING THERE   Middlebury is located on Route 7 about midway between Rutland and Burlington. It's served by bus through Vermont Transit (☎ **800/451-3292** or 802-388-4373).

VISITOR INFORMATION   The **Addison County Chamber of Commerce,** 2 Court St., Middlebury, VT 05753 (☎ **800/733-8376** or 802/388-7951; www.midvermont.com), is located in a handsome, historic white building just off the green, facing the Middlebury Inn. Brochures and assistance are available weekdays during business hours and weekends from early June to mid-October. Ask also for the map and guide to downtown Middlebury, published by the Downtown Middlebury Business Bureau, which lists shops and restaurants around town.

SEEING THE SIGHTS

The best place to begin a tour of Middlebury is the Addison County Chamber of Commerce (see above), where you can request the chamber's self-guided walking-tour brochure.

The historic **Otter Creek** district, set along a steep hillside by the rocky creek, is well worth exploring. While here, you can peruse top-flight Vermont crafts at the **Vermont State Crafts Center at Frog Hollow,** 1 Mill St. (☎ **802/388-3177**). The center, picturesquely situated overlooking tumbling Otter Creek, is open daily (closed Sundays in winter) and features the work of some 300 Vermont craftspeople, with exhibits ranging from extraordinary carved wood desks to metalwork to glass and pottery. The Middlebury center also features a pottery studio and a resident potter who's often busy at work. The Crafts Center also maintains shops in Manchester Village and at the Church Street Marketplace in Burlington. Visit the center's Web site for a listing of monthly exhibits: **www.froghollow.org.**

Beer hounds should schedule a stop at the **Otter Creek Brewing Co.,** 793 Exchange St. (☎ **800/473-0727**), for a tour (at 1, 3, and 5pm daily) and free samples of their well-regarded beverages, including the flagship Copper Ale and a robust Stovepipe Porter. The brewery opened in 1989; within a few years it had outgrown its old space and moved into the new 40-barrel brew house on 10 acres. The gift shop is open daily from 10am to 6pm.

Located atop a low ridge with beautiful views of both the Green Mountains to the east and farmlands rolling toward Lake Champlain in the west, prestigious **Middlebury College** has a handsome, well-spaced campus of gray limestone and white marble buildings that's best explored by foot. The architecture of the college, founded in 1800, is primarily colonial revival, which lends it a rather stern Calvinist demeanor. Especially appealing is the prospect from the marble Mead Memorial Chapel, built in 1917 and overlooking the campus green.

At the edge of campus is the **Middlebury College Center for the Arts,** which opened in 1992. This architecturally engaging center houses the **Middlebury College Museum of Art** (☎ 802/443-5000, ext. 5007), a small museum with a selective sampling of European and American art, both ancient and new. Classicists will savor the displays of Greek painted urns and vases; modern art aficionados can sample from the museum's permanent and changing exhibits. The museum is located on Route 30 and is open Tuesday to Friday from 10am to 5pm, weekends from noon to 5pm. Admission is free.

A couple of miles outside of Middlebury is the **Morgan Horse Farm** (☎ 802/388-2011), which is owned and administered by the University of Vermont. The farm dates back to the late 1800s and was for a time owned by the federal government, which in turn gave the farm to the university in 1951. Col. Joseph Battell, owner of the farm from the 1870s to 1906, is credited with preserving the Morgan breed, a horse of considerable beauty and stamina that has served admirably in war and exploration. The breed is now prized as show horses and family pleasure horses alike. The farm, with its 60 to 80 registered stallions, mares, and foals, is open for guided tours May through October from 9am to 4pm daily. There's also a picnic area and gift shop with loads of equine-themed items. Admission is $4 for adults, $3 for teens, $1 for children 5 to 12, and free for kids 4 and under. To reach the farm, take Route 125 to Weybridge Street (Route 23 north), and head north for three-quarters of a mile, then turn right at the sign for the farm and continue on approximately 2 miles.

OUTDOOR PURSUITS

HIKING   The Green Mountains roll down to Middlebury's eastern edge, making for easy access to the mountains. Stop by the **U.S. Forest Service's Middlebury Ranger District office,** south of town on Route 7 (☎ **802/388-4362**), for guidance and information on area trails and destinations. Ask for the brochure "Day Hikes on the Middlebury & Rochester Ranger Districts," which lists 14 hikes.

One recommended stroll for people of all abilities—and especially those of poetic sensibilities—is the **Robert Frost Interpretive Trail,** dedicated to the memory of New England's poet laureate. Frost lived in a cabin on a farm across the road for 23 summers. (The cabin is now a National Historic Landmark.) Located on Route 125 about 6 miles east of Middlebury, this relaxing loop trail is just a mile long, and excerpts of Frost's poems are placed on signs along the trail. Also posted is information about the trail's natural history. The trail, which is managed by the Green Mountain National Forest, offers pleasant access to the gentle woods of these lovely intermountain lowlands.

SKIING   Downhill skiers looking for a low-key, low-pressure mountain invariably head to **Middlebury College Snow Bowl** (☎ **802/388-4356**), near Middlebury Gap on Route 125 east of town. This historic ski area, founded in 1939, has a vertical drop of just over 1,000 feet served by three chairlifts. The college ski team uses the ski area for practice, but it's also open to the public at rates of about half what you'd pay at Killington. Adult tickets are $28 for weekends, $20 midweek; for students it's $20 all week; $6 for children under 6.

There's also cross-country skiing nearby at the **Rikert Ski Touring Center** (☎ **802/388-2759**) at Middlebury's Bread Loaf Campus on Route 125. The center offers 25 miles of machine-groomed trails through a lovely winter landscape. Adult ski passes are $10, students and children are $5.

WHERE TO STAY

Middlebury offers a handful of motels in addition to several inns. Two well-kept, inexpensive motels are located south of town on Route 7: The **Blue Spruce Motel,** 2428 Rte. 7 S., (☎ **800/640-7671** or 802/388-4091) and the **Greystone Motel,** 1395 Rte. 7 S., (☎ **802/388-4935**).

✪ **Blueberry Hill Inn.** Goshen-Ripton Rd., Goshen, VT 05733. ☎ **800/448-0707** or 802/247-6735. Fax 802/247-3983. www.blueberryhillinn.com. E-mail: info@blueberry-hillinn.com. 11 units. $190– $240 double. Rates include breakfast and dinner. MC, V.

The wonderfully homey Blueberry Hill Inn is in the heart of the Moosalamoo recreation area, where you'll find superb hiking, biking, canoeing, swimming, and cross-country skiing. It's located on a quiet road about half an hour southeast of Middlebury, and it's a delightful destination for those inclined toward spending time outdoors. The inn dates to 1813 and has been gracefully added to over the years, including a greenhouse walkway (appropriately called "The Jungle") that leads to the guest rooms, which are comfortable and cozy. The best of the lot is Norse Sky (the rooms are all named after types of blueberries), with skylights, a hardwood floor, and a handsome oak bed. Four rooms have sleeping lofts, perfect for families.

Dining: Meals are served family-style in a rustic dining room, with a great stone fireplace and homegrown herbs drying from the wooden beams. The menu changes with the season, but might feature an herb-crusted salmon or juniper and black pepper–crusted venison steak. The dining room is open to outside guests; the four-course meal (including hors d'oeuvres) is $35 per person (BYOB).

Amenities: The inn is situated on 180 acres and is surrounded by national forest laced with hiking and cross-country skiing trails. Lake swimming is just down the road, and there's a 10-person sauna for guests. Also: bike rentals, free coffee, and baby-sitting services are available.

Middlebury Inn and Motel. 14 Courthouse Sq., Middlebury, VT 05753. ☎ **800/ 842-4666** or 802/388-4961. www.middleburyinn.com. E-mail: midinnvt@sover.net. 80 units. A/C TV TEL. Midweek $88–$190 double; weekends $98–$210 double; $150–$300 suite. Rates include continental breakfast. AE, DC, DISC, MC, V. Pets allowed (limited; $6 additional per day).

The historic Middlebury Inn traces its roots back to 1827, when Nathan Wood built a brick public house he called the Vermont Hotel. It's come a long way since then and now contains 80 modern guest rooms equipped with most conveniences. The rooms are rather large and most come furnished with a sofa or upholstered chairs in addition to the bed; rooms are decorated in dark hues and colonial-reproduction furniture. The eight guest rooms in the Porterhouse Mansion next door also have a pleasant, historic aspect. An adjacent motel is decorated in an Early American motif, but it feels like veneer—underneath it's just a motel. Stick with the main inn if you're looking for a taste of history.

Dining: Three dining rooms offer breakfast, lunch, and dinner. Lunch includes a basic selection of sandwiches and salads ($4.50 to $6.95). Dinners tend toward traditional American fare (like meat loaf with mushroom gravy), although some entrees flirt with the mildy exotic (game ravioli or pesto-stuffed sirloin) Dinner entrees are well-priced at $9.95 to $16.95.

Swift House Inn. 25 Stewart Lane, Middlebury, VT 05753. ☎ **802/388-9925.** Fax 802/ 388-9927. 21 units (1 with detached bathroom). A/C TV TEL. $100–$185 double. Rates include continental breakfast. 2-night minimum stay some weekends. AE, CB, DC, DISC, MC, V.

The Swift House Inn is a compound of three graceful old homes set in a residential area just a few minutes' walk from the town green. The main Federal-style inn dates back to 1814; inside, it's decorated in a simple, historical style that still has a modern crispness. Guests rooms are well appointed with antique and reproduction furnishings. Especially appealing is the Swift Room, with its oversize bathroom, whirlpool, and private terrace. About half of the 21 rooms have fireplaces or whirlpools or both; all but two have TVs; most also have coffeemakers and hair dryers. Light sleepers may prefer the main inn or the Carriage House rather than the Gatehouse down the hill; the latter is on Route 7, and the truck noise can be a minor irritant at night.

Dining: The dining room is divided among three rooms. Regional fare is the specialty, including dishes like venison with burgundy and lentil sauce. Main courses are $7 to $22, with most in the $15-to-$17 range. Open daily in summer from 6 to 9:30pm; winter From Thursday to Saturday 5 to 9pm.

Amenities: Limited room service, steam room, sauna, safe.

WHERE TO DINE

Note that the two inns listed above have attractive dining rooms serving regional fare.

Woody's. 5 Bakery Lane (on Otter Creek just upstream from the bridge in the middle of town). ☎ **802/388-4182.** Reservations recommended on weekends and during college events. Lunch items $4.25–$7.95; main dinner courses $11.95–$17.95. AE, MC, V. Mon–Sat 11:30am–10pm, Sun 10:30am–9pm. Light menu only 3–5pm. Closed Tues in winter. PUB FARE/PASTA.

Woody's is not Olde New Englande. Set down a small alley in the middle of town, Woody's features dining on three levels overlooking the creek in an exuberantly retro interior with a huge neon clock, lots of brushed aluminum, soaring windows, and red-and-black checkered linoleum floors. It's the kind of fun, casual place destined to put you in a good mood the moment you walk in. Lunches include burgers, sandwiches, and salads, along with burritos and beer-steamed mussels. Dinner is heavy on the pasta selections (the Bourbon shrimp with linguine is popular), but also features appetizing selections from the grill, like Cajun-grilled salmon and a steak au poive with a brandy and three-peppercorn demi-glace.

7 Mad River Valley

The Mad River valley is one of Vermont's best-kept secrets. This scenic valley surrounding the towns of Warren and Waitsfield has something of a Shangri-La quality to it. In places, it has changed little since first settled in 1789 by Gen. Benjamin Wait and a handful of Revolutionary War veterans, including half a dozen that are said to have served as Minutemen at the battles of Concord Bridge and Lexington.

Since 1948, ski-related development has competed with the early farms that were the backbone of the region for two centuries. But the newcomers haven't been too pushy or overly obnoxious, at least so far. Save for a couple of telltale signs, you could drive Route 100 through the sleepy villages of Warren and Waitsfield and not realize that you've passed close to some of the choicest skiing in the state. The region hasn't fallen prey to unbridled condo or strip-mall developers, and the valley seems to have learned the lessons of haphazard development that afflicted Mount Snow and Killington to the south. Other towns could still learn a lot from Waitsfield: note the Mad River Green, a tidy strip mall disguised as an old barn on Route 100 just north of Route 17. It's scarcely noticeable from the main road. Longtime Vermont skiers say the valley today is similar to what Stowe used to be 25 years ago.

ESSENTIALS

GETTING THERE   Warren and Waitsfield straddle Route 100 between Killington and Waterbury. The nearest interstate access is from Exit 10 (Waterbury) on I-89; drive south on Route 100 for 14 miles to Waitsfield.

VISITOR INFORMATION   The **Sugarbush Chamber of Commerce,** P.O. Box 173, Waitsfield, VT 05673 (☎ **800/828-4748** or 802/469-3409), is on Route 100 in the General Wait House, next to the elementary school. It's open daily from 9am to 5pm during the busy seasons; during slow times expect limited hours and days.

SKIING

Sugarbush. Warren, VT 05674. ☎ **800/537-8427** for lodging, or 802/583-2381. www. sugarbush.com. Vertical drop: 2,650 ft. Lifts: 14 chairlifts (4 high-speed), 4 surface lifts. Skiable acreage: 432. Lift tickets: $49.

Sugarbush is part of the American Skiing Company empire, and its acquisition in 1995 led to $28 million in improvements, giving the ski area some flash and zip to broaden its classic New England ski resort appeal. The "new" Sugarbush announced its intentions by first linking the two main ski mountains—Lincoln Peak and Mount Ellen—with a 2-mile, 10-minute high-speed chairlift that crosses three ridges (no more irksome shuttle buses) and installing additional high-speed, detachable quad chairlifts at both mountains. Snowmaking has been significantly upgraded, and the improved slopes started generating some buzz. Happily, Sugarbush is still a low-key area with great intermediate cruising runs on the north slopes and some challenging, old-fashioned expert slopes on Castlerock. Sugarbush is a good choice if you find the sprawl of Killington overwhelming, but don't want to sacrifice great skiing in the search for a quieter and more intimate resort area.

Mad River Glen. Waitsfield, VT 05763. ☎ **802/496-3551.** www.madriver.com. E-mail: ski@madriver.com. Vertical drop: 2,000 ft. Lifts: 4 chairlifts. Skiable acreage: 115. Lift tickets: $29 midweek, $36 weekends, $38 holidays.

Mad River Glen is the curmudgeon of the Vermont ski world. Its motto is "Ski it if you can." High-speed detachable quads? Forget it. The main lift is a 1948 *single*-chair lift that creaks its way 1 mile to the summit. (It may receive national historic landmark status.) Snowmaking? Don't count on it. Only 15% of the terrain benefits from the fake stuff; the rest is dependent on Mother Nature. Snowboarding? Nope. It's forbidden at Mad River.

Mad River's slopes are twisting and narrow and hide some of the steepest drops you'll find in New England (nearly half of the slopes are classified as expert). Mad River Glen long ago attained the status of a cult mountain among serious skiers, and its fans seem bound and determined to keep it that way. Longtime owner Betsy Pratt sold the ski area to a cooperative of about 1,000 Mad River skiers in 1995, making it the only cooperative-owned ski area in the country. The new owners seem especially proud of the mountain's funky traditions (how *about* that single chair?) and say they're determined to maintain the spirit.

HIKING & BIKING

A rewarding 14-mile bike trip along paved roads begins at the village of Waitsfield. Park your car near the covered bridge, and follow East Warren Road past the Inn at Round Barn Farm and up into the hilly, farm-filled countryside. (Don't be discouraged by the unrelenting hill at the outset.) Near the village of Warren, turn right at Brook Road to connect back to Route 100. Return north on bustling but generally safe and often scenic Route 100 to Waitsfield.

Hikers in search of good exercise and a spectacular view should strike out for **Mount Abraham,** west of Warren. Drive west up Lincoln Gap Road (it leaves Route 100 just south of Warren Village), and continue until the crest, where you'll cross the intersection with the Long Trail. Park here and head north on the trail; about 2 miles along you'll hit the Battell Shelter. Push on another eight-tenths of a mile up a steep ascent to reach the panoramic views atop 4,006-foot Mount Abraham. Enjoy. Retrace your steps back to your car. Allow 4 or 5 hours for the round-trip hike.

For a less demanding adventure that still yields great views, head *south* from Lincoln Gap Road on the Long Trail. In about six-tenths of a mile, look for a short spur trail to **Sunset Rock** with sweeping westward vistas of the farms of the Champlain Valley, along with Lake Champlain and the knobby Adirondacks beyond. A round-trip hike requires a little more than an hour.

EXPLORING THE VALLEY

An unusual way to explore the region is atop an Icelandic pony. **The Vermont Icelandic Horse Farm** (☎ **802/496-7141**) specializes in tours on these small, sturdy, strong horses. Day and half-day rides are available, but to really appreciate both the countryside and the horses, you should sign up for one of the multiday treks. These range from 1 to 5 nights and include lodging at area inns, all your meals (lunches are either picnics or enjoyed at a local restaurant), your mount, and a guide to lead you through the lush hills around Waitsfield and Warren. In winter, there's also **skijoring,** that can best be described as waterskiing behind a horse. Call for pricing information and reservations.

The classic **Warren General Store** (☎ **802/496-3864**) anchors the former bustling timber town of Warren. Set along a tumbling stream, the store has uneven wooden floorboards, a potbellied stove, and shelf stock fully updated for the 1990s with a good selection of gourmet foods and wines. Get coffee or a sandwich at the back deli counter, and enjoy it on the deck overlooking the water. Afterward, browse upstairs, where you'll find an assortment of leather goods, clothing, and jewelry. The store is located in Warren Village just off Route 100 south of the Sugarbush Access Road.

WHERE TO STAY

Sugarbush isn't overrun with condos and lodges, although it has its share. Some 200 of the condos nearest the mountain are managed by the **Sugarbush Resort** (☎ 800/537-8427 or 802/583-3333), with accommodations ranging from one to four bedrooms. Guests have access to a slew of amenities, including a modern health club and five pools. The resort also manages the attractive Sugarbush Inn, right on the access road, with 46 hotel rooms and two restaurants. Shuttle buses deliver guests around the mountain, keeping driving to a minimum. During major winter holidays, there's a minimum stay of 5 days. Rates vary widely and most rooms are sold as packages that include lift tickets in winter; call for more information.

In spring of 1999, the resort began construction on a new Grand Hotel, a family-oriented hotel at the mountain's base that will offer amenities much like the other American Skiing Company Grand Hotels, such as those at Killington and Sunday River, Maine. Call ☎ 800/537-8427 for more information.

✪ **Inn at Round Barn Farm.** 661 E. Warren Rd., Waitsfield, VT 05673. ☎ **802/496-2276.** Fax 802/496-8832. www.innattheroundbarn.com. E-mail: roundbarn@madriver.com. 11 units. $135–$220 double. Rates include full breakfast. $20 surcharge on holidays and during foliage season; 3-night minimum stay foliage and holiday weekends. AE, DISC, MC, V. Closed Apr 15–30. No children under 15.

This ranks high among my favorite B&Bs in northern New England. Those seeking the romance of Vermont will find a surplus of it. You arrive after passing through a covered bridge just off Route 100; a couple of miles later you come upon a regal barn and farmhouse, set along a sloping hill with views of fields all around. The centerpiece of the inn is the eponymous Round Barn, a strikingly beautiful 1910 structure that's used variously for weddings, arts exhibits, and Sunday church services. Each guest room is furnished with an impeccable country elegance. The less expensive rooms are in the older part of the house, and are comfortable if small. The larger luxury rooms in the old attached horse barn feature stunning soaring ceilings under old log beams, and include extras like steam showers and gas fireplaces. They're worth a splurge.

Amenities: Indoor lap pool, 18-mile cross-country ski center, game rooms, guest safe, turndown service.

✪ **Inn at the Mad River Barn.** Rte. 17 (R.R. #1; P.O. Box 88), Waitsfield, VT 05673. ☎ **800/631-0466** or 802/496-3310. 15 units. TV. Summer $65 double; winter $95 double. Rates include breakfast. 2-day minimum stay holiday and winter weekends. AE, DISC, MC, V.

The Inn at the Mad River Barn, run by former Mad River Glen ski-area owner Betsy Pratt, is a classic, 1940s-style ski lodge that attracts a clientele nearly fanatical in its devotion to the place. It's best not to come here expecting anything fancy. Do come expecting to have some fun once you're settled in. It's all knotty pine, with spartanly furnished guest rooms and rustic common rooms where visitors feel at home putting their feet up. Most guests stay in a two-story barn behind the white clapboard main house; some stay at the annex up the lawn. In winter, guests can elect to get their dinners on the premises, served in boisterous family style. In summer, the mood is slightly more sedate (only breakfast is offered), but enhanced by a beautiful pool a short walk away in a grove of birches.

⚫ **The Pitcher Inn.** 275 Main St., Warren, VT 05674. ☎ **888/867-8424** or 802/
496-6350. Fax 802/496-6354. www.pitcherinn.com. E-mail: pitcher@madriver.com. 10 units
(including two 2-bedroom suites). A/C TV TEL. $200–$350 double; $400 suites. Rates include
full breakfast. 2-night minimum stay weekends, 3-night minimum holiday weekends, 5-night
minimum for Christmas. AE, MC, V. Children over 16 are welcome.

When the Pitcher Inn opened in December 1997, it instantly vaulted into the ranks
of the best half-dozen inns in northern New England. Set smack in the timeless village of Warren, this impressive structure was newly built from the ground up following a fire that leveled the previous home; only the barn (housing the two suites) is
original. But this architect-created inn seamlessly blends modern conveniences and
subtle whimsy with historic New England proportions and styling. The common areas
are appointed in a sort of American fusion style, with a little Colonial Revival, a little
Mission, and a little Adirondack sporting camp to cap it off. It melds perfectly. Be sure
to stop by the basement common room, called Tracks, to admire the impressive
stonework.

The guest rooms are equally eclectic: the cozy School Room has a quirky schoolhouse feel (the TV is hidden behind the Gilbert Stuart portrait of Washington); the
large Chester Arthur Room has presidential memorabilia set amid regal 19th century
furnishings, including a wood fireplace and a richly hued landscape over the massive
bed. Don't worry; none lapse into theme-park cute. All rooms have CD players; eight
have fireplaces (mostly wood-burning).

Dining: The dining room is an airy and bright amalgam of brick, granite, maple,
verdigris walls, Persian carpets, Mission-style lamps, and country Windsor chairs, with
a dash of modern art. (Like the rest of the inn, the styles blend together harmo-
niously.) The menu is ambitious and the New American regional meals typically hit
the mark. Look for entrees like rack of lamb with a maple glaze, pan-fried rabbit with
cranberry-vodka sauce, or salmon with a wild mushroom crust served with risotto rice
cakes. Entree prices range from $21 to $25.

West Hill House. W. Hill Rd. (R.R. #1, Box 292), Warren, VT 05674. ☎ **800/898-1427** or
802/496-7162. Fax 802/496-6443. www.westhillhouse.com. E-mail: westhill@madriver.com.
7 units. Summer, foliage, and ski seasons $100–$155 double; spring $90–$145 double. Rates
include full breakfast. 3-night minimum stay foliage and holiday weekends, 2-night minimum
on other weekends. AE, MC, V. No children under 10.

Nestled on a forested hillside along a lightly traveled country road, the West Hill Inn
offers the quintessential New England experience within a few minutes' commute to
the slopes at Sugarbush. Built in the 1850s, this farmhouse boasts a modern common
room, which offers a handsome fireplace for warmth in winter and an outdoor patio
for summer lounging. The guest rooms are well appointed in an updated country
style, and five have gas fireplaces. Although smaller, for character it's hard to beat the
two Hobbit-like rooms tucked under the eaves above a narrow staircase in the old part
of the home. The newer guest rooms over the living room include steam showers and
Jacuzzis. Country breakfasts are served around a large dining-room table, and the day's
first meal tends to be an event as much as it is nourishment.

WHERE TO DINE

The Common Man. German Flats Rd., Warren. ☎ 802/583-2800. Reservations recommended in season. Main courses $11.50–$21. AE, DISC, MC, V. Daily 6–9pm. Opens at
5:30pm on Sat and till 10pm on busier nights. Closed Mon from mid-Apr to mid-Dec.
CONTINENTAL.

The Common Man is located in a century-old barn, and the interior is soaring and
dramatic. Chandeliers, floral carpeting on the walls (weird, but it works), and candles
on the tables meld successfully and coax all but cold-hearted guests into a relaxed

frame of mind. You'll be halfway through the meal before you notice there are no windows. The menu strives to be as ambitious and appealing as the decor. It doesn't hit the mark as consistently as it once did, and guests often find themselves poking at a bland offering or two. Entrees range from roast duck served with raspberry vinegar and honey, to rainbow trout with sage leaves and pine nuts. The extravagant *Schneeballen* (vanilla ice cream with coconut and hot fudge) makes for a good conclusion.

The Den. Junction of Rtes. 100 and 17, Waitsfield. ☎ **802/496-8880.** Reservations not accepted. Lunch items $3.95–$6.95; main dinner courses $8.95–$13.95. AE, MC, V. Daily 11:30am–11pm. AMERICAN.

Good food, decent service, no frills. That's The Den in a nutshell. Since 1970 a local favorite for its well-worn, neighborly feel, it's the kind of spot where you can plop yourself down in a pine booth, help yourself to the salad bar while awaiting your main course, then cheer on the Red Sox (or Patriots or Celtics) on the tube over the bar. The menu offers the usual pub fare, with all manner of burgers, plus Reubens, roast-beef sandwiches, meal-size salads, fried chicken, bowls of chili, homemade soups, and pork chops with apple sauce and french fries.

John Eagan's Big World Pub. Rte. 100, Warren. ☎ **802/496-3033.** Reservations not accepted. Main courses $10.50–$15.50; burgers and sandwiches $6.25. AE, MC, V. Tues–Sun 5:30–9:30pm. GRILL/INTERNATIONAL.

Extreme skier John Eagan starred in 10 Warren Miller skiing films over the years, but *really* took a risk when he opened his own restaurant five years ago. Located in a 1970s-style motel dining room decorated with skiing mementos (including a bar made of ski sections signed by skiing luminaries like Tommy Moe), the Big World Pub compensates with a small but above-average pub menu that the chef pulls off with unexpected flair. Wood-grilled items are crowd pleasers, including the wood-grilled chicken breast glazed with Vermont cider, ginger, and lime. Also tasty (especially in the winter) is the Hungarian goulash, made with pork and sauerkraut.

8 Montpelier & Barre

✪ **Montpelier** is easily the most down-home, low-key state capital in the United States. There's a hint of that in every photo of the glistening gold dome of the state capitol. Rising up behind it isn't a bank of mirror-sided skyscrapers, but a thickly forested hill. Montpelier, it turns out, isn't a self-important center of politics, but a small town that happens to be home to state government.

The state capitol is worth a visit, as is the local art museum and historical society. But more than that, it's worth visiting just to experience a small, clean, New England town that's more than a little friendly. Montpelier centers on two main boulevards: State Street, that is lined with state government buildings, and Main Street, where many of the town's shops are located. It's all very compact, manageable, and cordial.

Nearby Barre (pronounced "Barry") is more commercial, but shares an equally vibrant past. Barre has a more commercial, blue-collar demeanor than Montpelier. The historic connection to the thriving granite industry is seen here and there, from the granite curbstones lining its long Main Street, to the signs for commercial establishments carved out of locally hewn rock. Barre attracted talented stone workers from Scotland and Italy (there's even a statue of Robert Burns), that gave the turn-of-the-century town a lively, cosmopolitan flavor.

ESSENTIALS

GETTING THERE   Montpelier is accessible via Exit 7 off I-89. For Barre, take Exit 8. Waterbury is located at Exit 10 off I-89. For bus service to Montpelier, contact

Central Vermont & the Champlain Valley

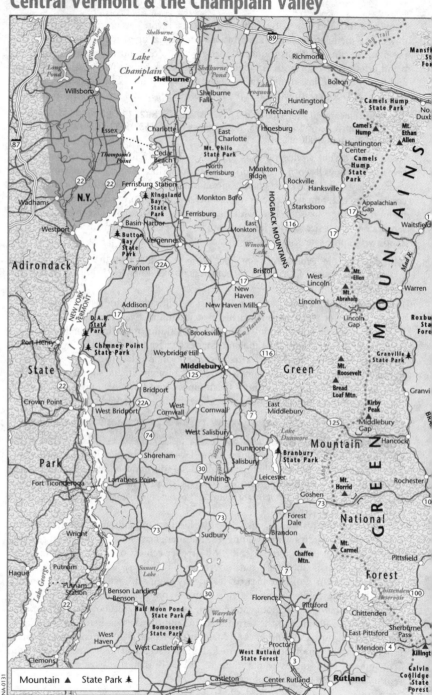

Mountain ▲   State Park ♣

NA-0131

500

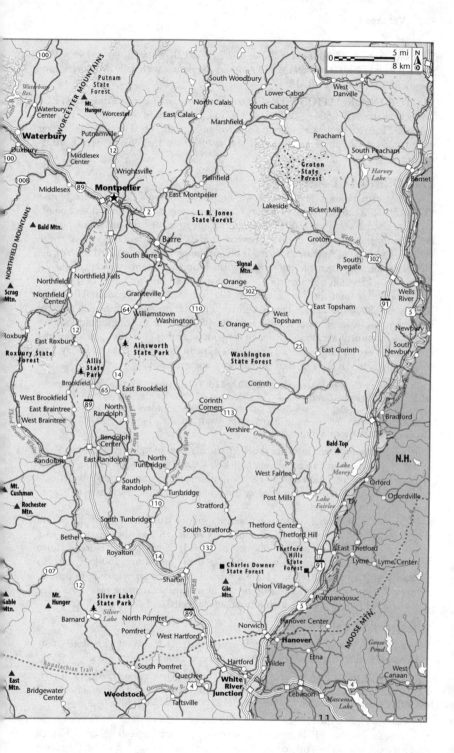

Vermont Transit (☎ 800/451-3292 or 802/223-7112). Waterbury is served by Vermont Transit (☎ 802/244-6943) and Amtrak's *Vermonter,* with daily departures from New York (☎ 800/USA-RAIL).

VISITOR INFORMATION   The **Central Vermont Chamber of Commerce,** P.O. Box 336, Barre, VT 05641 (☎ 802/229-5711), is located on Stewart Road off Exit 7 of I-89. Turn left at the first light; it's one-half mile on the left. The chamber is open weekdays 9am to 5pm. Information is also available on the Web at **www.central-vt.com.**

EXPLORING THE AREA

Start your exploration of Montpelier with a visit to the gold-domed **State House** (☎ 802/828-2228). A statue of Ethan Allen guards the doors. Three capitol buildings rose on this site since 1809; the present building retained the impressive portico designed during the height of Greek Revival style in 1836. It was modeled after the temple of Theseus in Athens, and is made of Vermont granite. Self-guided tours of the capitol are offered when the building is open, Monday to Friday (except holidays) 7:45am to 4:15pm; in summer, it's also open Saturdays 11am to 3pm.

A short stroll from the State House, at 109 State St., is the **Vermont Historical Society** (☎ 802/828-2291). This is a great spot to admire some of the rich tapestry of Vermont's history. The museum is housed in a replica of the elegant old Pavilion House, a prominent Victorian hotel, and contains a number of artifacts, including the gun once owned by Ethan Allen. The society's museum is open Tuesday to Friday 9am to 4:30pm, Saturday 9am to 4pm, and Sunday noon to 4pm.

Rock of Ages Quarry. Graniteville. ☎ 802/476-3119. www.rockofages.com. Tours $4 adults, $3.50 seniors 62 and over, $1.50 children 6–12, free for children under 6. Narrated tours June to mid-Oct 9:15am–3pm, visitor center May–Oct Mon–Sat 8:30am–5pm, Sun noon–5pm. Closed July 4. From Barre, drive south on Rte. 14, turn left at lights by McDonald's; watch for signs to quarry.

When in or around Barre, listen for the deep, throaty hum of industry. That's the Rock of Ages Quarry, set on a rocky hillside high above town near the aptly named hamlet of Graniteville. A free visitor's center presents informative exhibits, a video about quarrying, a glimpse at an old granite quarry (no longer active), and a selection of granite gifts.

For a look at the active quarry, sign up for a guided half-hour tour of the world's largest quarry (note the tour season and hours above). An old bus groans up to a viewer's platform high above the 500-foot, man-made canyon, where workers cleave huge slabs of fine-grained granite and hoist them out using 150-foot derricks anchored with a spider's web of 15 miles of steel cable. It's an operation to behold. Afterward, visitors are invited to stop by the nearby manufacturing plant to see the granite carved into memorials, architectural adornments, and other pieces.

WHERE TO STAY

Between Montpelier and Barre is an unlovely 6-mile stretch of road with motels, fast-food restaurants, and many of the other conveniences sought by travelers.

Capitol Plaza Hotel. 100 State St., Montpelier, VT 05602. ☎ 800/274-5252 or 802/223-5252. Fax 802/229-5427. www.capitolplaza.com. 46 units. A/C TV TEL. Midweek $82 double; weekends $92 double; foliage season $105 double. AE, DISC, MC, V.

The Capitol Plaza is the favored hotel of folks coming into town on business with the government, but is well located (across from the state capitol) to serve visitors exploring the town. The carpeted lobby is small and has a colonial cast to it; the rooms on the three upper floors also adopt a light, faux-colonial tone and feature the usual hotel amenities, including in-room coffeemakers. The hotel is nothing fancy, but it is clean, comfortable, and convenient. Plans call for adding several rooms by late 1999.

Dining: The hotel operates a locally popular steakhouse called J. Morgan's on the first floor, with steaks and other meats priced at $12.95 (for grilled Thai lamb) to $23.95 (for a 24-oz. porterhouse.) Less expensive dishes include pizza, pasta, and sandwiches. Open for all three meals daily.

Inn at Montpelier. 147 Main St., Montpelier, VT 05602. ☎ **802/223-2727.** Fax 802/223-0722. 19 units. A/C TV TEL. $99–$155 double (foliage season $119–$169). Rates include continental breakfast. AE, DC, DISC, MC, V.

Two historic in-town homes house guests at the Inn at Montpelier, and both offer superb accommodations with most major amenities. The main, cream-colored Federal-style inn, built in 1827, features a mix of historical and up-to-date furnishings, along with a sunny sitting room and deck off the rear of the second floor. The larger front rooms are nicely appointed, but so too are the much smaller rooms in the former servants' wing. Room 27 is especially pleasant and features a large private deck. The inn is a shade more antiseptic and Spartanly furnished than other historic inns I've visited, but it's certainly more intriguing and comfortable than any chain hotel.

WHERE TO DINE

Horn of the Moon. 8 Langdon St., Montpelier. ☎ **802/223-2895.** Reservations not accepted. Breakfast $2.50–$6; lunch $4–$6; dinner $6–$10. No credit cards (out-of-state checks OK). Tues–Sat 7am–9pm, Sun 9am–7pm (open Sun until 9pm summer and early fall). VEGETARIAN.

This relaxed, informal, and inexpensive restaurant overlooking a tributary of the Winooski was the first vegetarian restaurant in Vermont, and it remains one of the best. In fact, it's appealing enough to attract plenty of carnivores, drawn by the robust pastas, tasty sandwiches made on whole-wheat flat bread, and the Mexican-style dishes like burritos and tostados. If you're looking for a full three-course meal with dinner rolls and linens, you're better off around the corner at the Main Street Grill. But if you want wholesome, inexpensive food, get here early and get here often.

Main Street Grill & Bar. 118 Main St., Montpelier. ☎ **802/223-3188.** Reservations usually not necessary. Lunch items $3.75–$7.95; dinner entrees $5.95–$12.75. AE, DISC, MC, V. Mon–Fri 7–10am and 11:30am–2pm, Sat 8:30–10:30am and 11:30am–2pm, Sun 10am–2pm; daily 5:30–9pm. AMERICAN/ECLECTIC.

This airy, modern grill serves as classroom and ongoing exam for students of the New England Culinary Institute, which is located just down the block. It's not unusual to see knots of students, toques at a rakish angle, walking between the restaurant and class. Diners can eat in the first-level dining room, watching street life through the broad windows (in summer, there's seating on a narrow porch outside the windows), or burrow in the homey bar downstairs. Dishes change with the semester, but might include sautéed rainbow trout with rock shrimp, wood-grilled flank steak, or autumn squash ravioli. For memorable, upscale dining, head to the second-floor Chef's Table, which is also part of the culinary institute. Entrees here range from $15.25 to $18.75.

9 Stowe

Stowe is a wonderful destination, summer, fall, and winter. It was one of Vermont's first winter destination areas, but it has managed the decades-long juggernaut of growth reasonably well and with good humor. There are condo developments and strip mall–style restaurants, to be sure. In fact, this small town with a year-round population of just 3,400 boasts some 62 lodging establishments and more than 50 restaurants. But by and large it has managed to preserve its essential character quite well, including trademark views of the surrounding mountains and vistas across the fertile farmlands of the valley floor. Thanks to its history and charm, Stowe tends to attract a more upscale clientele than, say, Killington or Okemo, and the choice of lodging and dining is more interesting and diverse.

Stowe is quaint, compact, and home to what may be Vermont's most gracefully tapered church spire, located atop the Stowe Community Church. It's one of the most appealing of the ski areas in summer. Because the mountain is a few miles from the village, the town doesn't take on that woebegone emptiness that many ski areas do. You can actually park your car and enjoyably explore by foot or bike, which isn't the case at ski resorts that grew up around large parking lots and condo clusters.

Most of the development of recent decades has taken place along Mountain Road (Route 108), which runs northwest of the village to the base of Mount Mansfield and the Stowe ski area. Here you'll find an array of motels, restaurants, shops, bars, and even a three-screen cinema, with many establishments tastefully tucked out of sight. The road has all the convenience of a strip-mall area, but without the aesthetic blight.

The one complaint about Mountain Road: it invariably backs up at the end of the ski day in winter and on foliage weekends, and can make a trip into the village an interesting experiment in blood pressure management. Fortunately, a free trolley-bus connects the village with the mountain during ski season, so you can let your car get snowed in, and prevent outbreaks of village traffic from getting under your skin.

ESSENTIALS

GETTING THERE   Stowe is located on Route 100 north of Waterbury and south of Morrisville. In summer, Stowe may also be reached via Smugglers Notch on Route 108. This pass, which squeezes narrowly between the rocks and is not recommended for RVs or trailers, is closed in winter.

There is no direct train or bus service to Stowe. Travel to Waterbury, 10 miles south of Stowe, via **Vermont Transit** (☎ **800/451-3292** or 802-244-6943) or **Amtrak** (☎ **800/872-7245**), then connect to Stowe via rental car (Thrifty, ☎ **802/244-8800**), limo (Richard's Limousine Service, ☎ **800/698-3176** or 802/253-5600), or taxi (Peg's Pick Up, ☎ **800/370-9490** or 802/253-9490).

VISITOR INFORMATION   The **Stowe Area Association,** P.O. Box 1320, Stowe, VT 05672 (☎ **800/247-8693** or 802/253-7321), maintains a handy office on Main Street in the village center, which is open from 9am to 8pm Monday to Friday, and 10am to 5pm weekends (limited hours during slow times). Stowe's home page on the Internet may be found at **www.stoweinfo.com.**

The **Green Mountain Club** (☎ **802/244-7037**), a venerable statewide association devoted to building and maintaining backcountry trails, has a visitor's center on Route 100 between Waterbury and Stowe.

SUMMER OUTDOOR PURSUITS

Stowe's history is linked to winter recreation, but it's also an outstanding fair-weather destination, surrounded by lush, rolling green hills and open farmlands and towered over by craggy **Mount Mansfield,** Vermont's highest peak at 4,393 feet.

Deciding how to get atop Mount Mansfield is half the challenge. The **toll road** (☎ **802/253-7311**) traces its lineage back to the 19th century, when it served horse-drawn vehicles bringing passengers to the old hotel sited near the mountain's crown. (The hotel was demolished in the 1960s.) Drivers now twist their way up this road and park below the summit of Mansfield; a 2-hour hike along well-marked trails will bring you to the top with its unforgettable views. The toll road is open from late May to mid-October. The fare is $12 per car with up to six passengers, $2 per additional person. Ascending by foot or bicycle is free.

Another option is the Stowe **gondola** (☎ 802/253-7311), which whisks visitors to within 1½ miles of the summit at the Cliff House Restaurant. Hikers can explore the rugged, open ridgeline, then descend before twilight. The gondola runs from mid-June to mid-October and costs $10 round-trip for adults, $6 for children 6 to 12.

The budget route up Mount Mansfield (and to my mind the most rewarding), is on foot, and you have at least nine choices for an ascent. The easiest but least pleasing route is up the toll road. Other options require local guidance and a good map. Ask for information from knowledgeable locals (your inn might be of help), or stop by the Green Mountain Club headquarters, open weekdays, on Route 100 about 4 miles south of Stowe. GMC can also assist with advice on other area trails.

One of the most understated, most beloved local attractions is the **Stowe Recreation Path,** which winds 5.3 miles from behind the Stowe Community Church up the valley toward the mountain, ending behind the Topnotch Tennis Center. This exceptionally appealing pathway, completed in 1989, is heavily used by locals for transportation and exercise in summer; in winter, it serves as a cross-country ski trail. Connect to the pathway at either end or at points where it crosses side roads that lead to Mountain Road. No motorized vehicles or skateboards are allowed.

All manner of recreational paraphernalia is available for rent at **The Mountain Bike Shop** (☎ 802/253-7919), which is right on the Rec Path. This includes full-suspension demo bikes, baby joggers, and bike trailers. Basic bike rentals are $16 for 4 hours, which is plenty long enough to explore the path. The shop is on Mountain Road (across from the Golden Eagle Resort) and is open from 9am to 6pm daily in summer. (This is also a good spot for cross-country ski and snowshoe rentals in winter.)

Stowe also has an **in-line skate park** near the Spruce Peak base lodge, which is open daily from 10am to 5pm. It features a training loop, hockey area, half-pipe, spine ramp and slalom course. Rates are $10 for a day pass, or $15 for day pass and equipment rental. Half-day rates are also available. Call ☎ 802/253-3000 for more information.

Fans of paddle sports should head toward **Umiak Outdoor Outfitters,** located at 849 South Main St. in Stowe, ☎ 802/253-2317. The folks here offer guided river trips (flatwater or light rapids) and instruction (learn how to roll that kayak!), as well as canoe, kayak, and raft rentals ($25 to $35 per day).

SKIING
ALPINE SKIING

Stowe Mountain Resort. Stowe, VT 05672. ☎ 800/253-4754 for lodging or 802/ 253-3000. www.stowe.com. E-mail: stosales@sover.net. Vertical drop: 2,360 ft. Lifts: 1 gondola, 8 chairlifts (1 high-speed), 2 surface lifts. Skiable acreage: 480. Lift tickets: $54 holiday, $52 nonholiday.

Stowe was once *the* place to ski in New England—one of the first, one of the classiest, and one of the best ski resorts anywhere in the world. Killington, Sunday River, and Sugarloaf—among others—have all captured other superlatives, and never mind the Rocky Mountain resorts, that are much more accessible to easterners now than they ever were 50 years ago. But this historic resort, first developed in the 1930s, still has loads of charm and plenty of great runs. It's one of the best places for the full New England ski experience, and still offers great challenges to skiers. Especially notable are its legendary "Front Four" trails (National, Starr, Lift Line, and Goat), that have humbled more than a handful of skiers attempting to claw their way from intermediate to

The Story of Ben & Jerry

The doleful cows standing amid a bright-green meadow on Ben & Jerry's ice-cream pints have become almost a symbol for Vermont. But Ben & Jerry's cows—actually, they're Vermont artist Woody Jackson's cows—have also become a symbol for friendly capitalism ("hippie capitalism," as some prefer).

The founding of the company is a legend in business circles. Two friends from Long Island, New York, Ben Cohen and Jerry Greenfield, started up their company in Burlington in 1978 with $12,000 and a few mail-order lessons in ice-cream making. The pair experimented with the flavor samples they obtained free from salesmen and sold their products out of an old gas station in town. Embracing the outlook that work should be fun, they gave away free ice cream at community events, staged free outdoor films in summer, and plowed profits back into the community. This approach, along with the exceptional quality of their product, built a successful corporation with sales in the hundreds of millions of dollars.

The main factory in Waterbury, about 10 miles south of Stowe, is among the most popular tourist attractions in Vermont. The plant is located about a mile north of I-89 on Route 100, and the grounds have a festival-marketplace feel to them, despite the fact that there's no festival and no marketplace. During peak summer season, crowds mill about waiting for the 30-minute factory tours (the afternoon tours fill up quickly, so get there early if you want to avoid a long wait). Once you've got your ticket, browse the small ice-cream museum (learn the long, strange history of Cherry Garcia), buy a cone of your favorite flavor at the scoop shop, or lounge along the promenade, which is scattered with Adirondack chairs and picnic tables. Tours are $2 for adults, free for children under 12. For more information, call ☎ 802/244-8687.

expert. The mountain has four good, long lifts, that go from top to bottom—not the usual patchwork of shorter lifts you find at other ski areas.

CROSS-COUNTRY SKIING

Stowe is an outstanding destination for cross-country skiers, offering no fewer than four groomed ski areas with a combined total of 93 miles of trails traversing everything from gentle valley floors to challenging mountain peaks.

The **Trapp Family Lodge Cross-Country Ski Center,** on Luce Hill Road, 2 miles from Mountain Road (☎ **800/826-7000** or 802/253-8511; www.trappfamily.com), was the nation's first cross-country ski center. It remains one of the most gloriously situated in the Northeast, set atop a ridge with views across the broad valley and into the folds of the mountains flanking Mount Mansfield. The center features 36 miles of groomed trails on its 2,200 acres of rolling forestland. Rates are $12 for a trail pass, $13 for equipment rental, and $15 for a group lesson. A package of all three is $30.

The **Edson Hill Manor Ski Touring Center** (☎ **800/621-0284** or 802/253-8954) has 33 miles of wooded trails just off Mountain Road ($10 for a day pass). Also offering appealing ski touring are the **Stowe Mountain Resort Cross-Country Touring Center** (☎ **800/253-4754** or 802/253-7311), with 48 miles at the base of Mount Mansfield ($10, includes access to Tollhouse chairlift), and **Topnotch Resort** (☎ **800/451-8686** or 802/253-8585), with 15 miles of groomed trails in the forest flanking Mountain Road ($10).

WHERE TO STAY

Stowe has several motels of interest to budget travelers. The **Sun and Ski Motor Inn,** 1613 Mountain Rd., ☎ 800/448-5223 or 802/253-7159, has 26 serviceable but utilitarian units, all of which have air-conditioning, telephones, TVs, and small refrigerators. There's a year-round pool heated to 102 degrees, perfect for thawing after a cold day skiing. Rates are $65 to $140 for two.

The **Stowe Motel**, 2043 Mountain Rd., ☎ 800/829-7629 or 802/253-7629, offers 57 rooms spread among three buildings. It's a basic motel, but with rooms slightly larger than average and a bit more stylish and comfortable, with pine furniture, couches, and coffee tables. All rooms have TVs, telephones, small refrigerators and air-conditioning, and there's a Jacuzzi, heated pool (summer only), game room and (in winter) free use of snowshoes. Rates are $56 to $86 double ($98 to $116 during holidays). Add $10 to $20 for an efficiency unit. Winter ski packages are available.

Green Mountain Inn. Main St. (P.O. Box 60), Stowe, VT 05672. ☎ 800/253-7302 or 802/253-7301. Fax 802/253-5096. www.greenmountaininn.com. E-mail: grnmtinn@aol.com. 76 units. A/C TV TEL. $119–$209 double, $139–$219 foliage and Christmas. Discount in spring and late fall. Ask about packages. 2-night minimum stay summer/winter weekends and foliage. AE, DISC, MC, V. Pets allowed in some rooms; ask first.

This tasteful, historic structure sits right in the village. It's a sprawling place with 76 guest rooms spread through several buildings, but it feels far more intimate, with quirky narrow hallways and guest rooms tastefully decorated in an early-19th-century motif that befits the 1833 vintage of the main inn. About a dozen rooms feature Jacuzzis and/or gas fireplaces, and the new (late 1997) Mill House has nice-size rooms with small CD players, sofas, and Jacuzzis that open into the bedroom from behind folding wooden doors. Rooms also have those essential tools for weekend relaxing: wine glasses and a corkscrew. Note that some older rooms are heated with balky radiators, and a few of the guest rooms overlook noisy kitchen ventilators; ask when you book.

Dining: The Whip Bar and Grill is in the lower level of the main inn and is a cozy, classy grill with loads of pubby charm and a menu featuring a quirky selection ranging from burgers ($6.50) to filet mignon ($18.95) to sesame ginger chicken stir fry ($11.95). There's also a vegetarian menu (garden burgers, tempeh, tofu curry).

Amenities: Heated outdoor pool (summer), fitness club, Jacuzzi, sauna, library, lawn games, game room (air hockey, video games, Ping-Pong, billiards), limited room service, in-room massage, afternoon tea and cookies, safe-deposit boxes.

Stonehill Inn. 89 Houston Farm Rd. (just off Mountain Rd. midway between village and ski area), Stowe, VT 05672. ☎ 802/253-6282. www.stonehillinn.com. E-mail: stay@ stonehillinnn.com. 9 units. A/C TV. Winter $295–$385 double, spring–fall $250–$295, foliage & Christmas $425. Rates include full breakfast. 2-night minimum stay weekends and foliage season; 3-night minimum holiday weekends, 4-night minimum Christmas week. AE, DC, MC, V. Not suitable for children.

The Stonehill Inn brings a measure of contemporary elegance to Stowe. With just nine rooms, the newly opened (late 1998) inn offers personal service and a handy location, along with room amenities that include king-size beds, in-room safes, VCRs, and double-sided gas fireplaces that also front double Jacuzzis in the sizable bathrooms. (Note that there are no phones in the rooms, but a private phone booth allows guests to stay in touch.) The rooms have different color schemes and detailing, but are by and large identical in size and character, The high-ceilinged common rooms have fireplaces and billiard tables, and there's a well-stocked guest pantry with complimentary beverages and mixers. An outdoor hot tub provides guests with a relaxing soak. Breakfasts are in a bright morning room where every table is windowside; tasty hors d'oeuvres are set out each evening. Stonehill as yet lacks a patina of age or mature landscaping, but it will please those willing to forego timeworn character in exchange for quiet and a taste of luxury.

Stoweflake. Mountain Rd. (P.O. Box 369), Stowe, VT 05672. ☎ **800/253-2232** or 802/253-7355. Fax 802/253-6858. www.stoweflake.com. E-mail: stoweflk@sover.net. 95 units (includes 10 suites), plus 12 town houses. A/C TV TEL. $140–$220 double, suites $225–$295. Call for town-house or package info. 4-night minimum stay during holidays; 2-night minimum most weekends. AE, DC, DISC, MC, V.

Stoweflake is located on Mountain Road, which is 1.7 miles from the village, and recently has been playing catch-up with the more up-market Topnotch resort and spa. In 1998, this contemporary-style resort added a more luxurious east wing, including seven spacious new suites, and created a new spa and fitness club. The newer guest rooms are nicer than those at Topnotch—they're regally decorated and have amenities like two phones and wet bars. The spa and fitness facilities are perfectly adequate, but lack the sybaritic elegance of Topnotch (what, no waterfalls?). The fitness facilities include a decent-size fitness room with Cybex equipment, a squash/racquetball court, coed Jacuzzi, and a small indoor pool. The spa also offers a variety of treatments, including LaStone massage, which involves the application of smooth stones that are variously heated and iced. The resort has five categories of guest rooms in two wings; the "superior" rooms in the old wing are a bit cozy. They're OK for an overnight, but you're better off requesting "deluxe" or better if you're planning to stay a few days.

Dining: Charlie B's offers pub fare, including meat loaf, blackened chicken sandwiches, and pastas (dinner entrees $9.50 to $18.75). Next door is Winfield's, an attractive, richly hued setting in which to enjoy upscale resort fare along the lines of chicken saltimbocca, pan-seared rainbow trout, and roast duck with plum sauce ($16.50 to $21.50). One nice feature: both restaurants share an excellent wine list, with nearly 50 wines available by the glass.

Amenities: In addition to the spa and fitness center, there's a large outdoor pool set amid gardens, 2 tennis courts, a jogging trail, children's program, conference rooms, in-room massage, beauty salon, limited room service, laundry and dry-cleaning services, baby-sitting, safe-deposit boxes, and afternoon cookies and refreshments. For golfer's there's a practice facility and the adjacent Stowe Country Club.

Stowehof. 434 Edson Hill Rd. (P.O. Box 1139), Stowe, VT 05672. ☎ **800/932-7136** or 802/253-9722. Fax 802/253-7513. E-mail: stowehof1@aol.com. 50 units, 2 guest houses. A/C TV TEL. $80–$220 double. Rates include full breakfast. 4-night minimum stay during holidays, 2-night minimum some weekends. AE, DC, MC, V.

Stowehof's exterior architecture is mildly alarming in that aggressive neo-Tyrolean ski-chalet kind of way. But inside, the place comes close to magic—it's pleasantly woodsy, folksy, and rustic, with heavy beams and pine floors, ticking clocks, and massive maple tree trunks carved into architectural elements. Guests may feel a bit like characters in the Hobbit. The guest rooms are furnished simply, each decorated individually: Some are bold and festive with sunflower patterns, others subdued and quiet. Four have wood-burning fireplaces, and all have good views. Stowehof is situated high on a hillside and feels far removed from the hubbub of the valley floor.

Dining: Diners are served in a cozy, multilevel dining room, with entrees like ginger-roasted leg of venison, crab and shrimp cakes, and the house specialty, Wiener schnitzel. Entrees range from $17.95 to $22.95.

Amenities: Outdoor heated pool, 4 all-weather tennis courts, horseback riding (extra fee), game room, nearby jogging track, nature trails, business center, nearby health club, sauna, sundeck, dry-cleaning and laundry services, in-room massage, valet parking, safe. In winter there are sleigh rides (extra fee).

♦ Topnotch. 4000 Mountain Rd. (P.O. Box 1458), Stowe, VT 05672. ☎ **800/451-8686** or 802/253-8585. Fax 802/253-9263. www.topnotch-resort.com. E-mail: topnotch@sover. net. 92 units. A/C TV TEL. Ski season and midsummer $200–$300 double; $296–$600 suite. Off-season $160–$220 double; $210–$496 suite. Higher prices and 6-night minimum Christmas week. Town-home accommodations $185–$715 depending on season and size. AE, DC, DISC, MC, V. Pets allowed.

A boxy, uninteresting exterior hides a creatively designed interior at this upscale resort and spa on a knoll just off Mountain Rd. The main lobby is imaginatively conceived and furnished, with lots of stone and wood and an absolutely huge moose head hanging on the wall. There's even a telescope for watching skiers schuss down the slopes across the valley. The guest rooms, linked by long, motel-like hallways, are nicely appointed, if basic; ask for one of the top-floor rooms with cathedral ceilings. Ten rooms have wood-burning fireplaces; 18 have Jacuzzis.

Dining: Well-prepared continental dishes (grilled salmon, beef Wellington) are offered in the inn's stone-walled dining room. Entrees are priced from $18 to $26.

Amenities: Guests spend much of their time around the exceptionally appealing 60-foot indoor pool with bubbling fountain and 12-foot whirlpool. There's an outdoor pool for summer use as well. Activities arranged by the resort include horseback riding, fitness classes, massage, body treatments, and cross-country skiing. Other facilities include 10 indoor tennis courts, hot tub, Jacuzzi, nature trails, children's center, beauty salon, and a business center.

Trapp Family Lodge. 42 Trapp Hill Rd., Stowe, VT 05672. ☎ **800/826-7000** or 802/ 253-8511. Fax 802/253-5740. www.trappfamily.com. E-mail: info@trappfamily.com. 93 units. TV TEL. Winter $140–$225 double ($344-$384 during school vacation, includes meals); summer $140–$225 double. 5-night minimum stay Christmas week, 3-night minimum Presidents' week, and foliage season. AE, DC, DISC, MC, V. Depart Stowe village westward on Rte. 108; in 2 miles bear left at fork near white church; continue up hill following signs for lodge.

The Trapp Family of *Sound of Music* fame bought this sprawling farm high up in Stowe in 1942, just 4 years after fleeing the Nazi takeover of Austria. The descendants of Maria and Baron von Trapp continue to run this Tyrolean-flavored lodge. The original lodge burned in 1980, and some longtime guests still grouse that its replacement lacks the timeworn character of the old place. But it's a comfortable resort hotel, if designed more for efficiency than elegance. The guest rooms are a shade or two better than your standard hotel room, and most come with fine valley views and private balconies. Common areas with blonde wood and comfortably upholstered chairs abound and make for comfortable idling.

Dining: The restaurant offers well-prepared continental fare (Wiener schnitzel, lamb tenderloin). Dinner is prix fixe at $36; dinner and breakfast is $47 per person per day in addition to room rates. The informal Austrian Tea Room across the road from the main inn is open for lunch and offers three kinds of wurst and more.

Amenities: Fitness center, heated indoor pool, two outdoor pools (one for adults only), sauna, extensive cross-country ski and hiking trail network, game rooms, children's program, four clay tennis counts, in-room massage, baby-sitting, currency exchange (Canadian), courtesy shuttle to mountain for skiing, guest safe.

WHERE TO DINE

The **Harvest Market,** 1031 Mountain Rd. (☎ 802/253-3800), is the place for gourmet-to-go. Browse the Vermont products and exotic imports, then pick up some of the fresh-baked goods, like the pleasantly tart raspberry squares, to bring back to the ski lodge or take for a picnic along the bike path. The high prices may cause one's eyebrows to arch involuntarily, but if you're not traveling on a tight budget it's a good place to splurge.

✪ **Blue Moon Cafe.** 35 School St. ☎ **802/253-7006.** Reservations recommended. Main courses $15–$22. AE, CB, DC. DISC, MC, V. Daily 6–9:30pm. NEW AMERICAN.

The delectable crusty bread on the table and Frank Sinatra crooning in the background offer clues that this isn't your typical ski-area pub-fare restaurant. Located a short walk off Stowe's main street in an old village home accented with wood barn beams, the Blue Moon serves up the village's most reliably fine meals. The menu is always in play, changing every Friday. But count on at least one lamb, beef, and veggie dish, plus a couple of seafood offerings. Chef Jack Pickett has superb instincts for spicing and creates global inventive dishes like chicken with black beans and mango, or venison with a green tomato and chipotle sauce.

Mes Amis. 311 Mountain Rd. ☎ **802/253-8669.** Reservations not accepted. Dinner entrees $13.95–$16.95. DC, MC, V. Tues–Sun 5:30–10pm (open for appetizers at 4:30pm). BISTRO.

The uncommonly friendly Mes Amis is located in a cozy structure above Mountain Road, and not far from the village. It was once a British-style pub, but the new owners have done a nice job taking the half-timber Tudor decor and making it more broadly European. It's a quiet and friendly spot, and lacks even the smallest iota of pretension. The menu is rather limited (only five entrees), but the specials round out the offerings. The restaurant has three cozy dining rooms and a bar. Appetizers include smoked salmon on toast points and baked stuffed clams; entrees feature steaks and fish. The house specialty is a half-duck roasted with a hot-and-sweet sauce.

Miguel's Stowe-Away. Mountain Rd. ☎ **802/253-7574.** Reservations recommended weekends and peak ski season. Main courses $10–$15. AE, CB, DC, DISC, MC, V. Mon–Fri 5:30–10pm, Sat–Sun 5–10pm. MEXICAN/SOUTHWEST.

Located in an old farmhouse midway between the village and the mountain, Miguel's packs in locals who come for the tangiest Mexican and Tex-Mex food in the valley. Start off with a margarita or Vermont beer, then try out appetizers like the empanadas or the exceptionally flavorful chili verde. Follow up with fajitas or one of the filling combo plates. Like the big national chains, Miguel's has grown popular enough to offer its own brand of chips, salsa, and other products, that turn up in specialty food shops throughout the Northeast. Expect the place to be loud and boisterous on busy nights.

Mr. Pickwick's. 433 Mountain Rd. ☎ **802/253-7558.** Reservations accepted for parties of 8 or more only. Main courses, breakfast $3.95–$7.95, lunch $6.95–$12.95, dinner $11.95–$20.95 (mostly $14–$17). AE, MC, V. Daily 11am–1am. BRITISH PUB FARE.

As a matter of policy I refuse to consider any establishment with "Ye Olde" in its name. But I'm happy to make an exception for Mr. Pickwick's, a pub and restaurant that's part of Ye Old English Inne. It could justly be accused of being a theme park restaurant, with the theme being, well, ye olde Englande. But it's been run since 1983 with such creative gusto by British ex-pats Chris and Lyn Francis that it's hard not to enjoy yourself here. You can start by admiring the Union Jack tchotchkes and Anglo geegaws while relaxing at handsome wood tables at the booths (dubbed pews here). Then sample from the 150 beers (many British) before ordering off the menu, which includes house specialties like bangers and mashed (sausages and potatoes), fish and chips, and beef Wellington. For patriotic colonials who have yet to forgive the oppressive Brits, there's also burgers, salmon in potato crust, and an intriguing game menu that includes boar, rabbit, and kangaroo.

10 Burlington

Burlington is a vibrant college town that's continually, valiantly resisting the onset of middle age. It's the birthplace of hippies-turned-mega-corporation Ben & Jerry's. It elected a socialist mayor in 1981, Bernie Sanders, who's now Vermont's lone representative to the U.S. Congress. Burlington is also home to the eclectic rock band Phish, which has been anointed by many as the heir to the Grateful Dead hippie-rock tradition. And just look at the signs for offices as you wander downtown—an uncommonly high number seem to have the word "polarity" in them.

It's no wonder that Burlington has become a magnet for those seeking alternatives to big-city life with its big-city problems. The city has a superb location overlooking Lake Champlain to the Adirondacks of northern New York. To the east, visible on your way out of town, the Green Mountains rise dramatically, with two of the highest points (Mount Mansfield and Camel's Hump) rising above the undulating ridge.

In this century, Burlington turned its back for a time on its spectacular waterfront. Urban redevelopment focused on parking garages and high-rises; the waterfront lay fallow, open to development by light industry. In recent years the city has sought to regain a toehold along the lake, acquiring and redeveloping parts for commercial and recreational use. It's been successful in some sections, less so in others.

In contrast, the downtown is thriving. The pedestrian mall (Church Street) that has failed in so many other towns works here. As a result, the scale is skewed toward pedestrians in the heart of downtown. It's best to get out of your car as soon as feasible.

ESSENTIALS

GETTING THERE   Burlington is at the junction of I-89, Route 7, and Route 2.

Burlington International Airport, about 3 miles east of downtown, is served by **Continental Express** (☎ 800/732-6887), **United Airlines** (☎ 800/241-6522), **US Airways** (☎ 800/428-4322), and **Delta Connection** (☎ 800/345-3400).

Amtrak's *Vermonter* offers daily departures for Burlington from Washington, Baltimore, Philadelphia, New York, New Haven, and Springfield, Massachusetts. Call ☎ 800/872-7245 for more information.

Vermont Transit Lines (☎ 802/864-6811), with a depot at 345 Pine St., offers bus connections from Albany, Boston, Hartford, New York's JFK Airport, and other points in Vermont, Massachusetts, and New Hampshire.

VISITOR INFORMATION   The **Lake Champlain Regional Chamber of Commerce,** 60 Main St., Burlington, VT 05401 (☎ 802/863-3489), maintains an information center in a stout 1929 brick building on Main Street just up from the waterfront and a short walk from Church Street Market. The center is open weekdays from 8:30am to 5pm. On weekends, helpful maps and brochures are left in the entryway for visitors.

A seasonal information booth is also staffed summers on the Church Street Marketplace at the corner of Church and Bank streets. There's no phone. Information can also be requested via E-mail (**vermont@vermont.org**) or the Web (**www. vermont.org**).

EXPLORING BURLINGTON

✪ **Shelburne Museum.** Rte. 7 (P.O. Box 10), Shelburne, VT 05482. ☎ **802/985-3346.** www.shelburnemuseum.org. Summer admission (good for 2 consecutive days) $17.50 adults, $10.50 students, $7 children 6–14; winter tours $7 adults, $3 children. MC, V. Late May to late Oct daily 10am–5pm. Late Oct to mid-May daily tour at 1pm (reservations recommended).

Ethan Allen: Patriot and Libertine

In 1749, the governor of New Hampshire began giving away land to settlers willing to brave the howling wilderness of what is now Vermont. Two decades later, the New York State courts decreed those grants void, which opened the door for New York speculators to flood into the region vowing to push the original settlers out of the valleys and up into the Green Mountains.

Not too surprisingly, this didn't sit very well with those already there. They established a network of military units called the Green Mountain Boys, who promised to drive out the New Yorkers. A hale fellow named Ethan Allen headed up new militia, which launched a series of effective harrying raids against the impudent New Yorkers. Green Mountain Boys destroyed their homes, drove away their livestock, and chased the New York sheriffs back across the border.

The American Revolution soon intervened, and Ethan Allen and the Green Mountain Boys took up the revolutionary cause with a vigor. They helped sack Fort Ticonderoga in New York in 1775, rallied to the cause at the famed Battle of Bennington, and generally continued to make nuisances of themselves to the British effort throughout the war.

Allen's fame grew as word spread about him and his Green Mountain Boys. A hard-drinking, fierce-fighting, large-living sort of guy, Allen became a legend in his own time. One story claimed he could bite the head off a nail; another said that he was once bit by a rattlesnake, which promptly belched and died.

While Allen's apocryphal exploits lived on following his death in 1789, he also left a more significant legacy. Vermont's statehood in 1791 was due in large part to the independence and patriotism the region showed under Allen. And today you can't drive very far in Vermont without a reminder of Allen's historic presence—parks are named after him, inns boast that he once slept there, and Vermonters still tell the occasional story about his bawdy doings.

Established in 1947 by Americana collector Electra Havenmeyer Webb, the museum contains one of the nation's most outstanding collections of American decorative, folk, and fine art. The museum is spread over 45 beautiful acres 7 miles south of Burlington; the collections occupy some 37 buildings. The more mundane exhibits include quilts, early tools, decoys, and weather vanes. But the museum also collects and displays *whole* buildings from around New England and New York State. These include an 1890 railroad station, a lighthouse, a stagecoach inn, an Adirondack lodge, and a round barn from Vermont. There's even a 220-foot steamship, eerily landlocked on the museum's grounds. Spend a few hours here, and you're bound to come away with a richer understanding of regional culture. If you're planning to visit only one museum during your New England trip, this is the one.

The grounds also contain a museum shop, cafeteria, and picnic area. In winter, much of the museum is closed, but tours of selected collections are offered daily at 1pm. Dress warmly.

Ethan Allen Homestead. Rte. 127. ☎ **802/865-4556.** Admission $4 adults, $3 seniors, $2 children 6–16. Mid-May to mid-June daily 1–5pm. Mid-June to mid-Oct Mon–Sat 10am–5pm; Sun 1–5pm. Take Rte. 127 northward from downtown; look for signs.

A quiet retreat on one of the most idyllic, least developed stretches of the Winooski River, the Ethan Allen Homestead is a shrine to Vermont's favorite son. While Allen wasn't born in Burlington, he settled here later in life on property confiscated from a

Burlington

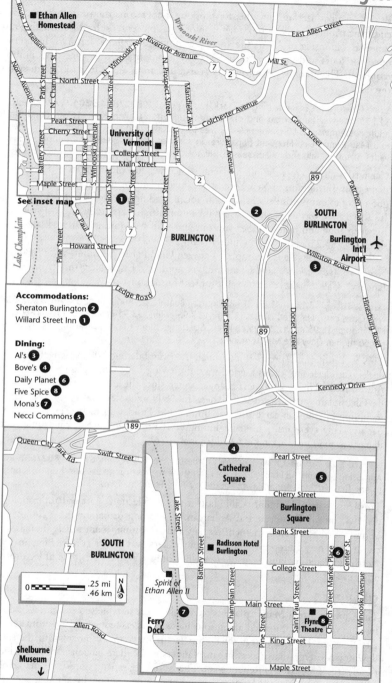

Accommodations:
Sheraton Burlington ❷
Willard Street Inn ❶

Dining:
Al's ❸
Bove's ❹
Daily Planet ❻
Five Spice ❽
Mona's ❼
Necci Commons ❺

Ethan Allen Homestead

University of Vermont

BURLINGTON

SOUTH BURLINGTON

Burlington Int'l Airport

Cathedral Square

Burlington Square

Radisson Hotel Burlington

Spirit of Ethan Allen II

Ferry Dock

Flynn Theatre

Shelburne Museum

Lake Champlain

0 .25 mi
.46 km

NA-0132

British sympathizer during the Revolution. The reconstructed farmhouse is an enduring tribute to this Vermont hero; an orientation center offers an intriguing multimedia accounting of Allen's life and other points of regional history. The house is open for tours mid-October to mid-May by appointment only (one day's notice is required). The grounds are open daily year-round from dawn to dusk. Admission to the park is free.

Lake Champlain Ferries. King St. Dock, Burlington. ☎ **802/864-9804.** www.ferries.com. $12.75 one-way fare for car and driver from Burlington to Port Kent; $6.50 round-trip for adult passengers; $2.50 children 6–12; free for children under 6. Burlington ferry operates mid-May to mid-Oct. Frequent departures in summer between 8am and 8:30pm. Schedule varies in spring, fall, and foliage season; call for current departure times. AE, MC, V.

Car ferries chug across the often placid, sometimes turbulent waters of Lake Champlain from Burlington to New York State between late spring and foliage season. It's a good way to cut out miles of driving if you're heading west toward the Adirondacks. It's also a good way to see the lake and the mountains on a pleasant, inexpensive cruise. Between June and mid-October you can also take a 90-minute narrated lake cruise; the cost is $7.25 adult, $3.75 children, under 6 free.

Ferries also cross Lake Champlain between Grande Isle, Vermont, and Plattsburgh, New York (year-round), and Charlotte, Vermont, and Essex, New York (April to early January). Call the above number for more information.

The Spirit of Ethan Allen II. Burlington Boathouse, Burlington. ☎ **802/862-8300.** www.soea.com. Narrated cruises (1½ hr.) $7.95 adults, $3.95 children 3–11. Sunset cruises (2½ hours) $8.95 adults, $4.95 children. Specialty cruises (dinner, brunch, mystery theater) priced higher. Daily late May to mid-Oct.

This is Burlington's premier tour boat. Accommodating 500 passengers on three decks, the sleek ship offers a good way of viewing Lake Champlain and the distant Adirondacks. The views haven't changed much since the area was explored by Samuel de Champlain, who first reached here in 1609. Food is available on all cruises, including all-you-can-eat buffets at dinner and Sunday brunch. The scenic cruise departs daily every other hour beginning at 10am through 4pm. The sunset cruise departs at 6:30pm. Parking is $2 additional.

Robert Hull Fleming Museum. 61 Colchester Ave. (UVM campus). ☎ **802/656-2090.** Admission $3 adult, $5 family, $2 seniors and students. Year-round Sat–Sun 1–5pm; Labor Day to Apr Tues–Fri 9am–4pm; May to Labor Day Tues–Fri noon–4pm.

This University of Vermont facility houses a fine collection of art and anthropological displays, mostly European and American. A selection of paintings by 20th-century Vermont artists are on permanent display, and exhibitions roam widely though world cultures. A new European and American gallery was under construction in 1999. Nearby metered parking available weekends only. Call for a schedule of lectures and other events.

SHOPPING

The **Church Street Marketplace** is one of the more notable success stories of downtown development. Situated along four blocks that extend southward from the austerely elegant 1816 Congregational church, the marketplace buzzes with the sort of downtown energy that makes urban planners everywhere envious. While decidedly trendy (there are Banana Republic and The Nature Company stores), the marketplace still makes room for used-book stores and homegrown shops. In summer, leave time to be entertained by drummers, pan-flutists, buskers, sidewalk vendors, and knots of young folks just hanging out.

OUTDOOR PURSUITS

On the downtown waterfront, look for the **Burlington Community Boathouse** (☎ 802/865-3377), a modern structure built with Victorian flair. A lot of summer action takes place at this city-owned structure and along the 900-foot boardwalk. You can rent a sailboat or rowboat, sign up for kayak or sculling lessons, or just wander around and enjoy the sunset.

Burlington's commitment to taking back its lake is best seen in the 9-mile ✪ **Burlington Bike Path,** that runs picturesquely along the shores of Lake Champlain to the mouth of the Winooski River. A superb way to spend a sunny afternoon, the paved bike route over a former rail bed passes through shady parklands and Burlington's backyards. Along the banks of the Winooski, you can admire the remains of an old bridge and scout around for marble chips.

Bike rentals are available downtown at the **Skirack,** 85 Main St. (☎ 802/658-3313), for $14 for 4 hours (enough time to do the whole trail), and up to $22 for a whole day. Skirack also rents in-line skates ($8 for 4 hr.), which are also commonly used on the bike path. **North Star Cyclery,** 100 Main St. (☎ 802/863-3832), also rents bicycles at comparable rates.

WHERE TO STAY

Burlington's motels are located along the two major access roads to the south and east. On Route 7 south of town, try the **Super 8 Motel** (1016 Shelburne Rd.; ☎ 800/800-8000 or 802/862-6421), the **Bel-Aire Motel** (111 Shelburne Rd.; ☎ 802/863-3116), or the **Town & Country Motel** (490 Shelburne Rd., ☎ 802/862-5786).

Clustered along Route 2 near I-89 and the airport are two chain hotels, the **Holiday Inn** (1068 Williston Rd.; ☎ 802/863-6363) and **Best Western** (1076 Williston Rd.; ☎ 800/371-1125 or 802/863-1125), along with the clean, budget-priced **Swiss Host Motel and Village** (1272 Williston Rd.; ☎ 800/326-5734 or 802/862-5734).

✪ **The Inn at Shelburne Farms.** Harbor Rd., Shelburne, VT 05482. ☎ **802/985-8498.** 24 units (7 units share 4 bathrooms). TEL. Spring and summer $95–$310 double; fall $105–$350 double. 2-night minimum stay weekends. AE, CB, DC, DISC, MC, V. Closed mid-Oct to mid-May.

The numbers behind this exceptional turn-of-the-century mansion on the shores of Lake Champlain tell the story: 60 rooms, 10 chimneys, 1,400 acres of land. Built in 1899 by William Seward and Lila Vanderbilt Webb, this sprawling Edwardian "farmhouse" is the place to fantasize about the lifestyles of the *truly* rich and famous. From the first glimpse of the mansion as you come up the winding drive, you'll know you've left the grim world behind. That's by design—noted landscape architect Frederick Law Olmsted had a hand in shaping the grounds, and noted forester Gifford Pinchot helped with the planting. The 24 guest rooms are splendidly appointed. The inn is owned and operated as part of a nonprofit environmental education center, with the emphasis on the sensitive stewardship of the agricultural resources.

Dining: Meals aren't included in the rates, but the Marble Restaurant on the property offers outstanding breakfasts and dinners, with a focus on contemporary regional cuisine. Chef David Hugo aims to showcase locally grown ingredients, with entrees such as pan-roasted chicken with a ragout of artichoke and lemon, and roasted rack of lamb with asparagus and Shelburne Farms cheddar. Entree prices range from $18 to $28.

Amenities: Tours of the farm, tennis court, lake for swimming, children's farmyard, nature trails, baby-sitting, afternoon tea.

Radisson Hotel Burlington. 60 Battery St., Burlington, VT 05401. ☎ **800/333-3333** or 802/658-6500. Fax 802/658-4659. 256 units. A/C TV TEL. Winter $99–$149 double; summer $139–$199 double. AE, CB, DC, ER, DISC, MC, V.

The nine-story Radisson offers the best views, as well as the best downtown location. As might be expected, it also offers the amenities of an upscale national hotel chain, including an indoor pool, covered parking, and two dining areas. Though built in 1976, renovations have kept the weariness at bay. Ask for a room with a lake view, which is far more dramatic than the downtown view. Families with kids might request one of the five cabana rooms that open up to the pool area.

Dining/Diversions: Seasons on the Lake offers great views and American and continental fare (rack of lamb, beef tournedos with béarnaise), with entrees priced from $16.95 to $21.95. A lounge and informal restaurant are located on the lobby level; weekends there's live comedy. For a quick bite or a drink, there's also the Oak Street Cafe off the lobby.

Amenities: Indoor pool, tiny fitness room, Jacuzzi, gift shop, concierge, dry-cleaning and laundry services, baby-sitting, newspaper delivery, limited room service, express checkout, courtesy car to airport, in-room safes, free business center.

Sheraton Burlington Hotel & Conference Center. 870 Williston Rd., Burlington, VT 05403. ☎ **800/325-3535** or 802/865-6600. Fax 802/865-6670. E-mail: sheratonvt@aol. com. 308 units. A/C TV TEL. $150–$195 double. AE, CB, DC, DISC, MC, V.

The largest conference facility in Vermont, the Sheraton also does a commendable job catering to individual travelers and families. This sprawling and modern complex just off the interstate, a 5-minutes drive east of downtown, features a sizable indoor garden area. The guest rooms all have two phones and in-room Nintendos (families take note); rooms in the newer addition (built in 1990) are a bit nicer, furnished in a simpler, lighter country style. Ask for a room facing east (no extra charge) to enjoy the views of Mount Mansfield and the Green Mountains.

Dining: G's, the complex's main restaurant, is located in and around an indoor garden, complete with gazebo, and serves three meals daily. The elaborate Sunday brunch is the best in town. Also serving meals is Tuckaway's, which features an English pub motif.

Amenities: Indoor pool with retractable skylights for summer, two Jacuzzis, a fitness room, outdoor sundeck. limited room service, concierge, secretarial services, courtesy cars, video rentals (extra charge), laundry service.

Willard Street Inn. 349 S. Willard St. (2 blocks south of Main St.), Burlington, VT 05401. ☎ **800/577-8712** or 802/651-8710. Fax 802/651-8714. www.willardstreetinn.com. E-mail: wstinn@vermontel.com. 15 units (3 share 1 bathroom; 1 with private hall bathroom). TEL. $85–$200 double. Rates include full breakfast. 2-night minimum stay weekends. AE, DC, DISC, MC, V.

This impressive inn, which opened in 1996, is a welcome addition to the Burlington lodging pool, which until recently had few alternatives to big, modern hotels and strip-mall motels. Located in a fine Queen Anne–style brick mansion near the university, the Willard Street Inn has soaring first-floor ceilings, cherry woodwork, and a beautiful window-lined breakfast room with a bold black-and-white tile floor. The home was originally built in 1881 by a bank president and served as a retirement home for a while before its conversion to an inn. Rooms in the former servants wing are more cozy than those in the core of the house, and the third-floor rooms are slightly less elegant. Among the best rooms are No. 12, which boasts a small sitting area and the best views of the lake, and No. 4, which is spacious, has a sizable private bathroom, and also features lake views.

WHERE TO DINE

✪ **Al's.** 1251 Williston Rd. (Rte. 2, just east of I-89), S. Burlington. ☎ **802/862-9203.** Sandwiches 75¢–$3.55. No credit cards. Mon–Wed 10:30am–11pm; Thurs–Sat 10:30am–midnight; Sun 11am–10pm. BURGER JOINT.

Two words: french fries.

✪ **Bove's.** 68 Pearl St. ☎ **802/864-6651.** Reservations not accepted. Sandwiches $1.30–$2.80; dinner items $3.85–$7.70. No credit cards. Tues–Sat 10am–9pm. ITALIAN.

A Burlington landmark since 1941, Bove's is a classic red-sauce-on-spaghetti joint just a couple of blocks from the Church Street Marketplace. The facade is stark black and white, its octagonal windows closed to prying eyes by Venetian blinds. Step through the doors and into a lost era; grab a seat at one of the vinyl-upholstered booths and browse the menu, which offers spaghetti with meat sauce, spaghetti with meatballs, spaghetti with sausage, and . . . well, you get the idea. The red sauce is rich and tangy; the garlic sauce packs enough garlic to knock you clear out of your booth.

Daily Planet. 15 Center St. ☎ **802/862-9647.** Reservations recommended for parties of 5 or more. Lunch items $4.95–$6.50; main dinner courses $5.95–$18.50 (mostly $12–$14). AE, DC, DISC, MC, V. Mon–Fri 11:30am–3pm; Sun–Thurs 5–9:30pm; Fri–Sat 5–10pm. Sept–May Sat–Sun brunch 11am–3pm. ECLECTIC.

This popular spot is usually brimming with college students and downtown workers evenings and weekends. But it's worth putting up with the mild mayhem for some of the more uncommonly creative food in town. The menu is eclectic, and the dishes better than the usual pub fare you might expect at a spot like this. Selections include burgers, muffuletta, grilled flank steak, Moroccan vegetable sauté, and the popular smoked salmon flat-bread pizza.

✪ **Five Spice.** 175 Church St. ☎ **802/864-4045.** Reservations recommended on weekends and in summer. Lunch items $5.25–$8.50; main dinner courses $7.95–$15.95. AE, CB, DC, DISC, MC, V. Mon–Sat 11:30am–10:30pm; Sun 11am–9:30pm. PAN-ASIAN.

Five Spice is the best of Burlington's bumper crop of Asian restaurants. Located upstairs and down in an intimate setting with rough wood floors and aquamarine wainscoting, Five Spice is a popular draw among college students and professors. But customers pour in for the exquisite food, not for the scene. The cuisine is multi-Asian, drawing on the best of Thailand, Vietnam, China, and beyond. Try the excellent hot and sour soup. Then gear up for Thai red snapper or the superior kung-pao chicken. The dish with the best name on the menu—Evil Jungle Prince with Chicken—is made with a light sauce featuring a combination of coconut milk, garlic, and lemongrass.

Mona's. 3 Main St. (in the Cornerstone Building). ☎ **802/658-6662.** Reservations recommended. Lunch items $3.95–$7.95; main dinner courses $9.95–$17.95 (mostly $12–$14). AE, CB, DC, MC, V. Mon–Thurs 11:30am–10pm, Fri–Sat 11:30am–11pm, Sun 10am–9pm. NEW AMERICAN.

This elegant but relaxed restaurant overlooking the waterfront is sleeker and more modern than the average Burlington bistro. Located next to the old train station at the foot of Main Street, Mona's is an up-tempo place rich with copper tones throughout. The ceiling in the first-floor jazz bar is made of copper and seems to emit a lurid, unearthly glow at sunset. For the best views of Lake Champlain and the Adirondacks, head to the upstairs dining room. In good weather, angle for a table on the 65-seat deck. The Mediterranean shrimp features shrimp, veggies and garlic served over pasta; meat lovers will enjoy the hand-cut sirloins or prime rib (try steaks with the portobello and oatmeal-stout sauce). Sundays (until 2pm) there's a lavish buffet brunch ($12.95), with selections ranging from the usual suspects (waffles and bagels) to vegetable tarts and marinated flank steak.

NECI Commons. 25 Church St. ☎ **802/862-6324.** Call before arrival for priority seating. Brunch $5.75–$6.95; lunch $5.50–$7.25; dinner $9.95–$14.50. AE, DC, DISC, MC, V Daily 11:30am–2pm and 5–9:30pm; Sun brunch 11am–3pm. BISTRO.

NECI Commons opened in 1997 and quickly attracted serious foodies from around the region. Yet another in the New England Culinary Institute empire (the Inn at Essex and Montpelier's Main Street Grill & Bar are others), this lively, spacious, and busy spot is also a training ground for aspiring chefs and restaurateurs. You can eat upstairs in the main dining room, which has soaring windows overlooking the Church Street Marketplace, or downstairs, where you can watch the chef-trainees prepare meals in the open kitchen. The fare is at once simple and creative: At Sunday brunch, there's a wood-fired breakfast pizza, featuring eggs, bacon, tomato, and cheddar. For dinner, look for sirloin served with the restaurant's famous Vermont cheddar potatoes or cassoulet with duck and garlic sausage. The prices are reasonable, and the service excellent.

BURLINGTON AFTER DARK

There's always something going on in the evening, although it might take a little snooping to find it. Burlington has a thriving local music scene. Check the local weeklies for information on festivals and concerts during your visit, and to find out who's playing at the clubs. On-line information about local music and arts events may be found at **www.bigheavyworld.com.** The three popular nightclubs listed below are located very near one another at the intersection of Main and Church streets.

Nectar's, 188 Main St. (☎ **802/658-4771**), is an odd amalgam—part funky cafeteria-style restaurant, part no-frills lounge. No wonder this is the place Phish got its start, and where the band occasionally shows up. Live bands play 7 days a week, and there's never a cover charge. On weekends it's packed with UVM students and abuzz with a fairly high level of hormonal energy. Look for the revolving neon sign (the last of its kind in Vermont).

Club Metronome, 188 Main St. (☎ **802/865-4563**), is a loud and loose nightspot that features a wide array of acts with a heavy dose of world beat. You can dance or shoot a game of pool (or do both at once, as seems popular). This is a good spot to sample some of the local talent pool, which runs quite deep. Cover is $3 to $15.

Club Extreme, 165 Church St. (☎ **802/660-2088**), formerly Club Toast, specializes in dance and hip-hop and targets a younger crowd. Cover ranges from nothing to $20, depending on the band.

For gay nightlife, head to **135 Pearl** (☎ **802/863-2343**), located naturally enough at 135 Pearl St. It's Burlington's only gay bar. You can get a bite to eat, dance to the DJ, or give karaoke a go (Wednesdays only). Open Monday to Thurs 7:30pm to 1am, Friday and Saturday from 5pm to 1am.

11 The Northeast Kingdom

Vermont's Northeast Kingdom has an edgy, wild, and remote character. Consisting of Orleans, Essex, and Caledonia counties, the region was given its memorable name in 1949 by Sen. George Aiken, who understood the area's allure at a time when few others paid it much heed. What gives this region its character is its stubborn, old-fashioned insularity.

In contrast to the dusky narrow valleys of southern Vermont, the Kingdom's landscape is open and spacious, with rolling meadows ending abruptly at the hard edge of

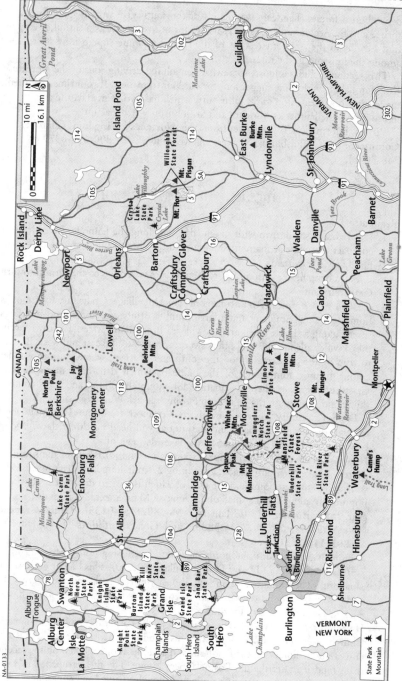

State Park ✦
Mountain ▲

NA-0133

dense boreal forests. The leafy woodlands of the south give way to spiky forests of spruce and fir. Accommodations and services for tourists aren't as plentiful or easy to find here as in the southern reaches of the state, but some superb inns are tucked among the hills and in the forests.

This section includes a loose, somewhat convoluted driving tour of the Northeast Kingdom, along with some suggestions for outdoor recreation. If your time is limited, make sure you at least stop in St. Johnsbury, which has two of my favorite attractions in the state—the Fairbanks Museum and St. Johnsbury Athenaeum.

Visitor information is available from the **Northeast Kingdom Chamber of Commerce** in St. Johnsbury; 357 Western Ave. Suite 2 (☎ **800/639-6379** or 802/748-3678).

Touring the Northeast Kingdom

Begin at:

1. **Hardwick,** a small town with rough edges set along the Lamoille River. It has a compact commercial main street, some quirky shops, and a couple of casual, family-style restaurants.

    From here, head north on Route 14 a little over 7 miles to the turnoff toward Craftsbury and:

2. **Craftsbury Common.** An uncommonly graceful village, Craftsbury Common is home to a small academy and a large number of historic homes and buildings spread along a sizable green and the village's broad main street. The town occupies a wide upland ridge and offers sweeping views to the east and west. Be sure to stop by the old cemetery on the south end of town, where you can wander among historic tombstones of the pioneers, which date back to the 1700s. Craftsbury is an excellent destination for mountain biking and cross-country skiing and is home to the region's finest inn (see below).

    From Craftsbury, continue north to reconnect to Route 14. You'll wind through the towns of Albany and Irasburg as you head north. At the village of Coventry, veer north on Route 5 to the lakeside town of:

3. **Newport.** This commercial outpost (population 4,400) is set on the southern shores of Lake Memphremagog, a stunning 27-mile-long lake that's just 2 miles wide at its broadest point and the bulk of which is located in Canada. Newport, improbably enough, has a small outlet zone on Main Street. Look for discounted gear from **Bogner** (150 Main St.; ☎ 802/334-0135), **Louis Garneau** (194 Main St.; ☎ 802/334-5885), and **Great Outdoors** (181 Main St.; ☎ 802/334-2831).

    From Newport, continue north on Route 5, crossing under I-91, for about 7 miles to the town of **Derby Line** (population 2,000). This border outpost has a handful of restaurants and antique shops; you can park and walk across the bridge to poke around the Canadian town of Rock Island without much hassle. Back in Derby Line, look for the

4. **Haskell Free Library and Opera House,** at the corner of Caswell Avenue and Church Street (☎ 802/873-3022). This handsome neoclassical building contains a public library on the first floor and an elegant opera house on the second that's modeled after the old Boston Opera House. The theater opened in 1904 with advertisements promoting a minstrel show featuring "new songs, new jokes, and beautiful electric effects." It's a beautiful theater, with a scene of Venice painted on the drop curtain and carved cherubim adorning the balcony.

What's most curious about the structure, however, is that it lies half in Canada and half in the United States. (The Haskell family donated the building jointly to the towns of Derby Line and Rock Island.) A thick black line runs beneath the seats of the opera house, indicating who's in the United States and who's in Canada. Because the stage is set entirely in Canada, apocryphal stories abound from the early days of frustrated U.S. officers watching fugitives perform on stage. More recently, the theater has been used for the occasional extradition hearing.

From Derby Line, retrace your path south on Route 5 to Derby Center and the juncture of Route 5A. Continue south on Route 5A to the town of Westmore on the shores of:

5. **Lake Willoughby.** This glacier-carved lake is best viewed from the north, with the shimmering sheet of water pinching between the base of two low mountains at the southern end. There's a distinctive Alpine feel to the whole scene, and this underappreciated lake is certainly one of the most beautiful in the Northeast. Route 5A along the eastern shore is lightly traveled and well suited to biking or walking. To ascend the two mountains by foot, see the "Outdoor Pursuits in the Northeast Kingdom" section, below.

Head southwest on Route 16, which departs from Route 5A just north of the lake. Follow Route 16 through the peaceful villages of Barton and Glover. A little over a mile south of Glover, turn left on Route 122. Very soon on your left, look for the farmstead that serves as home to the:

6. **Bread and Puppet Theater.** For the last 3 decades, Polish artist and performer Peter Schumann's Bread and Puppet Theater staged an elaborate annual summer pageant at this farm, attracting thousands. Attendees participated, watched, and lounged about the hillsides as huge, lugubrious, brightly painted puppets crafted of fabric and papier-mâché marched around the farm, acting out a drama that typically featured rebellion against tyranny of one form or another. It was like Woodstock without the music.

Alas, the summer event became so popular that it eventually overwhelmed the farm; for a brief spell, the event was held on secret dates that only diehard fans figured out. Starting in 1999, the theater opted to stage several shows throughout the season, hoping to spread out the mayhem. The schedule is still in an experimental phase; it's best to call ☎ 802/525-3031 for details.

Regardless of the pageant schedule, anytime between June and October you can visit a venerable, slightly tottering barn on the property that's home to the ✪ **Bread and Puppet Museum,** housing many of the puppets used in past events. This is a remarkable display and shouldn't be missed if you're anywhere near the area. Downstairs in the former cow-milking stalls are smaller displays, such as King Lear addressing his daughters, and a group of mournful washerwomen doing their laundry. Upstairs, the vast hayloft is filled to the eaves with soaring, haunting puppets, some up to 20 feet tall. The style is witty and eclectic; the barn seems a joint endeavor of David Lynch, Red Grooms, and Hieronymus Bosch. Admission is free, although donations are encouraged.

From Glover, continue south through serene farmlands to Lyndonville, where you pick up Route 5 south to:

7. **St. Johnsbury.** This town of 7,600 inhabitants is the largest in the Northeast Kingdom and is the major center of commerce. First settled in 1786, the town enjoyed a buoyant prosperity in the 19th century, largely stemming from the success of platform scales, invented here in 1830 by Thaddeus Fairbanks, and which are still manufactured here. The town, which has not suffered from the depredations of

tourist boutiques and brew pubs, has an abundance of fine commercial architecture in two distinct areas, which are joined by steep Eastern Avenue. The more commercial part of town lies along Railroad Street (Route 5) at the base of the hill. The more ethereal part of town, with the library, St. Johnsbury Academy, and a grand museum, is along Main Street at the top of the hill. The north end of Main Street is also notable for its grand residential architecture.

At the corner of Main and Prospect Streets in St. Johnsbury, look for:

8. ✪ The Fairbanks Museum (☎ **802/748-2372**). This imposing Romanesque red sandstone structure was constructed in 1889 to hold the collections of obsessive amateur collector Franklin Fairbanks, the grandson of the inventor of the platform scale. Fairbanks was once described as "the kind of little boy who came home with his pockets full of worms." In adulthood, his propensity to accumulate indiscriminately continued unabated. His artifacts include four stuffed bears, a huge moose with full antlers, art from Asia, and 4,500 stuffed native and exotic birds. And that's just the tip of it.

The soaring, barrel-vaulted main hall, reminiscent of an old-fashioned railway depot, embodies Victorian grandeur. Among the assorted clutter, look for the unique mosaics by John Hampson. Hampson crafted scenes of American history—such as Washington bidding his troops farewell—entirely of mounted insects. In the Washington scene, for instance, iridescent green beetles form the epaulets, and the regal great coat is comprised of hundreds of purple moth wings. Words fail me here; you must see these works, which alone are worth the price of admission.

The museum, at 1302 Main St., is open Monday to Saturday from 10am to 4pm (until 6pm in July and August), and Sunday from 1 to 5pm. Admission is $5 for adults, $4 for seniors, $3 for children 5 to 17, free for children under 5, and $12 per family (maximum of three adults, unlimited children).

Also in town, just south of the museum on Main Street:

9. ✪ The St. Johnsbury Athenaeum (☎ **802/748-8291**) is in an Edward Hopper–esque brick building with a truncated mansard tower and prominent keystones over the windows. This is the town's public library, but it also houses an extraordinary art gallery dating to 1873. It claims to be the oldest unadulterated art gallery in the nation, and I see no reason to question that claim.

Your first view of the gallery is spectacular: After winding through the cozy library with its ticking regulator clock, you round a corner and find yourself gazing across Yosemite National Park. This luminous 10-by-15-foot oil was created by noted Hudson River School painter Albert Bierstadt, and the gallery was built specifically to accommodate this work. (Not everyone was happy about the work moving here. "Now *The Domes* is doomed to the seclusion of a Vermont town, where it will astonish the natives," groused the *Boston Globe* at the time.) The natural light flooding in from the skylight above nicely enhances the painting.

Some 100 other works fill the walls. Most are copies of other paintings (a common teaching tool in the 19th century), but look for originals by other Hudson River School painters including Asher B. Durand, Thomas Moran, and Jasper Cropsey.

The Athenaeum is open Monday and Wednesday from 10am to 8pm; Tuesday, Thursday, and Friday from 10am to 5:30pm; and Saturday from 9:30am to 4pm. Admission is free, but donations are encouraged.

OUTDOOR PURSUITS IN THE NORTHEAST KINGDOM

HIKING   At the southern tip of Lake Willoughby, two rounded peaks rise above the lake's waters. These are the biblically named Mount Hor and Mount Pisgah, both of which lie within Willoughby State Forest. Both summits are accessible via footpaths that are somewhat strenuous but yield excellent views.

For **Mount Pisgah** (elevation 2,751 ft.), look for parking on the west side of Route 5A about 5.7 miles south of the junction with Route 16. The trail departs from across the road and runs 1.7 miles to the summit. To hike **Mount Hor** (elevation 2,648 ft.), drive 1.8 miles down the gravel road on the right side of the above-mentioned parking lot, veering right at the fork. Park at the small parking lot, and continue on foot past the parking lot a short distance until you spot the start of the trail. Follow the trail signs to the summit, a round-trip of about 3.5 miles.

MOUNTAIN BIKING   The Craftsbury ridge features several excellent variations for bikers in search of easy terrain. Most of the biking is on hard-packed dirt roads through sparsely populated countryside. The views are sensational, and the sense of being well out in the country very strong. The **Craftsbury Outdoor Center at Craftsbury Common** (☎ **800/729-7751** or 802/586-7767) rents mountain bikes and is an excellent source for maps and local information about area roads. Bike rentals are $25 per day. A small fee is charged for using bikes on the cross-country ski trail network.

CROSS-COUNTRY SKIING   The same folks who offer mountain biking at the Craftsbury Center also maintain 61 miles of groomed cross-country trails through the gentle hills surrounding Craftsbury. The trails, maintained by **Craftsbury Nordic** (☎ **800/729-7751** or 802/586-7767), are forgiving, old-fashioned trails that emphasize pleasing landscapes rather than fast action. Trail passes are $11 for adults, $5 for juniors 6 to 12, and $7 for seniors (discounts available midweek). **Highland Lodge** (☎ **802/533-2647**) on Caspian Lake offers 36 miles of trails (about 10 miles groomed) through rolling woodlands and fields.

ALPINE SKIING   **Jay Peak.** Rte. 242, Jay, VT 05859 (☎ **800/451-4449** for lodging, or 802/988-2611. E-mail: jaypeak@together.net). Vertical drop: 2,153 ft. Lifts: 1 tram, 4 chairlifts, 2 surface lifts. Skiable acreage: 300-plus. Lift tickets: $44.

Located just south of the Canadian border, Jay is Vermont's best ski mountain for those who get away just to ski and who prefer to avoid all the modern-day glitter and trappings that seem to clutter ski resorts elsewhere. (The lower lift prices also save you a few dollars a day.) While some new condo development has been taking place at the base of the mountain, the mountain still has the feeling of a remote, isolated destination, accessible by a winding road through unbroken woodlands.

More than half of Jay's 62 trails are for intermediate skiers. But experts haven't been left behind. Jay has developed extensive glade skiing, taking excellent advantage of its sizable natural snowfall, which averages more than 300 inches annually (more than any other New England ski area). Jay Peak's ski school emphasizes glade skiing, making it a fitting place to learn how to navigate these exciting, challenging trails that have cropped up at other New England ski areas in recent years.

WHERE TO STAY

Highland Lodge. Caspian Lake, Greensboro, VT 05841. ☎ **802/533-2647.** Fax 802/533-7494. E-mail: hlodge@connriver.net. 11 units, 11 cottages. $190–$230 double. Rates include breakfast and dinner. DISC, MC, V. Closed mid-Mar to May and mid-Oct to Christmas. From Hardwick, drive on Rte. 15 east 2 miles to Rte. 16; drive north 2 more miles to East Hardwick. Head west and follow signs to inn.

The Highland Lodge was built in the mid-19th century and has been accommodating guests since 1926. Located just across the road from lovely Caspian Lake, this lodge has 11 rooms furnished in a comfortable country style. Nearby are 11 cottages, fully equipped with kitchenettes. A stay here is supremely relaxing. The main activities include swimming and boating in the lake in summer, along with tennis on a clay court; in winter the lodge maintains its own cross-country ski area with 30 miles of groomed trail. Behind the lodge is an attractive nature preserve, which makes for quiet exploration.

Dining: The inn's welcoming dining room serves New England favorites, like Cornish game hen and crab gratin (open to outside guests, entrees $14.50 to $16.75).

✪ **Inn on the Common.** Craftsbury Common, VT 05827. ☎ **800/521-2233** or 802/586-9619. Fax 802/586-2249. www.innonthecommon.com. E-mail: info@innonthecommon.com. 16 units. $230–$250 double; foliage season $270–$290 double. Rates include breakfast and dinner ($30 less for breakfast only). 2-night minimum stay during foliage and Christmas week. AE, MC, V. Pets allowed by prior arrangement ($15 per visit).

This exceedingly handsome complex of three Federal-style buildings anchors the charming ridge-top village of Craftsbury Common. Innkeepers Penny and Michael Schmitt have run this place with panache since 1973 and have created a beautiful, comfortable inn that offers just the right measure of history and luxury. Guests can unwind in the nicely appointed common rooms or stroll the 15 acres of landscaped grounds. Five rooms have wood-burning fireplaces.

Dining: Dinner starts with cocktails at 6pm, then guests are seated family-style amid elegant Federal-era surroundings at 7:30pm. The menu changes nightly, but includes well-prepared contemporary American fare like pheasant breast with bourbon demi-glace or scallops with tomato and fresh basil served on linguini.

Amenities: Outdoor heated pool (summer only), clay tennis court, croquet, 250-video library. in-room massage, baby-sitting, nature trails, conference rooms. In winter there's cross-country skiing and snowshoeing.

New Hampshire 12

by Wayne Curtis

There are two ways to get New Hampshire old-timers riled up and spitting vinegar. First, tell them you think that Vermont is a great state. Then tell them you think it's a little weird that New Hampshire doesn't have a state income tax or sales tax.

At its most basic, New Hampshire defines itself by what it isn't, and that, more often than not, is Vermont—a state regarded by many locals as one of the few communist republics still remaining. No, New Hampshire is not Vermont, and they'll thank you not to confuse the two, despite some outward similarities.

Keep in mind that New Hampshire's state symbol is the Old Man of the Mountains, which is an actual site you can visit in the White Mountains. You'll see this icon just about everywhere you look—on state highway signs, on brochures, on state police cars. And it's an apt symbol for a state that relishes its cranky-old-man demeanor. New Hampshire has long been a magnet for folks who speak of government—especially "big government"—in tones normally reserved for bowel ailments. That "Live-Free-or-Die" license plate? It's for real. New Hampshire stands behind its words. This is a state that still regards zoning as a nefarious conspiracy to undermine property rights. Note that New Hampshire does not have a bottle-deposit law, or a law banning billboards. (Heathen Vermont has both, as does its other godless neighbor, Maine.)

New Hampshire savors its reputation as an embattled outpost of plucky and heroic independents fighting the good fight against intrusive laws and irksome bureaucrats. Without a state sales tax or state income tax, it's had to be creative. Many government services are funded through the "tourist tax" (an 8% levy on meals and rooms at restaurants and hotels) along with a hefty local property tax (the mere mention of which is another way to get locals riled up). In fact, candidates for virtually every office with the possible exception of dog-catcher must take "The Pledge," which means they'll vow to fight any effort to impose sales or income tax. To shirk The Pledge is tantamount to political suicide.

Get beyond New Hampshire's affable crankiness, though, and you'll find pure New England. Indeed, New Hampshire may represent the New England ethic distilled to its essence. At its core is a mistrust of outsiders, a premium placed on independence, a belief that government should be frugal above all else, and a laconic acceptance that, no matter what, you just can't change the weather. Travelers exploring the state with open eyes will find these attitudes in spades.

Travelers will also find wonderfully diverse terrain—from ocean beaches to the broad lakes to the region's impressive mountains. Without ever leaving the state's borders, you can toss a Frisbee on a sandy beach, ride bikes along quiet country lanes dotted with covered bridges, hike rugged granite hills blasted by some of the most severe weather in the world, and canoe on a placid lake in the company of moose and loons. You'll also find good food and country inns you won't want to ever leave. But most of all, you'll find vestiges of that feisty independence that has defined New England since the first settlers ran up their flag 3½ centuries ago.

1 Enjoying the Great Outdoors

BACKPACKING   The White Mountains of northern New Hampshire offer some of the most challenging and scenic backpacking in the Northeast. The best trails are located within 773,000-acre White Mountain National Forest, which encompasses several 5,000-plus–foot peaks and more than 100,000 acres of designated wilderness. Trails range from easy lowland walks along bubbling streams to demanding ridgeline paths buffeted by fierce winds. The **Appalachian Mountain Club** (☎ 603/466-2727) is an excellent source of general information about the New Hampshire outdoors, and their huts offer shelter in eight dramatically situated cabins that offer basic shelter and a certain Spartan comfort. Reservations are essential.

In addition, a number of three-sided Adirondack-style shelters are located throughout the backcountry on a first-come, first-served basis. Some are free; others have a small fee. Pitching a tent in the backcountry is free, subject to certain restrictions, and no permits are required. It's best to check with the forest headquarters (☎ 603/528-8721) or a district ranger station for rules and regulations. The Appalachian Trail passes through New Hampshire, entering the state at Hanover, running along the highest peaks of the White Mountains, and exiting into Maine along the Mahoosuc Range northeast of Gorham. The trail is well maintained, although it tends to attract teeming crowds along the highest elevations in summer.

Rental equipment—including sleeping bags and pad, tents, and packs—is available at **Eastern Mountain Sports** (☎ 603/356-5433), in North Conway, at reasonable rates.

BIKING   There's superb road biking throughout the state. The best advice is to bike the winding, twisting back roads. Southwest New Hampshire near Mount Monadnock offers a multitude of shady back roads for exploring, especially around Hancock and Greenfield.

The White Mountains have plenty of opportunities for mountain bikers; trails are open to bikers unless otherwise noted. Bikes are not allowed in wilderness areas. The upland roads outside of Jackson offer some superb country biking, as does the steep terrain around Franconia and Sugar Hill. **Great Glen Trails** (☎ 603/466-2333), near Mount Washington, and **Waterville Valley Base Camp** (☎ 800/468-2553), at the southwest edge of the park, both offer bike rentals and maintained mountain-bike trails for a fee. Waterville Valley also has lift-serviced mountain biking.

CAMPING   Car campers shouldn't have any problem finding a place to pitch a tent or park an RV, especially in the northern half of the state. The White Mountain National Forest maintains 20 campgrounds with a total of 819 sites (no hookups), some very small and personal, others quite large and noisy. Sites tend to be fairly easy to come by midweek, but on summer or foliage weekends, you're taking a chance if you arrive without reservations. For National Forest campground reservations, call the **National Recreation Reservation Service** (☎ 877/444-6777). There's an additional

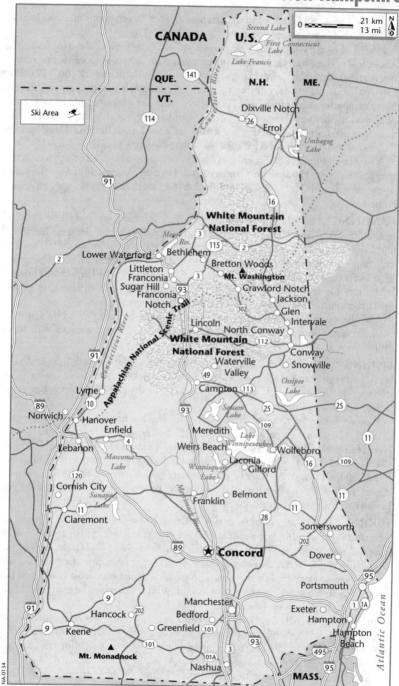

New Hampshire

CANADA
U.S.

Second Lake

First Connecticut Lake

Lake Francis

QUE.
VT.

N.H.

ME.

141

Ski Area

114

91

2

Lower Waterford

Littleton
Franconia
Sugar Hill
Franconia
Notch

Bethlehem

115

2

Moore
Res.

3

Dixville Notch
26
Errol

Umbagog
Lake

16

White Mountain
National Forest

Bretton Woods

Mt. Washington

93

Crawford Notch
Jackson
302
Glen
Intervale

Lincoln

North Conway

112

White Mountain
National Forest

91

Waterville
Valley

49

Campton 113

93

Squam
Lake

25

Conway
Snowville

Ossipee
Lake

25

Lyme
10

Norwich

Hanover
Enfield

89

Lebanon

4

Mascoma
Lake

Meredith

Weirs Beach

Laconia
Gilford

Lake
Winnipesaukee

109

Wolfeboro

16

109

Winnisquam
Lake

11

120

Cornish City

Sunapee
Lake

11

Claremont

Franklin

Belmont

Merrimack River

28

11

11

Somersworth

202

Dover

89

Concord

95

Portsmouth

9

Hancock 202

Manchester

Bedford

Exeter
Hampton

1 1A

91

9

Keene

Greenfield 101

3

93

Hampton
Beach

101

Mt. Monadnock

101A

Nashua

495

95

MASS.

Atlantic Ocean

Appalachian National Scenic Trail

Connecticut River

0   21 km
    13 mi

N

NA-0134

reservation fee of $8.65 added to the campground fee. Reservations may also be made via the Web at **www.reserveusa.com.**

Fifteen of New Hampshire's state parks allow camping (two of these for RVs only). About half of these parks are located in and around the White Mountains. For advance **reservations,** call the New Hampshire state park system, at ☎ **603/271-3628** between January and May; during the summer season call the campground directly. Some campgrounds are first-come, first served. A list of parks and phone numbers is published in the New Hampshire Visitor's Guide, distributed widely through information centers, or by contacting the **Office of Travel and Tourism Development,** P.O. Box 1856, Concord, NH 03302 (☎ **800/386-4664** or 603/271-2343).

New Hampshire also has more than 150 private campgrounds. For a free directory, contact the **New Hampshire Campground Owners Association,** P.O. Box 320, Twin Mountain, NH 03595 (☎ **800/822-6764** or 603/846-5511; www.ucampnh. com).

CANOEING   New Hampshire has a profusion of suitable rivers and lakes, and canoe rentals are widely available. Good flatwater paddling may be found along the Merrimack and Connecticut rivers in the southern parts of the state. Virtually any lake is good for canoeing, although beware of sudden squalls and northerly winds when crossing large lakes like vast Winnipesaukee. In the far north, 8,000-acre Lake Umbagog is home to bald eagles and loons, and is especially appealing for exploration by canoe. In general, the farther north you venture, the wilder and more remote the terrain.

Also the north, the Androscoggin River offers superb Class I–II white water and swift flat water upstream from Berlin; below, the river is faintly noxious with paper-mill pollution.

FISHING   A vigorous stocking program keeps New Hampshire's lakes and rivers lively with fish. Brook trout (about half of trout stocked), lake trout, and rainbow trout are in the waters. Other sportfish include small- and largemouth bass, land-locked salmon, and walleye.

Fishing licenses are required for freshwater fishing, but not for saltwater fishing. For detailed information on regulations, request the free *Freshwater Fishing Digest* from the **New Hampshire Fish and Game Department,** 2 Hazen Dr., Concord, NH 03301 (☎ **603/271-3211**). Fishing licenses for nonresidents range from $18.50 for 3 days to $27.50 for 15 days. Another helpful booklet, available free from the fish and game department, is *Fishing Waters of New Hampshire.* For on-line information, point your browser to www.wildlife.state.nh.us.

HIKING   The White Mountains alone offer 1,200 miles of trails; state parks and forests add considerably to the mileage. Serious hikers will want to bypass much of the state and beeline for the Whites. The essential guide to hiking trails is the Appalachian Mountain Club's *White Mountain Guide,* which contains up-to-date and detailed descriptions of every trail in the area. The guide is available at most book- and out-door shops in the state. See the section on the White Mountains later in this chapter for further suggestions on hikes.

In southwest New Hampshire, the premier hike is Mount Monadnock, said to be one of the world's two most popular hikes (second only to Mt. Fuji in Japan). This lone massif, rising regally above the surrounding hills, is a straightforward day hike accessible via several trails.

For other hiking opportunities outside the Whites, *50 More Hikes in New Hampshire* ($14.95), written by Daniel Doan and published by Backcountry Publications can be ordered through your bookstore, or directly from W. W. Norton & Co., Inc., 500 Fifth Ave,, New York, NY 10110, ☎ **800/233-4830.**

SKIING   New Hampshire offers a good selection of slopes, although in my opinion it doesn't compare with the quainter, more inclusive resorts of Vermont or Maine. But determined skiers can find everything from challenging steeps to gentle runs at some 20 downhill ski areas.

New Hampshire's forte are the small ski areas that cater to families. These include Gunstock, Black, Temple Mountain, Mount Sunapee, King Pine, and Pats Peak, all with vertical drops of around 1,500 feet or less. More challenging skiing is in the White Mountains region; the best areas here are Cannon Mountain, Loon Mountain, Waterville Valley, Wildcat, and Attitash Bear Peak, with vertical drops of 2,000 feet or so and feature services one would expect of a professional ski resort. **Ski NH** (☎ **800/ 887-5464,** or 603/745-9396 in N.H.) distributes a ski map and other information helpful in ski-trip planning. The same phone numbers provide recorded ski condition reports.

The state boasts some 26 cross-country ski centers, which groom a combined total of more than 500 miles of trails. The state's premier cross-country destination is the **Jackson** (☎ 603/383-9355), with 55 miles of groomed trail in and around an exceptionally scenic village in a valley near the base of Mount Washington. Other favorites include **Bretton Woods** (☎ 603/278-3307 or 603/278-5181) at the western entrance to Crawford Notch, also with more than 50 miles of groomed trails, and the spectacularly remote **Balsams/Wilderness** cross-country ski center (☎ **800/255- 0600** or 603/255-3951) in the northerly reaches of the state.

SNOWMOBILING   Snowmobilers will find nearly 6,000 miles of groomed, scenic snowmobile trails lacing the state, interconnected via a trail network maintained by local snowmobile clubs. All snowmobiles must be registered with the state; this costs $47 for nonresidents ($37 for residents) and can be done through any of the 248 off-highway recreational-vehicle agents in the state. More information may be obtained from the **New Hampshire Snowmobile Association,** 722 Rte. 3A, Bow, NH 03304 (☎ **603/224-8906**). On the Internet, try www.nhsa.com.

2 Portsmouth

A civilized, compact seaside city of bridges and brick and seagulls, ✪ **Portsmouth** is filled with elegant architecture. This bonsai-size city projects a strong and proud sense of its heritage without being overly precious about it.

Part of the city's appeal is its variety. Upscale coffee shops and fancy art galleries exist alongside old-fashioned barber shops and tattoo parlors. But the town still has a fundamental earthiness that serves as a tangy vinegar for the overly saccharine spots.

Portsmouth's history runs deep; this is instantly evident when walking through town. For the past three centuries, the city has served as a hub for the region's maritime trade. In the 1600s, Strawbery Banke (it wasn't renamed Portsmouth until 1653) was a center for the export of wood and dried fish to Europe. In the 19th century, it prospered as a center of regional trade. Across the river in Maine, the Portsmouth Naval Shipyard was founded in 1800 and evolved into a prominent base for the building, outfitting, and repair of U.S. Navy submarines. Today, Portsmouth's maritime tradition continues with a lively trade in bulk goods (look for scrap metal and minerals stockpiled along the shores of the Piscataqua River on Market Street); the city's de facto symbol is the tugboat, one or two of which are usually tied up near the waterfront's picturesque Tugboat Alley.

ESSENTIALS

GETTING THERE   Portsmouth is served by Exits 3 through 7 on I-95. The most direct access to downtown is via Market Street (Exit 7), which is the last New

Hampshire exit before crossing the river to Maine. By bus, Portsmouth is served by Concord Trailways and Vermont Transit.

VISITOR INFORMATION   The **Greater Portsmouth Chamber of Commerce,** 500 Market St., Portsmouth, NH 03802 (☎ **603/436-1118**), operates a tourist information center year-round between Exit 7 and downtown. Between Memorial Day and Columbus Day the center is open Monday to Wednesday 8:30am to 5pm, Thursday and Friday 8:30am to 7pm,, and Saturday and Sunday 10am to 4pm. The rest of the year, the center is open weekdays only 8:30am to 5pm. In summer the chamber staffs a second information booth at Market Square in the middle of the historic district.

PARKING   Most of Portsmouth can be easily reconnoitered on foot, so you need park only once. Parking can be tight in and around the historic district in summer. The municipal parking garage costs 50¢ per hour; look for signs pointing you there just west of Market Square off Congress Street. Strawbery Banke (see below) also offers limited parking for visitors.

A MAGICAL HISTORY TOUR

Portsmouth's 18th-century prosperity can be plainly seen in the regal Georgian-style homes that dot the city. Strawbery Banke occupies the core of the historic area, and is well worth visiting. If you don't have the budget, time, or inclination to visit Strawbery Banke, a walking tour will bring you past the most significant homes, many of which are maintained by various historical or colonial societies and are open to the public. A helpful map and brochure describing the key historic homes, entitled *The Portsmouth Trail: An Historic Walking Tour,* is available free at the city's information centers.

✪ **Strawbery Banke.** Hancock St., Portsmouth, NH 03802. ☎ **603/433-1106.** www.strawberybanke.org. Admission $12 adults, $11 seniors, $8 children 7–17, free for children under 7, $28 families. Apr–Oct daily 10am–5pm. Special events held first 2 weekends of Dec; otherwise closed Nov–Apr. Look for directional signs posted around town.

If Portsmouth were a festival of historic homes and buildings, Strawbery Banke would be the main stage. In 1958 the city planned to raze this venerable neighborhood, first settled in 1653, to make way for urban renewal. A group of local citizens resisted and won, establishing an outdoor history museum that's grown to be one of the largest in New England.

The museum today consists of 10 downtown acres and 46 historic buildings. Ten of these have been restored with period furnishings; eight others feature exhibits. (One admission fee buys access to all homes and exhibits.) While Strawbery Banke employs staffers to assume the character of historic residents (including Thomas Bailey Aldrich, a frequent early contributor to the *Atlantic Monthly*), the emphasis is more on the buildings, architecture, and historic accoutrement, and less on living history as practiced at Sturbridge Village or Plimoth Plantation in Massachusetts.

The neighborhood surrounds an open lawn (formerly a tidal creek), and has a settled, picturesque quality to it. You'll find three working crafts shops on the grounds, where you can watch coopers, boat builders, and potters at work. The most intriguing home may be the split-personality Drisco House, half of which depicts life in the 1790s, and half of which shows life in the 1950s, nicely demonstrating how houses grow and adapt to each era. The Shapiro House (opened in 1997) and illustrates the life of a Russian Jewish immigrant family from around 1919.

Portsmouth

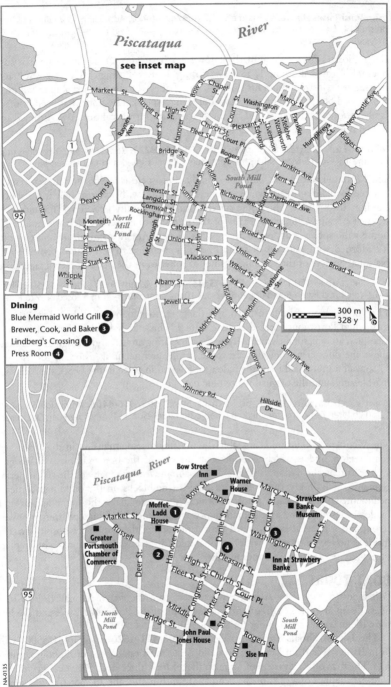

Piscataqua **River**

see inset map

Market St.

Bow St.
Chapel St.
Washington St.
Marcy St.
Russell St.
High St.
Court St.
Pleasant St.
Melcher
Franklin
Wentworth
Edward
Haynes Ave.
Deer St.
Hanover St.
Church St.
Court Pl.
Humphreys
Ct.
New Castle Ave.
Ridges Ct.
Fleet St.
Bridge St.
Rogers St.
Junkins Ave.
Kent St.
South Mill Pond
Middle St.
State St.
Summer St.
Richards Ave.
Rockingham St.
Sherburne Ave.
Clough Dr.

Brewster St.
Langdon St.
Cornwall St.
Rockingham St.
McDonough St.
Cabot St.
Union St.
Austin
Miller Ave.
Broad St.
Madison St.
Union St.
Lincoln Ave.
Broad St.
Dearborn St.
North Mill Pond
Monteith St.
Thornton St.
Burkitt St.
Stark St.
Whipple St.
Albany St.
Wibird St.
Park St.
Hawthorne St.
Jewell Ct.
Middle St.
Aldrich Rd.
Mendum
Thaxter Rd.
Fells Rd.
Monroe St.
Summit Ave.
Spinney Rd.
Hillside Dr.

95
Central
1
1
95

Dining
Blue Mermaid World Grill **2**
Brewer, Cook, and Baker **3**
Lindberg's Crossing **1**
Press Room **4**

0 | 300 m
328 y
N

Piscataqua **River**

Bow Street Inn
Warner House
Marcy St.
Strawbery Banke Museum
Moffet-Ladd House **1**
Market St.
Russell
Bow St.
Chapel St.
State St.
Court St.
Washington St. **3**
Cates St.
Greater Portsmouth Chamber of Commerce
Deer St.
Hanover St.
2
Daniel St.
4
Pleasant St.
Inn at Strawbery Banke
High St.
Church St.
Fleet St.
Congress
Court Pl.
Porter St.
Middle St.
State St.
Bridge St.
John Paul Jones House
Court St.
Rogers St.
Sise Inn
South Mill Pond
Junkins Ave.
North Mill Pond

NA-0135

John Paul Jones House. 43 Middle St. ☎ **603/436-8420**. Admission $5 adults, $2.50 children 6–14, free for children under 6. Mon–Sat 10am–4pm, Sun noon–4pm. Closed late Oct to May.

Revolutionary War hero John Paul Jones ("I have not yet begun to fight") was a boarder in this handsome 1758 home during the Revolutionary War. He was here to oversee the construction of his sloop, Ranger, believed to be the first ship to sail under the United States flag (there's a model of it on display). The home has been immaculately restored and maintained by the Portsmouth Historical Society; costumed tour guides offer tours of 45 minutes to an hour.

Moffatt-Ladd House. 154 Market St. ☎ **603/436-8221.** $5 adults, $2.50 children under 12. June 15–Oct 15 Mon–Sat 11am–5pm, Sun 1–5pm. Closed mid-Oct to mid-June.

The Moffatt-Ladd House, built for a family of prosperous merchants and traders, is as notable for its elegant garden as for the 1763 home, with its great hall and elaborate carvings throughout. The home stayed within one family between 1763 and 1913, when it became a museum. Many of the furnishings have never left the house. The home will especially appeal to aficionados of early American furniture and painting; it's adorned with portraits of some 15 family members. The home is owned by the National Society of the Colonial Dames of America in the State of New Hampshire.

Warner House. 150 Daniel St. ☎ **603/436-5909.** Admission $5 adults, $2.50 children 7–12, free for children 6 and under. Tues–Sat 10am–4pm, Sun 1–4pm. Closed Nov to June 1.

The Warner House, built in 1716, was the governor's mansion in the mid–18th century when Portsmouth served as state capital. This stately brick home with graceful Georgian architectural elements (note the alternating arched and triangular pediments above the dormer windows) is a favorite among architectural historians for its circa-1716 wall murals (said to be the oldest murals still in place in the U.S.), the early wall marbleizing, and the original white pine paneling.

Wentworth-Gardner House. 50 Mechanic St. ☎ **603/436-4406.** Admission $5 adults, $2.50 children 6–14, free for children 5 and under. Tues–Sun 1–4pm. Closed late Oct to early June.

The Wentworth-Gardner is arguably the most handsome mansion in the entire Seacoast region, and is widely considered to be one of the best examples of Georgian architecture in the nation. Built in 1760, the home features many of the classic period elements, including very pronounced quoins (the blocks on the building's corners), pedimented window caps, plank sheathing (meant to make the home appear as if made of masonry), and an elaborate doorway featuring Corinthian pilasters, a broken scroll, and a paneled door topped with a pineapple, the symbol of hospitality. The inside is no less impressive, with hand-painted Chinese wallpaper and a vast fireplace in the kitchen featuring a windmill spit.

BOAT TOURS

Portsmouth is especially attractive when seen from the water. A small fleet of tour boats tie up at Portsmouth, offering scenic tours of the Piscataqua River and the historic Isle of Shoals throughout the summer and fall.

The Isle of Shoals Steamship Co. (☎ 800/441-4620 or 603/431-5500) sails from Barker Wharf on Market Street and is the most established of the tour companies. The firm offers a variety of tours on the 90-foot, three-deck *Thomas Laighton* (it's a modern replica of a turn-of-the-century steamship) and the 70-foot *Oceanic*, which was especially designed for whale watching. Among the most popular excursions are to the Isle of Shoals, allowing passengers to disembark and wander about Star Island, a dramatic, rocky island that's part of an island cluster far out in the offshore swells.

Star Island has a rich history and today serves as the base for a summer religious institute. Reservations are strongly encouraged for this trip. Other popular trips include 6-hour whale-watching voyages and a sunset lighthouse cruise. Fares range from $9 to $25 for adults, $5 to $16 for children.

Portsmouth Harbor Cruises (☎ **800/776-0915** or 603/436-8084) specializes in tours of the historic Piscataqua River aboard the *Heritage*, a 49-passenger cruise ship with plenty of open deck space. Cruise by five old forts, or enjoy the picturesque tidal estuary of inland Great Bay, a scenic trip upriver from Portsmouth. Trips run daily, and reservations are suggested. Fares are $8.50 to $15 for adults, $6 to $9 for children.

SHOPPING

Portsmouth's compact historic district is home to dozens of boutiques offering unique items and antiques. A fine contemporary gallery featuring the work of area craftspeople, the elegant **N. W. Barrett Gallery,** 53 Market St. (☎ **603/431-4262**), offers up a classy selection of creative, exuberant crafts, including ceramic sculptures, glassware, lustrous woodworking, and a wide array of handmade jewelry.

Antiques stores are scattered around town. Among my favorites is **Victory Antiques,** 96 State St., (☎ **603/431-3046**), which has a limited yet eclectic selection, usually including furniture with the original paint. Some 25 dealers maintain cases here offering a good selection of china and glass.

The **Robert Lincoln Levy Gallery** operated by the New Hampshire Art Association, 136 State St., (☎ **603/431-4230**), has frequently changing exhibits and shows; it's a good destination to sample some of the fine art produced by New Hampshire artists.

City & Country, 50 Daniel St. (☎ **603/433-5353**), is a contemporary housewares store—a sort of Pottery Barn Lite—with a small but intriguing selection of glasses, table settings, flatware, and cooking implements, along with a mix of furniture and wrought-iron accessories.

Harbour Treats, 4 Market Square (☎ **603/431-3228),** is a chocoholic's paradise, with a good selection of homemade fudges, chocolates, and truffles. The chocolate turtles are a perennial local favorite.

Paradiza, 63 Penhallow St. (☎ **603/431-0180**), offers up an array of very clever greeting cards, along with exotica like soaps and bath products from Israel and Africa. Somewhat further down the knickknack food chain, **Marco Polo,** 89 Market St. (☎ **603/436-8338**) specializes in retro chic gifts, toys, and gadgets. This pleasantly cluttered shop stocks pink flamingos, refrigerator magnets, movie kitsch, candies, coffee mugs, and T-shirts, most of which are embellished with off-beat humor.

WHERE TO STAY

Portsmouth has a good selection of places to stay within walking distance of the downtown historic area. Less expensive, less stylish options include chain hotels at the edge of town near I-95. Among them are the **Anchorage Inn,** 417 Woodbury Ave. (☎ **603/431-8111**); **Susse Chalet,** 650 Borthwick Ave. (☎ **603/436-6363**); and the **Holiday Inn of Portsmouth** (☎ **603/431-8000**), at 300 Woodbury Ave.

Bow Street Inn. 121 Bow St., Portsmouth, NH 03801. ☎ **603/431-7760.** Fax 603/433-1680. 9 units. A/C TV TEL. Jan to mid-May $89–$119 double; mid-May to July 1 $105–$139 double; July 1 to Oct 31 $114–$149 double; Nov–Dec $99–$130 double. Rates include continental breakfast. 2-night minimum stay on some holidays. AE, DISC, MC, V.

This is a perfectly adequate destination for travelers willing to give up some charm in order to gain convenience. This former downtown brewery was made over in the 1980s in a bit of inspired adaptive reuse—condos occupy the top floor, and the respected **Seacoast Repertory Theatre** (☎ 603/433-4472) occupies the first. The second floor is the Bow Street Inn, a modern, nine-room hotel that offers great access to historic Portsmouth. The guest rooms, set off a somewhat sterile hallway, are clean, comfortable, small, and for the most part unexceptional in a contemporary motel sort of way. Only rooms 6 and 7 both feature good views of the harbor, and a premium is charged for these. Parking is on the street or at a nearby paid garage.

Inn at Strawbery Banke. 314 Court St., Portsmouth, NH 03801. ☎ **800/428-3933** or 603/436-7242. 7 units. A/C. Summer and early fall $100–$105 double; off-season $75–$80 double. Rates include full breakfast. 2-night minimum stay Oct weekends. AE, DISC, MC, V. "Well-behaved older children" are welcome.

The Inn at Strawbery Banke, located in a home built in the early 1800s on historic Court Street, is ideally located for exploring Portsmouth. Strawbery Banke is but a block away, and Market Square is just 2 blocks away. The inn has done a nice job taking a cozy antique home and making it comfortable for guests. Rooms are small but bright and feature stenciling, wooden interior shutters, and beautiful pine floors; one has a bathroom down the hall. There are two sitting rooms with TVs, and a dining room where a full breakfast is served.

✪ **Sise Inn.** 40 Court St., Portsmouth, NH 03801. ☎ and fax **603/433-1200.** E-mail: siseinn@cybertours.com. 34 units. A/C TV TEL. June–Oct $145–$225 double; Nov–May $110–$175 double. Rates include continental breakfast. AE, DC, MC, V.

The Sise Inn is a modern, elegant, small hotel in the guise of a country inn. This solid gray Queen Anne–style home with jade and cream trim overlooks the bustling intersection of Court and Middle streets, but inside it's a peaceful world removed from the buzz of town. The original home was built for a prominent merchant in 1881; the hotel addition was constructed in the 1980s. The effect is surprisingly harmonious, with the antique stained glass and copious oak trim meshing well with the more-contemporary elements. An elevator serves the three floors and there's modern carpeting throughout, but many of the rooms and suites feature antique armoires and an updated Victorian styling.

All rooms feature VCRs. Among the most sought-after rooms are Room 406, a suite with soaking tub and private sitting room, and Room 216 with its own sauna and lovely natural light. An elaborate continental breakfast is served in the huge old kitchen and adjoining sunroom, and there's usually something to snack on in the afternoon. This is a popular hotel for business travelers, but if you're on holiday you won't be made to feel out of place.

WHERE TO DINE

Portsmouth is blessed with two commendable places to satisfy a sweet tooth. **Ceres Bakery,** 51 Penhallow St. (☎ **603/436-6518**), is Portsmouth's original funky bakery, set off on a quiet side street. It's a tiny space with just a handful of tables, so you might be better off getting a cookie or slice of cake to go and then walking the few blocks to the waterfront rose gardens.

Cafe Brioche, 14 Market Square, (☎ **603/430-9225**) is more of a hangout, situated right on Market Square. It's often crowded with folks attracted not only by the central location, but also the delectable baked goods and buzz-inducing coffees.

✪ **Blue Mermaid World Grill.** The Hill (between Hanover and Deer sts. facing the municipal parking garage). ☎ **603/427-2583.** Reservations recommended for parties of 6 or more. Lunch items $5.75–$11.95; main dinner courses $10.25–$19.95 (most under $15). AE, DC, DISC, MC, V. Mon–Thurs 11:30am–9pm, Fri 11:30am–10pm, Sat noon–10pm; Sun 1–9pm. GLOBAL/ECLECTIC.

The Blue Mermaid ranks among my favorites in Portsmouth for its good food, good value, and good attitude. It's a short stroll from Market Square, in a historic area called The Hill, whose main feature today is a large parking lot and old homes converted to offices. It's not a pretentious place—Tom Waits drones on in the background—and the service is casual but professional. More locals than tourists congregate here. The menu is consistently adventurous in a low-key global kind of way—you might try Moroccan marinated lamb skewer, sea scallops with mango butter, or lobster quesadilla with corn and basil salsa. There's also seafood, burgers, and pizza from the wood grill.

Brewer, Cook, and Baker. 61 Washington St. ☎ **603/433-3309.** Sandwiches $3.50–$4.90. Daily 8:30am–4pm. CREATIVE SANDWICHES.

Housed in the 1791 Aaron Conant House (part of Strawbery Banke), BCB has the cheerful feel of a college-town sandwich shop. (You needn't pay Strawbery Banke admission to eat here.) It's a good destination for an easy lunch, although tables may be scarce at peak times during the summer. Sandwich selection includes roast beef with Swiss cheese and arugula with a horseradish sauce, and spicy Thai shrimp pocket with cashews.

Lindbergh's Crossing. 29 Ceres St. ☎ **603/431-0887.** Reservations recommended. Main courses $11–$22. AE, MC, V. Sun–Thurs 5:30–9:30pm; Fri–Sat 5:30–10pm. BISTRO.

If you're in the mood for seafood but have a more adventurous palate, head to this restaurant. Located in an old waterfront warehouse (the ooze on the walls is century-old linseed oil), this cozy, two-story restaurant has a bistro menu that's subtly creative without calling too much attention to itself. The seared scallops are served with asparagus tips and a basil tomato broth. The salmon is enlivened with sautéed leeks, sun-dried tomato, and a peppercorn crust. There's also beef tenderloin, roast pork, and a simple pasta with fresh vegetables. The preparation is the best in town, although it still comes up a bit short compared to Portland, Maine's better restaurants (about an hour north).

Press Room. 77 Daniel St. ☎ **603/431-5186.** Reservations not accepted. Sandwiches $3.25–$6.50; main courses $5.25–$9.95. AE, DISC, MC, V. Mon 5–11:45pm; Sun and Tues–Thurs 4–11:45pm, Fri–Sat 11:30am–11:45pm. TAVERN FARE.

Diners flock here more for the convivial atmosphere and the easy-on-the-budget prices than for creative cuisine. Opened in 1976, the Press Room likes to boast that it was the first in the area to serve Guinness Stout, and so it's appropriate that the atmosphere has a Gaelic charm. It's the sort of place where locals like to gather to debate the issues of the day and feel at home. As for character, it's got plenty. During winter and cool coastal days, a fire burns in the woodstove and quaffers flex their elbows at darts amid brick walls, pine floors, and heavy wooden beams overhead. Choose your meal from a basic bar menu, with inexpensive selections, including a variety of burgers, nachos, fish-and-chips, stir-fries, and a selection of salads.

3 Hanover & Environs

If your idea of New England involves a sweeping green edged with stately brick buildings, be sure to visit ✪ **Hanover,** a thriving university town agreeably situated in the Connecticut River valley. First settled in 1765, the town was home to early pioneers who were granted a charter by King George III to establish a college. The school was named after the second Earl of Dartmouth, the school's first trustee. Since its founding, Dartmouth College, the most northerly of the Ivy League schools, has had a large hand in shaping the community. One alumnus has aptly said of the school, "Dartmouth is the sort of place you're nostalgic for even if you've never been there."

Dartmouth has produced more than its share of illustrious alumni, including poet Robert Frost, Nelson Rockefeller, author Louise Erdrich, Robert Reich, former surgeon general and antitobacco crusader C. Everett Koop, and children's book author Dr. Seuss. Perhaps the most noted son of Dartmouth was the renowned 19th-century politician and orator, Daniel Webster. In arguing for the survival of Dartmouth College in a landmark case before the U.S. Supreme Court in 1816 (when two factions vied for control of the school), Webster offered his famous closing line: "It is a small college, gentlemen, but there are those who love it." This has served as an informal motto for school alumni ever since.

Today, a handsome, oversize village green marks the permeable border between college and town. In the summer, the green is an ideal destination for strolling and lounging. The best way to explore Hanover is by foot, so your first endeavor is to park your car, which can be trying during peak seasons. Try the municipal lots west of Main Street.

ESSENTIALS

GETTING THERE   Hanover is north of Lebanon, New Hampshire, and I-89 via Route 10 or Route 120. Amtrak serves White River Junction, Vermont, across the river.

VISITOR INFORMATION   Dartmouth College alumni and chamber volunteers maintain an **information center** (☎ 603/643-3512) on the green in the summer. It's open 7 days a week from June through September (9:30am to 5pm in July and August; 10am to 5pm in June and September.) In the off-season, head to the **Hanover Chamber of Commerce,** P.O. Box 5105, Hanover, NH 03755 (☎ 603/643-3115), located on Main Street across from the post office. It's open Monday through Friday 9am to 4:30pm.

SPECIAL EVENT   In mid-February, look for the massive, intricate ice sculptures from the Dartmouth Winter Carnival, held annually; contact **Dartmouth College** (☎ 603/646-1110) for more information on this traditionally beer-soaked event.

EXPLORING HANOVER

Hanover is a superb town to explore by foot, bike, and even canoe. Start by picking up a map of the campus, available at the Dartmouth information center on the green or at the Hanover Inn. (Free guided tours are also offered in the summer.) The expansive, leafy campus is a delight to walk through; be sure to stop by the Baker Memorial Library to view the murals by Latin American painter José Orozco. He painted *The Epic of American Civilization* while teaching here between 1932 and 1934. The huge murals wrap around a basement study room, and are as colorful as they are densely metaphorical. There's a helpful printed interpretation in a free brochure available at the front desk in the room.

Adjacent to the Hopkins Center is the **Hood Museum of Art** (☎ 603/646-2808). Although it houses one of the oldest college museums in the nation, it's a decidedly contemporary, open building, constructed in 1986. The austere, three-story structure displays selections from the permanent collection, including a superb selection of 19th-century American landscapes and a fine grouping of Assyrian reliefs dating from 883 to 859 B.C. The museum is open Tuesday, Thursday, Friday, and Saturday from 10am to 5pm, Wednesday from 10am to 9pm, and Sunday from noon to 5pm. Admission is free.

A fine way to spend a lazy afternoon is drifting along the Connecticut River in a canoe. Dartmouth's historic **Ledyard Canoe Club** (☎ 603/643-6709) is located just down the hill from the campus off West Wheelock Street (turn upstream at the

"An Aristocracy of Brains"

About a 25-minute drive south of Hanover is Cornish, the former site of a thriving arts colony. Artists and their followers flocked to this untroubled region in the late–19th century, and the subtle beauty of the area, still prevalent today, makes it abundantly clear why.

The first artistic immigrants to arrive were the painters and sculptors, who showed up in the late 1880s and early 1890s, building modest homes in the hills. They were followed by politicians and the affluent. Among those who populated the rolling hills that looked across the river toward Mount Ascutney were sculptor Daniel Chester French, painter Maxfield Parrish, and New Republic editor Herbert Crowley. Prominent visitors included Ethel Barrymore and presidents Woodrow Wilson and Theodore Roosevelt. A 1907 article in the *New York Daily Tribune* noted that artists made their homes in Cornish not "with the idea of converting it into a 'fashionable' summer resort, but rather to form there an aristocracy of brains and keep out that element which displays its lack of gray matter by an expenditure of money in undesirable ways."

The social allure eventually peaked, and the area lapsed into a peaceful slumber. Those who come here now do so for the beauty and seclusion, not for the gatherings and parties. Indeed, the country's most famous recluse—J. D. Salinger—lives in Cornish today.

The region is well worth visiting and exploring. At twilight, you can see where Maxfield Parrish found his inspiration for the rich, pellucid azure skies for which his prints and paintings are so noted.

The premier monument to the former arts colony is the ✪ **Saint-Gaudens National Historic Site** (☎ **603/675-2175**), located off Route 12A. Noted sculptor Augustus Saint-Gaudens first arrived in this valley in 1885, shortly after receiving an important commission to create a statue of Abraham Lincoln. A friend who owned several houses and considerable land in the Cornish area assured him he would find a surfeit of "Lincoln-shaped men" in the area. Saint-Gaudens came, and more or less stayed the rest of his life.

His home and studio, which he called "Aspet" after the village in Ireland where he was raised, is a superb place to learn more about this extraordinary artist. A brief tour of the house, which is kept as it was when Saint-Gaudens lived here, provides a brief introduction to the man. Visitors learn about Saint-Gaudens the artist at several outbuildings and on the grounds, where many replicas of his most famous statues are on display.

The 150-acre grounds also feature short nature trails, where visitors can explore the hilly woodlands, passing along streams and a millpond. The historic site is open daily from 9am to 4:30pm from late May through October. Admission is $4 for adults; free for children under 17.

bottom of the hill before crossing the river, then follow the signs to the clubhouse). While much of the club's focus is on competitive racing (the club has won 20 national titles since 1967), it's a good place to get a boat and explore the tree-lined river. It's open whenever the river temperature tops 50 degrees. Canoes and whitewater kayaks can be rented for $5 per hour, or $15 per day, with boat available first-come, first served. Summer hours are 9am to 8pm weekends, and 10am to 8pm weekdays. In spring and fall the club is open 10am to 6pm weekends, noon to 6pm weekdays.

KID STUFF

⭐ **Montshire Museum of Science.** Montshire Rd., Norwich, Vt. ☎ **802/649-2200.** Admission $5.50 adults, $4.50 children 3–17, free for children under 3. Daily 10am–5pm. Use Exit 13 off I-91 and head east; look for museum signs almost immediately.

This is not your average New England science museum of dusty stuffed animals in a creaky building in need of attention. Located just outside of Hanover on the New Hampshire side of the Connecticut River, the Montshire is a new, architecturally engaging, hands-on museum that draws kids back time and again. The Montshire took root in 1976, when area residents gathered up the leavings of Dartmouth's defunct natural-history museum and put them on display in a former bowling alley in Hanover. The museum grew and prospered, largely owing to the dedication of hundreds of volunteers. A decade ago, the museum moved to this beautiful 100-acre property sandwiched between I-91 and the river. Exhibits are housed in an open, soaring structure inspired by the region's barns. The museum contains some live animals, but it's mostly fun, interactive exhibits that involve kids deeply, teaching them the principles of math and science on the sly. A new exhibit is a computerized journey through the human body.

SHAKER LIFE

Southeast of Hanover in the town of Enfield is the Enfield Shaker Museum, a cluster of historic buildings on peaceful Lake Mascoma. "The Chosen Vale," as it was called by its first inhabitants, was founded in 1793; by the mid-1800s it had 350 members and 3,000 acres. From that peak, the community dwindled, and by 1927 the Shakers abandoned the Chosen Vale and sold the village lock, stock, and barrel.

Today, much of the property is either owned by the state of New Hampshire or the museum, which was founded in 1986. The village is picturesque and contains some extraordinary specimens of architecture; it's well worth stopping by for a self-guided walking tour and to view the small museum, which emphasizes Shaker industry rather than Shaker aesthetics.

After a few moments in the museum, ramble through the village and read about the buildings in the walking-tour guide (free with admission). Be sure to note the gardens and the communal grave. Across the road is a lovely hillside, where you can ascend to a former Shaker ceremonial area. The overall historic feel of the village is a tad compromised by a new condominium development along the lakeshores, although as these developments go the scale and design is quite sympathetic to the original village.

Dominating the village is the imposing **Great Stone Dwelling,** an austere but gracious building of granite erected between 1837 and 1841. When constructed, it was the tallest building north of Boston, and it remains the largest dwelling house in any of the Shaker communes. The Enfield Shakers lived and dined here, with as many as 150 Shakers at a time eating at long trestle tables. In 1997, the museum acquired the stone building, and in 1998 a new restaurant and inn opened to the public (see below).

The **Enfield Shaker Museum** (☎ 603/632-4346) is on Route 4A, and between Memorial Day and Columbus Day is open Monday to Saturday from 10am to 5pm, and Sunday from noon to 5pm. (The rest of the year it's open Saturday from 10am to 4pm and Sunday from noon to 4pm). Admission is $5 for adults, $3 for seniors, and $2.50 for children 10 to 18.

WHERE TO STAY

Several hotels and motels are located off the interstate in Lebanon and West Lebanon, about 5 miles south of Hanover. Try the **Airport Economy Inn** (☎ 800/433-3466

or 603/298-8888) at 45 Airport Rd. (Exit 20 off I-89); **Holiday Inn Express**
(☎ **603/448-5070**) 135 Route 120, (Exit 18 off I-89); the **Radisson Inn North
Country** (☎ **603/298-5906**) 25 Airport Rd.(Exit 20 off I-89); or **The Sunset**
(☎ **603/298-8721**), 305 N. Main St., (Exit 18 off I-89).

✪ **Hanover Inn.** Wheelock St. (P.O. Box 151), Hanover, NH 03755. ☎ **800/443-7024** or
603/643-4300. Fax 603/646-3744. www.hanoverinn.com. E-mail: hanover.inn@dartmouth.
edu. 92 units. A/C TV TEL. $227–$297 double. AE, DC, DISC, MC, V. Valet parking $5 per day.
Pets allowed.

The Hanover Inn was founded in 1780 and is New Hampshire's oldest continuing
business. But founder Gen. Ebenezer Brewster would be hard-pressed to recognize it
today. This large, modern hotel is thoroughly up-to-date; guests with laptops even have
on-line access to Dartmouth's mainframe. (The inn is owned and operated by Dartmouth College.) An expansion of the lobby in 1996 included a much-needed common
area, making this exceptionally well-run and well-maintained hotel all the more
inviting. Yet it has an old-world graciousness, and it's perfectly situated for exploring
the town. Rooms are priced according to size and view, and each is nicely furnished in
a contemporary colonial style. Most have canopied or four-poster beds and down comforters along with amenities like hair dryers, multiple phones, and bathrobes.

   Dining: The inn has two dining rooms; see "Where to Dine," below.

   Amenities: Valet parking, laundry/dry cleaning, safe-deposit boxes, turndown service, newspaper delivery, access to Dartmouth's fitness and athletic facilities.

Mary Keane House. Shaker Village, Enfield, NH 03748. ☎ **888/239-2153** or 603/
632-4241. E-mail: mary.keane@valley.net. 5 units. TV. $75–$135 double. Rates $10 higher
in foliage season. Rates include full breakfast. AE, MC, V. Pets allowed.

Situated at Lower Shaker Village about 25 minutes from Dartmouth, this is an ideal
spot for the gentle recuperation of a harried soul. Built in 1929 (two years after the
Shakers had abandoned the village), this two-story grayish-lavender Georgian Revival
doesn't share much with the Shaker village in architecture or spirit—in fact, it's filled
with lovely Victorian antiques, including a rosewood concert grand piano, which seem
to be anathema to the Shaker sensibility. But it's kept immaculately clean (something
the Shakers would appreciate), and it's right in the Shaker village, so guests can explore
the buildings and museum by day (the grounds are especially peaceful at twilight),
paddle the inn's canoes on Lake Mascoma, or swim at the small private beach.

Shaker Inn at the Great Stone Dwelling. Rte. 4, Enfield, NH 03748. ☎ **603/632-7810.**
www.theshakerinn.com. 24 units. $85–$165 double. Rates include breakfast. AE, CB, DC,
DISC, MC, V.

Part of the Enfield Shaker Museum, the Shaker Inn opened in 1998, and makes a
wonderful destination, especially for those who are curious about the Shakers or early
American history. The rooms are spread among the upper floors of the hulking stone
dwelling built by the Enfield Shaker community. It's an astounding edifice that was all
the more impressive when constructed in the late 1830s. Some of the rooms have original built-in Shaker cabinets (you can stow your socks in something that would bring
five figures at a New York auction house); others are furnished with reproductions. All
rooms are furnished with simple and attractive Shaker reproductions; the bigger and
more expensive rooms are on the lower floors. The inn is run by the same folks who
operate the Red Hill Inn in Center Harbor.

   Dining: The ground-floor restaurant (formerly the Shaker's dining hall) seats 150
and features upscale regional fare that draws on Shaker flavors and traditions,
including lamb with rosemary, duckling with a raspberry maple glaze, and sirloin with
smothered onions and a whiskey sauce. Entrees are priced from $13.50 to $23.95.

WHERE TO DINE

Daniel Webster Room. In the Hanover Inn, Wheelock St. ☎ **603/643-4300.** Reservations recommended. Breakfast items $4.25–$9.50; lunch items $6.95–$13.50; main dinner courses $15–$23. AE, DC, DISC, MC, V. Mon 7–10:30am, 11:30am–1:30pm, Tues–Fri 7–10:30am, 11:30am–1:30pm, 6–9pm, Sat 7–10:30am and 6–9pm, Sun 11:30am–1:30pm. CONTEMPO-RARY AMERICAN.

The neoclassical Daniel Webster Room of the Hanover Inn will appeal to those looking for exceptionally fine dining amid a formal New England atmosphere. The inn's proper dining room is reminiscent of a 19th-century resort hotel, with fluted columns, floral carpeting, and regal upholstered chairs. The dinner menu isn't exten-sive, but that doesn't make it any less appealing. Entrees range from oatmeal-crusted trout almondine with chanterelles and leeks to sautéed rabbit au jus. Diners can choose from an excellent selection of wines.

Off the inn's lobby is the more informal Zins, a wine bistro that serves some 30 wines by the glass. It's open daily from 11:30am to 10pm, and has lunches for under $10 and dinners like crispy half duck with glazed acorn squash and cider, and lobster and crab ravioli. Most dinner entrees are $13 to $15.

○ **La Poule à Dents.** Carpenter St. (off Main St. across from the Citgo station), Norwich, Vt. ☎ **802/649-2922.** Reservations recommended. Main courses $17.75–$25. AE, CB, DC, DISC, MC, V. Daily 6–10pm. FRENCH.

In the sleepy town of Norwich, Vermont, just across the river from Hanover, this place wakes up visitors with some of the region's most elegant and exquisite dining. Housed in a historic 1820 home, it's a perfect spot for a romantic meal or to celebrate a major occasion. The menu reads like the inventory of a Flemish still life capturing the bounty of the hunt. Begin your meal with an array of appealing appetizers, which range from Vermont quail to wild mushroom and boar sausage to hand-rolled pepper fettuccine with goat cheese, shiitake mushrooms, and thyme. But save room for the main courses, with appealing choices like baby pheasant with wild rice and a Pinot-Noir sauce, or loin of venison with braised red cabbage and a Riesling-and-stock reduction sauce flavored with juniper berries.

○ **Lou's.** 30 S. Main St. ☎ **603/643-3321.** Breakfast items $2.10–$6.50; lunch items $4.25–$6.95. AE, MC, V. Mon–Fri 6am–3pm, Sat 7am–5pm, Sun 7am–3pm. Bakery open for snacks until 5pm. BAKERY/COMFORT FOOD.

Lou's has been a Hanover institution since 1947, attracting vast crowds for breakfast on weekends and a steady clientele for lunch throughout the week. The mood is no-frills New Hampshire, with a black-and-white linoleum checkerboard floor, maple-and-vinyl booths, and a harried but efficient crew of waiters. Breakfast is served all day here (real maple syrup on your pancakes is $1 extra), and the sandwiches are huge and delicious, served on fresh-baked bread. This is definitely the place for breakfast or lunch in Hanover.

Monsoon. 13 Centerra Pkwy. (Rte. 120), Lebanon. ☎ **603/643-9227.** Main courses, lunch $5.95–$14.95 dinner $9.50–$13.95. Mon–Thurs 11:30am–2pm and 5–9pm, Fri 11:30am–2pm and 5–9:30pm, Sat–Sun 5–9:30pm. Follow Rte 120 south from Hanover to the Centerra Marketplace in Lebanon. PAN-ASIAN.

Monsoon was opened in 1998 by the same folks who run Sweet Tomatoes (in Lebanon and Burlington, Vt.), and it bills itself—accurately—as an "Asian bistro and satay bar." It's anything but traditional New England. Housed in a sleek, airy, and modern restaurant at the edge of upscale strip mall, it's boldly furnished with lami-nated wood and brushed steel. The menu is built around creative interpretations of Asian dishes, including appetizers of chicken, beef, and scallop satays with dipping sauces, and excellent lemongrass mussels. Wood-grilled entrees are the specialty, and include selections such as kaffir lime citrus salmon, and the improbable but tasty Thai cowboy steak. There's also a selection of filling Asian noodle dishes. Monsoon offers good value for budget-conscious diners.

4 The Lake Winnipesaukee Region

Lake Winnipesaukee is the state's largest lake, and sprawls immoderately across New Hampshire's central region just east of I-93. Oddly enough, when you're out on the lake, it rarely seems all that huge. That's because the 180-mile shoreline is convoluted and twisting, warped around dozens of inlets, coves, and bays, and further fragmented with some 274 islands. As a result, intermittent lake views from the shore give the illusion you're viewing a chain of smaller lakes and ponds rather than one massive body of water that measures 12 miles by 20 miles at its broadest points. (Incidentally, there's no agreement on the meaning of the lake's Indian name. Although "beautiful water in a high place" and "smile of the great spirit" are the most poetic interpretations, the more commonly accepted translation is "good outlet.")

How to best enjoy the lake? If you've got kids, settle in at Weirs Beach for a day or two, and take in the gaudy attractions. If you're looking for isolation, consider renting a lakeside cabin for a week or so on the eastern shore, track down a canoe or sailboat, then explore much the same way travelers did a century ago. If your time is limited, a driving tour around the lake with a few well-chosen stops will give you a nice taste of the region's woodsy flavor.

WESTERN SHORE

Lake Winnipesaukee's western shore has a more frenetic atmosphere than its sibling shore across the lake. That's partly for historic reasons—the main stage and rail routes passed along the western shore—and partly for modern reasons: I-93 runs west of the lake, serving as a sluice for harried visitors streaming in from the Boston megalopolis to the south. Laconia is the region's largest town. It has some attractive historic architecture and nice vistas, but also is home to an outsize measure of tacky sprawl and isn't really much of a tourist destination. Travelers are better off exploring farther north along the lakeshore, where you'll find plenty of diversions, especially for those with short attention spans.

ESSENTIALS

GETTING THERE Interstate access to the western shore is from I-93 at Exit 20 or Exit 23. From Exit 20, follow Route 3 north through Laconia to Weirs Beach. (It's less confusing and more scenic to stay on Business Route 3.) From Exit 23, drive 9 miles east on Route 104 to Meredith, then head either south on Route 3 to Route 11, or strike northeast on Route 25.

VISITOR INFORMATION The **Greater Laconia/Weirs Beach Chamber of Commerce,** 11 Veterans Square, Laconia, NH 03246 (☎ **603/524-5531**), maintains a seasonal information booth on Business Route 3 about halfway between Laconia and Weirs Beach. It's open daily in summer from 9am to 6pm. Information is also available year-round at the chamber's office at the **old railway station** in Laconia. It's open Monday to Friday from 9am to 5pm and on Saturday from 10am to 2pm.

The **Lakes Region Association,** P.O. Box 1545, Center Harbor, NH 03226 (☎ **888/925-2537** or 603/253-8555), doesn't maintain an information booth but is happy to send out a handy vacation kit with maps and extensive information about local attractions. Web information is available at www.lakesregion.org.

ENJOYING WEIRS BEACH

⭐ **Weirs Beach** is a compact resort town that reflects its Victorian heritage. Unlike beach towns that sprawl for miles, Weirs Beach clusters in that classic turn-of-the-century fashion along a boardwalk, which happens to be near a sandy beach. At the heart of the town is a working railroad that still connects to the steamship line—a nice throwback to an era when summer vacationers weren't dependent on cars. The town attracts a broad mix of visitors, from history and transportation buffs to beach nuts and young video-game warriors.

But most of all, it attracts families. Lots of families. In fact, Weirs Beach is an ideal destination for parents with kids possessed by an insatiable drive for new games and flashing lights. Families might start the morning at **Endicott Beach** (named after the Royal Governor of Massachusetts Bay Colony, who sent surveyors here in 1652), swimming in the clear waters of Winnipesaukee. Arrive early if you want to find public parking, which costs 50¢ an hour with a 5-hour maximum.

Afterward, stroll along the boardwalk into town, which offers a modest selection of penny arcades, bumper cars, jewelry outlets, leather shops, and tasty if unnutritious fare like crispy caramel corn.

Along the access roads to Weirs Beach are a number of activities that delight young kids and parents desperate to take some of the energy out of them. The **Surfcoaster** (☎ 603/366-4991) has a huge assortment of wave pools, water slides, and other moist diversions. It's on Route 11B just outside of Weirs Beach, and costs $18.95 for a day pass (adults or children). Also on Route 11B is **Daytona Fun Park** (☎ 603/366-5461), which has go-carts, minigolf, and batting cages. The **Weirs Beach Waterslide,** on Route 3 (☎ 603/366-5161), has four slides that produce varying levels of adrenaline ($2 per slide). And the **Funspot** (☎ 603/366-4377) will keep kids (and uninhibited adults) occupied with video games, candlepin bowling, and a driving range. Games are priced individually (e.g, bowling is $2.25 per game per person), or you can purchase the Supersaver, which gets you 125 tokens for $20.

EXPLORING BY RAIL & BY SAIL

Scenic train rides leave from town on the **Winnipesaukee Scenic Railroad** (☎ 603/279-5253 or 603/745-2135), which offers 1- and 2-hour excursions from Weirs Beach during the summer. It's an unusual way to enjoy views of lake and forest; kids are provided a hobo lunch packed in a bundle on a stick ($6.95). The two-hour ride is $8.50 for adults and $6.50 for children ages 4 to 11. The one-hour trip is $7.50 adult and $5.50 children.

After riding the rails, head out onto the waters on the stately ⭐ **M/V *Mount Washington,*** an exceptionally handsome 230-foot-long vessel with three decks and a capacity of 1,250 passengers (☎ 603/366-2628). This ship, by far the largest of the lake tour boats, is the best way to get to know Winnipesaukee, with excellent views of the winding shoreline and the knobby peaks of the White Mountains rising over the lake's north end. As many as four cruises a day are offered in summer, ranging from a 2½-hour excursion ($15 adults, $7 children 4 to 12) to a 3-hour dinner cruise ($29 to $39) that includes dinner and live entertainment on two decks. The dinner cruises offer different themes, but don't look for alternative rock; most are along the lines of classic rock, oldies nights, and country and western. The ship operates from the end of May to mid-October, departing from the train station in Weirs Beach. (You can't miss it when it's at the dock.)

WHERE TO STAY

The **Half Moon Motel and Cottages** (☎ 603/366-4494) is situated on a hillside overlooking the town and the lake beyond. It's a good choice if you're looking for the full 1940s experience. The cinder-block-walled rooms all have views, although they

Hog Heaven!

Laconia and Weirs Beach get very loud in mid-June, when some 150,000 motor-cyclists descend on the towns to fraternize, party, and race during what's become the legendary Motorcycle Week.

This bawdy event dates back to 1939, when motorcycle races were first staged at the newly built Belknap Gunstock Recreation Area. The annual gathering gained some unwelcome notoriety in 1965, when riots broke out involving bikers and locals. The mayor of Laconia attributed the problems to the Hell's Angels, claiming he had evidence that they had trained in Mexico before coming here to foment chaos. This peculiar episode was documented in Hunter S. Thompson's classic 1966 book, *The Hells Angels.*

Laconia and Weirs Beach eventually recovered from that unwanted publicity, and today bike races take place at the Loudon Speedway just north of Concord, and at the Gunstock Recreation Area, which hosts the Hill Climb. But the whole of the Weirs Beach area takes on a leather-and-beer carnival atmosphere through-out the week, with bikers cruising the main drag and enjoying one another's company until late at night. Many travelers would pay good money to avoid Weirs Beach at this time, but they'd be missing out on one of New England's more enduring annual phenomena.

tend toward, well, the monastic in their decor, with weary industrial carpeting and less-than-spanking-new beds. There's also a rather murky pool for splashing around. Summer rates are $69 to $79 double (premium charged Saturday and Motorcycle Week); rates start at $49 in the spring and fall.

✪ **Red Hill Inn.** Rte. 25B, Box 99M, Center Harbor, NH 03226. ☎ **800/573-3445** or 603/ 279-7001. Fax 603/279-7003. www.redhillinn.com. E-mail: info@redhillinn.com. 25 units (4 with shower or tub only). TEL. $105–$195 double; $195 cottage. Rates include full breakfast. 2-day minimum stay weekends. AE, CB, DC, DISC, MC, V. From Center Harbor, drive north-west 2.9 miles on Rte. 25B. Children over 5 are welcome.

The Red Hill Inn is tucked in the rolling hills between Winnipesaukee and Squam Lake but borrows more of its flavor from the mountains than the lakeshore. Housed in an architecturally austere three-story brick home dating from the turn of century, the inn looks down a long meadow toward a small complex of elegant green-and-red shingled farm buildings at the foot of a hill. Two of these have been converted into well-appointed guest quarters. Room prices are based on views and size (21 have wood-burning fireplaces), but my favorite room, the Kearsarge, is one of the least expensive, with a very private brick and chocolatey-brown paneled sitting room, off which lies a small bathroom with claw-foot tub.

Dining: The inn's dining room serves lunch, Sunday brunch, and dinner, with evening entrees such as rack of lamb with feta cheese and Dijon mustard, and roast duckling served with either an orange or cranberry glaze. Dinner entrees range from $10.95 to $22.95.

Amenities: Outdoor heated pool, outdoor hot tub (year-round).

Manor on Golden Pond. Rte. 3, Holderness, NH 03245. ☎ **800/545-2141** or 603/ 968-3348. Fax 603/968-2116. www.manorongoldenpond.com. 27 units. A/C TV TEL. Summer $210–$350 double; winter $150–$350. Rates include breakfast. AE, MC, V. 2-day minimum stay holidays and foliage season. No children under 12.

This regal stucco-and-shingle mansion, located a short drive north of Winnipesaukee in Holderness, was built between 1903 and 1907, and was owned by Life magazine editor Harold Fowler in the 1940s. Set on a low hill overlooking Squam Lake, the Manor is nicely situated on 14 landscaped acres studded with white pines that whisper in the breeze. Inside, it has the feel of an English manor house, with rich oak paneling, leaded windows, and mounted pheasants on the mantle. The guest rooms vary in size and decor—the larger, more expensive rooms are more creatively furnished and are far more inviting than the smaller, less expensive rooms in the first-floor wing. Innkeepers David and Bambi Arnold recently added four new cottages with views to the lake, all of which are open year-round.

Dining: Meals are served in three dark-hued dining rooms, including the former billiards hall with a beautiful green-tile fireplace. Meals are upscale New American, with main dishes changing nightly. Entrees might include a filet mignon with Boursin and chanterelles, or trout with a crab filling served in a sage-brown butter sauce. Wine selections are extensive. A five-course dinner is $50 per person ($38 for three courses).

Amenities: Boat house with canoes and private lakefront beach on 3 acres (nearby), pool, one clay tennis court (lights available for night play), croquet, horseshoes, volleyball, shuffleboard.

WHERE TO DINE

Kellerhaus (☎ 603/366-4466) is the classic house of sweets. Located in a storybook-like stone-and-half-timber structure on Route 3, a third of a mile north of Endicott Beach, this old-fashioned place overlooking the lake features a diet-busting ice-cream buffet where fanatics can select from a battery of toppings, including macaroon crunch, butterscotch, chocolate, and whipped cream. The smorgasbord is $3 to $6.25, depending on the number of scoops you begin with. There's also a sizable gift shop with homemade candies providing snacks for the road. The shop is open year-round; from Father's Day to Columbus Day it's open 8am to 11pm daily, with limited hours in the off-season (call first).

Hart's Turkey Farm Restaurant. At the junction of Rte. 3 and Rte. 104, Meredith. ☎ **603/279-6212.** Main courses $8.95–$17.95. AE, CB, DC, DISC, MC, V. Summer daily 11:15am–9pm; fall–spring daily 11:15am–8pm. TURKEY/AMERICAN.

Hart's Turkey Farm Restaurant is bad news if you're a turkey. On a typically busy day, this popular spot dishes up more than a ton of America's favorite bird, along with 4,000 dinner rolls and 1,000 pounds of potatoes. (Let's not even mention Thanksgiving.) Judging by name alone, Hart's Farm sounds more rural than it is. In fact, it's in a nondescript roadside building on a busy, nondescript part of Route 3. Inside, it's comfortable in a faux–Olde New Englande sort of way, and the service has that sort of rushed efficiency found in places where waitresses have been hoisting heavy trays for years. (Servers don't even blink when bus tours show up unannounced.) But diners don't return time and again to Harts for the charm. They come for turkey that's cooked moist and perfect every time.

Las Piñatas. 9 Veteran's Sq., Laconia. ☎ **603/528-1405.** Reservations recommended for parties of 5 or more. Lunch items $4–$8; main dinner courses $10–$15. AE, MC, V. Mon–Thurs 11am–2pm and 5–9pm, Fri–Sat 11am–2pm and 5–9:30pm, Sun 5–8pm. Closed Tues in winter. MEXICAN.

Armando Lezama first came to Laconia from Mexico City in 1979 as a high-school exchange student. He liked it. So he moved here with his family, opening one of the more authentic Mexican restaurants in New Hampshire. Housed in the handsome stone railroad station on the edge of Laconia's downtown, Las Piñatas has a good menu of Mexican dishes and frozen margaritas that seem especially tasty after a long day at the lake. The menu includes Mexican regulars like empanadas, tacos al carbón, and fajitas. Among the specialties are the delicious enchiladas de mole, made with the Lezamas' homemade mole sauce.

EASTERN SHORE

Winnipesaukee's east shore recalls Gertrude Stein's comment about Oakland: "There's no there there." Other than the low-key town of Wolfeboro, the east shore is mostly islands and coves, mixed forests and rolling hills, rocky farms and the occasional apple orchard. While it's a large lake, its waters are also largely inaccessible from this side. Old summer homes and new gated condominium communities occupy some of the best coves and points. But narrow roads do touch on the lake here and there, and most roads are nicely engineered for leisurely cruising.

ESSENTIALS

GETTING THERE   Lake Winnipesaukee's east shore is best explored on Route 28 (from Alton Bay to Wolfeboro) and Route 109 (from Wolfeboro to Moultonborough). From the south, Alton Bay can be reached via Route 11 from Rochester, or from Route 28, which intersects Routes 4 and 202 about 12 miles east of Concord.

VISITOR INFORMATION   The **Wolfeboro Chamber of Commerce**, P.O. Box 547, Wolfeboro, NH 03894 (☎ **800/516-5324** or 603/569-2200), offers regional travel information and advice from its offices in a converted railroad station at 32 Central Ave, 1 block off Main Street in Wolfeboro. It's open daily in summer 10am to 5pm, in the off-season 10am to 3pm Monday through Friday.

EXPLORING WOLFEBORO

The town of Wolfeboro claims to be the first summer resort in the United States, and the documentation makes a pretty good case for it. In 1763, John Wentworth, the nephew of a former governor, built a summer estate on what's now called Lake Wentworth, along with a road to it from Portsmouth. Wentworth didn't get to enjoy his holdings for long—his Tory sympathies forced him to flee when the political situation heated up in 1775. The house burned in 1820, but the site now attracts archaeologists.

Visitors are lured to **Wentworth State Beach** (☎ **603/569-3699**) not so much because of history but because of the attractive beach, refreshing lake waters, and shady picnic area. The park is located 5 miles east of Wolfeboro on Route 109.

The town of Wolfeboro (population 2,800) has a vibrant, homey downtown that's easily explored on foot. Park near Depot Square and the gingerbread Victorian train station, and stock up on brochures and maps at the Chamber of Commerce office inside. Behind the train station, running along the former tracks of the rail line, is the Russell C. Chase Bridge-Falls Path, a rail-trail that runs pleasantly along Back Bay to a set of small waterfalls.

For a superb view of the eastern shore, head 7 miles north of Wolfeboro on Route 109 to the Abenaki Tower. Look for a parking lot and wooden sign on the right side of the road at the crest of a hill. From the lot, it's an easy, 5-minute hike to the sturdy log tower, which rises about 60 feet high and is ascended by a steep staircase. (This is not a good destination for acrophobes.) Those who soldier on to the top are rewarded with excellent views of nearby coves, inlets, and the Belknap Mountains southwest of the lake.

A QUIRKY CASTLE

Castle in the Clouds. Rte. 171 (4 miles south of Rte. 25), Moultonborough. ☎ **800/ 729-2468** or 603/476-2352. Admission $8 adults, $7.50 seniors, $5 children 11–17. Mid-May to mid-June Sat–Sun 9am–5pm; mid-June to Labor Day daily 9am–5pm; Labor Day to 3rd week of Oct daily 9am–4pm. Closed Nov–Apr.

Cranky millionaire Thomas Gustav Plant built this eccentric stone edifice high atop a mountain overlooking Lake Winnipesaukee early in this century. Completed in 1913 at a cost of $7 million, the home is a sort of rustic San Simeon East, with orange roof tiles, cliff-hugging rooms, stained-glass windows, and unrivaled views of the surrounding hills and lakes. Visitors drive as far as the carriage house (nicely converted to a snack bar and restaurant), where they park and are taken in groups through the house by knowledgeable guides.

Even if the castle holds no interest, the 5,200-acre grounds are worth the admission price. The long access road is harrowingly narrow and winding (kids, don't try this in your mobile home!), with wonderful vistas and turnouts for stopping and exploring along the way. I'd advise taking your time on the way up; the separate exit road is fast, straight, and uninteresting. The grounds are also home to a bottled-water plant, and a microbrewery, both of which are open for tours.

WHERE TO STAY & DINE

Wolfeboro Inn. 90 N. Main St., Wolfeboro, NH 03894. ☎ **800/451-2389** or 603/ 569-3016. Fax 603/569-5375. www.wolfeboroinn.com. 44 units. A/C TV TEL. $79–$225 double. Rates include continental breakfast. Add $20 on weekends. 2-night minimum stay in peak season. AE, MC, V.

This small, elegant hotel strives to mix modern and traditional, and succeeds admirably in doing so. Located a short stroll from downtown Wolfeboro, the inn dates back to 1812 but was extensively expanded and updated in the mid-1980s. The modern lobby features a small atrium with wood beams, slate floor, and a brick fireplace, and has managed to retain an old-world elegance and grace. Comfortable guest rooms vary in size, and most are furnished with early American reproductions. The inn also has some nice extras, including its own 75-passenger excursion boat (a free trip is included in room rates). On the downside, for an inn of this elegance it has only a disappointing sliver of lakeshore and but a miniature beach for guests.

Dining/Diversions: The upscale 1812 Room serves regional and continental fare. Dinner entrees range from $12 to $22. The atmospheric Wolfe's Tavern has pewter tankards hanging from the low beams, 60 brands of beer, a sizable salad bar and a selection of basic pub fare. Prices run from $7 to $16.

Amenities: Beach swimming, conference rooms, nearby health club, concierge, limited room service, dry cleaning, laundry service, baby-sitting.

5 The White Mountains

The White Mountains are northern New England's undisputed outdoor-recreation capital. This cluster of ancient mountains is a sprawling, rugged playground that attracts kayakers, mountaineers, rock climbers, skiers, mountain bikers, bird-watchers, and hikers.

Especially hikers. The **White Mountain National Forest** encompasses some 773,000 acres of rocky, forested terrain, more than 100 waterfalls, dozens of remote backcountry lakes, and miles of clear brooks and cascading streams. An elaborate network of 1,200 miles of hiking trails dates back to the 19th century, when the urban gentry took to the mountains in droves to build character, build trails, and experience the raw sublimity of nature. Trails ranging from easy to extraordinarily demanding lace the hillside forests, run along remote valley rivers, and traverse barren, windswept ridgelines where the weather can change dramatically in less time than it takes to eat your lunch.

The spiritual center of the White Mountains is its highest point: 6,288-foot **Mount Washington,** an ominous, brooding peak that's often cloud-capped, and often mantled with snow early and late in the season. This blustery peak is accessible by cog railroad, car, and foot, making it one of the most popular spots in the region. You won't find wilderness here, but you will find a surfeit of natural drama.

Flanking this colossal peak are the brawny **Presidential Mountains,** a series of wind-blasted granite peaks named after U.S. presidents and offering spectacular views. Surrounding these are numerous other rocky ridges that lure hikers looking for challenges and a place to experience nature at its more elemental.

Travelers whose idea of fun doesn't involve steep cliffs or icy dips in mountain streams still have plenty of opportunity for milder adventures. A handful of major arteries provide easy access to mountain scenery. Route 302 carries travelers through North Conway and Crawford Notch to the pleasant towns of Bethlehem and Littleton. Route 16 travels from southern New Hampshire through congested North Conway before twisting up dramatic Pinkham Notch at the base of Mount Washington. Wide and fast, Route 2 skirts the northern edge of the mountains, offering wonderful views en route to the town of Jefferson. I-93 gets my vote for the most scenic interstate in northern New England, passing through spectacular Franconia Notch as it narrows to a two-lane road in deference to its natural surroundings (and local political will).

And finally, there's the **Kancamagus Highway,** linking Conway with Lincoln and providing some of the most spectacular White Mountain vistas in the region. Along the way, frequent roadside pull-offs and interpretive exhibits allow casual explorers to admire cascades, picnic along rivers, and enjoy sweeping mountain views. Several less-demanding nature hikes are also easily accessible from various roadside turnouts.

As for accommodations, it should be easy to find an area to suit your mood and inclinations. North Conway is the motel capital of the region, with hundreds of rooms, many quite charmless but usually offered at reasonable rates. The Loon Mountain and Waterville Valley areas have a sort of planned condo village graciousness that delights some travelers and creeps out others. Jackson, Franconia Notch, Crawford Notch, and the Bethlehem-Littleton area are the best destinations for old-fashioned hotels and inns.

BACKCOUNTRY FEES The White Mountain National Forest requires anyone using the backcountry—whether for hiking, mountain biking, picnicking, skiing, or any other activity—to pay a recreation fee. Anyone parking at a trailhead must display a backcountry permit on the dashboard of their car. The fees go to develop and maintain recreational facilities at the forest. Those lacking a permit face a fine. Permits are available at ranger stations and many stores in the region. Two permits are sold: an annual permit for $20, and a 7-day pass for $5. For information about the permit program, contact the **Forest Service's White Mountains office** at ☎ **603/528-8721.**

RANGER STATIONS & INFORMATION The Forest Service's **central White Mountains office** is at 719 Main St. in Laconia (☎ **603/528-8721**), which actually is near Lake Winnipesaukee. Your best general source of information the **Saco Ranger Station** (☎ **603/447-5448**) in Conway; the office is on the Kancamagus Highway just 100 yards west of Route 16. Other district offices are: **Androscoggin Ranger Station** (☎ **603/466-2713**), 80 Glen Rd. in Gorham; **Ammonoosuc Ranger Station** (☎ **603/869-2626**) Trudeau Road in Bethlehem; **Pemigewasset Ranger Station** (☎ **603/536-1310**) on Route 175 in Holderness, near the Plymouth town line. The

The White Mountains & Lake Country

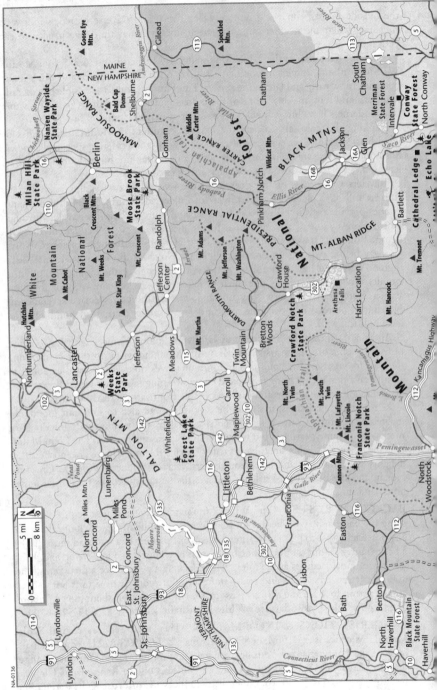

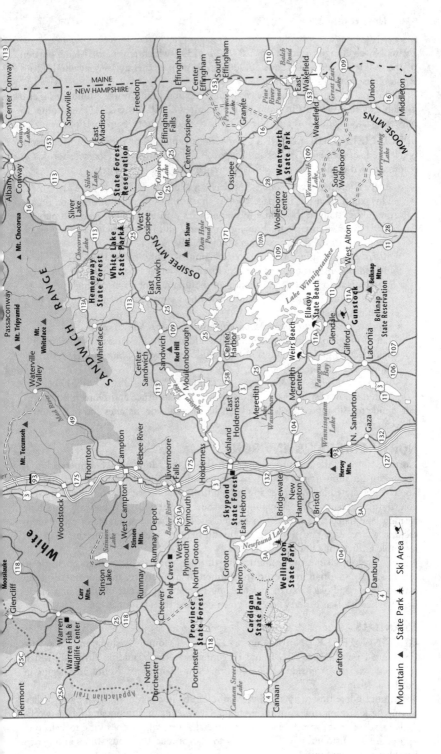

Evans Notch Ranger Station (☎ 207/824-2134), which covers the Maine portion of the White Mountains (about 50,000 acres), is in Bethel at 18 Mayville Rd., off Route 2 just north of town.

Additional information and advice about recreation in the White Mountains is also available at the **AMC's Pinkham Notch Camp** (☎ 603/466-2721) on Route 16 between Jackson and Gorham. The center is open daily from 6am to 10pm.

SPECIALIZED GUIDEBOOKS   For serious exploring of the White Mountains, you'll need supplemental guides and maps to keep you on track. Here's a short list of recommended guides, most of which are available at area bookstores:

- *AMC White Mountain Guide* (Appalachian Mountain Club, 1998, $21.95). This comprehensive 576-page book is chock full of detailed information on all the hiking trails in the White Mountains. It's printed in small type and published in a size suitable to throwing in a pack, and it comes with a handy set of maps. This is the definitive hiker's bible for the region.
- *50 Hikes in the White Mountains* (Backcountry Publications, 1994, $14). The fifth edition of this popular guide, written by Daniel Doan and Ruth Doan MacDougall, offers a good selection of mountain rambles in the high peaks region around Mount Washington. You'll find everything from easy strolls to overnight backpack trips.
- *Ponds & Lakes of the White Mountains* (Backcountry Publications, 1998, $16). The White Mountain high country is studded with dramatic tarns (many left by retreating glaciers). This 350-page guide by Steven D. Smith offers 68 trips to help get you there.
- *Waterfalls of the White Mountains* (Backcountry Publications, 1990, $17). Waterfall lovers will get their money's worth from Bruce and Doreen Bolnick's guide to 100 mountain waterfalls, including roadside cascades and backcountry cataracts.

NORTH CONWAY & ENVIRONS

North Conway is the commercial heart of the White Mountains. Shoppers adore it because of the profusion of outlets, boutiques, and restaurants along Routes 302 and 16. The two state highways overlap through town, and can be the source of considerable traffic back-ups. The shopping strip south of the village is basically one long turning lane flanked with outlet malls, motels, and chain restaurants of every architectural stripe. On rainy weekends and during the foliage season, the road can resemble a three-mile linear parking lot.

The village itself is trim and attractive (if often congested), with an open green, quaint shops, Victorian frontier-town commercial architecture, and a distinctive train station. It's a good place to park, stretch your legs, and find a cup of coffee or a snack. (Hint: There's a Ben & Jerry's off the green near the train station.)

ESSENTIALS

GETTING THERE   North Conway and the Mount Washington Valley are on Route 16 and Route 302. Route 16 connects to the Spaulding Turnpike, which intersects with I-95 outside of Portsmouth, New Hampshire. Route 302 begins in Portland, Maine.

Do not underestimate how bad the traffic can be in the Mount Washington Valley during peak visiting times, including holiday weekends in summer and foliage weekends in fall. I've seen traffic backups of several miles, which does little to help one appreciate the surroundings. Try valiantly to plan around these busy times in order to preserve your own sanity.

VISITOR INFORMATION   The **Mount Washington Valley Chamber of Commerce,** P.O. Box 2300, North Conway, NH 03860 (☎ **800/367-3364** or 603/356-3171), operates a seasonal information booth opposite the village green with brochures about attractions and inns. The staff can arrange for local accommodations. It's open daily in summer 9am to 6pm. In winter it's open weekends only. Information is also available on the web at www.4seasonresort.com.

The state of New Hampshire also operates an information booth with rest rooms and telephones at a vista with fine views of Mount Washington on Routes 16 and 302 north of North Conway.

RIDING THE RAILS

A unique way to view the mountainous landscape around North Conway is via train. The **Conway Scenic Railroad** (☎ **800/232-5251** or 603/356-5251; www.conwayscenic.com) offers regularly scheduled trips in comfortable cars pulled by either steam or sleek early diesel engines. Trips depart from an 1874 train station just off the village green, recalling an era when tourists arrived from Boston and New York to enjoy the country air for a month or two each summer. The 1-hour excursion heads south to Conway; the more scenic 1¾-hour trip heads north to the village of Bartlett. For a real show, sign up for the 5½-hour excursion through dramatic Crawford Notch, with stupendous views of the mountains from high along this beautiful glacial valley. You even get a great view of the remarkable Mount Washington Hotel. Ask also about the railway's dining excursions ($20.95 to $42.95 including lunch or dinner).

The train runs mid-April to mid-December, with more frequent trips scheduled daily in midsummer. Tickets are $8.50 to $17.50 for adults ($31 to $42 for Crawford Notch), $6 to $12.50 for children 4 to 12 ($16 to $27 for Crawford Notch). Kids under 4 ride free on the two shorter trips; there's a charge on the Crawford Notch trip. Reservations are accepted for the dining car and the Crawford Notch train.

SHOPPING

Consumers who find themselves suffering from mall withdrawal after being amidst all these trees and mountains can recuperate in North Conway very nicely, thank you. There are 200-plus shops along the strip, which extends about 3 miles northward from the junction of Route 302 and Route 16 in Conway in to the village of North Conway itself. It's a town planner's nightmare, but a shopper's paradise.

Among the more notable outlet clusters are **Outlet Village Plus** at Settler's Green, with better than 30 name-brand shops; the **Tanger Factory Outlet,** which hosts the popular L.L. Bean factory outlet; and **Willow Place,** with 11 shops like Dress Barn, Bed & Bath, and the Lingerie Factory. Other outlets scattered along the strip include Anne Klein, American Tourister, Izod, Dansk, Donna Karan, Levi's, Polo/Ralph Lauren, Reebok/Rockport, J. Crew, and Eddie Bauer. **Chuck Roast Mountainwear** (☎ **603/356-5589**), a North Conway–based manufacturer of outerwear, backpacks, and soft luggage, has a shop at the Mount Washington Outlet Center, the plaza next door to the L.L. Bean outlet.

For those setting out on a White Mountain expedition, outdoor equipment suppliers in town include **International Mountain Equipment** (☎ **603/356-7013**) and **Eastern Mountain Sports** (☎ **603/356-5433**), both on Main Street just north of the green. There's also **Ragged Mountain Equipment** (☎ **603/356-3042**), 3 miles north of town in Intervale on Routes 16 and 302.

SKIING

Cranmore Mountain Resort. N. Conway Village, NH 03860. ☎ **603/356-5544.** www.cranmore.com. Vertical drop: 1,200 ft. Lifts: 7 chairlifts (1 high-speed quad), 2 surface lifts. Skiable acreage: 192. Lift tickets: $29 all week.

Mount Cranmore is within walking distance of downtown North Conway, although it's far enough that you wouldn't want to try it in ski boots. The oldest operating ski area in New England, Mount Cranmore is unrepentantly old-fashioned and doesn't display an iota of pretense. It's not likely to challenge advanced skiers, but it will delight beginners and intermediates, as well as those who like the old-style New England cut of the trails. Prices were reduced in 1998, making it the best deal in the area for skiing.

WHERE TO STAY

Route 16 through North Conway is packed with basic motels, reasonably priced in the off-season (around $40 to $60), but more expensive in peak travel times such as summer and ski-season weekends, and fall foliage season. Fronting the commercial strip, these motels don't offer much in the way of a pastoral environment, but most are comfortable and conveniently located. Try the budget **School House Motel** (☎ 603/356-6829), with a heated outdoor pool; **The Yankee Clipper Motor Lodge** (☎ 800/343-5900 or 603/356-5736), with a pool and minigolf (the cheaper rooms lack phones); or the slightly pricier **Green Granite Inn** (☎ 800/468-3666 or 603/ 356-6901), with 88 rooms, whirlpool suites, and a free continental breakfast.

Albert B. Lester Memorial Hostel. 36 Washington St., Conway, NH 03818. ☎ **800/ 909-4776**, ext. 51 or 603/447-1001. Fax 603/447-3346. www.angel.net/~hostel. E-mail: hiconway@nxi.com. 45 beds. $16 per person, $45 for family rooms. Rates include continental breakfast. JCB, MC, V. Closed Nov 1–30. Turn north on Washington St. at the light in Conway; it's the 2nd house on the left.

Conveniently situated near the center of Conway Village, the Lester Hostel is the best choice for those traveling on a shoestring but not enamored of camping. Rooms in this gracious black-and-white farmhouse are set up hostel-style and accommodate 45 people (some family rooms are available). Not only will you save money here, but the congenial atmosphere offers a great way to swap tips on area trails and bike rides with newfound friends. You can borrow a bike or repair your own in the bike repair room. Music and impromptu performances are staged periodically at the new amphitheater, made of straw bales and packed earth. The hostel is open for check-in or checkout daily from 7:30 to 9:30am and 5 to 10pm.

Cranmore Inn. 80 Kearsarge St., N. Conway, NH 03860. ☎ **800/526-5502** or 603/ 356-5502. www.cranmoreinn.com. E-mail: cranmore@cranmoreinn.com. 18 units (3 with private hall bathrooms; 7 with showers only). Summer $69–$88 double; foliage season and ski weekends $89–$108 double; off-season $59–$78 double. Rates include full breakfast. 2-night minimum weekends, holidays, and foliage season. AE, MC, V.

The Cranmore Inn has the feel of a 19th-century boarding house—which is appropriate, since that's what it is. Open since 1863, this three-story Victorian home is hidden on a side street a short walk from North Conway's miniature downtown. Its distinguished heritage—it's the oldest continuously operating hotel in North Conway—adds considerable charm and quirkiness, but comes with some minor drawbacks, like uneven water pressure in the showers and some sinks with cracked or stained enamel. That said, I'd return here in a second because of its charm, its good value, and the warm hospitality of the innkeepers. There's also a heated outdoor pool in summer to cool off after a day of hiking.

Stonehurst Manor. Rte. 16 (1.2 miles north of N. Conway Village; P.O. Box 1937), N. Conway, NH 03860. ☎ **800/525-9100**. Fax 603/356-3217. www.stonehurstmanor.com. 24 units (2 with shared bathroom). A/C TV. $80–$140 double ($20–$30 surcharge during foliage season); $106–$166 double with breakfast and dinner included. 2-night minimum on weekends. AE, MC, V. Pets allowed ($25 extra).

This imposing, eclectic Victorian stone-and-shingle mansion is set amid white pines on a rocky knoll above Route 16. Oddly, it wouldn't seem at all out of place in either the south of France or the moors of Scotland. The immediate assumption is that it caters to the stuffy and affluent. But the main focus here is on outdoor adventure vacations, and it attracts a youngish crowd. My advice is to request one of the 14 rooms in the regal 1876 mansion itself (another 10 are in a comfortable but less elegant wing built in 1952). These mansion rooms are all individually furnished appropriately to the building's era.

Dining: See "Where to Dine," below.

Amenities: Outdoor pool, Jacuzzi, tennis court, nature trails.

✪ White Mountain Hotel and Resort. West Side Rd. (5.4 miles west of N. Conway; P.O. Box 1828), N. Conway, NH 03860. ☎ 800/533-6301 or 603/356-7100. 80 units. A/C TV TEL. Summer $129–$219 double; foliage season $149–$219 double; winter $79–$159 double; other times $59–$119 double. 2-night minimum on weekends. AE, DISC, MC, V.

This modern, refined resort has the best location of any lodge in North Conway. Sited at the base of dramatic White Horse Ledge near Echo Lake State Park and amid a contemporary golf-course community, the White Mountain Hotel was built in 1990 but borrows from the rich legacy of classic White Mountain resorts. Its designers have managed to take some of the more successful elements of a friendly country inn—a nice deck with a view, comfortable seating in the lobby, a clubby tavern area—and incorporate them into a thoroughly modern resort. Guest rooms are comfortably appointed with dark wood and an earthy maroon carpeting, and are a solid notch or two above standard hotel furnishings.

Dining: The pleasant Ledges Dining Room offers mountain panoramas through tall windows. Entrees include veal Oscar, shrimp stuffed with crabmeat, and charbroiled steaks, priced from $14.95 to $19.95.

Amenities: 9-hole golf course, two tennis courts, game rooms, outdoor heated pool, Jacuzzi, sauna, fitness center, nature trails, conference rooms, self-service Laundromat, limited room service, dry cleaning, laundry service, baby-sitting.

WHERE TO DINE

Bellini's. 33 Seavey St., N. Conway. ☎ 603/356-7000. Reservations not accepted. Main courses $11–$20. AE, CB, DC, DISC, MC, V. Sun–Mon and Wed–Thurs 5–10pm, Fri–Sat 5–11pm. Closed 2 weeks in Nov and 2 weeks during mud season. COUNTRY ITALIAN.

Bellini's has a fun, quirky interior that's more informal than its Victorian exterior might suggest. Inside it features Cinzano umbrellas and striped awnings, black-and-white–checkerboard floors, and huge potted plants—it's the kind of place to put you in a good mood right off. And the food, which runs the Italian gamut from fettuccine chicken pesto to braciola, can only further improve your spirits. Particularly good are the toasted raviolis. There's also Angus beef and limited fresh seafood.

Stonehurst Manor. Rte. 16 (1.2 miles north of the village), N. Conway. ☎ 800/525-9100 or 603/356-3113. Reservations recommended. Main courses $14.75–$21.75; pizza $9.95–$12.95. MC, V. Daily 5:30–10pm. AMERICAN/PIZZA.

The restaurant added wood-fired pizza to the menu when the owners noticed that inn guests arriving late on Friday nights from Boston didn't feel up to a full meal. So they started making pizza in a number of surprising variations (chicken sausage and wild mushrooms; grilled vegetables), and the word spread. Stonehurst's pizza has become a local institution, complementing the other dishes served here. Diners have a choice of four dining areas on the first floor of this 1876 mansion, and each area is decorated informally and comfortably. (The deep, overly low rattan chairs may have outlived their charm, however.) In addition to pizza, the chef serves up a raft of other creative dishes, including pit-smoked prime rib.

JACKSON & ENVIRONS

Jackson is like an eddy swirling gently on its own out of the flow of the tourist mainstream. Situated in a picturesque valley just off Route 16 about a 15-minute drive north of North Conway, Jackson still attracts plenty of travelers, but the rich history is strong enough here to absorb much of the tourist impact.

You enter Jackson, somewhat tentatively, on a single-lane covered bridge. The village center is tiny, but touches of old-world elegance remain here and there—vestiges of a time when Jackson was a favored destination for the East Coast upper middle class, who fled the summer heat in the cities to board at rambling wooden hotels or relax at shingled country homes.

With the Great Depression and the subsequent rise of the motel trade in the 1940s and 1950s, Jackson and its old-fashioned hostelries slipped into a long slumber. Then along came the 1980s, which brought developers in private helicopters, condo projects sprouting in fields where cows once roamed, and the resuscitation of the two vintage wooden hotels that didn't burn or collapse during the dark ages.

Thanks to a rebuilt golf course and one of the most elaborate and well-maintained cross-country ski networks in the country, Jackson is today again a thriving resort, both summer and winter. It's still out of the mainstream, and a peaceful spot quite distant in character from commercial North Conway. Settle into one of the old summer homes converted to an inn, park yourself on a rocker on a porch, and you'll suspect that not all that much has changed in the intervening century.

ESSENTIALS

GETTING THERE   Jackson is just off Route 16 about 11 miles north of North Conway. Look for the covered bridge on the right when heading north.

VISITOR INFORMATION   The **Jackson Chamber of Commerce,** P.O. Box 304, Jackson, NH 03846 (☎ **800/866-3334** or 603/383-9356), can answer your questions about area attractions or make lodging reservations for you.

EXPLORING MOUNT WASHINGTON

Mount Washington, located just north of Jackson in the national forest, is home to numerous superlatives. At 6,288 feet it's the highest mountain in the Northeast. (Mt. Mitchell in N.C. is slightly higher, robbing Mt. Washington of the "highest in the East" title.) It's said to have the worst weather in the world outside of the polar regions. It holds the world's record for the highest surface wind speed ever recorded—231 miles per hour, in 1934. Winds over 150 miles per hour are routinely recorded every month except June, July, and August, in part the result of the mountain's location at the confluence of three major storm tracks.

Mount Washington may also be the mountain with the most options for getting to the summit. Visitors can ascend by cog railroad (see the "Crawford Notch" section, below), by car, by guide-driven van, or by foot. There's an annual bike race and foot race to the summit, and each year winter mountaineers test their mettle by inching their way to the top outfitted with crampons and ice axes.

Despite the raw power of the weather, the summit of Mount Washington is not the best destination for those seeking wild and untamed wilderness. There's a train platform, a parking lot, a snack bar, a gift shop, a museum, and a handful of outbuildings, some of which house the weather observatory, which is staffed year-round. And there are the crowds, which can be thick on a clear day. Then again, on a clear day the views can't be beat, with vistas extending into four states and to the Atlantic Ocean.

The best place to learn about Mount Washington and its approaches is the rustic **Pinkham Notch Camp** (☎ **603/466-2721**), operated by the Boston-based Appalachian Mountain Club. Located at the crest of Route 16 between Jackson and Gorham, Pinkham Notch offers overnight accommodations and meals (see below), maps, a limited selection of outdoor supplies, and plenty of advice from the helpful staff. A number of hiking trails depart from Pinkham Notch, allowing for several loops and side trips.

About a dozen trails lead to the mountain's summit, ranging in length from 3.8 to 15 miles. (Detailed information is available from Pinkham Notch Camp.) The most direct and, in many ways, most dramatic trail is the Tuckerman Ravine Trail, which departs from Pinkham Notch. It's a full day's endeavor: healthy hikers should allow 4 to 5 hours for the ascent, an hour or two less for the return trip. Be sure to allow enough time to enjoy the dramatic glacial cirque of Tuckerman Ravine, which attracts extreme skiers to its snowy chutes and sheer drops as late as June, and often holds patches of snow well into summer.

The **Mount Washington Auto Road** (☎ **603/466-3988**) opened in 1861 as a carriage road, and has since remained one of the most popular White Mountain attractions. The steep, winding 8-mile road (it has an average grade of 12%) is partially paved and incredibly dramatic; your breath will be taken away at one curve after another. The ascent will test your iron will; the descent will test your car's brakes.

If you'd prefer to leave the driving to someone else, custom vans ascend throughout the day, allowing you to relax, enjoy the views, learn about the mountain from informed guides, and leave the fretting about overheating brakes to someone else.

The Auto Road, which is on Route 16 north of Pinkham Notch, is open mid-May to late October from 7:30am to 6pm (more limited hours early and late in the season). The cost for cars is $15 for vehicle and driver, and $6 for each additional adult ($4 for children 5 to 12). The fee includes an audiocassette featuring a narrator pointing out sights along the way (available in English, French, and German). The management has imposed some curious restrictions on automobiles; for instance, Acuras and Jaguars with automatic transmissions must show a "1" on the shifter to be allowed on the road, Saturns with automatic transmissions are limited to 300 pounds capacity (passengers and luggage), and no Lincoln Continentals from before 1969 are permitted.

Van tours are $20 for adults, $10 for children 5 to 12, including a half-hour stay on the summit. More information is available on the Web at www.mt-washington.com.

One additional note: The average temperature atop the mountain is 30°F. (The record low was −43°F, and the warmest temperature ever recorded atop the mountain, in August, was 72°.) Even in summer, visitors should come prepared for blustery, cold conditions.

Skiing

Cross-Country Skiing

Jackson regularly makes rankings in the top five cross-country ski resorts in the nation. The reason for that: the nonprofit **Jackson Ski Touring Foundation** (☎ **603/383-9355**), which created and now maintains the extensive trail network. The terrain around Jackson is wonderfully varied, with 93 miles of trails maintained by the foundation (56 miles are regularly groomed).

Start at the foundation headquarters in the middle of Jackson, then head right out the back door and ski through the village. Gentle trails traverse the valley floor, with more advanced trails winding up the flanking mountains. One-way ski trips with shuttles back to Jackson are also available; ask if you're interested. Given how extensive and well maintained the trails are, passes are a good value at $12 Saturdays and holidays, $10 all other days. Ski rentals are available in the ski center ($16 per day). More information is available on the Web at www.jacksonxc.com.

Alpine Skiing

Black Mountain. Jackson, NH 03846. ☎ **800/475-4669** or 603/383-4490. www.blackmt. com. Vertical drop: 1,100 ft. Lifts: 2 chairlifts, 2 surface lifts. Skiable acreage: 101. Lift tickets: $32 weekends, $20 weekdays.

Dating back to the 1930s, Black Mountain is one of the White Mountains' pioneer ski areas. It remains the quintessential family mountain—modest in size, thoroughly nonthreatening, and perfect for beginners. And the mountain offers some great views from the top, to boot. It feels a bit like you're skiing in a farmer's unused hayfield, which just adds to the charm. The mountain claims to have the first overhead lift in the country—the original lift featured shovel handles passing by on a cable, which skiers grabbed a hold of. The ski area offers lift-serviced tubing, which is popular among younger kids.

Wildcat. Rte. 16, Pinkham Notch, NH 03846. ☎ **800/255-6439** or 603/466-3326. www.skiwildcat.com. Vertical drop: 2,100 ft. Lifts: 1 gondola, 1 detachable high-speed quad, 4 chairlifts. Skiable acreage: 225. Lift tickets: $46 weekends and holidays, $39 weekdays.

Wildcat Mountain has a rich heritage as a venerable New England ski mountain. It also happens to offer the best mountain views of any ski area in the Whites. Situated on national forest land just across the valley from Mount Washington and Tuckerman Ravine, Wildcat has strong intermediate trails and some challenging expert slopes. This is skiing as it used to be—there's no base area clutter, just a simple ski lodge. While that also means there's no on-slope accommodations, you've got an abundance of choices within a 15-minute drive. Also ask about the occasional mid-week specials (such as two-for-one tickets) that can bring down the cost of skiing.

KID STUFF

Parents with young children who find majestic mountains about as interesting as watching C-Span can buy peace of mind at two area attractions. **StoryLand**, at the northern junction of Routes 16 and 302 (☎ **603/383-4293**), is filled with 30 acres of improbably leaning buildings, magical rides, fairy-tale creatures, and other enchanted beings. Kids can take a ride in a Pumpkin Coach, float in a swan boat, ride the watery Bamboo Chute, wander through a Dutch village, or spin on an antique carousel. A "sprayground" features a 40-foot water-spurting octopus—if they're so inclined, kids can get a good summer soaking. From Memorial Day to mid-June StoryLand is open weekends only 10am to 5pm; mid-June to Labor Day open daily from 9am to 6pm; and Labor Day to Columbus Day weekends only from 10am to 5pm. Admission, which includes all rides and entertainment, is $17 for visitors over 4 years old.

Next door is **Heritage New Hampshire** (☎ **603/383-9776**), which endeavors to make state history easily digestible for both adults and kids. It's an indoor theme park in a Georgian-style building with a theme of old-time New Hampshire. Visitors learn about the famous Concord Coach and hear prominent politician Daniel Webster discourse about his life and times. The attraction is open daily mid-May to mid-October from 9am until 5pm. Admission is $10 for adults, $4.50 for children 6 to 12, and free for children under 6.

WHERE TO STAY & DINE

Eagle Mountain House. Carter Notch Rd., Jackson, NH 03846. ☎ **800/966-5779** or 603/ 383-9111. Fax 603/383-0854. www.eaglemt.com. E-mail: reservations@eaglemt.com. 93 units.

TV TEL. Summer $89–$129 double; $129–$159 suite. Winter $69–$109 double; $99–$139 suite. Ask about package plans. AE, CB, DC, DISC, MC, V.

The Eagle Mountain House is a fine and handsome relic that happily survived the ravages of time, fire, and the capricious tastes of tourists. Built in 1916 and fully renovated in the 1980s, this five-story gleaming white wooden classic is set in an idyllic valley above the village of Jackson. The lobby is rich with earth tones, polished brass, and oak accenting. The guest rooms, set off wonderfully wide and creaky hallways, are furnished with a country pine look and feature stenciled blanket chests, pine armoires, and feather comforters.

Dining: There's a handsome oak tavern off the lodge for light snacks. The spacious, formal dining room seats about 150 guests and provokes a distinct "well-here-we-are!" sense of glee when one first settles in for dinner under the high ceilings. The menu features creative New England classics, with offerings like Maine lobster pie and roasted cranberry duck.

Amenities: 9-hole golf course, two tennis courts (one lit for night play), outdoor pool (summer), small health club, game room, conference rooms, dry cleaning, safe-deposit boxes.

✪ **Inn at Thorn Hill.** Thorn Hill Rd. (P.O. Box A), Jackson, NH 03846. ☎ **603/383-4242.** www.innatthornhill.com. E-mail: thornhll@ncia.net. 19 units (3 cottages). A/C TEL. $170–$270 double; foliage season and Christmas $195–$320 double; cottages $250–$320. Rates include breakfast and dinner. 2-night minimum on weekends, 3 nights some holidays. AE, DISC, MC, V. Children 10 and older are welcome.

This is a truly elegant inn. The classic shingle-style home was designed by scandal-plagued architect Stanford White in 1895 (alas, it is now sadly swathed in yellow siding). The Inn at Thorn Hill is just outside of the village center, surrounded by wooded hills that seem to greet it in a warm embrace. Inside, there's a comfortable Victorian feel, although mercifully sparing on the frilly stuff. The two sitting parlors are well-designed for lounging; cookies and tea are served here in the afternoon. There's also a TV room with jigsaw puzzles and a decent selection of books on the shelves. The hospitality is warm and top-notch. Three of the guest rooms have gas fireplaces.

Dining: The lovely dining room is decorated in what might be called Victorian great-aunt style, with rich green carpeting, press-backed oak chairs, and pink table-cloths. The inn serves what it dubbed "New England fusion," and you'll find Jackson's best meals here. The menu changes to reflect the seasons, but you might find entrees ($16.95 to $22.95) like ginger-cured pork tenderloin with a cranberry chutney.

Amenities: Outdoor pool, hot tub, sundeck, nature trails, conference rooms, babysitting, laundry service, turndown service, afternoon tea.

Joe Dodge Lodge at Pinkham Notch. Rte. 16, Pinkham Notch, N.H. (Mailing address: AMC, 5 Joy St., Boston, MA 02108). ☎ **603/466-2727.** 108 beds in bunk rooms of 2, 3, and 4 beds. All with shared bathroom. Peak season $47 per adult, $31 per child (discount for AMC members); off-peak $42 and $27. Rates include breakfast and dinner. MC, V. Children should be at least 3 years old.

Guests come to the Pinkham Notch Camp more for the camaraderie than the accommodations. Situated spectacularly at the base of Mount Washington and with easy access to numerous hiking and skiing trails, the lodge is operated like a tightly run Scandinavian youth hostel, with guests sharing bunk rooms and enjoying boisterous, filling meals (turkey, beef stew, baked chicken) at long family-style tables in the main lodge. The accommodations are Spartan and basic, but that's overcome by the often festive atmosphere. It's a place to meet others and swap information about what to do in the area. Limited private and family rooms are also available ($65 to $80).

CRAWFORD NOTCH

✪ **Crawford Notch** is a wild, rugged mountain valley that angles through the heart of the White Mountains. Within the notch itself lies plenty of legend and history. For years after its discovery by European settlers (Timothy Nash stumbled upon it in 1771), it was an impenetrable wilderness, creating a barrier to commerce by blocking trade between the upper Connecticut River valley and commercial harbors in Portland and Portsmouth. This was eventually surmounted by a plucky crew who hauled the first freight through.

Nathaniel Hawthorne immortalized the notch with a short story about a real-life tragedy that struck in 1826. One dark and stormy night (naturally), the Willey family fled its home when they heard an avalanche roaring toward the valley floor. As fate would have it, the avalanche divided above their home and spared the structure; the seven who fled were killed in tumbling debris. You can still visit the site today; watch for signs when driving through the notch.

The notch is accessible via Route 302, which is wide and speedy on the lower sections, becoming steeper as it approaches the narrow defile of the notch itself. Modern engineering has taken most of the kinks out of the road. The views up the cliffs from the road can be spectacular on a clear day; on an overcast or drizzly day, the effect is foreboding.

ESSENTIALS

GETTING THERE   Route 302 runs through Crawford Notch for approximately 25 miles between the towns of Bartlett and Twin Mountain.

VISITOR INFORMATION   **Twin Mountain Chamber of Commerce,** P.O. Box 194, Twin Mountain, NH 03595 (☎ **800/245-8946** or 603/846-5407), offers general information and lodging referrals at their information booth near the intersection of Routes 302 and 3. Open year-round. More information is available at www.twinmountain.org.

WATERFALLS & SWIMMING HOLES

Much of the mountainous land flanking Route 302 falls under the jurisdiction of **Crawford Notch State Park,** which was established in 1911 to preserve land that elsewhere had been decimated by overly aggressive logging. The headwaters of the Saco River form in the notch, and what's generally regarded as the first permanent trail up Mount Washington also departs from here. Several turnouts and trailheads invite a more leisurely exploration of the area. The trail network on both sides of Crawford Notch is extensive; consult the *AMC White Mountain Guide* for detailed information.

Engorged by snowmelt in the spring, the Saco River courses through the notch's granite ravines and winds past sizable boulders that have been left by retreating glaciers and crashed down from the mountainsides above. It's a popular destination among serious white-water boaters, and makes for a good spectator sport if you're here early in the season. During the lazy days of summer, the Saco offers several good swimming holes just off the highway. They're unmarked, but watch for local cars parked off the side of the road for no apparent reason, and you should be able to find your way to a good spot for soaking and splashing.

Up the mountain slopes that form the valley, hikers will spot a number of lovely waterfalls, some more easily accessible than others. A few to start with:

Arethusa Falls has the highest single drop of any waterfall in the state, and the trail to the falls passes several attractive smaller cascades. These are especially beautiful in the spring or after a heavy rain, when the falls are at their fullest. The trip can be done as a 2.6-mile round-trip to the falls and back on Arethusa Falls Trail, or as a 4.5-mile loop hike that includes views from stunning Frankenstein Cliffs. (These are named not after the creator of the famous monster, but after a noted landscape painter.) If you're arriving from the south, look for signs to the trail parking area shortly after passing the Crawford Notch State Park entrance sign. From the north, the trailhead is a half mile south of the Dry River Campground. At the parking lot, look for the sign and map to get your bearings, then cross the railroad tracks to start up the falls trail.

Another hike begins a short drive north on Route 302. Reaching tumultuous **Ripley Falls** requires an easy hike of a little more than 1 mile, round-trip. Look for the sign to the falls on Route 302 just north of the trailhead for Webster Cliff Trail. (If you pass the Willey House site, you've gone too far.) Drive in and park at the site of the Willey Station. Follow trail signs for the Ripley Falls Trail, and allow about a half hour to reach the cascades. The most appealing swimming holes are at the top of the falls.

Two attractive falls may be seen from the roadway at the head of the notch, just east of the crest. **Flume Cascades** and **Silver Cascades** tumble down the hills in white braids that are especially appealing during a misty summer rain. These falls were among the most popular sites in the region when tourists alighted at the train station about 1 mile away. They aren't as spectacular as the two mentioned above, but they're accessible if you're in a hurry. Travelers can park in the lots along the road's edge for a slower paced view.

A HISTORIC RAILWAY

✪ **Mount Washington Cog Railway.** Rte. 302, Bretton Woods. ☎ **800/922-8825** or 603/846-5404. Fare $44 adults, $30 children 6–12, free for children under 5. MC, V. Runs daily Memorial Day to late Oct, plus weekends in May. Frequent departures; call for schedule. Reservations recommended.

The cog railway was a marvel of engineering when it opened in 1869, and it remains so today. Part moving museum, part slow-motion roller-coaster ride, the cog railway steams to the summit with a determined "I think I can" pace of about 4 miles per hour. But there's still a *frisson* of excitement on the way up and back, especially when the train crosses Jacob's Ladder, a rickety-seeming trestle 25 feet high that angles upward at a grade of more than 37%. Passengers enjoy the expanding view on this 3-hour round-trip (there are stops to add water to the steam engine, to check the track switches, and to allow other trains to ascend or descend). There's also a 20-minute stop at the summit to browse around. Be aware that the ride is noisy and sulfurous, and you should dress expecting to acquire a patina of cinder and soot.

But it's hard to imagine anyone (other than those fearful of heights) not enjoying this trip—from kids marveling at the ratchety-ratchety noises and the thick plume of black smoke, to curious adults trying to figure out how the cog system works, to naturalists who get superb views of the bony, brawny uplands leading to Mount Washington's summit.

SKIING

Attitash Bear Peak. Rte. 302, Bartlett, NH 03812. ☎ **800/223-7669** or 603/374-2368. www.attitash.com. E-mail: info@attitash.com. Vertical drop: 1,750 ft. Lifts: 12 chairlifts (including 2 high-speed quads), 2 surface lifts. Skiable acreage: 273. Lift tickets: $48 weekends, $50 holidays, $42 weekdays.

Attitash Bear Peak is a good mountain for intermediate-to-advanced skiers, with a selection of great cruising runs and a handful of more challenging drops. The mountain includes two peaks: the 1,750-foot Attitash and the adjacent 1,450-foot Bear Peak. The main attraction here—in addition to the good skiing—are the great views of the White Mountains from the peaks; not much happens locally at night, so those looking for action typically head 15 minutes away to North Conway.

Bretton Woods. Rte. 302, Bretton Woods, NH 03575. ☎ 800/232-2972 or 603/278-3307. E-mail: skibw@brettonwoods.com. Vertical drop: 1,500 ft. Lifts: 5 chairlifts (including 1 high-speed quad), 3 surface lifts. Skiable acreage: 250. Lift tickets: $44 weekends and holidays, $36 weekdays.

Bretton Woods is solid beginner-to-intermediate mountain with a pleasant family atmosphere and great views of Mount Washington. The resort does a good job with kids, and offers some nice intermediate cruising runs and limited night skiing. There's even a speedy detachable quad chair, which skiers don't often find at resorts of this size. Accommodations are available on the mountain and nearby, but evening entertainment tends to revolve around hot tubs, TVs, and going to bed early. There's also an excellent cross-country ski center nearby. Plans call for expanding the ski area to include an adjacent mountain in 2000, with new lifts and additional acreage.

WHERE TO STAY & DINE

○ **Mount Washington Hotel.** Rte. 302, Bretton Woods, NH 03575. ☎ **800/258-0330** or 603/278-1000. www.mtwashington.com. 200 units. TEL. Midweek $210–$460 double; weekends and holidays $245–$495 double; suites up to $1,195. Rates include breakfast and dinner. Minimum stays required during holidays. AE, DISC, MC, V.

This five-story wooden resort, with its gleaming white clapboards and cherry-red roof, seems something out of a fable. Built in 1902 by railroad and coal magnate Joseph Stickney, the resort attracted luminaries like Babe Ruth, Thomas Edison, Woodrow Wilson, and silent-movie star Mary Pickford. In 1944 it hosted the famed Bretton Woods International Monetary Conference, which secured the dollar's role as the world's currency.

After large resorts fell out of fashion, the Mount Washington went through a succession of owners and fell on hard times. Threatened with demolition and put on the auction block in 1991, it was purchased for just over $3 million by a group of local business folks. The improvements are moving along nicely, but the hotel can still feel a bit shabby and threadbare in parts. The biggest change is slated for late 1999, when the hotel will be open through the winter following a $2 million upgrade (including replacing 800 windows with new double-panes!)

Guest rooms are furnished simply but comfortably but as with most other grand resorts, the Mount Washington was designed around public areas. Wide hallways and elegant common areas on the first floor invite strolling and indolence. A broad 900-foot wraparound veranda makes for relaxing afternoons.

Dining/Diversions: Meals are enjoyed in the impressive octagonal dining room, designed such that no guest would be slighted by being seated in a corner. (Jackets are requested for men at dinner.) A house orchestra provides entertainment during the dinner, and guests often dance between courses. The meals are delicious, with a continental bent but global influences. The fixed-price meal is $42 per person for outside visitors or non-MAP guests. There's live entertainment in the lounge.

Amenities: Concierge, baby-sitting, valet parking, safe-deposit boxes, 27-hole golf course, 12 red-clay tennis courts, indoor and outdoor pools, stables, game room, gift shop.

○ **Notchland Inn.** Rte. 302, Hart's Location, NH 03812. ☎ **800/866-6131** or 603/374-6131. Fax 603/374-6168. www.notchland.com. E-mail: notchland@aol.com. 12 units. $190–$240 double; foliage season and holidays $230–$280. Rates include breakfast and dinner. 2-night minimum on weekends; 3-night minimum some holidays. AE, DISC, MC, V. Children over 12 are welcome.

The inn appears just off Route 302 in a wild, remote section of the valley, looking every bit like a redoubt in a Sir Walter Scott novel. Built of hand-cut granite between 1840 and 1862, Notchland is classy yet informal, and perfectly situated for exploring the wilds of the White Mountains. All 12 guest rooms are tastefully appointed with antiques and traditional furniture, and all feature wood-burning fireplaces, high ceilings, and individual thermostats. Three rooms have Jacuzzis; two have soaking tubs.

Dining: Dinners in the bright, often noisy dining room are eclectic and nicely presented. Five-course dinners are served at 7pm, with a choice of three creative entrees or so each evening. These might include a Thai curry, five-pepper–crusted roast beef, or scallops with walnuts and a lime-ginger sauce. Dinners are available to the public (space permitting) at a fixed price of $32, not including tax, tip, or beverage.

Amenities: River swimming (just across the road), outdoor hot tub, nature trails, game room, baby-sitting by advance appointment.

WATERVILLE VALLEY & LOON MOUNTAIN

In the southwestern corner of the White Mountains are two ski resorts occupying attractive mountain valleys. **Waterville Valley,** which lies at the end of a 12-mile dead-end road, was the first to be developed. Incorporated as a town in 1829, Waterville Valley became a popular destination for summer travelers during the heyday of mountain travel late in the 19th century. Skiers first started descending the slopes in the 1930s after a few ski trails were hacked out of the forest by the Civilian Conservation Corps and local ski clubs. But it wasn't until 1965, when a skier named Tom Corcoran bought 425 acres in the valley, that Waterville began to assume its current modern air.

While the village has a decidedly manufactured character—it's also at a lower elevation than the ski area, requiring a drive or shuttle bus to the slopes—Corcoran's initial vision has kept the growth within bounds. The village is reasonably compact, with modern lodges, condos, and restaurants located within a loop road. In the center is the "Town Square," itself a sort of minor mall complex with a restaurant and a few shops. If there's any complaint, it's that Waterville Valley has the unnatural, somewhat antiseptic quality of planned communities everywhere.

One of the nicer features of Waterville Valley is the **Athletic Club,** an attractive and modern complex with cardiovascular equipment, tennis courts, racquetball, an Olympic-size pool, a good restaurant, and more. Admission to the complex is ostensibly "free" to valley hotel guests, who pay an involuntary 15% resort tax (13% in winter) on their hotel bills. (Combined with the sales tax, that adds up to a hefty 21% to 23% tax on room rates—rather steep for an ostensibly tax-free state.)

Some 25 miles to the north is **Loon Mountain,** which is located just outside the former paper-mill town of Lincoln. In summer a shorter route crosses Thornton Gap on Tripoli Road. The resort was first conceived in the early 1960s by Sherman Adams, a former New Hampshire governor and Eisenhower administration official. The mountain opened in 1966 and was quickly criticized for its mediocre skiing, but some upgrading and expanding since then has brought the mountain greater respect.

Loon has evolved from a friendly intermediate mountain served by a few motels to a friendly intermediate mountain served by dozens of condos and vast, modern hotels. At times it seems that Lincoln underwent not so much a development boom in the 1980s as a development spasm. Clusters of chicken-coop style homes and condos now blanket the lower hillsides of this narrow valley, and fast-food restaurants and strip-mall–style shops line Route 112 from I-93 to the mountain.

The Loon area includes the towns of Lincoln and North Woodstock, which flank I-93. North Woodstock has more of the feel of a town that's lived in year-round. Lincoln and the Loon Mountain base village are lively with skiers in the winter, but in the summer the area can have a post–nuclear fallout feel to it, with lots of homes but few people in evidence. The ambience is also compromised by that peculiar style of resort architecture that's simultaneously aggressive and bland.

ESSENTIALS

GETTING THERE   Waterville Valley is located 12 miles northwest of Exit 29 on I-93 via Route 49. Lincoln is accessible off I-93 on exits 32 and 33.

VISITOR INFORMATION   The **Waterville Valley Chamber of Commerce,** RFD #1, Box 1067, Campton, NH 03223 (☎ **800/237-2307** or 603/726-3804), staffs a year-round information booth on Route 49 in Campton, just off I-93. The **Lincoln-Woodstock Chamber of Commerce,** P.O. Box 358, Lincoln, NH 03251 (☎ **800/227-4191** or 603/745-6621), has an information office open daily at Depot Plaza on Route 112 in Lincoln.

The most comprehensive place for information about the region is the **White Mountains Visitor Center,** P.O. Box 10, North Woodstock, NH 03262 (☎ **800/ 346-3687** or 603/745-8720), located just east of Exit 32 on I-93. They'll send a visitor kit, and they offer brochures and answer questions from their center, which is open year-round from 8:30am to 5pm daily.

THE KANCAMAGUS HIGHWAY

The Kancamagus Highway—locally called "the Kanc"—is among the White Mountains' most spectacular drives. Officially designated a national scenic byway by the U.S. Forest Service, the 34-mile roadway joins Lincoln with Conway through 2,860-foot Kancamagus Pass. When the highway was built from 1960 to 1961, it opened up 100 square miles of wilderness—a move that irked preservationists but has proven very popular with folks who prefer their sightseeing by car.

The route begins and ends along wide, tumbling rivers on relatively flat plateaus. The two-lane road rises steadily to the pass. Several rest areas with sweeping vistas allow visitors to pause and enjoy the mountain views. The highway also makes a good destination for hikers; any number of day and overnight trips may be launched from the roadside. One simple, short hike along a gravel pathway (it's less than one-third mile each way) leads to **Sabbaday Falls,** a cascade that's especially impressive after a downpour. Six national forest campgrounds are also located along the highway.

To get the most out of the road, take your time and make frequent stops. Think of it as a scavenger hunt as you look for a covered bridge, cascades with good swimming holes, a historic home with a quirky story behind it, and spectacular mountain panoramas. All of these things and more are along the route.

SKIING

Loon Mountain. Lincoln, NH 03251. ☎ **800/227-4191** for lodging or 603/745-8111. www.loonmtn.com. Vertical drop: 2,100 ft. Lifts: 8 chairlifts (1 high-speed), 1 high-speed gondola, 1 surface lift. Skiable acreage: 250. Lift tickets: $47 weekends, $41 weekdays.

Located on U.S. Forest Service land, Loon has been stymied in past expansion efforts by environmental concerns regarding land use and water withdrawals from the river. Loon eventually got the go-ahead for expansion, and has undertaken a $12-million, 6-year effort to expand and reshape the ski mountain, add uphill capacity, and improve snowmaking. The expansion plans should reduce some of the congestion of this popular area and open up more room to roam. Today, most of the trails still cluster toward the bottom, and most are solid intermediate runs. Experts head to the north peak, which has a challenging selection of advanced trails served by a triple chairlift.

Waterville Valley. Waterville Valley, NH 03215. ☎ **800/468-2553** or 603/236-8311. www.waterville.com. E-mail: info@waterville.com. Vertical drop: 2,020 ft. Lifts: 8 chairlifts (2 high speed), 4 surface lifts. Skiable acreage: 255. Lift tickets: $46 weekends, $40 weekdays.

Waterville Valley is a classic intermediate skier's mountain. The trails are uniformly wide and well-groomed, and the ski area is compact enough that no one will get confused and end up staring down a double-diamond trail. In 1997 the mountain's new owners invested $4 million in improvements (including a second high-speed chair and more extensive snowmaking), making it a fine place to learn to ski or brush up on your skills. Advanced skiers have a selection of black diamond trails, but the selection and steepness doesn't begin to rival larger ski mountains.

WHERE TO STAY
In Waterville Valley
Guests at hotels in Waterville Valley pay an involuntary 15% resort tax (13% in winter) on their bills, which gains them admission to the Valley Athletic Club. If you don't plan to use the complex (at some hotels, that can mean an additional $30 a day), you might think about staying in Lincoln or North Woodstock.

Golden Eagle Lodge. Snowsbrook Rd., Waterville Valley, NH 03215. ☎ **800/910-4499** or 603/236-4600. Fax 603/236-4947. 118 units. TV TEL. Winter $89–$168 per unit midweek, $108–$198 weekend; summer $98–$188; spring $78–$148. Premium charged on holidays. Resort fee of 13–15% is additional. Minimum stay requirements on certain holidays. AE, DC, DISC, MC, V.

This dominating, contemporary condominium project is centrally located in the village, and from the outside the five-story shingle-and-stone edifice looks like one of the grand White Mountain resorts of the last century. Inside it's also regal in a cartoon-Tudor kind of way, with lots of stained wood and columns and tall windows to let in the views. The hotel accommodates two to six people in each one- or two-bedroom unit, which have kitchens and basic cookware (very handy given the dearth of available eateries during crowded times). While outwardly grand, some of the furnishings and construction feel low budget, which compromises the experience somewhat.

   Amenities: Indoor and outdoor pools, whirlpool, bike rental, nearby 9-hole golf course, game rooms, nearby indoor jogging track, nature trails, conference rooms, access to valley Athletic Club across the street, self-service Laundromat, sauna, outdoor and indoor tennis courts nearby.

Snowy Owl Inn. Village Rd., Waterville Valley, NH 03215. ☎ **800/766-9969** or 603/236-8383. Fax 603/236-4890. 80 units. TV TEL. Winter weekends $128–$158 double; $228 suite. Winter nonholiday midweek $98–$128 double; $188 suite. Summer $78–$108 double; $158 suite. Rates include continental breakfast and resort fee. Resort fee of 13–15% is additional. AE, DISC, MC, V.

The Snowy Owl will appeal to those who like the amiable character of a country inn but prefer modern conveniences like in-room hair dryers. A modern, four-story resort project near Town Square, the inn offers a number of dramatic touches like a towering fieldstone fireplace in the lobby (adorned with a moose head), a handsome octagonal indoor pool, and a curious rooftop observatory reached via spiral staircase. The rooms are a notch above basic motel-style rooms. A new manager came on board in 1997 and made a number of small but long-overdue improvements, reversing the several-year slide into dowdiness.

   Amenities: Indoor and outdoor pools, Jacuzzis, game room, VCR room, free access to the Athletic Club.

In Lincoln & North Woodstock
In addition to the places listed below, Lincoln offers a range of motels that will appeal to budget travelers. Among those worth seeking out are the **Kancamagus Motor**

Lodge (☎ 800/346-4205 or 603/745-3365), the **Mountaineer Motel** (☎ 800/356-0046 or 603/745-2235), and **Woodward's Motor Inn** (☎ 800/635-8968 or 603/745-8141).

Mountain Club at Loon. Rte. 112 (R.R. #1; Box 40), Lincoln, NH 03251. ☎ 800/229-7829 or 603/745-2244. Fax 603/745-2317. www.mtnclubonloon.com. 234 units. A/C TV TEL. Winter midweek $169–$399 double; weekend $209–$429 double; summer and off-season $114–$259 double. AE, DC, DISC, MC, V.

Set at the edge of Loon Mountain's slopes, the Mountain Club is a sprawling and contemporary resort built during the real-estate boom of the 1980s. It was managed for several years as a Marriott, and the decor tends to reflect its chain-hotel heritage. Guest rooms are designed to be rented either individually or as two-room suites; each pair features one traditional hotel-style bedroom with king-size bed, and one studio with a kitchen, sitting area, and a fold-down queen-size bed. The high room rates reflect the proximity to the slopes and the excellent health-club facilities connected to the hotel via covered walkway.

Dining: The resort features a lounge with pub-style noshing, and more upscale offerings at Rachel's Restaurant. Look for dishes like grilled salmon with tomatilla salsa, or seared duck breast with corn cakes. Entrees are priced from $10.95 to $16.95.

Amenities: Ski-out access, indoor and outdoor pools, year-round outdoor whirlpool, limited room service, concierge, health club and fitness facility (including basketball, walleyball, aerobics rooms), sauna, game room, Laundromat, and two outdoor tennis courts.

Wilderness Inn. Rte. 3, N. Woodstock, NH 03262. ☎ 800/200-9453 or 603/745-3890. E-mail: wildernessinn@juno.com. 7 units, 1 cottage (2 units share 1 hall bathroom). $50–$125 double. Rates include full breakfast. AE, MC, V. Located just south of Rte. 112. Pets allowed off-season in cottage ($10 fee).

The Wilderness Inn is located at the southern edge of North Woodstock village—it's not the wilderness that the name or the brochure might suggest. But it's a friendly, handsome bed-and-breakfast, with six guest rooms in a large bungalow-style home that dates to 1912. The interior features heavy timbers in classic Craftsman style, creaky maple floors, a somewhat spare mix of antiques and reproductions, and games to occupy an evening. Five rooms have TVs, the second floor rooms are air-conditioned, and there's a VCR and TV in the living room for all guests to enjoy. The breakfasts are righteously massive and very good.

Woodstock Inn. Main St. (P.O. Box 118), N. Woodstock, NH 03262. ☎ 800/321-3985 or 603/745-3951. Fax 603/745-3701. www.woodstockinnnh.com. 21 units (13 with private bathroom). A/C TV TEL. $55–$135 double; foliage season $75–$140 double. Rates include breakfast. AE, DISC, MC, V.

The Woodstock Inn has a Jekyll-and-Hyde appearance. In the front, it's a white Victorian with black shutters amid Woodstock's commercial downtown area—one of the few older inns in the land of condos and modern resorts. In the back, it's a modern, boisterous brew pub that serves up hearty fare along with robust ales (see "Where to Dine," below). The inn features 19 guest rooms spread among three houses. If you're on a tight budget, go for the shared-bathroom units in the main house and the nearby Deachman house; the slightly less personable Riverside building across the street offers rooms with private bathrooms, but at a premium. Rooms are individually decorated in a country Victorian style, furnished with both reproductions and antiques. Three have Jacuzzis.

WHERE TO DINE

Waterville Valley offers a limited selection of restaurants, which too often seem to be either closed for the night or too crowded. No one place is outstanding. The Athletic

Club has its own restaurant on the second floor, **Wild Coyote Grill** (☎ 603/ 236-4919), which offers regional favorites like potato-crusted salmon and grilled sirloin with mashed potatoes ($10.95 to $16.95). Decent pub fare (including commendable french fries) can be had in the **Red Fox Tavern** (☎ 603/236-8336) located in the basement of the Valley Inn.

The Lincoln–North Woodstock area is more capable of feeding the masses, but isn't known for haute cuisine. If you're in a condo or suite with an oven or microwave, your best option for a delicious, reasonably priced meal is at **Half Baked,** 43 Main St., North Woodstock (☎ 603/745-3811). The shop offers dinners to go from an old farmhouse just south of North Woodstock village—just reheat when you get back to your room. A half-dozen Greek triangles go for $3.95; homemade pasta is $2.50 a pound; a family-size lasagna is $29.50.

Woodstock Station. Main St. ☎ **603/745-3951.** Reservations accepted for Clement Room only. Breakfast items $3.95–$9.50; lunch and dinner items $5.50–$16 (dinner in Clement Room $10.95–$22.95). AE, DISC, MC, V. Clement Room daily 7–11:30am and 5:30–9:30pm; Woodstock Station daily 11:30am–10pm. PUB FARE/AMERICAN.

You've got a choice here: Dine amid the casually upscale Clement Room Grille on the enclosed porch of the Woodstock Inn, or head to the brew pub in the back, housed in an old train station. In the Clement Room there's an open grill and fare that aspires toward some refinement (for instance, ostrich quesadilla, cedar-plank salmon, stuffed sole, and roast duck). The pub has high ceilings, knotty pine, and a decor that draws on vintage winter recreational gear. The pub menu rounds up the usual suspects, like nachos, chicken wings, burgers, and pasta, none of which is prepared with much creative flair. Better are the porters, stouts, and brown and red ales, which are brewed on premises.

FRANCONIA NOTCH

Franconia Notch is rugged New Hampshire writ large. As travelers head north on I-93, the Kinsman Range to the west and the Franconia Range to the east begin to converge, and the road swells upward. Soon, the flanking mountain ranges press in on either side, forming tight and dramatic Franconia Notch, which offers little in the way of civilization but a whole lot in the way of natural drama. Most of the notch is included in a well-managed state park that to most travelers will be indistinguishable from the national forest. Travelers seeking the sublime should plan on a leisurely trip through the notch, allowing enough time to get out of the car and explore forests and craggy peaks.

ESSENTIALS

GETTING THERE I-93 runs through Franconia Notch, gearing down from four lanes to two (where it becomes the Franconia Notch Parkway) in the most scenic and sensitive areas of the park. Several roadside pull-outs and scenic attractions dot the route.

VISITOR INFORMATION Information on the park and surrounding area is available at the state-run **Flume Information Center** (☎ 603/823-5563) at Exit 1 off the parkway. The center is open daily in summer from 9am to 4:30pm. North of the notch, head to the **Franconia/Eaton/Sugar Hill Chamber of Commerce,** P.O. Box 780, Franconia, NH 03580 (☎ 603/823-5661), on Main Street next to the town hall. It's open spring through fall, Tuesday through Sunday from 10am to 5pm (days and hours often vary depending on staff availability).

EXPLORING FRANCONIA NOTCH STATE PARK

Franconia Notch State Park's 8,000 acres, nestled within the surrounding White Mountain National Forest, hosts an array of scenic attractions easily accessible from

I-93 and the Franconia Notch Parkway. For information on any of the follow attractions, contact the park offices (☎ **603/823-5563**).

Without a doubt, the most famous park landmark is the **Old Man of the Mountains,** located near Cannon Mountain. From the right spot on the valley floor, this 48-foot-high rock formation bears an uncanny resemblance to the profile of a craggy old man—early settlers said it was Thomas Jefferson. If it looks familiar, it's because this is the logo you see on all the New Hampshire state highway signs. The profile, which often surprises visitors by just how tiny it is when viewed from far below (bring binoculars), is best seen from the well-marked roadside viewing area at Profile Lake. In years past, harried tourists craning their necks to glimpse the Old Man while speeding onward resulted in some spectacular head-on collisions. Take your time and pull over. It's free.

The Flume is a rugged, 800-foot gorge through which the Flume Brook tumbles. The gorge, a hugely popular attraction in the mid–19th century, is 800 feet long, 90 feet deep, and as narrow as 20 feet at the bottom; visitors explore by means of a network of boardwalks and bridges. Early photos of the chasm show a boulder wedged in overhead; this was swept away in an 1883 avalanche. If you're looking for simple and quick access to natural grandeur, it's worth the money. Otherwise, set off into the mountains and seek your own drama with fewer crowds. Admission is $7 for adults, $4 for children 6 to 12.

Echo Lake is a picturesquely situated recreation area, with a 28-acre lake, a handsome swimming beach, and picnic tables scattered about all within view of Cannon Mountain on one side and Mount Lafayette on the other. A bike path runs alongside the lake and continues onward in both directions. Admission to the park is $2.50 for visitors over 12 years old.

For a high-altitude view of the region, set off for the alpine ridges on the **Cannon Mountain Tramway.** The old-fashioned cable car serves skiers in winter; in summer, it whisks up to 80 travelers at a time to the summit of the 4,180-foot mountain. Once at the top, you can strike out by foot along the Rim Trail for superb views. Be prepared for cool, gusty winds. The tramway costs $9 round-trip for adults, $5 for children 6 to 12. It's located at Exit 2 of the parkway.

HIKING

Hiking opportunities abound in the Franconia Notch area, ranging from demanding multi-day hikes high on exposed ridgelines to gentle valley walks. Consult AMC's *White Mountain Guide* for a comprehensive directory of area hiking trails.

A pleasant woodland detour of 2 hours or so can be found at the **Basin-Cascades Trail** (look for well-marked signs for the Basin off I-93 about 1½ miles north of the Flume). A popular roadside waterfall and natural pothole, the Basin attracts teeming crowds, but relatively few visitors continue on the trail to a series of cascades beyond. Look for signs for the trail, then head off into the woods. After about a half mile of easy hiking you'll reach **Kinsman Falls,** a beautiful 20-foot cascade. Continue on another half mile beyond that to Rocky Glen, where the stream plummets through a craggy gorge. Retrace your steps back to your car.

A POET'S PLACE

✪ **Robert Frost Farm.** Ridge Rd., Franconia. ☎ **603/823-5510.** Admission $3 adults, $1.50 children 6–15, free for children under 6. Late May to June Sat–Sun 1–5pm; July to mid-Oct Wed–Mon 1–5pm. Head south on Rte. 116 from Franconia 1 mile to Ridge Rd (gravel); follow signs a short way to the Frost House; park in lot below the house.

Robert Frost lived in New Hampshire between the ages of 10 and 45. "Nearly half my poems must actually have been written in New Hampshire," Frost said. "Every single person in my 'North of Boston' was a friend or acquaintance of mine in New Hampshire." The Frost Place is a humble farmhouse, where Frost lived simply with his family. Wandering the grounds, it's not hard to see how his granite-edged poetry evolved at the fringes of the White Mountains. First editions of Frost's works are on display; a slide show offers a glimpse into the poet's life, and a nature trail in the woods near the house is posted with excerpts from his poems.

SKIING

Cannon Mountain. Franconia Notch Pkwy., Franconia. ☎ **603/823-8800.** Vertical drop: 2,146 ft. Lifts: 80-person tram plus 4 chairlifts. Skiable acreage: about 200. Lift tickets: $39 weekend, $28 weekday.

This state-run ski area was once the place to ski in the East. One of New England's first ski mountains, Cannon remains famed for its challenging runs and exposed faces, and the mountain still attracts skiers serious about getting down the hill in style. Many of the old-fashioned New England–style trails are narrow and fun (if often icy, scoured by the notch's winds), and the enclosed tramway is an elegant way to get to the summit. There's no base scene to speak of; skiers tend to retire to inns around Franconia or retreat southward to the condo villages around Lincoln.

WHERE TO STAY & DINE

Franconia Inn. 1300 Easton Rd., Franconia, NH 03580. ☎ **800/473-5299** or 603/823-5542. Fax 603/823-8078. www.franconiainn.com. E-mail: info@franconiainn.com. 32 units. Midweek $86–$126 double; weekends $96–$136 double. Rates include breakfast. MAP rates also available. 3-night minimum on holiday weekends. Closed Apr to mid-May. AE, MC, V.

This is a pleasant inn that offers very good value. Owned by Alec and Richard Morris, two brothers who bought the inn in 1981, it's set along a quiet road in a bucolic valley 2 miles from the village of Franconia. The inn itself, built in 1934 after a fire destroyed the original 1886 inn, has a welcoming and informal feel to it, with wing-back chairs around the fireplace in one common room, and jigsaw puzzles half completed in the paneled library. Guest rooms are nicely appointed in a relaxed country fashion; three feature gas fireplaces and four have Jacuzzis. The inn is a haven for cross-country skiers—38 miles of groomed trails start right outside the front door.

Dining: The handsome first-floor dining room serves a delicious breakfast each morning and is open daily for dinner. The New American menu (entrees $14.95 to $18.95) includes dishes like rack of lamb dijonaise, portobello mushroom en papillote, and pepper-broiled salmon with dill.

Amenities: Heated pool, outdoor hot tub, four clay tennis courts, mountain bikes (free), game rooms, sauna, nearby golf course, tour desk, bridle trails and horse rentals, cross-country ski trails.

BETHLEHEM & LITTLETON

A century ago, **Bethlehem** was the same size as North Conway to the south, boasting an impressive number of sprawling resort hotels, summer homes, and even its own semiprofessional baseball team. (Joseph Kennedy, patriarch of the Kennedy clan, played for the team.) Bethlehem subsequently lost the race for the riches (or won, depending on your view of outlet shopping), and today is again a sleepy town high on a hillside.

Famed for its lack of ragweed and pollen, Bethlehem was once teeming with vacationers seeking respite from the ravages of hay fever. When antihistamines and air-conditioning appeared on the scene, the sufferers stayed home. Empty resorts burned down one by one. Around the 1920s, Bethlehem was discovered by Hasidim from New York City, who soon arrived in number to spend the summers in the remaining boarding houses. In fact, that tradition has endured, and it's not uncommon today to see resplendently bearded men in black walking the village streets or rocking on the porches of Victorian-era homes.

Nearby **Littleton,** set in a broad valley along the Ammonoosuc River, is the area's commercial hub, but it boasts a surfeit of small-town charm. The town's long main street has an eclectic selection of shops—you can buy a wrench, a foreign magazine or literary novel, locally brewed beer, pizza, whole foods, or camping supplies.

These two towns don't offer much in the way of must-see attractions, but both have good lodging, decent restaurants, and pleasant environs. Either town makes a peaceful alternative for travelers hoping to avoid the tourist bustle to the south.

ESSENTIALS

GETTING THERE   Littleton is best reached via I-93; get off at either Exit 41 or 42. Bethlehem is about 3 miles east of Littleton on Route 302. Get off I-93 at Exit 40 and head east. From the east, follow Route 302 past Twin Mountain to Bethlehem.

VISITOR INFORMATION   The **Bethlehem Chamber of Commerce,** P.O. Box 748, Bethlehem, NH 03574 (☎ **603/869-2151**), maintains an information booth in summer on Bethlehem's Main Street across from the town hall. The **Littleton Area Chamber of Commerce,** P.O. Box 105, Littleton, NH 03561 (☎ **603/444-6561**), offers information from its office at 120 Main St.

EXPLORING BETHLEHEM

Bethlehem once was home to 38 resort hotels, but little evidence of them remains today. For a better understanding of the town's rich history, track down a copy of *An Illustrated Tour of Bethlehem, Past and Present,* available at many shops around town. This unusually informative guide offers a glimpse into the town's past, bringing to life many of the most graceful homes and buildings. Bethlehem consists of Main Street and a handful of side streets. Several antiques stores clustered in what passes for downtown are worth browsing.

Just west of Bethlehem on Route 302 is **The Rocks** (☎ **603/444-6228**), a classic, Victorian gentleman's farm that today is the northern headquarters for the Society for the Protection of New Hampshire Forests. Set on 1,200 acres, this gracious estate was built in 1883 by John J. Glessner, an executive with the International Harvester Company. A well-preserved shingled house and an uncommonly handsome barn grace the grounds. Several hiking trails meander through meadows and woodlands on a gentle hillside, where visitors can enjoy open vistas of the wooded mountains across the rolling terrain. The Society operates a Christmas-tree farm here, as well as regular nature programs. Admission is free.

WHERE TO STAY

✪ **Adair.** 80 Guider Lane (just off Exit 40 on Rte. 93), Bethlehem, NH 03574. ☎ **888/ 444-2600** or 603/444-2600. Fax 603/444-4823. www.adairinn.com. E-mail: adair@con-nriver.net. 10 units. $140–$285 double. Rates include breakfast. 2-night minimum on summer weekends and foliage season. AE, MC, V. Children 12 and over welcome.

Adair opened in 1992, but remains one of New England's better kept secrets. Guests enter via a winding drive flanked by birches and stone walls to arrive at a peaceful Georgian Revival home dating from 1927 that seems far more regal than its years. The inn is set on 200 acres, including beautifully landscaped grounds around the home. Inside, the common rooms are open, elegant, and spacious. Downstairs is the memorable Granite Tap Room, a huge, wonderfully informal, granite-lined, stone-floored rumpus room with a VCR, antique pool table, fireplace, and self-service bar. The guest rooms are impeccably well-furnished with a mix of antiques and reproductions in a light country fashion. Six feature fireplaces. The best of the lot is the Kinsman suite with a Jacuzzi the size of a small swimming pool, and a petite balcony looking out toward the Dalton Range. New (in 1998) was a two-bedroom cottage on the grounds, which is available for a two night minimum stay. The innkeepers are Judy and Bill Whitman, who took over from the Banfield family in 1998.

Dining: See "Tim-Bir Alley," below.

Amenities: All-weather tennis court, nature trails, and game room with billiards.

Hearthside Village Cottage Motel. Rte. 302 (midway between Bethlehem Village and I-93), Bethlehem, NH 03574. ☎ **603/444-1000.** 16 cottages. TV. $54.95–$64.95 ($10 less in off-season). 2- or 3-day minimum during foliage season. MC, V. Closed mid-Oct to mid-May.

Hearthside Village is a quirky motel court that feels a bit like an installation by Red Grooms. A little bit weird and a little bit charming at the same time, Hearthside claims to be the first motel court built in New Hampshire. A colony of steeply gabled miniature homes, the village was built by a father and son in two construction bursts, the first in the 1930s, the second in the late 1940s. The six 1940s-era cottages are of somewhat better quality, with warm knotty-pine interiors. Many of the cottages have fireplaces (Duraflame-style logs only). There's a pool, an indoor playroom filled with toys for tots, and another recreation room with video games and Ping-Pong for older kids. Hasidic families often stay here in summer, which at times lends the place a somewhat cross-cultural quality.

Rabbit Hill Inn. Rte. 18, Lower Waterford, VT 05848. ☎ **800/762-8669** or 802/748-5168. Fax 802/748-8342. www.rabbithillinn.com. E-mail: info@rabbithillinn.com. 20 units. A/C. $235–$340 double. Rates include breakfast, dinner, afternoon tea, and service charge. 2-night minimum on weekends. AE, MC, V. Closed early Apr and early Nov. From I-93, take Rte. 18 northwest from Exit 44 for approximately 2 miles. Children over 12 are welcome.

A short hop across the Connecticut River from Littleton is the lost-in-time Vermont village of Lower Waterford with its perfect 1859 church and small library. Amid this cluster of buildings is the stately Rabbit Hill Inn, constructed in 1795. With its prominent gabled roof and imposing columns, the inn easily ranks among the most refined in the Connecticut River valley. More than half of the rooms have gas fireplaces, most have air-conditioning, and several feature Jacuzzis. The innkeepers go the extra mile to make this an appealing destination for couples in search of quiet romance.

Dining: Dinner is included in the rates, and the menu changes every 2 months. The menu is uncommonly creative. offering entrees like braised pheasant wrapped in bacon and served with a dried cherry nectarine cognac sauce, and beef tenderloin with a maple-molasses sauce. Proper attire is expected in the dining room. The public is welcome with reservations; a five-course meal costs $37 per person.

✪ **Thayers Inn.** Main St., Littleton, NH 03561. ☎ **800/634-8179** or 603/444-6469. 42 units (3 with shared bathroom, some with shower only). TV. $49.95–$79.95 double. AE, DC, DISC, MC, V.

President Ulysses S. Grant addressed a street-side crowd from one of the balconies under the grand eaves of Thayers Inn. You might try that, too, although it's not likely you'll be as successful at scaring up a crowd. Thayers is a clean, well-run hostelry in an impressive historic building. This solid 1850 inn has a variety of rooms furnished comfortably if basically on four floors. Each room is different (only some have TVs; ask if it's important to you), and guests are encouraged to poke around and see what's available before deciding on their evening quarters.

WHERE TO DINE

✪ **Tim-Bir Alley.** At Adair, Old Littleton Rd., Bethlehem. ☎ **603/444-6142.** Reservations recommended. Main courses $13.95–$18.50. No credit cards. Wed–Sun 5:30–9pm. Closed Apr, Nov, and Sun in off-season. REGIONAL/CONTEMPORARY.

The best dining in the White Mountains is at Tim-Bir Alley, housed in the area's most gracious country inn. Owners Tim and Biruta Carr have created an elegant and romantic setting, and prepare meals from ingredients that are wholesome and basic; even simple side dishes flirt with the remarkable. Diners might start with smoked chicken-tortilla soup or salmon pancakes with a spinach-olive pesto, then tuck into a main course of beef tournedos with smoked bacon and Cabernet sauce, or hoisin-ginger noodles with shrimp and bok choy. Save room for the superb desserts, which range from cranberry-almond cake with a warm honey sauce, to a chocolate-hazelnut pâté. Service can be a bit poky, so come expecting to enjoy a leisurely meal.

6 The North Country

I've been traveling to New Hampshire's North Country for more than 25 years, and it's come to serve as a touchstone for me. **Errol** is a town that regards change with high suspicion, something that held true even during the go-go times of the 1980s. The clean if basic Errol Motel is always there. The Errol Restaurant still serves the best homemade donuts north of Boston. And the land surrounding the town remains an outpost of rugged, raw grandeur that hasn't been at all compromised, as have many of the former wildlands to the south.

Of course, there's a problem with these lost-in-time areas. You drive for miles and see lots of spruce and pine, an infrequent bog, a glimpse of a shimmering lake, and— if you're lucky—a roadside moose chomping on sedges.

But there *is* plenty to do. White-water kayaking on the Androscoggin River. Canoeing on Lake Umbagog. Bicycling along the wide valley floors. And visiting one of the Northeast's grandest, most improbable turn-of-the-century resorts, which continues to thrive despite considerable odds.

ESSENTIALS

GETTING THERE   Errol is at the junction of Route 26 (accessible from Bethel, Maine) and Route 16 (accessible from Gorham, N.H.).

VISITOR INFORMATION   The **Northern White Mountains Chamber of Commerce,** 164 Main St., Berlin, NH 03570 (☎ **603/752-6060**), offers travel information from its offices weekdays between 8:30am and 4:30pm.

OUTDOOR PURSUITS

Dixville Notch State Park (☎ 603/788-2155) offers limited hiking, including a delightful 2-mile round-trip hike to Table Rock. Look for the small parking area just east of the Balsams resort on the edge of Lake Gloriette. The loop hike (it connects with a half-mile return along Route 26) ascends a scrabbly trail to an open rock with fine views of the resort and the flanking wild hills.

A great place to learn the fundamentals of white water is at **Saco Bound's Northern Waters** whitewater school (☎ 603/447-2177), located where the Errol bridge crosses the Androscoggin River. The school offers 2- to 5-day workshops in the art of getting downstream safely, if not dryly. Classes involve videos, dry-land training, and frequent forays onto the river—both at the Class I to III rapids at the bridge, and more forgiving rips downstream. The base camp is also a good place for last-minute boat supplies and advice for paddlers exploring the river on their own. Classes are $170 for 2 days, and $65 for each additional day up to five. The price includes camping fees.

Excellent lake canoeing may be found at Lake Umbagog, which sits between Maine and New Hampshire. The lake, which is home to the **Lake Umbagog Wildlife Refuge** (☎ **603/482-3415**), has some 40 miles of shoreline, most of which is wild and remote. Look for osprey and eagles, otter and mink. More than 20 primitive campsites are scattered around the shoreline and on the lake's islands. Starting in 1999, these backcountry campsites will be managed by New Hampshire parks department, with fees running around $20 per night. Contact **New Hampshire parks** at ☎ **603/ 271-3628** for more information.

WHERE TO STAY & DINE

✪ **Balsams Grand Resort Hotel.** Dixville Notch, NH 03576. ☎ **800/255-0600,** 800/255-0800 in N.H., or 603/255-3400. Fax 603/255-4221. www.thebalsams.com. E-mail: thebalsams@aol.com. 208 units. TEL. Winter $200–$350 double, including breakfast, dinner, and lift tickets; summer $275–$430 double, including all meals and entertainment; year-round $570–$650 suite. 4-night minimum on weekends July–Aug. AE, DISC, MC, V. Closed early Apr to late May and mid-Oct to Christmas.

Located on 15,000 private acres in a notch surrounded by 800-foot cliffs, the Balsams is a rare surprise hidden deep in the northern forest. The inn is but one of a handful of great resorts dating back to the 19th century still in operation, and its survival is all the more extraordinary given its remote location. What makes this Victorian grande dame even more exceptional has been its refusal to compromise or bend to the trend of the moment. Bathing suits and jeans are prohibited from the public areas, you'll be ejected from the tennis courts or golf course if you're not neatly attired, and men are required (not requested) to wear jackets at dinner. The resort has also maintained strict adherence to the spirit of the "American plan"—everything but booze is included in the room rate, from greens fees to tennis to boats on Lake Gloriette to evening enter-tainment in the three lounges. Even the lift tickets at the resort's downhill ski area are covered.

Dining/Diversions: Meals are superb. Especially famous is the sumptuous luncheon buffet, served in summer and featuring delightful salads, filling entrees like linguine with clam sauce and fried shrimp, and time-warp desserts (when did you last gorge on chocolate éclairs?). There are also three lounges.

Amenities: The resort is noted for its two golf courses (one 18-hole, one 9-hole). Also: concierge, limited room service, dry cleaning, laundry service, newspaper delivery, turndown service, baby-sitting, currency exchange, valet parking, six tennis courts, heated outdoor pool, 45 miles of groomed cross-country ski trails, bicycle rentals, game rooms, nature trails, children's programs, business center, conference rooms, sundeck, water-sports equipment, beauty salon, boutiques, shopping arcade.

✪ **Philbrook Farm Inn.** 881 North Rd. (off Rte. 2 between Gorham, N.H., and Bethel, Maine), Shelburne, NH 03581. ☎ **603/466-3831.** 18 units, 6 summer cottages (6 units have shared bathrooms). $115–$145 double, including full breakfast and dinner; cottages $600 weekly. No credit cards. Closed Apr and Nov to Dec 25. Pets allowed in cottages only.

The Philbrook Farm Inn is a New England classic, a period piece that can easily trace its lineage to the 19th century, when farmers opened their doors to summer travelers to earn some extra cash. Set on 1,000 acres between the Mahoosuc Range and the Androscoggin River, this country inn has been owned and operated by the Philbrook family continuously since 1853. The inn has expanded haphazardly, with additions in 1861, 1904, and 1934. As a result, the cozy guest rooms on three floors are eclectic—some have a country farmhouse feel, others a more Victorian flavor. Guests spend their days at leisure, swimming in the pool, playing croquet, exploring trails in the nearby hills. or just reading in the sun on the porch. Philbrook Farm is a wonderful retreat, well out of the tourist mainstream, and worthy of protection as a local cultural landmark.

Dining: The dining room has a farmhouse-formal feel to it; guests are assigned one table for their stay, and are served by waitresses in crisp white uniforms. Meals tend toward basic New England fare, with specialties like cod cakes and baked beans with brown bread.

Maine 13

by Wayne Curtis

Professional funny guy Dave Barry once suggested that Maine's state motto should be "Cold, but damp."

Cute, but true. There's spring, which tends to last a few blustery, rain-soaked days. There's November, in which Arctic winds alternate with gray sheets of rain. And then winter brings a character-building mix of blizzards and ice storms to the fabled coast. (The inland mountains are more or less blessed with uninterrupted snow.)

Ah, but then there's summer. Summer in Maine brings osprey diving for fish off wooded points; gleaming cumulus clouds building over the steely blue rounded peaks of the western mountains; and the haunting whoop of loons echoing off the dense forest walls bordering the lakes. It brings languorous days when the sun rises well before most visitors, and by 8am it seems like noontime. Maine summers bring a measure of gracious tranquillity, and a placid stay in the right spot can rejuvenate even the most jangled nerves.

The trick comes in finding that right spot. Those who arrive here without a clear plan may find themselves ruing their travel decision. Maine's Route 1 along the coast has its moments, but for the most part it's rather charmless—an amalgam of convenience stores, tourist boutiques, and restaurants catering to bus tours. Acadia National Park can be congested, Mount Katahdin's summit overcrowded, and some of the more popular lakes are obstacle courses of jet skis.

But Maine's size works to the traveler's advantage. Maine is roughly as large as the other five New England states combined. It has 3,500 miles of coastline, some 3,000 coastal islands, and millions of acres of undeveloped woodland. In fact, more than half of the state exists as "unorganized territories," where no town government exists, and the few inhabitants look to the state for basic services. With all this space and a little planning, you'll be able to find your piece of Maine.

1 Enjoying the Great Outdoors

BACKPACKING Compared to camping by canoe or sea kayak, backpacking opportunities are relatively limited in Maine. A few notable exceptions exist. The 2,000-mile Appalachian Trail, which begins at Maine's highest peak, is nothing short of spectacular as it passes through Maine. En route to Mount Katahdin, it winds through the "100-Mile Wilderness," a remote and bosky stretch where the trail crosses few roads and passes no settlements. It's the quiet habitat of loons and moose. Trail descriptions are available from the

Appalachian Trail Conference, P.O. Box 807, Harpers Ferry, WV 25425 (☎ 304/535-6331).

Another excellent destination is the 200,000-acre **Baxter State Park,** 64 Balsam Dr., Millinocket, ME 04462 (☎ **207/723-5140**), in the north-central part of the state. The park maintains about 180 miles of backcountry hiking trails and more than 25 backcountry sites, some accessible only by canoe. Most hikers coming to the park are intent on ascending 5,267-foot Mount Katahdin. But dozens of other peaks are well worth scaling, and just traveling through the deep woods hereabouts is a sublime experience. Reservations are required for backcountry camping, and many of the best spots fill up shortly after the first of the year. Reservations can be made by mail or in person, but not by phone.

Note that backcountry camping is not permitted at Acadia National Park.

BEACHES   Swimming at Maine's ocean beaches is for the hearty. Water temperatures rarely top 60°F even on the warmest days. See the section on the "South Coast," below, for more information.

BIKING   **Mount Desert Island** and **Acadia National Park** comprise the premier destination for bikers, especially mountain bikers looking for easy-riding terrain. The 57 miles of well-maintained carriage roads in the national park offer superb cruising through thick forests and to the tops of rocky knolls with ocean views. No cars are permitted on these grass and gravel lanes, so bikers and walkers have them to themselves. Mountain bikes may be rented in Bar Harbor, which has at least three bike shops. The Park Loop Road, while often crowded with slow-moving cars, offers one of the more memorable road-biking experiences in the state. The rest of Mount Desert Island is also good for road biking, especially on the quieter western half of the island.

BIRDING   Birders from southern and inland states should be able to lengthen their life lists along the **Maine Coast,** which attracts migrating birds cruising the Atlantic flyway and boasts populations of numerous native shorebirds, such as plovers (including the threatened piping plover), whimbrels, sandpipers, and dunlins. You'll see a surfeit of herring and great black-backed gulls along with the common tern; less frequently seen are Bonaparte's gull, laughing gull, jaegers, and the arctic tern. Far up the coast near Lubec, look for members of the alcid family, including razorbills and guillemots. Puffins (another alcid) nest on several offshore islands; tour boats to view puffins depart from Boothbay Harbor, Bar Harbor, and Jonesport.

CAMPING   Car campers in Maine have plenty of choices, from well-developed private campgrounds to primitive and remote sites. Baxter State Park and Acadia National Park tend to fill up the fastest, but there's no shortage of other options. Maine has nearly 62,000 acres in state parks (not including 200,000-acre Baxter), a dozen of which offer overnight camping. For more information about the state's parks, contact the **Department of Conservation,** State House Station #22, Augusta, ME 04333 (☎ 207/287-3821). To make **camping reservations** at any of 12 of the state park campgrounds, call between January and August (☎ 800/332-1501 in Maine or 207/287-3824). MasterCard and Visa are accepted. Campsite fees (with reservations) typically range from $13 to $19 for nonresidents.

On Maine's western border, the White Mountain National Forest offers superb camping at a handful of campgrounds in the rolling mountains of the Evans Notch area. Rates average about $12 per night. Contact **Evans Notch Ranger District,** 18 Mayville Rd., Bethel, ME 04217 (☎ 207/824-2134).

Maine also has more than 200 private campgrounds spread throughout the state, many offering full hookups for RVs. For a guide to the private campgrounds, contact

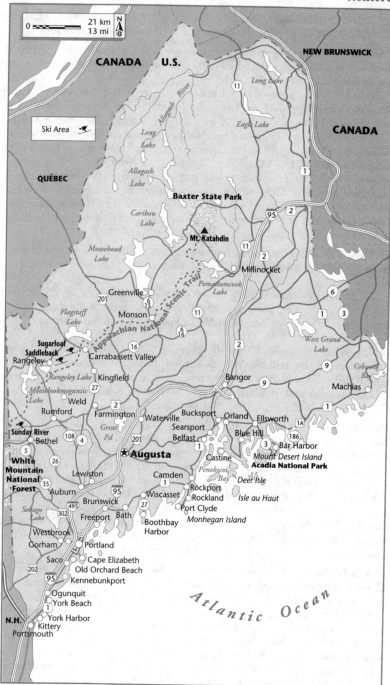

Maine

0 ___ 21 km
___ 13 mi
N

CANADA   U.S.

NEW BRUNSWICK

Long Lake

Ski Area

Allagash River

Long Lake

Eagle Lake

CANADA

QUÉBEC

11

Allagash Lake

1

Baxter State Park

Caribou Lake

Moosehead Lake

▲ Mt. Katahdin

11

95   2

Greenville

201

11

Millinocket

Pemadumcook Lake

6

Monson

13

11

16

Flagstaff Lake

6
18

1   3

Appalachian National Scenic Trail

Sugarloaf
Saddleback
Rangeley

Carrabassett Valley

2

West Grand Lake

9

Cobscook Bay

Kingfield

27

Rangeley Lake

Bangor

Machias

Mooselookmeguntic Lake

Weld

9

1

Rumford

2

Farmington

Waterville

Bucksport

Orland   Ellsworth

Sunday River
Bethel

108   4

Great Pd

201

Searsport

Blue Hill

1A

186

Bar Harbor

5

26

White
Mountain
National
Forest

Belfast

3

Mount Desert Island
Acadia National Park

35

Lewiston

★ **Augusta**

Castine

Auburn

Penobscot Bay

Deer Isle

Brunswick

95

Camden

1

Rockport

Sebago Lake

302

495

Freeport

Wiscasset

Rockland

Isle au Haut

Bath

27

Port Clyde

Westbrook

Monhegan Island

Gorham

Portland

Boothbay
Harbor

Saco

Cape Elizabeth

202

Old Orchard Beach

95

Kennebunkport

Ogunquit
York Beach

1

York Harbor

N.H.

Kittery

Portsmouth

A t l a n t i c   O c e a n

NA-0137

the **Maine Campground Owners Association,** 655 Main St., Lewiston, ME 04240 (☎ 207/782-5874; www.campmaine.com; E-mail: info@campmaine.com).

CANOEING   For many outdoor enthusiasts, Maine means canoeing. From the thousands of acres of lakes and ponds to the tumbling white water of mountain rivers, Maine is very alluring to serious paddlers.

The state's most popular long-distance excursion is the **Allagash Wilderness Waterway** canoe trip, which can be done end-to-end in 7 to 10 days. Some 80 camp-sites are spaced along the nearly 100-mile route, which includes a 9-mile stretch of Class I–II white water. For a map and brochure, contact the **Bureau of Parks and Recreation,** Maine Department of Conservation, State House Station #22, Augusta, ME 04333 (☎ 207/287-3821). The Allagash is also served by a number of outfitters, who can provide everything from a complete guide service to a simple car shuttle. You can't travel very far in Maine without stumbling upon a great canoe trip. Two excel-lent sources of information are the *AMC River Guide: Maine* and *Quiet Water Canoe Guide: Maine,* both published by the Appalachian Mountain Club, 5 Joy St., Boston, MA 02108.

FISHING   Maine draws anglers from throughout the Northeast who indulge their grand obsession on Maine's 6,000 lakes and ponds and its countless miles of rivers and streams.

For options on rustic fishing camps statewide, request one of the attractive brochures that describes more than 50 sporting camps between the Rangeley Lakes and Eagle Lake near Fort Kent from **Maine Sporting Camp Association,** P.O. Box 89, Jay, ME 04239.

Nonresident licenses are $50 for the season, or $21 for 3 days. Seven- and fifteen-day licenses are also available. You can purchase licenses at many outdoor shops or general stores. For a booklet of fishing regulations, contact the Fisheries Division at **Inland Fisheries and Wildlife,** 284 State St., Station # 41, Augusta, ME 04333 (☎ 207/287-5261).

HIKING   Maine is home to 10 peaks over 4,000 feet and trails abound. Acadia National Park offers superb and surprisingly tranquil hiking, given the huge popu-larity of the park. Happily for hikers, few visitors venture far from their cars, leaving the trail system relatively unpopulated. In western Maine, 50,000 acres of the White Mountains spill over the border from New Hampshire and boast an excellent network of trails. There are a number of pathways in and around Evans Notch that offer oppor-tunities for hikers of all levels. Finally, there's the dramatic Bigelow Range near the Sugarloaf/USA ski resort, which offers challenging trails and stunning vistas from high, blustery ridges. The Appalachian Trail traverses the range; a good source of trail information is in the AT guide (see "Backpacking," above).

SEA KAYAKING   Paddlers nationwide migrate to Maine in the summer for ✪ **world-class sea kayaking.** The 3,500 miles of rocky coastline and the thousands of off-shore islands have created a wondrous kayaker's playground. It's a sport that can be extremely dangerous (when the weather shifts, the seas can turn on you in a matter of min-utes), but can yield plenty of returns for those with the proper equipment and skills.

The nation's first long-distance water trail was created here in 1987 when the **Maine Island Trail** was established. This 325-mile waterway winds along the coast from Portland to Machias, and incorporates some 70 state and privately owned islands along the route. Members of the Maine Island Trail Association, a private nonprofit organization, help maintain and monitor the islands and in turn are granted permis-sion to visit and camp on them as long as they follow certain restrictions (for example, don't visit designated islands during seabird nesting season). Membership is $40 per year; contact the **Maine Island Trail Association,** P.O. Box C, Rockland, ME 04841 (☎ **207/596-6456** or 207/761-8225).

For novices, Maine has a number of kayak outfitters offering guided excursions ranging from an afternoon to a week. Outfitters include **Maine Island Kayak Co.,** 70 Luther St., Peaks Island, ME 04108 (☎ **207/766-2373**), and **Maine Sports Outfitters,** P.O. Box 956, Rockport, ME 04856 (☎ **800/722-0826** or 207/236-8797). Write or call to request information on upcoming trips.

SKIING   Maine has two major downhill ski resorts, as well as 10 smaller areas. The two big resorts, Sugarloaf and Sunday River, came under the same ownership in 1996, but both have distinct characters. **Sugarloaf** is compactly arrayed on a single large peak and offers the highest vertical drop in New England after Vermont's Killington. The resort's base area is self-contained like an established campus and is a big hit with families.

Sunday River seems to keep growing lengthwise along it undulating ridge—the local nickname for it is "Someday Bigger." It's a less established resort and its base area is still a bit rough around the edges—think of it as more of a brash community college. But it offers diverse skiing terrain and state-of-the-art snowmaking and grooming.

The medium and small mountains cater primarily to the local market but offer good alternatives for travelers who'd just as soon avoid the flash and crowds of the two larger areas. Of the midsize areas, **Shawnee Peak** and **Saddleback** have small resort complexes at or near their bases, and offer better bargains and fewer crowds; Shawnee Peak is open for night skiing until 10pm, 6 nights each week. **Mount Abram,** which is near Sunday River, has developed a solid reputation among telemark skiers. **Squaw Mountain** overlooking Moosehead Lake is the best choice for an old-fashioned bargain and features twisty, narrow trails and great views from the summit.

For a pamphlet with basic information about Maine's ski areas, contact **Ski Maine Association** (P.O. Box 7566, Portland, ME 04112; www.skimaine.com). The association maintains a recorded announcement of current downhill **ski conditions** statewide in season; call ☎ **800/533-9595** or 207/773-7669 in Maine.

Cross-country skiers have a glorious mix of terrain to choose from, although groomed cross-country ski areas aren't as extensive in Maine as in neighboring New Hampshire or Vermont. Sunday River, Saddleback, and Sugarloaf all have cross-country ski areas at or near their downhill complexes. For further information about cross-country ski areas in Maine, contact the **Maine Nordic Council** (☎ **800/ 754-9263**).

WHITE-WATER RAFTING   Maine's three northern rivers are dam-controlled, which means that good rafting is available throughout the season. The **Dead River** has a limited release schedule; it's opened only a half-dozen times for rafting in early summer and fall; smaller releases allow paddling in inflatable kayaks during the summer. The **Kennebec River** offers monstrous waves just below the dam, then tapers off into a gentle afternoon paddle as you float out of a scenic gorge. The west branch of the **Penobscot River** has a challenging, technical section called the Cribworks at the outset, several serious drops and falls after that, and dramatic views of Mount Katahdin along the route.

Raft Maine (☎ **800/723-8633** or 207/824-3694) is a trade association of white-water outfitters in Maine. Call their toll-free line and they'll connect you to one of their member outfitters. You can also learn more about rafting at their Web site, **www.raftmaine.com.**

WINDJAMMING   An ideal way to combine time in the outdoors with relative luxury and an easy-to-digest education in maritime history is aboard a windjammer cruise on the coast. Maine boasts a sizable fleet of vintage sailing ships that offer private cabins, meals, entertainment, and adventure. The ships range in size from 53 to 132 feet, and most are berthed around Rockland and Camden. You choose your adventure: an array of excursions are available, from simple overnights to weeklong expeditions gunkholing among Maine's thousands of scenic islands and coves. For information on windjamming vacations, contact **Maine Windjammer Association** (☎ **800/807-9463**).

2 The South Coast

Maine's southern coast runs roughly from the state line at Kittery to Portland, and is the destination of the great majority of travelers into the state (including many day trippers from the Boston area). While it will take some doing to find privacy and remoteness here, you'll will turn up at least two excellent reasons for a detour: the long, sandy beaches that are the region's hallmark, and the almost tactile sense of history in the coastal villages.

Thanks to quirks of geography, nearly all of Maine's sandy beaches are located in this 60-mile stretch of coastline. It's not hard to find a relaxing sandy spot, whether you prefer dunes and the lulling sound of the surf or the carny atmosphere of a festive beach town. The waves are dependent on the weather—during a good Northeast blow (especially prevalent in spring and fall) they pound the shores and threaten beach houses built decades ago. During the balmy days of midsummer the ocean can be as gentle as a farm pond, with barely audible waves lapping timidly at the shore.

One thing all beaches share in common: they're washed by the frigid waters of the Gulf of Maine. Except in the very young, who seem immune to blood-chilling temperatures, swimming sessions here tend to be very brief and often accompanied by shrieks, whoops, and agitated hand-waving. The beach season itself is also brief and intense, running from July 4th to Labor Day. Before and after, beach towns lapse into a lazy slumber.

KITTERY & THE YORKS

Driving into Maine from the south, as most visitors do, the first town you'll come to is **Kittery**. Kittery was once famous nationally for its naval yard (it's still operating), but regionally at least Kittery is now better known for the dozens of factory outlets that cluster here. (Why they chose to blossom here and not a couple of miles away in sales-tax-free New Hampshire remains an enduring mystery.) Maine has the second highest number of outlet malls in the nation (only California has more), and Kittery is home to a good many of them.

"The Yorks," just to the north, are comprised of three towns that share a name but little else. In fact, it's rare to find three such well-defined and diverse New England archetypes in such a compact area. **York Village** is redolent with early American history and architecture. **York Harbor** reached its zenith during America's late Victorian era, when wealthy urbanites constructed rambling cottages at the ocean's edge. **York Beach** has a turn-of-the-century beach town feel, with loud amusements, taffy shops, a modest zoo, and small gabled summer homes set in crowded enclaves near the beach.

ESSENTIALS

GETTING THERE   Kittery is accessible from I-95 or Route 1, with exits well marked. The Yorks are reached most easily from Exit 1 of the Maine Turnpike. From

Southern Maine Coast

5

26

117

Turner

Winthrop

North
Waterford

5

118

South Paris

4

11

202

Norway

495

201

117

Mechanic
Falls

Lewiston

Richmond

Lovell

Auburn

196

Lisbon
Falls

95

302

Bridgton

*Long
Lake*

11

26

136

Bath

Casco

Brunswick

5

117

Naples

11

*Saco
R.*

Gray

Freeport

Hiram

N. Windham

South Freeport

209

Cornish

*Sebago
Lake*

Yarmouth

Harpswell Center

35

South Harpswell

5

25

202

Westbrook

302

Bailey Island

*Casco
Bay*

Limerick

Portland

Hollis
Center

4

South Portland

To Nova Scotia
→

11

95

Cape
Elizabeth

Shapleigh

5

Old Orchard
Beach

*Saco
Bay*

Alfred

111

Saco

109

Sanford

Biddeford

TNPK.

202

4

109

1

MAINE

Kennebunk

North
Berwick

Kennebunkport

Rochester

95

Atlantic

Berwick

Wells

Ocean

Somersworth

Ogunquit

Dover

Cape Neddick

**New
Hampshire**

Maine

York Beach

Durham

Kittery

York Village

108

York Harbor

Portsmouth

0   16 km
10 mi.

N

1A

Exeter

NA-0138

the exit, look for Route 1A just south of the turnpike exit. This route connects all three York towns.

VISITOR INFORMATION   Travelers entering the state on I-95 can stock up on travel information for the region and beyond at the **Kittery Information Center** (☎ 207/439-1319), located at a well-marked rest area. Open 8am to 6pm in summer, 9am to 5pm year-round, it's amply stocked with brochures, and the helpful staff can answer most questions.

The **York Chamber of Commerce,** P.O. Box 417, York, ME 03909 (☎ 207/363-4422), operates an attractive, helpful information center at 571 Route 1, a short distance from the turnpike exit. It's open 9am to 5pm daily (until 6pm Fridays). A trackless trolley (a bus retrofitted to look like an old-fashioned trolley) regularly links all three York towns and provides a convenient way to explore without having to scare up parking spots at every stop. Hop the trolley at one of the well-marked stops for a 1-hour narrated tour ($3), or disembark along the way and explore by foot ($1.50 for a partial trip).

EXPLORING KITTERY

Kittery's consumer mecca is 4 miles south of York on Route 1. Some 120 factory outlets flank the highway, scattered among more than a dozen strip malls. Name-brand retailers include Champion, Anne Klein, Old Navy, Harry & David, Sunglass Hut, Tommy Hilfiger, Mikasa, J. Crew, Izod, Bose, and Black and Decker. The area can be tough to navigate in peak season owing to the four lanes of heavy summer traffic and capricious restrictions on turns. Information on current outlets is available from ☎ 888/548-8379, or on the web at www.thekitteryoutlets.com.

My advice: If you're headed north, wait until Freeport (60 miles away) to indulge your urge to acquire. In Freeport (as in Manchester, Vermont), you can park once and reconnoiter most of the outlet village on foot.

DISCOVERING LOCAL HISTORY

Old York Historical Society. Route 1A (York St.)., York. ☎ 207/363-4974. $6 adults, $2.50 children 6 to 16 includes admission to all buildings. Tues–Sat 10am–5pm; Sun 1–5pm. (Last tour leaves at 4pm.) Closed Oct–May.

John Hancock is famous for his oversize signature on the Declaration of Independence, his tenure as governor of Massachusetts, and the insurance company named after him. What's not so well known is his earlier checkered past as a businessman. Hancock was the proprietor of Hancock Wharf, a failed enterprise that's but one of the intriguing historic sites at York Village.

First settled in 1624, York Village has several early homes open to the public. Tickets are available at any of the properties, but a good place to start is **Jefferds Tavern,** across from the handsome old burying ground. Changing exhibits here document various facets of early life. Next door is the **School House,** furnished as it might have been in the last century. A 10-minute walk along lightly traveled Lindsay Road will bring you to **Hancock Wharf,** which is next door to the George Marshall Store. Also nearby is the **Elizabeth Perkins House** with its well-preserved Colonial Revival interiors.

The two don't-miss buildings in the society's collection are the intriguing **Old Gaol,** built in 1719 with its now-musty dungeons for criminals and debtors. The jail is the oldest surviving public building in the United States. Just down the knoll from the jail is the **Emerson-Wilcox House,** built in the mid-1700s. Added to periodically over the years, it's a virtual catalog of architectural styles and early decorative arts.

BEACHES

York Beach actually consists of two beaches—**Long Sands Beach** and **Short Sands Beach**—separated by a rocky headland and a small island capped by scenic **Nubble Light.** Both offer plenty of room for sunning and Frisbees when the tide is out. When the tide is in, they're both a bit cramped. Short Sands fronts the town of York Beach with its candlepin bowling and video arcades. It's the better bet for families traveling with kids who have short attention spans. Long Sands runs along Route 1A, across from a profusion of motels, summer homes, and convenience stores. Parking at both beaches is metered (50¢ per hour).

WHERE TO STAY

For basic accommodations, try York Beach, which has a proliferation of motels and guest cottages facing Long Sands Beach. Even with this abundance, it's advisable to reserve ahead during prime season. And don't expect any real bargains midsummer, even among the most basic of motels. Among those offering basic accommodation on or very near the beach are: **The Anchorage Inn** (☎ **207/363-5112**), **Sea Latch Motor Inn** (☎ **800/441-2993** or 207/363-4400), and the **Sunrise Motel** (☎ **800/ 242-0750** or 207/363-4542).

In Kittery

Inn at Portsmouth Harbor. 6 Water St., Kittery, ME 03904. ☎ **207/439-4040.** Fax 207/438-9286. www.innatportsmouth.com. E-mail: innph@cybertours.com. 6 units. TV TEL. May–Oct $125–$135 double; Nov–April $85–$125. Rates include full breakfast. 2-night minimum stay in summer, holidays. AE, MC, V.

The Inn at Portsmouth Harbor got new owners and a new name in late 1998—it used to be the Gundalow Inn—along with some sprucing up (all rooms now have TVs and telephones). But it's still the location that wins fans. This 1899 home is located just across the river from Portsmouth, New Hampshire, about a half-mile walk across the bridge. Guests here get a taste of small coastal town life, yet with access to the restaurants and shopping of the city. The rooms are tastefully restored and furnished with eclectic antiques; a first-floor common room and a small front porch allow guests to unwind with grace after a day's exertions.

In York

Dockside Guest Quarters. Harris Island (P.O. Box 205), York, ME 03909. ☎ **207/ 363-2868.** Fax 207/363-1977. www.docksidegq.com. E-mail: info@docksidegq.com. 25 units, 2 with shared bath. TV. Mid-June to early Sept, $69–$174 double. 2-night minimum July–Sept. DISC, MC, V. Closed weekdays Nov–May. Drive south on Rte. 103 from Rte. 1A in York Harbor; after bridge over York River, turn left and follow signs.

David and Harriet Lusty established this quiet retreat in 1954, and recent additions (mostly new cottages) haven't dulled the friendly, maritime flavor of the place. Situated on an island connected to the mainland by a small bridge, the inn occupies nicely landscaped grounds shady with maples and white pines. Five of the rooms are in the main house, built in 1885, but the bulk of the accommodations are in small, town house–style cottages constructed between 1968 and 1998. These are simply furnished, bright, and airy, and all have private decks that overlook the entrance to York Harbor. (Several rooms also offer woodstoves.)

Dining: The inn operates a locally popular restaurant on the property, serving traditional New England meals like broiled halibut, baked stuffed lobster, and braised lamb. Entrees are $13 to $17.

Amenities: Rowboats, badminton, croquet, ocean swimming.

Union Bluff Hotel. Beach St. (at the north end of Short Sands Beach), York Beach, ME 03910. ☎ **207/363-1333** or 800/833-0721 (out of state). www.unionbluff.com. 61 units. A/C TV TEL. Summer $98–$148 double; early fall $68–$88 double; spring and late fall $58–$78 double; winter $48–$68 double. $208 suite in season; $158 off-season. AE, DISC, MC, V.

Viewed from Short Sands Beach, the Union Bluff Hotel, with its stumpy turrets, dormers, and prominent porches, has the look and feel of an old-fashioned beach hotel. So it's a bit of a surprise to learn it was built in 1989 (the fifth hotel to rise on this site since the late 1800s). Inside is a generic-modern building with most amenities. Rooms have oak furniture, wall-to-wall carpeting, and small refrigerators. There's a comfortable and quiet deck on the top floor for getting away from it all (alas, no ocean view). Step outside and you're virtually at the beach and the Fun-O-Rama arcade with its candlepin bowling and banks of video games. (It can be noisy in the evening if your room faces this direction.) A newly acquired motel next door added 21 rooms to the mix, and are furnished simply. Stick to the main inn for the better views; the best rooms are the suites on the top floor, which offer beach vistas from sitting areas in the turrets.

Dining: On the ground floor there's a locally popular lounge and a restaurant; both are open only during the warmer months. The restaurant features American and Italian specialties, including pasta, burgers, and steamed lobsters.

WHERE TO DINE
In Kittery
✪ **Chauncey Creek Lobster Pier.** Chauncey Creek Rd., Kittery Point. ☎ 207/439-1030 or 439-9024. No reservations. Lobsters priced to market; other items $1.50–$8.95. Daily 11am–8pm (until 7pm during shoulder seaons); open Tues–Sun only after Labor Day. Closed Columbus Day–Mother's Day. Located between Kittery Point and York on Rte. 103; watch for signs. AE, DISC, MC, V.

It's not on the wild, open ocean, but Chauncey's remains one of the most scenic lobster pounds in the state, not the least because the Spinney Family, which has been selling lobsters here since the 1950s, takes such obvious pride in their place. You reach the pound by walking down a wooden ramp to the water's edge, where a broad deck and plenty of brightly painted picnic tables await.

Lobster, served hot and fresh, is the specialty, of course, but they also offer up steamed mussels (in wine and garlic) and clams. This is an a la carte place—buy a bag of potato chips and sodas while waiting for your lobsters to cook. There's a BYOB policy, and you can bring in any other food you want provided they don't sell it here. Afterward, wash up at the outdoor sink (labelled "finger bowl") on the deck.

In The Yorks
✪ **Cape Neddick Inn Restaurant.** 1233 Rte. 1, Cape Neddick. ☎ **207/363-2899.** Reservations recommended. Main courses $16–$28. DISC, MC, V. Summer daily 5:30–9:30pm; Sunday brunch 11:30am–3pm (mid-Oct to Mar only). Closed 1 or 2 days weekly during off-season (call ahead). REGIONAL/AMERICAN.

This fine inn has offered some of the consistently best dining in southern Maine since 1979, and continues to do so under current ownership. Located in an elegant structure on a relatively quiet stretch of Route 1, the Cape Neddick Inn has an open, handsome dining area that mixes traditional and modern. The old comes in the cozy golden glow of the room. The modern is the artwork, which changes frequently and showcases some of the region's better painters and sculptors.

The creative menu changes seasonally to make the most of local products. There's an extensive selection of appetizers, including a lobster roll with wasabi, and applewood-smoked seafood (smoked on premises) served tossed in an apple cider vinaigrette on Rhode Island johnnycakes. Depending on the season, main courses might include cod wrapped in smoked bacon and served on cabbage, or grilled rack of pork with firecracker shrimp on saffron basmati rice. Diners can select from more than 100 wines.

Goldenrod Restaurant. Railroad Road and Ocean Avenue, York Beach. ☎ 207/363-2621. www.thegoldenrod.com. Breakfast $2.10–$5.25; lunch and dinner entrees $1.75–$7.50. MC, V. Memorial Day to Labor Day daily 8am–10pm (until 9pm in June); Labor Day to Columbus Day Wed–Sun 8am–3pm. Closed Columbus Day to Memorial Day. FAMILY-STYLE.

This beach town classic is the place for local color—it's been a summer institution in York Beach since it first opened in 1896. It's easy to find: look for visitors gawking through plate-glass windows at the ancient taffy machines hypnotically churning out taffy in volumes enough (63 tons a year) to make busloads of dentists very wealthy. The restaurant is behind the taffy-and-fudge operation, and is low on frills and long on atmosphere. Diners sit on stout oak furniture around a stone fireplace, or at the marble soda fountain. There are dark beams overhead and the sort of linoleum floor you don't see much anymore. Breakfast offerings are the standards: omelets, waffles, griddle cakes and bakery items. Lunch is equally predictable American fare (soups, club sandwiches, hamburgers, hot dogs), but well presented. As for dinner, you'd probably be better served heading to some place more creative.

OGUNQUIT

Ogunquit is a bustling beachside town that's attracted vacationers and artists for more than a century. While notable for its abundant and elegant summer resort architecture, Ogunquit is most famous for its 3½-mile white-sand beach, backed by grassy dunes. The beach serves as the town's front porch, and everyone drifts over there at least once a day when the sun is shining.

Ogunquit's fame as an art colony dates to around 1890, when Charles H. Woodbury arrived and declared the place an "artist's paradise." He was followed by artists Walt Kuhn, Elihu Vedder, Yasuo Kuniyoshi, and Rudolph Dirks, who was best known for creating the "Katzenjammer Kids" comic strip.

In the current century, the town found quiet fame as a destination for gay travelers, at a time when being gay was not acknowledged in polite society. Ogunquit has retained its appeal for gays through the years, and visitors often find themselves at local enterprises run by gay entrepreneurs. However, the scene is low-key compared to Provincetown, Massachusetts. It's more like an understated family resort, where a good many family members just happen to be gay.

Despite the architectural gentility and the overall civility of the place, the town can feel overrun with tourists during the peak summer season, especially on weekends. The crowds are part of the allure for some Ogunquit regulars.

ESSENTIALS

GETTING THERE Ogunquit is located on Route 1 between York and Wells. It's accessible from either Exit 1 or Exit 2 of the Maine Turnpike.

VISITOR INFORMATION The **Ogunquit Welcome Center,** P.O. Box 2289, Ogunquit, ME 03907 (☎ 207/646-5533 or 207/646-2939), is located on Route 1 south of the village center. It's open daily 9am to 5pm Memorial Day to Columbus Day (until 8pm during the peak summer season) and weekdays during the off-season. On the Web, head to **www.ogunquit.org.**

GETTING AROUND The village of Ogunquit is centered around an intersection that seems fiendishly designed to cause massive traffic foul-ups in summer. Parking in and around the village is also tight and relatively expensive (expect to pay $6 per day or more). As a result, Ogunquit is best reconnoitered on foot or by bike.

A number of trackless trollies (with names like Dolly and Ollie—you get the idea) run all day long from mid-May to Columbus Day between Perkins Cove and the Wells town line to the north, with detours to the sea down Beach and Ocean streets. The cost is 50¢ per boarding; the driver can't make change. It's well worth the small expense to avoid the hassles of driving and parking.

EXPLORING THE TOWN

The village center is good for an hour or two of browsing among the boutiques, or sipping a cappuccino at one of the several coffee emporia.

From the village you can walk a mile to scenic Perkins Cove along **Marginal Way,** a mile-long oceanside pathway once used for herding cattle to pasture. Earlier in this century, the land was bought by a local developer who deeded the right-of-way to the town. The pathway, which is wide and well-maintained, departs across from the Sea-castles Resort on Shore Road. It passes tide pools, pocket beaches, and rocky, fissured bluffs, all of which are worth exploring. The seascape can be spectacular (especially after a storm), but Marginal Way can also be spectacularly crowded during fair weather weekends. To elude the crowds, I recommend heading out in the very early morning.

Perkins Cove, accessible either from Marginal Way or by driving south on Shore Road and veering left at the Y intersection, is a small, well-protected harbor that seems custom-designed for a photo opportunity. As such, it attracts visitors by the busload, carload, and boatload, and is often heavily congested. A handful of galleries, restaurants, and T-shirt shops catering to the tourist trade occupy a cluster of quaint buildings between the harbor and the sea. An intriguing pedestrian drawbridge is operated by whomever happens to be handy, allowing sailboats to come and go.

Perkins Cove is also home to a handful of deep-sea fishing and tour boat operators, who offer trips of various durations. Try the *Deborah Ann* (☎ 207/361-9501) for whale watching (two tours daily), or the *Ugly Anne* (☎ 207/646-7202) for deep-sea fishing. One last bit of advice: if crowds and tourist traps make you break out in a rash, steer well clear of Perkins Cove.

Not far from the cove is the **Ogunquit Museum of American Art,** 183 Shore Road (☎ 207/646-4909), one of the best small art museums in the nation. Set back from the road in a grassy glen overlooking the rocky shore, the museum's spectacular view initially overwhelms the artwork as visitors walk through the door. But stick around a few minutes—the changing exhibits in this architecturally engaging modern building of cement block, slate, and glass will get your attention soon enough, since the curators have a track record of staging superb shows and attracting national attention. (Be sure to note the bold, underappreciated work of Henry Strater, the Ogunquit artist who founded the museum in 1953.) A 1,400-square-foot wing opened in 1996, adding welcome new exhibition space. The museum is open July 1 to September 30 from 10:30am to 5pm Monday to Saturday, and 2 to 5pm on Sunday. Admission is $4 for adults, $3 for seniors and students, children under 12 are free.

BEACHES

Ogunquit's **main beach** is more than 3 miles long, and three paid parking lots (around $2 per hour) are located along its length. The most popular access point is at the foot of Beach Street, which connects to Ogunquit Village. The beach ends at a sandy spit, where the Ogunquit River flows into the sea, and offers changing rooms and a handful of informal restaurants. It's also the most crowded part of the beach. Less congested options are at **Footbridge Beach** (turn on Ocean Avenue off Route 1 north of the village center) and Moody Beach (turn on Eldridge Avenue in Wells).

WHERE TO STAY

Just a few steps from Ogunquit's main downtown intersection is the meticulously maintained **Studio East Motel,** 43 Main St. (☎ 207/646-7297). It's open April to mid-November, with peak season rates running $94 to $119 (from $39 in spring and early fall, and from $69 in early summer). Rooms are basic, but all have refrigerators; microwaves are available free to those staying 3 nights or more. A restaurant serving traditional New England fare is on the premises.

Beachmere Inn. Beachmere Rd., Ogunquit, ME 03907. ☎ **800/336-3983** or 207/646-2021. Fax 207/646-2231. www.beachmereinn.com. 53 units. A/C TV TEL. Peak season $110–$195, midseason $75–$140, off-season $65–$95. Rates include continental breakfast. 3-night minimum stay in summer. AE, CB, DC, DISC, MC, V. Closed mid-Dec to April.

Run by the same family since 1937, the Beachmere Inn sprawls across a grassy hillside (the inn occupies about 4 acres) and nearly every room has a view northward up Ogunquit's famous beach. Guests choose from two buildings. The Beachmere Victorian dates to the 1890s and is all turrets and porches. Next door is the dated but fun Beachmere South, a two-story motel-like structure done up in 1960s modern style, featuring concrete slathered with a stucco finish. The rooms are spacious (some are minisuites), interestingly angled, and all have private balconies or patios and great views. The beach is a short walk away via the Marginal Way pathway. When these rooms are filled, guests are offered rooms in the Bullfrog Cottage nearby. The five units are darker, lack views, and are less impressively furnished, but are spacious and popular with families.

Marginal Way House. Wharf Lane (P.O. Box 697), Ogunquit, ME 03907. ☎ **207/646-8801** or 207/363-6566 in winter. 30 units, 1 with private bathroom down the hall. A/C TV. Peak season $85–$175 double; shoulder seasons $42–$143 double. 2-night minimum stay holiday weekends. MC, V. Closed late Oct to mid-Apr. Pets allowed off-season.

If you travel for vistas, this is your place. Even if your room lacks a sweeping ocean view you've got the run of the lawn and the guest house porch, both of which overlook Ogunquit River to the beach and the sea beyond. This attractive compound centers around a four-story, mid-19th-century guest house, with summery, basic rooms that feature white painted furniture. Room 7 is the best, with a private porch and canopy and a drop-dead view. The guest house is surrounded by four more-or-less modern outbuildings, which lack charm but feature motel-style rooms that are clean, comfortable, and very, very bright. The whole affair is situated on a large, grassy lot on a quiet cul-de-sac. It's hard to believe that you're smack in the middle of Ogunquit, with both the beach and the village just a few minutes' walk away. All rooms have refrigerators; for longer stays one- and two-bedroom efficiencies are available.

Nellie Littlefield House. 9 Shore Rd., Ogunquit, ME 03907. ☎ **207/646-1692.** 8 units. A/C TV TEL. Peak season $140–$195, midseason $90–$140, off-season $75–$120. Rates include full breakfast. 2-night minimum stay weekends, 3-night minimum on holidays. DISC, MC, V. Closed late Oct to Apr. Children over 12 welcome.

This 1889 home stands impressively at the edge of Ogunquit's compact commercial district, and the prime location and the regal Queen Anne architecture are the main draws here. The updated carpeted rooms feature a mix of modern and antique reproduction furnishings, and several have refrigerators. Four rooms to the rear have private decks, but views are limited, mostly of the unlovely motel next door. The most spacious room? The third floor J. H. Littlefield suite, with two TVs and a Jacuzzi. The most unique? The circular Grace Littlefield room, located in the upper turret and overlooking the street. The basement features a compact fitness room with modern equipment.

WHERE TO DINE

✪ **Arrows.** Berwick Road. ☎ **207/361-1100.** Reservations strongly recommended. Main courses $29.95–$32.95. MC, V. May and Columbus Day to Thanksgiving Fri–Sun 6–9:30pm; June and Sept to Columbus Day Wed–Sun 6–9:30pm; July–Aug Tues–Sun 6–9:30pm. Closed late-Nov to Apr. Turn uphill at the Key Bank in the village; the restaurant is 1.9 miles on your right. NEW AMERICAN.

When owner/chefs Mark Gaier and Clark Frasier opened Arrows in 1988 they quickly put Ogunquit on the national culinary map. They've done so by not only creating an elegant and intimate atmosphere but by serving up some of the freshest, most innovative cooking in New England. The emphasis is on local products, sometimes very local. The salad greens are grown in gardens on the grounds, and much of the rest is grown or raised locally. The food transcends traditional New England, and is deftly prepared with exotic twists and turns. Frasier lived and traveled for a time in Asia, and his Far Eastern experiences tend to influence the menu, which changes nightly. Among the more popular recurrent dishes is the homemade prosciutto (hams are strung up around the restaurant to cure in the off-season) served with pears, toasted pumpkin seeds, and olive oil. The bento box includes marinated lamb brochettes, orange cabbage, and "strange flavored eggplant"; the grilled beef tenderloin is spiced with a Szechuan peppercorn marinade. The wine list is top-rate. Arrows isn't for the timid of wallet, but certainly will make for a special evening.

✪ **Hurricane.** Oarweed Rd., Perkins Cove. ☎ **207/646-6348** or 800/649-6348 (Me. & N.H. only). Reservations recommended. Lunch items mostly $9–$14; main dinner courses $16–$30. AE, DC, DISC, MC, V. Daily 11:30am–9:30pm (open until 10:30pm May–Oct). NEW AMERICAN.

Tucked away amid the T-shirt kitsch of Perkins Cove is one of southern Maine's classier dining experiences. The plain shingled exterior of the building, set along a curving, narrow lane, doesn't even hint at what you'll find inside. The narrow dining room is divided into two smallish halves, but soaring windows overlooking the Gulf of Maine lend a sense that the place is larger than it actually is. Hurricane's menu changes four times each year, but owner Brooks MacDonald is known for his consistently creative concoctions, like the appetizer of deviled Maine lobster cakes served with a tangy fresh salsa (so popular it's always available). At lunch look for salmon burgers or roasted wild mushrooms served over pasta with truffle oil. At dinner, there's delectable lobster cioppino, and a pistachio-coated veal chop with a light pomegranate sauce. Added bonus: Hurricane makes the best martinis in town.

THE KENNEBUNKS

"The Kennebunks" consist of the villages of **Kennebunk** and **Kennebunkport,** both situated along the shores of small rivers. The region was first settled in the mid-1600s and flourished after the American Revolution, when ship captains, ship builders, and prosperous merchants constructed the imposing, solid homes. The Kennebunks are famed for their striking historic architecture and expansive beaches.

ESSENTIALS

GETTING THERE   Kennebunk is located off Exit 3 of the Maine Turnpike. Kennebunkport is 3.5 miles southeast of Kennebunk on Port Road (Route 35).

VISITOR INFORMATION   The Kennebunk-Kennebunkport Chamber of Commerce, P.O. Box 740, Kennebunk, ME 04043 (☎ **800/982-4421** or 207/967-0857), can answer your questions year-round by phone or at their offices on

Route 9 next to Meserve's Market. The **Kennebunkport Information Center** (☎ 207/967-8600) is off Dock Square (next to Ben & Jerry's) and is open daily throughout the summer and fall.

The local trolley (bus) makes several stops in and around Kennebunkport and also serves the beaches. The fare is $6 per person per day, and includes unlimited trips.

EXPLORING KENNEBUNKPORT

Kennebunkport is the summer home of former President George Bush, whose family has summered here for much of this century. Given that, it has the tweedy, upper-crust feel that one might expect of the place. This historic village, whose streets were laid out during days of travel by foot and horse, is subject to monumental traffic jams around the town center. If the municipal lot off the square ($2 per hour) is full, head north on North St. a few minutes to the free long-term lot and catch the trolley back into town. Or walk—it's a pleasant walk of about 10 or 15 minutes from the lot to Dock Square.

Dock Square has a pleasantly wharflike feel to it, with low buildings of mixed vintages and styles (you'll find mansard, gabled, and hip roofs side by each), but the flavor is mostly clapboard and shingles. The boutiques in the area are attractive, and many feature creative artworks and crafts. But Kennebunkport's real attraction is found in the surrounding blocks, where the side streets are lined with one of the nation's richest assortments of early American homes. The neighborhoods are especially ripe with examples of Federal-style homes; many have been converted to bed-and-breakfasts (see "Where to Stay," below).

Aimless wandering is a good tactic for exploring Kennebunkport, but at the least make an effort to stop by the **Richard A. Nott House** (☎ 207/967-2751) in your travels. Situated on Maine Street at the head of Spring Street, this imposing Greek Revival house was built, 1853 and is a Victorian-era aficionado's dream. It remained untouched by the Nott family through the years, and was donated to the local historical society with the stipulation that it remain forever unchanged. It still boasts the original wallpaper, carpeting, and furnishings. It's open 1 to 4pm Tuesday to Friday from mid-June to mid-October. Admission is $3 adult, $2 children 6 to 12.

Ocean Drive from Dock Square to Walkers Point and beyond is lined with opulent summer homes overlooking surf and rocky shore. You'll likely recognize the former president's home at Walkers Point when you arrive. If it's not familiar from the several years it spent in the national spotlight, look for the crowds with telephoto lenses.

✪ **The Seashore Trolley Museum.** Log Cabin Rd., Kennebunkport. ☎ **207/967-2800.** www.gwi.net/trolley/. $7 adults, $4.50 children 6–16, $6 seniors, $22 family. Daily May to mid-Oct (10am–6pm during July & Aug; shorter hours otherwise); weekends only to late Oct. Closed Nov–April. Head north from Kennebunkport on North Street; look for signs.

A short drive north of Kennebunkport on Log Cabin Road is one of the quirkiest and more engaging museums in the state. This scrapyard-masquerading-as-a-museum ("world's oldest and largest museum of its type") was founded in 1939 to preserve a disappearing way of life, and today the collection contains more than 200 trolleys from around the world, including specimens from Glasgow, Moscow, San Francisco, and Rome. (Of course, there's also a streetcar named "Desire" from New Orleans.)

About 40 of the cars still operate, and the admission charge includes rides on a 2-mile track. The other cars, some of which still contain turn of the century advertising, are on display outdoors and in vast storage sheds. A good museum inspires awe and educates its visitors on the sly. This one does so deftly, and not until visitors are driving away are they likely to realize how much they learned about how America got around before there was a car in every garage.

BEACHES

The coastal area around Kennebunkport is home to several of the state's finest beaches. Southward across the river (technically this is Kennebunk although it's much closer to Kennebunkport) are **Gooch's Beach** and **Kennebunk Beach.** Head eastward on Beach Street. (from the intersection of Routes 9 and 35) and you'll soon wind into a handsome colony of eclectic shingled summer homes (some improbably grand, some modest). The narrow road twists past sandy beaches and rocky headlands. The area can be frightfully congested when traveling by car in the summer; avoid the local version of gridlock by traveling via foot or bike.

Goose Rocks Beach is north of Kennebunkport off Route 9 (watch for signs), and is the preferred destination for those who prefer crowds light, and are more drawn to beaches than the beach scene. You'll find an enclave of beach homes set amid rustling oaks just off a fine sand beach. Just offshore is a narrow barrier reef that has historically attracted flocks of geese—which in turn lent their name to the beach.

WHERE TO STAY

An unusual choice for budget accommodations is the **Franciscan Guest House,** Beach Street, (☎ 207/967-2011) a former dormitory on the 200-acre grounds of the St. Anthony's Monastery. The 60 rooms are basic and clean and have private baths; guests can stroll the attractive riverside grounds or walk over to Dock Square, about 10 minutes away. Rooms are $55 to $66. No credit cards; open mid-June to mid-September.

Captain Jefferds Inn. 5 Pearl St. (P.O. Box 691), Kennebunkport, ME 04046. ☎ **800/839-6844** or 207/967-2311. www.captainjefferdsinn.com. E-mail: capjeff@ captainjefferdsinn.com. 16 units. $105–$240 double. Rates include full breakfast. MC, V. 2-night minimum stay weekends July–Oct and holidays. Dogs $20 additional by advance reservation.

This 1804 Federal home surrounded by other historic homes was fully done over in 1997, and the new innkeepers have done a superb job in coaxing out the historic feel of the place while giving each room its own personality. Fine antiques abound throughout, and guests will need some persuading to come out of their wonderful rooms once they've settled in. Among the best are Manhattan, with a four-poster bed, fireplace, and beautiful afternoon light; and Assisi, with a restful indoor fountain and rock garden (sounds weird, but it works). The wide price range reflects the varying room sizes, but even the smallest rooms—like Katahdin—are comfortable and well beyond merely adequate. Bright common rooms on the first floor offer alluring lounging space; an elaborate breakfast is served before a fire on cool days, and on the terrace when summer weather permits.

✪ **Captain Lord.** Pleasant and Green sts. (P.O. Box 800), Kennebunkport, ME 04046. ☎ **207/967-3141.** Fax 207/967-3172. www.captainlord.com. E-mail: captain@biddeford. com. 16 units. A/C TEL. Summer and fall $199–$399 double; winter and spring $99–$299. Rates include full breakfast. 2-night minimum stay weekends and holidays year-round (some holidays 3-night minimum). DISC, MC, V. Children 10 and older welcome.

It's simple: This is the best building in Kennebunkport, in the best location, and furnished with the best antiques. It's also one of the most architecturally distinguished inns anywhere, housed in a pale-yellow Federal-style home that peers down a shady lawn toward the river. The adjective "stately" is laughably inadequate.

When you enter the downstairs reception area, you'll know immediately that this is the genuine article, with grandfather clocks and Chippendale highboys—and that's just the front hallway. Off the hall is a comfortable common area with piped-in classical music and a broad brick fireplace. Head up the elliptical staircase to the guest rooms, which are furnished with splendid antiques; 14 feature gas-burning fireplaces. If you're really looking to spoil yourself, book the first-floor Captain's Suite with king-size canopy bed, audio system, TV/VCR, whirlpool, exercise equipment, and shower with a multijet hydro-massage spa. The only complaint I've heard about this place is that it's too nice, too perfect, too friendly. That evidently puts some people on edge.

✪ **The Colony Hotel.** Ocean Ave. (about a mile from Dock Square; P.O. Box 511), Kennebunkport, ME 04046. ☎ **800/552-2363** or 207/967-3331. Fax 207/967-8738. www.the-colony hotel.com/maine. E-mail: info-me@thecolonyhotel.com. 125 units. TEL. $185–$355 double in July & August; off-season rates available. Rates include breakfast and dinner. 2-night minimum stay weekends and holidays in main hotel. AE, MC, V. Closed mid-Oct to mid-May. Pets allowed.

The Colony is one of the handful of oceanside resorts that has preserved intact the classic New England vacation experience. This gleaming white Georgian Revival (built in 1914) lords over the ocean and the mouth of the Kennebunk River. The three-story main inn has 105 rooms, most of which have been updated. The rooms are bright and cheery, simply furnished with summer cottage antiques. Rooms in two of the three outbuildings carry over the rustic elegance of the main hotel; the exception is the East House, a 1950s-era motor hotel at the back edge of the property with 20 charmless motel-style rooms.

Guest rooms lack TVs in the main inn, and that's by design. The Boughton family, which has owned the hotel since 1948, encourages guests to socialize in the evening downstairs in the lobby, on the porch, or at the shuffleboard court, which is lighted for night-time play. A staff naturalist leads guided coastal ecology tours Saturday mornings in July and August.

Dining/Diversions: The massive, pine-paneled dining room seats up to 400, and guests are assigned one table throughout their stay. Dinners begin with a relish tray, but quickly progress to creative regional entrees. On Fridays there's a lobster buffet, and Sunday a jazz brunch. Lunch is served poolside, and a pub menu is available for those seeking for lighter fare. The dining room is open to outsiders, with entrees priced $10 to $22. Live music is offered in the Marine Room lounge on weekends.

Amenities: Bike rental, putting green, game room, library, heated saltwater pool, small beach, conference rooms, poolside sundeck, cocktail lounge, gift shop, free refreshments in lobby, room service, social director, free newspaper, safe-deposit boxes. Health club 3 miles away for $6 fee.

The Tides Inn. Goose Rocks Beach, Kennebunkport, ME 04046. ☎ **207/967-3757.** 22 units (4 share 2 bathrooms). Peak season $165–$225 double with private bath (from $110 off season); $105 with shared bath (from $85 off season). 3-night minimum stay in peak season (mid-June to Labor Day, and all weekends). AE, MC, V. Closed mid-Oct to mid-May.

This is the best bet in the region for a quiet getaway. Located just across the street from Goose Rocks Beach, the Tides Inn is a yellow clapboard and shingle affair dating from 1899 that retains a seaside boarding house feel while providing up-to-date comfort. (Past guests have included Teddy Roosevelt and Arthur Conan Doyle.) The rooms tend toward the small side, but are comfortable and you can hear the lapping of surf from all of them. Among the brightest and most popular are rooms 11, 15, 24, and 29, some of which have bay windows and all of which have ocean views. The parlor has old wicker, TV, and chess for those rainy days. The pub is cozy and features a woodstove and dartboard.

Dining: The Belvedere Room offers upscale traditional dining in a Victorian setting with options such as rack of lamb, shellfish ragout, filet mignon, and boiled lobster. Entrees are $16.95 to $27.95. Less elaborate meals are served in the pub, including salads, burritos, and burgers ($4.50 to $10.25). Breakfast is also offered, but not included in room rates.

✪ **White Barn Inn.** Beach St. (¼ mile east of junction of Routes 9 and 35; P.O. Box 560), Kennebunkport, ME 04046. ☎ 207/967-2321. Fax 207/967-1100. www.whitebarninn. com. E-mail: innkeeper@whitebarninn.com. 24 units. A/C TEL. $160–$250 double, suites $350–$420. Rates include continental breakfast and afternoon tea. 2-night minimum stay weekends, 3-night minimum holiday weekends. AE, MC, V.

The White Barn Inn pampers its guests like no other in Maine. Upon checking in, guests are shown to one of the inn's parlors and offered sherry or brandy while valets in crisp uniforms gather luggage and park the cars. A tour of the inn follows, then guests are left to their own devices. They can avail themselves of the inn's free bikes (including a small fleet of tandems) to head to the beach, or walk cross the street and wander the quiet, shady pathways of St. Anthony's Franciscan Monastery. The rooms are individually decorated in a refined country style that's elegant without being obtrusive.

The inn has an atmosphere that's distinctly European, and the emphasis is on service. I'm not aware of any other inn of this size that offers as many unexpected niceties, like robes, fresh flowers in the rooms, bottled water, and turndown service at night. Nearly half the rooms have wood-burning fireplaces.

Dining: See "Where to Dine," below.

Amenities: Concierge, room service (breakfast only), free newspaper, in-room massage, twice-daily maid service, valet parking, guest safe, afternoon tea, outdoor heated pool, bicycles, nearby ocean beach, conference rooms, sundeck.

WHERE TO DINE

Grissini. 27 Western Ave., Kennebunkport. ☎ 207/967-2211. Reservations encouraged. Main courses $9.95–$15.95. AE, MC, V. Daily 5:30–9:30pm (limited hours and days in the off season; call first). TUSCAN.

Opened by the same folks who run the White Barn Inn, Grissini is a handsome trattoria that offers good value. The mood is rustic Italian writ large: Italian advertising posters line the walls of the soaring, barnlike space, and burning logs in the oversize fireplace takes the chill out of a cool evening. In fact, everything seems oversize, including the plates, flatware, and water goblets. The meals are also luxuriously size and nicely presented, and include a wide range of pastas and pizza, served with considerable flair. (The linguini tossed with seafood is simple, filling, and tasty.) The desserts are competent, not stellar, and include old friends like crème caramel and tiramisu.

Federal Jack's Restaurant and Brew Pub. Lower Village (south bank of Kennebunk River), Kennebunkport. ☎ 207/967-4322. www.shipyard.com. Lunch items $5.25–$12.95; main dinner courses $6.25–$21.95. AE, DISC, MC, V. Daily 11:30am–10pm. PUB FARE.

This light, airy, and modern restaurant is in a retail complex of recent vintage that sits a bit uneasily amid the scrappy boatyards lining the south bank of the Kennebunk River. From the second floor perch (look for a seat on the spacious deck in warm weather) you can gaze across the river toward the shops of Dock Square. The menu features bar food, including hamburgers, steamed mussels, and pizza, and everything is quite well prepared. Watch for specials like the grilled crab and Havarti sandwich. Don't leave without sampling the Shipyard ales, lagers, and porters brewed downstairs, which are among the best in New England. (Brewery tours available.) Consider the ale sampler, which provides tastes of various brews. Nontipplers can enjoy a zesty homemade root beer.

☺ **White Barn Inn.** Beach St., Kennebunkport. ☎ **207/967-2321**. Reservations recommended. Fixed-price dinner $67. AE, MC, V. Daily 6–9pm. Closed 2 weeks in Jan. REGIONAL/NEW AMERICAN.

The setting is magical. The restaurant (attached to an equally magical inn, see above) is housed in an ancient, rustic barn with a soaring interior. (The furnace runs nearly full time in winter to keep the space comfortable.) There's a copper-topped bar off to one side, rich leather seating in the waiting area, a pianist setting the mood, and an eclectic collection of country antiques displayed in the hayloft above. On the tables are floor-length tablecloths, and the chairs feature imported Italian upholstery. The service is impeccable, although those accustomed to more informal settings might find it overly attentive.

The excellent menu changes frequently, but depending on the season you might start with a lobster spring roll with daikon, carrots, snow peas and cilantro, then graduate to a crab-glazed poached fillet of halibut on sweet-pea puree, or pan-seared veal and venison on bacon-roasted butternut squash. Among the more popular dishes is the Maine lobster on homemade fettuccine with cognac coral butter sauce. Anticipate a meal to remember. The White Barn won't let you down.

3 Portland

Portland is Maine's largest city, and easily one of the more attractive and livable small cities on the East Coast—more like a large town than a small city. Strike up a conversation with a resident, and you're likely to get an earful about how easy it is to live here. You can buy superb coffee, see great movies, and get delicious pad thai to go. Yet it's still small enough to walk from one end of town to the other, and postal workers and bank clerks know your name soon after you move here. Despite its outward appearance of being an actual metropolis, Portland has a population of just 65,000, or roughly half that of Peoria, Ill.

ESSENTIALS

GETTING THERE Portland is located off the Maine Turnpike (I-95). Coming from the south, downtown is most easily reached by taking Exit 6A off the turnpike, then following I-295 to downtown. Exit at Franklin Street and follow this eastward until you arrive at the waterfront at the Casco Bay Lines terminal. Turn right on Commercial Street and you'll be at the lower edge of the Old Port. Continue on a few blocks to the visitor's center (see below).

Concord Trailways (☎ **800/639-3317** or 207/828-1151) and **Vermont Transit** (☎ **800/537-3330** or 207/772-6587) offer bus service to Portland from Boston and Bangor. The Vermont Transit bus terminal is located at 950 Congress St. Concord Trailways, which is a few dollars more expensive, usually offers movies and headsets on its trips. The Concord terminal is inconveniently located on Sewall Street (a 35-minute walk from downtown), but has plenty of free parking and is served by local buses from nearby Congress Street ($1 fare).

The **Portland International Jetport** is served by regularly scheduled flights on several airlines, including **Delta/Business Express** (☎ 800/638-7333), **Continental** (☎ 800/525-0280), **USAirways** (☎ 800/428-4322), **United** (☎ 800/241-6522), **Pine State** (☎ 207/353-6334), and **Northeast Airlines** (☎ 800/983-3247). The small and easily navigated airport is located just across the Fore River from downtown, although ongoing construction and tight parking can be frustrating at times. Metro buses ($1) connect the airport to downtown; cab fare runs about $12.

VISITOR INFORMATION   The **Convention and Visitor's Bureau of Greater Portland,** 305 Commercial St., Portland, ME 04101 (☎ **207/772-5800** or 207/772-4994), stocks a large supply of brochures and is happy to dispense information about local attractions, lodging, and dining. The center is open in summer weekdays 8am to 6pm and weekends 10am to 5pm; hours are shorter during the off-season. Ask for the free "Greater Portland Visitor Guide" with map.

EXPLORING THE CITY

Any visit to Portland should start with a stroll around the historic **Old Port.** Bounded by Commercial, Congress, Union, and Pearl streets, this several-square-block area near the waterfront contains the city's best commercial architecture, a plethora of fine restaurants, a mess of boutiques, and one of the thickest concentrations of bars you'll find anywhere. (The Old Port tends to transform as night lengthens, with the crowds growing younger and rowdier.) The narrow streets and intricate brick facades reflect the mid-Victorian era; most of the area was rebuilt following a devastating fire in 1866. Leafy, quaint Exchange Street is the heart of the Old Port, with other attractive streets running off and around it.

Flanking the Old Port on the two low hills are the downtown's main residential areas. Drive eastward on Congress Street up and over Munjoy Hill and you'll come to the **Eastern Promenade,** a 68-acre hillside park with broad, grassy slopes extending down to the water and superb views of Casco Bay and its islands. Atop Munjoy Hill is the **Portland Observatory,** a quirky shingled tower dating from 1807 and once used to signal which ships were coming into port. It was closed indefinitely for extensive repairs and restorations in 1995; call for an update (☎ 207/774-5561).

On the other end of the peninsula is the **Western Promenade.** (Follow Spring Street westward to Vaughan; turn right then take your first left on Bowdoin Street.) This narrow strip of lawn atop a forested bluff has views across the Fore River, which is lined with less-than-scenic light industry, to the White Mountains in the distance. It's a great spot to watch the sun set. Around the Western Prom are some of the grandest and most imposing houses in the city. A walk through the neighborhood reveals a wide array of architectural styles, from Italianate to shingle to stick.

✪ **Portland Public Market.** 25 Preble St. (½-block west of Monument Square). ☎ **207/228-2000.** Open year-round. Mon–Sat 9am–6pm, Sun 10am–5pm.

Portland's newest attraction, the Public Market opened in 1998 and features 30 vendors selling fresh foods and flowers, much of which is Maine grown. The architecturally distinctive building houses fishmongers, butchers, fresh fruit dealers, and a seafood cafe. It's a much-recommended spot for a quick snack, or just to sit and watch Portland pass by.

Children's Museum of Maine. 142 Free St. (next to the Portland Museum of Art). ☎ **207/828-1234.** Admission $5 per child or adult (under 1 year old free). MC, V. Mon–Sat 10am–5pm, Sun noon–5pm. Closed Mon–Tues fall–spring.

The centerpiece exhibit here is the camera obscura, a room-size "camera" located on the top floor of this stout, columned downtown building next to the art museum. Children gather around a white table in a dark room, where they see magically projected images that include cars driving on city streets and boats plying the harbor. The camera obscura never fails to enthrall, and it provides a memorable lesson in the workings of a lens—whether in a camera or an eye.

That's just one attraction; there's plenty more to do here, from running a supermarket checkout counter to sliding down the firehouse pole to piloting the mock space shuttle from a high cockpit. Leave time for lunch at the cafe, where you can

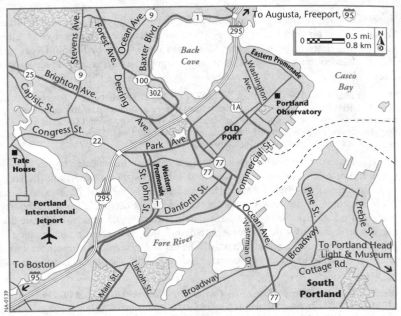

order up a peanut butter and jelly sandwich, a tall glass of milk, and an oatmeal cookie. Make a deal with your kids: they behave during a trip to the art museum, and they'll be rewarded with a couple of hours in their own museum.

✪ Portland Head Light & Museum. Fort Williams Park, 1000 Shore Rd., Cape Elizabeth. ☎ **207/799-2661.** www.portlandheadlight.com. Grounds free; museum admission $2 adults, $1 children 6–18. Park grounds open daily year-round sunrise to sunset (until 8:30pm in summer); museum open daily June–Oct 10am–4pm; open weekends only in spring and late fall. From Portland, follow State St. across the Fore River; continue straight on Broadway. At second light turn right on Cottage Rd., which becomes Shore Rd.; follow until you arrive at the park, on your left.

Just a 10-minute drive from downtown Portland, this 1794 lighthouse is one of the most picturesque in the nation. (You'll probably recognize it from its cameo role in numerous advertisements and calendars.) The light marks the entrance to Portland Harbor, and was occupied continuously from its construction until 1989, when it was automated and the graceful keeper's house (1891) converted to a small, town-owned museum focusing on the history of navigation. The lighthouse itself is still active and thus closed to the public, but visitors can stop by the museum, browse for lighthouse-themed gifts at the gift shop, wander the park grounds, and watch the sailboats and cargo ships come and go. The park has a pebble beach, grassy lawns with ocean vistas, and picnic areas well-suited for informal barbecues.

Portland Museum of Art. 7 Congress Sq. (corner of Congress and High streets). ☎ **207/775-6148.** www.portlandmuseum.org. E-mail: pma@maine.rr.com. Admission $6 adults, $5 students and seniors, $1 children 6–12. Free Fri 5–9pm. Tues–Wed and Sat–Sun 10am–5pm (June to mid-Oct also open Mon 10am–5pm), Thurs–Fri 10am–9pm.

This bold, modern museum was designed by I. M. Pei Associates in 1983, and displays selections from its own fine collections along with a parade of touring exhibits. The museum is particularly strong in American artists who had a connection to Maine, including Winslow Homer, Andrew Wyeth, and Edward Hopper, and has fine displays of early American furniture and crafts. The museum shares the Joan Whitney Payson Collection with Colby College (the college gets it one semester every other year). The collection also features wonderful European works by Renoir, Degas, and Picasso. Guided tours are daily at 2pm, and at 6pm on Thursday. A cafe serves light fare.

Victoria Mansion. 109 Danforth St. ☎ **207/772-4841.** $5 adults, $2 children under 18. May–Oct Tues–Sat 10am–4pm, Sun 1–5pm; tours offered at quarter past and quarter of each hour. Closed Nov–Apr, except for holiday tours from end of Nov to mid-Dec. From the Old Port, head west on Fore St., veer right on Danforth St. at light near Stonecoast Brewing; proceed 3 blocks to the mansion, at the corner of Park St.

Widely regarded as one of the most elaborate Victorian brownstone homes in existence, this mansion (also known as the Morse-Libby House) is a remarkable display of high Victorian style. Built between 1859 and 1863 for a Maine businessman who made a fortune in the New Orleans hotel trade, the towering, slightly foreboding home is a prime example of the Italianate style once in vogue. Inside, it appears that not a square inch of wall space was left unmolested by craftsmen or artisans (11 painters were hired to create the murals). The decor is ponderous and somber, but it offers an engaging look at a bygone era. A gift shop sells Victorian-themed gifts and books.

Wadsworth-Longfellow House & Center for Maine History. 489 Congress St. ☎ **207/879-0427.** www.mainehistory.com. Gallery and Longfellow house tour $5 adults, $1 children under 12. Gallery only $2 adults, $1 child. Longfellow House June–Oct Longfellow House daily 10am–4pm, gallery 10am–6pm; Nov–May gallery only Wed–Sat noon–4pm.

Maine Historical Society's "history campus" includes three widely varied buildings in the middle of downtown Portland. The austere brick Wadsworth-Longfellow House dates to 1785 and was built by Gen. Peleg Wadsworth, father of noted poet Henry Wadsworth Longfellow. It's furnished in an authentic early 19th century style, with many samples of Longfellow family furniture on display. Adjacent to the home is the Maine History Gallery, located in a garish post-modern building. Changing exhibits explore the rich texture of Maine history. Just behind the Longfellow house is the library of the Maine Historical Society, a popular destination among genealogists.

ON THE WATER

The 3.5-mile **Back Cove Pathway** loops around Portland's Back Cove, offering attractive views of the city skyline across the water, glimpses of Casco Bay, and a bit of exercise. The pathway is the city's most popular recreational facility; after work in summer, Portlanders flock here to walk, bike, jog, and windsurf (there's enough water 2½ hours before and after high tide). Part of the pathway shares a noisy bridge with I-295 and it can be a bit fulsome at a dead low tide, but when tides and weather cooperate it's hard to find a lovelier spot than the pathway along Baxter Boulevard.

The main parking lot is located across from Shop 'n Save Plaza at the water's edge. Take Exit 6 (Forest Avenue north) off I-295; turn right at the first light on Baxter Boulevard; at the next light turn right again and park in the lot ahead on the left.

Casco Bay Lines. Commercial and Franklin sts. ☎ **207/774-7871.** Fares vary depending on the run and season, but summer rates typically $5.25–$13.75 round trip. Frequent departures 6am–midnight.

Six of the Casco Bay islands have year-round populations and are served by scheduled ferries from downtown Portland. Except for Long Island, these are part of the city of Portland. The ferries offer an inexpensive way to view the bustling harbor and get a

Downtown Portland

Accommodation & Dining

- Back Bay Grill ➊
- Bella Cucina ➋
- Café Uffa! ➌
- Federal Spice ➒
- Fore Street ➑
- Katahdin ➍
- Portland Regency Hotel ➐
- Stone Coast Brewing Co. ➎
- Three Dollar Dewey's ➏

taste of Maine's islands. Trips range from a 20-minute (one-way) excursion to Peaks Island (the closest thing to an island suburb with 1,200 year-round residents), to the 5½-hour cruise to Bailey Island (connected by bridge to the mainland south of Brunswick) and back. All of the islands are well-suited for walking; Peaks Island has a rocky back shore that's easily accessible via the island's paved perimeter road (bring a picnic lunch). Cliff Island is the most remote of the bunch, and has a sedate turn-of-the-century island retreat character.

Eagle Island Tours. Long Wharf (Commercial St.) ☎ **207/774-6498.** $15 adults, $12 students, $9 children under 12 (plus state park fee of $1.50 adults, 50¢ children). One departure daily at 10am.

Eagle Island was the summer home of famed Arctic explorer and Portland native Robert E. Peary, who claimed in 1909 to be the first person to reach the North Pole. (His accomplishments have been the subject of exhaustive debates among Arctic scholars, some of whom insist he inflated his claims.) In 1904, Peary built a simple home on a remote, 17-acre island at the edge of Casco Bay; in 1912 he added flourishes in the form of two low stone towers. After his death in 1920 his family kept up the home, then later donated it to the state, which has since managed it as a state park. The home is open to the public, maintained much the way it was when Peary lived here. Island footpaths through the scant forest allow exploration to the open, seagull-clotted cliffs at the southern tip. Eagle Tours offers one trip daily from Portland. The 4-hour excursion includes a 1½-hour stopover on the island.

MINOR LEAGUE BASEBALL

Portland Sea Dogs. Hadlock Field, P.O. Box 636, Portland, ME 04104. ☎ **800/936-3647** or 207/879-9500. Tickets $4–$6. Season runs Apr to Labor Day.

The Portland Sea Dogs are the Double-A team affiliated with the 1997 World Champion Florida Marlins. The team plays throughout the summer at Hadlock Field, a small stadium near downtown that still retains an old-time feel despite aluminum benches and other updating. Activities are geared toward families, with lots of entertainment between innings and a selection of food that's a couple of notches above basic hot dogs and hamburgers. (Try the tasty french fries and grilled sausages.)

SIDE TRIPS

OLD ORCHARD BEACH   About 12 miles south of Portland is the unrepentantly honky-tonkish beach town of Old Orchard Beach, a venerable Victorian-era resort famed for its amusement park, pier, and long, sandy beach. Be sure to spend time and money on the stomach-churning rides at the beachside amusement park of **Palace Playland** (☎ **207/934-2001**), then walk on the 7-mile-long beach past the mid-rise condos that sprouted in the 1980s.

The beach is broad and open at low tide; at high tide, space to plunk your towel down is at a premium. In the evenings, teens and young adults dominate the town, spilling out of the video arcades and cruising the main strip. For dinner, do as the locals do and buy hot dogs and pizza and cotton candy; save your change for the arcades.

Old Orchard is just off Route 1 south of Portland. The quickest route is to leave the turnpike at Exit 5, then follow I-195 and the signs to the beach. Don't expect to be alone here: parking is tight, and the traffic can be horrendous during the peak summer months.

✪ SABBATHDAY LAKE SHAKER COMMUNITY   Route 26 from Portland to Norway is a speedy highway past new housing developments and through hilly farmland. At one point the road pinches through a cluster of stately historic buildings that stand proudly beneath towering shade trees. That's the Sabbathday Lake Shaker Community (☎ **207/926-4597**), the last active Shaker community in the nation. The half-dozen or so Shakers living here today still embrace the traditional Shaker beliefs and maintain a communal, pastoral way of life. The bulk of the community's income comes from the sale of herbs, which have been grown here since 1799.

Tours are offered daily in summer except on Sundays (when visitors are invited to attend Sunday services). Docents provide tours of the grounds and several of buildings, including the graceful 1794 meetinghouse. Exhibits in the buildings showcase the famed furniture handcrafted by the Shakers, and include antiques made by Shakers at other U.S. communes. You'll learn plenty about the Shaker ideology with its emphasis on simplicity, industry, and celibacy. After your tour, browse the gift shop for Shaker herbs and teas. Tours last either 1 hour ($5 adult, $2 children 6 to 12) or 1 hour and 45 minutes ($6.50 adult, $2.75 children). Open daily except Sunday, Memorial Day to Columbus Day from 10am to 4:30pm. The last tour is at 3:30pm.

The Shaker village is about 45 minutes from Portland. Head north on Route 26 (Washington Avenue in Portland). The village is 8 miles from Exit 11 (Gray) of the Maine Turnpike.

WHERE TO STAY

The **Holiday Inn** by the Bay, 88 Spring St. (☎ **207/775-2311**), offers great views of the harbor from about half the rooms, along with the usual chain-hotel creature comforts, including a ground-floor restaurant. Peak season rates are approximately $140 double.

Budget travelers may choose to seek accommodations near the Maine Mall in South Portland and off the Maine Turnpike near Westbrook—two areas that are patently charmless, but offer reasonable access to the attractions of downtown, about 10 minutes' drive away. Try **Days Inn** (☎ 207/772-3450), **Coastline Inn** (☎ 207/772-3838) near the mall, the **Super 8 Motel** (☎ 207/854-1881) or **Susse Chalet** (☎ 207/774-6101) off turnpike Exit 8.

The Danforth. 163 Danforth St., Portland, ME 04102. ☎ **800/991-6557** or 207/879-8755. Fax 207/879-8754. www.visionwork.com/danforth. E-mail: danforth@maine. rr.com. 10 units. A/C TV TEL. $115–$225 double. Rates include continental breakfast; discounts available in off-season. AE, MC, V. Pets allowed.

Located in an exceptionally handsome brick home constructed in 1821, The Danforth has been something of a work-in-progress since it first opened in 1994 with just two guest rooms. But it's fast closing in on its ultimate goal of becoming one of Portland's two most elegant small inns. (The Pomegranate is the other.) The guest rooms are handsomely decorated, many in rich and vibrant tones. The inn's extra touches are exceptional throughout, from working fireplaces in most guest rooms to the richly paneled basement billiards room to the direct-line phones in all rooms. Especially appealing is Room 1 with a sitting room and private second-floor deck, and Room 2 with high ceilings and superb morning light; rooms 5 and 6 are smaller, housed in the old servant's wing. The inn is located at the edge of the Spring Street Historic District, and is within a 10-minutes' walk of downtown attractions.

Amenities: Newspaper delivery, in-room massage, billiards room, bicycle rental, access to in-town health club.

Inn at Park Spring. 135 Spring St., Portland, ME 04101. ☎ **800/437-8511** or 207/774-1059. E-mail: psinn@javanet.com. 6 units. May–Oct $135–$145 double; Nov–April $95. Rates include an expanded continental breakfast and off-street parking. 2-night minimum stay weekends. AE, MC, V.

This small in-town B&B is housed in a comfortable, historic brick home dating back to 1835, and is well located for exploring the town on foot. The Portland Museum of Art is just 2 blocks away, the Old Port about 10 minutes, and great restaurants are all within easy walking distance. Guests can linger or watch TV in the front parlor, or chat at the table in the kitchen. The rooms are all corner rooms, and most are bright and sunny. Especially nice is "Spring," with its great morning light and wonderful views of the historic row houses on Park Street, and "Gables," on the third floor, which gets abundant afternoon sun.

✪ **Pomegranate Inn.** 49 Neal St., Portland, ME 04102. ☎ **800/356-0408** or 207/772-1006. Fax 207/773-4426. www.pomegranateinn.com. 8 units. A/C TV TEL. Summer and fall $135–$175 double; winter and spring $95–$135 double. Rates include full breakfast. 2-night minimum stay summer weekends; 4-night minimum at Christmas and Thanksgiving. AE, DISC, MC, V. On-street parking. From the Old Port, take Middle Street (which turns into Spring Street) to Neal Street in the West End (about 1 mile); turn right and proceed to inn. Children 16 and older are welcome.

This is Portland's most stunning B&B, and one of the best in northern New England. Housed in a handsome, dove-gray 1884 Italianate home in the architecturally distinctive Western Prom neighborhood, the interiors are wondrously decorated with whimsy and elegance—a combination that can be fatally cloying if attempted by someone without impeccably good taste. Look for the bold and exuberant wall paintings by a local artist, and the wonderfully eclectic antique furniture collected and tastefully arranged by owner Isabel Smiles. If you have the chance, peek in some of the unoccupied rooms—they're all different with painted floors and boisterous faux-marble woodwork. Most rooms have gas fireplaces; the best of the lot is in the carriage house, which has its own private terrace, kitchenette, and fireplace. The sit-down breakfasts in the cheery dining room are invariably creative and tasty. The inn is well-situated for exploring the West End, and downtown is about a 20-minute walk away.

Portland Regency Hotel. 20 Milk St., Portland, ME 04101. ☎ **800/727-3436** or 207/774-4200. Fax 207/775-2150. www.theregency.com. 95 units. A/C MINIBAR TV TEL. Summer $199–$249 double; off-season $159–$219. AE, CB, DISC, MC, V.

Centrally located on a cobblestone courtyard in the middle of the trendy Old Port, the Regency boasts the city's premier hotel location. But it's got more than location going for it—it's also one of the more architecturally striking and well-managed hotels in the state. Housed in a historic brick armory, the hotel offers a number of moderately size, modern guest rooms nicely appointed and furnished with all the expected upscale amenities. The one complaint I've heard is about the noise: the interior guest-room walls are a bit thin so noise travels from room to room, and on weekends the revelry in the Old Port streets can penetrate even the dense brick exterior walls.

Dining: The hotel is home to The Armory Restaurant, which serves breakfast, lunch, and dinner. Dinners include traditional favorites like steak au poive and surf-and-turf, with entree prices ranging from $16 to $25.

Amenities: Limited room service, valet parking, dry cleaning (Mon–Fri), baby-sitting (with prior notice), valet parking ($5), courtesy car to airport, safe-deposit boxes, Jacuzzi, sauna, fitness club, conference rooms, aerobics classes.

WHERE TO DINE
EXPENSIVE

Back Bay Grill. 65 Portland St. ☎ **207/772-8833.** Reservations encouraged. Main courses $17.50–$24.95. AE, DC, DISC, MC, V. Mon–Thurs 5:30–9:30pm, Fri–Sat 5:30–10:30pm. NEW AMERICAN.

Back Bay Grill offers an upscale, contemporary ambience amid a rather downscale neighborhood near the main post office. There's light jazz in the background, and bold artwork that goes several steps beyond mere atmosphere. The kitchen has been serving up some of Maine's most innovative meals for more than a decade, and has developed a loyal following. Diners might launch an evening with house-cured gravlax on tuna carpaccio, or Maine crab cakes with curry oil. Main dishes include creative pastas (e.g., herbed goat-cheese ravioli), along with more ambitious meals like sautéed halibut and a chorizo-saffron sauce, or herbed rack of lamb with figs and basil. If you're looking to sate your craving for lobster and expense is no object, there's a lobster tasting menu available on limited nights (call first) that includes four creative lobster dishes (such as lobster on asparagus risotto with a carrot-ginger jus) at a cost of $62 per person.

✪ Fore Street. 288 Fore St. ☎ **207/775-2717.** Reservations recommended. Main courses, $11.95–$21.95. AE, MC, V. Sun–Thurs 5:30–10pm, Fri–Sat until 10:30pm. CONTEMPORARY GRILL.

During the long summer evenings, light floods in through the huge sets of windows at this loftlike space; later at night, it takes on a more intimate glow with soft lighting against the brick walls and buttery wooden floors. But the place always feels bustling—the sprawling open kitchen is located in the middle of it all, filled with a team of chefs busy with stoking the wood-fired brick oven and grilling fish. And grilled foods are the specialty here. The menu is constantly in play, but you might start with the grilled calamari served with tomatoes and wild mushrooms or wood-fired pesto pizzetta, then move on to the baked halibut or turnspit-roasted Maine rabbit. There's always a selection of wonderfully grilled meals, including steak, chicken, duckling, or fresh fish steaks. Meals are consistently excellent here, and disappointments are rare.

Street & Co. 33 Wharf St. ☎ **207/775-0887.** Reservations recommended. Main courses $12.95–$20.95. AE, MC, V. Sun–Thurs 5:30–9:30pm, Fri–Sat until 10pm. MEDITERRANEAN/ SEAFOOD.

A pioneer establishment on now-trendy Wharf Street, Street & Co. specializes in seafood cooked just right. There's no smoke and mirrors—you pass the open kitchen as you're seated, and you can watch the talented chefs perform their magic in virtually no space. This intimate spot is a bit like something you might imagine stumbling onto while touring Provence: Low beams, dim lighting, and drying herbs hanging overhead nicely set the mood. Diners are seated at copper-topped tables, designed such that the waiters can deliver steaming skillets right from the stove. Looking for lobster? Try it grilled and served over linguini in a butter-garlic sauce. If you're partial to calamari, this is the place. They know how to cook it so it's perfectly tender, a knack that's been lost elsewhere. Street & Co. fills up early, so reservations are strongly recommended. One-third of the tables are reserved for walk-ins each night, so it can't hurt to ask if you're in the neighborhood. In summer, there's outdoor seating at tables along the cobblestone street.

MODERATE

Bella Cucina. 653 Congress St. ☎ **207/828-4033.** Reservations recommended. Main courses, $9–$17. AE, CB, DISC, MC, V. Daily 5–10pm. RUSTIC ITALIAN.

Situated in one of Portland's less elegant commercial neighborhoods, Bella Cucina sets an inviting mood with rich colors, soft lighting, and pinpoint spotlights over the tables that carve out alluring islands of light. The eclectic menu changes frequently but dances deftly between rustic Italian and regional, with options like a robust cioppino with haddock and lobster, and a mélange of veal, pork, and chicken served with a prosciutto and mushroom ragout. Three or four vegan entrees are always on hand. About half the seats are kept open for walk-ins, so take a chance and stop by even if you don't have reservations. There's a good selection of wines, and free parking evenings behind Joe's Smoke Shop.

Katahdin. 106 High St. ☎ **207/774-1740.** Reservations not accepted. Main courses $9.95–$15.95. DISC, MC, V. Tues–Thurs 5–9:30pm, Fri–Sat until 10:30pm. CREATIVE NEW ENGLAND

Katahdin is a lively, often noisy spot that prides itself on its eclectic cuisine. Artists on slim budgets dine on the nightly blue plate special, which typically features something basic like meat loaf or pan-fried catfish. Wealthy business folks one table over dine on more delicate fare, like the restaurant's noted crab cakes. Other recommended specialties include an appetizer of pan-seared oysters, and main courses of grilled sea scallops with a spicy lime vinaigrette or London broil marinated in a ginger, scallion, and garlic mix. Sometimes the kitchen nods, but for the most part, food is good at very reasonable prices. There's a bar in the dining room where you can enjoy Portland's best martini while waiting for a table.

INEXPENSIVE

Federal Spice. 225 Federal St. ☎ **207/774-6404.** Reservations not accepted. Main courses $2.50–$6. No credit cards. Mon–Sat 11am–9pm. WRAPS/GLOBAL.

This is Portland's best bet for a quick, cheap, and filling nosh. Located beneath a parking garage (just off Temple St.), Federal Spice is a breezy, informal spot with limited dining inside and a few tables outside. You'll find quesadillas, salads, and soft tacos here, along with the well-regarded wraps full of inventive, taste-bud-awakening stuffings (the curried coconut chicken is among the best). The yam fries are excellent, and will nicely accompany just about everything on the menu.

✪ **Silly's.** 40 Washington Ave. ☎ 207/772-0360. Lunch and dinner $1.25–$6.50; pizza $5.95–$16.90. MC, V. Mon–Sat 10am–10pm. Closed Sun. ECLECTIC & TAKEOUT.

Silly's is the favored cheap-eats joint among even jaded Portlanders. Situated on an aggressively charmless urban street, the interior is informal, bright and spunky, with a fine selection of mismatched 1950s-era dinettes and funky-retro accessories. The menu is creative and the selections tasty. A lot of the meals are served in hubcap-size pita bread (the shish-kabab roll-up is especially delicious), the pizza is superb, and there's beer on tap. Don't overlook the great mound of french fries, or the huge old-fashioned milkshakes and malts.

PORTLAND AFTER DARK

Portland is lively in the evenings, especially on summer weekends when the testosterone level in the Old Port seems to rocket into the stratosphere with young men and women prowling the dozens of bars and spilling out onto the streets.

Among the bars favored by locals are **Three-Dollar Dewey's** at the corner of Commercial and Union streets (try the great french fries), **Gritty McDuff's Brew Pub** on Fore Street near the foot of Exchange St., and **Brian Ború,** slightly out of the Old Port on Center St. All three bars are casual and pubby, with guests sharing long tables with new companions.

Beyond the active Old Port bar scene, a number of clubs offer a mix of live and recorded entertainment throughout the year. There's been considerable upheaval and turmoil among clubs and clubowners in recent years; check the free alternative paper, *Casco Bay Weekly*, for current venues, performers, and show times.

Among the more reliable spots for live music is **Stone Coast Brewing Co.,** 14 York St. (☎ 207/773-2337) a sizable brew pub in an old brick cannery at the edge of the Old Port. Downstairs there's a no-smoking bar and restaurant overlooking the brewery. Upstairs is "The Smoking Room," with pool tables, dart lanes, sales of hand-rolled cigars, and live music. Music features local acts, as well as touring bands. Cover charges range from $1 to $20, but is typically $3 to $5 for local and regional acts.

4 The Western Lakes & Mountains

Maine's western mountains comprise a rugged, brawny region that stretches northeast from the White Mountains to the Carrabassett Valley. It isn't as commercialized as the Maine coast, and the villages aren't as quaint as you'll find in Vermont's Green Mountains. But it has azure lakes, ragged forests of spruce, fir, and lichens, and rolling hills and mountains that take on a distinct sapphire hue during the summer hiking season.

Cultural amenities are few here, but natural amenities are legion. Hikers have the famed Appalachian Trail, which crosses into Maine in the Mahoosuc Mountains (near where Route 26 enters into N.H.) and follows rivers and ridgelines northeast to Bigelow Mountain and beyond. Canoeists and fishers head to the noted Rangeley Lakes area, a chain of deepwater ponds and lakes that has attracted sportsmen for more than a century. And in the winter, skiers can choose among several downhill ski areas, including the two largest in the state, Sunday River and Sugarloaf.

BETHEL

Until the mid-1980s, Bethel was a sleepy, 19th-century resort town with one of those friendly, family-oriented ski areas that seemed destined for certain extinction. Then a guy named Les Otten came along. This brash young entrepreneur bought Sunday River Ski Area and proceeded to make it into one of New England's most vibrant and successful ski destinations. (Otten subsequently acquired most of the other major ski areas in New England, including Killington, Attitash, Sugarbush, Sugarloaf, Mount Snow, and Waterville Valley, then set about buying western resorts.)

With the rise of Sunday River, the white-clapboard town of Bethel (located about 7 miles from the ski area) has been dragged into the modern era, although it hasn't yet taken on the artificial, packaged flavor of some other New England ski towns. The village (population 2,500) is still defined by the stoic buildings of the respected prep school Gould Academy, the broad village common, and the Bethel Inn, a turn-of-the-century resort that's managed to stay ahead of the tide by adding condos, but without losing its pleasant, timeworn character.

ESSENTIALS

GETTING THERE   Bethel is located at the intersection of Routes 26 and 2. It's accessible from the Maine Turnpike by heading west on Route 26 from Exit 11. From New Hampshire, drive east on Route 2 from Gorham.

VISITOR INFORMATION   The **Bethel Area Chamber of Commerce,** 30 Cross St., Bethel, ME 04217 (☎ **800/442-5826** for reservations, or 207/824-2282), has offices behind the Casablanca movie theater. It's open year-round Monday to Friday from 8am to 8pm, Saturday from 10am to 6pm, and Sunday noon to 5pm.

Across Route 2 from the chamber the **state tourism office** has paired up with the White Mountain National Forest district office to provide information. You can stock up on brochures from across the state and get information on local national forest activities, such as hiking and mountain biking. Open daily in summer 8am to 4:30pm (closed Wednesdays in winter). Call ☎ **207/824-4582.**

EXPLORING LOCAL HISTORY

Bethel's stately, historic homes ring the **Bethel Common,** a long, rectangular greensward created in 1807. The town's historic district encompasses some 27 homes, which represent a wide range of architectural styles popular in the 19th century. The oldest home in the district is the 1813 **Moses Mason House,** which is now a fine, small museum housing the collections and offices of the Bethel Historical Society (☎ 207/824-2908). The museum, at 14 Broad St., is open year-round 1 to 4pm Tuesday to Friday, and is also open weekends in July and August. Admission is $2 for adults and $1 for children.

OUTDOOR PURSUITS

Grafton Notch State Park

Grafton Notch straddles Route 26 as it angles northwest from Newry toward Errol, N.H. The 33-mile drive between the two towns is one of my favorites, both picturesque and dramatic. You initially pass through farmland in a fertile river valley before ascending through bristly forest to a handsome glacial notch hemmed in by rough, gray cliffs on the towering hillsides above. Foreboding Old Speck Mountain towers to the south; views of Lake Umbagog open to the north as you continue into New Hampshire. This route attracts few crowds, although it's popular with Canadians headed to the Maine Coast.

Public access to the park consists of a handful of roadside parking lots near scenic areas. The best of the bunch is **Screw Auger Falls,** where the Bear River drops through several small cascades before tumbling dramatically into a narrow and twisting gorge worn by glacial runoff through granite bedrock. Picnic tables dot the forested banks upriver of the falls, and kids seem inexorably drawn to splash and swim in the smaller pools on warm days.

Hiking

The **Appalachian Trail** crosses the Mahoosuc Mountains northwest of Bethel. Many of those who've hiked the entire 2,000-mile trail say this stretch is the most demanding on knees and psyches. The trail doesn't forgive; it generally foregoes switchbacks in favor of sheer ascents and descents. It's also hard to find water along the trail during dry weather. Still, it's worth the knee-pounding effort for the views and the unrivaled sense of remoteness.

One stretch crosses Old Speck Mountain, Maine's third highest peak. Views from the summit are all but nonexistent since the old fire tower closed a while back, but an easy-to-moderate spur trail ascends 800-foot cliff called "The Eyebrow" and provides a good vantage point for Bear River Valley and the rugged terrain of Grafton Notch. Look for the well-signed parking lot where Route 26 intersects the trail in Grafton Notch State Park. Park your car, then head south on the A.T. toward Old Speck; in 0.1 mile you'll intersect the Eyebrow Trail, which you can follow to the overlook.

The Appalachian Mountain Club's *Maine Mountain Guide* is highly recommended for detailed information about other area hikes.

Alpine Skiing

Sunday River Ski Resort. P.O. Box 450, Bethel, ME 04217. ☎ **800/543-2754** for lodging or 207/824-3000. www.sundayriver.com. E-mail: snowtalk@sundayriver.com. Vertical drop: 2,340 ft. Lifts: 15 chairlifts (4 high-speed), 3 surface lifts. Skiable acreage: 654. Lift tickets: $49 adults weekends, $47 weekdays; children under 5 ski free.

Sunday River has grown at stunning speed in recent years, and today competes in the same league as longtime New England winter resorts like Mount Snow and Killington. Unlike ski areas that have developed around a single tall peak, Sunday River has expanded along an undulating ridge about 3 miles wide that encompasses seven peaks. Just traversing the resort, stitching runs together with chairlift rides, can take an hour. As a result, you'll rarely get bored making the same run time and again. The descents offer something for virtually everyone, from steep bump runs to glade skiing to wide, wonderful intermediate trails. Sunday River is also blessed with plenty of water for snowmaking, and makes tons of the stuff using a snowmaking system it developed.

Unfortunately, superb skiing conditions are offset by an uninspiring base area. The lodges and condos are architecturally dull, and the less-than-delicate landscaping is of the sort created by graceless bulldozers. Efforts are underway to create a new village from scratch at the Jordan Bowl area, where more of a sense of community might develop. But that won't come to fruition until 2001 at the earliest.

Ski Mt. Abram. P.O. Box 120, Locke Mills, ME 04255. ☎ **207/875-5003.** Vertical drop: 1,030 ft. Lifts: 2 chairlifts, 3 T-bars. Skiable acreage: 135. Lift tickets: $31 weekends, $20 weekdays.

Mount Abram is a welcoming intermediate mountain that's perfect for families still ascending the learning curve. It has a friendly, informal atmosphere that's in sharp contrast with nearby bustling Sunday River. You don't have to expend much energy on logistics here planning when to meet up or at what base lodge. You don't have to expend nearly as much cash, either. The mountain features night skiing weekdays until 7pm, weekends until 9pm.

WHERE TO STAY

Bethel Inn. On the Common, Bethel, ME 04217. ☎ **800/654-0125** or 207/824-2175. www.bethelinn.com. 72 units. TV TEL. Summer $198–$360 double; winter $138–$260 double. Rates include breakfast and dinner. 2-night minimum on weekends in summer and ski season; 3-night minimum during winter school vacations. Ski packages available. AE, DC, DISC, MC, V. Pets allowed ($30 extra, one-time fee).

The Bethel Inn is a classic, old-fashioned resort set on 200 acres in the village. It has a quiet, settled air. This is appropriate, since it was built to house patients of Dr. John Gehring, who put Bethel on the map treating nervous disorders through a regimen of healthy country living, including a lot of wood splitting. (Bethel was once known as "the resting place of Harvard" for all the faculty treated here.) The quaint, homey rooms aren't terribly spacious, but they are welcoming and pleasingly furnished with country antiques. More luxurious are the 16 deluxe rooms and suites, added to the inn in late 1998. You give up some of the charm of the old inn, but gain elbow room.

Dining: The dining room remains the resort's Achilles' heel. It's promising at first, offering classic resort specialties like prime rib, shrimp scampi pesto, and cedar-planked salmon (main courses are $14 to $20 for outside guests). Alas, the preparation and service often fail to live up to the promise of these fine surroundings.

Amenities: Fitness center with an outdoor heated pool (open year-round), whirlpool, sauna, golf course, tennis, cross-country skiing, shuttle to ski areas, laundry service, baby-sitting, guest safe. Also: lake swimming at the inn's Lake House, picturesquely located amid pines on a small lake a short drive away.

Black Bear Bed & Breakfast. Sunday River Rd. (P.O. Box 55), Bethel, ME 04217. ☎ **207/824-0908.** www.bbearbandb.com. E-mail: bbearinn@megalink.net. 6 units. $60–$80 double. Rates include breakfast. 2-night minimum stay on ski season weekends. AE, MC, V. Closed May.

This 1830s farmhouse is located a short drive beyond the turn-off to Sunday River ski area, and is a great choice for those seeking a casual spot to rest up between ski runs or hiking trips. The rooms vary in size but are each furnished in a simple country style with pine and oak furniture, and with lots of daylight through oversize old windows. The common room is a good spot sit around the woodstove and chat with other guests or innkeepers Faith Spath and Phil Buell, as is the hot tub just off the deck. But the chief amenity is the location: it's on eight acres in a lovely dead-end valley. You can be on the ski slopes in winter within five minutes, yet it feels like you're far off in the country by nightfall. In summer, guests can splash around in the river, or set off on great mountain-bike and hiking rambles up the valley into the national forest.

Jordan Grand Resort Hotel. Sunday River Rd., (P.O. Box 450), Bethel, ME 04217. ☎ **800/543-2754** or 207/824-5000. Fax 207/824-2111. www.sundayriver.com. 195 units. A/C TV TEL. Ski season $155–$225 double, off-season $105–$120. AE, DC, DISC, MC, V.

The Jordan Grand is the anchor for new development slated for the far-flung Jordan Bowl area. Right now, though, the place feels miles away from the rest of the resort, largely because it is—even the staff makes "The Shining" jokes about its remoteness. It's a modern if sprawling hotel that offers little in the way of a personal touch or flair, but boasts a great location for skiers who want to be first on the slopes each morning. Owing to the quirky terrain, parking is inconvenient and you often have to walk great distances to your room (opt for the valet parking). The rooms are simply furnished in a durable condo style (145 have kitchen facilities), and many are quite spacious; most have balconies. It's a popular destination with families, so this isn't the best choice couples seeking a quiet getaway.

Dining: Sunday River has stepped up efforts to improve its food service, and the two restaurants here suggest that it's succeeding. Breakfast and dinner are served daily at the Grand Avenue Cafe, which offers up tasty meals like Jack Daniels duck and sautéed lobster (entrees $14.95 to $24.95). Sliders is at the distant other end of the hotel and faces the slopes. Upgraded pub fare (meat loaf, beef stew, big and sloppy hamburgers) is reasonably priced and large-proportioned. Prices are $5.95 to $8.95.

Amenities: Outdoor heated pool (year-round), Jacuzzis, sauna, steam room, fitness room, children's center, conference rooms, business center, valet parking, in-room massage, limited room service, concierge, washer-dryer, dry cleaning, baby-sitting, safe-deposit boxes.

The Victoria. 32 Main St., Bethel, ME 04217. ☎ **888/774-1235** or 207/824-8060. www.victoria-inn.com. E-mail: erickate@megalink.net. 15 units (including 4 family suites). A/C TV TEL. $105–$175 double; $250–$350 loft rooms. Rates include full breakfast. 2-night minimum stay weekends and holidays. MC, V. Pets allowed with prior approval.

Newly opened in 1998, The Victoria marks the welcome rehabilitation of one of the village's most prominent structures. Built in 1895 and damaged by lightning a few years ago, the inn has been superbly restored, complete with antique lighting fixtures, period furniture, and the original formidable oak doors guarding the entryway. The guest rooms have a luxurious William Morris feel, with richly patterned wallpaper and handmade duvet covers. Room 1 is the luxurious master suite, with a turret window and a sizable bathroom; Room 3 is the only room with wood floors (the others are carpeted), but has a tiny bathroom. Most intriguing are the four loft rooms in the attached carriage house, each with gas fireplace, Jacuzzi, and soaring ceiling revealing old beams. These are perfect for families, with spare beds in lofts over the main rooms. Room 7 has spiral stairs leading to bunk beds; Room 9 has a separate sitting room with TV. All guests have access to a bright sitting area with woodstove on the second floor of the carriage house.

Dining: The inn's two dining rooms are stately and handsome, as one would expect in this elaborate manse. Dinner is served nightly except Tuesday, with entrees including breast of duck with a raspberry coulis and bordelaise sauce, and grilled salmon with a crabmeat and red pepper garnish. Reservations are requested; entree prices range from $11.95 (spinach manicotti) to $22.95 (veal chop).

WHERE TO DINE

Many restaurants are open only in ski season. It's best to call ahead in summer. In addition to the informal establishments listed below, don't overlook **The Victoria** (see above) for the best upscale dining in the village. It's open year-round.

Great Grizzly/Matterhorn. Sunday River Rd. ☎ **207/824-6271** or 207/824-6836. Pizza $7.95 and up; other entrees $6.95–$16.95. MC, V. Pizza from 3pm–10pm; steakhouse menu from 5pm. STEAKHOUSE/BRICK-OVEN PIZZA.

These two restaurants share a handsome new timber-frame structure on the Sunday River Road just a couple of minutes from the ski area. It's casual and relaxed, with pool table, pinball and a handsome metal-top bar. You'll get two menus after you settle in: Great Grizzly offers mostly steaks. Matterhorn specializes in wood-fired pizza, and they're very, very good. The atmosphere is more relaxed and the food significantly better than at the Sunday River Brewing Co. a couple of miles down the road, and the beer-on-tap selection doesn't suffer much for not being a brew pub. It was unclear at press time if this spot will be open at all in summer; call ahead to avoid disappointment.

Sunday River Brewing Company. Rte. 2 (at Sunday River Rd.), Bethel. ☎ **207/824-4253.** Reservations not accepted. Main courses $5.95–$15.95 (most $7–$9). AE, MC, V. Daily 11:30am–12:30am. PUB FARE.

Sunday River Brewing Co. opened this modern and boisterous brew pub on prime real estate at the corner of Route 2 and the Sunday River access road. This is a good choice if your primary objective is to quaff robust ales and porters. The brews are awfully good; the food (burgers, nachos, chicken wings) doesn't strive for any culinary heights, and certainly doesn't achieve any. If you want good pub fare, you're better off headed up Sunday River Road a piece to try Great Grizzly/Matterhorn. Come early if you're looking for a quiet evening; it gets loud later in the evening when bands take the stage.

RANGELEY LAKES

Mounted moose heads on the walls, log cabins tucked into spruce forest, and cool August mornings that sometimes require not one sweater but two are the stuff of the Rangeley Lakes region. Although Rangeley Lake and its eponymous town are at the heart of the region, its borders extend much further, consisting of a series of lakes that feed into and flow out of the main lake.

The town of **Rangeley** (population 1,063) is the regional center for outdoor activities. It offers a handful of motels and restaurants, a bevy of fishing guides, and a smattering of shops, but little else. Easy-to-visit attractions in the Rangeley area are few, and most regular visitors and residents seem determined to keep it that way. The wise visitor rents a cabin or takes a room at a lodge, then explores the area with the slow pace that seems custom-made for the region. Rangeley is Maine's highest town at 1,546 feet, and usually remains quite cool throughout the summer.

ESSENTIALS

GETTING THERE   Rangeley is 122 miles north of Portland, and 39 miles northwest of Farmington on Route 4.

VISITOR INFORMATION   The **Rangeley Lakes Region Chamber of Commerce,** P.O. Box 317, Rangeley, ME 04970 (☎ **800/685-2537** or 207/864-5364), maintains an information booth in town at a small park near the lake that's open year-round Monday to Saturday from 9am to 5pm.

ODD SCIENCE

✪ **Orgonon.** Dodge Pond Rd. (3½ miles west of Rangeley off Rte. 4). ☎ **207/864-3443.** Admission $3 adults, free for children under 12. Open July and Aug Tues–Sun 1–5pm; Sept Sun only 1–5pm.

Among the few historic sites in Maine relating to the 20th century is Orgonon, former home of controversial Viennese psychiatrist Wilhelm Reich (1897–1957). Reich was an associate of Sigmund Freud during the early days of psychoanalysis. Like Freud, Reich believed that underlying sexual tension governed much of our behavior. But Reich took Freud's work a few steps further, building on the hypothesis that pent-up sexual energy—a sort of psychological blockage—resulted in numerous neuroses.

Reich settled in Rangeley in 1942, where he developed the science of "orgonomy." According to Reich, living matter was animated by a sort of life force called "orgone." This floated freely in the atmosphere and was blue (which Reich believed explained the hue of the sky). To cure orgone imbalances he invented orgone energy boxes, which were said to gather and concentrate ambient orgone. These boxes were just big enough to sit in, and featured 6-inch walls of metal and asbestos.

Reich was sentenced to federal prison for matters related to the interstate transport of his orgone boxes. He died in prison in 1957. While many dismissed Reich's theories as quackery, he still has serious and dedicated adherents, including those who maintain the museum in his memory.

Orgonon, built in 1948 of native fieldstone, has a spectacular view of Dodge Pond and is built in the distinctive American Modern style, which stands apart from the local rustic-lodge motif. Visitors on the 1-hour guided tour of the estate and the architecturally distinctive home can view the orgone boxes along with other intriguing inventions.

OUTDOOR PURSUITS

CANOEING   The Rangeley Lakes area is a canoeist's paradise. Azure waters, dense forests, and handsome hills are all part of the allure. Rangeley Lake has a mix of wild forest and classic old cottages lining the lakeshore. The southeast coves ofMooselookmeguntic Lake suffered an unfortunate period of haphazard development during the 1980s, but much of the shore, especially along the west shore, is still very attractive.

HIKING   The Appalachian Trail crosses Route 4 about 10 miles south of Rangeley. A strenuous but rewarding hike is along the trail northward to the summit of **Saddleback Mountain,** a 10-mile round-trip that ascends through thick forest and past remote ponds to open, arcticlike terrain with fine views of the surrounding mountains and lakes. Saddleback actually consists of two peaks over 4,000 feet (hence the name). Be prepared for sudden shifts in weather, and for the high winds that often rake the open ridgeline.

An easier 1-mile hike may be found at **Bald Mountain** near the village of Oquossuc, on the northeast shore of Mooselookmeguntic Lake. (Look for the trailhead 1 mile south of Haines Landing on Bald Mountain Road). The views have grown over in recent years, but you can still catch glimpses of the clear blue waters from above.

ALPINE SKIING   **Saddleback Ski Area.** P.O. Box 490, Rangeley, ME 04970. ☎ 207/864-5671. Vertical drop: 1,830 ft. Lifts: 2 double chairs, 3 T-bars. Skiable acreage: 100. Lift tickets: $42 weekends; $27 midweek.

With only two chairlifts, Saddleback qualifies as a small mountain. But Saddleback has an unexpectedly big-mountain feel. It offers a vertical drop of just 1,830 feet, but what makes Saddleback so appealing is its rugged alpine setting (the Appalachian Trail runs across the high, mile-long ridge above the resort) and the old-fashioned trails. Saddleback offered glade skiing and narrow, winding trails well before the bigger ski areas sought to re-create these old-fashioned slopes.

WHERE TO STAY & DINE

Rangeley Inn. P.O. Box 160, Rangeley, ME 04907. ☎ **800/666-3687** or 207/864-3341. Fax 207/864-3634. www.rangeleyinn.com. E-mail: rangeinn@rangeley.org. 50 units. TV (in motel units only). $69–$119 double. 2-night minimum stay winter weekends. AE, DISC, MC, V. Limited pets allowed ($8 extra per night).

The architecturally eclectic Rangeley Inn dominates Rangeley's miniature downtown. Parts of this old-fashioned, blue-shingled hotel date back to 1877, but the main wing was built in 1907, with additions in the 1920s and the 1940s. A 15-unit motel annex was built more recently behind the inn on Haley Pond, but those looking for creaky floors and a richer sense of local heritage should request a room in the main, three-floor inn. Some rooms in the motel have woodstoves, kitchenettes, or whirlpools; in the inn you'll find a handful of rooms with claw-foot tubs perfect for an evening's soaking.

Dining: The gracious, old-worldish dining room serves hearty, filling meals; less formal fare is available in the Rangeley Inn Tavern. During the heavy tour season (especially fall), bus groups tend to dominate.

CARRABASSETT VALLEY

The Carrabassett Valley can be summed up in six words: big peaks, wild woods, deep lakes. The crowning jewel of the region is Sugarloaf Mountain, Maine's second highest peak at 4,237 feet. Distinct from nearby peaks because of its pyramidal shape, the mountain has been developed for skiing and offers the largest vertical drop in Maine, the best selection of activities daytime and night, and a wide range of accommodations within easy commuting distance.

While Sugarloaf draws the lion's share of visitors, it's not the only game in town. Nearby **Kingfield** is an attractive, historic town with a fine old hotel; it has more of the character of an Old West outpost than of classic New England. Other valley towns offering limited services for travelers include **Eustis, Stratton,** and **Carrabassett Valley.**

Outside the villages and ski resort, it's all rugged hills, tumbling streams, and spectacular natural surroundings. The muscular mountains of the **Bigelow Range** provide terrain for some of the state's best hiking. And Flagstaff Lake is the place for flat-water canoeing amid majestic surroundings.

ESSENTIALS

GETTING THERE   Kingfield and Sugarloaf are on Route 27. Skiers debate over the best route from the turnpike. Some exit at Auburn and take Route 4 north to Route 27; others exit in Augusta and take Route 27 straight through. It's a toss-up time-wise, but exiting at Augusta is marginally more scenic.

Maine Tour and Travel (☎ **800/649-5071**) offers shuttle service from state airports to the mountain.

VISITOR INFORMATION   The **Sugarloaf Area Chamber of Commerce** (☎ **207/235-2100**) offers information from its offices 9½ miles north of Kingfield on Route 27. The office is open year-round; their goal is to be open daily 10am to 4pm, but that may vary. The chamber can book lodgings in and around Sugarloaf; call ☎ **800/843-2732.** For accommodations on the mountain, contact Sugarloaf directly (see below).

SKIING

Alpine Skiing

Sugarloaf/USA. RR #1, Box 5000, Carrabassett Valley, ME 04947. ☎ **800/843-5623** or 207/237-2000. www.sugarloaf.com. Vertical drop: 2,820 ft. Lifts: 13 chairlifts, including 2 high-speed quads; 1 surface lift. Skiable acreage: 1,400 (snowmaking on 475 acres). Lift tickets: $49 adults weekends; $47 weekdays.

Sugarloaf is Maine's big mountain, with the highest vertical drop in New England after Vermont's Killington. And thanks to quirks of geography, it actually feels bigger than it is. From the high, open snowfields (which account for much of Sugarloaf's huge skiable acreage) or the upper advanced runs like Bubblecuffer or White Nitro, skiers develop vertigo looking down at the valley floor. Sugarloaf attracts plenty of experts to its hard-core runs, but it's also a fine intermediate mountain with great cruising runs. A gentle bunny slope extends down through the village; the "green" slopes on the mountain itself are a bit more challenging. The main drawback comes in the form of wind. Sugarloaf seems to get buffeted regularly, with the higher lifts often closed due to gusting.

Cross-Country Skiing

The **Sugarloaf Ski Touring Center** (☎ **207/237-6830**) offers 57 miles of groomed trails that weave through the village at the base of the mountain and into the low hills covered with scrappy woodlands along the Carrabassett River. The trails are impeccably groomed for striding and skating, and wonderful views open here and there to Sugarloaf Mountain and the Bigelow Range. The base lodge is simple and attractive, all knotty pine with a cathedral ceiling, and features a cafeteria, towering stone fireplace, and a well-equipped ski shop. Trail fees are $15 daily for adults; $10 for seniors and children 12 and under. The center is located on Route 27 about 1 mile south of the Sugarloaf access road. A shuttle bus serves the area in winter.

HIKING

The 12-mile Bigelow Range has some of the most dramatic high-ridge hiking in the state, a close second to Mount Katahdin. It consists of a handful of lofty peaks, with Avery Peak (the east peak) offering the best views. On exceptionally clear days, hikers can see Mount Washington to the southwest and Mount Katahdin to the northeast.

A strenuous but rewarding hike for fit hikers is the 10.3-mile loop that begins at the **Fire Warden's Trail.** (The trailhead is at the washed-out bridge on Stratton Brook Pond Road, a rugged dirt road that leaves eastward from Route 27 about 2.3 miles north of the Sugarloaf access road.) Follow the Fire Warden's Trail up the steep ridge to the junction with the **Appalachian Trail**. Head south on the AT, which tops the West Peak and South Horn, two open summits with stellar views. One-quarter mile past Horns Pond, turn south on **Horns Pond Trail** and descend back to the Fire Warden's Trail to return to your car. Allow about 8 hours for the loop; a topographical map and hiking guide are strongly recommended.

Detailed directions for these hikes and many others in the area may be found in the AMC's *Maine Mountain Guide.*

OTHER OUTDOOR PURSUITS

Sugarloaf's 18-hole **golf course** (☎ 207/237-2000) is often ranked the number-one golf destination in the state by experienced golfers, who are lured here by the Robert Trent Jones, Jr., course design and dramatic mountain backdrop. Sugarloaf hosts a well-respected golf school during the season.

Other outdoor activities are located in and around the **Sugarloaf Outdoor Center** (☎ 207/237-6830). Through the center, you can arrange for fly-fishing lessons, a mountain-bike excursion at the resort's mountain-bike park (rentals available), or hiking or white-water rafting in the surrounding mountains and valleys.

WHERE TO STAY

For convenience, nothing beats staying right on the mountain in winter. Many of the **slopeside condos** are booked through the Sugarloaf/USA Inn (☎ 800/843-5623 or 207/237-2000). Units are spread throughout the base area and are of varying vintage and opulence. All guests have access to the Sugarloaf Sports and Fitness Center.

The Herbert. Main St. (P.O. Box 67), Kingfield, ME 04947. ☎ 800/843-4372 or 207/265-2000. www.byme.com. E-mail: herbert@somtel.com. 32 units. $59 double midweek, $89 weekend, $98 holiday. Rates include continental breakfast. 3-night minimum during holidays. AE, DC, DISC, MC, V. Pets allowed.

The Herbert has the feel of a classic North Woods hostelry—sort of Dodge City by way of Alaska. Built in downtown Kingfield in 1918, the three-story hotel featured all of the finest accoutrements when it was built, including fumed oak paneling and incandescent lights in the lobby (look for the original brass fixtures), a classy dining room, and comfortable rooms. The rooms are furnished in a fairly simple and basic style, featuring flea-market antiques and some newer additions. The Herbert is located about 15 miles from the slopes at Sugarloaf/USA.

Dining: The open but intimate dining room off the lobby of the hotel recalls the days when hotels served the best meals in town. The chef offers interpretations of regional classics, like venison medallions with shiitake mushrooms, and haddock baked with feta cheese. Entrees are $13.95 to $19.95.

5 The Mid-Coast

Veteran Maine travelers contend this part of the coast is fast losing its native charm—it's too commercial, too developed, too much like the rest of the United States. The grousers do have a point, especially regarding Route 1's roadside, but get off the main roads and you'll find pockets where you can catch glimpses of another Maine. Among the sights back road travelers will stumble upon are quiet inland villages, dramatic coastal scenery, and a rich sense of history, especially maritime history.

The best source of information for the region in general is found at the **Maine State Information Center** (☎ **207/846-0833**) just off Exit 17 of I-95 in Yarmouth. This state-run center is stocked with hundreds of brochures and free newspapers, and is staffed with a helpful crew that can provide information on the entire state, but is particularly well-informed about the mid-coast region.

Note that just across the road is the **DeLorme Map Store** (☎ **888/227-1656**). Here you'll find a broad assortment of maps, including the firm's trademark state atlases and a line of CD-ROM map products. The lobby is dominated by a massive rotating globe, constructed on a scale of 1:1,000,000.

FREEPORT

If Freeport were a mall (and that's not a far-fetched analogy), **L.L. Bean** would be the anchor store. It's the business that launched Freeport, elevating its status from just another town off the interstate to one of the two outlet capitals of Maine (the other is Kittery). Freeport still has the form of a classic Maine village, but it's a village that's been largely taken over by the national fashion industry. Most of the old homes and stores have been converted to upscale shops, and now sell name-brand clothing and housewares. Banana Republic occupies an exceedingly handsome brick Federal-style home; even the McDonald's is in a tasteful, understated Victorian farmhouse—you really have to look for the golden arches.

While a number of more modern structures have been built to accommodate the outlet boom, strict planning guidelines have managed to preserve much of the local charm, at least in the village section. Huge parking lots off Main Street are hidden from view, making this one of the more aesthetically pleasing places to shop. But even with these large lots, parking can be scarce during the peak season, especially on rainy summer days when every cottage-bound tourist between York and Camden decides that a trip to Freeport is a winning idea. Bring a lot of patience, and expect teeming crowds if you come at a busy time.

ESSENTIALS

GETTING THERE   Freeport is on Route 1, but is most commonly reached via I-95 from either Exit 19 or 20.

VISITOR INFORMATION   The **Freeport Merchants Association,** P.O. Box 452, Freeport, ME 04032 (☎ **800/865-1994** or 207/865-1212) publishes a map and directory of businesses, restaurants, and overnight accommodations. The free map is available widely around town at stores and restaurants, or contact the association to have them send you one.

WHERE TO STAY

Harraseeket Inn. 162 Main St., Freeport, ME 04032. ☎ **800/342-6423** or 207/865-9377. www.stayfreeport.com. E-mail: harraseeke@aol.com. 84 units. A/C TV TEL. Summer and fall $165–$265 double; spring and early summer $130–$250; winter $100–$235. Rates include breakfast buffet. Take Exit 20 off I-95 to Main St. AE, DC, DISC, MC, V.

The Harraseeket Inn is a large, thoroughly modern hotel 2 blocks north of L.L. Bean. It's to the inn's credit that you could drive down Main Street and not notice it. A late-19th-century home is the soul of the hotel, but most of the rooms are in later additions built in 1989 and 1997. Guests can relax in the well-regarded dining room, in the common room with the baby grand player piano, or in the homey Broad Arrow Tavern with its wood-fired oven and grill. The guest rooms are on the large side and tastefully done, with quarter-canopy beds and a nice mix of contemporary and antique furniture. All have hair dryers and coffee makers; about a quarter have gas or wood-burning fireplaces, and more than half feature single or double whirlpools.

Dining: There are two restaurants on the premises. The Maine Dining Room offers New American dining with an emphasis on local ingredients; entree prices are $13 to $26. The Broad Arrow Tavern has a more informal setting with a less ambitious menu, which includes an array of pizzas and pasta; entrees range from $10 to $21.

Amenities: Concierge, limited room service, dry cleaning, laundry service, safe-deposit boxes, indoor heated lap pool, business center, conference rooms.

○ **Maine Idyll Motor Court.** 325 Route 1, Freeport, ME 04032. ☎ **207/865-4201.** 20 cottages. TV. $44–$70 double (2- and 3-bedroom cottages $68–$90). No credit cards (checks OK). Closed early Nov to late April. Pets allowed.

The 1932 Maine Idyll Motor Court is a Maine classic—a cluster of 20 cottages scattered about a grove of beech and oak trees. Each has a tiny porch, wood-burning fireplace (birch logs provided), TV, modest kitchen facilities (no ovens), and timeworn furniture. The cabins are not lavishly sized, but are comfortable and spotlessly clean. If you need a phone, you're out of luck—the cabins lack them, and there's no pay phone on the premises (the owners are good about letting guests use the office phone if they're in a pinch). The only interruption to an idyll here is the omnipresent sound of traffic: I-95 is just through the trees on one side, Route 1 on the other side. Get past the drone, and you'll find very good value for the money here.

WHERE TO DINE

Harraseeket Lunch & Lobster. Main St., South Freeport. ☎ **207/865-4888.** No reservations. Lobsters market price (typically $8–$11). No credit cards. Daily 11:30am to 8:30pm. Closed mid-Oct to May 1. From I-95 take Exit 17 and head north on Route 1; turn right on S. Freeport Rd. at the huge Indian statue; continue to stop sign in South Freeport; turn right to waterfront. From Freeport take South St. (off Bow St.) to Main St. in South Freeport; turn left to water. LOBSTER POUND.

Located at a boatyard on the Harraseeket River about 10 minutes drive from Freeport's main shopping district, this lobster pound is an especially popular destination on sunny days—although with its heated dining room, it's a worthy destination any time. Order a crustacean according to how hungry you are (from 1 pound on up), then take in the river view from the deck while waiting for your number to be called. Be prepared for big crowds; a good alternative is to come in late afternoon between the crushing lunch and dinner hordes.

Jameson Tavern. 115 Main St.; ☎ **207/865-4196.** Reservations encouraged. Lunch main courses, taproom $5.25–$9.95; dining room $5.25–$10.95; dinner $10.95–$19.95. AE, CB, DC, DISC, MC, V. Taproom daily 11am–11pm; dining room daily 11:30am–10pm. AMERICAN.

Located in a handsome, historic farmhouse literally in the shadow of L.L. Bean (it's just north of the store), the Jameson Tavern touts itself as the birthplace of Maine. In 1820 the papers were signed here legally separating Maine from Massachusetts. Today, it's a dual restaurant under the same ownership. As you enter the door you can head left to the historic Tap Room, a compact, often crowded spot filled with the smell of fresh-popped popcorn. (You're best off outside on the brick patio if the weather's good.) Meals here include fare like crab-cake burgers, lobster croissants, and a variety of build-your-own burgers. The other part of the house is the Dining Room, which is rather more formal in a country-colonial sort of way. Meals here are more sedate and gussied up, with an emphasis on steak and hearty fare. (This isn't a spot for dieters.) While not overly creative, the meals in both the dining room and taproom will hit the spot if you've worked up one of those fierce hungers peculiar to marathon shopping adventures.

BRUNSWICK & BATH

Brunswick and Bath are two handsome and historic towns that share a strong commercial past. Many travelers heading up Route 1 pass through both towns eager to reach the areas with higher billing on the marquee. That's a shame, for both are well worth the detour to sample the sort of slower pace that's being lost elsewhere.

Brunswick was once home to several mills along the Androscoggin River; these have since been converted to offices and the like, but Brunswick's broad Maine Street still bustles with activity. (Idiosyncratic traffic patterns can lead to snarls of traffic in the late afternoon, when local business let out.) Brunswick is also home to Bowdoin College, one of the nation's most respected small colleges. The school was founded in 1794, offered its first classes eight years later, and has since amassed an illustrious roster of prominent alumni, including Nathaniel Hawthorne, Henry Wadsworth Longfellow, Franklin Pierce, and arctic explorer Robert E. Peary. Civil War hero Joshua Chamberlain served as president of the college after the war.

Eight miles to the east, **Bath** is pleasantly situated on the broad Kennebec River, and is a noted center of shipbuilding. The first U.S.-built ship was constructed downstream at the Popham Bay colony in the early–17th century; in the years since, shipbuilders have constructed more than 5,000 ships hereabouts. Bath shipbuilding reached its heyday in the late–19th century, but the business of shipbuilding continues to this day. Bath Iron Works is one of the nation's preeminent boatyards, constructing and repairing ships for the U.S. Navy. The scaled-down military has left Bath shipbuilders in a somewhat tenuous state, but it's still common to see the steely gray ships in the dry dock (the best view is from the bridge over the Kennebec), and the towering red-and-white crane moving supplies and parts around the yard.

ESSENTIALS

GETTING THERE Brunswick and Bath are both situated on Route 1. Brunswick is accessible via Exits 22 and 23 off I-95. If you're bypassing Brunswick and heading north up Route 1 to Bath or beyond, continue up I-95 and exit at the "coastal connector" exit in Topsham, which avoids some of the slower going through Brunswick.

For bus service from Portland or Boston, contact **Vermont Transit** (☎ 800/451-3292) or **Concord Trailways** (☎ 800/639-3317).

VISITOR INFORMATION The **Bath-Brunswick Region Chamber of Commerce,** 59 Pleasant Street, Brunswick, ME 04011 (☎ 207/725-8797 or 207/443-9751) offers information and lodging assistance Monday to Friday 8:30am to 5pm from its offices near downtown Brunswick. The chamber also staffs an information center 10am to 7pm daily in summer on Route 1 between Brunswick and Bath.

SPECIAL EVENT In early August look for posters for the ever-popular ✪ **Maine Festival** (☎ 207/772-9012), which takes place at Thomas Point Beach between Brunswick and Bath. What started as a sort of counterculture celebration of Maine people and crafts has evolved and grown to a hugely popular mainstream event. Performers from throughout Maine gather at this pretty coveside park (it's a private campground the rest of the summer), and put on shows from noon past dark throughout the first weekend in August. Displays of crafts, artwork, and the products of small Maine businesses are also on display. An admission fee is charged.

SEEING THE SIGHTS

In Brunswick

Bowdoin College Museum of Art. Walker Art Building, Bowdoin College. ☎ 207/725-3275. Free admission. Tues–Sat 10am–5pm, Sun 2–5pm.

This stern, neoclassical building on the Bowdoin campus was designed by the prominent architectural firm of McKim, Mead, and White. While the collection is small, it has a number of exceptionally fine paintings, along with early furniture and artifacts from classical antiquity. The artists include Andrew and N. C. Wyeth, Marsden Hartley, Winslow Homer, and John Singer Sargent. The older upstairs galleries have soft, diffused lighting from skylights high above; it feels a bit as if you're underwater. The basement galleries, which feature temporary exhibits (almost all are excellently conceived), are modern and spacious.

Peary-MacMillan Arctic Museum. Hubbard Hall, Bowdoin College. ☎ **207/725-3416.** Free admission. Tues–Sat 10am–5pm, Sun 2–5pm.

While Admiral Robert E. Peary (class of 1887) is better known for his accomplishments (he "discovered" the North Pole at age 53 in 1909), Donald MacMillan (class of 1898) also racked up an impressive string of achievements in Arctic research and exploration. You can learn about both men and the wherefores of Arctic exploration in this altogether manageable museum on the Bowdoin campus. The front room features mounted animals from the Arctic, including some impressive polar bears. A second room outlines Peary's historic 1909 expedition, complete with excerpts from Peary's journal. The last room includes varied displays of Inuit arts and crafts, some historic, some modern. This compact museum can be visited in about 20 minutes or so; the art museum (see above) is just next door.

In Bath

Maine Maritime Museum & Shipyard. 243 Washington St. ☎ **207/443-1316.** Admission $8 adult, $5.50 child 6–17, $24 family. Daily 9:30am–5pm.

On the shores of the Kennebec River, this museum (it's just south of Bath Iron Works) features a wide array of displays and exhibits related to the boatbuilder's art. It's sited at the former shipyard of Percy and Small, which built some 42 schooners in the late 19th and early 20th century. The largest wooden ship ever built in America—the 329-foot *Wyoming*—was constructed on this lot in 1909.

The centerpiece of the museum is the handsomely modern Maritime History Building. Here, you'll find changing exhibits of maritime art and artifacts. (There's also a gift shop with a great selection of books about ships.) The 10-acre property houses a fleet of additional displays, including an intriguing exhibit on lobstering and a complete boat building shop. Here, you can watch handsome wooden boats take shape in this active program. Kids enjoy the play area (they can search for pirates from the crow's nest of the play boat). Be sure to wander down to the docks on the river to see what's tied up, or to inquire about river cruises (extra charge).

WHERE TO STAY

The three places listed below are all located at a distance from Bath or Brunswick, but are worth the little bit of extra effort because they each offer a taste of classic coastal Maine. For comfortable in-town accommodations in Brunswick, try the **Brunswick Bed & Breakfast** (165 Park Row, Brunswick, ME 04011☎ **800/299-4914** or 207/729-4914), with eight rooms in a Federal home on the green ($87 to $125 double).

In Bath, try the very Victorian **Galen C. Moses House** (1009 Washington St., Bath, ME 04530, ☎ **888/442-8771** or 207/442-8771), whose exterior is done up exuberantly in plum and teal ($69 to $129 double).

✪ **Driftwood Inn & Cottages.** Washington Ave., Bailey Island, ME 04003. ☎ **207/ 833-5461,** off-season ☎ 508/947-1066. 18 double units, 9 single units, 6 cottages (most units share hallways baths). $70–$75 double; weekly $360 per person including breakfast and dinner; cottages $475–$550 per week. No credit cards. Open late May to mid-Oct; dining room open late June–Labor Day.

The oceanside Driftwood Inn dates back to 1910 and is a coastal New England classic. A rustic summer retreat on three acres at the end of a dead-end road, the inn is a compound of four weathered, shingled buildings and a handful of housekeeping cottages on a rocky, oceanside property. The spartan rooms of time-aged pine have a simple turn-of-the-century flavor that hasn't been gentrified in the least. Most rooms share bathrooms down the hall, but some have private sinks and toilets. Your primary company will be the constant sound of surf surging in and ebbing out of the fissured rocks. The inn has an old saltwater pool and porches with wicker furniture to while away the afternoons; bring plenty of books and board games.

Dining: The dining room serves basic fare (roasts, fish, etc.) in a wonderfully austere setting overlooking the sea; meals are extra, although a weekly American plan is available. Dining is open to outside guests if you call ahead.

Grey Havens. Seguinland Rd., Georgetown Island, ME 04548. ☎ **207/371-2616.** Fax 207/ 371-2274. 13 units, 2 with private hall bathrooms. $100–$205 double. Rates include continental breakfast. MC, V. Closed mid-Nov to early Apr. From Rte. 1 head south on Rte. 127 then follow signs for Reid State Park; watch for inn on left. No children under 7.

Located on Georgetown Island off the beaten track southeast of Bath, Grey Havens is worth seeking out if you're in mind of a place to idly watch the ocean while you unwind. This graceful, 1904 shingled home with prominent turrets sits on a high, rocky bluff overlooking the sea. Inside, it's all richly mellowed pine paneling, and a spacious common room where you can relax in cozy chairs in front of the cobblestone fireplace while listening to classical music. The guest rooms are simply but comfortably furnished. In the turret rooms, the managers have even placed binoculars to help guests better monitor the comings and goings on the water. The oceanfront rooms command a premium, but are worth it. (If you're looking to save a few dollars, ask for an oceanfront room that has a private bath just across the hall.) Guests have the run of the old kitchen and can use the inn's canoe and bikes to explore the outlying area. One caveat: The inn has been only lightly modernized, which means rather thin walls. If you have loud neighbors, you'll learn more about their lives than you may care to know.

Sebasco Harbor Resort. Route 217, Sebasco Estates, ME 04565. ☎ **800/225-3819** or 207/389-1161. Fax 207/389-2004. www.sebasco.com. E-mail: info@sebasco.com. 115 units. TEL. July to Labor Day $186–$326 double; May–June $146–$298; Sept–Oct $156–$306. Rates include breakfast and dinner. 15% service charge additional. 2-night minimum stay weekends. AE, DISC, MC, V. Closed late Oct to early May. South from Bath 11 miles on Rt. 209; look for Rte. 217 and signs for Sebasco.

Sebasco is a grand old seaside resort under new and vigorous management that's fighting a generally successful battle against time and irrelevance. It's a self-contained resort of the sort that flourished 50 years ago, and today is being rediscovered by families. Some guests have been coming here for 60 years and love the timelessness of it; newcomers are starting to visit now that much of it has benefited from a facelift.

The 664-acre grounds remain the real attraction here—guests enjoy sweeping ocean views, a lovely seaside pool, and great walks around well-cared-for property. The guest rooms, it should be noted, are adequate rather than elegant, and may seem a bit short of the mark given the high prices charged. Most lack a certain style—especially the 40 rooms in the old inn, which are dated, and I don't mean that in a good way. (The small wooden decks on many rooms are a plus, though.) Better are the quirky rooms in the octagonal Lighthouse Building—rooms #12 and #20 have among the best views in the state. Most (not all) rooms have TVs; ask first if it's important to you. If you're coming for more than 2 days, it's probably best to book a cottage, which come in all sorts and sizes.

Dining/Diversions: The Pilot House Dining Room is airy, contemporary, and the best place to enjoy the sunsets. You'll find white linens and a jackets-recommended-on-men policy; the menu is contemporary resort style, with dishes like grilled swordfish with a pesto butter, and prime rib with a Parmesan Yorkshire pudding. The dining room is open to the public ($28 fixed price). Another restaurant, Ledges, is a more informal spot downstairs that serves from a lighter menu.

Amenities: Swimming in outdoor saltwater pool and ocean, 9-hole golf course, tennis courts, hot tub, sauna, health club, bay cruises, canoe and kayak rentals, shuffleboard, snack bar, children's center and programs, video games, candlepin bowling, movies, nature trails, sailing lessons, bike rentals. Popham Beach is 5 miles away.

WHERE TO DINE

✪ **Robinhood Free Meetinghouse.** Robinhood Rd., Robinhood. ☎ **207/371-2188.** Reservations encouraged. Main courses $16–$23. AE, DISC, MC, V. Daily May–Oct 5:30–9pm; limited days late fall–spring; call first. FUSION.

Chef Michael Gagne is ambitious. His menu features between 30 and 40 entrees, and they're wildly eclectic—from Thai grilled vegetables to Wiener schnitzel to salmon en papillote. Ordering from the menu almost seems like playing stump the chef: Let's see you make *this!*

And you know what? Gagne always hits his notes and rarely serves a mediocre meal. You just can't go wrong here. Gagne has attracted legions of dedicated local followers, who appreciate the extraordinary attention paid to detail. Carbonated water and slices of citrus are served at every table. Foam baffles are glued discreetly to the underside of the seats to dampen the echoes in the sparsely decorated, immaculately restored 1855 Greek Revival Meetinghouse. Even the sorbet served between courses is homemade. Eating here is not an inexpensive proposition, but it offers tremendous value for the price.

Five Islands Lobster Co. Rte. 127, Georgetown. ☎ **207/371-2990.** No reservations. $5–$8 per lobster; 75¢ for corn on the cob. MC, V. Daily 11am–8pm in July & August; shorter hours during the off-season. Closed Columbus Day to Mother's Day. LOBSTER POUND.

The drive alone makes this lobster pound a worthy destination. It's located about 12 miles south of Route 1 down winding Route 127, past bogs and spruce forests with glimpses of azure ocean inlets. (Head south from Woolwich, which is just across the bridge from Bath.) Drive until you pass a cluster of clapboard homes, then keep going until you can't go any farther.

Wander out to the wharf with its unbeatable island views, and place your order. This is a down-home affair, owned jointly by local lobstermen and the proprietors of Grey Havens, a local inn (see above). While you're awaiting your lobster, you can wander next door to the Love Nest Snack Bar for extras like soda or the killer onion rings (you get a huge basketful for $2.75). Gather up your grub and settle in at one of the wharf picnic tables, or head over to the grassy spots at the edge of the dirt parking lot. And bring some patience: despite its edge-of-the-world feel, the lobster pound draws steady traffic and it can be crowded on weekends.

BOOTHBAY HARBOR

Boothbay Harbor, 11 miles south of Route 1, is a small and scenic town that seems to exert an outsize allure on passing tourists. This former fishing port was discovered in the last century by wealthy rusticators who built imposing seaside homes and retreated here in summer to avoid the swelter of the cities along the eastern seaboard.

Having embraced the tourist dollar, the harborfront village never really looked back, and in more recent years it has emerged one of the premier destinations of travelers in search of classic coastal Maine. This embrace has had an obvious impact. The village has been discovered by bus tours, which has in turn attracted kitschy shops and a slew of mediocre restaurants that all seem to specialize in baked stuffed haddock. Note that Boothbay Harbor is very much a summer town; by and large it shutters up shortly after Labor Day.

If Boothbay Harbor is stuck in a time warp, it's Tourist Trap (ca. 1974) bland and boxy motels hem in the harbor, and side-by-side boutiques hawk the same mass market trinkets (Beanie Babies, T-shirts emblazoned with puffins). Despite it all, there's still an affable charm that manages to rise above the clutter and cheese, especially on foggy days when the horns bleat mournfully at the harbor's mouth.

ESSENTIALS

GETTING THERE   Boothbay Harbor is south of Route 1 on Route 27. Coming from the west, look for signs shortly after crossing the Sheepscot River at Wiscasset.

VISITOR INFORMATION   As befits a town where tourism is a major industry, Boothbay has three visitor information centers in and around town, reflecting the importance of the travel dollars to the region. At the intersection of Route 1 and Route 27 is a **visitor center** that's open May through October and is a good place to stock up on brochures. A mile before you reach the village is the seasonal **Boothbay Information Center** on your right (open June to October). If you zoom past it or it's closed, don't fret. The year-round **Boothbay Harbor Region Chamber of Commerce,** P.O. Box 356, Boothbay Harbor, ME 04538 (☎ **207/633-2353**) is at the intersection of Route 27 and Route 96.

EXPLORING BOOTHBAY HARBOR

Compact Boothbay Harbor, clustered along the water's edge, is ideal for exploring by foot. (The trick is parking, which in midsummer will require either persistence or the forking over of a few dollars.) Pedestrians naturally gravitate to the long, narrow **footbridge** across the harbor, first built in 1901, but it's more of a destination than a link—other than some restaurants and motels, there's really not much on the other side. The winding, small streets that weave through the town also offer plenty of boutiques and shops that cater to the tourist trade and offer decent browsing.

If dense fog or rain socks in the harbor, bide your time at the vintage **Romar Bowling Lanes** (☎ **207/633-5721**). This log-and-shingle building near the footbridge has a harbor view and has been distracting travelers with the promise of traditional New

England candlepin bowling since 1946. On rainy summer days, the wait for one of the eight lanes can be up to an hour. While you're waiting you can play pool and video games, or order a root beer float from the snack bar. It's not hard to find. You'll hear pins crashing, shrieks of victory, and howls of despair from various points around the town.

Marine Resources Aquarium. McKown Point Rd., West Boothbay Harbor. ☎ **207/633-9542.** $2.50 adult, $2 children 5–18. Daily 10am–5pm. Closed after Columbus Day to just before Memorial Day.

Operated by the state's Department of Marine Resources, this compact aquarium offers context for life in the sea that surrounds Boothbay and beyond. You can view rare albino and blue lobsters, and get your hands wet at a 20-foot touch tank—a sort of petting zoo of the slippery and slimy. Parking is tight at aquarium, which is located on a point across the water from Boothbay Harbor. A free shuttle bus (look for the Rocktide trolley) connects downtown with the aquarium and runs frequently throughout the summer.

BOAT TOURS

The best way to see the timeless Maine coast around Boothbay is on a boat tour. Nearly two dozen tour boats berth at the harbor or nearby, offering a range of trips ranging from an hour's outing to a full-day excursion to Monhegan Island. You can even observe puffins at their rocky colonies far offshore.

Balmy Day Cruises (☎ 207/633-2284) runs several trips from the harbor, including an all-day excursion to Monhegan Island on the 65-foot *Balmy Days II* (this allows passengers about 4 hours to explore the island before returning—see "Monhegan Island" section below). The Monhegan trip is $29 (children $18). The company also offers harbor tours and 2-hour dinner cruises with onboard meals of chicken, lobster roll, and steamed lobster; harbor tours are $8.50; and dinner cruises are approximately $22. If you'd rather be sailing, ask about the 90-minute cruises on the *Bay Lady,* a 15-passenger Friendship sloop ($18).

Windborne Cruises (☎ **207/882-1020**) sails from Smuggler's Cove Motel on Route 96, about 2 miles south of East Boothbay. Passengers report that Capt. Roger Marin is a great storyteller and captivates his temporary crew with local tales. Marin can accommodate just six passengers on the 40-foot *Tribute,* a handsome Block Island sailboat. Two-hour cruises depart at 11am and 3pm, and cost $25 per person. You can also charter the boat for a half day ($200) or full day ($375), with both options including lunch.

The most personal way to see the harbor is via sea kayak. **Tidal Transit Kayak Co.** (☎ **207/633-7140**), offers morning, afternoon, and sunset tours of the harbor for $30 (sunset's the best bet). Kayaks may also be rented for $12 an hour, or $50 per day. Tidal Transit is open daily in summer (except when it rains) on the waterfront at 47 Townshend Avenue (walk down the alley).

WHERE TO STAY

Five Gables Inn. Murray Hill Rd. (P.O. Box 335, East Boothbay, ME 04544. ☎ **800/451-5048** or 207/633-4551. www.fivegablesinn.com. E-mail: info@fivegablesinn.com. 16 units. TEL. $100–$170 double. Rates include breakfast buffet. MC, V. Closed Nov to mid-May. Drive through East Boothbay on Rte. 96; turn right after crest of hill on Murray Hill Rd. Children 12 and older are welcome.

The handsome Five Gables Inn was painstakingly restored just over a decade ago, and now sits proudly amid a small colony of summer homes on a quiet road above a peaceful cove. It's nicely isolated from the confusion and hubbub of Boothbay Harbor; the activity of choice here is to sit on the deck and enjoy the glimpses of the water through the trees. It's a good base for bicycling—you can pedal down to Ocean Point or in to town. It's also handy to the Lobsterman's Wharf for good, informal dining. The rooms are pleasantly appointed, and five have fireplaces that burn manufactured logs. The common room is nicely furnished in an upscale country style. The breakfast buffet is an inviting affair, with offerings like tomato-basil frittata, cornbread with bacon and green onions, and blueberry-stuffed French toast.

Newagen Seaside Inn. Route 27 (P.O. Box 68), Cape Newagen, ME 04552. E-mail: seaside@wiscasset.net. ☎ **800/654-5242** or 207/633-5242. 26 units. $120–$200 double. Rates include breakfast. MC, V. Closed late Sept to mid-June. Located on south tip of Southport Island; take Rte. 27 from Boothbay Harbor and continue on until the inn sign.

This 1940s-era resort has seen more glamorous days, but it's still a superb small, low-key resort offering stunning ocean views and walks in a fragrant spruce forest. The inn is housed in a low, wide, white-shingled building that's furnished simply with country pine furniture. There's a classically austere dining room, narrow cruise-ship-like hallways with pine wainscotting, and a lobby with a fireplace. The rooms are plain and the inn is a bit threadbare in spots, but never mind that. Guests flock here for the 85-acre oceanside grounds filled with decks, gazebos, and walkways that border on the magical. It's hard to convey the magnificence of the ocean views, which may be the best of any inn in Maine.

Dining: The handsome, simple dining room with ocean views offers a menu with traditional New England fare and a selection of more creative additions (entrees $10 to $25). Closed Tuesday for dinner.

Amenities: Freshwater and saltwater pools, badminton, horseshoes, tennis, sundeck, free rowboats.

Spruce Point Inn. Atlantic Ave. (P.O. Box 237), Boothbay Harbor, ME 04538. ☎ **800/553-0289** or 207/633-4152. www.sprucepointinn.com. E-mail: thepoint@sprucepointinn. com. 72 units. TV TEL. July–Aug $195–$310 double; shoulder seasons $95–$250. 2-night minimum weekends; 3-nights holidays. AE, DC, DISC, MC, V. Closed mid-Oct to Memorial Day. Turn seaward on Union St. in Boothbay Harbor; proceed 2 miles to the inn. Pets allowed ($50 deposit, $100 cleaning fee).

The Spruce Point Inn was originally built as a hunting and fishing lodge in the 1890s, and evolved into a summer resort in 1912. After years of quiet neglect, it has benefited greatly from a makeover that's been ongoing since the late 1980s. A number of new units have been built on the grounds in the late 1990s; they match the older buildings architecturally, and blend in seamlessly. (Another dozen units are slated for construction by late 1999.) Those looking for historic authenticity may be disappointed. Those seeking modern resort facilities (Jacuzzis, carpeting, updated furniture) along with accenting to provide a bit of historic flavor, will be delighted.

Anyway, it's hard to imagine anyone being let down by the 15-acre grounds, situated on an rocky point facing west across the harbor. Guests typically fill their time idling in the Adirondack chairs, or partaking of more strenuous activities include croquet, shuffleboard, tennis on clay courts, or swimming. New for 1999 are children's programs to accommodate the growing number of families destined here. Note also that rates have dropped this year, reflecting that meals are no longer included.

Dining: Diners are seated in an elegant formal dining room (men are requested to wear jackets) and enjoy wonderful sunset views across the mouth of Boothbay Harbor as they peruse the evening menu. The menu features adaptations of traditional New England meals. Appetizers include crab cakes with three sauces; sautéed mussels; and a signature cabbage-and-lobster soup with fresh dandelion. Main courses might include pan-roasted filet mignon, or lobster with a bay stuffing of scallops. Entrees range from $15 to $25.

Amenities: Two outdoor pools (one heated), Jacuzzi, two outdoor clay tennis courts, fitness center, lawn games (shuffleboard, tetherball, etc.), sundeck, conference rooms, self-service Laundromat, concierge, dry cleaning, laundry service, in-room massage, baby-sitting, safe, game room, free shuttle to Boothbay.

Topside. McKown Hill, Boothbay Harbor, ME 04538. ☎ **207/633-5404.** 25 units. TEL. July 1–Labor Day $65–$150 double (most rooms $85); May–June and Sept–Oct $50–$80 double. Rates include continental breakfast. DISC, MC, V. Closed mid-Oct to mid-May.

The old gray house on the hilltop looming over the dated motel buildings may bring to mind the Bates Motel, especially when a full moon is overhead. But get over that. Because Topside offers spectacular ocean views at a reasonable price from a quiet hilltop compound located right in downtown Boothbay. The inn itself—a former boarding house for shipyard workers—features several comfortable rooms, furnished with an odd mix of antiques and contemporary furniture. At the edge of the inn's lawn are two outbuildings housing basic motel units. These are on the small side, furnished simply and basically with dated paneling and some unfortunate furniture. (You definitely won't find this hotel profiled in *House Beautiful.*) Rooms 9 and 14 have the best views, but most rooms offer a glimpse of the water, and many have decks or patios. All guests have access to the wonderful lawn and the endless views, and the Reed family, which owns and operates the inn, is accommodating and friendly.

WHERE TO DINE

When wandering through Boothbay Harbor, watch for "King" Brud and his famous **hot-dog cart.** Brud started selling hot dogs in town in 1943, and he's still at it. Dogs are $1. He's usually at the corner of McKown and Commercial streets from 10 am till 4 pm from June through October.

Those wishing for innovative dining should also consider (in addition to Christopher's Boathouse, below) the **Spruce Point Inn,** listed above.

Boothbay Region Lobstermen's Co-op. Atlantic Ave., Boothbay Harbor. ☎ **207/633-4900.** No reservations. Fried and grilled foods $1.25–$8.75; dinners $6.50–$9.95. No credit cards. Open daily May to mid-Oct 11:30am–8:30pm. By foot: cross footbridge and turn right; follow road for ⅓ mile to co-op. SEAFOOD.

"We are not responsible if the seagulls steal your food" reads the sign at the ordering window of this casual, harborside lobster joint. And that sets the tone pretty well. Situated across the harbor from downtown Boothbay, the lobstermen's co-op offers no-frills lobster and seafood. This is the best pick from among the cluster of usually dependable lobster-in-the-rough places that line the waterfront nearby. You order at a pair of windows, then pick up your meal and carry your tray to either the picnic tables on the dock or inside a garagelike two-story prefab building. Lobsters are priced to market (figure $8 to $10), with extras like corn on the cob for 95¢. A bank of soda machines provides liquid refreshment. This is a fine place for a lobster on a sunny day, but it's uninteresting at best in rain or fog.

○ **Christopher's Boathouse.** 25 Union St., Boothbay Harbor. ☎ **207/633-6565.** Reservations recommended during peak season. Main courses $16.75–$22.50. MC, V. Daily 5–9pm (until 9:30pm Fri–Sat). CREATIVE AMERICAN/WOOD GRILL.

Christopher's opened in Boothbay Harbor in 1998 and offers a welcome change from the generally unexciting fare found elsewhere around town. Scenically located at the head of the harbor, the restaurant is open, bright, and modern, and a handful of lucky diners get a tremendous view up the harbor. (There's also outside deck dining when the weather is good.) The chef has a superb touch with spicy flavors, and deftly combines the expected with the unexpected (to wit: lobster and mango bisque with spicy lobster wontons.) The meals from the wood grill are excellent, and include an Asian-spiced tuna with Caribbean salsa, and a barbecue-spiced flank steak. Christopher's is a popular destination in the summer months; make a reservation to avoid disappointment.

MONHEGAN ISLAND

Brawny, wild, and remote, ✪ **Monhegan Island** is Maine's premier island destination. Visited by Europeans as early as 1497 (although some historians insist that earlier Norsemen carved primitive runes on neighboring Manana Island), the island was first settled by fishermen attracted to the sea's bounty in the offshore waters. Starting in the 1870s and continuing to the present day, noted artists discovered the island and came to stay for a spell. Their roster included Rockwell Kent (the artist most closely associated with the island), George Bellows, Edward Hopper, and Robert Henri. The artists gathered in the kitchen of the lighthouse to chat and drink coffee; it's said that the wife of the lighthouse keeper accumulated a tremendously valuable collection of paintings. Today, Jamie Wyeth, scion of the Wyeth clan, claims the island as his part-time home.

It's not hard to figure why artists have been attracted to the place: there's a mystical quality to it, from the thin light to the startling contrasts of the dark cliffs and the foamy white surf. There's also a remarkable sense of tranquillity to this place, which can only help focus one's inner vision.

If you have the time, I'd strongly recommend an overnight on the island at one of the several hostelries. Day trips are popular and easily arranged, but the island's true character doesn't start to emerge until the last day boat sails away and the quiet, rustic appeal of the island starts to percolate back to the surface.

ESSENTIALS

GETTING THERE Access to Monhegan Island is via boat from either New Harbor, Boothbay Harbor, or Port Clyde. The hour-and-ten-minute trip from Port Clyde is the favored route among longtime island visitors. The trip from this rugged fishing village is very picturesque as it passes the Marshall Point Lighthouse and a series of spruce-clad islands before setting out on the open sea.

Two boats make the run to Monhegan from Port Clyde. The *Laura B.* is a doughty workboat (building supplies and boxes of food are loaded on first; passengers fill in the available niches on the deck and in the small cabin). A newer boat—the faster, passenger-oriented *Elizabeth Ann*—also makes the run, offering a large heated cabin and more seating. You'll need to leave your car behind, so pack light and wear sturdy shoes. The fare is $25 round-trip for adults; $12 for children 2 to 12 years old. Reservations are advised: **Monhegan Boat Line,** P.O. Box 238, Port Clyde, ME 04855 (☎ 207/372-8848; www.monheganboat.com). Parking is available near the dock for an additional $4 per day.

VISITOR INFORMATION Monhegan Island has no formal visitor's center, but it's small and friendly enough that you can make inquiries of just about anyone you meet on the island pathways. The clerks at the ferry dock in Port Clyde are also quite helpful. Be sure to pick up the inexpensive map of the island's hiking trail at the boat ticket office or at the various shops around the island.

Because wildfire could destroy this breezy island in short order, smoking is prohibited outside the village.

EXPLORING MONHEGAN

Walking is the chief activity on the island, and it's genuinely surprising how much distance you can cover on these 700 acres (about 1½ miles long and ½ mile wide). The village clusters tightly around the harbor; the rest of the island is mostly wildland, laced with some 17 miles of trails. Much of the island is ringed with high, open bluffs atop fissured cliffs. Pack a picnic lunch and hike the perimeter trail, and plan to spend much of the day just sitting and reading, or enjoying the surf rolling in against the cliffs. During one lazy afternoon on a bluff near the island's southern tip, I spotted a half-dozen whale spouts over the course of a half hour, but never did agree with my friend whether it was one whale or several.

Birding is a popular activity in the spring and fall. Monhegan Island is on the Atlantic flyway, and a wide variety of birds stop at the island along their migration routes. Swapping stories of the day's sightings is a popular activity at island inns and B&Bs.

The sole attraction on the island is the **Monhegan Museum,** located next to the 1824 lighthouse on a high point above the village. The museum, open from July through September, has a quirky collection of historic artifacts and provides some context for this rugged island's history. Also near the lighthouse is a small and select art museum that opened in 1998, featuring the works of Rockwell Kent and other island artists.

The spectacular view from the grassy slope in front of the lighthouse is the real prize. The vista sweeps across a marsh, past one of the island's most historic hotels, past melancholy Manana Island and across the sea beyond. Get here early if you want a good seat for the sunset; it seems most visitors to the island congregate here after dinner to watch the sinking of the sun. (Another popular place is the island's southern tip, where the wreckage of the *D. T. Sheridan,* a coal barge, washed up in 1948.)

WHERE TO STAY & DINE

Monhegan House. Monhegan Island, ME 04852. ☎ **800/599-7983** or 207/594-7983. 33 units, all with shared bath. $90 double. AE, DISC, MC, V. Closed Columbus Day to Memorial Day.

The handsome Monhegan House has been accommodating guests since 1870, and it has the comfortable, worn patina of a venerable lodging house. The accommodations at this four-floor walk-up are austere but comfortable; there are no closets, and everyone uses clean dormitory-style bathrooms. The downstairs lobby with fireplace is a welcome spot to sit and take the fog-induced chill out of your bones (even in August it can be cool here). The front deck is a nice place to lounge and keep a close eye on the comings and goings of the village. The restaurant offers three meals a day, with a selection of filling but simple meat and fish dishes, along with vegetarian entrees. Main courses range in price from about $9 to $16.

Trailing Yew. Monhegan Island, ME 04852. ☎ **207/596-0440.** 37 units in four buildings (all but 1 share bathrooms). $116 double, including breakfast, dinner, taxes, and tips. No credit cards. Closed mid-Oct to mid-May. Pets allowed.

At the end of long summer afternoons, guests congregate near the flagpole in front of the main building of this rustic hillside compound. They sit in Adirondack chairs or chat with newfound friends. But mostly they're waiting for the ringing of the bell, which signals them in for dinner, as if at summer camp. Inside, guests sit around long tables, introduce themselves to their neighbors, then pour an iced tea and wait for the delicious, family-style dinner. (You're given a choice, including vegetarian options, but my advice is to opt for the fresh fish whenever its available.)

The Trailing Yew, which has been taking in guests since 1929, is a friendly, informal place, popular with hikers and birders (meals are a great time to swap tales of sightings) who tend to make fast friends here amid the welcome adversity of Monhegan Island. Guest rooms are eclectic and simply furnished in a pleasantly dated summer-home style; only one of the four guest buildings has electricity (most but not all bathrooms have electricity); guests in rooms without electricity are provided a kerosene lamp and instructions in its use (bring a flashlight just in case).

6 Penobscot Bay

Traveling eastward along the Maine Coast, those who pay attention to such things will notice they're suddenly heading almost due north around Rockland. The culprit behind this geographic quirk is Penobscot Bay, a sizable bite out of the Maine Coast that forces a lengthy northerly detour to cross the head of the bay where the Penobscot River flows in at Bucksport.

You'll find some of Maine's most distinctive coastal scenery in this area, dotted with broad offshore islands and high hills rising above the blue bay. Although the mouth of Penobscot Bay is occupied by two large islands, its waters can still churn with vigor when the tides and winds conspire.

Penobscot Bay's western shore gets a heavy stream of tourist traffic, especially along Route 1 through the scenic village of Camden. Nonetheless, this is a good destination to get a taste of the Maine coast. Services for travelers are abundant, although during the peak season a small miracle will be required to find a weekend guest room without a reservation.

ROCKLAND & ENVIRONS

Located on the southwest edge of Penobscot Bay, Rockland has long been proud of its brick-and-blue-collar waterfront town reputation. Built around the fishing industry, Rockland historically dabbled in tourism on the side. But with the decline of the fisheries and the rise of the tourist economy in Maine, the balance has shifted—in the last decade, Rockland has been colonized by creative restaurateurs and innkeepers and other small-business folks who are painting it with an unaccustomed gloss.

There's a small park on the waterfront from which the fleet of windjammers comes and goes (see below), but more appealing than Rockland's waterfront is its commercial downtown—it's basically one long street lined with sophisticated historic brick architecture. If it's picturesque harbor towns you're seeking, head to Camden, Rockport, Port Clyde, or Stonington. But Rockland makes a great base for exploring this beautiful coastal region, especially if you have a low tolerance for trinkets and tourist hordes.

ESSENTIALS

GETTING THERE   Route 1 passes directly through Rockland. Rockland's tiny airport is served by **Colgan Air** (☎ **800/272-5488** or 207/596-7604) with daily flights from Boston and Bar Harbor. **Concord Trailways** (☎ **800/639-3317**) offers bus service from Rockland to Bangor and Portland.

VISITOR INFORMATION   The **Rockland/Thomaston Area Chamber of Commerce,** P.O. Box 508, Rockland, ME 04841 (☎ **800/562-2529** or 207/596-0376; E-mail rtacc@midcoast.com) staffs an information desk at Harbor Park. It's open daily 9am to 5pm Memorial Day to Labor Day; Monday to Saturday until Columbus Day; and weekdays only the rest of the year.

TWO FINE MUSEUMS

Farnsworth Museum. 352 Main St., Rockland. ☎ **207/596-6457.** E-mail: farnsworth@ midcoast.com. $9 adults, $8 seniors, $5 students 18 and older, free for 17 and under (prices discounted $1 in winter). MC, V. Summer 9am–5pm daily; winter Tues–Sat 10am–5pm, Sun 1–5pm.

Penobscot Bay

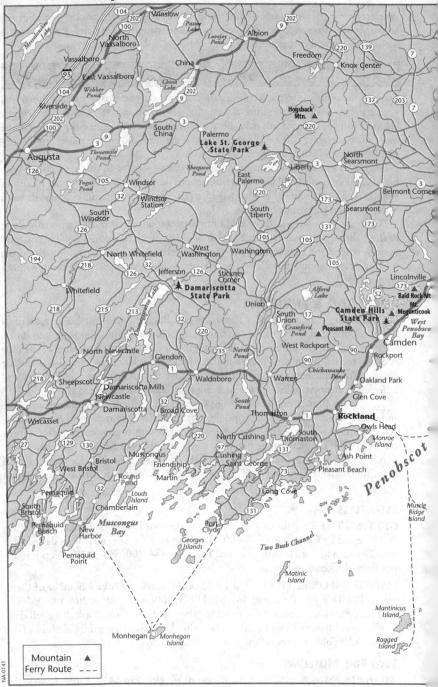

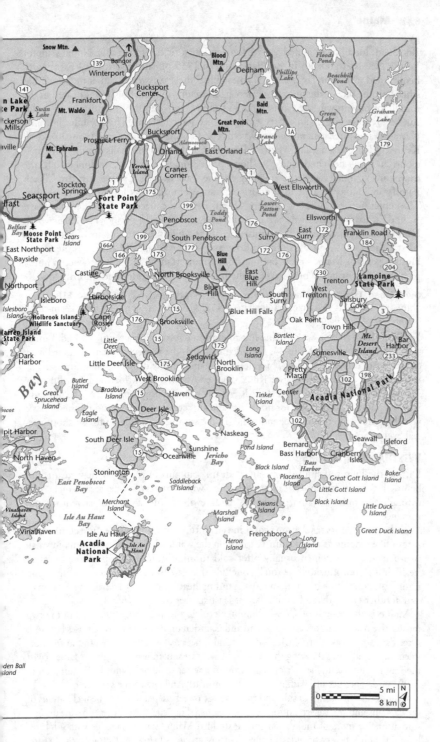

Snow Mtn. ▲

139
Winterport

↑ TO
Bangor

141

Blood
Mtn. ▲

Dedham

Flood
Pond

Phillips
Lake

Beachhill
Pond

n Lake
e Park

Frankfort

Mt. Waldo ▲

1A

Bucksport
Center

46

Bald
Mtn. ▲

Green
Lake

Graham
Lake

ckerson
Mills

sville

Mt. Ephraim ▲

Prospect Ferry

Bucksport

Great Pond
Mtn. ▲

1A

Branch
Lake

180

179

Orland

East Orland

Alamoosook
Lake

Cranes
Corner

1

West Ellsworth

Verona
Island

Stockton
Springs

1

175

Searsport

fast

Fort Point
State Park

199

Toddy
Pond

Lower
Patton
Pond

176

Ellsworth

1

Penobscot

15

Surry

East
Surry

172

Franklin Road

3

184

Belfast
Bay

Moose Point
State Park

Sears
Island

199

South Penobscot

177

172

176

East Northport

166A

166

175

Blue
Hill ▲

230

Trenton

204

Lamoine
State Park

Bayside

Castine

North Brooksville

East
Blue
Hill

West
Trenton

South
Surry

Salsbury
Cove

Northport

Isleboro

Harborside

Blue
Hill

Blue Hill Falls

Oak Point

Town Hill

3

Islesboro
Island

Holbrook Island
Wildlife Sanctuary

Cape
Rosier

176

Brooksville

15

Bartlett
Island

Somesville

Mt.
Desert
Island

Bar
Harbor

arren Island
State Park

Little
Deer
Isle

15

Sedgwick

175

Long
Island

Pretty
Marsh

233

Dark
Harbor

Little Deer Isle

175

North
Brooklin

Center

102

198

Bay

Butler
Island

West Brooklin

Tinker
Island

Acadia National Park

Great
Sprucehead
Island

Bradbury
Island

15

Haven

Blue Hill Bay

102

scot
y

Eagle
Island

Deer Isle

pit Harbor

South Deer Isle

Naskeag

Pond Island

Bernard
Bass Harbor

Seawall

Isleford

North Haven

15

Sunshine

Oceanville

Jericho
Bay

Black Island

Bass
Harbor

Great Gott Island

Cranberry
Isles

Baker
Island

Stonington

Placenta
Island

Little Gott Island

East Penobscot
Bay

Saddleback
Island

Swans
Island

Black Island

Little Duck
Island

Vinalhaven
Island

Merchant
Island

Marshall
Island

Great Duck Island

Vinalhaven

Isle Au Haut
Bay

Isle Au Haut

Acadia
National
Park

Isle Au
Haut

Heron
Island

Frenchboro

Long
Island

den Ball
sland

0

5 mi

8 km

N

Rockland, for all its rough edges, has long and historic ties to the arts. Noted sculptor Louise Nevelson grew up in Rockland, and in 1935 philanthropist Lucy Farnsworth bequeathed a fortune large enough to establish the Farnsworth Museum, which has since become one of the most respected art museums in New England. Located in the middle of downtown, the Farnsworth has superb collections of paintings and sculptures by renown American artists with a connection to Maine. This includes not only Nevelson and three generations of Wyeths (N. C., Andrew, and Jamie), but Rockwell Kent, Childe Hassam, and Maurice Prendergast. The exhibit halls are modern, spacious, and well-designed, and the shows professionally prepared. In June 1998, the museum expanded with the opening of the **Farnsworth Center for the Wyeth Family** in Maine, housed in the former Pratt Memorial Methodist Church nearby. The center houses Andrew and Betsy Wyeth's personal collection of Maine-related art.

The Farnsworth also owns two other buildings open to the public. The **Farnsworth Homestead,** located behind the museum, offers a glimpse into the life of prosperous coastal Victorians. And a 25-minute drive away in the village of Cushing is the **Olson House,** perhaps Maine's most famous home, immortalized in Andrew Wyeth's noted painting, "Christina's World." Ask at the museum for directions and information.

Owls Head Transportation Museum. Rte. 73, Owls Head. ☎ **207/594-4418.** www.ohtm.org. $6 adults, $5 seniors, $4 children 5–12, $16 families. April–Oct daily 10am–5pm; Nov–March daily 10am–4pm.

You don't have to be a car or plane nut to enjoy a day at this museum, located 3 miles south of Rockland on Route 73. Founded in 1974, the museum has an extraordinary collection of cars, motorcycles, bicycles, and planes, nicely displayed in a tidy, hangar-like building at the edge of the Knox County Airport. Look for the beautiful early Harley Davidson, and the sleek Rolls Royce Phantom dating from 1929. The museum is also a popular destination for hobbyists and tinkerers, who drive and fly their classic vehicles here for frequent weekend rallies in the summer. Call ahead to ask about special events.

WINDJAMMER TOURS

During the long transition from sail to steam, captains of the fancy new steamships belittled the old-fashioned sailing ships as "windjammers." The term stuck, and through a curious metamorphosis the name evolved into a term of adventure and romance.

Today, windjammer vacations combine adventure with limited creature comforts—sort of like lodging at a backcountry cabin on the water. Guests typically bunk in small two-person cabins, which usually offer cold running water and a porthole to let in fresh air, but not much else. (You'll conclude this isn't like a stay at a fancy inn upon noting that one ship's brochure boasts "standing headroom in all 15 passenger cabins," and another crows that all cabins "are at least six feet by eight feet.")

Maine is the capital of ✪ **windjammer cruising** in the United States, and the two most active Maine harbors are **Rockland** and **Camden** on Penobscot Bay. Cruises last from three days to a week, during which these handsome, creaky vessels poke around the tidal inlets and small coves that ring the beautiful bay. It's a superb way to explore Maine's coast the way it's historically been explored—from the water looking inland. Rates run around $100 per day per person, with modest discounts early and late in the season.

Cruises vary from ship to ship and from week to week, depending on the inclinations of the captains and the vagaries of the Maine weather. The "standard" cruise often features a stop at one or more of the myriad spruce-studded Maine islands (perhaps with a lobster bake on shore), hearty breakfasts enjoyed sitting at tables below decks (or perched cross-legged on the sunny deck), and a palpable sense of maritime history as these handsome ships scud through frothy waters. A windjammer vacation demands you use all your senses, to smell the tang of the salt air, to hear the rhythmic creaking of the masts in the evening, and to feel the frigid ocean waters as you leap in for a bracing dip.

About a dozen windjammers offer cruises in the Penobscot Bay region during the summer season (many migrate south to the Caribbean for the winter). The ships vary widely in size and vintage, and guest accommodations range from cramped and rustic to reasonably spacious and well-appointed. Ideally, you'll have a chance to look at a couple of ships to find one that suits you before signing up.

If that's not practical, call ahead to the **Maine Windjammer Association** (☎ **800/ 807-9463**) and request a packet of brochures, which allow comparison shopping. If you're hoping for a last-minute cruise, stop by the chamber of commerce office at the Rockland waterfront (see above) and ask if any berths are available.

WHERE TO STAY

Capt. Lindsey House Inn. 5 Lindsey St., Rockland, ME 04841. ☎ **800/523-2145** or 207/ 596-7950. 9 units. A/C TV TEL. Peak season $95–$170 double; Columbus Day–Memorial Day $65–$110. Rates include continental breakfast. AE, DISC, MC, V.

The three-story, brick Capt. Lindsey House is located just a couple minutes' walk from the Farnsworth Museum It was originally was erected as a hotel in 1835, but went through several subsequent incarnations, including headquarters of the Rockland Water Co. (The inn's front desk is where folks once paid their water bills.) Guests enter through a doorway a few steps off Rockland's Main St., and enter into an opulent first-floor common area done up in rich tones, handsome dark-wood paneling, and a well-selected mix of antique and contemporary furniture. The upstairs rooms are also tastefully decorated in a contemporary country style, generally with bold, modern colors and patterns applied to traditional design. Even the smaller rooms like Room 4 are well done (this in a sort of steamship nouveau style); the rooms on the third floor all feature yellow pine floors and antique oriental carpets. All rooms have nice details, like handmade bedspreads, hair dryers, down comforters, and bathrobes. Reliable pub fare is available at the Waterworks next door, which is owned by the same people who own the inn.

East Wind Inn. P.O. Box 149, Tenants Harbor, ME 04860. ☎ **800/241-8439** or 207/ 372-6366. Fax 207/372-6320. www.eastwindinn.com. E-mail: info@eastwindinn.com. 26 units, 7 with shared bath. Summer $90–$132 double, $165–$275 suites and apartments. Off-season $55–$99 double. Rates include full breakfast. 2-night minimum stay on suites and apts. AE, DISC, MC, V. Closed Dec–Apr. Drive south on Rte. 131 from Thomaston to Tenants Harbor; turn left at post office. Pets allowd by reservation ($10 extra). Children 12 and older welcome.

The inn itself, formerly a sail loft, is perfectly situated next to the harbor with water views from all rooms and the long porch. It's a classic seaside hostelry with busy wall-paper, simple colonial reproduction furniture, and tidy rooms. (The 10 guest rooms across the way at a former sea captain's house have most of the private baths.) The atmosphere is relaxed almost to the point of ennui and the service good.

Dining: Traditional New England fare is served in an Edwardian-era dining room. The seafood is usually your best bet; the baked haddock is always popular. Entrees are priced $11.95 to $17.95.

Samoset Resort. Rockport, ME 04856. ☎ **800/341-1650** (outside Maine) or 207/ 594-2511. www.samoset.com. E-mail: info@samoset.com. 150 hotel units, plus 72 town-house units. A/C TV TEL. Early July to Labor Day $215–$265 double ($315 suite), fall $155–$215 ($260), winter $99–$140 ($175), May to mid-June $135–$180 ($220), mid-June to early July $175–$245 ($285). Meals not included; ask about MAP packages. AE, CB, DC, DISC, MC, V.

The Samoset is a wonderful destination for those wishing for a self-contained resort that offers contemporary styling, ocean views, and lots of golf. This modern resort is located on 230 spacious acres at the mouth of Rockland Harbor. Both the hotel and town houses are surrounded by the handsome golf course, which opens up expansive views from most every window on the property. The lobby is constructed of massive timbers (recovered from an old grain silo in Portland), and the guest rooms all have balconies or terraces. Golfers love the place—it's been called Pebble Beach East—and families will always find plenty of activities for kids (there's a summer camp during high season at $40 additional per day, and baby-sitting the rest of the year). The resort also has the best sunset stroll in the state—you can ramble across the golf course to a breakwater that leads out to a picturesque lighthouse. The one downside: for the high price charged, the staff may be less polished than you would expect.

Dining: The Samoset offers four dining areas, including the Clubhouse Grill, Breakwater Cafe, and the Poolhouse. The centerpiece restaurant is Marcel's, where specialty dinners are prepared tableside. These include lobster flambé, rack of lamb for two, and steak Diane. Prices for main courses at Marcel's range from $14 to $29.

Amenities: 18-hole golf course, indoor and outdoor pools, modern health club, hot tub, sauna, indoor video golf driving range, 4 tennis courts (night play), jogging and walking trails, children's program, business center, gift shops, courtesy car, valet parking, massage, free newspaper, concierge, laundry and dry-cleaning service, baby-sitting, safe, and safe-deposit boxes.

WHERE TO DINE

✪ **Cafe Miranda.** 15 Oak St., Rockland. ☎ **207/594-2034.** Reservations strongly encouraged. Main courses $9.50–$16.50. DISC, MC, V. Tues–Sat 5:30–9:30pm. WORLD CUISINE.

Hidden away on a side street, this tiny, contemporary restaurant features a huge menu with big flavors. The fare draws liberally from cuisines from around the globe ("It's comfort food for whatever planet you're from," says owner-chef Kerry Altiero), and given its wide-ranging culinary inclinations it comes as something of a surprise just how well-prepared everything is. The char-grilled pork and shrimp cakes served with a ginger-lime-coconut sauce are superb. Other creative entrees include barbecue pork ribs with a smoked jalapeño sauce, and Indian almond chicken. (The menu changes often, so don't set your heart on these dishes in particular.) Cafe Miranda provides some of the best value for the buck of any restaurant in Maine. There's also an outdoor seating area, called Karmen's Patio, which serves light fare in season from 11:30am onward. Beer and wine is available.

✪ CAMDEN

Camden is quintessential coastal Maine. Set at the foot of the wooded Camden Hills on a picturesque harbor that no Hollywood movie set could improve, the affluent village of Camden has attracted the gentry of the eastern seaboard for more than a century. The elaborate mansions of the moneyed set still dominate the shady side streets (many have been converted into bed-and-breakfasts), and Camden is possessed of a grace and sophistication that eludes many other coastal towns.

Nor have Camden's charms gone unnoticed. The village and the surrounding communities have become a haven for retired U.S. Foreign Service and CIA personnel, and has attracted its share of summering corporate bigwigs, including former Apple Computer C.E.O. John Sculley. More recently, the town received an economic injection from the rapid growth of MBNA, a national credit card company that has restored historic buildings and contributed significantly to Camden's current prosperity (this explains the high number of clean-cut young men in white shirts and ties you may see in and around town).

On the downside: all this attention and Camden's growing appeal to bus tours is having a deleterious impact, say some longtime visitors. The merchandise at the shops seems to be trending downward to appeal to a lower common denominator, and the constant summer congestion distracts somewhat from the village's inherent charm. If you don't come expecting a pristine and undiscovered village, you're likely to enjoy the place all the more.

ESSENTIALS

GETTING THERE   Camden is located on Route 1. Coming from the south, travelers can shave a few minutes off their trip by turning left on Route 90, 6 miles past Waldoboro, bypassing Rockland. The most traffic-free route from southern Maine is to Augusta via the Maine Turnpike, then via Route 17 to Route 90 to Route 1.

Concord Trailways (☎ 800/639-3317) offers bus service from Camden to Bangor and Portland.

VISITOR INFORMATION   The **Rockport-Camden-Lincolnville Chamber of Commerce,** P.O. Box 919, Camden, ME 04843 (☎ 800/223-5459 or 207/236-4404) dispenses helpful information from its center at the Public Landing in Camden. The chamber is open year-round weekdays from 9am to 5pm and Saturdays 10am to 5pm. In summer, it's also open Sundays 10am to 4pm.

EXPLORING CAMDEN

Camden Hills State Park (☎ 207/236-3109) is located about a mile north of the village center on Route 1. This 6,500-acre park features an oceanside picnic area, camping at 112 sites, a winding toll road up 800-foot Mount Battie with spectacular views from the summit, and a variety of well-marked hiking trails. The day use fee is $2 adult, 50¢ for children 5 to 11.

One easy hike I can recommend highly is an ascent to the ledges of **Mount Megunticook,** preferably early in the morning before the crowds have amassed and when the mist still lingers in the valleys. Leave from near the campground and follow the well-maintained trail to these open ledges, which requires only about 30 to 45 minutes' exertion. Spectacular, almost improbable, views of the harbor await, as well as glimpses inland to the gentle vales. Depending on your stamina and desires, you can continue on the park's trail network to Mount Battie, or into the less-trammeled woodlands on the east side of the Camden Hills.

For a view from the water back to the hills, **Maine Sports Outfitters** (☎ 800/722-0826 or 207/236-8797) offers sea-kayaking tours of Camden's scenic harbor. The standard tour lasts two hours and costs $30, and takes paddlers out to Curtis Island at the outer edge of the harbor. This beginners tour is offered three or four times daily, and is an easy, delightful way to get a taste of the area's maritime culture. Longer trips and instruction are also available. The outfitter's main shop, located on Route 1 in Rockport, has a good selection of outdoor gear and is worth a stop for outdoor enthusiasts gearing up for local adventures or heading on to Acadia.

WHERE TO STAY

Despite the preponderance of B&Bs, the total number of guest rooms is limited relative to the number of visitors, and during peak season lodging is tight. It's best to reserve well in advance. You might also try **Camden Accommodations and Reservations** (☎ 800/236-1920), which offers assistance with everything from booking rooms at local B&Bs to finding cottages for seasonal rental.

If the inns and B&Bs listed below are booked up or too pricey, a handful of area motels and hotels may be able to accommodate you. South of the village center are the **Cedar Crest Motel** (115 Elm St.; ☎ 800/422-4964 or 207/236-4839), a handsome compound with coffee shop and a shuttle-bus connection downtown; and longtime mainstay **Towne Motel** (68 Elm St.; ☎ 207/236-3377), which is within walking distance of the village. Also right in town, just across the footbridge, is the modern if generic **Best Western Camden Riverhouse Hotel** (11 Tannery Lane; ☎ **800/755-7483** or 207/236-0500), which has an indoor pool and fitness center. Finally, there's camping at Camden Hills State Park (see "Exploring Camden," above).

Cedarholm Cottages. Route 1, Lincolnville Beach, ME 04849. ☎ **207/236-3886.** 6 units (includes 3 two-bedroom cottages). TV. Oceanfront cottages $225–$300 double (up to four guests); oceanview cottages $80–$135 double. Rates include breakfast. 2-night minimum in some cottages. MC, V.

Cedarholm began as a small cottage court with four simple cottages just north of Camden along Route 1. It was operated more or less as a hobby. Then Joyce and Barry Jobson—the daughter of the former owner and her husband—took over in 1995, built a road down to the 460 feet of dramatic cobblestone shoreline, and constructed two modern, steeply gabled cedar cottages, each with two bedrooms. These are uniquely wonderful places, with great detailing like pocket doors, cobblestone fireplaces, handsome kitchenettes, and Jacuzzis. They're easily among the region's most quiet and peaceful retreats. Guests staying up the hill in the smaller, older (but recently updated) cottages can still wander down to the shore and lounge on the common deck overlooking the upper reaches of Penosbscot Bay. It's noisier up above, where it's closer to Route 1, and the prices reflect that.

Inn at Sunrise Point. Rte. 1 (P.O. Box 1344), Camden, ME 04843. ☎ **800/435-6278** or 207/236-7716. Fax 207/236-0820. www.sunrisepoint.com. E-mail: info@sunrisepoint.com. 7 units (4 in cottages). TV TEL. $175–$225 rooms; $250–$350 cottages. Rates include a full breakfast. AE, MC, V. Closed Nov to late May. No children.

This peaceful, private sanctuary 4 miles north of Camden Harbor seems a world apart from the bustling town. The service is crisp and helpful, and the setting can't be beat. Situated on the edge of Penobscot Bay down a long, tree-lined gravel road, the Inn at Sunrise Point consists of a cluster of contemporary but classic shingled buildings set amid a nicely landscaped yard. The predominant sounds here are of birds and waves lapping at the cobblestone shore. A granite bench and Adirondack chairs on the front lawn to allow guests to enjoy the bay view; breakfasts are served in a sunny conservatory. Guest rooms are spacious and comfortable and full of amenities, including VCRs and individual heat controls. The cottages are at the deluxe end of the scale, and all feature double Jacuzzis, fireplaces, wet bars, and private decks.

✪ **Maine Stay.** 22 High St., Camden, ME 04843. ☎ **207/236-9636.** www.mainestay.com. E-mail: innkeeper@mainestay.com. 8 units. $100–$145 double including breakfast; discounts during the off-season. AE, MC, V. Children over age 10 welcome.

The Maine Stay is Camden's premier bed-and-breakfast. Located in a home dating to 1802 but expanded in Greek Revival style in 1840, the Maine Stay is a classic slate-roofed New England homestead set in a shady yard within walking distance of both downtown and Camden Hills State Park. The eight guest rooms on three floors all have ceiling fans and are distinctively furnished with antiques and special decorative touches. My favorite: the downstairs Carriage House Room, which is away from the buzz of traffic on Route 1 and boasts its own stone patio.

The downstairs common rooms are perfect for unwinding, and the country kitchen is open to guests at all times. Hikers can set out on trails right from the yard into the Camden Hills. Perhaps the most memorable part of a stay here, however, will be the hospitality of the three hosts—Peter Smith, his wife Donny, and her twin sister, Diana Robson. The trio is genuinely interested in their guests' well-being, and they offer dozens of day trip suggestions, which are conveniently printed out from the inn's computer for guests to take with them. A major makeover in 1998 to 1999 created a roomy new suite on the top floor, along with other upgrades and subtle improvements.

✪ **Norumbega**. 61 High St., Camden, ME 04843. ☎ **207/236-4646** Fax 207/236-0824. www.norumbegainn.com. 13 units. TV TEL. July to mid-Oct $155–$450 double; mid-May to June and late Oct, $125–$375; Nov to mid-May $99–$295. Rates include full breakfast and evening refreshments. 2-night minimum stay weekends and holidays. AE, DISC, MC, V. Children over 7 years of age are welcome.

You'll have no problem finding Norumbega. Just head north of the village and look for travelers pulled over taking photos of this Victorian-era stone castle overlooking the bay. The 1886 structure is both wonderfully eccentric and finely built, full of wondrous curves and angles throughout. There's extravagant carved-oak woodwork in the lobby, and a stunning oak and mahogany inlaid floor. The downstairs billiards room is the place to pretend you're a 19th-century railroad baron. (Or an information-age baron—the home was owned for a time by Hodding Carter III.)

Guest rooms have been meticulously restored and furnished with antiques. Five of the rooms have fireplaces, and the three "garden level rooms" (they're off the downstairs billiards room) have private decks. Two rooms rank among the finest and in this country—the Library Suite, housed in the original two-story library with interior balcony, and the sprawling Penthouse with its superlative views. The inn is big enough to ensure privacy, but also intimate enough for you to get to know the other guests—mingling often occurs at breakfast, at the optional evening social hour, and in the afternoon, when the inn puts out its famous fresh-baked cookies.

Whitehall Inn. 52 High St., Camden, ME 04843. ☎ **800/789-6565** or 207/236-3391. Fax 207/236-4427. www.whitehall-inn.com. E-mail: stay@whitehall-inn.com. 50 units (8 units share 4 bathrooms). July to late Oct $140–$180 double, including breakfast and dinner ($110–$150 with breakfast only). Discounts in late May and June. AE, MC, V. Closed late Oct to late May.

The Whitehall is a venerable Camden establishment, the sort of place you half expect to find the young Cary Grant in a blue blazer tickling the ivories on the 1904 Steinway in the lobby. Set at the edge of town on Route 1 in a structure that dates to 1834, this three-story inn has a striking architectural integrity with its columns, gables and long roofline. This is the place you think of when you think of the classic New England summer inn. The only downside is its location on Route 1—the traffic noise tends to persist through the evening then start up early in the morning. (Ask for a room away from the road.)

Inside, the antique furnishings—including the handsome Seth Thomas clock, Oriental carpets, and cane-seated rockers on the front porch—are impeccably well cared for. Guest rooms are simple but appealing; only some rooms have phones. The Whitehall also occupies a minor footnote in the annals of American literature—a young local poet recited her poems here for guests in 1912, stunning the audience with her eloquence. Her name? Edna St. Vincent Millay.

Dining: The Whitehall's dining room boasts a slightly faded glory and service that occasionally limps along, but remains a good destination for reliable New England fare like veal with sweet vermouth, sage, and prosciutto; or baked haddock stuffed with Maine shrimp. (Entrees are $15 to $18.) And, of course, there's always boiled Maine lobster.

Amenities: Tennis court, tour desk, nature trails, conference rooms, baby-sitting, guest safe, afternoon tea.

WHERE TO DINE

Peter Ott's. 16 Bayview St., Camden. ☎ **207/236-4032.** Reservations not accepted. Main courses $13.95–$22.95 (most $14–$16). MC, V. Daily 5:30–9:30pm during season; usually closed 1 night weekly off-season; call first. AMERICAN.

Peter Ott's has attracted a steady stream of satisfied local customers and repeat-visitor yachtsmen since it opened smack in the middle of Camden in 1974. While it poses as a steak house with its simple wooden tables and chairs and its manly meat dishes (like char-broiled Black Angus with mushrooms and onions, and sirloin steak dijonaise), it's grown beyond that to satisfy more diverse tastes. In fact, the restaurant offers some of the better prepared seafood in town, including a pan-blackened seafood sampler and grilled salmon served with a lemon caper sauce. Be sure to leave room for the specialty coffees and its famous desserts, like the lemon-almond crumb tart.

Sea Dog Brewing Co. 43 Mechanic St. Camden. ☎ **207/236-6863.** Reservations not accepted. Main courses $6.95–$12.95. AE, DISC, MC, V. Daily 11:30am–9pm (kitchen closed 2–5pm off-season). Located at Knox Mill 1 block west of Elm St. PUB FARE.

This is one of a handful of brew pubs that have found quick acceptance in Maine, and it makes a reasonable destination for quick pub food like nachos or hamburgers. It won't set your taste buds dancing, but it will satisfy basic cravings. On the ground floor of an old woolen mill that's been renovated by MBNA (a national credit-card company), the restaurant has a pleasing, comfortable atmosphere with its booths, handsome bar, and views through tall windows of the old millrace. And the beers are consistently excellent, although some suffer from regrettable cute names (e.g., Old Gollywobbler Brown Ale).

The Waterfront. Bayview St. on Camden Harbor. ☎ **207/236-3747.** No reservations accepted. Main courses, lunch $6.95–$13.95; dinner $12.95–$22.95. AE, MC, V. Daily 11:30am–2:30pm and 5–9pm. SEAFOOD.

The Waterfront disproves the restaurant rule of thumb that "the better the view, the worse the food." Here you can watch multimillion-dollar yachts and handsome wind-jammers come and go (angle for a harborside seat on the deck), yet still be impressed by the food. The house specialty is fresh seafood of all kinds. Lunch and dinner menus are an enterprising mix of old-favorites and creative originals. On the old-favorites side are fried clams, crab cakes, boiled lobster, and a fisherman's platter piled with fried seafood. On the more adventurous side, is black sesame shrimp salad (served on noodles with a Thai vinaigrette), or seafood linguini with shrimp, mussels, squid, and caramelized balsamic onions. More earthbound fare for nonseafood eaters includes burgers, pitas, and strip steaks.

7 Blue Hill Peninsula

The Blue Hill Peninsula is a backroads paradise. If you're of a mind to get lost on country lanes that suddenly dead-end at the sea or inexplicably start to loop back on themselves, this is the place. In contrast to the western shores of Penobscot Bay, the Blue Hill Peninsula has more of a lost-in-time character. The roads are hilly, winding, and narrow, passing through leafy forests, along venerable saltwater farms, and touching on the edge of an azure inlet here or there. By and large it's overlooked by the majority of Maine's visitors, especially those who like their itineraries well-structured and their destinations clear and simple.

CASTINE & ENVIRONS

Castine gets my vote for the most settled and gracious village in Maine. It's not so much the stunningly handsome and meticulously maintained mid-19th-century homes that fill the side streets. Nor is it the location on a quiet peninsula, 16 miles south of RV-clotted Route 1.

No, what lends ✪ **Castine** its charm are the splendid, towering elm trees, which still overarch many of the village streets. Before Dutch elm disease ravaged the nation's tree-lined streets, much of America once looked like this, and it's easy to slip into a debilitating nostalgia for this most graceful tree, even if you're too young to remember America of the elms. Through perseverance and a measure of luck, Castine has managed to keep several hundred elms alive, and it's worth the drive here for these alone.

For American history buffs, Castine offers much more. This outpost served as a strategic town in various battles between British, Dutch, French, and feisty colonials in the centuries following its settlement in 1613. It was occupied by each of those groups at some point, and historical personages like Miles Standish and Paul Revere passed through during one epoch or another. The town has a dignified, aristocratic bearing, and it somehow seems appropriate that Tory-dominated Castine welcomed the British with open arms during the Revolution.

ESSENTIALS

GETTING THERE   Castine is located 16 miles south of Route 1. Turn south on Route 175 in Orland (east of Bucksport) and follow this to Route 166, which winds its way to Castine. Route 166A offers an alternate route along Penobscot Bay.

VISITOR INFORMATION   Castine lacks a formal information center, but the clerk at the **Town Office** (☎ 207/326-4502) is often helpful with local questions.

EXPLORING CASTINE

One of the town's more intriguing attractions is the **Wilson Museum** (days, ☎ 207/326-8753, or between 5 and 9pm call the curator at ☎ 207/326-8545) on Perkins St., an attractive and quirky anthropological museum constructed in 1921. This small museum contains the collections of John Howard Wilson, an archaeologist and collector of prehistoric artifacts from around the globe. His gleanings are neatly arranged in a staid, classical arrangement of the sort that proliferated in the late-19th and early–20th centuries. The museum is open from end of May to the end of September daily except Monday 2 to 5pm; admission is free.

Next door is the **John Perkins House,** Castine's oldest home. It was occupied by the British during the Revolution and the War of 1812, and a tour features demonstrations of old-fashioned cooking techniques. The Perkins House is open July and August on Wednesday and Sunday only from 2 to 5pm. Admission is $2.

Castine is also home to the **Maine Maritime Academy** (☎ 207/326-8545), which trains sailors for the rigors of life at sea. The campus is on the western edge of the village, and the *S. S. Maine,* the hulking gray training ship, is often docked in Castine, threatening to overwhelm the village with its sheer size. Free, half-hour tours of the ship are offered in summer (assuming the ship is in port) from 10am to noon, and 1pm to 4pm.

WHERE TO STAY

Castine Harbor Lodge. Perkins St (P.O. Box 215), Castine, ME 04421. ☎ 207/326-4861. 9 units (2 share 1 bathroom; 1 with private hall bathroom). $75–$115 double. Rates include continental breakfast. DC, DISC, MC, V. Closed Nov–May. Pets allowed.

This is a great spot for families. Housed in a grand 1893 mansion (the only inn on the water in Castine), it's run with an informal good cheer that allow kids to feel at home amid the regal architecture. The main parlor is dominated by a Ping-Pong table, and there's Scrabble and Nintendo if you but look. The front porch has views that extend across the bay to the Camden Hills, and is one of the best places to unwind in all of

Maine. The spacious rooms are eclectically furnished, with some antiques and some modern. Two of the guest rooms share an adjoining bathroom—of note to traveling families. The family dog is welcome. And if you're not traveling with a family? It's still a great spot if you prefer a well-worn comfort to high-end elegance. Last word: the bathrooms have the best views of any in the state.

Castine Inn. Main St. (P.O. Box 41), Castine, ME 04421. ☎ **207/326-4365.** Fax 207/326-4570. www.castineinn.com. E-mail: relax@castineinn.com. 19 units. $85–$135 double ($210 suite). Rates include full breakfast. 2-night minimum stay July–Aug. MC, V. Closed mid-Dec to May. Children 8 and older are welcome.

The Castine Inn is a Maine Coast rarity—a hotel that was originally built as a hotel (not as a residence), in this case in 1898. This handsome cream-colored village inn, designed in an eclectic Georgian-Federal–Revival style, has a fine front porch and attractive gardens. Inside, the lobby takes its cue from the 1940s, with wingback chairs and loveseats and a fireplace in the parlor. There's also an intimate, dark lounge decked out in rich green hues, reminiscent of an Irish pub. The guest rooms on the two upper floors are attractively if unevenly furnished in early-American style—the innkeepers are revamping the rooms one by one to an even gloss, even adding luxe touches. Until they're all renovated, it may be wise to ask to view the available rooms before you sign in.

Dining: The elegant dining room serves up Castine's best fare, and some of the best food in the state. Chef/owner Tom Gutow served a stint at Bouley in New York, and isn't timid about experimenting with local meats and produce, almost always to good effect. The menu changes nightly with ingredients varying by the season, but you might expect to find dishes such as lobster with wild mushrooms, leeks, corn and a tarragon sauce; or veal sweetbreads spiced with cloves and served with a soy honey glaze. Entrees range from $17 to $24.

Pentagöet Inn. Main St. (P.O. Box 4), Castine, ME 04421. ☎ **800/845-1701** or 207/326-8616. Fax 207/326-9382. www.pentagoet.com. E-mail: pentagoet@hypernet.com. 16 units, 2 with private hallway bathrooms. $99–$129 double, including buffet breakfast. 2-night minimum stay in peak season. MC, V. Closed third week of Oct through early May. Pets allowed by reservation. Suitable for children 12 and older.

Here's the big activity at the Pentagöet: Sit on the wraparound front porch on cane-seated rockers and watch the slow-paced activity on Main Street. That's not likely to be overly appealing to those looking for a fast-paced vacation, but it's the perfect salve for someone seeking respite from urban life. This quirky yellow and green 1894 structure with its prominent turret is tastefully furnished downstairs with hardwood floors, oval braided rugs, and a woodstove. It's comfortable without being overly elegant, professional without being chilly, personal without being overly intimate. High tea is served to guests each afternoon, as are cocktails and canapés in the evening.

The rooms on the upper two floors of the main house are furnished eclectically, with a mix of antiques and old collectibles. The five guest rooms in the adjacent Perkins Street building—a more austere Federal-era house—are furnished simply and feature painted floors. There's no air-conditioning, but all rooms have ceiling or window fans.

WHERE TO DINE

The best dinner in town is at the **Castine Inn** (see above). For lunch or more informal dinner fare.

Dennett's Wharf. Sea St. (next to the Town Dock). ☎ **207/326-9045.** Reservations recommended in summer and for parties of 6 or more. Lunch $5.50–$17.95; dinner $8.95–$17.95. Daily 11am–midnight. Closed mid-Oct to Apr 30. PUB FARE. AE, DISC, MC, V.

Located in a soaring waterfront sail loft with dollar bills tacked all over the high ceiling, Dennett's Wharf offers upscale bar food amid a lively setting leavened with a good selection of microbrews. If the weather's decent, there's outside dining under a bright yellow awning with superb harbor views. Look for grilled sandwiches, roll-ups, and salads at lunch; dinner includes lobster, stir-fry, and steak teriyaki. And how did all those bills get on the ceiling? Ask your server. It will cost you exactly $1 to find out.

DEER ISLE

Deer Isle is well off the beaten path, but worth the long detour from Route 1 if your tastes run to pastoral countryside with a nautical edge. Loopy, winding roads cross through forest and farmland, and travelers are rewarded with sudden glimpses of the sun-dappled ocean and mint-green coves. An occasional settlement crops up now and again.

Deer Isle doesn't cater exclusively to tourists, as many coastal regions do. It's still occupied by fifth-generation fishermen, farmers, long-time rusticators, and artists who prize their seclusion. The village of **Deer Isle** has a handful of inns and galleries, but its primary focus is to serve locals and summer residents, not transients. The village of **Stonington**, on the southern tip, is a rough-hewn sea town. Despite serious incursions the past five years by galleries and enterprises dependent on seasonal tourism, it remains dominated in spirit by fishermen and the occasional quarry worker.

ESSENTIALS

GETTING THERE   Deer Isle is accessible via several winding country roads from Route 1. Coming from the west, head south on Route 175 off Route 1 in Orland, then connect to Route 15 to Deer Isle. From the east, head south on Route 172 to Blue Hill, where you can pick up Route 15. Deer Isle is connected to the mainland via a high, narrow, and graceful suspension bridge, built in 1938, which can be somewhat harrowing to cross in high winds.

VISITOR INFORMATION   The **Deer Isle-Stonington Chamber of Commerce** (☎ 207/348-6124) staffs a seasonal information booth just beyond the bridge on Little Deer Isle. The booth is open daily in summer from 10 am to 4 pm, depending on volunteer availability.

EXPLORING DEER ISLE

Deer Isle, with its network of narrow roads to nowhere, is ideal for perfunctory rambling. It's a pleasure to explore by car, and is also inviting to travel by bike, although hasty and careening fishermen in pickups can make this unnerving at times. Especially tranquil is the narrow road between Deer Isle and Sunshine to the east. Plan to stop and explore the rocky coves and inlets along the way. To get here, head toward Stonington on Route 15 and just south of the village of Deer Isle, turn east toward Stinson Neck and continue along this scenic byway for about 10 miles over bridges and causeways.

Along this road watch for the **Haystack Mountain School of Crafts** (☎ 207/ 348-2306). The campus of this respected summer crafts school is visually stunning. Designed in the 1960s by Edward Larrabee Barnes, the campus is set on a steep hillside overlooking the cerulean waters of Jericho Bay. Barnes cleverly managed to play up the views while respecting the delicate landscape by building a series of small buildings on pilings that seem to float above the earth. The classrooms and studios are linked by boardwalks, many of which are connected to a wide central staircase, ending at the "Flag Deck," a sort of open-air commons just above the shoreline.

The buildings and classrooms are closed to the public, but summer visitors are welcome to walk to the Flag Deck and stroll the nature trail adjacent to the campus.

There's also one public tour weekly on Wednesday at 1pm, during which you can catch glimpses of the studios. Donations are appreciated. Call for further information.

Stonington, at the very southern tip of Deer Isle, consists of one commercial street that wraps along the harbor's edge. While bed-and-breakfasts and boutiques have made inroads here recently, it's still mostly a rough-and-tumble waterfront town with strong links to the sea, and you're likely to observe lots of activity in the harbor as lobstermen come and go. If you hear industrial sounds emanating from just offshore, that's probably the stone quarry on Crotch Island, which has been supplying architectural granite to builders nationwide for more than a century.

You can learn more about the stone industry at **the Deer Isle Granite Museum** on Main Street (☎ **207/367-6331**). The tiny storefront museum features some historical artifacts from the quarry's golden years, but the real draw is a working diorama (eight foot by fifteen) of Crotch Island as it would have appeared around 1900. It features a little railroad, little boats, and little cranes moving little stones around. Kids under 10 years old find it endlessly fascinating. The museum is open from late May through August daily 10am to 5pm. (Sunday it opens at 1pm). Admission is free; donations are requested.

◆ DAY TRIP TO ISLE AU HAUT

Rocky and remote Isle au Haut offers the most unusual hiking and camping experience in northern New England. This 6-x-3 mile island, located 6 miles south of Stonington, was originally named Ille Haut—or High Island—in 1604 by French explorer Samuel de Champlain. The name and its pronunciation evolved—today, it's generally pronounced "aisle-a-ho"—but the island itself has remained steadfastly unchanged over the centuries.

About half of the island is owned by the National Park Service and maintained as an outpost of Acadia National Park (see section 8 later in this chapter). A 60-passenger "mailboat" makes a stop in the morning and late afternoon at Duck Harbor, allowing for a solid day of hiking while still returning to Stonington by nightfall. At Duck Harbor the NPS also maintains a cluster of five Adirondack-style lean-tos, which are available for overnight camping. (Advance reservations are essential. Contact **Acadia National Park,** Bar Harbor, ME 04609, or call ☎ **207-288-3338.**

A network of hiking trails radiates from Duck Harbor. Be sure to ascend the island's highest point, 543-foot **Duck Harbor Mountain,** for exceptional views of the Camden Hills to the west and Mount Desert Island to the east. Nor should you miss the **Cliff or Western Head trails,** which track along high, rocky bluffs and coastal outcroppings capped with damp, tangled fog forests of spruce. The trails periodically descend to cobblestone coves, which issue forth a deep rumble with every incoming wave. A hand-pump near Duck Harbor provides drinking water, but be sure to bring food and other refreshments in a daypack.

The other half of the island is privately owned, some by fishermen who can trace their island ancestry back three centuries, and some by summer rusticators whose forebears discovered the bucolic splendor of Isle au Haut in the 1880s. The summer population of the island is about 300, with about 50 die-hards remaining year-round. The mailboat also stops at the small harborside village, which has a few old homes, a handsome church, and tiny schoolhouse, post office, and store. Day-trippers will be better served ferrying straight to Duck Harbor.

The **mail boat** (☎ **207/367-5193** or 207/367-6516) to Isle au Haut leaves from the pier at the end of Sea Breeze Ave. in Stonington. In summer (mid-June to mid-September), the *Miss Lizzie* departs for the village of Isle au Haut daily at 7am,

11:30am, and 4:30pm; the *Mink* departs for Duck Harbor daily at 10am and 4:30pm. (Limited trips to Isle au Haut the remainder of the year.) The round trip boat fare is $24 for adults to either the village or Duck Harbor. Children under 12 are $10. Reservations are not accepted; it's best to arrive about a half-hour before departure.

WHERE TO STAY

✪ **Goose Cove Lodge.** Goose Cove Rd (P.O. Box 40), Sunset, ME 04683. ☎ **207/ 348-2508**. Fax 207/348-2624. 25 units. High season (including breakfast and dinner) $160–$286 double. Low-season (including full breakfast) $98–$185 double. 2-night minimum stay July–Aug, 1-week minimum in cottages. MC, V. Closed mid-Oct to mid-May.

A rustic compound adjacent to a nature preserve on a remote coastal point, Goose Cove Lodge is a superb destination for families and lovers of the outdoors. Exploring the grounds offers an adventure every day. You can hike out at low tide to salty Barred Island, or take a guided nature hike on any of five trails. You can mess around in boats in the cove (the inn has kayaks and canoes), or borrow one of the inn's bikes for an excursion. And after dinner there's astronomy. When fog or rain puts a damper on things, curl up with a book in front of a fireplace (20 of the rooms offer fireplaces or Franklin stoves). Two new (1997) architecturally designed modern cottages sleep six, and are available through the winter. My favorites? Elm and Linnea, cozy cabins tucked privately in the woods on a rise overlooking the beach.

Dining: Meals here are excellent—far above what you would expect to find at the end of a remote dirt road. Each evening begins with a cocktail hour at 5:30pm in the lodge, followed by dinner. The maple-floored dining room wraps in a semicircle around the living room, and guests, seated family style, dine while enjoying views of the cove and distant islands. There's always a vegetarian option at dinner, along with one or two other entrees, like beef tenderloin with a pepper crust and horseradish spaetzle, or salmon with wild mushroom couscous and white truffle essence. The dining room is open to the public; come for lunch on the deck, or for dinner if space permits (reservations essential; fixed-price $33; Sunday $25).

Inn on the Harbor. Main St. (P.O. Box 69), Stonington, ME 04681. ☎ **800/942-2420** or 207/367-242. Fax 207/367-2420. 14 units. TV TEL. $100–$125 double. Rates include continental breakfast. AE, DISC, MC, V. Closed Jan to mid-Apr. Children 12 and older welcome.

This appealingly quirky waterfront inn has the best location in town—perched over the harbor and right on the main street. In its former incarnation (called the Captain's Quarters) the inn was funky, with small rooms and 1970s-era furnishings. Under new management, rooms have been enlarged (with the loss of several) and nicely appointed with antiques and sisal carpets. Yet spread about a handful of buildings, with the spacious wooden deck overlooking the harbor, the place still retains an unconventional charm.

Guests swap notes about their rooms over complimentary sherry and wine served in the reception room in the late afternoon. A sign of the times: there's an espresso bar open afternoons. This is a great location for resting up before or after a kayak expedition, or a good base for a day trip out to Isle au Haut. All rooms except the suite, located across town in the innkeeper's home, feature in-room phones. The inn also operates a restaurant a short walk away called the Cafe Atlantic, which features seafood, pasta, and beef (prime rib on weekends) with entrees priced at $11 to $17.

Pilgrim's Inn. Deer Isle, ME 04627. ☎ **207/348-6615**. www.pilgrimsinn.com. 13 units, 2 cottages (3 rms with shared bathroom). $160–$215 double. Rates include breakfast and dinner. (B&B rates available; call for info.) MC, V. Closed mid-Oct to mid-May (cottages open year-round). Children 10 and older are welcome.

Set just off a town road and between an open bay and a millpond, this is a historic, handsomely renovated inn in a lovely setting. This four-story, gambrel-roofed structure will especially appeal to those intrigued by early American history. The inn was built in 1793 by Ignatius Haskell, a prosperous sawmill owner. His granddaughter opened the home to boarders, and it's been housing summer guests ever since. The interior is tastefully decorated in a style that's informed by early Americana, but not beholden to historic authenticity. The guest rooms are well-appointed with antiques and painted in muted colonial colors; especially intriguing are the rooms on the top floor with impressive diagonal beams. Two nearby cottages are also available. Activities here include strolling around the village, using the inn's bikes to explore (free), and taking scenic drives. Ask about birdwatching weekends in May.

Dining: Dinners start with cocktails and hors d'oeuvres in the common room at 6pm, followed by one seating at 7pm in the adjacent barn dining room. Only one entree is served, but the creative American cuisine is not likely to disappoint. You might feast on tenderloin of beef with lobster risotto, or a bouillabaisse made of locally caught seafood. Dinner is open to the public by reservation at a fixed price of $29.50.

WHERE TO DINE

For fine dining, check out **Goose Cove Lodge** or the **Pilgrim's Inn** (see above.) For more basic fare:

Fisherman's Friend. School St., Stonington. ☎ **207/367-2442.** Reservations recommended peak season and weekends. Sandwiches $2–$6; dinner entrees $7–$15. No credit cards. Daily 11am–9pm. Closed Nov–Mar. Located up the hill from the harbor past the Opera House. SEAFOOD.

This lively, boisterous restaurant is usually as crowded as it is unpretentious. Simple tables fill a large room, and long-experienced waitresses hustle about to keep up with demand. The menu typically includes a wide range of fresh fish, prepared in a variety of styles. (The locals seem to like it fried.) If you find yourself beset with a fierce craving for lobster, do yourself a favor and bypass the same-old-same-old boiled lobster with bib. Instead, head straight for the lobster stew, which is brimming with meaty lobster chunks and is flavored perfectly. It's not a light meal, but travelers often find themselves making excuses to linger in Stonington the next day to indulge in yet another hearty bowl of stew. Bring your own wine, beer, or cocktails.

BLUE HILL

Blue Hill, population 1,900, is fairly easy to find—just look for gently domed, eponymous Blue Hill Mountain, which lords over the northern end of Blue Hill Bay. Set between the mountain and the bay is the quiet and historic town of Blue Hill, which clusters along the bay shore and a burbling stream. There's never much going on in town. And that seems to be exactly what attracts summer visitors back time and again—and may explain why two excellent bookstores are located here. Many old-money families still maintain retreats set along the water or in the rolling inland hills, but Blue Hill offers several excellent choices for lodging if you're not well endowed with local relatives. It's a good destination for an escape, and will especially appeal to those deft at crafting their own entertainment.

ESSENTIALS

GETTING THERE   Blue Hill is located southeast of Ellsworth on Route 172. Coming from the west, head south on Route 15, 5 miles east of Bucksport (it's well-marked with road signs).

VISITOR INFORMATION   Blue Hill does not maintain a visitor information booth. Look for the "Blue Hill, Maine" brochure and map at state information centers, or write the **Blue Hill Chamber of Commerce,** P.O. Box 520, Blue Hill, ME 04614. The staff at area inns and restaurants are usually able to answer any questions you might have.

EXPLORING BLUE HILL

A good way to start your exploration is to ascend the open summit of **Blue Hill Mountain,** from which you'll have superb views of the azure bay and the rocky balds on nearby Mount Desert Island. To reach the trailhead from the village, drive north on Route 172, then turn west (left) on Mountain Road at the Blue Hill Fairgrounds. Drive 0.8 mile and look for the well-marked trail. An ascent of the "mountain" (elevation 940 feet) is about a mile, and requires about 45 minutes. Bring a picnic lunch and enjoy the vistas.

Blue Hill has traditionally attracted more than its fair share of artists, especially, it seems, potters. On Union Street, stop by **Rowantrees Pottery** (☎ 207/374-5535), which has been a Blue Hill institution for more than half a century. The shop was founded by Adelaide Pearson, who was inspired to pursue pottery as a career after a conversation with Mahatma Gandhi in India. Rowantrees' pottery is richly hued, and the potters who've succeeded Pearson continue to use glazes made from local resources.

Another inventive shop, the family-run **Rackliffe Pottery** on Ellsworth Rd. (☎ 207/374-2297), uses native clay and lead-free glazes, and the bowls, vases, and plates produced here have a lustrous, silky feel to them. Visitors are welcome to watch the potters at work. Both shops are open year-round.

Even if you've never been given to swooning over historic homes, you owe yourself a visit to the intriguing **Parson Fisher House** (contact Blue Hill Tea & Tobacco, ☎ 207/374-2161, for information), located on Routes 176 and 15, a half-mile west of the village. Fisher, Blue Hill's first permanent minister, was a rustic version of a Renaissance man when he settled here in 1796. Educated at Harvard, Fisher not only delivered sermons in six different languages, including Aramaic, but was a writer, painter, and minor inventor whose energy was evidently boundless. On a tour of his home, which he built in 1814, you can see a clock with wooden works he made, and samples of the books he not only wrote but published and bound himself.

Parson Fisher House is open from July to mid-September daily except Sunday from 2 pm to 5 pm. Admission is $2 adults, children under 12 are free.

WHERE TO STAY

Blue Hill Inn. Union St. (P.O. Box 403), Blue Hill, ME 04614. ☎ **207/374-2844.** Fax 207/ 374-2829. www.bluehillinn.com. E-mail: bluhilin@downeast.net. 12 units. $140–$190 double; suite $200–$260. Rates include breakfast and dinner. 2-night minimum stay in summer. DISC, MC, V. Closed Dec to mid-May. Children 13 and older are welcome.

The Blue Hill Inn has been hosting travelers since 1840. Situated on one of Blue Hill's busy streets and within walking distance of most everything, this Federal-style inn features a convincing colonial American motif throughout, with the authenticity enhanced by creaky floors and doorjambs slightly out of true. Innkeepers Mary and Don Hartley have furnished all the rooms pleasantly with antiques and down comforters; four rooms feature wood-burning fireplaces. A more contemporary suite is located in an adjacent building, which features cathedral ceiling, fireplace, kitchen, and deck. Ask about packages that include kayaking, hiking, or sailing.

Dining: The one part of the inn that doesn't feel old is the dining room, which is built in a shedlike addition to the old house. But the superb country French-style cooking of chef Andre Strong makes up for the less interesting atmosphere. The meals are made chiefly with local, organic ingredients. Among the creative dishes are lobster with a vanilla beurre blanc and roast duck with green peppercorn sauce. The wine selection is excellent. The fixed-price dinner ($30) is served Wednesday to Sunday and is open to the public; reservations required.

✪ **John Peters Inn.** Rte. 176 E. (P.O. Box 916), Blue Hill, ME 04614. ☎ **207/374-2116.** www.johnpetersinn.com. E-mail: jpi@downeast.net. 14 units. $105–$165 double. Rates include full breakfast. MC, V. Closed Nov–Apr.

The long and narrow dirt driveway of the John Peters Inn sends a signal that you're entering into another world. You ascend a gentle hill between a row of stately maples; to the right are glimpses of the bay, to the left is the handsome 1810 home that, with its later architectural embellishments, could be a modest antebellum plantation home.

Inside, it's strictly New England and decorated in antiques with an uncommon elegance and an eye to detail by the innkeepers. There's nothing grand here—it's all simple early American style done with exceptionally good taste. The guest rooms, nine of which boast fireplaces and four of which have private phones, all feature loveseats or sofas, and it's hard to tear yourself away from them. But do try. The inn sits on 25 lovely shorefront acres, and has been lightly landscaped—to do more would be to gild the lily. There's also an unheated outdoor pool that will appeal mostly to those of stout constitution, and a rowboat, sailboat, and canoe for low-key exploring. Breakfast in the simply decorated dining room is a sublime treat, with offerings like freshly squeezed orange juice, poached eggs with asparagus, lobster omelets, and a variety of waffles.

WHERE TO DINE

✪ **Firepond.** Main St., Blue Hill. ☎ **207/374-9970.** Reservations recommended. Lunch $4–$12; dinner entrees $16–$30 (mostly $18–$20). DISC, MC, V. Daily, lunch 11:30am–2:30pm, happy hour (light fare) 3–5pm; dinner 5–9:30pm. Closed Nov to mid-May. ECLECTIC.

It's located right in the village of Blue Hill, a drop-dead gorgeous restaurant that happens to serve exceptionally fine food. Ideally sited along a small stream in a former blacksmith's shop, Firepond has old-pine floors and its lavish decor flirts with a Martha-Stewart-run-amok look, but it pulls back in the nick of time and carries its elegance unusually well. The best seats are downstairs in the covered porch overhanging the stream, but it's hard to go wrong anywhere here for setting a romantic mood. If you're not sure this is the place for you, try this: Stop by the handsome bar with its wrought-iron stools for a drink and an appetizer. The odds are you'll decide that staying for dinner is a good idea. Meals are adventurous. Traditional regional fare updated for the 1990s dominates, and the restaurant is noted for its fresh-fish specials, which change daily. You might also find wild boar, ostrich, or rack of New Zealand lamb. They also serve plain boiled lobster in response to customer demand, but what's the point in ordering that? Be adventurous, and expect your meal to be prepared with a deft touch.

Jonathan's. Main St., Blue Hill. ☎ **207/374-5226.** Reservations recommended. Main courses, $15.95–$21.95. MC, V. Daily 5–9:30pm. Closed Mon–Tues Nov–May. ECLECTIC.

Located in the middle of Blue Hill, Jonathan's appeals to almost everyone—from the younger local crowd to the old-money summer denizens. The background music is jazz or light rock, the service brisk and professional, and the wine list extensive and creative. Guests choose between the barnlike back room with its comfortable knotty-pine feel, or the less elegant front room facing Main Street, and done up in green tablecloths, captain's chairs, and booths of white pine. The menu changes frequently, but among typical dishes are churrasco (a Cuban-style marinated flank steak with

Caribbean condiments), mixed grill of quail, rabbit, and venison sausage, and a simple poached salmon with dill sauce. Appetizers run along the lines of warm smoked mussel and chèvre salad, or Indonesian shrimp satay.

8 Mount Desert Island & Acadia National Park

Mount Desert Island is home to spectacular Acadia National Park, and for many visitors the two places are one and the same. Yes, visitors to Acadia drive the economy, and their presence defines the spirit of Maine's largest island. And the park does contain the most dramatic coastal real estate on the eastern seaboard.

Yet the park holdings are only part of the appeal of this immensely popular island, which is connected to the mainland via a short, two-lane causeway. Beyond the parklands are scenic harborside villages and remote backcountry roads, quaint B&Bs and unusually fine restaurants, oversize 19th-century summer "cottages" and the unrepentant tourist trap of Bar Harbor. Those who arrive on the island expecting untamed wilderness invariably leave disappointed. Those who understand that Acadia National Park is but one chapter (albeit a very large one) in the intriguing story of Mount Desert Island will enjoy their visit thoroughly.

Mount Desert (pronounced "de-*sert*") is divided into two lobes separated by Somes Sound, the only legitimate fjord in the continental U.S. (A fjord is a valley carved by a glacier that subsequently filled with rising ocean water.) Those with a poetic imagination see Mount Desert shaped as lobster, with one large claw and one small. Most of the parkland is on the meatier east claw, although large swaths of park exist on the leaner west claw as well. The eastern side is more developed, with Bar Harbor the center of commerce and entertainment. The western side has a more quiet, settled air, and teems more with wildlife than tourists. The island isn't huge—it's only about 15 miles from the causeway to the southernmost tip at Bass Harbor Head—and visitors can do a lot of adventuring in such a compact space. The best plan is to take it slow, exploring whenever possible by foot, bicycle, canoe, or kayak.

ACADIA NATIONAL PARK

It's not hard to fathom why Acadia is consistently one of the biggest draws in the U.S. national park system. The park's landscape is a rich tapestry of rugged cliffs, restless ocean, and deep, silent woods. Acadia's landscape, like so much of the rest of northern New England, was carved by glaciers some 18,000 years ago. A mile-high ice-sheet shaped the land by scouring valleys into their distinctive U shapes, rounding many of the once-jagged peaks, and depositing huge boulders about the landscape, such as the famous 10-foot-high "Bubble Rock," which appears to be perched precariously on the side of South Bubble Mountain.

The park's more recent roots can be traced back to the 1840s, when noted Hudson River School painter Thomas Cole packed his sketchbooks and easels for a trip to this remote island, then home to a small number of fishermen and boat-builders. His stunning renditions of the surging surf pounding against coastal granite were later displayed in New York and triggered an early tourism boom as urbanites flocked to the island to "rusticate." By 1872, national magazines were touting Eden (Bar Harbor's name until 1919) as a desirable summer resort. It attracted the attention of wealthy industrialists, and soon became summer home to Carnegies, Rockefellers, Astors, and Vanderbilts, who built massive summer cottages with literally dozens of rooms (one "cottage" even boasted 28 bathrooms). More recently, lifestyle doyenne Martha Stewart bought a multimillion dollar hilltop compound originally built for Edsel Ford.

By early in this century, the huge popularity and growing development of the island began to concern its most ardent supporters. Boston textile heir and conservationist George Dorr and Harvard president Charles Eliot, aided by the largesse of John D. Rockefeller Jr., started acquiring large tracts for the public's enjoyment. These parcels were eventually donated to the federal government, and in 1919 the public land was designated Lafayette National Park, the first national park east of the Mississippi. Renamed Acadia in 1929, the park has grown to encompass nearly half the island, with holdings scattered about piecemeal here and there.

Rockefeller purchased and donated about 11,000 acres—about one-third of the park. He's also responsible for one of the park's most extraordinary features. Around 1905 a dispute erupted over whether to allow noisy new motorcars on to the island. Resident islanders wanted these new conveniences to boost their mobility; John D. Rockefeller Jr., whose fortune was from the oil industry (students of irony take note), strenuously objected, preferring the tranquillity of the car-free island. Rockefeller went down to defeat on this issue, and the island was opened to cars in 1913. In response, the multimillionaire set about building an elaborate 57-mile system of private carriage roads, featuring a dozen gracefully handcrafted stone bridges. These roads, open today only to pedestrians, bicyclists, and equestrians, are concentrated most densely around Jordan Pond, but also ascend to some of the most scenic open peaks and wind through sylvan valleys.

ESSENTIALS

GETTING THERE   Acadia National Park is reached from the town of Ellsworth via Route 3. If you're coming from southern Maine, you can avoid the coastal congestion along Route 1 by taking the Maine Turnpike to Bangor, picking up I-395 to Route 1A, then continuing south on Route 1A to Ellsworth. While this looks longer on the map, it's by far the quickest route in summer.

Daily flights from Boston to the airport in Trenton, just across the causeway from Mt. Desert Island, are offered year-round by Continental affiliate **Colgan Air** (☎ **800/523-3273** or 207/667-7171).

In summer, **Concord Trailways** (☎ **800/639-3317**) offers seasonal van service between Bangor (including an airport stop), Ellsworth, and Bar Harbor. Reservations are required.

ENTRY POINTS & FEES   A 1-week park pass, which includes unlimited trips on Park Loop Road, costs $10 per car; no extra charge per passenger. (No daily pass is available.) The main point of entry to Park Loop Road, the park's most scenic byway, is at the visitor center at **Hulls Cove.** Mount Desert Island consists of an interwoven network of park and town roads, allowing visitors to enter the park at numerous points. A glance at a park map (available at the visitor center) will make these access points self-evident. The entry fee is collected at a toll booth on Park Loop Road ½-mile north of Sand Beach.

VISITOR CENTERS   Acadia staffs two visitor centers. The **Thompson Island Information Center** (☎ **207/288-3411**) on Route 3 is the first you'll pass as you enter Mount Desert Island. This center is maintained by the local chambers of commerce, but park personnel are often on hand to answer inquiries. It's open May through mid-October, and is a good stop for general lodging and restaurant information.

If you're primarily interested in information about the park itself, continue on Route 3 to the National Park Service's **Hulls Cove Visitor Center** about 7.5 miles beyond Thompson Island. This attractive stone-walled center includes professionally prepared park service displays, such as a large relief map of the island, natural history exhibits, and a short introductory film. You can also request free brochures

Mount Desert Island/Acadia National Park

about hiking trails and the carriage roads, or purchase postcards and more detailed guidebooks. The center is open mid-April through October. Information is also available year-round, by phone or in person, from the park's **headquarters** (☎ **207/ 288-3338**) on Route 233 between Bar Harbor and Somesville.

Your questions might also be answered in advance on the park's web page at **www.nps.gov/acad/anp.html.**

PARK ACCOMMODATIONS The national park itself offers no overnight accommodations other than two campgrounds (see below). But visitors don't have to go far to find a room. That's especially true of Bar Harbor, which is teeming with motels and inns. The rest off the island also has a good if scattered selection of places to spend the night. See the "Where to Stay" sections, below.

SEASONS Visit Acadia in September if you can. Between Labor Day and the foliage season of early October, the days are often warm and clear, the nights have a crisp northerly tang, and you can avoid the hassles of congestion, crowds, and pesky insects. Not that the park is empty in September. Bus tours seem to proliferate at that time, which results in crowds at the most popular sites. Not to worry: If you walk just a minute or two off the road you can find solitude and an agreeable peacefulness. Hikers and bikers have the trails and carriage roads to themselves.

Summer, of course, is peak season at Acadia. Weather is perfect for just about any outdoor activity in July and August. Most days are warm (in the 70s or 80s), with afternoons frequently cooler than mornings owing to ocean breezes. While sun seems to be the norm, come prepared for rain and fog, both frequent visitors to the Maine coast. And once or twice each summer a heat wave will settle into the area, producing temperatures in the 90's, dense haze, and stifling humidity, but this rarely lasts more than two or three days. Soon enough, a brisk north wind will blow in from the Canadian Arctic, churning up the waters and forcing visitors into sweaters at night. Sometime during the last two weeks of August, a cold wind will blow through at night and you'll smell the approach of autumn, with winter not far behind.

Winter is increasingly popular among travelers who enjoy cross-country skiing on the carriage roads. Be aware, though, that snow is inconsistent and services are very much limited in the off-season.

AVOIDING THE CROWDS   Early fall is the best time to miss out on the mobs yet still enjoy the weather. If you do come mid-summer, try to venture out in the early morning and or early evening to see the most popular spots, like the Thunder Hole or the summit of Cadillac Mountain. Setting off into the woods at every opportunity is also a good strategy. About four out of five visitors restrict their tours to the loop road and a handful of other major attractions, leaving the Acadia backcountry open for more adventurous spirits.

The best guarantee of solitude is to head to the more remote outposts managed by Acadia, especially Isle au Haut and Schoodic Peninsula, located across the bay to the east. Ask for more information at the visitor's centers.

REGULATIONS   The usual national park rules apply. Guns may not be used in the park; if you have a gun, it must be "cased, broken down, or otherwise packaged against use." Fires and camping are allowed only at designated areas. Pets must be on a leash at all times. Seat belts must be worn in the national park (this is a federal law). Don't remove anything from the park, either man-made or natural; this includes cobblestones from the shore.

RANGER PROGRAMS   Frequent ranger programs are offered throughout the year. These include talks at campground amphitheaters and tours of various locations around the island. Examples are the Otter Point nature hike, Mr. Rockefeller's bridges walk, Frenchman Bay cruise (rangers provide commentary on commercial trips; make reservations with commercial tour boat owners), and a discussion of changes in Acadia's landscape. Ask for a schedule of events or more information at either of the two visitor's centers or campgrounds.

SEEING THE HIGHLIGHTS

Try to allow 3 or 4 days at a minimum for visiting the park. If you're passing through just briefly, at least try to work in at least three of the four following activities.

☼ DRIVE THE PARK LOOP ROAD   This almost goes without saying, since it's the park's premier attraction. This 20-mile road runs along the island's eastern shore, then loops inland along Jordan Pond and Eagle Lake. The road runs high along the shoulders of dramatic coastal mountains, then dips down along the boulder-strewn coastlines. The dark granite is broken by the spires of spruce and fir, and the earthy tones contrast sharply with the frothy white surf and the steely, azure sea. The two-lane road is one-way along the coastal stretches; the right-hand lane is set aside for parking, so it's easy to make frequent stops to admire the vistas.

Ideally, visitors will make at least two trips on the loop road. The first is for the sheer exhilaration and to suss out the lay of the land. On the second trip, plan to stop frequently, leaving your car behind while you set off on trails and wander down to the coastline.

Attractions along the coastal loop include: scenic **Sand Beach**, the only sand beach on the island; **Thunder Hole**, a shallow oceanside cavern into which the surf surges, compresses, and bursts out with an explosive force and a concussive sound (young kids seem to be endlessly mesmerized by this); and **Cadillac Mountain**, the highest point on the island at 1,530 feet, and the place in the United States first touched by the sun during much of the year. The mountaintop is accessible by car along an old carriage road, but the parking lot at the summit is often crowded and drivers testy. You're better off hiking to the top, or scaling a more remote peak.

HIKE A MOUNTAIN   This quintessential Acadia experience shouldn't be missed. The park is studded with low "mountains" (they'd be called hills elsewhere) that offer superb views over the island and the open ocean. The trails weren't simply hacked out of the hillside; many were crafted by experienced stonemasons and others with high aesthetic intent. The routes aren't the most direct, or the easiest to build. But they're often the most scenic, taking advantage of fractures in the rocks, picturesque ledges, and sudden vistas. See "Hiking" below for suggested climbs.

BIKE A CARRIAGE ROAD   The 57 miles of carriage roads built by John D. Rockefeller, Jr. are among the park's most extraordinary hidden treasures. (See the introduction above for a brief history.) While built for horse and carriage, these grass-and-gravel roads are ideal for cruising by mountain bike. Park near Jordan Pond and plumb the tree-shrouded lanes that lace the area, and take time to admire the stonework on the uncommonly fine bridges. Afterward, stop for tea and popovers at the **Jordan Pond House,** which has been a popular island destination for over a century, although it's unlikely as much Lycra was in evidence 100 years ago. For bike rentals, see "Mountain Biking," below.

EAT A LOBSTER   The best lobster restaurants are those right on the water, where there's no pretension or fills. The ingredients for a proper feed at a local lobster pound are a pot of boiling water, a tank of lobsters, some well-worn picnic tables, a good view, and a six-pack of Maine beer. Among the best are **Beal's Lobster Pier** (☎ 207/244-7178) in Southwest Harbor, which is one of the oldest pounds in the area. **Thurston's Lobster Pound** (☎ 207/244-7600) in tiny Bernard (across the water from Bass Harbor) was atmospheric enough to be used as a backdrop for the Stephen King miniseries "Storm of the Century"; it's a fine place to linger toward dusk. **Abel's Lobster Pound** (☎ 207/276-5827) on Route 198, 5 miles north of Northeast Harbor overlooks the deep blue waters of Somes Sound; eat at picnic tables under the pines or indoors at the restaurant. It's quite a bit pricier than other lobster restaurants at first glance, but they don't charge for the extras like many other lobster joints and some visitors claim that lobsters here are more succulent.

On the mainland just north of the causeway is the wonderful **Oak Point Lobster Pound** (☎ 207/667-6998). This is off the beaten path (although still popular and often crowded), where you can enjoy your lobster with a sensational view of the island's rocky hills. To get here, turn west off Route 3 onto Route 230 before crossing to Mount Desert, then continue 4 miles to the restaurant.

OUTDOOR PURSUITS

CARRIAGE RIDES   Carriage rides are offered by **Wildwood Stables** (☎ 207/276-3622), a national park concessioner located a half-mile south of Jordan Pond House. The one-hour Day Mountain trip departs three times daily, yields wonderful views, and costs $13 for adults, $7 for children 6 to 12, and $4 for children 2 to 5. Longer tours and charters are also available, as is a special carriage designed to accommodate handicapped passengers; reservations are encouraged.

HIKING   Acadia National Park has 120 miles of hiking trails in addition to the carriage roads. The **Hulls Cove Visitor Center** offers a one-page chart of area hikes;

combined with the park map, this is all you'll need since the trails are well-maintained and well-marked. It's not hard to cobble together loop hikes to make your trips more varied. Coordinate your hiking with the weather; if it's damp or foggy, you'll stay drier and warmer strolling the carriage roads. If it's clear and dry, head for the highest peaks with the best views.

- Among my favorite trails is the **Dorr Ladder Trail,** which departs from Route 3 near The Tarn just south of the Sieur de Monts entrance to the Loop Road. This trail begins with a series of massive stone steps ascending along the base of a vast slab of granite, then passes through crevasses (not for the wide of girth) and up ladders affixed to the granite. The views east and south are superb.

- An easy lowland hike is **around Jordan Pond,** with the northward leg along the pond's east shore on a hiking trail, and the return via carriage road. It's mostly level, with the total loop measuring just over 3 miles. At the north end of Jordan Pond, consider heading up the prominent, oddly symmetrical mounds called The Bubbles. These detours shouldn't take much more than 20 minutes each; look for signs off the Jordan Pond Shore Trail.

- On the western side of the island, an ascent of **Acadia Mountain** and return takes about an hour and a half, but hikers should schedule in some time for lingering while they enjoy the view of Somes Sound and the smaller islands off Mount Desert's southern shores. This 2.5-mile loop hike begins off Route 102 at a trailhead 3 miles south of Somesville. Head eastward through rolling mixed forest, then begin an ascent over ledgy terrain. Be sure to visit both the east and west peaks (the east peak has the better views), and look for hidden balds in the summit forest that open up to unexpected vistas.

✪ **MOUNTAIN BIKING**   Acadia's **carriage roads** (see introduction, above) offer some of the most scenic, relaxing mountain biking anywhere in the United States. The 57 miles of grassy lanes and gravel roads were maintained by John D. Rockefeller, Jr. until his death in 1960, but afterward they became somewhat shaggy and overgrown. A major restoration effort was launched in 1990, and the roads today are superbly restored and maintained. Where the carriage roads cross private land (generally between Seal Harbor and Northeast Harbor), they are closed to mountains bikes.

A decent map of the carriage roads is available free at the park's visitor's center. More detailed guidebooks are sold at area bookstores.

Mountain bikes may be rented along Cottage Street in Bar Harbor, with rates around $15 to $17 for a full day, $10 to $12 for a half day. Most bike shops include locks and helmets as basic equipment, but ask what's included before you rent. Also ask about closing times, since you'll be able to get a couple extra hours in with a later-closing shop. **Bar Harbor Bicycle Shop** (☎ 207/288-3886) at 141 Cottage St. gets my vote for the most convenient and friendliest; you might also try **Acadia Outfitters** (☎ 207/288-8118) at 106 Cottage St., or **Acadia Bike & Coastal Kayak** (☎ 207/ 288-9605) at 48 Cottage St.

ROCK CLIMBING   Many of the oceanside rock faces attract experienced rock climbers, as much for the beauty of the climbing areas as the challenge of the climbs. For curious novices, **Acadia Mountain Guides** (☎ 207/288-8186) offers rock climbing lessons and guide services, ranging from a half-day introduction to rock climbing to intensive workshops on self-rescue and instruction on how to lead climbs. The Bar Harbor shop is located at the corner of Main and Mount Desert streets.

SEA KAYAKING   Experienced sea kayakers flock to Acadia to test their paddling skills along the surf at the base of rocky cliffs, to venture out to the offshore islands, and to probe the still, silent waters of Somes Sound. Novice sea kayakers also come to

Acadia to try their hand for the first time with guided tours, which are offered by several outfitters. Many new paddlers have found their inaugural experiences gratifying; others have complained that the quantity of paddlers taken out on quick tours during peak season make the experience a little too much like a cattle drive to truly enjoy. Ask how many paddlers have already signed up if crowding is an issue for you. (Insider tip: rainy days can be magical on the water and surprisingly dry once you're sealed inside a kayak; you're also likely to have a much less crowded experience.) You can turn up a variety of tours, ranging from a 2½-hour harbor tour to a 7-hour full-day tour by contacting the following guide services: **Acadia Outfitters** (☎ **207/288-8118**) at 106 Cottage St.; **Coastal Kayaking Tours** (☎ **207/288-9605**) at 48 Cottage St., and **National Park Sea Kayak Tours** (☎ **207/288-0342**) at 137 Cottage St. Rates range from $34 per person for a 2-hour harbor tour, to $65 for a full-day excursion.

CAMPING

The National Park Service maintains two campgrounds within Acadia National Park. Both are extremely popular; during July and August expect both to fill by early to midmorning.

The more popular of the two is **Blackwoods** (☎ **207/288-3274**), located on the island's eastern side. Access is from Route 3, 5 miles south of Bar Harbor. Bikers and pedestrians have easy access to the loop road from the campground via a short trail. The campground has no public showers, but an enterprising business just outside the campground entrance offers clean showers for a modest fee. Camping fees are $14 and limited reservations are accepted; **reservations** may be made up to 5 months in advance by calling ☎ **800/365-2267**. (This is to a national reservation service, whose contract is revisited from time to time by the park service; if it's nonworking, call the campground directly to ask for the current toll-free reservation number.)

Seawall (☎ **207/244-3600**) is on the quieter, western half of the island near the fishing village of Bass Harbor. This is a good base for road biking, and several short coastal hikes are within easy striking distance. Many of the sites are walk-ins, which require carrying your gear a hundred yards or so to the site. The campground is open late May through September on a first-come, first-served basis. In general, if you get here by 9 or 10am, you'll be pretty much assured of a campsite, especially if you're a tent camper. No showers, but they're available nearby. The fee is $14 for those arriving by car, $10 for those coming by foot or bike.

Private campgrounds handle the overflow. The region from Ellsworth south boasts some 14 private campgrounds, which offer varying amenities. The **Thompson Island Information Center** (☎ 207/288-3411) posts up-to-the-minute information on which campgrounds still have vacancies; it's a good first stop for those arriving without camping reservations.

BAR HARBOR

Bar Harbor's historical roots are in the grand resort era of the late–19th century. The region was discovered by wealthy rusticators, drawn by landscape paintings exhibited in Boston and New York. Later, sprawling hotels and boarding houses cluttered the shores and hillsides as the newly affluent middle class flocked here in summer by steamboat and rail from eastern seaboard cities. When the resort was at its zenith near the turn of the last century, Bar Harbor had rooms enough to accommodate some 5,000 visitors. Along with the hotels and guest houses, hundreds of cottages were built by the wealthiest rusticators who came here season after season.

The tourist business continued to grow through the early part of the 1900s, then all but collapsed as the Great Depression and the growing popularity of automobile travel doomed the era of the extended vacation. Bar Harbor was dealt a further blow in 1947 when a fire, fueled by an unusually dry summer and fierce northwest winds, leveled many of the most opulent cottages and much of the rest of the town. (To this day, no one knows with any certainty how the fire started.) The fire destroyed five hotels, 67 grand cottages, and 170 homes. In all, some 17,000 acres of the island were burned. Downtown Bar Harbor was spared, and many of the in-town mansions along the oceanfront were missed by the conflagration.

After a period of quiet slumber (some storefronts were still boarded up as late as the 1970s), Bar Harbor has been rejuvenated and rediscovered in recent years as visitors have poured in to this area, followed by entrepreneurs who opened dozens of restaurants, shops, and boutiques. The less charitable regard Bar Harbor as just another tacky tourist mecca. And it does have some of those traits—the downtown hosts a proliferation of T-shirt vendors, ice-cream-cone shops, and souvenir palaces. Crowds spill off the sidewalk and into the street in midsummer, and the traffic and congestion can be truly appalling. Yet Bar Harbor's vibrant history, distinguished architecture, refusal to sprawl, and beautiful location along Frenchman Bay allow it to rise above being only a diversion for tourists.

Most of the island's inns, motels, and B&Bs are located here, as are dozens of fine restaurants, making it a desirable base of operations. Bar Harbor is also the best destination for the usual supplies and services; there's a decent grocery store and Laundromat, and you can stock up on all the necessities of life.

ESSENTIALS

GETTING THERE   Bar Harbor is located on Route 3 about 10 miles southeast of the causeway. Seasonal bus service is available in summer; for schedules contact **Vermont Transit** (☎ **800/451-3292** or 800/642-3133) or **Concord Trailways** (☎ **800/ 639-3317**).

VISITOR INFORMATION   The **Bar Harbor Chamber of Commerce,** P.O. Box 158, Bar Harbor, ME 04609 (☎ **207/288-5103;** www.acadia.net/bhcc) stockpiles a huge amount of information about local attractions at its offices at 93 Cottage Street. Write, call or E-mail (bhcc@acadia.net) in advance for a full guide to area lodging and attractions.

EXPLORING BAR HARBOR

Wandering the compact downtown on foot is a good way to get a taste of the town. Among the best views in town are those from the foot of Main St. at grassy **Agamont Park,** which overlooks the town pier and Frenchman Bay. From here, set off past the Bar Harbor Inn on the **Shore Path,** a winding, wide trail that follows the shoreline for a short distance along a public right of way. The pathway passes in front of many of the elegant summer homes (some converted to inns), offering a superb vantage point to view the area's architecture.

From the path, you'll also have an open view of **The Porcupines,** a cluster of spruce-studded islands just offshore. This is a good spot to witness the powerful force of glacial action. The south-moving glacier ground away at the islands, creating a gentle slope facing north. On the south shore, away from the glacial push (glaciers simply melted when they retreated north), is a more abrupt, clifflike shore. The resulting islands look like a small group of porcupines migrating southward—or so early visitors imagined.

One of downtown's less obvious attractions is the **Criterion Theater** (☎ 207/ 288-3441), a movie house built in 1932 in a classic art-deco style and which so far avoided the degradation of multiplexification. The 900-seat theater, located on Cottage

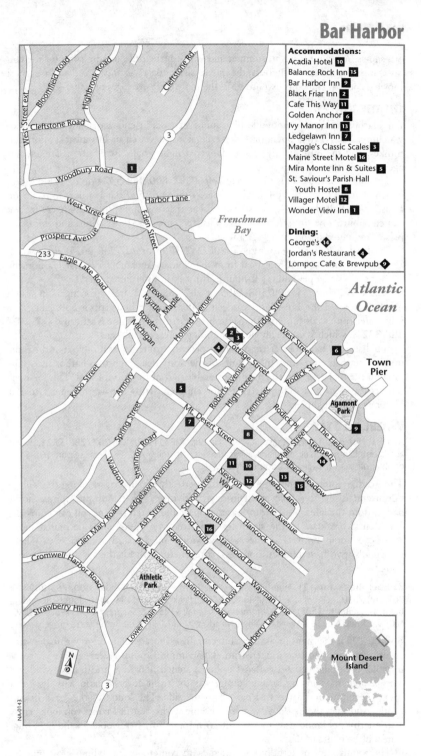

Bar Harbor

Accommodations:
Acadia Hotel **10**
Balance Rock Inn **15**
Bar Harbor Inn **9**
Black Friar Inn **2**
Cafe This Way **11**
Golden Anchor **6**
Ivy Manor Inn **13**
Ledgelawn Inn **7**
Maggie's Classic Scales **3**
Maine Street Motel **16**
Mira Monte Inn & Suites **5**
St. Saviour's Parish Hall
   Youth Hostel **8**
Villager Motel **12**
Wonder View Inn **1**

Dining:
George's **14**
Jordan's Restaurant **4**
Lompoc Cafe & Brewpub **9**

Frenchman Bay

Atlantic Ocean

Town Pier

Agamont Park

Athletic Park

Mount Desert Island

NA-0143

St., shows first-run movies in summer and is worth the price of admission for the fantastic if somewhat faded interiors; the movie is secondary. As once was the case at most movie palaces, it still costs extra to sit in the more exclusive loges upstairs.

ON THE WATER

Bar Harbor makes a memorable base for several ocean endeavors, including whale watching. Several tour operators offer excursions in search of humpbacks, finbacks, minkes, and the infrequently seen endangered right whale. Reservations are encouraged during July and August.

The largest of the fleet is the *Friendship V* (☎ 800/942-5374 or 207/288-2386), which operates from the Holiday Inn wharf 1 mile north of Bar Harbor. Tours are on a fast, twin-hulled three-level excursion boat that can hold 200 passengers in two heated cabins. The tours run 3 hours plus; the cost is $31 per adult, and the ticket price is refunded if you fail to see a whale.

Sea Bird Watcher Company (☎ 800/247-3794 or 207/288-2025) runs whale-and-puffin tours on a 72-foot boat from the Golden Anchor Pier in Bar Harbor; the 4-hour tour is $33 per adult; a 2-hour puffin trip is also offered for $18.

Whale Watcher (☎ 800/508-1499 or 207/288-3322) takes passengers in search of whales aboard the 116-foot, two-deck *Atlantis*. The 3-hour trip is $30. The same folks offer somewhat more rustic bay tours aboard the 42-foot **Katherine** (☎ 207/288-3322), which is especially popular among younger children.

You'll stop to haul lobster traps and inspect the contents, and look at and handle urchins, starfish, and other inhabitants of the briny deep. Spotting harbor seals sunning on the rocks is often the most memorable part of the trip for kids. The 1½-hour tour costs $16.75 for adults, $12.75 for children. Trips depart from next to Bar Harbor's municipal pier.

WHERE TO STAY

Acadia Hotel. 20 Mt. Desert St., Bar Harbor, ME 04609. ☎ **207/288-5721.** www.acadiahotel.com. E-mail: acadiahotel@acadia.net. 10 units. A/C TV. Peak season $65–$135 double; off-season $45–$115 double. MC, V.

The Acadia Hotel is a good budget choice, perfectly situated overlooking the Village Green and easily accessible to all in-town activities. This handsome, simple home dating from the late 19th century has a wraparound porch (where you can enjoy the continental breakfast in the summer) and attractive guest rooms decorated in an aggressive floral motif. The rooms vary widely in size and amenities; two have whirlpools, two have phones, one has a kitchenette. Ask for the specifics when you book.

Balance Rock Inn. 21 Albert Meadow, Bar Harbor, ME 04609. ☎ **800/753-0494** or 207/288-2610.. 21 units. A/C MINIBAR TV TEL. Peak season $195–$410 double, including breakfast (suites to $525); early summer and late fall $125–$255; spring $95–$195. AE, DISC, MC, V. Closed Nov to early May. Albert Meadow is off Main St. at Butterfield's grocery store.

Built in 1903, the mansion is an architecturally elaborate affair of gray shingles with cream, maroon, and forest green trim. The common rooms are expansive yet comfortable, with pilasters and coffered ceilings, arched doorways and leaded windows. The favored spot among serious loungers is the front covered patio with its green wicker furniture and a recessed bar off to the side. The sound of the sea drifts up gently. And then there's the view, which is among the best in Maine: you look across a wonderful pool, and down a verdant lawn framed by hardwoods to the rich, blue waters of Frenchman Bay.

The rooms are wonderfully appointed, with contemporary styling; most may be reached by elevator, and many feature whirlpool baths or fireplaces. About half are done up in softer, floral decor, and half in darker, more masculine tones. The top floor rooms (in the former attic) tend to be a bit tighter with odd angles, but are still bright and comfortable. Among the most outstanding rooms: Room 304 with a private roof deck and sauna ($275), and the deluxe suite (no. 408) with full kitchen, outside deck, and upstairs Jacuzzi with spectacular ocean view ($525). The inn also features a fitness center in an air-conditioned carriage house on the property. Some Frommer's readers have complained about lackluster service, which in some cases has not measured up to the room rates.

The Bar Harbor Inn. Newport Drive (P.O. Box 7), Bar Harbor, ME 04609. ☎ **800/ 248-3351** or 207/288-3351. www.barharborinn.com. 153 units. A/C TV TEL. Peak season $155–$395 double; spring and late fall $75–$199. Rates include continental breakfast. AE, DISC, MC, V. Closed Dec to late March.

The Bar Harbor Inn, located just off Agamont Park, manages to nicely mix traditional and contemporary. Situated on shady waterfront grounds just a minute's stroll from downtown boutiques (it's also at the start of the Shore Path), the inn offers both convenience and gracious charm. The main shingled inn, which dates back to the turn of the century, has a settled, old-money feel, with its semicircular dining room with ocean views, and the button-down elegance of the lobby. The guest rooms, located in the main inn and two additional structures, are decidedly more contemporary. Guest rooms in the Oceanfront and Main Inn both offer spectacular views of the bay, and many have private balconies; the less expensive Newport building lacks views but is comfortable and up-to-date. The inn offers attractive packages in the shoulder seasons.

Dining: The inn's semiformal dining room serves up well-regarded meals along with one of the best ocean views in town. Entrees include charred tuna with a pineapple kiwi salsa, and boneless lamb loin with wild mushrooms. Prices are $16.95 to $22.95. An outdoor grill, serving simpler fare like chowders, salads, and boiled lobster, overlooks the bay and is open daily for lunch and dinner.

Amenities: Heated outdoor pool, hot tub, morning newspaper, conference space, limited room service, afternoon coffee and cookies.

The Colony. Route 3, (P.O. Box 56) Hulls Cove, ME 04644. ☎ **800/524-1159** or 207/ 288-3383. 55 units. $60–$90 double. AE, DC, DISC, MC, V. Closed mid-Oct to early June.

The Colony is a classic motor court consisting of a handful of motel rooms and a battery of 55 cottages arrayed around a long green. It will be most appreciated by those with a taste for retro chic; others might decide to look for something with more modern amenities. The rooms are furnished in a simple '70s style that won't win any awards for decor, but all are comfortable; many have kitchenettes. It's situated just across Route 3 from a cobblestone beach, and a 10-minute drive from Bar Harbor. The Colony offers one of the better values on the island.

Ivy Manor Inn. 194 Main St. Bar Harbor, ME 04609. ☎ **207/288-2138.** E-mail: ivy-manor@acadia.net. 7 units. A/C TV TEL. Mid-May to mid-Oct $150–$275 double; mid-Oct to mid-Mar $85–$135 double; mid-Mar to mid-May $85–$185 double. Rates include full breakfast. AE, DISC, MC, V. 2-night minimum stay holiday weekends. Children over 12 welcome.

The Ivy Manor opened in 1997 and is one of Bar Harbor's newest additions to the upscale lodging pool. Located in a 1940s-era Tudor-style house that was once home and office of a doctor, the Ivy Manor was thoroughly done over in an understated French Victorian style, mostly in lush, rich colors like burgundy. The rooms are nicely sized; most are carpeted and furnished with attractive, tasteful antiques from the innkeeper's collection. Some rooms have antique claw-foot tubs; others have small outdoor sitting decks (none with views to speak of). Among the best rooms are no. 6—a small suite with a private sitting room and small fireplace—and no. 1, the honey-

Pillow Talk

Bar Harbor is the bedroom community for Mount Desert Island, with hundreds of hotel, motel, and inn rooms. While varied in size, shape, cost, and decor, all share one thing in common: they're filled during the busy days of mid-summer. Even the most basic of rooms can be expensive in July and August; it will require a small miracle to find a motel for less than $60, and bed-and-breakfasts start at about $85. It's essential to book your room as early as possible.

A number of modern hotels and motels cluster along Route 3 just northwest of the village center; this is your best bet if you arrive without reservations. Don't despair if you can't book a room in any of the fine establishments reviewed on the adjacent pages, there are still dozens of other good options, including those listed below.

The Acadia Inn (98 Eden St.; ☎ **800/638-3636** or 207/288-3500) is a modern if unintriguing three-story hotel on busy Route 3, with amenities including a playground, outdoor pool, and Jacuzzi. The village is 5 minutes away by foot. Peak season rates are $139 to $159 and include continental breakfast.

The Golden Anchor (55 West St.; ☎ **800/328-5033** or 207/288-5033) is smack on the waterfront, with some rooms looking across the harbor toward the town pier and others out to Bar Island. (Less expensive rooms have no view.) There's a pool and hot tub right at the harbor's edge, and an oceanfront dining room that serves basic fare. Peak season rates range from $110 to $165.

The Town Motel and Guest House (12 Atlantic Ave., 800/458-8644 or 207/288-5548) has both comfortable motel rooms and inn rooms in a Victorian manor; it's located within walking distance of downtown attractions. Peak season rates are $92 to $140.

The **Park Entrance Oceanfront Motel** (Route 3; ☎ **800/288-9703** or 207/288-9703) is nicely situated on 10 handsome waterfront acres close to the

moon room with an imposing walnut headboard and matching armoire. All rooms have small TVs. Leave time for a cocktail in the cozy first-floor lounge after you return from your day's outing.

Dining: Michelle's. See "Where to Dine," below.

Ledgelawn Inn. 66 Mt. Desert St., Bar Harbor, ME 04609. ☎ **800/274-5334** or 207/288-4596. Fax 207/288-9968. 33 units. TV TEL. July and August $95–$245 double. Rates include full breakfast. Discounts off-season. AE, DISC, MC, V. Closed late Oct to early May. Pets allowed ($15 a day extra).

If you want a great location and more flair than a motel, this is a good bet. This hulking cream and maroon 1904 "cottage" sits on a village lot amid towering oaks and maples, and has a mid-century elegance to it, although updated with modern amenities; on the property you'll find a small, no-frills pool, and some rooms have air-conditioning. The Ledgelawn first gets your attention with a handsome sun porch lounge with a full bar, and when you first set foot here you half expect to find Bogart flirting with Bacall in a corner. The guest rooms all vary somewhat as to size and mood, but all are comfortably if not stylishly furnished with antiques and reproductions. Some rooms feature fireplaces that burn Duraflame-style logs; others have bathrooms wedged into small spaces.

Maples Inn. 16 Roberts Ave., Bar Harbor, ME 04609. ☎ **207/288-3443.** E-mail: maplesinn@acadia.net. 6 units, 1 with private hall bathroom. Mid-June to mid-Oct $90–$150 park visitor's center. The inn has an attractive private pier and cobblestone beach, and an outdoor swimming pool and Jacuzzi. Summer rates are $129 to $159; suites are $169 to $299.

Great views greet guests at the **Atlantic Eyrie Lodge** (Highbrook Rd., ☎ 207/288-9786), perched on a hillside above Route 3. Peak rates are $99 to $153. Some units have kitchenettes and balconies; all share access to the ocean-view pool.

The Aurora Motel (51 Holland Ave.; ☎ 800/841-8925 or 207/288-3771) is nicely situated downtown, has 10 basic rooms decorated in a modern country style, and offers easy access to the village for rates of $80 to $96.

Convenient to the Nova Scotia ferry on nicely landscaped grounds is the family-friendly **Bar Harbor Motel** (100 Eden St; ☎ 800/388-3453 or 207/288-3453), which has a heated outdoor pool and a small playground. Two-bedroom units for families are $135 in midsummer; standard rooms run $102 to $112.

Those looking for a bit more quiet and who don't feel the need to be right downtown have a good option in the **Edgewater Motel and Cottages** (off Route 3, Salisbury Cove; ☎ 207/288-3491). The 11 cottages are just up from the water's edge (the name doesn't lie), where you can enjoy the early morning sun with your morning coffee, and prowl around watery crevices at low tide. Rates are $78 to $105 during peak season, which offer good value.

Reputable motels and hotels offering at least some rooms under $100 include the conveniently located, budget-priced **Villager Motel,** (207 Main St.; ☎ 207/288-3211) a family-run motel with 63 rooms; the 79-room **Wonder View Inn,** (50 Eden St.; ☎ 800/341-1553 or 207/288-3358) with sweeping bay views (pets welcome); and the downtown **Maine Street Motel,** (315 Main St.; ☎ 800/333-3188 or 207/288-3188).

double, off-season $60–$95 double. Rates include full breakfast. DISC, MC, V. 2-night minimum stay holiday weekends. Children 10 and over are welcome.

The Maples is a popular destination among those attracted to outdoor activities. You'll often find guests swapping stories of the day's adventure on the handsome front porch, or lingering over breakfast to compare notes about the best hiking trails. The rather modest (by Bar Harbor standards) yellow farmhouse-style home is tucked away on a leafy sidestreet among other B&Bs; it's an easy walk downtown to a movie or dinner. The innkeepers have a good way of making guests comfortable, with board games and paperbacks scattered about, and down comforters in all rooms. The rooms aren't huge, but you're not likely to feel cramped either. (The suite with fireplace is the largest.) Breakfasts—including dishes like Bananas Holland America—are appropriately filling for a full day outdoors.

Mira Monte Inn. 69 Mount Desert St., Bar Harbor, ME 04609. ☎ 800/553-5109 or 207/288-4263. Fax 207/288-3115. E-mail: mburns@acadia.net. 12 units, 3 suites. A/C TV TEL. $135–$165 double, $195–$205 suites. Rates include breakfast. 2-night minimum stay in midsummer. AE, DC, DISC, MC, V. Closed Nov–May (suites available by week in winter).

A stay at this impressive grayish-green Italianate mansion, built in 1864, feels a bit like a trip to grandmother's house—a grandmother who inherited most of her furniture from her grandmother. The antiques are more intriguing than elegant, and the common rooms are furnished in a pleasant country Victorian style. The 2-acre grounds, located within a few minutes' walk of Bar Harbor's restaurants and attractions, are attractively landscaped and include a cutting garden to keep the house in flowers. There's a nice brick terrace away from the street, which makes a fine place to enjoy breakfast on warm summer mornings. The guest rooms are blessed with a profusion of balconies and fireplaces—most rooms have one or the other; many have both. The room styles vary widely; some are heavy on the Victorian, others have the bright and airy feel of a country farmhouse. If you're a light sleeper, avoid the rooms facing Mount Desert Street; those facing the gardens in the rear are far more peaceful. Families should inquire about the suites in the adjacent outbuilding.

WHERE TO DINE

Café This Way. 14½ Mt. Desert St. ☎ **207/288-4483.** Reservations recommended for dinner. Main courses, breakfast $3.25–$5.95, dinner $11–$18. MC, V. Summer daily 7–11am (8am–1pm Sun), and 6–9pm. Closed for dinner and open for lunch in winter. CONTEMPORARY CAFE.

Café This Way has the feel of a casually hip coffee house, and is much more airy than one might guess upon first looking at this cottage tucked on a side street across from the village green. Bookshelves line one wall, and there's a small bar tucked in a nook. The breakfasts are excellent and mildly sinful, with offerings like eggs Benedict with spinach, artichoke and tomato. The red-skinned potatoes are crispy and delicious; the robust coffee requires two creamers to lighten it. Dinners are equally appetizing, with tasty dishes like butternut squash ravioli, crab cakes with a tequila-lime sauce, and filet mignon grilled with fresh basil. This is the kind of place I love, where they know how to do great things with relatively simple ingredients.

✪ **George's.** 7 Stephens Lane. ☎ **207/288-4505.** Reservations recommended. Entrees $24; appetizer, entree & dessert packages $33–$36. AE, DISC, MC, V. Daily 5:30–10pm; shorter hours after Labor Day. Closed Nov to early May. CONTEMPORARY MEDITERRANEAN.

George's takes some sleuthing to find, but it's worth the effort. Because this is one of Bar Harbor classics, offering fine dining in informal surroundings for nearly two decades. (It's located in the small clapboard cottage behind Main Street's First National Bank.) George's captures the joyous feel of summer nicely with four smallish dining rooms (and plenty of open windows) and additional seating on the terrace outside, which is the best place to watch the gentle dusk settle over town. The service is upbeat, and the meals wonderfully prepared. All entrees sell for one price ($24), and include salad, vegetable, and potato or rice. You won't go wrong with the basic choices, like steamed lobster or roast chicken, but you're even better off opting for the more adventurous fare like lobster strudel or the house specialty lamb in its many incarnations, including charcoal-grilled lamb tenderloin and rolled lamb stuffed with wild mushrooms.

Lompoc Cafe and Brewpub. 36 Rodick St. ☎ **207/288-9392.** Reservations not accepted. Sandwiches $4.50–$6.50; dinner $8.95–$15.95. MC, V. May–Nov daily 11:30am–1am. Closed Dec–April. AMERICAN/ECLECTIC.

The Lompoc Cafe has a well-worn, neighborhood bar feel to it, and it's little wonder that waiters from around Bar Harbor congregate here after hours. The cafe consists of three sections—there's the original bar, a tidy beer garden just outside (try your hand at bocce), and a small and open barnlike structure at the garden's edge to handle the overflow. The on-site brewery produces several unique beers, including a blueberry ale (intriguing concept, but ask for a sample before you order a full glass), and the smooth Coal Porter, available in sizes up to the 20-ounce "fatty." Whisky drinkers will be busy here: the Lompoc claims the largest selection of single-malts north of Boston. Bar menus are usually yawn-inducing, but this one has some pleasant surprises, like the

Persian plate (hummus and grape leaves), Szechuan eggplant wrap, and crab and shrimp cakes. A number of vegetarian entrees are offered. Live music is offered some evenings, when there's a small cover charge.

Maggie's Classic Scales. 6 Summer St. ☎ **207/288-9007.** Reservations recommended in July and August. Main courses $12.95–$20.95. DISC, MC, V. Daily 5–10pm. Closed mid-Oct to mid-June. SEAFOOD.

The slogan for Maggie's is "notably fresh seafood," and the place invariably delivers on that understated promise. (Only fish caught off the island is used.) It's a causally elegant spot tucked off Cottage St., good for a romantic evening with soothing music and good service. Appetizers include smoked salmon and charbroiled shrimp brochettes. Main courses range from basic boiled lobster and crabmeat-stuffed sole, to more adventurous offerings like Maine seafood provencal and sautéed scallops with fresh corn, bacon, and peppers. The servings are usually quite sizable. Desserts are homemade and well worth leaving room for.

Michelle's. 194 Main St. ☎ **207/288-0038.** Reservations recommended during peak season. Main courses $19–$42 (mostly $24–$28). Daily 6:30–9:30pm. Closed late Oct to early May. FRENCH. AE. MC, V.

Michelle's is located in the graceful Ivy Manor Inn (see above), and soon caught the attention of the state's gourmands when it opened in 1997. The three dining rooms are elegant and set out with fresh roses and candles (there's outside seating when the weather's good). The extensive menu elaborates on traditional French cuisine with New England twists. The appetizers ($7 to $16) include smoked salmon layered with a chervil mousse, and foie gras with black truffle. Main courses are elaborate affairs, with dishes like chateaubriand for two carved at the table, and oven roasted duckling with a ragout of cranberries and apricot. Appropriately for Bar Harbor, the seafood selection is extensive. The "chilled seafood bounty" for two ($80) should sate any craving for local fare from the sea; it includes lobster, mussels, clams, oyster, scallops and crab.

ELSEWHERE ON THE ISLAND

There's plenty to explore outside of Acadia National Park and Bar Harbor. Quiet fishing villages, deep woodlands, and unexpected ocean views are among the jewels that turn up when one peers beyond the usual places.

ESSENTIALS

GETTING AROUND   The east half of the island is best navigated on Route 3, which forms the better part of a loop from Bar Harbor through Seal Harbor and past Northeast Harbor before returning up the eastern shore of Somes Sound. Route 102 and Route 102A provide access to the island's western half.

VISITOR INFORMATION   The best source of information on the island is at the **Thompson Island Information Center** (☎ 207/288-3411) on Route 3 just south of the causeway connecting Mount Desert Island with the mainland. Another reliable source of local information is **Mount Desert Chamber of Commerce,** P.O. Box 675, Northeast Harbor, ME 04662 (☎ 207/276-5040).

EXPLORING THE REST OF THE ISLAND

On the tip of the eastern lobe of Mount Desert Island is the staid, prosperous community of **Northeast Harbor,** long one of the favored retreats among the Eastern Seaboard's upper crust. Those without personal invitations to come as house guests will need to be satisfied with glimpses of the shingled palaces set in the fragrant spruce forests and along the rocky shore. But the village itself is worth investigating. Situated on a scenic, narrow harbor, with the once-grand Asticou Inn at its head, Northeast Harbor is possessed of a refined sense of elegance that's best appreciated by finding a vantage point, then sitting and admiring.

One of the best, least publicized places for enjoying views of the harbor is from the understatedly spectacular ✪ **Asticou Terraces** (☎ 207/276-5130). Finding the parking lot can be tricky: head one-half mile east (toward Seal Harbor) on Route 3 from the junction with Route 198, and look for the small gravel lot on the water side of the road with a sign reading ASTICOU TERRACES. Park here, cross the road on foot, and set off up a magnificent path made of local rock that ascends the sheer hillside with expanding views of the harbor and the town. This pathway, with its precise stonework and the occasional bench and gazebo, is one of the nation's hidden marvels of landscape architecture. Created by Boston landscape architect Joseph Curtis, who summered here for many years prior to his death in 1928, the pathway seems to blend in almost preternaturally with its spruce-and-fir surroundings, as if it were created by an act of God rather than of man. Curtis donated the property to the public for quiet enjoyment.

Continue on the trail at the top of the hillside and you'll soon arrive at **Curtis's cabin** (open to the public daily in summer), behind which lies the formal **Thuya Gardens,** which are as manicured as the terraces are natural. These wonderfully maintained gardens, designed by noted landscape architect Charles K. Savage, attract flower enthusiasts, students of landscape architecture, and local folks looking for a quiet place to rest. It's well worth the trip. A donation of $2 is requested of visitors to the garden; the terraces are free.

WHERE TO STAY

✪ **Claremont.** P.O. Box 137, Southwest Harbor, ME 04679. ☎ 800/244-5036 or 207/ 244-5036. 30 inn rooms, 12 cottages. TEL. July to Labor Day $135–$145 double (including breakfast), $160–$200 double (including breakfast and dinner); off-season from $95 double. Cottages: July–Labor Day $158–$198 double; off-season $100–$140 double. 3-day minimum stay on cottages. No credit cards. Closed mid-Oct to early June.

Early prints of the Claremont, built in 1884, show an austere four-story wooden building with a single severe gable overlooking Somes Sound from a low, grassy rise. And the place hasn't changed all that much since then. The Claremont offers nothing fancy or elaborate, just simple, classic New England grace. It's wildly appropriate that the state's most high-profile and combative croquet tournament takes place here annually in early August; all those folks in their whites seem right at home. The common areas and dining rooms are pleasantly appointed in an affable country style. There's a library with rockers, a fireplace, and jigsaw puzzles waiting to be assembled. Two other fireplaces in the lobby take the chill out of the morning air.

Most of the guest rooms are bright and airy, furnished with antiques and some old furniture that doesn't quite qualify as "antique." The bathrooms are modern. Guests opting for the full meal plan at the inn are given preference in reserving rooms overlooking the water; it's almost worth it, although dinners can be lackluster. There's also a series of cottages, available for a 3-day minimum. Some are set rustically in the piney woods; others offer pleasing views of the sound.

Dining: The dining room is open nightly. Meals are mainly reprises of American classics like salmon, grilled lamb, and steamed lobster; guests report being underwhelmed by the kitchen. The dining room is open to the public; entrees are $17 to $22.

Amenities: One clay tennis court, rowboats, bicycles (free to guests), croquet court.

Inn at Southwest. 371 Main St. (P.O. Box 593), Southwest Harbor, ME 04679. ☎ 207/ 244-3835. www.acadia.net/iaswh. E-mail: innatsw@acadia.net. 9 units, 2 with private hall bathrooms. Summer and early fall $95–$145 double; off-season $65–$105. Rates include full breakfast. DISC, MC, V. Closed Nov–Apr.

Innkeeper Jill Lewis acquired the architecturally quirky Inn at Southwest in 1995, and she's done a fine job making this mansard-roofed Victorian a hospitable place. There's a decidedly turn-of-the-century air to this elegant home, but it's restrained on the frills. The guest rooms are named after Maine lighthouses, and are furnished with both contemporary and antique furniture. All rooms have ceiling fans and down comforters. Among the most pleasant rooms is Blue Hill Bay on the third floor, with its large bath, sturdy oak bed and bureau, and glimpses of the scenic harbor. Breakfasts offer ample reason to rise and shine, featuring specialties like vanilla Belgian waffles with raspberry sauce, and crab potato bake.

✪ **Lindenwood Inn.** 118 Clark Point Rd. (P.O. Box 1328), Southwest Harbor, ME 04679. ☎ **207/244-5335.** 22 units (some with shower only), 1 suite. July and August $95–$185 double; Sept to mid-Oct $85–$165 double; mid-Oct to June $75–$145. Suite $30 additional. Rates include full breakfast. AE, MC, V.

The Lindenwood offers a refreshing change from the fusty, overly draperied inns that tend to proliferate along Maine's coast. Housed in a handsome 1902 Queen Anne–style home at the harbor's edge, the inn features rooms that are modern and uncluttered, the colors simple and bold. The adornments are relatively few (those that do exist are mostly from the innkeeper's collection of African and Pacific art and artifacts), but clean lines and bright natural light more than create a relaxing mood—you'll even begin to view the cobblestone doorstops as works of art. Especially appealing is the spacious suite, which features great harbor views. If you're on a tighter budget, ask for a room in the annex, housed in an 1883 home just a minute's walk down the block. The rooms are somewhat less expansive and more simply decorated, but still offer nice touches (like bright halogen reading lamps) and make a superb base from which to explore the area. Eight of the rooms feature fireplaces; most also have telephones, but ask when you book if this is important to you.

Dining: The Lindenwood's dining room attracted serious attention from around the island when it started offering dinner in 1996, but it was closed in the summer of 1998 following some unexpected turnover in kitchen staff. Innkeeper Jim King was anticipating reopening the dining room in 1999 as of press time, but it's safest to call first.

Amenities: Jacuzzi, heated outdoor pool, boat dock.

WHERE TO DINE

Jordan Pond House. Park Loop Rd., Acadia National Park (near Seal Harbor). ☎ **207/ 276-3316.** Advance reservations not accepted; call before arriving to hold table. Lunch $6.25–$12.75, afternoon tea $5.75–$6.75; dinner $9.25–$17.50. AE, DISC, MC, V. Mid-May to late Oct daily 11:30am–8pm (until 9pm July–Aug). AMERICAN.

The secret to the Jordan Pond House? Location, location, location. The restaurant traces its roots back to 1847, when an early farm was established on this picturesque property at the southern tip of a pond looking toward The Bubbles, a pair of towering, glacially sculpted mounds. The spot first caught on during the local mania for tea-houses in the late–19th century. But tragedy struck in 1979 when the original structure and its birch-bark dining room was destroyed by fire. A more modern, two-level dining room was built in its place—it's got less charm, but it still has the location. If the weather's agreeable, ask for a seat on the lawn with its unrivaled views. Afternoon tea is a hallowed Jordan Pond House tradition. Ladies-Who-Lunch sit next to Mountain-Bikers-Who-Wear-Lycra, and everyone feasts on the huge, tasty popovers and strawberry jam served with a choice of teas or fresh lemonade. Dinners are reasonably priced, and include classic resort entrees like prime rib, steamed lobster, and baked scallops with a crumb topping.

Keenan's. Route 102A, Bass Harbor. ☎ **207/244-3403.** Reservations suggested for parties of five or more. Sandwiches and main courses $5–$17. No credit cards. Summers Tues–Sun 4:30–10pm; weekends only off-season. SEAFOOD.

This classic, informal seafood shack at a fork in the road is one of those local secrets that most travelers zip right by without a second thought. But do yourself a favor and make an effort to stop here and order up some of the best seafood value for your money. The fried clams are well-prepared, and the spicy gumbo packs a kick. If you're of a mind to gorge on seafood, go with the seafood sampler, which includes lobster, crab, mussels, clams, and corn, all for around $17, which is what you'd pay for a lobster alone at some of the snootier coastal joints.

Restaurant XYZ. Shore Rd., Manset. ☎ **207/244-5221.** Reservations recommended. Main courses $13–$15. MC, V. Daily in summer 5:30–9pm; limited hours (usually weekends only) shoulder seasons. Closed Columbus Day to Memorial Day. MEXICAN.

Restaurant XYZ doesn't promise much at first: it's on the ground floor beneath a run-of-the-mill motel overlooking the harbor, and the interior is adorned with kitschy imports from Mexico that might best be described as "stuff." But the food! Drawing on the traditions of central Mexico and the Yucatan, the fare here is spicy, earthy, and tangy. Don't look for thin sauces and melted cheese. Expect a remarkably savory mole (especially good with chicken), and a chipotle salsa that sings. Start with one of the stand-out margaritas (made with fresh lime juice), and then head straight to the main courses. (The appetizers don't offer especially good value.) Among the more notable entrees are the pork dishes, including *tatemado* (a pork loin baked with guajillo and ancho chiles), and Yucatan-style pork rubbed with achiote paste and marinated with citrus before baking. Aficionados of authentic Mexican cooking will be delightfully surprised to find such excellent dining deep in the home turf of boiled lobster and fried clams.

9 The Moosehead Lake Region

Thirty-two miles long and five miles across at its widest point, Moosehead Lake is Maine's largest lake, and it's a great destination for hikers, boaters, and canoeists. The lake was historically the center of the region's logging activity; that ownership preserved the lake and kept it largely unspoiled by housing developments. Timber companies still own much of the lakeside property (although the state has acquired significant amounts in recent years), and the 350-mile shoreline is mostly unbroken second- or third-growth forest. The second-home building frenzy of the 1980s had an obvious impact on the southern reaches of the lake, but the woody shoreline has absorbed most of the boom quite gracefully.

The first thing to know about the lake is that it's not meant to be seen by car. There are some great views from a handful of roads—especially from Route 6/15 as you near Rockwood, and from the high elevations on the way to Lily Bay—but for the most part the roads are a distance from the shores, and offer uninteresting driving. To see the lake at its best you should plan to get out on the water by steamship or canoe, or fly above it on a charter floatplane.

Greenville is the de facto capital of Moosehead Lake, scenically situated at the southern tip. Most services are located here, and you can stock up on groceries and camping supplies. The descent into Greenville on Route 6/15 is becoming a bit cluttered with commercial strip development, but the town is still holding on to its remote, woodsy flavor.

ESSENTIALS

GETTING THERE   Greenville is 158 miles from Portland. Take the turnpike to the Newport exit (Exit 39) and head north on Route 7/11 to Route 23 in Dexter, following that northward to Route 6/15 near Sangerville. Follow this to Greenville.

VISITOR INFORMATION   The Moosehead Lake Chamber of Commerce, P.O. Box 581, Greenville, ME 04441 (☎ **207/695-2702**), maintains an information booth that's open daily Memorial Day to mid-October from 10am to 4pm just south of the village on Route 6/15. (It's closed on Wednesday and Sunday the rest of the year.) Information is also available via e-mail: moose@moosehead.net.

HIKING

An inviting local hike is **Mount Kineo,** a sheer, broad cliff that rises from the shores of Moosehead. This hike is only accessible by water; near the town of Rockwood, look for signs advertising shuttles across the lake to Kineo (folks offering this service seem to change from year to year, so ask around). Once across, you can explore the grounds of the famed old Kineo Mountain House (alas, the grand, 500-guest-room hotel was demolished in 1938), then cut across the golf course and follow the shoreline to the trail that leads to the 1,800-foot summit. The views from the cliffs are dazzling; one hiker I know says he has no problems on any mountain except Kineo, which afflicts him each time with vertigo. Be sure to continue on the trail to the old fire tower, which you can ascend for a hawk's-eye view of the region.

WHITE-WATER RAFTING

Big waves and boiling drops await rafters on the hairy run through **Kennebec Gorge** at the headwaters of the Kennebec River, located southwest of Greenville.

A number of commercial white-water outfits offer trips throughout the summer at a cost of about $75 to $115 per person. **Northern Outdoors,** P.O. Box 100, The Forks, ME 04985 (☎ **800/765-7238;** www.northernoutdoors.com), is the oldest of the bunch, and offers rock climbing, mountain biking, and fishing expeditions as well, plus snowmobiling in winter. Other reputable rafting companies to check with include **Wilderness Expeditions,** P.O. Box 41, Rockwood, ME 04478 (☎ **800/ 825-9453**), which is affiliated with the rustic Birches Resort, and the **New England Outdoor Center,** P.O. Box 669, Millinocket, ME 04462 (☎ **800/766-7238**).

MOOSEHEAD BY STEAMSHIP & FLOATPLANE

During the lake's golden days of tourism in the late 19th century, visitors could come to the lake by train from New York or Washington, then connect with steamship to the resorts and boarding houses around the lake. A vestige of that era is found at the **Moosehead Marine Museum** (☎ 207/695-2716) in Greenville. A new museum building opened along the shores in 1999 (replacing the old museum, which was in a former gas station), and features exhibits that suggest the grandeur of life on the lake in the last century.

But the museum's showpiece is the SS *Katahdin,* a 115-foot steamship that's been cruising Moosehead's waters since 1914. The regal two-deck ship (it's now run by diesel rather than steam) offers a variety of sightseeing tours, including a weekly excursion up the lake to the site of the former Kineo Mountain House. Fares vary depending on the length of the trip, and range from $17 to $25 for adults, and $9 to $14 for children 6 and over (children under 6 go free). Admission to the museum exhibits is $3 for adults, under 12 free.

WHERE TO STAY

Greenville Inn. Norris St., Greenville, ME 04441. ☎ **888/695-6000** or 207/695-2206. www.greenvilleinn.com. E-mail: gvlinn@moosehead.net. 6 units, 6 cottages. Summer $115–$148 double; $118–$148 cottage; $195 suite. Off-season $85–$125 double; $98–$118 cottage; $175 suite. Rates include continental breakfast buffet. 2-night minimum stay holiday weekends. DISC, MC, V. No children under 8.

This handsome 1895 lumber baron's home sits regally on a hilly side street in a residential neighborhood a short walk from Greenville's commercial district. The interiors are manly and sumptuous, with wonderful cherry and mahogany woodworking and a lovely stained-glass window of a pine tree over the stairwell. There's a handsome small bar, where you can order up a cocktail or Maine beer, then sit in front of the fire or retreat to the front porch to watch the evening sun slip over Squaw Mountain and the lake. The rooms vary in size (the new master suite with lake views is the best—and most expensive), but all are richly appointed. Four new cottages were built on the property in 1995, adding to the two already there. The trim cottages are furnished in a light summer-cottage style and have views of the lake.

Dining: The dinners served in the elegant dining room are delicious. The menu features continental fare with a regional twist, with entrees like roast duck breast with blueberry sauce, or lobster in puff pastry with a tarragon sauce. The popovers are delectable and roughly the size of a football. The restaurant is open for dinner daily late May through October; entrees range from $17 to $28, with most under $20.

The Lodge at Moosehead Lake. Lily Bay Rd. (P.O. Box 1167), Greenville, ME 04441. ☎ **207/695-4400.** Fax 207/695-2281. www.lodgeatmooseheadlake.com. E-mail: lodge@moosehead.net. 8 units. A/C TV. $175–$395 double. Rates include full breakfast (also include dinner in winter and spring). 2-night minimum stay. DISC, MC, V. Located 2½ miles north of Greenville on Lily Bay Rd. (head north through blinker). Children 16 and older are welcome.

The Lodge at Moosehead is housed in a wonderful 1917 home constructed high on a hillside for a wealthy summer rusticator. The inn offers a mix of woodsy and modern; think Disneyland does the North Woods. The guest rooms are all carpeted, but there's Adirondack-style stick furnishings mixed in with wing-back chairs and antique English end tables. The dining room, where a full breakfast is served year-round (so is dinner in the winter), has a brisk, modern feel to it in contrast to much of the rest of the inn. The hosts are especially proud of the beds they offer guests. Those in the main lodge are hand-carved by local artist Joe Bolf; the suites in the carriage house feature unique swinging beds, suspended from the ceiling by chains.

Little Lyford Pond Camps. P.O. Box 340, Greenville, ME 04441. ☎ **207/280-0016.** www.midmaine.com/~islander/lyford. 8 log cabins (each with private outhouse). $170 double. Rates include all meals. Accessible by logging road in summer; by snowmobile or ski-plane in winter. 2-night minimum stay on weekends and holidays. No credit cards. Closed spring and late fall/early winter. Pets allowed.

This venerable backwoods logging camp is one of the most welcoming and comfortable spots in the North Woods. Guests stay in cozy log cabins originally built to house loggers in the 1870s, each with a small woodstove, propane lantern, cold running water, a private outhouse, and plenty of rustic charm. The more spacious main lodge has books to browse and board games for the evening, and is where guest gather to eat. During the day, activities aren't hard to find, from fishing or canoeing at the two ponds situated down a short trail, or hiking the Appalachian Trail to Gulf Hagas, just 2 miles away. In winter, the cross-country skiing on the lodging's private network is superb.

New England in Depth

by Wayne Curtis

Reduced to simplest terms, New England consists of two regions: Boston and Not-Boston.

Boston, of course, is in the same league as other major metropolitan areas nationwide, and boasts many of the same amenities: first-class hotels, elegant historic and modern architecture, and world-class restaurants. Of all U.S. cities, Boston has perhaps the richest and most complex history, ranging from the days of America's settlement in the 17th century through the War of Independence in 1776 and on into the nation's cultural renaissance in the mid– and late–19th century. The Boston area is also a national seat of education, with dozens of prestigious colleges and universities in or near the city including Harvard, MIT, Wellesley, and Boston University. .

The extensive territory of Not-Boston arcs widely, from the Connecticut and Rhode Island shoreline through the rolling Berkshire Mountains of western Massachusetts on through the Green and White Mountains and into the vast state of Maine. (Some purists insist that southern Connecticut should be cut loose from New England since many of its towns are bedroom communities for New York City, whose cultural and economic tides strongly influence the local ebb and flow.)

The Not-Boston region, while widely spread, traces it roots back to a Puritan ethic, and its longtime residents still tend to display shared traits and values, like a stubborn independence, a respect for thrift, and an almost genetic mistrust of outsiders. (In Vermont, you're not considered a native until at least a couple of generations have passed. "If a kitten is born in an oven, you don't call it a biscuit," goes the saying.)

New England's legendary aloofness is important to keep in mind when visiting the area. Because getting to know the region requires equal amounts of patience and persistence. New England doesn't wear its attractions on its sleeve. It keeps its best destinations hidden in valleys and on the side streets of small villages. Your most memorable experience might come in cracking open a boiled lobster at a pound marked only with a scrawled paper sign, or exploring a cobblestone Boston alley that's not on the maps. There's no Disneyland or Space Needle or Grand Canyon here. New England is the sum of dozens of smaller attractions, and resists being defined by a few big ones.

Which isn't to say that New England lacks attractions. It has the mansions of Newport, the endless beaches of Cape Cod, the rolling Green Mountains of Vermont, the craggy White Mountains of New Hampshire, and magnificent Acadia National Park on the Maine

Coast. It has wonderful, lost-in-time towns like New Preston, Connecticut and Woodstock, Vermont. But attempting to explore New England as a "connect-the-dots" endeavor linking the major sights with long drives is a surefire recipe for disappointment. It's better to plan a slower itinerary that allows you to enjoy the desultory trips between destinations, to explore the little villages and quiet byways. What you'll find mostly is an inviting blend of history, both human and natural.

Some writers maintain that New England's character is still informed by a grim Calvinist doctrine, which decrees nothing will change one's fate and that hard work is a moral virtue. The New Englander's dull acceptance that the Boston Red Sox will never be victorious is often trotted out as evidence of the region's enduring Calvinism, as is the inhabitants' perverse celebration of the often brutish climate.

But that's not to say travelers should expect rock-hard mattresses and nutritional but tasteless meals. On the contrary, luxurious country inns and restaurants serving food rivaling what you'll find in Manhattan have become part of the landscape in the past two decades. Be sure to visit these places. But to get the most out of your trip, leave enough time to spend an afternoon rocking and reading on a broad inn porch, or to wander out of town on an abandoned county road with no particular destination in mind.

"There's nothing to do here," an inn manager in Vermont once explained to me. "Our product is indolence." That's an increasingly rare commodity these days. Take the time to savor it.

1 New England Today

It's a common question, so don't be embarrassed about asking it. You might be on Martha's Vineyard, or traveling through a pastoral Vermont valley, or exploring an island off the Maine coast. You'll see houses and people. And you'll wonder: "What do these people do to earn a living?"

As recently as a few decades ago, the answer was probably this: living off the land. They might have fished the seas, harvested timber in the forest, operated a truck farm, or managed a gravel pit. Of course, many still do operate such businesses, but this work is no longer the economic mainstay it once was. Today, scratch a rural New Englander and you're just as likely to find an editor for a magazine that's published in Boston or New York, a farmer who grows specialized produce for gourmet restaurants, or a banking consultant who handles business by fax and e-mail. And you'll find lots of folks dependent on tourism—innkeepers and motel owners and restaurateurs and shopkeepers.

This change in the economy is but one of the tectonic shifts facing the region. The most visible and more wracking change involves development and growth. A region long familiar with economic poverty, the recent prosperity has threatened to bring to New England that curious sort of homogenization that has marked much of the nation. Instead of distinctive downtowns and courthouse squares, the landscape in New England is starting to look a lot like suburban landscapes everywhere—a pastiche of strip malls dotted with fast-food chains and big-box stores like Wal-Mart and Home Depot.

New England towns have long maintained their strong identity in the face of considerable pressure. The region has always taken a quiet pride in its low-key, practical approach to life. In smaller communities, town meetings are still the preferred form of government. Residents gather in a public place in town, usually in the grim season of February or March, and vote on the important issues of the day, like funding for their schools, road improvements, and, at times, symbolic gestures, such as declaring their town a nuclear-free zone. "Use it up, wear it out, make do, or do without" is a well-worn phrase that aptly sums up the attitude of many in New England.

New England is still figuring out how best to balance the principles of growth and conservation—how to allow the economy to edge into the modern age, without sacrificing those qualities that make New England such a distinctive place.

Development is a hot but not necessarily inflammatory issue—this isn't like the property rights movement in the West, where residents are manning the barricades and taking hostages for the cause. (At least not yet.) Few seem to think that development should be allowed at all costs. And few seem to think that the land should be preserved at all costs.

Pinching off all development means the offspring of longtime New England families will have no jobs, and New England will be fated to spend its days as a sort of quaint theme park. But if development continues unabated, many of the characteristics that make New England unique—and attract tourist dollars—will vanish. Will the Berkshires or the Maine Coast be able to sustain its tourism industry if they're blanketed with strip malls and fast-food joints, making it look like every other place in the nation? Not likely. The question is how to respect the conservation ethic while leaving room for growth. And that question won't be resolved in the near future.

New England's heady five-year economic boom in the late 1980s, which fueled much of the debate over development, slowed in the 1990s, making the issue less urgent but no less critical. Commentators point out that other social changes on the horizon could raise new conflicts. The rise of the information culture will make it increasingly likely that those telecommuters and info-entrepreneurs will settle in remote and pristine villages, running their businesses via modem and satellite. How will these affluent migrants adapt to clear cutting in the countryside or increasing numbers of tour buses cruising their village greens?

Change doesn't come rapidly to New England. But there's a lot to sort out, and friction will certainly build, one strip mall at a time.

2 History 101

Viewed from a distance, New England's history mirrors that of its namesake, England. The region rose from nowhere to gain tremendous historical prominence, captured a good deal of overseas trade, and became an industrial powerhouse and center for creative thought. And then the party ended relatively abruptly, as commerce and culture sought more fertile grounds to the west and south.

To this day, New England refuses to be divorced from its past. Walking through Boston, layers of a varied history are evident at every turn, from the church steeples that remain powerful icons of colonial times (despite being dwarfed by glass-sided skyscrapers), to verdant parklands that bespeak the refined sensibility of the late Victorian era.

History is even more inescapable in off-the-beaten track New England. Travelers in Downeast Maine, northern New Hampshire, Connecticut's Litchfield Hills, the Berkshires of

Dateline

- **1000–1015** Viking explorers land in Canada, and may or may not have sailed southward to New England. Evidence is spotty.
- **1497** John Cabot, seeking to establish trade for England, reaches the island of New-foundland in Canada and sails south as far as Maine.
- **1602** Capt. Bartholomew Gosnold lands on the Massachusetts coast. Names Cape Cod, Martha's Vineyard, and other locations.
- **1604** French colonists settle on an island on the St. Croix River between present-day Maine and New Brunswick. They leave after a single miserable winter.

continues

- **1614** Capt. John Smith maps the New England coast, names the Charles River after King Charles I of England and calls the area a paradise.

- **1616** Smallpox kills large numbers of Indians between Maine and Rhode Island.

- **1620** The Mayflower carrying some 100 colonists (including many Pilgrims, fleeing religious persecution in England), arrives at Cape Cod.

- **1630** Colonists led by John Winthrop establish the town of Boston, named after an English village.

- **1635–36** Roger Williams is exiled from Massachusetts for espousing liberal religious ideas; he founds the city of Providence, Rhode Island.

- **1636** Harvard College founded to educate young men for the ministry.

- **1638** America's first printing press established in Cambridge.

- **1648** First labor unions established by coopers and shoemakers in Boston.

- **1675–76** Native Americans attack colonists throughout New England in what is known as King Philip's war.

- **1692** The Salem witch trials take place. Twenty people (including 14 women) are executed before the hysteria subsides.

- **1704** America's first regularly published newspaper, the *Boston News Letter*, is founded.

- **1713** The first schooner, a distinctively American sailing ship, is designed and built in Gloucester, Massachusetts.

- **1764** "Taxation without representation" is denounced in reaction to the Sugar Act.

- **1770** Five colonists are killed outside what is now the Old State House in an incident known as the Boston Massacre.

continues

Massachusetts and much of Vermont will find clues to what Henry Wadsworth Longfellow called "the irrevocable past" every way they turn, from stone walls running through now-dense woods, to spectacular Federal style homes standing alone in the countryside.

Here's a brief overview of some historical episodes and trends that shaped New England:

INDIGENOUS CULTURE Native Americans have inhabited New England since about 7,000 B.C. While New York's Iroquois Indians had a presence in Vermont, New England was inhabited chiefly by Algonquins known as Abenakis ("people of the dawn"), who lived a nomadic life, moving with the seasons and travelling to areas where food was abundant. What is now Boston was home to several Algonquin tribes, who dwelled along the coast and rivers; Connecticut was home to some 16 Algonquin tribes, who dubbed the region Quinnetukut.

THE COLONIES The colonization of the region began in earnest with the arrival of the Pilgrims at Plymouth Rock in 1620. The Pilgrims—a religious group that had split from the Church of England—established the first permanent colony, although it came at a hefty price: half the group perished during the first harsh winter. But the colony took root, and thrived over the years in part thanks to helpful Indians.

The success of the Pilgrims lured other settlers from England, who established a constellation of small towns outside of Boston that became the Massachusetts Bay Colony. Roger Williams was expelled from the colony for his religious beliefs; he founded the city of Providence, Rhode Island. Other restless colonists expanded their horizons in search of lands for settlement. Throughout the 17th century colonists from Massachusetts pushed northward into what is now New Hampshire and Maine, and southward into Connecticut. The first areas to be settled were lands near protected harbors along the coast, and on navigable waterways.

The more remote settlements came under attack in the 17th and early 18th centuries in a series of raids by the Indians against the British settlers—conducted both independently and in concert with the French. These proved temporary setbacks; colonization continued apace throughout New England into 18th century.

THE AMERICAN REVOLUTION Starting around 1765 Great Britain launched a series of ham-handed economic policies to reign in the increasingly feisty colonies in America. These included a direct tax—the Stamp Act—to pay for a standing army (created largely to curb the thriving colonial trade in smuggled goods). The crackdown provoked strong resistance. Under the banner of "No taxation without representation," disgruntled colonists engaged in a series of riots, resulting in the Boston Massacre of 1770, when five protesting colonists were fired upon and killed by British soldiers.

In 1773 the most infamous protest took place in Boston. The British had imposed the Tea Act (the right to collect duties on tea imports), which prompted a group of colonists dressed as Mohawk Indians to board three British ships and dump 342 chests of tea into the harbor. This well known incident was dubbed the Boston Tea Party.

Hostilities reached a peak in April 1775, when the British sought to quell burgeoning unrest in Massachusetts. A contingent of British soldiers was sent to Lexington to seize military supplies and arrest two high-profile rebels—John Hancock and Samuel Adams. The militia formed by the colonists exchanged gunfire with the British, thereby igniting the revolution ("the shot heard 'round the world.").

Notable battles in New England included the Battle of Bunker Hill outside Boston, which the British won but at tremendous cost; and the Battle of Bennington in Vermont, in which the colonists prevailed, thereby ending the British strategy of dividing the colonies and fighting on one front then the other. Hostilities formally ended in February 1783, and in September, Britain recognized the United States as a sovereign nation.

FARMING & TRADE As the new republic matured, economic growth in New England followed two tracks. Residents of inland communities survived by clearing the land for farming and trading in furs. Vermont in particular has always been an agrarian state, and remains a prominent dairy producer to this day. (It's no coincidence that Ben & Jerry's ice cream is manufactured here.)

Meanwhile, on the coast, the region prospered as boat yards sprang up from Connecticut through Maine, and ship captains made tidy fortunes trading lumber for sugar and rum in the

- **1773** British ships are raided by colonists poorly disguised as Indians during the Boston Tea Party. More than 300 chests of tea are dumped into the harbor from three British ships.
- **1775** On April 18 Paul Revere and William Dawes spread the word that the British are marching toward Lexington and Concord. The next day the "shot heard round the world" is fired. On June 17 the British win the Battle of Bunker Hill but suffer heavy casualties.
- **1783** Treaty of Paris signed, formally concluding the American Revolution
- **1788** Connecticut becomes the fifth, Massachusetts the sixth, and New Hampshire the ninth state to formally join the union.
- **1790** Rhode Island becomes the 13th state and the final colony to ratify the constitution.
- **1791** The short-lived Republic of Vermont (1777–91) ends and the state of Vermont joins the union.
- **1812** War of 1812 with England batters New England economy.
- **1814** The nation's first textile mill is built, in Waltham, Massachusetts.
- **1820** Maine, formerly a district of Massachusetts, becomes a state.
- **1835** Samuel Colt of Connecticut develops the six-shooter pistol.
- **1861** Massachusetts Institute of Technology founded.
- **1892** America's first gasoline-powered automobile is built in Chicopee, Massachusetts.
- **1897** First Boston Marathon is run; Boston completes first American subway.
- **1903** The first World Series is played; Boston Red Sox win.

New England in Depth

continues

- **1918** The Red Sox celebrate another World Series victory. For the next eight decades (and counting) they fail to repeat this feat.
- **1930** America's Cup sailing race first held in Newport, Rhode Island.
- **1930s** The Great Depression devastates New England's already reeling industrial base.
- **1938** A major hurricane sweeps into New England, killing hundreds and destroying countless buildings and trees.
- **1942** A fire at Boston's Cocoanut Grove nightclub kills 491 people.
- **1946** John F. Kennedy is elected to Congress to represent Boston's first congressional district.
- **1957** Boston Celtics win their first NBA championship, laying the groundwork for a reign that will eventually capture 16 championships.
- **1963** New Hampshire becomes first state to establish a lottery to support education.
- **1966** Edward Brooke of Massachusetts becomes the first African American elected to the U.S. Senate since Reconstruction.
- **1972** Maine's Indians head to court, claiming the state illegally seized their land in violation of a 1790 act. They settle eight years later for $81.5 million.
- **1974** In Connecticut Ella Grasso becomes the first elected woman governor.

Caribbean. Trade was dealt a severe blow and coastal economies sent into a tailspin following the Embargo Act of 1807 (which sharply limited trade), but commerce eventually recovered and New England ships could be encountered everywhere around the globe. Even ice became a valued commodity—entrepreneurs from Maine and Massachusetts shipped tons of ice in insulated ships to the Caribbean, Brazil, and even India. More adventurous traders made the hazardous voyage to the Orient, bringing back lacquered furniture and delicate Chinese paintings, some of which turn up in country auctions to this day.

The growth of the railroad throughout New England in the mid–19th century was another boon. The train opened up much of the interior, and led to towns springing up overnight, like White River Junction in Vermont. The rail lines allowed local resources—such as the fine marbles and granites from Vermont—to be easily shipped to markets to the south.

INDUSTRY New England's industrial revolution found seed around the time of the embargo of 1807. Barred from importing English fabrics, Americans had to build their own textile mills to obtain cloth. Other common household products were also manufactured domestically, especially shoes, which became an industrial mainstay for decades. Towns like Lowell, Massachusetts, Lewiston, Maine, and Manchester, New Hampshire became centers of textile and shoe production. In Connecticut, the manufacture of arms and clocks emerged as lasting and major industries.

Industry no longer plays the prominent role it once did in New England—manufacturing first moved to the southern United States, then overseas. The main manufacturing centers include computer makers around Boston, and paper mills in Maine, but far more New England residents are today employed by service providers and government than by manufacturers.

TOURISM In the mid– and late–19th century New Englanders discovered a new cash crop: the tourist. All along the eastern seaboard it became fashionable for the gentry and eventually the working class to set out for excursions to the mountains and the shore. The White Mountains of New Hampshire were among the first regions to benefit from this boom. By the mid–19th century, farmhouses were being converted to inns to accommodate those seeking inspiration in the clear mountain air. By later in the century, tourists were venturing throughout the region in search of the picturesque and sublime. "Summer" became a verb. Regions like the Berkshires, Vermont's Green Mountains, the southern Maine Coast, and Block Island were lifted by the tide of summer visitors.

The 19th-century tourism wave crested in the 1890s in Newport, Rhode Island, and Bar Harbor, Maine, both of which were flooded by the affluent who spent time in their extravagant mansions (the mansions were called, not convincingly, "cottages.") The middle class also embraced leisure vacations en mass at the end of the century, setting off to the sea and mountains to rusticate in summer boarding houses and hotels. Several grand resort hotels from tourism's golden era still host summer travelers in the region.

ECONOMIC DOWNTURN   While the railways allowed New England to thrive in the mid–19th century, the train played an equally central role in undermining its prosperity. The driving of the Golden Spike in 1869 in Utah, linking America's Atlantic and Pacific coasts by rail, was heard loud and clear in New England, and it had a discordant ring. Transcontinental rail meant farmers and manufacturers could ship goods from the fertile Great Plains and California to faraway markets, making it harder for New England's hardscrabble farmers and antiquated, water-powered industries to survive. Likewise, the coastal shipping trade, already in difficult straits, was dealt a fatal blow by this new transportation network. And the tourists set their sights on the Rockies and other stirring western sites.

Beginning in the late–19th century and accelerating through much of the early 20th, New England lapsed into an extended economic slumber. As early as the 1870s, families commonly walked away from their farmhouses (there was no market for resale), and set off for regions with more promising opportunities. The abandoned, decaying farmhouse became almost an icon for New England, and vast tracts of open farmland were reclaimed by forest. With the rise of the automobile, the grand resorts further succumbed, and many closed their doors as inexpensive motels siphoned off their business.

During the Great Depression, historian Bernard DeVoto toured New England. Of the depressed milltown of Fall River, Massachusetts, he wrote, "To spend a day in Fall River is to realize how limited were the imaginations of the poets who have described hell."

BOOM TIMES   Toward the end of the current century, much of New England has ridden an unexpected wave of prosperity, which peaked in the late 1980s. During that decade, a massive real-estate boom shook the region, driving land prices sky high as prosperous buyers from New York and Boston—fueled by tremendous growth in the financial services and computer industries—acquired vacation homes or retired to the most alluring areas, like the Maine Coast and regions near ski mountains in Vermont. Tourism also rebounded as harried urbanites of the Eastern seaboard opted for shorter, more frequent vacations closer to home.

Travelers to the more remote regions will discover that many communities never benefitted from the boom at all; they're still waiting to rebound from the economic malaise of earlier in this century. Especially hard-hit have been places like Northeastern Vermont and far Downeast Maine, where residents still depend on local resources—timber, fisheries, and farmland—to eke out a living. Although areas within the orbit of Boston have remained economically vigorous well in the mid- and late-1990s, prosperity remains elusive for the more distant villages.

3 New England Style

When folks talk of New England "style," the conversation inevitably veers toward church steeples and white clapboard. But New England style transcends those iconic objects. Spend enough time here, and you'll realize

A Literary Legacy

New Englanders have generated whole libraries, some of it literature, from the earliest days of hellfire-and-brimstone Puritan sermons to Stephen King's horror novels set in fictional Maine villages.

Among the more enduring writings from New England's earliest days are the poems of Massachusetts Bay Colony resident Anne Bradstreet (1612?–1672), and the sermons and essays of Increase Mather (1639–1723) and his son, Cotton Mather (1663–1728), both of whom sought to reconcile science with religion.

After the American Revolution, Hartford dictionary writer Noah Webster (1758–1843) issued a call to American writers: "America must be as independent in literature as she is in politics, as famous for arts as for arms." He struck an early blow for pragmatism by taking the "u" out of British words like "labour" and honour.

Nathaniel Hawthorne's (1804–64) tales captivated a public eager for a native literature. His most famous story, *The Scarlet Letter,* is a tale about morality set in 17th-century Boston, but he wrote numerous other books that wrestled with themes of sin and guilt, often set in the emerging republic. Among his best known works are *The House of the Seven Gables, Twice-Told Tales,* and *The Marble Faun.*

Henry Wadsworth Longfellow (1807–82), the Portland, Maine, poet who settled in Cambridge (his house is a landmark and open to visitors) caught the attention of the public with evocative narrative poems focusing on distinctly American subjects. His popular works included *The Courtship of Miles Standish, Paul Revere's Ride,* and *Hiawatha.* Poetry in the mid–19th century was the equivalent of Hollywood movies today—Longfellow could be considered his generation's Steven Spielberg (apologies to literary scholars).

The zenith of New England literature occurred in the mid– and late–19th century with the Transcendentalist movement. These exalted writers and thinkers included Ralph Waldo Emerson (1803–82),

New England style is defined by its scale, which is at once very grand and very human.

You can see this appealing scale in the way man's creations relate almost perfectly to the landscape—the way a slender church spire rises from a wooded valley floor, or a silo from a hilltop farm. You'll find it in the way handsome homes cluster around a village green, or low block of row houses curves toward the waterfront in a coastal city.

The building blocks of New England style, of course, are its early homes. You can often trace the evolution of a town by its architecture, as styles evolve from basic structures to elaborate Victorian mansions. The primer below should aid with basic identification.

- **Colonial** (1600–1700). The New England house of the 17th century was a simple, boxy affair, often covered in shingles or rough clapboards. Don't look for ornamentation; these homes were designed for basic shelter from the elements, and are often marked by prominent stone chimneys. Your best destinations for viewing the very earliest kind of homes are at Plimoth Plantation, which features replicas of dwellings that one might have found here in 1627. A handful of original homes dating from this era may still be found around the region; Salem, near Boston, is rich with them. Another good

Margaret Fuller (1813–50), Bronson Alcott (1799–1888), and Henry David Thoreau (1817–62). They fashioned a way of viewing nature and society that was uniquely American. They rejected the rigid doctrines of the Puritans, and found sustenance in self-examination, the glories of nature, and a celebration of individualism. Perhaps the best known work to emerge from this period was Thoreau's *Walden, or, Life in the Woods.*

Among other New England writers who left a lasting mark on American literature was Emily Dickinson (1830–86), a native of Amherst, Massachusetts, whose precise and enigmatic poems placed her in the front rank of American poets. James Russell Lowell (1819–91) of Cambridge, Massachusetts, was an influential poet, critic, and editor. Later poets were imagist Amy Lowell (1874–1925) from Brookline, Massachusetts, and Edna St. Vincent Millay (1892–1950), from Camden, Maine.

Bestselling *Uncle Tom's Cabin,* the book Abraham Lincoln half-jokingly accused of starting the Civil War, was written by Harriet Beecher Stowe (1811–86) in Brunswick, Maine. She lived much of her life as a neighbor of Mark Twain (himself an adopted New Englander) in Hartford, Connecticut. Another bestseller was the children's book, *Little Women,* written by Louisa May Alcott (1832–88), whose father, Bronson, was part of the Transcendentalist movement.

New England's later role in the literary tradition may best be symbolized by the poet, Robert Frost (1874–1963). This exceptionally gifted writer, who some believe was the greatest poet of this century, was born in California but lived his life in Massachusetts, New Hampshire, and Vermont. In the New England landscape and community he found a lasting grace and rich metaphors for life. (Among his most famous lines: "Two roads diverged in a wood, and I— / I took the one less traveled by, / And that has made all the difference.")

example is the Sherburne House (ca. 1695), at Strawbery Banke in Portsmouth, New Hampshire.

- **Georgian** (1700–1800). Ornamentation comes into play in the Georgian style, which draws heavily on classical symmetry. Georgian buildings were in vogue in England at the time, and were embraced by the affluent colonists. Look for Palladian windows, formal pilasters, and elaborate projecting pediments over the main doorway. Some homes like Portsmouth's impressive Wentworth-Gardner House were made of wood but designed to look like masonry.

  Georgian homes are commonly found throughout the region. Deerfield, in the Pioneer Valley, is a good destination for seeing early Georgian homes; Providence, Rhode Island, and Portsmouth, New Hampshire, have abundant examples of later Georgian styles.

- **Federal** (1780–1820). Federal homes (sometimes called Adams homes) may best represent the New England ideal. Spacious yet austere, Federal homes are often rectangular or square, with low pitched roofs and little ornament on the front, although carved swags or other embellishments are frequently seen near the roof line. Look for fan windows and chimneys bracketing the building. Excellent federal-style homes are found throughout the region, many of which were built during the period of exceptional prosperity prior to the Embargo of 1807. Kennebunkport, Maine, is rich with federal homes set in tranquil neighborhoods.

- **Greek Revival** (1820–1860). The most easy-to-identify Greek Revival homes feature a bold projecting portico with massive columns, like a part of the Parthenon grafted onto an existing home. The less dramatic homes may have subtle pilasters, or simply be oriented such that the gable faces the street, accenting the triangular pediment. Greek Revival didn't catch on in New England quite the way it did elsewhere in the South, but some fine examples exist, notably in Newfane, Vermont, which is a virtual museum of Greek Revival architecture.

- **Carpenter Gothic & Gothic Revival** (1840–1880). The second half of the 19th century brought a wave of Gothic Revival homes and cottages, which borrowed their aesthetic from the English country home. The 1846 Henry C. Bowen Cottage in Woodstock, Connecticut, is a superb example; aficionados of this style and its later progeny featuring gingerbread trim owe themselves a trip to Oak Bluffs at Martha's Vineyard, where compact, clustered cottages of a historic Methodist meeting ground are festooned with scrollwork and exuberant architectural flourishes.

- **Victorian** (1860–1900). This is a catchall term for the jumble of mid- to late–19th century architectural styles that emphasized complexity and opulence. Perhaps the best known Victorian style—almost a caricature—is the tall and narrow Addams-Family-style house with mansard roof and prickly roof cresting. You'll find these scattered throughout the region. A notable example of this is author Stephen King's house in Bangor, Maine.

  The Victorian style also includes squarish **Italianate** homes with wide eaves and unusual flourishes; among the best examples are the huge brownstone Victoria Mansion in Portland, and the domed and pinnacled Samuel Colt House in Hartford.

- **Shingle Style** (1880–1900). This uniquely New England style arose in late–19th century, and quickly became the preferred style for vacation homes among the affluent on Cape Cod, Maine, and even eastern Long Island. These homes are marked by a profusion of gables, roofs, and porches, and were typically covered with shingles from roofline to foundation. Shingle-style homes project a sense of leisure and wealth. Look for Shingle-style homes in coastal communities that flourished during the heyday of 19th-century summer rusticating.

- **Modern** (1900–present). In the late 1930s, Boston became a center for the stark **International Style** with the appointment of Bauhaus veteran Walter Gropius to the faculty at Harvard. Some of the region's more intriguing experiments in this style are found on the MIT and Harvard campuses in Cambridge, including Gropius's Campus Center and Eero Saarinen's Kresge Auditorium. For the most part, however, New England architecture is defined by historical styles dating from the 19th century and earlier.

  Among the native architectural styles to watch for is the classic, continuous New England farmhouse. These tend to be huge and rambling, with the old barn connected to the main house by one or two intermediary buildings. This setup allowed the farmer to perform his barn chores in winter without having to brave the frigid winds. This style—locally called "big house, little house, back house, barn"—not only describes a building style, but was part of a well-known jump-rope rhyme. These farmhouses are relatively common throughout the region.

  In your travels, always bear in mind that New England is best appreciated when you're out of your car. Driving through a wonderful village, circling the green twice before heading onward, seems somehow unclean, like showing up at a wedding in sweaty gym clothes. You really need to get out and stretch your legs, if just for a few minutes, to really appreciate the human scale of many of these towns. Take the time to walk the tree-lined streets, or wander into a venerable church. These minor adventures inexplicably feel comforting and serene, as if you're coming home after a long journey, even if you've never been to New England before.

4 A Taste of New England

The quintessential New England meal is the clambake. If you're adventurous, here's how it's done: Start by digging a deep pit at the beach. Build a roaring fire of driftwood and throw in some beach stones to absorb the heat. Cover the hot ashes and stone with a layer of seaweed, then throw in lobsters. Add more seaweed, then corn on the cob, then another layer of seaweed followed by clams and a final topping of seaweed. Let sit. When the clams have opened, dig everything up and serve with lots of fresh butter. (A less gritty, easier version can be made in a large stockpot on your stove. Or easier still, ask around in your travels—some restaurants and inns feature clambakes during the summer.)

All along the New England's coast—from southern Connecticut to far Downeast Maine—you'll be tempted by seafood in its various forms. Fried claims are a filling specialty along the southern New England coast—you can get them by the bucket at divey clam houses along remote coves and busy highways. They're tasty, but not entirely wholesome if you're watching your waistline or nutritional intake. (A friend of mine once likened eating fried clams to consuming a bucket of grout followed by a shot of Mazola.) The more upscale seafood restaurants offer fresh fish cooked over a grill, or gently sautéed.

Live lobster can be bought literally off the boat at lobster shacks, especially along the Maine coast. The setting is usually rustic—maybe a couple of picnic tables and a shed where huge vats of water are kept at a low boil. A lobster dinner might include corn on the cob or some seafood chowder, and typically costs around $10 or $12 per person.

Inland, take time to sample the local products. This includes delectable maple syrup, of course, which is sold at farmhouses and farmstands throughout the northern reaches of the region. (Look for the homemade signs tacked to a tree at the end of a driveway.) Check the label for Grade A syrup certification—it's lighter and sweeter than the heavier, more tart Grade B. Cheese is a Vermont specialty, especially the strong cheddar produced throughout the state. Look also for Vermont's famed apple cider, and Maine's wild blueberries.

Throughout in the summer small farmers across New England set up stands at the end of their driveways offering fresh produce straight from the garden. Don't pass these by. You can usually find fresh berries, delicious fruits, and sometimes home-cooked breads that make excellent snacks on the road. These stands are rarely tended; just leave your money in the coffee can.

Restauranteurs haven't overlooked New England's bounty. Many fine restaurants throughout the region serve up delicious meals consisting of local ingredients—some places even tend their own gardens for fresh greens and herbs. Some of the best restaurants are set well outside of the cities, borrowing from the French tradition of classic country inns serving superior food in pastoral settings. Talented chefs have taken basic ingredients that would have been familiar to the Pilgrims and adapted them to more adventurous palates. I'm thinking of some of the fine meals I've enjoyed while researching this guide, such as curried pumpkin soup, venison medallions with shiitake mushrooms, and wild boar with juniper berries.

But you don't have to have a hefty budget to enjoy the local foods. A number of regional classics fall under the "road food" category. Here's an abbreviated field guide:

Beans: Boston is forever linked with baked beans (hence the nickname "Beantown"), and the sweet, earthy beans are popular throughout the region. A New England Saturday night supper traditionally consists of baked beans and brown bread, and some diners still offer up beans with breakfast. (Try them!)

Moxie: Early in this century Moxie outsold Coca-Cola. Part of its allure was the fanciful story behind its 1885 creation: A traveler named Lieutenant Moxie was said to have observed South American Indians consuming the sap of a native plant, which gave them extraordinary strength. The drink was "re-created" by Maine native and Massachusetts resident Dr. Augustin Thompson, who marketed it nationwide. It's still a popular drink in New England (it's now manufactured by former rival Coca-Cola), although some folks liken the taste to a combination of medicine and topsoil.

Muffins: These have long been a New England institution. A blueberry muffin is the classic choice, but a wide variety of fresh-baked muffins is available at bakeries, restaurants, and convenience stores throughout the region. At some traditional restaurants, blueberry muffins are even served with dinner.

Lobster rolls: Lobster rolls consist of lobster meat plucked from the shell, mixed with just enough mayonnaise to hold it all together, then served on a hot-dog roll. They're available at roadside stands and restaurants throughout Maine.

Necco Wafers: Still made in Cambridge by the New England Confectionery Company, these powdery wafers of tangy hard candy haven't changed a bit since they were first manufactured in 1847. (It's the nation's oldest continuously produced candy.) Still wrapped in crinkly waxed paper, they're as good as they ever were. The factory no longer offers tours, but the candies are available widely throughout the region.

Pies: New Englanders are serious about their pies, and it remains a popular dessert (and sometimes breakfast) throughout the region. Apple, blueberry, and mincemeat and the traditional favorites, but you can usually find a good selection of cream pies as well.

Finally, no survey of comestibles would be complete without mention of something to wash it all down: beer. New England has more microbreweries than any other region outside of the Pacific Northwest—Maine alone had nearly two dozen at last count. Even remote towns are getting their own brew pubs, leaving some to wonder if a shakeout is overdue.

Popular brew pubs that should rank high on the list for those making a barley-and-hops pilgrimage through New England include the Great Providence Brewing Co., the Commonwealth Brewing Co. (Boston's first brew pub), the Portsmouth Brewery, Federal Jack's Brewpub (Kennebunkport, Me.), Vermont Pub & Brewery (Burlington), and the Windham Brewery at the Latchis Grille (Brattleboro). That's just the tip of the iceberg, but it's a good start.

5 Recommended Reading

Travelers hoping to broaden their understanding of the region need not look much further than the many excellent bookstores (both new and used) they'll find scattered throughout the region. Among my favorite books about New England:

In the Memory House by Howard Mansfield (Fulcrum Publishing, 1993). This finely written book by a New Hampshire author provides a penetrating look at New England's sometimes estranged relationship with its own past. First published in 1993 and available in paperback.

Inventing New England by Dona Brown (Smithsonian Institute Press, 1995). A University of Vermont professor tells the extraordinary tale of the rise of 19th century tourism in New England in this uncommonly well-written study.

Lobster Gangs of Maine by James M. Acheson (1988). This exhaustively researched book answers every question you'll have about the lobsterman's life, and then some.

North Woods: An Inside Look at the Nature of Forests in the Northeast, by Peter J. Marchand (Appalachian Mountain Club). This slim volume (just 141 pages) contains a fine, easily readable overview of the ecology of the surprisingly complex northern forest. First published in 1987 and still available in paperback.

Serious Pig by John Thorne with Matt Lewis Thorne (North Point Press, 1996). The way to a region's character is through its stomach. The Thornes' finely crafted essays on regional cooking—mostly about Maine—are exhaustive in their coverage of chowder, beans, pie, and more.

GUIDE BOOKS
INDIVIDUAL GUIDES

Frommer's Great Outdoors Guide to New England by Stephen Jermanok (Macmillan Travel, 1999). Where to go and what to do if your interests include hiking, canoeing, kayaking, swimming, skiing, or anything else having to do with the outdoors.

Guide to Writer's Homes in New England by Miriam Levine (Applewood Books, 1989). Bookish pilgrims will get the lowdown on a literary homes in New England, including the Mark Twain and Harriet Beecher Stowe houses in Connecticut.

Hot Showers: Maine Coast Lodgings for Kayakers and Sailors by Lee Bumsted (Audenreed Press, 1997). This comprehensive and thoroughly researched guide is useful for boaters (what other guide tells you which tides are best to avoid seaweed?), but also handy for folks who simply want to be on the water.

National Audubon Society Field Guide to New England by Peter Alden and Brian Cassie. Published in 1998, this is the best all-purpose guide to the natural attractions you'll come across in your travels, and touches on geology, birds, mushrooms, and whales, among other subjects.

New England Beach Guide by Ellen Ruggles (Pleasant Street Press). This 1996 guide offers directions and insight into more than 400 beaches open to the public from Maine through Connecticut.

New England Camping by Carol Connare and Stephen Gorman (Foghorn Press). This exhaustive guide (more than 500 pages) gives the lowdown on 815 public and private campgrounds throughout the region, complete with directions, prices, and brief notes on what sort of facilities you'll find.

Sloan's Green Guide to Antiquing in New England edited by Lisa Freeman (Globe Pequot Press). This is the essential guide for serious antiques hounds, with concise listings of locations and contents of 2,500 antique stores.

SERIES GUIDES

25 Bicycle Tours (Countryman Press). One of the trickiest parts of day touring by bike is finding routes that stay away from traffic and busy roads. The authors of this series have done the hard lifting. Regions include Cape Cod and the Islands, Maine, New Hampshire, and Vermont. (Mountain bike tour guides are also available for Massachusetts and Vermont.)

AMC River Guides and *Quiet Water Canoe Guides.* This series of paddle guides published by the Appalachian Mountain Club in Boston covers all the major (and many of the minor) waterways in all six New England states. The River guides focus on white-water paddling; the Quiet Water guides on flatwater.

Fifty Hikes series. Each of these guides provides descriptions and maps of, well, 50 hikes in each region they cover. Most are a bit more ambitious than the outings described in the Nature Walks series, but hikers of all abilities will find inviting options. Regions covered include: Connecticut, Maine Mountains, Southern and Coastal Maine, Massachusetts, Vermont, New Hampshire, and the White Mountains.

Nature Walks series. Another AMC series, Nature Walks highlights low-key adventures ranging from strolls to hikes that will bring travelers into close contact with New England's ecosystem and wildlife. Titles include White Mountains, New Hampshire Lakes Region, Southern New Hampshire, Eastern Massachusetts, Central Massachusetts, The Berkshire Hills, Southern Vermont, Northern Vermont, Southern Maine, and Northern Maine.

Frommer's Online Directory

By Michael Shapiro

Michael Shapiro is the author of
Internet Travel Planning (Globe Pequot Press).
Bruce Gerstman contributed some of the
Massachusetts listings to this directory.

Frommer's Online Directory is a new feature designed to help you take advantage of the Internet to better plan your trip. Part I lists general Internet resources that can make any trip easier, such as sites for booking airline tickets. Please keep in mind that this is not a comprehensive list, but rather a discriminating selection of useful sites to get you started. In Part II you'll find some top online guides for New England.

1 Top Travel Planning Web Sites

The top online travel agencies, including Expedia, Preview Travel, and Travelocity, offer an array of tools that are valuable even if you don't book online. You can check flight schedules, hotel availability, car rental prices, or even get paged if your flight is delayed.

While online agencies have come a long way over the past few years, they don't always yield the best price. Unlike a travel agent, they're unlikely to tell you that you can save money by flying a day earlier or a day later. On the other hand, if you're looking for a bargain fare, you might find something online that an agent wouldn't dig up—a travel agent may not find it worthwhile spending half an hour trying to find you the best deal. On the Net you can be your own agent and take all the time you want.

Online booking sites aren't the only places to book airline tickets—all major airlines have their own Web sites and often offer incentives, such as bonus frequent flyer miles or Net-only discounts, for buying online. These incentives have helped airlines capture the majority of the online booking market. According to Jupiter Communications, online agencies such as Travelocity booked about 80 percent of tickets purchased online in 1996, but by 1999 airline sites (such as **www.ual.com**) were projected to own about 60 percent of the online market, with online agencies' share of the pie dwindling each year.

Below are the Web sites for the major airlines serving New England's airports and for regional airlines serving Cape Cod and the islands. These sites offer schedules, flight booking, and most have pages where you can sign up for E-mail alerts on weekend deals.

American www..americanair.com
Cape Air www.flycapeair.com
Comair www.fly-comair.com
Continental www.flycontinental.com

Looking & Booking Online

Far more people look online than book online, partly due to fear of putting their credit cards through on the Net. Though secure encryption has made this fear less justified, there's no reason why you can't find a flight online and then book it by calling a toll-free number or contacting your travel agent. To be sure you're in secure mode when you book online, look for a little icon of a key (in Netscape) or a padlock (Internet Explorer) at the bottom of your Web browser.

Delta **www.delta-air.com**
Island Airlines **www.nantucket.net**
Nantucket Airlines **www.nantucketairlines.com**
New England Airlines **www.users.ids.net**
Northwest **www.nwa.com**
Southwest **www.iflyswa.com**
TWA **www.nwa.com**
United **www.ual.com**
US Airways **www.usair.com**

WHEN SHOULD YOU BOOK ONLINE?

Online booking is not for everyone. If you prefer to let others handle your travel arrangements, one call to an experienced travel agent should suffice. But if you want to know as much as possible about your options, the Net is a good place to start, especially for bargain hunters.

The most compelling reason to use online booking is to take advantage of last-minute specials, such as American Airlines' weekend deals or other Internet-only fares that must be purchased online. Another advantage is that you can cash in on incentives for booking online, such as rebates or bonus frequent flyer miles.

Online booking works best for trips within North America—it's not for those with a complex international itinerary. If you require follow-up services, such as itinerary changes, use a travel agent. Though Expedia and some other online agencies employ travel agents available by phone, these sites are geared primarily for self-service.

LEADING BOOKING SITES

Below are listings for the top travel booking sites. The starred selections are the most useful and best-designed sites.

Cheap Tickets. **www.cheaptickets.com**
Essentials: Discounted rates on domestic and international airline tickets and hotel rooms.

Sometimes discounters such as Cheap Tickets have exclusive deals that aren't available through more mainstream channels. Registration at Cheap Tickets requires inputting a credit card number before getting started, which is one reason many people elect to call the company's toll-free number rather than booking online. Cheap Tickets actually regards this policy as a selling point, arguing that "lookers" who don't intend to buy will be scared off by its "credit card first" approach and won't bog down the site with their queries. Despite its misguided credit card policy, Cheap Tickets is worth the effort because its fares can be lower than those offered by its competitors.

✪ Expedia. **expedia.com**
Essentials: Domestic and international flight hotel and rental car booking; late-breaking travel news, destination features and commentary from travel experts; deals on cruises and vacation packages. Free registration is required for booking.

Take a Look at Frommer's Site

We highly recommend Arthur Frommer's Budget Travel Online (**www. frommers.com**) as an excellent travel planning resource. Of course, we're a little biased, but you will find indispensable travel tips, reviews, monthly vacation giveaways, and online booking.

Subscribe to Arthur Frommer's Daily Newsletter (**www.frommers.com/ newsletters**) to receive the latest travel bargains and inside travel secrets in your mailbox every day. You'll read daily headlines and articles from the dean of travel himself, highlighting last-minute deals on airfares, accommodations, cruises, and package vacations. You'll also find great travel advice by checking our Tip of the Day or Hot Spot of the Month.

Search our Destinations archive (**www.frommers.com/destinations**) of more than 200 domestic and international destinations for great places to stay, tips for traveling there, and what to do while you're there. Once you've researched your trip, you might try our online reservation system (**www.frommers.com/book-travelnow**) to book your dream vacation at affordable prices.

Expedia makes it easy to handle flight, hotel and car booking on one itinerary, so it's a good place for one-stop shopping. Expedia's hotel search offers crisp, zoomable maps to pinpoint most properties; click on the camera icon to see images of the rooms and facilities. But like many online databases, Expedia focuses on the major chains, such as Hilton and Hyatt, so don't expect to find too many one-of-a-kind resorts or B&Bs here.

Once you're registered (it's only necessary to do this once from each computer you use), you can start booking with the Roundtrip Fare Finder box on the home page, which expedites the process. After selecting a flight, you can hold it until midnight the following day or purchase online. If you think you might do better through a travel agent, you'll have time to try to get a lower price. And you may do better with a travel agent because Expedia's computer reservation system does not include all airlines. Most notably absent are some leading budget carriers, such as Southwest Airlines. (Note: At press time, Travelocity was the only major booking service that included Southwest.)

Expedia's World Guide, offering destination information, has a glaring weakness— it takes a lot of page views to get very little information. However, Expedia compensates by linking to other Microsoft Network services, such as its Sidewalk city guides, which offer entertainment and dining advice for many of the cities it covers.

Preview Travel. www.previewtravel.com
Essentials: Domestic and international flight, hotel and rental car booking; Travel Newswire lists fare sales; deals on cruises and vacation packages. Free (one-time) registration is required for booking. Preview offers express booking for members but at press time this feature was buried below the fold on Preview's reservation page.

Preview features the most inviting interface for booking trips, though the wealth of graphics involved can make the site somewhat slow to load. Use Farefinder to quickly find the lowest current fares on flights to dozens of major cities. Carfinder offers a similar service for rental cars, but you can only search airport locations, not city pick-up sites. To see the lowest fare for your itinerary, input the dates and times for your route and see what comes up.

Preview has a great feature called the "Best Fare Finder"—after a search for the best deal on your itinerary, it will check flights that are a bit later or earlier to see if it might be cheaper to fly at a different time. While these searches have become quite sophisticated, they still occasionally overlook deals that might be uncovered by a top-notch travel agent. It might be worthwhile, after searching online, to call an agent to see if you can get a better price.

With Preview's Fare Alert feature, you can set fares for up to three routes and you'll receive E-mail notices when the fare drops below your target amount. For example, you could tell Preview to alert you when the fare from Chicago to Boston drops below $250. If it does, you'll get an E-mail telling you the current fare.

Minor quibbles: When you search for a fare, hotel or car—at least when we went to press—Preview launches an annoying little "Please Wait" window that gets in the way of the main browser window even when your results begin to appear. The hotel search feature is intuitive, but the images and maps aren't as crisp as those at Expedia. Also: all sorts of extraneous information (such as NYC public school locations), irrelevant to most travelers, is on the maps.

Note to AOL Users: You can book flights, hotels, rental cars and cruises on AOL at keyword: Travel. The booking software is provided by Preview Travel and is similar to Preview on the Web. Use the AOL "Travelers Advantage" program to earn a 5% rebate on flights, hotel rooms and car rentals.

Priceline.com. www.priceline.com

Launched in 1998 with a $10 million ad campaign, Priceline lets you "name your price" for domestic and international airline tickets. In other words, you select a route and dates, guarantee with a credit card, and make a bid for what you're willing to pay. If one of the airlines in Priceline's database has a fare that's lower than your bid, your credit card will automatically be charged for a ticket.

However, you can't say *when* you want to fly—you have to accept any flight leaving between 6am and 10pm, and you may have to make a stopover. No frequent flyer miles are awarded, and tickets are non-refundable and non-exchangeable. Priceline can be good for travelers who have to take off on short notice (and who are thus unable to qualify for advance purchase discounts). But be sure to shop around first—if you overbid, you'll be required to purchase the ticket and Priceline will pocket the difference.

Travelocity. www.travelocity.com

Essentials: Domestic and international flight, hotel and rental car booking; deals on cruises and vacation packages. Travel Headlines spotlights latest bargain airfares. Free (one-time) registration is required for booking.

Travelocity almost got it right. Its Express Booking feature enables travelers to complete the booking process more quickly than they could at Expedia or Preview, but Travelocity gums up the works with a page called "Featured Airlines." Big placards of several featured airlines compete for your attention—if you want to see the fares for all available airlines, click the much smaller box at the bottom of the page labeled "Book a Flight."

Some have worried that Travelocity, which is owned by American Airlines' parent company AMR, directs bookings to American. This doesn't seem to be the case— I've booked there dozens of times and have always been directed to the cheapest listed flight, whatever the airline. But the "Featured Airlines" page does seem to be Travelocity's way of trying to cash in with ads and incentives for booking certain airlines. There are rewards for choosing one of the featured airlines—you'll get 1,500 bonus frequent flyer miles if you book through United's site, for example, but the site doesn't tell you about other airlines that might be cheaper. If the United flight costs $150 more than the best deal on another airline, it's not worth spending the extra money for a relatively small number of bonus miles.

On the plus side, Travelocity has some leading-edge techie tools for modern travelers. Exhibit A is Fare Watcher E-mail, an "intelligent agent" that keeps you informed of the best fares offered for the city pairs (round-trips) of your choice. Whenever the fare changes by $25 or more, Fare Watcher will alert you by E-mail. Exhibit B is Flight Paging—if you own an alphanumeric pager with national access that can receive E-mail, Travelocity's paging system can alert you if your flight is delayed. Finally, though Travelocity doesn't include every budget airline, it does include Southwest, the leading U.S. budget carrier.

FINDING LODGINGS ONLINE

While the services above offer hotel booking, on a site devoted primarily to lodging you may find properties that aren't listed on more general online travel agencies. You won't find some of the kinds of accommodations, such as bed and breakfast inns, which appear on the specialized sites on the more mainstream booking services. Other services, such as TravelWeb, offer weekend deals on major chain properties, which cater to business travelers and have more empty rooms on weekends.

All Hotels on the Web. www.all-hotels.com
Well, this site doesn't include all the hotels on the Web, but it does have tens of thousands of listings throughout the world. Bear in mind that each hotel listed has paid a small fee of ($25 and up) for placement, so it's not an objective list but more like a book of online brochures.

Go Camping America. www.gocampingamerica.com/main.html
An extensive listing of RV parks and campgrounds for the U.S. (and some Canadian provinces), organized by state. The listings include dates of operation, number of sites, hookup availability, tent sites, and modem access. Some campgrounds offer "online brochures" which, like printed brochures, put the best possible face on a place.

Hotel Reservations Network. www.180096hotel.com
Bargain room rates at hotels in more than two dozen U.S. and international cities. The cool thing is that HRN pre-books blocks of rooms in advance, so sometimes it has rooms—at discount rates—at hotels that are "sold out."

InnSite. www.innsite.com
B&B listings for inns in all 50 U.S. states and dozens of countries around the globe.
Find an inn at your destination, have a look at images of the rooms, check prices and availability, and then send E-mail to the innkeeper if you have further questions. This is an extensive directory of bed and breakfast inns but only includes listings if the proprietor submitted one (note: it's free to get an inn listed). The descriptions are written by the innkeepers and many listings link to the inn's own Web sites, where you can find more information and images.

Places to Stay. www.placestostay.com
Mostly one-of-a-kind places in the U.S. and abroad that you might not find in other directories, with a focus on resort accommodations. Again, listing is selective—this isn't a comprehensive directory, but can give you a sense of what's available at different destinations.

✪ TravelWeb. www.travelweb.com
TravelWeb lists more than 16,000 hotels worldwide, focusing on chains such as Hyatt and Hilton, and you can book almost 90 percent of these online. TravelWeb's Click-It Weekends, updated each Monday, offers weekend deals at many leading hotel chains. TravelWeb is the online home for Pegasus Systems, which provides transaction processing systems for the hotel industry.

LAST-MINUTE DEALS AND OTHER ONLINE BARGAINS

There's nothing airlines hate more than flying with lots of empty seats. The Net has enabled airlines to offer last-minute bargains to entice travelers to fill those seats. Most of these are announced on Tuesday or Wednesday and are valid for travel the following weekend, but some can be booked weeks or months in advance. You can sign up for weekly E-mail alerts at airlines' sites (For airlines' Web site addresses, see above) or check sites such as WebFlyer (see below) that compile lists of these bargains. To make it easier, visit a site (see below) that will round up all the deals and send them in one convenient weekly E-mail. But last-minute deals aren't the only online bargains—other sites can help you find value even if you can't wait until the eleventh hour.

☺ 1travel.com. www.1travel.com

Deals on domestic and international flights, cruises, hotels, and all-inclusive resorts such as Club Med. 1travel.com's Saving Alert compiles last-minute air deals so you don't have to scroll through multiple E-mail alerts. A feature called "Drive a little using low-fare airlines" helps map out strategies for using alternate airports to find lower fares. And Farebeater searches a database that includes published fares, consolidator bargains and special deals exclusive to **1travel.com.** *Note:* The travel agencies listed by 1travel.com have paid for placement.

BestFares. www.bestfares.com

Bargain-seeker Tom Parsons lists some great deals on airfares, hotels, rental cars and cruises, but the site is poorly organized. News Desk is a long list of hundreds of bargains but they're not broken down into cities or even countries, so it's not easy to find what you're looking for. If you have time to wade through it, you might find a good deal. Some material is available only to paid subscribers.

Go4less.com. www.go4less.com

Specializing in last-minute cruise and package deals, Go4less has some eye-popping offers, such as off-peak Caribbean cruises for under $100 per day. The site has a clean design but the bargains aren't organized by destination. However you avoid sifting through all this material by using the Search box and entering vacation type, destination, month and price.

Smarter Living. www.smarterliving.com

Best known for its E-mail dispatch of weekend deals on 20 airlines, Smarter Living also keeps you posted about last-minute bargains on everything from Windjammer Cruises to flights to Iceland.

☺ WebFlyer. www.webflyer.com

WebFlyer is the ultimate online resource for frequent flyers and also has an excellent listing of last-minute air deals. Click on "Deal Watch" for a round-up of weekend deals on flights, hotels and rental cars from domestic and international suppliers.

TRAVELER'S TOOLKIT

Seasoned travelers usually carry some essential items to make their trips easier. Following is a selection of online tools to smooth your journey.

Handy Tip

While most people learn about last-minute weekend deals from E-mail, it can be best to find out precisely when these deals become available and check airlines' Web sites at this time. To find out when deals become available, check the pages devoted to these deals on airlines' Web pages. Because they are limited, these deals can vanish within hours, sometimes even minutes, so it pays to log on as soon as they are posted.

Check E-mail at Internet Cafés While Traveling

Until a few years ago, most travelers who checked their E-mail while traveling carried a laptop, but this posed some problems. Not only are laptops expensive, but they can be difficult to configure, incur expensive connection charges, and are attractive to thieves. Thankfully, Web-based free E-mail programs have made it much easier to check your mail.

Just open an account at a freE-mail provider, such as Hotmail (**hotmail.com**) or Yahoo! Mail (**mail.yahoo.com**) and all you'll need to check your mail is a Web connection, easily available at Net cafés and copy shops around the world. After logging on, just point the browser to **www.hotmail.com,** enter your username and password and you'll have access to your mail.

Internet cafés have become ubiquitous, so for a few dollars an hour you'll be able to check your mail and send messages back to colleagues, friends and family. If you already have a primary E-mail account, you can set it to forward mail to your freE-mail account while you're away. FreE-mail programs have become enormously popular (Hotmail claims more than 10 million members), because they enable everyone, even those who don't own a computer, to have an E-mail address they can check wherever they log onto the Web.

At **www.netcafeguide.com,** you can locate Internet cafés at hundreds of locations around the globe.

ATM Locators:
Visa (www.visa.com/pd/atm/). MasterCard (www.mastercard.com/atm)
Find ATMs in hundreds of cities in the U.S. and around the world. Both include maps for some locations and list airport ATM locations, some with maps. *Tip:* You'll usually get a better exchange rate using ATMs than exchanging traveler's checks at banks.

CultureFinder. www.culturefinder.com
Up-to-date listings for plays, opera, classical music, dance, film and other cultural events in more than 1300 U.S. cities. Enter the dates you'll be in a city and get a list of events. You can purchase tickets online. Also see FestivalFinder (**www.festivalfinder.com**) for more than 1500 rock, folk, reggae, blues, and bluegrass festivals throughout North America.

Intellicast. www.intellicast.com
Weather forecasts for all 50 states and cities around the world.

✪ MapQuest. www.mapquest.com
Specializing in U.S. maps, MapQuest enables you to zoom in on a destination, calculate step-by-step driving directions between any two U.S. points, and locate restaurants, hotels and other attractions on maps.

Trip.com. www.trip.com
A business travel site where you can find out when an airborne flight is scheduled to arrive. Click on "Guides and Tools" to peruse airport maps for more than 40 domestic cities.

2 Top Sites for New England

Because New England is such a vast and varied area, it's not possible to list all the valuable Web sites for this fascinating region. Instead, this list includes some of the best places to start, organized by state, with a general category for all of New England at the top.

NEW ENGLAND GENERAL SITES

About.com. www.about.com
This extensive list of links, categorized by state, includes sections for sightseeing, dining, shopping, lodging and camping. The links are culled by a "guide" who writes short features on the region, such as "Top New England Events." Some Miningco.com pages have an amateurish feel, but the New England section is well done and includes pointers to many worthwhile Web sites.

NewEngland.com. www.newengland.com
Produced by Yankee magazine, this is a superb guide to lodging, dining and events. But you'll find much more, such as driving tours, a B&B finder with more than 600 inns, and an updated guide to New England's fall foliage.

Visit New England. www.visitnewengland.com
An extensive collection of links to Web sites covering New England's attractions, events, tours, shopping, dining, lodging and much more. The descriptions aren't quite as detailed or as informed as those in this book, but the links make this site valuable.

CONNECTICUT

Connecticut Campground Owners Association. www.campconn.com
A nice round-up, organized by region, of more than 100 places to camp. Many of the listings, which include address, phone and number of campsites, link to a campground's own Web site, where you can get more information.

Connecticut Magazine. www.connecticutmag.com
This print-magazine companion includes an extensive dining guide. For ideas on what to do, click on "Bored?"—though it's hard to take seriously its list of Connecticut's Top 50 Web Sites because Connecticut Magazine includes itself.

Connecticut Tourism. www.tourism.state.ct.us
An extensive guide to attractions, outdoor recreation, lodging, and events throughout the state. Most listings link to external sites, for example the mention of Berkshire Balloons links to that company's Web site. Quick Trips includes sections on romantic getaways, golf, family fun, and Amistad trails.

Let's Eat Out. www.letseatout.com
With unpaid (thus more objective) listings for about 2,400 restaurants, Let's Eat Out attempts to include all restaurants (except for take-out joints). Search for restaurants by name, type of cuisine, or location.

Mystic Seaport. www.mystic.org
A nicely designed guide to one of America's most popular historic seaports. The site includes the program for the annual Sea Music Festival, when renowned musicians play from the decks of tall ships.

Visit Connecticut. www.visitconnecticut.com
An extensive, well organized guide to attractions, parks, shopping and dining, from Visit New England.

MAINE

Acadia National Park. www.nps.gov/acad
Preserved in 1919, Acadia was the first U.S. national park east of the Mississippi. This site from the National Park Service includes recommended activities, events and attractions, camping and lodging options, and trail information.

For AOL Users

Digital City: Hartford. Keyword: Hartford
Produced in association with local newspapers, this is primarily a guide for locals, but has information on dining, shopping and entertainment that's valuable to visitors as well. Digital City: Hartford is also available on the Web at (**www.digitalcity.com/hartford**).

✪ **Destination Maine. www.destinationmaine.com**
A literate introduction to the state including a calendar of events, a section on museums and galleries, and reflections on fishing in Maine's remote wilderness areas. If you're wondering whether to trek up north, this is the type of site that may just inspire you to make the journey.

L.L. Bean. www.llbean.com/about/retail
Visit the store that made Freeport famous and see the catalog come alive. L.L. Bean, named for founder Leon Leonwood Bean, is open 24 hours a day to accommodate the 3.5 million visitors who drop in each year.

Maine Event Scheduler. maineevents.com
A roundup of events throughout the state, organized by month. The site doesn't seem to have all the important events, but this list can help you find an enjoyable family outing such as Boothbay Harbor's Scottish Festival.

✪ **Maine Resource Guide. maineguide.com**
An extensive guide, broken down by region, to lodgings, dining, activities and attractions. Much of the information is hosted by other sites, for example, to learn about Maine Island Kayak Company, you'll be directed to that outfitter's site. On its own site, Maine Resource Guide covers attractions such as Bar Harbor, Acadia National Park, and Bangor.

Maine's Great Camping Areas. www.campmaine.com
An extensive listing of Maine campgrounds, sorted by region. If a campground has its own Web site, you'll find a link to it so you can get more information. The listings on Maine's Great Camping Areas include address, phone and a brief description with numbers of campsites, tents-only areas, facilities, and more.

✪ **Visit Maine. www.visitmaine.com**
An up-to-date listing of activities including boating, shopping, and historical sites from the Maine Office of Tourism. Perhaps the best thing about this site is the extensive calendar of events (**www.visitmaine.com/calendar.html**).

Visit Portland: Vacation Planning. www.visitportland.com/vaca.html
This solid all-around site, from the Portland Convention & Visitor's Bureau, is a good place to learn about Maine's largest city. You'll find lodging and dining listings, but the restaurants are listed alphabetically, rather than by type of cuisine. Hotels are organized by region, which is helpful. Other sections list points of interest, shopping, events, and outdoor adventures.

MASSACHUSETTS

BerkshireWeb. www.berkshireweb.com
A guide to activities (such as kid stuff), lodging (including B&Bs), and dining (with reviews of some restaurants). You'll also find sections on shopping, culture and nightlife. Also see the Berkshires Visitors Bureau at (**www.berkshires.org**).

⭕ Boston.com (from the Boston Globe). **www.boston.com**

An excellent all-around site featuring entertainment listings, weather, and city events. The most valuable section for visitors is Going Out/Arts, which includes listings for dining, movies, music, and other arts performances. Reviews and calendar listings from the Boston Globe can help you make informed choices about how to spend your evenings. The Globe's Calendar Choice is updated every Thursday and includes critics' top picks for the coming week.

Boston Insider. **www.theinsider.com/boston**

Tips on theater, museums and books, geared to budget travelers. Peruse city photographs and reviews of the editors' favorite restaurants.

⭕ Boston Phoenix. **www.bostonphoenix.com**

Critical reviews of theater productions, restaurants, movies, dance and art exhibits from this alternative weekly create an excellent city guide. The gay, lesbian and bisexual section includes articles, clubs and event listings. Also see The Best: Boston Phoenix (**www.bostonphoenix.com/supplements/the_best/index.html**), where editors share their favorite things to do, including all kinds of entertainment, nightlife, shopping, hiking and more.

⭕ Boston Sidewalk. **boston.sidewalk.com**

Occasionally delivered with humor, Sidewalk covers the arts, movies, outdoor recreation, local shopping, and weekend getaways. Listings on theater, music, dance, museums, and night clubs update regularly. Editorial packages highlight neighborhoods to explore and ways for visitors to pass the time, from skiing to stand-up comedy. Most of the reviews, which are usually uncritical, originate from staff writers and contributors.

BostonUSA: Greater Boston Convention and Visitors Bureau.
   www.bostonusa.com

Search by location for lodging, dining, museums, theater and nightlife. Also find details about expos, parades, transportation, cruises and sports. Read about bargains for museums and activities that could help you stay within your budget.

Cape Cod Chamber of Commerce. **capecodchamber.org**

Click on "Vacation Planning" for a beach guide, events calendar, and information on dining, lodging, shopping and top attractions.

CapeCod.com. **www.capecod.com**

A basic guide to the region with uncritical restaurant assessments, lodging advice, suggestions for activities for adults and kids, and a calendar of events.

CuisineNet: Boston. **www.cuisinenet.com/restaurant/boston**

Listings and reviews for Boston and 15 other U.S. cities. Each restaurant has a capsule review compiled by CuisineNet and ratings based on surveys received from site users.

Destination Plymouth. **www.visit-plymouth.com**

These listings and descriptions of hotels, restaurants, local events, and shopping create Plymouth's most extensive online guide.

Martha's Vineyard Chamber of Commerce. **www.mvy.com**

Though not comprehensive, this guide has some useful listings for dining, lodging (including campgrounds and weekly rentals), boating, biking and other things to do.

Welcome to Massachusetts. **www.mass-vacation.com**

From the Massachusetts Office of Travel and Tourism comes a clean, well-organized guide to destinations, lodging, events, outdoor adventures and trip planning. The trip

---

For AOL Users

Digital City: Boston. **AOL Keyword: Boston**
Maps, weather forecasts, sports, restaurant and listings and reviews. You can depend on a Bostonian perspective because much of the information comes from local newspapers. Scroll down to the Inside Boston section which includes personalized "Best of" and "Worst of" guides. Digital City is also available on the Web at (**www.digitalcity.com**).

---

planning section includes attractions listed by category and by region. A regional listing of campgrounds tops off this online guide.

Wicked Good Guide to Boston. www.boston-online.com/wicked.html
Seeking the wickedest bagel in town, or want to learn the local lingo? Discover obscure and alternative places to visit with Wicked's Bizzaro Guide.

NEW HAMPSHIRE

Dartmouth College. www.dartmouth.edu
An orientation to the campus and calendar of events can help you plan a visit to this Ivy League college.

New Hampshire Campgrounds. www.ucampnh.com
A directory of about 150 campgrounds and information on camping in New Hampshire, from the New Hampshire Campground Owners Association. You'll also find information on boating, fishing and hunting.

New Hampshire Newspapers. ajr.newslink.org/nhnews.html
Links to daily newspapers in Concord, Portsmouth and Manchester, as well as other papers throughout the state.

New Hampshire Office of Travel & Tourism. www.visitnh.gov
A boosterish guide from this official agency with information on everything from kids' activities to maple sugaring. The best part of this site is the hundreds of links to other Web sites; the worst part is that it loads slowly because of it includes large images.

NH Parks and Recreation. www.nhparks.state.nh.us
Learn about state parks, trails and even a ski area on this official government site. There's also a campground directory with maps with reservation information. Also see the Parks Bureau at (**www.nhparks.state.nh.us/parkops.html**) for more on camping, beaches and historic sites.

Visit New Hampshire. www.visitnewengland.com/newhamp
An extensive site where you can search by region (Dartmouth, White Mountains, etc.) or by category (lodging, dining, shopping, outdoors, attractions, etc.).

White Mountains, New Hampshire. www.whitemtn.org
Though this is a clunky site, it offers listings of attractions and events for the White Mountains, as well as a fall foliage guide for the region.

RHODE ISLAND

Best Read Guide: Newport. www.newportri.com
Featuring an excellent calendar of events, this site also includes attractions, dining, lodging and shopping advice.

DiningOut.com. www.diningout.com
While this isn't the most smartly designed site, it does have quite a few dining options for New England. Search by type of cuisine or geographically, but remember these are paid listings, so take any recommendations with a grain of salt.

Providence Journal. www.projo.com
Local news, sports and entertainment from Providence's daily newspaper. You'll also find a ski guide, a round-up of local nightspots, and discussion forums you can join. The "computer user's guide to RI" includes links to local sites for tourism and outdoor recreation, among other categories.

Visit Rhode Island. www.visitri.com
An extensive, all-around guide to the smallest state in the union, including dining, lodging, attractions and shopping. Many of the attractions have images and links, for example, the listing for Hammersmith Farm links to that attraction's own Web site. Visit Rhode Island includes many sub-sites, such as Visit Newport (**www.visitnewport.com**).

VERMONT

Brewpubs and Microbreweries.
   www.vermont.com/travel/attractions/beerindex.html
A guide to 17 establishments throughout the state, from Vermont.com.

Rural Vermont. www.ruralvermont.com
This site has been described as "smelling like apple cider and tasting like maple syrup." Anyway, it's a fine place to get a sense of Vermont, offering an extensive calendar of events as well as the opportunity to chat online with the locals.

This Is Vermont. www.thisisvermont.com
A homespun guide to dining, lodging, shopping and recreation in southern Vermont. You'll also find a museum directory, local lore, and an events calendar.

Vermont Life. www.vtlife.com
The online edition of this long-published print magazine includes a calendar of arts and music events.

Vermont's Northeast Kingdom Guide. www.vermonter.com/nek
Learn more about outdoor recreation, shopping and lodging in one of Vermont's most breathtaking regions.

Vermont State Parks. www.state.vt.us/anr/fpr/parks
This official government site includes a locator map, reservation information, fees, and just about everything else you might want to know about camping in Vermont.

Virtual Vermont. www.virtualvermont.com
Notable for its extensive calendar of events, this site also includes information on hiking, biking, camping, golf, museums and more.

Visit Vermont. www.visitnewengland.com/vermont
An extensive guide to the Green Mountain state including dining, lodging, attractions and shopping. Other categories include boating, skiing, events and outdoors; many of the listings have links to relevant Web sites.

Index

Page numbers in italics refer to maps.

Index

WHEREVER YOU TRAVEL, *H*ELP IS NEVER FAR AWAY.

From planning your trip to providing travel assistance along the way, American Express® Travel Service Offices are always there to help you do more.

New England

CONNECTICUT
New Haven Travel Service, Inc. (R)
195 Church St. 11th Floor
New Haven
203/772-0600

American Express Travel Service
One Landmark Sq.
111 Broad St.
Stamford
203/359-4244

MAINE
American Express Travel Service
480 Congress St.
Portland
201/772-8450

MASSACHUSETTS
American Express Travel Service
One State St. Ground Level
Boston
617/723-8400

Swain's Travel, Inc. (R)
35 Old South Rd.
Nantucket
508/228-3201

NEW HAMPSHIRE
American Express Travel Service
1117 Elm St.
Manchester
603/668-7171

RHODE ISLAND
Pearson Travel (R)
93 Dyer St.
Providence
401/274-2900

VERMONT
Milne Travel (R)
17 Court St.
Middlebury
802/388-6600

do more AMERICAN EXPRESS

Travel

www.americanexpress.com/travel

American Express Travel Service Offices are located throughout the United States. For the office nearest you, call 1-800-AXP-3429.